Financial Aid
for Native Americans
1997-1999

ESSENTIAL FINANCIAL AID DIRECTORIES
PUBLISHED BY REFERENCE SERVICE PRESS

College Students' Guide to Merit and Other No-Need Funding, 1996-1998
More than 1,200 funding opportunities for currently-enrolled or returning college students are described in this award-winning directory. 366 pages. ISBN 0-918276-30-6. $29.95, plus $4.50 shipping.

Directory of Financial Aids for Women, 1997-1999
Nearly 1,800 funding programs set aside for women are described in this biennial directory, which *School Library Journal* calls "the cream of the crop." 579 pages. ISBN 0-918276-52-7. $45, plus $4.50 shipping.

Financial Aid for African Americans, 1997-1999
1,500 scholarships, fellowships, loans, grants, and internships open to African Americans are described in this new directory from Reference Service Press. 512 pages. ISBN 0-918276-56-X. $35, plus $4.50 shipping.

Financial Aid for Asian Americans, 1997-1999
This is the source to use if you are looking for financial aid for Asian Americans; nearly 1,100 funding opportunities are described. 382 pages. ISBN 0-918276-57-8. $30, plus $4.50 shipping.

Financial Aid for Hispanic Americans, 1997-1999
More than 1,400 funding programs open to Americans of Mexican, Puerto Rican, Central American, or other Latin American heritage are described here. 494 pages. ISBN 0-918276-58-6. $32.50, plus $4.50 shipping.

Financial Aid for Native Americans, 1997-1999
Detailed information is provided on nearly 1,800 funding opportunities open to American Indians, Native Alaskans, and Native Pacific Islanders. 618 pages. ISBN 0-918276-59-4. $35, plus $4.50 shipping.

Financial Aid for Research and Creative Activities Abroad, 1996-1998
Described here are 1,300 funding programs (scholarships, fellowships, grants, etc.) available to support research, professional, or creative activities abroad. 452 pages. ISBN 0-918276-34-9. $45, plus $4.50 shipping.

Financial Aid for Study and Training Abroad, 1996-1998
This directory, which *Children's Bookwatch* calls "invaluable," describes more than 900 financial aid opportunities available to support study abroad. 345 pages. ISBN 0-918276-35-7. $38.50, plus $4.50 shipping.

Financial Aid for the Disabled and Their Families, 1996-1998
Named one of the "Best Reference Books of the Year" by *Library Journal,* this directory describes in detail more than 900 funding opportunites. 350 pages. ISBN 0-918276-36-5. $39.50, plus $4.50 shipping.

Financial Aid for Veterans, Military Personnel, and Their Dependents, 1996-1998
According to *Reference Book Review,* this directory (with its 1,000 entries) is "the most comprehensive guide available on the subject." 322 pages. ISBN 0-918276-37-3. $39.50, plus $4.50 shipping.

High School Seniors' Guide to Merit and Other No-Need Funding, 1996-1998
Here's your guide to 1,000 funding programs that *never* look at income level when making awards to college-bound high school seniors. 340 pages. ISBN 0-918276-29-2. $25.95, plus $4.50 shipping.

Money for Graduate Students in the Humanities, 1996-1998
Use this directory to identify nearly 900 funding opportunities available to support graduate study, training, research, and creative activities in the humanities. 298 pages. ISBN 0-918276-31-4. $37.50, plus $4.50 shipping.

Money for Graduate Students in the Sciences, 1996-1998
Described here are nearly 1,300 funding opportunities set aside just for students interested in working on a graduate degree in the sciences. 420 pages. ISBN 0-918276-32-2. $45, plus $4.50 shipping.

Money for Graduate Students in the Social Sciences, 1996-1998
If you are looking for funding to support graduate study or research in the social sciences, this is the directory to use (1,000 funding programs are described). 330 pages. ISBN 0-918276-33-0. $40, plus $4.50 shipping.

Financial Aid
for Native Americans
1997-1999

First Edition

Gail Ann Schlachter
R. David Weber

A List of: Scholarships, Fellowships, Loans, Grants, Awards, and Internships Open Primarily or Exclusively to Native Americans

Reference Service Press
El Dorado Hills, California

ISBN: 0-918276-59-4

10 9 8 7 6 5 4 3 2 1

Reference Service Press
El Dorado Hills Business Park
5000 Windplay Drive, Suite 4
El Dorado Hills, CA 95762
(916) 939-9620
Fax: (916) 939-9626
E-mail: findaid@aol.com

Manufactured in the United States of America

Contents

Sources of Information on:

Indexes **527**

About the Authors **617**

Introduction

PURPOSE OF THE DIRECTORY

For years, numerous directories have been prepared to identify and describe general financial aid programs (those open to all segments of society), but they never covered more than a few of the programs designed primarily or exclusively for minority groups. As a result, advisors, librarians, scholars, researchers, and students frequently were unaware of the extensive array of financial aid programs established with minorities in mind. Then, in 1984, this changed. Reference Service Press began issuing the biennial *Directory of Financial Aids for Minorities,* the only up-to-date and comprehensive listing of funding opportunities available to African Americans, Asian Americans, Hispanic Americans, and Native Americans.

The praise for this landmark work has been unanimous. *RQ* called it "the only one of its kind." The Grantsmanship Center labeled the *Directory* "a must for every organization serving minorities!" In the view of *Choice,* "the entire work is carefully conceived and highly usable." *Small Press* perhaps best summed up the critics' views: "It is hard to imagine what else might be needed."

Every year since the *Directory* began, the funds available to minorities have increased steadily. And, so has the size of the *Directory!* By the 1995-1997 edition, the compilation had more than 2,000 program entries, nearly 700 pages, and a two-inch spine. In the past two years, despite certain steps taken by the federal and state governments to discourage funding for minorities, the number of programs set aside for these groups has grown at an even faster rate. By 1997, this proliferation of funding programs made it completely impractical for us to continue the *Directory's* original single-volume format.

As a result, the editors at Reference Service Press had to decide how best to divide the material: by type of program, by subject coverage, or by ethnic group? The feedback from numerous librarian and user surveys consistently and enthusiastically favored a division by ethnic group, since most fund-seekers referred to programs in only one ethnic category. In response to this user feedback, we have decided to replace the *Directory of Financial Aids for Minorities* with a four-volume *Minority Funding Set.* Each volume in the set focuses on a different ethnic group (and can be purchased separately or as part of the set):

> *Financial Aid for African Americans:* describes funding opportunities open to Black/African Americans.

> *Financial Aid for Asian Americans:* describes funding opportunities open to Americans of Chinese, Japanese, Korean, Vietnamese, Filipino, or other Asian ancestry.

> *Financial Aid for Hispanic Americans:* describes funding opportunities open to Americans with Mexican, Puerto Rican, Cuban, or other Latin American origins.

> *Financial Aid for Native Americans:* describes funding opportunities open to American Indians, Native Alaskans, and Native Pacific Islanders (including Native Hawaiians and Samoans).

SCOPE OF THE DIRECTORY

This first edition of *Financial Aid for Native Americans* will help American Indians, Native Alaskans (including Eskimos and Aleuts), and Native Pacific Islanders (including Native Hawaiians and Samoans) tap into the billions of dollars available to them, as minorities, to support study, research, creative activities, past accomplishments, future projects, professional development, and work experience. The listings cover every major subject area, are sponsored by more than 750 different private and public agencies and organizations, and are open to Native Americans at any level—from high school through postdoctorate and professional. This approach is unique. No other single source focuses solely on programs open exclusively to Native Americans or to minority pools that specifically include Native Americans.

In addition to its comprehensive coverage, *Financial Aid for Native Americans* offers several other unique features. Covered here are hundreds of funding opportunities not listed in other sources. Unlike other funding directories, which generally follow a straight alphabetical arrangement, this one groups entries by both type and recipient group, thus facilitating your search for appropriate programs. The same convenience is offered in the indexes, where title, organization, geographic, subject, and deadline date entries are each subdivided by recipient group and type of program. In addition, we have tried to anticipate all the ways you might wish to search for funding; we organized the volume so you can identify programs not only by type and recipient group, but by specific subject, sponsoring organization, program title, residency requirements, where the money can be spent, and even deadline date. Plus, we've included all the information you'll need to decide if a program is right for you: purpose, eligibility requirements, financial data, duration, special features, limitations, number awarded, and application date. You even get fax numbers, toll-free numbers, and e-mail addresses (when available), along with complete contact information.

COMPILATION OF THE DIRECTORY

To compile the first edition of *Financial Aid for Native Americans,* we first reviewed and updated all relevant programs included in the last edition of the *Directory of Financial Aids for Minorities.* Next, we collected updated information on all programs open to Native Americans that were added to Reference Service Press' funding database since the last edition of the *Directory.* Then, we searched extensively for new program leads in a variety of sources, including printed directories, news reports, journals, newsletters, house organs, annual reports, and sites on the Internet.

Finally, we contacted the sponsoring organizations identified in this process (up to four times in writing and, if necessary, up to 3 times by telephone) and requested descriptions of their funding programs so we could prepare the entries for this book (no information was taken from secondary sources). Unfortunately, despite our best efforts, some sponsoring organizations failed to respond to our data requests; consequently, their programs are not included in this edition of the directory.

ARRANGEMENT OF THE DIRECTORY

Financial Aid for Native Americans is divided into three separate sections: descriptions of nearly 1,800 funding opportunities open to Native Americans, an annotated bibliography of directories listing general financial aid programs, and a set of six indexes.

Financial Aid Programs Open to Native Americans. The first section of the directory describes 1,776 funding opportunities open exclusively to Native Americans or to minority pools that specifically include Native Americans. The programs described here are sponsored by more than 750 government agencies, professional organizations, corporations, sororities and fraternities, foundations, religious groups, educational associations, and military/veterans organizations. They are open to Native Americans at any level (high school through postdoctoral) for education, research, travel, training, career development, or innovative effort. All areas of the sciences, social sciences, and humanities are covered. The focus is on programs open to American citizens or permanent residents and tenable in the United States.

Entries in this section are grouped in the following six categories to facilitate your search for a specific kind of financial assistance (e.g., a scholarship for undergraduate study, a grant for independent research, an award for outstanding literary achievement).

> *Scholarships:* Programs that support studies at the undergraduate level in the United States. Usually no return of service or repayment is required. For information on funding for research on the undergraduate level, see the Grants category below.

SAMPLE ENTRY

(1) **[1212]**

(2) **NATIVE AMERICAN COMMUNITY SCHOLAR AWARDS**

(3) Smithsonian Institution
Attn: Office of Fellowships and Grants
955 L'Enfant Plaza, Suite 7000
MRC 902
Washington, DC 20560
(202) 287-3271   Fax: (202) 287-3691
E-mail: siofg@sivm.si.edu

(4) **Purpose** To provide opportunities for Native Americans to pursue projects related to Native American topics at the Smithsonian Institution.

(5) **Eligibility** Native Americans who are formally or informally related to a Native American community are eligible to apply. Applicants may be students at any level or independent scholars, but they must undertake a project that is related to a Native American topic and requires the use of Native American resources at the Smithsonian Institution.

(6) **Financial data** Subsistence of $75 per day and travel allowances are provided.

(7) **Duration** Up to 12 weeks.

(8) **Special features** Projects are carried out in association with the Smithsonian's research staff.

(9) **Limitations** Fellows are required to be in residence at the Smithsonian for the duration of the fellowship.

(10) **Number awarded** Varies each year.

(11) **Deadline** Applications are accepted year-round, but it is advisable to submit a completed application at least 3 months prior to the proposed date of appointment.

DEFINITION

(1) **Entry number:** Consecutive number assigned to the references and used to index the entry.

(2) **Program title:** Title of scholarship, fellowship, loan, grant, award, or internship.

(3) **Sponsoring organization:** Name, address, and telephone number, toll-free number, fax number and/or e-mail address (when information was supplied) for organization sponsoring the program.

(4) **Purpose:** Objectives of program and/or sponsoring institution.

(5) **Eligibility:** Qualifications required of applicants.

(6) **Financial data:** Financial details of the program, including fixed sum, average amount, or range of funds offered, expenses for which funds may and may not be applied, and cash-related benefits supplied (e.g., room and board).

(7) **Duration:** Period for which support is provided; renewal prospects.

(8) **Special features:** Any unusual (generally nonmonetary) benefits or features associated with the program.

(9) **Limitations:** Any unusual restrictions or requirements associated with the program.

(10) **Number awarded:** Total number of recipients each year or other specified period.

(11) **Deadline:** The month by which applications must be submitted.

Fellowships: Programs that support studies on the graduate or postgraduate level in the United States. Usually no return of service or repayment is required. For information on funding for research on the graduate, postgraduate, or postdoctoral levels, see the Grants category below.

Loans: Programs that provide money that eventually must be repaid—with or without interest. Forgivable loans (along with scholarship/loans) are also covered here.

Grants: Programs that provide funds to support Native Americans' innovative efforts, travel, projects, creative activities, or research on any level (from undergraduate to postdoctorate, professional, or other). In a number of cases, proposals may be submitted by institutions or organizations only; in others, individual minority group members may submit proposals directly.

Awards: Competitions, prizes, and honoraria granted in recognition or support of Native Americans' creative work and public service. Prizes received solely as the result of entering contests are excluded.

Internships: Work experience programs for Native American undergraduates, graduate students, and postgraduates. Only salaried positions are described.

Each of these six categories is further divided into four minority groupings: American Indians, Native Alaskans (including Eskimos and Aleuts), Native Pacific Islanders (including Native Hawaiians and Samoans), and Native Americans in General. Within each of the minority-group subdivisions, entries appear alphabetically by program title. Programs that supply more than one type of assistance or assistance to more than one specific group are listed in all relevant subsections. For example, both undergraduate and graduate students may apply for the American Indian Scholarships, so the program is described in the scholarship and in the fellowship sections. Similarly, since the Phillips Fund Grant for Native American Research is open specifically to American Indians and Native Alaskans, it is included in both of these recipient subsections.

Each program entry has been designed to provide a concise profile that includes information (when available) on program title, organization address and telephone numbers (including toll-free, fax, and e-mail), purpose, eligibility, remuneration, duration, special features, limitations, number of awards, and application deadline. (Refer to the sample on p. xi).

The information reported for each of the programs in this section was supplied in response to questionnaires distributed through the beginning of 1997. While this listing is intended to be as comprehensive as possible, some sponsoring organizations did not respond to our research inquiry and, consequently, are not included in this edition of the directory.

The focus of the directory is on noninstitution-specific programs open exclusively to Native Americans or to minority pools that specifically include Native Americans. Excluded from this listing are:

Awards for which American citizens would be ineligible: Programs open only to nationals from other countries (e.g., Canada) are not covered.

Awards tenable only outside the United States: Since there are comprehensive and up-to-date directories that describe the available funding for study and research abroad (see the Annotated Bibliography section), only programs that fund activities in the United States are covered here.

Minority programs that specifically exclude Native Americans: Programs that are open to specific minority groups, but not to Native Americans (e.g., programs only for Hispanic Americans), are excluded.

Programs that are open equally to all segments of the population: See the Annotated Bibliography section for the names of publications that list and describe these unrestricted programs.

Programs administered by individual academic institutions solely for their own students: The directory identifies "portable" programs—ones that can be used at any number of schools. Financial aid administered by individual schools specifically for their currently-enrolled students is not covered. Write directly to the schools you are considering to get information on their offerings.

Annotated Bibliography of General Financial Aid Directories.   While this directory is the only comprehensive and current listing of financial aid programs available to Native Americans, there are numerous other publications that describe the thousands of resources open equally to all segments of American society. The second section of the directory provides an annotated list of the 60 key directories published in the past five years or so that any individual (Native American or not) can use to locate additional sources of financial assistance. The directories are listed by coverage (scholarships, fellowships and loans; grants; awards and prizes; internships and other work experience programs; and financial assistance to special groups). Each entry contains basic bibliographic information and an annotation specifying scope, arrangement, publication history, and special features of the source. If a more comprehensive listing of available directories is required, the reader is directed to the evaluative guide published by Reference Service Press: *How to Find Out About Financial Aid: A Guide to Over 400 Directories Listing Scholarships, Fellowships, Loans, Grants, Awards and Internships.*

Indexes.   The directory's six indexes facilitate the search for appropriate financial aid opportunities. Program Title, Sponsoring Organization, Residency, Tenability, Subject, and Calendar Indexes follow a word-by-word alphabetical arrangement and refer the user to the appropriate entry by number.

Program Title Index.   This index lists alphabetically all references and cross-references to the scholarships, fellowships, loans, grants, awards, and internships covered in the first section of *Financial Aid for Native Americans.* Since one program can be listed in several subsections (e.g., a program providing assistance to American Indian *and* Native Hawaiian undergraduate *and* graduate students is listed in four subsections), each entry number in the index has been coded to indicate both program type (e.g., scholarship, loan, internship) and availability (e.g., American Indians, Native Americans in General). By using this coding system, readers can avoid duplicate entries and turn directly to the programs that match their financial needs.

Sponsoring Organization Index.   This index provides an alphabetical listing of the 768 organizations sponsoring financial aid programs listed in the first section of the directory. As in the Program Title Index, entry numbers have been coded to indicate program type and availability.

Residency Index.   This index identifies the residency requirements of the financial aid programs listed in the directory. Index entries (city, county, state, province, region, country, continent) are arranged alphabetically (word by word). To facilitate access, the 150 geographic terms in the index are subdivided by program type and eligibility. Use this index when you are looking for money available to Native Americans in a particular geographic area.

Tenability Index.   This index identifies the geographic locations where the funding programs listed in the directory may be used. Index entries (city, county, state, province, region, country, continent) are arranged alphabetically (word by word) and subdivided by program type and eligibility. Use this index when you are looking for money to support your activities in a particular geographic area.

Subject Index.   This index allows the reader to identify by subject both the funding opportunities available to Native Americans (first section of the directory) and the directories listing general financial aid opportunities (second section). More than 300 different subject terms are listed. Extensive "see" and "see also" references facilitate the search for appropriate financial aid programs.

Calendar Index.   To assist fundseekers who often must work within specific time constraints, the Calendar Index identifies financial aid programs by filing date. The Calendar is arranged by applicant group and divided by program type (e.g., scholarship, loan, internship) and month during which the deadline falls. Filing dates can and quite often do vary from year to year; consequently, this index should be used only as a guide for deadlines beyond mid-1999. It is important to note that not all sponsoring organizations supplied information on application deadline, so some of the programs described in the directory are not listed here.

HOW TO USE THE DIRECTORY

To Locate Programs Open to Individuals from Specific Native American Groups.   To bring programs with similar eligibility requirements together, each type of program chapter in the directory (e.g., Scholarships, Grants) is subdivided by up to four availability subsections: American Indians, Native Alaskans, Native Pacific Islanders, and Native Americans in General. When browsing through the directory, you should always check at least two of these subsections: the specific group or groups that best represent your background (e.g., Native Alaskans) *and* the Native Americans in General subsection (which lists programs open equally to members of any of the specific Native Americans groups). *Financial Aid for Native Americans* is the only volume in Reference Service Press' *Minority Funding Set* to utilize this two-level organizational structure (the listings for African Americans, Asian Americans, and Hispanic Americans are grouped only by program title), because only Native Americans have a sizeable number of programs for specific subgroups.

To Locate Programs Offering a Particular Type of Assistance.   If you are looking for programs offering a particular type of financial aid (e.g., a scholarship for undergraduate courses, a grant for independent research, an award for outstanding literary achievement), first read the definitions of the various program types on page x and then turn to the appropriate category in the first section of the directory (scholarships, fellowships, loans, grants, awards, or internships) and read through all the entries in the subsections that apply. Since programs with multiple purposes are listed in every appropriate location, each of these subsections functions as a self-contained entity. In fact, you can browse through any of the sections or subsections in the directory without first consulting an index.

To Locate a Particular Financial Aid Program.   If you know the name of a particular financial aid program, and the type of assistance offered by the program (scholarship, fellowship, grant, etc.), and the availability (e.g., American Indians, Native Pacific Islanders), then go directly to the appropriate category in the first section of the directory, where you will find the program profiles arranged alphabetically by title. But be careful: program titles can be misleading. For example, the Indian Fellowship Program is also open to undergraduates; the John Carter Brown Library Associates Fellowship is a grant; and the Muscogee (Creek) Nation Tribal Funds Grant Program is actually a scholarship. So, if you are looking for a specific program and do not find it in the subsection you have checked, be sure to refer to the Program Title Index to see if it is covered elsewhere in the directory. To save time, always check the Program Title Index first if you know the name of a specific award but are not sure under which subsection it has been listed.

To Locate Programs Sponsored by a Particular Organization.   The Sponsoring Organization Index makes it easy to determine agencies that provide financial assistance to Native Americans or to identify specific financial aid programs offered by a particular organization. Each entry number in the index is coded to identify program type and availability, so that you can easily target appropriate entries.

To Locate Programs Open to Native Americans from or Tenable in a Particular City, State, or Country.   The Residency Index identifies financial aid programs open to residents of a particular city, county, state, region, or country. The Tenability Index shows where the money can be spent. "See" and "see also" references are used liberally in both indexes, and index entries for a particular geographic area are subdivided by both type of program (scholarships, fellowships, loans, grants, awards, internships) and eligible group.

To Locate Financial Aid Programs Open to Native Americans in a Particular Subject Area.   Turn to the Subject Index first if you are interested in identifying by subject either financial aid programs for Native Americans or directories that list programs open to all segments of the population. To facilitate your search, the type of reference indexed (scholarships, fellowships, loans, grants, awards, internships, or directories) and the recipient group are clearly identified. Extensive cross-references are provided.

To Locate Financial Aid Programs Open to Native Americans by Deadline Date.   If you are working with specific time constraints and want to weed out the financial aid programs whose filing dates you won't be able to meet, turn first to the Calendar Index and check the program references listed under recipient group, program type, and month. Remember, not all sponsoring organizations supplied deadline information, so not all programs are indexed in this section. To identify every relevant financial aid program, regardless of filing date, read through all the entries in each of the program categories (Scholarships, Fellowships, etc.) and availability subsections (American Indians, Native Americans in General) that apply.

To Locate Financial Aid Programs Open to All Segments of the Population.   Only programs available to Native Americans are listed in this publication. However, there are thousands of other programs that are open equally to all segments of the population. To identify these programs, use the publications described in the second section of the directory (access to these sources is also provided through the Subject Index), talk to your local librarian, check with your financial aid office on campus, or use a computerized scholarship or grant search service.

PLANS TO UPDATE THE DIRECTORY

This volume, covering 1997-1999, is the first edition of *Financial Aid for Native Americans.* The next biennial edition will cover the years 1999-2001 and will be issued in early 1999.

OTHER RELATED PUBLICATIONS

In addition to *Financial Aid for Native Americans,* Reference Service Press publishes several other titles dealing with fundseeking, including the award-winning *Directory of Financial Aids for Women; Financial Aid for the Disabled and Their Families;* and *Financial Aid for Veterans, Military Personnel, and Their Dependents.* Since each of these titles focuses on a separate population group, there is little duplication in the listings. For more information on Reference Service Press' publications, write to the company at 5000 Windplay Drive, Suite 4, El Dorado Hills, CA 95762, fax us at (916) 939-9626, or send us an e-mail at findaid@aol.com.

RSP ONLINE

Since 1995, a portion of Reference Service Press' extensive financial aid database has been available online, through the consumer service America Online. Use "RSP Funding Focus" on this service to update and augment the listings in this edition of the *Financial Aid for Native Americans.*

ACKNOWLEDGEMENTS

A debt of gratitude is owed all the organizations that contributed information to the first edition of *Financial Aid for Native Americans.* Their generous cooperation has helped to make this publication a current and comprehensive survey of awards.

Financial Aid Programs
Open to Native Americans

- Scholarships
- Fellowships
- Loans
- Grants
- Awards
- Internships

Scholarships

American Indians ●
Native Alaskans ●
Native Pacific Islanders ●
Native Americans in General ●

Described here are 379 funding programs open to Native Americans that are available to pursue studies on the undergraduate level in the United States. Usually no return of service or repayment is required. Of these listings, 137 are open to American Indians, 16 to Native Alaskans, 17 to Native Pacific Islanders, and 209 to Native Americans in General. Note: other funding opportunities for Native American undergraduates are also described in the Loans, Grants, Awards, and Internships sections. So, if you are looking for a particular program and don't find it in this section, be sure to check the Program Title Index to see if it is covered elsewhere in the directory.

American Indians

[1]
AAIA DISPLACED HOMEMAKER SCHOLARSHIPS

Association on American Indian Affairs, Inc.
Attn: Scholarship Coordinator
P.O. Box 268
Sisseton, SD 57262
(605) 698-3998

Purpose To provide financial assistance for Native American mid-life homemakers, both men and women, who are trying to complete their college education.

Eligibility Eligible are Native American college students who have special needs as heads of household, single parents, or displaced homemakers. Applications include an essay outlining the applicant's life experience, 2 letters of recommendation, a personal monthly budget (including child care cost, food, transportation, and other expenses), the most recent financial aid award letter, a copy of either a certificate of degree of Indian blood or a tribal enrollment card, and a transcript.

Financial data Awards are intended to assist recipients with child care, transportation, and some basic living expenses.

Duration Up to 3 years.

Number awarded Varies each year.

Deadline August of each year.

[2]
ADOLPH VAN PELT SCHOLARSHIPS

Association on American Indian Affairs, Inc.
Attn: Scholarship Coordinator
P.O. Box 268
Sisseton, SD 57262
(605) 698-3998

Purpose To provide financial assistance to Native American students interested in postsecondary education.

Eligibility Applicants must be Native American students interested in undergraduate or graduate education. Selection is based on merit and financial need. Applications include an essay (1 to 2 pages) describing educational goals, a budget of educational costs and resources, a copy of a certificate of at least one-quarter Indian blood or of registration with a federally-recognized Indian tribe, and the most recent transcript.

Financial data The award is $500 for the first year, $600 for the second year, $700 for the third year, and $800 for the fourth year. Monies are paid directly to accredited educational institutions to be used for tuition, books, and other academic-related expenses.

Duration 1 year; renewable if academic progress is satisfactory.

Special features Recipients may attend any accredited college or university of their choice level.

Deadline May of each year.

[3]
AISF GRANTS

American Indian Scholarship Fund
c/o Native American Student Programs
University of California at Riverside
224 Costo Hall
Riverside, CA 92521
(909) 787-4143

Purpose To provide financial assistance to Native Americans interested in attending college in California.

Eligibility Native American undergraduate and graduate students are eligible to apply if they can prove Indian blood (by tribal enrollment or birth certificate) and are currently enrolled in a college or university in California. Financial need must be documented.

Financial data The amount awarded varies, depending upon the needs of the recipient.

Duration 1 year; may be renewed.

Number awarded 1 or more each year.

Deadline Applications may be submitted at any time.

[4]
AL QOYAWAYMA AWARD FOR EXCELLENCE IN ARTS AND SCIENCE

American Indian Science and Engineering Society
Attn: Scholarship Department
5661 Airport Boulevard
Boulder, CO 80301
(303) 939-0023   E-mail: ascholar@spot.colorado.edu

Purpose To help artistically-talented American Indian science and engineering students on the undergraduate or graduate school level meet the financial demands of going to college.

Eligibility To be eligible for this scholarship, the applicant must have applied for the A.T. Anderson Memorial Scholarship Program and have met the following requirements: a full-time student at the undergraduate or graduate level, a member of the American Indian Science and Engineering Society, at least one-quarter Indian, in financial need, and pursuing a double major in science or engineering and a degree in the arts. Evidence of the student's excellence in art and engineering is taken from the A.T. Anderson Memorial Scholarship Program application.

Financial data The stipend is $1,500.

Duration 1 year.

Special features This award is sponsored by the George Bird Grinnell American Indian Children's Education Foundation. It honors Al Qöyawayma, a distinguished engineer, renowned Hopi artist, and 1 of the founders of the American Indian Science and Engineering Society.

Number awarded 1 or more each year.

Deadline June of each year.

[5]
ALL INDIAN PUEBLO COUNCIL JOBS TRAINING PARTNERSHIP ACT

All Indian Pueblo Council, Inc.
Attn: JTPA Department
3939 San Pedro NE, Suite D
P.O. Box 3256
Albuquerque, NM 87190
(505) 884-3820   Fax: (505) 883-7682

Purpose To provide employment and training to selected Pueblo Indians.

Eligibility Eligible to apply are enrolled and verified members of the Isleta and San Felipe Pueblos who are unemployed, underemployed, or economically disadvantaged.

Financial data Tuition and other services are offered to recipients.

Duration Up to 1 year.

Special features This program provides short-term employment within the pueblo work force for eligible individuals, as well as vocational training.

[6]
ALL INDIAN PUEBLO COUNCIL SCHOLARSHIP GRANT PROGRAM

All Indian Pueblo Council, Inc.
Attn: Scholarship Program
3939 San Pedro NE, Suite D
P.O. Box 3256
Albuquerque, NM 87190
(505) 884-3820   Fax: (505) 883-7682

Purpose To provide financial assistance for postsecondary education to Pueblo Indians.

Eligibility Eligible to apply are enrolled and verified members of the following Indian Pueblos: Cochiti, Jemez, Sandia, and Santa Ana. Applications must be accompanied by an official transcript of the last school attended (high school or college), a letter of admission from an accredited college or university, 2 letters of recommendation, a certificate of Indian blood, a certificate of tribal verification, and a copy of the student's eligibility for a federal Pell Grant that shows financial need and that the applicant has exhausted all other possible sources of aid.

Financial data The amount awarded varies, depending upon the recipient's financial need.

Duration 1 academic year; renewable.

Deadline February for the summer or fall terms; October for the spring term.

[7]
AMERICAN CHEMICAL SOCIETY SCHOLARS PROGRAM

American Chemical Society
Attn: Membership Division
1155 16th Street, N.W.
Washington, DC 20036
(202) 872-6250   (800) 227-5558
Fax: (202) 776-8003

Purpose To provide financial assistance to underrepresented minority students with a strong interest in chemistry and a desire to pursue a career in a chemically-related science.

Eligibility This program is open to 1) high school seniors planning to enter college in the following fall; 2) college students who are currently or planning to pursue full-time study in a chemically-related field; 3) community college graduates and transfer students who plan to study for the baccalaureate degree in chemistry, biochemistry, chemical engineering, toxicology, materials science, environmental science, and other programs of study with a strong component of chemistry; 4) community college freshmen majoring in a 2-year chemical technology program. Applicants must be African American, Hispanic/Latino, American Indian, or Alaskan Native. Selection is based on academic merit and financial need.

Financial data Scholarships for freshmen and sophomores are up to $2,500 per year; for juniors and seniors, the awards are up to $5,000 per year.

Duration 1 year only.

Special features This program was formerly known as the American Chemical Society Minority Scholars Program.

Number awarded Approximately 200 each year.

Deadline February of each year.

[8]
AMERICAN INDIAN HERITAGE FOUNDATION SCHOLARSHIP

American Indian Heritage Foundation
6051 Arlington Boulevard
Falls Church, VA 22044-2788
(202) INDIANS   (703) 237-7500
Fax: (703) 532-1921

Purpose To provide financial assistance to Native American students interested in pursuing postsecondary education.

Eligibility Native American high school graduates are eligible to apply if they have been accepted by an institution of higher education, are U.S. citizens, demonstrate financial need, and provide information on tribal affiliation and grade point average.

Financial data The amount awarded varies up to a maximum of $1,000.

Duration The scholarships are granted annually.

Number awarded 1 or more each year.

[9]
AMERICAN INDIAN SCHOLARSHIPS

National Society, Daughters of the American Revolution
Attn: Scholarship Committee
1776 D Street, N.W.
Washington, DC 20006-5392
(202) 628-1776

Purpose To provide supplementary financial assistance to Native American students who wish to pursue postsecondary education in any field in either vocational, undergraduate, or graduate school.

Eligibility Native American high school graduates who wish to attend college are eligible to apply. Scholarships are awarded on the basis of financial need, academic achievement, and ambition. Applicants must have at least a 2.75 grade point average. Graduate students are eligible but undergraduate students receive preference.

Financial data The stipend is $500. The funds are paid directly to the recipient's college.

Duration This is a 1-time award.

Deadline July of each year for fall term; November of each year for spring term.

[10]
ARDELL BJUGSTAD MEMORIAL SCHOLARSHIP

South Dakota Board of Regents
Attn: Scholarship Committee
207 East Capitol Avenue
Pierre, SD 57501-3159
(605) 773-3455   Fax: (605) 773-5320

Purpose To provide financial assistance to Native Americans in South and North Dakota who are graduating from high school and preparing for a career in agriculture.

Eligibility This program is open to high school seniors who are preparing to enter college and are planning to major in agricultural sciences, agribusiness, agricultural production, or natural resources. They must be enrolled members of a federally recognized tribe whose reservations are located in North or South Dakota and they must be residents of those states. Selection is based on academic achievement.

Financial data The stipend is $500; funds are allocated to the institution for distribution to the student.

Duration 1 year.

Number awarded 1 each year.

Deadline February of each year.

[11]
A.T. ANDERSON MEMORIAL SCHOLARSHIP PROGRAM

American Indian Science and Engineering Society
Attn: Scholarship Department
5661 Airport Boulevard
Boulder, CO 80301
(303) 939-0023   E-mail: ascholar@spot.colorado.edu

Purpose To help talented American Indian science and engineering students meet the financial demands of going to college.

Eligibility To be eligible for a scholarship, the applicant must be a full-time student at the undergraduate or graduate level, attending an accredited 4-year college or university or a 2-year college leading to a 4-year degree, a member of the American Indian Science and Engineering Society who can furnish proof of tribal enrollment, and majoring in health sciences, engineering, science, natural resources, mathematics, business, or math and science secondary education. Recipients are selected on the basis of academic achievement, leadership potential, financial need, and commitment to helping other American Indians.

Financial data The annual stipend is $1,000 for undergraduates and $2,000 for graduate students.

Duration 1 year; may be renewed.

Special features This program was launched in 1983 in memory of A.T. Anderson, a Mohawk and a chemical engineer who worked with Albert Einstein. Anderson was 1 of the society's founders and was the society's first executive director.

Number awarded Varies; generally, 200 or more each year, depending upon the availability of funds from corporate and other sponsors.

Deadline June of each year.

[12]
BECHTEL UNDERGRADUATE FELLOWSHIP AWARD

National Action Council for Minorities in Engineering
3 West 35th Street
New York, NY 10001-2281
(212) 279-2626   Fax: (212) 629-5178

Purpose To provide financial assistance for education in construction engineering to underrepresented minority students.

Eligibility Engineering students who are African American, Latino, or American Indian are eligible for this award. Candidates must be sophomores with a minimum grade point average of 3.0 nominated by their deans. Selection is based on high academic achievement and interest in a corporate career in construction engineering.

Financial data The stipend is $5,000 per year.

Duration 2 years.

Special features Funding for this program is provided by the Bechtel Foundation. Fellows also receive an internship and a mentor.

Number awarded 1 each year.

[13]
BIA HIGHER EDUCATION GRANT PROGRAM

Bureau of Indian Affairs
Attn: Area Education Programs Administrator
4149 Highline Boulevard, Suite 380
Oklahoma City, OK 73108
(405) 945-6051   Fax: (405) 945-6057

Purpose To provide financial assistance for postsecondary education to undergraduate and graduate students who belong to certain federally recognized Indian tribes.

Eligibility Students who are members of recognized Indian tribes are eligible to apply. The tribes served by this office are: Seneca-Cayuga, Quapaw, Modoc, Iowa of Kansas and Nebraska, and Fort Still Apache. Applicants must be enrolled or planning to enroll in an accredited college or university and must be able to demonstrate financial need. Priority is given to students residing near or within the boundary of an Indian reservation. Graduate study is included only if money is available after all qualified undergraduate students have been funded. All students must achieve and maintain a cumulative grade point average of at least 2.0.

Financial data The amount awarded varies, up to a maximum of $2,000 per year. The exact amount depends upon the financial needs of the recipient.

Duration 1 year; may be renewed for up to 3 additional years.

Special features Funds may be used for either part-time or full-time study.

Limitations Aid for summer school is available only to juniors and seniors.

Number awarded Varies each year.

Deadline June of each year for fall term; October of each year for spring term; April of each year for summer school.

[14]
BLACKFEET ADULT VOCATIONAL TRAINING GRANTS

Blackfeet Nation
P.O. Box 850
Browning, MT 59417
(406) 338-7539   Fax: (406) 338-7530

Purpose To provide financial assistance for vocational training to members of the Blackfeet Tribe.

Eligibility Applicants must be enrolled members of a federally recognized tribe between the ages of 18 and 35 in need of training to obtain reasonable and satisfactory employment. Recipients must be willing to accept full-time employment as soon as possible after completion of training. Grants are awarded according to the following priorities: 1) Blackfeet Tribal members residing on or near the Blackfeet Reservation; 2) Blackfeet Tribal members residing off the Blackfeet Reservation; 3) members of other federally recognized tribes (as funding permits); and 4) second training grant applicants (as funding permits).

Financial data The amount awarded varies, depending upon the recipient's educational requirements and financial needs. The maximum for an unmarried student with no dependents is $2,800 per year and for a student with 2 or more dependents $3,500. Funds are sent to the school's financial aid officer.

Duration Up to 24 months (36 months for registered nursing students) of full-time training.

Number awarded Varies each year.

Deadline February of each year; March for summer term.

[15]
BLACKFEET HIGHER EDUCATION PROGRAM

Blackfeet Nation
P.O. Box 850
Browning, MT 59417
(406) 338-7539   Fax: (406) 338-7530

Purpose To provide financial assistance for undergraduate education to members of the Blackfeet Tribe.

Eligibility Applicants must be enrolled members of the Blackfeet Tribe and be enrolled or accepted for enrollment in an academically recognized college or university pursuing an undergraduate degree. Selection is based on academic record (normally a high school grade point average of at least 2.25) and financial need. Scholarships are awarded according to the following priority: 1) renewal of grants to students currently funded who are in good academic and financial aid standing and submitted application packet on time; 2) college seniors not currently funded who can graduate within the current academic year; 3) 2-year degree graduates who apply within 1 year of earning their associates degree; 4) high school seniors who apply within 1 year of earning their high school diploma; 5) applicants previously funded who are in good academic and financial aid standing and submit application packet in a timely manner; and 6) candidates who submit late applications (supported only if funding permits).

Financial data The amount awarded varies, depending upon the recipient's educational requirements and financial needs. The maximum for an unmarried student with no dependents is $2,800 per year and for a student with 2 or more dependents $3,500. Funds are sent to the school's financial aid officer.

Duration 1 year; may be renewed to a total of 10 semesters or 15 quarters.

Limitations Recipients must enroll as full-time students and earn no less than 12 credit hours per term with a grade point average of no less than 2.0 as freshmen, 2.2 as sophomores, 2.4 as juniors, and 2.6 as seniors. Students who attend private schools or institutions outside of Montana must pay the difference in tuition, unless no comparable program exists in Montana public institutions.

Number awarded Varies each year.

Deadline February of each year; March for summer term.

[16]
BURLINGTON NORTHERN SANTA FE FOUNDATION SCHOLARSHIP

American Indian Science and Engineering Society
Attn: Scholarship Department
5661 Airport Boulevard
Boulder, CO 80301
(303) 939-0023   E-mail: ascholar@spot.colorado.edu

Purpose To provide financial assistance to outstanding Native American high school seniors interested in pursuing postsecondary education.

Eligibility Applicants must be accepted as full-time students at an accredited 4-year college or university, or a 2-year college with a program leading to an academic degree. They must be student members of the American Indian Science and Engineering Society who can furnish proof of tribal enrollment. Residence in the service area of the Burlington Northern and Santa Fe Railway (Arizona, Colorado, Kansas, Minnesota, Montana, New Mexico, North Dakota, Oklahoma, Oregon, South Dakota, Washington or San Bernardino County, California) is also required. Winners are selected on the basis of strong academic performance in high school, with award preference given to the study of any of the sciences (medical, engineering, other natural and physical sciences) or administration (business, education, or health).

Financial data The award ranges from $1,250 to $2,500 per year.

Duration 1 year; renewable up to 3 additional years or until the bachelor's degree requirements are completed, whichever occurs first.

Special features Funds for the program are provided by the Burlington Northern Santa Fe Foundation. The program is administered by the American Indian Science and Engineering Society.

Number awarded 5 new awards are made each year.

Deadline March of each year.

[17]
CERT SCHOLARSHIPS

Council of Energy Resource Tribes
Attn: Student Services Coordinator
1999 Broadway, Suite 2600
Denver, CO 80202-5726
(303) 297-2378   Fax: (303) 296-5690

Purpose To provide financial assistance to Native American students who are interested in pursuing postsecondary education (on either the undergraduate or graduate level).

Eligibility Indian high school graduates who are preparing to enter college may enroll in the Tribal Resource Institute in Business, Engineering, and Science (TRIBES) program, an intensive 7-week summer college-level math, science, and Indian studies program. TRIBES graduates are eligible to receive these scholarships throughout their undergraduate and graduate education. Also eligible are participants in the Council of Energy Resource Tribes (CERT) Summer Internship Program.

Financial data Costs of instruction, activities, and room and board for the summer institute are paid by the TRIBES program. The amount of the college scholarships is $1,000.

Duration 1 year.

Deadline July of each year.

[18]
CHEROKEE NATION HIGHER EDUCATION UNDERGRADUATE GRANT PROGRAM

Cherokee Nation of Oklahoma
Attn: Higher Education Program
P.O. Box 948
Tahlequah, OK 74465
(918) 456-0671   (800) 256-0671

Purpose To provide financial assistance for postsecondary education to undergraduate students who belong to the Cherokee Nation of Oklahoma.

Eligibility High school graduates who are members of the Cherokee Nation of Oklahoma or the United Keetoowah Band of Cherokee Indians are eligible to apply if they are enrolled or planning to enroll in a fully accredited postsecondary institution and can demonstrate financial need. Applicants must be studying or planning to study for an associate of arts, associate of science, or baccalaureate degree; study for applied science certificates or vocational/technical training is not funded. Applicants must also apply for financial aid at the institution they attend, and and must also be eligible to receive federal Pell grants.

Financial data The amount awarded varies, depending upon the educational requirements and financial needs of the recipient. These grants are intended only to supplement the federal aid package.

Duration 1 year; may be renewed.

Number awarded Approximately 450 to 500 students can be supported each year.

Deadline March of each year.

[19]
CHEYENNE AND ARAPAHO FEDERAL AID GRANTS

Cheyenne and Arapaho Tribes of Oklahoma
Attn: Department of Education
P.O. Box 38
Concho, OK 73022
(405) 262-0345   (800) 247-4612
Fax: (405) 262-0745

Purpose To provide financial assistance to Cheyenne-Arapaho tribal members who are interested in pursuing postsecondary education.

Eligibility To be eligible, applicants must be at least one-quarter degree of Cheyenne-Arapaho Indian, high school graduates (or the equivalent), approved for admission by a college or university, and in financial need. Applicants may either be enrolled or planning to enroll in a postsecondary school. The vast majority of students assisted under this program are at the undergraduate level, although graduate and/or married students are eligible for consideration and assistance. Summer and part-time students may apply as well, as long as application is made well in advance of enrollment and is accompanied by an official need evaluation.

Financial data The amount of the award depends on the need of the applicant. In addition, Merit Scholars who earn a grade point average of 3.0 to 3.49 during a semester receive an incen-

tive award of $75, Outstanding Scholars who earn a grade point average of at least 3.5 during a semester receive an incentive award of $150, graduate students who earn at least a 3.5 grade point average receive $250, students who complete an associate's degree receive $75, and students who complete a baccalaureate degree receive $150.

Duration 1 year; renewable.

Number awarded 40 to 80 each year.

Deadline May of each year for fall semester; October for spring semester; and March for summer session.

[20]
CHIEF MANUELITO SCHOLARSHIP PROGRAM

Navajo Nation
Attn: Scholarship and Financial Assistance Program
P.O. Drawer 1870
Window Rock, AZ 86515-1870
(520) 871-7640   (800) 243-2956

Purpose To provide financial assistance to academically superior members of the Navajo Nation who are interested in pursuing undergraduate education.

Eligibility Enrolled members of the Navajo Nation are eligible to apply if they are graduating high school seniors planning to attend an accredited college or university. Selection is based solely upon college entrance test scores and high school grade point average. Applicants must have the following minimum combinations of ACT score and GPA: 20 and 3.6, 21 and 3.5, 22 and 3.4, 23 and 3.3, 24 and 3.2, 25 and 3.1, or 26 and 3.0.

Financial data The amount awarded varies.

Duration 1 year.

Deadline April of each year.

[21]
CHOCTAW NATION HIGHER EDUCATION PROGRAM

Choctaw Nation
Attn: Higher Education Department
P.O. Drawer 1210
Durant, OK 74702-1210
(405) 924-8280   (800) 522-6170 (within OK)

Purpose To provide financial assistance to Choctaw Indians who are interested in pursuing postsecondary education.

Eligibility Applicants must be at least one-quarter Choctaw or mixed with another federally recognized tribe to equal one-quarter Indian blood. They must be high school seniors or graduates who are interested in going on to college. Graduate students may receive assistance if funds are available.

Financial data Funds will cover the unmet need, up to $1,600 per year; for students attending a private college or university or a school outside of Oklahoma, the Choctaw Nation will fund 50 percent of the unmet need, up to the maximum of $1,600 per year.

Duration 1 year; may be renewed for up to 4 additional years as long as the recipient enrolls in at least 12 hours per semester with a minimum grade point average of 2.0.

Limitations Students must be working on a college degree.

Number awarded Varies each year.

Deadline March of each year.

[22]
COLORADO SOCIETY OF CPAS ETHNIC DIVERSITY SCHOLARSHIPS

Colorado Society of Certified Public Accountants
Attn: Educational Foundation
7979 East Tufts Avenue, Suite 500
Denver, CO 80237-2843
(303) 773-2877   (800) 523-9082

Purpose To provide financial assistance to minority students in Colorado who are studying accounting.

Eligibility This program is open to African American, Hispanic, Asian American, and Native American Indian students planning to major in accounting at a college or university in Colorado at the associate, baccalaureate, or graduate level. Applicants must have a grade point average of at least 3.0. Selection is based on grade point average and financial need.

Financial data The stipend is $750.

Duration 1 year; nonrenewable.

Number awarded 2 each year.

Deadline February of each year.

[23]
CONTINENTAL SOCIETY, DAUGHTERS OF INDIAN WARS SCHOLARSHIP

Continental Society, Daughters of Indian Wars
Attn: Scholarship Chair
206 Springdale Drive
LaGrange, GA 30240

Purpose To provide financial assistance to Native American college students who are interested in preparing for a career in education.

Eligibility Applicants must be certified tribal members of a federally recognized tribe, plan to prepare for a career in education or the social services, plan to work on a reservation, be a junior at an accredited college, have earned at least a 3.0 grade point average, and carry at least 10 quarter hours or 8 semester hours. Selection is based primarily on academic achievement and commitment to the field of study; financial need is not necessary but is considered.

Financial data The stipend is $500.

Duration 1 year; may be renewed.

Number awarded 1 each year.

Deadline June of each year.

[24]
CREEK NATION HIGHER EDUCATION UNDERGRADUATE GRANT PROGRAM

Creek Nation of Oklahoma
Attn: Higher Education Program
P.O. Box 580
Okmulgee, OK 74447
(918) 756-8700

Purpose To provide educational grants to aid Creek undergraduate students who are interested in pursuing postsecondary studies.

Eligibility Eligible to apply are Creek students of any degree of Indian blood who are attending or plan to attend an accredited institution of higher learning. Financial need must be demonstrated.

Financial data The amount awarded varies, up to a maximum of $2,000 per year. The exact amount depends upon the financial needs of the recipient. Full-time students may use these funds to pay for tuition and fees, books and supplies, room and board, transportation, and personal expenses (including medical and child care). Part-time students (less than 12 credits) may use their funds for tuition, fees, and books, not to exceed the in-state cost at a 2- or 4-year college or university.

Duration 1 year; may be renewed for a maximum of 10 semesters of funding as long as the recipient enrolls in at least 15 hours per term and maintains a minimum grade point average of 2.0.

Special features The Creek Nation of Oklahoma administers the Higher Education Program. This program expends funds appropriated by Congress for the education of Indian students.

Limitations Recipients who withdraw from school are suspended until they have financed themselves for 1 full semester and passed 12 credit hours with at least a grade point average of 2.0.

Number awarded Varies each year.

Deadline May of each year.

[25]
CULTURALLY DIVERSE INSTITUTIONS UNDERGRADUATE STUDENT FELLOWSHIPS

Environmental Protection Agency
Attn: Office of Research and Development
National Center for Environmental Research and Quality
   Assurance
401 M Street, S.W.
Washington, DC 20460
(800) 490-9194

Purpose To provide financial assistance to students in culturally diverse 4-year colleges who are interested in majoring in fields related to the environment.

Eligibility Applicants for this program must be U.S. citizens or permanent residents who are enrolled full time with a minimum grade point average of 3.0 in a 4-year accredited institution that meets the definition of the Environmental Protection Agency (EPA) as a culturally diverse institution: Historically Black Colleges and Universities (HBCUs), members of the Hispanic Association of Colleges and Universities (HACU), and members of the American Indian Consortium for Higher Education (AICHE). Students must be majoring in environmental science, physical sciences, biological sciences, computer science, environmental health, social sciences, mathematics, or engineering. They must be available to work as interns at an EPA facility during the summer between their junior and senior years.

Financial data The fellowship provides payment of tuition and fees, an annual book allowance of $250, and an annual stipend of $1,125. During the summer internship, students receive up to $600 in relocation support and up to $5,000 as a stipend to cover living expenses.

Duration 2 years: the final 2 years of baccalaureate study, including 12 weeks during the summer between those years.

Special features This program began in 1982.

Number awarded Approximately 25 each year.

Deadline February of each year.

[26]
DEPARTMENT OF ENERGY MINORITY TECHNICAL EDUCATION PROGRAM

Department of Energy
Attn: Office of Economic Impact and Diversity
Forrestal Building, Room 5B-110, ED-2
1000 Independence Avenue, S.W.
Washington, DC 20585
(202) 586-5876

Purpose To provide financial support to programs for minority students who are interested in energy-related careers.

Eligibility This program is open to 2-year colleges which have at least 25 percent minority enrollment and a history of graduating students in mathematics, computer sciences, life sciences, or engineering. The institutions may use the funds to enhance their energy-related technical and academic curricula; establish linkages with high schools, other community colleges, and 4-year universities; and provide financial assistance to financially needy honors students pursuing energy-related careers.

Financial data Grants average $50,000 per year.

Duration 1 year; renewable.

Special features Currently, 8 colleges are participating in this program: American Samoa Community College of Pago Pago, American Samoa, for Native Pacific Islanders; Eugenio Maria de Hostos Community College of Bronx, New York, for Puerto Ricans; Fort Peck Community College of Poplar, Montana, for American Indians; Greenville Technical College of Greenville, South Carolina, for African Americans; Houston Community College, of Houston, Texas, for Mexican Americans; Luna Vocational Technical Institute of Las Vegas, New Mexico, for Mexican Americans and American Indians; Maui Community College of Kahului, Hawaii, for Asian Americans, Native Hawaiians, and Native Pacific Islanders; and Salish Kootenai College of Pablo, Montana, for American Indians. Students interested in participating in this program should first contact the address above to obtain names, addresses, and telephone numbers of administrators at each of the participating colleges, and then contact the college.

Deadline Deadline dates vary; contact the college for further information.

[27]
EIGHT NORTHERN INDIAN PUEBLO COUNCIL SCHOLARSHIP PROGRAM

Eight Northern Indian Pueblo Council, Inc.
Attn: Scholarship Program
P.O. Box 969
San Juan Pueblo, NM 87566
(505) 753-1808   (800) 750-1808

Purpose To provide financial assistance for the postsecondary education of members of the Eight Northern Indian Pueblos.

Eligibility Enrolled members of the Eight Northern Indian Pueblos (Taos, Tesuque, San Ildefonso, Nambe, Santa Clara, Pojoaque, Picuris, and San Juan) are eligible to apply if they are enrolled or planning to enroll in an undergraduate or graduate course of study. Applicants must have at least a 2.0 grade point average. They may major in any subject area. Financial need is considered in determining the amount of the award.

Financial data The amount awarded varies, depending upon the recipient's financial need. Generally, scholarships range between $1,000 and $1,800 per year.

Duration 1 year; may be renewed for up to 4 additional years.

Limitations Recipients must enroll in school on a full-time basis.

Number awarded Varies each year.

Deadline February for the fall term; October for the spring term.

[28]
EISENHOWER TRIBAL COLLEGES INITIATIVES

Department of Transportation
Attn: Federal Highway Administration
National Highway Institute
901 North Stuart Street, Suite 300
Arlington, VA 22203
(703) 235-0538   Fax: (703) 235-0593

Purpose To provide financial assistance for Native American students and faculty in transportation-related fields at tribal colleges.

Eligibility This program identifies transportation activities at tribal colleges in order to provide fellowships to Native American students and faculty for further study.

Financial data Fellows receive the full cost of education, including tuition and fees.

Duration 1 year.

Number awarded Varies each year.

Deadline February of each year.

[29]
EMERGENCY AID AND HEALTH PROFESSIONS SCHOLARSHIP PROGRAM

Association on American Indian Affairs, Inc.
Attn: Scholarship Coordinator
P.O. Box 268
Sisseton, SD 57262
(605) 698-3998

Purpose To provide emergency financial aid to Native Americans pursuing college-level education.

Eligibility Applicants must be American Indians or Alaskan Natives who are currently enrolled as full-time undergraduates in an institution of higher education and facing an educationally related emergency. Applications must be accompanied by a certificate of degree of Indian blood, a 1- to 2-page essay describing the specific nature of the emergency need, a budget of educational costs and resources, and the most recent copy of a transcript.

Financial data The grants range between $50 and $300, depending on need and the availability of funds.

Limitations Because of the emergency nature of these funds, scholarships cannot be granted in advance. Students must apply after they begin college classes.

Number awarded Varies each year.

Deadline Requests may be submitted any time after the applicant begins college or college-level technical/vocational classes.

[30]
EPA TRIBAL LANDS ENVIRONMENTAL SCIENCE SCHOLARSHIP

American Indian Science and Engineering Society
Attn: Scholarship Department
5661 Airport Boulevard
Boulder, CO 80301
(303) 939-0023   E-mail: ascholar@spot.colorado.edu

Purpose To provide financial assistance to outstanding college students interested in studying environmental or related sciences.
Eligibility Applicants must be full-time juniors, seniors, or graduate students with a minimum grade point average of 2.5 majoring in biochemistry, biology, chemical engineering, chemistry, environmental economics, environmental science, entomology, hydrology, or related environmental disciplines. A certificate of Indian blood is not required, but applications must include a 250-word essay on the candidate's personal commitment to environmental protection on tribal lands and a brief statement explaining how and when knowledge of tribal culture was acquired.
Financial data The award is $4,000 per year.
Duration 1 year; renewable upon reapplication.
Special features Funds for the program are provided by the Environmental Protection Agency. The program is administered by the American Indian Science and Engineering Society.
Deadline June of each year.

[31]
FALMOUTH INSTITUTE SCHOLARSHIP

Falmouth Institute, Inc.
Attn: Scholarship Administrator
3918 Prosperity Avenue, Suite 302
Fairfax, VA 22031
(703) 641-9100   Fax: (703) 641-1558

Purpose To provide financial assistance for postsecondary education to American Indian high school seniors.
Eligibility Applicants must be American Indian high school students planning to attend a 2-year or 4-year accredited school of higher education. Proof of tribal enrollment and high school transcripts are required. Selection is based on scholastic achievement and financial need.
Financial data The stipend is $1,000.
Duration 1 year.
Number awarded 1 each year.
Deadline April of each year.

[32]
FLORIDA EMPLOYMENT AND TRAINING PROGRAM

Florida Governor's Council on Indian Affairs
P.O. Box 10449
Tallahassee, FL 32302-2449
(800) 322-9186

Purpose To provide financial assistance to needy Native Americans in Florida or Georgia who are interested in obtaining additional education or training.
Eligibility Unemployed, underemployed, or economically disadvantaged Native Americans (Native Hawaiians, Alaskan Natives, American Indians) are eligible to apply for this support. The Florida Governor's Council on Indian Affairs provides this service for 63 of the 67 counties in Florida and all of the state of Georgia.

Financial data Tuition and other services are offered to recipients.
Duration Up to 1 year.
Special features Funds may be used for a vocational-technical degree, an A.A. or Associate Degree, GED preparation, or adult education.
Number awarded Varies each year.

[33]
FOND DU LAC CRITICAL PROFESSIONS PROGRAM

Fond du Lac Tribal Council
Attn: Bonnie Wallace
105 University Road
Cloquet, MN 55720
(218) 879-4691   (800) 365-1613
Fax: (218) 879-7839

Purpose To provide financial assistance to Indian students who wish to pursue a course of study leading to an undergraduate or graduate degree in business administration, natural resources or forestry, computer programming, urban or rural planning, or elementary or secondary school teaching.
Eligibility Applicants must be enrolled members of the Fond du Lac Tribal Council of the Minnesota Chippewa Tribe, and full-time students. Applicants are evaluated on academic record, leadership ability, and commitment.
Financial data Award varies; graduate students receive $650 per month (plus $90 per dependent) and undergraduate students receive $450 per month (plus $90 per dependent). Funds are disbursed directly to the recipient's institution of higher education.
Duration 1 quarter/semester; renewable if the applicant remains a full-time student and is in good standing (good standing means at least a 2.5 cumulative grade point average for undergraduate work or a 3.0 for graduate work). Financial need must be demonstrated.
Limitations Applicants must demonstrate a commitment to work for a tribal government or in an Indian community for 2 years after graduation.
Number awarded Varies each year.
Deadline Applications are accepted at any time.

[34]
FOND DU LAC SCHOLARSHIP PROGRAM

Fond du Lac Tribal Council
Attn: Bonnie Wallace
105 University Road
Cloquet, MN 55720
(218) 879-4691   (800) 365-1613
Fax: (218) 879-7839

Purpose To provide financial assistance to Minnesota Chippewa Tribe high school graduates who are interested in postsecondary education.
Eligibility Applicants must be at least one-quarter Indian ancestry, residents of Minnesota for at least 1 year, high school graduates or the equivalent, and enrolled members of the Fond du Lac Tribal Council of the Minnesota Chippewa Tribe or eligible for enrollment. Financial need is required.
Financial data Up to $3,000 per year, depending on need.
Duration 1 year; may be renewed.
Special features Applicants for this program must also apply for financial aid administered by their institution and any other aid for which they may be eligible (e.g., work-study, Social Security,

veteran's benefits). Recipients may attend a college, university, or vocational school.

Number awarded Varies each year.

Deadline For vocational school students, at least 8 weeks before school starts; for college or university students, June of each year.

[35]
GRAND PORTAGE CRITICAL PROFESSIONS PROGRAM

Grand Portage Tribal Council
Attn: Rosie Novitsky
P.O. Box 428
Grand Portage, MN 55605
(218) 475-0121   Fax: (218) 475-2455

Purpose To provide financial assistance to Indian students who wish to pursue a course of study leading to an undergraduate or graduate degree in business administration, natural resources or forestry, computer programming, urban or rural planning, or elementary or secondary school teaching.

Eligibility Applicants must be enrolled members of the Grand Portage Tribal Council of the Minnesota Chippewa Tribe, and full-time students. Applicants are evaluated on academic record, leadership ability, and commitment.

Financial data Award varies; graduate students receive $650 per month (plus $90 per dependent) and undergraduate students receive $450 per month (plus $90 per dependent). Funds are disbursed directly to the recipient's institution of higher education.

Duration 1 quarter/semester; renewable if the applicant remains a full-time student and is in good standing (good standing means at least a 2.5 cumulative grade point average for undergraduate work or a 3.0 for graduate work). Financial need must be demonstrated.

Limitations Applicants must demonstrate a commitment to work for a tribal government or in an Indian community for 2 years after graduation.

Number awarded Varies each year.

Deadline Applications are accepted at any time.

[36]
GRAND PORTAGE SCHOLARSHIP PROGRAM

Grand Portage Tribal Council
Attn: Rosie Novitsky
P.O. Box 428
Grand Portage, MN 55605
(218) 475-0121   Fax: (218) 475-2455

Purpose To provide financial assistance to Minnesota Chippewa Tribe high school graduates who are interested in postsecondary education.

Eligibility Applicants must be at least one-quarter Indian ancestry, residents of Minnesota for at least 1 year, high school graduates or the equivalent, and enrolled members of the Grand Portage Tribal Council of the Minnesota Chippewa Tribe or eligible for enrollment. Financial need is required.

Financial data Up to $3,000 per year, depending on need.

Duration 1 year; may be renewed.

Special features Applicants for this program must also apply for financial aid administered by their institution and any other aid for which they may be eligible (e.g., work-study, Social Security, veteran's benefits). Recipients may attend a college, university, or vocational school.

Number awarded Varies each year.

Deadline For vocational school students, at least 8 weeks before school starts; for college or university students, June of each year.

[37]
HEADLANDS INDIAN HEALTH CAREERS PARTICIPANT GRANTS

University of Oklahoma Health Sciences Center
Basic Sciences Education Building, Room 200
P.O. Box 26901
Oklahoma City, OK 73190-3040
(405) 271-2250   Fax: (405) 271-2254

Purpose To increase the science and mathematics background and communication skills of Native American students who are interested in preparing for careers as health professionals.

Eligibility Native American students interested in health careers are eligible to apply for this program if they are presently in their senior year of high school or freshmen year of college and have completed at least 2 years of algebra and 2 science courses with a minimum grade point average of 2.5. Selection is based on expressed plans to enter the health sciences, academic performance in science and mathematics, and motivation and aptitude for pursuing a health science career.

Financial data Each participant is provided with free room, board, and tuition during the program, as well as round-trip airfare and a stipend of $500.

Duration 8 weeks during the summer.

Special features The Headlands program is held on the campus of the University of Oklahoma in Norman. The program provides a science and mathematics enrichment and reinforcement program, consisting of mini-block courses in biology, chemistry, physics, calculus, writing, and other communication skills. Courses are designed to increase the students' background and skills so they are better prepared for required college-level math and science course work in pre-health programs.

Limitations High school seniors must provide evidence of acceptance into college.

Number awarded Varies; approximately 30 each year.

Deadline March of each year.

[38]
HEALTH CAREERS OPPORTUNITY PROGRAM GRANTS

Health Resources and Services Administration
Attn: Bureau of Health Professions
Division of Disadvantaged Assistance
Parklawn Building, Room 8A09
5600 Fishers Lane
Rockville, MD 20857
(301) 443-4493   Fax: (301) 443-6343
E-mail: bbrooks@hrsa.ssw.dhhs.gov

Purpose To provide financial support for education in health professions to students from disadvantaged backgrounds.

Eligibility This program is open to schools of allopathic medicine, osteopathic medicine, public health, dentistry, veterinary medicine, optometry, pharmacy, allied health, chiropractic and podiatric medicine, and public and nonprofit private schools which offer graduate programs in clinical psychology. Health professions schools are eligible if they identify a cohort of at least 7 disadvantaged students who applied but were not accepted to a health professions school; allied health schools are eligible if they identify a cohort of at least 5 disadvantaged students who have completed an undergraduate degree with a significant science focus and made a late decision to enter an allied health professions school and are in pursuit of a baccalaureate level degree in physical therapy, physician assistant, respiratory therapy, medical technology, or occupational therapy. Applicants must provide the designated students with a program of rigorous science and other education experiences and then admit the students who successfully complete the program or arrange for their admission to another health professions or allied health school. Recipient schools must also provide the students with a prematriculation summer program to ease their transition into the health professions or allied health school, and with counseling and advice on financial aid to assist them to complete successfully their education. Individuals from a disadvantaged background are those who come from an environment that has inhibited them from obtaining the knowledge, skill, and abilities to enroll in and graduate from a health professions school or allied health program, or who come from a low-income family (ranging from an annual income below $10,200 for a family of 1 to $26,700 for a family of 6).

Financial data Approximately $30.1 million is available for this program each year, of which $18.5 million is for continuing grants and $11.6 million is available for new grants, averaging $199,000 each. Of the appropriated funds each year, 20 percent must be obligated for stipends to disadvantaged students of exceptional financial need who are students at schools of allopathic medicine, osteopathic medicine, or dentistry; 10 percent must be obligated to community-based programs (including Indian tribes and Alaska Native villages); and 70 percent must be obligated for grants and contracts to institutions of higher education. Students receive a stipend during their participation in the program.

Duration Grants to institutions are up to 3 years; for students, the program is 1 year, including 6 to 8 weeks in the summer.

Number awarded Approximately 58 new projects are funded each year.

Deadline February of each year.

[39]
HEALTH PROFESSIONS PREGRADUATE SCHOLARSHIP PROGRAM

Indian Health Service
Attn: Scholarship Program
Twinbrook Metro Plaza, Suite 100
12300 Twinbrook Parkway
Rockville, MD 20852
(301) 443-6197   Fax: (301) 443-6048

Purpose To provide financial support for American Indian students interested in pursuing postsecondary education in pre-medicine or pre-dentistry.

Eligibility Applicants must be American Indians or Alaska Natives; be high school graduates or the equivalent; have the capacity to complete a health professions course of study; and be enrolled or accepted for enrollment in a baccalaureate degree program for pre-medicine or pre-dentistry. Applicants must provide verification from a school official (preferably for an undergraduate curriculum leading to a bachelor's degree in premedicine and represent 12 credit hours per semester/quarter/term, or the equivalent of full-time study at the applicant's school). Selection is based on academic performance, work experience and community background, faculty/employer recommendations, and applicant's reasons for seeking the scholarship. Recipients must

intend to serve Indian people upon completion of professional health care education as a health care provider in the discipline for which the student is enrolled at the pregraduate level.

Financial data Awards provide for payment of a monthly stipend to cover living expenses including room and board, tuition and required fees, and all other reasonable educational expenses; the total award is approximately $15,000 per year. Recent annual funding available for this and the Health Professions Preparatory Scholarship Program was approximately $1,380,000 for continuation awards and $2,190,000 for new awards.

Duration 1 year; may be renewed for up to 3 additional years.

Number awarded Varies; in a recent year, 238 awards (of which 92 were continuing) were made under this and the Health Professions Preparatory Scholarship Program.

Deadline March of each year.

[40]
HEALTH PROFESSIONS PREPARATORY SCHOLARSHIP PROGRAM

Indian Health Service
Attn: Scholarship Program
Twinbrook Metro Plaza, Suite 100
12300 Twinbrook Parkway
Rockville, MD 20852
(301) 443-6197   Fax: (301) 443-6048

Purpose To provide financial assistance to Native American students who need compensatory preprofessional education to qualify for enrollment in a health professions school.

Eligibility Applicants must be American Indians or Alaska Natives; be high school graduates or the equivalent; have the capacity to complete a health professions course of study; and be enrolled or accepted for enrollment in a compensatory or preprofessional general education course or curriculum. The qualifying fields of study include pre-medical technology, pre-dietetics, pre-nursing, pre-pharmacy, pre-physical therapy, and pre-social work. Recipients must intend to serve Indian people upon completion of professional health care education as a health care provider in the discipline for which the student is enrolled at the pregraduate level.

Financial data Awards provide for payment of a monthly stipend to cover living expenses including room and board, tuition and required fees, and all other reasonable educational expenses; the total award is approximately $15,000 per year. Recent annual funding available for this and the Health Professions Pregraduate Scholarship Program was approximately $1,380,000 for continuation awards and $2,190,000 for new awards.

Duration 1 year; renewable.

Number awarded Varies; in a recent year, 238 awards (of which 92 were continuing) were made under this and the Health Professions Pregraduate Scholarship Program.

Deadline March of each year.

[41]
HEALTH PROFESSIONS RECRUITMENT PROGRAM SUMMER ROTATION

Yakama Indian Nation
Attn: Higher Education Programs
Department of Human Services
P.O. Box 151
Toppenish, WA 98948
(509) 865-5121, ext. 533   (800) 543-2802
Fax: (509) 865-6994

Purpose To provide work experience to American Indians who are interested in preparing for a career in the health sciences.

Eligibility This program is open to enrolled members of a federally recognized tribe who live on or near the Yakama Indian Reservation. They may be high school seniors or college students. They must be interested in preparing for a career in the health field.

Financial data The participants receive a bi-weekly stipend.

Duration Summer months.

Special features This program is designed to give participants an opportunity to observe professional health care providers at work. The students work with health professionals at a local hospital and in a clinic. In addition, participants receive assistance with college applications, personal counseling, academic advising, career counseling, and tutorial services.

Number awarded Varies each year.

[42]
HEALTH PROFESSIONS SCHOLARSHIP PROGRAM

Indian Health Service
Attn: Scholarship Program
Twinbrook Metro Plaza, Suite 100
12300 Twinbrook Parkway
Rockville, MD 20852
(301) 443-6197   Fax: (301) 443-6048

Purpose To provide financial support to students enrolled in health professions and allied health professions programs.

Eligibility Applicants must be at least high school graduates and be enrolled in a full-time study program leading to a degree in a health-related professions school within the United States. Even though non-Indian students may apply for this program, the Indian Health Care Improvement Act (P.L. 94-437) requires that priority for the awards be given to Indian and Native Alaskan applicants. Both the number of Indian applicants and the level of appropriations limit the availability of scholarship awards to non-Indians. Qualifying fields of study include associate degree nurse, chemical dependency counseling, clinical psychology (Ph.D. only), computer science (B.S.), dentistry, dietician (B.S.), civil engineering (B.S.), health education (master's only), health records, medical technology (B.S.), medical social work (master's only), allopathic and osteopathic medicine, nurse practitioner, nurse midwife, B.S. nurse, M.S. nurse, optometry, para-optometric, pharmacy (B.S.), physician assistant (B.S.), physical therapy, podiatry (D.P.M.), public health (M.P.H. only), public health nutrition (master's only), radiologic therapy (associate and B.S.), respiratory therapy (associate), and sonography.

Financial data Awards provide for payment of a monthly stipend to cover living expenses, including room and board, tuition and required fees, and all other reasonable educational expenses; the total award is approximately $18,000. In a recent year, approximately $6,300,000 was available for continuation awards and $1,860,751 for new awards.

Duration 1 year; may be renewed for up to 3 additional years.

Limitations Upon completion of their program of study, recipients are required to provide payback service of 1 year for each year of scholarship support at the Indian Health Service, 1 of 638 tribal health programs, an urban health program, or in private practice serving a substantial number of Indians.

Number awarded Varies; In a recent year, 350 continuing and 103 new awards were provided.

Deadline April of each year.

[43]
HELEN GOUGH SCHOLARSHIP

Helen Gough Scholarship Foundation
c/o Karen Colbenson, Chair
P.O. Box 69
Stanley, ND 58784-0069
(701) 628-2955   Fax: (701) 628-3975

Purpose To provide financial assistance for educational purposes to members of the Three Affiliated Tribes of the Fort Berthold Reservation in North Dakota.

Eligibility Applicants must be enrolled members of the Three Affiliated Tribes of the Fort Berthold Reservation in North Dakota, interested in education beyond the high school level, 18 years of age or older, and full-time undergraduate or graduate students in good academic standing.

Financial data The amount awarded varies, depending upon the funds available; generally, the stipend does not exceed $500.

Duration 1 quarter, 1 semester, or 1 year; renewable.

Number awarded Varies each year depending upon the availability of funds; in recent years, approximately 25 awards have been made.

Deadline May of each year.

[44]
HOPI EDUCATIONAL ENRICHMENT GRANT

Hopi Tribe
Attn: Education Director
P.O. Box 123
Kykotsmovi, AZ 86039
(520) 734-2441   (800) 762-9630

Purpose To provide financial assistance to Hopi students who have an opportunity to participate in a special leadership activity or event.

Eligibility This program is open to Hopi Indians (enrolled tribal members) in grades 4 through college. They must have an opportunity to participate in a special activity or event that enhances leadership/personal skills or provides educational or pre-college experiences.

Financial data The amount awarded varies, depending upon the needs of the recipient.

Special features Examples of appropriate activities or events include: math camps, pre-college orientations, and conferences.

Deadline Applications may be submitted at any time.

Number awarded Varies each year.

[45]
HOPI PRIVATE HIGH SCHOOL SCHOLARSHIP
Hopi Tribe
Attn: Education Director
P.O. Box 123
Kykotskmovi, AZ 86039
(520) 734-2441   (800) 762-9630

Purpose To provide financial assistance to students of Hopi Indians who are interested in attending a private high school.

Eligibility Applicants must be an enrolled member of the Hopi Tribe. They must meet the following grade point averages: entering freshmen must have an 8th grade average of 3.5; continuing high school students must have at least a 3.25 average. Selection is based on academic ability.

Financial data The stipend is $1,000 per semester.

Duration 1 year; may be renewed.

Limitations Recipients must attend an accredited private high school.

Number awarded 2 each year.

[46]
HOPI SCHOLARSHIP
Hopi Tribe
Attn: Education Director
P.O. Box 123
Kykotskmovi, AZ 86039
(520) 734-2441   (800) 762-9630

Purpose To provide financial assistance to students of Hopi ancestry who are pursuing an undergraduate, graduate, or postgraduate degree.

Eligibility This program is open to students who are pursuing an associate, baccalaureate, graduate, or postgraduate degree. Applicants must be an enrolled member of the Hopi Tribe. Entering freshmen must be in the top 10 percent of their graduating class or score at least 21 on the ACT or score at least 930 on the SAT. Undergraduate students must have at least a 3.0 grade point average. Graduate, postgraduate, and professional students must have at least a 3.2 grade point average for all graduate course work. Selection is based on academic merit.

Financial data The stipend is $1,000 per semester.

Duration 1 year; may be renewed.

Limitations Recipients must attend school on a full-time basis.

Number awarded Varies each year.

[47]
HOPI SUPPLEMENTAL GRANT
Hopi Tribe
Attn: Education Director
P.O. Box 123
Kykotskmovi, AZ 86039
(520) 734-2441   (800) 762-9630

Purpose To provide financial assistance to students of Hopi ancestry who are pursuing an undergraduate, graduate, or postgraduate degree.

Eligibility This program is open to students who are pursuing an associate, baccalaureate, graduate, or postgraduate degree. Applicants must be an enrolled member of the Hopi Tribe. They must be able to demonstrate financial need. Entering freshmen must have a 2.0 high school grade point average or a minimum composite score of 45 percent on the GED exam. Continuing stu-

dents must have at least a 2.0 grade point average for all college work.

Financial data Up to $4,000 per semester and up to $2,750 for the summer session.

Duration 1 year; may be renewed.

Special features This grant is awarded as a secondary source of financial aid to eligible students.

Limitations Recipients must attend school on a full-time basis.

Number awarded Varies each year.

[48]
HOPI TRIBAL PRIORITY SCHOLARSHIP
Hopi Tribe
Attn: Education Director
P.O. Box 123
Kykotskmovi, AZ 86039
(520) 734-2441   (800) 762-9630

Purpose To encourage Hopi students to get a degree in an area of interest to the Hopi Tribe.

Eligibility This program is open to enrolled members of the Hopi tribe. They must be college juniors or seniors or graduate students. Their degree must be in a subject area that is of priority interest to the Hopi Tribe. These areas include: law, natural resources, education, medicine, health, engineering, or business. This is a highly competitive scholarship. Selection is based on academic merit and the likelihood that the applicants will use their training and expertise to tribal goals and objectives.

Financial data The amount awarded varies, depending upon the needs of the recipient.

Duration 1 year; may be renewed.

Limitations Recipients must attend school on a full-time basis.

Number awarded Varies each year.

[49]
HOPI TUITION/BOOK SCHOLARSHIP
Hopi Tribe
Attn: Education Director
P.O. Box 123
Kykotskmovi, AZ 86039
(520) 734-2441   (800) 762-9630

Purpose To provide financial assistance to students of Hopi ancestry who are pursuing an undergraduate, graduate, or postgraduate degree.

Eligibility This program is open to students who are pursuing an associate, baccalaureate, graduate, or postgraduate degree. Applicants must be an enrolled member of the Hopi Tribe. They must be pursuing a postsecondary degree for at least 1 of the following reasons: personal growth, career enhancement, career change, and/or continuing education. Both full- and part-time students may apply. Financial need is not required, but students must have applied for federal aid before applying for this award.

Financial data The scholarship covers the cost of tuition/fees and books.

Duration 1 year; may be renewed.

Number awarded Varies each year.

[50]
HUALAPAI EMPLOYMENT ASSISTANCE PROGRAM

Hualapai Tribal Council
Attn: Education Director
P.O. Box 179
Peach Springs, AZ 86434-0179
(602) 769-2216

Purpose To provide financial assistance to Hualapai Tribe Indians who are interested in obtaining a diploma, certificate, or associate of arts degree at a vocational/technical/junior college.

Eligibility Enrolled members of the Hualapai Tribe aged 18 and older are eligible to apply if they have graduated from high school (or earned the GED) and plan to attend a junior/technical/community college on a full-time basis (at least 12 credit hours).

Financial data A total of $11,000 is distributed each year.

Duration 1 year; may be renewed to a maximum of 24 months for vocational/occupation training or to a maximum of 36 months for registered nurse training.

Number awarded Limited number each year.

Deadline Applications must be submitted at least 2 weeks before each term begins.

[51]
HUALAPAI HIGHER EDUCATION GRANTS

Hualapai Tribal Council
Attn: Education Director
P.O. Box 179
Peach Springs, AZ 86434-0179
(602) 769-2216

Purpose To provide financial assistance for members of the Hualapai Tribe who are interested in pursuing undergraduate education.

Eligibility Enrolled members of the Hualapai Tribe are eligible to apply if they have graduated from high school (or earned the GED) and plan to attend college full time (at least 12 credit hours per term). Grants are awarded in the following priority order: 1) continuing students in good standing; 2) incoming freshmen; 3) adults who have previously attended or taken college classes; 4) adults never attending college; 5) graduate students; 6) repeating or probationary students.

Financial data Up to $5,000 per year.

Duration 1 year; may be renewed.

Special features Recipients may pursue any area of study.

Number awarded Varies each year.

Deadline Applications must be submitted at least 4 weeks before each term.

[52]
INCENTIVE GRANTS PROGRAM

National Action Council for Minorities in Engineering
3 West 35th Street
New York, NY 10001-2281
(212) 279-2626   Fax: (212) 629-5178

Purpose To provide funding to universities for scholarships to minority students in engineering.

Eligibility Colleges and universities with engineering curricula may submit requests for scholarship funds from this Incentive Grants Program of the National Action Council for Minorities in Engineering (NACME). To be eligible, the schools must have 1 or more programs approved by the Accreditation Board for Engineering Technology, have a minimum of 100 minority engineering majors or at least a 5 percent minority representation in engineering, and be able to show progress in retaining and graduating minority engineers. Students selected for the awards by the recipient school must be African Americans, Hispanics, or American Indians; U.S. citizens or permanent residents; enrolled full-time in an undergraduate engineering program; in need of financial assistance; and entering freshman or transfer students to an engineering program with at least a 2.5 grade point average.

Financial data The grant to the recipient school is determined by the percentage of upper-division minority enrollment and the number of minority engineering graduates produced by that institution. In general, NACME grants to participating schools range from $5,000 to $40,000. Recipient schools use NACME funds to award no less than $250 and no more than $2,500 a year to any qualifying minority student. In all, NACME allocates nearly $2 million per year in grants to be distributed by these schools.

Duration 1 year; may be renewed up to 3 additional years.

Special features Students interested in this program should contact the address above for a list of participating schools. NACME was formed in 1980 by the consolidation of the Minority Engineering Education Effort, the National Fund for Minority Engineering Students, and some of the functions of the Committee on Minorities in Engineering.

Number awarded In a recent year, 66 institutions received these grants for distribution to 1,389 students.

Deadline Varies by participating institution.

[53]
INDIAN FELLOWSHIP PROGRAM

Department of Education
Attn: Office of Elementary and Secondary Education
Office of Indian Education
Portals Building, Room 4300
600 Independence Avenue, S.W.
Washington, DC 20202-6335
(202) 260-1683   E-mail: Indian_Fellowships@ed.gov

Purpose To provide financial assistance to graduate students and selected undergraduate students who are Native Americans interested in preparing for careers in medicine, law, engineering, natural resources, business administration, education, psychology, and related fields.

Eligibility American Indian students who are attending or have been accepted for admission at an accredited institution of higher learning and working toward 1) a graduate degree in medicine, law, education, psychology, clinical psychology, or related fields or 2) a graduate or undergraduate degree in natural resources, business administration, engineering, or related fields may apply. All applicants must be U.S. citizens and Indians. By federal government definition, this means that applicants must be 1) a member of a tribe, band, or other organized group of Indians (including those tribes, bands, or groups terminated since 1940 and those recognized by the state in which they reside); 2) a descendant in the first or second degree of any individual described above; 3) considered by the Secretary of the Interior to be an Indian for any purpose or be an Eskimo, Aleut, or other Alaska Native; or 4) a member of an organized Indian group that received a grant under the Indian Education Act of 1988. Selection is based on academic record (60 points), letters of recommendation (15 points), and an essay on career goals, why the chosen field of study will benefit Indian people, life experiences and personal and family expectations that will enhance the applicant's anticipated career accomplishments, and anticipated commitment to providing service to Indian people (25 points).

Financial data Fellowships are intended to provide full financing for a student's educational expenses or to supplement other sources of financial aid.

Duration Up to 2 years for a master's degree; up to 4 years for an undergraduate or doctorate degree. Each year's renewal is dependent upon appropriations from Congress and satisfactory performance by the fellow.

Special features Up to 10 percent of the awards are to persons receiving training in guidance counseling with a specialty in the area of alcohol and substance abuse counseling and education.

Limitations Individuals receiving assistance under this program are required to perform work related to the training received and that benefits Indian people, or repay all or a prorated part of the assistance received. This payback must begin within 6 months from the date of the completion of the training and is equivalent to the total period of time for which training was actually received.

Number awarded Varies; approximately 60 continuation and 550 new awards are made each year.

Deadline January of each year.

[54]
INDIAN NURSE SCHOLARSHIP AWARDS

National Society of the Colonial Dames of America
Attn: National Patriotic Service Committee
c/o Mrs. Leslie N. Boney, Jr.
2305 Gillette Drive
Wilmington, NC 28403
(910) 763-6013

Purpose To provide financial assistance to Native Americans interested in preparing for a career in nursing.

Eligibility To be eligible for this scholarship, candidates must be Native Americans, be high school graduates (or the equivalent), be enrolled full time in an accredited school, be in the nursing program, be within 2 years of completing the course for which the scholarship is being given, have maintained the scholastic average required by their school, be recommended by their counselor or school officer, not be receiving an Indian Health Service Scholarship, have a career goal directly related to the needs of the Indian people, and be in financial need.

Financial data The stipends are $500, $750, or $1,000 per year. Funds are to be used for tuition or fees. The money is sent directly to the recipient's school.

Duration 1 year; those students who continue to meet the eligibility requirements and have been recommended for continuation are given priority consideration for additional periods of support.

Special features This program was established in 1928.

Number awarded A small number each year.

[55]
INTERNATIONAL ORDER OF THE KING'S DAUGHTERS AND SONS NORTH AMERICAN INDIAN SCHOLARSHIP PROGRAM

International Order of the King's Daughters and Sons
c/o Headquarters Office
34 Vincent Avenue
P.O. Box 1017
Chautauqua, NY 14722-1017
(716) 357-4951

Purpose To provide supplemental aid to Native American students interested in pursuing postsecondary education.

Eligibility There are no restrictions as to tribal affiliation or degree of Indian blood. However, applicants or their parents must have a reservation registration and number. Only 1 member of a family is eligible in any 1 year. Selection is based on scholastic standing, demonstrated leadership ability, community service, character, and financial need.

Financial data Grants are intended to provide supplemental aid only and do not exceed $500 each.

Duration 1 year.

Special features Further information is also available from Mrs. Harry E. Stuard, Jr., 5451 Cameo Court, Pleasanton, CA 94588, (510) 847-0105.

Limitations Funds may be used to support vocational, technical, or college training; graduate education is excluded.

Number awarded Approximately 50 each year.

Deadline April of each year.

[56]
JOHNNY STRICKLAND MEMORIAL SCHOLARSHIP

Metrolina Native American Association
2601-A East Seventh Street
Charlotte, NC 28204
(704) 331-4818　　　　　　Fax: (704) 331-9501

Purpose To provide financial assistance to Native Americans in North Carolina who are interested in continuing their college education.

Eligibility Applicants must be Native American enrolled or planning to enroll in a 4-year college or university. They must be enrolled for full-time study.

Financial data The stipend is $500.

Duration 1 year; may be renewed.

Special features This scholarship is named in honor of the Chairman of the Board of the Metrolina Native American Association who died of a heart attack in 1994 at the age of 36.

Number awarded 1 each year.

Deadline April of each year.

[57]
LEECH LAKE CRITICAL PROFESSIONS PROGRAM

Leech Lake Tribal Council
Attn: Carol Jenkins
Route 3, Box 100
Cass Lake, MN 56633
(218) 335-8252　　　　　　(800) 711-0443
Fax: (218) 335-8309

Purpose To provide financial assistance to Indian students who wish to pursue a course of study leading to an undergraduate or graduate degree in business administration, natural resources or forestry, computer programming, urban or rural planning, or elementary or secondary school teaching.

Eligibility Applicants must be enrolled members of the Leech Lake Tribal Council of the Minnesota Chippewa Tribe, and full-time students. Applicants are evaluated on academic record, leadership ability, and commitment.

Financial data Award varies; graduate students receive $650 per month (plus $90 per dependent) and undergraduate students receive $450 per month (plus $90 per dependent). Funds are disbursed directly to the recipient's institution of higher education.

Duration 1 quarter/semester; renewable if the applicant remains a full-time student and is in good standing (good standing means at least a 2.5 cumulative grade point average for undergraduate work or a 3.0 for graduate work). Financial need must be demonstrated.

Limitations Applicants must demonstrate a commitment to work for a tribal government or in an Indian community for 2 years after graduation.

Number awarded Varies each year.

Deadline Applications are accepted at any time.

[58]
LEECH LAKE SCHOLARSHIP PROGRAM

Leech Lake Tribal Council
Attn: Carol Jenkins
Route 3, Box 100
Cass Lake, MN 56633
(218) 335-8252   (800) 711-0443
Fax: (218) 335-8309

Purpose To provide financial assistance to Minnesota Chippewa Tribe high school graduates who are interested in postsecondary education.

Eligibility Applicants must be at least one-quarter Indian ancestry, residents of Minnesota for at least 1 year, high school graduates or the equivalent, and enrolled members of the Leech Lake Tribal Council of the Minnesota Chippewa Tribe or eligible for enrollment. Financial need is required.

Financial data Up to $3,000 per year, depending on need.

Duration 1 year; may be renewed.

Special features Applicants for this program must also apply for financial aid administered by their institution and any other aid for which they may be eligible (e.g., work-study, Social Security, veteran's benefits). Recipients may attend a college, university, or vocational school.

Number awarded Varies each year.

Deadline For vocational school students, at least 8 weeks before school starts; for college or university students, June of each year.

[59]
LOUIE LEFLORE/GRANT FOREMAN SCHOLARSHIPS

Cherokee Nation of Oklahoma
Attn: Higher Education Program
P.O. Box 948
Tahlequah, OK 74465
(918) 456-0671   (800) 256-0671 (within OK)

Purpose To provide financial assistance to Native American high school graduates who are interested in postsecondary education.

Eligibility Applicants must be members of 1 of the Five Civilized Tribes who reside in Oklahoma and in the respective tribal service area. They must be high school graduates, interested in pursuing nursing or other health-related careers, and able to demonstrate financial need.

Financial data The stipend is $650.

Duration 1 year; may not be renewed.

Special features This scholarship is rotated among the Five Tribes: the Cherokee Nation, the Muscogee (Creek) Nation, the Choctaw Nation, the Seminole Nation, and the Chickasaw Nation.

Number awarded 1 each year.

Deadline June of each year.

[60]
MALKI MUSEUM SCHOLARSHIPS

Malki Museum, Inc.
Morongo Indian Reservation
P.O. Box 578
Banning, CA 92220
(909) 849-7289

Purpose To provide financial assistance to California Indians who are interested in pursuing postsecondary education.

Eligibility Students of California Indian ancestry are eligible to apply if they provide 1) proof of enrollment with a southern California Indian tribe or proof of one-quarter Indian blood from a southern California tribe, 2) verification of acceptance or enrollment at any accredited institution of higher learning as a full-time student, and 3) a statement of financial need.

Financial data The stipends are small: generally, between $150 and $300 per quarter or semester. The funds are to be used to pay the costs of books and other fees associated with college attendance.

Duration 1 quarter or semester; renewable.

Special features The Malki Museum is the first all-Indian museum on a California Indian reservation.

Number awarded Varies; generally, 2 to 3 per year.

Deadline Applications may be submitted at any time; the Board of Directors meets the last Thursday of each month to consider applications.

[61]
MARK ULMER NATIVE AMERICAN SCHOLARSHIP

Triangle Native American Society
P.O. Box 26841
Raleigh, NC 27611-6841
(919) 662-9197

Purpose To provide financial assistance to Native Americans in North Carolina who are interested in continuing their college education.

Eligibility Eligible to apply are American Indians who 1) have been North Carolina residents for at least 1 year; 2) are rising college sophomores, juniors, or seniors with at least a 2.0 grade point average; 3) are enrolled as a full-time student for the next semester/quarter in 1 of the schools in the University of North Carolina system; 4) can demonstrate financial need; 5) and can demonstrate leadership and community involvement.

Financial data The stipend is $500.

Duration 1 year; recipients may reapply.

Number awarded Varies each year.

Deadline May of each year.

[62]
MASSACHUSETTS INDIAN ASSOCIATION SCHOLARSHIP FUND

Massachusetts Indian Association
c/o Marjorie Findlay
245 Rockland Road
Carlisle, MA 01741

Purpose To provide financial assistance to Native Americans interested in pursuing postsecondary education.

Eligibility Native American high school students anywhere in the United States may apply for these scholarships if they have a tribal number, are in good academic standing, and can demonstrate financial need.

Financial data The stipends range up to $500 for undergraduate students and $1,000 for graduate students. The funds are intended to supplement other aid by paying for books, lab fees, and other course-related expenses. Grants may be used for tuition, if necessary.

Duration 1 year; may be renewed.

Number awarded 50 each year.

Deadline January and September of each year.

[63]
MASSACHUSETTS NATIVE AMERICAN TUITION WAIVER PROGRAM

Higher Education Coordinating Council
McCormack Building
One Ashburton Place, Room 1401
Boston, MA 02108-1696
(617) 727-7785   Fax: (617) 727-6397

Purpose To provide financial assistance for the postsecondary education of Massachusetts residents who are Native Americans.

Eligibility Applicants for these scholarships must have been permanent legal residents of Massachusetts for at least 1 year and certified by the Bureau of Indian Affairs as Native Americans. They may not be in default of any federal student loan.

Financial data Eligible students are exempt from any tuition payments toward an undergraduate degree or certificate program at public colleges or universities in Massachusetts.

Duration Up to 4 academic years, for a total of 130 semester hours.

Special features Recipients may enroll either part- or full-time in a Massachusetts public-supported institution.

Number awarded Varies each year.

[64]
MENOMINEE INDIAN TRIBE ADULT VOCATIONAL TRAINING PROGRAM

Menominee Indian Tribe of Wisconsin
Attn: Tribal Education Office
P.O. Box 910
Keshena, WI 54135
(715) 799-5110

Purpose To provide financial assistance to Menominee Indians who are interested in obtaining a diploma or certificate (1-year program) or associate of arts (2-year program) at a vocational/technical/junior college.

Eligibility Grants are available to adult students who are one-fourth or more degree Menominee, are enrolled or accepted for enrollment in an appropriate postsecondary school, and are in

financial need. Individuals who do not possess at least one-fourth degree Menominee blood quantum but meet the following criteria are eligible for this program: 1) possess a minimum of one-eighth Menominee blood and 2) possess one-fourth degree Indian blood. Preference is given to applicants in this order: those who live on or near the Menominee Reservation, those who live in Wisconsin and have been accepted for enrollment in an accredited institution in Wisconsin, and those who live in the United States and have been accepted for enrollment in an accredited institution in the United States outside of Wisconsin.

Financial data Up to $2,200 each year.

Duration The maximum training period for Adult Vocational Training students is 24 months. Training for nursing is 36 months. Renewal awards require the student to maintain a minimum grade point average of 2.0 and to carry at least 12 credits per term.

Limitations Part-time study is not supported under this program.

Deadline February of each year.

[65]
MENOMINEE INDIAN TRIBE HIGHER EDUCATION PROGRAM

Menominee Indian Tribe of Wisconsin
Attn: Tribal Education Office
P.O. Box 910
Keshena, WI 54135
(715) 799-5110

Purpose To provide financial assistance to Menominee Indians who are interested in pursuing postsecondary studies.

Eligibility Funds are available to students who are at least one-quarter degree Menominee Indians and are enrolled or accepted for enrollment in accredited colleges or universities. Individuals who do not possess at least one-quarter degree Menominee blood quantum but meet the following criteria are also eligible: 1) possess a minimum of one-eighth Menominee blood and 2) possess one-quarter degree Indian blood. Preference is given to applicants in this order: continuing undergraduate students in good standing; new undergraduates, awarded on a first come, first served basis; late applicants, depending on the availability of funds; second term applicants, only on projected availability of funds; and graduate and professional students, considered only if funds are available after all worthy Menominee undergraduates are selected.

Financial data Up to $2,200 per year for full-time students, for tuition, books, and fees only. Part-time students are also eligible for assistance, but the maximum funding available to students is $11,000 of combined part-time/full-time study.

Duration Up to 10 semesters.

Number awarded Varies each year.

Deadline February of each year.

[66]
MESCALERO APACHE TRIBAL SCHOLARSHIP

Mescalero Apache Tribe
Attn: Tribal Education Department
P.O. Box 176
Mescalero, NM 88340
(505) 671-4494

Purpose To provide financial assistance for undergraduate or graduate education to members of the Mescalero Apache Tribe.

Eligibility Enrolled members of the Mescalero Apache Tribe are eligible to apply if they are high school seniors, high school graduates, or currently-enrolled college students, have earned at least a 2.0 grade point average, and are interested in going to a college, university, vocational, or graduate school.

Financial data The amount awarded varies, up to $6,000 per year.

Duration 1 year; may be renewed for up to 3 additional years.

Number awarded Varies each year.

Deadline June for the fall term; October for the spring term.

[67]
METROLINA NATIVE AMERICAN ASSOCIATION EMPLOYMENT AND TRAINING PROGRAM

Metrolina Native American Association
2601-A East Seventh Street
Charlotte, NC 28204
(704) 331-4818   Fax: (704) 331-9501

Purpose To provide financial assistance to needy Native Americans in North Carolina who are interested in obtaining additional education or training.

Eligibility Native Americans or Alaskan Natives who are unemployed, underemployed, or economically disadvantaged are eligible to apply for this support if they reside in the service area of the Metrolina Native American Association of 10 counties (Cabarrus, Catawba, Cleveland, Gaston, Iredell, Lincoln, Mecklenburg, Rowan, Stanley, or Union) in North Carolina.

Financial data Tuition assistance and other services are offered to recipients.

Duration Up to 1 year.

Special features Funds may be used for a vocational/technical degree, an associate degree, GED preparation, or adult education.

Number awarded Varies each year.

[68]
MICHIGAN INDIAN TUITION WAIVER PROGRAM

Michigan Commission on Indian Affairs
Attn: Department of Civil Rights
P.O. Box 30026
611 West Ottawa, North Tower, Third Floor
Lansing, MI 48913-1070
(517) 373-0654   Fax: (517) 335-1642

Purpose To provide financial assistance to Native American high school graduates who are interested in attending college in Michigan.

Eligibility Eligible students must have one-quarter or more quantum blood Indian, as certified by tribal association and verified by the Michigan Commission on Indian Affairs; enrolled or eligible to enroll full time, part time, or in summer school at a public postsecondary institution in Michigan as an undergraduate or graduate student; and a legal resident of Michigan for not less than 12 consecutive months.

Financial data Students in the program receive free tuition at any Michigan public 2-year or 4-year college or university.

Duration 1 year; renewable.

[69]
MILLE LACS CRITICAL PROFESSIONS PROGRAM

Mille Lacs Tribal Council
Attn: Melissa Hill
HCR 67, Box 242
Onamia, MN 56359
(612) 532-4714   Fax: (320) 532-4209

Purpose To provide financial assistance to Indian students who wish to pursue a course of study leading to an undergraduate or graduate degree in business administration, natural resources or forestry, computer programming, urban or rural planning, or elementary or secondary school teaching.

Eligibility Applicants must be enrolled members of the Mille Lacs Tribal Council of the Minnesota Chippewa Tribe, and full-time students. Applicants are evaluated on academic record, leadership ability, and commitment.

Financial data Award varies; graduate students receive $650 per month (plus $90 per dependent) and undergraduate students receive $450 per month (plus $90 per dependent). Funds are disbursed directly to the recipient's institution of higher education.

Duration 1 quarter/semester; renewable if the applicant remains a full-time student and is in good standing (good standing means at least a 2.5 cumulative grade point average for undergraduate work or a 3.0 for graduate work). Financial need must be demonstrated.

Limitations Applicants must demonstrate a commitment to work for a tribal government or in an Indian community for 2 years after graduation.

Number awarded Varies each year.

Deadline Applications are accepted at any time.

[70]
MILLE LACS SCHOLARSHIP PROGRAM

Mille Lacs Tribal Council
Attn: Melissa Hill
HCR 67, Box 242
Onamia, MN 56359
(612) 532-4714   Fax: (320) 532-4209

Purpose To provide financial assistance to Minnesota Chippewa Tribe high school graduates who are interested in postsecondary education.

Eligibility Applicants must be at least one-quarter Indian ancestry, residents of Minnesota for at least 1 year, high school graduates or the equivalent, and enrolled members of the Mille Lacs Tribal Council of the Minnesota Chippewa Tribe or eligible for enrollment. Financial need is required.

Financial data Up to $3,000 per year, depending on need.

Duration 1 year; may be renewed.

Special features Applicants for this program must also apply for financial aid administered by their institution and any other aid for which they may be eligible (e.g., work-study, Social Security, veteran's benefits). Recipients may attend a college, university, or vocational school.

Number awarded Varies each year.

Deadline For vocational school students, at least 8 weeks before school starts; for college or university students, June of each year.

[71]
MINNESOTA INDIAN SCHOLARSHIP PROGRAM
Minnesota State Department of Education
Attn: Indian Education
1819 Bemidji Avenue
Bemidji, MN 56601
(218) 755-2926

Purpose To provide financial assistance to Native Americans in Minnesota who are interested in pursuing undergraduate or graduate education.

Eligibility Applicants must be at least one-fourth degree Indian ancestry; members of a recognized Indian tribe; at least high school graduates (or approved equivalent); accepted by an accredited college, university, or vocational school in Minnesota; and residents of Minnesota for at least 1 year.

Financial data The scholarships range from $500 to $3,000, depending upon financial need. The average award is $1,450. Awards are paid directly to the student's school or college, rather than to the student.

Duration 1 year; renewable for an additional 4 years.

Limitations Recipients must maintain a minimum grade point average of 2.0, earn 12 credits per quarter, and send official grade transcripts to the office for review after each quarter or semester.

Deadline There is no deadline, but students are encouraged to apply as early as possible before starting their postsecondary school program as scholarships are awarded on a first-come, first-served basis.

[72]
MINORITY PRESENCE GRANTS (GENERAL PROGRAM II)
North Carolina State Education Assistance Authority
Attn: Scholarship and Grant Services
P.O. Box 2688
Chapel Hill, NC 27515-2688
(919) 549-8614   Fax: (919) 549-8481

Purpose To increase the presence of minority students at each University of North Carolina constituent institution.

Eligibility The grants are available to North Carolina residents taking at least 3 hours of degree-credit course work per semester at 1 of the University of North Carolina system schools who are Native Americans or other minority students. Applicants must be able to demonstrate financial need.

Financial data The amount of the award depends upon the financial need of the recipient and the availability of funds.

Duration 1 year; may be renewed up to 3 additional years.

Limitations Students must submit applications to the constituent institution's financial aid office rather than directly to the North Carolina State Education Assistance Authority.

Number awarded Varies each year.

Deadline Deadline dates vary; check with the specific constituent institution.

[73]
MISS INDIAN USA SCHOLARSHIP PROGRAM
American Indian Heritage Foundation
6051 Arlington Boulevard
Falls Church, VA 22044-2788
(202) INDIANS   (703) 237-7500
Fax: (703) 532-1921

Purpose To recognize and reward the most beautiful and talented Native American women.

Eligibility Native American women aged 18 to 26 are eligible to enter this national contest if they are high school graduates and have never been married, cohabited with the opposite sex, been pregnant, or had children.

Financial data The National Miss Indian USA and her Court Members receive $12,000 in scholarships.

Duration This competition is held annually.

Special features The program involves a week long competition in the Washington, D.C. metropolitan area that includes seminars, interviews, cultural presentations, and many public appearances.

Limitations An application fee of $25 is required.

Deadline February of each year.

[74]
MONTANA INDIAN STUDENT FEE WAIVER
Montana Guaranteed Student Loan Program
2500 Broadway
Helena, MT 59620-3103
(406) 444-6570

Purpose To provide financial assistance to Montana Indian students interested in pursuing postsecondary education.

Eligibility Eligible to apply are Native American students (one-quarter Indian blood or more) who have been bona fide residents of Montana for at least 1 year prior to application, have graduated from an accredited high school or federal Indian school, and can demonstrate financial need.

Financial data Tuition is waived for recipients at all schools of the Montana University System.

Duration 1 year; renewable.

Number awarded Up to 48 each year.

[75]
MUSCOGEE (CREEK) NATION TRIBAL FUNDS GRANT PROGRAM
Creek Nation of Oklahoma
Attn: Higher Education Program
P.O. Box 580
Okmulgee, OK 74447
(918) 756-8700

Purpose To provide financial assistance to enrolled citizens of the Muscogee (Creek) Nation attending an accredited college or university.

Eligibility All enrolled citizens of the Muscogee (Creek) Nation are eligible to apply (with no minimum blood quantum required) if they are enrolled or planning to enroll in an accredited college or university.

Financial data $400 per academic year for full-time students (12 credit hours or more per semester) and $200 per academic year for part-time students (less than 12 hours). The award may be used to supplement other financial aid sources.

Duration 1 year; may be renewed up to 3 additional years (as long as the recipient maintains at least a 2.5 grade point average).

Limitations Recipients who withdraw from school or earn less than a 1.5 grade point average are suspended until they have financed themselves for 1 full semester and passed 12 credit hours with at least a grade point average of 2.0.

Number awarded Varies each year.

Deadline June of each year.

[76]
MUSCOGEE (CREEK) NATION TRIBAL INCENTIVE GRANT PROGRAM

Creek Nation of Oklahoma
Attn: Higher Education Program
P.O. Box 580
Okmulgee, OK 74447
(918) 756-8700

Purpose To provide financial assistance to enrolled citizens of the Muscogee (Creek) Nation attending an accredited college or university.

Eligibility All enrolled citizens of the Muscogee (Creek) Nation are eligible to apply (with no minimum blood quantum required) if they are enrolled or planning to enroll in an accredited college or university and have earned at least a 3.0 grade point average.

Financial data Full time students: $200 per semester/quarter; part-time students: $100 per semester/quarter.

Duration 1 semester; may be renewed for up to 7 additional semesters.

Limitations Recipients who withdraw from school are suspended until they have financed themselves for 1 full semester and passed 12 credit hours with an acceptable grade point average.

Number awarded Varies each year.

Deadline June of each year.

[77]
NACME CORPORATE SCHOLARS PROGRAM

National Action Council for Minorities in Engineering
3 West 35th Street
New York, NY 10001-2281
(212) 279-2626   Fax: (212) 629-5178

Purpose To support exceptional underrepresented minority students in preparing for careers at the frontier of engineering technology.

Eligibility This program is open to African Americans, Latinos, and American Indians who are currently enrolled full time in an undergraduate engineering program, are U.S. citizens or permanent residents, and have demonstrated engineering leadership potential.

Financial data This program provides students with scholarships of up to $5,000 per year, depending on their financial need, and paid internships.

Duration 1 year; may be renewed if recipients maintain at least a 2.5 grade point average.

Special features This program also offers R&D work experience, academic and career mentoring, summer internships, and professional development opportunities. The National Action Council for Minorities in Engineering (NACME) supports corporate mentors with a broad range of appropriate training. Recipients attend a leadership development seminar, the cost of which is

underwritten by sponsoring companies. The program was started in 1991.

Number awarded Varies; generally, more than 60 each year.

[78]
NACME SUSTAINING FELLOWS AWARD

National Action Council for Minorities in Engineering
3 West 35th Street
New York, NY 10001-2281
(212) 279-2626   Fax: (212) 629-5178

Purpose To provide financial assistance for education in engineering to underrepresented minority students.

Eligibility Engineering students who are African American, Latino, or American Indian are eligible for this award. Candidates must have completed the first year of college and be nominated by their dean. Selection is based on high academic achievement and interest in a career in engineering.

Financial data The stipend is $5,000 per year.

Duration 1 year; may be renewed if the recipient maintains a minimum grade point average of 3.0.

Number awarded 1 each year.

[79]
NATIVE AMERICAN EDUCATION GRANTS

Presbyterian Church (U.S.A.)
Attn: Office of Financial Aid for Studies
100 Witherspoon Street, Room M042
Louisville, KY 40202-1396
(502) 569-5776   Fax: (502) 569-5018

Purpose To provide financially needy Native American students with support to continue their college education.

Eligibility Alaska Native and Native American students pursuing full-time postsecondary education are eligible to apply if they are members of the Presbyterian Church (U.S.A.), are U.S. citizens, have completed at least 1 semester of work at an accredited institution of higher education, and can demonstrate financial need.

Financial data Stipends range from $200 to $1,500, depending upon the recipient's financial need.

Duration 1 year; may be renewed upon documentation of continued financial need and satisfactory academic progress.

Number awarded Varies each year.

Deadline May of each year.

[80]
NATIVE AMERICAN LEADERSHIP IN EDUCATION (NALE) PROGRAM

Native American Scholarship Fund
8200 Mountain Road, N.E., Suite 203
Albuquerque, NM 87110-7835
(505) 262-2351   Fax: (505) 262-0534

Purpose To provide financial assistance to American Indian paraprofessionals in the education field who wish to return to school.

Eligibility Paraprofessionals working in the schools are eligible to apply for this program if they 1) have at least a quarter Indian blood; 2) are members of a U.S. tribe that is either federally-recognized, state-recognized, or terminated; 3) are interested in returning to college to complete their undergraduate degrees and/or earn credentials as teachers, counselors, or administrators; 4) have been admitted to or are enrolled in college; 5) have grade point averages of at least 3.0 and scores on the SAT of at least 950 or ACT of at least 23; and 6) have applied for all other sources of funding for which they are eligible. They must attend an accredited 4-year college or university, but may be entering freshmen, undergraduate students, graduate students, or Ph.D. candidates. Awards are based on merit and the potential of the applicant to improve the lives of Indian people; financial need is not a consideration. Students with no clear goals are discouraged from applying.

Financial data The amount awarded varies but is generally at least $500 in the form of grants, loans, or a combination of both.

Duration 1 year; may be renewed.

Number awarded Varies; generally, 15 or more each year.

Deadline April of each year for fall terms; September of each year for spring and winter terms; March of each year for summer school.

[81]
NATIVE AMERICAN SEMINARY SCHOLARSHIPS

Presbyterian Church (U.S.A.)
Attn: Office of Financial Aid for Studies
100 Witherspoon Street, Room M042
Louisville, KY 40202-1396
(502) 569-5776   Fax: (502) 569-5018

Purpose To provide financial assistance to Native American students interested in preparing for church occupations.

Eligibility Native American and Alaska Native students may apply for the award if they are U.S. citizens or permanent residents, can demonstrate financial need, are in good academic standing, and are in 1 of the following 3 categories: 1) theological student enrolled as an inquirer or candidate by a presbytery of the Presbyterian Church (U.S.A.), preparing for a church occupation, and enrolled in a theological institution approved by the students' Committee on Preparation for Ministry; 2) Presbyterian Church (U.S.A.) member enrolled in a program of theological education by extension, such as the NATEC; or 3) inquirer, candidate, minister, or member of the Presbyterian Church (U.S.A.) in other church occupations pursuing an approved program of continuing education.

Financial data The amounts of the awards depend on the availability of funds.

Number awarded Varies each year.

[82]
NAVAJO NATION SCHOLARSHIP AND FINANCIAL ASSISTANCE PROGRAM

Navajo Nation
Attn: Scholarship and Financial Assistance Program
P.O. Drawer 1870
Window Rock, AZ 86515-1870
(520) 871-7640   (800) 243-2956

Purpose To provide financial assistance to members of the Navajo Nation who are interested in pursuing undergraduate or graduate education.

Eligibility Enrolled members of the Navajo Nation are eligible to apply if they meet 1 of the following requirements: 1) are ranked in the top 30 percent of their class; 2) achieved an ACT score of at least 17; 3) have accumulated 12 college credit hours with a grade point average of at least 2.0; or 4) have a General Education Development (GED) score of at least 55. Applications must

be accompanied by a certificate of Indian blood, a high school or college transcript, a letter of admission from an accredited postsecondary institution, and a financial need analysis.

Financial data The amount awarded varies, depending upon the needs of the recipient.

Duration 1 year; may be renewed.

Deadline April of each year for fall semester; September of each year for winter quarter or spring semester; March of each year for summer session.

[83]
NETT LAKE/BOIS FORTE CRITICAL PROFESSIONS PROGRAM

Nett Lake/Bois Forte Tribal Council
Attn: Joanne Donald
P.O. Box 16
Nett Lake, MN 55772
(218) 757-3107   Fax: (218) 757-3118

Purpose To provide financial assistance to Indian students who wish to pursue a course of study leading to an undergraduate or graduate degree in business administration, natural resources or forestry, computer programming, urban or rural planning, or elementary or secondary school teaching.

Eligibility Applicants must be enrolled members of the Nett Lake/Bois Forte Tribal Council of the Minnesota Chippewa Tribe and full-time students. Applicants are evaluated on academic record, leadership ability, and commitment.

Financial data Award varies; graduate students receive $650 per month (plus $90 per dependent) and undergraduate students receive $450 per month (plus $90 per dependent). Funds are disbursed directly to the recipient's institution of higher education.

Duration 1 quarter/semester; renewable if the applicant remains a full-time student and is in good standing (good standing means at least a 2.5 cumulative grade point average for undergraduate work or a 3.0 for graduate work). Financial need must be demonstrated.

Limitations Applicants must demonstrate a commitment to work for a tribal government or in an Indian community for 2 years after graduation.

Number awarded Varies each year.

Deadline Applications are accepted at any time.

[84]
NETT LAKE/BOIS FORTE SCHOLARSHIP PROGRAM

Nett Lake/Bois Forte Tribal Council
Attn: Joanne Donald
P.O. Box 16
Nett Lake, MN 55772
(218) 757-3107   Fax: (218) 757-3118

Purpose To provide financial assistance to Minnesota Chippewa Tribe high school graduates who are interested in postsecondary education.

Eligibility Applicants must be at least one-quarter Indian ancestry, residents of Minnesota for at least 1 year, high school graduates or the equivalent, and enrolled members of the Nett Lake/Bois Forte Tribal Council of the Minnesota Chippewa Tribe or eligible for enrollment. Financial need is required.

Financial data Up to $3,000 per year, depending on need.

Duration 1 year; may be renewed.

Special features Applicants for this program must also apply for financial aid administered by their institution and any other aid for which they may be eligible (e.g., work-study, Social Security, veteran's benefits). Recipients may attend a college, university, or vocational school.

Number awarded Varies each year.

Deadline For vocational school students, at least 8 weeks before school starts; for college or university students, June of each year.

[85]
NEW YORK AID TO NATIVE AMERICANS

New York State Education Department
Attn: Native American Education Unit
Education Building, Room 543
Albany, NY 12234
(518) 474-0537

Purpose To provide financial assistance to Native American New York residents to attend postsecondary institutions within the state.

Eligibility Student aid is available to Native Americans who meet these qualifications: are on official tribal rolls of a New York State tribe or are the child of an enrolled member; are residents of New York State; and are graduates of an accredited high school or hold a New York State General Equivalency Diploma or are enrolled in college credit programs working for the State High School Equivalency Diploma. Recipients must be accepted by an approved accredited postsecondary institution within New York State.

Financial data The stipend is $775 per semester for full-time study (at least 12 credit hours per semester or 24 credit hours per year); students registering for less than full-time study are funded on a prorated basis. Funding is available for summer course work on a special needs basis. Monies expended for summer school are deducted from the recipient's maximum entitlement.

Duration 1 year; renewable for up to 3 additional years (4 additional years for specific programs requiring 5 years to complete degree requirements).

Limitations Remedial, noncredit, or college preparation courses are not fundable.

Number awarded Varies; approximately 500 each year.

Deadline July of each year for the fall semester; December of each year for spring semester; May of each year for summer session.

[86]
NEW YORK STATE REGENTS PROFESSIONAL OPPORTUNITY SCHOLARSHIPS

New York State Education Department
Attn: Bureau of Postsecondary Grants Administration
Cultural Education Center
Albany, NY 12230
(518) 486-1319

Purpose To expand educational opportunities for underrepresented minority and economically disadvanataged students interested in pursuing professional careers.

Eligibility Candidates must be U.S. citizens or permanent residents and legal residents of New York for 1 year prior to application. The law requires that awards be made to eligible candidates in the following order: first priority is given to any candidate who is economically disadvantaged and a minority group member historically underrepresented in the professions (Black Americans, Hispanic Americans, Native Americans, or Alaskan Natives); second priority is given to any candidate who is a minority group member underrepresented in the professions; and third priority is given to any candidate who is enrolled in or a graduate of 1 of these state-supported opportunity programs: Search for Education, Elevation and Knowledge (SEEK) or College Discovery at City University; Educational Opportunity Program (EOP) in the State University system; or Higher Education Opportunity Program (HEOP) at an independent college.

Financial data The stipends range from $1,000 to $5,000 per year, depending on income.

Duration Up to 4 years.

Special features Scholarships are available for study in the following areas: accounting (baccalaureate level), architecture (baccalaureate or master's), chiropractic medicine (doctoral), dental hygiene (associate), engineering (baccalaureate), landscape architecture (baccalaureate or master's), law (juris doctoral), nursing (baccalaureate), occupational therapy (baccalaureate or master's), occupational therapy assistant (associate), ophthalmic dispensing (associate), optometry (doctoral), pharmacy (baccalaureate), physical therapist assistant (associate), physical therapy (baccalaureate or master's), physicians assistant (baccalaureate or master's), psychology (doctoral), social work (master's), speech-language pathology/audiology (master's), and veterinary medicine (doctoral).

Limitations No award can exceed the actual cost of attendance. After completion of their professional studies, scholarship holders are required to practice in New York for 12 months for each annual payment received.

Number awarded 220 each year.

Deadline January of each year.

[87]
NORBERT S. HILL, JR. LEADERSHIP AWARD

American Indian Science and Engineering Society
Attn: Scholarship Department
5661 Airport Boulevard
Boulder, CO 80301
(303) 939-0023   E-mail: ascholar@spot.colorado.edu

Purpose To help talented American Indian science and engineering students meet the financial demands of going to college.

Eligibility To be eligible for this scholarship, the applicant must have applied for the A.T. Anderson Memorial Scholarship Program and have met the following requirements: a full-time student at the undergraduate or graduate level, a member of the American Indian Science and Engineering Society, at least one-quarter Indian, in financial need, and majoring in the sciences, health-related fields, business, natureal resources, engineering, and math and science secondary education. Evidence of the student's outstanding leadership is taken from the A.T. Anderson Memorial Scholarship Program application. The leadership should be manifest not only in the local chapter of the American Indian Science and Engineering Society, but also in the campus and community, particularly as it relates to American Indian youth mentoring and motivation.

Financial data The stipend is $1,500.

Duration 1 year.

Number awarded 1 or more each year.

Deadline June of each year.

[88]
NORMAN TECUBE SR. HIGHER EDUCATION FUND

Jicarilla Apache Tribe
Attn: Higher Education Program
P.O. Box 507
Dulce, NM 87528-0507
(505) 759-3316

Purpose To provide financial assistance for undergraduate or graduate education to members of the Jicarilla Apache tribe.

Eligibility Enrolled members of the Jicarilla Apache tribe are eligible to apply if they are attending either undergraduate or graduate school. Recipients may enroll in any accredited postsecondary school and may major in any subject area.

Financial data The amount awarded varies, up to a maximum of $1,800 per year. Funds may not be used for extra-curricular activities, trips out of the United States, non-credit courses, or unnecessary tools.

Duration 1 year; may be renewed.

Special features This program was formerly called the Chester E. Faris Higher Education Fund.

Number awarded Varies each year.

Deadline February for fall semester or academic year applications; September of each year for spring semester applications.

[89]
NORTH CAROLINA INCENTIVE SCHOLARSHIP AND GRANT PROGRAM FOR NATIVE AMERICANS—MERIT-BASED SCHOLARSHIPS

North Carolina Commission of Indian Affairs
North Carolina Department of Administration
217 West Jones Street
Raleigh, NC 27603-1336
(919) 733-5998   Fax: (919) 733-1207

Purpose To provide financial assistance to American Indians who are interested in studying at a university in North Carolina.

Eligibility Applicants must 1) be Native Americans; 2) be high school graduates who ranked in the top half of their graduating class or graduates of community colleges who have been accepted as a new transfer student; 3) be accepted for enrollment and enroll for a minimum of 15 credit hours per term at a constituent institution of the University of North Carolina that awards the scholarship; 4) apply for need-based financial aid to allow for a reduction in the amount required from this program; 5) be classified as North Carolina residents for tuition purposes; and 6) perform approved public service at least 6 hours per week as a freshman and 8 hours per week as a sophomore, junior, or senior.

Financial data The stipend is $3,000 per year.

Duration 1 year; may be renewed up to 3 additional years provided the recipient achieves at least a 2.0 grade point average by the end of the freshman year, 2.5 at the end of the sophomore year, and 3.0 by the end of the junior year.

Number awarded Varies each year.

Deadline Applications are available from the participating institutions (listed above). Deadline dates vary by institution; check with the specific school you wish to attend to determine the current schedule.

[90]
NORTH CAROLINA INCENTIVE SCHOLARSHIP AND GRANT PROGRAM FOR NATIVE AMERICANS—NEED-BASED GRANTS

North Carolina Commission of Indian Affairs
North Carolina Department of Administration
217 West Jones Street
Raleigh, NC 27603-1336
(919) 733-5998   Fax: (919) 733-1207

Purpose To provide financial assistance to American Indians who are interested in studying at a university in North Carolina.

Eligibility Applicants must be American Indians, as defined by this program: "An individual who maintains cultural identification as an American Indian through membership in an Indian tribe recognized by the State of North Carolina or by the federal government or through other tribal affiliation or community recognition." They must be enrolled or planning to enroll as undergraduate students in 1 of the following North Carolina schools: Appalachian State University, East Carolina University, Elizabeth City State University, Fayetteville State University, North Carolina A&T State University, North Carolina Central University, North Carolina School of the Arts, North Carolina State University at Raleigh, Pembroke State University, University of North Carolina at Asheville, University of North Carolina at Chapel Hill, University of North Carolina at Charlotte, University of North Carolina at Greensboro, University of North Carolina at Wilmington, Western Carolina University, or Winston-Salem State University. Also eligible are students enrolled in a doctoral program at North Carolina State University, the University of North Carolina at Chapel Hill, or the University of North Carolina at Greensboro. All applicants must be classified as North Carolina residents for tuition purposes and be able to demonstrate financial need.

Financial data For undergraduates, the maximum award is $700 full-time study or a prorated amount for part-time study; the maximum award for doctoral students is $5,000. The actual amount depends on financial need of the recipient.

Duration 1 year; may be renewed up to 3 additional years.

Special features Recipients may be full- or part-time students. Stipends are reduced proportionately for part-time students.

Number awarded Varies; in recent years, approximately 250 undergraduates and 6 doctoral students have received awards.

Deadline Applications are available from the participating institutions (listed above). Deadline dates vary by institution; check with the specific school you wish to attend to determine the current schedule.

[91]
NORTH DAKOTA INDIAN SCHOLARSHIP PROGRAM

North Dakota University System
Attn: North Dakota Indian Scholarship Program
State Capitol, 10th Floor
600 East Boulevard Avenue
Bismarck, ND 58505-0230
(701) 328-2166

Purpose To provide financial assistance to Native American students in North Dakota colleges and universities.

Eligibility Applicants must be at least one-quarter degree Indian blood, residents of North Dakota or enrolled members of a tribe resident in North Dakota, accepted as full-time undergraduate students by an institution of higher learning or vocational education in North Dakota, and in good health and good character. Students with at least a 3.5 grade point average may apply for a merit award based primarily on their grades rather than on financial need; students with a grade point average below 3.5 may apply for a regular award if they can demonstrate financial need. The awards to merit scholarship recipients receive priority funding and are generally larger than regular awards.

Financial data The amount of the stipend varies from $600 to $2,000 depending on scholastic ability, funds available, total number of applicants, and financial need. The award is divided into semester or quarter payments. The money is to be used to pay registration, health fees, board, room, books, and other necessary items handled by the institution. Any remaining balance may be used to cover the student's personal expenses.

Duration 1 academic year; renewable up to 3 additional years, if the recipient maintains a 2.0 grade point average and continues to be in financial need.

Number awarded Varies; approximately 100 each year.

Deadline July of each year.

[92]
NORTHERN ARAPAHO TRIBAL SCHOLARSHIP

Sky People Higher Education
P.O. Box 8480
Ethete, WY 82520
(307) 332-5286   Fax: (307) 332-9104

Purpose To provide financial assistance to members of the Northern Arapaho Tribe who are interested in postsecondary education.

Eligibility This program is open to anyone who can certify at least one-fourth or more degree Northern Arapaho Indian Blood, but preference is given to enrolled members of the Northern Arapaho tribe. Funding priorities are 1) college seniors ready to graduate; 2) continuing students with a grade point average of 2.25 or better; 3) high school or GED graduates; and 4) late applicants.

Financial data The amount of the awards depends on the financial need of the recipients.

Duration 1 year; may be renewed for a total of 5 academic years.

Special features The scholarships may be used at any accredited college, university, or vocational/technical school.

Limitations Recipients must attend college full time.

Number awarded Varies each year.

Deadline May of each year for the fall semester; November of each year for the spring semester; February of each year for summer school.

[93]
NORTHERN CHEYENNE ADULT VOCATIONAL TRAINING PROGRAM

Tribal Council of the Northern Cheyenne
c/o Northern Cheyenne Agency
P.O. Box 307
Lame Deer, MT 59043
(406) 477-6467

Purpose To provide financial assistance to Northern Cheyenne tribal members who are interested in pursuing vocational training.

Eligibility Applicants must be enrolled members of the Northern Cheyenne tribe, be between the ages of 18 and 35, be high school graduates or have obtained a high school equivalency before applying, and be enrolled or accepted in a Bureau of Indian Affairs-approved school. Northern Cheyennes are not required to reside on the Northern Cheyenne Reservation; other eligible Indian members may qualify for this assistance if they reside on the Northern Cheyenne Reservation. The applicant must intend to pursue a full-time trade or vocational program that can be completed in 3 to 24 months and that will prepare the student for employment. Selection is based on academic achievement, educational goals, need for financial support, choice of school, and plans after graduation. Awards are made according to the following priorities: 1) renewal of grants to continuing students in good standing; 2) new applicants who are enrolled Northern Cheyenne residing on or near the Northern Cheyenne Indian Reservation; 3) enrolled Northern Cheyenne new applicants who reside outside the service area of the reservation; 4) other Indian enrolled tribal members residing on the Northern Cheyenne Indian Reservation; and 5) individuals requesting retraining.

Financial data Funding under this program is supplemental to any other income. Grants are intended to cover living expenses, tuition, books, supplies related directly to the course, and child care. Transportation costs to training sites off the reservation are provided for the student and eligible family members. Medical coverage is provided by the Northern Cheyenne Indian Health Service for the duration of the training period.

Duration Up to 24 months for vocational training; up to 36 months for nursing training.

Special features Individuals can request support for retraining, provided they can supply a physician's statement explaining why the applicant cannot continue in the present occupation.

Limitations Recipients must complete at least 12 units each semester or quarter with at least a 2.0 grade point average. Recipients who voluntarily discontinue training without prior approval from the tribe or because of poor attendance or academic performance are not eligible for continued financial assistance.

Number awarded Varies each year.

Deadline February for fall quarter/semester; September for winter quarter/spring semester/spring quarter; March for summer school.

[94]
NORTHERN CHEYENNE HIGHER EDUCATION PROGRAM

Tribal Council of the Northern Cheyenne
c/o Northern Cheyenne Agency
P.O. Box 307
Lame Deer, MT 59043
(406) 477-6467

Purpose To provide financial assistance to Northern Cheyenne high school graduates who are interested in pursuing postsecondary education.

Eligibility Applicants must be at least high school graduates (or seniors about to graduate) who are enrolled Northern Cheyenne tribal members, can show financial need, and have been accepted for enrollment at an accredited college or university in a program leading to an associate or baccalaureate degree. Graduate study may be approved if all undergraduate applicants have been approved and funds are still available. Selection is based on academic achievement, educational goals, financial need, choice of school, and plans after graduation.

Financial data The stipend is intended to supplement all other available sources of funding. The scholarship must be used for tuition, subsistence, required fees, and textbooks.

Duration 1 year; may be renewed if the recipient maintains a 2.0 grade point average and completes at least 14 quarter or 16 semester units as a freshman and sophomore and at least 16 quarter or 18 semester units as a junior or senior.

Limitations Recipients who reside in Montana are expected to attend a postsecondary institution in the state. They must pay the difference in cost between Montana public postsecondary schools and private or out-of-state schools, if they elect to attend either of those. An exception is made if no comparable course of study exists in a Montana public institution. Eligible Northern Cheyenne Indians residing out of state are subject to the same regulation; however, they may enroll in a Montana institution of higher learning if there is no comparable course of study at a public institution in their home state.

Number awarded Varies each year.

Deadline February for fall quarter/semester; September for winter quarter/spring semester/spring quarter; March for summer school.

[95]
ONEIDA CONFERENCES PROGRAM

Oneida Nation of Wisconsin
Attn: Higher Education Office
P.O. Box 365
Oneida, WI 54155-0365
(414) 869-4333   (800) 236-2214, ext. 4333
Fax: (414) 869-4039

Purpose To provide financial assistance for conference attendance to members of the Oneida Nation of Wisconsin.

Eligibility This program is open to Oneida students who wish to participate in an appropriate educational experience which directly pertains to their field of study or vocation, especially those which are directed toward the Native American experience.

Financial data Up to $500 for direct costs may be granted.

Duration These are 1-time grants.

Number awarded Varies each year.

Deadline Applications may be submitted at any time, but at least 20 days prior to the conference date.

[96]
ONEIDA FELLOWSHIP PROGRAM

Oneida Nation of Wisconsin
Attn: Higher Education Office
P.O. Box 365
Oneida, WI 54155-0365
(414) 869-4333   (800) 236-2214, ext. 4333
Fax: (414) 869-4039

Purpose To provide financial assistance for postsecondary education to members of the Oneida Nation of Wisconsin.

Eligibility This program is open to full-time Oneida students accepted into a degree program, in pursuit of professions determined critical within the tribal structure.

Financial data This program provides for payment of tuition and a stipend.

Limitations In return for this assistance, recipients are required to fulfill a service obligation of employment with the tribal organization.

Number awarded Varies each year.

Deadline May of each year.

[97]
ONEIDA MANAGEMENT OPPORTUNITY PROGRAM

Oneida Nation of Wisconsin
Attn: Higher Education Office
P.O. Box 365
Oneida, WI 54155-0365
(414) 869-4333   (800) 236-2214, ext. 4333
Fax: (414) 869-4039

Purpose To provide financial assistance to employees of the Oneida Tribe who wish to obtain a college degree.

Eligibility Applicants must be employees of the Oneida Tribe of Wisconsin who require a college degree to fill key management positions within the tribal structure.

Financial data The program provides tuition and required text books.

Duration 1 year.

Number awarded Vares each year.

Deadline May of each year for fall term; September of each year for spring term.

[98]
ONEIDA SHORT-TERM TRAINING PROGRAM

Oneida Nation of Wisconsin
Attn: Higher Education Office
P.O. Box 365
Oneida, WI 54155-0365
(414) 869-4333   (800) 236-2214, ext. 4333
Fax: (414) 869-4039

Purpose To provide financial assistance for short-term training programs to members of the Oneida Nation of Wisconsin.

Eligibility Applicants must be enrolled members of the Oneida Nation who wish to participate in short-term, career enrichment training opportunities that are approved by the state but ineligible for all other funding resources.

Financial data Up to $500 for direct costs may be granted.

Duration These are 1-time grants.

Number awarded Varies each year.

Deadline Applications may be submitted at any time, but at least 20 days prior to the beginning of training.

[99]
ONEIDA TRIBE ADULT VOCATIONAL TRAINING PROGRAM

Oneida Nation of Wisconsin
Attn: Higher Education Office
P.O. Box 365
Oneida, WI 54155-0365
(414) 869-4333   (800) 236-2214, ext. 4333
Fax: (414) 869-4039

Purpose To provide financial assistance to members of the Oneida Tribe of Wisconsin who are interested in earning a vocational, technical, or junior college degree.

Eligibility Enrolled members of the Oneida Tribe of Wisconsin who have been accepted into an accredited vocational program are eligible to apply for this aid. They must demonstrate financial need and plan to pursue training on a full-time basis.

Financial data Up to $3,000 per year.

Duration Up to 25 months (36 months for nurses training), as long as the recipient maintains a full-time program and a minimum grade point average of 2.0.

Number awarded Varies each year, depending upon the funds available.

Deadline The Financial Aid Form and the Indian Scholarship Application must be submitted by March for the fall term, by August for the spring term, and by April for the summer term.

[100]
ONEIDA TRIBE EMERGENCY PROGRAM

Oneida Nation of Wisconsin
Attn: Higher Education Office
P.O. Box 365
Oneida, WI 54155-0365
(414) 869-4333   (800) 236-2214, ext. 4333
Fax: (414) 869-4039

Purpose To provide emergency financial assistance to members of the Oneida Tribe of Wisconsin who are pursuing postsecondary education.

Eligibility Enrolled members of the Oneida Tribe of Wisconsin who are attending an accredited college or university may apply for this assistance if they are confronting an emergency financial situation that threatens to interrupt their educational goal or if their needs are not being met by the Oneida Tribe Higher Education or Adult Vocational Training Programs. Applicants may request either a grant or a loan; tribal officials will decide whether to award a grant or loan depending on applicants' financial hardship, nature of the emergency, and other information provided.

Financial data Up to $500.

Duration These are 1-time awards.

Number awarded Varies each year, depending upon the funds available and the number of applications.

Deadline Applications may be submitted at any time.

[101]
ONEIDA TRIBE HIGHER EDUCATION PROGRAM

Oneida Nation of Wisconsin
Attn: Higher Education Office
P.O. Box 365
Oneida, WI 54155-0365
(414) 869-4333   (800) 236-2214, ext. 4333
Fax: (414) 869-4039

Purpose To provide financial assistance to members of the Oneida Tribe of Wisconsin who are interested in attending college.

Eligibility Enrolled members of the Oneida Tribe of Wisconsin who have been accepted into an accredited 4-year college or university are eligible to apply for this aid. They must demonstrate financial need and a minimum grade point average of 2.0.

Financial data Up to $3,000 per year.

Duration 1 semester; recipients may reapply for up to 9 additional semesters until they complete their undergraduate degree.

Number awarded Varies each year, depending upon the funds available.

Deadline The Financial Aid Form and the Indian Scholarship Application must be submitted by March for the fall term, by August for the spring term, and by April for the summer term.

[102]
ONEIDA TRIBE/RADISSON INN SCHOLARSHIP

Oneida Nation of Wisconsin
Attn: Higher Education Office
P.O. Box 365
Oneida, WI 54155-0365
(414) 869-4333   (800) 236-2214, ext. 4333
Fax: (414) 869-4039

Purpose To provide financial assistance to members of the Oneida Tribe who are enrolled in an accredited hospitality management program.

Eligibility Applicants must enrolled members of the Oneida Tribe of Wisconsin who are attending a 4-year college or university in a hotel/restaurant management program.

Financial data The stipend is $1,000.

Duration 1 year.

Special features Funds for this program are provided by the Radisson Inn.

Limitations An internship is required as part of the program.

Number awarded 5 each year.

Deadline July of each year for fall term; October of each year for spring term.

[103]
ONEIDA TRUST SCHOLARSHIP

Oneida Nation of Wisconsin
Attn: Higher Education Office
P.O. Box 365
Oneida, WI 54155-0365
(414) 869-4333   (800) 236-2214, ext. 4333
Fax: (414) 869-4039

Purpose To provide financial assistance for postsecondary education to members of the Oneida Tribe.

Eligibility Applicants must be enrolled members of the Oneida Tribe of Wisconsin who have been accepted into an accredited college or university or privately owned, operated, and recognized institution. Undergraduates must have a minimum grade point average of 2.5 and graduate students must be admitted with a cumulative grade point average of at least 2.75 and must then maintain at least a 3.0 grade point average. This fund should be considered a resource of last resort; all traditional resources must be expended, unavailable, or depleted.

Financial data The maximum stipend is $500 per semester.

Duration 1 semester; may be renewed for 1 additional semester.

Special features Recipients are expected to return to the Oneida Tribe to share their acquired knowledge, experience, and education to benefit the Oneida Tribe as a whole.

Number awarded Varies each year.

Deadline August of each year for fall term; November of each year for spring term.

[104]
OSAGE TRIBAL EDUCATION COMMITTEE PROGRAM

Osage Tribal Education Committee
c/o Oklahoma Area Education Office
4149 Highline Boulevard, Suite 380
Oklahoma City, OK 73108
(405) 945-6051   Fax: (405) 945-6057

Purpose To provide financial assistance for postsecondary education to undergraduate and graduate Osage students.

Eligibility This program is open to students enrolled in accredited postsecondary educational programs at the college, university, or technical/vocational level who can prove Osage Indian blood. Applicants may be candidates for an associate, baccalaureate, or graduate degree.

Financial data The amount of the award depends on the financial need of the recipient.

Duration 1 year; may be renewed for up to 3 additional years.

Number awarded Varies each year.

Deadline June of each year for fall term; December of each year for spring term; April of each year for summer school.

[105]
PHILIP D. REED UNDERGRADUATE FELLOWSHIP IN ENVIRONMENTAL ENGINEERING

National Action Council for Minorities in Engineering
3 West 35th Street
New York, NY 10001-2281
(212) 279-2626   Fax: (212) 629-5178

Purpose To provide financial assistance for education in environmental engineering to underrepresented minority students.

Eligibility Engineering sophomores who are African American, Latino, or American Indian are eligible to be nominated by their deans for this award. Selection is based on high academic achievement and interest in environmental engineering.

Financial data The stipend is $5,000 per year.

Duration 1 year; may be renewed for 1 additional year if the recipient maintains a minimum grade point average of 3.0.

Special features Funding for this program, which began in 1996, is provided by the Philip D. Reed Foundation. The program may include internships, mentors, and undergraduate research.

Number awarded 1 or 2 each year.

[106]
POLINGAYSI QOYAWAYMA AWARD

American Indian Science and Engineering Society
Attn: Scholarship Department
5661 Airport Boulevard
Boulder, CO 80301
(303) 939-0023   E-mail: ascholar@spot.colorado.edu

Purpose To provide financial assistance to Indian educators who wish to teach in a Native community or at the college level.

Eligibility To be eligible for this scholarship, the applicant must have applied for the A.T. Anderson Memorial Scholarship Program and have met the following requirements: a full-time student at the undergraduate or graduate level, a member of the American Indian Science and Engineering Society, at least one-quarter Indian, in financial need, and pursuing a teaching degree in order to teach mathematics or science in a Native community or an advanced degree for personal improvement or teaching at the college level.

Financial data The stipend is $1,000.

Duration 1 year.

Special features This award honors Polingaysi (Elizabeth) Qöyawayma, an outstanding pioneer American Indian educator.

Number awarded 1 or more each year.

Deadline June of each year.

[107]
PUEBLO OF ACOMA HIGHER EDUCATION GRANT PROGRAM

Pueblo of Acoma
Attn: Higher Education Coordinator
P.O. Box 307
Acoma, NM 87034
(505) 552-6604   Fax: (505) 552-6600

Purpose To provide financial assistance to Pueblo of Acoma high school graduates who are interested in postsecondary education.

Eligibility Applicants must be enrolled citizens of the Pueblo of Acoma, residents of New Mexico, high school seniors or graduates, enrolled or planning to enroll in an accredited college or university, and in financial need.

Financial data The amount awarded varies, depending upon the recipient's financial need. Generally, scholarships range between $1,000 and $1,800 per year.

Duration 1 year; may be renewed for up to 3 additional years.

Number awarded Varies each year.

Deadline February for the fall term; August for the spring term.

[108]
RICHARD AND JESSIE BARRINGTON EDUCATIONAL FUND

Wells Fargo Bank
Attn: Special Investment Services
P.O. Box 20160
Long Beach, CA 90801
(310) 901-4117   (800) 352-3705

Purpose To provide financial assistance for postsecondary education to Washoe Indians.

Eligibility Eligible to apply are enrolled members of the Washoe Tribe who reside in California or Nevada and who need financial assistance to attend college for vocational education, undergraduate study, or graduate work.

Financial data Up to $5,000 is awarded each year.

Duration 1 year; may be renewed.

Special features Interested applicants may also contact the Washoe Tribe of Nevada and California Education Department (919 Highway 395 South, Gardnerville, NV 89410; telephone: (702) 265-4191) for more information or an application.

Number awarded Varies each year.

[109]
ROBERT W. BROCKSBANK LEADERSHIP AWARD

Council on Career Development for Minorities
Attn: Chief Operating Officer
1341 West Mockingbird Lane, Suite 722 East
Dallas, TX 75247
(214) 631-3677   Fax: (214) 905-2046

Purpose To provide financial assistance to underrepresented ethnic minority members who demonstrate outstanding academic achievement.

Eligibility This competition is open only to those sophomore African American, Hispanic American, and American Indian students who have participated in the Corporate Orientation Programs (CORPs) of the Council on Career Development for Minorities (CCDM). Each year, the CCDM selects the most outstanding leadership project from each group of CORP students and awards the winner this scholarship.

Financial data The recipient is awarded a $1,000 stipend, applicable to the next year's tuition.

Duration 1 year.

Special features The CORPs are weekend seminars usually conducted in 5 different regions of the country each year; they provide minority students with an orientation to the business world through interaction with management executives. Students should check with their campus career planning and placement office to learn if their school will be participating in 1 of CCDM's CORP programs in the near future and if they are eligible to apply for participation.

Number awarded 1 each year.

[110]
ROBERT W. BROCKSBANK SCHOLARSHIP

American Indian Science and Engineering Society
Attn: Scholarship Department
5661 Airport Boulevard
Boulder, CO 80301
(303) 939-0023   E-mail: ascholar@spot.colorado.edu

Purpose To help talented American Indian science and engineering students on the undergraduate or graduate school level meet the financial demands of going to college.

Eligibility To be eligible for this scholarship, the applicant must have applied for the A.T. Anderson Memorial Scholarship Program and have met the following requirements: a full-time student at the undergraduate or graduate level, a member of the American Indian Science and Engineering Society, at least one-quarter Indian, in financial need, and pursuing a degree in the sciences, engineering, health-related fields, business, natural resources, and math and science secondary education. Candidates should exemplify strong leadership skills and a determination for achieving excellence in the academic arena, as well as in the community.

Financial data The stipend is $1,500.

Duration 1 year.

Special features This award is sponsored by Karin Brocksbank. It honors Robert W. Brocksbank, a distinguished member of the American Indian Science and Engineering Society who served as the chairman of the Corporate Advisory Board for a number of years.

Number awarded 1 or more each year.

Deadline June of each year.

[111]
SANTO DOMINGO SCHOLARSHIP PROGRAM

Santo Domingo Tribe
Attn: Scholarship Program
P.O. Box 99
Santo Domingo Pueblo, NM 87052
(505) 465-2214, ext. 227

Purpose To provide financial assistance for undergraduate education to members of the Santo Domingo Tribe.

Eligibility Applicants must at least one-quarter degree of the Santo Domingo Tribe (students residing on the reservation are given priority) and high school seniors or graduates with at least a 2.0 grade point average. Scholarships may be used at any accredited college or university in pursuit of a bachelor or associate of science/arts degree. Students in vocational, technical, or associate of applied science programs are not eligible.

Financial data The amount awarded depends on the financial need of the recipient, up to $1,800 per year.

Duration 1 year; may be renewed for up to 3 additional years if the recipient maintains full-time status and a 2.0 grade point average.

Number awarded Varies each year.

Deadline February for the fall or summer terms; October for the spring term.

[112]
SCHUYLER M. MEYER, JR. SCHOLARSHIP FUND

American Indian Science and Engineering Society
Attn: Scholarship Department
5661 Airport Boulevard
Boulder, CO 80301
(303) 939-0023   E-mail: ascholar@spot.colorado.edu

Purpose To provide financial assistance to undergraduate or graduate Indian students who are single parents.

Eligibility This program is open to American Indian full-time undergraduate and graduate students who are single parents, with a minor child residing in the same household. Applicants must be at least one-quarter American Indian or recognized as a member of a tribe. All fields of study are eligible and students must demonstrate financial need.

Financial data The stipend is $1,000.

Duration 1 year; may be renewed.

Special features This award is sponsored by the George Bird Grinnell American Indian Children's Education Foundation and administered by the American Indian Science and Engineering Society.

Number awarded 1 or more each year.

Deadline June of each year.

[113]
S.D. BECHTEL JR. FOUNDATION FELLOWS

National Action Council for Minorities in Engineering
3 West 35th Street
New York, NY 10001-2281
(212) 279-2626   Fax: (212) 629-5178

Purpose To provide financial assistance for education in engineering to underrepresented minority students.

Eligibility Engineering students who are African American, Latino, or American Indian are eligible for this award. Candidates must be sophomores with a minimum grade point average of 3.0

nominated by their dean. Selection is based on high academic achievement and interest in a corporate career in engineering.
Financial data The stipend is $5,000 per year.
Duration 2 years.
Number awarded 1 each year.

[114]
SEMINOLE AND MICCOSUKEE INDIAN SCHOLARSHIP PROGRAM

Florida Department of Education
Attn: Office of Student Financial Assistance
State Programs—255 Collins
Tallahassee, FL 32399-0400
(904) 487-0049

Purpose To provide financial assistance to Florida's Seminole and Miccosukee Indians who wish to pursue postsecondary education.
Eligibility Scholarships are awarded to Florida residents who hold certification of membership or eligibility of membership in the Seminole Indian Tribe of Florida or the Miccosukee Indian Tribe of Florida and who meet the following criteria: are Florida residents; have complied with registration requirements of the Selective Service System; have participated in the college-level communication and computation skills test (CLAST) program; are enrolled as either a graduate or undergraduate student at an eligible public or private college or university in Florida for at least 1 credit hour per term; demonstrate financial need; and are not in default or owing repayment on any federal or state grant, loan, or scholarship program.
Financial data The amount of the award depends on the recommendation by the respective tribe, but may not exceed the annual cost of education for 4 years of undergraduate study or 2 years of graduate study.
Duration 1 year; renewable, provided recipient continues to demonstrate academic progress by meeting all academic and other requirements set by the college or university attended.
Number awarded Varies each year.
Deadline June of each year.

[115]
SENECA NATION OF INDIANS HIGHER EDUCATION PROGRAM

Seneca Nation of Indians
Attn: Higher Education Program
8183 Center Road
P.O. Box 231
Salamanca, NY 14779
(716) 945-1790

Purpose To provide financial assistance to Seneca Nation members who are interested in pursuing postsecondary education.
Eligibility Enrolled members of the Seneca Nation are eligible to apply if they are interested in pursuing postsecondary education and are in financial need. They must be accepted in an accredited program of study.
Financial data Up to $4,000. Family income and size determine the exact amount of the award.
Duration Up to 5 years of study, through the attainment of a master's degree.
Number awarded Varies each year.

Deadline Applications may be submitted at any time.

[116]
SHOSHONE TRIBAL SCHOLARSHIP PROGRAM

Shoshone Higher Education Program
P.O. Box 628
Fort Washakie, WY 82514
(307) 332-3538

Purpose To provide financial assistance to members of the Shoshone Tribe who are interested in undergraduate or graduate education.
Eligibility Enrolled members of the Eastern Shoshone Tribe are eligible to apply. They must be able to demonstrate financial need. The tribal program provides funding for students who do not qualify for the Bureau of Indian Affairs (BIA) Higher Education Program or the BIA Adult Vocational Training Program. Aid is provided to students enrolled in 2-year or 4-year degree programs, in vocational training, or in extension type college courses.
Financial data Up to $1,100 per year for junior college students; up to $2,200 per year for college and graduate students.
Duration 1 year; may be renewed.
Limitations Recipients must attend college full time.
Number awarded Varies; generally, at least 60 each year.
Deadline April or November of each year.

[117]
SILVER EAGLE INDIAN SCHOLARSHIP

American Legion Auxiliary
Attn: Department Secretary
1718 State Street
North Las Vegas, NV 89030-7260

Purpose To provide financial assistance for postsecondary education to the dependents of American Indian veterans.
Eligibility Eligible to apply are the children or grandchildren of American Indian veterans. The applicant must have been born in Nevada.
Financial data The stipend is $200.
Duration 1 year.
Number awarded 1 each year.

[118]
SOCIETY OF ACTUARIES SCHOLARSHIPS FOR MINORITY STUDENTS

Society of Actuaries
Attn: Minority Scholarship Coordinator
475 North Martingale Road, Suite 800
Schaumburg, IL 60173-2226
(847) 706-3543   Fax: (847) 706-3599

Purpose To provide financial assistance to minority undergraduate students who are interested in pursuing actuarial careers.
Eligibility This program is open to African Americans, Hispanics, and Native North Americans who are U.S. citizens or have a permanent resident visa. Before applying for this program, students should have taken Exam 100 of the Actuarial Examinations, the Scholastic Assessment Test, or the ACT Assessment. Applicants must be admitted to a college or university offering either a program in actuarial science or courses that will prepare the students for an actuarial career. Scholarships are awarded on the basis of individual merit and financial need.

Financial data The amount of the award is determined by a committee of members of the sponsors. There is no limit to the size of the scholarship.

Duration 1 year; may be renewed.

Special features This program is jointly sponsored by the Society of Actuaries and the Casualty Actuarial Society.

Number awarded There is no limit to the number of scholarships awarded.

Deadline April of each year.

[119]
SOUTH DAKOTA SPACE GRANT CONSORTIUM FELLOWSHIPS AND ASSISTANTSHIPS

South Dakota Space Grant Consortium
c/o South Dakota School of Mines and Technology
Graduate Education and Research Office
501 East St. Joseph Street
Rapid City, SD 57701-3995
(605) 394-2291   Fax: (605) 394-6061
E-mail: psmith@nimbus.ias.sdsmt.edu

Purpose To provide support for space-related activities in South Dakota.

Eligibility This program is open to faculty, graduate students, and undergraduate students at member institutions of the South Dakota Space Grant Consortium (South Dakota School of Mines and Technology and South Dakota State University). Activities include summer faculty fellowships at the EROS Data Center in Sioux Falls, graduate fellowships, and undergraduate assistantships. Participants must be U.S. citizens. Underrepresented groups, primarily Native Americans and women, are especially encouraged to participate.

Financial data Approximately $70,000 per year is available to support the program.

Special features This program is funded by the U.S. National Aeronautics and Space Administration (NASA).

Number awarded Varies each year.

[120]
SOUTHEAST NEW MEXICO MINORITY AND HANDICAPPED TEACHERS' LOAN-FOR-SERVICE PROGRAM

New Mexico Commission on Higher Education
Attn: Financial Aid and Student Services
10668 Cerrillos Road
P.O. Box 15910
Santa Fe, NM 87506-5910
(505) 827-7383   (800) 279-9777 (within NM)
E-mail: highered@che.state.nm.us

Purpose To provide financial assistance to underrepresented minority and disabled residents of designated counties in southeastern New Mexico who are interested in becoming teachers in that area.

Eligibility Eligible to apply for this program are ethnic minorities and people with disabilities who are current or former residents of Lea, Otero, Eddy, Chaves, or Roosevelt Counties of New Mexico. Applicants must declare an intent to provide service at public schools in 1 of those counties and must be U.S. citizens or permanent residents.

Financial data This is a loan-for-service program in which the amount of the loan (up to $4,000 per year, depending on financial need) may be wholly or partially forgiven upon completion of service as an educator in the designated New Mexico counties.

Duration 1 year; may be renewed.

Number awarded Varies each year.

[121]
SPRINT/CAROLINA TELEPHONE SCHOLARSHIP PROGRAM

North Carolina Community College System
Attn: Student Support Services
200 West Jones Street
Raleigh, NC 27603-1379
(919) 733-7051   Fax: (919) 733-0680

Purpose To provide financial assistance to North Carolina residents studying at publicly-supported technical or vocational schools in the state.

Eligibility Applicants must be North Carolina residents enrolled in technical or vocational schools in the service area of Carolina Telephone and Telegraph Company. Priority is given to minorities (defined by Carolina Telephone as Blacks, Spanish Surname Americans, American Indians/Native Alaskans, Orientals) and "displaced workers." Selection is based on scholastic achievements, individual financial need, participation in outside activities, and demonstrated interest in a technical or vocational career.

Financial data The stipend is $550 per year.

Duration 1 year; may be renewed 1 additional year.

Limitations There are no special application forms for the scholarship. Students apply to their local community college, not to the system office. Each eligible school selects its own recipients from applicants meeting the above criteria.

Number awarded 70 each year.

[122]
STUDENT OPPORTUNITY SCHOLARSHIPS FOR ETHNIC MINORITY GROUPS

Presbyterian Church (U.S.A.)
Attn: Office of Financial Aid for Studies
100 Witherspoon Street, Room M042
Louisville, KY 40202-1396
(502) 569-5776   Fax: (502) 569-5018

Purpose To provide financial assistance for educational purposes to Presbyterian members of racial/ethnic minority groups.

Eligibility To be eligible, students must be from racial/ethnic minority groups (Asian American, African American, Hispanic American, Native American, Alaska Native), unable to pursue postsecondary education without financial assistance, high school seniors entering college as full-time students, U.S. citizens or permanent residents, and members of the Presbyterian Church (U.S.A.).

Financial data Amount varies; stipends range from $100 to $1,400 per year, depending upon the financial need of the recipient.

Duration 1 year; renewable if the recipient continues to need financial assistance and demonstrates satisfactory academic progress.

Number awarded Varies each year.

Deadline March of each year.

[123]
TECHFORCE PREENGINEERING PRIZE

National Action Council for Minorities in Engineering
3 West 35th Street
New York, NY 10001-2281
(212) 279-2626   Fax: (212) 629-5178

Purpose To recognize and reward outstanding underrepresented minority high school seniors who are planning to pursue a career in engineering.

Eligibility This program is open to African American, Latino, and American Indian high school seniors who have demonstrated academic excellence, leadership skills, and commitment to engineering as a career.

Financial data Semifinalists receive $500 per year, primary finalists receive $1,000 per year, and top scholars receive the 3M Engineering Award of an additional $2,500 per year.

Duration Semifinalists: 1 year; primary finalists: 4 years; 3M Engineering Award recipients: 4 years.

Number awarded 10 semifinalists, 10 primary finalists, and 2 3M Engineering Award recipients each year.

[124]
THUNDERBIRD FOUNDATION SCHOLARSHIP

Red Cloud Indian Art Show
Heritage Center, Inc.
Box 100
Pine Ridge, SD 57770
(605) 867-5491

Purpose To provide financial assistance for the education of Native American artists.

Eligibility Young Native American tribal members (18 years of age or older) who submit artistic works to the Red Cloud Indian Art Show are considered for this award.

Financial data A total of $5,000 in art scholarships is awarded, at the discretion of the Red Cloud Indian Art Show judges, to show participants.

Duration The award is presented annually.

Number awarded Varies each year.

Deadline May of each year.

[125]
UNITED SOUTH AND EASTERN TRIBES SCHOLARSHIP FUND

United South and Eastern Tribes
Attn: Scholarship Fund
711 Stewarts Ferry Pike, Suite 100
Nashville, TN 37214
(615) 872-7900   Fax: (615) 872-7417

Purpose To provide supplemental financial assistance to Native Americans who are in the United South and Eastern Tribes service area and are interested in pursuing postsecondary education.

Eligibility Eligible to apply are Native American students who are enrolled members of 1 of the following United South and Eastern Tribes: Chitimacha Tribe of Louisiana; Coushatta Tribe of Louisiana; Eastern Band of Cherokees (North Carolina); Mississippi Band of Choctaws; Miccosukee Tribe of Florida; Passamaquoddy–Indian Township (Maine); Passamaquoddy–Pleasant Point (Maine); Penobscot Nation (Maine); Mohegan Tribe of Connecticut; Seminole Tribe of Florida; Seneca Nation (New York); St.

Regis Band of Mohawks (New York); Houlton Band of Maliseet (Maine); Jena Band of Choctaw (Louisiana); Poarch Band of Creeks (Alabama); Narragansett Tribe (Rhode Island); Tunica–Biloxi Tribe of Louisiana; Mashantucket Pequot Tribe (Connecticut); Wampanoag (Aquinnah) Tribe of Gay Head (Massachusetts); Alabama–Coushatta Tribe of Texas; Oneida Nation (New York); Aroostook Band of Micmacs (Maine); or Catawba Nation (South Carolina). Applicants must have current enrollment or acceptance in a postsecondary educational institution, satisfactory scholastic standing, and demonstrated need for additional funding.

Financial data The award is $500 and is meant to supplement other funding sources.

Duration 1 year.

Number awarded Varies each year.

Deadline April of each year.

[126]
UNTO THESE HILLS EDUCATIONAL FUND SCHOLARSHIP

Unto These Hills Educational Fund, Inc.
P.O. Box 398
Cherokee, NC 28719
(704) 497-2111

Purpose To provide financial assistance to Cherokee Indians who are interested in pursuing postsecondary education at the undergraduate level.

Eligibility Scholarships are available only to students who are enrolled members of the Eastern Bank of Cherokee Indians, Cherokee, North Carolina or to students whose parents are enrolled members of the Eastern Bank of Cherokee. The student must provide the selection committee with information to establish tribal enrollment. Selection is based on scholastic aptitude, achievement, career ambitions, and the relative financial need of the student.

Financial data Scholarships are awarded in the amount of $500 each. They may be used for undergraduate study only.

Duration 1 year; may be renewed.

Special features This fund was established in the memory of the late Suzanne M. Davis, who was the costume designer for "Unto These Hills." The organization was originally chartered as the Suzanne M. Davis Educational Fund, Inc., but in 1979 the name of the organization was changed to Unto These Hills Educational Fund, Inc.

Number awarded 8 to 10 each year.

Deadline April of each year.

[127]
WASHINGTON STATE AMERICAN INDIAN ENDOWED SCHOLARSHIP PROGRAM

Washington Higher Education Coordinating Board
917 Lakeridge Way
P.O. Box 43430
Olympia, WA 98504-3430
(360) 753-7843   Fax: (360) 753-7808
TDD: (360) 753-7809

Purpose To provide financial assistance to American Indian students in Washington State.

Eligibility American Indian students who are Washington residents are eligible for this program if they have close social and cultural ties to an American Indian tribe and/or community in the state and agree to use their education to benefit other American Indians. They must demonstrate financial need and be enrolled, or intend to enroll, at a Washington state college or university on a full-time basis; all qualified applicants are considered, but upper-division and graduate students receive priority. Students who are involved in an academic program that includes any religious worship, exercise, or instruction or the pursuit of any degree in religious, seminarian, or theological academic studies are not eligible.

Financial data The amount of the award depends on the need of the recipient.

Duration 1 year.

Special features This program was created by the Washington legislature in 1990 with an appropriation to an endowment fund with matching contributions from tribes, individuals, and organizations.

Number awarded Varies each year, depending on the availability of funds; in a recent year, 13 scholarships were provided.

Deadline May of each year.

[128]
WHITE EARTH CRITICAL PROFESSIONS PROGRAM

White Earth Tribal Council
Attn: Jeanne McDougall
P.O. Box 70
Naytahwaush, MN 56566
(218) 935-5554   (800) 950-3248
Fax: (218) 935-2593

Purpose To provide financial assistance to Indian students who wish to pursue a course of study leading to an undergraduate or graduate degree in business administration, natural resources or forestry, computer programming, urban or rural planning, or elementary or secondary school teaching.

Eligibility Applicants must be enrolled members of the White Earth Tribal Council of the Minnesota Chippewa Tribe, and full-time students. Applicants are evaluated on academic record, leadership ability, and commitment.

Financial data Award varies; graduate students receive $650 per month (plus $90 per dependent) and undergraduate students receive $450 per month (plus $90 per dependent). Funds are disbursed directly to the recipient's institution of higher education.

Duration 1 quarter/semester; renewable if the applicant remains a full-time student and is in good standing (good standing means at least a 2.5 cumulative grade point average for undergraduate work or a 3.0 for graduate work). Financial need must be demonstrated.

Limitations Applicants must demonstrate a commitment to work for a tribal government or in an Indian community for 2 years after graduation.

Number awarded Varies each year.

Deadline Applications are accepted at any time.

[129]
WHITE EARTH SCHOLARSHIP PROGRAM

White Earth Tribal Council
Attn: Jeanne McDougall
P.O. Box 70
Naytahwaush, MN 56566
(218) 935-5554   (800) 950-3248
Fax: (218) 935-2593

Purpose To provide financial assistance to Minnesota Chippewa Tribe high school graduates who are interested in postsecondary education.

Eligibility Applicants must be at least one-quarter Indian ancestry, residents of Minnesota for at least 1 year, high school graduates or the equivalent, and enrolled members of the White Earth Tribal Council of the Minnesota Chippewa Tribe or eligible for enrollment. Financial need is required.

Financial data Up to $3,000 per year, depending on need.

Duration 1 year; may be renewed.

Special features Applicants for this program must also apply for financial aid administered by their institution and any other aid for which they may be eligible (e.g., work-study, Social Security, veteran's benefits). Recipients may attend a college, university, or vocational school.

Number awarded Varies each year.

Deadline For vocational school students, at least 8 weeks before school starts; for college or university students, June of each year.

[130]
WILLIAM R. HEARST TECHFORCE ENDOWMENT SCHOLARSHIP

National Action Council for Minorities in Engineering
3 West 35th Street
New York, NY 10001-2281
(212) 279-2626   Fax: (212) 629-5178

Purpose To provide financial assistance for engineering education to underrepresented minority high school seniors.

Eligibility High school seniors who are African American, Latino, or American Indian are eligible for this award. They must be proposing to study engineering at the university level. Selection is based on academic excellence, leadership skills, and a commitment to a career in engineering.

Financial data The stipend is $2,500 per year.

Duration 1 year; may be renewed for up to 3 additional years if the recipient maintains a minimum grade point average of 3.0.

Special features This program, which began in 1995, is funded by the William Randolph Hearst Foundation.

Number awarded 2 each year.

[131]
WISCONSIN NATIVE AMERICAN STUDENT GRANTS

Wisconsin Higher Educational Aids Board
131 West Wilson Street
P.O. Box 7885
Madison, WI 53707-7885
(608) 267-2206   Fax: (608) 267-2808

Purpose To provide financial aids for higher education to Native Americans in Wisconsin.

Eligibility Wisconsin residents who have at least 25 percent Native American blood (of a certified tribe or band) are eligible to apply if they are able to demonstrate financial aid and are interested in attending college on the undergraduate or graduate school level. Applicants must attend a Wisconsin institution, either public, independent, or proprietary. They may be enrolled either full or part time.

Financial data Up to $1,100 per year. Additional funds are available on a matching basis from the U.S. Bureau of Indian Affairs.

Duration Up to 5 years.

Deadline Generally, applications can be submitted at any time.

[132]
YAKAMA ADULT VOCATIONAL TRAINING PROGRAM

Yakama Indian Nation
Attn: Higher Education Programs
Department of Human Services
P.O. Box 151
Toppenish, WA 98948
(509) 865-5121, ext. 540   (800) 543-2802
Fax: (509) 865-6994

Purpose To provide financial assistance to Yakama Indians who are interested in acquiring technical training by attending an accredited vocational school, college, or trade institute.

Eligibility Yakama Indians who are at least 18 years of age, at least high school seniors, members of the Yakama Indian tribe, residents of the Yakima Indian Nation service area for the last 6 months, and unemployed or underemployed are eligible to apply for this program.

Financial data The amount awarded depends on the recipient's need.

Duration 1 year; may be renewed.

Special features In addition to financial assistance, this program provides career guidance and vocational training.

Number awarded Varies each year.

Deadline Applications may be submitted at any time.

[133]
YAKAMA COLLEGE STUDENT ASSISTANCE PROGRAM

Yakama Indian Nation
Attn: Higher Education Programs
Department of Human Services
P.O. Box 151
Toppenish, WA 98948
(509) 865-5121   (800) 543-2802
Fax: (509) 865-6994

Purpose To provide financial assistance to Yakama Indians who wish to pursue postsecondary education.

Eligibility This program is open to enrolled members of U.S. Indian tribes; preference is given to enrolled Yakama members. Applicants must be high school seniors or graduates (or GED recipients), accepted to a college or university as full-time students, and in financial need.

Financial data These awards are based on unmet need. "Unmet need" is established from information the students and/or parents submit on official financial aid forms (FAFSA or ACT Financial Aid Form).

Duration 1 year; may be renewed.

Special features The Yakama Nation through the Bureau of Indian Affairs provides this assistance to students to pursue a 2-year or 4-year professional degree in any field.

Number awarded Varies each year.

Deadline June of each year for fall quarter or semester; October of each year for winter quarter or spring semester; January of each year for spring quarter; April of each year for summer term.

[134]
YAKAMA INCENTIVE AWARDS PROGRAM

Yakama Indian Nation
Attn: Higher Education Programs
Department of Human Services
P.O. Box 151
Toppenish, WA 98948
(509) 865-5121   (800) 543-2802
Fax: (509) 865-6994

Purpose To recognize and reward the outstanding academic achievement of Yakama Indians.

Eligibility Yakama Indian college students who maintain excellent academic and attendance performance during the year are eligible to apply.

Financial data Monetary awards are presented to college students based on cumulative grade point average, course level, and class level.

Duration The awards are presented annually.

Number awarded Varies each year.

[135]
YAKAMA TRIBAL SCHOLARSHIP

Yakama Indian Nation
Attn: Higher Education Programs
Department of Human Services
P.O. Box 151
Toppenish, WA 98948
(509) 865-5121   (800) 543-2802
Fax: (509) 865-6994

Purpose To provide financial assistance to Yakama tribe members interested in pursuing undergraduate or graduate education.

Eligibility Eligible to apply are Yakama students of one-quarter or more blood quantum. They must be at least high school graduates and enrolled or planning to enroll in a postsecondary institution. Applicants must have at least a 2.0 grade point average. Scholarships are awarded on the basis of academic achievement rather than financial need.

Financial data Eligible undergraduate students receive $1,000 per year; graduate students receive $2,000 per year. Part-time students receive funding for tuition, books, and transportation; this amount may never exceed the Tribal Scholarship amount.

Duration 1 year; may be renewed.

Limitations Before being awarded the scholarship, recipients must attend an orientation session. Students who drop out of school after receiving scholarship awards must refund the Yakama Tribal Scholarships before being granted additional funding. Tuition amounts kept by the student's college do not count against student refunds.

Number awarded Varies each year.

Deadline June of each year for fall quarter or semester; October of each year for winter quarter or spring semester; January of each year for spring quarter; April of each year for summer term.

[136]
ZUNI EMPLOYMENT ASSISTANCE PROGRAM

Zuni Tribe
Attn: Department of Higher Education
P.O. Box 339
Zuni, NM 87327
(505) 782-4481, ext. 482   Fax: (505) 782-2700

Purpose To provide financial assistance for vocational education to members of the Zuni tribe.

Eligibility Enrolled members of the Zuni tribe are eligible to apply if they are high school seniors or graduates, have earned at least a 2.0 grade point average, and are interested in pursuing a certificate program at a vocational/technical institution. Applicants must have applied for all other potential sources of financial aid.

Financial data The amount awarded depends on the need of the recipient and the availability of funds.

Duration 1 year; may be renewed.

Number awarded Because of limited funding, students who qualify for this aid are kept on a waiting list and funds are dispensed on a first come, first served basis.

Deadline Applications may be submitted at any time.

[137]
ZUNI HIGHER EDUCATION PROGRAM

Zuni Tribe
Attn: Department of Higher Education
P.O. Box 339
Zuni, NM 87327
(505) 782-4481, ext. 482   Fax: (505) 782-2700

Purpose To provide financial assistance for postsecondary education to members of the Zuni tribe.

Eligibility Enrolled members of the Zuni tribe are eligible to apply if they are high school seniors or graduates, have earned at least a 2.0 grade point average, and are interested in pursuing a college degree, including associate, bachelor's, master's, or doctorate.

Financial data The amount awarded depends on the need of the recipient, up to $1,800 per year.

Duration 1 year; may be renewed.

Number awarded Varies each year.

Deadline March for the summer session, May for the fall term, and September for the spring term.

Native Alaskans

[138]
AMERICAN CHEMICAL SOCIETY SCHOLARS PROGRAM

American Chemical Society
Attn: Membership Division
1155 16th Street, N.W.
Washington, DC 20036
(202) 872-6250   (800) 227-5558
Fax: (202) 776-8003

Purpose To provide financial assistance to underrepresented minority students with a strong interest in chemistry and a desire to pursue a career in a chemically-related science.

Eligibility This program is open to 1) high school seniors planning to enter college in the following fall; 2) college students who are currently or planning to pursue full-time study in a chemically-related field; 3) community college graduates and transfer students who plan to study for the baccalaureate degree in chemistry, biochemistry, chemical engineering, toxicology, materials science, environmental science, and other programs of study with a strong component of chemistry; 4) community college freshmen majoring in a 2-year chemical technology program. Applicants must be African American, Hispanic/Latino, American Indian, or Alaskan Native. Selection is based on academic merit and financial need.

Financial data Scholarships for freshmen and sophomores are up to $2,500 per year; for juniors and seniors, the awards are up to $5,000 per year.

Duration 1 year only.

Special features This program was formerly known as the American Chemical Society Minority Scholars Program.

Number awarded Approximately 200 each year.

Deadline February of each year.

[139]
EMERGENCY AID AND HEALTH PROFESSIONS SCHOLARSHIP PROGRAM

Association on American Indian Affairs, Inc.
Attn: Scholarship Coordinator
P.O. Box 268
Sisseton, SD 57262
(605) 698-3998

Purpose To provide emergency financial aid to Native Americans pursuing college-level education.

Eligibility Applicants must be American Indians or Alaskan Natives who are currently enrolled as full-time undergraduates in an institution of higher education and facing an educationally related emergency. Applications must be accompanied by a certificate of degree of Indian blood, a 1- to 2-page essay describing the specific nature of the emergency need, a budget of educational costs and resources, and the most recent copy of a transcript.

Financial data The grants range between $50 and $300, depending on need and the availability of funds.

Limitations Because of the emergency nature of these funds, scholarships cannot be granted in advance. Students must apply after they begin college classes.

Number awarded Varies each year.

Deadline Requests may be submitted any time after the applicant begins college or college-level technical/vocational classes.

[140]
FLORIDA EMPLOYMENT AND TRAINING PROGRAM

Florida Governor's Council on Indian Affairs
P.O. Box 10449
Tallahassee, FL 32302-2449
(800) 322-9186

Purpose To provide financial assistance to needy Native Americans in Florida or Georgia who are interested in obtaining additional education or training.

Eligibility Unemployed, underemployed, or economically disadvantaged Native Americans (Native Hawaiians, Alaskan Natives, American Indians) are eligible to apply for this support. The Florida Governor's Council on Indian Affairs provides this service for 63 of the 67 counties in Florida and all of the state of Georgia.

Financial data Tuition and other services are offered to recipients.

Duration Up to 1 year.

Special features Funds may be used for a vocational-technical degree, an A.A. or Associate Degree, GED preparation, or adult education.

Number awarded Varies each year.

[141]
HEALTH CAREERS OPPORTUNITY PROGRAM GRANTS

Health Resources and Services Administration
Attn: Bureau of Health Professions
Division of Disadvantaged Assistance
Parklawn Building, Room 8A09
5600 Fishers Lane
Rockville, MD 20857
(301) 443-4493   Fax: (301) 443-6343
E-mail: bbrooks@hrsa.ssw.dhhs.gov

Purpose To provide financial support for education in health professions to students from disadvantaged backgrounds.

Eligibility This program is open to schools of allopathic medicine, osteopathic medicine, public health, dentistry, veterinary medicine, optometry, pharmacy, allied health, chiropractic and podiatric medicine, and public and nonprofit private schools which offer graduate programs in clinical psychology. Health professions schools are eligible if they identify a cohort of at least 7 disadvantaged students who applied but were not accepted to a health professions school; allied health schools are eligible if they identify a cohort of at least 5 disadvantaged students who have completed an undergraduate degree with a significant science focus and made a late decision to enter an allied health professions school and are in pursuit of a baccalaureate level degree in physical therapy, physician assistant, respiratory therapy, medical technology, or occupational therapy. Applicants must provide the designated students with a program of rigorous science and other education experiences and then admit the students who successfully complete the program or arrange for their admission to another health professions or allied health school. Recipient schools must also provide the students with a prematriculation summer program to ease their transition into the health professions or allied health school, and with counseling and advice on financial aid to assist them to complete successfully their education. Individuals from a disadvantaged background are those who come from an environment that has inhibited them from obtaining the knowledge, skill, and abilities to enroll in and graduate from a health professions school or allied health program, or who come from a low-income family (ranging from an annual income below $10,200 for a family of 1 to $26,700 for a family of 6).

Financial data Approximately $30.1 million is available for this program each year, of which $18.5 million is for continuing grants and $11.6 million is available for new grants, averaging $199,000 each. Of the appropriated funds each year, 20 percent must be obligated for stipends to disadvantaged students of exceptional financial need who are students at schools of allopathic medicine, osteopathic medicine, or dentistry; 10 percent must be obligated to community-based programs (including Indian tribes and Alaska Native villages); and 70 percent must be obligated for grants and contracts to institutions of higher education. Students receive a stipend during their participation in the program.

Duration Grants to institutions are up to 3 years; for students, the program is 1 year, including 6 to 8 weeks in the summer.

Number awarded Approximately 58 new projects are funded each year.

Deadline February of each year.

[142]
HEALTH PROFESSIONS PREGRADUATE SCHOLARSHIP PROGRAM

Indian Health Service
Attn: Scholarship Program
Twinbrook Metro Plaza, Suite 100
12300 Twinbrook Parkway
Rockville, MD 20852
(301) 443-6197   Fax: (301) 443-6048

Purpose To provide financial support for American Indian students interested in pursuing postsecondary education in pre-medicine or pre-dentistry.

Eligibility Applicants must be American Indians or Alaska Natives; be high school graduates or the equivalent; have the capacity to complete a health professions course of study; and be enrolled or accepted for enrollment in a baccalaureate degree program for pre-medicine or pre-dentistry. Applicants must provide verification from a school official (preferably for an undergraduate curriculum leading to a bachelor's degree in premedicine and represent 12 credit hours per semester/quarter/term, or the equivalent of full-time study at the applicant's school). Selection is based on academic performance, work experience and community background, faculty/employer recommendations, and applicant's reasons for seeking the scholarship. Recipients must intend to serve Indian people upon completion of professional health care education as a health care provider in the discipline for which the student is enrolled at the pregraduate level.

Financial data Awards provide for payment of a monthly stipend to cover living expenses including room and board, tuition and required fees, and all other reasonable educational expenses; the total award is approximately $15,000 per year. Recent annual funding available for this and the Health Professions Preparatory Scholarship Program was approximately $1,380,000 for continuation awards and $2,190,000 for new awards.

Duration 1 year; may be renewed for up to 3 additional years.

Number awarded Varies; in a recent year, 238 awards (of which 92 were continuing) were made under this and the Health Professions Preparatory Scholarship Program.

Deadline March of each year.

[143]
HEALTH PROFESSIONS PREPARATORY SCHOLARSHIP PROGRAM

Indian Health Service
Attn: Scholarship Program
Twinbrook Metro Plaza, Suite 100
12300 Twinbrook Parkway
Rockville, MD 20852
(301) 443-6197   Fax: (301) 443-6048

Purpose To provide financial assistance to Native American students who need compensatory preprofessional education to qualify for enrollment in a health professions school.

Eligibility Applicants must be American Indians or Alaska Natives; be high school graduates or the equivalent; have the capacity to complete a health professions course of study; and be enrolled or accepted for enrollment in a compensatory or pre-professional general education course or curriculum. The qualifying fields of study include pre-medical technology, pre-dietetics, pre-nursing, pre-pharmacy, pre-physical therapy, and pre-social work. Recipients must intend to serve Indian people upon completion of professional health care education as a health care provider in the discipline for which the student is enrolled at the pre-graduate level.

Financial data Awards provide for payment of a monthly stipend to cover living expenses including room and board, tuition and required fees, and all other reasonable educational expenses; the total award is approximately $15,000 per year. Recent annual funding available for this and the Health Professions Pregraduate Scholarship Program was approximately $1,380,000 for continuation awards and $2,190,000 for new awards.

Duration 1 year; renewable.

Number awarded Varies; in a recent year, 238 awards (of which 92 were continuing) were made under this and the Health Professions Pregraduate Scholarship Program.

Deadline March of each year.

[144]
HEALTH PROFESSIONS SCHOLARSHIP PROGRAM

Indian Health Service
Attn: Scholarship Program
Twinbrook Metro Plaza, Suite 100
12300 Twinbrook Parkway
Rockville, MD 20852
(301) 443-6197   Fax: (301) 443-6048

Purpose To provide financial support to students enrolled in health professions and allied health professions programs.

Eligibility Applicants must be at least high school graduates and be enrolled in a full-time study program leading to a degree in a health-related professions school within the United States. Even though non-Indian students may apply for this program, the Indian Health Care Improvement Act (P.L. 94-437) requires that priority for the awards be given to Indian and Native Alaskan applicants. Both the number of Indian applicants and the level of appropriations limit the availability of scholarship awards to non-Indians. Qualifying fields of study include associate degree nurse, chemical dependency counseling, clinical psychology (Ph.D.

only), computer science (B.S.), dentistry, dietician (B.S.), civil engineering (B.S.), health education (master's only), health records, medical technology (B.S.), medical social work (master's only), allopathic and osteopathic medicine, nurse practitioner, nurse midwife, B.S. nurse, M.S. nurse, optometry, para-optometric, pharmacy (B.S.), physician assistant (B.S.), physical therapy, podiatry (D.P.M.), public health (M.P.H. only), public health nutrition (master's only), radiologic therapy (associate and B.S.), respiratory therapy (associate), and sonography.

Financial data Awards provide for payment of a monthly stipend to cover living expenses, including room and board, tuition and required fees, and all other reasonable educational expenses; the total award is approximately $18,000. In a recent year, approximately $6,300,000 was available for continuation awards and $1,860,751 for new awards.

Duration 1 year; may be renewed for up to 3 additional years.

Limitations Upon completion of their program of study, recipients are required to provide payback service of 1 year for each year of scholarship support at the Indian Health Service, 1 of 638 tribal health programs, an urban health program, or in private practice serving a substantial number of Indians.

Number awarded Varies; In a recent year, 350 continuing and 103 new awards were provided.

Deadline April of each year.

[145]
HOWARD ROCK FOUNDATION SCHOLARSHIPS

Howard Rock Foundation
1577 C Street, Suite 304
Anchorage, AK 99501
(907) 274-5400   (800) 478-2332 (within AK)
Fax: (907) 263-9971

Purpose To provide financial assistance to Native Alaskans who are interested in pursuing a college degree.

Eligibility This program is open to Native Alaskans who are shareholders in a village corporation or tribal government that belongs to the Alaska Village Initiative (formerly the Community Enterprise Development Corporation of Alaska). The applicant must have attended high school in Alaska, be able to demonstrate financial need, be enrolled as a full-time student in an accredited undergraduate or graduate program at a college or university, and be majoring in a field of study that promotes the economic well-being of life for residents of rural Alaska.

Financial data Varies; recently, undergraduate scholarships have been $2,500 and graduate fellowships have been $5,000.

Duration 1 year; may be renewed.

Special features Recipients may attend school anywhere in the United States. This program began as the Bush Development Fund, created by the Community Enterprise Development Corporation of Alaska (CEDC) in 1986. In 1992 the name was changed to Howard Rock Foundation.

Number awarded Varies; recently 4 undergraduate and 1 graduate scholarships have been awarded each year.

Deadline February of each year.

[146]
INDIAN FELLOWSHIP PROGRAM

Department of Education
Attn: Office of Elementary and Secondary Education
Office of Indian Education
Portals Building, Room 4300
600 Independence Avenue, S.W.
Washington, DC 20202-6335
(202) 260-1683   E-mail: Indian_Fellowships@ed.gov

Purpose To provide financial assistance to graduate students and selected undergraduate students who are Native Americans interested in preparing for careers in medicine, law, engineering, natural resources, business administration, education, psychology, and related fields.

Eligibility American Indian students who are attending or have been accepted for admission at an accredited institution of higher learning and working toward 1) a graduate degree in medicine, law, education, psychology, clinical psychology, or related fields or 2) a graduate or undergraduate degree in natural resources, business administration, engineering, or related fields may apply. All applicants must be U.S. citizens and Indians. By federal government definition, this means that applicants must be 1) a member of a tribe, band, or other organized group of Indians (including those tribes, bands, or groups terminated since 1940 and those recognized by the state in which they reside); 2) a descendant in the first or second degree of any individual described above; 3) considered by the Secretary of the Interior to be an Indian for any purpose or be an Eskimo, Aleut, or other Alaska Native; or 4) a member of an organized Indian group that received a grant under the Indian Education Act of 1988. Selection is based on academic record (60 points), letters of recommendation (15 points), and an essay on career goals, why the chosen field of study will benefit Indian people, life experiences and personal and family expectations that will enhance the applicant's anticipated career accomplishments, and anticipated commitment to providing service to Indian people (25 points).

Financial data Fellowships are intended to provide full financing for a student's educational expenses or to supplement other sources of financial aid.

Duration Up to 2 years for a master's degree; up to 4 years for an undergraduate or doctorate degree. Each year's renewal is dependent upon appropriations from Congress and satisfactory performance by the fellow.

Special features Up to 10 percent of the awards are to persons receiving training in guidance counseling with a specialty in the area of alcohol and substance abuse counseling and education.

Limitations Individuals receiving assistance under this program are required to perform work related to the training received and that benefits Indian people, or repay all or a prorated part of the assistance received. This payback must begin within 6 months from the date of the completion of the training and is equivalent to the total period of time for which training was actually received.

Number awarded Varies; approximately 60 continuation and 550 new awards are made each year.

Deadline January of each year.

[147]
METROLINA NATIVE AMERICAN ASSOCIATION EMPLOYMENT AND TRAINING PROGRAM

Metrolina Native American Association
2601-A East Seventh Street
Charlotte, NC 28204
(704) 331-4818   Fax: (704) 331-9501

Purpose To provide financial assistance to needy Native Americans in North Carolina who are interested in obtaining additional education or training.

Eligibility Native Americans or Alaskan Natives who are unemployed, underemployed, or economically disadvantaged are eligible to apply for this support if they reside in the service area of the Metrolina Native American Association of 10 counties (Cabarrus, Catawba, Cleveland, Gaston, Iredell, Lincoln, Mecklenburg, Rowan, Stanley, or Union) in North Carolina.

Financial data Tuition assistance and other services are offered to recipients.

Duration Up to 1 year.

Special features Funds may be used for a vocational/technical degree, an associate degree, GED preparation, or adult education.

Number awarded Varies each year.

[148]
NATIVE AMERICAN EDUCATION GRANTS

Presbyterian Church (U.S.A.)
Attn: Office of Financial Aid for Studies
100 Witherspoon Street, Room M042
Louisville, KY 40202-1396
(502) 569-5776   Fax: (502) 569-5018

Purpose To provide financially needy Native American students with support to continue their college education.

Eligibility Alaska Native and Native American students pursuing full-time postsecondary education are eligible to apply if they are members of the Presbyterian Church (U.S.A.), are U.S. citizens, have completed at least 1 semester of work at an accredited institution of higher education, and can demonstrate financial need.

Financial data Stipends range from $200 to $1,500, depending upon the recipient's financial need.

Duration 1 year; may be renewed upon documentation of continued financial need and satisfactory academic progress.

Number awarded Varies each year.

Deadline May of each year.

[149]
NATIVE AMERICAN SEMINARY SCHOLARSHIPS

Presbyterian Church (U.S.A.)
Attn: Office of Financial Aid for Studies
100 Witherspoon Street, Room M042
Louisville, KY 40202-1396
(502) 569-5776   Fax: (502) 569-5018

Purpose To provide financial assistance to Native American students interested in preparing for church occupations.

Eligibility Native American and Alaska Native students may apply for the award if they are U.S. citizens or permanent residents, can demonstrate financial need, are in good academic standing, and are in 1 of the following 3 categories: 1) theological student enrolled as an inquirer or candidate by a presbytery of the Presbyterian Church (U.S.A.), preparing for a church occupation, and enrolled in a theological institution approved by the students' Committee on Preparation for Ministry; 2) Presbyterian Church (U.S.A.) member enrolled in a program of theological education by extension, such as the NATEC; or 3) inquirer, candidate, minister, or member of the Presbyterian Church (U.S.A.) in other church occupations pursuing an approved program of continuing education.

Financial data The amounts of the awards depend on the availability of funds.

Number awarded Varies each year.

[150]
NEW YORK STATE REGENTS PROFESSIONAL OPPORTUNITY SCHOLARSHIPS

New York State Education Department
Attn: Bureau of Postsecondary Grants Administration
Cultural Education Center
Albany, NY 12230
(518) 486-1319

Purpose To expand educational opportunities for underrepresented minority and economically disadvantaged students interested in pursuing professional careers.

Eligibility Candidates must be U.S. citizens or permanent residents and legal residents of New York for 1 year prior to application. The law requires that awards be made to eligible candidates in the following order: first priority is given to any candidate who is economically disadvantaged and a minority group member historically underrepresented in the professions (Black Americans, Hispanic Americans, Native Americans, or Alaskan Natives); second priority is given to any candidate who is a minority group member underrepresented in the professions; and third priority is given to any candidate who is enrolled in or a graduate of 1 of these state-supported opportunity programs: Search for Education, Elevation and Knowledge (SEEK) or College Discovery at City University; Educational Opportunity Program (EOP) in the State University system; or Higher Education Opportunity Program (HEOP) at an independent college.

Financial data The stipends range from $1,000 to $5,000 per year, depending on income.

Duration Up to 4 years.

Special features Scholarships are available for study in the following areas: accounting (baccalaureate level), architecture (baccalaureate or master's), chiropratic medicine (doctoral), dental hygiene (associate), engineering (baccalaureate), landscape architecture (baccalaureate or master's), law (juris doctoral), nursing (baccalaureate), occupational therapy (baccalaureate or master's), occupational therapy assistant (associate), ophthalmic dispensing (associate), optometry (doctoral), pharmacy (baccalaureate), physical therapist assistant (associate), physical therapy (baccalaureate or master's), physicians assistant (baccalaureate or master's), psychology (doctoral), social work (master's), speech-language pathology/audiology (master's), and veterinary medicine (doctoral).

Limitations No award can exceed the actual cost of attendance. After completion of their professional studies, scholarship holders are required to practice in New York for 12 months for each annual payment received.

Number awarded 220 each year.

Deadline January of each year.

[151]
SOCIETY OF ACTUARIES SCHOLARSHIPS FOR MINORITY STUDENTS

Society of Actuaries
Attn: Minority Scholarship Coordinator
475 North Martingale Road, Suite 800
Schaumburg, IL 60173-2226
(847) 706-3543   Fax: (847) 706-3599

Purpose To provide financial assistance to minority undergraduate students who are interested in pursuing actuarial careers.

Eligibility This program is open to African Americans, Hispanics, and Native North Americans who are U.S. citizens or have a permanent resident visa. Before applying for this program, students should have taken Exam 100 of the Actuarial Examinations, the Scholastic Assessment Test, or the ACT Assessment. Applicants must be admitted to a college or university offering either a program in actuarial science or courses that will prepare the students for an actuarial career. Scholarships are awarded on the basis of individual merit and financial need.

Financial data The amount of the award is determined by a committee of members of the sponsors. There is no limit to the size of the scholarship.

Duration 1 year; may be renewed.

Special features This program is jointly sponsored by the Society of Actuaries and the Casualty Actuarial Society.

Number awarded There is no limit to the number of scholarships awarded.

Deadline April of each year.

[152]
SPRINT/CAROLINA TELEPHONE SCHOLARSHIP PROGRAM

North Carolina Community College System
Attn: Student Support Services
200 West Jones Street
Raleigh, NC 27603-1379
(919) 733-7051   Fax: (919) 733-0680

Purpose To provide financial assistance to North Carolina residents studying at publicly-supported technical or vocational schools in the state.

Eligibility Applicants must be North Carolina residents enrolled in technical or vocational schools in the service area of Carolina Telephone and Telegraph Company. Priority is given to minorities (defined by Carolina Telephone as Blacks, Spanish Surname Americans, American Indians/Native Alaskans, Orientals) and "displaced workers." Selection is based on scholastic achievements, individual financial need, participation in outside activities, and demonstrated interest in a technical or vocational career.

Financial data The stipend is $550 per year.

Duration 1 year; may be renewed 1 additional year.

Limitations There are no special application forms for the scholarship. Students apply to their local community college, not to the system office. Each eligible school selects its own recipients from applicants meeting the above criteria.

Number awarded 70 each year.

[153]
STUDENT OPPORTUNITY SCHOLARSHIPS FOR ETHNIC MINORITY GROUPS

Presbyterian Church (U.S.A.)
Attn: Office of Financial Aid for Studies
100 Witherspoon Street, Room M042
Louisville, KY 40202-1396
(502) 569-5776   Fax: (502) 569-5018

Purpose To provide financial assistance for educational purposes to Presbyterian members of racial/ethnic minority groups.

Eligibility To be eligible, students must be from racial/ethnic minority groups (Asian American, African American, Hispanic American, Native American, Alaska Native), unable to pursue postsecondary education without financial assistance, high school seniors entering college as full-time students, U.S. citizens or permanent residents, and members of the Presbyterian Church (U.S.A.).

Financial data Amount varies; stipends range from $100 to $1,400 per year, depending upon the financial need of the recipient.

Duration 1 year; renewable if the recipient continues to need financial assistance and demonstrates satisfactory academic progress.

Number awarded Varies each year.

Deadline March of each year.

Native Pacific Islanders

[154]
AAJA HAWAII CHAPTER SCHOLARSHIPS

Asian American Journalists Association—Hawaii Chapter
P.O. Box 22592
Honolulu, HI 96823

Purpose To provide financial assistance to Asian/Pacific Islander students in Hawaii who are interested in careers in broadcast or print journalism.

Eligibility These scholarships are open to Asian/Pacific Islander students in Hawaii who are planning a career in broadcast or print journalism. Applicants may be high school seniors, college undergraduates, or graduate students. Selection is based on academic achievement, financial need, writing or broadcasting skills, recommendations, and essays on their career goals and responsibility to their Asian heritage.

Financial data Stipends are up to $1,000.

Duration 1 year; may be renewed.

Number awarded 2 each year.

Deadline April of each year.

[155]
AAJA LOS ANGELES GENERAL SCHOLARSHIPS

Asian American Journalists Association—Los Angeles
    Chapter
231 East Third Street
Los Angeles, CA 90013
(213) 206-0169   Fax: (818) 570-9300

Purpose To provide financial assistance to Asian/Pacific

Islander students in southern California who are interested in careers in journalism.

Eligibility These scholarships are open to Asian/Pacific Islander students who are planning a career in broadcast, photo, or print journalism. Applicants may be high school seniors, college undergraduates, or graduate students who are either permanently residing in or attending a school in the southern California region. They do not need to be a journalism, photojournalism, or communications major, but applicants must show serious intent to pursue a journalism career. Selection is based on commitment to the field of journalism, scholastic achievement, journalistic ability and potential, a sensitivity to Asian American issues demonstrated by community involvement, and financial need.

Financial data Stipends are up to $2,000.

Duration 1 year; may be renewed.

Number awarded At least 5 each year.

Deadline April of each year.

[156]
AAJA–NEWHOUSE NATIONAL SCHOLARSHIPS

Asian American Journalists Association
1765 Sutter Street, Room 1000
San Francisco, CA 94115-3217
(415) 346-2051   Fax: (415) 346-6343
E-mail: HienN@aaja.org

Purpose To provide financial assistance for study in print journalism to undergraduate and graduate students, especially Asian Pacific Americans.

Eligibility This program is open to all students, but especially welcomes applications from historically underrepresented Asian Pacific American groups, including Southeast Asians, South Asians, Koreans, Filipinos, and Pacific Islanders. Applicants may be graduating high school seniors who declare journalism as a major or undergraduate or graduate students pursuing a degree in journalism and a career in print journalism. Selection is based on scholastic ability, commitment to journalism, sensitivity to Asian American issues as demonstrated by community involvement, journalistic ability, and financial need.

Financial data The grant is $2,000 per year.

Duration 4 years for a graduating high school senior; 1 year for current undergraduate or graduate students.

Special features This program began in 1994; it is funded by Newhouse News Service and administered by the Asian American Journalists Association.

Number awarded 1 each year to a graduating high school senior; several each year to current undergraduate and graduate students.

Deadline April of each year.

[157]
AHAHUI KALAKAUA SCHOLARSHIPS

Ahahui Kalakaua Association of Hawaiian Civic Clubs
c/o Violet Hughes
1330 36th Avenue
San Francisco, CA 94122

Purpose To provide financial assistance to students of Hawaiian ancestry who live in California and are interested in pursuing a college education (on the undergraduate or graduate level).

Eligibility Financially needy students of Hawaiian ancestry who were born in Hawaii or have parents who were born in Hawaii are eligible to apply if they are interested in pursuing postsecondary education and live in northern California (north of Monterey, Kings, Tulare, and Inyo counties).

Financial data Stipends range from $150 to $750.

Duration 1 year.

Limitations Requests for applications must be accompanied by a $2 fee.

Number awarded Varies each year.

Deadline April of each year.

[158]
ASIAN PACIFIC WOMEN'S NETWORK SCHOLARSHIPS

Asian Pacific Women's Network
Attn: Scholarship Committee
P.O. Box 86995
Los Angeles, CA 90086
(213) 891-6040   (909) 596-5331
Fax: (909) 596-5331

Purpose To encourage Asian/Pacific women to pursue life change through academic, vocational, trade, or other skill development programs.

Eligibility Eligible to apply are women of Asian or Pacific Island ancestry who are 1) residents of 1 of the 5 southern California counties (Los Angeles, Orange, Riverside, San Bernardino, or Ventura), 2) interested in pursuing further education (graduate or undergraduate) or training (vocational or trade), and 3) accepted into a college, university, vocational, or trade school. Women from immigrant and refugee backgrounds are particularly encouraged to apply, as are women returning to school after raising their children, making a mid-career change, and pursuing leadership training.

Financial data The stipend is $1,000.

Duration 1 year.

Limitations Finalists must provide financial data and participate in a personal interview.

Number awarded 4 each year.

Deadline June of each year.

[159]
BLOSSOM KALAMA EVANS MEMORIAL FUND

Hawai'i Community Foundation
900 Fort Street Mall, Suite 1300
Honolulu, HI 96813
(808) 566-5570   Fax: (808) 521-6286

Purpose To provide financial assistance to Hawaiians who are interested in studying Hawaiian language or Hawaiian Studies.

Eligibility Eligible to apply are residents of Hawaii who are college juniors, seniors, or graduate students majoring in either Hawaiian Studies or Hawaiian language. Applicants must demonstrate financial need and academic achievement (at least a 3.0 grade point average). Preference is given to applicants of Hawaiian ancestry. Applicants must write an essay describing their interests and goals in pursuing Hawaiian Studies or language and how they plan to use their studies to contribute to the community. Members of the Hawaiian Girls Golf Association are not eligible.

Financial data The amount awarded varies, depending upon the needs of the recipient.

Deadline February of each year.

[160]
DEPARTMENT OF ENERGY MINORITY TECHNICAL EDUCATION PROGRAM

Department of Energy
Attn: Office of Economic Impact and Diversity
Forrestal Building, Room 5B-110, ED-2
1000 Independence Avenue, S.W.
Washington, DC 20585
(202) 586-5876

Purpose To provide financial support to programs for minority students who are interested in energy-related careers.

Eligibility This program is open to 2-year colleges which have at least 25 percent minority enrollment and a history of graduating students in mathematics, computer sciences, life sciences, or engineering. The institutions may use the funds to enhance their energy-related technical and academic curricula; establish linkages with high schools, other community colleges, and 4-year universities; and provide financial assistance to financially needy honors students pursuing energy-related careers.

Financial data Grants average $50,000 per year.

Duration 1 year; renewable.

Special features Currently, 8 colleges are participating in this program: American Samoa Community College of Pago Pago, American Samoa, for Native Pacific Islanders; Eugenio Maria de Hostos Community College of Bronx, New York, for Puerto Ricans; Fort Peck Community College of Poplar, Montana, for American Indians; Greenville Technical College of Greenville, South Carolina, for African Americans; Houston Community College, of Houston, Texas, for Mexican Americans; Luna Vocational Technical Institute of Las Vegas, New Mexico, for Mexican Americans and American Indians; Maui Community College of Kahului, Hawaii, for Asian Americans, Native Hawaiians, and Native Pacific Islanders; and Salish Kootenai College of Pablo, Montana, for American Indians. Students interested in participating in this program should first contact the address above to obtain names, addresses, and telephone numbers of administrators at each of the participating colleges, and then contact the college.

Deadline Deadline dates vary; contact the college for further information.

[161]
FLORIDA EMPLOYMENT AND TRAINING PROGRAM

Florida Governor's Council on Indian Affairs
P.O. Box 10449
Tallahassee, FL 32302-2449
(800) 322-9186

Purpose To provide financial assistance to needy Native Americans in Florida or Georgia who are interested in obtaining additional education or training.

Eligibility Unemployed, underemployed, or economically disadvantaged Native Americans (Native Hawaiians, Alaskan Natives, American Indians) are eligible to apply for this support. The Florida Governor's Council on Indian Affairs provides this service for 63 of the 67 counties in Florida and all of the state of Georgia.

Financial data Tuition and other services are offered to recipients.

Duration Up to 1 year.

Special features Funds may be used for a vocational-technical degree, an A.A. or Associate Degree, GED preparation, or adult education.

Number awarded Varies each year.

[162]
IDA M. POPE MEMORIAL TRUST SCHOLARSHIPS

Kamehameha Schools
Attn: Financial Aid Department
1887 Makuakane Street
Honolulu, HI 96817-1887
(808) 842-8216   Fax: (808) 841-0660

Purpose To provide financial assistance to Native Hawaiian women who are interested in pursuing postsecondary education.

Eligibility Native Hawaiian women who have graduated from high school in Hawaii are eligible to apply if they can demonstrate academic excellence and financial need. They must be pursuing undergraduate degrees at accredited 2-year or 4-year colleges in Hawaii.

Financial data The amount awarded varies, depending upon the financial need of the recipient; recent awards averaged $571.

Duration 1 year; may be renewed.

Special features Native Hawaiian means any descendant of the aboriginal inhabitants of the Hawaiian islands prior to 1778.

Number awarded Varies; in a recent year, 70 students received these scholarships.

Deadline February of each year.

[163]
JOHN ROSS FOUNDATION SCHOLARSHIPS

Hawai'i Community Foundation
900 Fort Street Mall, Suite 1300
Honolulu, HI 96813
(808) 566-5570   Fax: (808) 521-6286

Purpose To provide financial assistance to residents of Hawaii's Big Island who are interested in attending college and returning to the Island.

Eligibility This program is open to residents of Hawaii's Big Island; preference is given to those born on and with ancestors from this area who plan to remain or return to the Big Island (applicants should write about this in their personal statement). They may plan to study on the undergraduate (preferred) or graduate school level. They must be able to demonstrate academic achievement (at least a 3.0 grade point average), good moral character, and financial need. In addition to filling out the standard application form, they must write a short statement, indicating why they want to attend college, their course of study, and their career goals.

Financial data A stipend is awarded.

Duration The scholarship is awarded annually.

Special features Recipients may attend college in Hawaii or on the mainland.

Number awarded 1 or more each year.

Deadline February of each year.

[164]
KAIULANI HOME FOR GIRLS TRUST SCHOLARSHIP

Hawai'i Community Foundation
900 Fort Street Mall, Suite 1300
Honolulu, HI 96813
(808) 566-5570   Fax: (808) 521-6286

Purpose To provide financial support for the undergraduate or graduate education of young Hawaiian women.

Eligibility By court order, preference is given to girls of Hawaiian or part-Hawaiian descent. However, girls of other racial back-

grounds are encouraged to apply and will not be excluded. Applicants must be residents of Hawaii, have graduated from a public or private high school with a minimum grade point average of 3.0, and be enrolled or intend to enroll full time in an accredited business school, community college, 4-year college, or university. In addition, applicants must demonstrate financial need.

Financial data Grants range from $200 to $1,500 per year.

Duration 1 year; renewable.

Special features Awards are tenable either in Hawaii or on the mainland. The fund was established with property formerly used to provide boarding home facilities for young women of Hawaiian ancestry.

Number awarded Approximately 75 each year.

Deadline February of each year.

[165]
KAMEHAMEHA SCHOOLS BISHOP ESTATE SCHOLARSHIPS

Kamehameha Schools
Attn: Financial Aid Department
1887 Makuakane Street
Honolulu, HI 96817-1887
(808) 842-8216   Fax: (808) 841-0660

Purpose To provide financial assistance to Native Hawaiians who are interested in pursuing postsecondary education.

Eligibility Native Hawaiians (or part Hawaiians) who have graduated from high school in Hawaii are eligible to apply if they can demonstrate academic excellence and financial need. They must be pursuing undergraduate or graduate degrees at accredited 2-year or 4-year colleges in Hawaii; graduate students may attend out-of-state schools if their major field of study is not available in Hawaii. Students who graduated from the Kamehameha Schools are not eligible to apply.

Financial data The amount awarded varies, depending upon the financial need of the recipient; recently, the average award was $3,214.

Duration 1 year; may be renewed.

Special features Native Hawaiian means any descendant of the aboriginal inhabitants of the Hawaiian islands prior to 1778.

Number awarded Varies; in a recent year, 1,630 students received these scholarships.

Deadline February of each year.

[166]
NATIVE HAWAIIAN HEALTH SCHOLARSHIP PROGRAM

Health Resources and Services Administration
Attn: Bureau of Primary Health Care
Division of Scholarships and Loan Repayments
4350 East-West Highway, 10th Floor
Bethesda, MD 20814
(301) 594-4400   (800) 435-6464
(808) 842-8562   Fax: (301) 594-4981

Purpose To provide financial assistance to Native Hawaiians for training in health professions in exchange for service in a federally designated health professional shortage area (HPSA) in Hawaii.

Eligibility Applicants must be Native Hawaiians training in allopathic or osteopathic medicine, dentistry, clinical psychology, registered nursing, nurse midwifery, psychiatric nursing, public health/community nursing, social work, dental hygienist, physician assistant, or master of public health degree. Recipients must agree to serve in a federally designated HPSA in Hawaii on completion of training.

Financial data A stipend and other reasonable costs are paid directly to the scholar and full tuition is paid directly to the health professional school.

Duration 1 year; may be renewed for up to 3 additional years.

Limitations Participants are obligated to provide full-time clinical primary health care services to populations in federally-designated, high-priority HPSAs (these include Native Hawaiian health centers and medical facilities of the Federal Bureau of Prisons). Participants incur 1 year of obligated service in the National Health Service Corps for each full or partial year of support provided under this program. The minimum service obligation is 2 years.

Number awarded Varies each year, depending upon the funding available.

Deadline March of each year.

[167]
NATIVE HAWAIIAN HIGHER EDUCATION PROGRAM

Department of Education
Attn: Office of Postsecondary Education
Division of Higher Education Incentive Programs
Portals Building, Suite C-80
600 Independence Avenue, S.W.
Washington, DC 20202-5329
(202) 260-3608   Fax: (202) 260-7615

Purpose To provide direct grants for a program of graduate and undergraduate fellowship assistance to Native Hawaiian students.

Eligibility Native Hawaiian private nonprofit educational organizations or educational entities with experience in developing or operating Native Hawaiian programs or programs of instruction conducted in the Native Hawaiian language are eligible. They may apply for funding for the following activities: 1) full or partial scholarship support for Native Hawaiian students enrolled at 2- or 4-year degree granting institutions of higher education with awards to be based on academic potential and financial need; 2) full or partial fellowship support for Native Hawaiian students enrolled at graduate degree granting institutions of higher education with priority given to providing fellowship support for professions in which Native Hawaiians are underrepresented and with fellowship awards to be based on academic potential and financial need; 3) counseling and support services for students receiving financial assistance under this program; 4) college preparation and guidance counseling at secondary school level for students who may be eligible for support under this program; 5) appropriate research and evaluation of the activities authorized under this program; and 6) implementation of faculty development programs for the improvement and matriculation of Native Hawaiian students.

Financial data Awards to institutions range up to $1,400,000 and average $467,000; awards to students are established by the institutions.

Duration Up to 5 years.

Limitations Students must apply directly to the institution, not to the Department of Education. For a list of participating institutions, write to the address above.

Number awarded 2 to 4 each year.

Deadline July of each year.

[168]
PETER IMAMURA MEMORIAL SCHOLARSHIP

Asian American Journalists Association—Los Angeles
    Chapter
244 South San Pedro Street, Room 411
Los Angeles, CA 90012
(213) 426-4525

Purpose To provide financial assistance to Asian/Pacific Islander students in southern California who are interested in careers in journalism.

Eligibility These scholarships are open to Asian/Pacific Islander students who are planning a career in broadcast, photo, or print journalism. Applicants may be high school seniors, college undergraduates, or graduate students who are either permanently residing in or attending a school in the southern California region. They do not need to be a journalism, photojournalism, or communications major, but applicants must show serious intent to pursue a journalism career. Selection is based on commitment to the field of journalism, scholastic achievement, journalistic ability and potential, a sensitivity to Asian American issues demonstrated by community involvement, and financial need.

Financial data The stipend is up to $1,000.

Duration 1 year.

Special features This award honors a former reporter at the *Riverside Press-Enterprise* and editor of the *Pacific Citizen*.

Number awarded 1 each year.

Deadline April of each year.

[169]
ROSEMARY & NELLIE EBRIE FOUNDATION SCHOLARSHIPS

Hawai'i Community Foundation
900 Fort Street Mall, Suite 1300
Honolulu, HI 96813
(808) 566-5570   Fax: (808) 521-6286

Purpose To provide financial assistance to Hawaii residents of Hawaiian descent who are interested in studying on the undergraduate or graduate school level.

Eligibility This program is open to Hawaii residents who 1) were born on the Big Island of Hawaii, 2) have been long-term residents of the Big Island, and 3) are of Hawaiian ancestry. They must be interested in pursuing an academic degree on the undergraduate or graduate school level and must be able to demonstrate academic achievement (at least a 3.0 grade point averag), good moral character, and financial need. In addition to filling out the standard application form, they must write a short statement, indicating why they want to attend college, their course of study, and their career goals.

Financial data A stipend is awarded.

Duration The scholarship is awarded annually.

Special features Recipients may attend college in Hawaii or on the mainland.

Number awarded 1 or more each year.

Deadline February of each year.

[170]
WAIALUA HAWAIIAN CIVIC CLUB SCHOLARSHIPS

Waialua Hawaiian Civic Club
P.O. Box 396
Haleiwa, HI 96712

Purpose To provide financial assistance for undergraduate education to Hawaiian natives residing in the Waialua, Haleiwa, and Waimea areas.

Eligibility Eligible for these scholarships are students of Hawaiian ancestry attending Waialua School. Students attending other schools are also eligible if their parents are members of the Waialua Hawaiian Civic Club. College students whose parents are not members of the Waialua Hawaiian Civic Club but who reside in the district of the Waialua Hawaiian Civic Club are also eligible. All applicants must have a grade point average of 2.0 or better and be attending secondary school, junior college, nursing school, business college, technical school, or university. Selection is based on attitude and motivation toward higher education, attendance record, character, physical health and health habits, recommendations, and an interview. potential to succeed, and financial need.

Financial data The annual award is $100 for secondary school students and $200 for postsecondary students.

Duration 1 year; may be renewed.

Special features The Waialua Hawaiian Civic Club was chartered in 1934 and has been providing scholarships since then.

Number awarded Varies each year, depending on the availability of funds.

Deadline April of each year.

Native Americans in General

[171]
ABC NATIVE AMERICAN GRANTS

American Baptist Financial Aid Program
Attn: Educational Ministries, ABC/USA
P.O. Box 851
Valley Forge, PA 19482-0851
(800) ABC-3USA, ext. 2067   Fax: (610) 768-2056

Purpose To provide financial assistance to Native American students interested in preparing for a ministerial career.

Eligibility This program is open to Native Americans who are American Baptists and interested in preparing for ministerial service.

Financial data Partial tuition scholarships are offered.

Duration 1 year.

Special features This program is offered in cooperation with the TEE program: Theological Education by Extension.

Number awarded Varies each year.

[172]
AEROSPACE ILLINOIS SPACE GRANT CONSORTIUM PROGRAM

Aerospace Illinois Space Grant Consortium
c/o University of Illinois at Urbana-Champaign
College of Engineering
Aeronautical and Astronomical Engineering
306F Talbot Lab
104 South Wright Street
Urbana, IL 61801
(217) 244-7646   Fax: (217) 244-0720
E-mail: solomon@uxh.cso.uiuc.edu

Purpose To provide financial support for space-related academic activities in Illinois.

Eligibility Aerospace Illinois has established 4 program elements: 1) undergraduate/high school teaching and research, to attract undergraduates and secondary school students to modern aerospace science and engineering; 2) training in graduate research, through research experiences focused on aerospace science and engineering; 3) outreach and public service, to employ the region's extensive existing public educational information networks and outreach programs to provide a window to the highest quality student populations with emphasis on minorities, women, and persons with disabilities; and 4) fellowships with industry, to add substantially to the national aerospace science and engineering pool. Currently, 2 of the Aerospace Illinois member institutions (University of Illinois at Urbana-Champaign and Illinois Institute of Technology) use funding for aerospace engineering, 2 member institutions (University of Chicago and Northwestern University) use funding for aerospace sciences, 2 affiliate institutions (Southern Illinois University and Western Illinois University) use funding for teacher education and training, 1 affiliate institution (McDonnell-Douglas Corporation) uses funding for research initiatives, and 1 affiliate institution (Argonne National Laboratory) uses funding for research and K-12 education. Students, teachers, researchers, and others interested in Aerospace Illinois activities should contact the institutions to obtain further information on program opportunities. Aerospace Illinois is a component of the U.S. National Aeronautics and Space Administration (NASA) Space Grant program.

Financial data Awards depend on the availability of funds and the nature of the proposal.

Duration Depends on the program.

Special features This program is funded by NASA.

Number awarded Varies each year.

[173]
AIA MINORITY/DISADVANTAGED SCHOLARSHIP PROGRAM

American Institute of Architects
Attn: Scholarship Program Director
1735 New York Avenue, N.W.
Washington, DC 20006-5292
(202) 626-7511   Fax: (202) 626-7420

Purpose To provide financial assistance to students from minority and/or disadvantaged backgrounds who would not otherwise have the opportunity to be enrolled in professional architectural studies.

Eligibility Students from minority and/or disadvantaged backgrounds who are high school seniors, students in junior college or technical school, or enrolled in the first year of professional study are eligible for this award. Initially, candidates must be nominated by 1 of the following organizations or persons: an individual architect or firm, a local chapter of the American Institute of Architects (AIA), a community design center, a guidance counselor or teacher, the dean or administrative head of an accredited school of architecture, or the director of a community or civic organization. Candidates must gain admission to an accredited school of architecture before the award can be accepted. Students who have completed 1 or more years of a standard college curriculum are not eligible. Applicants must write an essay describing the reasons they are interested in becoming an architect and provide documentation of academic excellence and financial need; selection is based primarily on financial need.

Financial data Awards vary, depending upon individual need. The exact amount is determined by the program director and the AIA's scholarship committee after a review of the nominee's financial statement and consultation with the director of financial aid at the student's school. Efforts are made to secure matching or supplementary funds from other sources to defray the scholarship costs.

Duration 9 months; may be renewed for up to 2 additional years.

Special features This program is offered jointly by the American Architectural Foundation and the AIA.

Number awarded 20 each year.

Deadline Nominations are due by December of each year; final applications must be submitted by January of each year.

[174]
AL MEDORO SCHOLARSHIP

BDA International
Attn: Scholarships
145 West 45th Street, Suite 1100
New York, NY 10036-4008
(212) 376-6222   Fax: (212) 376-6202

Purpose To provide financial assistance to ethnically diverse undergraduate students who are pursuing a career in the design of electronic media.

Eligibility Eligible to apply are undergraduate students who have attended at least 2 quarters or semesters of college and are majoring in graphic design, emphasizing electronic media, such as design in television, video, or computer-related media. A goal of this scholarship is to promote a more diverse community of design students, drawing from all ethnic groups. Applicants must prepare several graphic projects as part of the application process.

Financial data The stipend is $4,000 per year for tuition. The winner also receives complimentary transportation, conference registration, and housing to attend the award ceremony at the organization's conference and exposition.

Duration 1 year; recipients may reapply.

Special features This scholarship is provided by the BDA Foundation, the educational foundation of the Broadcast Designers' Association (BDA) International. Applicants automatically receive a 1-year BDA International student membership. This scholarship is named after 1982-1983 BDA President Al Medoro and is intended to inspire those individuals who might not otherwise consider electronic media design as a potential career path.

Number awarded 1 each year.

Deadline March of each year.

[175]
ALABAMA SPACE GRANT CONSORTIUM TEACHER EDUCATION SCHOLARSHIP PROGRAM

Alabama Space Grant Consortium
c/o University of Alabama in Huntsville
Materials Science Building, Room 205
Huntsville, AL 35899
(205) 890-6028   Fax: (205) 890-6061
E-mail: jcgregory@matsci.uah.edu
E-mail: jfreasoner@matsci.uah.edu

Purpose To provide financial assistance for undergraduate study to students at universities participating in the Alabama Space Grant Consortium who wish to pursue careers as teachers of science or mathematics.

Eligibility This program is open to students enrolled in or accepted for enrollment at 1 of the 6 universities participating in the Alabama Space Grant Consortium: University of Alabama in Huntsville, Alabama A&M University, University of Alabama, University of Alabama at Birmingham, University of South Alabama, and Auburn University. Applicants must declare their intent to enter the teacher certification program on a track to qualify them to teach in a pre-college setting. Priority is given to those majoring in science, mathematics, or earth/space/environmental science. Applicants should have a grade point average of at least 3.0 and must be U.S. citizens. Individuals from underrepresented groups—specifically African Americans, Hispanics, American Indians, Pacific Islanders, Asian Americans, people with disabilities, and women of all races—are encouraged to apply.

Financial data The stipend is $1,000 per year.

Duration 1 year; nonrenewable.

Number awarded Approximately 15 each year.

Deadline April of each year.

[176]
ALABAMA SPACE GRANT CONSORTIUM UNDERGRADUATE SCHOLARSHIP PROGRAM

Alabama Space Grant Consortium
c/o University of Alabama in Huntsville
Materials Science Building, Room 205
Huntsville, AL 35899
(205) 890-6028   Fax: (205) 890-6061
E-mail: jcgregory@matsci.uah.edu
E-mail: jfreasoner@matsci.uah.edu

Purpose To provide financial assistance for undergraduate study related to the space sciences at universities participating in the Alabama Space Grant Consortium.

Eligibility This program is open to full-time students entering their junior or senior year at 1 of the 6 universities participating in the Alabama Space Grant Consortium: University of Alabama in Huntsville, Alabama A&M University, University of Alabama, University of Alabama at Birmingham, University of South Alabama, and Auburn University. Applicants must be studying in a field related to space, including the physical, natural, and biological sciences, engineering, education, economics, business, sociology, behavioral sciences, computer science, communications, law, international affairs, and public administration. They must be U.S. citizens. Individuals from underrepresented groups—specifically African Americans, Hispanics, American Indians, Pacific Islanders, Asian Americans, persons with disabilities, and women of all races—are encouraged to apply. Interested students should submit a completed application with a career goal statement, personal references, a brief resume, and transcripts. Selection is based on 1) academic qualifications, 2) quality of the career goal statement, and 3) an assessment of the applicant's motivation for a career in aerospace.

Financial data The stipend is $1,000 per year.

Duration 1 year; may be renewed 1 additional year.

Number awarded Approximately 25 each year.

Deadline February of each year.

[177]
ALBUQUERQUE JOURNAL PUBLISHERS' SCHOLARSHIP FUND FOR MINORITIES

Albuquerque Journal
7777 Jefferson Street, N.E.
Albuquerque, NM 87109-4360
(505) 823-7777

Purpose To provide financial assistance and work experience to minority students in journalism at universities in New Mexico.

Eligibility This program is open to minority students majoring or minoring in journalism at 1 of 4 universities in New Mexico: University of New Mexico, New Mexico State University, Eastern New Mexico University, or New Mexico Highlands University.

Financial data The scholarship is $2,000; the recipient also receives a paid internship and moving expenses.

Duration 1 year.

Special features This program is funded by the *Albuquerque Journal,* where the internship takes place, but applications are submitted through the 4 universities.

Number awarded 1 each year.

Deadline February of each year.

[178]
AMELIA KEMP MEMORIAL SCHOLARSHIP

Women of the Evangelical Lutheran Church in America
Attn: Scholarships
8765 West Higgins Road
Chicago, IL 60631-4189
(312) 380-2730   (800) 638-3522, ext. 2747
Fax: (312) 380-2419   E-mail: womnelca@elca.org

Purpose To provide financial assistance to lay women of color who are members of Evangelical Lutheran Church of America (ELCA) congregations and who wish to pursue postsecondary education on the undergraduate, graduate, professional, or vocational school level.

Eligibility These scholarships are aimed at ELCA lay women of color who are at least 21 years of age and have experienced an interruption of at least 2 years in their education since high school. They must demonstrate high academic potential, Christian commitment, realistic goals, and significant financial need. This program is only available to U.S. citizens who are studying for a career other than ordination, the diaconate, or church-certified professions.

Financial data The stipends range up to $2,000.

Duration 1 year; may be renewed for 1 additional year.

Number awarded Varies each year, depending upon the funds available.

Deadline March of each year.

[179]
AMERICAN DENTAL HYGIENISTS' ASSOCIATION INSTITUTE MINORITY SCHOLARSHIP

American Dental Hygienists' Association
Attn: Institute for Oral Health
444 North Michigan Avenue, Suite 3400
Chicago, IL 60611
(312) 440-8900

Purpose To provide financial assistance to minority group students enrolled in certificate/associate, baccalaureate, master's, or doctoral programs in dental hygiene leading to licensure as a dental hygienist.

Eligibility Applicants must be members of groups currently underrepresented in the dental hygiene profession; these include Native Americans, African Americans, Hispanics, Asians, and males (who are not required to be members of a minority group). Applicants must be American citizens and have completed 1 year in a dental hygiene curriculum with at least a 3.0 grade point average. They must intend to be full-time students during the academic year for which they are applying. Financial need of at least $1,500 must be documented.

Financial data The amount of the scholarship generally will be based on the tuition charged at the student's institution plus $250 for books and supplies, or the applicant's assessed need, whichever is less. The maximum award is $1,500.

Duration 1 year; nonrenewable.

Number awarded 2 each year.

Deadline May of each year.

[180]
AMERICAN METEOROLOGICAL SOCIETY INDUSTRY UNDERGRADUATE SCHOLARSHIPS

American Meteorological Society
Attn: Fellowship/Scholarship Coordinator
45 Beacon Street
Boston, MA 02108-3693
(617) 227-2426, ext. 235   E-mail: sarmstrg@ametsoc.org

Purpose To encourage outstanding undergraduate students to pursue careers in the atmospheric and related oceanic and hydrologic sciences.

Eligibility Students in the following fields are encouraged to apply: atmospheric sciences, oceanography, hydrology, chemistry, computer sciences, engineering, environmental sciences, mathematics, and physics. Applicants must be entering their junior year, pursuing a full-time course of study leading to a baccalaureate degree in the atmospheric, oceanic, or hydrologic sciences, or pursuing a baccalaureate degree in science or engineering with a clear intent to pursue a career in the atmospheric or related oceanic or hydrologic sciences after completion of graduate study. Candidates must have a minimum grade point average of 3.0, and must be U.S. citizens or permanent residents. The American Meteorological Society (AMS) encourages applications from women, minorities, and students with disabilities. Awards are based on merit and potential for accomplishment in the field.

Financial data The stipend is $2,000 per academic year.

Duration 9 months; may be renewed for the final year of undergraduate study.

Limitations Requests for an application must be accompanied by a self-addressed stamped envelope.

Number awarded 12 each year.

Deadline February of each year.

[181]
AMERICAN METEOROLOGICAL SOCIETY MINORITY SCHOLARSHIPS

American Meteorological Society
Attn: Fellowship/Scholarship Coordinator
45 Beacon Street
Boston, MA 02108-3693
(617) 227-2426, ext. 235   E-mail: sarmstrg@ametsoc.org

Purpose To provide financial assistance to underrepresented minority students entering college and planning to major in meteorology or some aspect of atmospheric sciences.

Eligibility Candidates must be entering their freshman year of college and be planning to pursue careers in the atmospheric or related oceanic and hydrologic sciences. They must be minority students traditionally underrepresented in the sciences. Applications must include an official high school transcript showing grades from the past 3 years, a letter of recommendation from a high school teacher or guidance counselor, and a copy of scores from an SAT or similar national entrance exam.

Financial data The stipend is $3,000 per year.

Duration 1 year; may be renewed for the second year of college study.

Limitations Requests for an application must be accompanied by a self-addressed stamped envelope.

Number awarded 3 each year.

Deadline January of each year.

[182]
AMERICAN PHILOLOGICAL ASSOCIATION MINORITY SCHOLARSHIP

American Philological Association
c/o Department of Classics
College of the Holy Cross
Worcester, MA 01610
(508) 793-2203   Fax: (508) 793-3428

Purpose To prepare minority students for graduate work in classics.

Eligibility Eligible to apply are minority (African American, Hispanic American, Asian American, and Native American) undergraduate students who desire to engage in summer study as preparation for graduate work in classics. Applicants may propose participation in summer programs in Italy, Greece, Egypt, or other classical center; language training at institutions in the United States or Canada; or other relevant courses of study. Selection is based on academic qualifications, especially in classics with demonstrated ability in at least 1 classical language; quality of the proposal for study; and financial need. Applications must be endorsed by a member of the American Philological Association (APA).

Financial data The award is $3,000.

Duration 1 summer.

Special features Information is also available from Elizabeth Keitel, Department of Classics, University of Massachusetts, Amherst, MA 0131, (413) 545-5777, Fax: (413) 545-6137, E-mail: eek@classics.umass.edu.

Number awarded 1 each year.

Deadline February of each year.

[183]
AMS 75TH ANNIVERSARY SCHOLARSHIP

American Meteorological Society
Attn: Fellowship/Scholarship Coordinator
45 Beacon Street
Boston, MA 02108-3693
(617) 227-2426, ext. 235   E-mail: sarmstrg@ametsoc.org

Purpose To provide financial assistance to students majoring in meteorology or some aspect of atmospheric sciences.

Eligibility Candidates must be entering their final undergraduate year and be majoring in meteorology or some aspect of the atmospheric or related oceanic and hydrologic sciences. They must intend to make atmospheric or related sciences their career. Applicants must be U.S. citizens or permanent residents, enrolled full time in an accredited U.S. institution, and have a cumulative grade point average of at least 3.0. Selection is based on academic excellence and achievement. The American Meteorological Society (AMS) encourages applications from women, minorities, and students with disabilities.

Financial data The stipend is $2,000.

Duration 1 year.

Limitations Requests for an application must be accompanied by a self-addressed stamped envelope.

Number awarded 1 each year.

Deadline June of each year.

[184]
ARTS DANCE COMPETITION SCHOLARSHIPS

National Foundation for Advancement in the Arts
800 Brickell Avenue, Suite 500
Miami, FL 33131
(305) 377-1148   (800) 970-ARTS
E-mail: nfaa@artbank.com

Purpose To recognize and reward outstanding high school student dancers or choreographers.

Eligibility Applicants must be U.S. citizens or permanent residents who are graduating high school seniors or, if not enrolled in high school, are 17 or 18 years old. Dancers should have several years of concentrated study and choreographers should have a record of serious interest and production extending over at least 1 year. Acceptable categories are ballet, choreography, jazz, modern, tap, and additional (such as African, East Indian, Native American, Irish Step, and Spanish); applicants may enter 1 or more of the categories. Applicants submit videotapes showing up to 2 minutes of technique, up to 2 minutes of solo performance, and a brief full-face shot, half-body shot, and full-body shot at the end of the tape. Selection is based on presence, technique, musicality and phrasing, and artistry. On the basis of the tapes, judges invite award winners to Miami for the final competitions. An Affirmative Action Panel works with other panels to ensure minority and special needs applicants are equitably evaluated, and special arrangements are made to permit full participation by applicants with special needs.

Financial data First-level awards are $3,000 each, second level $1,500, third level $1,000, fourth level $500, and fifth level $100; honorable mentions receive $100 awards but are not invited to Miami.

Duration The competition is held annually.

Special features ARTS (Arts Recognition and Talent Search) is sponsored by the National Foundation for Advancement in the Arts, which is funded by many corporations, foundations, and individuals. The names of all ARTS applicants are provided to 100 participating colleges, universities, and professional institutions that have $3 million in scholarships available for ARTS applicants.

Limitations The application fee is $25 for early applications and $35 for regular applications.

Number awarded Up to 20 award candidates compete in Miami; an unlimited number of honorable mention awards are made to candidates who are not invited to Miami.

Deadline Early applications must be submitted by May of each year; regular applications are due by September of each year.

[185]
ARTS JAZZ COMPETITION SCHOLARSHIPS

National Foundation for Advancement in the Arts
800 Brickell Avenue, Suite 500
Miami, FL 33131
(305) 377-1148   (800) 970-ARTS
E-mail: nfaa@artbank.com

Purpose To recognize and reward outstanding high school student jazz musicians.

Eligibility Applicants must be graduating high school seniors (including both U.S. and foreign citizens) or, if not enrolled in high school, are 17 or 18 years old. Candidates submit an audiotape of 20 to 30 minutes (15 to 30 minutes for vocalists) in 1 or more of the categories of keyboard, violin, viola, cello, double bass, guitar, flute, oboe, clarinet, saxophone, trumpet, trombone, percussion, vocalist, or composer. Selection is based on improvisation, tone production, technique, diction, rhythm, intonation, interpretation, and phrasing. On the basis of the audiotapes, judges select award winners to come to Miami for the final competitions. An Affirmative Action Panel works with other panels to ensure minority and special needs applicants are equitably evaluated, and special arrangements are made to permit full participation by applicants with special needs.

Financial data First-level awards are $3,000 each, second level $1,500, third level $1,000, fourth level $500, and fifth level $100; honorable mentions receive $100 awards but are not invited to Miami.

Duration The competition is held annually.

Special features ARTS (Arts Recognition and Talent Search) is sponsored by the National Foundation for Advancement in the Arts and the International Association of Jazz Educators (IAJE); funding is provided by many corporations, foundations, and individuals. Candidates who are invited to participate in ARTS Week are named Clifford Brown/Stan Getz Fellows and also attend and perform at the annual convention of IAJE. The names of all ARTS applicants are provided to 100 participating colleges, universities, and professional institutions that have $3 million in scholarships available for ARTS applicants.

Limitations The application fee is $25 for early applications and $35 for regular applications.

Number awarded Up to 5 award candidates compete in Miami; an unlimited number of honorable mention awards are made to candidates who are not invited to Miami.

Deadline Early applications must be submitted by May of each year; regular applications are due by September of each year.

[186]
ARTS MUSIC COMPETITION SCHOLARSHIPS

National Foundation for Advancement in the Arts
800 Brickell Avenue, Suite 500
Miami, FL 33131
(305) 377-1148   (800) 970-ARTS
E-mail: nfaa@artbank.com

Purpose To recognize and reward outstanding high school student musicians.

Eligibility Applicants must be U.S. citizens or permanent residents who are graduating high school seniors or, if not enrolled in high school, are 17 or 18 years old. They may compete in the following categories: classical instruments (each instrument is a separate category), popular piano, and composition. Selection in the performance categories is based on tone production, technique, rhythm, intonation, interpretation, and phrasing; selection in the composition category is based on musical ideas, musical structure, and control of medium. Applicants submit audiotapes for each category entered, and judges select award winners to come to Miami for the final competitions. An Affirmative Action Panel works with other panels to ensure minority and special needs applicants are equitably evaluated, and special arrangements are made to permit full participation by applicants with special needs.

Financial data First-level awards are $3,000 each, second level $1,500, third level $1,000, fourth level $500, and fifth level $100; honorable mentions receive $100 awards but are not invited to Miami.

Duration The competition is held annually.

Special features ARTS (Arts Recognition and Talent Search) is sponsored by the National Foundation for Advancement in the Arts which is funded by many corporations, foundations, and individuals. The names of all ARTS applicants are provided to 100 participating colleges, universities, and professional institutions that have $3 million in scholarships available for ARTS applicants.

Limitations The application fee is $25 for early applications and $35 for regular applications.

Number awarded Up to 20 award candidates compete in Miami; an unlimited number of honorable mention awards are made to candidates who are not invited to Miami.

Deadline Early applications must be submitted by May of each year; regular applications are due by September of each year.

[187]
ARTS PHOTOGRAPHY COMPETITION SCHOLARSHIPS

National Foundation for Advancement in the Arts
800 Brickell Avenue, Suite 500
Miami, FL 33131
(305) 377-1148   (800) 970-ARTS
E-mail: nfaa@artbank.com

Purpose To recognize and reward outstanding high school student photographers.

Eligibility Applicants must be U.S. citizens or permanent residents who are graduating high school seniors, or, if not enrolled in high school, are 17 or 18 years old. Competitors may submit any form of photography, including color, black-and-white, mixed media, non-silver processes, documentary, etc. Entries consist of a portfolio of 10 slides, 5 of which tell a story or are thematically related. Selection criteria include original thinking, an artistic commitment, and a willingness to take creative risks. On the basis of the portfolios, judges select award recipients to come to Miami for the final competitions. An Affirmative Action Panel works with other panels to ensure minority and special needs applicants are equitably evaluated, and special arrangements are made to permit full participation by applicants with special needs.

Financial data First-level awards are $3,000 each, second level $1,500, third level $1,000, fourth level $500, and fifth level $100; honorable mentions receive $100 awards but are not invited to Miami.

Duration The competition is held annually.

Special features ARTS (Arts Recognition and Talent Search) is sponsored by the National Foundation for Advancement in the Arts which is funded by many corporations, foundations, and individuals. This photography category is sponsored by photographer Nancy Ellison and her husband, William D. Rollnick. The names of all ARTS applicants are provided to 100 participating colleges, universities, and professional institutions that have $3 million in scholarships available for ARTS applicants.

Limitations The application fee is $25 for early applications and $35 for regular applications.

Number awarded Up to 10 award candidates compete in Miami; an unlimited number of honorable mention awards are made to candidates who are not invited to Miami.

Deadline Early applications must be submitted by May of each year; regular applications are due by September of each year.

[188]
ARTS THEATER COMPETITION SCHOLARSHIPS

National Foundation for Advancement in the Arts
800 Brickell Avenue, Suite 500
Miami, FL 33131
(305) 377-1148   (800) 970-ARTS
E-mail: nfaa@artbank.com

Purpose To recognize and reward outstanding high school student actors.

Eligibility Applicants must be U.S. citizens or permanent residents who are graduating high school seniors, or, if not enrolled in high school, are 17 or 18 years old. Competition is in either spoken acting only or in spoken and musical theater acting. Applicants submit a videotape containing 2 auditions, each 2 minutes in length: 1 from a play published before 1910 and 1 from a play published in or after 1910. The 2 auditions should represent a maximum contrast (such as comedy/serious, verse/prose, representational/naturalistic, etc.) and, for candidates in musical theater acting, 1 must be spoken and 1 may be a selection from a musical play. Selection is based on the actor's ability to demonstrate concentration, control of material, flexibility and versatility of voice, movement, and expression. On the basis of the videotapes, judges select award recipients to come to Miami for the final competitions. An Affirmative Action Panel works with other panels to ensure minority and special needs applicants are equitably evaluated, and special arrangements are made to permit full participation by applicants with special needs.

Financial data First-level awards are $3,000 each, second level $1,500, third level $1,000, fourth level $500, and fifth level $100; honorable mentions receive $100 awards but are not invited to Miami.

Duration The competition is held annually.

Special features ARTS (Arts Recognition and Talent Search) is sponsored by the National Foundation for Advancement in the Arts which is funded by many corporations, foundations, and individuals. The names of all ARTS applicants are provided to 100

participating colleges, universities, and professional institutions that have $3 million in scholarships available for ARTS applicants.

Limitations The application fee is $25 for early applications and $35 for regular applications.

Number awarded Up to 20 award candidates compete in Miami; an unlimited number of honorable mention awards are made to candidates who are not invited to Miami.

Deadline Early applications must be submitted by May of each year; regular applications are due by September of each year.

[189]
ARTS VISUAL ARTS COMPETITION SCHOLARSHIPS

National Foundation for Advancement in the Arts
800 Brickell Avenue, Suite 500
Miami, FL 33131
(305) 377-1148   (800) 970-ARTS
E-mail: nfaa@artbank.com

Purpose To recognize and reward outstanding high school student artists.

Eligibility Applicants must be U.S. citizens or permanent residents who are graduating high school seniors or, if not enrolled in high school, are 17 or 18 years old. There are 2 categories of competition; in the first, which includes ceramics, costume design, drawing, graphic design, jewelry making, painting, printmaking, sculpture, textile and fiber design, and theater set design, candidates submit 10 slides, illustrating a minimum of 5 of their original works; in the other category, applicants submit a VHS cassette videotape of up to 10 minutes for which they had primary creative responsibility; the work may have been produced on film but must be transferred to videotape. Selection in both categories is based on imagination, competence, and the skillful use of materials. On the basis of the slides or videotapes, judges select award winners to come to Miami for the final competitions. An Affirmative Action Panel works with other panels to ensure minority and special needs applicants are equitably evaluated, and special arrangements are made to permit full participation by applicants with special needs.

Financial data First-level awards are $3,000 each, second level $1,500, third level $1,000, fourth level $500, and fifth level $100; honorable mentions receive $100 awards but are not invited to Miami.

Duration The competition is held annually.

Special features ARTS (Arts Recognition and Talent Search) is sponsored by the National Foundation for Advancement in the Arts which is funded by many corporations, foundations, and individuals. The names of all ARTS applicants are provided to 100 participating colleges, universities, and professional institutions that have $3 million in scholarships available for ARTS applicants.

Limitations The application fee is $25 for early applications and $35 for regular applications.

Number awarded Up to 20 award candidates compete in Miami; an unlimited number of honorable mention awards are made to candidates who are not invited to Miami.

Deadline Early applications must be submitted by May of each year; regular applications are due by September of each year.

[190]
ARTS VOICE COMPETITION SCHOLARSHIPS

National Foundation for Advancement in the Arts
800 Brickell Avenue, Suite 500
Miami, FL 33131
(305) 377-1148   (800) 970-ARTS
E-mail: nfaa@artbank.com

Purpose   To recognize and reward outstanding high school student singers.

Eligibility   Applicants must be U.S. citizens or permanent residents who are graduating high school seniors or, if not enrolled in high school, are 17 or 18 years old. They must compete in either classical voice (soprano, mezzo soprano, contralto, tenor, baritone, bass) or popular music vocals. Selection is based on tone production, technique, diction, rhythm, intonation, interpretation, and phrasing. Applicants submit audiotapes for each category entered, and judges select award winners to come to Miami for the final competitions. An Affirmative Action Panel works with other panels to ensure minority and special needs applicants are equitably evaluated, and special arrangements are made to permit full participation by applicants with special needs.

Financial data   First-level awards are $3,000 each, second level $1,500, third level $1,000, fourth level $500, and fifth level $100; honorable mentions receive $100 awards but are not invited to Miami.

Duration   The competition is held annually.

Special features   ARTS (Arts Recognition and Talent Search) is sponsored by the National Foundation for Advancement in the Arts which is funded by many corporations, foundations, and individuals. The names of all ARTS applicants are provided to 100 participating colleges, universities, and professional institutions that have $3 million in scholarships available for ARTS applicants.

Limitations   The application fee is $25 for early applications and $35 for regular applications.

Number awarded   Up to 5 award candidates compete in Miami; an unlimited number of honorable mention awards are made to candidates who are not invited to Miami.

Deadline   Early applications must be submitted by May of each year; regular applications are due by September of each year.

[191]
ARTS WRITING COMPETITION SCHOLARSHIPS

National Foundation for Advancement in the Arts
800 Brickell Avenue, Suite 500
Miami, FL 33131
(305) 377-1148   (800) 970-ARTS
E-mail: nfaa@artbank.com

Purpose   To recognize and reward outstanding high school student writers.

Eligibility   Applicants must be U.S. citizens or permanent residents who are graduating high school seniors, or, if not enrolled in high school, are 17 or 18 years old. Competitors may enter portfolios in 1 or more of these categories: poetry (up to 6 poems in up to 10 pages), short story—fiction (up to 3 stories in up to 16 pages), play or script for film or television (up to 3 scripts for dramatic performance in any medium in up to 20 pages), selection from a novel (up to 20 pages, preceded by a description of the complete work and how the excerpt fits into it), or expository (up to 3 essays in up to 16 pages). Selection is based on language, originality, imagination, and overall excellence. On the basis of the portfolios, award winners are invited to Miami for the final competitions. An Affirmative Action Panel works with other

panels to ensure minority and special needs applicants are equitably evaluated, and special arrangements are made to permit full participation by applicants with special needs.

Financial data   First-level awards are $3,000 each, second level $1,500, third level $1,000, fourth level $500, and fifth level $100; honorable mention recipients receive $100 awards but are not invited to Miami.

Duration   The competition is held annually.

Special features   ARTS (Arts Recognition and Talent Search) is sponsored by the National Foundation for Advancement in the Arts which is funded by many corporations, foundations, and individuals. The names of all ARTS applicants are provided to 100 participating colleges, universities, and professional institutions that have $3 million in scholarships available for ARTS applicants.

Limitations   The application fee is $25 for early applications and $35 for regular applications.

Number awarded   Up to 20 award candidates compete in Miami; an unlimited number of honorable mention awards are made to candidates who are not invited to Miami.

Deadline   Early applications must be submitted by May of each year; regular applications are due by September of each year.

[192]
ASBURY PARK PRESS SCHOLARSHIP IN THE MEDIA FOR MINORITY STUDENTS

Asbury Park Press
Attn: Scholarship Committee
3601 Highway 66
P.O. Box 1550
Neptune, NJ 07754-1551
(908) 922-6000, ext. 4262   Fax: (908) 922-4818

Purpose   To provide financial assistance to minority students from selected counties in New Jersey who are interested in postsecondary education in the field of communications.

Eligibility   Graduating minority high school students from Monmouth County, New Jersey and Ocean County, New Jersey are eligible to apply if they are seeking a career in the field of communications, including reporting, broadcasting, marketing, and advertising. Also eligible are college students entering their junior year with a demonstrated commitment to a newspaper reporting or editing career; preference is given to students from New Jersey or attending New Jersey colleges.

Financial data   The award is $2,000.

Duration   1 year; may be renewed for 1 additional year (with continued satisfactory work).

Special features   Recipients are offered an internship at the Asbury Park Press for 1 summer.

Number awarded   3 each year: 1 to a high school senior from Monmouth County, 1 to a high school senior from Ocean County, and 1 to a current college student entering the junior year.

Deadline   April of each year.

[193]
ATLANTA ASSOCIATION OF MEDIA WOMEN SCHOLARSHIP

Atlanta Association of Media Women
P.O. Box 4132
Atlanta, GA 30302

Purpose   To provide financial assistance to minority women in Georgia interested in studying mass communications on the undergraduate level.

Eligibility Minority women currently enrolled in a postsecondary institution in Georgia are eligible to apply if they are majoring in mass communications and need financial assistance to complete their studies.

Financial data The amount awarded varies, but each stipend is at least $1,000.

Duration 1 year.

Limitations Recipients must attend a college or university in Georgia.

Deadline March of each year.

[194]
BACCALAUREATE DEGREE COMPLETION PROGRAM (BDCP)

U.S. Navy
Attn: Naval Education and Training Program Management
  Support Activity
6490 Saufley Field Road
Pensacola, FL 32509-5204
(904) 452-1806   (800) USA-NAVY

Purpose To provide incentives to students from minority or educationally underprivileged backgrounds to continue their education and receive commissions in the Navy following graduation.

Eligibility Eligible are students in junior college, community college, or 4-year college in any major who wish to serve in the Navy as officers following receipt of the bachelor's degree. They must be under the age of 25 at the expected date of commissioning. Preference is given to minority students or those from an educationally underprivileged background.

Financial data Participants become active reserve enlisted Navy personnel and receive the pay of an E-3 seaman, or about $1,000 per month; the exact amount depends on the local cost of living and other factors.

Duration Until completion of a bachelor's degree.

Special features Following graduation, participants in this program attend officer candidate school or aviation officer candidate school for 4 months and are commissioned as Navy ensigns. They have an active duty service obligation that varies from 4 to 7 years, depending upon specialization within the Navy. Further information is available from local Navy recruiters or Navy Recruiting Command, 801 North Randolph Street, Arlington, VA 22203-1991.

Number awarded Varies each year.

[195]
BARNETT BANK OF PALM BEACH COUNTY MINORITY STUDENT SCHOLARSHIP

Community Foundation for Palm Beach and Martin Counties
324 Datura Street, Suite 340
West Palm Beach, FL 33401-5431
(561) 659-6800   Fax: (561) 832-6542

Purpose To provide financial assistance to minority high school seniors in Florida who are interested in preparing for a career in business.

Eligibility Applicants must be minority residents of Palm Beach, Martin, or Hendry Counties. Priority is given to economically disadvantaged students in good academic standing who intend to major in business.

Financial data The amount awarded varies but is approximately $1,000 per year.

Duration 4 years.

Special features The funds for this program, established in 1986, are provided by the Barnett Bank of Palm Beach County.

Number awarded 1 each year.

Deadline February of each year.

[196]
BIRDELL CHEW MOORE SCHOLARSHIP AWARD

Watts Health Foundation, Inc.
Attn: Health Education and Promotion
10300 South Compton Avenue
Los Angeles, CA 90002
(213) 564-1163   Fax: (213) 563-6378

Purpose To provide financial assistance to minority students interested in preparing for a career in health and human services.

Eligibility Applicants must be high school seniors, be Los Angeles County residents, have at least a 2.5 grade point average, and be interested in studying health and human services (or related studies, excluding veterinary medicine) in college. Selection is based on merit, scholastic ability, letters of recommendation, financial need, and a personal interview.

Financial data A total of $50,000 is distributed each year. Funds must be used to pay for tuition , books, supplies, transportation, housing, and other academically-related expenses.

Duration 1 year; may be renewed.

Number awarded Up to 50 each year.

Deadline April of each year.

[197]
BREAKTHROUGH TO NURSING SCHOLARSHIPS FOR ETHNIC PEOPLE OF COLOR

National Student Nurses' Association
555 West 57th Street, Suite 1327
New York, NY 10019
(212) 581-2215   Fax: (212) 581-2368

Purpose To provide financial assistance to minority students who wish to prepare for careers in nursing.

Eligibility Minority (Black, Native American, Spanish surname, Asian, or Polynesian) undergraduate students currently enrolled in state-approved schools of nursing or pre-nursing associate degree, baccalaureate, diploma, generic doctorate, and generic master's programs. Although graduate students in other disciplines are eligible if they wish to study nursing or pre-nursing, no monies can be used for graduate education in nursing. Selection is based on academic achievement, financial need, and involvement in student nursing organizations and community health activities related to health care.

Financial data The stipend awarded ranges from $1,000 to $2,500.

Duration 1 year.

Limitations Applications must be accompanied by a $10 processing fee.

Number awarded 13 to 15 each year.

Deadline January of each year.

[198]
BROADENED OPPORTUNITY FOR OFFICER SELECTION AND TRAINING (BOOST)

U.S. Navy
Attn: Naval Education and Training Program Management
    Support Activity
6490 Saufley Field Road
Pensacola, FL 32509-5204
(904) 452-1806   (800) USA-NAVY

Purpose   To provide preparatory training for civilians and Navy personnel who wish to participate in the Navy ROTC program but are not yet fully qualified to do so.

Eligibility   Applicants must be high school graduates between the ages of 17 and 21 who earned a minimum score on the Scholastic Assessment Test (SAT) of 390 verbal and 460 mathematics or on the American College Testing (ACT) of 19 English and 21 mathematics. Married civilian applicants and enlisted members below paygrade E-4 (petty officer third class) may have no more than 2 dependents. Single people with dependent children are not eligible to enlist in the Navy. Applicants must also meet the general physical standards for all NROTC scholarship programs, and have no record of conviction by a civil court (for other than minor traffic offenses). Minorities or others from deprived educational backgrounds are especially encouraged to apply.

Financial data   Participants receive regular Navy pay while they attend BOOST school.

Duration   The program consists of 9 to 12 months of college preparatory training in mathematics, science, English, and computer science.

Special features   Students who successfully complete the BOOST Program are guaranteed to receive an NROTC scholarship. Those who are not successful in completing BOOST school may either receive a discharge from naval service or continue on active duty and complete the 4-year active duty service obligation. BOOST school is located in Newport, Rhode Island. Marines may also apply for BOOST school to prepare for NROTC or the Marine Corps Enlisted Commissioning Education Program (MECEP). For further information on this program, civilians may contact their local Navy recruiter or Navy Recruiting Command, 801 North Randolph Street, Arlington, VA 22203-1991; current enlisted Navy personnel may contact the Navy Campus officer at their installation or the Program for Afloat College Education (PACE) officer aboard ship.

Deadline   Civilians must complete their applications by April of each year; current Naval personnel by November of each year.

[199]
BUSH LEADERSHIP FELLOWS PROGRAM

Bush Foundation
E-900 First National Bank Building
332 Minnesota Street
St. Paul, MN 55101-1387
(612) 227-0891   Fax: (612) 297-6485

Purpose   To provide educational and/or internship experiences to strongly motivated individuals in midcareer to prepare them for higher-level responsibilities.

Eligibility   Men and women in mid-career who are between the ages of 28 and 54 and are deemed likely to advance to leading positions in architecture, business, engineering, farming, forestry, government, journalism, law, law enforcement, social work, theology, trade unionism, and in the administration of arts, education, health, or scientific organizations are eligible to apply. Applicants

must have substantial standing in their fields, at least 5 years of work experience, residency in Minnesota, North Dakota, South Dakota, or the 26 northern and western Wisconsin counties that fall within the Ninth Federal Reserve District, and American citizenship or permanent resident status. The application may be either for a long term, involving a policy-level internship experience and often leading to an academic degree, or for a short term, to enroll in university programs to enhance managerial skills on a non-degree basis. Members of minority groups are particularly encouraged to apply.

Financial data   Long-term fellows receive monthly stipends and short-term fellows receive weekly stipends; the amount of the stipends is intended to cover basic living expenses. In addition, all fellows receive reimbursement for 50 percent of their tuition charges up to $8,000 plus 80 percent of tuition charges over $8,000.

Duration   From 4 to 18 months for long-term awards; from 3 to 10 weeks for short-term awards.

Special features   Awards are for full-time study and internships anywhere in the United States. This program began in 1965; the shorter awards were added in 1973.

Limitations   Fellowships are not awarded for applicants who are already enrolled as full-time students, part-time study combined with full- or part-time employment, academic research, publications, or design and development of service programs or projects. Fellowships are unlikely to be awarded for unstructured internships, full-time study plans built on academic programs designed primarily for part-time students, programs intended to meet the coninuing education requirements for professional certification, completion of basic educational requirements for non-administrative jobs or professions, segments of degree programs that cannot be completed within or near the end of the fellowship period, or projects that might more properly be the subjects of grant proposals from organizations.

Number awarded   Approximately 35 each year.

Deadline   November of each year for long-term fellowships; February of each year for short-term fellowships.

[200]
CANFIT PROGRAM SCHOLARSHIPS

California Adolescent Nutrition and Fitness Program
2140 Shattuck Avenue, Suite 610
Berkeley, CA 94704
(510) 644-1533   (800) 200-3131
Fax: (510) 644-1535

Purpose   To provide financial assistance to minority undergraduate and graduate students who are studying nutrition or physical education in California.

Eligibility   Eligible to apply are American Indians/Alaska Natives, African Americans, Asians/Pacific Islanders, and Latinos/Hispanics who are enrolled in either: 1) an approved master's or doctoral graduate program in nutrition, public health nutrition, or physical education or in the American Dietetic Association Approved Preprofessional Practice Program at an accredited university in California; or, 2) an approved bachelor's level program in nutrition or physical education at an accredited (WASC) college or university in California. Graduate student applicants must have completed 12 to 15 units of graduate course work and have at least a 3.0 cumulative grade point average; undergraduate applicants must have completed 50 semester units or the equivalent of college credits and have at least a 2.5 cumulative grade point average. Selection is based on financial need, academic goals, and community nutrition or physical education activities.

Financial data Graduate stipends are $1,000 each and undergraduate stipends are $500 per year.

Special features A goal of the California Adolescent Nutrition and Fitness (CANFit) program is to improve the nutritional status and physical fitness of California's low-income multi-ethnic youth aged 10 to 14. By offering these scholarships, the program hopes to encourage more students to consider careers in adolescent nutrition and fitness.

Number awarded 5 graduate scholarships and 10 undergraduate scholarships are available each year.

Deadline March of each year.

[201]
CAROLE SIMPSON SCHOLARSHIP

Radio and Television News Directors Foundation
1000 Connecticut Avenue, N.W., Suite 615
Washington, DC 20036
(202) 659-6510   Fax: (202) 223-4007

Purpose To provide financial assistance to an outstanding student whose career objective is electronic journalism.

Eligibility Eligible are sophomore or more advanced undergraduate or graduate students enrolled in an electronic journalism sequence at an accredited or nationally recognized college or university. Applications must include 1 to 3 examples of reporting or producing skills on audio or video cassette tapes (no more than 15 minutes total), a statement explaining why the candidate seeks a career in broadcast or cable journalism, and a letter of endorsement from a faculty sponsor that verifies that the applicant has at least 1 year of school remaining. Minority undergraduate students receive preference.

Financial data The scholarship is $2,000, paid in semi-annual installments of $1,000 each.

Duration 1 year.

Special features An expense-paid trip to the Radio-Television News Directors Association Annual International Convention is also provided.

Limitations Previous winners of any RTNDF scholarship or internship are not eligible.

Number awarded 1 each year.

Deadline February of each year.

[202]
CHARLOTTE W. NEWCOMBE SCHOLARSHIPS AT PRESBYTERIAN COLLEGES

Charlotte W. Newcombe Foundation
35 Park Place
Princeton, NJ 08542-6918
(609) 924-7022

Purpose To provide scholarship grants to Presbyterian Church-related colleges with small endowments that serve a significant number of minority and/or economically disadvantaged students.

Eligibility Presbyterian Church-related colleges that serve minority and/or disadvantaged student populations are eligible to apply for grants. The percentage of needy students in the student body, the location of the college, and the size of the college's endowment are considered in the selection process. The colleges use the grants to underwrite scholarships for minority and economically disadvantaged students on their campuses. For a cur-

rent list of the 14 colleges offering these scholarships, write to the foundation.

Financial data The amount awarded to the colleges varies; generally, the average grant is $15,000 per year. The colleges individually determine the amounts awarded in the student scholarships.

Duration 1 year; may be renewed.

Special features The colleges that receive these grants offer scholarships to selected students from economically depressed areas and/or minority students. The students are selected on the basis of financial need, not on the basis of academic merit or athletic ability.

Limitations The colleges may not offer scholarships as an enticement to increase enrollment. Students interested in the scholarship program should apply directly to the colleges receiving grants, not to the foundation. The colleges must submit 2 progress reports during the grant period, in December and in the following April.

Deadline March of each year.

[203]
CHICAGO SUN-TIMES MINORITY SCHOLARSHIP AND INTERNSHIP PROGRAM

Chicago Sun-Times
Attn: Assistant to the Executive Editor
401 North Wabash Avenue
Chicago, IL 60611
(312) 321-3000

Purpose To provide financial assistance to minority college students in the Chicago area who are interested in preparing for a career in print journalism.

Eligibility Minority students are eligible to apply if they are entering their junior year in college, graduated from a Chicago-area high school or have lived in the Chicago metropolitan area for at least 5 years, and have demonstrated an interest in print journalism.

Financial data Students selected for this program receive a $1,500 scholarship plus a paid internship.

Duration The program provides a scholarship in the junior year, a paid internship during the summer between the junior and senior years, and a renewal of the scholarship in the senior year if the recipient maintains a 3.0 grade point average.

Special features The Chicago metropolitan area includes Cook, DuPage, Kane, Lake, McHenry, and Will counties in Illinois and Lake and Porter counties in Indiana. Recipients may use the scholarship at any school of their choosing. For the summer internships, assignments are available in reporting, editing, graphics, or photography.

Number awarded 1 or more each year.

Deadline March of each year.

[204]
CHIPS QUINN SCHOLARS PROGRAM

Freedom Forum
Attn: Journalism Scholarships Committee
1101 Wilson Boulevard
Arlington, VA 22209
(703) 528-0800   Fax: (703) 528-7766

Purpose To provide work experience, career mentoring, and scholarship support to minority college students who are majoring in journalism.

Eligibility Deans of all journalism schools in the country are each invited to nominate 1 junior-year journalism student for this program. Students must also apply for an internship for the summer following their junior year.

Financial data Students chosen for this program receive a travel stipend to attend a spring workshop at the Freedom Forum in Arlington, Virginia and, upon completion of the internship, a $1,000 scholarship.

Duration 1 year, including the summer internship.

Special features Students are invited to the workshop at the Freedom Forum at the end of their junior year and then work as an intern during the summer at a newspaper where they are linked with a mentor editor. This program was established in 1990 in memory of the late John D. Quinn Jr., managing editor of the *Poughkeepsie Journal.* Funding is provided by the Freedom Forum, formerly the Gannett Foundation.

Number awarded Varies each year; in a recent year, 36 scholarships were awarded through this program.

Deadline January of each year.

[205]
CHRYSLER CORPORATION SCHOLARSHIP

Society of Women Engineers
120 Wall Street, 11th Floor
New York, NY 10005-3902
(212) 509-9577　　　　　　　Fax: (212) 509-0224
E-mail: 71764.743@compuserve.com

Purpose To provide financial assistance to minority undergraduate women majoring in engineering or computer science.

Eligibility Applicants must be sophomore, junior, or senior women who are minorities or other members of an underrepresented group in the fields of engineering and computer science.

Financial data The stipend is $1,750.

Duration 1 year.

Special features This program was established in 1995.

Number awarded 1 each year.

Deadline January of each year.

[206]
CHSPA/DENVER METRO MEDIA ALLIANCE DIVERSITY SCHOLARSHIP

Colorado High School Press Association
Attn: Executive Director
Campus Box 287
School of Journalism and Mass Communication
University of Colorado
Boulder, CO 80309
(303) 492-5045

Purpose To provide financial assistance for postsecondary education to minority journalism students in Colorado.

Eligibility This program is open to members of recognized ethnic minorities who are publication members of the Colorado High School Press Association (CHSPA) with at least 1 year of experience on a school newspaper or yearbook staff. Applicants must be high school seniors planning to attend any accredited Colorado institution with a journalism program. Selection is based on quality of published work in the school newspaper or yearbook, the application letter, teacher recommendations, and grades.

Financial data The stipend is $750.

Duration 1 year; nonrenewable.

Number awarded 1 each year.

Deadline January of each year.

[207]
CIA TUITION ASSISTANCE PROGRAM

Central Intelligence Agency
Attn: Personnel Representative
P.O. Box 12727
Arlington, VA 22209-8727
(703) 351-2028　　　　　　　(800) JOBS CIA

Purpose To provide tuition assistance to undergraduate and graduate students who participate in Central Intelligence Agency (CIA) internship programs.

Eligibility Eligible to apply are undergraduate and graduate students who are participating as interns in any of these 3 programs: the CIA Summer Internship (primarily for minorities and people with disabilities), the CIA Student Trainee Program (for undergraduate students), or the CIA Graduate Studies Program (for graduate students). Applicants must maintain at least a 2.75 grade point average, be enrolled in a minimum of 12 hours of course work, and have completed 2 work tours and be scheduled for a third tour as an intern (graduate fellows must have completed 1 work tour). Assistance is granted to those interns whom the CIA is willing to hire as staff employees within 60 days following the completion of their degree requirements.

Financial data The stipend is $2,000 per program (undergraduate or graduate); students with a grade point average above 3.5 receive an additional payment of $500 per program.

Duration 1 year as an undergraduate and 1 year as a graduate student.

Limitations Recipients must agree to return to the CIA as a staff employee for a 1-year period for each program in which tuition assistance is accepted.

Number awarded Varies each year.

[208]
CIA UNDERGRADUATE SCHOLAR PROGRAM

Central Intelligence Agency
Attn: Personnel Representative
P.O. Box 12727
Arlington, VA 22209-8727
(703) 351-2028　　　　　　　(800) JOBS CIA

Purpose To provide financial assistance to minority or disabled undergraduates who are interested in completing their postsecondary education and gaining work experience at the Central Intelligence Agency (CIA).

Eligibility Graduating high school seniors, particularly minorities from inner city neighborhoods and people with disabilities, are eligible for this program. They must be U.S. citizens, be 18 years of age by May 1 of their senior year, achieve a score of at least 1,000 on the SAT or 21 on the ACT, have a high school grade point average of 2.75 or higher, demonstrate financial need, and meet the same employment standards as permanent CIA employees. Recipients must attend an accredited college or university as full-time students in a 4- or 5-year program, majoring in computer science, engineering, economics, foreign languages (non-romance), or foreign area studies.

Financial data The scholarships provide a yearly salary at the GS-2 to GS-5 levels and up to $15,000 per school year for tuition, fees, books, and supplies. Travel to Washington D.C. and a housing allowance while there are also provided.

Duration Up to 5 years of study; up to 4 years of summer internships.

Special features During the summer, recipients work for the CIA in the Washington, D.C. metropolitan area.

Limitations After graduation, participants are eligible for promotion to a general professional entry grade level as a CIA employee (GS-7 level). They must work for the agency for a period of 1 1/2 times the length of their college career.

Number awarded Varies each year.

Deadline Applications must be submitted by the end of the first semester of senior year in high school or, for students who do not meet the age requirement, by the end of the first semester as a college freshman (usually December of each year).

[209]
CLAIRE B. SCHULTZ SCHOLARSHIP FUND

Community Foundation for Palm Beach and Martin Counties
324 Datura Street, Suite 340
West Palm Beach, FL 33401-5431
(561) 659-6800   Fax: (561) 832-6542

Purpose To provide financial assistance to students from selected areas of Florida.

Eligibility Eligible are graduating seniors from high schools in Palm Beach County who demonstrate financial need. Special preference is given to students who are either disabled or a member of a minority group.

Financial data The amount of the award varies.

Special features Ms. Schultz established this fund in 1989.

Limitations This fund is not currently active.

Number awarded 1 each year.

Deadline February of each year.

[210]
COLGATE "BRIGHT SMILES, BRIGHT FUTURES" MINORITY SCHOLARSHIPS

American Dental Hygienists' Association
Attn: Institute for Oral Health
444 North Michigan Avenue, Suite 3400
Chicago, Il 60611
(312) 440-8900

Purpose To provide financial assistance to minority group students enrolled in doctoral, master's, baccalaureate, or certificate/associate programs in dental hygiene.

Eligibility Applicants must be members of groups currently underrepresented in the dental hygiene profession; these include Native Americans, African Americans, Hispanics, Asians, and males. Applicants must have completed at least 1 year in a dental hygiene curriculum, have earned at least a 3.0 grade point average, and be able to demonstrate financial need of at least $1,500. They must intend to be full-time students in the academic year for which they are applying.

Financial data The amount of the scholarship generally will be based on the tuition charged at the student's institution, plus $250 for books and supplies, or the applicant's assessed need, whichever is less. The maximum award is $1,500.

Duration 1 year.

Special features These scholarships are sponsored by the Colgate-Palmolive Company.

Number awarded 2 each year.

Deadline May of each year.

[211]
COLGATE MINORITY SCHOLARSHIPS

American Dental Hygienists' Association
Attn: Institute for Oral Health
444 North Michigan Avenue, Suite 3400
Chicago, Il 60611
(312) 440-8900

Purpose To provide financial assistance to minority group students enrolled in doctoral, master's, baccalaureate, or certificate/associate programs in dental hygiene.

Eligibility Applicants must be members of groups currently underrepresented in the dental hygiene profession; these include Native Americans, African Americans, Hispanics, Asians, and males. Applicants must be have completed at least 1 year in a dental hygiene curriculum, have earned at least a 3.0 grade point average, and be able to demonstrate financial need of at least $1,500. They must intend to be full-time students in the academic year for which they are applying.

Financial data The amount of the scholarship generally is based on the tuition charged at the student's institution, plus $250 for books and supplies, or the applicant's assessed need, whichever is less. The maximum award is $1,500.

Duration 1 year.

Special features These scholarships are sponsored by Colgate Oral Pharmaceuticals.

Number awarded 6 each year.

Deadline May of each year.

[212]
COLLEGE GENERAL DISTRIBUTION GRANTS

American Baptist Financial Aid Program
Attn: Educational Ministries, ABC/USA
P.O. Box 851
Valley Forge, PA 19482-0851
(800) ABC-3USA, ext. 2067   Fax: (610) 768-2056

Purpose To provide funding to American Baptist related colleges and universities for financial aid to minority students.

Eligibility This program provides funding to the 16 American Baptist related colleges and universities to support financial aid to American Baptist minority students. Preference is given to newly enrolled students; aid is based on financial need. Students interested in the program should contact the address above to obtain the names and addresses of participating colleges and universities.

Financial data The amount of the grants depends on the availability of funds; 50 percent of the total dollars go to the 5 predominantly minority colleges and universities; the other 50 percent is divided among the remaining schools based on the number of minority students enrolled and percentage of student body they represent.

Duration The colleges and universities establish the terms of the scholarships they offer.

Number awarded Varies each year.

[213]
COLORADO DIVERSITY GRANTS

Colorado Commission on Higher Education
1300 Broadway, Second Floor
Denver, CO 80203
(303) 866-2723   Fax: (303) 860-9750

Purpose To provide financial assistance for undergraduate education to residents of Colorado who are nontraditional students.

Eligibility Eligible for the program are residents of Colorado who are enrolled or accepted for enrollment in eligible postsecondary institutions in Colorado. The program is designed for the following categories of students: first generation college students, economically disadvantaged students, single parents, nontraditional students, students enrolled in a nontraditional gender program, adult students with career changes due to employment, and ethnic minority students. Applicants must be able to demonstrate financial need.

Financial data The amount of assistance varies, to a maximum of $5,000 per year.

Duration 1 year; renewable.

Special features Applications are available either from the address above or from the financial aid office of eligible Colorado institutions.

Number awarded Varies each year.

Deadline Each participating institution sets its own deadlines.

[214]
CONCERNED PARENTS OF NOVATO SCHOLARSHIPS

Concerned Parents of Novato
P.O. Box 1906
Novato, CA 94948

Purpose To provide financial assistance to minority high school students who live in Novato, California and are interested in pursuing postsecondary education.

Eligibility Graduating minority high school seniors who are students attending the Novato Unified School District or residents of Novato and attending college outside the area are eligible to apply. Selection is based on academic achievement, school/community involvement, and scholastic record.

Financial data The stipends range from $200 to $500.

Duration 1 year.

Number awarded 1 or more each year.

Deadline April of each year.

[215]
CORNING CULINARY STUDENT SCHOLARSHIP

International Association of Culinary Professionals
    Foundation
Attn: Director of Administration
304 West Liberty Street, Suite 201
Louisville, KY 40202
(502) 587-7953   Fax: (502) 589-3602

Purpose To offer financial assistance to minorities who are interested in preparing for a career in the culinary arts.

Eligibility This program is open to minority students who can demonstrate financial need. They must have an outstanding leadership and academic record and plan to pursue a career in the culinary arts field.

Financial data The stipend is $1,000.

Duration 1 year.

Special features Recipients may use the award to pay for tuition in the program of their choice.

Limitations 1 each year.

Deadline May of each year.

[216]
CORPORATE-SPONSORED SCHOLARSHIPS FOR MINORITY UNDERGRADUATE STUDENTS WHO MAJOR IN PHYSICS

American Physical Society
One Physics Ellipse
College Park, MD 20740-3844
(301) 209-3200   Fax: (301) 209-0865

Purpose To provide financial assistance to minority group students interested in studying physics on the undergraduate level.

Eligibility Any African American, Hispanic American, or Native American U.S. citizen who plans to major in physics and who is a high school senior or college freshman or sophomore may apply. A selection committee recommended by the association's Committee on Minorities in Physics and appointed by the association's president selects the scholarship recipients and the host institutions. The selection committee also arranges for a physicist to provide appropriate mentor guidance for each scholarship recipient. The scholarships are awarded in 2 modes: institutionally attached scholarships and portable scholarships. The institutionally attached scholarships are assigned to institutions with historically or predominantly Black, Hispanic, or Native American enrollment. The portable scholarships allow recipients to enroll in programs of their choice. It is anticipated that in any award year, half of the scholarships will be institutionally attached and half will be portable.

Financial data Each scholarship consists of $2,000 awarded to the student for tuition, room, and board, and $500 awarded to the host department. The scholarships may be supplemented in some cases by a work-study program arranged by the corporate sponsor with the scholarship recipient and with the concurrence of the association's selection committee.

Duration 1 year; renewable for 1 additional year with the approval of the APS selection committee.

Special features APS conducts the scholarship program in conjunction with the Corporate Associates of the American Institute of Physics. Each scholarship is sponsored by a corporation, which is normally designated as the sponsor. A corporation generally sponsors from 1 to 10 scholarships, depending upon its size and the utilization of physics in the business.

Number awarded Varies; generally, 6 new and 11 renewed scholarships each year.

Deadline February of each year.

[217]
COX MINORITY JOURNALISM SCHOLARSHIP PROGRAM

Cox Enterprises, Inc.
Attn: Scholarship Administrator
P.O. Box 4689
Atlanta, GA 30302
(404) 526-5151

Purpose To provide work experience and financial assistance to minority high school graduates in areas served by Cox Enterprises newspapers.

Eligibility Applicants must be financially needy racial minorities who are enrolled as seniors in public high schools in the city selected for the particular year and who plan to attend college in the same city. They must have at least a 3.0 grade point average and an interest in journalism. Applications include an essay of 500 words or more on "Why I Want a Career in the Newspaper Industry."

Financial data All educational expenses are paid for 4 years of college, including room, board, books, and tuition. A variety of part-time newspaper work experiences will be offered while the student attends college and (full time) during the summer. The approximate total value of the award is $40,000.

Duration The scholarship is awarded for 4 years. The recipient is expected to intern for approximately 20 hours weekly throughout the 4 years of college.

Special features Employment at 1 of Cox Enterprises, Inc. newspapers is offered upon successful completion of the program. The scholarship rotates on an annual basis among the different cities where Cox Enterprises owns and operates newspapers; headquarters of the corporation are in Atlanta.

Number awarded 1 each year.

Deadline April of each year.

[218]
DAVID A. DEBOLT TEACHER SHORTAGE SCHOLARSHIPS

Illinois Student Assistance Commission
Attn: Scholarship and Grant Services
1755 Lake Cook Road
Deerfield, IL 60015-5209
(708) 948-8550
(800) 899-ISAC (within IL, IA, IN, MO, and WI)

Purpose To provide financial assistance to students in Illinois who are interested in training or retraining for a teaching career in academic shortage areas.

Eligibility Eligible for support under this program are Illinois residents who are enrolled or planning to enroll in an Illinois institution of higher education to pursue careers as public preschool, elementary, and secondary school teachers in designated teacher shortage disciplines. Priority is given to minority students.

Financial data This programs pays tuition and fees, room and board, or a commuter allowance at academic institutions in Illinois, to a maximum of $5,000. Funds are paid directly to the school. This is a scholarship/loan program. Recipients must agree to take a teaching position in Illinois within 2 years of graduation and must remain in that position for at least 3 years. Recipients who fail to honor this work obligation must repay the award.

Duration 1 year; may be renewed.

Number awarded Varies each year.

Deadline April of each year.

[219]
THE DAY SCHOLARSHIP FOR MINORITY JOURNALISTS

The Day Publishing Company
47 Eugene O'Neill Drive
P.O. Box 1231
New London, CT 06320-1231
(203) 442-2200, ext. 238

Purpose To provide financial assistance and work experience in journalism for minorities who live or attend college in eastern Connecticut.

Eligibility Minorities (African Americans, Latinos, Asian Americans, or Native Americans) who live or attend school in eastern Connecticut may apply if they are interested in journalism as a career. Applicants may be 1) high school seniors who will enroll as college freshmen in the fall following application or 2) current college students. A minimum high school or college grade point average of 2.5 is required.

Financial data Recipients receive up to $10,000 in scholarship money and paid internships during school breaks.

Duration 4 years.

Special features During the internship periods, which may begin as early as the summer after high school graduation, students participate in the newsroom training program, receive special attention from editors and a mentor, and undergo a formal evaluation regularly. Upon graduation from college, recipients are offered an entry-level job and are expected to work at The Day for 2 years.

Number awarded Varies each year.

Deadline February of each year.

[220]
DELAWARE NASA SPACE GRANT UNDERGRADUATE TUITION SCHOLARSHIPS

Delaware Space Grant Consortium
c/o University of Delaware
Bartol Research Institute
217 Sharp Laboratory
Newark, DE 19716-4793
(302) 831-8116   Fax: (302) 831-1843
E-mail: sherry@brivs2.bartol.udel.edu

Purpose To provide financial support to undergraduate students in Delaware involved in space-related studies.

Eligibility This program is open to undergraduate students in aerospace engineering and space science-related fields studying at member institutions of the Delaware Space Grant Consortium. U.S. citizenship is required. As a component of the U.S. National Aeronautics and Space Administration (NASA) Space Grant program, this program encourages applications from women, minorities, and persons with disabilities.

Financial data This program provides tuition assistance.

Duration 1 year; may be renewed.

Special features This program is funded by NASA.

Number awarded In a recent year, 6 students received these scholarships.

Deadline March of each year.

[221]
DETROIT FREE PRESS MINORITY JOURNALISM SCHOLARSHIP

Detroit Free Press
Attn: Publishers Office
321 West Lafayette Boulevard
Detroit, MI 48226
(313) 222-6400   (800) 678-6400
Fax: (313) 222-8874

Purpose To encourage outstanding minority high school seniors in the circulation area of the *Detroit Free Press* to prepare for a newspaper career.

Eligibility This program is open to minority high school seniors in the newspaper's circulation area who plan to become writers, editors, or photojournalists. They must have earned at least a 3.0 grade point average and plan to major in journalism in college. Selection is based on academic record, journalism-related extracurricular activities, recommendations, and a 5-page essay on why the applicant wants to become a journalist.

Financial data The first-place winner receives $1,000 and the second-place winner receives $750.

Duration 1 year.

Special features The first-place winner is automatically considered for the 4-year Knight-Ridder Minority Scholarship Program.

Number awarded At least 3 each year.

Deadline January of each year.

[222]
DOW JONES NEWSPAPER FUND BUSINESS REPORTING PROGRAM

Dow Jones Newspaper Fund
P.O. Box 300
Princeton, NJ 08543-0300
(609) 452-2820   (800) DOWFUND
Fax: (609) 520-5804
E-mail: newsfund@wsf.dowjones.com

Purpose To provide work experience and financial assistance to minority college students who are interested in careers in journalism.

Eligibility Minority college sophomores and juniors who are U.S. citizens are eligible to apply if they are interested in careers in journalism and summer internships at daily newspapers as business reporters.

Financial data Interns receive regular wages from the newspapers for which they work and a $1,000 scholarship at the successful completion of the summer of work.

Duration 3 months for the summer internship; 1 year for the scholarship.

Number awarded Up to 12 each year.

Deadline November of each year.

[223]
DR. PEDRO GRAU UNDERGRADUATE SCHOLARSHIP

American Meteorological Society
Attn: Fellowship/Scholarship Coordinator
45 Beacon Street
Boston, MA 02108-3693
(617) 227-2426, ext. 235   E-mail: sarmstrg@ametsoc.org

Purpose To provide financial assistance to students majoring in meteorology or some aspect of atmospheric sciences.

Eligibility Candidates must be entering their final undergraduate year and be majoring in meteorology or some aspect of the atmospheric or related oceanic and hydrologic sciences. They must intend to make atmospheric or related sciences their career. Applicants must be U.S. citizens or permanent residents, enrolled full time in an accredited U.S. institution, and have a cumulative grade point average of at least 3.0. Selection is based on academic excellence and achievement. The American Meteorological Society (AMS) encourages applications from women, minorities, and students with disabilities.

Financial data The stipend is $2,500.

Duration 1 year.

Special features This scholarship honors the memory of Dr. Pedro Grau y Triana, a medical doctor, legislator, inventor, and businessman with a special interest in tropical hurricanes. His daughter, Mrs. Manon Rodriguez, funded these scholarships in order to have more effort and resources devoted to atmospheric research.

Limitations Requests for an application must be accompanied by a self-addressed stamped envelope.

Number awarded 1 each year.

Deadline June of each year.

[224]
DURACELL—NATIONAL URBAN LEAGUE SCHOLARSHIP AND INTERN PROGRAM

National Urban League
Attn: Scholarship Coordinator
500 East 62nd Street, 10th Floor
New York, NY 10021-8379
(212) 310-9212

Purpose To assist and encourage outstanding minority students who are interested in completing their college education in the areas of engineering, sales, marketing, manufacturing operations, finance, or business administration.

Eligibility Eligible to apply are minority students who are pursuing full-time studies leading to a bachelor's degree at an accredited institution of higher learning. They must be juniors or third-year students at the time the scholarship award begins, rank within the top 25 percent of their class when the application is submitted, and be majoring in the areas of engineering, sales, marketing, manufacturing operations, finance, or business administration. Applications must be submitted to a local Urban League office. These applications are screened and sent to the appropriate National Urban League regional office. Each regional office may nominate up to 4 potential scholarship recipients who meet the competition criteria. The National Urban League interviews each of the semifinalists to select the 10 finalists. In the final step of the selection process, Duracell and the National Urban League review the 10 finalists and select the 5 winners.

Financial data The $10,000 scholarships are divided equally between the junior and senior years of the winners (in amounts of $5,000 per school year).

Duration 2 years.

Special features During the summer between the junior and senior years, scholarship recipients work as interns at a Duracell USA facility; many recipients have accepted employment opportunities at Duracell.

Limitations The stipends are sent directly to the recipient's college or university; the school is custodian of the funds and disburses the money consistent with the purposes of the program.

Number awarded 5 each year.

Deadline Applications must be submitted to local Urban League offices by April of each year.

[225]
ED BRADLEY SCHOLARSHIP

Radio and Television News Directors Foundation
1000 Connecticut Avenue, N.W., Suite 615
Washington, DC 20036
(202) 659-6510   Fax: (202) 223-4007

Purpose To provide financial assistance to an outstanding student whose career objective is electronic journalism.

Eligibility Eligible are sophomore or more advanced undergraduate or graduate students enrolled in an electronic journalism sequence at an accredited or nationally recognized college or university. Applications must include 1 to 3 examples of reporting or producing skills on audio or video cassette tapes (no more than 15 minutes total), a statement explaining why the candidate seeks a career in broadcast or cable journalism, and a letter of endorsement from a faculty sponsor that verifies that the applicant has at least 1 year of school remaining. Minority students receive preference.

Financial data The scholarship is $5,000, paid in semi-annual installments of $2,500 each.

Duration 1 year.

Special features An expense-paid trip to the Radio-Television News Directors Association Annual International Convention is also provided.

Limitations Previous winners of any RTNDF scholarship or internship are not eligible.

Number awarded 1 each year.

Deadline February of each year.

[226]
EDUCATIONAL ADVANCEMENT SCHOLARSHIPS FOR GENERIC STUDENTS

American Association of Critical-Care Nurses
Attn: Department of Research
101 Columbia
Aliso Viejo, CA 92656-1491
(714) 362-2000   (800) 809-CARE, ext. 376
Fax: (714) 362-2020   E-mail: aacninfo@vta.net

Purpose To assist members of the American Association of Critical-Care Nurses (AACN) who are working on a degree in nursing.

Eligibility Registered nurses who are current members of the AACN or National Student Nurses' Association (NSNA) may apply if they have a cumulative grade point average of 3.0 or better and are enrolled in an accredited B.S.N. program. This program is intended for students who are not yet licensed as an R.N.,

although they may be licensed as an L.V.N. or L.P.N. Applicants must be entering their junior or senior year. At least 20 percent of these awards are allocated for ethnic minorities.

Financial data The stipend is $1,500. The funds are sent directly to the recipient's college or university and may be used only for tuition or fees.

Duration 1 year; recipients may reapply.

Special features This scholarship is administered by the NSNA; for further information, write to that association at 555 West 57th Street, New York, NY 10019.

Deadline January of each year.

[227]
EDWARD D. STONE, JR. AND ASSOCIATES MINORITY SCHOLARSHIP

Landscape Architecture Foundation
Attn: Scholarship Program
4401 Connecticut Avenue, N.W., Suite 500
Washington, DC 20008-2302
(202) 686-8337   Fax: 202) 686-1001

Purpose To provide financial assistance to minority college students who wish to study landscape architecture.

Eligibility This program is open to African American, Hispanic, and minority college students of other cultural and ethnic backgrounds, if they are entering their final 2 years of undergraduate study in landscape architecture. Applicants must submit a 500-word essay on a design or research effort they wish to pursue (explaining how it will contribute to the advancement of the profession and to their ethnic heritage), 4 to 8 35mm color slides or black-and-white photographs of their best work, and 2 letters of recommendation. Selection is based on professional experience, community involvement, extracurricular activities, and financial need.

Financial data The stipend is $1,000.

Duration 1 year.

Number awarded 2 each year.

Deadline March of each year.

[228]
EDWARD DEZULUETA GREENEBAUM FUND SCHOLARSHIP

James G.K. McClure Educational and Development Fund, Inc.
Attn: Executive Director
Sugar Hollow Farm
11 Sugar Hollow Lane
Fairview, NC 28730
(704) 628-2114

Purpose To provide financial assistance to students in western North Carolina who are interested in attending college.

Eligibility Applications may be submitted by students from the following counties in North Carolina: Allegheny, Ashe, Avery, Buncombe, Burke, Caldwell, Cherokee, Clay, Graham, Haywood, Henderson, Jackson, Macon, Madison, McDowell, Mitchell, Polk, Rutherford, Swain, Transylvania, Watauga, or Yancey. They must be entering the freshman class of a 4-year college or university in North Carolina. Selection is based on academic promise, Christian character, and financial need. A special effort is made to offer scholarships to minority students from the region and to students entering into nursing or other health-care careers.

Financial data The stipend is $2,500 per year.

Duration 4 years.
Number awarded 1 each year.
Deadline April of each year.

[229]
ELEANOR CURRY AWARD FOR GIRLS AND YOUNG WOMEN

Peninsula Community Foundation
1700 South El Camino Real, Suite 300
San Mateo, CA 94402-3049
(415) 358-9369   Fax: (415) 358-9817

Purpose To provide financial assistance to women in California who wish to pursue postsecondary education.

Eligibility Young women residents of San Mateo County, California between the ages of 16 and 26 are eligible to apply for this award if they have graduated from high school (or will shortly) and are interested in pursuing postsecondary education. The program is designed for women who have dropped out of school for reasons beyond their control, or have undergone unusual hardships to remain in school. Special attention is given to applications from minorities, persons with disabilities, or individuals interested in nontraditional areas of study.

Financial data Up to $500 per year is available to recipients.
Duration 1 year; recipients may reapply.
Special features This award was established in 1983.
Number awarded Up to 5 each year.
Deadline March of each year.

[230]
ETHNIC DIVERSITY SCHOLARSHIPS

Colorado Society of Certified Public Accountants
7979 East Tufts Avenue, Suite 500
Denver, CO 80237-2843
(303) 773-2877   (800) 523-9082 (within CO)

Purpose To provide funding to minority high school seniors in Colorado who are interested in majoring in accounting.

Eligibility These scholarships are available to high school seniors of color in Colorado who plan on majoring in accounting at a community college, college, or university in Colorado. Selection is based on academic achievement.

Financial data The stipend is $750.
Duration 1 year.
Number awarded 2 each year.
Deadline February of each year.

[231]
ETHNIC MINORITY BACHELOR'S SCHOLARSHIPS

Oncology Nursing Foundation
501 Holiday Drive
Pittsburgh, PA 15220-2749
(412) 921-7373   Fax: (412) 921-6565
E-mail: onsmain@nauticom.net

Purpose To provide financial assistance to ethnic minorities for undergraduate studies in nursing.

Eligibility The candidate must 1) be a registered nurse with a demonstrated interest in and commitment to cancer nursing; 2) be enrolled in an undergraduate nursing degree program at an NLN-accredited school of nursing (the program must have application to oncology nursing); 3) have a current license to practice as a registered nurse; 4) not have previously received a bachelor's scholarship from the Oncology Nursing Foundation; and 5) be a member of an ethnic minority group (Native American, African American, Asian American, Pacific Islander, Hispanic/Latino, or other ethnic minority background).

Financial data The stipend is $2,000.
Duration 1 year.
Limitations At the end of each year of scholarship participation, recipients must submit a summary describing their educational activities.
Number awarded 3 each year.
Deadline January of each year.

[232]
EXTENDED OPPORTUNITY PROGRAMS AND SERVICES GRANTS

California Community Colleges
Attn: EOPS Program Coordinator
1107 Ninth Street
Sacramento, CA 95814
(916) 445-8752

Purpose To provide financial assistance to disadvantaged students attending community colleges in California.

Eligibility To receive support under this program, students must be residents of California, be enrolled full time in a California community college, not have completed more than 70 units of course work in any combination of postsecondary institutions, be educationally disadvantaged, and be able to demonstrate financial need. Up to 10 percent of the EOPS students at each college may enroll for only 9 units; students with disabilities may enroll for fewer units, based on their disability. Educationally disadvantaged students include those who are not qualified to enroll in the minimum level English or mathematics course at their college, did not graduate from high school or obtain the GED, graduated from high school with a grade point below 2.5, previously enrolled in remedial education, or met other factors described in their college's plan, such as first generation college student, member of underrepresented group at the college, or English not the primary language.

Financial data Up to $900 per year or the amount of a recipient's unmet financial need, whichever is less.
Duration 1 year; may be renewed.
Special features EOPS students are also eligible for other support in the form of counseling, tutoring, registration assistance, orientation, child care, transportation, and cultural activities.
Limitations Students apply to their community college, not to the sponsoring organization.
Number awarded Varies each year.
Deadline Varies by participating institution.

[233]
FEL-PRO AUTOMOTIVE TECHNICIANS SCHOLARSHIP PROGRAM

Fel-Pro Incorporated
7450 North McCormick Boulevard
Box C1103
Skokie, IL 60076-8103
(847) 674-7700   Fax: (847) 568-1902

Purpose To provide financial assistance to college-level students pursuing careers as automotive technicians.

Eligibility High school seniors or graduates are eligible to apply if they are currently enrolled or planning to enroll in a full-time course of study in automotive technology at any accredited postsecondary institution in the United States or Canada. Minorities and women are strongly encouraged to apply. Eligible fields of study include auto, diesel, heavy equipment, and agricultural equipment mechanics. Ineligible majors include auto body, engineering, automotive design, aviation mechanics, and business management. Selection is based on educational performance and potential, work experience, extracurricular activities, and career commitment. Financial need is not considered.

Financial data The stipend is $500 per year; funds may be used to cover tuition, fees, books, or supplies at accredited institutions offering educational courses leading to certification in automotive technology.

Duration 1 year; may be renewed for 1 additional year.

Special features FEL-PRO is a leading manufacturer of gaskets and sealing products. The scholarship program is administered by the Citizens' Scholarship Foundation of America, Inc., 1505 Riverview Road, P.O. Box 297, St. Peter, MN 56082, (507) 931-1682, Fax: (507) 931-9168.

Number awarded Up to 270 each year. The number of awards to each ethnic group and to females is at least in direct proportion to the number of applications received from each ethnic group and from female applicants.

Deadline April of each year.

[234]
FFA MINORITY SCHOLARSHIPS

National FFA Center
Attn: Scholarship Office
P.O. Box 15160
5632 Mt. Vernon Memorial Highway
Alexandria, VA 22309-0160
(703) 360-3600   Fax: (703) 360-5524

Purpose To provide financial assistance to minority high school seniors and graduates who are interested in studying agriculture in college.

Eligibility Applicants must be FFA members who are interested in pursuing a college degree in an area of agriculture. They must be members of 1 of the following ethnic groups: African Americans, Asian Americans or Pacific Islanders, Hispanic Americans, or Native Americans. High school seniors and graduates are eligible to apply from any state, Puerto Rico, the U.S. Virgin Islands, or the District of Columbia.

Financial data Scholarships are either $10,000 or $5,000. Funds are paid directly to the recipient.

Duration 1 year; may be renewed for up to 3 additional years, if the recipients attend college full time and maintain at least a 2.0 grade point average.

Number awarded 4 each year: 1 of $10,000 and 3 of $5,000.

Deadline February of each year.

[235]
FLEET SCHOLARS WORK/STUDY SCHOLARSHIP PROGRAM

Fleet Bank of Maine
Attn: Education Finance Manager
P.O. Box 1280
Portland, ME 04104
(207) 874-5102

Purpose To provide financial assistance to minority high school students in Maine who are interested in working on a college degree.

Eligibility This program is open to minority high school seniors graduating from public, private or parochial high schools in Maine. Selection is based on academic record and financial need.

Financial data The stipend is $1,000 per year.

Duration 1 year; may be renewed for up to 3 additional years as long as the recipient maintains a minimum grade point average of 3.0.

Special features During the summer, recipients are encouraged to work (full- or part-time), but employment at Fleet Bank is not mandatory. Upon graduation from college, they are eligible to enroll in Fleet Bank's management training program.

Number awarded 4 each year.

Deadline March of each year.

[236]
FLORIDA MINORITY PARTICIPATION IN LEGAL EDUCATION (MPLE) PRE-LAW SCHOLARSHIP PROGRAM

Florida Education Fund
18350 NW Second Avenue, Third Floor
Miami, FL 33169
(305) 654-7133   Fax: (305) 654-7135

Purpose To provide financial assistance to minority pre-law students in Florida.

Eligibility This program is open to U.S. citizens who are members of historically disadvantaged minority groups that are underrepresented in the membership of the Florida Bar (African Americans, Hispanics, and Native Americans), who are enrolled as pre-law juniors or seniors at Florida colleges and universities, and who plan to continue as law students at 1 of the 6 participating law schools in Florida (Nova Southeastern—Shepard Broad Law Center, Florida State University College of Law, St. Thomas University School of Law, Stetson University College of Law, University of Florida College of Law, or University of Miami School of Law).

Financial data The stipend is $6,146 per year.

Duration 1 year; may be renewed for 1 additional year.

Special features This program is intended to identify and prepare a group of future candidates for the Minority Participation in Legal Education (MPLE) Scholarship Program.

Number awarded Approximately 17 each year.

[237]
FOREIGN AFFAIRS FELLOWSHIP PROGRAM

Woodrow Wilson National Fellowship Foundation
Attn: Foreign Affairs Fellowship Program
5 Vaughn Drive, Suite 300
P.O. Box 2437
Princeton, NJ 08543-2437
(609) 452-7007   Fax: (609) 452-0066

Purpose To provide financial assistance for the education of students interested in pursuing a career with the Foreign Service of the Department of State.

Eligibility Applicants must be U.S. citizens in the sophomore year of undergraduate study at an accredited 4-year college or university with a cumulative grade point average of at least 3.2. They must plan to pursue graduate study in the field of international affairs and a career in the Foreign Service. Selection is based on general qualifications, academic performance, interest in a career in the Foreign Service, financial need, and potential for success in the program. Special emphasis is given to promoting knowledge, awareness of, and interest in employment with the Foreign Service among minority students. Children of State Department employees are not eligible.

Financial data Fellows receive support for college tuition, fees, room, board, and books during the final 2 years of undergraduate study and the first year of graduate work. Their graduate institution provides similar support during the second year of graduate study, depending upon financial need. For the summer institute and the internships, travel expenses and stipends are paid. The overseas internship includes medical insurance. Married fellows receive additional funding for university room and board, but are themselves responsible for travel and accommodations for their spouse and family during the institute and the internships.

Duration 4 years: the final 2 years of undergraduate study and the first 2 years of graduate work (provided the student maintains a minimum 3.2 grade point average).

Special features Each May, the fellows participate in orientation and training sessions in Washington, D.C. to help prepare them for Foreign Service careers. During the summer between their junior and senior years, they attend a 6- to 8-week summer institute in a graduate school of public policy and international affairs, with courses in international relations, public policy, policy analysis, policy modules, economics, calculus, and communication skills. During the summer following graduation, they are assigned to an internship at an overseas post of the State Department. Between the first and second year of graduate school, they serve a summer internship in the Department of State in Washington, D.C. This program is funded by the State Department and administered by the Woodrow Wilson National Fellowship Foundation.

Limitations Fellows must commit to a minimum of 4 and a half years of service in an appointment as a Foreign Service Officer following the second year of graduate study. Candidates who do not successfully complete the program and Foreign Service entry requirements must reimburse the Department of State for expenses paid under the fellowship.

Number awarded Approximately 10 each year.

Deadline February of each year.

[238]
FORT WAYNE NEWS-SENTINEL MINORITY SCHOLARSHIP

Fort Wayne News-Sentinel
Attn: Assistant Managing Editor
600 West Main Street
P.O. Box 102
Fort Wayne, IN 46801
(219) 461-8417

Purpose To provide financial assistance to minority high school seniors in the circulation area of the *Fort Wayne News-Sentinel* who are interested in journalism as a career.

Eligibility This program is open to minority high school seniors from the newspaper's circulation area planning to study journalism at the college of their choice.

Financial data The award is $500.

Duration 1 year.

Special features The winner of this scholarship is nominated to compete for the Knight-Ridder Minority Scholarship Program that offers awards of $5,000 per year for up to 4 years.

Number awarded 1 each year.

Deadline November of each year.

[239]
GARTH REEVES JR. MEMORIAL SCHOLARSHIPS

Society of Professional Journalists—South Florida Chapter
c/o Gina Carroll
Miami Herald
One Herald Plaza
Miami, FL 33132-1693
(305) 376-2710

Purpose To provide financial assistance for education of South Florida minority students interested in journalism as a career.

Eligibility Minority students committed to careers in print or broadcast journalism are eligible for these scholarships if they reside in South Florida or are enrolled in or accepted for enrollment in a college or university in that area. Selection is based on scholastic achievement, extracurricular activities in journalism, and financial need. Both undergraduate and graduate students are eligible.

Financial data The stipend ranges from $300 to $1,500 per year, depending upon the recipient's educational requirements and financial need.

Duration 1 year.

Number awarded 10 or more each year.

Deadline February of each year.

[240]
GEORGE M. BROOKER COLLEGIATE SCHOLARSHIP FOR MINORITIES

Institute of Real Estate Management Foundation
Attn: Foundation Coordinator
430 North Michigan Avenue
Chicago, IL 60611-4090
(312) 329-6008   Fax: (312) 661-0217

Purpose To provide financial assistance to minorities interested in preparing (on the undergraduate or graduate level) for a career in the real estate management industry.

Eligibility This program is open to undergraduate and graduate minority students majoring in real estate, preferably with an emphasis on management, asset management, or related fields. Applicants must be interested in entering a career in real estate management upon graduation. They must have earned at least a 3.0 grade point average in their major, have completed at least 2 college courses in real estate, and write an essay (up to 500 words) on why they want to follow a career in real estate management. U.S. citizenship is required.

Financial data The stipend for undergraduates is $1,000; the stipend for graduate students is $2,500.

Duration 1 year; nonrenewable.

Number awarded 3 each year: 2 undergraduate awards and 1 graduate award.

Deadline March of each year.

[241]
GOLDEN STATE MINORITY SCHOLARSHIPS

Golden State Minority Foundation
Attn: Scholarship Information
1055 Wilshire Boulevard, Suite 1115
Los Angeles, CA 90017-2431
(213) 482-6300   (800) 666-4763
Fax: (213) 482-6305

Purpose To stimulate and encourage high academic performance among California minority students; to provide qualified minority students with financial assistance to pursue studies in business or a related field.

Eligibility Candidates for the scholarship must be currently enrolled as full-time students at a 4-year accredited college or university as juniors, seniors, or graduate students; be majoring in business administration, economics, life insurance, or a related field; have a grade point average of at least 3.0; be a qualified underrepresented ethnic minority (African American, Latino, or Native American); attend school or be a resident of California; be a U.S. citizen or permanent legal resident; and, if employed, be working no more than 28 hours per week.

Financial data Scholarships are intended to be supplemental funds.

Duration The scholarships are awarded annually.

Special features The foundation was established by Golden State Mutual Insurance Company and is the first public foundation to be created by a major Black financial institution.

Number awarded In any given academic year, scholarships awarded to a particular minority group approximate in percentages that group's numeric proportion of the national minority population.

Deadline For southern California, March of each year; for northern California, October of each year.

[242]
GULF COAST RESEARCH LABORATORY MINORITY SUMMER GRANT PROGRAM

Mississippi Office of State Student Financial Aid
3825 Ridgewood Road
Jackson, MS 39211-6453
(601) 982-6589   (800) 327-2980 (within MS)

Purpose To provide financial assistance to minority students who wish to study or conduct research in the marine and environmental sciences in Mississippi.

Eligibility Eligible are Mississippi residents who are minority students seeking to attend classes or conduct independent study or research at the Gulf Coast Research Laboratory.

Financial data Grants for the 4-week program provide $750 to the institution and $100 to the student; grants for the 5-week program provide $900 to the institution and $125 to the student; grants for the 10-week program provide $1,800 to the institution and $250 to the student.

Duration Up to 10 weeks, during the summer.

Number awarded Varies each year.

Deadline May of each year.

[243]
HANA SCHOLARS PROGRAM

United Methodist Church
Attn: Office of Loans and Scholarships
1001 19th Avenue South
P.O. Box 871
Nashville, TN 37202-0871
(615) 340-7344   Fax: (615) 340-7048

Purpose To provide financial assistance to outstanding United Methodist Hispanic, Asian, and Native American undergraduate and graduate full-time college students.

Eligibility Applicants must be born of Hispanic, Asian, or Native American parentage, be active members of the United Methodist Church for at least 1 year prior to applying, be citizens or permanent residents of the United States, demonstrate academic ability, have a commitment to their ethnic community and their careers, be able to demonstrate financial need, and be enrolled as juniors, seniors, or graduate students in accredited academic institutions in the United States.

Financial data The stipend depends on the availability of funds and the need of the recipient.

Duration 1 year; students must reapply in following years to be considered for further aid. Undergraduate students are eligible to receive support for up to 2 years; graduate students for up to 3 years.

Limitations Applicants may accept Hispanic, Asian, Native American (HANA) awards only if they are not receiving any other major United Methodist scholarship for the same academic year. When asked, recipients will be expected to participate in such related activities as: serving as HANA interpreters within their local church, conference, or region; sharing information about their educational activities with other scholars and higher education personnel; and attending HANA seminars, institutes, consultations, or other similar activities.

Deadline March of each year.

[244]
HARRY AND BERTHA BRONSTEIN SCHOLARSHIP FUND

Community Foundation for Palm Beach and Martin Counties
324 Datura Street, Suite 340
West Palm Beach, FL 33401-5431
(561) 659-6800   Fax: (561) 832-6542

Purpose To provide financial assistance to minority and other high school students in Palm Beach County, Florida who are interested in going to college.

Eligibility This program is open to high school seniors in Palm Beach County who are interested in going to college and can demonstrate financial need. Preference is given to minorities and persons with disabilities.

Financial data The amount awarded varies but is generally at least $1,000.

Duration 1 year.
Number awarded 1 each year.
Deadline February of each year.

[245]
HEALTH CAREERS OPPORTUNITY PROGRAM GRANTS

Health Resources and Services Administration
Attn: Bureau of Health Professions
Division of Disadvantaged Assistance
Parklawn Building, Room 8A09
5600 Fishers Lane
Rockville, MD 20857
(301) 443-4493   Fax: (301) 443-6343
E-mail: bbrooks@hrsa.ssw.dhhs.gov

Purpose To provide financial support for education in health professions to students from disadvantaged backgrounds.
Eligibility This program is open to schools of allopathic medicine, osteopathic medicine, public health, dentistry, veterinary medicine, optometry, pharmacy, allied health, chiropractic and podiatric medicine, and public and nonprofit private schools which offer graduate programs in clinical psychology. Health professions schools are eligible if they identify a cohort of at least 7 disadvantaged students who applied but were not accepted to a health professions school; allied health schools are eligible if they identify a cohort of at least 5 disadvantaged students who have completed an undergraduate degree with a significant science focus and made a late decision to enter an allied health professions school and are in pursuit of a baccalaureate level degree in physical therapy, physician assistant, respiratory therapy, medical technology, or occupational therapy. Applicants must provide the designated students with a program of rigorous science and other education experiences and then admit the students who successfully complete the program or arrange for their admission to another health professions or allied health school. Recipient schools must also provide the students with a prematriculation summer program to ease their transition into the health professions or allied health school, and with counseling and advice on financial aid to assist them to complete successfully their education. Individuals from a disadvantaged background are those who come from an environment that has inhibited them from obtaining the knowledge, skill, and abilities to enroll in and graduate from a health professions school or allied health program, or who come from a low-income family (ranging from an annual income below $10,200 for a family of 1 to $26,700 for a family of 6).
Financial data Approximately $30.1 million is available for this program each year, of which $18.5 million is for continuing grants and $11.6 million is available for new grants, averaging $199,000 each. Of the appropriated funds each year, 20 percent must be obligated for stipends to disadvantaged students of exceptional financial need who are students at schools of allopathic medicine, osteopathic medicine, or dentistry; 10 percent must be obligated to community-based programs (including Indian tribes and Alaska Native villages); and 70 percent must be obligated for grants and contracts to institutions of higher education. Students receive a stipend during their participation in the program.
Duration Grants to institutions are up to 3 years; for students, the program is 1 year, including 6 to 8 weeks in the summer.
Number awarded Approximately 58 new projects are funded each year.
Deadline February of each year.

[246]
HERCULES MINORITY ENGINEERS DEVELOPMENT PROGRAM

Hercules Incorporated
Attn: Human Resources Department
Hercules Plaza
1313 North Market Street
Wilmington, DE 19894-0001
(302) 594-5000

Purpose To provide financial assistance for minority students interested in pursuing careers in engineering.
Eligibility Eligible are minority group members who have completed at least 1 semester of university study before applying, are interested in careers in engineering, have earned a 3.0 grade point average, and attend 1 of the 5 schools participating in the program (Georgia Institute of Technology, University of Michigan, North Carolina State University, University of Virginia, and University of Utah).
Financial data The scholarship stipend is $4,000 per year.
Duration 1 year; renewable for up to 3 additional years.
Special features Recipients are eligible to work as interns during the summer months throughout their undergraduate years. Information about the scholarship/internship program can be obtained by writing to Hercules Incorporated or contacting the participating university.
Limitations Candidates must be nominated by their Dean of Engineering.
Deadline Varies from school to school.

[247]
HIGHER EDUCATION MULTICULTURAL SCHOLARS PROGRAM

Department of Agriculture
Attn: Cooperative State Research, Education, and Extension
     Service
Office of Science and Education Resources Development
South Agriculture Building, Room 3433
1400 Independence Avenue, S.W.
Washington, DC 20250-2251
(202) 720-1973   E-mail: jgilmore@reeusda.gov

Purpose To provide grants to universities for scholarships to minority students in agriculture.
Eligibility This program is open to all U.S. colleges and universities offering baccalaureate degree programs in any discipline of the food and agricultural sciences, or offering a D.V.M. degree. Funding is provided to the institutions to provide financial aid to full-time students pursuing a baccalaureate degree in a discipline of the food and agricultural sciences or a D.V.M. degree. Students must be U.S. citizens newly recruited to their course of study and from a racial or ethnic group traditionally underrepresented in the food and agricultural sciences (Blacks, Hispanics, American Indians or Alaskan Natives, and Asians or Pacific Islanders). Students at 2-year institutions may participate in this program if their institution has an articulation or bridging agreement with an eligible 4-year institution. Fields of study include agriculture, conservation and renewable natural resources, forestry, veterinary medicine, home economics, and closely allied disciplines. Students must apply directly to a participating university or college for these scholarships; for a list, contact the address above.
Financial data Grants to institutions range from $40,000 to $100,000, and average $50,000. Institutions may offer stipends

to students of up to $5,750 per year, of which $4,500 is provided by this program and $1,250 is provided by the university from non-federal matching funds. Institutions also receive an annual cost-of-education allowance of $500 per year for each scholar supported by a grant.

Duration Grants to institutions are made up to 5 years, but students may be supported only up to 4 years.

Number awarded From 30 to 40 grants to institutions are made each year; each participating college or university must support from 2 to 5 students.

Deadline Institutions must submit grant applications by October of each year; each institution sets its own deadlines for students. Beginning with FY 1998, applications from institutions will be accepted only in even-numbered years.

[248]
HOWARD H. HANKS, JR. SCHOLARSHIP IN METEOROLOGY

American Meteorological Society
Attn: Fellowship/Scholarship Coordinator
45 Beacon Street
Boston, MA 02108-3693
(617) 227-2426, ext. 235   E-mail: sarmstrg@ametsoc.org

Purpose To provide financial assistance to students majoring in meteorology or some aspect of atmospheric sciences.

Eligibility Candidates must be entering their final undergraduate year and be majoring in meteorology or some aspect of the atmospheric or related oceanic and hydrologic sciences. They must intend to make the atmospheric or related sciences their career. Applicants must be U.S. citizens or permanent residents, enrolled full time in an accredited U.S. institution, and have a cumulative grade point average of at least 3.0. Selection is based on academic excellence and achievement. The American Meteorological Society (AMS) encourages applications from women, minorities, and students with disabilities.

Financial data The stipend is $700.

Duration 1 year.

Special features This scholarship honors Howard H. Hanks, Jr., vice-president of Weather Corporation of America until his death in an airplane crash in 1969. Funding is provided by William J. Hartnett, president of Weather Corporation of America.

Limitations Requests for an application must be accompanied by a self-addressed stamped envelope.

Number awarded 1 each year.

Deadline June of each year.

[249]
HOWARD T. ORVILLE SCHOLARSHIP IN METEOROLOGY

American Meteorological Society
Attn: Fellowship/Scholarship Coordinator
45 Beacon Street
Boston, MA 02108-3693
(617) 227-2426, ext. 235   E-mail: sarmstrg@ametsoc.org

Purpose To provide financial assistance to students majoring in meteorology or some aspect of atmospheric sciences.

Eligibility Candidates must be entering their final undergraduate year and be majoring in meteorology or some aspect of the atmospheric or related oceanic and hydrologic sciences. They must intend to make atmospheric or related sciences their career. Applicants must be U.S. citizens or permanent residents, be

enrolled full time in an accredited U.S. institution, and have a cumulative grade point average of at least 3.0. Selection is based on academic excellence and achievement. The American Meteorological Society (AMS) encourages applications from women, minorities, and students with disabilities.

Financial data The stipend is $2,000.

Duration 1 year.

Special features This scholarship honors Howard T. Orville, head of the Naval Aerological Service from 1940 to 1950, president of the American Meteorological Society in 1948 and 1949, and chairman of the Advisory Committee on Weather Control in 1953.

Limitations Requests for an application must be accompanied by a self-addressed stamped envelope.

Number awarded 1 each year.

Deadline June of each year.

[250]
HUGH A. MCMANUS JR. MEMORIAL SCHOLARSHIP FUND

Massachusetts AFL-CIO
8 Beacon Street, Third Floor
Boston, MA 02108
(617) 227-8260   Fax: (617) 227-2010

Purpose To provide financial assistance for certain high school seniors in Massachusetts who are interested in pursuing postsecondary education.

Eligibility Applicants must be residents of the greater Lynn, Massachusetts area (Lynn, Peabody, Salem, Saugus, Lynnfield, Nahant, Swampscott, and Marblehead). Only children of members of IUE Local 201 are eligible for 1 of the scholarships; the other is limited to minority children of members of that local.

Financial data The stipend is $500.

Duration 1 year.

Number awarded 2 each year: 1 specifically designated for a minority child of an IUE union member and 1 specifically designated for a child of an IUE union member.

Deadline January of each year.

[251]
"I HAVE A DREAM" FOUNDATION SCHOLARSHIPS

"I Have a Dream" Foundation
330 Seventh Avenue
New York, NY 10001
(212) 293-5480   Fax: (212) 293-5478

Purpose To assure the college education of minority and disadvantaged elementary school students from selected inner-city locations.

Eligibility In selected cities, "I Have a Dream" (IHAD) Foundation programs adopt whole classes of second and third graders in either a public housing project or a public school in which at least 75 percent of the students qualify for the free or reduced lunch program. Once a class has been adopted by a sponsor, its members receive year-round academic and social support throughout their elementary and high school years. Upon graduation from high school, IHAD provides scholarships to each of the students ready to pursue a college education.

Financial data Full or partial tuition scholarships are awarded to all students adopted by the program who meet the graduation/college attendance requirements.

Duration 1 semester; renewed as long as the recipient meets the requirements of the program.

Special features The IHAD Foundation was started by Eugene Lang in 1981 in New York. Today, there are 160 projects in 61 cities and 28 states, serving approximately 12,000 disadvantaged children.

[252]
IDAHO MINORITY AND "AT RISK" STUDENT SCHOLARSHIP

Idaho Board of Education
Len B. Jordan Office Building
650 West State Street, Room 307
P.O. Box 83720
Boise, ID 83720-0037
(208) 334-2270   Fax: (208) 334-2632
E-mail: csmith@osbe.state.id.us

Purpose To help talented disabled and other "at risk" students in Idaho pursue a college education.

Eligibility This program focuses on talented students who may be at risk of failing to meet their ambitions because of physical, economic, or cultural limitations. Applicants must be high school graduates, Idaho residents, and meet at least 3 of the following 5 requirements: 1) have a disability; 2) be a member of an ethnic minority group historically underrepresented in higher education; 3) have a substantial financial need; 4) be a first-generation college student; 5) be a migrant farm worker or a dependent of farm workers.

Financial data The stipend is up to $2,700 per year.

Duration 1 year; may be renewed.

Special features This program was established in 1991 by the Idaho state legislature. Information is available from high school counselors and financial aid offices of colleges and universities in Idaho.

Limitations Recipients must plan to attend or be attending 1 of 8 participating postsecondary institutions in the state on a full-time basis.

Number awarded Varies each year.

[253]
IDAHO SPACE GRANT CONSORTIUM HIGHER EDUCATION AND RESEARCH PROGRAM

Idaho Space Grant Consortium
c/o University of Idaho
College of Engineering
Mechanical Engineering
Moscow, ID 83844-1011
(208) 885-7018   Fax: (208) 885-6645
E-mail: rgill@uidaho.edu

Purpose To provide financial assistance for study and research in space-related fields to students and faculty at member institutions of the Idaho Space Grant Consortium.

Eligibility This program is open to students and faculty at the University of Idaho, Boise State University, Idaho State University, and other member institutions of the Idaho Space Grant Consortium. Faculty members may apply for funding to travel to facilities of the U.S. National Aeronautics and Space Administration (NASA) or other aerospace related agencies/industries to obtain research funding. Students may apply for scholarships, assistantships, or fellowships for space related programs. U.S. citizenship is required. As a component of the NASA Space Grant program,

the Idaho Space Grant Consortium encourages participation by women, minorities, and persons with disabilities.

Financial data The amounts of the awards depend on the availability of funds and the nature of the proposal.

Duration Depends on the nature of the proposal.

Special features This program is funded by NASA.

Number awarded Varies each year. Since it began in 1991, this program has awarded 33 faculty research initiation awards, 21 scholarships, and 6 fellowships.

[254]
INDEPENDENT COLLEGES OF SOUTHERN CALIFORNIA SCHOLARSHIP PROGRAM

Southern California Edison Company
Attn: Scholarship Committee
1190 Durfee Avenue
South El Monte, CA 91733
(818) 302-0284

Purpose To provide financial assistance to minority high school students who plan to attend a 4-year college in California.

Eligibility High school seniors who live or attend a school in an area served by Southern California Edison may apply for this scholarship if they belong to an underrepresented ethnic group and plan to attend 1 of the Independent Colleges of Southern California as a full-time undergraduate student. Applicants must be U.S. citizens or permanent residents, be the first generation in their family to attend college, and demonstrate financial need. Selection is based on academic performance, extracurricular activities, and demonstrated leadership skills.

Financial data The stipend is $20,000.

Duration 4 years.

Number awarded 2 each year.

Deadline February of each year.

[255]
INDIANA PROFESSIONAL CHAPTER OF SPJ MINORITY SCHOLARSHIP

Society of Professional Journalists—Indiana Chapter
c/o Bill Bridges
Franklin College
501 East Monroe Street
Franklin, IN 46131
(317) 738-8196

Purpose To provide financial assistance for undergraduate education to minority students in Indiana who are pursuing a career in journalism.

Eligibility This program is open to minority residents of Indiana who are majoring in journalism as undergraduate students at any college or university in Indiana. Selection is based on academic performance.

Financial data The stipend is $2,000.

Duration 1 year.

Number awarded 1 each year.

[256]

INDIANA SPACE GRANT CONSORTIUM FELLOWSHIPS

Indiana Space Grant Consortium
c/o Purdue University
School of Aeronautics and Astronautics
1282 Grissom Hall
West Lafayette, IN 47907-1282
(317) 494-5135   Fax: (317) 494-0307
E-mail: andrisan@ecn.purdue.edu

Purpose To provide financial support to students in Indiana interested in pursuing space-related studies.

Eligibility This program is open to students interested in pursuing space-related programs at Purdue University or the University of Notre Dame. U.S. citizenship is required. The Indiana Space Grant Consortium is a component of the U.S. National Aeronautical and Space Administration (NASA) Space Grant program, which encourages participation by women, minorities, and persons with disabilities.

Financial data Each year, $25,000 is available for fellowships at each of the 2 universities.

Special features This program is funded by NASA.

Number awarded Each participating university determines how to allocate its funds.

Deadline Deadline dates are established by the participating universities; contact the address above for information on the programs at each institution.

[257]

INFORMATION HANDLING SERVICES/SAE WOMEN ENGINEERS COMMITTEE SCHOLARSHIP

Society of Automotive Engineers
Attn: Educational Relations
400 Commonwealth Drive
Warrendale, PA 15096-0001
(412) 772-8534   E-mail: lorile@sae.org

Purpose To provide financial support to women and minorities for postsecondary education in engineering.

Eligibility Applicants must be U.S. citizens who intend to earn a degree in engineering; they must be high school seniors with a 3.0 grade point average accepted into an ABET accredited engineering program. The program is designed to increase the diversity of membership of the Society of Automotive Engineers, especially by promoting the participation and leadership of women.

Financial data This scholarship is $1,500.

Duration 1 year.

Special features Funding for this program is provided by Information Handling Services, Inc., of Englewood, Colorado.

Limitations Candidates must include a $5 processing fee with their applications.

Number awarded 1 each year.

Deadline November of each year.

[258]

IRENE RYAN ACTING SCHOLARSHIPS

Kennedy Center American College Theater Festival
Attn: Producing Director
Education Department
Kennedy Center
Washington, DC 20566
(202) 416-8857   Fax: (202) 416-8802
E-mail: skshaffer@mail.kennedy-center.org

Purpose To recognize and reward outstanding college performers with scholarships for their continuing education.

Eligibility Eligible are students enrolled in any accredited junior or senior college in the United States or in countries contiguous to the continental United States. Participants must appear as actors in plays produced by their college and entered in 1 of the 8 regional festivals of the Kennedy Center American College Theater Festival (KC/ACTF). From each of the regional festivals, 2 winners and their acting partners are invited to the national festival at the John F. Kennedy Center for the Performing Arts in Washington, D.C. to participate in an "Evening of Scenes." Scholarships are awarded to outstanding student performers at each regional festival and from the "Evening of Scenes."

Financial data Regional winners receive $500 scholarships; national winners receive $2,500 scholarships; the best partner receives a special award. All scholarship monies are paid directly to the institutions designated by the recipients and may be used for any field of study.

Duration The competition is held annually.

Special features These awards have been presented since 1972 by the Irene Ryan Foundation of Encino, California. The national finalists are eligible to receive a fellowship to participate in the National Stage Combat Workshop conducted by the Society of American Fight Directors and to receive a Classical Acting Award of Excellence. Minority national finalists are eligible to receive an apprenticeship to participate in an 11-week workshop at the Williamstown Theatre Festival in the Berkshire Hills of northwestern Massachusetts.

Limitations The sponsoring college or university must pay a registration fee of $250 for each production.

Number awarded The number of regional winners varies each year; at the national festival "Evening of Scenes," 2 performers and 1 best partner receive awards.

Deadline The regional festivals are held in January and February of each year; the national festival is held in April of each year. Application deadlines are set within each region.

[259]

JACKIE ROBINSON SCHOLARSHIP

Jackie Robinson Foundation
Attn: Scholarship Program
3 West 35th Street, 11th Floor
New York, NY 10001-2204
(212) 290-8600

Purpose To provide financial assistance to minorities interested in pursuing postsecondary education.

Eligibility To apply for the scholarship, students must be members of an ethnic minority group, U.S. citizens, high school seniors, and accepted to a 4-year college or university. They must be able to demonstrate high academic achievement, financial need, and leadership potential.

Financial data Up to $5,000 per year.

Duration 4 years.

Special features The program also offers personal and career counseling on a year-round basis, a week of interaction with other scholarship students from around the country, and assistance in obtaining summer jobs and permanent employment after graduation. It was established in 1973 by a grant from Chesebrough-Pond.

Number awarded 100 or more each year.

Deadline March of each year.

[260]
JAMES B. BLACK COLLEGE SCHOLARSHIPS

Pacific Gas and Electric Company
c/o Citizens' Scholarship Foundation of America
1505 Riverview Road
P.O. Box 297
St. Peter, MN 56082

Purpose To provide financial assistance for postsecondary education to African American, Hispanic, and Native American students in California who have succeeded in spite of overwhelming obstacles.

Eligibility Deserving minority and other students who have achieved academic success despite disadvantages are eligible to apply if they are high school seniors residing in the service territory of Pacific Gas and Electric Company (PG&E). They must be interested in majoring in engineering, computer science, math, finance, or economics. Selection is based on test scores, academic performance, leadership and participation in school and community activities, work experience, a statement of career and educational aspirations and goals, and an outside appraisal. Within each of the 4 PG&E regions, 3 of the first-place awards and 1 of the runner-up scholarships are reserved for African American, Hispanic, or Native American students; 1 of the first-place awards and 1 of the runner-up scholarships are open to students of all ethnic backgrounds.

Financial data First-place winners receive $4,000. Runners-up receive $1,000.

Duration Runners-up receive a 1-time award. First-place winners receive $1,000 a year for 4 years.

Number awarded 24 each year: 6 (4 first-place awards and 2 runner-up scholarships) in each of the 4 PG&E service regions.

Deadline November of each year.

[261]
JAMES G.K. MCCLURE EDUCATIONAL AND DEVELOPMENT FUND SCHOLARSHIPS

James G.K. McClure Educational and Development Fund, Inc.
Attn: Executive Director
Sugar Hollow Farm
11 Sugar Hollow Lane
Fairview, NC 28730
(704) 628-2114

Purpose To provide financial assistance to students in western North Carolina who are interested in attending college.

Eligibility Applications may be submitted by students from the following counties in North Carolina: Allegheny, Ashe, Avery, Buncombe, Burke, Caldwell, Cherokee, Clay, Graham, Haywood, Henderson, Jackson, Macon, Madison, McDowell, Mitchell, Polk, Rutherford, Swain, Transylvania, Watauga, or Yancey. They must be entering the freshman class of 1 of the following schools: Asheville-Buncombe Community Technical College, Appalachian

State University, Berea College, Blue Ridge Community College, Brevard College, Caldwell Community College, East Tennessee State, Gardner-Webb College, Haywood Community College, Isothermal Community College, Lees-McRae College, Mars Hill College, Mayland Community College, McDowell Community College, Montreat-Anderson College, North Carolina School of the Arts, North Carolina State University, Southwestern Community College, Tri-County Community College, University of North Carolina-Asheville, University of North Carolina-Greensboro, Warren Wilson College, Western Carolina University, Western Piedmont Community College, Wilkes Community College, and Young Harris College. Selection is based on academic promise, Christian character, and financial need. A special effort is made to offer scholarships to minority students from the region and to students entering into nursing or other health-care careers. Students facing a sudden and catastrophic financial problem may apply for a hardship grant to finish their course of study.

Financial data Awards for 4-year colleges and universities are either $750 or $1,500 per year; stipends at technical or community colleges are $300 per year; hardship scholarships and minority scholarships are $1,000 per year. Funds are paid directly to the recipient's college.

Duration 1 year; may be renewed.

Number awarded Varies; in a recent year, the fund awarded 39 scholarships to 4-year institutions for a total of $44,700, 22 scholarships to community colleges for $6,600, 25 health careers scholarships (to both 4-year and 2-year institutions) for $9,300, 1 designated minority scholarship (although some of the other scholarships went to minorities), and 1 hardship scholarship.

Deadline April of each year.

[262]
JASCO TOOLS INCENTIVE PROGRAM

Rochester Area Foundation
335 East Main Street, Suite 402
Rochester, NY 14604
(716) 325-4353   Fax: (716) 546-5069

Purpose To provide financial assistance to minorities in the Rochester, New York area who are interested in pursuing postsecondary education.

Eligibility Minority high school students are eligible for consideration if they are interested in going on to college and are residents of Genesee, Livingston, Monroe, Ontario, Orleans, and Wayne counties.

Financial data The stipend is $3,000 and must be used to pay for college-related expenses.

Duration 1 year; may be renewed.

Special features The funding for this program comes from Jasco Tools.

Limitations Applications for these scholarships are available only from high school counselors.

Number awarded Varies each year.

[263]
JIMMY A. YOUNG MEMORIAL SCHOLARSHIPS

American Respiratory Care Foundation
Attn: Administrative Coordinator
11030 Ables Lane
Dallas, TX 75229-4593
(214) 243-2272

Purpose To provide financial assistance to minority college students interested in becoming respiratory therapists.

Eligibility Applicants must be of minority origin, be enrolled in an accredited respiratory therapy program, have completed a minimum of 1 semester/quarter of the program, have earned at least a 3.0 grade point average, and be U.S. citizens or applicants for U.S. citizenship. Applications include 6 copies of an original referenced paper on some aspect of respiratory care and letters of recommendation attesting to 1) approval of the candidate's paper, 2) candidate's worthiness for the scholarship, and 3) candidate's potential for a career in the profession of respiratory care. The foundation prefers that the candidates be nominated by a school or program, but any student may initiate a request for sponsorship by a school (in order that a deserving candidate is not denied the opportunity to compete simply because the school does not initiate the application).

Financial data The stipend is $1,000.

Duration 1 year.

Number awarded 1 each year.

Deadline June of each year.

[264]
JOHN AND MURIEL LANDIS SCHOLARSHIP AWARD

American Nuclear Society
Attn: Scholarship Program
555 North Kensington Avenue
La Grange Park, IL 60525
(708) 352-6611   Fax: (708) 352-0499

Purpose To provide financial assistance to undergraduate or graduate students who are interested in pursuing a career in nuclear-related fields.

Eligibility To be eligible, applicants must be undergraduates or graduate students at colleges or universities located in the United States who are pursuing, or planning to pursue, a career in nuclear science, nuclear engineering, or a related field. In addition, applicants must have a greater than average financial need. Minorities and women are especially encouraged to apply. Selection is primarily based on financial need and potential for academic and professional success.

Financial data The stipend is $3,000, to be used to defray educational costs, including tuition, books, fees, and room and board.

Duration 1 year.

Limitations Applicants must be sponsored by an American Nuclear Society local section, division, technical group, committee, student branch, or organization member. If a student does not know of a sponsoring organization, the ANS will help to establish contact. Augmentation of this scholarship program with matching or supplemental funds by the sponsoring organization is encouraged (though not required). Requests for an application must be accompanied by a self-addressed stamped envelope.

Number awarded 8 each year.

Deadline February of each year.

[265]
JOSEPH EHRENREICH SCHOLARSHIPS

National Press Photographers Foundation
3200 Croasdaile Drive, Suite 306
Durham, NC 27705
(919) 383-7246   (800) 289-6772

Purpose To encourage and help disadvantaged and minority students—as well as others with evidence of talent—to continue their education in photojournalism.

Eligibility To be eligible, students must have completed 1 year at a recognized 4-year college or university having courses in photojournalism. They must be full-time students with at least half a year of undergraduate schooling remaining, have satisfactory scholastic grades, be able to document financial need, and intend to pursue a career in journalism. Nominations and applications may be made by students, interested instructors, or members of the National Press Photographers Association. Nominees and applicants need not be journalism majors, but they must show aptitude and potential in the making or use of photographs in communication. Applications must be accompanied by representative examples of the applicant's work. For student photographers, a minimum of 6 8x10 prints are required. For students working in picture editing, at least 3 examples of recent work should be included. This program is not limited to minority students, but their applications are given special attention.

Financial data The stipend is $1,000 per year.

Duration 1 year; nonrenewable.

Special features This program is named for the president of Ehrenreich Photo-Optical industries, importer of Nikon cameras and lenses. Further information is available from Mike Smith, Detroit Free Press, 321 Lafayette Boulevard, Detroit, MI 48231, (313) 222-8893. Recipients may attend school in the United States or Canada.

Number awarded 5 each year.

Deadline February of each year.

[266]
KANSAS ETHNIC MINORITY SCHOLARSHIP PROGRAM

Kansas Board of Regents
700 S.W. Harrison Street, Suite 1410
Topeka, KS 66603-3760
(913) 296-3517

Purpose To provide financial assistance to minority students who are interested in attending college in Kansas.

Eligibility Eligible to apply are minority Kansas residents designated according to the following ethnic groups: American Indian or Alaskan Native, Asian or Pacific Islander, Black, and Hispanic. Applicants may be current college students (enrolled in community colleges, colleges, or universities in Kansas) but high school seniors graduating in the current year receive priority consideration. Minimum academic requirements include 1 of the following: 1) ACT score of 21 or SAT score of 816; 2) cumulative grade point average of 3.0; 3) high school rank in upper one-third; 4) completion of Regents Recommended Curriculum (4 years of English, 3 years of mathematics, 3 years of science, 3 years of social studies, and 2 years of foreign language); 5) selection by National Merit Corporation in any category; or 6) selection by College Board as a Hispanic Scholar.

Financial data The stipend is up to $1,500, depending on financial need and availability of state funds.

Duration 1 year; may be renewed for up to 3 additional years (4 additional years for designated 5-year programs) if the recipient maintains a 2.0 cumulative grade point average and has financial need.

Number awarded Approximately 200 each year.

Deadline March of each year.

[267]
KANSAS TEACHER SCHOLARSHIP

Kansas Board of Regents
700 S.W. Harrison Street, Suite 1410
Topeka, KS 66603-3760
(913) 296-3517

Purpose To provide financial assistance to high school seniors, high school graduates, and selected undergraduates who are interested in preparing for a career as a teacher in Kansas.

Eligibility This program is open to Kansas residents who plan to enter the teaching profession in specific curriculum areas, currently special education (85 percent of the awards), science (8 percent of the awards), and foreign language (7 percent of the awards). Minimum selection criteria include: 1) intention to enroll in 1 of the specified curricular areas of a teacher education program; 2) completion of the Regents Recommended Curriculum (4 years of English, 3 years of mathematics, 3 years of science, 3 years of social studies, and 2 years of foreign language); 3) ACT or SAT score; 4) high school grade point average; 5) high school class rank; 6) college transcript (for college-enrolled applicants); and 7) letter of recommendation from college or university official (for college-enrolled applicants). Special consideration is given to minority applicants because minorities continue to be underrepresented in the teaching profession in Kansas schools.

Financial data Participants receive $5,000 per year. This is a scholarship/loan program. Recipients must teach in Kansas 1 year for every year of funding received, or they must repay the amount received at 15 percent interest.

Duration 1 year; may be renewed for up to 3 additional years or up to 4 additional years for designated 5-year courses of study requiring graduate work.

Number awarded Approximately 100 each year.

Deadline March of each year.

[268]
KEN INOUYE MEMORIAL SCHOLARSHIP

Society of Professional Journalists—Los Angeles Chapter
c/o Daniel E. Garvey
Scholarship Chair
9951 Barcelona Lane
Cypress, CA 90631-3759

Purpose To provide financial assistance to minority undergraduate and graduate students in southern California who are interested in pursuing careers in journalism.

Eligibility Minority college juniors, seniors, or graduate students who are interested in careers in journalism or communications (but not public relations, advertising, or publicity) are eligible to apply if they are residents of or attending school in Los Angeles, Ventura, or Orange Counties, California. Selection is based on evidence of unusual accomplishment and potential to advance in a news career; financial need is considered if 2 applicants are similarly qualified.

Financial data The stipend is $1,000 per year.

Duration 1 year.

Number awarded 1 each year.

Deadline February of each year.

[269]
KENTUCKY SPACE GRANT CONSORTIUM UNDERGRADUATE SCHOLARSHIPS

Kentucky Space Grant Consortium
c/o Western Kentucky University
Department of Physics and Astronomy, TCCW 246
Hardin Planetarium and Astrophysical Observatory
1 Big Red Way
Bowling Green, KY 42101-3576
(502) 745-4156   Fax: (502) 745-6471
E-mail: ksgc@wkuvx1.wku.edu

Purpose To provide financial assistance for undergraduate education in space-related fields to students in Kentucky.

Eligibility This program is open to undergraduate students at member institutions of the Kentucky Space Grant Consortium (Centre College, Eastern Kentucky University, Kentucky State University, Morehead State University, Murray State University, Northern Kentucky University, Thomas More College, Transylvania University, University of Kentucky, University of Louisville, and Western Kentucky University). Applicants must be enrolled in a baccalaureate degree program in a space-related field or teaching specialization. As part of the program, a faculty member must agree to serve as a mentor on a research project. U.S. citizenship is required. The Kentucky Space Grant Consortium is a component of the U.S. National Aeronautics and Space Administration (NASA) Space Grant program, which encourages participation by women, minorities, and persons with disabilities.

Financial data The stipend is $3,000 per year, with an additional $500 for use in support of the student's mentored research project. Preference is given to applicants from schools which agree to waive tuition for the scholar as part of the program.

Duration 1 year; may be renewed.

Special features This program is funded by NASA.

Number awarded Varies each year.

Deadline March of each year.

[270]
KNIGHT-RIDDER MINORITY SCHOLARSHIP PROGRAM

Knight-Ridder, Inc.
One Herald Plaza
Miami, FL 33132-1609
(305) 376-3800

Purpose To provide financial assistance to minority students who are interested in going to college to prepare for a career in journalism.

Eligibility Graduating minority high school seniors are eligible to apply if they are attending a school in an area served by Knight-Ridder and are interested in majoring in journalism in college. Candidates first apply to their local Knight-Ridder newspaper and compete for local scholarships; selected winners are then nominated for this award.

Financial data The stipend is $5,000.

Duration 1 year; may be renewed for up to 3 additional years, based on the recipient's academic performance.

Special features Scholarship recipients are offered an internship opportunity at a Knight-Ridder newspaper during the summer.

Limitations At the end of the program, recipients must work at a Knight-Ridder newspaper for 1 year.

Number awarded 4 each year.

[271]
KNIGHT-RIDDER SCHOLARSHIP FOR NATIVE AMERICAN JOURNALISTS

Knight-Ridder, Inc.
c/o Linda Fullerton
St. Paul Pioneer Press
345 Cedar Street
St. Paul, MN 55101-1057
(612) 228-5465   (800) 950-9080

Purpose To provide financial assistance to Native American students who are interested in going to college to prepare for a career in journalism.

Eligibility This program is open to Native American students interested in pursuing a newspaper journalism career. The recipient is required to work as a paid intern during the summer at a Knight-Ridder newspaper, and is eligible to apply for other Knight-Ridder scholarships.

Financial data The stipend is $5,000.

Duration 1 year.

Number awarded 1 each year.

Deadline March of each year.

[272]
KNTV MINORITY SCHOLARSHIP

KNTV Television
Attn: Janet Neill
645 Park Avenue
San Jose, CA 95110
(408) 286-1111   Fax: (408) 295-5461

Purpose To provide financial assistance for postsecondary education to minority students in selected areas of California who are interested in preparing for a career in television.

Eligibility This program is open to minority students who are residents of Monterey, San Benito, Santa Clara, and Santa Cruz counties. Applicants should be high school seniors or college freshmen, sophomores, or juniors. They should be majoring (or planning to major) in television production, journalism, or a related field (e.g., marketing, public relations, advertising, or graphics), able to demonstrate financial need, and planning to attend college in California on a full-time basis (at least 12 semester units). Selection is based on interest in television, financial need, involvement in the community, academic achievement, and career aspirations.

Financial data The stipend is $1,000.

Duration 1 year.

Special features Recipients have the option of 8 weeks of paid summer employment at KNTV in San Jose.

Number awarded 2 each year.

Deadline April of each year.

[273]
LASPACE SCHOLARS PROGRAM

Louisiana Space Consortium
c/o Louisiana State University
Physics and Astronomy
277 Nicholson Hall
Baton Rouge, LA 70803-4001
(504) 388-8697   Fax: (504) 388-1222
E-mail: wefel@phepds.dnet.nasa.gov

Purpose To provide financial assistance to students working on an undergraduate degree in an aerospace-related discipline at a college or university belonging to the Louisiana Space Consortium (LaSPACE).

Eligibility This program is open to U.S. citizens working on a baccalaureate degree as full-time students in an aerospace-related field at 1 of the LaSPACE member schools: Dillard University, Grambling State University L.S.U. Agricultural Center, Louisiana State University and A&M College, Louisiana Tech University, Loyola University, McNeese State University, Northwestern State University of Louisiana, Northeast Louisiana University, Southern University and A&M College, Southern University at New Orleans, Southern University at Shreveport, Tulane University, University of New Orleans, University of Southwestern Louisiana, Xavier University of Louisiana. LaSPACE is a component of the U.S. National Aeronautics and Space Administration (NASA) Space Grant program, which encourages participation by women, minorities, and persons with disabilities.

Financial data The stipend is $2,500 per year, to be used for tuition, fees, books, and expenses related to the educational program.

Duration 1 year; renewable for up to 3 additional years.

Special features Funding for this program is provided by NASA.

Number awarded Depends on the availability of funds.

[274]
LAWRENCE WADE JOURNALISM FELLOWSHIP

Heritage Foundation
Attn: Selection Committee
214 Massachusetts Avenue, N.E.
Washington, DC 20002
(202) 546-4400

Purpose To provide financial assistance and work experience to college students who are interested in a career in journalism.

Eligibility This program is open to undergraduate or graduate students who are currently enrolled full time and are interested in a career as a journalist upon graduation. Applicants need not be majoring in journalism, but they must submit writing samples of published news stories, editorial commentaries, or broadcast scripts. Preference is given to candidates who are Asian Americans, African Americans, Hispanic Americans, or Native Americans.

Financial data The winner receives a $1,000 scholarship and participates in a 10-week salaried internship at the Foundation.

Number awarded 1 each year.

Deadline February of each year.

[275]
LEADERSHIP FOR DIVERSITY SCHOLARSHIP

California School Library Association
1499 Old Bayshore Highway, Suite 142
Burlingame, CA 94010
(415) 692-2350   Fax: (415) 692-4956

Purpose To encourage minority students to get a credential as a library media teacher in California.

Eligibility This program is open to students who are members of a traditionally underrepresented group enrolled in a college or university library media teacher credential program in California. Applicants must intend to work as a library media teacher in a California school library media center for a minimum of 3 years. Financial need is considered in awarding the scholarship.

Financial data The stipend is $1,000.

Duration 1 year.

Special features The California School Library Association was formerly named the California Media Library Educators Association.

Number awarded 1 each year.

Deadline May of each year.

[276]
LEO BURNETT COMPANY SCHOLARSHIP

National FFA Center
Attn: Scholarship Office
P.O. Box 15160
5632 Mt. Vernon Memorial Highway
Alexandria, VA 22309-0160
(703) 360-3600   Fax: (703) 360-5524

Purpose To provide financial assistance to minorities for the study of agriculture in college.

Eligibility Eligible to apply are Native American, Asian American, African American, or Hispanic American FFA members who are planning to pursue a college degree in any area of agriculture. Scholarships are available to FFA members who are either high school seniors or high school graduates preparing to enroll in their first year of education beyond high school. Preference is given to applicants from the Midwest.

Financial data The stipends are $1,000 and $2,000 per year. Funds are paid directly to the recipient.

Duration 1 year.

Special features Funding for these scholarships is provided by Leo Burnett Company, Inc.

Number awarded 2 $2,000 scholarships and 1 $1,000 scholarship each year.

Deadline February of each year.

[277]
LEONARD M. PERRYMAN COMMUNICATIONS SCHOLARSHIP FOR ETHNIC MINORITY STUDENTS

United Methodist Communications
Attn: Public Media Division
P.O. Box 320
Nashville, TN 37202-0320
(615) 742-5405   Fax: (615) 742-5404

Purpose To provide financial assistance to minority students who are interested in careers in religious communications.

Eligibility Applicants must be minority juniors or seniors who are attending accredited institutions of higher education and are interested in pursuing careers in religious communications. For the purposes of this program, "communications" is meant to cover audiovisual, electronic, and print journalism. Selection is based on Christian commitment and involvement in the life of the church, academic achievement, journalistic experience, clarity of purpose, and professional potential as a religious journalist.

Financial data The stipend is $2,500 per year.

Duration 1 year.

Special features The scholarship may be used at any accredited institution of higher education.

Number awarded 1 each year.

Deadline February of each year.

[278]
LOS ANGELES PHILHARMONIC FELLOWSHIPS FOR EXCELLENCE IN DIVERSITY

Los Angeles Philharmonic
Attn: Education Department
135 North Grand Avenue
Los Angeles, CA 90012
(213) 972-0703

Purpose To identify, nurture, and support talented minority instrumentalists in the southern California area.

Eligibility Applicants must reside (or have parents who reside) in southern California, be between the ages of 16 and 30, and be musicians from historically underrepresented communities: African American, Asian American, Native American, or Latino. Live auditions are required. Applications must include all of the following materials: federal tax form, letter of recommendation from a noted musical authority, a recent photograph, and a brief biographical statement (including career goals).

Financial data Fellowships range from $500 to $2,000; individual awards are determined on the basis of talent and financial circumstances. Funds are to be used to underwrite specific 1-time costs, such as tuition at an accredited institution, travel expenses for audition or solo appearances, instrument purchase, or participation in a summer music festival.

Duration The competition is held annually.

Special features Previous applicants and fellowship winners may reapply.

Number awarded Varies each year.

Deadline April of each year.

[279]
LOUISVILLE COMMUNITY FOUNDATION EDUCATIONAL OPPORTUNITY SCHOLARSHIP FUND

Louisville Community Foundation
Attn: President
Waterfront Plaza, Suite 1110
325 West Main Street
Louisville, KY 40202
(502) 585-4649   Fax: (502) 587-7484

Purpose To provide financial assistance for education at all levels to students in Kentucky.

Eligibility This program is open to "high risk," especially minority, families in Louisville or Jefferson County to support educational expenses from preschool through college. Selection is based on financial need and a 150-word essay on personal and career goals.

Financial data The amount awarded varies but generally is $500 or more.
Duration 1 year.

[280]
MAERC STUDENT FELLOWSHIPS

Associated Western Universities
Attn: MAERC Program
4190 South Highland Drive, Suite 211
Salt Lake City, UT 84124
(801) 273-8904   Fax: (801) 277-5632

Purpose To identify, encourage, and support outstanding college students in California and Texas who are enrolled in science or engineering programs.

Eligibility This program is open to students who are enrolled in science or engineering programs at the Los Angeles, Northridge, or San Diego campuses of the California State University system or at the University of Texas at Austin. Applicants must have junior standing by the start date of the fellowship, a grade point average of 2.5 or better, and U.S. citizenship. Selection is based on academic program and performance, promise of success in the program, demonstrated leadership qualities, career interests and goals, extracurricular activities, and compatibility of applicant's research interests with those of the host facilities. Underrepresented minorities, women, and the physically challenged are especially encouraged to apply.

Financial data The stipend is $400 per month during the academic year and $1,000 per month during the summer. Other benefits during the academic year are tuition and fees up to $1,500 per year and research assistance up to $1,000 per year; during the summer the program provides round-trip travel to the U.S. Department of Energy (DOE) facility and a relocation allowance of $200 per month ($380 in California).

Duration Initially, 12 months (9 months during the academic year and 10 weeks in the summer); renewable to a maximum of 24 months depending on year in school and satisfactory performance.

Special features The Minority Access to Energy-Related Research Careers (MAERC) program is sponsored by DOE and administered by Associated Western Universities. Participants spend the academic year at their home campus and the summer in a research practicum appointment at 1 of the participating DOE facilities: Idaho National Engineering Laboratory (Idaho Falls, Idaho); Lawrence Berkeley Laboratory (Berkeley, California); Los Alamos National Laboratory (Los Alamos, New Mexico); or National Renewable Energy Laboratory (Golden, Colorado).

Deadline March of each year.

[281]
MARC UNDERGRADUATE STUDENT TRAINING IN ACADEMIC RESEARCH (U-STAR) PROGRAM

National Institutes of Health
Attn: National Institute of General Medical Sciences
Director, Minority Access to Research Careers Program
Natcher Building, Suite 2AS43C
45 Center Drive MSC 6200
Bethesda, MD 20892-6200
(301) 594-3900   Fax: (301) 480-2753
E-mail: at21z@nih.gov

Purpose To increase the number of well-prepared minority students who can compete successfully for entry into graduate programs in the biomedical sciences, and to assist minority institutions in developing strong undergraduate science curricula to stimulate interest in biomedical research.

Eligibility To be eligible for this program, an applicant institution must be a public or private nonprofit university, 4-year college, or other institution offering baccalaureate degrees and have a student enrollment with a significant proportion of minorities underrepresented in the biomedical sciences (African Americans, Hispanic Americans, Native Americans, and Pacific Islanders). The institutions receive support to provide science courses and biomedical research training for students at the junior or senior level, who are selected by the institutions on the basis of both their academic achievements and their commitment to pursue a doctoral degree in an area of biomedical science.

Financial data Grants provide a stipend of $7,656 per year for trainees, as well as full tuition, fees, and trainee-related expenses. The sponsoring institutions may apply for funds to cover allowable costs.

Duration Up to 5 years; renewable.

Special features This program is part of the Minority Access to Research Careers (MARC) program of the National Institute of General Medical Sciences. It was formerly known as the MARC Honors Undergraduate Research Training Program. The National Institutes of Health (NIH) designates it as 1 of the T34 Awards.

Number awarded Varies; averages 5 new awards each year.

Deadline April and December of each year.

[282]
MARILYN LLOYD SCHOLARSHIP PROGRAM

Oak Ridge Institute for Science and Education
Attn: Science/Engineering Education Division
P.O. Box 117
Oak Ridge, TN 37831-0117
(423) 576-0128   (423) 576-9272
(800) 569-7749   Fax: (423) 576-3643
E-mail: mlloydsp@orau.gov

Purpose To provide financial assistance for undergraduate study and work experience in areas of interest to the U.S. Department of Energy (DOE).

Eligibility This program is open to students at designated participating universities (write to the address above for a list of these) who are working on an associates's or bachelor's degree with a major in science or engineering and a minor in risk assessment, political science, public policy, economics, law, or business administration. All programs operated by the Science/Engineering Education Division (SEED) of Oak Ridge Institute for Science and Education (ORISE) seek to broaden the participation of minorities, women, and persons with disabilities in science and engineering careers.

Financial data Participants receive a monthly stipend of $600 and payment of tuition and fees.

Duration The program provides tuition support for 2 years with a 3-month summer practicum.

Special features Participants intern at DOE headquarters or operations offices. This program is funded by DOE and administered by ORISE/SEED.

Number awarded Varies each year.

Deadline May of each year.

[283]
MARK J. SCHROEDER SCHOLARSHIP IN METEOROLOGY

American Meteorological Society
Attn: Fellowship/Scholarship Coordinator
45 Beacon Street
Boston, MA 02108-3693
(617) 227-2426, ext. 235   E-mail: sarmstrg@ametsoc.org

Purpose To provide financial assistance to students majoring in meteorology or some aspect of atmospheric sciences.

Eligibility Candidates must be entering their final undergraduate year and be majoring in meteorology or some aspect of the atmospheric or related oceanic and hydrologic sciences. They must intend to make atmospheric or related sciences their career. Applicants must be U.S. citizens or permanent residents, enrolled full time in an accredited U.S. institution, and have a cumulative grade point average of at least 3.0. Selection is based on academic excellence, financial need, and achievement. The American Meteorological Society (AMS) encourages applications from women, minorities, and students with disabilities.

Financial data The stipend is $3,000.

Duration 1 year.

Limitations Requests for an application must be accompanied by a self-addressed stamped envelope.

Number awarded 1 each year.

Deadline June of each year.

[284]
MARTIN LUTHER KING, JR. MEMORIAL SCHOLARSHIP FUND

California Teachers Association
Attn: Human Rights Department
1705 Murchison Drive
P.O. Box 921
Burlingame, CA 94011-0921
(415) 697-1400

Purpose To provide financial assistance to racial-ethnic minority group members in California needing a graduate year to prepare for leadership roles in education.

Eligibility Applicants must be members of a racial-ethnic minority group; U.S. citizens and California residents; college juniors, seniors, or graduate students pursuing a college degree or credential for a teaching-related career in public education in an accredited institution of higher education; and either active members of the California Teachers Association (CTA), members of the Student CTA, or dependents of active, retired, or deceased CTA members.

Financial data Stipends vary each year, depending upon the amount of contributions received and the financial need of individual recipients.

Duration The fellowship is awarded annually.

Number awarded Varies; up to 7 each year.

Deadline March of each year.

[285]
MARY'S PENCE GRANT PROGRAM

Mary's Pence
P.O. Box 29078
Chicago, IL 60629-9078
(708) 499-3771

Purpose To provide funding for projects in the Americas that empower Catholic women.

Eligibility Eligible to apply are Catholic women in the United States who are working toward societal or ecclesial structures that improve or empower the lives of women. Eligible programs include 1) direct service with women that in some way brings self-empowerment and change to their lives; 2) promotion of ecclesial and societal change of oppressive structures; 3) theological studies that promote pastoral alternatives or influence change; or 4) studies in other disciplines that directly impact the lives of women. Special priority is given to requests that focus on the needs of economically disadvantaged women as well as ministries created and managed by women of color. Grants are restricted to projects, programs, or courses of study for ministry in the Americas.

Financial data Grants are provided up to $3,000 for direct service and up to $1,500 for study.

Duration These are 1-time grants; the funds are distributed in October.

Special features The program (which began in 1987) is named for the 3 Marys in scripture.

Number awarded Varies, depending on the availability of funds.

Deadline June of each year.

[286]
MCI INTERNATIONAL SCHOLARSHIPS

MCI International
c/o Julie Peterson, Project Coordinator
Weinberg, Harris & Associates
200 South President Street, Suite 206
Baltimore, MD 21202
(410) 962-7246   (800) MCI-GRAD
Fax: (410) 962-7249

Purpose To provide financial assistance to bilingual high school seniors from certain cities for postsecondary studies in designated curricula.

Eligibility Eligible to apply are high school seniors who attend public schools in New York City, Chicago, Miami, Washington, D.C., San Francisco, or Los Angeles and who are fluent in 2 or more languages. Applicants must be planning to pursue postsecondary studies at a 2-year or 4-year accredited college or technical school on a full-time basis and must demonstrate an interest in studying telecommunications, computer science, international or general business, engineering, communications, or marketing. Selection is based on academic record, SAT scores, an essay, and fluency in 2 or more languages.

Financial data Stipends are $5,000.

Number awarded A total of 60 scholarships are awarded: 10 to students in each of the 6 participating cities.

Deadline January of each year.

[287]
MESBEC PROGRAM

Native American Scholarship Fund
8200 Mountain Road, N.E., Suite 203
Albuquerque, NM 87110-7835
(505) 262-2351   Fax: (505) 262-0534

Purpose To provide financial assistance to Native American students interested in pursuing postsecondary education.

Eligibility Native American students (with at least a quarter Indian blood and members of a U.S. tribe that is federally-recognized, state-recognized, or terminated) are eligible to apply for this program if they are majoring in the 1 of the following fields: mathematics, engineering, science, business administration, education, or computer science. They should have a grade point average of at least 3.0 and scores on the SAT of at least 950 or ACT of at least 23 and must apply for all other sources of funding for which they are eligible. Applicants should demonstrate clear goals and plan to earn a 4-year or graduate degree. Awards are based on merit and the potential of the applicant to improve the lives of Indian people; financial need is not a consideration.

Financial data The amount awarded varies but is generally at least $500, in the form of grants, loans, or a combination of both.

Duration 1 year; may be renewed.

Special features MESBEC is an acronym that stands for the priority areas of this program: mathematics, engineering, science, business, education, and computers.

Number awarded Varies; generally, 30 to 35 each year.

Deadline April of each year for fall terms; September of each year for spring and winter terms; March of each year for summer school.

[288]
MINNESOTA NURSING GRANTS FOR PERSONS OF COLOR

Minnesota Higher Education Services Office
Capitol Square Building
550 Cedar Street, Suite 400
St. Paul, MN 55101
(612) 296-3974   (800) 657-3866 (within MN)
Fax: (612) 297-8880   E-mail: info@heso.state

Purpose To provide financial assistance for persons of color in Minnesota who wish to pursue nursing education.

Eligibility Minnesota residents who are U.S. citizens and Asian-Pacific American, African American, American Indian, or Hispanic American (Latino, Chicano, or Puerto Rican) may apply for these grants if they are entering or enrolled at a Minnesota school, college, or nursing program that leads to licensure as a registered nurse or advanced nursing education. Recipients must be willing to practice in Minnesota for at least 3 years following licensure.

Financial data The amount of the award depends on the need of the recipient, but ranges from from $2,000 to $4,000.

Duration 1 year.

Number awarded Varies each year.

[289]
MINNESOTA SPACE GRANT CONSORTIUM SCHOLARSHIPS AND FELLOWSHIPS

Minnesota Space Grant Consortium
c/o University of Minnesota
Department of Aerospace Engineering and Mechanics
107 Akerman Hall
110 Union Street S.E.
Minneapolis, MN 55455
(612) 626-9295   Fax: (612) 626-1558
E-mail: mnsgc@aem.umn.edu

Purpose To provide financial assistance for postsecondary study in space-related science and engineering fields to students in Minnesota.

Eligibility This program is open to graduate and undergraduate students at institutions that are affiliates of the Minnesota Space Grant Consortium (Augsburg College, Bethel College, Bemidji State University, College of St. Catherine, Fond du Lac Community College, Macalaster College, Normandale Community College, University of Minnesota at Duluth, and University of Minnesota at Twin Cities). U.S. citizenship is required. The Minnesota Space Grant Consortium is a component of the U.S. National Aeronautics and Space Administration (NASA) Space Grant program, which encourages participation by women, minorities, and persons with disabilities.

Financial data The amounts of the awards are set by each of the participating institutions, which augment funding from this program with institutional resources.

Duration 1 year; renewable.

Special features This program is funded by NASA.

Number awarded Varies; more than $50,000 is available from this program each year for scholarships and fellowships.

Deadline Participating institutions set their own deadlines; contact the above for information on the names and addresses of the responsible administrators at the respective institutions.

[290]
MINORITY GEOSCIENCE UNDERGRADUATE SCHOLARSHIPS

American Geological Institute
Attn: Director, AGI Minority Geoscience Scholarships
4220 King Street
Alexandria, VA 22302-1507
(703) 379-2480   Fax: (703) 379-7563

Purpose To provide financial assistance to underrepresented minority undergraduate students interested in pursuing a degree in the geosciences.

Eligibility Awards are limited to geoscience majors who are U.S. citizens and members of the following underrepresented ethnic minority groups: Blacks, Hispanics, and Native Americans (American Indians, Eskimos, Hawaiians, and Samoans). The term "geosciences" is used to refer to study in the fields of geology, geophysics, hydrology, meteorology, physical oceanography, planetary geology, and earth-science education. Selection is based on academic excellence, financial need, and probable future success in the geosciences profession.

Financial data Up to $10,000 per year.

Duration 1 academic year; renewable if the recipient maintains satisfactory performance.

Special features Funding for this program is provided by a grant from the National Science Foundation.

Number awarded Varies; approximately 40 each year.
Deadline January of each year.

[291]
MINORITY OPPORTUNITIES THROUGH SCHOOL TRANSFORMATION (MOST) PROGRAM SUMMER INSTITUTES

American Sociological Association
Attn: Minority Affairs Program
1722 N Street, N.W.
Washington, DC 20036-2981
(202) 833-3410, ext. 322/321   Fax: (202) 785-0146
TDD: (202) 872-0486   E-mail: minority.affairs@asanet.org

Purpose To provide funding to minority undergraduate students who are interested in preparing for a career in sociology.

Eligibility Minority undergraduate students are invited to apply if they will have completed their sophomore year by the time the program begins, are thinking about going on to graduate school in sociology after graduation, and want to prepare for that future activity.

Financial data Participants receive a $1,000 stipend, travel reimbursement, and room and board at 1 of the top graduate departments in the United States for the duration of the program. The host universities change each year; recently, they were the University of Nebraska and the University of California at Santa Barbara.

Duration 8 weeks during the summer.

Special features This summer training program involves an intensive introduction to the arena of graduate sociology, including course work for credit, training seminars focusing on the practice of doing sociology, the development of mentor/student relationships that can carry over into graduate studies, and exposure to career opportunities available to professional sociologists. Further, this program provides an opportunity for the recipients to develop a relationship with the American Sociological Association (ASA) that might continue with further monetary support through the association's graduate-level Minority Fellowship Program. Other components of the ASA MOST program include outreach at undergraduate and graduate levels to increase the number of minorities entering graduate study in sociology, evaluation and revision of the curriculum to better prepare minority students for a career in sociology, mentoring programs at 12 undergraduate and 6 Ph.D. conferring institutions, and efforts to develop a departmental climate that is sensitive to issues of diversity and multiculturalism. The MOST program, funded by the Ford Foundation, began in 1994.

Number awarded In recent years, 38 students annually have participated in MOST summer institutes.

[292]
MINORITY PRESENCE GRANTS (GENERAL PROGRAM II)

North Carolina State Education Assistance Authority
Attn: Scholarship and Grant Services
P.O. Box 2688
Chapel Hill, NC 27515-2688
(919) 549-8614   Fax: (919) 549-8481

Purpose To increase the presence of minority students at each University of North Carolina constituent institution.

Eligibility The grants are available to North Carolina residents taking at least 3 hours of degree-credit course work per semester at 1 of the University of North Carolina system schools who are Native Americans or other minority students. Applicants must be able to demonstrate financial need.

Financial data The amount of the award depends upon the financial need of the recipient and the availability of funds.

Duration 1 year; may be renewed up to 3 additional years.

Limitations Students must submit applications to the constituent institution's financial aid office rather than directly to the North Carolina State Education Assistance Authority.

Number awarded Varies each year.

Deadline Deadline dates vary; check with the specific constituent institution.

[293]
MINORITY SCHOLARSHIP AWARD FOR COLLEGE STUDENTS IN CHEMICAL ENGINEERING

American Institute of Chemical Engineers
Attn: Coordinator of Student Chapter Activities
345 East 47th Street
New York, NY 10017-2395
(212) 705-7840

Purpose To provide financial assistance for study in chemical engineering to underrepresented minority college students.

Eligibility Eligible are undergraduate student members of the American Institute of Chemical Engineers (AIChE) who are also members of a disadvantaged minority group that is underrepresented in chemical engineering (African Americans, Hispanics, and Native Americans). Each AIChE chapter may nominate 1 member. Selection is based on academic record, participation in AIChE student and professional activities, career objectives and plans, and financial need.

Financial data Each scholarship is $1,000.

Duration 1 year.

Number awarded 3 each year.

Deadline Nominations must be submitted by April of each year.

[294]
MINORITY SCHOLARSHIP AWARD FOR INCOMING COLLEGE FRESHMEN IN CHEMICAL ENGINEERING

American Institute of Chemical Engineers
Attn: Coordinator of Student Chapter Activities
345 East 47th Street
New York, NY 10017-2395
(212) 705-7840

Purpose To provide financial assistance for study in chemical engineering to incoming college minority freshmen.

Eligibility Eligible are members of a disadvantaged minority group that is underrepresented in chemical engineering (African Americans, Hispanics, and Native Americans) who are graduating high school seniors planning to enroll in a 4-year university with a major in chemical engineering. Students must be nominated by an American Institute of Chemical Engineers (AIChE) local section. Selection is based on academic record, participation in school and/or necessary work activities, reasons for choosing chemical engineering, and financial need.

Financial data Each scholarship is $1,000.

Duration 1 year.

Number awarded 2 each year.

Deadline Nominations must be submitted by April of each year.

[295]
MINORITY TEACHERS OF ILLINOIS SCHOLARSHIP PROGRAM

Illinois Student Assistance Commission
Attn: Scholarship and Grant Services
1755 Lake Cook Road
Deerfield, IL 60015-5209
(708) 948-8550
(800) 899-ISAC (within IL, IA, IN, MO, and WI)

Purpose To provide funding to minority students in Illinois who plan to become teachers at the preschool, elementary, or secondary level.

Eligibility Applicants must be Illinois residents, U.S. citizens or eligible noncitizens, members of a minority group (African American, Hispanic American, Asian American, or Native American), and high school graduates or holders of a General Educational Development (GED) certificate. They must be enrolled in college full time at the sophomore level or above, have at least a 2.5 grade point average, not be in default on any student loan, and be enrolled or accepted for enrollment in a teacher education program.

Financial data Up to $5,000 per year.

Duration 1 year.

Special features This is a scholarship/loan program. Recipients agree to teach full time 1 year for each year of support received. The teaching agreement may be fulfilled at a public, private, or parochial preschool, elementary school, or secondary school in Illinois; at least 30 percent of the student body at those schools must be minority.

Limitations If the teaching commitment is not fulfilled, the scholarship converts to a loan, and the student must repay the entire amount plus interest.

Number awarded Varies each year.

Deadline July of each year.

[296]
MISSOURI MINORITY TEACHER EDUCATION SCHOLARSHIP PROGRAM

Missouri Department of Elementary and Secondary
   Education
P.O. Box 480
Jefferson City, MO 65102-0480
(573) 751-1668

Purpose To provide financial assistance to minority high school graduates and college students in Missouri who are interested in preparing for a teaching career in mathematics or science.

Eligibility Applicants for this program must 1) be Missouri residents; 2) be African American, Asian American, Hispanic American, or Native American; 3) be high school graduates, college students, or individuals with a baccalaureate degree returning to an approved mathematics or science teacher education program; 4) rank in the top 25 percent of their high school class, or score at or above the 75th percentile on the ACT or SAT examination, or have 30 college hours with a grade point average of 3.0 or better; 5) enroll as full-time students in an approved mathematics or science teacher education program in Missouri; and 6) commit to teach mathematics or science in Missouri public schools for 5 years.

Financial data The stipend is $3,000 per year. This is a scholarship/loan program. The amount of the recipient's potential obligation is reduced by 20 percent for each year of teaching science

or mathematics in the state. Recipients who fail to honor part or all of the 5-year teaching requirement must repay the balance.

Duration Up to 4 years.

Number awarded Varies each year.

[297]
MISSOURI TEACHER EDUCATION SCHOLARSHIP PROGRAM

Missouri Department of Elementary and Secondary
   Education
P.O. Box 480
Jefferson City, MO 65102-0480
(573) 751-1668

Purpose To provide financial assistance to high school seniors, high school graduates, and college students in Missouri who are interested in preparing for a teaching career.

Eligibility This program is open to graduating high school seniors, high school graduates, and lower-division college students who are Missouri residents, ranked in the top 15 percent of their high school class or scored in the top 15 percent on a national standardized test, and are entering or already enrolled at a teacher education program in a 4-year college or university in Missouri. Selection is based on class rank, ACT/SAT scores, school and community activities, leisure activities, leadership ability, employment experiences, essays, and recommendations. Special consideration is given to applicants who desire to teach in Missouri's urban areas or in certain "critical need" fields. Males, minorities, and nontraditional students are encouraged to apply. Each year, 15 percent of the scholarships are reserved for minority students.

Financial data The stipend is $2,000 (half of the award is paid by the state of Missouri and the other half is paid by the participating college or university). This is a scholarship/loan program. The amount of the recipient's potential obligation is reduced by 20 percent for each year of teaching in the state. Recipients who fail to honor part or all of the 5-year teaching requirement must repay the balance.

Duration 1 year; nonrenewable.

Number awarded Varies; generally, at least 200 each year.

Deadline February of each year.

[298]
MODESTO BEE MINORITY SCHOLARSHIP PROGRAM

Modesto Bee
Attn: Executive Editor
1325 H Street
P.O. Box 5256
Modesto, CA 95352
(209) 578-2350

Purpose To provide financial assistance to minority high school seniors in the Modesto area who are interested in preparing for a career in journalism.

Eligibility This program is open to high school seniors who are enrolled in college for the following fall, have maintained a 2.5 grade point average in college, live and attend high school in the Modesto Bee's home delivery circulation area, supply samples of journalistic work, have worked in journalism-related jobs, write an autobiography of up to 1,000 words, and sign a statement of intent to pursue a college education and work toward a career in journalism.

Financial data The stipend is $500.
Duration 1 year.
Number awarded 2 each year.
Deadline February of each year.

[299]
MONTANA SPACE GRANT CONSORTIUM SCHOLARSHIP PROGRAM

Montana Space Grant Consortium
c/o Montana State University
Physics Department
AJM Johnson Hall
Bozeman, MT 59717-0350
(406) 994-4223   Fax: (406) 994-4452
E-mail: msgc@orion.physics.montana.edu

Purpose To provide financial assistance to students in Montana who are interested in working on an undergraduate degree in the space sciences and/or engineering.
Eligibility This program is open to undergraduate students in Montana pursuing studies in fields related to space sciences and engineering. Priority is given to students who have been involved in aerospace-related research. U.S. citizenship is required. The Montana Space Grant Consortium is a component of the U.S. National Aeronautics and Space Administration (NASA) Space Grant program, which encourages participation by women, minorities, and persons with disabilities.
Financial data The amount awarded varies.
Duration 1 year.
Special features Funding for this program is provided by NASA.
Number awarded 8 to 12 each year.

[300]
MORRIS SCHOLARSHIP

Morris Scholarship Fund
206 Sixth Avenue
Midland Building, Room 900
Des Moines, IA 50309-4015
(515) 282-8192   Fax: (515) 282-9117

Purpose To provide financial assistance to minority students in Iowa who are interested in careers in law, journalism, education, or communications.
Eligibility Minority students (Blacks, Asian/Pacific Islanders, Hispanics, or American Indian/Alaskan Natives) are eligible to apply if they are interested in studying 1) journalism, education, or communications at the undergraduate or graduate level or 2) law at the graduate level. Recipients may be residents of any state and may be attending any U.S. college or university, but preference is given to Iowa residents who are attending an Iowa college or university. Selection is based on academic achievement, community service, and financial need.
Financial data Stipends range from $750 to $1,250 per year.
Duration 1 year; may be renewed.
Special features The scholarship is named in honor of the J.B. Morris family, who were founders of the Iowa branches of the National Association for the Advancement of Colored People and published the Iowa Bystander newspaper.
Number awarded 10 to 20 each year.
Deadline January of each year.

[301]
NACA MULTICULTURAL SCHOLARSHIP PROGRAM

National Association for Campus Activities
Attn: Educational Foundation
13 Harbison Way
Columbia, SC 29212-3401
(803) 732-6222   Fax: (803) 749-1047

Purpose To provide financial assistance to minority students who wish to attend training workshops, regional conferences, or national conventions sponsored by the National Association for Campus Activities (NACA).
Eligibility This program is open to ethnic minorities (Black, Latino, Native American, Asian American, or Pacific Islander) who wish to participate in NACA-sponsored summer or winter workshops, regional conferences, or the national convention. Selection is based on past and present involvement in campus activities, potential involvement in campus activities in the immediate future, professional development objectives, and financial need.
Financial data Awards provide for conference or workshop registration only; travel is not included.
Number awarded Up to 3 each year.
Deadline April of each year.

[302]
NATIONAL HEALTH SERVICE CORPS SCHOLARSHIP PROGRAM

Health Resources and Services Administration
Attn: Bureau of Primary Health Care
National Health Service Corps Program
2070 Chain Bridge Road, Suite 450
Vienna, VA 22182-2536
(703) 821-8955   (800) 221-9393

Purpose To provide financial assistance to primary health care scholars willing to serve in a federally designated health professional shortage area on completion of training.
Eligibility The following requirements must be met by applicants to be eligible for these awards: U.S. citizenship or permanent residency, full-time enrollment in an accredited school or program in the United States or its possessions, and a demonstrated potential for providing primary health care services, including allopathic and osteopathic medicine (with a specialty in family medicine, general pediatrics, general internal medicine, or obstetrics/gynecology), family nurse practitioner, nurse midwife, and physician assistant (either baccalaureate or master's level). Preference is given to applicants who have participated in the federal Scholarship Program for Students of Exceptional Financial Need at their medical schools, come from a disadvantaged background, and have characteristics that increase the probability they will continue to practice in a health professional shortage area (HPSA) after they have completed their service obligation.
Financial data The stipend is $817 per month. In addition, the program makes a direct payment to each participant's school for tuition and fees and a single additional payment toward other reasonable educational expenses (e.g., books, clinical supplies, laboratory expenses, uniforms, graduation fees, and clinical rotational travel). Participants incur 1 year of obligated service in the National Health Service Corps for each full or partial year of support provided under this program. The minimum service obligation is 2 years.
Duration 1 year; may be renewed for up to 3 additional years.
Special features This scholarship was first offered in 1978/9. It is the successor to the Public Health and National Health Ser-

vice Corps Scholarship Training Program, which was in effect from 1973/4 to 1977/8.

Limitations Participants are obligated to provide full-time clinical primary health care services to populations in federally-designated, high-priority HPSAs (these include the Indian Health Service or medical facilities of the Federal Bureau of Prisons).

Number awarded Varies each year, depending upon the funding available. In a recent year, 220 scholarships were awarded.

Deadline March of each year.

[303]
NATIONAL HEART, LUNG, AND BLOOD INSTITUTE SHORT-TERM RESEARCH TRAINING FOR MINORITY STUDENTS PROGRAM

National Institutes of Health
Attn: National Heart, Lung, and Blood Institute
Division of Lung Diseases
Two Rockledge Center, Room 10112
6701 Rockledge Drive MSC 7952
Bethesda, MD 20892-7952
(301) 435-0222   Fax: (301) 480-1046
E-mail: mr50w@nih.gov

Purpose To enable research institutions to provide opportunities for underrepresented minority students at the undergraduate and graduate level to become exposed to biomedical research in areas relevant to cardiovascular, pulmonary, and hematologic diseases through a short-term research experience.

Eligibility Applications may be submitted by non-federal, domestic, for-profit and nonprofit, public and private organizations, such as universities, colleges, medical schools, and units of state and local government. Racial/ethnic minority individuals, women, and persons with disabilities are particularly encouraged to apply as program directors. The proposal must support short-term research training experiences of minority undergraduate students, minority students in health professional schools, and minority graduate students. The grantee institution is responsible for selection and appointment of trainees. Special attention should be given to the recruitment of individuals from minority groups that are underrepresented nationally in the biomedical and behavioral sciences (Blacks, Hispanics, American Indians, Alaska Natives, and Pacific Islanders). Trainees must have successfully completed at least 1 undergraduate year at an accredited school or university (including baccalaureate schools of nursing) or have successfully completed 1 semester at a school of medicine, optometry, osteopathy, dentistry, veterinary medicine pharmacy, or public health, or an institution with an accredited graduate program. Trainees appointed to the program need not be from the grantee institution, but may include a number of minority students from other institutions, schools, colleges, or universities.

Financial data The award provides salary support to the trainees of $834 per month, as well as up to $125 per trainee per month for other training costs (supplies, tuition, fees, etc.), up to $500 per trainee for travel to and from the training site, and up to $250 per month per trainee for housing at the training site.

Duration Grants to institutions are for 5 years; students receive support for 2 to 3 months.

Special features Students interested in this program should check with the office of sponsored research at their institution to see if such programs are available. They may also contact the address above to obtain a list of participating institutions.

Number awarded Varies each year; each institutional grant supports 4 to 24 students per year.

Deadline August of each year.

[304]
NATIVE AMERICAN JOURNALISTS ASSOCIATION SCHOLARSHIPS

Native American Journalists Association
Attn: College Scholarships
1433 East Franklin Avenue, Suite 11
Minneapolis, MN 55404-2135
(612) 874-8833   Fax: (612) 874-9007

Purpose To provide financial assistance to Native American undergraduates who are interested in majoring in journalism in college.

Eligibility Native American students pursuing a degree in journalism or a related field are eligible. Applications include proof of enrollment in a federal or state recognized tribe, work samples (including printed works and photographs), grade transcripts showing an above average grade point average, a personal statement that demonstrates financial need and the student's reasons for pursuing a career in journalism, and a letter of recommendation from an academic advisor or a member of the community that attests to the applicant's ability to complete the desired education.

Financial data The scholarships provide $2,500 for broadcast journalism or $2,000 for print or photojournalism.

Duration 1 year.

Number awarded 6 each year: 2 in broadcast journalism and 4 in print or photojournalism.

[305]
NEBRASKA SPACE GRANT COURSE WORK AWARDS

Nebraska Space Grant Consortium
c/o UNO Aviation Institute
Allwine Hall 422
University of Nebraska at Omaha
Omaha, NE 68182-0508
(402) 554-3772   (800) 858-8648
Fax: (402) 554-3781   E-mail: nasa@cwis.unomaha.edu

Purpose To fund aerospace-related study on the undergraduate and graduate school level for students in Nebraska.

Eligibility This program is open to all eligible undergraduate and graduate students at the following schools in Nebraska: University of Nebraska at Omaha, University of Nebraska at Lincoln, University of Nebraska at Kearney, University of Nebraska Medical Center, Creighton University, Western Nebraska Community College, Chadron State College, College of St. Mary, Metro Community College, and Nebraska Indian Community College. Applicants must be U.S. citizens and working on a degree in an aerospace-related area as full-time students during the spring and fall semesters or half-time during the summer session. Special attention is given to applications submitted by women, underrepresented minorities, and individuals with disabilities.

Financial data The amount of the award depnds on the scope of the proposal and the qualifications of the applicant.

Duration Academic awards are 1 year; summer awards are for the summer months. Both awards are renewable.

Special features Recipients enroll in courses in an approved aviation/aerospace course of study. Funding for this program is provided by the National Aeronautics and Space Administration.

Limitations Recipients must submit a progress report each semester on the progress of their course work to a designated faculty monitor. Failure to provide that report disqualifies the student from reapplying for a renewal fellowship.

[306]
NEW JERSEY EDUCATIONAL OPPORTUNITY FUND GRANTS

Commission on Higher Education
Attn: Educational Opportunity Fund
20 West State Street, Seventh Floor
CN 542
Trenton, NJ 08625-0542
(609) 292-4310   (800) 792-8670 (within NJ)

Purpose To provide financial assistance for undergraduate or graduate education in New Jersey to students from educationally disadvantaged backgrounds.

Eligibility Students from educationally disadvantaged backgrounds with demonstrated financial need who have been legal residents of New Jersey for at least 12 consecutive month are eligible. Applicants must be from families with annual incomes below specified limits, ranging from $14,940 for a household size of 1 to $50,780 for a household size of 8. They must be attending or accepted for attendance as full-time undergraduate or graduate students at institutions of higher education in New Jersey. To apply, students must fill out the Free Application for Federal Student Aid. Some colleges may also require students to complete the College Scholarship Service's (CSS) Financial Aid Form to apply for institutional aid.

Financial data Undergraduate grants range from $200 to $2,100 and graduate grants from $200 to $2,650, depending on the type of institution and financial need.

Duration 1 year; renewable annually (based on satisfactory academic progress and continued eligibility).

Special features This is a campus-based program; each college or university has its own specific criteria for admission and program participation; students should contact the Educational Opportunity Fund (EOF) director at their institution for specific admissions information and requirements for participating in the program. Participants are also eligible for supportive services such as counseling, tutoring, and developmental course work.

Deadline September of each year.

[307]
NEWSDAY SCHOLARSHIP IN COMMUNICATIONS FOR MINORITIES

Newsday
Attn: Public Affairs Manager
235 Pinelawn Road
Melville, NY 11747-4250
(516) 843-2173   (212) 308-2961
Fax: (516) 843-5424

Purpose To provide financial assistance to minority students from selected areas of New York who are interested in pursuing a career in communications.

Eligibility Minority (African American, Latino American, Asian American, and Native American) students graduating from high schools in Queens or Long Island (Nassau or Suffolk counties) planning to attend a 4-year college or university in the United States and interested in communications are eligible to apply. Students must in the top 10 percent of their graduating class and

have demonstrated exceptional ability in the field of print or broadcast journalism.

Financial data Scholarships are $4,000 and $1,000.

Duration 1 year; nonrenewable.

Number awarded 2 each year: 1 of $4,000 and 1 of $1,000.

Deadline April of each year.

[308]
NORTH CAROLINA COMMUNITY COLLEGE SCHOLARSHIP PROGRAM

North Carolina Community College System
Attn: Student Support Services
200 West Jones Street
Raleigh, NC 27603-1379
(919) 733-7051   Fax: (919) 733-0680

Purpose To provide financial assistance to Black Americans and other minorities attending community colleges in North Carolina.

Eligibility Applicants must be North Carolina residents enrolled at least part time in a curriculum program at 1 of the 58 institutions in North Carolina's community college system. Awards are granted according to the following priorities: 1) students with the greatest financial need; 2) minorities, defined as Blacks, American Indians, Spanish Surname Americans, Native Alaskans, and Orientals; 3) Black American students enrolled in college transferable curriculum programs; 4) displaced persons seeking new job skills; and 5) women in nontraditional curricula. Other factors considered in the selection process are scholastic achievement and participation in instruction and community activities.

Financial data The stipend is $556.50 per year.

Duration 1 year; may be renewed.

Limitations There are no special application forms for the scholarships. Students apply to their local community college, not to the system office. Each eligible school selects its own recipients from applicants meeting the above criteria.

Number awarded 575 each year.

[309]
NORTH CAROLINA TEACHING FELLOWS PROGRAM

North Carolina Teaching Fellows Commission
Koger Center, Cumberland Building
3739 National Drive, Suite 210
Raleigh, NC 27612
(919) 781-6833   Fax: (919) 781-6527

Purpose To provide financial assistance to high school seniors and graduates in North Carolina who wish to prepare for a career in teaching.

Eligibility Applicants must be North Carolina residents, interested in preparing for a career as a teacher, and accepted for enrollment at 1 of the following schools in North Carolina: Appalachian State University, East Carolina University, Elon College, Meredith College, North Carolina A&T University, University of North Carolina at Asheville, North Carolina Central University, North Carolina State University, Pembroke State University, University of North Carolina at Chapel Hill, University of North Carolina at Charlotte, University of North Carolina at Greensboro, University of North Carolina at Wilmington, or Western Carolina University. Selection is based on academic record, SAT scores, class standing, writing ability, community service, extracurricular activities, and recommendations. A particular goal of the program is to recruit and retain greater numbers of male and minority teacher education candidates in North Carolina.

Financial data The stipend is $5,000. This is a scholarship/loan program; 1 year of work as a teacher in North Carolina cancels 1 year of support under this program. Recipients who fail to honor the work obligation must repay the balance at 10 percent interest.

Duration 1 year; renewable for up to 3 additional years.

Number awarded Up to 400 each year.

[310]
NORTHERN CALIFORNIA CHEVRON MERIT AWARD

Independent Colleges of Northern California
225 Bush Street, Suite 1185
San Francisco, CA 94104
(415) 543-0556

Purpose To recognize and reward the outstanding classroom, school, and community achievements of high school seniors planning to major in business or the sciences at an independent college in northern California.

Eligibility Students who have an outstanding record of academic achievement, leadership, and participation in school and community activities and are interested in attending an independent college in northern California are invited to apply for these awards. Minorities and women are particularly encouraged to apply.

Financial data The stipend is $2,000 per year.

Duration 4 years for entering freshmen.

Special features Funding for this program is supplied by Chevron U.S.A. Inc.

Number awarded 8 each year. In even-numbered years, awards are for freshmen entering the following schools: College of Notre Dame, Fresno Pacific College, Holy Names College, Menlo College, or Stanford University. In odd-numbered years, the awards are for students entering: Dominican College of San Rafael, Golden Gate University, Monterey Institute of International Studies (for upper-division or graduate students), Pacific Union College, University of the Pacific, or Mills College.

Deadline February of each year.

[311]
NORTHWEST JOURNALISTS OF COLOR SCHOLARSHIP AWARDS

Northwest Journalists of Color
c/o Janet Tu
The Seattle Times
P.O. Box 70
Seattle, WA 98111
(206) 464-2272

Purpose To provide financial assistance to minority students from Washington state who are interested in careers in journalism.

Eligibility These scholarships are open to minority students from Washington state who are planning a career in broadcast, photo, or print journalism. Applicants may be high school seniors or college undergraduates who are residents of Washington State, although they may attend college anywhere in the country. Students are not required to major in journalism, but they should have a strong interest in the subject.

Financial data Stipends are up to $1,000.

Duration 1 year; may be renewed.

Special features This program is sponsored by the Seattle chapters of the Asian American Journalists Association, the National Association of Black Journalists, the Latino Media Association, and the Native American Journalists Association.

Number awarded Varies each year.

Deadline May of each year.

[312]
NURSING EDUCATION OPPORTUNITIES FOR INDIVIDUALS FROM DISADVANTAGED BACKGROUNDS

Health Resources and Services Administration
Attn: Bureau of Health Professions
Division of Nursing
Parklawn Building, Room 9-46
5600 Fishers Lane
Rockville, MD 20857
(301) 443-5763   Fax: (301) 443-8586

Purpose To provide grants to schools of nursing to meet the costs of special projects to increase nursing education opportunities for individuals from disadvantaged backgrounds.

Eligibility Public and private nonprofit schools of nursing may apply for these grants to 1) identify, recruit, and select individuals from disadvantaged backgrounds; 2) facilitate the entry of such individuals into schools of nursing; 3) provide counseling or other services designed to assist such individuals to complete their nursing education; 4) provide, for a period prior to the entry of each individuals into the regular course of education at a school of nursing, preliminary education designed to assist them to complete successfully such regular course of education; 5) provide training, information, or advice to the faculty of such schools with respect to encouraging such individuals to complete the programs of nursing education in which the individuals are enrolled; 6) publicize, especially to licensed vocational or practical nurses, existing sources of financial aid available to persons enrolled in schools of nursing or who are undertaking training necessary to qualify them to enroll in such schools; and 7) pay stipends for such individuals for any period of nursing education. Individuals from disadvantaged backgrounds are defined as those who 1) come from an environment that has inhibited the individual from obtaining the knowledge, skill, and abilities required to enroll in and graduate from a health professions school; or 2) come from a family with a low income, currently established as less than $10,200 for a family with 1 dependent, ranging to less than $26,700 for a family with 6 dependents.

Financial data For the past several years, $19.3 million in grants annually have been provided through this program; average grants have been $170,400.

Duration 1 year; may be renewed.

Special features Applications for the stipends provided through this program are submitted directly to schools which have received grants for that purpose; for a list of such schools, contact the address above.

Number awarded 122 awards were granted over the past 5 years.

Deadline December of each year.

[313]
NURSING SPECIAL PROJECT GRANTS

Health Resources and Services Administration
Attn: Bureau of Health Professions
Division of Nursing
Parklawn Building, Room 9-46
5600 Fishers Lane
Rockville, MD 20857
(301) 443-6193   Fax: (301) 443-8586

Purpose To provide grants to schools of nursing to improve nursing practice through projects that increase the knowledge and skills of nursing personnel, enhance their effectiveness in primary health care delivery, and increase the number of qualified nurses.

Eligibility Public and private nonprofit schools of nursing may apply for these grants to 1) expand enrollment in professional nursing programs, especially schools that provide clinical training in the provision of primary health care in publicly-funded urban or rural outpatient facilities, home health agencies, public health agencies, or rural hospitals; 2) provide primary health care in non-institutional settings; 3) provide continuing education for nurses in medically underserved communities; or 4) offer fellowships for payment of tuition and fees to nursing paraprofessionals, especially those who are economically disadvantaged or members of minority groups underrepresented among registered nurses and who wish to transition to status as professional nurses. Preference is given to institutions that 1) provide students with clinical training in the provision of primary health care in outpatient facilities, home health agencies, public health agencies, or rural hospitals; 2) offer generic baccalaureate programs and R.N. completion programs; 3) demonstrate either substantial progress over the last 3 years or a significant experience of 10 or more years in enrolling and graduating trainees from those minority or low-income populations identified as at-risk of poor health outcomes; and 4) offer continuing education programs for nurses from medically underserved communities to increase their knowledge and skills in care of persons who are HIV positive or who have AIDS. Nursing paraprofessionals who are seeking assistance under this program may contact the address above to obtain a list of the current grantees offering fellowships.

Financial data In recent years, $10.3 million in grants has been provided through this program annually; the average award has been $159,000. The institutions that receive funding through this program determine the amounts they wish to devote to financial aid for students.

Duration Up to 3 years for the initial grant; renewable.

Number awarded Recently, 60 awards have been granted each year.

Deadline February of each year.

[314]
OHIO NEWSPAPERS FOUNDATION JOURNALISM SCHOLARSHIPS

Ohio Newspapers Foundation
1335 Dublin Road, Suite 216-B
Columbus, OH 43215-7038
(614) 486-6677

Purpose To provide financial assistance for college education to minority students in Ohio planning to pursue careers in journalism.

Eligibility This program is open to high school seniors in Ohio who are members of minority groups and planning to pursue careers in journalism. Applicants must have a minimum high school grade point average of 2.5, demonstrate writing ability, and plan to attend a college or university in Ohio.

Financial data The award is $1,000.

Duration 1 year.

Number awarded 2 each year.

Deadline March of each year.

[315]
OHIO SPACE GRANT CONSORTIUM JUNIOR SCHOLARSHIP

Ohio Space Grant Consortium
c/o Ohio Aerospace Institute
22800 Cedar Point Road
Cleveland, OH 44142
(216) 962-3032   (800) 828-OSGC
Fax: (216) 962-3120   E-mail: osgc@oai.org

Purpose To encourage American citizens to pursue a baccalaureate degree in aerospace-related engineering and science at major universities in Ohio.

Eligibility These fellowships are available to U.S. citizens who expect to complete the requirements for a bachelor of science degree in an aerospace-related discipline (aeronautical engineering, aerospace engineering, chemical engineering, computer engineering and science, control engineering, electrical engineering, engineering mechanics, industrial engineering, manufacturing engineering, materials science and engineering, mechanical engineering, physics, petroleum engineering, and systems engineering) 2 years after applying. They must be attending 1 of the following participating universities in Ohio: University of Akron, Case Western Reserve University, Central State University, University of Cincinnati, Cleveland State University, University of Dayton, Ohio State University, Ohio University, University of Toledo, Wilberforce University, or Wright State University. Members of groups underrepresented in science and engineering (including women, minorities, and persons with disabilities) are particularly encouraged to apply. Selection is based on academic record, recommendations, and a personal statement of career goals and anticipated benefits from the Space Grant program; the statement should also discuss plans for a research laboratory experience.

Financial data The stipend is $2,000.

Duration 1 year.

Special features These scholarships are funded through the National Space Grant College and Fellowship Program, administered by the National Aeronautics and Space Administration (NASA) with matching funds provided by the member universities, the Ohio Aerospace Institute, and private industry.

Deadline January of each year.

[316]
OHIO SPACE GRANT CONSORTIUM SENIOR SCHOLARSHIP

Ohio Space Grant Consortium
c/o Ohio Aerospace Institute
22800 Cedar Point Road
Cleveland, OH 44142
(216) 962-3032   (800) 828-OSGC
Fax: (216) 962-3120   E-mail: osgc@oai.org

Purpose To encourage American citizens to pursue a baccalaureate degree in aerospace-related engineering and science at major universities in Ohio.

Eligibility These fellowships are available to U.S. citizens who expect to complete the requirements for a bachelor of science degree in an aerospace-related discipline (aeronautical engineering, aerospace engineering, chemical engineering, computer engineering and science, control engineering, electrical engineering, engineering mechanics, industrial engineering, manufacturing engineering, materials science and engineering, mechanical engineering, physics, petroleum engineering, and systems engineering) 1 year after applying. They must be attending 1 of the following participating universities in Ohio: University of Akron, Case Western Reserve University, Central State University, University of Cincinnati, Cleveland State University, University of Dayton, Ohio State University, Ohio University, University of Toledo, Wilberforce University, or Wright State University. Members of groups underrepresented in science and engineering (including women, minorities, and persons with disabilities) are particularly encouraged to apply. Applicants must propose a research project to be conducted during the scholarship period in a campus laboratory. Selection is based on academic record, recommendations, the proposed research project, and a personal statement of career goals and anticipated benefits from the Space Grant program.

Financial data The stipend is $3,000.

Duration 1 year.

Special features These scholarships are funded through the National Space Grant College and Fellowship Program, administered by the National Aeronautics and Space Administration (NASA) with matching funds provided by the member universities, the Ohio Aerospace Institute, and private industry.

Limitations Scholars are required to describe their research at an annual spring research symposium sponsored by the consortium.

Deadline January of each year.

[317]
OKLAHOMA FUTURE TEACHERS SCHOLARSHIP PROGRAM

Oklahoma State Regents for Higher Education
500 Education Building
State Capitol Complex
Oklahoma City, OK 73105-4503
(405) 524-9153   Fax: (405) 524-9230

Purpose To provide financial assistance to Oklahoma residents who are interested in teaching (particularly in teacher shortage fields) in Oklahoma.

Eligibility Candidates for this program are nominated by institutions of higher education in Oklahoma. Nominees must be high school seniors, high school graduates, or currently-enrolled undergraduate or graduate students. They must 1) rank in the top 15 percent of their high school graduating class; 2) place at least at the 85th percentile on the ACT or SAT either for their class as a whole or for a subdivision of Black Non-Hispanic, Hispanic, Native American, or Asian; 3) have been admitted into a professional education program at an accredited Oklahoma institution of higher education; or 4) have achieved an undergraduate record of outstanding success as defined by the institution. Recipients must agree to teach in critical shortage areas in the state upon graduation. These areas change periodically but in the past have included (for all applicants) special education, science, and foreign languages; (for graduate students) counseling, library/media

specialist, and speech and language pathology; and (for renewal applicants) early childhood education and mathematics.

Financial data Full-time students receive up to $1,500 per year if they have completed 60 hours or more and up to $1,000 if they have completed fewer than 60 hours; part-time students receive up to $750 per year if they have completed 60 hours or more and up to $500 per year if they have completed fewer than 60 hours. Funds are paid directly to the institution on the student's behalf. This is a scholarship/loan program; recipients must agree to teach in Oklahoma public schools for 3 years following graduation and licensure.

Duration 1 year; may be renewable for up to 3 additional years as long as the recipient maintains a grade point average of at least 2.5.

Number awarded 100 or more each year.

Deadline Participating institutions set their own deadline dates, but must forward applications and prioritized nominations to the State Regents by June of each year.

[318]
OKLAHOMA STATE REGENTS ACADEMIC SCHOLARS PROGRAM

Oklahoma State Regents for Higher Education
500 Education Building
State Capitol Complex
Oklahoma City, OK 73105-4503
(405) 524-9153   Fax: (405) 524-9230

Purpose To provide financial assistance to outstanding high school seniors and recent graduates in Oklahoma.

Eligibility High school seniors or graduates from any state automatically are eligible for this funding if they have been named a National Merit Scholar, a National Merit Scholar Finalist, a National Achievement Scholar, a National Achievement Scholar Finalist, a National Hispanic Scholar, a National Hispanic Honorable Mention Awardee, or a Presidential Scholar. In addition, Oklahoma residents can be eligible for support under this program if they have scored within the 99.5 to 100 percentile levels on the SAT or ACT; those percentiles apply to the total student population as well as to separate subdivisions—male, female, Black Non-Hispanic, Native American, Hispanic, Asian-Pacific Islander, and White Non-Hispanic. Applicants must apply within 27 months of their high school graduation date.

Financial data The program provides funding for tuition, fees, room and board, and textbooks. The exact amount of funding awarded varies each year but is currently $5,000 per year for students at the University of Oklahoma, Oklahoma State University, or University of Tulsa, $3,500 per year for students at other 4-year public or private colleges or universities in Oklahoma, or $3,100 per year for students at Oklahoma 2-year colleges.

Duration Up to 5 years of undergraduate study as long as the recipient remains a full-time student with a minimum grade point average of 3.25.

Special features Recipients may enroll in either public or private schools.

Limitations Recipients must attend a school in Oklahoma.

Deadline September of each year.

[319]
OMEGA BOYS CLUB SCHOLARSHIP

Omega Boys Club
P.O. Box 884463
San Francisco, CA 94188-4463
(415) 826-8664   (800) SOLDIER
Fax: (415) 826-8673

Purpose To provide financial assistance to inner-city minority students in the San Francisco area who are interested in pursuing a college education.

Eligibility Minorities in the San Francisco area are eligible to apply if they are members of the Omega Boys Club, are high school seniors, are in financial need, and are interested in attending college (particularly a traditionally Black college/university). Both males and females are eligible.

Financial data Up to $6,000 per year (the average award is $3,000).

Duration 1 year; may be renewed for up to 3 additional years.

Number awarded Approximately 30 each year.

[320]
OREGON CHEVRON MERIT AWARD

Oregon Independent College Foundation
121 Southwest Salmon Street, Suite 1130
Portland, OR 97204
(503) 227-7568

Purpose To recognize and reward the outstanding classroom, school, and community achievements of high school seniors planning to major in business or the sciences at an independent college in Oregon.

Eligibility Students who have an outstanding record of academic achievement, leadership, and participation in school and community activities and are interested in attending an independent college in Oregon are invited to apply for these awards. Minorities and women are particularly encouraged to apply.

Financial data The stipend is $2,000 per year.

Duration 4 years for entering freshmen.

Special features Funding for this program is supplied by Chevron U.S.A. Inc.

Number awarded 8 each year.

Deadline February of each year.

[321]
ORNL PROFESSIONAL INTERNSHIP PROGRAM

Oak Ridge Institute for Science and Education
Attn: Science/Engineering Education Division
P.O. Box 117
Oak Ridge, TN 37831-0117
(423) 576-3427   (423) 576-3426
(800) 569-7749   Fax: (423) 576-3643
E-mail: pipornl@orau.gov   E-mail: gpipornl@orau.gov

Purpose To provide financial assistance for postsecondary study and practical research experience at Oak Ridge National Laboratory (ORNL).

Eligibility This program is open to U.S. citizens or permanent residents at least 18 years of age who are currently enrolled in an accredited U.S. college or university in an academic program leading to an associate, baccalaureate, or graduate degree. High school seniors are eligible if they have been accepted in an associate or baccalaureate program. Students should be pursuing studies in chemistry, computer science, civil engineering, environmental engineering, hydrogeology, mechanical engineering, environmental science, geology, or hydrology. A cumulative grade point average of at least 2.5 is required. All programs operated by the Science/Engineering Education Division (SEED) of Oak Ridge Institute for Science and Education (ORISE) seek to broaden the participation of minorities, women, and persons with disabilities in science and engineering careers.

Financial data Participants receive tuition and fees for off-campus courses related to the research experience during the appointment period. Monthly stipends range from $1,000 to $1,300 for undergraduates or $1,300 to $1,400 for graduate students. Travel expenses for a single round trip from the student's campus to the research center are also reimbursed.

Duration 3 to 12 consecutive months.

Special features Interns are assigned individual research projects that relate to their academic majors, career goals, and the ongoing research and development missions of ORNL: to carry out applied research and engineering development in energy production and conservation technologies as well as experimental and theoretical research in the physical and life sciences to advance fundamental knowledge and to lay the foundation for technology development. A secondary mission is to address other nationally important issues, such as environmental protection and waste management and non-nuclear defense technologies, when such work is closely related to the primary mission. This program is funded by Oak Ridge National Laboratory but managed and operated by ORISE/SEED.

Number awarded Varies each year.

Deadline February of each year for programs to begin in May or June; May of each year for programs to begin in August or September; September of each year for programs to begin in January.

[322]
OSGC EDUCATION PROGRAM

Oklahoma Space Grant Consortium
c/o University of Oklahoma
College of Geosciences
Oklahoma Climatological Survey
100 East Boyd, Suite 1210
Norman, Oklahoma 73019-0628
(405) 325-1240   Fax: (405) 325-2550
E-mail: vduca@geoadm.gen.uoknor.edu

Purpose To provide support for programs in Oklahoma that increase participation of underrepresented minority and women students in aerospace-related studies at the undergraduate and graduate level.

Eligibility This program is open to undergraduate and graduate students at member and affiliate institutions of the Oklahoma Space Grant Consortium (OSGC)—Oklahoma State University, the University of Oklahoma, Cameron University, and Langston University. U.S. citizenship is required. The OSGC is a component of the U.S. National Aeronautics and Space Administration (NASA) Space Grant program, which encourages participation by women, minorities, and persons with disabilities.

Financial data Financing depends on the availability of funds.

Special features This program is funded by NASA. For information on the program at each participating university, contact the address above.

[323]
PAUL H. KUTSCHENREUTER SCHOLARSHIP

American Meteorological Society
Attn: Fellowship/Scholarship Coordinator
45 Beacon Street
Boston, MA 02108-3693
(617) 227-2426, ext. 235   E-mail: sarmstrg@ametsoc.org

Purpose   To provide financial assistance to students majoring in meteorology or some aspect of atmospheric sciences.

Eligibility   Candidates must be entering their final undergraduate year and be majoring in meteorology or some aspect of the atmospheric or related oceanic and hydrologic sciences. They must intend to make atmospheric or related sciences their career. Applicants must be U.S. citizens or permanent residents, enrolled full time in an accredited U.S. institution, and have a cumulative grade point average of at least 3.0. Selection is based on academic excellence, achievement, and financial need. The American Meteorological Society (AMS) encourages applications from women, minorities, and students with disabilities.

Financial data   The stipend is $5,000.

Duration   1 year.

Special features   This scholarship honors the late Paul H. Kutschenreuter, who served as deputy director of the U.S. Weather Bureau, assistant administrator of the Environmental Science Services Administration, U.S. delegate to numerous World Meteorological Organization (WMO) meetings, and president of the Commission of Synoptic Meteorology of the WMO.

Limitations   Requests for an application must be accompanied by a self-addressed stamped envelope.

Number awarded   1 each year.

Deadline   June of each year.

[324]
PHI DELTA KAPPA SCHOLARSHIP GRANTS FOR PROSPECTIVE EDUCATORS

Phi Delta Kappa International
Attn: Director of Chapter Programs
408 North Union
P.O. Box 789
Bloomington, IN 47402-0789
(812) 339-1156   (800) 766-1156
Fax: (812) 339-0018

Purpose   To provide financial assistance to students who are interested in becoming teachers.

Eligibility   Eligible to apply are high school seniors who are in the upper third of their classes and interested in attending college and preparing for a teaching career. Selection is based on scholastic achievement, letters of recommendation, written expression, interest in a teaching or professional education career, and school and community activities. Applicants must submit a 750-word essay on a topic that changes annually; a recent topic asked what educators and communities might do to reduce the level of school violence.

Financial data   Stipends are $1,000 and $2,000.

Duration   1 year.

Number awarded   48 each year: 47 for $1,000 and 1 for $2,000. At least 4 scholarships awarded each year are set aside specifically for minority recipients: 1 each for an African American, Hispanic, Native American, and Asian American.

Deadline   January of each year.

[325]
PHILADELPHIA INQUIRER JOURNALISM CAREER DEVELOPMENT WORKSHOP SCHOLARSHIPS

Philadelphia Inquirer
Attn: Lucia Herndon
400 North Broad Street
P.O. Box 8263
Philadelphia, PA 19101
(215) 854-5724

Purpose   To provide financial assistance for college education to outstanding participants in a journalism workshop.

Eligibility   Minority high school juniors and seniors from Pennsylvania, New Jersey, and Delaware participate in a journalism workshop at the *Philadelphia Inquirer*. College scholarships are awarded to the most promising students.

Financial data   Each scholarship is $1,500.

Special features   During the workshops, students learn about newspaper journalism from *Inquirer* editors, reporters, and photographers.

Number awarded   About 30 students participate in the workshop and 2 of them receive college scholarships.

[326]
PITTSBURGH ENERGY TECHNOLOGY CENTER PROFESSIONAL INTERNSHIP PROGRAM

Oak Ridge Institute for Science and Education
Attn: Science/Engineering Education Division
P.O. Box 117
Oak Ridge, TN 37831-0117
(423) 576-3427   (423) 576-3426
(800) 569-7749   Fax: (423) 576-3643
E-mail: pippetc@orau.gov   E-mail: gpippetc@orau.gov

Purpose   To provide financial assistance for postsecondary study and practical research experience at the Pittsburgh Energy Technology Center.

Eligibility   This program is open to U.S. citizens or permanent residents at least 18 years of age who are currently enrolled in an accredited U.S. college or university in an academic program leading to an associate, baccalaureate, or graduate degree. High school seniors are eligible if they have been accepted to an associate or baccalaureate program. Students should be pursuing studies in chemistry, computer science, engineering, environmental sciences, mathematics, statistics, geology, or physics. A cumulative grade point average of at least 2.5 is required. All programs operated by the Science/Engineering Education Division (SEED) of Oak Ridge Institute for Science and Education (ORISE) seek to broaden the participation of minorities, women, and persons with disabilities in science and engineering careers.

Financial data   Participants receive tuition and fees for off-campus courses related to the research experience during the appointment period. Monthly stipends range from $1,000 to $1,300 for undergraduates or $1,300 to $1,400 for graduate students. Travel expenses for a single round trip from the student's campus to the research center are also reimbursed.

Duration   3 to 12 consecutive months.

Special features   Interns are assigned individual research projects that relate to their academic majors, career goals, and the ongoing research and development missions of the Pittsburgh Energy Technology Center in multidisciplinary coal-related research and development. This program is funded by the Office of Fossil Energy of the U.S. Department of Energy and administered by ORISE/SEED.

Number awarded Varies each year.

Deadline February of each year for programs to begin in May or June; May of each year for programs to begin in August or September; September of each year for programs to begin in January.

[327]
PRSA MULTICULTURAL AFFAIRS SCHOLARSHIPS

Public Relations Society of America
Attn: Educational Affairs Department
33 Irving Place
New York, NY 10003-2376
(212) 460-1474

Purpose To provide financial assistance to minority college students who are interested in preparing for a career in public relations.

Eligibility Minority students who are at least juniors in college are eligible to apply if they are attending an accredited 4-year college or university full time, can demonstrate financial need, and have earned at least a 3.0 grade point average. Membership in the Public Relations Student Society of America is preferred but not required. A major or minor in public relations is preferred; students who attend a school that does not offer a public relations degree or program must be enrolled in a communications degree program.

Financial data The stipend is $1,500.

Duration 1 year.

Number awarded 2 each year.

Deadline April of each year.

[328]
PUBLIC POLICY AND INTERNATIONAL AFFAIRS JUNIOR YEAR SUMMER INSTITUTES

Woodrow Wilson National Fellowship Foundation
Attn: Program in Public Policy and International Affairs
5 Vaughn Drive, Suite 300
P.O. Box 2434
Princeton, NJ 08543-2434
(609) 452-7007   Fax: (609) 452-0066

Purpose To enable minority students to participate in special summer institutes to help prepare them for graduate work in public policy and international affairs.

Eligibility Applicants must members of minority groups historically underrepresented in public policy and international affairs careers (especially African Americans, Alaska Natives, Asian Americans, Hispanic Americans, Native Americans, and Pacific Islanders) who are in the junior year of college with at least 1 full semester of course work remaining before graduation. They must be U.S. citizens or permanent residents and demonstrate a strong interest in continuing on to graduate study in public policy and international affairs by participating in a special summer institute.

Financial data Funding covers student housing and meals in a university facility, travel costs (if the student meets appropriate financial eligibility requirements), and a stipend of $1,000.

Duration 7 weeks, during the summer between the junior and senior year of college.

Special features Recent institutes were held at 5 locations: the Woodrow Wilson School of Public and International Affairs at Princeton University, the Graduate School of Public Policy at the University of California at Berkeley, the School of Public Affairs at the University of Maryland, the Graduate School of Public

Affairs and the Henry M. Jackson School of International Studies at the University of Washington, and (jointly) the School of Public Policy at the University of Michigan and the Graduate School of International Studies at the University of Denver. At each of the institutes, students study policy analysis, economics, quantitative methods, computer skills, and communication skills (oral and written); participate in discussions with a variety of speakers, including career placement officers and specialists familiar with foreign and domestic policy issues; receive mentoring and counseling on graduate school choices, GRE standardized-test preparation and the graduate application process, and advice about academic course preparation for graduate school; participate in extracurricular activities such as formal lectures and brown bag lunches with policy practitioners as well as optional trips to nearby museums, theaters, sports, and social events; and meet with representatives and admissions officers from public policy and international affairs graduate schools. Funding for this program is provided by the Ford Foundation, Rockefeller Foundation, Philip D. Clark Foundation, and Edna McConnell Clark Foundation.

Limitations Applications are submitted directly to the participating institute.

Number awarded Varies each year.

Deadline March of each year.

[329]
RACIAL ETHNIC EDUCATIONAL SCHOLARSHIP PROGRAM

Synod of the Trinity (Presbyterian Church)
Attn: Social and Racial Justice Ministry Unit
3040 Market Street
Camp Hill, PA 17011-4599
(717) 737-0421   Fax: (717) 737-8211

Purpose To assist racial minority students who could benefit from postsecondary education, but who need financial aid to do so.

Eligibility Persons applying for aid must be members of a racial minority group (Asian, African American, Hispanic, or Native Americans); residents of Pennsylvania, West Virginia, or the Presbytery of Upper Ohio Valley (Belmont, Harrison, Jefferson, Monroe, and Columbiana counties); and be accepted or enrolled as a full-time undergraduate student at an accredited undergraduate or vocational school. Financial aid is given only after the Synod has determined that an applicant is eligible and that family resources are insufficient to meet college costs. Recipients may be of any religious persuasion.

Financial data Awards depend on the need of the recipient; the larger grants are awarded to students with the greatest financial need and the least ability to cover educational costs.

Duration 1 year; may be renewed.

Limitations Students may not apply for this program and the Synod of the Trinity Educational Scholarship Program.

Number awarded Varies each year.

Deadline February of each year.

[330]
RACINE EDUCATION COUNCIL AWARDS

Racine Education Council
310 Fifth Street, Room 101
Racine, WI 53403
(414) 634-9200   Fax: (414) 631-5606

Purpose To provide financial assistance for postsecondary education to minority and low-income youths living in Racine, Wisconsin.

Eligibility Only minority group members and low-income youths who are residents of Racine (for at least 1 year) and/or graduates of a local high school are eligible to apply.

Financial data Stipend amounts vary, depending upon the needs of each student. All grants are made to the students through their respective schools.

Duration The awards are granted annually.

Special features To date, more than 3,700 students have participated in this program: 75 percent Black, 12 percent Spanish, and 13 percent nonminority students. Priority is given to grant recipients for Racine's Summer Employment Program, which assists economically disadvantaged youths (between the ages of 17 and 21) in obtaining summer jobs within the city's industrial or business community.

Number awarded Approximately 125 per year.

Deadline June and October of each year.

[331]
RCA ETHNIC SCHOLARSHIP FUND

Reformed Church in America
Attn: Policy, Planning, and Administration Services
475 Riverside Drive, Room 1814
New York, NY 10115
(212) 870-3243   Fax: (212) 870-2499

Purpose To provide assistance to minority student members of the Reformed Church in America (RCA) who are interested in pursuing postsecondary education.

Eligibility An applicant must be a member of a minority group (American Indian, African American, Hispanic, or Pacific and Asian American), be admitted to a college or other institution of higher learning, and be a member of an RCA congregation or be admitted to an RCA college. Priority is given to applicants who will enter undergraduate colleges or universities or students enrolled in undergraduate occupational training programs. Selection is based primarily on financial need.

Financial data Amount varies, depending upon individual need; the minimum award is $500, payable directly to the institution.

Duration 1 academic year; may be renewed.

Number awarded Several each year.

Deadline April of each year.

[332]
REAL ESTATE AND LAND USE INSTITUTE SCHOLARSHIPS FOR MINORITIES

Real Estate and Land Use Institute
Attn: Scholarship Selection Committee
7750 College Town Drive, Suite 102
Sacramento, CA 95826-2344
(916) 278-4823   Fax: (916) 278-4500

Purpose To provide financial assistance to minority and disadvantaged students in California who are interested in a career in real estate.

Eligibility Eligible to apply are minority and disadvantaged students at any of the 22 California State University campuses who are enrolled at least half-time or majoring in a program aimed at a career in real estate. Financial need must be demonstrated. Minority undergraduates must have a minimum grade point average of 2.25, non-minority undergraduates 2.5, and graduates 3.0.

Financial data A total of $60,300 in scholarships is offered each year; individual awards range from $375 to $600 per quarter or $603 to $935 per semester.

Duration 1 year; may be renewed.

Number awarded Varies; generally, at least 20 each year.

Deadline April of each year.

[333]
RICHARD S. SMITH SCHOLARSHIP

United Methodist Church
Attn: National Youth Ministry Organization
P.O. Box 840
Nashville, TN 37202-0840
(615) 340-7184   Fax: (615) 340-7516
E-mail: nymo@aol.com

Purpose To provide financial assistance to minority high school seniors or graduates who wish to prepare for a church-related career.

Eligibility Minority students who are beginning college are eligible to apply if they are members of the United Methodist Church, have been active in their local church for at least 1 year, can demonstrate financial need, have maintained a "C" average throughout high school, and are interested in pursuing a church-related career after graduation.

Financial data The stipend is up to $1,000.

Duration 1 year; nonrenewable.

Deadline May of each year.

[334]
ROBERT A. HINE MEMORIAL SCHOLARSHIP

Southern California Edison Company
Attn: Scholarship Committee
1190 Durfee Avenue
South El Monte, CA 91733
(818) 302-0284

Purpose To provide financial assistance to minority high school students who plan to attend a 4-year college in California.

Eligibility High school seniors who live or attend a school in an area served by Southern California Edison may apply for this scholarship if they belong to an underrepresented ethnic group and plan to attend a California 4-year college as a full-time undergraduate student. Applicants must be U.S. citizens or permanent residents. Selection is based on leadership skills, educational performance, and extracurricular activities; preference is given to students with financial need.

Financial data The stipend is $20,000.

Duration 4 years.

Number awarded 1 each year.

Deadline January of each year.

[335]
ROSEWOOD FAMILY SCHOLARSHIP FUND

Florida Department of Education
Attn: Office of Student Financial Assistance
State Programs—255 Collins
Tallahassee, FL 32399-0400
(904) 487-0049

Purpose To provide financial assistance for undergraduate education to needy minority students who wish to study in Florida.

Eligibility Minority students from any state who wish to attend state universities, public community colleges, or public postsecondary vocational/technical schools in Florida may apply. Preference is given to descendants of African American Rosewood families. Financial need must be demonstrated.

Financial data Awards cover the actual costs of tuition and fees, up to $4,000 per year.

Duration 1 year; may be renewed.

Limitations It is expected that all available scholarships will be awarded to descendants of Rosewood families.

Number awarded 25 each year.

Deadline March of each year.

[336]
SACRAMENTO BEE MINORITY MEDIA SCHOLARSHIPS

Sacramento Bee
Attn: Community Relations Department
P.O. Box 15779
Sacramento, CA 95852
(916) 321-1794   Fax: (916) 321-1783

Purpose To provide financial assistance to Sacramento-area minority students who are actively pursuing a course of study leading to a career in the mass media.

Eligibility Applicants must be minority high school or college students residing in the Sacramento Bee circulation area (Sacramento, Placer, Yolo, and western El Dorado counties of California) although they need not be attending a college or university in the state. They must have a demonstrated interest in pursuing a career in the mass media and a minimum grade point average of 3.0.

Financial data Stipends range from $1,000 to $4,000.

Duration 1 year; may be renewed.

Number awarded Up to 12 each year.

Deadline March of each year.

[337]
SAN JOSE MERCURY NEWS MINORITY SCHOLARSHIP

San Jose Mercury News
Attn: Human Resources Department
750 Ridder Park Drive
San Jose, CA 95190
(408) 271-3689

Purpose To provide financial assistance to minority students interested in pursuing careers in journalism and newspaper management.

Eligibility Minority high school seniors in the San Francisco/San Jose area are eligible to apply if they are interested in majoring in journalism or communications in college. They must have professional experience or high school newspaper/yearbook experience, be nominated by their journalism advisor or teacher, send up to 5 samples of their work, and submit a 500-word essay on why they want to pursue a career in journalism or newspaper management.

Financial data The stipend is $500.

Duration 1 year; may be renewed for up to 3 additional years.

Special features The *Mercury News* selects its winners by February of each year and submits their applications to the Knight-Ridder Minority Scholarship Program. These winners are given the chance to compete for a 4-year Knight-Ridder scholarship/internship and the promise of a job in journalism upon graduation. The internship takes place at a Knight-Ridder paper in the recipient's community; interns work each year, during the summer.

Number awarded 2 each year.

Deadline December of each year.

[338]
SAVANNAH RIVER SITE PROFESSIONAL INTERNSHIP PROGRAM

Oak Ridge Institute for Science and Education
Attn: Science/Engineering Education Division
P.O. Box 117
Oak Ridge, TN 37831-0117
(423) 576-3427   (423) 576-3426
(800) 569-7749   Fax: (423) 576-3643
E-mail: pipsrs@orau.gov   E-mail: gpipsrs@orau.gov

Purpose To provide financial assistance for postsecondary study and practical research experience at the Savannah River Site in Aiken, South Carolina.

Eligibility This program is open to U.S. citizens or permanent residents at least 18 years of age who are currently enrolled in an accredited U.S. college or university in an academic program leading to an associate, baccalaureate, or graduate degree. High school juniors and seniors are also eligible. Students should be pursuing studies in chemistry, computer science, engineering, environmental sciences, geology, or physics. A cumulative grade point average of at least 2.5 is required. All programs operated by the Science/Engineering Education Division (SEED) of Oak Ridge Institute for Science and Education (ORISE) seek to broaden the participation of minorities, women, and persons with disabilities in science and engineering careers.

Financial data Participants receive tuition and fees for off-campus courses related to the research experience during the appointment period. Monthly stipends range from $800 to $1,300 for high school students and undergraduates or $1,300 to $1,400 for graduate students. Travel expenses for a single round trip from the student's campus to the research center are also reimbursed.

Duration 3 to 12 consecutive months.

Special features Interns are assigned individual research projects that relate to their academic majors, career goals, and the ongoing research and development missions of the Savannah River Site, which conducts research and development in support of the production of plutonium-239 and tritium for national defense purposes. Graduate students may utilize this program to conduct research for their theses or dissertations. This program is funded by the Savannah River Site and administered by ORISE/SEED.

Number awarded Varies each year.

Deadline February of each year for programs to begin in May or June; May of each year for programs to begin in August or September; September of each year for programs to begin in January.

[339]
SCHOLARSHIPS FOR DISADVANTAGED STUDENTS GRANTS

Health Resources and Services Administration
Attn: Bureau of Health Professions
Division of Student Assistance
Parklawn Building, Room 8-34
5600 Fishers Lane
Rockville, MD 20857
(301) 443-4776   Fax: (301) 443-0846

Purpose To provide financial support for full-time financially needy disadvantaged health professions students who are enrolled in accredited schools.

Eligibility Eligible to submit grant requests are accredited schools of medicine, nursing, osteopathic medicine, dentistry, pharmacy, podiatric medicine, optometry, veterinary medicine, public health, or allied health (baccalaureate and graduate degree programs of dental hygiene, medical laboratory technology, occupational therapy, physical therapy, and radiologic technology), and graduate programs in clinical psychology. They must be carrying out a program for recruiting and retaining students from disadvantaged backgrounds, including racial and ethnic minorities, and carrying out a program for recruiting and retaining minority faculty. Recipient institutions must use the funds received through this program to offer scholarships to students who are U.S. citizens, nationals, or permanent residents and who meet the definition of an individual from a disadvantaged background (either 1) individuals who come from an environment that has inhibited them from obtaining the knowledge, skill, and abilities required to enroll in and graduate from a health professions school, or from a program providing education or training in allied health professions, or 2) individuals who come from a family with low income, ranging from less than $10,200 for a family with 1 dependent to less than $26,700 for a family with 6 dependents). Applicant institutions must also have programs to 1) ensure that adequate instruction regarding minority health issues is provided for in the curricula of the school; 2) enter into agreements with 1 or more health clinics providing services to a significant number of individuals who are from disadvantaged backgrounds, including members of minority groups, for the purpose of providing students of the school with experience in providing clinical services to such individuals; 3) enter into arrangements with 1 or more public or nonprofit institutions of higher education (feeder schools) for the purpose of carrying out programs regarding the educational preparation of disadvantaged students, including minority students, into the health professions, and the recruitment of disadvantaged students, including minority students, into the health professions; and 4) establish a mentor program for assisting disadvantaged students, including minority students, regarding the completion of the educational requirements for degrees from the school. Students apply directly to their academic institution for support. For a list of schools participating in this program, contact the address above.

Financial data With these grants, schools award students funds to cover the costs of tuition and other reasonable educational expenses including fees, books, laboratory expenses and other costs of attending school. Scholarships cannot exceed a student's financial need. Of the funds available, 30 percent are set aside for schools that provide scholarships only for nurses.

Duration 1 year; may be renewed.

Number awarded Varies each year.

Deadline Deadline dates vary but are usually in June; check the *Federal Register* for the current schedule.

[340]
SCHOLARSHIPS FOR MINORITY ACCOUNTING STUDENTS

American Institute of Certified Public Accountants
1211 Avenue of the Americas
New York, NY 10036-8775
(212) 596-6270   Fax: (212) 596-6213

Purpose To provide financial assistance to underrepresented minority students interested in studying accounting.

Eligibility Undergraduate applicants must be minority students who are enrolled full time, have completed at least 30 semester hours of college work, are majoring in accounting with an overall grade point average of at least 3.0, and are U.S. citizens or permanent residents. Minority students who are interested in a graduate degree must be 1) in a 5-year accounting program; 2) an undergraduate accounting major currently accepted in a master's-level accounting, business administration, finance, or taxation program; or 3) any undergraduate major currently accepted in a master's-level accounting program. Selection is based primarily on merit (academic achievement); financial need is evaluated as a secondary criteria. For purposes of this program, the American Institute of Certified Public Accountants (AICPA) considers minority students as those of Black, Native American/Alaskan Native, or Pacific Island races, or of Hispanic ethnic origin.

Financial data Up to $5,000 per year.

Duration 1 year; may be renewed, if recipients are making satisfactory progress toward graduation.

Special features These scholarships are granted by the institute's Minority Educational Initiatives Committee.

Number awarded Up to 100 each year.

Deadline June of each year.

[341]
SNPA FOUNDATION ADOPT-A-STUDENT MINORITY SCHOLARSHIP PROGRAM

Southern Newspaper Publishers Association
Attn: Foundation
P.O. Box 28875
Atlanta, GA 30358
(404) 256-0444

Purpose   To provide financial assistance to minority students in areas served by member newspapers of the Southern Newspaper Publishers Association (SNPA) Foundation.

Eligibility   Newspapers that are members of the Association and its Foundation may nominate graduating high school seniors who are racial minorities and have at least a 2.0 grade point average. Students must take the SAT or ACT exams; be admitted to any 4-year college, community college, or trade school that is acceptable to the nominating newspaper; plan to study journalism, business, advertising, graphic arts, or any other discipline that can be used in the newspaper industry; and submit an essay of no more than 500 words on "Why I want to work for a newspaper." High school seniors interested in this program should contact their local newspaper; for a list of members of the Association, write to the address above.

Financial data   Students receive annual scholarships of $1,000 from the newspaper that nominates them and $2,000 from the Foundation.

Duration   4 years.

Limitations   Applications are not accepted directly from students or colleges.

Number awarded   Currently, 11 students are sponsored by the Foundation.

Deadline   Nominations must be submitted by March of each year.

[342]
SOUTH CAROLINA SPACE GRANT CONSORTIUM COMMUNITY COLLEGE SCHOLARSHIPS

South Carolina Space Grant Consortium
c/o College of Charleston
Department of Geology
58 Coming Street
Charleston, SC 29424
(803) 953-5463   Fax: (803) 953-5446
E-mail: mcolgan@jove.cofc.edu

Purpose   To provide financial assistance for space-related study to students in South Carolina who are transferring from a community college to a 4-year university.

Eligibility   This program is open to students who have graduated from a community college in South Carolina and have enrolled at a member institution of the South Carolina Space Grant Consortium (the University of Charleston, Clemson University, the University of South Carolina, and South Carolina State University). The participating community colleges are Trident Tech, Greenville Tech, Orangeburg-Calhoun Tech, and Midlands Tech. The South Carolina Space Grant Consortium is a component of the U.S. National Aeronautics and Space Administration (NASA) Space Grant program, which encourages the participation of women, minorities, and persons with disabilities.

Financial data   The stipend is $500 per year.

Duration   1 year.

Special features   This program is funded by NASA.

Number awarded   Varies each year.

[343]
SOUTH CAROLINA SPACE GRANT CONSORTIUM UNDERGRADUATE SCHOLARSHIPS

South Carolina Space Grant Consortium
c/o College of Charleston
Department of Geology
58 Coming Street
Charleston, SC 29424
(803) 953-5463   Fax: (803) 953-5446
E-mail: mcolgan@jove.cofc.edu

Purpose   To provide financial assistance for space-related study to undergraduate students in South Carolina.

Eligibility   This program is open to undergraduate students at member institutions of the South Carolina Space Grant Consortium (the University of Charleston, Clemson University, the University of South Carolina, South Carolina State University, and the University of the Virgin Islands). Applicants must be interested in space-related studies, although students from engineering, geology, biology, and physics are eligible to apply. U.S. citizenship is required. The South Carolina Space Grant Consortium is a component of the U.S. National Aeronautics and Space Administration (NASA) Space Grant program, which encourages the participation of women, minorities, and persons with disabilities.

Financial data   Stipends up to $2,500 per year are available.

Duration   1 year.

Special features   This program is funded by NASA.

Number awarded   Varies each year.

[344]
SOUTHERN CALIFORNIA CHEVRON MERIT AWARD

Independent Colleges of Southern California
411 West Fifth Street, Suite 1000
Los Angeles, CA 90013-1001
(213) 627-7091

Purpose   To recognize and reward the outstanding classroom, school, and community achievements of high school seniors (or entering graduate school students) planning to major in business or the sciences at an independent college in southern California.

Eligibility   Students who have an outstanding record of academic achievement, leadership, and participation in school and community activities and are interested in attending an independent college in southern California are invited to apply for these awards. Minorities and women are particularly encouraged to apply.

Financial data   The stipend is $2,000 per year.

Duration   4 years for entering freshmen; 2 years for entering graduate students.

Special features   Funding for this program is supplied by Chevron U.S.A. Inc.

Number awarded   8 each year. In even-numbered years, awards are for freshmen entering the following schools: Claremont McKenna College, Loyola Marymount University, Mount St. Mary's College, Occidental College, Scripps College, University of Redlands, Whittier College, and Claremont Graduate School (first-year graduate students). In odd-numbered years, the awards are for students entering: Chapman University, Harvey Mudd College, Pepperdine University, Pitzer College, Pomona College, University of La Verne, University of San Diego, Westmont College, and Claremont Graduate School (first-year graduate students).

Deadline February of each year.

[345]
SOUTHERN CALIFORNIA EDISON COMMUNITY COLLEGE ACHIEVEMENT AWARDS

Southern California Edison Company
Attn: Scholarship Committee
1190 Durfee Avenue
South El Monte, CA 91733
(818) 302-0284

Purpose To provide financial assistance to community college students in southern California.

Eligibility Full-time community college students who live or attend school in an area served by Southern California Edison may apply for these scholarships if they are members of an underrepresented ethnic or disadvantaged group. Applicants must be U.S. citizens or permanent residents with a minimum 2.5 grade point average and sufficient transferable units to enter a California 4-year college or university as a junior in the following fall, planning to become secondary school teachers of mathematics or science. Selection is based on career objectives, academic achievements, and desire for a continued education.

Financial data The stipend is $6,000, of which $2,000 is a post-baccalaureate stipend for the credential year.

Duration 3 years.

Limitations Applicants must be nominated by the Financial Aid Officer of their community college.

Number awarded 20 each year.

Deadline February of each year.

[346]
STAN BECK FELLOWSHIP

Entomological Society of America
Attn: Executive Director
9301 Annapolis Road
Lanham, MD 20706-3115
(301) 731-4535   Fax: (301) 731-4538

Purpose To assist "needy" students at any level of their science education.

Eligibility All society members are eligible to nominate candidates for this fellowship. Nominees must be "needy" students at any level of their science education. For the purposes of this program, need may be based on physical limitations, or economic, minority, or environmental conditions.

Financial data The fellowship is $4,000 per year.

Duration The award is presented annually.

Limitations Recipients are expected to be present at the society's annual meeting, where the award will be presented.

Number awarded 1 or more each year.

Deadline August of each year.

[347]
STANFORD SUMMER RESEARCH PROGRAM IN BIOMEDICAL SCIENCES

Stanford University
Attn: School of Medicine
Office of Graduate Affairs
M.S.O.B. Room 309
Stanford, CA 94305-5501
(415) 723-9455   E-mail: SSRPBS@list.stanford.edu

Purpose To provide underrepresented minority undergraduate students with a summer research experience at Stanford University in biological and biomedical sciences.

Eligibility This program is open to undergraduates at any university in the country who are Black/African American, Chicano/Latino, Puerto Rican, Native American, or Pacific Islander. Applicants must have at least 1 year of undergraduate education remaining before graduation and should be planning to prepare for and enter Ph.D. programs in the biological and biomedical sciences.

Financial data The program provides a stipend, room and board, and transportation to and from the San Francisco bay area.

Duration 8 weeks, during the summer.

Special features The program provides a rigorous research experience with comprehensive mentoring and advising.

Deadline February of each year.

[348]
STANLEY E. JACKSON SCHOLARSHIP AWARD FOR ETHNIC MINORITY GIFTED/TALENTED STUDENTS WITH DISABILITIES

Foundation for Exceptional Children
1920 Association Drive
Reston, VA 22091
(703) 620-1054

Purpose To provide financial assistance to gifted minority students with disabilities interested in pursuing postsecondary education or training.

Eligibility Applicants must possess demonstrated or potential gifted and talented abilities in 1 or more of the following categories: general intellectual ability, specific academic aptitude, creativity, leadership, or visual or performing arts. They must be disabled, financially needy, anticipating enrollment for the first time in full-time postsecondary education or training, and a member of an ethnic minority group (e.g., Asian, Afro-American, Hispanic, or Native American).

Financial data The stipend is $1,000.

Duration 1 year; may not be renewed.

Special features Candidates must submit a 250-word statement of philosophical, educational, and occupational goals as part of the application process. Scholarships may be used for 2- or 4-year undergraduate college programs or for vocational or fine arts training programs.

Number awarded 1 each year.

Deadline January of each year.

[349]
STANLEY E. JACKSON SCHOLARSHIP AWARD FOR ETHNIC MINORITY STUDENTS WITH DISABILITIES

Foundation for Exceptional Children
1920 Association Drive
Reston, VA 22091
(703) 620-1054

Purpose To provide financial assistance to minority students with disabilities interested in pursuing postsecondary education or training.

Eligibility Applicants must be students with disabilities who intend to enroll for the first time on a full-time basis in a college, university, vocational/technical school, or fine arts institute and are able to document financial need. Only minority (Afro-American, Asian, Native American, or Hispanic) students are eligible for the award.

Financial data The stipend is $1,000.

Duration 1 year; may not be renewed.

Special features Candidates must submit a 250-word statement of philosophical, educational, and occupational goals as part of the application process. Scholarships may be used for 2- or 4-year undergraduate college programs or for vocational or fine arts training programs.

Number awarded 1 each year.

Deadline January of each year.

[350]
STUDENT CEC/FEC ETHNIC DIVERSITY SCHOLARSHIP

Council for Exceptional Children
Attn: Coordinator of Student Activities
1920 Association Drive
Reston, VA 22091
(703) 620-3660   (800) 845-6232
Fax: (703) 264-9494   TDD: (703) 620-3660

Purpose To provide financial assistance to ethnic minority students who wish to pursue a career in special education.

Eligibility Eligible are student members of the Council for Exceptional Children (CEC), citizens of the United States or Canada, members of an ethnic minority group (African American or Black, American Indian, Alaska Native, Native Canadian, Hispanic, Asian, or Pacific Islander), and juniors, seniors, or graduate students enrolled in an accredited college or university majoring in special education with a grade point average of at least 2.5. Applications include documentation of financial need, a list of Student CEC and/or other activities relating to individuals with disabilities, and a brief biography explaining why the applicant chose special education as a career and plans for accomplishments as a special education teacher.

Financial data The stipend is $500.

Duration 1 year; nonrenewable.

Special features This program is administered by the Student CEC; the scholarship committee includes representatives of the Foundation for Exceptional Children (FEC) and the chair of the Student CEC Ethnic and Multicultural Concerns Committee.

Number awarded 1 each year.

Deadline December of each year.

[351]
SYNOD OF THE TRINITY EDUCATIONAL SCHOLARSHIP PROGRAM

Synod of the Trinity (Presbyterian Church)
Attn: Social and Racial Justice Ministry Unit
3040 Market Street
Camp Hill, PA 17011-4599
(717) 737-0421   Fax: (717) 737-8211

Purpose To assist disadvantaged Presbyterian students who could benefit from postsecondary education, but who need financial aid to do so.

Eligibility Persons applying for aid must be economically disadvantaged; members of the Presbyterian Church (USA) or attending a Presbyterian Church (USA) college; residents of Pennsylvania, West Virginia, or the Presbytery of Upper Ohio Valley (Belmont, Harrison, Jefferson, Monroe, and Columbiana counties); and accepted or enrolled as a full-time undergraduate student at an accredited undergraduate or vocational school. Priority is given to applicants entering or enrolled at Synod-related colleges (Beaver, Davis and Elkins, Grove City, Lafayette, Waynesburg, Westminster, and Wilson). Financial aid is given only after the Synod has determined that an applicant is eligible and that family resources are insufficient to meet college costs.

Financial data Awards depend on the need of the recipient; the larger grants are awarded to students with the greatest financial need and the least ability to cover educational costs.

Duration 1 year; may be renewed.

Limitations Students may not apply for this program and the Racial Ethnic Educational Scholarship Program of the Synod of the Trinity.

Number awarded Varies each year.

Deadline February of each year.

[352]
TAMPA BAY PROFESSIONAL CHAPTER OF SPJ SCHOLARSHIP

Society of Professional Journalists—Tampa Bay Chapter
c/o Don Richards
WFLA Radio
4002 Grandy Boulevard
Tampa, FL 33611

Purpose To provide financial assistance for undergraduate education to minority students in Florida who are pursuing a career in journalism.

Eligibility This program is open to minority residents of Florida who are majoring in journalism as undergraduate students or intend to pursue a career in journalism. Selection is based on need and academic performance.

Financial data The stipend is $1,000.

Duration 1 year.

Number awarded 1 each year.

[353]
TENNESSEE MINORITY TEACHING FELLOWS PROGRAM

Tennessee Student Assistance Corporation
Parkway Towers
404 James Robertson Parkway, Suite 1950
Nashville, TN 37243-0820
(615) 741-1346   (800) 342-1663 (within TN)

Purpose To encourage talented minority Tennesseans to enter the teaching field.

Eligibility This program is open to minority residents of Tennessee who are entering college freshmen at a college in Tennessee. Applicants must be U.S. citizens with a 2.5 high school cumulative grade point average and a score of 18 on the ACT test, 850 on the SAT, or a ranking in the top 25 percent of their high school graduating class.

Financial data The stipend is $5,000 per year.

Duration 1 year; may be renewed for up to 3 additional years.

Limitations This is a scholarship/loan program; recipients incur an obligation to teach at the K-12 level in a Tennessee public school 1 year for each year the award is received.

Number awarded 19 each year.

Deadline May of each year.

[354]
TEXAS FIFTH-YEAR ACCOUNTANCY SCHOLARSHIP PROGRAM

Texas Higher Education Coordinating Board
Attn: Division of Student Services
P.O. Box 12788, Capitol Station
Austin, TX 78711-2788
(512) 483-6340   TDD: (800) 735-2988

Purpose To provide financial assistance to accounting students students attending school in Texas.

Eligibility This program is open to both residents and nonresidents of Texas. Applicants must be enrolled as fifth year accounting students on at least a half-time basis and confirm their intent to take the written examination conducted by the Texas State Board of Public Accountancy for the purpose of granting a certificate as a certified public accountant. They must have a grade point average equal to that required for graduation. Selection is based on financial need, ethnic or racial minority status, and scholastic ability and performance.

Financial data The award equals the lesser of unmet financial need or $3,000.

Duration 1 year.

Special features Information and application forms may be obtained from the director of financial aid at the public college or university in Texas the applicant attends. This program began in 1996.

Limitations Study must be conducted in Texas; funds cannot be used to support attendance at an out-of-state institution.

[355]
TEXAS MINORITY LEADERS IN EDUCATION SCHOLARSHIP PROGRAM

Southwestern Bell Foundation
1 Bell Plaza, Room 3040
Dallas, TX 75202
(214) 464-4521

Purpose To provide financial assistance to minorities enrolled at selected colleges or universities in Texas who plan a career in education in Texas.

Eligibility This program is open to minority students who have attained at least junior status in college, have earned at least a 3.0 grade point average, can demonstrate financial need, are committed to preparing for a career in education, and are currently enrolled in 1 of the private schools that are members of the Texas Independent College Fund or in 1 of the public universities in the state.

Financial data The stipend is $2,000 per year at private institutions or $1,000 per year at public universities.

Duration 1 year; will be renewed if the student maintains the academic standards set by the college or university, continues in full-time status, and applies for renewal of funding after the junior year.

Limitations Applications must be submitted through the student's school rather than directly to the foundation.

Deadline Deadline dates vary; check with the participating school you are attending.

[356]
TEXAS SCHOLARSHIP PROGRAM FOR ETHNIC MINORITIES IN NURSING

Texas Higher Education Coordinating Board
Attn: Division of Student Services
P.O. Box 12788, Capitol Station
Austin, TX 78711-2788
(512) 483-6340   TDD: (800) 735-2988

Purpose To provide financial assistance for Texas minorities who are interested in preparing for a career in the nursing field.

Eligibility This program is open to minority undergraduate or graduate students who are residents of Texas and enrolled at least half time in a program leading to licensure as an L.V.N. (licensed vocational nurse) or in an associate, bachelor, or graduate degree program in professional nursing.

Financial data Up to $1,500 for L.V.N. students; up to $2,000 for A.D.N. (associate degree in nursing) students; up to $3,000 for B.S.N. (bachelor's degree in nursing) or graduate students.

Duration 1 academic year.

Special features This program was established in 1990.

Number awarded Varies; in a recent year, 20 of these scholarships were awarded to L.V.N. students and 53 to A.D.N., B.S.N., and graduate students.

Deadline Applicants should contact the financial aid director at the vocational or professional nursing school in which they plan to enroll for appropriate deadline dates.

[357]
TEXAS SPACE GRANT CONSORTIUM SCHOLARSHIPS

Texas Space Grant Consortium
Attn: Public Service Programs
2901 North IH 35, Suite 200
Austin, TX 78722-2348
(512) 471-3583   Fax: (512) 471-3585
E-mail: fowler@utcsr.ae.utexas.edu

Purpose To provide financial assistance for undergraduate study at Texas universities in the fields of space science and engineering.

Eligibility Applicants must be U.S. citizens, be eligible for financial assistance, and be registered for full-time study as seniors in an undergraduate program at 1 or more of the following participating universities: Baylor University, Lamar University, Prairie View A&M University, Rice University, Southern Methodist University, Texas A&M University at Kingsville, Texas A&M University, Texas Christian University, Texas Southern University, Texas Tech University, University of Houston, University of Houston/Clear Lake, University of Houston/Downtown, University of Texas at Arlington, University of Texas at Austin, University of Texas at Dallas, University of Texas at El Paso, University of Texas at San Antonio, University of Texas Health Science Center at Houston, University of Texas Health Science Center at San Antonio, University of Texas Medical Branch at Galveston, University of Texas/Pan American, University of Texas Southwestern Medical Center, and West Texas A&M University. Students apply to their respective university representative; each representative then submits up to 3 candidates into the statewide selection process. Special attention is paid to applications submitted by persons with disabilities, women, and underrepresented minorities (African Americans, Hispanic Americans, Native Americans, and Pacific Islanders). Fellowships are awarded competitively, on the basis of above-average performance in academics, examples of intent to participate in space education and/or research experience, leadership qualities, and participation by members of underrepresented groups in science and engineering.

Financial data The award is $1,000.

Duration 1 year.

Special features This program is funded by the National Aeronautics and Space Administration.

Number awarded Approximately 20 each year.

Deadline February of each year.

[358]
TEXAS STATE SCHOLARSHIP PROGRAM FOR ETHNIC RECRUITMENT

Texas Higher Education Coordinating Board
Attn: Division of Student Services
P.O. Box 12788, Capitol Station
Austin, TX 78711-2788
(512) 483-6340   TDD: (800) 735-2988

Purpose To provide financial assistance to educationally deprived students of a minority race in Texas who are capable of college-level work.

Eligibility To qualify, entering minority freshmen must be Texas residents, have attained an SAT score of at least 750 or an ACT score of at least 17; new transfer students must have a grade point average of at least 2.5 as undergraduates or 3.0 as graduate students. They must plan to enroll as a full-time graduate or undergraduate student in a Texas 4-year college or university and

be a member of an ethnic group comprising less than 40 percent of that school's enrollment.

Financial data The maximum award is $2,000 per year.

Duration 1 academic year; may be renewed as long as undergraduates maintain a grade point average of 2.5 and graduate students 3.0.

Number awarded Varies; in a recent year, 556 of these scholarships were awarded.

Deadline Applicants should contact the financial aid director or minority recruitment officer at the public senior college in which they plan to enroll for appropriate deadline dates.

[359]
TRANSPORTATION PLANNING DIVISION SCHOLARSHIP

American Planning Association
Attn: Assistant for Divisions, Fellowships and Council
     Administration
1776 Massachusetts Avenue, N.W.
Washington, DC 20036-1904
(202) 872-0611   (800) 800-1589
Fax: (202) 872-0643

Purpose To provide financial assistance to minority undergraduate and graduate students specializing in transportation planning.

Eligibility This program is open to undergraduate and graduate students who are enrolled in an accredited planning program, are specializing in transportation planning, and are members of a minority group. Candidates must be nominated by their program chair.

Financial data The stipend is $2,500.

Duration 1 year.

Number awarded 1 or 2 each year.

Deadline May of each year.

[360]
UNDERGRADUATE SCHOLARSHIP PROGRAM FOR INDIVIDUALS FROM DISADVANTAGED BACKGROUNDS

National Institutes of Health
Attn: Loan Repayment and Scholarship Programs
Federal Building, Room 604
7550 Wisconsin Avenue MSC 9015
Bethesda, MD 20892-9015
(800) 528-7689   Fax: (301) 496-0840
TTY: (888) 352-3001   E-mail: kk10b@nih.gov

Purpose To provide financial assistance for undergraduate education in the life sciences to students from disadvantaged backgrounds.

Eligibility Eligible are U.S. citizens, nationals, and permanent residents who are enrolled or accepted for enrollment as full-time students at qualified accredited institutions of higher education and planning to pursue a career in biomedical research. Applicants must meet a definition of disadvantaged, that they either 1) come from an environment that inhibited (but did not prevent) them from obtaining the knowledge, skills, and ability required to enroll in an undergraduate institution; or 2) come from a family with an annual income below $10,200 for a 1-person family, ranging to below $26,700 for families of 6 or more. First priority is given to applicants who have demonstrated good academic performance, state a career goal of pursuing biomedical/biobehavioral research, and have characteristics which support the likelihood they will complete their service obligations. Second priority is given to individuals who are underrepresented in biomedical/biobehavioral research including women, individuals from minority groups, or persons with disabilities.

Financial data Stipends are available up to $20,000 per year, to be used for tuition, educational expenses such as books and lab fees, and qualified living expenses while attending a college or university. Recipients incur a service obligation to work as an employee of the National Institutes of Health (NIH) in Bethesda, Maryland for 10 consecutive weeks (during the summer) during the sponsored year and, upon graduation, for 12 months for each academic year of scholarship support. The NIH 12-month employment obligation may be deferred during enrollment in graduate or medical school.

Duration 1 year; may be renewed for up to 3 additional years.

Number awarded 15 each year.

[361]
UNITED CHURCH OF CHRIST SPECIAL HIGHER EDUCATION PROGRAM

United Church of Christ
Attn: Commission for Racial Justice
700 Prospect Avenue East
Cleveland, OH 44115-1110
(216) 736-2169 Fax: (216) 736-2171

Purpose To provide financial assistance for postsecondary education to minority undergraduate students.

Eligibility Undergraduate students are eligible to apply for this support if they are African Americans, Native Americans, Asian Americans, or Hispanics and have financial need. Members of the United Church of Christ (UCC), especially those participating in the UCC Matching Program, receive priority, as do students at UCC-related colleges. Applicants who do not have large financial assistance packages, and who are not outstanding athletes or scholars, also receive priority.

Financial data Awards range from $150 to $250 per semester.

Duration 1 semester; may be renewed.

Special features The United Church of Christ's Commission on Racial Justice offers recipients assistance in locating other sources of financial aid, tutorials, and other special services beneficial to their well-being while in college. It also counsels students on adjusting to college life and parents on the dynamics of higher education, including the availability and acquisition of financial aid and the procedures for filing applications.

Number awarded Up to 200 each year.

Deadline July of each year for fall; December of each year for spring.

[362]
UNITED METHODIST ETHNIC MINORITY SCHOLARSHIPS

United Methodist Church
Attn: Office of Loans and Scholarships
1001 19th Avenue South
P.O. Box 871
Nashville, TN 37202-0871
(615) 340-7344 Fax: (615) 340-7048

Purpose To provide financial assistance to minority students interested in pursuing postsecondary education.

Eligibility Applicants must be born of Native American, Asian, Pacific Islander, African, or Hispanic parentage (at least 1 parent) and be active in the United Methodist Church. They must be recommended by their pastor, American citizens or permanent residents, enrolled or accepted for enrollment in undergraduate studies in an accredited institution of higher education, and able to establish financial need.

Financial data The amount awarded depends upon need, costs, and total number of awards granted.

Duration 1 year; recipients may reapply.

Special features These awards are funded from a percentage of the World Communion Offering received annually by the church on the first Sunday in October.

Deadline April of each year.

[363]
UNITED METHODIST PUBLISHING HOUSE MERIT SCHOLARSHIP PROGRAM

United Methodist Church
Attn: Office of Loans and Scholarships
1001 19th Avenue South
P.O. Box 871
Nashville, TN 37202-0871
(615) 340-7344 Fax: (615) 340-7048

Purpose To recognize and support superior academic effort by ethnic minorities who are interested in professional lay employment with the United Methodist Church and with the United Methodist Publishing House.

Eligibility Ethnic minority students who are enrolled in full-time undergraduate study are eligible to apply if they are planning on pursuing a career with the United Methodist Church (and particularly the Publishing House) upon graduation. They must be U.S. citizens enrolled as sophomores, juniors, or seniors at a college or university related to the United Methodist Church with a grade point average of at least 2.7.

Financial data Up to $5,000 per year.

Duration 1 year; may be renewed.

Special features Recipients also work as interns at the United Methodist Publishing House.

Deadline March of each year.

[364]
UPS SCHOLARSHIP FOR MINORITY STUDENTS

Institute of Industrial Engineers
25 Technology Park/Atlanta
Norcross, GA 30092-2988
(770) 449-0460 (800) 494-0460
Fax: (770) 441-3295

Purpose To provide financial assistance to minority undergraduate students who wish to study industrial engineering at any school in the United States, Canada, or Mexico.

Eligibility Eligible are minority undergraduate students enrolled in any school in the United States and its territories, Canada, or Mexico, provided the school's engineering program is accredited by an agency recognized by the Institute of Industrial Engineers (IIE) and the student is pursuing a full-time course of study in industrial engineering with a grade point average of 3.4 and at least 5 full quarters or 3 full semesters remaining until graduation. Nominees must be IIE members. Selection is based on scholastic ability, character, leadership, potential service to the industrial engineering profession, and need for financial assistance.

Financial data These scholarships are $2,500.
Duration 1 year.
Limitations Students may not apply directly for these awards; they must be nominated by the head of their industrial engineering department.
Number awarded 1 each year.
Deadline November of each year.

[365]
UTAH CAREER TEACHING SCHOLARSHIPS

Utah State Office of Education
250 East Fifth South
Salt Lake City, UT 84111
(801) 538-7741

Purpose To provide financial assistance to undergraduate students interested in becoming elementary or secondary school teachers.
Eligibility Applicants must be either graduates of Utah high schools who are recommended by local superintendents or teacher education students currently enrolled in Utah's public colleges or universities. Minority students are particularly encouraged to apply. Selection is based on teaching potential, scholastic ability, financial need, and cultural background.
Financial data Full tuition is paid for each recipient.
Duration Up to 4 years.
Limitations Recipients must agree to teach in Utah public schools after graduation.
Number awarded Up to 50 graduating seniors from Utah high schools are selected each year and up to 40 teacher education students are selected each year (they must have completed at least 1 year of college courses at the following schools: Westminster College, Brigham Young University, Southern Utah University, University of Utah, Utah State University, or Weber State University).
Deadline March of each year.

[366]
VIRGINIA SPACE GRANT COMMUNITY COLLEGE SCHOLARSHIP PROGRAM

Virginia Space Grant Consortium
c/o Old Dominion University Peninsula Center
2713-D Magruder Boulevard
Hampton, VA 23666-1563
(757) 865-0726   Fax: (757) 865-7965
E-mail: vsgc@pen.k12.va.us

Purpose To provide financial assistance for education in space-related fields to students at community colleges in Virginia.
Eligibility This program is open to students currently enrolled in a program of study at a Virginia community college who are U.S. citizens and who have completed at least the first semester of their program with a grade point average of at least 3.0. Awards are generally made to full-time students but part-time students demonstrating academic merit are also eligible. Applicants can be enrolled in any program that includes course work related to an understanding of or interest in technological fields supporting aerospace. A particular goal of the program is to increase the participation of underrepresented minorities, women, and persons with disabilities in aerospace-related, high technology careers.
Financial data The maximum stipend is $1,500.
Duration 1 year; nonrenewable.

Special features This program is funded by the U.S. National Aeronautics and Space Administration (NASA).
Number awarded Up to 10 each year.
Deadline March of each year.

[367]
VIRGINIA SPACE GRANT TEACHER EDUCATION SCHOLARSHIP PROGRAM

Virginia Space Grant Consortium
c/o Old Dominion University Peninsula Center
2713-D Magruder Boulevard
Hampton, VA 23666-1563
(757) 865-0726   Fax: (757) 865-7965
E-mail: vsgc@pen.k12.va.us

Purpose To provide financial assistance for college education to students in Virginia planning a career as science, mathematics, or technology educators.
Eligibility This program is open to full-time undergraduate students at 1 of the Virginia Space Grant Colleges (College of William and Mary, Hampton University, Old Dominion University, the University of Virginia, and Virginia Polytechnic Institute and State University). Applicants may apply while seniors in high school or sophomores in a community college, with the award contingent on their matriculation at a Space Grant college and entrance into a teacher certification program. Students currently enrolled in a Space Grant college can apply when they declare their intent to enter the teacher certification program. Students enrolled in a career transition program leading to a degree in education are also eligible to apply. Applicants must be U.S. citizens with a grade point average of at least 3.0. Since an important purpose of this program is to increase the participation of underrepresented groups (African Americans, Hispanics, Native Americans, women, and persons with disabilities) in science, mathematics, and technology education, the Virginia Space Grant Consortium especially encourages applications from those students.
Financial data The maximum stipend is $1,000.
Duration 1 year; nonrenewable.
Special features This program is funded by the U.S. National Aeronautics and Space Administration (NASA).
Number awarded Up to 12 each year.
Deadline March of each year.

[368]
VIRGINIA UNDERGRADUATE STUDENT FINANCIAL ASSISTANCE (LAST DOLLAR) PROGRAM

State Council of Higher Education for Virginia
Attn: Financial Aid Office
James Monroe Building
101 North 14th Street
Richmond, VA 23219-3659
(804) 786-1690   Fax: (804) 225-2604
TDD: (804) 371-8017   E-mail: fainfo@pcmail.schev.edu

Purpose To provide financial assistance to minority undergraduate students enrolled in Virginia colleges or universities.
Eligibility Eligible to apply for this program are minority undergraduate students who are enrolled at least half-time for the first time (as freshmen) in state-supported 2-year or 4-year colleges or universities in Virginia. They must be enrolled in a degree-granting program. Financial need is required.
Financial data The stipends range from $400 to the cost of full-time tuition and fees.

Duration 1 year.
Number awarded Varies each year.
Deadline Deadline dates vary by school.

[369]
VSGC UNDERGRADUATE SCHOLARSHIPS

Vermont Space Grant Consortium
c/o University of Vermont
College of Engineering and Mathematics
119 Votey Building
Burlington, VT 05405-0156
(802) 656-1936   Fax: (802) 656-8802
E-mail: keller@emba.uvm.edu

Purpose To provide financial assistance for undergraduate study in space-related fields to students in Vermont.

Eligibility Applicants for these scholarships must be 1) Vermont residents and U.S. citizens; 2) a graduating senior in a Vermont high school, or a current undergraduate enrolled in a degree program in a Vermont institution of higher education; 3) planning to attend an institution of higher education within the state of Vermont during the year of the proposed scholarship; 4) planning to pursue a professional career which has direct relevance to the U.S. aerospace industry and the goal of the National Aeronautics and Space Administration (NASA), including mathematics, physics, engineering, and other basic sciences. Selection is based on academic standing, letters of recommendation, and an essay detailing career goals. The Vermont Space Grant Consortium (VSGC) is a component of the NASA Space Grant program, which encourages participation by women, minorities, and persons with disabilities.

Financial data The stipend is $1,500 per year.
Duration 1 year.
Special features This program is funded by NASA.
Number awarded Up to 10 each year.
Deadline February of each year.

[370]
WASHINGTON CHEVRON MERIT AWARD

Independent Colleges of Washington
600 Tower Building
1809 Seventh Avenue
Seattle, WA 98101
(206) 623-4494

Purpose To recognize and reward the outstanding classroom, school, and community achievements of high school seniors planning to major in business or the sciences at an independent college in Washington.

Eligibility Students who have an outstanding record of academic achievement, leadership, and participation in school and community activities and are interested in attending an independent college in Washington are invited to apply for these awards. Minorities and women are particularly encouraged to apply.

Financial data The stipend is $2,000 per year.
Duration 4 years for entering freshmen.
Special features Funding for this program is supplied by Chevron U.S.A. Inc.
Number awarded 8 each year.
Deadline February of each year.

[371]
WASHINGTON STATE NEED GRANT

Washington Higher Education Coordinating Board
917 Lakeridge Way
P.O. Box 43430
Olympia, WA 98504-3430
(360) 753-7850   Fax: (360) 753-7808
TDD: (360) 753-7809

Purpose To assist needy and disadvantaged Washington residents in obtaining a postsecondary education in 1 of Washington's 2-year or 4-year public or private colleges or universities, selected proprietary schools, or 1 of the 6 public vocational-technical institutions.

Eligibility To be eligible for the award, a student must be needy or disadvantaged, a resident of Washington, enrolled or accepted for enrollment as at least a half-time undergraduate student, and a U.S. citizen or in the process of becoming one. Applicants may not be pursuing a degree in theology.

Financial data $570 per year is awarded to recipients living away from home; $300 per year to recipients living with their parents.

Duration 1 academic year; renewal possible for up to 3 additional years.

Special features Consideration is automatic with the institution's receipt of the student's completed financial aid application. This program began in 1969.

Number awarded In a recent year, approximately 38,000 students received more than $46 million in benefits from this program.

Deadline Varies according to the participating institution; generally in October of each year.

[372]
WASHINGTON STATE TUITION AND FEE WAIVER PROGRAM

Washington Higher Education Coordinating Board
917 Lakeridge Way
P.O. Box 43430
Olympia, WA 98504-3430
(360) 753-7850   Fax: (360) 753-7808
TDD: (360) 753-7809

Purpose To provide financial assistance to needy or disadvantaged Washington residents who are interested in attending college in the state.

Eligibility This program is open to Washington residents who are disadvantaged and need financial assistance to attend a public 2- or 4-year college or university in Washington. The application for this program is automatic, if the student applies for financial aid from a public Washington State institution.

Financial data Public colleges and universities in Washington waive all or part of the tuition for students who qualify for this program. More than $7 million is distributed annually; the average fee waiver is worth approximately $1,000.

Duration 1 year; may be renewed.

Special features This program was created by the Washington legislature in 1971.

Number awarded Varies; generally, at least 7,100 per year.

[373]
WILLIAM E. MCKNIGHT SCHOLARSHIP

Rochester Area Foundation
335 East Main Street, Suite 402
Rochester, NY 14604
(716) 325-4353   Fax: (716) 546-5069

Purpose To provide financial assistance to minorities in the Rochester, New York area who are interested in pursuing postsecondary education.

Eligibility Minority high school students are eligible for consideration if they are interested in going on to college and are residents of Genesee, Livingston, Monroe, Ontario, Orleans, and Wayne counties.

Financial data The amount awarded varies, depending upon the needs of the recipient.

Duration 1 year; renewable.

Limitations Applications for these scholarships are available only from high school counselors.

Number awarded 1 each year.

[374]
WISCONSIN MINORITY RETENTION GRANTS

Wisconsin Higher Educational Aids Board
131 West Wilson Street
P.O. Box 7885
Madison, WI 53707-7885
(608) 267-2206   Fax: (608) 267-2808

Purpose To provide financial assistance to minorities in Wisconsin who are interested in pursuing postsecondary education.

Eligibility Black Americans, Hispanic Americans, and Native Americans in Wisconsin are eligible to apply if they are enrolled as sophomores, juniors, seniors, or fifth-year undergraduates in a 4-year nonprofit institution or as second-year students in a 2-year program at a public vocational institution in the state. The grant also includes students who were admitted to the United States after December 31, 1975, and who are either a former citizen of Laos, Vietnam, or Cambodia or whose ancestor was a citizen of 1 of those countries. They must be nominated by their institution and be able to demonstrate financial need.

Financial data Up to $2,500 per year.

Duration Up to 4 years.

Special features The Wisconsin Higher Educational Aids Board administers this program for students in private nonprofit institutions and public vocational institutions. The University of Wisconsin has a similar program for students attending any of the branches of that system.

Limitations Eligible students should apply through their school's financial aid office.

Number awarded Varies each year.

Deadline Deadline dates vary by institution; check with your school's financial aid office.

[375]
WISCONSIN SPACE GRANT CONSORTIUM UNDERGRADUATE SCHOLARSHIPS

Wisconsin Space Grant Consortium
Attn: Program Office
333 Architecture and Urban Planning Building
2131 East Hartford Avenue
University of Wisconsin at Milwaukee
P.O. Box 413
Milwaukee, WI 53201-0413
(414) 229-3878   Fax: (414) 229-6976
E-mail: wsgc@csd.uwm.edu

Purpose To provide financial support to undergraduate students at universities participating in the Wisconsin Space Grant Consortium.

Eligibility This program is open to undergraduate students enrolled at 1 of the universities participating in the Wisconsin Space Grant Consortium: Alverno College, University of Wisconsin at Milwaukee, University of Wisconsin at Madison, College of the Menominee Nation, Marquette University, Carroll College, Lawrence University, Milwaukee School of Engineering, Northland College, Beloit College, Medical College of Wisconsin, St. Norbert College, University of Wisconsin at LaCrosse, University of Wisconsin at Green Bay, University of Wisconsin at Parkside, University of Wisconsin at Whitewater, or Ripon College. Applicants must be U.S. citizens; be enrolled full time in a baccalaureate program related to space science, aerospace, or interdisciplinary space studies; and have at least a 3.0 grade point average. The consortium especially encourages applications from minorities, women, and the physically challenged. Selection is based on academic performance and potential for success.

Financial data Stipends up to $1,500 per year are available.

Duration 1 academic year.

Special features Funding for this program is provided by the U.S. National Aeronautics and Space Administration.

Number awarded Varies; generally, at least 30 each year.

Deadline March of each year.

[376]
WISCONSIN TALENT INCENTIVE PROGRAM (TIP) GRANTS

Wisconsin Higher Educational Aids Board
131 West Wilson Street
P.O. Box 7885
Madison, WI 53707-7885
(608) 266-2206   Fax: (608) 267-2808

Purpose To provide supplemental grant awards to minority, disabled and other nontraditional students in Wisconsin during their postsecondary schooling.

Eligibility To be eligible for a grant, a student must be a Wisconsin resident, be a first-year (freshman) student, and possess at least 2 of the following characteristics: 1) be a member of a minority group (Hispanic, Native American, Indian, Black, or Asian American); 2) be a student with a disability, be a first-generation postsecondary student, or be currently or formerly incarcerated in a correctional institution; 3) be a dependent student whose expected parents' contribution is $2,000 or less; 4) be a student who is or will be enrolled in a special academic support program due to insufficient preparation; 5) be a member of a family receiving welfare benefits; 6) be a member of a family whose parent is ineligible for unemployment compensation and has no current income from employment.

Financial data Up to $1,800 is awarded, based on relative need.

Duration Up to 10 semesters.

Special features Additional information is available from the Wisconsin Educational Opportunity Program, 101 West Pleasant Street, Bottlehouse Atrium, Milwaukee, WI 53212.

Number awarded Varies each year.

[377]
WOMEN AND MINORITIES IN ADMINISTRATION SCHOLARSHIP

Illinois Student Assistance Commission
Attn: Scholarship and Grant Services
1755 Lake Cook Road
Deerfield, IL 60015-5209
(708) 948-8550
(800) 899-ISAC (within IL, IA, IN, MO, and WI)

Purpose To provide financial aid to minorities and women in Illinois who are interested in preparing for a career in educational administration.

Eligibility Minorities (Blacks, Hispanics, Asian Americans, American Indians, and Alaskan Natives) and women who are residents of Illinois are eligible to apply for this program if they are college students or graduates and interested in enrolling in an approved administrative certification program in a senior institution in Illinois.

Financial data This program covers all tuition and fees (except revenue bond fees). Funds are paid directly to the participant's school (rather than directly to the participant).

Duration 1 semester or quarter; may be renewed.

Number awarded Varies; this program is awarded on a first-come, first-served basis, with priority to renewal applications, until all available funds are allocated.

Deadline July of each year for fall semester or quarter; November of each year for spring semester or winter quarter; February of each year for spring quarter; May of each year for summer term.

[378]
WOODLAKE FUND

Women's Foundation
340 Pine Street, Suite 302
San Francisco, CA 94104
(415) 837-1113   Fax: (415) 837-1144
E-mail: womensfoun@igc.apc.org

Purpose To provide financial assistance for college education to women of color from East Palo Alto, California.

Eligibility Women of color in East Palo Alto may apply for scholarships from this fund. Applicants may be average students, but must be highly motivated and otherwise unable to pursue an education beyond high school.

Financial data Amounts of the awards depend on the financial need of the recipient and availability of funds.

Number awarded Varies each year.

[379]
XEROX TECHNICAL MINORITY SCHOLARSHIP PROGRAM

Xerox Corporation
Attn: College Relations Manager
800 Phillips Road, 205-99E
Webster, NY 14580
(716) 422-7689

Purpose To provide financial assistance for minorities interested in postsecondary education in the sciences and/or engineering.

Eligibility Minorities enrolled full time in the following science and engineering degree programs at the baccalaureate level or above are eligible to apply: chemical engineering, computer engineering and science, electrical engineering, materials sciences, mechanical engineering, civil engineering, optical engineering, physics, and imaging.

Financial data The program provides annual tuition grants of up to $4,000 for undergraduates and $5,000 for graduate students.

Duration 1 or more years for the scholarship.

Deadline September of each year.

Fellowships

American Indians ●
Native Alaskans ●
Native Pacific Islanders ●
Native Americans in General ●

Described here are 349 funding programs open to Native Americans that are available to be used to pursue studies on the graduate, postgraduate, or postdoctoral level in the United States. Usually no return of service or repayment is required. Of these listings, 72 are open to American Indians, 14 to Native Alaskans, 17 to Native Pacific Islanders, and 246 to Native Americans in General. Note: other funding opportunities for graduate, postgraduate, and postdoctoral Native Americans are also described in the Loans, Grants, Awards, and Internships sections. So, if you are looking for a particular program and don't find it in this section, be sure to check the Program Title Index to see if it is covered elsewhere in the directory.

American Indians

[380]
ADOLPH VAN PELT SCHOLARSHIPS
Association on American Indian Affairs, Inc.
Attn: Scholarship Coordinator
P.O. Box 268
Sisseton, SD 57262
(605) 698-3998

Purpose To provide financial assistance to Native American students interested in postsecondary education.

Eligibility Applicants must be Native American students interested in undergraduate or graduate education. Selection is based on merit and financial need. Applications include an essay (1 to 2 pages) describing educational goals, a budget of educational costs and resources, a copy of a certificate of at least one-quarter Indian blood or of registration with a federally-recognized Indian tribe, and the most recent transcript.

Financial data The award is $500 for the first year, $600 for the second year, $700 for the third year, and $800 for the fourth year. Monies are paid directly to accredited educational institutions to be used for tuition, books, and other academic-related expenses.

Duration 1 year; renewable if academic progress is satisfactory.

Special features Recipients may attend any accredited college or university of their choice level.

Deadline May of each year.

[381]
AISF GRANTS
American Indian Scholarship Fund
c/o Native American Student Programs
University of California at Riverside
224 Costo Hall
Riverside, CA 92521
(909) 787-4143

Purpose To provide financial assistance to Native Americans interested in attending college in California.

Eligibility Native American undergraduate and graduate students are eligible to apply if they can prove Indian blood (by tribal enrollment or birth certificate) and are currently enrolled in a college or university in California. Financial need must be documented.

Financial data The amount awarded varies, depending upon the needs of the recipient.

Duration 1 year; may be renewed.

Number awarded 1 or more each year.

Deadline Applications may be submitted at any time.

[382]
AL QOYAWAYMA AWARD FOR EXCELLENCE IN ARTS AND SCIENCE
American Indian Science and Engineering Society
Attn: Scholarship Department
5661 Airport Boulevard
Boulder, CO 80301
(303) 939-0023   E-mail: ascholar@spot.colorado.edu

Purpose To help artistically-talented American Indian science and engineering students on the undergraduate or graduate school level meet the financial demands of going to college.

Eligibility To be eligible for this scholarship, the applicant must have applied for the A.T. Anderson Memorial Scholarship Program and have met the following requirements: a full-time student at the undergraduate or graduate level, a member of the American Indian Science and Engineering Society, at least one-quarter Indian, in financial need, and pursuing a double major in science or engineering and a degree in the arts. Evidence of the student's excellence in art and engineering is taken from the A.T. Anderson Memorial Scholarship Program application.

Financial data The stipend is $1,500.

Duration 1 year.

Special features This award is sponsored by the George Bird Grinnell American Indian Children's Education Foundation. It honors Al Qöyawayma, a distinguished engineer, renowned Hopi artist, and 1 of the founders of the American Indian Science and Engineering Society.

Number awarded 1 or more each year.

Deadline June of each year.

[383]
AMERICAN INDIAN SCHOLARSHIPS
National Society, Daughters of the American Revolution
Attn: Scholarship Committee
1776 D Street, N.W.
Washington, DC 20006-5392
(202) 628-1776

Purpose To provide supplementary financial assistance to Native American students who wish to pursue postsecondary education in any field in either vocational, undergraduate, or graduate school.

Eligibility Native American high school graduates who wish to attend college are eligible to apply. Scholarships are awarded on the basis of financial need, academic achievement, and ambition. Applicants must have at least a 2.75 grade point average. Graduate students are eligible but undergraduate students receive preference.

Financial data The stipend is $500. The funds are paid directly to the recipient's college.

Duration This is a 1-time award.

Deadline July of each year for fall term; November of each year for spring term.

[384]
ARROW GRADUATE SCHOLARSHIP PROGRAM

Arrow, Inc.
1000 Connecticut Avenue, N.W., Suite 1204
Washington, DC 20036
(202) 296-0685   Fax: (202) 659-4377

Purpose To provide financial assistance to Native American graduate students in any field.

Eligibility Applicants for this program must 1) be enrolled members (or possess at least a quarter Indian blood) from a federally-recognized American Indian tribe or Alaska Native group; 2) be attending an accredited U.S. graduate school; 3) be pursuing a master's or doctoral degree as full-time students; and 4) apply for campus-based aid through the federal financial aid process. Students in all fields are eligible, although 1 scholarship is reserved each year for a student pursuing an advanced degree in nursing.

Financial data The amounts of the awards depends on the availability of funds and the needs of the applicants; in recent years, approximately $20,000 has been available for fellowships.

Duration 1 year.

Special features Arrow, Inc. was founded in 1949 and is dedicated to the advancement of the American Indian. Its range of projects embraces direct aid, education, health, training, and resource development. It recently decided to concentrate its financial aid activities to these large fellowships for Indian graduate students. The program is administered by the American Indian Graduate Center, 4520 Montgomery Boulevard, N.E., Suite #1-B, Albuquerque, NM 87109-1291, (505) 881-4584, Fax: (505) 884-0427.

Number awarded At least 5 each year.

[385]
A.T. ANDERSON MEMORIAL SCHOLARSHIP PROGRAM

American Indian Science and Engineering Society
Attn: Scholarship Department
5661 Airport Boulevard
Boulder, CO 80301
(303) 939-0023   E-mail: ascholar@spot.colorado.edu

Purpose To help talented American Indian science and engineering students meet the financial demands of going to college.

Eligibility To be eligible for a scholarship, the applicant must be a full-time student at the undergraduate or graduate level, attending an accredited 4-year college or university or a 2-year college leading to a 4-year degree, a member of the American Indian Science and Engineering Society who can furnish proof of tribal enrollment, and majoring in health sciences, engineering, science, natural resources, mathematics, business, or math and science secondary education. Recipients are selected on the basis of academic achievement, leadership potential, financial need, and commitment to helping other American Indians.

Financial data The annual stipend is $1,000 for undergraduates and $2,000 for graduate students.

Duration 1 year; may be renewed.

Special features This program was launched in 1983 in memory of A.T. Anderson, a Mohawk and a chemical engineer who worked with Albert Einstein. Anderson was 1 of the society's founders and was the society's first executive director.

Number awarded Varies; generally, 200 or more each year, depending upon the availability of funds from corporate and other sponsors.

Deadline June of each year.

[386]
BIA HIGHER EDUCATION GRANT PROGRAM

Bureau of Indian Affairs
Attn: Area Education Programs Administrator
4149 Highline Boulevard, Suite 380
Oklahoma City, OK 73108
(405) 945-6051   Fax: (405) 945-6057

Purpose To provide financial assistance for postsecondary education to undergraduate and graduate students who belong to certain federally recognized Indian tribes.

Eligibility Students who are members of recognized Indian tribes are eligible to apply. The tribes served by this office are: Seneca-Cayuga, Quapaw, Modoc, Iowa of Kansas and Nebraska, and Fort Still Apache. Applicants must be enrolled or planning to enroll in an accredited college or university and must be able to demonstrate financial need. Priority is given to students residing near or within the boundary of an Indian reservation. Graduate study is included only if money is available after all qualified undergraduate students have been funded. All students must achieve and maintain a cumulative grade point average of at least 2.0.

Financial data The amount awarded varies, up to a maximum of $2,000 per year. The exact amount depends upon the financial needs of the recipient.

Duration 1 year; may be renewed for up to 3 additional years.

Special features Funds may be used for either part-time or full-time study.

Limitations Aid for summer school is available only to juniors and seniors.

Number awarded Varies each year.

Deadline June of each year for fall term; October of each year for spring term; April of each year for summer school.

[387]
CERT SCHOLARSHIPS

Council of Energy Resource Tribes
Attn: Student Services Coordinator
1999 Broadway, Suite 2600
Denver, CO 80202-5726
(303) 297-2378   Fax: (303) 296-5690

Purpose To provide financial assistance to Native American students who are interested in pursuing postsecondary education (on either the undergraduate or graduate level).

Eligibility Indian high school graduates who are preparing to enter college may enroll in the Tribal Resource Institute in Business, Engineering, and Science (TRIBES) program, an intensive 7-week summer college-level math, science, and Indian studies program. TRIBES graduates are eligible to receive these scholarships throughout their undergraduate and graduate education. Also eligible are participants in the Council of Energy Resource Tribes (CERT) Summer Internship Program.

Financial data Costs of instruction, activities, and room and board for the summer institute are paid by the TRIBES program. The amount of the college scholarships is $1,000.

Duration 1 year.

Deadline July of each year.

[388]
CHEROKEE NATION GRADUATE SCHOLARSHIP AWARD

Cherokee Nation of Oklahoma
Attn: Higher Education Program
P.O. Box 948
Tahlequah, OK 74465
(918) 456-0671   (800) 256-0671 (within OK)

Purpose To provide financial assistance for graduate education to college graduates who belong to the Cherokee Nation of Oklahoma.

Eligibility Graduate students who are members of the Cherokee Nation of Oklahoma or the Keetoowah Band of Cherokee Indians are eligible to apply. Awards are granted in 3 categories: 1) full-time students (first priority); 2) part-time students (second priority); and 3) special awards, for students working on certification in such work-related areas as teaching or administration or students having a baccalaureate degree but needing additional hours in certain work-related areas (third priority). Funding for applicants pursuing a Ph.D. degree are considered if funds are available after funding eligible master's program applicants.

Financial data Awards are $500 per semester for full-time students and $250 per semester for part-time students and special awards.

Duration 1 semester; renewable 1 additional semester if the recipient maintains a 3.0 grade point average.

Limitations Applications for summer funding and for second undergraduate, master's, or doctoral degrees are not considered.

Number awarded Varies, depending upon the funds available.

Deadline May of each year.

[389]
CHEYENNE AND ARAPAHO FEDERAL AID GRANTS

Cheyenne and Arapaho Tribes of Oklahoma
Attn: Department of Education
P.O. Box 38
Concho, OK 73022
(405) 262-0345   (800) 247-4612
Fax: (405) 262-0745

Purpose To provide financial assistance to Cheyenne-Arapaho tribal members who are interested in pursuing postsecondary education.

Eligibility To be eligible, applicants must be at least one-quarter degree of Cheyenne-Arapaho Indian, high school graduates (or the equivalent), approved for admission by a college or university, and in financial need. Applicants may either be enrolled or planning to enroll in a postsecondary school. The vast majority of students assisted under this program are at the undergraduate level, although graduate and/or married students are eligible for consideration and assistance. Summer and part-time students may apply as well, as long as application is made well in advance of enrollment and is accompanied by an official need evaluation.

Financial data The amount of the award depends on the need of the applicant. In addition, Merit Scholars who earn a grade point average of 3.0 to 3.49 during a semester receive an incentive award of $75, Outstanding Scholars who earn a grade point average of at least 3.5 during a semester receive an incentive award of $150, graduate students who earn at least a 3.5 grade point average receive $250, students who complete an associate's degree receive $75, and students who complete a baccalaureate degree receive $150.

Duration 1 year; renewable.

Number awarded 40 to 80 each year.

Deadline May of each year for fall semester; October for spring semester; and March for summer session.

[390]
CHOCTAW NATION HIGHER EDUCATION PROGRAM

Choctaw Nation
Attn: Higher Education Department
P.O. Drawer 1210
Durant, OK 74702-1210
(405) 924-8280   (800) 522-6170 (within OK)

Purpose To provide financial assistance to Choctaw Indians who are interested in pursuing postsecondary education.

Eligibility Applicants must be at least one-quarter Choctaw or mixed with another federally recognized tribe to equal one-quarter Indian blood. They must be high school seniors or graduates who are interested in going on to college. Graduate students may receive assistance if funds are available.

Financial data Funds will cover the unmet need, up to $1,600 per year; for students attending a private college or university or a school outside of Oklahoma, the Choctaw Nation will fund 50 percent of the unmet need, up to the maximum of $1,600 per year.

Duration 1 year; may be renewed for up to 4 additional years as long as the recipient enrolls in at least 12 hours per semester with a minimum grade point average of 2.0.

Limitations Students must be working on a college degree.

Number awarded Varies each year.

Deadline March of each year.

[391]
COLORADO SOCIETY OF CPAS ETHNIC DIVERSITY SCHOLARSHIPS

Colorado Society of Certified Public Accountants
Attn: Educational Foundation
7979 East Tufts Avenue, Suite 500
Denver, CO 80237-2843
(303) 773-2877   (800) 523-9082

Purpose To provide financial assistance to minority students in Colorado who are studying accounting.

Eligibility This program is open to African American, Hispanic, Asian American, and Native American Indian students planning to major in accounting at a college or university in Colorado at the associate, baccalaureate, or graduate level. Applicants must have a grade point average of at least 3.0. Selection is based on grade point average and financial need.

Financial data The stipend is $750.

Duration 1 year; nonrenewable.

Number awarded 2 each year.

Deadline February of each year.

[392]
ECIM SCHOLARSHIPS

Episcopal Church Center
Attn: Domestic and Foreign Missionary Society
815 Second Avenue
New York, NY 10017-4594
(212) 922-5293   (800) 334-7626, ext. 5293
Fax: (212) 867-0395

Purpose To provide financial assistance to Native Americans interested in theological education within the Episcopal Church in the United States of America (ECUSA).

Eligibility Applicants must be seminarians of American Indian/Alaska Native descent attending an accredited Episcopal institution.

Financial data The amount of the award depends on the needs of the recipient and the availability of funds.

Special features The Episcopal Council of Indian Ministries (ECIM) also awards the David Oakerhater Merit Fellowship to a middler with outstanding achievement and the Oakerhater Award of $2,500 to a seminarian pursuing a Ph.D.

Number awarded Varies each year.

Deadline May of each year.

[393]
EIGHT NORTHERN INDIAN PUEBLO COUNCIL SCHOLARSHIP PROGRAM

Eight Northern Indian Pueblo Council, Inc.
Attn: Scholarship Program
P.O. Box 969
San Juan Pueblo, NM 87566
(505) 753-1808   (800) 750-1808

Purpose To provide financial assistance for the postsecondary education of members of the Eight Northern Indian Pueblos.

Eligibility Enrolled members of the Eight Northern Indian Pueblos (Taos, Tesuque, San Ildefonso, Nambe, Santa Clara, Pojoaque, Picuris, and San Juan) are eligible to apply if they are enrolled or planning to enroll in an undergraduate or graduate course of study. Applicants must have at least a 2.0 grade point average. They may major in any subject area. Financial need is considered in determining the amount of the award.

Financial data The amount awarded varies, depending upon the recipient's financial need. Generally, scholarships range between $1,000 and $1,800 per year.

Duration 1 year; may be renewed for up to 4 additional years.

Limitations Recipients must enroll in school on a full-time basis.

Number awarded Varies each year.

Deadline February for the fall term; October for the spring term.

[394]
EISENHOWER TRIBAL COLLEGES INITIATIVES

Department of Transportation
Attn: Federal Highway Administration
National Highway Institute
901 North Stuart Street, Suite 300
Arlington, VA 22203
(703) 235-0538   Fax: (703) 235-0593

Purpose To provide financial assistance for Native American students and faculty in transportation-related fields at tribal colleges.

Eligibility This program identifies transportation activities at tribal colleges in order to provide fellowships to Native American students and faculty for further study.

Financial data Fellows receive the full cost of education, including tuition and fees.

Duration 1 year.

Number awarded Varies each year.

Deadline February of each year.

[395]
ELI LILLY GRADUATE SCHOLARSHIPS

Society for Advancement of Chicanos and Native Americans
   in Science
1156 High Street
University of California at Santa Cruz
Santa Cruz, CA 95064
(408) 459-4272   Fax: (408) 459-3156
E-mail: sacnas@cats.ucsc.edu

Purpose To provide financial assistance for graduate study in biology or organic chemistry to Chicano or Native American students.

Eligibility Chicano and Native American students who are junior or senior undergraduate students accepted to enter graduate school are eligible to apply. They must be planning to pursue a research degree (M.S. or Ph.D.) in biology or organic chemistry.

Financial data The stipend is $1,250.

Duration 1 year; nonrenewable.

Special features Funding for these scholarships is provided by Eli Lilly Company.

Number awarded 2 each year.

[396]
EPA TRIBAL LANDS ENVIRONMENTAL SCIENCE SCHOLARSHIP

American Indian Science and Engineering Society
Attn: Scholarship Department
5661 Airport Boulevard
Boulder, CO 80301
(303) 939-0023   E-mail: ascholar@spot.colorado.edu

Purpose To provide financial assistance to outstanding college students interested in studying environmental or related sciences.

Eligibility Applicants must be full-time juniors, seniors, or graduate students with a minimum grade point average of 2.5 majoring in biochemistry, biology, chemical engineering, chemistry, environmental economics, environmental science, entomology, hydrology, or related environmental disciplines. A certificate of Indian blood is not required, but applications must include a 250-word essay on the candidate's personal commitment to environmental protection on tribal lands and a brief statement explaining how and when knowledge of tribal culture was acquired.

Financial data The award is $4,000 per year.

Duration 1 year; renewable upon reapplication.

Special features Funds for the program are provided by the Environmental Protection Agency. The program is administered by the American Indian Science and Engineering Society.

Deadline June of each year.

[397]
FOND DU LAC CRITICAL PROFESSIONS PROGRAM

Fond du Lac Tribal Council
Attn: Bonnie Wallace
105 University Road
Cloquet, MN 55720
(218) 879-4691   (800) 365-1613
Fax: (218) 879-7839

Purpose To provide financial assistance to Indian students who wish to pursue a course of study leading to an undergraduate or graduate degree in business administration, natural resources or forestry, computer programming, urban or rural planning, or elementary or secondary school teaching.

Eligibility Applicants must be enrolled members of the Fond du Lac Tribal Council of the Minnesota Chippewa Tribe, and full-time students. Applicants are evaluated on academic record, leadership ability, and commitment.

Financial data Award varies; graduate students receive $650 per month (plus $90 per dependent) and undergraduate students receive $450 per month (plus $90 per dependent). Funds are disbursed directly to the recipient's institution of higher education.

Duration 1 quarter/semester; renewable if the applicant remains a full-time student and is in good standing (good standing means at least a 2.5 cumulative grade point average for undergraduate work or a 3.0 for graduate work). Financial need must be demonstrated.

Limitations Applicants must demonstrate a commitment to work for a tribal government or in an Indian community for 2 years after graduation.

Number awarded Varies each year.

Deadline Applications are accepted at any time.

[398]
GEM M.S. ENGINEERING FELLOWSHIP PROGRAM

National Consortium for Graduate Degrees for Minorities in Engineering and Science (GEM)
P.O. Box 537
Notre Dame, IN 46556
(219) 631-7778   Fax: (219) 287-1486
E-mail: GEM.1@nd.edu

Purpose To provide financial assistance to minority graduate students in engineering with fellowships and paid summer internships.

Eligibility Criteria for selection are: American citizenship; specific ethnicity—those ethnic minorities underrepresented in the engineering profession: American Indians, Black Americans, Mexican Americans, Puerto Ricans, and other Hispanic Americans; enrolled as at least a junior in an accredited engineering discipline with a minimum grade point average of 2.8; and an academic record that indicates the ability to pursue graduate studies in engineering. Recipients must attend 1 of the 75 GEM member universities that offer a master's degree.

Financial data The fellowship pays tuition and fees and a stipend of $6,000 per academic year. In addition, each participant receives a salary during the summer work assignment as a GEM Summer Intern, making the value of the total award between $20,000 and $40,000. Employer members reimburse GEM participants for travel expenses to and from the summer work site.

Duration Up to 3 semesters or 4 quarters, plus a summer work internship lasting 10 to 14 weeks for up to 3 summers, depending on whether the student applies as a junior, senior, or college graduate; recipients begin their internship upon acceptance into the program and work each summer until completion of their master's degree.

Special features During the summer internship, each fellow is assigned an engineering project in a research setting. Each project is based on the fellow's interest and background and is carried out under the supervision of an experienced engineer. At the conclusion of the internship, each fellow writes a project report.

Limitations Recipients must seek the master's degree in the same engineering discipline as their baccalaureate degree.

Number awarded More than 200 each year.

Deadline November of each year.

[399]
GEM PH.D. ENGINEERING FELLOWSHIP PROGRAM

National Consortium for Graduate Degrees for Minorities in Engineering and Science (GEM)
P.O. Box 537
Notre Dame, IN 46556
(219) 631-7778   Fax: (219) 287-1486
E-mail: GEM.1@nd.edu

Purpose To provide opportunities for minority students to obtain a Ph.D. degree in engineering.

Eligibility Criteria for selection include: American citizenship; specific ethnicity underrepresented in engineering—American Indians, Black Americans, Mexican Americans, Puerto Ricans, and other Hispanic Americans; currently enrolled as a graduate student in engineering or recent recipient of a graduate degree in engineering with a minimum grade point average of 3.0; and an academic record that indicates the ability to pursue doctoral studies in engineering.

Financial data The stipend is $12,000 per year, plus tuition and fees; the total value of the award is between $60,000 and $100,000.

Duration 3 to 5 years.

Special features This program is valid only at 1 of 67 participating GEM member universities; for a list, write to the address above. The fellowship award is designed to support the student in the first year of the doctoral program without working. Subsequent years are subsidized by the respective university and will usually include either a teaching or research assistantship.

Number awarded Varies; approximately 24 each year.

Deadline November of each year.

[400]
GEM PH.D. SCIENCE FELLOWSHIP PROGRAM

National Consortium for Graduate Degrees for Minorities in Engineering and Science (GEM)
P.O. Box 537
Notre Dame, IN 46556
(219) 631-7778   Fax: (219) 287-1486
E-mail: GEM.1@nd.edu

Purpose To provide opportunities for minority students to obtain a Ph.D. degree in the natural sciences (chemistry, physics, earth sciences, mathematics, biological sciences, and computer sciences).

Eligibility Criteria for selection include: American citizenship; specific ethnicity underrepresented in the natural sciences—American Indians, Black Americans, Mexican Americans, Puerto Ricans, and other Hispanic Americans; enrolled as at least a junior in an accredited science discipline with a minimum grade point average of 3.0; and an academic record that indicates the ability to pursue doctoral studies in the natural sciences.

Financial data The stipend is $12,000 per year, plus tuition and fees. In addition, there is a summer internship program that provides a salary and reimbursement for travel expenses to and from the summer work site. The total value of the award is between $60,000 and $100,000, depending upon academic status at time of application, summer employer, and graduate school attended.

Duration 3 to 5 years for the fellowship; 12 weeks for at least 1 summer for the internship. Fellows selected as juniors or seniors intern each summer until entrance to graduate school; fellows selected after college graduation intern at least 1 summer.

Special features This program is valid only at 1 of 53 participating GEM member universities; for a list, write to the address above. The fellowship award is designed to support the student in the first year of the doctoral program without working. Subsequent years are subsidized by the respective university and will usually include either a teaching or research assistantship.

Limitations Recipients must participate in the GEM summer internship; failure to agree to accept the internship cancels the fellowship. Recipients must enroll in the same scientific discipline as their undergraduate major.

Number awarded Varies; approximately 30 each year.

Deadline November of each year.

[401]
GRADUATE FELLOWSHIPS FOR AMERICAN INDIAN AND ALASKAN NATIVE STUDENTS

American Indian Graduate Center
4520 Montgomery Boulevard, NE, Suite 1-B
Albuquerque, NM 87109-1291
(505) 881-4584   Fax: (505) 883-6694

Purpose To provide financial assistance to Native American students interested in pursuing graduate education.

Eligibility To apply, students must be one-quarter or more Indian blood, from a federally-recognized American Indian tribe or Alaska Native group. They must be enrolled as full-time students in a graduate or professional school in the United States pursuing a master's or doctoral degree. Selection is based on academic achievement, financial need, and desire to perform community service after graduation. Preference is not given to any field of study.

Financial data Awards are based on each applicant's unmet financial need, and range from $250 to $3,000 per year.

Duration 1 academic year and summer school, if funds are available; recipients may reapply.

Limitations Since this a supplemental program, applicants must apply in a timely manner for campus-based aid at the college they are attending to be considered for this program. Failure to apply will disqualify an applicant.

Number awarded Varies; generally, more than 400 each year, representing 90 to 120 tribes from at least 25 states.

Deadline May of each year.

[402]
GRAND PORTAGE CRITICAL PROFESSIONS PROGRAM

Grand Portage Tribal Council
Attn: Rosie Novitsky
P.O. Box 428
Grand Portage, MN 55605
(218) 475-0121   Fax: (218) 475-2455

Purpose To provide financial assistance to Indian students who wish to pursue a course of study leading to an undergraduate or graduate degree in business administration, natural resources or forestry, computer programming, urban or rural planning, or elementary or secondary school teaching.

Eligibility Applicants must be enrolled members of the Grand Portage Tribal Council of the Minnesota Chippewa Tribe, and full-time students. Applicants are evaluated on academic record, leadership ability, and commitment.

Financial data Award varies; graduate students receive $650 per month (plus $90 per dependent) and undergraduate students receive $450 per month (plus $90 per dependent). Funds are disbursed directly to the recipient's institution of higher education.

Duration 1 quarter/semester; renewable if the applicant remains a full-time student and is in good standing (good standing means at least a 2.5 cumulative grade point average for undergraduate work or a 3.0 for graduate work). Financial need must be demonstrated.

Limitations Applicants must demonstrate a commitment to work for a tribal government or in an Indian community for 2 years after graduation.

Number awarded Varies each year.

Deadline Applications are accepted at any time.

[403]
HEALTH CAREERS OPPORTUNITY PROGRAM GRANTS

Health Resources and Services Administration
Attn: Bureau of Health Professions
Division of Disadvantaged Assistance
Parklawn Building, Room 8A09
5600 Fishers Lane
Rockville, MD 20857
(301) 443-4493   Fax: (301) 443-6343
E-mail: bbrooks@hrsa.ssw.dhhs.gov

Purpose To provide financial support for education in health professions to students from disadvantaged backgrounds.

Eligibility This program is open to schools of allopathic medicine, osteopathic medicine, public health, dentistry, veterinary medicine, optometry, pharmacy, allied health, chiropractic and podiatric medicine, and public and nonprofit private schools which offer graduate programs in clinical psychology. Health professions schools are eligible if they identify a cohort of at least 7 disadvantaged students who applied but were not accepted to a health professions school; allied health schools are eligible if they identify a cohort of at least 5 disadvantaged students who have completed an undergraduate degree with a significant science focus and made a late decision to enter an allied health professions school and are in pursuit of a baccalaureate level degree in physical therapy, physician assistant, respiratory therapy, medical technology, or occupational therapy. Applicants must provide the designated students with a program of rigorous science and other education experiences and then admit the students who successfully complete the program or arrange for their admission to another health professions or allied health school. Recipient schools must also provide the students with a prematriculation summer program to ease their transition into the health professions or allied health school, and with counseling and advice on financial aid to assist them to complete successfully their education. Individuals from a disadvantaged background are those who come from an environment that has inhibited them from obtaining the knowledge, skill, and abilities to enroll in and graduate from a health professions school or allied health program, or who come from a low-income family (ranging from an annual income below $10,200 for a family of 1 to $26,700 for a family of 6).

Financial data Approximately $30.1 million is available for this program each year, of which $18.5 million is for continuing grants and $11.6 million is available for new grants, averaging $199,000 each. Of the appropriated funds each year, 20 percent must be obligated for stipends to disadvantaged students of exceptional financial need who are students at schools of allopathic medicine, osteopathic medicine, or dentistry; 10 percent must be obligated to community-based programs (including Indian tribes and Alaska Native villages); and 70 percent must be obligated for grants and contracts to institutions of higher education. Students receive a stipend during their participation in the program.

Duration Grants to institutions are up to 3 years; for students, the program is 1 year, including 6 to 8 weeks in the summer.

Number awarded Approximately 58 new projects are funded each year.

Deadline February of each year.

[404]
HEALTH PROFESSIONS SCHOLARSHIP PROGRAM

Indian Health Service
Attn: Scholarship Program
Twinbrook Metro Plaza, Suite 100
12300 Twinbrook Parkway
Rockville, MD 20852
(301) 443-6197   Fax: (301) 443-6048

Purpose To provide financial support to students enrolled in health professions and allied health professions programs.

Eligibility Applicants must be at least high school graduates and be enrolled in a full-time study program leading to a degree in a health-related professions school within the United States. Even though non-Indian students may apply for this program, the Indian Health Care Improvement Act (P.L. 94-437) requires that priority for the awards be given to Indian and Native Alaskan applicants. Both the number of Indian applicants and the level of appropriations limit the availability of scholarship awards to non-Indians. Qualifying fields of study include associate degree nurse, chemical dependency counseling, clinical psychology (Ph.D. only), computer science (B.S.), dentistry, dietician (B.S.), civil engineering (B.S.), health education (master's only), health records, medical technology (B.S.), medical social work (master's only), allopathic and osteopathic medicine, nurse practitioner, nurse midwife, B.S. nurse, M.S. nurse, optometry, paraoptometric, pharmacy (B.S.), physician assistant (B.S.), physical therapy, podiatry (D.P.M.), public health (M.P.H. only), public health nutrition (master's only), radiologic therapy (associate and B.S.), respiratory therapy (associate), and sonography.

Financial data Awards provide for payment of a monthly stipend to cover living expenses, including room and board, tuition and required fees, and all other reasonable educational expenses; the total award is approximately $18,000. In a recent year,

approximately $6,300,000 was available for continuation awards and $1,860,751 for new awards.

Duration 1 year; may be renewed for up to 3 additional years.

Limitations Upon completion of their program of study, recipients are required to provide payback service of 1 year for each year of scholarship support at the Indian Health Service, 1 of 638 tribal health programs, an urban health program, or in private practice serving a substantial number of Indians.

Number awarded Varies; In a recent year, 350 continuing and 103 new awards were provided.

Deadline April of each year.

[405]
HOPI SCHOLARSHIP

Hopi Tribe
Attn: Education Director
P.O. Box 123
Kykotskmovi, AZ 86039
(520) 734-2441   (800) 762-9630

Purpose To provide financial assistance to students of Hopi ancestry who are pursuing an undergraduate, graduate, or postgraduate degree.

Eligibility This program is open to students who are pursuing an associate, baccalaureate, graduate, or postgraduate degree. Applicants must be an enrolled member of the Hopi Tribe. Entering freshmen must be in the top 10 percent of their graduating class or score at least 21 on the ACT or score at least 930 on the SAT. Undergraduate students must have at least a 3.0 grade point average. Graduate, postgraduate, and professional students must have at least a 3.2 grade point average for all graduate course work. Selection is based on academic merit.

Financial data The stipend is $1,000 per semester.

Duration 1 year; may be renewed.

Limitations Recipients must attend school on a full-time basis.

Number awarded Varies each year.

[406]
HOPI SUPPLEMENTAL GRANT

Hopi Tribe
Attn: Education Director
P.O. Box 123
Kykotskmovi, AZ 86039
(520) 734-2441   (800) 762-9630

Purpose To provide financial assistance to students of Hopi ancestry who are pursuing an undergraduate, graduate, or postgraduate degree.

Eligibility This program is open to students who are pursuing an associate, baccalaureate, graduate, or postgraduate degree. Applicants must be an enrolled member of the Hopi Tribe. They must be able to demonstrate financial need. Entering freshmen must have a 2.0 high school grade point average or a minimum composite score of 45 percent on the GED exam. Continuing students must have at least a 2.0 grade point average for all college work.

Financial data Up to $4,000 per semester and up to $2,750 for the summer session.

Duration 1 year; may be renewed.

Special features This grant is awarded as a secondary source of financial aid to eligible students.

Limitations Recipients must attend school on a full-time basis.

Number awarded Varies each year.

[407]
HOPI TRIBAL PRIORITY SCHOLARSHIP

Hopi Tribe
Attn: Education Director
P.O. Box 123
Kykotskmovi, AZ 86039
(520) 734-2441 (800) 762-9630

Purpose To encourage Hopi students to get a degree in an area of interest to the Hopi Tribe.

Eligibility This program is open to enrolled members of the Hopi tribe. They must be college juniors or seniors or graduate students. Their degree must be in a subject area that is of priority interest to the Hopi Tribe. These areas include: law, natural resources, education, medicine, health, engineering, or business. This is a highly competitive scholarship. Selection is based on academic merit and the likelihood that the applicants will use their training and expertise to tribal goals and objectives.

Financial data The amount awarded varies, depending upon the needs of the recipient.

Duration 1 year; may be renewed.

Limitations Recipients must attend school on a full-time basis.

Number awarded Varies each year.

[408]
HOPI TUITION/BOOK SCHOLARSHIP

Hopi Tribe
Attn: Education Director
P.O. Box 123
Kykotskmovi, AZ 86039
(520) 734-2441 (800) 762-9630

Purpose To provide financial assistance to students of Hopi ancestry who are pursuing an undergraduate, graduate, or post-graduate degree.

Eligibility This program is open to students who are pursuing an associate, baccalaureate, graduate, or postgraduate degree. Applicants must be an enrolled member of the Hopi Tribe. They must be pursuing a postsecondary degree for at least 1 of the following reasons: personal growth, career enhancement, career change, and/or continuing education. Both full- and part-time students may apply. Financial need is not required, but students must have applied for federal aid before applying for this award.

Financial data The scholarship covers the cost of tuition/fees and books.

Duration 1 year; may be renewed.

Number awarded Varies each year.

[409]
HUALAPAI HIGHER EDUCATION GRANTS

Hualapai Tribal Council
Attn: Education Director
P.O. Box 179
Peach Springs, AZ 86434-0179
(602) 769-2216

Purpose To provide financial assistance for members of the Hualapai Tribe who are interested in pursuing undergraduate education.

Eligibility Enrolled members of the Hualapai Tribe are eligible to apply if they have graduated from high school (or earned the GED) and plan to attend college full time (at least 12 credit hours per term). Grants are awarded in the following priority order: 1) continuing students in good standing; 2) incoming freshmen; 3) adults who have previously attended or taken college classes; 4) adults never attending college; 5) graduate students; 6) repeating or probationary students.

Financial data Up to $5,000 per year.

Duration 1 year; may be renewed.

Special features Recipients may pursue any area of study.

Number awarded Varies each year.

Deadline Applications must be submitted at least 4 weeks before each term.

[410]
INDIAN FELLOWSHIP PROGRAM

Department of Education
Attn: Office of Elementary and Secondary Education
Office of Indian Education
Portals Building, Room 4300
600 Independence Avenue, S.W.
Washington, DC 20202-6335
(202) 260-1683 E-mail: Indian_Fellowships@ed.gov

Purpose To provide financial assistance to graduate students and selected undergraduate students who are Native Americans interested in preparing for careers in medicine, law, engineering, natural resources, business administration, education, psychology, and related fields.

Eligibility American Indian students who are attending or have been accepted for admission at an accredited institution of higher learning and working toward 1) a graduate degree in medicine, law, education, psychology, clinical psychology, or related fields or 2) a graduate or undergraduate degree in natural resources, business administration, engineering, or related fields may apply. All applicants must be U.S. citizens and Indians. By federal government definition, this means that applicants must be 1) a member of a tribe, band, or other organized group of Indians (including those tribes, bands, or groups terminated since 1940 and those recognized by the state in which they reside); 2) a descendant in the first or second degree of any individual described above; 3) considered by the Secretary of the Interior to be an Indian for any purpose or be an Eskimo, Aleut, or other Alaska Native; or 4) a member of an organized Indian group that received a grant under the Indian Education Act of 1988. Selection is based on academic record (60 points), letters of recommendation (15 points), and an essay on career goals, why the chosen field of study will benefit Indian people, life experiences and personal and family expectations that will enhance the applicant's anticipated career accomplishments, and anticipated commitment to providing service to Indian people (25 points).

Financial data Fellowships are intended to provide full financing for a student's educational expenses or to supplement other sources of financial aid.

Duration Up to 2 years for a master's degree; up to 4 years for an undergraduate or doctorate degree. Each year's renewal is dependent upon appropriations from Congress and satisfactory performance by the fellow.

Special features Up to 10 percent of the awards are to persons receiving training in guidance counseling with a specialty in the area of alcohol and substance abuse counseling and education.

Limitations Individuals receiving assistance under this program are required to perform work related to the training received and that benefits Indian people, or repay all or a prorated part of the assistance received. This payback must begin within 6 months from the date of the completion of the training and is equivalent to the total period of time for which training was actually received.

Number awarded Varies; approximately 60 continuation and 550 new awards are made each year.

Deadline January of each year.

[411]
INDIAN PROFESSIONAL DEVELOPMENT GRANTS

Department of Education
Attn: Office of Elementary and Secondary Education
Office of Indian Education
Portals Building, Room 4300
600 Independence Avenue, S.W.
Washington, DC 20202-6335
(202) 260-3774   (800) 501-5795

Purpose To provide financial assistance for development of programs for education of Indians.

Eligibility Applications may be submitted by institutions of higher education, including Indian institutions of higher education; state or local educational agencies, in consortium with an institution of higher education; or an Indian tribe or organization in consortium with an institution of higher education. Funds must be used to develop programs that improve the skills of qualified Indian individuals; increase the number of qualified Indian individuals in professions that serve Indian persons; or support training programs for qualified Indian persons to become teachers, administrators, teacher aides, social workers, and ancillary educational personnel. Activities may include, but are not limited to, continuing programs, symposia, workshops, conferences, and direct financial support. Grants for training educational personnel may be for preservice or inservice training. For individuals who are being trained to enter any field other than education, the training received must be in a program resulting in a graduate degree.

Financial data Grants range from $75,000 to $275,000 and average approximately $200,000. For project participants receiving training, the stipend maximum is $1,000 per month for full-time students with a dependent allowance of $125 per month.

Duration Up to 5 years.

Limitations Individuals receiving assistance under this program are required to perform work related to the training received and that benefits Indian people, or repay all or a prorated part of the assistance received. This payback must begin within 6 months from the date of the completion of the training and is equivalent to the total period of time for which training was actually received.

Number awarded Approximately 5 each year.

Deadline August of each year.

[412]
JOHN CARTER BROWN LIBRARY SHORT-TERM RESEARCH FELLOWSHIPS

John Carter Brown Library
Brown University
P.O. Box 1894
Providence, RI 02912
(401) 863-2725   E-mail: Karen_DeMaria@Brown.edu

Purpose To support scholars interested in conducting research at the John Carter Brown Library, which is renowned for its collection of historical sources pertaining to the Americas prior to 1830.

Eligibility These fellowships are open to Americans and foreign nationals who are engaged in pre- or postdoctoral or independent research. Graduate students must have passed their preliminary examinations at the time of application.

Financial data The stipend is $1,000 per month.

Duration From 2 to 4 months.

Special features Among the emphases of the library's holdings are works dealing with Native Americans in North and South America, colonial architecture books, economic history, maritime history, and works on the adaptation of religion and religious institutions to the New World.

Limitations Fellows are expected to be in regular residence at the library and to participate in the intellectual life of Brown University for the duration of the program.

Number awarded 15 to 17 each year.

Deadline January of each year.

[413]
LEECH LAKE CRITICAL PROFESSIONS PROGRAM

Leech Lake Tribal Council
Attn: Carol Jenkins
Route 3, Box 100
Cass Lake, MN 56633
(218) 335-8252   (800) 711-0443
Fax: (218) 335-8309

Purpose To provide financial assistance to Indian students who wish to pursue a course of study leading to an undergraduate or graduate degree in business administration, natural resources or forestry, computer programming, urban or rural planning, or elementary or secondary school teaching.

Eligibility Applicants must be enrolled members of the Leech Lake Tribal Council of the Minnesota Chippewa Tribe, and full-time students. Applicants are evaluated on academic record, leadership ability, and commitment.

Financial data Award varies; graduate students receive $650 per month (plus $90 per dependent) and undergraduate students receive $450 per month (plus $90 per dependent). Funds are disbursed directly to the recipient's institution of higher education.

Duration 1 quarter/semester; renewable if the applicant remains a full-time student and is in good standing (good standing means at least a 2.5 cumulative grade point average for undergraduate work or a 3.0 for graduate work). Financial need must be demonstrated.

Limitations Applicants must demonstrate a commitment to work for a tribal government or in an Indian community for 2 years after graduation.

Number awarded Varies each year.

Deadline Applications are accepted at any time.

[414]
LORETTA V. METOXEN SCHOLARSHIP

Oneida Nation of Wisconsin
Attn: Higher Education Office
P.O. Box 365
Oneida, WI 54155-0365
(414) 869-4333   (800) 236-2214, ext. 4333
Fax: (414) 869-4039

Purpose To provide financial assistance for postsecondary education to graduating high school senior members of the Oneida Tribe.

Eligibility Enrolled members of the Oneida Tribe of Wisconsin who are graduating high school students accepted into a college or university. Selection is based on citizenship, respect, academics, and the knowledge of Oneida Land Claims.

Financial data The stipend is $200.

Duration 1 year.

Number awarded 1 each year.

Deadline May of each year.

[415]
MASSACHUSETTS INDIAN ASSOCIATION SCHOLARSHIP FUND

Massachusetts Indian Association
c/o Marjorie Findlay
245 Rockland Road
Carlisle, MA 01741

Purpose To provide financial assistance to Native Americans interested in pursuing postsecondary education.

Eligibility Native American high school students anywhere in the United States may apply for these scholarships if they have a tribal number, are in good academic standing, and can demonstrate financial need.

Financial data The stipends range up to $500 for undergraduate students and $1,000 for graduate students. The funds are intended to supplement other aid by paying for books, lab fees, and other course-related expenses. Grants may be used for tuition, if necessary.

Duration 1 year; may be renewed.

Number awarded 50 each year.

Deadline January and September of each year.

[416]
MENOMINEE INDIAN TRIBE HIGHER EDUCATION PROGRAM

Menominee Indian Tribe of Wisconsin
Attn: Tribal Education Office
P.O. Box 910
Keshena, WI 54135
(715) 799-5110

Purpose To provide financial assistance to Menominee Indians who are interested in pursuing postsecondary studies.

Eligibility Funds are available to students who are at least one-quarter degree Menominee Indians and are enrolled or accepted for enrollment in accredited colleges or universities. Individuals who do not possess at least one-quarter degree Menominee blood quantum but meet the following criteria are also eligible: 1) possess a minimum of one-eighth Menominee blood and 2) possess one-quarter degree Indian blood. Preference is given to applicants in this order: continuing undergraduate students in good standing; new undergraduates, awarded on a first come, first served basis; late applicants, depending on the availability of funds; second term applicants, only on projected availability of funds; and graduate and professional students, considered only if funds are available after all worthy Menominee undergraduates are selected.

Financial data Up to $2,200 per year for full-time students, for tuition, books, and fees only. Part-time students are also eligible for assistance, but the maximum funding available to students is $11,000 of combined part-time/full-time study.

Duration Up to 10 semesters.

Number awarded Varies each year.

Deadline February of each year.

[417]
MESCALERO APACHE TRIBAL SCHOLARSHIP

Mescalero Apache Tribe
Attn: Tribal Education Department
P.O. Box 176
Mescalero, NM 88340
(505) 671-4494

Purpose To provide financial assistance for undergraduate or graduate education to members of the Mescalero Apache Tribe.

Eligibility Enrolled members of the Mescalero Apache Tribe are eligible to apply if they are high school seniors, high school graduates, or currently-enrolled college students, have earned at least a 2.0 grade point average, and are interested in going to a college, university, vocational, or graduate school.

Financial data The amount awarded varies, up to $6,000 per year.

Duration 1 year; may be renewed for up to 3 additional years.

Number awarded Varies each year.

Deadline June for the fall term; October for the spring term.

[418]
MICHIGAN INDIAN TUITION WAIVER PROGRAM

Michigan Commission on Indian Affairs
Attn: Department of Civil Rights
P.O. Box 30026
611 West Ottawa, North Tower, Third Floor
Lansing, MI 48913-1070
(517) 373-0654   Fax: (517) 335-1642

Purpose To provide financial assistance to Native American high school graduates who are interested in attending college in Michigan.

Eligibility Eligible students must have one-quarter or more quantum blood Indian, as certified by tribal association and verified by the Michigan Commission on Indian Affairs; enrolled or eligible to enroll full time, part time, or in summer school at a public postsecondary institution in Michigan as an undergraduate or graduate student; and a legal resident of Michigan for not less than 12 consecutive months.

Financial data Students in the program receive free tuition at any Michigan public 2-year or 4-year college or university.

Duration 1 year; renewable.

[419]
MILLE LACS CRITICAL PROFESSIONS PROGRAM

Mille Lacs Tribal Council
Attn: Melissa Hill
HCR 67, Box 242
Onamia, MN 56359
(612) 532-4714   Fax: (320) 532-4209

Purpose To provide financial assistance to Indian students who wish to pursue a course of study leading to an undergraduate or graduate degree in business administration, natural resources or forestry, computer programming, urban or rural planning, or elementary or secondary school teaching.

Eligibility Applicants must be enrolled members of the Mille Lacs Tribal Council of the Minnesota Chippewa Tribe, and full-time students. Applicants are evaluated on academic record, leadership ability, and commitment.

Financial data Award varies; graduate students receive $650 per month (plus $90 per dependent) and undergraduate students receive $450 per month (plus $90 per dependent). Funds are disbursed directly to the recipient's institution of higher education.

Duration 1 quarter/semester; renewable if the applicant remains a full-time student and is in good standing (good standing means at least a 2.5 cumulative grade point average for undergraduate work or a 3.0 for graduate work). Financial need must be demonstrated.

Limitations Applicants must demonstrate a commitment to work for a tribal government or in an Indian community for 2 years after graduation.

Number awarded Varies each year.

Deadline Applications are accepted at any time.

[420]
MINNESOTA INDIAN SCHOLARSHIP PROGRAM

Minnesota State Department of Education
Attn: Indian Education
1819 Bemidji Avenue
Bemidji, MN 56601
(218) 755-2926

Purpose To provide financial assistance to Native Americans in Minnesota who are interested in pursuing undergraduate or graduate education.

Eligibility Applicants must be at least one-fourth degree Indian ancestry; members of a recognized Indian tribe; at least high school graduates (or approved equivalent); accepted by an accredited college, university, or vocational school in Minnesota; and residents of Minnesota for at least 1 year.

Financial data The scholarships range from $500 to $3,000, depending upon financial need. The average award is $1,450. Awards are paid directly to the student's school or college, rather than to the student.

Duration 1 year; renewable for an additional 4 years.

Limitations Recipients must maintain a minimum grade point average of 2.0, earn 12 credits per quarter, and send official grade transcripts to the office for review after each quarter or semester.

Deadline There is no deadline, but students are encouraged to apply as early as possible before starting their postsecondary school program as scholarships are awarded on a first-come, first-served basis.

[421]
NATIVE AMERICAN LEADERSHIP IN EDUCATION (NALE) PROGRAM

Native American Scholarship Fund
8200 Mountain Road, N.E., Suite 203
Albuquerque, NM 87110-7835
(505) 262-2351   Fax: (505) 262-0534

Purpose To provide financial assistance to American Indian paraprofessionals in the education field who wish to return to school.

Eligibility Paraprofessionals working in the schools are eligible to apply for this program if they 1) have at least a quarter Indian blood; 2) are members of a U.S. tribe that is either federally-recognized, state-recognized, or terminated; 3) are interested in returning to college to complete their undergraduate degrees

and/or earn credentials as teachers, counselors, or administrators; 4) have been admitted to or are enrolled in college; 5) have grade point averages of at least 3.0 and scores on the SAT of at least 950 or ACT of at least 23; and 6) have applied for all other sources of funding for which they are eligible. They must attend an accredited 4-year college or university, but may be entering freshmen, undergraduate students, graduate students, or Ph.D. candidates. Awards are based on merit and the potential of the applicant to improve the lives of Indian people; financial need is not a consideration. Students with no clear goals are discouraged from applying.

Financial data The amount awarded varies but is generally at least $500 in the form of grants, loans, or a combination of both.

Duration 1 year; may be renewed.

Number awarded Varies; generally, 15 or more each year.

Deadline April of each year for fall terms; September of each year for spring and winter terms; March of each year for summer school.

[422]
NATIVE AMERICAN SEMINARY SCHOLARSHIPS

Presbyterian Church (U.S.A.)
Attn: Office of Financial Aid for Studies
100 Witherspoon Street, Room M042
Louisville, KY 40202-1396
(502) 569-5776   Fax: (502) 569-5018

Purpose To provide financial assistance to Native American students interested in preparing for church occupations.

Eligibility Native American and Alaska Native students may apply for the award if they are U.S. citizens or permanent residents, can demonstrate financial need, are in good academic standing, and are in 1 of the following 3 categories: 1) theological student enrolled as an inquirer or candidate by a presbytery of the Presbyterian Church (U.S.A.), preparing for a church occupation, and enrolled in a theological institution approved by the students' Committee on Preparation for Ministry; 2) Presbyterian Church (U.S.A.) member enrolled in a program of theological education by extension, such as the NATEC; or 3) inquirer, candidate, minister, or member of the Presbyterian Church (U.S.A.) in other church occupations pursuing an approved program of continuing education.

Financial data The amounts of the awards depend on the availability of funds.

Number awarded Varies each year.

[423]
NAVAJO NATION SCHOLARSHIP AND FINANCIAL ASSISTANCE PROGRAM

Navajo Nation
Attn: Scholarship and Financial Assistance Program
P.O. Drawer 1870
Window Rock, AZ 86515-1870
(520) 871-7640   (800) 243-2956

Purpose To provide financial assistance to members of the Navajo Nation who are interested in pursuing undergraduate or graduate education.

Eligibility Enrolled members of the Navajo Nation are eligible to apply if they meet 1 of the following requirements: 1) are ranked in the top 30 percent of their class; 2) achieved an ACT score of at least 17; 3) have accumulated 12 college credit hours with a grade point average of at least 2.0; or 4) have a General Education Development (GED) score of at least 55. Applications must be accompanied by a certificate of Indian blood, a high school or college transcript, a letter of admission from an accredited postsecondary institution, and a financial need analysis.

Financial data The amount awarded varies, depending upon the needs of the recipient.

Duration 1 year; may be renewed.

Deadline April of each year for fall semester; September of each year for winter quarter or spring semester; March of each year for summer session.

[424]
NETT LAKE/BOIS FORTE CRITICAL PROFESSIONS PROGRAM

Nett Lake/Bois Forte Tribal Council
Attn: Joanne Donald
P.O. Box 16
Nett Lake, MN 55772
(218) 757-3107   Fax: (218) 757-3118

Purpose To provide financial assistance to Indian students who wish to pursue a course of study leading to an undergraduate or graduate degree in business administration, natural resources or forestry, computer programming, urban or rural planning, or elementary or secondary school teaching.

Eligibility Applicants must be enrolled members of the Nett Lake/Bois Forte Tribal Council of the Minnesota Chippewa Tribe and full-time students. Applicants are evaluated on academic record, leadership ability, and commitment.

Financial data Award varies; graduate students receive $650 per month (plus $90 per dependent) and undergraduate students receive $450 per month (plus $90 per dependent). Funds are disbursed directly to the recipient's institution of higher education.

Duration 1 quarter/semester; renewable if the applicant remains a full-time student and is in good standing (good standing means at least a 2.5 cumulative grade point average for undergraduate work or a 3.0 for graduate work). Financial need must be demonstrated.

Limitations Applicants must demonstrate a commitment to work for a tribal government or in an Indian community for 2 years after graduation.

Number awarded Varies each year.

Deadline Applications are accepted at any time.

[425]
NEW MEXICO GRADUATE SCHOLARSHIP PROGRAM

New Mexico Commission on Higher Education
Attn: Financial Aid and Student Services
10668 Cerrillos Road
P.O. Box 15910
Santa Fe, NM 87506-5910
(505) 827-7383   (800) 279-9777 (within NM)
E-mail: highered@che.state.nm.us

Purpose To provide financial assistance for graduate education to underrepresented groups in New Mexico.

Eligibility Applicants for this program must be New Mexico residents who are members of underrepresented groups, particularly minorities and women. Preference is given to 1) students enrolled in business, engineering, computer science, mathematics, agriculture and 2) American Indian students enrolled in any graduate program. All applicants must be U.S. citizens or perma-

nent residents enrolled in graduate programs at public institutions of higher education in New Mexico.

Financial data The stipend is up to $7,200 per year.

Duration 1 year; may be renewed.

Special features Information is available from the dean of graduate studies at the participating New Mexico public institution.

Number awarded Varies each year, depending on the availability of funds.

[426]
NEW MEXICO MINORITY DOCTORAL ASSISTANCE STUDENT LOAN-FOR-SERVICE PROGRAM

New Mexico Commission on Higher Education
Attn: Financial Aid and Student Services
10668 Cerrillos Road
P.O. Box 15910
Santa Fe, NM 87506-5910
(505) 827-7383   (800) 279-9777 (within NM)
E-mail: highered@che.state.nm.us

Purpose To provide financial assistance to underrepresented minorities and women who reside in New Mexico and are interested in pursuing graduate study in selected fields.

Eligibility Eligible to apply for this program are ethnic minorities and women who have received a baccalaureate and/or master's degree from a state-supported 4-year higher education institution in New Mexico; wish to pursue a doctoral degree at an eligible sponsoring New Mexico institution in mathematics, engineering, the physical or life sciences, or any other academic discipline in which ethnic minorities and women are demonstrably underrepresented in New Mexico colleges and universities; and are willing after obtaining their degree to teach at an institution of higher education in the state. Applicants must be U.S. citizens and New Mexico residents.

Financial data This is a loan-for-service program in which the amount of the loan (up to $25,000 per year) may be wholly or partially forgiven upon completion of service as a college instructor in New Mexico.

Duration 1 year; may be renewed for up to 2 additional years for students who enter with a master's degree or up to 3 additional years for students who begin with a baccalaureate degree.

Special features Sponsoring institutions nominate candidates to the Commission on Higher Education for these awards.

Limitations Recipients must agree to teach at the college/university level in New Mexico upon completion of their doctoral degree. If the sponsoring institution where the recipient completes the degree is unable to provide a tenure-track position, it must arrange placement at another alternate and mutually-acceptable New Mexico public postsecondary instutition.

Number awarded Up to 12 each year.

Deadline March of each year.

[427]
NEW YORK STATE REGENTS HEALTH CARE OPPORTUNITY SCHOLARSHIPS

New York State Education Department
Attn: Bureau of Postsecondary Grants Administration
Cultural Education Center
Albany, NY 12230
(518) 486-1319

Purpose To provide financial assistance to minority or educationally disadvantaged students who are beginning or enrolled in an approved program in medicine or dentistry.

Eligibility Candidates must be U.S. citizens or permanent residents and legal residents of New York for 1 year prior to application. The law requires that awards be made to eligible candidates in the following order: first priority is given to any candidate who is economically disadvantaged and a minority group member historically underrepresented in the professions (Black Americans, Hispanic Americans, Native Americans, or Alaskan Natives); second priority is given to any candidate who is a minority group member underrepresented in the professions; and third priority is given to any candidate who is enrolled in or a graduate of 1 of these state-supported opportunity programs: Search for Education, Elevation and Knowledge (SEEK) or College Discovery at City University; Educational Opportunity Program (EOP) in the State University system; or Higher Education Opportunity Program (HEOP) at an independent college.

Financial data Scholarship holders receive from $1,000 to $10,000 per year, depending on income.

Duration Up to 4 years.

Limitations No award can exceed the actual cost of attendance. After completion of their professional studies, scholarship holders are required to practice 12 months for each annual payment received, including at least 24 months in a designated physician-shortage area in New York.

Number awarded 100 each year; 80 of the awards are made for medicine and 20 for dentistry.

Deadline February of each year.

[428]
NEW YORK STATE REGENTS PROFESSIONAL OPPORTUNITY SCHOLARSHIPS

New York State Education Department
Attn: Bureau of Postsecondary Grants Administration
Cultural Education Center
Albany, NY 12230
(518) 486-1319

Purpose To expand educational opportunities for underrepresented minority and economically disadvanataged students interested in pursuing professional careers.

Eligibility Candidates must be U.S. citizens or permanent residents and legal residents of New York for 1 year prior to application. The law requires that awards be made to eligible candidates in the following order: first priority is given to any candidate who is economically disadvantaged and a minority group member historically underrepresented in the professions (Black Americans, Hispanic Americans, Native Americans, or Alaskan Natives); second priority is given to any candidate who is a minority group member underrepresented in the professions; and third priority is given to any candidate who is enrolled in or a graduate of 1 of these state-supported opportunity programs: Search for Education, Elevation and Knowledge (SEEK) or College Discovery at City University; Educational Opportunity Program (EOP) in the State University system; or Higher Education Opportunity Program (HEOP) at an independent college.

Financial data The stipends range from $1,000 to $5,000 per year, depending on income.

Duration Up to 4 years.

Special features Scholarships are available for study in the following areas: accounting (baccalaureate level), architecture (baccalaureate or master's), chiropratic medicine (doctoral), dental hygiene (associate), engineering (baccalaureate), landscape architecture (baccalaureate or master's), law (juris doctoral), nursing (baccalaureate), occupational therapy (baccalaureate or master's), occupational therapy assistant (associate), ophthalmic dispensing (associate), optometry (doctoral), pharmacy (baccalaureate), physical therapist assistant (associate), physical therapy (baccalaureate or master's), physicians assistant (baccalaureate or master's), psychology (doctoral), social work (master's), speech-language pathology/audiology (master's), and veterinary medicine (doctoral).

Limitations No award can exceed the actual cost of attendance. After completion of their professional studies, scholarship holders are required to practice in New York for 12 months for each annual payment received.

Number awarded 220 each year.

Deadline January of each year.

[429]
NORBERT S. HILL, JR. LEADERSHIP AWARD

American Indian Science and Engineering Society
Attn: Scholarship Department
5661 Airport Boulevard
Boulder, CO 80301
(303) 939-0023   E-mail: ascholar@spot.colorado.edu

Purpose To help talented American Indian science and engineering students meet the financial demands of going to college.

Eligibility To be eligible for this scholarship, the applicant must have applied for the A.T. Anderson Memorial Scholarship Program and have met the following requirements: a full-time student at the undergraduate or graduate level, a member of the American Indian Science and Engineering Society, at least one-quarter Indian, in financial need, and majoring in the sciences, health-related fields, business, natureal resources, engineering, and math and science secondary education. Evidence of the student's outstanding leadership is taken from the A.T. Anderson Memorial Scholarship Program application. The leadership should be manifest not only in the local chapter of the American Indian Science and Engineering Society, but also in the campus and community, particularly as it relates to American Indian youth mentoring and motivation.

Financial data The stipend is $1,500.

Duration 1 year.

Number awarded 1 or more each year.

Deadline June of each year.

[430]
NORMAN TECUBE SR. HIGHER EDUCATION FUND

Jicarilla Apache Tribe
Attn: Higher Education Program
P.O. Box 507
Dulce, NM 87528-0507
(505) 759-3316

Purpose To provide financial assistance for undergraduate or graduate education to members of the Jicarilla Apache tribe.

Eligibility Enrolled members of the Jicarilla Apache tribe are eligible to apply if they are attending either undergraduate or graduate school. Recipients may enroll in any accredited postsecondary school and may major in any subject area.

Financial data The amount awarded varies, up to a maximum of $1,800 per year. Funds may not be used for extra-curricular activities, trips out of the United States, non-credit courses, or unnecessary tools.

Duration 1 year; may be renewed.

Special features This program was formerly called the Chester E. Faris Higher Education Fund.

Number awarded Varies each year.

Deadline February for fall semester or academic year applications; September of each year for spring semester applications.

[431]
NORTH CAROLINA INCENTIVE SCHOLARSHIP AND GRANT PROGRAM FOR NATIVE AMERICANS—NEED-BASED GRANTS

North Carolina Commission of Indian Affairs
North Carolina Department of Administration
217 West Jones Street
Raleigh, NC 27603-1336
(919) 733-5998   Fax: (919) 733-1207

Purpose To provide financial assistance to American Indians who are interested in studying at a university in North Carolina.

Eligibility Applicants must be American Indians, as defined by this program: "An individual who maintains cultural identification as an American Indian through membership in an Indian tribe recognized by the State of North Carolina or by the federal government or through other tribal affiliation or community recognition." They must be enrolled or planning to enroll as undergraduate students in 1 of the following North Carolina schools: Appalachian State University, East Carolina University, Elizabeth City State University, Fayetteville State University, North Carolina A&T State University, North Carolina Central University, North Carolina School of the Arts, North Carolina State University at Raleigh, Pembroke State University, University of North Carolina at Asheville, University of North Carolina at Chapel Hill, University of North Carolina at Charlotte, University of North Carolina at Greensboro, University of North Carolina at Wilmington, Western Carolina University, or Winston-Salem State University. Also eligible are students enrolled in a doctoral program at North Carolina State University, the University of North Carolina at Chapel Hill, or the University of North Carolina at Greensboro. All applicants must be classified as North Carolina residents for tuition purposes and be able to demonstrate financial need.

Financial data For undergraduates, the maximum award is $700 full-time study or a prorated amount for part-time study; the maximum award for doctoral students is $5,000. The actual amount depends on financial need of the recipient.

Duration 1 year; may be renewed up to 3 additional years.

Special features Recipients may be full- or part-time students. Stipends are reduced proportionately for part-time students.

Number awarded Varies; in recent years, approximately 250 undergraduates and 6 doctoral students have received awards.

Deadline Applications are available from the participating institutions (listed above). Deadline dates vary by institution; check with the specific school you wish to attend to determine the current schedule.

[432]
NORTHERN CHEYENNE HIGHER EDUCATION PROGRAM

Tribal Council of the Northern Cheyenne
c/o Northern Cheyenne Agency
P.O. Box 307
Lame Deer, MT 59043
(406) 477-6467

Purpose To provide financial assistance to Northern Cheyenne high school graduates who are interested in pursuing postsecondary education.

Eligibility Applicants must be at least high school graduates (or seniors about to graduate) who are enrolled Northern Cheyenne tribal members, can show financial need, and have been accepted for enrollment at an accredited college or university in a program leading to an associate or baccalaureate degree. Graduate study may be approved if all undergraduate applicants have been approved and funds are still available. Selection is based on academic achievement, educational goals, financial need, choice of school, and plans after graduation.

Financial data The stipend is intended to supplement all other available sources of funding. The scholarship must be used for tuition, subsistence, required fees, and textbooks.

Duration 1 year; may be renewed if the recipient maintains a 2.0 grade point average and completes at least 14 quarter or 16 semester units as a freshman and sophomore and at least 16 quarter or 18 semester units as a junior or senior.

Limitations Recipients who reside in Montana are expected to attend a postsecondary institution in the state. They must pay the difference in cost between Montana public postsecondary schools and private or out-of-state schools, if they elect to attend either of those. An exception is made if no comparable course of study exists in a Montana public institution. Eligible Northern Cheyenne Indians residing out of state are subject to the same regulation; however, they may enroll in a Montana institution of higher learning if there is no comparable course of study at a public institution in their home state.

Number awarded Varies each year.

Deadline February for fall quarter/semester; September for winter quarter/spring semester/spring quarter; March for summer school.

[433]
ONEIDA TRUST SCHOLARSHIP

Oneida Nation of Wisconsin
Attn: Higher Education Office
P.O. Box 365
Oneida, WI 54155-0365
(414) 869-4333   (800) 236-2214, ext. 4333
Fax: (414) 869-4039

Purpose To provide financial assistance for postsecondary education to members of the Oneida Tribe.

Eligibility Applicants must be enrolled members of the Oneida Tribe of Wisconsin who have been accepted into an accredited college or university or privately owned, operated, and recognized institution. Undergraduates must have a minimum grade point average of 2.5 and graduate students must be admitted with a cumulative grade point average of at least 2.75 and must then maintain at least a 3.0 grade point average. This fund should be considered a resource of last resort; all traditional resources must be expended, unavailable, or depleted.

Financial data The maximum stipend is $500 per semester.

Duration 1 semester; may be renewed for 1 additional semester.

Special features Recipients are expected to return to the Oneida Tribe to share their acquired knowledge, experience, and education to benefit the Oneida Tribe as a whole.

Number awarded Varies each year.

Deadline August of each year for fall term; November of each year for spring term.

[434]
OSAGE TRIBAL EDUCATION COMMITTEE PROGRAM

Osage Tribal Education Committee
c/o Oklahoma Area Education Office
4149 Highline Boulevard, Suite 380
Oklahoma City, OK 73108
(405) 945-6051　　　　　　　Fax: (405) 945-6057

Purpose To provide financial assistance for postsecondary education to undergraduate and graduate Osage students.

Eligibility This program is open to students enrolled in accredited postsecondary educational programs at the college, university, or technical/vocational level who can prove Osage Indian blood. Applicants may be candidates for an associate, baccalaureate, or graduate degree.

Financial data The amount of the award depends on the financial need of the recipient.

Duration 1 year; may be renewed for up to 3 additional years.

Number awarded Varies each year.

Deadline June of each year for fall term; December of each year for spring term; April of each year for summer school.

[435]
POLINGAYSI QOYAWAYMA AWARD

American Indian Science and Engineering Society
Attn: Scholarship Department
5661 Airport Boulevard
Boulder, CO 80301
(303) 939-0023　　　E-mail: ascholar@spot.colorado.edu

Purpose To provide financial assistance to Indian educators who wish to teach in a Native community or at the college level.

Eligibility To be eligible for this scholarship, the applicant must have applied for the A.T. Anderson Memorial Scholarship Program and have met the following requirements: a full-time student at the undergraduate or graduate level, a member of the American Indian Science and Engineering Society, at least one-quarter Indian, in financial need, and pursuing a teaching degree in order to teach mathematics or science in a Native community or an advanced degree for personal improvement or teaching at the college level.

Financial data The stipend is $1,000.

Duration 1 year.

Special features This award honors Polingaysi (Elizabeth) Qöyawayma, an outstanding pioneer American Indian educator.

Number awarded 1 or more each year.

Deadline June of each year.

[436]
PRE-LAW SUMMER INSTITUTE FOR AMERICAN INDIANS AND ALASKA NATIVES

American Indian Law Center, Inc.
Attn: Director
P.O. Box 4456, Station A
Albuquerque, NM 87196
(505) 277-5462　　　　　　　Fax: (505) 277-1035

Purpose To prepare Native Americans to be successful law students and successful lawyers at a pre-law summer institute.

Eligibility To be eligible, Native Americans (American Indians and Alaska Natives) must have completed their undergraduate degrees, taken the LSAT, and applied to law schools accredited by the American Bar Association. They must be enrolled members of a federally-recognized Indian tribe.

Financial data Students receive funding to cover tuition, textbooks, personal expenses, and some travel; the amount of funding depends on the number of qualified participants who are admitted, but is usually at least $1,200 plus $200 for travel.

Duration 8 weeks during the summer.

Special features The institute is conducted at the University of New Mexico School of Law. Participants take courses in Indian law, constitutional law, criminal law, and other subjects. Funding is provided by the U.S. Bureau of Indian Affairs.

Number awarded Between 25 and 40 each year.

Deadline March of each year.

[437]
PROGRAM FOR MINORITY RESEARCH TRAINING IN PSYCHIATRY

American Psychiatric Association
Attn: Office of Research
1400 K Street, N.W.
Washington, DC 20005
(202) 682-6225　　　　　　　(800) 852-1390

Purpose To provide financial assistance to minority medical students and residents interested in psychiatric research.

Eligibility This program is open to underrepresented minorities (American Indians, Blacks/African Americans, Hispanics, and Pacific Islanders) at 3 levels: medical students, residents, and graduates of residency programs. All candidates must be interested in training at research-intensive departments of psychiatry in major U.S. medical schools. Training sites with excellence as demonstrated by research facilities and resources, funded research, research faculty (including minority researchers), and successful training history are considered preferable.

Financial data Annual stipends are $10,008 for medical students, from $19,608 to $28,200 for residents, and up to $32,300 for post-residency fellows. Other benefits include travel funds to attend the annual meeting of the American Psychiatric Association (APA) or the American College of Neuropsychopharmacology, and limited tuition assistance for full-time trainees to attend specific courses that are required as part of their training.

Duration For medical students, 2 to 6 months, either during an elective period or as a summer experience; for residents, 3 to 6 months within or outside the home institution, although a year of full-time research training is also possible; for post-residency fellows, 2 years, although a third year is possible if appropriate to a trainee's career development.

Special features   This program is funded by the National Institute of Mental Health and administered by the APA.

Number awarded   Varies each year.

Deadline   Medical students and residents seeking less than 1 year of training may apply at any time, but at least 3 months before the proposed training is to begin; medical students seeking summer training should apply by March of each year; residents seeking a year or more of training and post-residency fellows should apply by November of each year.

[438]
PURCELL POWLESS SCHOLARSHIP FUND

Oneida Nation of Wisconsin
Attn: Higher Education Office
P.O. Box 365
Oneida, WI 54155-0365
(414) 869-4333   (800) 236-2214, ext. 4333
Fax: (414) 869-4039

Purpose   To provide financial assistance for graduate education to members of the Oneida Tribe.

Eligibility   Enrolled members of the Oneida Tribe of Wisconsin who are attending graduate school majoring in economics or business are eligible for this scholarship. Applicants must demonstrate financial need and must have applied for all other sources of aid.

Financial data   The scholarship provides the cost of tuition, required books, and related fees.

Duration   1 year.

Limitations   Recipients are expected to provide technical assistance to the Oneida Nation following completion of their graduate study.

Number awarded   1 each year.

Deadline   August of each year for fall term; November of each year for spring term.

[439]
ROBERT W. BROCKSBANK SCHOLARSHIP

American Indian Science and Engineering Society
Attn: Scholarship Department
5661 Airport Boulevard
Boulder, CO 80301
(303) 939-0023   E-mail: ascholar@spot.colorado.edu

Purpose   To help talented American Indian science and engineering students on the undergraduate or graduate school level meet the financial demands of going to college.

Eligibility   To be eligible for this scholarship, the applicant must have applied for the A.T. Anderson Memorial Scholarship Program and have met the following requirements: a full-time student at the undergraduate or graduate level, a member of the American Indian Science and Engineering Society, at least one-quarter Indian, in financial need, and pursuing a degree in the sciences, engineering, health-related fields, business, natural resources, and math and science secondary education. Candidates should exemplify strong leadership skills and a determination for achieving excellence in the academic arena, as well as in the community.

Financial data   The stipend is $1,500.

Duration   1 year.

Special features   This award is sponsored by Karin Brocksbank. It honors Robert W. Brocksbank, a distinguished member of the American Indian Science and Engineering Society who served as the chairman of the Corporate Advisory Board for a number of years.

Number awarded   1 or more each year.

Deadline   June of each year.

[440]
SCHUYLER M. MEYER, JR. SCHOLARSHIP FUND

American Indian Science and Engineering Society
Attn: Scholarship Department
5661 Airport Boulevard
Boulder, CO 80301
(303) 939-0023   E-mail: ascholar@spot.colorado.edu

Purpose   To provide financial assistance to undergraduate or graduate Indian students who are single parents.

Eligibility   This program is open to American Indian full-time undergraduate and graduate students who are single parents, with a minor child residing in the same household. Applicants must be at least one-quarter American Indian or recognized as a member of a tribe. All fields of study are eligible and students must demonstrate financial need.

Financial data   The stipend is $1,000.

Duration   1 year; may be renewed.

Special features   This award is sponsored by the George Bird Grinnell American Indian Children's Education Foundation and administered by the American Indian Science and Engineering Society.

Number awarded   1 or more each year.

Deadline   June of each year.

[441]
SEMINOLE AND MICCOSUKEE INDIAN
SCHOLARSHIP PROGRAM

Florida Department of Education
Attn: Office of Student Financial Assistance
State Programs—255 Collins
Tallahassee, FL 32399-0400
(904) 487-0049

Purpose   To provide financial assistance to Florida's Seminole and Miccosukee Indians who wish to pursue postsecondary education.

Eligibility   Scholarships are awarded to Florida residents who hold certification of membership or eligibility of membership in the Seminole Indian Tribe of Florida or the Miccosukee Indian Tribe of Florida and who meet the following criteria: are Florida residents; have complied with registration requirements of the Selective Service System; have participated in the college-level communication and computation skills test (CLAST) program; are enrolled as either a graduate or undergraduate student at an eligible public or private college or university in Florida for at least 1 credit hour per term; demonstrate financial need; and are not in default or owing repayment on any federal or state grant, loan, or scholarship program.

Financial data   The amount of the award depends on the recommendation by the respective tribe, but may not exceed the annual cost of education for 4 years of undergraduate study or 2 years of graduate study.

Duration 1 year; renewable, provided recipient continues to demonstrate academic progress by meeting all academic and other requirements set by the college or university attended.

Number awarded Varies each year.

Deadline June of each year.

[442]
SENECA NATION OF INDIANS HIGHER EDUCATION PROGRAM

Seneca Nation of Indians
Attn: Higher Education Program
8183 Center Road
P.O. Box 231
Salamanca, NY 14779
(716) 945-1790

Purpose To provide financial assistance to Seneca Nation members who are interested in pursuing postsecondary education.

Eligibility Enrolled members of the Seneca Nation are eligible to apply if they are interested in pursuing postsecondary education and are in financial need. They must be accepted in an accredited program of study.

Financial data Up to $4,000. Family income and size determine the exact amount of the award.

Duration Up to 5 years of study, through the attainment of a master's degree.

Number awarded Varies each year.

Deadline Applications may be submitted at any time.

[443]
SEQUOYAH GRADUATE FELLOWSHIPS FOR AMERICAN INDIANS AND ALASKAN NATIVES

Association on American Indian Affairs, Inc.
Attn: Scholarship Coordinator
P.O. Box 268
Sisseton, SD 57262
(605) 698-3998

Purpose To provide financial assistance to Native Americans interested in pursuing graduate education.

Eligibility American Indian and Alaskan Native graduate students who are enrolled members of their tribes and are able to provide proof of enrollment are eligible to apply. Applicants must submit a certificate of degree of Indian blood, a 1- to 2-page essay describing educational goals, the most recent copy of a transcript, a budget of educational costs and resources, and 2 letters of recommendation.

Financial data The stipend is $1,500 per year.

Duration 1 year; may be renewed.

Number awarded 10 each year.

Deadline September of each year.

[444]
SHOSHONE TRIBAL SCHOLARSHIP PROGRAM

Shoshone Higher Education Program
P.O. Box 628
Fort Washakie, WY 82514
(307) 332-3538

Purpose To provide financial assistance to members of the Shoshone Tribe who are interested in undergraduate or graduate education.

Eligibility Enrolled members of the Eastern Shoshone Tribe are eligible to apply. They must be able to demonstrate financial need. The tribal program provides funding for students who do not qualify for the Bureau of Indian Affairs (BIA) Higher Education Program or the BIA Adult Vocational Training Program. Aid is provided to students enrolled in 2-year or 4-year degree programs, in vocational training, or in extension type college courses.

Financial data Up to $1,100 per year for junior college students; up to $2,200 per year for college and graduate students.

Duration 1 year; may be renewed.

Limitations Recipients must attend college full time.

Number awarded Varies; generally, at least 60 each year.

Deadline April or November of each year.

[445]
SOUTH DAKOTA SPACE GRANT CONSORTIUM FELLOWSHIPS AND ASSISTANTSHIPS

South Dakota Space Grant Consortium
c/o South Dakota School of Mines and Technology
Graduate Education and Research Office
501 East St. Joseph Street
Rapid City, SD 57701-3995
(605) 394-2291   Fax: (605) 394-6061
E-mail: psmith@nimbus.ias.sdsmt.edu

Purpose To provide support for space-related activities in South Dakota.

Eligibility This program is open to faculty, graduate students, and undergraduate students at member institutions of the South Dakota Space Grant Consortium (South Dakota School of Mines and Technology and South Dakota State University). Activities include summer faculty fellowships at the EROS Data Center in Sioux Falls, graduate fellowships, and undergraduate assistantships. Participants must be U.S. citizens. Underrepresented groups, primarily Native Americans and women, are especially encouraged to participate.

Financial data Approximately $70,000 per year is available to support the program.

Special features This program is funded by the U.S. National Aeronautics and Space Administration (NASA).

Number awarded Varies each year.

[446]
SUBSTANCE ABUSE FELLOWSHIP FOR MINORITY NURSES

American Nurses Association
Attn: Minority Fellowship Programs
600 Maryland Avenue, S.W., Suite 100 West
Washington, DC 20024-2571
(202) 651-7244   Fax: (202) 789-1413

Purpose To provide financial assistance for pre- and postdoctoral training to nurses pursuing careers in substance abuse prevention, intervention, or comorbidity in minority communities.

Eligibility Applications will be accepted from registered nurses who are members of an ethnic or racial minority group, including but not limited to African Americans, Hispanics, American Indians, Asian Americans, Pacific Islanders and/or others who can demonstrate a commitment to careers in psychiatric nursing, related to ethnic minority mental health. Applicants must be U.S. citizens or permanent residents, registered nurses, members of the American Nurses Association (ANA), and holders of master's degrees pursuing a doctoral degree or postdoctoral training. Students specializing in the following areas of research are encouraged to apply: psychosocial, behavioral, and psychological factors that contribute to alcohol, tobacco, and other drug use; development and testing of intervention strategies designed to improve clinical treatment outcomes for minority populations; and psychosocial and other coping mechanisms designed to prevent or ameliorate substance abuse.

Financial data Awards include a stipend to defray the cost of living; the amounts of awards depend on the availability of funds. This is a scholarship/loan program; recipients of these awards must agree to provide clinical services to underserved populations for a period of time equal to the length of support, within 2 years after termination of such support.

Duration Up to 3 years.

Special features Funds for this program are provided by the Substance Abuse and Mental Health Services Administration.

Deadline January of each year.

[447]
WASHINGTON STATE AMERICAN INDIAN ENDOWED SCHOLARSHIP PROGRAM

Washington Higher Education Coordinating Board
917 Lakeridge Way
P.O. Box 43430
Olympia, WA 98504-3430
(360) 753-7843   Fax: (360) 753-7808
TDD: (360) 753-7809

Purpose To provide financial assistance to American Indian students in Washington State.

Eligibility American Indian students who are Washington residents are eligible for this program if they have close social and cultural ties to an American Indian tribe and/or community in the state and agree to use their education to benefit other American Indians. They must demonstrate financial need and be enrolled, or intend to enroll, at a Washington state college or university on a full-time basis; all qualified applicants are considered, but upper-division and graduate students receive priority. Students who are involved in an academic program that includes any religious worship, exercise, or instruction or the pursuit of any degree in religious, seminarian, or theological academic studies are not eligible.

Financial data The amount of the award depends on the need of the recipient.

Duration 1 year.

Special features This program was created by the Washington legislature in 1990 with an appropriation to an endowment fund with matching contributions from tribes, individuals, and organizations.

Number awarded Varies each year, depending on the availability of funds; in a recent year, 13 scholarships were provided.

Deadline May of each year.

[448]
WHITE EARTH CRITICAL PROFESSIONS PROGRAM

White Earth Tribal Council
Attn: Jeanne McDougall
P.O. Box 70
Naytahwaush, MN 56566
(218) 935-5554   (800) 950-3248
Fax: (218) 935-2593

Purpose To provide financial assistance to Indian students who wish to pursue a course of study leading to an undergraduate or graduate degree in business administration, natural resources or forestry, computer programming, urban or rural planning, or elementary or secondary school teaching.

Eligibility Applicants must be enrolled members of the White Earth Tribal Council of the Minnesota Chippewa Tribe, and full-time students. Applicants are evaluated on academic record, leadership ability, and commitment.

Financial data Award varies; graduate students receive $650 per month (plus $90 per dependent) and undergraduate students receive $450 per month (plus $90 per dependent). Funds are disbursed directly to the recipient's institution of higher education.

Duration 1 quarter/semester; renewable if the applicant remains a full-time student and is in good standing (good standing means at least a 2.5 cumulative grade point average for undergraduate work or a 3.0 for graduate work). Financial need must be demonstrated.

Limitations Applicants must demonstrate a commitment to work for a tribal government or in an Indian community for 2 years after graduation.

Number awarded Varies each year.

Deadline Applications are accepted at any time.

[449]
WISCONSIN NATIVE AMERICAN STUDENT GRANTS

Wisconsin Higher Educational Aids Board
131 West Wilson Street
P.O. Box 7885
Madison, WI 53707-7885
(608) 267-2206   Fax: (608) 267-2808

Purpose To provide financial aids for higher education to Native Americans in Wisconsin.

Eligibility Wisconsin residents who have at least 25 percent Native American blood (of a certified tribe or band) are eligible to apply if they are able to demonstrate financial aid and are interested in attending college on the undergraduate or graduate school level. Applicants must attend a Wisconsin institution, either public, independent, or proprietary. They may be enrolled either full or part time.

Financial data Up to $1,100 per year. Additional funds are available on a matching basis from the U.S. Bureau of Indian Affairs.

Duration Up to 5 years.

Deadline Generally, applications can be submitted at any time.

[450]
YAKAMA TRIBAL SCHOLARSHIP
Yakama Indian Nation
Attn: Higher Education Programs
Department of Human Services
P.O. Box 151
Toppenish, WA 98948
(509) 865-5121   (800) 543-2802
Fax: (509) 865-6994

Purpose To provide financial assistance to Yakama tribe members interested in pursuing undergraduate or graduate education.
Eligibility Eligible to apply are Yakama students of one-quarter or more blood quantum. They must be at least high school graduates and enrolled or planning to enroll in a postsecondary institution. Applicants must have at least a 2.0 grade point average. Scholarships are awarded on the basis of academic achievement rather than financial need.
Financial data Eligible undergraduate students receive $1,000 per year; graduate students receive $2,000 per year. Part-time students receive funding for tuition, books, and transportation; this amount may never exceed the Tribal Scholarship amount.
Duration 1 year; may be renewed.
Limitations Before being awarded the scholarship, recipients must attend an orientation session. Students who drop out of school after receiving scholarship awards must refund the Yakama Tribal Scholarships before being granted additional funding. Tuition amounts kept by the student's college do not count against student refunds.
Number awarded Varies each year.
Deadline June of each year for fall quarter or semester; October of each year for winter quarter or spring semester; January of each year for spring quarter; April of each year for summer term.

[451]
ZUNI HIGHER EDUCATION PROGRAM
Zuni Tribe
Attn: Department of Higher Education
P.O. Box 339
Zuni, NM 87327
(505) 782-4481, ext. 482   Fax: (505) 782-2700

Purpose To provide financial assistance for postsecondary education to members of the Zuni tribe.
Eligibility Enrolled members of the Zuni tribe are eligible to apply if they are high school seniors or graduates, have earned at least a 2.0 grade point average, and are interested in pursuing a college degree, including associate, bachelor's, master's, or doctorate.
Financial data The amount awarded depends on the need of the recipient, up to $1,800 per year.
Duration 1 year; may be renewed.
Number awarded Varies each year.
Deadline March for the summer session, May for the fall term, and September for the spring term.

Native Alaskans

[452]
ALASKA LIBRARY ASSOCIATION SCHOLARSHIP FOR GRADUATE LIBRARY STUDIES
Alaska Library Association
Attn: Aja Markel Razumny
Alaska State Library
P.O. Box 110571
Juneau, AK 99811-0571
(907) 465-2458   Fax: (907) 465-2665

Purpose To provide financial assistance to Alaska residents who are interested in working on a library degree and, upon graduation, working in a library in Alaska.
Eligibility This program is open to applicants who are Alaska residents; have earned a bachelor's degree or higher from an accredited college or university; are eligible for acceptance or are currently enrolled in an accredited graduate degree program in library and information science; are or will be full-time students during the academic year, semester, or quarter for which the scholarship is awarded; and are willing to make a commitment to work in an Alaskan library for at least 1 year after graduation as a paid employee or volunteer. Preference is given to applicants meeting the federal definition of Alaska native ethnicity.
Financial data The stipend is $2,000.
Duration 1 year.
Number awarded 1 each year.
Deadline January of each year.

[453]
ARROW GRADUATE SCHOLARSHIP PROGRAM
Arrow, Inc.
1000 Connecticut Avenue, N.W., Suite 1204
Washington, DC 20036
(202) 296-0685   Fax: (202) 659-4377

Purpose To provide financial assistance to Native American graduate students in any field.
Eligibility Applicants for this program must 1) be enrolled members (or possess at least a quarter Indian blood) from a federally-recognized American Indian tribe or Alaska Native group; 2) be attending an accredited U.S. graduate school; 3) be pursuing a master's or doctoral degree as full-time students; and 4) apply for campus-based aid through the federal financial aid process. Students in all fields are eligible, although 1 scholarship is reserved each year for a student pursuing an advanced degree in nursing.
Financial data The amounts of the awards depends on the availability of funds and the needs of the applicants; in recent years, approximately $20,000 has been available for fellowships.
Duration 1 year.
Special features Arrow, Inc. was founded in 1949 and is dedicated to the advancement of the American Indian. Its range of projects embraces direct aid, education, health, training, and resource development. It recently decided to concentrate its financial aid activities to these large fellowships for Indian graduate students. The program is administered by the American Indian

Graduate Center, 4520 Montgomery Boulevard, N.E., Suite #1-B, Albuquerque, NM 87109-1291, (505) 881-4584, Fax: (505) 884-0427.

Number awarded At least 5 each year.

[454]
ECIM SCHOLARSHIPS

Episcopal Church Center
Attn: Domestic and Foreign Missionary Society
815 Second Avenue
New York, NY 10017-4594
(212) 922-5293   (800) 334-7626, ext. 5293
Fax: (212) 867-0395

Purpose To provide financial assistance to Native Americans interested in theological education within the Episcopal Church in the United States of America (ECUSA).

Eligibility Applicants must be seminarians of American Indian/Alaska Native descent attending an accredited Episcopal institution.

Financial data The amount of the award depends on the needs of the recipient and the availability of funds.

Special features The Episcopal Council of Indian Ministries (ECIM) also awards the David Oakerhater Merit Fellowship to a middler with outstanding achievement and the Oakerhater Award of $2,500 to a seminarian pursuing a Ph.D.

Number awarded Varies each year.

Deadline May of each year.

[455]
GRADUATE FELLOWSHIPS FOR AMERICAN INDIAN AND ALASKAN NATIVE STUDENTS

American Indian Graduate Center
4520 Montgomery Boulevard, NE, Suite 1-B
Albuquerque, NM 87109-1291
(505) 881-4584   Fax: (505) 883-6694

Purpose To provide financial assistance to Native American students interested in pursuing graduate education.

Eligibility To apply, students must be one-quarter or more Indian blood, from a federally-recognized American Indian tribe or Alaska Native group. They must be enrolled as full-time students in a graduate or professional school in the United States pursuing a master's or doctoral degree. Selection is based on academic achievement, financial need, and desire to perform community service after graduation. Preference is not given to any field of study.

Financial data Awards are based on each applicant's unmet financial need, and range from $250 to $3,000 per year.

Duration 1 academic year and summer school, if funds are available; recipients may reapply.

Limitations Since this a supplemental program, applicants must apply in a timely manner for campus-based aid at the college they are attending to be considered for this program. Failure to apply will disqualify an applicant.

Number awarded Varies; generally, more than 400 each year, representing 90 to 120 tribes from at least 25 states.

Deadline May of each year.

[456]
HEALTH CAREERS OPPORTUNITY PROGRAM GRANTS

Health Resources and Services Administration
Attn: Bureau of Health Professions
Division of Disadvantaged Assistance
Parklawn Building, Room 8A09
5600 Fishers Lane
Rockville, MD 20857
(301) 443-4493   Fax: (301) 443-6343
E-mail: bbrooks@hrsa.ssw.dhhs.gov

Purpose To provide financial support for education in health professions to students from disadvantaged backgrounds.

Eligibility This program is open to schools of allopathic medicine, osteopathic medicine, public health, dentistry, veterinary medicine, optometry, pharmacy, allied health, chiropractic and podiatric medicine, and public and nonprofit private schools which offer graduate programs in clinical psychology. Health professions schools are eligible if they identify a cohort of at least 7 disadvantaged students who applied but were not accepted to a health professions school; allied health schools are eligible if they identify a cohort of at least 5 disadvantaged students who have completed an undergraduate degree with a significant science focus and made a late decision to enter an allied health professions school and are in pursuit of a baccalaureate level degree in physical therapy, physician assistant, respiratory therapy, medical technology, or occupational therapy. Applicants must provide the designated students with a program of rigorous science and other education experiences and then admit the students who successfully complete the program or arrange for their admission to another health professions or allied health school. Recipient schools must also provide the students with a prematriculation summer program to ease their transition into the health professions or allied health school, and with counseling and advice on financial aid to assist them to complete successfully their education. Individuals from a disadvantaged background are those who come from an environment that has inhibited them from obtaining the knowledge, skill, and abilities to enroll in and graduate from a health professions school or allied health program, or who come from a low-income family (ranging from an annual income below $10,200 for a family of 1 to $26,700 for a family of 6).

Financial data Approximately $30.1 million is available for this program each year, of which $18.5 million is for continuing grants and $11.6 million is available for new grants, averaging $199,000 each. Of the appropriated funds each year, 20 percent must be obligated for stipends to disadvantaged students of exceptional financial need who are students at schools of allopathic medicine, osteopathic medicine, or dentistry; 10 percent must be obligated to community-based programs (including Indian tribes and Alaska Native villages); and 70 percent must be obligated for grants and contracts to institutions of higher education. Students receive a stipend during their participation in the program.

Duration Grants to institutions are up to 3 years; for students, the program is 1 year, including 6 to 8 weeks in the summer.

Number awarded Approximately 58 new projects are funded each year.

Deadline February of each year.

[457]
HEALTH PROFESSIONS SCHOLARSHIP PROGRAM

Indian Health Service
Attn: Scholarship Program
Twinbrook Metro Plaza, Suite 100
12300 Twinbrook Parkway
Rockville, MD 20852
(301) 443-6197   Fax: (301) 443-6048

Purpose To provide financial support to students enrolled in health professions and allied health professions programs.

Eligibility Applicants must be at least high school graduates and be enrolled in a full-time study program leading to a degree in a health-related professions school within the United States. Even though non-Indian students may apply for this program, the Indian Health Care Improvement Act (P.L. 94-437) requires that priority for the awards be given to Indian and Native Alaskan applicants. Both the number of Indian applicants and the level of appropriations limit the availability of scholarship awards to non-Indians. Qualifying fields of study include associate degree nurse, chemical dependency counseling, clinical psychology (Ph.D. only), computer science (B.S.), dentistry, dietician (B.S.), civil engineering (B.S.), health education (master's only), health records, medical technology (B.S.), medical social work (master's only), allopathic and osteopathic medicine, nurse practitioner, nurse midwife, B.S. nurse, M.S. nurse, optometry, para-optometric, pharmacy (B.S.), physician assistant (B.S.), physical therapy, podiatry (D.P.M.), public health (M.P.H. only), public health nutrition (master's only), radiologic therapy (associate and B.S.), respiratory therapy (associate), and sonography.

Financial data Awards provide for payment of a monthly stipend to cover living expenses, including room and board, tuition and required fees, and all other reasonable educational expenses; the total award is approximately $18,000. In a recent year, approximately $6,300,000 was available for continuation awards and $1,860,751 for new awards.

Duration 1 year; may be renewed for up to 3 additional years.

Limitations Upon completion of their program of study, recipients are required to provide payback service of 1 year for each year of scholarship support at the Indian Health Service, 1 of 638 tribal health programs, an urban health program, or in private practice serving a substantial number of Indians.

Number awarded Varies; In a recent year, 350 continuing and 103 new awards were provided.

Deadline April of each year.

[458]
HOWARD ROCK FOUNDATION SCHOLARSHIPS

Howard Rock Foundation
1577 C Street, Suite 304
Anchorage, AK 99501
(907) 274-5400   (800) 478-2332 (within AK)
Fax: (907) 263-9971

Purpose To provide financial assistance to Native Alaskans who are interested in pursuing a college degree.

Eligibility This program is open to Native Alaskans who are shareholders in a village corporation or tribal government that belongs to the Alaska Village Initiative (formerly the Community Enterprise Development Corporation of Alaska). The applicant must have attended high school in Alaska, be able to demonstrate financial need, be enrolled as a full-time student in an accredited undergraduate or graduate program at a college or university, and be majoring in a field of study that promotes the economic well-being of life for residents of rural Alaska.

Financial data Varies; recently, undergraduate scholarships have been $2,500 and graduate fellowships have been $5,000.

Duration 1 year; may be renewed.

Special features Recipients may attend school anywhere in the United States. This program began as the Bush Development Fund, created by the Community Enterprise Development Corporation of Alaska (CEDC) in 1986. In 1992 the name was changed to Howard Rock Foundation.

Number awarded Varies; recently 4 undergraduate and 1 graduate scholarships have been awarded each year.

Deadline February of each year.

[459]
INDIAN FELLOWSHIP PROGRAM

Department of Education
Attn: Office of Elementary and Secondary Education
Office of Indian Education
Portals Building, Room 4300
600 Independence Avenue, S.W.
Washington, DC 20202-6335
(202) 260-1683   E-mail: Indian_Fellowships@ed.gov

Purpose To provide financial assistance to graduate students and selected undergraduate students who are Native Americans interested in preparing for careers in medicine, law, engineering, natural resources, business administration, education, psychology, and related fields.

Eligibility American Indian students who are attending or have been accepted for admission at an accredited institution of higher learning and working toward 1) a graduate degree in medicine, law, education, psychology, clinical psychology, or related fields or 2) a graduate or undergraduate degree in natural resources, business administration, engineering, or related fields may apply. All applicants must be U.S. citizens and Indians. By federal government definition, this means that applicants must be 1) a member of a tribe, band, or other organized group of Indians (including those tribes, bands, or groups terminated since 1940 and those recognized by the state in which they reside); 2) a descendant in the first or second degree of any individual described above; 3) considered by the Secretary of the Interior to be an Indian for any purpose or be an Eskimo, Aleut, or other Alaska Native; or 4) a member of an organized Indian group that received a grant under the Indian Education Act of 1988. Selection is based on academic record (60 points), letters of recommendation (15 points), and an essay on career goals, why the chosen field of study will benefit Indian people, life experiences and personal and family expectations that will enhance the applicant's anticipated career accomplishments, and anticipated commitment to providing service to Indian people (25 points).

Financial data Fellowships are intended to provide full financing for a student's educational expenses or to supplement other sources of financial aid.

Duration Up to 2 years for a master's degree; up to 4 years for an undergraduate or doctorate degree. Each year's renewal is dependent upon appropriations from Congress and satisfactory performance by the fellow.

Special features Up to 10 percent of the awards are to persons receiving training in guidance counseling with a specialty in the area of alcohol and substance abuse counseling and education.

Limitations Individuals receiving assistance under this program are required to perform work related to the training received and that benefits Indian people, or repay all or a prorated part of the assistance received. This payback must begin within 6 months from the date of the completion of the training and is equivalent to the total period of time for which training was actually received.

Number awarded Varies; approximately 60 continuation and 550 new awards are made each year.

Deadline January of each year.

[460]
JOHN CARTER BROWN LIBRARY SHORT-TERM RESEARCH FELLOWSHIPS

John Carter Brown Library
Brown University
P.O. Box 1894
Providence, RI 02912
(401) 863-2725   E-mail: Karen_DeMaria@Brown.edu

Purpose To support scholars interested in conducting research at the John Carter Brown Library, which is renowned for its collection of historical sources pertaining to the Americas prior to 1830.

Eligibility These fellowships are open to Americans and foreign nationals who are engaged in pre- or postdoctoral or independent research. Graduate students must have passed their preliminary examinations at the time of application.

Financial data The stipend is $1,000 per month.

Duration From 2 to 4 months.

Special features Among the emphases of the library's holdings are works dealing with Native Americans in North and South America, colonial architecture books, economic history, maritime history, and works on the adaptation of religion and religious institutions to the New World.

Limitations Fellows are expected to be in regular residence at the library and to participate in the intellectual life of Brown University for the duration of the program.

Number awarded 15 to 17 each year.

Deadline January of each year.

[461]
NATIVE AMERICAN SEMINARY SCHOLARSHIPS

Presbyterian Church (U.S.A.)
Attn: Office of Financial Aid for Studies
100 Witherspoon Street, Room M042
Louisville, KY 40202-1396
(502) 569-5776   Fax: (502) 569-5018

Purpose To provide financial assistance to Native American students interested in preparing for church occupations.

Eligibility Native American and Alaska Native students may apply for the award if they are U.S. citizens or permanent residents, can demonstrate financial need, are in good academic standing, and are in 1 of the following 3 categories: 1) theological student enrolled as an inquirer or candidate by a presbytery of the Presbyterian Church (U.S.A.), preparing for a church occupation, and enrolled in a theological institution approved by the students' Committee on Preparation for Ministry; 2) Presbyterian Church (U.S.A.) member enrolled in a program of theological education by extension, such as the NATEC; or 3) inquirer, candidate, minister, or member of the Presbyterian Church (U.S.A.) in other church occupations pursuing an approved program of continuing education.

Financial data The amounts of the awards depend on the availability of funds.

Number awarded Varies each year.

[462]
NEW YORK STATE REGENTS HEALTH CARE OPPORTUNITY SCHOLARSHIPS

New York State Education Department
Attn: Bureau of Postsecondary Grants Administration
Cultural Education Center
Albany, NY 12230
(518) 486-1319

Purpose To provide financial assistance to minority or educationally disadvantaged students who are beginning or enrolled in an approved program in medicine or dentistry.

Eligibility Candidates must be U.S. citizens or permanent residents and legal residents of New York for 1 year prior to application. The law requires that awards be made to eligible candidates in the following order: first priority is given to any candidate who is economically disadvantaged and a minority group member historically underrepresented in the professions (Black Americans, Hispanic Americans, Native Americans, or Alaskan Natives); second priority is given to any candidate who is a minority group member underrepresented in the professions; and third priority is given to any candidate who is enrolled in or a graduate of 1 of these state-supported opportunity programs: Search for Education, Elevation and Knowledge (SEEK) or College Discovery at City University; Educational Opportunity Program (EOP) in the State University system; or Higher Education Opportunity Program (HEOP) at an independent college.

Financial data Scholarship holders receive from $1,000 to $10,000 per year, depending on income.

Duration Up to 4 years.

Limitations No award can exceed the actual cost of attendance. After completion of their professional studies, scholarship holders are required to practice 12 months for each annual payment received, including at least 24 months in a designated physician-shortage area in New York.

Number awarded 100 each year; 80 of the awards are made for medicine and 20 for dentistry.

Deadline February of each year.

[463]
NEW YORK STATE REGENTS PROFESSIONAL OPPORTUNITY SCHOLARSHIPS

New York State Education Department
Attn: Bureau of Postsecondary Grants Administration
Cultural Education Center
Albany, NY 12230
(518) 486-1319

Purpose To expand educational opportunities for underrepresented minority and economically disadvanataged students interested in pursuing professional careers.

Eligibility Candidates must be U.S. citizens or permanent residents and legal residents of New York for 1 year prior to application. The law requires that awards be made to eligible candidates in the following order: first priority is given to any candidate who is economically disadvantaged and a minority group member historically underrepresented in the professions (Black Americans,

Hispanic Americans, Native Americans, or Alaskan Natives); second priority is given to any candidate who is a minority group member underrepresented in the professions; and third priority is given to any candidate who is enrolled in or a graduate of 1 of these state-supported opportunity programs: Search for Education, Elevation and Knowledge (SEEK) or College Discovery at City University; Educational Opportunity Program (EOP) in the State University system; or Higher Education Opportunity Program (HEOP) at an independent college.

Financial data The stipends range from $1,000 to $5,000 per year, depending on income.

Duration Up to 4 years.

Special features Scholarships are available for study in the following areas: accounting (baccalaureate level), architecture (baccalaureate or master's), chiropratic medicine (doctoral), dental hygiene (associate), engineering (baccalaureate), landscape architecture (baccalaureate or master's), law (juris doctoral), nursing (baccalaureate), occupational therapy (baccalaureate or master's), occupational therapy assistant (associate), ophthalmic dispensing (associate), optometry (doctoral), pharmacy (baccalaureate), physical therapist assistant (associate), physical therapy (baccalaureate or master's), physicians assistant (baccalaureate or master's), psychology (doctoral), social work (master's), speech-language pathology/audiology (master's), and veterinary medicine (doctoral).

Limitations No award can exceed the actual cost of attendance. After completion of their professional studies, scholarship holders are required to practice in New York for 12 months for each annual payment received.

Number awarded 220 each year.

Deadline January of each year.

[464]
PRE-LAW SUMMER INSTITUTE FOR AMERICAN INDIANS AND ALASKA NATIVES

American Indian Law Center, Inc.
Attn: Director
P.O. Box 4456, Station A
Albuquerque, NM 87196
(505) 277-5462   Fax: (505) 277-1035

Purpose To prepare Native Americans to be successful law students and successful lawyers at a pre-law summer institute.

Eligibility To be eligible, Native Americans (American Indians and Alaska Natives) must have completed their undergraduate degrees, taken the LSAT, and applied to law schools accredited by the American Bar Association. They must be enrolled members of a federally-recognized Indian tribe.

Financial data Students receive funding to cover tuition, textbooks, personal expenses, and some travel; the amount of funding depends on the number of qualified participants who are admitted, but is usually at least $1,200 plus $200 for travel.

Duration 8 weeks during the summer.

Special features The institute is conducted at the University of New Mexico School of Law. Participants take courses in Indian law, constitutional law, criminal law, and other subjects. Funding is provided by the U.S. Bureau of Indian Affairs.

Number awarded Between 25 and 40 each year.

Deadline March of each year.

[465]
SEQUOYAH GRADUATE FELLOWSHIPS FOR AMERICAN INDIANS AND ALASKAN NATIVES

Association on American Indian Affairs, Inc.
Attn: Scholarship Coordinator
P.O. Box 268
Sisseton, SD 57262
(605) 698-3998

Purpose To provide financial assistance to Native Americans interested in pursuing graduate education.

Eligibility American Indian and Alaskan Native graduate students who are enrolled members of their tribes and are able to provide proof of enrollment are eligible to apply. Applicants must submit a certificate of degree of Indian blood, a 1- to 2-page essay describing educational goals, the most recent copy of a transcript, a budget of educational costs and resources, and 2 letters of recommendation.

Financial data The stipend is $1,500 per year.

Duration 1 year; may be renewed.

Number awarded 10 each year.

Deadline September of each year.

Native Pacific Islanders

[466]
AAJA HAWAII CHAPTER SCHOLARSHIPS

Asian American Journalists Association—Hawaii Chapter
P.O. Box 22592
Honolulu, HI 96823

Purpose To provide financial assistance to Asian/Pacific Islander students in Hawaii who are interested in careers in broadcast or print journalism.

Eligibility These scholarships are open to Asian/Pacific Islander students in Hawaii who are planning a career in broadcast or print journalism. Applicants may be high school seniors, college undergraduates, or graduate students. Selection is based on academic achievement, financial need, writing or broadcasting skills, recommendations, and essays on their career goals and responsibility to their Asian heritage.

Financial data Stipends are up to $1,000.

Duration 1 year; may be renewed.

Number awarded 2 each year.

Deadline April of each year.

[467]
AAJA LOS ANGELES GENERAL SCHOLARSHIPS

Asian American Journalists Association—Los Angeles Chapter
231 East Third Street
Los Angeles, CA 90013
(213) 206-0169   Fax: (818) 570-9300

Purpose To provide financial assistance to Asian/Pacific Islander students in southern California who are interested in careers in journalism.

Eligibility These scholarships are open to Asian/Pacific Islander students who are planning a career in broadcast, photo, or print journalism. Applicants may be high school seniors, college undergraduates, or graduate students who are either permanently residing in or attending a school in the southern California region. They do not need to be a journalism, photojournalism, or communications major, but applicants must show serious intent to pursue a journalism career. Selection is based on commitment to the field of journalism, scholastic achievement, journalistic ability and potential, a sensitivity to Asian American issues demonstrated by community involvement, and financial need.

Financial data Stipends are up to $2,000.

Duration 1 year; may be renewed.

Number awarded At least 5 each year.

Deadline April of each year.

[468]
AAJA–NEWHOUSE NATIONAL SCHOLARSHIPS

Asian American Journalists Association
1765 Sutter Street, Room 1000
San Francisco, CA 94115-3217
(415) 346-2051   Fax: (415) 346-6343
E-mail: HienN@aaja.org

Purpose To provide financial assistance for study in print journalism to undergraduate and graduate students, especially Asian Pacific Americans.

Eligibility This program is open to all students, but especially welcomes applications from historically underrepresented Asian Pacific American groups, including Southeast Asians, South Asians, Koreans, Filipinos, and Pacific Islanders. Applicants may be graduating high school seniors who declare journalism as a major or undergraduate or graduate students pursuing a degree in journalism and a career in print journalism. Selection is based on scholastic ability, commitment to journalism, sensitivity to Asian American issues as demonstrated by community involvement, journalistic ability, and financial need.

Financial data The grant is $2,000 per year.

Duration 4 years for a graduating high school senior; 1 year for current undergraduate or graduate students.

Special features This program began in 1994; it is funded by Newhouse News Service and administered by the Asian American Journalists Association.

Number awarded 1 each year to a graduating high school senior; several each year to current undergraduate and graduate students.

Deadline April of each year.

[469]
AHAHUI KALAKAUA SCHOLARSHIPS

Ahahui Kalakaua Association of Hawaiian Civic Clubs
c/o Violet Hughes
1330 36th Avenue
San Francisco, CA 94122

Purpose To provide financial assistance to students of Hawaiian ancestry who live in California and are interested in pursuing a college education (on the undergraduate or graduate level).

Eligibility Financially needy students of Hawaiian ancestry who were born in Hawaii or have parents who were born in Hawaii are eligible to apply if they are interested in pursuing postsecondary education and live in northern California (north of Monterey, Kings, Tulare, and Inyo counties).

Financial data Stipends range from $150 to $750.

Duration 1 year.

Limitations Requests for applications must be accompanied by a $2 fee.

Number awarded Varies each year.

Deadline April of each year.

[470]
ASIAN PACIFIC WOMEN'S NETWORK SCHOLARSHIPS

Asian Pacific Women's Network
Attn: Scholarship Committee
P.O. Box 86995
Los Angeles, CA 90086
(213) 891-6040   (909) 596-5331
Fax: (909) 596-5331

Purpose To encourage Asian/Pacific women to pursue life change through academic, vocational, trade, or other skill development programs.

Eligibility Eligible to apply are women of Asian or Pacific Island ancestry who are 1) residents of 1 of the 5 southern California counties (Los Angeles, Orange, Riverside, San Bernardino, or Ventura), 2) interested in pursuing further education (graduate or undergraduate) or training (vocational or trade), and 3) accepted into a college, university, vocational, or trade school. Women from immigrant and refugee backgrounds are particularly encouraged to apply, as are women returning to school after raising their children, making a mid-career change, and pursuing leadership training.

Financial data The stipend is $1,000.

Duration 1 year.

Limitations Finalists must provide financial data and participate in a personal interview.

Number awarded 4 each year.

Deadline June of each year.

[471]
BLOSSOM KALAMA EVANS MEMORIAL FUND

Hawai'i Community Foundation
900 Fort Street Mall, Suite 1300
Honolulu, HI 96813
(808) 566-5570   Fax: (808) 521-6286

Purpose To provide financial assistance to Hawaiians who are interested in studying Hawaiian language or Hawaiian Studies.

Eligibility Eligible to apply are residents of Hawaii who are college juniors, seniors, or graduate students majoring in either Hawaiian Studies or Hawaiian language. Applicants must demonstrate financial need and academic achievement (at least a 3.0 grade point average). Preference is given to applicants of Hawaiian ancestry. Applicants must write an essay describing their interests and goals in pursuing Hawaiian Studies or language and how they plan to use their studies to contribute to the community. Members of the Hawaiian Girls Golf Association are not eligible.

Financial data The amount awarded varies, depending upon the needs of the recipient.

Deadline February of each year.

[472]
EPISCOPAL ASIAN AMERICAN MINISTRY LEADERSHIP DEVELOPMENT FUND

Episcopal Church Center
Attn: Domestic and Foreign Missionary Society
815 Second Avenue
New York, NY 10017-4594
(212) 922-5293   (800) 334-7626, ext. 5293
Fax: (212) 867-0395

Purpose To provide financial assistance to Asian Americans interested in theological education within the Episcopal Church in the United States of America (ECUSA).

Eligibility Applicants must be students of Asian or Pacific Islands descent sponsored by their diocese. They must be pursuing theological education leading to ordination in the ECUSA or in another branch of the Anglican Communion, or ordained clergy pursuing courses of continuing education to improve their ministry skills.

Financial data The amount of the award depends on the needs of the recipient and the availability of funds.

Number awarded Varies each year.

Deadline May of each year.

[473]
JOHN ROSS FOUNDATION SCHOLARSHIPS

Hawai'i Community Foundation
900 Fort Street Mall, Suite 1300
Honolulu, HI 96813
(808) 566-5570   Fax: (808) 521-6286

Purpose To provide financial assistance to residents of Hawaii's Big Island who are interested in attending college and returning to the Island.

Eligibility This program is open to residents of Hawaii's Big Island; preference is given to those born on and with ancestors from this area who plan to remain or return to the Big Island (applicants should write about this in their personal statement). They may plan to study on the undergraduate (preferred) or graduate school level. They must be able to demonstrate academic achievement (at least a 3.0 grade point average), good moral character, and financial need. In addition to filling out the standard application form, they must write a short statement, indicating why they want to attend college, their course of study, and their career goals.

Financial data A stipend is awarded.

Duration The scholarship is awarded annually.

Special features Recipients may attend college in Hawaii or on the mainland.

Number awarded 1 or more each year.

Deadline February of each year.

[474]
KAIULANI HOME FOR GIRLS TRUST SCHOLARSHIP

Hawai'i Community Foundation
900 Fort Street Mall, Suite 1300
Honolulu, HI 96813
(808) 566-5570   Fax: (808) 521-6286

Purpose To provide financial support for the undergraduate or graduate education of young Hawaiian women.

Eligibility By court order, preference is given to girls of Hawaiian or part-Hawaiian descent. However, girls of other racial backgrounds are encouraged to apply and will not be excluded. Applicants must be residents of Hawaii, have graduated from a public or private high school with a minimum grade point average of 3.0, and be enrolled or intend to enroll full time in an accredited business school, community college, 4-year college, or university. In addition, applicants must demonstrate financial need.

Financial data Grants range from $200 to $1,500 per year.

Duration 1 year; renewable.

Special features Awards are tenable either in Hawaii or on the mainland. The fund was established with property formerly used to provide boarding home facilities for young women of Hawaiian ancestry.

Number awarded Approximately 75 each year.

Deadline February of each year.

[475]
KAMEHAMEHA SCHOOLS BISHOP ESTATE SCHOLARSHIPS

Kamehameha Schools
Attn: Financial Aid Department
1887 Makuakane Street
Honolulu, HI 96817-1887
(808) 842-8216   Fax: (808) 841-0660

Purpose To provide financial assistance to Native Hawaiians who are interested in pursuing postsecondary education.

Eligibility Native Hawaiians (or part Hawaiians) who have graduated from high school in Hawaii are eligible to apply if they can demonstrate academic excellence and financial need. They must be pursuing undergraduate or graduate degrees at accredited 2-year or 4-year colleges in Hawaii; graduate students may attend out-of-state schools if their major field of study is not available in Hawaii. Students who graduated from the Kamehameha Schools are not eligible to apply.

Financial data The amount awarded varies, depending upon the financial need of the recipient; recently, the average award was $3,214.

Duration 1 year; may be renewed.

Special features Native Hawaiian means any descendant of the aboriginal inhabitants of the Hawaiian islands prior to 1778.

Number awarded Varies; in a recent year, 1,630 students received these scholarships.

Deadline February of each year.

[476]
NATIVE HAWAIIAN HEALTH SCHOLARSHIP PROGRAM

Health Resources and Services Administration
Attn: Bureau of Primary Health Care
Division of Scholarships and Loan Repayments
4350 East-West Highway, 10th Floor
Bethesda, MD 20814
(301) 594-4400   (800) 435-6464
(808) 842-8562   Fax: (301) 594-4981

Purpose To provide financial assistance to Native Hawaiians for training in health professions in exchange for service in a federally designated health professional shortage area (HPSA) in Hawaii.

Eligibility Applicants must be Native Hawaiians training in allopathic or osteopathic medicine, dentistry, clinical psychology, registered nursing, nurse midwifery, psychiatric nursing, public health/community nursing, social work, dental hygienist, physician assistant, or master of public health degree. Recipients must agree to serve in a federally designated HPSA in Hawaii on completion of training.

Financial data A stipend and other reasonable costs are paid directly to the scholar and full tuition is paid directly to the health professional school.

Duration 1 year; may be renewed for up to 3 additional years.

Limitations Participants are obligated to provide full-time clinical primary health care services to populations in federally-designated, high-priority HPSAs (these include Native Hawaiian health centers and medical facilities of the Federal Bureau of Prisons). Participants incur 1 year of obligated service in the National Health Service Corps for each full or partial year of support provided under this program. The minimum service obligation is 2 years.

Number awarded Varies each year, depending upon the funding available.

Deadline March of each year.

[477]
NATIVE HAWAIIAN HIGHER EDUCATION PROGRAM

Department of Education
Attn: Office of Postsecondary Education
Division of Higher Education Incentive Programs
Portals Building, Suite C-80
600 Independence Avenue, S.W.
Washington, DC 20202-5329
(202) 260-3608   Fax: (202) 260-7615

Purpose To provide direct grants for a program of graduate and undergraduate fellowship assistance to Native Hawaiian students.

Eligibility Native Hawaiian private nonprofit educational organizations or educational entities with experience in developing or operating Native Hawaiian programs or programs of instruction conducted in the Native Hawaiian language are eligible. They may apply for funding for the following activities: 1) full or partial scholarship support for Native Hawaiian students enrolled at 2- or 4-year degree granting institutions of higher education with awards to be based on academic potential and financial need; 2) full or partial fellowship support for Native Hawaiian students enrolled at graduate degree granting institutions of higher education with priority given to providing fellowship support for professions in which Native Hawaiians are underrepresented and with fellowship awards to be based on academic potential and financial need; 3) counseling and support services for students receiving financial assistance under this program; 4) college preparation and guidance counseling at secondary school level for students who may be eligible for support under this program; 5) appropriate research and evaluation of the activities authorized under this program; and 6) implementation of faculty development programs for the improvement and matriculation of Native Hawaiian students.

Financial data Awards to institutions range up to $1,400,000 and average $467,000; awards to students are established by the institutions.

Duration Up to 5 years.

Limitations Students must apply directly to the institution, not to the Department of Education. For a list of participating institutions, write to the address above.

Number awarded 2 to 4 each year.

Deadline July of each year.

[478]
PETER IMAMURA MEMORIAL SCHOLARSHIP

Asian American Journalists Association—Los Angeles
  Chapter
244 South San Pedro Street, Room 411
Los Angeles, CA 90012
(213) 426-4525

Purpose To provide financial assistance to Asian/Pacific Islander students in southern California who are interested in careers in journalism.

Eligibility These scholarships are open to Asian/Pacific Islander students who are planning a career in broadcast, photo, or print journalism. Applicants may be high school seniors, college undergraduates, or graduate students who are either permanently residing in or attending a school in the southern California region. They do not need to be a journalism, photojournalism, or communications major, but applicants must show serious intent to pursue a journalism career. Selection is based on commitment to the field of journalism, scholastic achievement, journalistic ability and potential, a sensitivity to Asian American issues demonstrated by community involvement, and financial need.

Financial data The stipend is up to $1,000.

Duration 1 year.

Special features This award honors a former reporter at the *Riverside Press-Enterprise* and editor of the *Pacific Citizen*.

Number awarded 1 each year.

Deadline April of each year.

[479]
PROGRAM FOR MINORITY RESEARCH TRAINING IN PSYCHIATRY

American Psychiatric Association
Attn: Office of Research
1400 K Street, N.W.
Washington, DC 20005
(202) 682-6225   (800) 852-1390

Purpose To provide financial assistance to minority medical students and residents interested in psychiatric research.

Eligibility This program is open to underrepresented minorities (American Indians, Blacks/African Americans, Hispanics, and Pacific Islanders) at 3 levels: medical students, residents, and graduates of residency programs. All candidates must be interested in training at research-intensive departments of psychiatry in major U.S. medical schools. Training sites with excellence as demonstrated by research facilities and resources, funded research, research faculty (including minority researchers), and successful training history are considered preferable.

Financial data Annual stipends are $10,008 for medical students, from $19,608 to $28,200 for residents, and up to $32,300 for post-residency fellows. Other benefits include travel funds to attend the annual meeting of the American Psychiatric Association (APA) or the American College of Neuropsychopharmacology, and limited tuition assistance for full-time trainees to attend specific courses that are required as part of their training.

Duration For medical students, 2 to 6 months, either during an elective period or as a summer experience; for residents, 3 to 6 months within or outside the home institution, although a year of full-time research training is also possible; for post-residency fellows, 2 years, although a third year is possible if appropriate to a trainee's career development.

Special features This program is funded by the National Institute of Mental Health and administered by the APA.

Number awarded Varies each year.

Deadline Medical students and residents seeking less than 1 year of training may apply at any time, but at least 3 months before the proposed training is to begin; medical students seeking summer training should apply by March of each year; residents seeking a year or more of training and post-residency fellows should apply by November of each year.

[480]
ROSEMARY & NELLIE EBRIE FOUNDATION SCHOLARSHIPS

Hawai'i Community Foundation
900 Fort Street Mall, Suite 1300
Honolulu, HI 96813
(808) 566-5570   Fax: (808) 521-6286

Purpose To provide financial assistance to Hawaii residents of Hawaiian descent who are interested in studying on the undergraduate or graduate school level.

Eligibility This program is open to Hawaii residents who 1) were born on the Big Island of Hawaii, 2) have been long-term residents of the Big Island, and 3) are of Hawaiian ancestry. They must be interested in pursuing an academic degree on the undergraduate or graduate school level and must be able to demonstrate academic achievement (at least a 3.0 grade point averag), good moral character, and financial need. In addition to filling out the standard application form, they must write a short statement, indicating why they want to attend college, their course of study, and their career goals.

Financial data A stipend is awarded.

Duration The scholarship is awarded annually.

Special features Recipients may attend college in Hawaii or on the mainland.

Number awarded 1 or more each year.

Deadline February of each year.

[481]
SAMUEL R. WALLIS MEMORIAL SCHOLARSHIP

Wilcox Hospital Foundation
3420 Kuhio Highway
Lihue, HI 96766
(808) 245-1198   Fax: (808) 245-1171

Purpose To provide financial assistance to medical students from Hawaii.

Eligibility Eligible to apply for this support are Hawaii residents who are working on a medical degree or nonresidents attending medical school in Hawaii. Preference is given to Native Hawaiians and/or students from Kauai or the island of Hawaii who plan to practice medicine in Hawaii.

Financial data The stipend is $2,000.

Duration 1 year.

Number awarded 3 each year.

Deadline April of each year.

[482]
SUBSTANCE ABUSE FELLOWSHIP FOR MINORITY NURSES

American Nurses Association
Attn: Minority Fellowship Programs
600 Maryland Avenue, S.W., Suite 100 West
Washington, DC 20024-2571
(202) 651-7244   Fax: (202) 789-1413

Purpose To provide financial assistance for pre- and postdoctoral training to nurses pursuing careers in substance abuse prevention, intervention, or comorbidity in minority communities.

Eligibility Applications will be accepted from registered nurses who are members of an ethnic or racial minority group, including but not limited to African Americans, Hispanics, American Indians, Asian Americans, Pacific Islanders and/or others who can demonstrate a commitment to careers in psychiatric nursing, related to ethnic minority mental health. Applicants must be U.S. citizens or permanent residents, registered nurses, members of the American Nurses Association (ANA), and holders of master's degrees pursuing a doctoral degree or postdoctoral training. Students specializing in the following areas of research are encouraged to apply: psychosocial, behavioral, and psychological factors that contribute to alcohol, tobacco, and other drug use; development and testing of intervention strategies designed to improve clinical treatment outcomes for minority populations; and psychosocial and other coping mechanisms designed to prevent or ameliorate substance abuse.

Financial data Awards include a stipend to defray the cost of living; the amounts of awards depend on the availability of funds. This is a scholarship/loan program; recipients of these awards must agree to provide clinical services to underserved populations for a period of time equal to the length of support, within 2 years after termination of such support.

Duration Up to 3 years.

Special features Funds for this program are provided by the Substance Abuse and Mental Health Services Administration.

Deadline January of each year.

Native Americans in General

[483]
ABC NATIVE AMERICAN GRANTS

American Baptist Financial Aid Program
Attn: Educational Ministries, ABC/USA
P.O. Box 851
Valley Forge, PA 19482-0851
(800) ABC-3USA, ext. 2067   Fax: (610) 768-2056

Purpose To provide financial assistance to Native American students interested in preparing for a ministerial career.

Eligibility This program is open to Native Americans who are American Baptists and interested in preparing for ministerial service.

Financial data Partial tuition scholarships are offered.

Duration 1 year.

Special features This program is offered in cooperation with the TEE program: Theological Education by Extension.

Number awarded Varies each year.

[484]
ADVANCED INDUSTRIAL CONCEPTS MATERIALS SCIENCE PROGRAM

Oak Ridge Institute for Science and Education
Attn: Science/Engineering Education Division
P.O. Box 117
Oak Ridge, TN 37831-0117
(423) 576-9279   (423) 576-2194
(800) 569-7749   Fax: (423) 576-3643
E-mail: aicmsp@orau.gov

Purpose To provide financial assistance to selected minorities for graduate study and work experience in materials science and related disciplines.

Eligibility This program is open to African American or Native American graduating seniors and graduate students who have not completed their first year. They must be enrolled or planning to enroll in an accredited U.S. institution with a major in materials science, materials engineering, metallurgical engineering, polymer science and engineering, ceramic engineering, chemical engineering, or chemistry.

Financial data Participants receive a monthly stipend of $1,200, a dislocation allowance of $300 during the research appointment, and payment of tuition and fees up to $6,000 per year.

Duration 12 months; renewable to 24 months.

Special features The program includes a research appointment at Oak Ridge National Laboratory (ORNL) in Tennessee. This program is funded by ORNL and administered by the Science/Engineering Education Division (SEED) of Oak Ridge Institute for Science and Education (ORISE).

Number awarded Varies each year.

Deadline February of each year.

[485]
AEJMC COMMUNICATION THEORY AND METHODOLOGY DIVISION MINORITY DOCTORAL SCHOLARSHIP

Association for Education in Journalism and Mass
    Communication
c/o Executive Director
College of Journalism
University of South Carolina
1621 College Street
Columbia, SC 29208-0251
(803) 777-2005   Fax: (803) 777-4728
E-mail: aejmchq@univscvm.csd.scarolina.edu

Purpose To provide financial assistance for minorities who are interested in working on a doctorate in mass communication.

Eligibility Applicants must be members of the association or the Communication Theory and Methodology Division and be enrolled in a Ph.D. program in mass communication. They must submit 2 letters of recommendation, a resume, and a brief letter outlining their research interests and career plans.

Financial data The amount awarded ranges from $1,000 to $1,300.

Duration 1 year.

Special features For the name and address of the current chair of the Communication Theory and Methodology committee, write or call the address above.

Number awarded 1 or more each year.

[486]
AEROSPACE ILLINOIS SPACE GRANT CONSORTIUM PROGRAM

Aerospace Illinois Space Grant Consortium
c/o University of Illinois at Urbana-Champaign
College of Engineering
Aeronautical and Astronomical Engineering
306F Talbot Lab
104 South Wright Street
Urbana, IL 61801
(217) 244-7646   Fax: (217) 244-0720
E-mail: solomon@uxh.cso.uiuc.edu

Purpose To provide financial support for space-related academic activities in Illinois.

Eligibility Aerospace Illinois has established 4 program elements: 1) undergraduate/high school teaching and research, to attract undergraduates and secondary school students to modern aerospace science and engineering; 2) training in graduate research, through research experiences focused on aerospace science and engineering; 3) outreach and public service, to employ the region's extensive existing public educational information networks and outreach programs to provide a window to the highest quality student populations with emphasis on minorities, women, and persons with disabilities; and 4) fellowships with industry, to add substantially to the national aerospace science and engineering pool. Currently, 2 of the Aerospace Illinois member institutions (University of Illinois at Urbana-Champaign and Illinois Institute of Technology) use funding for aerospace engineering, 2 member institutions (University of Chicago and Northwestern University) use funding for aerospace sciences, 2 affiliate institutions (Southern Illinois University and Western Illinois University) use funding for teacher education and training, 1 affiliate institution (McDonnell-Douglas Corporation) uses funding for research initiatives, and 1 affiliate institution (Argonne National Laboratory) uses funding for research and K-12 education. Students, teachers, researchers, and others interested in Aerospace Illinois activities should contact the institutions to obtain further information on program opportunities. Aerospace Illinois is a component of the U.S. National Aeronautics and Space Administration (NASA) Space Grant program.

Financial data Awards depend on the availability of funds and the nature of the proposal.

Duration Depends on the program.

Special features This program is funded by NASA.

Number awarded Varies each year.

[487]
AICPA FELLOWSHIPS FOR MINORITY DOCTORAL STUDENTS

American Institute of Certified Public Accountants
1211 Avenue of the Americas
New York, NY 10036-8775
(212) 596-6270   Fax: (212) 596-6213

Purpose To enable more minorities to enter or advance in the field of teaching accounting at the college level.

Eligibility To be eligible, an applicant must be a minority student who has applied to and/or been accepted into a doctoral program with a concentration in accounting, has earned a master's degree or completed a minimum of 3 years of full-time work in the practice of accounting, is attending or planning to attend full time and work consistently to attain a Ph.D. degree, and agrees not to accept responsibility for teaching more than 1 course as a teaching assistant or working more than 25 percent as a research assistant. In selecting the recipient, financial need is considered. All applicants must be U.S. citizens. For purposes of this program, the American Institute of Certified Public Accountants (AICPA) considers minority students as those of Black, Native American/Alaskan Native, or Pacific Island races, or of Hispanic ethnic origin.

Financial data   The stipend is $12,000 per year.

Duration   1 year; may be renewed up to 3 additional years.

Deadline   March of each year.

[488]
ALABAMA SPACE GRANT CONSORTIUM GRADUATE FELLOWSHIP PROGRAM

Alabama Space Grant Consortium
c/o University of Alabama in Huntsville
Materials Science Building, Room 205
Huntsville, AL 35899
(205) 890-6028   Fax: (205) 890-6061
E-mail: jcgregory@matsci.uah.edu
E-mail: jfreasoner@matsci.uah.edu

Purpose   To provide financial assistance for graduate study or research related to the space sciences at universities participating in the Alabama Space Grant Consortium.

Eligibility   This program is open to graduate students enrolled at 1 of the 6 universities participating in the Alabama Space Grant Consortium: University of Alabama in Huntsville, Alabama A&M University, University of Alabama, University of Alabama at Birmingham, University of South Alabama, and Auburn University. Applicants must be studying in a field related to space, including the physical, natural, and biological sciences, engineering, education, economics, business, sociology, behavioral sciences, computer science, communications, law, international affairs, and public administration. They must be U.S. citizens. Individuals from underrepresented groups—specifically African Americans, Hispanics, American Indians, Pacific Islanders, Asian Americans, people with disabilities, and women of all races—are encouraged to apply. Interested students should submit a completed application form, description of the proposed research, a schedule, a budget, a list of references, a vitae, and undergraduate and graduate transcripts. Selection is based on 1) academic qualifications, 2) quality of the proposed research program and its relevance to the aerospace science and technology program of the National Aeronautics and Space Administration (NASA), 3) quality of the proposed interdisciplinary approach, 4) merit of the proposed utilization of a NASA center to carry out the objectives of the program, 5) prospects for completing the project within the allotted time, and 6) applicant's motivation for a career in aerospace.

Financial data   The award for 12 months includes $16,000 for a student stipend and up to $4,000 for a tuition/student research allowance.

Duration   Up to 36 months.

Number awarded   Varies; generally, 10 to 12 each year.

Deadline   February of each year.

[489]
ALBERT W. DENT STUDENT SCHOLARSHIP

American College of Healthcare Executives
One North Franklin Street, Suite 1700
Chicago, IL 60606-3491
(312) 424-2800   Fax: (312) 424-0023

Purpose   To increase the enrollment of minority students in healthcare management on the graduate school level.

Eligibility   Applicants must be student associate members in the American College of Healthcare Executives, accepted or currently enrolled in a healthcare management graduate program approved by the Accrediting Commission on Education for Health Services Administration, in financial need, U.S. or Canadian citizens, and members of a minority group.

Financial data   The stipend is $3,000.

Duration   1 year.

Special features   The program was established and named in honor of Dr. Albert W. Dent, the foundation's first Black fellow and president emeritus of Dillard University.

Number awarded   Varies each year.

Deadline   March of each year.

[490]
AMELIA KEMP MEMORIAL SCHOLARSHIP

Women of the Evangelical Lutheran Church in America
Attn: Scholarships
8765 West Higgins Road
Chicago, IL 60631-4189
(312) 380-2730   (800) 638-3522, ext. 2747
Fax: (312) 380-2419   E-mail: womnelca@elca.org

Purpose   To provide financial assistance to lay women of color who are members of Evangelical Lutheran Church of America (ELCA) congregations and who wish to pursue postsecondary education on the undergraduate, graduate, professional, or vocational school level.

Eligibility   These scholarships are aimed at ELCA lay women of color who are at least 21 years of age and have experienced an interruption of at least 2 years in their education since high school. They must demonstrate high academic potential, Christian commitment, realistic goals, and significant financial need. This program is only available to U.S. citizens who are studying for a career other than ordination, the diaconate, or church-certified professions.

Financial data   The stipends range up to $2,000.

Duration   1 year; may be renewed for 1 additional year.

Number awarded   Varies each year, depending upon the funds available.

Deadline   March of each year.

[491]
AMERICAN DENTAL HYGIENISTS' ASSOCIATION INSTITUTE MINORITY SCHOLARSHIP

American Dental Hygienists' Association
Attn: Institute for Oral Health
444 North Michigan Avenue, Suite 3400
Chicago, IL 60611
(312) 440-8900

Purpose   To provide financial assistance to minority group students enrolled in certificate/associate, baccalaureate, master's, or doctoral programs in dental hygiene leading to licensure as a dental hygienist.

Eligibility Applicants must be members of groups currently underrepresented in the dental hygiene profession; these include Native Americans, African Americans, Hispanics, Asians, and males (who are not required to be members of a minority group). Applicants must be American citizens and have completed 1 year in a dental hygiene curriculum with at least a 3.0 grade point average. They must intend to be full-time students during the academic year for which they are applying. Financial need of at least $1,500 must be documented.

Financial data The amount of the scholarship generally will be based on the tuition charged at the student's institution plus $250 for books and supplies, or the applicant's assessed need, whichever is less. The maximum award is $1,500.

Duration 1 year; nonrenewable.

Number awarded 2 each year.

Deadline May of each year.

[492]
AMERICAN ECONOMIC ASSOCIATION/FEDERAL RESERVE SYSTEM MINORITY FELLOWSHIP PROGRAM

American Economic Association
Attn: Committee on the Status of Minority Groups in the Economics Profession
c/o The Brookings Institution
1775 Massachusetts Avenue, N.W.
Washington, DC 20036-2188
(202) 797-6000   Fax: (202) 797-6004

Purpose To provide financial assistance to underrepresented minority economics doctoral students who are about to begin their dissertation research.

Eligibility Applicants must be U.S. citizens who are Black, Hispanic, or Native American and are enrolled in an accredited doctoral program in economics in the United States where they have completed their comprehensive examinations and are about to begin their dissertation research. Preference is given to applicants whose areas of concentration are of special interest to the Federal Reserve System (e.g., financial markets and monetary policy, nonfinancial macroeconomics, forecasting, banking markets and financial structure, regional studies, the external sector of the U.S. economy, the economics of other countries, foreign exchange markets, and international banking and financial markets). Selection is based on academic performance.

Financial data The stipend is $900 per month during the academic year. Institutions nominating candidates must agree to provide a tuition waiver without requiring research or teaching assistantship.

Special features Recipients are assigned an advisor from the Federal Reserve System and given the opportunity to complete an internship at the Federal Reserve Board or a Federal Reserve Bank.

Limitations Because of uncertainty about the legal status of affirmative action programs, new applications are not currently being solicited for this program.

Deadline February of each year.

[493]
AMERICAN METEOROLOGICAL SOCIETY INDUSTRY GRADUATE FELLOWSHIPS

American Meteorological Society
Attn: Fellowship/Scholarship Coordinator
45 Beacon Street
Boston, MA 02108-3693
(617) 227-2426, ext. 235   E-mail: sarmstrg@ametsoc.org

Purpose To encourage students entering their first year of graduate school to pursue an advanced degree in the atmospheric and related oceanic and hydrologic sciences.

Eligibility Students in the following fields are encouraged to apply: atmospheric sciences, oceanography, hydrology, chemistry, computer sciences, engineering, environmental sciences, mathematics, and physics. Applicants must be in the first year of graduate school, pursuing a full-time course of study in the atmospheric, oceanic, or hydrologic sciences, and a U.S. citizen or permanent resident. The Society encourages applications from women, minorities, and students with disabilities. Awards are based on academic performance and plans to pursue a career in meteorology or a related science.

Financial data The stipend is $15,000 per academic year.

Duration 9 months.

Special features This program was initiated in 1991. Corporations who have supported the program include: Cray Research, Inc., PRC Inc., Hughes Information Technology Company, Unisys Corporation, Government Systems Group, ITT Aerospace Communications Division, Space Systems/Loral, Martin Marietta Astro Space, GTE's Federal Systems Division, and NOAA's Office of Global Programs. Most industry-sponsored fellowship recipients have the opportunity to work at the corporation that granted their award during the summer following the academic year of their award. The summer employment opportunities are coordinated by AMS.

Limitations Requests for an application must be accompanied by a self-addressed stamped envelope.

Number awarded Varies; approximately 8 each year.

Deadline February of each year.

[494]
AMERICAN POLITICAL SCIENCE ASSOCIATION PH.D. FELLOWSHIPS FOR MINORITY STUDENTS

American Political Science Association
1527 New Hampshire Avenue, N.W.
Washington, DC 20036
(202) 483-2512   Fax: (202) 483-2657

Purpose To provide financial assistance to underrepresented minorities interested in pursuing a graduate degree in political science.

Eligibility This program is open to African American, Latino(a), and Native American graduates of baccalaureate institutions in the United States planning to enroll in a doctoral program in the following academic year. Applicants must be U.S. citizens with a record of outstanding academic achievement in political science and other related courses.

Financial data The stipend is $6,000 per year.

Duration 1 year.

Special features In addition to the fellows who receive stipends from this program, fellows without stipend are recommended for admission and financial support to every doctoral political science program in the country.

Number awarded 5 each year: 3 African Americans, 1 Latino(a), and 1 Native American.
Deadline October of each year.

[495]
AMERICAN SPEECH-LANGUAGE-HEARING FOUNDATION YOUNG SCHOLARS AWARD FOR MINORITY STUDENTS

American Speech-Language-Hearing Foundation
Attn: Director of Programs and Corporate Development
10801 Rockville Pike
Rockville, MD 20852
(301) 897-5700   Fax: (301) 571-0457

Purpose To provide financial assistance to minority graduate students in communication sciences and disorders programs.
Eligibility This program is open to full-time graduate students who are enrolled in communication sciences and disorders programs, with preference given to a student who is a racial/ethnic minority and a U.S. citizen. Selection is based on academic promise and outstanding academic achievement. Master's (but not doctoral) candidates must be enrolled in an ASHA Educational Standards Board (ESB) accredited program.
Financial data The stipend is $2,000.
Duration 1 year.
Number awarded 1 each year.
Deadline June of each year.

[496]
ANDREW W. MELLON FELLOWSHIPS IN HUMANISTIC STUDIES

Woodrow Wilson National Fellowship Foundation
Attn: Director
5 Vaughn Drive, Suite 300
CN 5329
Princeton, NJ 08543-5329
(609) 452-7007   Fax: (609) 452-0066
E-mail: jacquie@woodrow.org

Purpose To provide financial assistance for the first year of graduate studies in the humanities.
Eligibility Any college senior or recent graduate who has not yet begun graduate study, is a U.S. citizen or permanent resident, and is applying to a program leading to a Ph.D. in a humanistic field is encouraged to compete. Eligible fields of study are: American studies, art history, classics, comparative literature, cultural anthropology, English literature, foreign language and literature, history, history and philosophy of science, musicology, philosophy, political philosophy, and religion. Persons who are or have been enrolled in graduate or professional study following the bachelor's degree or who hold a master's degree are not eligible. Previously unsuccessful candidates are not considered a second time. Interviews are required for those candidates who are being considered seriously. Selection is based on academic record, Graduate Record Exam scores, and future promise. Particular attention is paid to applications submitted by minorities.
Financial data The stipend is $13,750 plus tuition and required fees. Payment is made to the recipient in 2 equal installments, in September and in January.
Duration 1 academic year.
Special features This program is funded by the Andrew W. Mellon Foundation and administered by the Woodrow Wilson National Fellowship Foundation.

Limitations Fellows are expected to carry a full course load. They may not accept supplementary institutional awards or hold teaching assistantships during the period of the fellowship.
Number awarded 80 each year.
Deadline December of each year.

[497]
APPLIED HEALTH PHYSICS FELLOWSHIP PROGRAM

Oak Ridge Institute for Science and Education
Attn: Science/Engineering Education Division
P.O. Box 117
Oak Ridge, TN 37831-0117
(423) 576-9279   (423) 576-2194
(800) 569-7749   Fax: (423) 576-3643
E-mail: ahpfp@orau.gov

Purpose To provide funding for graduate study and work experience in applied health physics (radiation protection).
Eligibility This program is open to students working on a master's degree in applied health physics at universities participating in this program (for a list of participating schools, write to the address above). Applicants must be U.S. citizens or permanent residents with a baccalaureate degree in either the life or physical sciences, engineering, or mathematics. All programs operated by the Science/Engineering Education Division (SEED) of Oak Ridge Institute for Science and Education (ORISE) seek to broaden the participation of minorities, women, and persons with disabilities in science and engineering careers.
Financial data Fellows receive full payment of tuition and fees and a stipend of $14,400 per year. An additional $300 per month is paid during the practicum period. A $1,000 annual allowance is paid to the recipient's university.
Duration Up to 24 months.
Special features Participants perform a research practicum as interns at various U.S. Department of Energy (DOE) research facilities for 3 months during the summer between the 2 years of the program. This program is funded by DOE and administered by ORISE/SEED.
Number awarded Varies each year.
Deadline January of each year.

[498]
ASME GRADUATE TEACHING FELLOWSHIP

American Society of Mechanical Engineers
Attn: Director, Engineering Education
345 East 47th Street
New York, NY 10017-2392
(212) 705-7177

Purpose To encourage outstanding graduate students to pursue a doctorate in mechanical engineering and to select engineering education as a profession.
Eligibility This program is open to U.S. citizens or permanent residents who hold an undergraduate degree from an ABET-accredited program, belong to the American Society of Mechanical Engineers, are currently employed as a teaching assistant, and are pursuing a doctorate in mechanical engineering. Applications from women and minorities are particularly encouraged.
Financial data Fellowship stipends are $5,000 per year.
Duration 1 year; may be renewed for up to 3 years.
Deadline October of each year.

[499]
ASTRA MERCK ADVANCED RESEARCH TRAINING AWARDS

American Digestive Health Foundation
7910 Woodmont Avenue, Suite 700
Bethesda, MD 20814-3015
(301) 654-2635   Fax: (301) 654-5920

Purpose To provide funding to M.D.s for research training in an area of gastrointestinal or liver function.

Eligibility Applicants must be M.D.s currently holding a gastro-enterology-related fellowship at an accredited North American institution. They must be committed to an academic career; have completed 2 years of research at the time they use this award; be sponsored by a member of the American Gastroenterological Association (AGA) who directs a gastroenterology-related unit that is engaged in research training in a North American medical school, affiliated teaching hospital, or research institute; and be cosponsored by the director of a basic research laboratory (or other comparable laboratory) who is committed to the training and development of the applicant. Individuals who hold a Ph.D. degree are not eligible. Minorities and women investigators are strongly encouraged to apply. Selection is based on novelty, feasibility and significance of the proposal, attributes of the candidate, record and commitment of the sponsors, and the institutional environment.

Financial data The stipend is $36,000 per year. Funds are to be used as salary support for the recipient. Indirect costs are not allowed.

Duration 2 years.

Special features This training can be considered the equivalent of the practical training ordinarily provided in a Ph.D. program. This award is administered by the American Digestive Health Foundation (ADHF) and sponsored by the AGA and with support from Astra Merck Inc.

Limitations Finalists for the award are interviewed. Although the host institution may supplement the award, the applicant may not concurrently hold a similar training award or grant from another organization. All publications coming from work funded by this program must acknowledge the support of the award.

Number awarded 6 each year.

Deadline September of each year.

[500]
AT&T COOPERATIVE RESEARCH FELLOWSHIP PROGRAM

AT&T Bell Laboratories
Attn: CRFP Manager
101 Crawfords Corner Road
P.O. Box 3030
Holmdel, NJ 07733-3030
(908) 949-2943

Purpose To develop scientific and engineering ability among members of minority groups currently underrepresented in the sciences.

Eligibility Outstanding Blacks, Hispanics, and Native American Indians who are college seniors and interested in pursuing a Ph.D. degree in chemistry, chemical engineering, electrical engineering, information science, materials sciences, mathematics, mechanical engineering, physics, or statistics are eligible to apply.

Financial data This program covers tuition and fees, a textbook allowance, a $13,200 annual stipend, and conference travel.

Recipients also participate in a summer internship at AT&T and receive housing, a salary, and transportation during that time.

Duration 1 academic year plus a summer internship; may be renewed.

Special features During the summer preceding graduate work, fellowship recipients are employed at AT&T Bell Laboratories and are assigned an appropriate research mentor.

Number awarded 9 to 12 each year.

Deadline January of each year.

[501]
BEHAVIORAL SCIENCES RESEARCH TRAINING FELLOWSHIPS

Epilepsy Foundation of America
Attn: Department of Research and Professional Education
4351 Garden City Drive
Landover, MD 20785
(301) 459-3700   (800) EFA-1000
Fax: (301) 577-2684   TDD: (800) 332-2070
E-mail: postmaster@efa.org

Purpose To offer qualified individuals an opportunity to develop expertise in the area of epilepsy research related to the behavioral sciences through training and involvement in an epilepsy research project.

Eligibility Individuals who have received their doctoral degree in a field of the behavioral sciences by the time the fellowship begins and desire additional postdoctoral research experience in epilepsy may apply. Appropriate fields of study for applications in the behavioral sciences include sociology, social work, psychology, anthropology, nursing, political science, and others relevant to epilepsy research and practice. Special attention is given to applications submitted by women and minorities.

Financial data Up to $30,000 per year, depending upon the experience and qualifications of the applicant and the scope and duration of the proposed project.

Duration 1 year.

Limitations The project must be carried out at an approved facility. Research must be conducted in the United States.

Number awarded Varies each year.

Deadline February of each year.

[502]
BOARD OF GOVERNORS MEDICAL SCHOLARSHIP PROGRAM

North Carolina State Education Assistance Authority
Attn: Scholarship and Grant Services
P.O. Box 2688
Chapel Hill, NC 27515-2688
(919) 549-8614   Fax: (919) 549-8481

Purpose To provide financial assistance to minority and economically disadvantaged students interested in medical education in North Carolina.

Eligibility Students must be nominated for this program. Nominees must be residents of North Carolina, be minority or economically disadvantaged students, express an intent to practice medicine in North Carolina, and be accepted or plan to enroll in 1 of the 4 medical schools in North Carolina: Bowman Gray School of Medicine at Wake Forest University, Duke University School of Medicine, East Carolina University School of Medicine, and the University of North Carolina at Chapel Hill School of Medicine.

Financial data Each scholarship provides a stipend of $5,000 a year, plus tuition and mandatory fees.

Duration 1 year; renewable up to 3 additional years, provided the recipient makes satisfactory academic progress, continues to have financial need, and remains interested in medical practice in North Carolina.

Number awarded 20 each year.

[503]
BUSH LEADERSHIP FELLOWS PROGRAM

Bush Foundation
E-900 First National Bank Building
332 Minnesota Street
St. Paul, MN 55101-1387
(612) 227-0891   Fax: (612) 297-6485

Purpose To provide educational and/or internship experiences to strongly motivated individuals in midcareer to prepare them for higher-level responsibilities.

Eligibility Men and women in mid-career who are between the ages of 28 and 54 and are deemed likely to advance to leading positions in architecture, business, engineering, farming, forestry, government, journalism, law, law enforcement, social work, theology, trade unionism, and in the administration of arts, education, health, or scientific organizations are eligible to apply. Applicants must have substantial standing in their fields, at least 5 years of work experience, residency in Minnesota, North Dakota, South Dakota, or the 26 northern and western Wisconsin counties that fall within the Ninth Federal Reserve District, and American citizenship or permanent resident status. The application may be either for a long term, involving a policy-level internship experience and often leading to an academic degree, or for a short term, to enroll in university programs to enhance managerial skills on a non-degree basis. Members of minority groups are particularly encouraged to apply.

Financial data Long-term fellows receive monthly stipends and short-term fellows receive weekly stipends; the amount of the stipends is intended to cover basic living expenses. In addition, all fellows receive reimbursement for 50 percent of their tuition charges up to $8,000 plus 80 percent of tuition charges over $8,000.

Duration From 4 to 18 months for long-term awards; from 3 to 10 weeks for short-term awards.

Special features Awards are for full-time study and internships anywhere in the United States. This program began in 1965; the shorter awards were added in 1973.

Limitations Fellowships are not awarded for applicants who are already enrolled as full-time students, part-time study combined with full- or part-time employment, academic research, publications, or design and development of service programs or projects. Fellowships are unlikely to be awarded for unstructured internships, full-time study plans built on academic programs designed primarily for part-time students, programs intended to meet the coninuing education requirements for professional certification, completion of basic educational requirements for non-administrative jobs or professions, segments of degree programs that cannot be completed within or near the end of the fellowship period, or projects that might more properly be the subjects of grant proposals from organizations.

Number awarded Approximately 35 each year.

Deadline November of each year for long-term fellowships; February of each year for short-term fellowships.

[504]
BUSH PRINCIPALS' PROGRAM

Bush Foundation
E-900 First National Bank Building
332 Minnesota Street
St. Paul, MN 55101-1387
(612) 227-0891   Fax: (612) 297-6485

Purpose To improve principals' skills in such areas as teacher supervision, curriculum design, community-school relationships, and program evaluation.

Eligibility Elementary and secondary school principals in Minnesota are eligible for this mid-career program; also eligible are Minnesota teachers whose work qualifies them as "leaders." Candidates must have at least 5 years of experience with at least 8 years remaining before retirement. Minorities and women are specifically encouraged to apply.

Financial data The amount awarded is established annually.

Duration 34 days of formal instruction spread over a 2-year period. The sessions vary in length from 3 to 12 days.

Special features The primary mode of instruction is the case method of analysis. Faculty in the program act as advisors to participants during the time between formal sessions, when principals work on special school improvement projects within their own districts. The funds for this program come from a grant from the Bush Foundation to the Strategic Management Research Center at the University of Minnesota, Carlson School of Management. Inquiries about this program may also be sent to the center, at 832 Management and Economics Building, University of Minnesota, 271 19th Avenue South, Minneapolis, MN 55455, (612) 624-5845.

Number awarded 21 principals and 7 teacher "leaders" each year.

Deadline October of each year.

[505]
C. CLYDE FERGUSON LAW SCHOLARSHIP

Commission on Higher Education
Attn: Educational Opportunity Fund
20 West State Street, Seventh Floor
CN 542
Trenton, NJ 08625-0542
(609) 292-4310   (800) 792-8670 (within NJ)

Purpose To provide financial assistance to disadvantaged and minority students who want to study law in New Jersey.

Eligibility Applicants must be disadvantaged students or members of an ethnic minority group that has been historically underrepresented in the legal profession. Applicants must be New Jersey residents for at least 12 months before receiving the award. They must plan to enroll full time in the Minority Student Program at Rutgers University School of Law at Newark, Rutgers University School of Law at Camden, or Seton Hall Law School. Applicants may be former or current undergraduate recipients of the New Jersey Educational Opportunity Fund (EOF) grant or students who would have met the undergraduate EOF grant eligibility requirements. Financial need must be demonstrated.

Financial data Awards are based on financial need. In no case, however, can awards exceed the maximum amount of tuition, fees, room, and board charged at Rutgers University School of Law at Newark.

Duration 1 year; may be renewed.

[506]
CALIFORNIA GRADUATE FELLOWSHIP PROGRAM

California Student Aid Commission
Attn: Customer Service Division
P.O. Box 510845
Sacramento, CA 94245-0845
(916) 445-0880

Purpose To provide financial assistance to California graduate students who are interested in becoming college faculty.

Eligibility Applicants must plan to pursue a graduate degree at an accredited California graduate school. They must demonstrate their intent to become a college or university faculty member, be legal California residents (must not be in California solely for the purpose of attending college), take the appropriate graduate examination, and be in financial need. For dependent students and independent students with dependents, the income ceiling is $68,000 per year and asset ceiling is $42,000. For independent students without dependents (other than a spouse), the income ceiling is $24,000 for married students and $21,000 for unmarried students with an asset ceiling of $20,000. Selection is based on undergraduate and graduate grades, test scores, and extent of disadvantaged background.

Financial data The amounts change annually. Currently, new awards are $882 at the California State University system, $1,669 at the University of California system, and up to $6,490 at independent colleges in California.

Duration 1 year; may be renewed.

Limitations Recipients must attend school at least half time.

Number awarded Approximately 300 each year.

Deadline February of each year.

[507]
CALIFORNIA PSYCHOLOGICAL ASSOCIATION FOUNDATION MINORITY SCHOLARSHIP PROGRAM

California Psychological Association Foundation
Attn: Administrator
1022 G Street
Sacramento, CA 95814
(916) 325-9786   Fax: (916) 325-9790

Purpose To provide financial assistance to minority students interested in pursuing a graduate degree in psychology in California.

Eligibility Applicants must be full-time first-year graduate students who are enrolled or accepted in a doctoral-level psychology program at an accredited California school. Membership in 1 of the following ethnic groups is required: Black/African American, Hispanic/Latino, Asian/Asian American, American Indian/Alaskan Native, or Pacific Islander. Priority is given to graduate students who meet the following criteria: demonstrate involvement and leadership in community activities, have focused on ethnic minority issues as part of their graduate program, demonstrate financial need, and plan to work with direct delivery of services to a culturally diverse population in either private or public settings.

Financial data The stipend is $2,500.

Duration 1 year.

Special features This program was established in 1991.

Number awarded 2 or more each year.

Deadline October of each year.

[508]
CALIFORNIA SPACE GRANT FELLOWSHIP PROGRAM

California Space Grant Consortium
c/o University of California at San Diego
California Space Institute
9500 Gilman Drive, 0524
La Jolla, CA 92093
(619) 534-5869   Fax: (619) 534-7840
E-mail: mwiskerchen@ucsd.edu

Purpose To provide financial assistance for graduate study in space-related science, engineering, and technology at branches of the University of California.

Eligibility This program is open to graduate students in space-related science, engineering, and technology at 7 of the campuses of the UC system. U.S. citizenship is required. As the California element of the Space Grant program of the U.S. National Aeronautics and Space Administration (NASA), this program encourages applications from underrepresented ethnic or gender groups and by persons with disabilities.

Financial data The annual stipend is $10,000.

Duration 1 year.

Special features This program is funded by NASA.

Number awarded 10 each year: 2 at Berkeley, 1 at Irvine, 2 at Los Angeles, 1 at Riverside, 2 at San Diego, 1 at Santa Barbara, and 1 at Santa Cruz.

Deadline Each of the participating UC campuses sets its own deadline.

[509]
CALIFORNIA STATE LIBRARY MULTI-ETHNIC RECRUITMENT SCHOLARSHIPS

California State Library
Attn: Library Development Services
900 N Street
P.O. Box 942837
Sacramento, CA 94237-0001
(916) 653-6822   (800) 654-0183
E-mail: klow@library.ca.gov

Purpose To provide financial assistance to minorities in California who are interested in pursuing a degree or gaining greater work experience in public librarianship.

Eligibility Applicants must be members of an ethnic minority group underrepresented in the library profession (Asian/Pacific Islander, Black/African American, Hispanic, and American Indian) seeking a master's degree in library and information science at an accredited graduate library school in California. Selection is based on an essay (75 percent) and previous experience in working with an ethnic community (25 percent). Candidates must be nominated by a public library, academic library, cooperative library system, or accredited graduate library school in California.

Financial data Up to $6,000 each year. Funds are awarded to the sponsoring library or library school, which may charge up to 10 percent of the scholarship monies for administrative overhead.

Duration 1 year; may be renewed for 1 additional year, although first priority is given to first time applicants.

Special features Recipients are assigned an internship in a public library that serves a predominately ethnic community or conduct research in an area of public librarianship that makes a contribution toward the improvement of library services to ethnic minority populations in California.

Number awarded Up to 8 each year.

Deadline Students must submit their applications to the sponsoring graduate library school, library, or library system by March of each year; the library system or library submits the application packets to the library school the student will be attending by April of each year; the library school submits the formal application to the State Library by May of each year.

[510]
CANFIT PROGRAM SCHOLARSHIPS

California Adolescent Nutrition and Fitness Program
2140 Shattuck Avenue, Suite 610
Berkeley, CA 94704
(510) 644-1533   (800) 200-3131
Fax: (510) 644-1535

Purpose To provide financial assistance to minority undergraduate and graduate students who are studying nutrition or physical education in California.

Eligibility Eligible to apply are American Indians/Alaska Natives, African Americans, Asians/Pacific Islanders, and Latinos/Hispanics who are enrolled in either: 1) an approved master's or doctoral graduate program in nutrition, public health nutrition, or physical education or in the American Dietetic Association Approved Preprofessional Practice Program at an accredited university in California; or, 2) an approved bachelor's level program in nutrition or physical education at an accredited (WASC) college or university in California. Graduate student applicants must have completed 12 to 15 units of graduate course work and have at least a 3.0 cumulative grade point average; undergraduate applicants must have completed 50 semester units or the equivalent of college credits and have at least a 2.5 cumulative grade point average. Selection is based on financial need, academic goals, and community nutrition or physical education activities.

Financial data Graduate stipends are $1,000 each and undergraduate stipends are $500 per year.

Special features A goal of the California Adolescent Nutrition and Fitness (CANFit) program is to improve the nutritional status and physical fitness of California's low-income multi-ethnic youth aged 10 to 14. By offering these scholarships, the program hopes to encourage more students to consider careers in adolescent nutrition and fitness.

Number awarded 5 graduate scholarships and 10 undergraduate scholarships are available each year.

Deadline March of each year.

[511]
CAREER DEVELOPMENT GRANTS

American Association of University Women
Attn: Educational Foundation
2201 North Dodge Street
Iowa City, IA 52243-4030
(319) 337-1716   Fax: (319) 337-1204

Purpose To provide financial assistance to women in the early stages of graduate studies to reenter the work force, change careers, or advance their current careers.

Eligibility This program is open to women who are U.S. citizens or permanent residents, have earned a bachelor's degree, received their most recent degree more than 4 years ago, and plan to pursue course work at a fully accredited 2- or 4-year college or university (or a technical school that is licensed, accredited, or approved by the Veteran Affairs Department). Special

consideration is given to qualified members of the American Association of University Women (AAUW), women of color, women pursuing their first terminal degrees, and women pursuing degrees in nontraditional fields.

Financial data The awards range from $1,000 to $5,000. The funds are to be used for tuition, fees, books, local transportation, and dependent care.

Duration 1 year, beginning in July; nonrenewable.

Limitations Candidates eligible for other fellowship programs of the AAUW are not eligible for these grants. Doctoral students may apply for funding only for course work, not for dissertation research or writing.

Number awarded 75 each year.

Deadline December of each year.

[512]
CARLEY—CANOYER—CUTLER FELLOWSHIP IN CONSUMER STUDIES

American Association of Family and Consumer Sciences
Attn: Awards, Fellowships and Grants Office
1555 King Street
Alexandria, VA 22314
(703) 706-4600   Fax: (703) 706-HOME

Purpose To provide financial assistance to minority and international students interested in graduate study in consumer affairs.

Eligibility Members of U.S. minority groups or international students interested in pursuing consumer studies at the graduate level are eligible to apply.

Financial data The stipend is $2,000 to $3,000. When the fellowship is awarded to an international student, cooperating colleges agree to remit an amount of tuition and/or fees equal to at least $500.

Duration The fellowship is awarded periodically, when enough interest has been earned on the fund.

Special features The fellowship honors Verna Carley and Helen Canoyer. It was established by Virginia F. Cutler.

Limitations Students living in the United States must send $15 with each request for fellowship materials. International students residing outside the United States at the time of application are not required to pay the fee.

Number awarded 1 each year the fellowship is offered.

Deadline January of each year the fellowship is offered.

[513]
CAROLE SIMPSON SCHOLARSHIP

Radio and Television News Directors Foundation
1000 Connecticut Avenue, N.W., Suite 615
Washington, DC 20036
(202) 659-6510   Fax: (202) 223-4007

Purpose To provide financial assistance to an outstanding student whose career objective is electronic journalism.

Eligibility Eligible are sophomore or more advanced undergraduate or graduate students enrolled in an electronic journalism sequence at an accredited or nationally recognized college or university. Applications must include 1 to 3 examples of reporting or producing skills on audio or video cassette tapes (no more than 15 minutes total), a statement explaining why the candidate seeks a career in broadcast or cable journalism, and a letter of endorsement from a faculty sponsor that verifies that the applicant has at least 1 year of school remaining. Minority undergraduate students receive preference.

Financial data The scholarship is $2,000, paid in semi-annual installments of $1,000 each.

Duration 1 year.

Special features An expense-paid trip to the Radio-Television News Directors Association Annual International Convention is also provided.

Limitations Previous winners of any RTNDF scholarship or internship are not eligible.

Number awarded 1 each year.

Deadline February of each year.

[514]
CAY DRACHNIK MINORITIES FUND FOR THE PURCHASE OF BOOKS

American Art Therapy Association, Inc.
1202 Allanson Road
Mundelein, IL 60060
(847) 949-6064   Fax: (847) 566-4580

Purpose To help to pay for the books needed by minority students working on a degree in art therapy.

Eligibility This program is open to minority students accepted or enrolled in a graduate art therapy program approved by the American Art Therapy Association. They should demonstrate financial need. Applications must include transcripts, 2 letters of reference, a student financial information form, and a 2-page essay that contains a brief biography and a statement of career goals.

Financial data $200 for the purchase of books.

Duration 1 year.

Deadline June of each year.

[515]
CHARLES A. EASTMAN DISSERTATION FELLOWSHIP FOR NATIVE AMERICAN SCHOLARS

Dartmouth College
Attn: Assistant Dean of Graduate Studies
6062 Wentworth, Room 305
Hanover, NH 03755-3526
(603) 646-2107

Purpose To provide funding to Native American doctoral students who are interested in working on their dissertation at Dartmouth College.

Eligibility This program is open to U.S. citizens of Native American descent who are planning a career in college or university teaching. They must have completed all other Ph.D. requirements and be interested in working on their dissertation at Dartmouth College.

Financial data The stipend is $25,000. In addition, fellows receive office space, library privileges, and a $2,500 research allowance.

Duration 1 year, beginning in September.

Special features The fellows are affiliated with a department or program at Dartmouth College.

Limitations Fellows are expected to be in residence at Dartmouth College for the duration of the program and to complete their dissertation during that time. They are also expected to teach a course, either as the primary instructor or as part of a team.

Number awarded 1 each year.

Deadline March of each year.

[516]
CIA TUITION ASSISTANCE PROGRAM

Central Intelligence Agency
Attn: Personnel Representative
P.O. Box 12727
Arlington, VA 22209-8727
(703) 351-2028   (800) JOBS CIA

Purpose To provide tuition assistance to undergraduate and graduate students who participate in Central Intelligence Agency (CIA) internship programs.

Eligibility Eligible to apply are undergraduate and graduate students who are participating as interns in any of these 3 programs: the CIA Summer Internship (primarily for minorities and people with disabilities), the CIA Student Trainee Program (for undergraduate students), or the CIA Graduate Studies Program (for graduate students). Applicants must maintain at least a 2.75 grade point average, be enrolled in a minimum of 12 hours of course work, and have completed 2 work tours and be scheduled for a third tour as an intern (graduate fellows must have completed 1 work tour). Assistance is granted to those interns whom the CIA is willing to hire as staff employees within 60 days following the completion of their degree requirements.

Financial data The stipend is $2,000 per program (undergraduate or graduate); students with a grade point average above 3.5 receive an additional payment of $500 per program.

Duration 1 year as an undergraduate and 1 year as a graduate student.

Limitations Recipients must agree to return to the CIA as a staff employee for a 1-year period for each program in which tuition assistance is accepted.

Number awarded Varies each year.

[517]
CIC PREDOCTORAL FELLOWSHIPS

Committee on Institutional Cooperation
302 East John Street
Champaign, IL 61820-5698
(217) 333-8475   Fax: (217) 244-7127
E-mail: cic@uiuc.edu

Purpose To increase the number of underrepresented minority group members (Native Americans, African Americans, Mexican Americans, and Puerto Ricans) among Ph.D. degree recipients in the physical sciences.

Eligibility Applicants must be American citizens who are racial minority students seeking doctorates in the physical sciences (including mathematics and engineering). Applicants must be planning to enroll (but must not be currently enrolled) in a university affiliated with the Committee on Institutional Cooperation (CIC): University of Chicago, University of Illinois at Chicago, University of Illinois at Urbana-Champaign, Indiana University, Indiana University/Purdue University at Indianapolis, University of Iowa, University of Michigan, Michigan State University, University of Minnesota, Northwestern University, Ohio State University, Pennsylvania State University, Purdue University, University of Wisconsin at Madison, or University of Wisconsin at Milwaukee.

Financial data Each award provides for full tuition plus an annual stipend of at least $11,000.

Duration 4 years.

Special features Major funding for this program is provided by the Lilly Endowment, the Andrew W. Mellon Foundation, the General Electric Foundation, and the home CIC graduate school of each Fellow.

Limitations Fellowships are tenable at member institutions only. Currently enrolled graduate students at CIC university campuses are not eligible to apply.

Number awarded About 40 each year.

Deadline November of each year.

[518]
CIVILIAN RADIOACTIVE WASTE MANAGEMENT FELLOWSHIP PROGRAM

Oak Ridge Institute for Science and Education
Attn: Science/Engineering Education Division
P.O. Box 117
Oak Ridge, TN 37831-0117
(423) 241-2890   (423) 576-2600
(800) 569-7749   Fax: (423) 576-3643
E-mail: crwmfp@orau.gov

Purpose To provide graduate study and research opportunities in fields related to the management of spent nuclear fuel and high-level radioactive wastes.

Eligibility This program is open to graduate students who are working on a master's or doctoral degree in earth sciences, engineering, materials sciences, or radiation sciences at participating schools (for a list of these schools, write to the address above). Application should be made before or during the first year of graduate school. All programs operated by the Science/Engineering Education Division (SEED) of Oak Ridge Institute for Science and Education (ORISE) seek to broaden the participation of minorities, women, and persons with disabilities in science and engineering careers.

Financial data Participants receive an annual stipend of $14,400, plus an additional $300 per month during their practicum. Participants are also paid for some of their travel and tuition and fees up to $8,000 per year.

Duration 1 year; may be renewed for up to 4 additional years.

Special features Participants intern at various U.S. Department of Energy (DOE) research facilities. This program is funded by the DOE's Office of Civilian Radioactive Waste Management and administered by ORISE/SEED.

Number awarded Varies each year.

Deadline January of each year.

[519]
CLA SCHOLARSHIP FOR MINORITY STUDENTS IN MEMORY OF EDNA YELLAND

California Library Association
717 K Street, Suite 300
Sacramento, CA 95814-3477
(916) 447-8541   Fax: (916) 447-8394

Purpose To provide financial assistance to students of ethnic origin who are interested in pursuing a career in library or information science.

Eligibility To be eligible, students must be of ethnic origin (American Indian, African American/Black, Mexican American/Chicano, Latino/Hispanic, Asian American, Pacific Islander, or Filipino), show financial need, be a California resident, be a U.S. citizen or permanent U.S. resident, and be enrolled or accepted for enrollment in a master's program in an accredited graduate library school in California.

Financial data Amount varies; generally, $2,000 per year.

Duration 1 academic year.

Special features This fellowship is named for the executive secretary of the California Library Association from 1947 to 1963 who worked to promote the goals of the California Library Association and the profession. Until 1985, it was named the Edna Yelland Memorial Scholarship.

Number awarded 1 or 2 each year.

Deadline May of each year.

[520]
CLINICAL TRAINING FELLOWSHIP FOR MINORITY NURSES

American Nurses Association
Attn: Minority Fellowship Programs
600 Maryland Avenue, S.W., Suite 100 West
Washington, DC 20024-2571
(202) 651-7244   Fax: (202) 789-1413

Purpose To provide financial assistance to nurses pursuing careers as psychiatric/mental health nurses who serve a minority population.

Eligibility Applications will be accepted from registered nurses who are members of an ethnic or racial minority group, including but not limited to African Americans, Hispanics, American Indians, Asian Americans, Pacific Islanders and/or who can demonstrate a commitment to careers in psychiatric nursing, related to ethnic minority mental health. Applicants must be U.S. citizens or permanent residents, registered nurses, members of the American Nurses Association (ANA), and holders of master's degrees pursuing a doctoral degree. Students specializing in the following areas of research are encouraged to apply: basic and clinical research on the nature, prevention, and treatment of mental disorders affecting ethnic/racial minority populations; clinical studies of ethnic/racial minority populations at high risk for clinical disorders; and cross-cultural, cross-ethnic and/or cross-racial studies in psychopathology, etc.

Financial data Awards include a stipend to defray the cost of living; the amounts of awards depend on the availability of funds. This is a scholarship/loan progam; recipients of these awards must agree to provide clinical services to underserved populations for a period of time equal to the length of support, within 2 years after termination of such support.

Duration Up to 3 years.

Special features Funds for this program are provided by the Substance Abuse and Mental Health Services Administration.

Deadline January of each year.

[521]
CLINICAL TRAINING FELLOWSHIP IN PSYCHOLOGY

American Psychological Association
Attn: Minority Fellowship Program
750 First Street, N.E.
Washington, DC 20002-4242
(202) 336-6027   Fax: (202) 336-6012
TDD: (202) 336-6123   E-mail: mfp@apa.org

Purpose To increase the number of ethnic and racial minorities who complete doctoral programs as psychology clinicians.

Eligibility Applicants must be U.S. citizens or permanent residents, enrolled full time in an accredited doctoral program, committed to a career in psychology related to ethnic minority mental health, and members of an ethnic minority group, including but not limited to African Americans, Hispanics, American Indians, Alaskan Natives, Asian Americans, and Pacific Islanders. Students specializing in clinical concerns (such as prevention and treatment of problems affecting ethnic minority populations) as well as students specializing in clinical, school, and counseling psychology are encouraged to apply. Students of any other specialty will be considered if they plan careers in which their training will lead to delivery of psychological services or the conduct of clinical research relevant to ethnic minority populations. Selection is based on clinical and/or research potential, scholarship, writing ability, ethnic minority identification, knowledge of broad issues in psychology, and professional commitment. Students of clinical and counseling psychology and students working on a master's degree only are ineligible.

Financial data The stipend is $834 per month. In some cases, the fellowship may pay for tuition, fees, and pre-selection travel.

Duration 1 academic or calendar year; may be renewed for up to 2 additional years.

Special features Funding is provided by the U.S. Substance Abuse and Mental Health Services Administration.

Limitations Recipients are obligated to provide clinical services to underserved populations within 24 months after the completion of their training and for a period equal to the length of the award. This obligation may not be fulfilled in private clinical practice.

Deadline January of each year.

[522]
COLGATE "BRIGHT SMILES, BRIGHT FUTURES" MINORITY SCHOLARSHIPS

American Dental Hygienists' Association
Attn: Institute for Oral Health
444 North Michigan Avenue, Suite 3400
Chicago, Il 60611
(312) 440-8900

Purpose To provide financial assistance to minority group students enrolled in doctoral, master's, baccalaureate, or certificate/associate programs in dental hygiene.

Eligibility Applicants must be members of groups currently underrepresented in the dental hygiene profession; these include Native Americans, African Americans, Hispanics, Asians, and males. Applicants must have completed at least 1 year in a dental hygiene curriculum, have earned at least a 3.0 grade point average, and be able to demonstrate financial need of at least $1,500. They must intend to be full-time students in the academic year for which they are applying.

Financial data The amount of the scholarship generally will be based on the tuition charged at the student's institution, plus $250 for books and supplies, or the applicant's assessed need, whichever is less. The maximum award is $1,500.

Duration 1 year.

Special features These scholarships are sponsored by the Colgate-Palmolive Company.

Number awarded 2 each year.

Deadline May of each year.

[523]
COLGATE MINORITY SCHOLARSHIPS

American Dental Hygienists' Association
Attn: Institute for Oral Health
444 North Michigan Avenue, Suite 3400
Chicago, Il 60611
(312) 440-8900

Purpose To provide financial assistance to minority group students enrolled in doctoral, master's, baccalaureate, or certificate/associate programs in dental hygiene.

Eligibility Applicants must be members of groups currently underrepresented in the dental hygiene profession; these include Native Americans, African Americans, Hispanics, Asians, and males. Applicants must be have completed at least 1 year in a dental hygiene curriculum, have earned at least a 3.0 grade point average, and be able to demonstrate financial need of at least $1,500. They must intend to be full-time students in the academic year for which they are applying.

Financial data The amount of the scholarship generally is based on the tuition charged at the student's institution, plus $250 for books and supplies, or the applicant's assessed need, whichever is less. The maximum award is $1,500.

Duration 1 year.

Special features These scholarships are sponsored by Colgate Oral Pharmaceuticals.

Number awarded 6 each year.

Deadline May of each year.

[524]
COLORADO LIBRARY MINORITY SCHOLARSHIP

Colorado Council on Library Development
c/o Dr. Camila Alire
Auraria Library
Lawrence at 11th Street
Denver, CO 80204
(303) 556-3521   Fax: (303) 556-3528

Purpose To provide financial encouragement to library science students in Colorado who are committed to developing services and programs to meet the needs of ethnic minorities.

Eligibility This program is open to students enrolled in an accredited master's degree program in library science who are Colorado residents, are citizens or residents of the United States, and have demonstrated a commitment of service to a traditional ethnic minority community. Library experience is desirable but not required. Applicants must be committed to working 2 years in a Colorado public library after graduating with a master's degree in library science.

Financial data The stipend is $3,000.

Duration 1 year for full-time students; 2 years for part-time students.

Special features Recipients may attend school on either a full-time or part-time basis.

Limitations If a recipient does not complete the library degree, the scholarship must be repaid.

Number awarded 1 each year.

Deadline May of each year.

[525]
CONSORTIUM FOR GRADUATE STUDY IN MANAGEMENT FELLOWSHIPS

Consortium for Graduate Study in Management
200 South Hanley Road, Suite 1102
St. Louis, MO 63105-3415
(314) 935-5614   E-mail: cgsm@wuolin.wustl.edu

Purpose To accelerate the entry of racial minorities into managerial positions in business.

Eligibility Eligible to apply are African Americans, Hispanic Americans (Chicanos, Cubans, Dominicans, and Puerto Ricans), and Native Americans who have graduated from college and are interested in a career in business. An undergraduate degree in business or economics is not required. Applicants must be U.S. citizens and planning to pursue a Master's of Business Administration degree at 1 of the Consortium's schools: University of California at Berkeley, Indiana University, University of Michigan, New York University, University of North Carolina at Chapel Hill, University of Rochester, University of Southern California, University of Texas at Austin, University of Virginia, Washington University, or University of Wisconsin at Madison. Preference is given to applicants under 31 years of age.

Financial data The fellowship provides full tuition and required fees. Summer internships with the consortium's cooperative sponsors, providing paid practical experience, are also offered.

Duration Up to 4 semesters.

Limitations Fellowships are tenable at member schools only.

Number awarded Varies; approximately 180 each year.

Deadline January of each year.

[526]
C.R. BARD FOUNDATION PRIZE

National Medical Fellowships, Inc.
Attn: Scholarships and Programs
110 West 32nd Street, 8th Floor
New York, NY 10001-3205
(212) 714-1007

Purpose To recognize and reward the outstanding talents and future potential of a graduating underrepresented medical student who intends to practice in the field of cardiology or urology.

Eligibility This award is open to senior African American, Native American, Mexican American, and mainland Puerto Rican students enrolled in accredited U.S. medical schools and planning to pursue careers in cardiology or urology. Candidates must be nominated by their medical schools during their senior year. Selection is based on academic achievement, leadership, and potential to make significant contributions in their field.

Financial data This honor includes a certificate of merit and a $5,000 stipend.

Duration 1 year; nonrenewable.

Special features This award was established in 1996 by C.R. Bard, Inc., a developer, manufacturer, and marketer of cardiovascular, urological, and surgical products.

Number awarded 1 each year.

Deadline Nominations are requested in January of each year.

[527]
CRUSADE SCHOLARSHIP PROGRAM

United Methodist Church
Attn: General Board of Global Ministries
475 Riverside Drive, Suite 1470
New York, NY 10115
(212) 870-3660   (800) 654-5929

Purpose To provide financial assistance to minority and foreign students who are interested in pursuing graduate education for leadership within the United Methodist Church.

Eligibility This program is open to ethnic and racial minority graduate students (African Americans, Hispanic Americans, Pacific/Asian Americans, and Native Americans) who are enrolled in school full time and are U.S. citizens or permanent residents. They may be seeking an M.Div., M.A., Ph.D., D.D.S., M.D., M.Ed., M.B.A., or other graduate degree. Applicants must be members of the United Methodist Church and preparing to commit themselves for leadership in mission to church and society.

Financial data The amount awarded varies, depending upon the availability of funds.

Duration Up to 3 years.

Special features These awards are funded by the World Communion Offering received in United Methodist churches on the first Sunday in October.

Number awarded Varies each year.

Deadline January of each year.

[528]
CSU FORGIVABLE LOAN/DOCTORAL INCENTIVE PROGRAM

California State University
c/o Office of the Chancellor
400 Golden Shore, Suite 222
Long Beach, CA 90802-4275
(310) 985-2692

Purpose To increase the number of minorities, women, and persons with disabilities with doctoral degrees in selected fields of study of particular interest and relevance to the California State University (CSU) system, and to increase the likelihood that those people will seek teaching careers within the CSU system.

Eligibility Applicants must be minorities, women, or persons with disabilities who are new or continuing full-time students enrolled in a doctoral program, whether affiliated with a CSU campus or not. Selection is based on: 1) potential for success—the applicant's potential to complete an approved doctoral program and compete successfully for a CSU tenure-track faculty position; considerations include the applicant's academic record, professional qualifications, and motivations to teach in the CSU, as well as the quality of the proposed doctoral field and the probable need for faculty in the candidate's field; this criterion is given greatest weight; 2) underrepresentation—the degree of underrepresentation in the national pool of doctoral recipients and in the CSU tenure-track faculty in the area of study proposed by the applicant; special consideration is given to applicants with backgrounds that are underrepresented in the natural sciences, engineering, computer science, and mathematics, although consideration is given to applicants in all fields where such underrepresentation exists; persons with disabilities are considered underrepresented in all fields; 3) faculty sponsor's plan of support—the plan submitted by a full-time tenured CSU faculty member who advises and supports the candidate throughout doctoral study.

Financial data   Participants receive up to $10,000 per year. The loans are converted to fellowships at the rate of 20 percent of the total loan amount for each postdoctoral year that the program participant teaches, for up to 5 years. Thus, the entire loan will be forgiven after the recipient has taught full time for 5 years on a CSU campus. Recipients who do not teach on a CSU campus or who discontinue full-time studies will be required to repay the total loan amount within a 15-year period at the rate established for other student loans. The minimum repayment required for a $30,000 loan is approximately $300 per month to amortize the 8 percent per annum loan over a 15-year period. Waiver of loan obligations can be made in those exceptional cases where graduate work was discontinued for valid reasons and where repayment of the loan would cause an unnecessary or undue hardship.

Duration   Up to 3 years.

Number awarded   Varies each year.

Deadline   February of each year.

[529]
CT&M DIVISION MINORITY DOCTORAL STUDENT SCHOLARSHIP

Association for Education in Journalism and Mass
   Communication
c/o Dr. Wayne Wanta
School of Journalism and Communication
1275 University of Oregon
Eugene, OR 97403-1275

Purpose   To provide financial assistance to a minority doctoral student in journalism.

Eligibility   Applicants must be minority students (U.S. citizens or permanent residents) enrolled in a Ph.D. program in mass communications. Their program should reflect the interests of the Communication Theory and Methodology (CT&M) Division of the Association for Education in Journalism and Mass Communication (AEJMC). Applicants need not be members of AEJMC of the CT&M Division.

Financial data   The stipend is $1,200.

Duration   1 year.

Number awarded   1 each year.

Deadline   May of each year.

[530]
DAVID A. DEBOLT TEACHER SHORTAGE SCHOLARSHIPS

Illinois Student Assistance Commission
Attn: Scholarship and Grant Services
1755 Lake Cook Road
Deerfield, IL 60015-5209
(708) 948-8550
(800) 899-ISAC (within IL, IA, IN, MO, and WI)

Purpose   To provide financial assistance to students in Illinois who are interested in training or retraining for a teaching career in academic shortage areas.

Eligibility   Eligible for support under this program are Illinois residents who are enrolled or planning to enroll in an Illinois institution of higher education to pursue careers as public preschool, elementary, and secondary school teachers in designated teacher shortage disciplines. Priority is given to minority students.

Financial data   This programs pays tuition and fees, room and board, or a commuter allowance at academic institutions in Illinois, to a maximum of $5,000. Funds are paid directly to the school. This is a scholarship/loan program. Recipients must agree to take a teaching position in Illinois within 2 years of graduation and must remain in that position for at least 3 years. Recipients who fail to honor this work obligation must repay the award.

Duration   1 year; may be renewed.

Number awarded   Varies each year.

Deadline   April of each year.

[531]
DEPARTMENT OF DEFENSE AUGMENTATION AWARDS FOR SCIENCE AND ENGINEERING RESEARCH TRAINING

Air Force Office of Scientific Research
Attn: Directorate of Academic and International Affairs
110 Duncan Avenue, Room B115
Bolling Air Force Base, DC 20332-8080
(202) 767-4969   Fax: (202) 767-5012
E-mail: jan.cerveny@afosr.af.mil

Purpose   To provide supplemental funding to recipients of research grants from the Department of Defense (DoD) so they can include students as research assistants on their projects.

Eligibility   This program is open to investigators operating under ongoing DoD research grants. They may apply for this additional funding to provide support for graduate students to serve as research assistants on their projects, and to involve undergraduate and precollege students in their work. Students must be U.S. citizens or nationals whose research is directly related to the investigator's DoD-sponsored research and who are in addition to students normally accommodated by the parent grant. Graduate students normally are supported for the third through fifth year of education, following 1 to 2 years of required course work and the successful completion of a qualifying examination. Proposals are encouraged from Historically Black Colleges and Universities and other Minority Institutions, as defined by federal regulations. All proposers are encouraged to use funding from this program to recruit students from groups underrepresented among U.S. citizens holding advanced degrees in science and engineering, including ethnic minorities (Black, Hispanic, American Indian, Alaskan Eskimo/Aleut, or American Samoan, Micronesian, Guamian, and Northern Marianian), women, and persons with disabilities. Increased funding allowances for persons with disabilities are considered to offset special education expenses.

Financial data   The program provides graduate students' tuition and fees (at the normal research assistant rate), salary, and the cost of research training required for the advanced degree; research training costs vary greatly depending on the institution, discipline, and nature of the research. For undergraduate and precollege students, awards cover salary and research operating costs associated with the students' participation but do not cover tuition or fees.

Duration   Grants are for 3 years.

Special features   This program is also available through the Office of Naval Research, 800 North Quincy Street, Arlington, VA 22217-5660; the Army Research Office, 4300 South Miami Boulevard, P.O. Box 12211, Research Triangle Park, NC 27709-2211; and the Ballistic Missile Defense Organization, 7100 Defense, BMDO-TRI, The Pentagon: Mail Room 1E117, Washington, DC 20310-7100. Students interested in this program should contact 1 of the sponsoring agencies to obtain a list of principal investigators currently holding appropriate grants.

Number awarded Varies; a total of approximately $45 million is available through this program each year, distributed through the Air Force Office of Scientific Research ($12 million), Army Research Office ($11 million), Ballistic Missile Defense Organization ($5 million), and Office of Naval Research ($17 million).

Deadline November of each year.

[532]
DEPARTMENT OF ENERGY DISTINGUISHED POSTDOCTORAL RESEARCH PROGRAM

Oak Ridge Institute for Science and Education
Attn: Science/Engineering Education Division
P.O. Box 117
Oak Ridge, TN 37831-0117
(423) 576-9934   (423) 576-3192
(800) 569-7749   Fax: (423) 576-3643
E-mail: doedprp@orau.gov

Purpose To provide financial assistance for postdoctoral research and training in energy-related engineering, physical sciences, and computer sciences.

Eligibility Applicants must have completed a doctoral degree within the past 3 years and be proposing a program of research and training in computer sciences, physical sciences, engineering, and other scientific disciplines related to energy. Awards are tenable at laboratories in the United States that are affiliated with or supported by the U.S. Department of Energy (DOE); for a list of those, contact the address above. All programs operated by the Science/Engineering Education Division (SEED) of Oak Ridge Institute for Science and Education (ORISE) seek to broaden the participation of minorities, women, and persons with disabilities in science and engineering careers.

Financial data The stipend is $52,800 per year; reimbursement for inbound travel, moving, travel to 2 domestic scientific meetings per year, and medical insurance are also provided.

Duration 1 year; renewable.

Special features This program is funded by the DOE Office of Science Education Programs and administered by ORISE/SEED.

Number awarded Varies each year.

Deadline December of each year.

[533]
DISSERTATION FELLOWSHIP ON PEACE AND SECURITY IN A CHANGING WORLD

Social Science Research Council
810 Seventh Avenue
New York, NY 10019
(212) 377-2700   Fax: (212) 377-2727

Purpose To support doctoral research and training on the implications for security issues of worldwide cultural, social, economic, military, and political changes.

Eligibility The competition is open to researchers who are finishing course work, examinations, or similar requirements for the doctoral degree (Ph.D. or its equivalent), but desire to undertake training that adds a new competence to the disciplinary skills that they already have. Applicants should be nearing completion of all requirements for the Ph.D. except the dissertation at the time of application. They must propose to make substantial revisions in their dissertation plans during the course of this fellowship. There are no citizenship, residency, or nationality requirements. Applicants must be working in the social/behavioral sciences (including history and foreign area studies), the humanities, or the physi-

cal and biological sciences. Minorities and women are particularly encouraged to apply.

Financial data The stipend, up to $17,500, is appropriate for the cost of living where the fellow will be working.

Duration In most cases, 2 years.

Special features The Social Science Research Council administers this program with funds provided by the John D. and Catherine T. MacArthur Foundation as part of its Program in International Peace and Security Studies. Training may occur in any setting of the recipient's choice, in any nation, and may consist of formal course work, tutorials, internships, senior apprenticeships, or supervised study with senior faculty.

Limitations The program requires and enables researchers to add to their present specialty a competence in a different area and to apply their newly-enhanced skills to specific research projects. The fellowships are not designed for and will not support programs for which the applicant is already prepared by prior experience and training. Fellows must devote full time to the fellowship and are not permitted to be otherwise employed.

Number awarded Approximately 7 each year.

Deadline November of each year.

[534]
DOCTORAL FELLOWSHIPS IN SOCIAL WORK FOR ETHNIC MINORITY STUDENTS PREPARING FOR LEADERSHIP ROLES IN MENTAL HEALTH AND/OR SUBSTANCE ABUSE

Council on Social Work Education
Attn: Minority Fellowship Program
1600 Duke Street, Suite 300
Alexandria, VA 22314-3421
(703) 683-8080

Purpose To increase the number of racial minority members in the mental health fields.

Eligibility Applicants must be American citizens or permanent residents who have been underrepresented in the field of social work. These include but are not limited to the following groups: American Indians/Alaskan Natives, Asian/Pacific Islanders (e.g. Chinese, East Indians and other South Asians, Filipinos, Hawaiians, Japanese, Koreans, and Samoans), Blacks, and Hispanics (e.g. Mexicans/Chicanos, Puerto Ricans, Cubans, Central or South Americans). Selection is based upon potential for assuming leadership roles in mental health, a commitment to a career providing mental health and/or substance abuse services to ethnic minority clients and communities, and potential for success in doctoral studies. To be eligible for consideration, applicants must have already earned a master's degree in social work.

Financial data Awards provide a monthly stipend and some tuition support. A payback provision requires recipients to engage in clinical services in specific areas of need for a period of time equal to the length of support; such service could include teaching, consultation, research, or a combination of those.

Duration 1 academic year; renewable for 1 additional year if funds are available and the recipient achieves satisfactory progress toward the degree objectives.

Special features This program is funded by the Center for Mental Health Services of the Substance Abuse and Mental Health Services Administration.

Limitations The fellowship is to be used to pursue doctoral studies/research only.

Deadline February of each year.

[535]
DOCTORAL FELLOWSHIPS IN SOCIAL WORK FOR ETHNIC MINORITY STUDENTS SPECIALIZING IN MENTAL HEALTH RESEARCH

Council on Social Work Education
Attn: Minority Fellowship Program
1600 Duke Street, Suite 300
Alexandria, VA 22314-3421
(703) 683-8080

Purpose To increase the number of racial minority members in mental health research.

Eligibility Applicants must be American citizens or permanent residents who have been underrepresented in the field of social work. These include but are not limited to the following groups: American Indians/Alaskan Natives, Asian/Pacific Islanders (e.g. Chinese, East Indians and other South Asians, Filipinos, Hawaiians, Japanese, Koreans, and Samoans), Blacks, and Hispanics (e.g. Mexicans/Chicanos, Puerto Ricans, Cubans, Central or South Americans). Selection is based upon a desire to acquire a mastery of sound research skills and a commitment to future research activity and a career in mental health research. To be eligible for consideration, applicants must have already earned a master's degree in social work and be enrolled in or planning to enroll in a doctoral program in social work as full-time students.

Financial data Awards provide a monthly stipend and some tuition support.

Duration 1 academic year; renewable for 1 additional year if funds are available and the recipient achieves satisfactory progress toward the degree objectives.

Special features This program is funded by the National Institute of Mental Health of the National Institutes of Health.

Deadline February of each year.

[536]
DOCTORAL TRAINEESHIPS IN AGING RESEARCH

American Psychological Association
Attn: Minority Fellowship Program
750 First Street, N.E.
Washington, DC 20002-4242
(202) 336-6027　　　　　　Fax: (202) 336-6012
TDD: (202) 336-6123　　　　E-mail: mfp@apa.org

Purpose To provide financial assistance to minority students who are interested in completing a doctorate in gerontology.

Eligibility Racial and ethnic minorities who are interested in earning a doctorate in gerontology are eligible to apply. They must be American citizens or permanent visa residents and be enrolled full time in an accredited academic program leading to a doctoral degree in psychology with a specialty in gerontology. Applicants must be members of an ethnic minority group, including but not limited to African Americans, American Indians, Alaskan Natives, Asian Americans, Hispanics, Pacific Islanders, and/or persons who demonstrate a commitment to research careers related to ethnic minority gerontology. Students specializing in such research areas as social, personality, biopsychology, developmental, quantitative, industrial/organization, cognitive, educational, experimental, and neuropsychology are encouraged to apply; students of other psychology specialties may apply if they plan careers in gerontology research.

Financial data The stipend is $834 per month. In some cases, the fellowship may pay for tuition, fees, and pre-selection travel.

Duration 1 year; may be renewed for up to 2 additional years.

Special features This program is funded by the National Institute on Aging of the National Institutes of Health and administered by the American Psychological Association.

Number awarded 1 or more each year.

Deadline January of each year.

[537]
DOROTHY DANFORTH COMPTON FELLOWSHIPS

Institute for the Study of World Politics
1755 Massachusetts Avenue, N.W.
Washington, DC 20036

Purpose To provide funding to underrepresented minority students interested in preparing for a career in world affairs.

Eligibility This program is open to African American, Hispanic American, and Native American students pursuing a master's or doctoral degree in preparation for a career in world affairs (as scholars or practitioners). Applicants should be U.S. citizens pursuing degrees from U.S. institutions. Ph.D. candidates who have completed their course work and are engaged in dissertation research should submit an application and cover letter. Students pursuing a master's degree or a Ph.D. degree (but are not yet at the dissertation stage) should submit an application form, a curriculum vitae, a statement of plans for a career in world affairs, standardized test scores, and letters of recommendation.

Financial data The amount awarded varies, depending upon the status and needs of the recipient.

Duration 1 year.

Special features The Institute for the Study of World Politics (ISWP) awards fellowships to students of political science, economics, international relations, and history as long as the work relates to political, economic, and social issues that affect the security, well-being, and dignity of peoples of the world. Dissertation level doctoral student applicants are also considered for ISWP Doctoral Dissertation Fellowships.

Limitations Telephone inquiries are not accepted.

Number awarded Varies each year.

Deadline February of each year for applicants engaged in dissertation research; March of each year for applicants engaged in work at the master's or pre-dissertation Ph.D. level.

[538]
DOROTHY DANFORTH COMPTON MINORITY FELLOWSHIPS

Danforth Foundation
231 South Bemiston Avenue, Suite 1080
St. Louis, MO 63105-1996
(314) 862-6200　　　　　　Fax: (314) 862-2003

Purpose To provide financial assistance to minority graduate students attending universities supported by Danforth Foundation grants who wish to be college teachers.

Eligibility Black American, Hispanic American, and Native American college graduates who are interested in becoming college teachers are eligible to apply for support if they are attending or planning to attend 1 of the following 10 universities: Brown University, University of Chicago, Columbia University, Howard University, Stanford University, University of Texas at Austin, University of California at Los Angeles, Vanderbilt University, University of Washington, or Yale University.

Financial data Each of the 10 universities has received grants of up to $300,000 from the Danforth Foundation to distribute to fellowship recipients.

Duration 1 year; renewable for 2 additional years.

Special features Recipients attend local and regional meetings featuring minority scholars that deal with problems and interests of importance to the students and their teachers.

Number awarded Since 1979, 47 fellows have completed their Ph.D.s and 46 are teaching in a college or university.

Deadline Students interested in participating in this program should contact 1 of the universities listed above for application information and materials.

[539]
DU PONT PHARMA/AFPE MINORITIES FELLOWSHIP IN PHARMACEUTICS

American Foundation for Pharmaceutical Education
One Church Street, Suite 202
Rockville, MD 20850-4158
(301) 738-2160   Fax: (301) 738-2161

Purpose To encourage minority students with no more than 3 years remaining of graduate school to continue their studies and earn a Ph.D. in pharmaceutics.

Eligibility This program is open to minority students who have no more than 3 years remaining to complete a Ph.D. degree in a graduate program administered by or affiliated with a college of pharmacy. Applicants must be U.S. citizens or permanent residents.

Financial data The regular stipend is $6,000 per year.

Duration 1 year; may be renewed up to 2 additional years.

Special features This fellowship is offered as part of the industry-oriented fellowship program of the American Foundation for Pharmaceutical Education (AFPE).

Number awarded 1 each year.

Deadline February of each year.

[540]
ED BRADLEY SCHOLARSHIP

Radio and Television News Directors Foundation
1000 Connecticut Avenue, N.W., Suite 615
Washington, DC 20036
(202) 659-6510   Fax: (202) 223-4007

Purpose To provide financial assistance to an outstanding student whose career objective is electronic journalism.

Eligibility Eligible are sophomore or more advanced undergraduate or graduate students enrolled in an electronic journalism sequence at an accredited or nationally recognized college or university. Applications must include 1 to 3 examples of reporting or producing skills on audio or video cassette tapes (no more than 15 minutes total), a statement explaining why the candidate seeks a career in broadcast or cable journalism, and a letter of endorsement from a faculty sponsor that verifies that the applicant has at least 1 year of school remaining. Minority students receive preference.

Financial data The scholarship is $5,000, paid in semi-annual installments of $2,500 each.

Duration 1 year.

Special features An expense-paid trip to the Radio-Television News Directors Association Annual International Convention is also provided.

Limitations Previous winners of any RTNDF scholarship or internship are not eligible.

Number awarded 1 each year.

Deadline February of each year.

[541]
ELCA EDUCATIONAL GRANT PROGRAM

Evangelical Lutheran Church in America
Attn: Director for Theological Education, Division of Ministry
8765 West Higgins Road
Chicago, IL 60631-4195
(312) 380-2870

Purpose To provide financial assistance to members of the Evangelical Lutheran Church (ELCA) in America for the development of theological education.

Eligibility All applicants must be active members of the ELCA who are pursuing advanced academic theological education degrees (Ph.D., Th.D.) with the intent to teach in the field of theological education. Priority is given to women and minority applicants.

Financial data The amount of the grant depends upon the financial need of the applicant.

Number awarded Varies each year.

Deadline March of each year.

[542]
ELEANOR ROOSEVELT TEACHER FELLOWSHIPS

American Association of University Women
Attn: Educational Foundation
2201 North Dodge Street
Iowa City, IA 52243-4030
(319) 337-1716   Fax: (319) 337-1204

Purpose To increase the effectiveness of women teachers who are responsible for mathematics and science courses or at-risk girls.

Eligibility Women public school teachers with at least 3 consecutive years of full-time teaching experience in grades K through 12 are eligible to apply if they are responsible for mathematics, science, or technology courses for at-risk girls and are committed to creating gender equity in schools. Applicants must be U.S. citizens or permanent residents. This fellowship is designed for those who will return to teaching for at least 3 years after the fellowship year. Women of color are strongly encouraged to apply.

Financial data The amount awarded varies from $1,000 to $10,000, depending upon the recipient's proposed sabbatical program. Funds can be used by the recipients to pay for graduate study, thesis research, or course work that will improve their expertise.

Duration 1 year, beginning in July.

Special features This program was established in 1990. It is part of the foundation's Eleanor Roosevelt Fund for Women and Girls.

Number awarded 15 each year.

Deadline January of each year.

[543]
ENVIRONMENTAL SCIENCE AND MANAGEMENT FELLOWS PROGRAM

National Urban Fellows, Inc.
55 West 44th Street, Suite 600
New York, NY 10036
(212) 921-9400   Fax: (212) 921-9572

Purpose To provide mid-career executives and scientists who are women, minorities, or members of socially disadvantaged groups with an opportunity to enhance their skills through a program of academic study and professional experience in the administrative, technical, and scientific realms of environmental protection and management.

Eligibility Eligible to apply are U.S. citizens who have a bachelor's degree, have 3 years of full-time work experience in an administrative or managerial capacity, have demonstrated exceptional ability and leadership potential, meet academic admission requirements, have a high standard of integrity and work ethic, and are willing to relocate for the duration of the fellowship year.

Financial data The fellowship provides a stipend, tuition, and other program-related expenses.

Duration 2 years.

Special features The program begins with an academic year of study in environmental sciences at Duke University in Durham, North Carolina. Following this, fellows spend 12 months in mentorship assignments as special assistants to key executives and scientists in the environmental protection and conservation community. A summer session at Duke following the mentorship concludes the program. Fellows who successfully complete all requirements are granted a master of science degree from Tufts.

Number awarded Varies; approximately 15 each year.

Deadline February of each year.

[544]
EPILEPSY FOUNDATION OF AMERICA RESEARCH TRAINING FELLOWSHIPS

Epilepsy Foundation of America
Attn: Department of Research and Professional Education
4351 Garden City Drive
Landover, MD 20785
(301) 459-3700   (800) EFA-1000
Fax: (301) 577-2684   TDD: (800) 332-2070
E-mail: postmaster@efa.org

Purpose To offer qualified individuals the opportunity to develop expertise in epilepsy research through training and involvement in an epilepsy research project.

Eligibility Application is open to physicians or Ph.D. neuroscientists who are interested in a postdoctoral research experience. The proposed research may be either basic or clinical but must address a question of fundamental importance. A clinical training component is not required. Preference is given to applicants whose proposals have a pediatric or developmental emphasis. Special attention is given to applications from minorities and women.

Financial data The stipend is $40,000.

Duration 1 year.

Limitations The fellowship must be carried out at a facility where there is an ongoing epilepsy research program. Research must be conducted in the United States.

Number awarded Approximately 3 each year.

Deadline August of each year.

[545]
EPILEPSY FOUNDATION OF AMERICA RESEARCH/CLINICAL TRAINING FELLOWSHIPS

Epilepsy Foundation of America
Attn: Department of Research and Professional Education
4351 Garden City Drive
Landover, MD 20785
(301) 459-3700   (800) EFA-1000
Fax: (301) 577-2684   TDD: (800) 332-2070
E-mail: postmaster@efa.org

Purpose To offer qualified individuals the opportunity to develop expertise in clinical epilepsy and epilepsy research through training experience and involvement in an epilepsy research project.

Eligibility Applications are open to individuals who have received their M.D. degree and completed residency training. The proposed research may be either basic or clinical, but there must be a substantial clinical training component of the program. Emphasis is placed on individuals who will be trained in research in epilepsy rather than use epilepsy as a tool in their research in other fields. Special attention is given to applications submitted by women and minorities.

Financial data The stipend is $40,000.

Duration 1 year.

Limitations The fellowship must be carried out at a facility where there is an ongoing epilepsy research program. Research must be conducted in the United States.

Number awarded Approximately 7 each year.

Deadline August of each year.

[546]
ETHNIC MINORITY MASTER'S SCHOLARSHIPS

Oncology Nursing Foundation
501 Holiday Drive
Pittsburgh, PA 15220-2749
(412) 921-7373   Fax: (412) 921-6565
E-mail: onsmain@nauticom.net

Purpose To provide financial assistance to ethnic minorities for master's degree studies in nursing.

Eligibility The candidate must 1) be a registered nurse with a demonstrated interest in and commitment to cancer nursing; 2) be enrolled in a graduate nursing degree program at an NLN-accredited school of nursing (the program must have application to oncology nursing); 3) not have previously received a master's scholarship from the Oncology Nursing Foundation; 4) have a current license to practice as a registered nurse; and 5) be a member of an ethnic minority group (Native American, African American, Asian American, Pacific Islander, Hispanic/Latino, or other ethnic minority background).

Financial data The stipend is $3,000.

Duration 1 year.

Special features Recipients may attend school on a part-time or full-time basis.

Limitations At the end of each year of scholarship participation, recipients must submit a summary describing their educational activities.

Number awarded 2 each year.

Deadline January of each year.

[547]
FACULTY DEVELOPMENT FELLOWSHIP PROGRAM
Department of Education
Attn: Office of Postsecondary Education
Division of Higher Education Incentive Programs
Portals Building, Suite C-80
600 Independence Avenue, S.W.
Washington, DC 20202-5329
(202) 260-3209

Purpose To provide grants to institutions of higher education to fund fellowships for individuals from underrepresented minority groups to enter or continue in the higher education professorate.

Eligibility Applications may be submitted by institutions of higher education, consortia of institutions, and consortia of institutions and nonprofit organizations if they have a demonstrated record of enhancing the access to graduate education of individuals from underrepresented minority groups. Funds must be used to award the following types of fellowships: 1) prospective faculty development fellowships, for talented baccalaureate degree recipients from underrepresented minority groups who wish to obtain a doctoral degree and enter the higher education professorate; 2) experienced faculty development fellowships, for talented faculty from underrepresented minority groups who wish to continue in the higher education professorate and obtain a doctoral degree; and 3) faculty professional development fellowships, for talented faculty from underrepresented minority groups who wish to participate in short-term professional development programs, including seminars, conferences, and workshops, specifically designed to enhance their skills and careers, but not for study leading to a doctoral degree. Preference is given to applications for projects that provide each fellow with a tuition waiver and a minimum $2,000 in support beyond the stipend received by each fellow. Institutions may award fellowships to underrepresented minorities who are U.S. citizens, nationals, or permanent residents, or residing in the United States for other than a temporary purpose and intending to become citizens or permanent residents.

Financial data Grantee institutions may pay each fellow a level of support equal to the provided by the National Science Foundation graduate fellowships (currently $14,400 per year) or the fellow's demonstated level of financial need, whichever is less.

Duration Prospective or experience faculty development fellowships: up to 5 years; faculty professional development fellowships: up to 3 years.

Special features Recipients of prospective and experienced faculty development fellowships must enter into an agreement with the grantee in which they agree to teach full time, within 5 years after completing the doctoral degree for which the fellowship was awarded, for a period of not less than 1 year for each year for which financial assistance was received; experienced faculty development fellows must agree to teach in a public or private nonprofit institution of higher education that has a significant minority enrollment. Fellows who fail to comply with that agreement must repay the amount of the grant funds received, prorated according to the fraction of the teaching obligation not completed, with interest. Repayment of fellowship funds may be deferred while the recipient is serving in the armed forces (up to 3 years), temporarily and totally disabled (up to 3 years), providing care for an immediate member of the family who is disabled (up to 1 year), enrolled as a full-time doctoral student and making satisfactory progress toward a degree, serving as a Peace Corps volunteer, seeking and unable to find employment (up to 1 year), or engaged in full-time employment as an elementary or secondary school teacher. The obligation will be cancelled in case of the recipient's death or permanent and total disability.

Limitations Prospective fellows must apply directly to recipient institutions, not to the Department of Education.

Number awarded Varies each year.

Deadline Application dates vary; for current information, check the *Federal Register.*

[548]
FERMI NATIONAL ACCELERATOR LABORATORY GRADUATE FELLOWSHIPS FOR MINORITY STUDENTS
Fermi National Accelerator Laboratory
Attn: Manager, Equal Opportunity Office
MS 117
P.O. Box 500
Batavia, IL 60510
(708) 840-4633   E-mail: sist@fnal.gov

Purpose To provide financial assistance for graduate study in physics to underrepresented minority students.

Eligibility Historically underrepresented minorities in the sciences (Hispanics, African Americans, and Native Americans) are eligible to apply if they are pursuing or graduate study in physics. Normally, applicants will have participated as undergraduates in Fermilab Summer Internships in Science and Technology for Minority Students.

Financial data The program provides assistance with tuition and fees, a stipend of up to $600 per month, and summer employment with Fermilab.

Duration 1 year; may be renewed up to 3 additional years.

Special features Fermilab scientists are assigned to all recipients as advisors to aid their progress in graduate school.

Limitations Although students may attend graduate schools of their choice, Fermilab helps them in making their applications and evaluating their preparation.

Number awarded Varies each year.

Deadline February of each year.

[549]
FINANCIAL ASSISTANCE FOR DISADVANTAGED HEALTH PROFESSIONS STUDENTS GRANTS
Health Resources and Services Administration
Attn: Bureau of Health Professions
Division of Student Assistance
Parklawn Building, Room 8-34
5600 Fishers Lane
Rockville, MD 20857
(301) 443-4776   Fax: (301) 443-0846

Purpose To provide financial support for disadvantaged health professions students who are enrolled in accredited medical schools.

Eligibility Eligible to submit grant requests are accredited schools (private or public) of medicine, osteopathic medicine, or dentistry. They must request funds for students at their institutions who are from a disadvantaged background and can demonstrate exceptional financial need; these students must be working on a degree in medicine, osteopathic medicine, or dentistry. Disadvantaged individuals are defined as those who 1) come from an environment that has inhibited the individual from obtaining the knowledge, skill, and abilities required to enroll in and graduate from a health professions school; or 2) come from a family with a low income, currently set at less than $10,200 for a family with 1 dependent, ranging to less than $26,700 for a family with 6 dependents. Applicant institutions must be carrying out programs to recruit and retain minority students and faculty.

Financial data With these grants, schools award students funds to cover the costs of tuition and other reasonable educational expenses including fees, books, laboratory expenses and other costs of attending school. In return for this support, students of medicine and osteopathic medicine must agree to enter and complete residency training in primary care and to practice in primary care for 5 years after completing a residency training program. Students of dentistry must agree to practice in general dentistry for 5 years after completing residency training.

Duration 1 year; may be renewed.

Special features Students apply directly to their academic institution for support. For a list of schools participating in this program, contact the address above.

Number awarded Varies each year.

Deadline Deadline dates vary but are usually in June; check the *Federal Register* for the current schedule.

[550]
FLEMMIE P. KITTRELL FELLOWSHIP FOR MINORITIES

American Association of Family and Consumer Sciences
Attn: Awards, Fellowships, and Grants Office
1555 King Street
Alexandria, VA 22314
(703) 706-4600   Fax: (703) 706-HOME

Purpose To provide financial assistance for graduate study in home economics to minority women in the United States and developing countries.

Eligibility Minority women in the United States and developing countries who are interested in pursuing an advanced degree in home economics are eligible to apply.

Financial data The stipend is $3,000. When the fellowship is awarded to an international student, cooperating colleges agree to remit an amount of tuition and/or fees equal to at least $500.

Duration The fellowship is awarded periodically (when funding is available).

Special features The fellowship honors Kittrell, who served for 27 years as the chair of the Home Economics Department (now the School of Human Ecology) at Howard University and pioneered in the development of international cooperation in home economics in Africa and India. The fellowship is made possible through an annual gift from the J.C. Penney Company, Inc.

Limitations Students living in the United States must send $15 with each request for fellowship materials. No application fee is assessed international students residing outside the United States at the time of application.

Number awarded 1 each year the fellowship is offered.

Deadline January of each year the fellowship is offered.

[551]
FLORIDA MINORITY PARTICIPATION IN LEGAL EDUCATION (MPLE) SCHOLARSHIP PROGRAM

Florida Education Fund
18350 NW Second Avenue, Third Floor
Miami, FL 33169
(305) 654-7133   Fax: (305) 654-7135

Purpose To increase the number of historically underrepresented minority attorneys practicing in Florida by providing financial aid to minority law students in the state.

Eligibility This program is open to U.S. citizens who are members of historically disadvantaged minority groups that are underrepresented in the membership of the Florida Bar (African Americans, Hispanics, and Native Americans), who hold or will receive a bachelor's degree from a regionally accredited college or university, and who have taken or will take the Law School Admission Test. Applicants must have been accepted at 1 of the 6 participating law schools in Florida (Nova Southeastern—Shepard Broad Law Center, Florida State University College of Law, St. Thomas University School of Law, Stetson University College of Law, University of Florida College of Law, or University of Miami School of Law). They must plan to practice law in Florida for a period of time equal to the amount of time for which the student receives assistance from this program.

Financial data The annual award is $13,972 at public law schools or $19,000 at private law schools.

Duration 1 year; may be renewed for 2 additional years if the recipient maintains satisfactory performance and normal progress toward the J.D. degree.

Limitations Since this program is intended to increase minority enrollment at the 6 participating law schools, currently enrolled students are not eligible to apply.

Number awarded 200 over each 3-year cycle.

[552]
FLORIDA SPACE GRANT CONSORTIUM FELLOWSHIP PROGRAM

Florida Space Grant Consortium
c/o University of Florida
Department of Astronomy
405 Space Sciences Research Building
Gainesville, FL 32611-2055
(352) 392-6750   Fax: (352) 392-3456
E-mail: fsgc@astro.ufl.edu

Purpose To provide financial assistance for graduate space studies at universities participating in the Florida Space Grant Consortium.

Eligibility Eligible to be nominated for this program are U.S. citizens who are enrolled in aerospace-related doctoral studies at universities participating in the Florida Space Grant Consortium: Embry-Riddle Aeronautical University, Florida State University, University of Miami, Florida Atlantic University, Florida A&M University, University of North Florida, Florida Institute of Technology, University of Central Florida, University of South Florida, Florida International University, University of Florida, and University of West Florida. The Florida Space Grant Consortium is a component of the U.S. National Aeronautics and Space Administration (NASA) Space Grant program, which encourages participation by women, minorities, and persons with disabilities.

Financial data Each fellow receives a $12,000 stipend and a supplementary summer traineeship stipend from a participating industry, government, or private laboratory.

Duration Up to 3 years.

Special features Fellows work during the summer in a government, industry, or private laboratory. This program is funded by NASA.

Number awarded 6 each year.

Deadline February of each year.

[553]
FOCUS PROFESSIONS GROUP FELLOWSHIPS

American Association of University Women
Attn: Educational Foundation
2201 North Dodge Street
Iowa City, IA 52243-4030
(319) 337-1716   Fax: (319) 337-1204

Purpose To provide financial assistance to minority women who are interested in entering designated fields with traditionally low female participation.

Eligibility Women from minority groups that have been historically underrepresented in designated fields are eligible to apply. They must be graduate students in 1 of the following fields: business administration (M.B.A., 2-year, and executive programs only), law (J.D.), or medicine (M.D. or D.O.). Eligible minority candidates are African Americans, Mexican Americans, Puerto Ricans, other Latinas, Native Americans, Alaska Natives, Asian Americans, and Pacific Islanders. Applicants must be U.S. citizens or permanent residents. Special consideration is given to applicants who show professional promise in innovative or neglected areas of research and/or practice in public interest concerns.

Financial data The stipends range from $5,000 to $9,500 for full-time study.

Duration 1 year.

Special features This program is part of the American Association of University Women's Selected Professions Fellowships program. There are no restrictions on the age of the applicant or the place of study (among accredited U.S. institutions).

Deadline December of each year for all applicants except for M.B.A. candidates, who must submit their applications by January of each year.

[554]
FORD FOUNDATION POSTDOCTORAL FELLOWSHIPS FOR MINORITIES

National Research Council
Attn: Fellowship Office
2101 Constitution Avenue
Washington, DC 20418
(202) 334-2860   Fax: (202) 334-3419
E-mail: infofell@nas.edu

Purpose To help members of minority groups already engaged in college or university teaching to develop as scholars in their respective fields and to acquire the professional associations that will make them more effective and productive when they resume academic employment.

Eligibility Applicants must be citizens or nationals of the United States by the application deadline date; be members of 1 of the following ethnic minority groups: Black/African Americans, Mexican Americans/Chicanos, Native Pacific Islanders (Micronesians or Polynesians), Puerto Ricans, Alaskan Natives (Eskimo or Aleut), or Native American Indians; and have earned within the preceding 7 years a Ph.D. or Sc.D. degree in 1 of the eligible fields (behav-

ioral and social sciences, humanities, engineering, mathematics, physical sciences, life sciences, and interdisciplinary programs). Awards are not made to candidates in professional fields, including medicine, law, social work, library science, business administration, management, fine arts, performing arts, speech pathology, audiology, health sciences, personnel and guidance, public health, home economics, and education. Selection is based on achievement and ability as evidenced by academic records and quality of proposed plan of study or research.

Financial data The stipend is $25,000; in addition, fellows receive a travel and relocation allowance up to $3,000. Most institutions receive a $2,000 cost-of-research allowance to provide partial support for the fellow's study and research program. The allowance is prorated for tenure less than 12 months. Finally, each fellow's employing institution is given a $2,500 grant-in-aid for the fellow's use once the fellowship tenure is completed. The employing institution is expected to match the grant. These funds are designated to be used for the fellow's research expenditures.

Duration Up to 12 months. Tenable at any appropriate nonprofit U.S. institution, including a research university, government laboratory, privately-sponsored nonprofit institute, or center for advanced study (such as the Woodrow Wilson Center for Scholars, the Institute for Advanced Study, the Center for Advanced Study in the Behavioral Sciences, the Newberry Library, or the University of Wisconsin's Institute for Research on Poverty), as long as it is an institution other than that from which the candidate applies.

Limitations Fellows may not accept another major fellowship while they are being supported by this program. Applicants who wish to affiliate with institutions outside the United States must provide evidence of the particular benefits that would accrue from affiliation with a foreign center.

Number awarded Varies; approximately 25 each year.

Deadline January of each year.

[555]
FORD FOUNDATION PREDOCTORAL FELLOWSHIP PROGRAM FOR MINORITIES

National Research Council
Attn: Fellowship Office
2101 Constitution Avenue
Washington, DC 20418
(202) 334-2872   Fax: (202) 334-3419
E-mail: infofell@nas.edu

Purpose To increase minority presence in the arts and sciences on college and university faculties.

Eligibility These fellowships are intended for minority students (Black/African American, Puerto Rican, Mexican American/Chicano, Alaskan Native, Native Pacific Islander, or Native American Indian) who plan to work toward the Ph.D. or Sc.D. degree and who are at or near the beginning of their graduate studies. Eligible to apply are college seniors, first-year graduate students, or others who have completed a limited amount of graduate work. Candidates must not have completed more than 30 semester hours, 45 quarter hours (or the equivalent) of graduate-level study in the fields supported by the program. All applicants must take the GRE General Test. Awards are made for study in research-based doctoral programs in the behavioral and social sciences, humanities, engineering, mathematics, physical sciences, and biological sciences, or for interdisciplinary programs comprised of 2 or more eligible disciplines. The fellowships are tenable at any accredited nonprofit institution of higher education in the United States that offers Ph.D.s or Sc.D.s in the fields eligible for support.

Financial data The stipend to the recipient is $12,000 per year and to the host institution is $6,000 per year. In addition, the foundation provides $1,000 to the recipient's undergraduate department to be used to encourage minorities to consider graduate study and academic careers.

Duration 1 year; may be renewed for up to 2 additional years.

Special features The competition for this program is conducted by the National Research Council on behalf of the Ford Foundation. Applicants who merit receiving the fellowship but to whom awards cannot be made because of insufficient funds are given Honorable Mentions; this recognition does not carry with it a monetary award but honors applicants who have demonstrated substantial academic achievement. The National Research Council will publish a list of those Honorable Mentions who wish their names publicized.

Limitations Awards are not made in such areas as business administration and management, home economics, health sciences, public health, library science, personnel and guidance, social work, speech pathology and audiology, fine arts and performing arts, or education. In addition, awards are not made for work leading to terminal master's degrees, doctorates in education, Doctor of Fine Arts degrees, joint degree programs such as M.D./Ph.D. or M.F.A./Ph.D., or professional degrees in such areas as medicine, law, or business. Fellows may not accept remuneration from another fellowship or similar external award while on this program; however, supplementation from institutional funds, educational benefits from the Veterans Administration, or educational incentive funds may be received concurrently with Ford Foundation support. Predoctoral fellows are required to submit an interim progress report 6 months after the start of the fellowship and a final report at the end of the 12 month tenure.

Number awarded Approximately 50 each year.

Deadline November of each year.

[556]
FOREIGN AFFAIRS FELLOWSHIP PROGRAM

Woodrow Wilson National Fellowship Foundation
Attn: Foreign Affairs Fellowship Program
5 Vaughn Drive, Suite 300
P.O. Box 2437
Princeton, NJ 08543-2437
(609) 452-7007   Fax: (609) 452-0066

Purpose To provide financial assistance for the education of students interested in pursuing a career with the Foreign Service of the Department of State.

Eligibility Applicants must be U.S. citizens in the sophomore year of undergraduate study at an accredited 4-year college or university with a cumulative grade point average of at least 3.2. They must plan to pursue graduate study in the field of international affairs and a career in the Foreign Service. Selection is based on general qualifications, academic performance, interest in a career in the Foreign Service, financial need, and potential for success in the program. Special emphasis is given to promoting knowledge, awareness of, and interest in employment with the Foreign Service among minority students. Children of State Department employees are not eligible.

Financial data Fellows receive support for college tuition, fees, room, board, and books during the final 2 years of undergraduate study and the first year of graduate work. Their graduate institution provides similar support during the second year of graduate study, depending upon financial need. For the summer institute and the internships, travel expenses and stipends are paid. The overseas internship includes medical insurance. Married fellows receive additional funding for university room and board, but are themselves responsible for travel and accommodations for their spouse and family during the institute and the internships.

Duration 4 years: the final 2 years of undergraduate study and the first 2 years of graduate work (provided the student maintains a minimum 3.2 grade point average).

Special features Each May, the fellows participate in orientation and training sessions in Washington, D.C. to help prepare them for Foreign Service careers. During the summer between their junior and senior years, they attend a 6- to 8-week summer institute in a graduate school of public policy and international affairs, with courses in international relations, public policy, policy analysis, policy modules, economics, calculus, and communication skills. During the summer following graduation, they are assigned to an internship at an overseas post of the State Department. Between the first and second year of graduate school, they serve a summer internship in the Department of State in Washington, D.C. This program is funded by the State Department and administered by the Woodrow Wilson National Fellowship Foundation.

Limitations Fellows must commit to a minimum of 4 and a half years of service in an appointment as a Foreign Service Officer following the second year of graduate study. Candidates who do not successfully complete the program and Foreign Service entry requirements must reimburse the Department of State for expenses paid under the fellowship.

Number awarded Approximately 10 each year.

Deadline February of each year.

[557]
FRANKLIN C. MCLEAN AWARD

National Medical Fellowships, Inc.
Attn: Scholarships and Programs
110 West 32nd Street, 8th Floor
New York, NY 10001-3205
(212) 714-1007

Purpose To recognize and reward the outstanding academic achievement, leadership, and community service of senior medical school minority students.

Eligibility This award is open to senior African American, Native American, Mexican American, and mainland Puerto Rican students enrolled in accredited U.S. medical schools. Financial need is not a consideration. Candidates must be nominated by their medical schools during the summer preceding their senior year.

Financial data This honor includes a certificate of merit and a $3,000 award.

Duration 1 year; nonrenewable.

Special features This award, the first award offered by the National Medical Fellowship, was established in 1968 in memory of the Chicago bone physiologist who founded the organization.

Number awarded 1 each year.

Deadline June of each year.

[558]
FREDRIKSON & BYRON FOUNDATION MINORITY SCHOLARSHIPS

Fredrikson & Byron Foundation
1100 International Centre
900 Second Avenue South
Minneapolis, MN 55402-3397
(612) 347-7000   Fax: (612) 347-7077

Purpose To provide financial assistance to minority law students and to increase the number of minority lawyers practicing in the Twin Cities area of Minnesota.

Eligibility African American, Asian American/Pacific Islander, Hispanic American, and Native American students enrolled in their first year of law school are eligible to apply (they must be currently enrolled and in the second semester of their first year at the time of application). Selection is based on academic performance and potential. Financial need is not considered.

Financial data The fellowship stipend is $5,000.

Duration 1 year.

Number awarded Up to 2 each year.

Deadline February of each year.

[559]
FUND FOR GRADUATE EDUCATION

Presbyterian Church (U.S.A.)
Attn: Office of Financial Aid for Studies
100 Witherspoon Street, Room M042
Louisville, KY 40202-1396
(502) 569-5776   Fax: (502) 569-5018

Purpose To provide financial assistance to minority and women church members who plan to teach at the college or seminary level and wish to pursue a doctoral degree.

Eligibility This program is open to women and members of minority racial/ethnic groups who wish to teach at the college or seminary level and/or assume comparable positions of professional leadership within the church. Applicants must be enrolled in a Ph.D./St.D./Th.D./Ed.D. program in an accredited graduate institution, preparing for or already engaged in teaching/administrative positions in a college or theological school of the Presbyterian Church (U.S.A.), a communicant member of that church, and able to demonstrate financial need. Students must be endorsed by a letter of recommendation from a minister as well as a faculty member or administrator of their own school.

Financial data Amount varies, depending upon the availability of funds.

Duration 1 year; renewable.

Number awarded Varies each year.

Deadline April of each year.

[560]
GARTH REEVES JR. MEMORIAL SCHOLARSHIPS

Society of Professional Journalists—South Florida Chapter
c/o Gina Carroll
Miami Herald
One Herald Plaza
Miami, FL 33132-1693
(305) 376-2710

Purpose To provide financial assistance for education of South Florida minority students interested in journalism as a career.

Eligibility Minority students committed to careers in print or broadcast journalism are eligible for these scholarships if they reside in South Florida or are enrolled in or accepted for enrollment in a college or university in that area. Selection is based on scholastic achievement, extracurricular activities in journalism, and financial need. Both undergraduate and graduate students are eligible.

Financial data The stipend ranges from $300 to $1,500 per year, depending upon the recipient's educational requirements and financial need.

Duration 1 year.

Number awarded 10 or more each year.

Deadline February of each year.

[561]
GEORGE A. STRAIT MINORITY STIPEND

American Association of Law Libraries
53 West Jackson Boulevard, Suite 940
Chicago, IL 60604
(312) 939-4764   Fax: (312) 431-1097

Purpose To provide financial assistance to minority college seniors or college graduates who are interested in becoming law librarians.

Eligibility Applicants must be members of a minority group; seniors, college graduates, or matriculated graduate library school students with an interest in law librarianship; citizens of the United States or Canada (or able to submit evidence of becoming naturalized at the beginning of the award period); interested in and able to demonstrate an aptitude for law library work; and able to show financial need. Preference is given to applicants with previous service to law librarianship.

Financial data The stipend is $3,500.

Duration 1 year.

Number awarded 1 each year.

Deadline March of each year.

[562]
GEORGE M. BROOKER COLLEGIATE SCHOLARSHIP FOR MINORITIES

Institute of Real Estate Management Foundation
Attn: Foundation Coordinator
430 North Michigan Avenue
Chicago, IL 60611-4090
(312) 329-6008   Fax: (312) 661-0217

Purpose To provide financial assistance to minorities interested in preparing (on the undergraduate or graduate level) for a career in the real estate management industry.

Eligibility This program is open to undergraduate and graduate minority students majoring in real estate, preferably with an emphasis on management, asset management, or related fields. Applicants must be interested in entering a career in real estate management upon graduation. They must have earned at least a 3.0 grade point average in their major, have completed at least 2 college courses in real estate, and write an essay (up to 500 words) on why they want to follow a career in real estate management. U.S. citizenship is required.

Financial data The stipend for undergraduates is $1,000; the stipend for graduate students is $2,500.

Duration 1 year; nonrenewable.

Number awarded 3 each year: 2 undergraduate awards and 1 graduate award.

Deadline March of each year.

[563]
GERBER PRIZE FOR EXCELLENCE IN PEDIATRICS

National Medical Fellowships, Inc.
Attn: Scholarships and Programs
110 West 32nd Street, 8th Floor
New York, NY 10001-3205
(212) 714-1007

Purpose To recognize and reward an underrepresented minority medical student who will pursue a career in pediatric medicine.

Eligibility Candidates must be African Americans, Mexican Americans, Native Americans, or mainland Puerto Ricans who are seniors at 1 of the following allopathic medical schools in Michigan: University of Michigan Medical School, Michigan State University School of Human Medicine, Michigan State University College of Osteopathic Medicine, or Wayne State University School of Medicine. They must be nominated by the medical school dean and chair of the department of pediatrics at the medical school in which they are enrolled, be able to demonstrate academic achievement, plan to pursue a career in pediatric medicine, and meet the requirements of pediatric residence programs.

Financial data The award is $2,000.

Duration The competition is held annually.

Special features This award was established in 1990.

Number awarded 1 each year.

Deadline Nominations are due in January of each year.

[564]
GLOBAL CHANGE GRADUATE FELLOWSHIPS

Oak Ridge Institute for Science and Education
Attn: Science/Engineering Education Division
P.O. Box 117
Oak Ridge, TN 37831-0117
(423) 576-9655   (423) 576-7009
(800) 569-7749   Fax: (423) 576-3643
E-mail: gfglobal@orau.gov

Purpose To provide funding for graduate study and work experience in various aspects of global change.

Eligibility This program is open to graduate students in atmospheric sciences, meteorology, ecology, ocean sciences, biology, and other scientific disciplines related to global change. Applicants must be enrolled in master's or doctoral programs at universities participating in this program (for a list of participating schools, write to the address above). All programs operated by the Science/Engineering Education Division (SEED) of Oak Ridge Institute for Science and Education (ORISE) seek to broaden the participation of minorities, women, and persons with disabilities in science and engineering careers.

Financial data Fellows receive full payment of tuition and fees and a stipend of $14,400 per year. An additional $300 per month is paid during the research experience. A $1,000 annual allowance is paid to the recipient's university.

Duration 1 year; renewable.

Special features Participants perform a required collaborative research experience as interns at either a U.S. Department of Energy (DOE) or other government agency global change research facility. This program is funded by DOE's Office of Energy Research, Environmental Sciences Division, Office of Health and Environmental Research, and administered by ORISE/SEED.

Number awarded Varies each year.

Deadline January of each year.

[565]
GOALS FELLOWSHIPS

Industrial Relations Council on GOALS
P.O. Box 4363
East Lansing, MI 48826-4363
(517) 351-6122   (800) 344-6257

Purpose To provide funding for minority students who are interested in obtaining a master's degree in labor/industrial relations.

Eligibility Applicants must be U.S. citizens and members of 1 of the racial/ethnic groups that are underrepresented in labor/industrial relations: African Americans, Hispanics, Native Hawaiians, Native Alaskans, or Native Americans. They must have earned an undergraduate degree in 1 of the social sciences (e.g. economics, psychology, sociology, political science) that provides appropriate preparation for graduate study in labor/industrial relations, and be interested in attending 1 of the schools participating in this program: Cornell University, Georgia State, University of Illinois at Urbana-Champaign, Loyola University of Chicago, University of Massachusetts at Amherst, Michigan State University, University of Minnesota, University of Oregon, Ohio State University, Rutgers University, University of South Carolina, West Virginia University, or the University of Wisconsin at Madison.

Financial data The fellowship pays tuition, fees, and a stipend of up to $7,800 per academic year.

Duration 1 year; may be renewed for a second year if satisfactory progress is being made toward the degree.

Special features The Industrial Relations Council on Graduate Opportunities for Advanced Level Studies (GOALS) is a cooperative effort by the 13 consortium universities, 32 major American corporations, and the AFL-CIO.

Limitations Fellows may not work for pay during the school year.

Number awarded At least 10 each year.

Deadline Applications for these fellowships may be submitted after acceptance by 1 of the participating graduate schools; application deadlines for the schools vary, so candidates should check with the school they wish to attend.

[566]
GOLDEN STATE MINORITY SCHOLARSHIPS

Golden State Minority Foundation
Attn: Scholarship Information
1055 Wilshire Boulevard, Suite 1115
Los Angeles, CA 90017-2431
(213) 482-6300   (800) 666-4763
Fax: (213) 482-6305

Purpose To stimulate and encourage high academic performance among California minority students; to provide qualified minority students with financial assistance to pursue studies in business or a related field.

Eligibility Candidates for the scholarship must be currently enrolled as full-time students at a 4-year accredited college or university as juniors, seniors, or graduate students; be majoring in business administration, economics, life insurance, or a related field; have a grade point average of at least 3.0; be a qualified underrepresented ethnic minority (African American, Latino, or

Native American); attend school or be a resident of California; be a U.S. citizen or permanent legal resident; and, if employed, be working no more than 28 hours per week.

Financial data Scholarships are intended to be supplemental funds.

Duration The scholarships are awarded annually.

Special features The foundation was established by Golden State Mutual Insurance Company and is the first public foundation to be created by a major Black financial institution.

Number awarded In any given academic year, scholarships awarded to a particular minority group approximate in percentages that group's numeric proportion of the national minority population.

Deadline For southern California, March of each year; for northern California, October of each year.

[567]
GRADUATE FELLOWSHIP PROGRAM IN BILINGUAL EDUCATION

Department of Education
Attn: Office of Bilingual Education and Minority Languages
    Affairs
Switzer Building, Room 5086
600 Independence Avenue, S.W.
Washington, DC 20202-6510
(202) 205-9727

Purpose To provide financial assistance for graduate and post-doctoral education in areas related to programs of study for limited English proficient (LEP) persons.

Eligibility Institutions of higher education offering degrees beyond the baccalaureate level in areas related to programs for LEP children and youth may apply for these grants. Funds must be used to provide fellowships to graduate students and post-doctoral scholars in such areas as teacher training, program administration, research and evaluation, and curriculum development. Applicants for fellowships under this program must be U.S. citizens, nationals, or permanent residents; have been accepted for enrollment as full-time students in an approved course of study; be proficient in English and, if applicable, another language; have an excellent academic record; be planning to enter or return to a career in service to LEP children and youth after completion of their studies; and have experience in providing services to, teaching in, or administering programs for LEP children and youth.

Financial data The amounts of the grants to institutions depend on the nature of the applications and the availability of funds. Awards to students may provide for tuition and fees, books (up to $300 per year), travel directly related to the program of study (up to $250 per year), and a stipend of up to $500 per month. Postdoctoral scholars may receive a stipend up to $40,000 and assistance for publications, research and scholarly materials, research-related travel, and fees up to $5,000.

Duration Students who maintain satisfactory progress in master's degree or postdoctoral programs may be awarded fellowships for a maximum of 2 1-year periods; students in doctoral programs may receive 3 1-year fellowships.

Limitations Grants are made only to institutions of higher education, not to individuals; students apply to the university they plan to attend. Fellows must, within 6 months of completing their studies or postdoctoral project, work as bilingual educators for a period of time that they receive assistance under the fellowship.

A fellow who does not work in a prescribed activity must repay the full amount of the fellowship with interest.

Deadline Deadlines vary annually; check the *Federal Register* for the current schedule.

[568]
GRANTS FOR RESIDENCY TRAINING AND ADVANCED EDUCATION IN THE GENERAL PRACTICE OF DENTISTRY

Health Resources and Services Administration
Attn: Bureau of Health Professions
Division of Associated, Dental and Public Health Professions
Parklawn Building, Room 8-101
5600 Fishers Lane
Rockville, MD 20857
(301) 443-6896   Fax: (301) 443-1164

Purpose To provide funding to dental schools for initiation, expansion, or improvement of programs in general dentistry residency training.

Eligibility This program is open to accredited public or non-profit private schools of dentistry or postgraduate dental training institutions located in the United States or its possessions. Funding may be used to 1) plan, develop, and operate an approved residency program in the general practice of dentistry or an approved advanced educational program in the general practice of dentistry; 2) provide financial assistance to participants in such a program who are in need of financial assistance and who plan to specialize in the practice of general dentistry; 3) fund innovative, nontraditional models for the provision of postdoctoral general dentistry training. Selection criteria include the degree to which the project proposes to attract, maintain, and graduate minority and disadvantaged students. Students who are interested in receiving aid through this program should contact the address above to obtain a list of the institutions that are current grant recipients.

Financial data Recently, $3,720,000 per year has been available for this program, including $2,178,000 for continuation support and $1,542,000 for new competing awards; the average competing grant has been $100,000. Institutions that receive grants determine the amounts to award as financial assistance.

Duration Up to 3 years.

Number awarded Varies each year; in recent years, 11 new competing grants have been awarded annually.

Deadline December of each year.

[569]
GRANTS FOR THE MINORITY FELLOWSHIP FACULTY PROGRAM

Health Resources and Services Administration
Attn: Bureau of Health Professions
Division of Disadvantaged Assistance
Parklawn Building, Room 8A09
5600 Fishers Lane
Rockville, MD 20857
(301) 443-3680   Fax: (301) 443-5242
E-mail: bbrooks@hrsa.ssw.dhhs.gov

Purpose To provide grants to institutions for funding fellowships to underrepresented minority faculty members in health professions schools.

Eligibility Eligible applicants for this program are schools of medicine, allopathic and osteopathic medicine, dentistry, veterinary medicine, optometry, podiatric medicine, pharmacy, public health, health administration, clinical psychology, and other public or private nonprofit health or educational entities. They must be submitting proposals to 1) identify, recruit, and select individuals from underrepresented minorities in health professions; 2) provide such individuals with the skills necessary to enable them to secure an academic career including pedagogical skills, program administration, the design and conduct of research, grant writing, and publications; 3) provide services designed to assist such individuals in their preparation for an academic career, including the provision of mentors; and 4) provide health services to rural or medically underserved populations. Applicant institutions must provide an assurance that they will make available fellowships to qualified individuals. Fellowship recipients must 1) be U.S. citizens, nationals, or permanent residents; 2) have completely satisfied any other obligation for health professional service which is owed under an agreement with the federal government, state government, or other entity prior to beginning the period of service under this program; 3) be from an underrepresented minority in the health professions; 4) have at a minimum appropriate advanced preparation (such as a master's or doctoral degree in a health profession) and special skills necessary to enable that individual to teach and practice; 5) not have been a member of the faculty of any school at any time during the 18-month period preceding the date on which the individual submits a request for the fellowship; and 6) become a member of the faculty of the applicant institution.

Financial data Each fellowship includes a stipend in an amount not exceeding 50 percent of the regular salary of a similar faculty member, or $30,000, whichever is less. The applicant institution must make available $1 for every $1 of federal funds received under the fellowship.

Duration The fellowship must be for a minimum of 2 years; federal support, however, is provided only for the first year; the applicant institution (school) is required to support the fellow for the second year at a level not less than the total of federal and institutional funds awarded for the first year.

Number awarded Varies each year.

Deadline February of each year.

[570]
GULF COAST RESEARCH LABORATORY MINORITY SUMMER GRANT PROGRAM

Mississippi Office of State Student Financial Aid
3825 Ridgewood Road
Jackson, MS 39211-6453
(601) 982-6589   (800) 327-2980 (within MS)

Purpose To provide financial assistance to minority students who wish to study or conduct research in the marine and environmental sciences in Mississippi.

Eligibility Eligible are Mississippi residents who are minority students seeking to attend classes or conduct independent study or research at the Gulf Coast Research Laboratory.

Financial data Grants for the 4-week program provide $750 to the institution and $100 to the student; grants for the 5-week program provide $900 to the institution and $125 to the student; grants for the 10-week program provide $1,800 to the institution and $250 to the student.

Duration Up to 10 weeks, during the summer.

Number awarded Varies each year.

Deadline May of each year.

[571]
HANA SCHOLARS PROGRAM

United Methodist Church
Attn: Office of Loans and Scholarships
1001 19th Avenue South
P.O. Box 871
Nashville, TN 37202-0871
(615) 340-7344   Fax: (615) 340-7048

Purpose To provide financial assistance to outstanding United Methodist Hispanic, Asian, and Native American undergraduate and graduate full-time college students.

Eligibility Applicants must be born of Hispanic, Asian, or Native American parentage, be active members of the United Methodist Church for at least 1 year prior to applying, be citizens or permanent residents of the United States, demonstrate academic ability, have a commitment to their ethnic community and their careers, be able to demonstrate financial need, and be enrolled as juniors, seniors, or graduate students in accredited academic institutions in the United States.

Financial data The stipend depends on the availability of funds and the need of the recipient.

Duration 1 year; students must reapply in following years to be considered for further aid. Undergraduate students are eligible to receive support for up to 2 years; graduate students for up to 3 years.

Limitations Applicants may accept Hispanic, Asian, Native American (HANA) awards only if they are not receiving any other major United Methodist scholarship for the same academic year. When asked, recipients will be expected to participate in such related activities as: serving as HANA interpreters within their local church, conference, or region; sharing information about their educational activities with other scholars and higher education personnel; and attending HANA seminars, institutes, consultations, or other similar activities.

Deadline March of each year.

[572]
HEALTH CAREERS OPPORTUNITY PROGRAM GRANTS

Health Resources and Services Administration
Attn: Bureau of Health Professions
Division of Disadvantaged Assistance
Parklawn Building, Room 8A09
5600 Fishers Lane
Rockville, MD 20857
(301) 443-4493   Fax: (301) 443-6343
E-mail: bbrooks@hrsa.ssw.dhhs.gov

Purpose To provide financial support for education in health professions to students from disadvantaged backgrounds.

Eligibility This program is open to schools of allopathic medicine, osteopathic medicine, public health, dentistry, veterinary medicine, optometry, pharmacy, allied health, chiropractic and podiatric medicine, and public and nonprofit private schools which offer graduate programs in clinical psychology. Health professions schools are eligible if they identify a cohort of at least 7 disadvantaged students who applied but were not accepted to a health professions school; allied health schools are eligible if they identify a cohort of at least 5 disadvantaged students who have completed an undergraduate degree with a significant science focus and made a late decision to enter an allied health professions school and are in pursuit of a baccalaureate level degree in physical therapy, physician assistant, respiratory therapy, medical technology, or occupational therapy. Applicants must provide the designated students with a program of rigorous science and other education experiences and then admit the students who successfully complete the program or arrange for their admission to another health professions or allied health school. Recipient schools must also provide the students with a prematriculation summer program to ease their transition into the health professions or allied health school, and with counseling and advice on financial aid to assist them to complete successfully their education. Individuals from a disadvantaged background are those who come from an environment that has inhibited them from obtaining the knowledge, skill, and abilities to enroll in and graduate from a health professions school or allied health program, or who come from a low-income family (ranging from an annual income below $10,200 for a family of 1 to $26,700 for a family of 6).

Financial data Approximately $30.1 million is available for this program each year, of which $18.5 million is for continuing grants and $11.6 million is available for new grants, averaging $199,000 each. Of the appropriated funds each year, 20 percent must be obligated for stipends to disadvantaged students of exceptional financial need who are students at schools of allopathic medicine, osteopathic medicine, or dentistry; 10 percent must be obligated to community-based programs (including Indian tribes and Alaska Native villages); and 70 percent must be obligated for grants and contracts to institutions of higher education. Students receive a stipend during their participation in the program.

Duration Grants to institutions are up to 3 years; for students, the program is 1 year, including 6 to 8 weeks in the summer.

Number awarded Approximately 58 new projects are funded each year.

Deadline February of each year.

[573]
HIGHER EDUCATION MULTICULTURAL SCHOLARS PROGRAM

Department of Agriculture
Attn: Cooperative State Research, Education, and Extension
  Service
Office of Science and Education Resources Development
South Agriculture Building, Room 3433
1400 Independence Avenue, S.W.
Washington, DC 20250-2251
(202) 720-1973   E-mail: jgilmore@reeusda.gov

Purpose To provide grants to universities for scholarships to minority students in agriculture.

Eligibility This program is open to all U.S. colleges and universities offering baccalaureate degree programs in any discipline of the food and agricultural sciences, or offering a D.V.M. degree. Funding is provided to the institutions to provide financial aid to full-time students pursuing a baccalaureate degree in a discipline of the food and agricultural sciences or a D.V.M. degree. Students must be U.S. citizens newly recruited to their course of study and from a racial or ethnic group traditionally underrepresented in the food and agricultural sciences (Blacks, Hispanics, American Indians or Alaskan Natives, and Asians or Pacific Islanders). Students at 2-year institutions may participate in this program if their institution has an articulation or bridging agreement with an eligible 4-year institution. Fields of study include agriculture, conservation and renewable natural resources, forestry, veterinary medicine, home economics, and closely allied disciplines. Students must apply directly to a participating univer-

sity or college for these scholarships; for a list, contact the address above.

Financial data Grants to institutions range from $40,000 to $100,000, and average $50,000. Institutions may offer stipends to students of up to $5,750 per year, of which $4,500 is provided by this program and $1,250 is provided by the university from non-federal matching funds. Institutions also receive an annual cost-of-education allowance of $500 per year for each scholar supported by a grant.

Duration Grants to institutions are made up to 5 years, but students may be supported only up to 4 years.

Number awarded From 30 to 40 grants to institutions are made each year; each participating college or university must support from 2 to 5 students.

Deadline Institutions must submit grant applications by October of each year; each institution sets its own deadlines for students. Beginning with FY 1998, applications from institutions will be accepted only in even-numbered years.

[574]
HOLLY A. CORNELL SCHOLARSHIP

American Water Works Association
Attn: Scholarship Coordinator
6666 West Quincy Avenue
Denver, CO 80235-3098
(303) 794-7711, ext. 6210   Fax: (303) 794-7310

Purpose To encourage outstanding minority and female students to pursue advanced training in the field of water supply and treatment.

Eligibility Minority and female students who anticipate completing the requirements for a master's degree in engineering no sooner than December of the following year are eligible. Students who have been accepted into graduate school but have not yet begun graduate study are encouraged to apply. Recipients of the Larson Aquatic Research Support (LARS) MS Scholarship are not considered for this program. Selection is based on the quality of the applicant's academic record and the potential to provide leadership in the field of water supply and treatment.

Financial data The stipend is $5,000.

Duration 1 year.

Special features Funding for this program comes from the consulting firm CH2M Hill.

Limitations The association reserves the right not to make an award for any year in which an outstanding candidate is not identified.

Number awarded 1 each year.

Deadline December of each year.

[575]
HOWARD HUGHES MEDICAL INSTITUTE PREDOCTORAL FELLOWSHIPS IN BIOLOGICAL SCIENCES

National Research Council
Attn: Fellowship Office
2101 Constitution Avenue
Washington, DC 20418
(202) 334-2872   Fax: (202) 334-3419
E-mail: infofell@nas.edu

Purpose To provide funding for students (particularly minorities and women) interested in pursuing graduate education in the biological sciences.

Eligibility This is an international program: both American citizens and foreign nationals may apply; foreign nationals must study at a U.S. institution but U.S. citizens may study in the United States or abroad. Applicants must be able to demonstrate superior scholarship, be able to show great promise for future achievement, and be interested in working full time toward a Ph.D. or Sc.D. degree in the biological sciences (biochemistry, biophysics, biostatistics, cell biology, developmental biology, epidemiology, genetics, immunology, mathematical and computational biology, microbiology, molecular biology, neuroscience, pharmacology, physiology, structural biology, or virology). The program is aimed at students who are at or near the beginning of their graduate program; those eligible at the time of application may be college seniors, college graduates with no or limited postbaccalaureate graduate study in the biological sciences, and first-year graduate students. Minorities underrepresented in the sciences (Blacks, Hispanics, Native Alaskans, Native Americans, and Native Pacific Islanders) and women are particularly encouraged to apply.

Financial data The stipends are $15,000. In addition, there is a cost-of-education allowance, payable to the host institution, of $15,000 (up to $12,800 in lieu of tuition and assessed fees and $2,200 for the direct benefit of the fellow for health insurance, books and supplies, a computer and computer-related expenses, travel to scientific meetings, tuition for special summer courses, or secretarial or clerical services relevant to the program of study).

Duration 3 years; may be renewed for up to 2 additional years.

Special features This program is administered by the National Research Council; the Howard Hughes Medical Institute selects the recipients.

Number awarded Varies; generally, 80 each year.

Deadline November of each year.

[576]
IDAHO SPACE GRANT CONSORTIUM HIGHER EDUCATION AND RESEARCH PROGRAM

Idaho Space Grant Consortium
c/o University of Idaho
College of Engineering
Mechanical Engineering
Moscow, ID 83844-1011
(208) 885-7018   Fax: (208) 885-6645
E-mail: rgill@uidaho.edu

Purpose To provide financial assistance for study and research in space-related fields to students and faculty at member institutions of the Idaho Space Grant Consortium.

Eligibility This program is open to students and faculty at the University of Idaho, Boise State University, Idaho State University, and other member institutions of the Idaho Space Grant Consortium. Faculty members may apply for funding to travel to facilities of the U.S. National Aeronautics and Space Administration (NASA) or other aerospace related agencies/industries to obtain research funding. Students may apply for scholarships, assistantships, or fellowships for space related programs. U.S. citizenship is required. As a component of the NASA Space Grant program, the Idaho Space Grant Consortium encourages participation by women, minorities, and persons with disabilities.

Financial data The amounts of the awards depend on the availability of funds and the nature of the proposal.

Duration Depends on the nature of the proposal.

Special features This program is funded by NASA.

Number awarded Varies each year. Since it began in 1991, this program has awarded 33 faculty research initiation awards, 21 scholarships, and 6 fellowships.

[577]
ILLINOIS CONSORTIUM FOR EDUCATIONAL OPPORTUNITY PROGRAM

Southern Illinois University Carbondale
Attn: Director of ICEOP
Woody Hall C-224
Carbondale, IL 62901-4716
(618) 453-4558

Purpose To increase the participation of minority students in graduate school programs in Illinois.

Eligibility To be eligible for this award, an applicant must be a resident of Illinois, a U.S. citizen or permanent resident, a recipient of an earned baccalaureate degree, of above-average academic ability, admitted to a graduate or professional degree program at a participating institution in Illinois, in financial need, and a member of an underrepresented minority group—African Americans, Hispanics, Native Americans, and Asian Americans (but only in those disciplines where they are underrepresented).

Financial data The stipend is $10,000 per year for full-time students or $5,000 per year for part-time students.

Duration Up to 2 years for master's and professional degree students; up to 4 years for doctoral students.

Special features The intent of this program is to increase the number of minorities employed in faculty and administrative positions in postsecondary institutions and in state agencies and governing boards in Illinois. It was established by the Illinois General Assembly in 1985 and may be utilized at 33 participating institutions in Illinois.

Limitations Award recipients must agree to accept a position, in teaching or administration, in an Illinois postsecondary educational institution, on an Illinois higher education governing or coordinating board staff, or as an employee in Illinois in an education related capacity, for a period equal to the number of years of the award. Recipients failing to fulfill the conditions of the award are required to repay 20 percent of the total award.

Deadline February of each year.

[578]
ILLINOIS MINORITY GRADUATE INCENTIVE PROGRAM

Southern Illinois University Carbondale
Attn: Director of IMGIP
Woody Hall C-224
Carbondale, IL 62901
(618) 453-4558

Purpose To increase the number of underrepresented minority students pursuing doctoral degrees in science, mathematics, and engineering at graduate schools in Illinois.

Eligibility To be considered for this program, an applicant must be a U.S. citizen or permanent resident, a member of an underrepresented minority group (African American, Hispanic, Native American), a recipient of an earned baccalaureate degree, and accepted for admission to a doctoral program in the life sciences, physical sciences, mathematics, or engineering at a participating school in Illinois: Illinois Institute of Technology, Illinois State University, Loyola University of Chicago, Northern Illinois University, Northwestern University, University of Chicago, Rush University,

University of Illinois at Chicago, University of Illinois at Urbana-Champaign, and Southern Illinois University at Carbondale.

Financial data In addition to full tuition and fees, each fellow receives an annual stipend of $12,500 and an annual $1,500 allowance for books, supplies, equipment, and travel. Upon completion of the degree and acceptance of appropriate employment, fellows are eligible to receive a $15,000 placement incentive.

Duration 1 year; may be renewed for up to 2 additional years.

Special features This program was established in 1985 and is funded by a Higher Education Cooperation Act grant from the Illinois State Board of Higher Education.

Limitations Each fellow must sign a letter of intent agreeing to seek and accept appropriate employment at an Illinois college or university upon completion of the doctoral degree.

Number awarded Varies; generally, about 5 each year.

Deadline February of each year.

[579]
INDIANA SPACE GRANT CONSORTIUM FELLOWSHIPS

Indiana Space Grant Consortium
c/o Purdue University
School of Aeronautics and Astronautics
1282 Grissom Hall
West Lafayette, IN 47907-1282
(317) 494-5135   Fax: (317) 494-0307
E-mail: andrisan@ecn.purdue.edu

Purpose To provide financial support to students in Indiana interested in pursuing space-related studies.

Eligibility This program is open to students interested in pursuing space-related programs at Purdue University or the University of Notre Dame. U.S. citizenship is required. The Indiana Space Grant Consortium is a component of the U.S. National Aeronautical and Space Administration (NASA) Space Grant program, which encourages participation by women, minorities, and persons with disabilities.

Financial data Each year, $25,000 is available for fellowships at each of the 2 universities.

Special features This program is funded by NASA.

Number awarded Each participating university determines how to allocate its funds.

Deadline Deadline dates are established by the participating universities; contact the address above for information on the programs at each institution.

[580]
INDIVIDUAL DENTIST SCIENTIST AWARDS

National Institutes of Health
Attn: National Institute of Dental Research
Division of Extramural Research
Natcher Building, Room 4AN-18J
45 Center Drive MSC 6402
Bethesda, MD 20892-6402
(301) 594-2618   Fax: (301) 480-8318
E-mail: jl46d@nih.gov

Purpose To provide financial support to doctoral students interested in pursuing careers in basic, biomedical, behavioral, and clinical oral health research.

Eligibility Applications for this program may be submitted on behalf of the candidates by domestic, public or private dental schools or institutions affiliated with a dental school. Candidates must be pursuing Ph.D. basic science and research experiences to facilitate transition to a research career. They may already hold a D.D.S. degree. Preference is given to candidates with advanced clinical knowledge and skills in a recognized dental specialty or who have received 2 or more years of formal post-D.D.S. clinical development in a non-specialty recognized field. Minorities and women are particularly encouraged to apply.

Financial data Starting salaries are based on relevant experience, ranging from $26,500 for no experience to a maximum of $39,226 with 10 or more years of experience. In addition, the institute allows $15,000 per year for research development support such as tuition, fees, and books related to career development; research expenses for supplies, equipment, and technical personnel; travel to research meetings or training; and statistical services including personnel and computer time.

Duration 5 years; nonrenewable.

Special features The National Institutes of Health (NIH) designates this program as the K15 Awards.

Number awarded Varies each year.

Deadline January, May, and September of each year.

[581]
INDIVIDUAL EAST EUROPEAN LANGUAGE TRAINING GRANTS

American Council of Learned Societies
228 East 45th Street
New York, NY 10017-3398
(212) 697-1505   Fax: (212) 949-8058
E-mail: grants@acls.org

Purpose To provide financial assistance for study of eastern European languages.

Eligibility Applicants must be citizens or permanent legal residents of the United States who hold at least a 4-year college degree; graduate students, postdoctoral scholars, and professionals are eligible. Grants are provided for first- or second-year study of any eastern European language (except the languages of the Independent States of the Former Soviet Union) at universities in the United States or eastern Europe. The awards are intended for people who will use the eastern European languages in their academic or other professional careers. Applications are particularly invited from women and members of minority groups.

Financial data The stipend is $2,000 for study in the United States or $2,500 for study in eastern Europe.

Duration Summer months.

Special features This program is sponsored jointly by the American Council of Learned Societies (ACLS) and the Social Science Research Council, funded by the U.S. Department of State but administered by ACLS.

Number awarded Varies each year.

Deadline January of each year.

[582]
INDIVIDUAL PREDOCTORAL NATIONAL RESEARCH SERVICE AWARDS FOR M.D./PH.D. FELLOWS

National Institutes of Health
Attn: National Institute on Alcohol Abuse and Alcoholism
Office of Scientific Affairs
Willco Building, Suite 409
6000 Executive Boulevard MSC 7003
Bethesda, MD 20892-7003
(301) 443-2890   Fax: (301) 443-6077
E-mail: jv24p@nih.gov

Purpose To provide financial assistance for students enrolled in an M.D./Ph.D. program who plan careers in mental health, drug abuse and addiction, and alcohol abuse research.

Eligibility Applicants must be 1) U.S. citizens or permanent residents of the United States; 2) enrolled in an M.D./Ph.D. program at an approved medical school; 3) accepted in a related scientific Ph.D. program; and 4) supervised by a mentor in that scientific discipline when the application is submitted. Normally, students apply during the first year of medical school, but applications may be submitted at any stage of medical study. Applicants must be proposing a course of study to prepare themselves to conduct research in areas of demonstrable mental health, drug abuse and addition, or alcohol abuse relevance and document that the proposed graduate program offers them an opportunity to develop expert research skills and knowledge. Racial/ethnic minority individuals, women, and persons with disabilities are especially encouraged to apply.

Financial data The annual stipend is $10,008; fellows may also request funds for tuition and fees. The institution may receive an allowance of $2,000 per fellow per 12-month period to help defray such expenses as research supplies, equipment, travel to scientific meetings, and related items.

Duration Up to 6 years.

Special features This award is offered by 3 of the institutes within the National Institutes of Health (NIH): the National Institute on Alcohol Abuse and Alcoholism (NIAAA), the National Institute on Drug Abuse (NIDA), and the National Institute of Mental Health (NIMH). Information is available from various components of those 3 institutes. The NIH designates this program as the F30 Awards.

Number awarded Varies each year.

Deadline April, August, or December of each year.

[583]
INDUSTRIAL HYGIENE GRADUATE FELLOWSHIP PROGRAM

Oak Ridge Institute for Science and Education
Attn: Science/Engineering Education Division
P.O. Box 117
Oak Ridge, TN 37831-0117
(423) 576-9655   (423) 576-7009
(800) 569-7749   Fax: (423) 576-3643
E-mail: indhyggf@orau.gov

Purpose To provide financial assistance for graduate study and work experience in the area of industrial hygiene.

Eligibility This program is open to students at designated participating universities (write to the address above for a list of these) who are working on a master's degree in industrial hygiene. All programs operated by the Science/Engineering Education Division (SEED) of Oak Ridge Institute for Science and Education (ORISE) seek to broaden the participation of minorities, women, and persons with disabilities in science and engineering careers.

Financial data Participants receive a monthly stipend of $1,300 plus $400 per month during the practicum period. In addition, there is an annual $1,500 academic allowance.

Duration 2 years.

Special features Participants intern at a U.S. Department of Energy (DOE) research facility. This program is funded by DOE's Office of Health, Industrial Hygiene Programs Division and administered by ORISE/SEED.

Number awarded Varies each year.

Deadline January of each year.

[584]
INSTITUTIONAL DENTIST SCIENTIST AWARDS

National Institutes of Health
Attn: National Institute of Dental Research
Division of Extramural Research
Natcher Building, Room 4AN-18J
45 Center Drive MSC 6402
Bethesda, MD 20892-6402
(301) 594-2618   Fax: (301) 480-8318
E-mail: jl46d@nih.gov

Purpose To provide dentists with advanced clinical training to prepare them to become researchers.

Eligibility Dental institutions may obtain funding under this program in order to provide support to dentists who wish to pursue career development experiences leading to research independence. Program directors at the institutions select candidates who have already attained a D.D.S., D.M.D., or equivalent degree but who normally have not started postgraduate clinical training. Candidates must intend to pursue a program that includes didactic and supervised basic, clinical, or behavioral research experiences which result in the Ph.D. degree, and advanced clinical training in either a recognized clinical specialty or equivalent dental clinical discipline. The program strongly encourages the recruitment and retention of women and underrepresented minorities for this program.

Financial data Starting salaries are based on relevant experience, ranging from $26,500 for no experience to a maximum of $39,226 with 10 or more years of experience. In addition, the institute allows $15,000 per year for research development support such as tuition, fees, and books related to career development; research expenses for supplies, equipment, and technical personnel; travel to research meetings or training; and statistical services including personnel and computer time.

Duration 5 years.

Special features Currently, 9 institutions are participating in this program: the University of Alabama at Birmingham, the University of California at San Francisco, the University of Connecticut Health Center, the University of Iowa, the Harvard School of Dental Medicine, the University of Minnesota, the State University of New York at Buffalo, the University of Rochester, and the University of Washington. The National Institutes of Health (NIH) designates this program as the K16 Awards.

Number awarded 18 each year: 2 at each of the 9 participating schools of dentistry.

Deadline Application deadlines are established by each dental school participating in the program.

[585]
INTERNATIONAL PREDISSERTATION FELLOWSHIP PROGRAM ADVANCED DISCIPLINARY TRAINING FELLOWSHIPS

Social Science Research Council
810 Seventh Avenue
New York, NY 10019
(212) 377-2700   Fax: (212) 377-2727

Purpose To provide funding for the training of talented graduate students in the social sciences who are planning research and teaching careers oriented to the developing world.

Eligibility Applications are sought from students enrolled in Ph.D. programs in the economics, political science, psychology, or sociology at 23 participating schools: University of California at Berkeley, University of California at Los Angeles, University of California at San Diego, University of Chicago, Columbia University, Cornell University, Duke University, Harvard University, University of Illinois at Urbana-Champaign, Indiana University, Massachusetts Institute of Technology, Michigan State University, University of Michigan, University of Minnesota, University of North Carolina at Chapel Hill, Northwestern University, University of Pennsylvania, Princeton University, Stanford University, University of Texas at Austin, University of Washington, University of Wisconsin at Madison, and Yale University. Applicants should be in the early stages of their training and should demonstrate an interest in combining disciplinary skills with area and language studies. This program is directed at students with an exceptionally strong background who wish to acquire advanced theoretical and methodological training at their U.S. university that will provide them with a more sophisticated understanding of their discipline. Recipients should ultimately plan to conduct dissertation research in or on Africa, Central Asia and the Caucasus, China, Latin America, the Caribbean, the Near and Middle East, South Asia, and Southeast Asia. Minorities and women are particularly encouraged to apply.

Financial data Fellowships provide support for advanced study at a U.S. university.

Duration 12 months.

Special features Fellows are invited to participate in a conference with other fellows and, in some instances, in a region-specific workshop with graduate students in the developing world. The conferences and workshops promote interdisciplinary dialogue on theoretical and methodological issues on an international scale, and encourage international cooperation and collaboration. This program is funded by the Ford Foundation and jointly administered by the Social Science Research Council and the American Council of Learned Societies.

Limitations Awards are not tenable for dissertation research itself.

Deadline Application deadlines are established by the participating universities.

[586]
INTERNATIONAL PREDISSERTATION FELLOWSHIP PROGRAM STANDARD FELLOWSHIPS

Social Science Research Council
810 Seventh Avenue
New York, NY 10019
(212) 377-2700   Fax: (212) 377-2727

Purpose To provide funding for the training of talented graduate students in the social sciences who are planning research and teaching careers oriented to the developing world.

Eligibility Applications are sought from students enrolled in Ph.D. programs in the social sciences at 23 participating schools: University of California at Berkeley, University of California at Los Angeles, University of California at San Diego, University of Chicago, Columbia University, Cornell University, Duke University, Harvard University, University of Illinois at Urbana-Champaign, Indiana University, Massachusetts Institute of Technology, Michigan State University, University of Michigan, University of Minnesota, University of North Carolina at Chapel Hill, Northwestern University, University of Pennsylvania, Princeton University, Stanford University, University of Texas at Austin, University of Washington, University of Wisconsin at Madison, and Yale University. The program is aimed primarily at graduate students in economics, political science, psychology, and sociology, but is open to students in the other social science disciplines as well. Applicants should be in the early stages of their training and should demonstrate an interest in combining disciplinary skills with area and language studies. The intent is to encourage students to undertake dissertation research in or on Africa, Central Asia and the Caucasus, China, Latin America, the Caribbean, the Near and Middle East, South Asia, and Southeast Asia. Minorities and women are particularly encouraged to apply.

Financial data Fellowships typically support a combination of language training, overseas study, and course work in area studies, in addition to living stipends and international travel expenses.

Duration 12 months of support over a 2-year period.

Special features Fellows are invited to participate in a conference with other fellows and, in some instances, in a region-specific workshop with graduate students in the developing world. The conferences and workshops promote interdisciplinary dialogue on theoretical and methodological issues on an international scale, and encourage international cooperation and collaboration. This program is funded by the Ford Foundation and jointly administered by the Social Science Research Council and the American Council of Learned Societies.

Limitations Awards are not tenable for dissertation research itself.

Deadline Application deadlines are established by the participating universities.

[587]
IRVING GRAEF MEMORIAL SCHOLARSHIP

National Medical Fellowships, Inc.
Attn: Scholarships and Programs
110 West 32nd Street, 8th Floor
New York, NY 10001-3205
(212) 714-1007

Purpose To recognize and reward third-year minority medical school students' outstanding academic achievement, leadership, and community service.

Eligibility This competition is open only to third-year minority medical school students who received financial assistance from National Medical Fellowships during their second year. For the purposes of this program, "minority" is defined as African American, Native American, Mexican American, and mainland Puerto Rican students. Candidates must be able to demonstrate outstanding academic achievement and leadership. They must be nominated by their medical schools in the summer before the students' third year. The Graef family reviews candidates' dossiers and selects the student most deserving of the award.

Financial data This honor includes a certificate of merit and an annual stipend of $2,000.

Duration 1 year; renewable in the fourth year of medical school, if the recipient continues in good academic standing.

Special features This program is named in honor of an active National Medical Fellowship board member who was also an associate professor of clinical medicine at New York University's School of Medicine. It was established in 1978.

Number awarded 1 each year.

Deadline Nominations are usually requested in July of each year.

[588]
JOHN AND MURIEL LANDIS SCHOLARSHIP AWARD

American Nuclear Society
Attn: Scholarship Program
555 North Kensington Avenue
La Grange Park, IL 60525
(708) 352-6611   Fax: (708) 352-0499

Purpose To provide financial assistance to undergraduate or graduate students who are interested in pursuing a career in nuclear-related fields.

Eligibility To be eligible, applicants must be undergraduates or graduate students at colleges or universities located in the United States who are pursuing, or planning to pursue, a career in nuclear science, nuclear engineering, or a related field. In addition, applicants must have a greater than average financial need. Minorities and women are especially encouraged to apply. Selection is primarily based on financial need and potential for academic and professional success.

Financial data The stipend is $3,000, to be used to defray educational costs, including tuition, books, fees, and room and board.

Duration 1 year.

Limitations Applicants must be sponsored by an American Nuclear Society local section, division, technical group, committee, student branch, or organization member. If a student does not know of a sponsoring organization, the ANS will help to establish contact. Augmentation of this scholarship program with matching or supplemental funds by the sponsoring organization is encouraged (though not required). Requests for an application must be accompanied by a self-addressed stamped envelope.

Number awarded 8 each year.

Deadline February of each year.

[589]
JOHN HUGHLINGS JACKSON RESEARCH/CLINICAL TRAINING FELLOWSHIPS

Epilepsy Foundation of America
Attn: Department of Research and Professional Education
4351 Garden City Drive
Landover, MD 20785
(301) 459-3700   (800) EFA-1000
Fax: (301) 577-2684   TDD: (800) 332-2070
E-mail: postmaster@efa.org

Purpose To offer qualified individuals the opportunity to develop expertise in clinical epilepsy and epilepsy research through training experience and involvement in an epilepsy research project.

Eligibility Applications are open to individuals who have received their M.D. degree and completed residency training. The proposed research may be either basic or clinical, but there must be an equal emphasis on clinical training and clinical epileptology. Special attention is given to applications submitted by women and minorities.

Financial data The stipend is $30,000.

Duration 1 year.

Limitations The fellowship must be carried out at a facility where there is an ongoing epilepsy research program. Research must be conducted in the United States.

Number awarded Varies each year.

Deadline August of each year.

[590]
JOINTLY SPONSORED NIH PREDOCTORAL TRAINING PROGRAM IN THE NEUROSCIENCES

National Institutes of Health
Attn: National Institute of Neurological Disorders and Stroke
Division of Fundamental Neurosciences and Developmental Disorders
Federal Building, Room 916
7550 Wisconsin Avenue MSC 9170
Bethesda, MD 20892-9170
(301) 496-5745   Fax: (301) 402-1501
E-mail: rb175y@nih.gov

Purpose To provide support to institutions for programs of predoctoral training in the neurosciences.

Eligibility This program is open to domestic, nonprofit, private or public institutions with the staff and facilities required for the proposed program of research training. The research training program director at the institution is responsible for the selection and appointment of trainees, who must have received a baccalaureate degree and be training at the postbaccalaureate level in a program leading to a Ph.D. in the neurosciences. All candidates must be U.S. citizens or permanent citizens. Institutions must give particular attention to recruiting individuals from minority groups that are underrepresented nationally in biomedical and behavioral research (African Americans, Hispanics, Native Americans, Alaskan Natives, and Pacific Islanders).

Financial data For trainees, the annual stipend is $10,008. Institutions may apply for training costs (such as staff salaries, consultant costs, equipment, research supplies, and staff travel) of up to $1,500 per year per trainee; up to $125 per month to offset the cost of tuition, fees, travel, supplies, and other expenses for each short-term health professional research training position; and an indirect cost allowance of 8 percent of total allowable direct costs or actual indirect costs, whichever is less.

Duration 5 years; may be renewed.

Special features This program is jointly administered by 8 components of the National Institutes of Health (NIH): the National Institute on Aging, the National Institute of Child Health and Human Development, the National Institute on Deafness and Other Communication Disorders, the National Institute of Dental Research, the National Institute of General Medical Sciences, the National Institute of Mental Health, the National Institute of Neurological Disorders and Stroke, and the National Institute of Nursing Research. The NIH administers this program as part of its National Research Service Award Institutional Research Training Grants (T32).

Number awarded Varies each year.

Deadline Letters of intent must be submitted by February of each year and applications are due by May.

[591]
KALA SINGH MEMORIAL SCHOLARSHIP

American Speech-Language-Hearing Foundation
Attn: Director of Programs and Corporate Development
10801 Rockville Pike
Rockville, MD 20852
(301) 897-5700   Fax: (301) 571-0457

Purpose To provide financial assistance for graduate education to international or minority students who are interested in working on a graduate degree in communication sciences and disorders.

Eligibility Applicants must be college graduates who are accepted for graduate study in the United States in a communication sciences and disorders program or enrolled as a full-time graduate student. The fund gives priority to a foreign or minority (American Indian, Alaskan Native, Asian, Pacific Islander, Black, Hispanic) student. Students who previously received a scholarship from the American Speech-Language-Hearing Foundation are not eligible.

Financial data The award is $2,000.

Duration The award is granted annually.

Number awarded 1 each year.

Deadline June of each year.

[592]
KANSAS ETHNIC MINORITY FELLOWSHIP

Kansas Board of Regents
700 S.W. Harrison Street, Suite 1410
Topeka, KS 66603-3760
(913) 296-3517

Purpose To encourage minorities to attend graduate school in Kansas.

Eligibility This program is open to Kansas residents. Applicants must be Asian American, African American, Hispanic American or Native American. They must be enrolled or accepted in a graduate school in Kansas. Financial need must be documented.

Financial data A minimum of $8,000 per year for full-time study. This is a scholarship/loan program; recipients must seek employment in a Kansas educational institution upon graduation, working 1 year for each year of support; if they fail to do so, they must repay the fellowship at 15 percent interest.

Duration 1 year; may be renewed.

Limitations Recipients must attend school on a full-time basis and may now work during enrollment.

Number awarded Varies each year.

[593]
KEN INOUYE MEMORIAL SCHOLARSHIP

Society of Professional Journalists—Los Angeles Chapter
c/o Daniel E. Garvey
Scholarship Chair
9951 Barcelona Lane
Cypress, CA 90631-3759

Purpose To provide financial assistance to minority undergraduate and graduate students in southern California who are interested in pursuing careers in journalism.

Eligibility Minority college juniors, seniors, or graduate students who are interested in careers in journalism or communications (but not public relations, advertising, or publicity) are eligible to apply if they are residents of or attending school in Los Ange-

les, Ventura, or Orange Counties, California. Selection is based on evidence of unusual accomplishment and potential to advance in a news career; financial need is considered if 2 applicants are similarly qualified.

Financial data The stipend is $1,000 per year.

Duration 1 year.

Number awarded 1 each year.

Deadline February of each year.

[594]
KENTUCKY SPACE GRANT CONSORTIUM GRADUATE FELLOWSHIPS

Kentucky Space Grant Consortium
c/o Western Kentucky University
Department of Physics and Astronomy, TCCW 246
Hardin Planetarium and Astrophysical Observatory
1 Big Red Way
Bowling Green, KY 42101-3576
(502) 745-4156   Fax: (502) 745-6471
E-mail: ksgc@wkuvx1.wku.edu

Purpose To provide financial assistance for graduate education in space-related fields to students in Kentucky.

Eligibility This program is open to graduate students at member institutions of the Kentucky Space Grant Consortium (Centre College, Eastern Kentucky University, Kentucky State University, Morehead State University, Murray State University, Northern Kentucky University, Thomas More College, Transylvania University, University of Kentucky, University of Louisville, and Western Kentucky University). Applicants must be enrolled in a graduate degree program in a space-related field or teaching specialization. As part of the program, a faculty member must agree to serve as a mentor on a research project. U.S. citizenship is required. The Kentucky Space Grant Consortium is a component of the U.S. National Aeronautics and Space Administration (NASA) Space Grant program, which encourages participation by women, minorities, and persons with disabilities.

Financial data The stipend is $16,000 per year, with an additional $2,000 for use in support of the student's mentored research project. Preference is given to applicants from schools which agree to waive tuition for the fellow as part of the program.

Duration 1 year; may be renewed.

Special features This program is funded by NASA.

Number awarded Varies each year.

Deadline March of each year.

[595]
LASPACE FELLOWS PROGRAM

Louisiana Space Consortium
c/o Louisiana State University
Physics and Astronomy
277 Nicholson Hall
Baton Rouge, LA 70803-4001
(504) 388-8697   Fax: (504) 388-1222
E-mail: wefel@phepds.dnet.nasa.gov

Purpose To provide financial assistance to students working on a graduate degree in an aerospace-related discipline at a college or university belonging to the Louisiana Space Consortium (LaSPACE).

Eligibility This program is open to U.S. citizens working on a master's or doctoral degree in an aerospace-related field at 1 of the LaSPACE member schools: Dillard University, Grambling

State University L.S.U. Agricultural Center, Louisiana State University and A&M College, Louisiana Tech University, Loyola University, McNeese State University, Northwestern State University of Louisiana, Northeast Louisiana University, Southern University and A&M College, Southern University at New Orleans, Southern University at Shreveport, Tulane University, University of New Orleans, University of Southwestern Louisiana, Xavier University of Louisiana. LaSPACE is a component of the U.S. National Aeronautics and Space Administration (NASA) Space Grant program, which encourages participation by women, minorities, and persons with disabilities.

Financial data The stipend is $15,000 per year for students working on a master's degree and $17,500 per year for students working on a doctorate.

Duration 1 year; renewable for up to 3 years for master's degree students and up to 5 years for Ph.D. students.

Special features Fellows work with an established aerospace researcher and are expected to describe the work in a yearly written report and in seminars presented to various audiences. Funding for this program is provided by NASA.

Number awarded Depends on the availability of funds.

[596]
LAWRENCE WADE JOURNALISM FELLOWSHIP

Heritage Foundation
Attn: Selection Committee
214 Massachusetts Avenue, N.E.
Washington, DC 20002
(202) 546-4400

Purpose To provide financial assistance and work experience to college students who are interested in a career in journalism.

Eligibility This program is open to undergraduate or graduate students who are currently enrolled full time and are interested in a career as a journalist upon graduation. Applicants need not be majoring in journalism, but they must submit writing samples of published news stories, editorial commentaries, or broadcast scripts. Preference is given to candidates who are Asian Americans, African Americans, Hispanic Americans, or Native Americans.

Financial data The winner receives a $1,000 scholarship and participates in a 10-week salaried internship at the Foundation.

Number awarded 1 each year.

Deadline February of each year.

[597]
LEADERSHIP FOR DIVERSITY SCHOLARSHIP

California School Library Association
1499 Old Bayshore Highway, Suite 142
Burlingame, CA 94010
(415) 692-2350   Fax: (415) 692-4956

Purpose To encourage minority students to get a credential as a library media teacher in California.

Eligibility This program is open to students who are members of a traditionally underrepresented group enrolled in a college or university library media teacher credential program in California. Applicants must intend to work as a library media teacher in a California school library media center for a minimum of 3 years. Financial need is considered in awarding the scholarship.

Financial data The stipend is $1,000.

Duration 1 year.

Special features The California School Library Association was formerly named the California Media Library Educators Association.

Number awarded 1 each year.

Deadline May of each year.

[598]
LITA/LSSI MINORITY SCHOLARSHIP

American Library Association
Attn: Library and Information Technology Association
50 East Huron Street
Chicago, IL 60611-2795
(312) 280-4270   (800) 545-2433, ext. 4270
TDD: (312) 944-7298   Fax: (312) 280-3257
E-mail: tbarbee@ala.org

Purpose To provide financial assistance to minority students interested in preparing for a career in library automation.

Eligibility Applicants must be American or Canadian citizens, interested in pursuing a master's degree in library/information science (with a focus on library automation), and a member of 1 of the following ethnic groups: American Indian, Alaskan Native, Asian or Pacific Islander, African American, or Hispanic. The award is based on academic excellence, leadership potential, evidence of a commitment to a career in library automation and information technology, and prior activity and experience in those fields. Economic need is considered when all other criteria are equal.

Financial data The stipend is $2,500.

Duration 1 year.

Special features This scholarship is funded by Library Systems & Services, Inc. (LSSI) and administered by the Library and Information Technology Association (LITA) of the American Library Association.

Number awarded 1 each year.

Deadline March of each year.

[599]
LITA/OCLC MINORITY SCHOLARSHIP

American Library Association
Attn: Library and Information Technology Association
50 East Huron Street
Chicago, IL 60611-2795
(312) 280-4270   (800) 545-2433, ext. 4270
TDD: (312) 944-7298   Fax: (312) 280-3257
E-mail: tbarbee@ala.org

Purpose To provide financial assistance to minority students interested in preparing for a career in library automation.

Eligibility Applicants must be American or Canadian citizens, interested in pursuing a master's degree in library/information science (with a focus on library automation), and a member of 1 of the following ethnic groups: American Indian, Alaskan Native, Asian or Pacific Islander, African American, or Hispanic. The award is based on academic excellence, leadership potential, evidence of a commitment to a career in library automation and information technology, and prior activity and experience in those fields. Economic need is considered when all other criteria are equal.

Financial data The stipend is $2,500.

Duration 1 year.

Special features This fellowship was awarded for the first time in 1991. The funding for the program comes from OCLC.

Number awarded 1 each year.
Deadline March of each year.

[600]
LOEB FELLOWSHIP IN ADVANCED ENVIRONMENTAL STUDIES

Graduate School of Design
Harvard University
48 Quincy Street
Cambridge, MA 02138
(617) 495-9345   Fax: (617) 495-8949

Purpose To prepare postdoctoral individuals for professional studies in architecture, landscape architecture, and urban planning and design.

Eligibility This program is open to accomplished midcareer professionals in design, environmental, and related fields. Normally, only U.S. citizens working in the United States are eligible. Although there are no specific background requirements, applicants must have worked professionally for at least 5 years. Persons with full-time academic positions are free to apply, but have lower priority in the selection process. The program encourages the participation of members of minority groups.

Financial data The program provides fellows with round-trip airfare and a fixed allowance for incidental expenses. In addition, all applicants are expected to ask their employers to maintain all or part of their regular salaries during the fellowship period. Stipends are available only when no other financial aid is available.

Duration Fellowships are granted for either full-time or part-time participation. Part-time fellowships are usually limited to persons living within a 2-hour airline distance of Cambridge; they are encouraged to spend at least 2 days per week at Harvard during 1 academic semester or the academic year. Full-time fellows are expected to obtain a leave of absence in order to participate in the program (for 1 semester or the entire academic year).

Special features Fellows are given access to all of Harvard's facilities, including individual offices and the libraries. They may audit courses at the Graduate School of Design or Harvard's other graduate schools. Fellows are eligible to draw up a list of potential guest speakers from within Harvard and the Boston professional community; these guests are invited to dinner at the program's headquarters for informal meetings that promote and stimulate professional and intellectual interests. A fully furnished house is available near the Graduate School of Design for the use of all fellows during the academic year.

Limitations Personal secretarial and other office services are not provided. Fellows must attend orientation sessions, receptions, and functions held for guests invited by the fellowship group. They must also give talks and slide presentations, advise students on their papers and theses, and serve on occasion as consultants in courses and studies. Before the end of the term, fellows are required to prepare a written report describing their activities (courses, readings, research projects) and their contributions to the school.

Number awarded Generally, 8 to 12 fellowships are granted per year.

Deadline January of each year.

[601]
LOS ANGELES PHILHARMONIC FELLOWSHIPS FOR EXCELLENCE IN DIVERSITY

Los Angeles Philharmonic
Attn: Education Department
135 North Grand Avenue
Los Angeles, CA 90012
(213) 972-0703

Purpose To identify, nurture, and support talented minority instrumentalists in the southern California area.

Eligibility Applicants must reside (or have parents who reside) in southern California, be between the ages of 16 and 30, and be musicians from historically underrepresented communities: African American, Asian American, Native American, or Latino. Live auditions are required. Applications must include all of the following materials: federal tax form, letter of recommendation from a noted musical authority, a recent photograph, and a brief biographical statement (including career goals).

Financial data Fellowships range from $500 to $2,000; individual awards are determined on the basis of talent and financial circumstances. Funds are to be used to underwrite specific 1-time costs, such as tuition at an accredited institution, travel expenses for audition or solo appearances, instrument purchase, or participation in a summer music festival.

Duration The competition is held annually.

Special features Previous applicants and fellowship winners may reapply.

Number awarded Varies each year.

Deadline April of each year.

[602]
LOUISE GILES MINORITY SCHOLARSHIP

American Library Association
Attn: Office for Library Personnel Resources
50 East Huron Street
Chicago, IL 60611-2795
(312) 280-4281   (800) 545-2433, ext. 4281
TDD: (312) 944-7298   Fax: (312) 280-3256
E-mail: pjackson@ala.org

Purpose To encourage members of minority groups to train for a career in librarianship.

Eligibility The program is open to worthy American or Canadian students who are members of a principal minority group: American Indian or Alaska Native, Asian or Pacific Islander, African American, or Hispanic. The recipient must agree to enter a formal program of graduate study leading to a master's degree at a graduate library education program accredited by the American Library Association. Selection is based on academic excellence, leadership qualities, and evidence of a commitment to a career in librarianship.

Financial data The amount of the award is $3,000.

Duration 1 year.

Limitations Applicants cannot have already completed more than 12 semester hours toward a master's degree in library science.

Number awarded Varies, depending upon the total amount of contributed funds each year.

Deadline December of each year.

[603]
MAGNETIC FUSION ENERGY TECHNOLOGY FELLOWSHIP PROGRAM

Oak Ridge Institute for Science and Education
Attn: Science/Engineering Education Division
P.O. Box 117
Oak Ridge, TN 37831-0117
(423) 576-9558   (423) 576-2600
(800) 569-7749   Fax: (423) 576-3643
E-mail: mfetfp@orau.gov

Purpose To provide funding for graduate study and work experience in magnetic fusion energy technology.

Eligibility Applications are generally submitted before the student has received a bachelor's degree or during the first year of graduate school. Applicants should be working or planning to work on a doctorate in the physical sciences, mathematics, or engineering at participating universities (for a list of these schools, write to the address above). All programs operated by the Science/Engineering Education Division (SEED) of Oak Ridge Institute for Science and Education (ORISE) seek to broaden the participation of minorities, women, and persons with disabilities in science and engineering careers.

Financial data The stipend is $15,600 per year. An additional $200 per month is paid during the practicum period. Tuition and fees are covered. Some travel money is available.

Duration 1 year; may be renewed for up to 4 additional years.

Special features Participants intern at various research facilities of the U.S. Department of Energy (DOE). This program is funded by DOE's Office of Fusion Energy and administered by ORISE/SEED.

Number awarded Varies each year.

Deadline January of each year.

[604]
MAGNETIC FUSION SCIENCE FELLOWSHIP PROGRAM

Oak Ridge Institute for Science and Education
Attn: Science/Engineering Education Division
P.O. Box 117
Oak Ridge, TN 37831-0117
(423) 576-9558   (423) 576-2600
(800) 569-7749   Fax: (423) 576-3643
E-mail: magfsfp@orau.gov

Purpose To provide funding for graduate study and work experience in magnetic fusion science.

Eligibility Applications are generally submitted before or during the first year of graduate school. Applicants should be working or planning to work on a doctorate in the physical sciences, mathematics, or engineering at participating universities (for a list of these schools, write to the address above). All programs operated by the Science/Engineering Education Division (SEED) of Oak Ridge Institute for Science and Education (ORISE) seek to broaden the participation of minorities, women, and persons with disabilities in science and engineering careers.

Financial data The stipend is $15,600 per year. An additional $200 per month is paid during the practicum period. Tuition and fees are covered. Some travel money is available.

Duration 1 year; may be renewed for up to 3 additional years.

Special features Participants intern at various research facilities of the U.S. Department of Energy (DOE). This program is funded by DOE's Office of Fusion Energy and administered by ORISE/SEED.

Number awarded Varies each year.

Deadline January of each year.

[605]
MANHATTAN THEATRE CLUB PLAYWRITING FELLOWSHIPS

Manhattan Theatre Club
Attn: Literary Assistant
453 West 16th Street
New York, NY 10011
(212) 645-5590, ext. 161   Fax: (212) 691-9106

Purpose To provide funding to emerging playwrights (at the beginning of their careers) who are interested in developing their craft, identifying their career goals, and learning about the tools needed to realize those goals.

Eligibility To be eligible, writers must be 35 years of age or under. They must have completed their formal education (either undergraduate or graduate) by the time the fellowship begins. Applicants must submit 1 writing sample (full-length dramatic works are preferred), a resume, a statement of purpose, and 1 letter of recommendation. Preference is given to New York-based writers from diverse cultural and minority backgrounds who can demonstrate financial need. Selection is based on quality of work, financial need (must be documented), dedication to theater, and potential for growth as artists and professionals as the result of this program.

Financial data Each fellowship consists of: a commission of $5,000 for a new play, a production assistantship with a stipend of $1,500, and $3,500 for living and other expenses.

Duration 1 year, beginning in September.

Special features Fellows observe rehearsals for plays presented at the club each season, receive professional guidance from the club's script department staff, and are given access to the resources available through the club and its network of theater professionals.

Number awarded 2 each year.

Deadline February of each year.

[606]
MARILYN LLOYD FELLOWSHIP PROGRAM

Oak Ridge Institute for Science and Education
Attn: Science/Engineering Education Division
P.O. Box 117
Oak Ridge, TN 37831-0117
(423) 576-9279   (423) 576-2194
(800) 569-7749   Fax: (423) 576-3643
E-mail: mlloydfl@orau.gov

Purpose To provide financial assistance for graduate study and work experience in areas of interest to the U.S. Department of Energy (DOE).

Eligibility This program is open to students at designated participating universities (write to the address above for a list of these) who are working on a master's degree with a major in science or engineering and a minor in risk assessment, political science, public policy, economics, law, or business administration. All programs operated by the Science/Engineering Education Division (SEED) of Oak Ridge Institute for Science and Education (ORISE) seek to broaden the participation of minorities, women, and persons with disabilities in science and engineering careers.

Financial data Participants receive a monthly stipend of $1,200 and payment of tuition and fees.

Duration The program provides tuition support for 2 years with a 3-month summer practicum.

Special features Participants intern at DOE headquarters or operations offices. This program is funded by DOE and administered by ORISE/SEED.

Number awarded Varies each year.

Deadline May of each year.

[607]
MARTIN LUTHER KING, JR. MEMORIAL SCHOLARSHIP FUND

California Teachers Association
Attn: Human Rights Department
1705 Murchison Drive
P.O. Box 921
Burlingame, CA 94011-0921
(415) 697-1400

Purpose To provide financial assistance to racial-ethnic minority group members in California needing a graduate year to prepare for leadership roles in education.

Eligibility Applicants must be members of a racial-ethnic minority group; U.S. citizens and California residents; college juniors, seniors, or graduate students pursuing a college degree or credential for a teaching-related career in public education in an accredited institution of higher education; and either active members of the California Teachers Association (CTA), members of the Student CTA, or dependents of active, retired, or deceased CTA members.

Financial data Stipends vary each year, depending upon the amount of contributions received and the financial need of individual recipients.

Duration The fellowship is awarded annually.

Number awarded Varies; up to 7 each year.

Deadline March of each year.

[608]
MARY LITTY MEMORIAL FELLOWSHIP

Epilepsy Foundation of America
Attn: Department of Research and Professional Education
4351 Garden City Drive
Landover, MD 20785
(301) 459-3700   (800) EFA-1000
Fax: (301) 577-2684   TDD: (800) 332-2070
E-mail: postmaster@efa.org

Purpose To provide financial assistance for vocational rehabilitation students to work on an epilepsy study project.

Eligibility Vocational rehabilitation or rehabilitation counseling students may apply for these fellowships to carry out a project at a U.S. institution where there are ongoing programs of study or training in epilepsy. A preceptor must accept responsibility for supervision of the student and the project. Applications from women and minorities are especially encouraged.

Financial data Stipends are $2,000.

Duration 3 months.

Special features These fellowships are also known as the Behavior Sciences Student Fellowships.

Number awarded Varies each year.

Deadline February of each year.

[609]
MASGC GRADUATE FELLOWSHIPS

Massachusetts Space Grant Consortium
c/o MIT
Building 33, Room 208
77 Massachusetts Avenue
Cambridge, MA 02139
(617) 258-5546   Fax: (617) 253-0823
E-mail: halaris@mit.edu

Purpose To provide funding for space-related graduate study at institutions in Massachusetts.

Eligibility This program is open to graduate students at institutions that are members of the Massachusetts Space Grant Consortium (MASGC). Applicants must be pursuing research and study in space-related science or engineering fields. U.S. citizenship is required. Selection is based on academic achievement and interest in space science or space engineering. MASGC is a component of the U.S. National Aeronautics and Space Administration (NASA) Space Grant program, which encourages participation by women, minorities, and persons with disabilities.

Financial data The fellowships provide full tuition plus a stipend.

Duration 1 academic year.

Special features This program is funded by NASA.

Number awarded Varies each year.

Deadline December of each year.

[610]
MATHEMATICAL SCIENCES POSTDOCTORAL RESEARCH FELLOWSHIPS

National Science Foundation
Attn: Directorate for Mathematical and Physical Sciences
Division of Mathematical Sciences
4201 Wilson Boulevard, Room 1025
Arlington, VA 22230
(703) 306-1870   Fax: (703) 306-0555
E-mail: msprf@nsf.gov

Purpose To provide financial assistance for postdoctoral research training in mathematics.

Eligibility To become fellows, candidates must 1) be U.S. citizens, nationals, or permanent residents; 2) have earned a Ph.D. in a mathematical science or have had research training and experience equivalent to that represented by such a Ph.D.; 3) have held the Ph.D. for no more than 5 years; and 4) not have previously held any other postdoctoral fellowship from the National Science Foundation (NSF). They must be proposing to conduct a program of postdoctoral research training at an appropriate nonprofit U.S. institution, including government laboratories, national laboratories, and privately sponsored nonprofit institutes, as well as institutions of higher education. A senior scientist at the institution must indicate availability for consultation and agreement to work with the fellow. Women, underrepresented minorities, and persons with disabilities are strongly encouraged to apply.

Financial data The stipend is $2,750 per full-time month or $1,375 per half-time month, for a total of $66,000. In addition, the fellow receives an allowance of $4,500 to defray research costs (travel, publication costs, and other research-related items) and the institution receives an allowance of $4,500 as partial reimbursement for expenses incurred in support of the research (space, supplies, equipment, secretarial assistance, etc.).

Duration The program provides support for 2 9-month academic years and 6 summer months, for a total of 24 months of support. Fellows have 2 options for the academic years' stipend: full-time support for any 18 academic-year months in a 3-year period, in intervals not shorter than 3 consecutive months, or a combination of full-time and half-time support over a period of 3 academic years, usually 1 academic year full-time and 2 academic years half-time. Not more than 2 summer months' support may be received in any calendar year.

Special features Under certain circumstances, it may be desirable for portions of the work to be done at foreign institutions. Approval to do so must be obtained in advance from both the sponsoring senior scientist and the NSF.

Number awarded 30 to 40 each year.

Deadline October of each year.

[611]
MATHEMATICAL SCIENCES UNIVERSITY–INDUSTRY POSTDOCTORAL RESEARCH FELLOWSHIPS

National Science Foundation
Attn: Directorate for Mathematical and Physical Sciences
Division of Mathematical Sciences
4201 Wilson Boulevard, Room 1025
Arlington, VA 22230
(703) 306-1870   Fax: (703) 306-0555
E-mail: uicrp@nsf.gov

Purpose To provide financial assistance to recent doctoral recipients in mathematics who wish to broaden their knowledge, experience, and research perspectives by exposure to industrial environments.

Eligibility Candidates to become fellows must 1) be U.S. citizens, nationals, or permanent residents; 2) be eligible to be appointed as a research associate or assistant professor at the institution submitting the proposal; 3) have earned a Ph.D. in a mathematical science or have had research training and experience equivalent to that represented by such a Ph.D.; 4) have held the Ph.D. for no more than 7 years; 5) not hold a tenured position at any academic institution; and 6) not have previously held any other postdoctoral fellowship from the National Science Foundation (NSF). Applications must be submitted by a university principal investigator who will serve as scientific mentor to a fellow with an industrial sponsor. The proposal may either identify the prospective postdoctoral fellow or present a plan for recruiting the fellows. Principal investigators are encouraged to submit proposals that include women, underrepresented minorities, and persons with disabilities as postdoctoral fellows, or whose recruitment plans include strategies for identifying highly qualified postdoctoral fellows from those groups. Selection is based on the quality of the proposed research to be conducted at both the academic and industrial sites, the qualifications of and commitment by both the faculty mentor and the industrial sponsor, the appropriateness of the academic/industrial interaction, and the impact of the proposed training on the professional development of the postdoctoral fellow.

Financial data The total award is $111,000, of which $71,000 is provided by the National Science Foundation and $40,000 by the industrial sponsor. The award includes a stipend allowance for the fellow of $80,000 ($40,000 per year) plus a fringe benefit allowance of $16,000 ($8,000 per year), an allowance of $4,500 for the sponsoring institution in lieu of indirect costs, a research allowance of $4,500 for the fellow to be used for travel, publication costs, and other research-related expenses, and an allow-

ance of $6,000 for the faculty mentor for research expenses related to the industrial partnership.

Duration 2 years.

Number awarded Varies each year.

Deadline November of each year.

[612]
MAYNARD INSTITUTE EDITING PROGRAM FOR MINORITY JOURNALISTS

Robert C. Maynard Institute for Journalism Education
1211 Preservation Park Way
Oakland, CA 94612
(510) 891-9202   Fax: (510) 891-9565

Purpose To provide assistance to journalists who want to excel as copy editors or assignment editors.

Eligibility Applicants must have at least 1 year of experience in print media. Although the program emphasizes significant non-white representation, participation is also open to white journalists. Each applicant must complete the program application and submit a 1,000-word autobiographical essay and an 800-word critique of the daily newspaper the candidate works for or reads regularly. Semifinalists are invited for testing and interviewing by a selection panel of experienced daily newspaper editors and officers of the Robert C. Maynard Institute for Journalism Education.

Financial data Successful candidates receive transportation to the University of Arizona in Tucson, tuition, and housing. Transportation and expenses for interviews are also covered. Candidates not receiving salaries from sponsoring newspapers receive a $200-a-week stipend. Sponsoring newspapers cover transportation from Tucson to the city in which the newspaper is located. The program does not pay for: required books, meals, or other incidental expenses; transportation from Tucson to the participant's home city at the end of the program; or transportation of family or relocation of belongings.

Duration 8 weeks, beginning in June.

Special features During the 8-week program, participants work as editors on the program's newspaper and on the copy desks of the Tucson newspapers. Participants work under the guidance of veteran daily newspaper editors. They use video display terminals and learn the basics and fine points of copy editing, headline writing, newspaper layout and design, city desk operations, photo editing, libel law, and newspaper production. Management training is also provided during the session; instruction includes assessment of management and leadership skills, group discussions, problem-solving exercises in newsroom management, and information on newsroom finances. After completing the session, participants go on to copy desk jobs at sponsoring daily newspapers. Those not sponsored by a newspaper are matched to newspapers and sent on 1 or more interviews before the program begins. The Robert C. Maynard Institute for Journalism Education was incorporated in 1977 as the Institute for Journalism Education; it was renamed in 1993 in honor of the late *Oakland Tribune* owner who co-founded the nonprofit corporation.

Limitations Newspapers wishing to guarantee a copy desk job for a selected candidate are asked to pay a fee of $2,500. During the 8-week session, participants are required to live in apartments provided by the program. Family members may not accompany them.

Number awarded 10 to 12 each session.

Deadline February of each year.

[613]
MAYNARD INSTITUTE MANAGEMENT TRAINING PROGRAM

Robert C. Maynard Institute for Journalism Education
1211 Preservation Park Way
Oakland, CA 94612
(510) 891-9202   Fax: (510) 891-9565

Purpose To provide training to newspaper managers so they can operate effectively and creatively in a multicultural work force and marketplace.

Eligibility Applications are encouraged from professionals in the middle-management ranks of all operating departments of newspapers (both the business and editorial sides). Preference is given to individuals with at least 5 years of experience in the field (as well as some management background and high potential for success). Applicants must have the written endorsements of their employers. Special consideration is given to applications from racial minority groups.

Financial data Sponsoring newspapers pay a training fee of $5,000 per participant, continue the fellow's salary during the program, and cover the cost of transportation to and from Northwestern University (where the Management Training Center is located). The institute supplies housing and some meals during the periods of study at Northwestern. The program provides travel to and from the field sites and pays housing at the sites.

Duration 2 months in the summer.

Special features This program began in 1984. Participants spend 5 1/2 weeks at Northwestern, learning about financial management, capital budgeting, leadership styles, business decisions, business ethics, and organizational behavior. They spend 2 1/2 weeks at field-site newspapers. The Robert C. Maynard Institute for Journalism Education was incorporated in 1977 as the Institute for Journalism Education; it was renamed in 1993 in honor of the late *Oakland Tribune* owner who co-founded the nonprofit corporation. For candidates who do not have a sponsoring newspaper employer, scholarships are available from the National Association of Hispanic Journalists, the National Association of Black Journalists, and the Asian American Journalists Association; those scholarships pay the $5,000 training fee.

Limitations Program participants are not permitted to have family or friends accompany or stay with them during the program.

Number awarded Up to 20 each year.

Deadline April of each year.

[614]
MCKNIGHT JUNIOR FACULTY DEVELOPMENT FELLOWSHIP PROGRAM

Florida Education Fund
201 East Kennedy Boulevard, Suite 1525
Tampa, FL 33602
(813) 272-2772   Fax: (813) 272-2784

Purpose To provide minority and women junior faculty at colleges and universities in Florida with an opportunity to earn a graduate degree or conduct independent research.

Eligibility This program is open to minorities (especially African Americans) and women in underrepresented fields. Applicants should have between 2 and 6 years of service as faculty members in a Florida public or private university, 4-year college, or community college and should not have obtained tenure (the non-tenure requirement does not apply to community college faculty). They must desire to spend a year away from their teaching duties in order to pursue graduate course work, work on a doctoral dissertation, or conduct independent research. Faculty in all fields of study are eligible, but applications are especially encouraged in agriculture, biology, business administration, chemistry, computer science, engineering, marine biology, mathematics, physics, and psychology.

Financial data The recipient's institution receives $15,000 to cover the necessary teaching replacement cost. The recipient continues to receive full pay and benefits.

Duration 1 year.

Number awarded 20 each year.

Deadline January of each year.

[615]
MEDICAL INFORMATICS RESEARCH TRAINING AWARDS

National Institutes of Health
Attn: National Library of Medicine
Division of Extramural Programs
Building 38A, Suite 5S-522
Bethesda, MD 20894
(301) 496-4221   Fax: (301) 402-0421
E-mail: rd57e@nih.gov

Purpose To provide financial assistance to pre- and postdoctoral students who wish to pursue research training on the use of computers and telecommunications to manage health information.

Eligibility This program is open to students at both the predoctoral and postdoctoral level who wish to pursue a program of research training in medical informatics, the interaction of computers and telecommunications with biomedicine. Candidates may apply either to selected institutions which have received grants from the National Library of Medicine (NLM) of the National Institutes of Health (NIH) to operate such programs or directly to the NLM to pursue a program of research training with a mentor and institution of their own choice. All applicants must be U.S. citizens, nationals, or permanent residents. Applications from minority individuals and women are strongly encouraged.

Financial data Annual stipends for predoctoral fellows are $10,008; for postdoctoral fellows, the annual stipend ranges from $19,608 to $32,300 per year, depending on the years of postdoctoral experience.

Duration 1 to 3 years.

Special features Currently, the funded sites are at Baylor/Rice, Columbia, Harvard/MIT/Tufts, North Carolina/Duke, Minnesota, Missouri, Oregon, Pittsburgh, Stanford, and Yale; for the name and address of the program director at each of the institutions, contact the address above. The NIH designates these fellowships as F38 Awards.

Number awarded Varies each year.

Deadline Each of the funded institutions sets its own application deadlines. For students applying directly to the NLM, applications must be submitted by April, August, and December of each year.

[616]
MENTORED CLINICAL SCIENTIST DEVELOPMENT AWARDS

National Institutes of Health
Attn: Office of Extramural Research
Extramural Outreach and Information Resources Office
6701 Rockledge Drive, Room 6207
MSC 7910
Bethesda, MD 20892-7910
(301) 435-0714   Fax: (301) 480-8443
E-mail: asknih@odrockm1.od.nih.gov

Purpose To provide financial support for specialized study to clinically trained professionals who are committed to a career in research and have the potential to develop into independent investigators.

Eligibility This program is open to candidates who 1) have a clinical degree or its equivalent; 2) can identify a mentor with extensive research experience; and 3) are willing to spend a minimum of 75 percent of full-time professional effort conducting research and research career development activities for the period of the award. Applications may be submitted on behalf of candidates by domestic, non-federal organizations, public or private, such as medical, dental, or nursing schools or other institutions of higher education. Minorities and women are particularly encouraged to apply. Candidates must be U.S. citizens or permanent residents.

Financial data This program provides salary and fringe benefits for the candidate only; each component establishes its own salary limits on career awards. Each appointee is allowed up to $20,000 per year for tuition, fees, and books related to career development; research expenses, such as supplies, equipment, and technical personnel; travel to research meetings or training; and statistical services including personnel and computer time. Indirect costs are reimbursed at 8 percent of modified total direct costs, or at the actual indirect cost rate, whichever is less.

Duration 3 to 5 years.

Special features Awards under this program are available from 15 agencies of the National Institutes of Health (NIH): the National Institute on Aging, the National Institute on Alcohol Abuse and Alcoholism, the National Institute of Allergy and Infectious Diseases, the National Institute of Arthritis and Musculoskeletal and Skin Diseases, the National Cancer Institute, the National Institute of Child Health and Human Development, the National Institute on Deafness and Other Communication Disorders, the National Institute of Dental Research, the National Institute of Diabetes and Digestive and Kidney Diseases, the National Institute on Drug Abuse, the National Institute of Environmental Health Sciences, the National Eye Institute, the National Heart, Lung, and Blood Institute, the National Institute of Mental Health, and the National Institute of Neurological Disorders and Stroke. The names and addresses of staff people at each agency are available from the address above. The NIH designates this program as the K08 Awards.

Number awarded Varies each year.

Deadline January, May, or September of each year.

[617]
MERRITT-PUTNAM RESEARCH/CLINICAL TRAINING FELLOWSHIPS

Epilepsy Foundation of America
Attn: Department of Research and Professional Education
4351 Garden City Drive
Landover, MD 20785
(301) 459-3700   (800) EFA-1000
Fax: (301) 577-2684   TDD: (800) 332-2070
E-mail: postmaster@efa.org

Purpose To offer qualified individuals the opportunity to develop expertise in clinical epilepsy and epilepsy research through training experience and involvement in an epilepsy research project.

Eligibility Applications are open to individuals who have received their M.D. degree and completed residency training. The proposed research may be either basic or clinical, but there must be an equal emphasis on clinical training and clinical epileptology. Special attention is given to applications submitted by women and minorities.

Financial data The stipend is $40,000.

Duration 1 year.

Limitations The fellowship must be carried out at a facility where there is an ongoing epilepsy research program. Research must be conducted in the United States.

Number awarded Varies each year.

Deadline August of each year.

[618]
MESBEC PROGRAM

Native American Scholarship Fund
8200 Mountain Road, N.E., Suite 203
Albuquerque, NM 87110-7835
(505) 262-2351   Fax: (505) 262-0534

Purpose To provide financial assistance to Native American students interested in pursuing postsecondary education.

Eligibility Native American students (with at least a quarter Indian blood and members of a U.S. tribe that is federally-recognized, state-recognized, or terminated) are eligible to apply for this program if they are majoring in the 1 of the following fields: mathematics, engineering, science, business administration, education, or computer science. They should have a grade point average of at least 3.0 and scores on the SAT of at least 950 or ACT of at least 23 and must apply for all other sources of funding for which they are eligible. Applicants should demonstrate clear goals and plan to earn a 4-year or graduate degree. Awards are based on merit and the potential of the applicant to improve the lives of Indian people; financial need is not a consideration.

Financial data The amount awarded varies but is generally at least $500, in the form of grants, loans, or a combination of both.

Duration 1 year; may be renewed.

Special features MESBEC is an acronym that stands for the priority areas of this program: mathematics, engineering, science, business, education, and computers.

Number awarded Varies; generally, 30 to 35 each year.

Deadline April of each year for fall terms; September of each year for spring and winter terms; March of each year for summer school.

[619]

METROPOLITAN LIFE FOUNDATION AWARDS PROGRAM FOR ACADEMIC EXCELLENCE IN MEDICINE

National Medical Fellowships, Inc.
Attn: Scholarships and Programs
110 West 32nd Street, 8th Floor
New York, NY 10001-3205
(212) 714-1007

Purpose To provide financial assistance to underrepresented minority medical students.

Eligibility Students must be nominated by their medical school deans. They must be 1) African American, mainland Puerto Rican, Mexican American, or Native American medical students in their second or third year, 2) enrolled in medical schools located in (or residents of) the following cities only: Phoenix, Arizona; San Francisco, California; Los Angeles, California; Denver, Colorado; Washington, D.C.; Miami, Florida; Tampa/St. Petersburg, Florida; Atlanta, Georgia; Aurora/Chicago, Illinois; Wichita, Kansas; Boston, Massachusetts; St. Louis, Missouri; Metropolitan New York, New York (including northern New Jersey and lower Connecticut); Tulsa, Oklahoma; Philadelphia, Pennsylvania; Pittsburgh, Pennsylvania; Scranton, Pennsylvania; Warwick/Providence, Rhode Island; Greenville, South Carolina; Austin, Texas; Dallas/Fort Worth, Texas; or Houston, Texas; and 3) able to demonstrate financial need, outstanding academic achievement, leadership, and potential for distinguished contributions to medicine.

Financial data The stipend is $3,500.

Duration 1 year; nonrenewable.

Special features The funding for this program is provided by the Metropolitan Life Foundation of New York, New York.

Number awarded Up to 14 each year.

Deadline Nominations are requested in August of each year.

[620]

MFT MINORITY FELLOWSHIP PROGRAM

American Association for Marriage and Family Therapy
Attn: Research and Education Foundation
1133 15th Street, N.W., Suite 300
Washington, DC 20005-2710
(202) 452-0109   Fax: (202) 223-2329

Purpose To provide financial assistance to minority students enrolled in graduate and post-degree training programs in marital and family therapy.

Eligibility Eligible to apply are minority students (including African Americans, Hispanics, Native Americans, Asian Americans, and Pacific Islanders) enrolled in university graduate education programs or post-degree institutes that provide training in marital and family therapy. They must be citizens of the United States or Canada and show promise in and commitment to a career in marital and family therapy education, research, or practice.

Financial data Each stipend is generally $1,500 (plus conference expenses).

Duration 1 year.

Special features Award winners are invited to attend the annual conference of the American Association for Marriage and Family Therapy (AAMFT); expenses for attending the conference are covered by AAMFT. This program began in 1986.

Number awarded Up to 3 each year.

Deadline April of each year.

[621]

MINNESOTA NURSING GRANTS FOR PERSONS OF COLOR

Minnesota Higher Education Services Office
Capitol Square Building
550 Cedar Street, Suite 400
St. Paul, MN 55101
(612) 296-3974   (800) 657-3866 (within MN)
Fax: (612) 297-8880   E-mail: info@heso.state

Purpose To provide financial assistance for persons of color in Minnesota who wish to pursue nursing education.

Eligibility Minnesota residents who are U.S. citizens and Asian-Pacific American, African American, American Indian, or Hispanic American (Latino, Chicano, or Puerto Rican) may apply for these grants if they are entering or enrolled at a Minnesota school, college, or nursing program that leads to licensure as a registered nurse or advanced nursing education. Recipients must be willing to practice in Minnesota for at least 3 years following licensure.

Financial data The amount of the award depends on the need of the recipient, but ranges from from $2,000 to $4,000.

Duration 1 year.

Number awarded Varies each year.

[622]

MINNESOTA SPACE GRANT CONSORTIUM SCHOLARSHIPS AND FELLOWSHIPS

Minnesota Space Grant Consortium
c/o University of Minnesota
Department of Aerospace Engineering and Mechanics
107 Akerman Hall
110 Union Street S.E.
Minneapolis, MN 55455
(612) 626-9295   Fax: (612) 626-1558
E-mail: mnsgc@aem.umn.edu

Purpose To provide financial assistance for postsecondary study in space-related science and engineering fields to students in Minnesota.

Eligibility This program is open to graduate and undergraduate students at institutions that are affiliates of the Minnesota Space Grant Consortium (Augsburg College, Bethel College, Bemidji State University, College of St. Catherine, Fond du Lac Community College, Macalaster College, Normandale Community College, University of Minnesota at Duluth, and University of Minnesota at Twin Cities). U.S. citizenship is required. The Minnesota Space Grant Consortium is a component of the U.S. National Aeronautics and Space Administration (NASA) Space Grant program, which encourages participation by women, minorities, and persons with disabilities.

Financial data The amounts of the awards are set by each of the participating institutions, which augment funding from this program with institutional resources.

Duration 1 year; renewable.

Special features This program is funded by NASA.

Number awarded Varies; more than $50,000 is available from this program each year for scholarships and fellowships.

Deadline Participating institutions set their own deadlines; contact the above for information on the names and addresses of the responsible administrators at the respective institutions.

[623]
MINORITY ACCESS TO RESEARCH CAREERS (MARC) FACULTY PREDOCTORAL FELLOWSHIPS

National Institutes of Health
Attn: National Institute of General Medical Sciences
Director, Minority Access to Research Careers Program
Natcher Building, Suite 2AS43C
45 Center Drive MSC 6200
Bethesda, MD 20892-6200
(301) 594-3900   Fax: (301) 480-2753
E-mail: at21z@nih.gov

Purpose To enable faculty at minority institutions to complete the Ph.D. degree in the biomedical sciences.

Eligibility Institutions with student enrollments drawn substantially from minorities may nominate faculty who lack the Ph.D. degree for these awards. Nominees must have been full-time faculty members in biomedically-related science or mathematics for at least 3 years at the institution, which may be a university, 4-year college, or health professional school. Fellows may train at any nonprofit private or public institution in the United States with suitable facilities, but are expected to return to their sponsoring institutions after completion of their fellowships.

Financial data The fellowships provide payment of tuition and fees, a stipend that is based on the applicant's current salary but that may not exceed $20,700 per year, and an allowance of $2,000 to help defray the cost of supplies and permit limited travel.

Duration Up to 5 years.

Special features The National Institutes of Health (NIH) designates these fellowships as part of the F34 program.

Deadline April or December of each year.

[624]
MINORITY ACCESS TO RESEARCH CAREERS (MARC) PREDOCTORAL FELLOWSHIPS

National Institutes of Health
Attn: National Institute of General Medical Sciences
Director, Minority Access to Research Careers Program
Natcher Building, Suite 2AS43C
45 Center Drive MSC 6200
Bethesda, MD 20892-6200
(301) 594-3900   Fax: (301) 480-2753
E-mail: at21z@nih.gov

Purpose To increase the number of well-prepared minority students who are pursuing research training in the biomedical sciences.

Eligibility These fellowships are awarded, on a highly competitive basis, to distinguished graduates of the MARC Undergraduate Student Training in Academic Research Program. Support is provided for specified Ph.D. programs in the biomedical sciences or combined M.D./Ph.D. programs. Students enrolled in medical or other professional schools are not eligible, unless they are enrolled in an M.D./Ph.D. or other combined professional degree/Ph.D. program.

Financial data The fellowships provide payment of tuition and fees, a stipend of $10,008 per year, and an allowance of $2,000 to help defray the cost of supplies and permit limited travel.

Duration Up to 5 years.

Deadline April or December of each year.

[625]
MINORITY DENTAL STUDENT SCHOLARSHIP

ADA Endowment and Assistance Fund
211 East Chicago Avenue, Suite 820
Chicago, IL 60611-2678
(312) 440-2567

Purpose To provide financial assistance to minority Americans who wish to enter the field of dentistry.

Eligibility Applicants must be U.S. citizens from a minority group that is currently underrepresented in the dental profession: Native American Indians, Black African Americans, or Hispanics; they must have a grade point average of at least 2.5. To be eligible, they must have been accepted as a first- or second-year student at a dental school in the United States accredited by the Commission on Dental Accreditation. Selection is based upon academic achievement, a written summary of personal and professional goals, letters of reference, and demonstrated financial need.

Financial data The amount of the stipend is $2,000; it is sent directly to the student's financial aid office to be used to cover tuition, fees, books, supplies, and living expenses.

Duration 1 year.

Special features This program is the result of the merger in 1992 of the minority dental scholarship programs of the ADA Endowment and Assistance Fund and the American Fund for Dental Health. Funding support is provided by Colgate-Palmolive.

Limitations Students receiving a full scholarship from any other source are ineligible to receive this scholarship.

Number awarded Varies each year.

Deadline June of each year.

[626]
MINORITY FELLOWSHIP PROGRAM IN GENERAL SOCIOLOGY

American Sociological Association
Attn: Minority Affairs Program
1722 N Street, N.W.
Washington, DC 20036-2981
(202) 833-3410, ext. 322/321   Fax: (202) 785-0146
TDD: (202) 872-0486   E-mail: minority.affairs@asanet.org

Purpose To provide financial assistance to minority doctoral candidates in sociology.

Eligibility These fellowships are available to American citizens or permanent residents who are Blacks/African Americans, Latinos (e.g., Chicanos, Puerto Ricans, Cubans), American Indians or Alaskan Natives, Asian Americans (e.g., Southeast Asian, Japanese, Chinese, Korean), or Pacific Islanders (e.g., Filipino, Samoan, Hawaiian, Guamanian). The competition is open to students beginning or continuing study in sociology at the doctoral level. Selection is based on commitment to research, academic achievement, scholarship, writing ability, research potential, and financial need.

Financial data The stipend is $10,008 per year; candidates who have completed all course work and who have been advanced to degree candidacy may receive a dissertation grant of up to $5,000.

Duration 1 year; renewable for 5 additional years.

Number awarded 1 or 2 each year.

Deadline December of each year.

[627]
MINORITY FELLOWSHIP PROGRAM IN MENTAL HEALTH

American Sociological Association
Attn: Minority Affairs Program
1722 N Street, N.W.
Washington, DC 20036-2981
(202) 833-3410, ext. 322/321   Fax: (202) 785-0146
TDD: (202) 872-0486   E-mail: minority.affairs@asanet.org

Purpose To provide financial assistance to minority doctoral candidates in sociology who are interested in conducting research on mental health issues relating to minority groups.

Eligibility These fellowships are available to American citizens or permanent residents who are Blacks/African Americans, Latinos (e.g., Chicanos, Puerto Ricans, Cubans), American Indians or Alaskan Natives, Asian Americans (e.g., Southeast Asian, Japanese, Chinese, Korean), or Pacific Islanders (e.g., Filipino, Samoan, Hawaiian, Guamanian). The competition is open to students beginning or continuing study in sociology at the doctoral level. Selection is based on commitment to research in mental health and mental illness, scholarship, writing ability, research potential, and financial need.

Financial data The stipend is $10,008 per year; candidates who have completed all course work and who have been advanced to degree candidacy may receive a dissertation grant of up to $5,000.

Duration 1 year; renewable for 5 additional years.

Special features This program is funded by a grant from the U.S. National Institute of Mental Health, a component of the National Institutes of Health.

Limitations Upon completion of their studies, recipients are expected to engage in mental health and mental illness research and/or teaching for a period equal to the period of support beyond 12 months.

Number awarded 10 each year.

Deadline December of each year.

[628]
MINORITY GEOSCIENCE GRADUATE SCHOLARSHIPS

American Geological Institute
Attn: Director, AGI Minority Geoscience Scholarships
4220 King Street
Alexandria, VA 22302-1507
(703) 379-2480   Fax: (703) 379-7563

Purpose To provide financial assistance to underrepresented minority graduate students interested in pursuing a degree in the geosciences.

Eligibility Awards are limited to geoscience graduate students who are U.S. citizens and members of the following underrepresented ethnic minority groups: Blacks, Hispanics, and Native Americans (American Indians, Eskimos, Hawaiians, and Samoans). The term "geosciences" is used to refer to study in the fields of geology, geophysics, hydrology, meteorology, physical oceanography, planetary geology, and earth-science education. Selection is based on academic excellence, financial need, and probable future success in the geosciences profession.

Financial data Up to $4,000 per year.

Duration 1 academic year; renewable if the recipient maintains satisfactory performance.

Special features Funding for this program comes from geoscience industries, professional societies, and individuals.

Deadline January of each year.

[629]
MINORITY JOURNALISM EDUCATORS FELLOWSHIP

American Press Institute
Attn: Fellowship Program Coordinator
11690 Sunrise Valley Drive
Reston, VA 22091-1498
(703) 620-3611   Fax: (703) 620-5814
E-mail: vcju07a@prodigy.com

Purpose To provide financial support to minority college-level journalism educators who are interested in attending American Press Institute (API) seminars.

Eligibility Nominations are invited from all schools and departments of journalism and mass communications. Eligible to be nominated are college-level minority journalism educators who wish to attend API seminars. Each API seminar is designed for a particular specialty or problem.

Financial data The fellowship covers tuition, room, and meals.

Special features The program includes a 10-day seminar followed by a 1-month internship in a newspaper or broadcast newsroom.

Number awarded 1 each year.

Deadline Nominations must be submitted by November of each year.

[630]
MINORITY MEDICAL FACULTY DEVELOPMENT PROGRAM

Robert Wood Johnson Foundation
College Road East and U.S. Route 1
P.O. Box 2316
Princeton, NJ 08543-2316
(609) 452-8701

Purpose To provide financial support and continued training for minority physicians who are interested in academic careers in biomedical research, clinical investigation, or health services research.

Eligibility African American, Mexican American, Native American, and mainland Puerto Rican physicians residing in the United States are eligible to apply if they have completed or will have completed formal clinical training. Applicants must be U.S. citizens with outstanding academic backgrounds and a commitment to academic medicine. Preference is given to physicians who have recently completed their clinical training and are seeking advanced research training.

Financial data The stipend is $50,000 per year, plus a $25,000 annual research allowance.

Duration 2 years; renewable for an additional 2 years.

Special features Fellows study and conduct research under the supervision of a senior faculty member located at any academic center in the United States that is noted for the training of young faculty and that offers research opportunities of interest to the fellow.

Limitations An interview is required.

Number awarded Up to 12 each year.

Deadline March of each year.

[631]
MINORITY POSTDOCTORAL RESEARCH FELLOWSHIPS

National Science Foundation
Attn: Directorate for Biological Sciences
Division of Biological Infrastructure
4201 Wilson Boulevard, Room 615
Arlington, VA 22230
(703) 306-1469   E-mail: ckimsey@nsf.gov

Purpose To provide financial assistance for postdoctoral research training to minority scientists in the biological, social, economic, and behavioral sciences.

Eligibility Eligible to apply are underrepresented minorities (African Americans, Hispanics, Native Pacific Islanders, and Native Americans) who are American citizens or permanent residents and will complete their doctorate within a year or have completed it within the previous 4 years but have not completed more than 2 years of postdoctoral support. They must be proposing research training that falls within the program areas of the National Science Foundation (NSF) Directorate for Biological Sciences or the Directorate for Social, Behavioral, and Economic Sciences to be conducted at any appropriate nonprofit U.S. or foreign institution (government laboratory, institution of higher education, national laboratory, or public or private research institute), but not at the same institution where the doctorate was obtained.

Financial data The program provides a stipend of $28,000 per year, an institutional allowance of $4,000 for partial reimbursement of indirect research costs (space, equipment, general purpose supplies, and fringe benefits), and a special allowance of $8,000 for direct research costs (scientific supplies, research-related travel, publication expenses, and other research-related costs).

Duration 2 years; applicants who propose to spend their 2-year tenure at a foreign institution may apply for a third year of support at an appropriate U.S. institution.

Special features Information on the programs from the Directorate for Social, Behavioral, and Economic Sciences is available at (703) 306-1733.

Number awarded Approximately 12 each year.

Deadline November of each year.

[632]
MISSOURI SPACE GRANT CONSORTIUM GRADUATE FELLOWSHIPS

Missouri Space Grant Consortium
c/o University of Missouri at Rolla
College of Engineering
Mechanical and Aerospace Engineering and Engineering
    Mechanics
101 Mechanical Engineering Building
Rolla, Mo 65401-0249
(314) 341-4671   Fax: (314) 341-4607
E-mail: bpaul@umr.edu

Purpose To provide financial assistance for graduate students in Missouri pursuing a degree in an aerospace field.

Eligibility This program is open to graduate students pursuing a degree in an aerospace field at member institutions of the Missouri Space Grant Consortium (Southwest Missouri State University, University of Missouri at Columbia, University of Missouri at Rolla, University of Missouri at St. Louis, or Washington University). Selection is based on academic records, recommendation

letters fro sponsoring faculty, student publications and academic achievements, and a statement of interest. U.S. citizenship is required. The Missouri Space Grant Consortium is a component of the U.S. National Aeronautics and Space Administration (NASA), which encourages participation by women, minorities, and persons with disabilities.

Financial data The maximum funding is $12,500 per year.

Duration 1 year.

Special features This program is funded by NASA.

Number awarded 4 or more each year.

[633]
MIT COMMUNITY FELLOWS PROGRAM

Massachusetts Institute of Technology
Department of Urban Studies and Planning
77 Massachusetts Avenue, Room 9-320
Cambridge, MA 02139
(617) 253-3216   Fax: (617) 253-2654
E-mail: bjr@MIT.edu

Purpose To provide midcareer community activists of color with a year of study, reflection, and research to enhance their effectiveness in future work on youth development issues.

Eligibility This program invites participation from community activists of color (Afro-Americans, Hispanics, Asians, and Native Americans). Candidates fall into 3 categories: 1) people working on youth concerns at the local government level, sponsored by their government office; 2) people coming from youth health projects funded by the W.K. Kellogg Foundation; and 3) people working with youth at the community level. All applicants should have a distinguished record as community practitioners whose primary concern is the development of communities of color in the United States.

Financial data For people working at the local government level, their agency grants a paid leave of absence to participate in the program and the Ford Foundation supplements their income with a modest stipend for local housing, research, and travel. For the second group of participants, the W.K. Kellogg Foundation provides a small supplemental stipend in addition to the support they receive from their agencies. Candidates not working for a local government or a Kellogg-supported community organization must seek funding from their agency or from local foundations.

Duration 9 months, beginning in August.

Special features Fellows take part in orientation modules, semester-long courses, and seminars in computers, writing, organizational management, negotiating techniques, creative problem-solving, program planning, proposal writing, fund-raising, media, economics, team building, and organizing. A great deal of their time is spent on creating or refining a youth project which they implement upon returning to their communities.

Limitations Fellows must be in residence in Cambridge for the duration of the fellowship program except for 2 return visits (in October and in January) to their community to solicit input on their project.

Number awarded 10 to 12 each year.

Deadline February of each year.

[634]

MLA SCHOLARSHIP FOR MINORITY STUDENTS

Medical Library Association
Attn: Professional Development Department
6 North Michigan Avenue, Suite 300
Chicago, IL 60602-4805
(312) 419-9094   Fax: (312) 419-8950

Purpose To assist minority students interested in pursuing a career in medical librarianship.

Eligibility Racial minority students (Asians, African Americans, Hispanics, Native Americans, or Pacific Islanders) who are entering a graduate program in librarianship or have completed less than half of their academic requirements for the master's degree in library science and are interested in pursuing a career in medical librarianship may apply. Selection is based on academic record, letters of reference, professional potential, and the applicant's statement of career objectives. The program is open to both U.S. and Canadian citizens.

Financial data The stipend is $2,000.

Duration 1 year.

Number awarded 1 each year.

Deadline November of each year.

[635]

MONTANA SPACE GRANT CONSORTIUM FELLOWSHIP PROGRAM

Montana Space Grant Consortium
c/o Montana State University
Physics Department
AJM Johnson Hall
Bozeman, MT 59717-0350
(406) 994-4223   Fax: (406) 994-4452
E-mail: msgc@orion.physics.montana.edu

Purpose To provide financial assistance to students in Montana who are interested in working on a graduate degree in the space sciences and/or engineering.

Eligibility This program is open to graduate students in Montana pursuing studies in fields related to space sciences and engineering. Priority is given to students who have been involved in aerospace-related research. U.S. citizenship is required. The Montana Space Grant Consortium is a component of the U.S. National Aeronautics and Space Administration (NASA) Space Grant program, which encourages participation by women, minorities, and persons with disabilities.

Financial data The amount awarded varies; stipends average $9,000.

Duration 1 year.

Special features Funding for this program is provided by NASA.

Number awarded 3 to 4 each year.

[636]

MORRIS SCHOLARSHIP

Morris Scholarship Fund
206 Sixth Avenue
Midland Building, Room 900
Des Moines, IA 50309-4015
(515) 282-8192   Fax: (515) 282-9117

Purpose To provide financial assistance to minority students in Iowa who are interested in careers in law, journalism, education, or communications.

Eligibility Minority students (Blacks, Asian/Pacific Islanders, Hispanics, or American Indian/Alaskan Natives) are eligible to apply if they are interested in studying 1) journalism, education, or communications at the undergraduate or graduate level or 2) law at the graduate level. Recipients may be residents of any state and may be attending any U.S. college or university, but preference is given to Iowa residents who are attending an Iowa college or university. Selection is based on academic achievement, community service, and financial need.

Financial data Stipends range from $750 to $1,250 per year.

Duration 1 year; may be renewed.

Special features The scholarship is named in honor of the J.B. Morris family, who were founders of the Iowa branches of the National Association for the Advancement of Colored People and published the Iowa Bystander newspaper.

Number awarded 10 to 20 each year.

Deadline January of each year.

[637]

NASA GRADUATE STUDENT FELLOWSHIPS IN EARTH SYSTEM SCIENCE

National Aeronautics and Space Administration
Attn: Earth System Science Fellowship Program
Code Y
700 Virginia Avenue, S.W., Suite 700
Washington, DC 20024

Purpose To provide financial assistance to graduate students in earth system science.

Eligibility This program is open to students accepted or enrolled in a full-time M.Sc. and/or Ph.D. program at accredited U.S. universities. Applicants must be involved in interdisciplinary programs involving the study of the earth as a system. Priority topics include seasonal-to-interannual climate prediction, long-term climate variability, land cover change and global productivity, atmospheric ozone, and natural hazards. U.S. citizens and permanent residents are given preference, although the program is not restricted to them. Students with disabilities and from underrepresented minority groups (African Americans, Native Americans, Alaskan Natives, Mexican Americans, Puerto Ricans, and Native Pacific Islanders) are especially urged to apply.

Financial data This stipend is $20,000 per year, to be used to defray living and educational expenses, tuition, and fees. An additional allowance of $2,000 may be provided for the faculty advisor's use in support of the student's research.

Duration 1 year; may be renewed for up to 2 additional years.

Special features This program was established in 1990. Beginning in 1996, the National Aeronautics and Space Administration (NASA) combined the earth science portion of its Graduate Student Researchers Program (GSRP), supported by the NASA Education Division, and the Graduate Student Fellowship in Global Change Research, supported by the Office of Mission to Planet Earth (MTPE), to establish this program. For further information on the GSRP program, contact the Office of Human Resources and Education, Code FE, Headquarters Room 4D45, Washington, DC 20546-0001, (202) 358-1517, Fax: (202) 358-4068, E-mail: anurrid@hq.nasa.gov; for further information on the MTPE program, contact the Office of Mission to Planet Earth, Code YS, Headquarters Room 5Q13, Washington, DC 20546-0001, (202) 358-0273, Fax: (202) 358-2770, E-mail: gasrar@hq.gov.

Limitations Applications for paleo-climate related study are discouraged.

Number awarded 3 to 8 master's fellowships through the GSRP program and up to 40 Ph.D. fellowships through the MTPE program are awarded each year.

Deadline March of each year.

[638]
NASA/DESGC GRADUATE STUDENT FELLOWSHIPS

Delaware Space Grant Consortium
c/o University of Delaware
Bartol Research Institute
217 Sharp Laboratory
Newark, DE 19716-4793
(302) 831-8116   Fax: (302) 831-1843
E-mail: sherry@brivs2.bartol.udel.edu

Purpose To provide financial support to graduate students in Delaware involved in space-related studies.

Eligibility This program is open to graduate students in Delaware embarking on or involved in aerospace-related research, technology, or design. U.S. citizenship is required. The Delaware Space Grant Consortium (DESGC) is a component of the U.S. National Aeronautics and Space Administration (NASA) Space Grant program, which encourages applications from women, minorities, and persons with disabilities.

Financial data This program provides tuition and stipends.

Duration 1 year; may be renewed.

Special features This program is funded by NASA.

Number awarded In a recent year, 4 students received these fellowships.

Deadline March of each year.

[639]
NATIONAL ASSOCIATION OF SCHOOLS OF PUBLIC AFFAIRS AND ADMINISTRATION DIVERSITY DOCTORAL AWARDS PROGRAM

National Association of Schools of Public Affairs and
    Administration
Attn: Executive Director
1120 G Street, N.W., Suite 730
Washington, DC 20005
(202) 628-8965   Fax: (202) 626-4978

Purpose To provide financial assistance to minorities who are interested in working on a doctorate in public affairs and administration.

Eligibility There are 38 universities participating in this program. These schools have agreed to provide funding to underrepresented minorities interested in working on a Ph.D. in public affairs and administration. The participating schools are: American University, Arizona State University, Auburn University, Carnegie Mellon University, Cleveland State University, Florida Atlantic University, Florida International University, Florida State University, George Washington University, Harvard University, Indiana University, Kent State University, Michigan State University, Mississippi State University, New York University, Northern Illinois University, Nova University, Ohio State University, Pennsylvania State University, Princeton University, St. Louis University, Syracuse University, Texas A&M University, Texas Tech University, University of Akron, University of Alabama, University of Albany, University of Chicago, University of Colorado, University of Delaware, University of Georgia, University of Kansas, University of

Maryland, University of Massachusetts, University of Michigan, University of Pittsburgh, University of Southern California, University of Utah, University of Virginia, Virginia Commonwealth University, and Virginia Polytechnic Institute and State University. At most of the participating schools, U.S. citizenship is required. Admission requirements vary by school. In general, schools look for evidence of research and scholastic ability.

Financial data The amount awarded varies by school. Most schools waive tuition and offer stipends that range between $6,000 and $10,000 per year.

Duration 1 year; may be renewed.

Number awarded 1 or more at each of the participating schools.

Deadline Application dates vary by school.

[640]
NATIONAL DEFENSE SCIENCE AND ENGINEERING GRADUATE FELLOWSHIP PROGRAM

Department of Defense
c/o Battelle
200 Park Drive, Suite 211
P.O. Box 13444
Research Triangle Park, NC 27709-3444
(919) 549-8505   Fax: (919) 549-8205
E-mail: ndseg@aro-emh1.army.mil

Purpose To provide financial assistance for doctoral study in areas of science and engineering that are of military importance.

Eligibility Graduate students in the following specialties are eligible: aeronautical and astronautical engineering; biosciences, including toxicology; chemical engineering; chemistry; cognitive, neural, and behavioral sciences; computer science; electrical engineering; geosciences, including terrain, water, and air; manufacturing sciences and engineering, including industrial engineering; materials science and engineering; mathematics; mechanical engineering; naval architecture and ocean engineering; oceanography; and physics, including optics. Applicants must be U.S. citizens or nationals at or near the beginning of their graduate study planning to pursue a doctoral degree in 1 of the indicated specialties. Applications are encouraged from women, underrepresented minorities (American Indians, Blacks, Hispanics, Native Alaskans, and Pacific Islanders), and persons with disabilities. Selection is based on all available evidence of ability, including academic records, letters of recommendation, and GRE scores.

Financial data The annual stipend is $17,000 for the first year, $18,000 for the second year; and $189000 for the third year; the program also pays the recipient's institution full tuition and required fees (not to include room and board) and $2,000 per year to the fellow's department. An additional allowance may be considered for a student with a disability.

Duration 3 years, as long as satisfactory academic progress is maintained.

Special features This program is sponsored by the U.S. Army, Navy, Air Force, and Advanced Research Projects Agency. Recipients do not incur any military or other service obligation.

Number awarded Approximately 90 each year.

Limitations Recipients must attend school on a full-time basis.

Deadline January of each year.

[641]
NATIONAL HEALTH SERVICE CORPS SCHOLARSHIP PROGRAM

Health Resources and Services Administration
Attn: Bureau of Primary Health Care
National Health Service Corps Program
2070 Chain Bridge Road, Suite 450
Vienna, VA 22182-2536
(703) 821-8955   (800) 221-9393

Purpose To provide financial assistance to primary health care scholars willing to serve in a federally designated health professional shortage area on completion of training.

Eligibility The following requirements must be met by applicants to be eligible for these awards: U.S. citizenship or permanent residency, full-time enrollment in an accredited school or program in the United States or its possessions, and a demonstrated potential for providing primary health care services, including allopathic and osteopathic medicine (with a specialty in family medicine, general pediatrics, general internal medicine, or obstetrics/gynecology), family nurse practitioner, nurse midwife, and physician assistant (either baccalaureate or master's level). Preference is given to applicants who have participated in the federal Scholarship Program for Students of Exceptional Financial Need at their medical schools, come from a disadvantaged background, and have characteristics that increase the probability they will continue to practice in a health professional shortage area (HPSA) after they have completed their service obligation.

Financial data The stipend is $817 per month. In addition, the program makes a direct payment to each participant's school for tuition and fees and a single additional payment toward other reasonable educational expenses (e.g., books, clinical supplies, laboratory expenses, uniforms, graduation fees, and clinical rotational travel). Participants incur 1 year of obligated service in the National Health Service Corps for each full or partial year of support provided under this program. The minimum service obligation is 2 years.

Duration 1 year; may be renewed for up to 3 additional years.

Special features This scholarship was first offered in 1978/9. It is the successor to the Public Health and National Health Service Corps Scholarship Training Program, which was in effect from 1973/4 to 1977/8.

Limitations Participants are obligated to provide full-time clinical primary health care services to populations in federally-designated, high-priority HPSAs (these include the Indian Health Service or medical facilities of the Federal Bureau of Prisons).

Number awarded Varies each year, depending upon the funding available. In a recent year, 220 scholarships were awarded.

Deadline March of each year.

[642]
NATIONAL HEART, LUNG, AND BLOOD INSTITUTE MINORITY INSTITUTIONAL RESEARCH TRAINING PROGRAM

National Institutes of Health
Attn: National Heart, Lung, and Blood Institute
Division of Heart and Vascular Diseases
Two Rockledge Center, Room 9204
6701 Rockledge Drive MSC 7940
Bethesda, MD 20892-7940
(301) 435-0530   Fax: (301) 480-1454
E-mail: mc63a@nih.gov

Purpose To train pre- and postdoctoral students in minority schools that have the potential to develop a meritorious program in cardiovascular, pulmonary, or hematologic research for research careers in areas relevant to these diseases.

Eligibility Minority institutions seeking this support may be schools of medicine, osteopathy, dentistry, or veterinary medicine in which students of minority underrepresented groups (including African Americans, Hispanics, American Indians, Alaska Natives, or Pacific Islanders) comprise a majority or significant proportion of the enrollment. Eligible schools must have the ongoing staff and facilities required for the proposed program. The minority institution must identify and collaborate with a research center that has strong, well-established cardiovascular, pulmonary, or hematologic research and research training programs. Cooperation between institutions is needed to provide each student trainee with a mentor who is recognized as an accomplished investigator in cardiovascular, pulmonary, or hematologic research and who will assist the advisor at the minority institution in the trainee's development and research plan. All students to be trained under the program must be U.S. citizens, noncitizen nationals, or permanent residents at the time of appointment; predoctoral candidates must have a baccalaureate degree and be training at the graduate level in a relevant biomedical scientific area with made a strong commitment to complete a doctoral degree; postdoctoral candidates must have a doctoral degree or equivalent in a biomedical or behavioral science and must show evidence of a strong interest in a cardiovascular, pulmonary, or hematologic research career. Selection is based upon adequacy of faculty, facilities, and resources for the proposed research training (at both the minority institution and the research center); adequacy of the cooperative arrangements between the minority institution and the research center; commitment of the relevant faculty and the 2 institutions to the goals of the training program; and procedures for evaluation of the impact of the program on the trainees involved.

Financial data Predoctoral students receive an annual stipend of $10,008; postdoctoral candidates receive an annual stipend that ranges from $19,608 to $32,300, depending on the years of postdoctoral experience. Institutions receive an allowance for training related costs of $1,500 per year for predoctoral students and $2,500 per year for postdoctoral candidates, as well as tuition and fees and travel expenses (to $800 per trip).

Duration Trainees are encouraged to be appointed to the training for at least 2 years.

Special features Students interested in this program apply directly to the university; for a list of the currently participating institutions, contact the address above.

Limitations Students may not spend more than 50 percent of their time at the research training center over the course of the year, including a period of intensive research over the summer.

Number awarded Up to 3 each year.

Deadline August of each year.

[643]
NATIONAL HEART, LUNG, AND BLOOD INSTITUTE MINORITY SCHOOL FACULTY DEVELOPMENT AWARD

National Institutes of Health
Attn: National Heart, Lung, and Blood Institute
Division of Lung Diseases
Two Rockledge Center, Room 10112
6701 Rockledge Drive MSC 7952
Bethesda, MD 20892-7952
(301) 435-0222   Fax: (301) 480-1046
E-mail: mr50w@nih.gov

Purpose To encourage the development of faculty investigators at minority schools in areas relevant to cardiovascular, pulmonary, and hematologic diseases.

Eligibility Candidates for this award are minority school faculty members who are U.S. citizens, noncitizen nationals, or permanent residents at the time of application; have a doctoral degree or equivalent in a biomedical science; wish to receive specialized training in cardiovascular, pulmonary, or blood research; and have the background and potential to benefit from the training. Each candidate must identify and complete arrangements with a nearby mentor (within approximately 100 miles) who is recognized as an accomplished investigator in the research area proposed and who will provide guidance for the awardee's development and research plans. For the purposes of this program, "minority school" is defined as a medical or nonmedical college, university, or equivalent school in which 1) students of minority ethnic groups (including but not limited to African Americans, Hispanics, Native Americans, and Asian or Pacific Islanders) comprise a majority or significant proportion of the school's enrollment; 2) there is a commitment to the special encouragement of minority faculty, students, and investigators; and 3) few or no members of its faculty are actively engaged in biomedical research.

Financial data The awardee receives salary support of up to $50,000 per year plus fringe benefits for 5 years. The actual amount of support awarded is based on the recipient's current salary and must be consistent with the established salary structure of the minority institution for persons of equivalent qualifications, experience, and rank. Support for up to 10 percent of the mentor's salary during the summer experience may also be awarded. In addition, up to $20,000 per year will be provided for research support. These research funds may be used for equipment, supplies, travel, tuition and fees, and other related costs (e.g., personnel, publication costs, computer costs).

Duration 2 to 3 months during the summer and quarter time during the academic year for up to 5 years.

Special features Support is also available through the Division of Heart and Vascular Diseases and the Division of Blood Diseases and Resources.

Number awarded Up to 15 each year.

Deadline August of each year.

[644]
NATIONAL HEART, LUNG, AND BLOOD INSTITUTE SHORT-TERM RESEARCH TRAINING FOR MINORITY STUDENTS PROGRAM

National Institutes of Health
Attn: National Heart, Lung, and Blood Institute
Division of Lung Diseases
Two Rockledge Center, Room 10112
6701 Rockledge Drive MSC 7952
Bethesda, MD 20892-7952
(301) 435-0222   Fax: (301) 480-1046
E-mail: mr50w@nih.gov

Purpose To enable research institutions to provide opportunities for underrepresented minority students at the undergraduate and graduate level to become exposed to biomedical research in areas relevant to cardiovascular, pulmonary, and hematologic diseases through a short-term research experience.

Eligibility Applications may be submitted by non-federal, domestic, for-profit and nonprofit, public and private organizations, such as universities, colleges, medical schools, and units of state and local government. Racial/ethnic minority individuals, women, and persons with disabilities are particularly encouraged to apply as program directors. The proposal must support short-term research training experiences of minority undergraduate students, minority students in health professional schools, and minority graduate students. The grantee institution is responsible for selection and appointment of trainees. Special attention should be given to the recruitment of individuals from minority groups that are underrepresented nationally in the biomedical and behavioral sciences (Blacks, Hispanics, American Indians, Alaska Natives, and Pacific Islanders). Trainees must have successfully completed at least 1 undergraduate year at an accredited school or university (including baccalaureate schools of nursing) or have successfully completed 1 semester at a school of medicine, optometry, osteopathy, dentistry, veterinary medicine pharmacy, or public health, or an institution with an accredited graduate program. Trainees appointed to the program need not be from the grantee institution, but may include a number of minority students from other institutions, schools, colleges, or universities.

Financial data The award provides salary support to the trainees of $834 per month, as well as up to $125 per trainee per month for other training costs (supplies, tuition, fees, etc.), up to $500 per trainee for travel to and from the training site, and up to $250 per month per trainee for housing at the training site.

Duration Grants to institutions are for 5 years; students receive support for 2 to 3 months.

Special features Students interested in this program should check with the office of sponsored research at their institution to see if such programs are available. They may also contact the address above to obtain a list of participating institutions.

Number awarded Varies each year; each institutional grant supports 4 to 24 students per year.

Deadline August of each year.

[645]
NATIONAL LAWYERS GUILD SUMMER PROJECTS

National Lawyers Guild
126 University Place, Fourth Floor
New York, NY 10013
(212) 627-2656 Fax: (212) 627-2404
E-mail: nlgno@igc.apc.org

Purpose To provide law students with direct experience in progressive legal work, encouraging careers in fields of law dedicated to using the legal system in the service of justice.

Eligibility This program is open to law students, legal workers, and lawyers interested in working with civil rights and poverty law groups. Women and ethnic minorities are particularly encouraged to apply.

Financial data Interns receive a $2,000 stipend. Recipients are encouraged to seek other funding sources, including law school work-study and fellowship programs.

Duration 10 weeks during the summer; renewable the following year.

Special features Summer Project programs are located throughout the country, in rural and urban areas. Interns have the opportunity to work on issues concerning Central American and Haitian refugees, farm worker rights, union democracy, opposition to the death penalty and inhumane prison conditions, women's economic and reproductive rights, unemployment rights, Philippine solidarity work, the farm crisis, voting rights, Native American treaty rights, Asian American housing and job rights, and workplace health and safety. Among the participating agencies are: Association of Community Organizations for Reform Now, Asian Law Caucus, California Center for Law and the Deaf, Michigan Migrant Legal Assistance Project, and the Native American Rights Fund.

Number awarded Approximately 20 each year.

Deadline February of each year.

[646]
NATIONAL RESEARCH SERVICE AWARD INSTITUTIONAL RESEARCH TRAINING GRANTS

National Institutes of Health
Attn: Office of Extramural Research
Extramural Outreach and Information Resources Office
6701 Rockledge Drive, Room 6207
MSC 7910
Bethesda, MD 20892-7910
(301) 435-0714 Fax: (301) 480-8443
E-mail: asknih@odrockm1.od.nih.gov

Purpose To provide funding to institutions to develop or enhance research training opportunities for individuals, selected by the institution, who are training for careers in specified areas of biomedical and behavioral research.

Eligibility This program is open to domestic, nonprofit, private or public institutions with the staff and facilities required for the proposed program of research training. The research training program director at the institution is responsible for the selection and appointment of trainees, who may be in 1 of 3 categories: 1) predoctoral, for trainees who have received a baccalaureate degree and are training at the postbaccalaureate level in a program leading to the Ph.D. in areas of basic biomedical and behavioral sciences or in an equivalent research doctoral degree program; 2) postdoctoral, for trainees who have received a Ph.D., M.D., or comparable doctoral degree and wish to pursue specialized training to meet national research priorities in the biomedical and behavioral sciences; or 3) short-term health professional, for health professional students who have completed at least 1 quarter in a program leading to a clinical doctorate and wish to engage in biomedical and/or behavioral research during the summer or other "off-quarter" periods. All candidates must be U.S. citizens or permanent citizens. Institutions must give particular attention to recruiting individuals from minority groups that are underrepresented nationally in biomedical and behavioral research (African Americans, Hispanics, Native Americans, Alaskan Natives, and Pacific Islanders).

Financial data For predoctoral trainees, the annual stipend is $10,008; health professional trainees receive the same stipend, prorated at $834 per month. For postdoctoral trainees, the award provides an annual stipend based on the number of years of postdoctoral experience, ranging from $19,608 for less than 1 year to $32,300 for 7 or more years. Institutions may apply for training costs (such as staff salaries, consultant costs, equipment, research supplies, and staff travel) of up to $1,500 per year per predoctoral trainee or $2,500 per year per postdoctoral trainee; up to $125 per month to offset the cost of tuition, fees, travel, supplies, and other expenses for each short-term health professional research training position; and an indirect cost allowance of 8 percent of total allowable direct costs or actual indirect costs, whichever is less.

Duration Awards may be made for up to 5 years and are renewable. Predoctoral and postdoctoral trainee appointments are normally made in 12-month increments with support for additional years dependent on satisfactory progress and the continued availability of funds. Health professional traineeships are for 2 to 3 months.

Special features This award is offered by all funding Institutes and Centers of the National Institutes of Health (NIH) as part of the National Research Service Award (NRSA) program, originally established in 1974. The NIH designates this program as the T32 Awards.

Limitations The initial 12 months of NRSA postdoctoral support carries a service payback requirement, which can be fulfilled by continued training under the award or by engaging in other health-related research training, health-related research, or health-related teaching. Fellows who fail to fulfill the payback requirement of 1 month of acceptable service for each month of the initial 12 months of support received must repay all funds received with interest.

Number awarded Varies each year.

Deadline January, May, and September of each year; some Institutes accept applications only once each year; contact the address above for further information.

[647]
NATIONAL RESEARCH SERVICE AWARD SENIOR FELLOWSHIPS

National Institutes of Health
Attn: Office of Extramural Research
Extramural Outreach and Information Resources Office
6701 Rockledge Drive, Room 6207
MSC 7910
Bethesda, MD 20892-7910
(301) 435-0714 Fax: (301) 480-8443
E-mail: asknih@odrockm1.od.nih.gov

Purpose To provide mentored research training for experienced scientists who wish to make major changes in the direction of their research careers.

Eligibility Applications for this program may be submitted on behalf of the candidates by a sponsoring institution which may be private (profit or nonprofit) or public, including a federal laboratory. Individuals requesting foreign-site training must justify the particular suitability of the foreign site, based on the nature of the facilities and/or training opportunity, rather than a domestic institution. Only in cases where there are clear scientific advantages will foreign training be supported. Candidates must have received a Ph.D., D.D.S., D.M.D., or equivalent degree from an accredited domestic or foreign institution and must have had at least 7 subsequent years of relevant research experience. Applications from minorities and women are particularly encouraged.

Financial data Salaries are determined individually, based on the salary or remuneration which the individual would have received from the home institution, but may not exceed $32,300 per year. Institutional allowances for tuition, fees, individual health insurance, research supplies, equipment, travel to scientific meetings, and related items are up to $3,000 for nonfederal sponsoring institutions and $2,000 for federal laboratories. The initial 12 months of postdoctoral support carries a service payback requirement, which can be fulfilled by continued training under the award or by engaging in other health-related research training, health-related research, or health-related teaching. Fellows who fail to fulfill the payback requirement of 1 month of acceptable service for each month of the initial 12 months of support received must repay all funds received with interest.

Duration 5 years; nonrenewable.

Special features The National Institutes of Health (NIH) designates this program as the F33 Awards. It is offered by 8 components of the NIH: the National Institute on Aging, the National Institute on Alcohol Abuse and Alcoholism, the National Institute of Allergy and Infectious Diseases, the National Institute of Arthritis and Musculoskeletal and Skin Diseases, the National Cancer Institute, the National Institute of Child Health and Human Development, the National Institute on Deafness and Other Communication Disorders, and the National Institute of Dental Research.

Number awarded Varies each year.

Deadline April, August, and December of each year.

[648]
NATIONAL RESEARCH SERVICE AWARDS FOR INDIVIDUAL PREDOCTORAL FELLOWS

National Institutes of Health
Attn: National Institute on Alcohol Abuse and Alcoholism
Office of Scientific Affairs
Willco Building, Suite 409
6000 Executive Boulevard MSC 7003
Bethesda, MD 20892-7003
(301) 443-2890   Fax: (301) 443-6077
E-mail: jv24p@nih.gov

Purpose To provide funding for doctoral research training in areas of behavioral, biomedical, or social science that deal with alcohol, drug abuse, and mental health.

Eligibility Applicants must be U.S. citizens or permanent residents enrolled in a program leading to a research doctorate such as the Ph.D. or D.Sc. at a domestic or foreign nonprofit private or public institution, including a federal laboratory. This program is not available for study leading to the M.D., D.O., D.D.S., Psy.D., or similarly professional degrees. Women and minorities are especially encouraged to apply.

Financial data The annual stipend is $10,008; fellows may also request funds for tuition and fees. The institution may receive an

allowance of $3,000 ($2,000 at federal laboratories) per fellow per 12-month period to help defray such expenses as research supplies, equipment, travel to scientific meetings, and related items.

Duration Up to 5 years.

Special features This award is offered by 3 of the institutes within the National Institutes of Health (NIH): the National Institute on Alcohol Abuse and Alcoholism (NIAAA), the National Institute on Drug Abuse (NIDA), and the National Institute of Mental Health (NIMH). Information is available not only from the address above, but from other components of those 3 institutes. The NIH designates this program as the F31 Awards.

Number awarded Varies each year.

Deadline April, August, or December of each year.

[649]
NATIONAL RESEARCH SERVICE AWARDS FOR RESEARCH TRAINING IN PRIMARY MEDICAL CARE

Health Resources and Services Administration
Attn: Bureau of Health Professions
Division of Medicine
Parklawn Building, Room 9A-20
5600 Fishers Lane
Rockville, MD 20857
(301) 443-1467

Purpose To provide grants to institutions to offer opportunities for training for future researchers and academicians in primary medical care.

Eligibility Accredited public or private nonprofit schools of medicine, osteopathic medicine, or dentistry, or public or private nonprofit hospitals or other entities may apply for these grants. They may use the funds to provide fellowships to facilitate the training of primary care researchers in the problems, methods, and settings that have been to date inadequately pursued and utilized in the United States. Trainees must be U.S. citizens, nationals, or permanent residents who have received a Ph.D., Ed.D., Sc.D., D.Pharm., D.D.S., M.D., D.O., or equivalent degree and who propose to engage in full-time research or training in primary medical care. Applications must include a plan to recruit, admit, and train underrepresented minority postdoctoral trainees (Alaskan Natives, Blacks, Hispanics, Native Americans, and Pacific Islanders) and separately address the efforts of the program to recruit, admit, and train women for research careers. Students interested in this program should write to the address above to obtain a list of institutions currently offering fellowships.

Financial data Recently, a total of $3,357,899 per year was awarded to institutions for research training as part of this program. Fellowships paid to the postdoctoral trainees depend on the years of relevant postdoctoral experience, ranging from $19,608 for no experience to $32,300 for 7 or more years of experience. Institutional costs of up to $3,000 per full-time trainee may be requested to defray costs of other training related expenses, such as staff salaries, consultant costs, equipment, research supplies, and staff travel.

Duration Grants to institutions are provided for up to 5 years; individual trainees may receive up to 3 years of support.

Limitations Awards are made only to institutions, not to individuals; the institutions recruit and select individual trainees. Recipients of individual support must pay back the federal government by engaging in health related biomedical, behavioral, or primary medical care research, teaching, or a combination of those activities for a period of time equal to the total period of support in excess of the initial 12 months of support.

Number awarded Recently, 23 institutions annually received grants through this program and provided training to 77 fellows.
Deadline April of each year.

[650]
NATIONAL URBAN/RURAL FELLOWS PROGRAM

National Urban Fellows, Inc.
55 West 44th Street, Suite 600
New York, NY 10036
(212) 921-9400   Fax: (212) 921-9572
Purpose To provide mid-career minority and women public sector professionals an opportunity to strengthen leadership skills through an academic program coupled with a mentorship.
Eligibility Eligible to apply are U.S. citizens who have a bachelor's degree, have 3 years of full-time work experience in an administrative or managerial capacity, have demonstrated exceptional ability and leadership potential, meet academic admission requirements, have a high standard of integrity and work ethic, and are willing to relocate for the duration of the fellowship year.
Financial data The stipend is up to $20,000. The program also provides full payment of tuition fees, a relocation allowance of $500, and reimbursement for program related travel.
Duration 14 months.
Special features The program begins with a semester of study at Bernard M. Baruch College of the City University of New York. Following this, fellows spend 9 months in mentorship assignments as special assistants to governors, mayors, city managers, or county administrators of urban and rural organizations. Fellows who successfully complete all requirements are granted a master's of public administration from Bernard M. Baruch College.
Number awarded Varies; approximately 20 each year.
Deadline February of each year.

[651]
NATIVE AMERICAN SEMINARY AWARD

United Methodist Church
Attn: Office of Loans and Scholarships
1001 19th Avenue South
P.O. Box 871
Nashville, TN 37202-0871
(615) 340-7344   Fax: (615) 340-7048
Purpose To provide financial assistance to Native American students at United Methodist schools of theology.
Eligibility Applicants must be full-time degree candidates in a United Methodist school of theology, active members of the United Methodist Church for at least 3 years, able to demonstrate financial need, citizens or permanent residents of the United States, born of Native American parentage (at least 1 parent), and affiliated with a Native American tribal organization.
Financial data The amount awarded varies, depending upon the needs of the recipient. Funds must be used only for graduate study.
Duration 1 year; may be renewed.
Deadline April of each year.

[652]
NBC MINORITY FELLOWSHIP PROGRAM IN BROADCASTING

National Broadcasting Company
Attn: Employee Relations
30 Rockefeller Plaza, Suite 1678
New York, NY 10112
(212) 836-5523   Fax: (212) 836-5520
Purpose To provide financial assistance for minority students interested in pursuing a graduate degree in journalism, business, or communications.
Eligibility Minority college graduates seeking a graduate degree in journalism, business, or communications are eligible. Specific universities are invited to nominate students who have distinguished themselves through academic work, extracurricular activities, and work experience. Candidates must be U.S. citizens or permanent residents, demonstrate financial need and academic achievement at the undergraduate level, be enrolled in a graduate school of journalism or communications, and have an interest in broadcasting or related industries.
Financial data Stipends up to $8,000 are provided.
Duration 1 academic year.
Number awarded 1 each year. Since its inception, the program has awarded more than 80 minority fellowships.
Deadline The deadline date varies by institution; check directly with the school you wish to attend.

[653]
NCAA ETHNIC MINORITY POSTGRADUATE SCHOLARSHIP PROGRAM

National Collegiate Athletic Association
Attn: Director of Professional Development
6201 College Boulevard
Overland Park, KS 66211-2422
(913) 339-1906
Purpose To provide funding for ethnic minorities who are interested in pursuing graduate education in athletics.
Eligibility Minorities who have been accepted in a National Collegiate Athletic Association (NCAA) member institution's sports administration program or a related program (that will lead to a career in athletics) are eligible to apply if they are U.S. citizens, have performed with distinction as a student-body member at their respective undergraduate institution, and are entering the first semester or term of their postgraduate studies. Especially considered are the applicant's involvement in extracurricular activities, course work, commitment to pursuing a career in intercollegiate athletics, and promise for success. Financial need is not a factor in granting these scholarships.
Financial data The stipend is $6,000; funds are paid to the college or university of the recipient's choice.
Duration 1 year; nonrenewable.
Number awarded 10 each year.
Deadline February of each year.

[654]
NEBRASKA SPACE GRANT COURSE WORK AWARDS

Nebraska Space Grant Consortium
c/o UNO Aviation Institute
Allwine Hall 422
University of Nebraska at Omaha
Omaha, NE 68182-0508
(402) 554-3772   (800) 858-8648
Fax: (402) 554-3781   E-mail: nasa@cwis.unomaha.edu

Purpose To fund aerospace-related study on the undergraduate and graduate school level for students in Nebraska.

Eligibility This program is open to all eligible undergraduate and graduate students at the following schools in Nebraska: University of Nebraska at Omaha, University of Nebraska at Lincoln, University of Nebraska at Kearney, University of Nebraska Medical Center, Creighton University, Western Nebraska Community College, Chadron State College, College of St. Mary, Metro Community College, and Nebraska Indian Community College. Applicants must be U.S. citizens and working on a degree in an aerospace-related area as full-time students during the spring and fall semesters or half-time during the summer session. Special attention is given to applications submitted by women, underrepresented minorities, and individuals with disabilities.

Financial data The amount of the award depnds on the scope of the proposal and the qualifications of the applicant.

Duration Academic awards are 1 year; summer awards are for the summer months. Both awards are renewable.

Special features Recipients enroll in courses in an approved aviation/aerospace course of study. Funding for this program is provided by the National Aeronautics and Space Administration.

Limitations Recipients must submit a progress report each semester on the progress of their course work to a designated faculty monitor. Failure to provide that report disqualifies the student from reapplying for a renewal fellowship.

[655]
NEUROSCIENCE TRAINING FELLOWSHIP

American Psychological Association
Attn: Minority Fellowship Program
750 First Street, N.E.
Washington, DC 20002-4242
(202) 336-6027   Fax: (202) 336-6012
TDD: (202) 336-6123   E-mail: mfp@apa.org

Purpose To provide financial assistance to minority students who are interested in completing a doctorate in neuroscience.

Eligibility Underrepresented racial and ethnic minorities (including but not limited to African Americans, Alaskan Natives, Mexican Americans, Native Americans, Pacific Islanders, and Puerto Ricans) who are interested in earning a doctorate in psychology are eligible to apply. They must be American citizens or permanent visa residents, be enrolled full time in an accredited doctoral program, and be committed to a research career in neuroscience. Students who wish to pursue a research career in such areas as basic brain research related to normal and abnormal functions and behavior, including research on humans, vertebrate and invertebrate animals, and isolated biological systems may apply. This program is also open to underrepresented postdoctoral minority candidates.

Financial data The stipend depends on the number of years of research experience. The fellowship also provides travel funds to visit universities being considered for graduate training and to attend the annual meeting of the Society for Neuroscience. Many universities also provide tuition support as part of the program; recently, the average annual combined award was $18,780 per year and the minimum was $10,008.

Duration 1 year; may be renewed for up to 2 additional years for predoctoral students or up to 1 additional year for postdoctorates.

Special features The program was established in 1987. It is funded by the U.S. National Institute of Mental Health of the National Institutes of Health and administered by the American Psychological Association. As part of the program, participants receive summer training at the Marine Biological Laboratory in Woods Hole, Massachusetts and the McDonnell Foundation Summer Institute in Cognitive Neuroscience at the University of California at Davis.

Limitations Students who receive a federally-funded grant from another source may not also accept funds from this program.

Number awarded 1 or more each year.

Deadline January of each year.

[656]
NEW HAMPSHIRE SPACE GRANT CONSORTIUM FELLOWSHIPS

New Hampshire Space Grant Consortium
c/o University of New Hampshire
Institute for the Study of Earth, Oceans, and Space
Morse Hall
Durham, NH 03824-3525
(603) 862-0094   Fax: (603) 862-1915
E-mail: nhspacegrant@unh.edu

Purpose To provide financial assistance for graduate study in space-related fields to students in New Hampshire.

Eligibility This program is open to graduate students at member institutions of the New Hampshire Space Grant Consortium (Dartmouth College and the University of New Hampshire). Applicants must be studying space physics, astrophysics, astronomy, or aspects of computer science, engineering, earth sciences, ocean sciences, atmospheric sciences, or life sciences which utilize space technology and/or adopt a planetary view of the global environment. U.S. citizenship is required. The New Hampshire Space Grant Consortium is a component of the U.S. National Aeronautics and Space Administration (NASA) Space Grant program, which encourages participation by women, minorities, and persons with disabilities.

Financial data Awards provide stipend and tuition support.

Duration At Dartmouth, awards are for 1 quarter and are renewable; at the University of New Hampshire, awards are for 12 months.

Special features This program is funded by NASA.

Number awarded Varies each year.

Deadline January of each year.

[657]
NEW YORK SPACE GRANT CONSORTIUM GRADUATE FELLOWSHIPS

New York Space Grant Consortium
c/o Cornell University
Astronomy Department
512 Space Sciences Building
Ithaca, NY 14853-6801
(607) 255-4935　　　　　　　Fax: (607) 255-9817
E-mail: terzian@astrosun.tn.cornell.edu

Purpose To provide financial assistance for graduate study in space-related fields at designated universities in New York.

Eligibility This program is open to graduate students at Cornell University, City College of the City University of New York, Clarkson University, or Columbia University. Applicants must be studying space related fields, including aerospace engineering, astronomy, electrical engineering, geological sciences, and mechanical engineering. U.S. citizenship is required. The New York Space Grant Consortium is a component of the U.S. National Aeronautics and Space Administration (NASA) Space Grant program, which encourages participation by women, minorities, and persons with disabilities.

Financial data The amounts of the awards depends on the availability of funding.

Duration 1 year.

Special features This program is funded by NASA.

Number awarded Varies each year.

[658]
NMF SCHOLARSHIPS

National Medical Fellowships, Inc.
Attn: Scholarships and Programs
110 West 32nd Street, 8th Floor
New York, NY 10001-3205
(212) 714-1007

Purpose To provide financial assistance to underrepresented minority medical students.

Eligibility This fellowship is open students enrolled in the first or second year of medical school. Applicants must be U.S. citizens enrolled in accredited M.D. and D.O. degree-granting programs in the United States who are African American, Mexican American, Native American, or mainland Puerto Rican. Selection is based on academic achievement, leadership, and community service. Financial need must be demonstrated.

Financial data The amount of the award depends on the student's total resources (including parental and spousal support), cost of education, and receipt of additional scholarships; in a recent year, individual awards ranged from $500 to $4,250; the average award was $1,676.

Duration 1 year for first-year students; may be renewed for the second year only.

Limitations A personal interview is required of all applicants.

Number awarded Varies each year; in recent years, approximately 600 students have received support.

Deadline July of each year for new applicants; April of each year for renewal applicants.

[659]
NPSC GRADUATE FELLOWSHIPS

National Physical Science Consortium
c/o Ms. L. Nan Snow, Executive Director
New Mexico State University
O'Loughlin House on University Boulevard
Box 30001, Department 3NPS
Las Cruces, NM 88003-8001
(505) 646-6038　　　　　　　(800) 952-4118
Fax: (505) 646-6097　　　　　E-mail: npsc@nmsu.edu

Purpose To provide financial assistance to underrepresented minorities and women interested in pursuing graduate study in astronomy, chemistry, computer science, geology, materials sciences, mathematics, or physics.

Eligibility To be eligible, applicants must be either 1) an African American, Hispanic, American Indian, Eskimo, Aleut, or Polynesian or 2) a female. In addition, they must be a U.S. citizen; have earned at least a 3.0 cumulative grade point average through the senior year in college; and be able to pursue doctoral study at a participating member university of the National Physical Science Consortium (NPSC). For a list of participating universities, write to the address above. Students who are completing a master's degree at an institution that does not offer a Ph.D. in their discipline are also eligible, but students currently enrolled in a master's or Ph.D. program at an institution that offers the Ph.D. in the student's field are not eligible.

Financial data The fellowship pays tuition and fees plus an annual stipend of $12,500 during the first 4 years and $15,000 during the fifth and sixth years. It also provides on-site paid summer employment to enhance technical experience. The exact value of the fellowship depends on academic standing, summer employment, and graduate school attended.

Duration Up to 6 years.

Special features Among the employers in the internship part of the program are: Argonne, Lawrence Berkeley, Lawrence Livermore, Los Alamos, and Sandia National Laboratories; National Security Agency; Ford Motor Company; Department of Energy; Jet Propulsion Laboratory; IBM; Polaroid; Xerox Corporation; the National Aeronautics and Space Administration and its Ames, Goddard Space, Johnson Space, Kennedy Space, Langley Research, Lewis Research, Marshall Space, and Stennis Space centers; Navajo Nation; Clorox Corporation; and the National Institute of Standards and Technology.

Number awarded Varies each year.

Deadline November of each year.

[660]
NSEP AREA AND LANGUAGE STUDIES DOCTORAL FELLOWSHIPS

Academy for Educational Development
1875 Connecticut Avenue, N.W., Suite 900
Washington, DC 20009-1202
(202) 884-8285　　　　　　　(800) 498-9360
Fax: (202) 884-8408　　　　　E-mail: nsep@aed.org

Purpose To help support outstanding students who are pursuing doctoral studies and are interested in developing expertise in languages, cultures, and area studies of countries less commonly studied by Americans.

Eligibility This program is open to doctoral students (or students applying to a doctoral program) who are U.S. citizens, enrolled in or applying to an accredited school in the United States, and interested in earning a doctorate with a specialization in a foreign language and culture of an area of the world that is critical to national security and economic competitiveness. Part-time students are eligible to be considered for the fellowship, but they must be enrolled in a degree program. Selection is based on demonstrated academic excellence; a comprehensive, clear, concise, feasible proposal for study; a plan to develop or reinforce language competence; leadership potential and community involvement; evidence of ability to adapt to a different cultural environment; and integration of proposed program into academic and career goals. Applications from individuals from traditionally underrepresented groups (women and minorities) are especially encouraged.

Financial data Fellowships for the study of critical foreign languages and areas at the doctoral level support part or all of the costs of that study. The maximum funding is $25,000 per year.

Duration Up to 3 years.

Special features Study outside the United States is strongly encouraged. This program is part of the National Security Education Program (NSEP), funded by the National Security Education Act, and administered by the Academy for Educational Development.

Limitations All fellowships must include study of a language other than English and the corresponding culture that is appropriate for the degree program in which the student is enrolled. The program supports study abroad in areas of the world critical to national security; study will not be supported in most cases in western Europe, Canada, Australia, or New Zealand. Fellowship recipients incur a service obligation and must agree to work for the federal government or in the field of education subsequent to the fellowship period. These fellowships were not awarded in the 1996 and 1997 competition cycles, but will be competed again in 1998 and 1999.

Number awarded Varies; generally, at least 300 per year.

Deadline December of each year.

[661]
NSEP GRADUATE ENHANCEMENT FELLOWSHIPS

Academy for Educational Development
1875 Connecticut Avenue, N.W., Suite 900
Washington, DC 20009-1202
(202) 884-8285   (800) 498-9360
Fax: (202) 884-8408   E-mail: nsep@aed.org

Purpose To help support outstanding students who are pursuing graduate studies and are interested in developing expertise in languages, cultures, and area studies of countries less commonly studied by Americans.

Eligibility This program is open to graduate students in professional and other disciplines who are interested in introducing an international component to their degree studies by focusing on an area of the world that is critical to national security and economic competitiveness. Applicants must be U.S. citizens, enrolled in or applying to an accredited graduate school in the United States, and interested in internationalizing their educational experience or in enhancing an existing internationally-focused program. Part-time students are eligible to be considered for the fellowship, but they must be enrolled in a degree program. Selection is based on demonstrated academic excellence; a comprehensive, clear, concise, feasible proposal for study; a plan to develop or reinforce language competence; leadership potential and community involvement; evidence of ability to adapt to a different cultural environment; and integration of proposed program into academic and career goals. Applications from individu-

als from traditionally underrepresented groups (women and minorities) are especially encouraged.

Financial data The normal domestic stipend is $2,000 per semester; the stipend for overseas study is up to $10,000 per semester.

Duration Up to 2 years.

Special features Study outside the United States is strongly encouraged. This program is part of the National Security Education Program (NSEP), funded by the National Security Education Act, and administered by the Academy for Educational Development.

Limitations All fellowships must include study of a language other than English and the corresponding culture that is appropriate for the degree program in which the student is enrolled. The program supports study abroad in areas of the world critical to national security; study will not be supported in most cases in western Europe, Canada, Australia, or New Zealand. Fellowship recipients incur a service obligation and must agree to work for the federal government or in the field of education subsequent to the fellowship period.

Number awarded Varies; generally, at least 300 per year.

Deadline December of each year.

[662]
NSF GRADUATE FELLOWSHIPS

Oak Ridge Associated Universities
Attn: NSF Graduate Research Fellowship Program
P.O. Box 3010
Oak Ridge, TN 37831-3010
(423) 241-4300   Fax: (423) 241-4513
E-mail: nsfgrfp@orau.gov

Purpose To provide financial assistance to women, minorities, persons with disabilities, and others interested in working on a master's or doctoral degree in sciences, mathematics, and engineering.

Eligibility The program is open only to citizens or nationals of the United States who have not completed more than 20 semester/30 quarter hours or the equivalent of study; individuals may apply during the senior year of college or in the first year of graduate school. Applicants may propose to study engineering, mathematical sciences, computer and information science and engineering, chemistry, earth sciences, physics, astronomy, psychology, life sciences, or social sciences. Women, minorities, and persons with disabilities are specifically encouraged to apply.

Financial data The stipend is $14,400 per year, plus a $9,500 cost-of-education allowance given to the recipient's institution. In addition, there is a $1,000 Special International Research Travel Allowance for 3 months or more of research in countries outside of the United States.

Duration 12 months; may be renewed for up to 2 additional years.

Special features Fellows may choose as their fellowship institution any appropriate nonprofit U.S. or foreign institution of higher education. Oak Ridge Associated Universities administers the program for the National Science Foundation.

Limitations Awards are not made in clinical, business, or management fields; in other education programs of any kind; in history or social work; for work leading to medical, dental, law, public health, or practice-oriented professional degrees, or for joint science-professional degree programs.

Number awarded Approximately 850 each year.

Deadline November of each year.

[663]
NSF MINORITY GRADUATE FELLOWSHIPS

Oak Ridge Associated Universities
Attn: NSF Graduate Research Fellowship Program
P.O. Box 3010
Oak Ridge, TN 37831-3010
(423) 241-4300 Fax: (423) 241-4513
E-mail: nsfgrfp@orau.gov

Purpose To increase the number of practicing scientists and engineers who are members of ethnic minority groups that traditionally have been underrepresented in the advanced levels of the nation's science and engineering talent pool.

Eligibility This program is open to applicants who are citizens or nationals of the United States and who are members of an ethnic minority group underrepresented in the advanced levels of the U.S. science and engineering pool (e.g., American Indian, Black/African American, Native Alaskan (Eskimo or Aleut), Native Pacific Islander (Polynesian or Micronesian), or Hispanic). Persons who hold permanent resident status are not eligible to apply. These fellowships are intended for students in the early stages of their graduate study in science or engineering (or such related fields as mathematics, social sciences, and the history and philosophy of science). In general, those eligible to apply are college seniors, first-year graduate students, and others who have completed a limited amount of graduate study. Specifically, eligibility is limited to those individuals who have completed no more than 30 semester hours, 45 quarter hours, or the equivalent of graduate study. The fields supported by this program include: engineering, mathematical sciences, computer and information science and engineering, chemistry, earth sciences, physics, astronomy, psychology, life sciences, or social sciences. Applicants who have earned a medical degree (e.g., MD, DDS, DVM) are ineligible.

Financial data Fellows receive $14,400. In addition, a $1,000 Special International Research Travel Allowance is available (for at least 3 months of full-time research at a foreign site). The program also provides fellowship institutions, on behalf of each fellow, a cost-of-education allowance ($9,500) to cover all tuition costs and assessed fees. Fellows are also eligible to receive a Mentoring Assistantship ($500 a month for up to 3 months), to participate in summer research.

Duration 9 to 12 months; renewable for up to 2 additional years.

Special features Recipients may use their fellowship at appropriate institutions in the United States or abroad. Oak Ridge Associated Universities administers this program on behalf of the National Science Foundation.

Limitations After an award is made, a major change in course of study or institution to be attended by the fellow requires prior approval of the National Science Foundation.

Number awarded Approximately 150 each year.

Deadline November of each year.

[664]
NUCLEAR ENGINEERING AND HEALTH PHYSICS FELLOWSHIP PROGRAM

Oak Ridge Institute for Science and Education
Attn: Science/Engineering Education Division
P.O. Box 117
Oak Ridge, TN 37831-0117
(423) 576-9558 (423) 576-2600
(800) 569-7749 Fax: (423) 576-3643
E-mail: nehpfp@orau.gov

Purpose To provide funding for graduate study and research experience in nuclear science and engineering or health physics.

Eligibility This program is open to highly capable students who are interested in working on a master's or doctoral degree in nuclear science, nuclear engineering, or health physics at a participating university (for a list of participating schools, write to the address above). Applications are usually submitted during the senior year of undergraduate school. Applicants may not be enrolled in or have been previously enrolled in a full-time graduate program at the time of application. All programs operated by the Science/Engineering Education Division (SEED) of Oak Ridge Institute for Science and Education (ORISE) seek to broaden the participation of minorities, women, and persons with disabilities in science and engineering careers.

Financial data The stipend is $14,400 per year. An additional $300 per month is paid during the practicum period. Tuition and fees are covered. Some travel money is available.

Duration 1 year; may be renewed for up to 4 additional years.

Special features Participants intern at various research facilities of the U.S. Department of Energy (DOE). This program is funded by DOE's Office of Nuclear Energy and administered by ORISE/SEED.

Number awarded Varies each year.

Deadline January of each year.

[665]
OAK RIDGE NATIONAL LABORATORY POSTDOCTORAL RESEARCH ASSOCIATES PROGRAM

Oak Ridge Institute for Science and Education
Attn: Science/Engineering Education Division
P.O. Box 117
Oak Ridge, TN 37831-0117
(423) 241-2877 (423) 576-4805
(800) 569-7749 Fax: (423) 576-3643
E-mail: ornlprap@orau.gov

Purpose To provide financial assistance for postdoctoral research and training in a broad range of science and engineering activities related to basic sciences, energy, and environment.

Eligibility Applicants must have completed a doctoral degree within the past 5 years in engineering, life sciences, physical sciences, earth sciences, environmental sciences, mathematics, computer sciences, or other scientific disciplines. Awards are tenable at Oak Ridge National Laboratory in Tennessee. All programs operated by the Science/Engineering Education Division (SEED) of Oak Ridge Institute for Science and Education (ORISE) seek to broaden the participation of minorities, women, and persons with disabilities in science and engineering careers.

Financial data The stipend is based on research area and degree; reimbursement for inbound travel and moving are also provided.

Duration 1 year; renewable.

Special features This program is funded by Oak Ridge National Laboratory and administered by ORISE/SEED.
Number awarded Varies each year.
Deadline Applications may be submitted at any time.

[666]
OHIO SPACE GRANT CONSORTIUM DOCTORAL FELLOWSHIP

Ohio Space Grant Consortium
c/o Ohio Aerospace Institute
22800 Cedar Point Road
Cleveland, OH 44142
(216) 962-3032   (800) 828-OSGC
Fax: (216) 962-3120   E-mail: osgc@oai.org

Purpose To encourage American citizens to pursue a doctorate in aerospace-related engineering and science at major universities in Ohio.
Eligibility These fellowships are available to U.S. citizens enrolled in a doctoral program in an aerospace-related discipline (aeronautical engineering, aerospace engineering, chemical engineering, computer engineering and science, control engineering, electrical engineering, engineering mechanics, industrial engineering, manufacturing engineering, materials science and engineering, mechanical engineering, physics, petroleum engineering, and systems engineering) at 1 of the participating universities in Ohio: University of Akron, Case Western Reserve University, University of Cincinnati, Cleveland State University, University of Dayton, Ohio State University, Ohio University, University of Toledo, or Wright State University. Members of groups underrepresented in aerospace disciplines (including women, minorities, and persons with disabilities) are particularly encouraged to apply. Selection is based on academic achievement, recommendations, academic background, and the relevance of the applicant's research interests and experience.
Financial data The stipend is $18,000 per year plus tuition at the university attended. Also provided is up to $2,400 per year for reimbursement to the fellow of personal expenses related to research at NASA and up to $500 per year as reimbursement to the dissertation advisor for expenses related to travel to the NASA center for meetings with the fellow.
Duration Up to 3 years.
Special features These fellowships are funded through the National Space Grant College and Fellowship Program, administered by the National Aeronautics and Space Administration (NASA) with matching funds provided by the member universities, the Ohio Aerospace Institute, and private industry.
Limitations Recipients are required to conduct a significant portion of their doctoral research in residence at NASA Lewis Research Center/Ohio Aerospace Institute or at another appropriate approved NASA center.
Number awarded 3 each year.
Deadline January of each year.

[667]
OHIO SPACE GRANT CONSORTIUM MASTER'S FELLOWSHIP

Ohio Space Grant Consortium
c/o Ohio Aerospace Institute
22800 Cedar Point Road
Cleveland, OH 44142
(216) 962-3032   (800) 828-OSGC
Fax: (216) 962-3120   E-mail: osgc@oai.org

Purpose To encourage American citizens to pursue a master's degree in aerospace-related engineering and science at major universities in Ohio.
Eligibility These fellowships are available to U.S. citizens enrolled in a master's degree program in an aerospace-related discipline (aeronautical engineering, aerospace engineering, chemical engineering, computer engineering and science, control engineering, electrical engineering, engineering mechanics, industrial engineering, manufacturing engineering, materials science and engineering, mechanical engineering, physics, petroleum engineering, and systems engineering) at 1 of the following participating universities in Ohio: University of Akron, Case Western Reserve University, University of Cincinnati, Cleveland State University, University of Dayton, Ohio State University, Ohio University, University of Toledo, or Wright State University. Members of groups underrepresented in aerospace-related disciplines (including women, minorities, and persons with disabilities) are particularly encouraged to apply. Selection is based on academic achievement, recommendations, academic background, and the relevance of the applicant's research interests and experience.
Financial data The stipend is $14,000 per academic year plus tuition at the university attended.
Duration Up to 18 months.
Special features These fellowships are funded through the National Space Grant College and Fellowship Program, administered by the National Aeronautics and Space Administration (NASA) with matching funds provided by the member universities, the Ohio Aerospace Institute, and private industry.
Number awarded 5 each year.
Deadline January of each year.

[668]
OKLAHOMA FUTURE TEACHERS SCHOLARSHIP PROGRAM

Oklahoma State Regents for Higher Education
500 Education Building
State Capitol Complex
Oklahoma City, OK 73105-4503
(405) 524-9153   Fax: (405) 524-9230

Purpose To provide financial assistance to Oklahoma residents who are interested in teaching (particularly in teacher shortage fields) in Oklahoma.
Eligibility Candidates for this program are nominated by institutions of higher education in Oklahoma. Nominees must be high school seniors, high school graduates, or currently-enrolled undergraduate or graduate students. They must 1) rank in the top 15 percent of their high school graduating class; 2) place at least at the 85th percentile on the ACT or SAT either for their class as a whole or for a subdivision of Black Non-Hispanic, Hispanic, Native American, or Asian; 3) have been admitted into a professional education program at an accredited Oklahoma institution of higher education; or 4) have achieved an undergraduate record of outstanding success as defined by the institution. Recipients

must agree to teach in critical shortage areas in the state upon graduation. These areas change periodically but in the past have included (for all applicants) special education, science, and foreign languages; (for graduate students) counseling, library/media specialist, and speech and language pathology; and (for renewal applicants) early childhood education and mathematics.

Financial data Full-time students receive up to $1,500 per year if they have completed 60 hours or more and up to $1,000 if they have completed fewer than 60 hours; part-time students receive up to $750 per year if they have completed 60 hours or more and up to $500 per year if they have completed fewer than 60 hours. Funds are paid directly to the institution on the student's behalf. This is a scholarship/loan program; recipients must agree to teach in Oklahoma public schools for 3 years following graduation and licensure.

Duration 1 year; may be renewable for up to 3 additional years as long as the recipient maintains a grade point average of at least 2.5.

Number awarded 100 or more each year.

Deadline Participating institutions set their own deadline dates, but must forward applications and prioritized nominations to the State Regents by June of each year.

[669]
OKLAHOMA MINORITY DOCTORAL STUDY GRANT PROGRAM

Oklahoma State Regents for Higher Education
500 Education Building
State Capitol Complex
Oklahoma City, OK 73105-4503
(405) 524-9143   Fax: (405) 524-9230

Purpose To increase the number of faculty and administrative staff from minority groups in the Oklahoma State System of Higher Education.

Eligibility This program is open to United States citizens who are of a disproportionately underrepresented minority group and are enrolled or accepted for enrollment as doctoral students at an Oklahoma institution of higher education. Candidates must be nominated by the dean of their instituiton.

Financial data The maximum stipend is $6,000 each year, paid directly to the student. This is a scholarship/loan program; recipients must agree to teach in a state system institution for a minimum of 1 year for each year of assistance received.

Duration 1 year; renewable.

Number awarded Varies each year.

Deadline May of each year.

[670]
OKLAHOMA MINORITY PROFESSIONAL STUDY GRANT PROGRAM

Oklahoma State Regents for Higher Education
500 Education Building
State Capitol Complex
Oklahoma City, OK 73105-4503
(405) 524-9143   Fax: (405) 524-9230

Purpose To increase the number of qualified professionals from minority groups in Oklahoma in the areas of medicine, dentistry, law, veterinary medicine, and optometry.

Eligibility Applicants must be United States citizens who are of a disproportionately underrepresented minority group and have completed minimum professional school admission requirements

at an accredited college or university. Priority is given to Oklahoma residents who are attending or have graduated from an accredited Oklahoma college or university; next consideration is given to Oklahoma residents who are attending or have graduated from an accredited out-of-state institution. Only after all eligible Oklahoma candidates have won awards under the program may nonresident candidates be accepted. Students must provide evidence that they have been accepted for admission to or have made satisfactory progress in a professional degree program at the University of Oklahoma Health Sciences Center, the Oklahoma College of Osteopathic Medicine and Surgery, the Oklahoma State University College of Veterinary Medicine, the University of Oklahoma College of Law, or the Northeastern State University College of Optometry.

Financial data The maximum stipend is $4,000 each year, paid directly to the student in 8 monthly installments.

Duration This fellowship may be applied toward the first 2 years of professional study, if the student is enrolled as a full-time professional student and maintains satisfactory progress toward the degree.

Number awarded Varies each year.

Deadline May of each year.

[671]
OLD DOMINION UNIVERSITY PRESIDENT'S GRADUATE FELLOWSHIP

Old Dominion University
Attn: Office of Research, Economic Development and
    Graduate Studies
New Administration Building, Room 210
Norfolk, VA 23529-0013
(804) 683-3460   Fax: (804) 683-3004

Purpose To provide financial support to minorities and women working toward their terminal degree who are willing to serve in a tenure-track faculty position at Old Dominion University.

Eligibility This program is open to women and minorities who show strong potential for success in advanced graduate study and whose academic disciplines correspond to the programmatic needs of Old Dominion University. Candidates may be undergraduate or master's-level students. They must be enrolled in or accepted into a graduate program leading to a terminal degree (generally at a university other than Old Dominion). All applicants must be U.S. citizens. Fellowships are awarded on the basis of the individual's potential to contribute to their chosen discipline as a faculty member at Old Dominion.

Financial data Participants are given a non-tenure track faculty appointment with the appropriate academic department at Old Dominion University. Financial support will be negotiated but may include not only tuition and fees but also a stipend of up to one half of the non-tenured faculty salary, health coverage, and travel and research assistance. Every recipient is required to sign a program agreement with Old Dominion University which contains, among other items, an interest-bearing promissory note which will be cancelled upon successful completion of 3 years of employment with the University in a tenure-track faculty position. If a fellow fails to complete the degree within the program terms, or serves the University for fewer than 3 years because of unsatisfactory performance resulting in either involuntary or voluntary termination of employment, the portion of the note and interest which remains unfilled must be repaid.

Duration Up to 5 years.

Special features Upon completion of the terminal degree, fellows assume a tenure-track position in the designated department at Old Dominion University.
Deadline February of each year.

[672]
ONE-YEAR-ON-CAMPUS PROGRAM

Sandia National Laboratories
Attn: Staffing Specialist
Department 3535
P.O. Box 5800
Albuquerque, NM 87185-1023
(505) 844-3441   E-mail: pacover@sandia.gov

Purpose To enable minority students to obtain a master's degree in engineering or computer science and also work at Sandia National Laboratories.
Eligibility This program is open to minority students with a baccalaureate degree in engineering or computer science and a minimum grade point average of 3.2. Participants must apply to 3 of the following schools: University of Arizona, University of California at Berkeley, University of California at Davis, University of California at Los Angeles, Cal Tech, University of Texas at Austin, Georgia Tech, Cornell, University of Michigan, University of New Mexico, New Mexico State University, University of Oklahoma, Purdue, University of Southern California, Stanford, University of Wisconsin, or University of Washington. They must be prepared to obtain a master's degree within 1 year. The fields of study (not all fields are available at all participating universities) include computer science, electrical engineering, mechanical engineering, civil engineering, chemical engineering, nuclear engineering, materials sciences, and petroleum engineering. Applicants must be interested in working at the laboratories during the summer between graduation from college and the beginning of their graduate program, and then following completion of their master's degree.
Financial data Participants receive a competitive salary while working at the laboratories on a full-time basis and a stipend while attending school.
Duration 1 year.
Special features During their summer assignment, participants work at the laboratories, either in Albuquerque, New Mexico or in Livermore, California. Upon successful completion of the program, they return to Sandia's hiring organization as a full-time member of the technical staff. This program began in 1968.
Limitations Application to schools where students received their undergraduate degree is not recommended. After the schools accept an applicant, the choice of a school is made jointly by the laboratories and the participant.
Number awarded Varies each year; since the program began, more than 330 engineers and computer scientists have gone to work at Sandia with master's degrees.

[673]
OREGON STATE BAR SCHOLARSHIP PROGRAM

Oregon State Bar
Attn: Affirmative Action Program
5200 SW Meadows Road
P.O. Box 1689
Lake Oswego, OR 97035-0889
(503) 620-0222   (800) 452-8260 (within OR)
Fax: (503) 684-1366

Purpose To provide financial assistance to minority students in Oregon who are currently attending law school.
Eligibility This program is open to minority (African American, Asian, Hispanic, Native American) law students with financial need who attend an Oregon law school and plan to practice law in Oregon upon graduation.
Financial data The amount awarded varies, depending upon the needs of the recipient. Funds are credited to the recipient's law school tuition account.
Duration 1 year; recipients may reapply.
Limitations Recipients are encouraged to contribute monetarily to the Oregon State Bar's affirmative action program once they become employed.
Number awarded Varies each year.

[674]
ORNL PROFESSIONAL INTERNSHIP PROGRAM

Oak Ridge Institute for Science and Education
Attn: Science/Engineering Education Division
P.O. Box 117
Oak Ridge, TN 37831-0117
(423) 576-3427   (423) 576-3426
(800) 569-7749   Fax: (423) 576-3643
E-mail: pipornl@orau.gov   E-mail: gpipornl@orau.gov

Purpose To provide financial assistance for postsecondary study and practical research experience at Oak Ridge National Laboratory (ORNL).
Eligibility This program is open to U.S. citizens or permanent residents at least 18 years of age who are currently enrolled in an accredited U.S. college or university in an academic program leading to an associate, baccalaureate, or graduate degree. High school seniors are eligible if they have been accepted in an associate or baccalaureate program. Students should be pursuing studies in chemistry, computer science, civil engineering, environmental engineering, hydrogeology, mechanical engineering, environmental science, geology, or hydrology. A cumulative grade point average of at least 2.5 is required. All programs operated by the Science/Engineering Education Division (SEED) of Oak Ridge Institute for Science and Education (ORISE) seek to broaden the participation of minorities, women, and persons with disabilities in science and engineering careers.
Financial data Participants receive tuition and fees for off-campus courses related to the research experience during the appointment period. Monthly stipends range from $1,000 to $1,300 for undergraduates or $1,300 to $1,400 for graduate students. Travel expenses for a single round trip from the student's campus to the research center are also reimbursed.
Duration 3 to 12 consecutive months.
Special features Interns are assigned individual research projects that relate to their academic majors, career goals, and the ongoing research and development missions of ORNL: to carry out applied research and engineering development in energy production and conservation technologies as well as experimental

and theoretical research in the physical and life sciences to advance fundamental knowledge and to lay the foundation for technology development. A secondary mission is to address other nationally important issues, such as environmental protection and waste management and non-nuclear defense technologies, when such work is closely related to the primary mission. This program is funded by Oak Ridge National Laboratory but managed and operated by ORISE/SEED.

Number awarded Varies each year.

Deadline February of each year for programs to begin in May or June; May of each year for programs to begin in August or September; September of each year for programs to begin in January.

[675]
OSGC EDUCATION PROGRAM

Oklahoma Space Grant Consortium
c/o University of Oklahoma
College of Geosciences
Oklahoma Climatological Survey
100 East Boyd, Suite 1210
Norman, Oklahoma 73019-0628
(405) 325-1240   Fax: (405) 325-2550
E-mail: vduca@geoadm.gen.uoknor.edu

Purpose To provide support for programs in Oklahoma that increase participation of underrepresented minority and women students in aerospace-related studies at the undergraduate and graduate level.

Eligibility This program is open to undergraduate and graduate students at member and affiliate institutions of the Oklahoma Space Grant Consortium (OSGC)—Oklahoma State University, the University of Oklahoma, Cameron University, and Langston University. U.S. citizenship is required. The OSGC is a component of the U.S. National Aeronautics and Space Administration (NASA) Space Grant program, which encourages participation by women, minorities, and persons with disabilities.

Financial data Financing depends on the availability of funds.

Special features This program is funded by NASA. For information on the program at each participating university, contact the address above.

[676]
PATRICIA ROBERTS HARRIS FELLOWSHIPS

Department of Education
Attn: Office of Postsecondary Education
Division of Higher Education Incentive Programs
Portals Building, Suite C-80
600 Independence Avenue, S.W.
Washington, DC 20202-5329
(202) 260-3608   Fax: (202) 260-7615
E-mail: cosette_ryan@ed.gov

Purpose To provide grants to institutions of higher education for the support of graduate and professional education students who are in financial need and who are women and minorities underrepresented in the academic field of study.

Eligibility Accredited institutions of higher learning with graduate or professional programs leading to advanced degrees are eligible to apply. Recipient institutions must use these funds to provide fellowships to minorities and women who wish to undertake graduate and professional study in academic fields in which they

have been historically underrepresented. Interested students apply directly to the institution they plan to attend.

Financial data Fellows receive stipends up to $14,400 per year, depending upon financial need; their institutions receive up to $9,493 per year. Awards to institutions range from $23,893 to $597,325 for 1 to 25 fellow participants.

Duration 1 year or longer.

Limitations No grant funds are awarded directly to students by the Department of Education. Because the president has not requested funding for this program, no applications are currently being accepted.

Number awarded Varies; recently, 57 institutions received grants to award 259 new fellowships and 50 institutions received continuation awards to support 180 continuing fellows.

Deadline July of each year.

[677]
PITTSBURGH ENERGY TECHNOLOGY CENTER PROFESSIONAL INTERNSHIP PROGRAM

Oak Ridge Institute for Science and Education
Attn: Science/Engineering Education Division
P.O. Box 117
Oak Ridge, TN 37831-0117
(423) 576-3427   (423) 576-3426
(800) 569-7749   Fax: (423) 576-3643
E-mail: pippetc@orau.gov   E-mail: gpippetc@orau.gov

Purpose To provide financial assistance for postsecondary study and practical research experience at the Pittsburgh Energy Technology Center.

Eligibility This program is open to U.S. citizens or permanent residents at least 18 years of age who are currently enrolled in an accredited U.S. college or university in an academic program leading to an associate, baccalaureate, or graduate degree. High school seniors are eligible if they have been accepted to an associate or baccalaureate program. Students should be pursuing studies in chemistry, computer science, engineering, environmental sciences, mathematics, statistics, geology, or physics. A cumulative grade point average of at least 2.5 is required. All programs operated by the Science/Engineering Education Division (SEED) of Oak Ridge Institute for Science and Education (ORISE) seek to broaden the participation of minorities, women, and persons with disabilities in science and engineering careers.

Financial data Participants receive tuition and fees for off-campus courses related to the research experience during the appointment period. Monthly stipends range from $1,000 to $1,300 for undergraduates or $1,300 to $1,400 for graduate students. Travel expenses for a single round trip from the student's campus to the research center are also reimbursed.

Duration 3 to 12 consecutive months.

Special features Interns are assigned individual research projects that relate to their academic majors, career goals, and the ongoing research and development missions of the Pittsburgh Energy Technology Center in multidisciplinary coal-related research and development. This program is funded by the Office of Fossil Energy of the U.S. Department of Energy and administered by ORISE/SEED.

Number awarded Varies each year.

Deadline February of each year for programs to begin in May or June; May of each year for programs to begin in August or September; September of each year for programs to begin in January.

[678]
PLANNING FELLOWSHIPS

American Planning Association
Attn: Assistant for Divisions, Fellowships and Council
 Administration
1776 Massachusetts Avenue, N.W.
Washington, DC 20036-1904
(202) 872-0611   (800) 800-1589
Fax: (202) 872-0643

Purpose To support underrepresented minority students enrolled in master's degree programs at recognized planning schools.

Eligibility Candidates must be nominated by a planning school or department that is recognized by the National Education Development Committee of the American Planning Association. Students are eligible to be nominated if they are or will be enrolled in full-time programs for the master of city planning or equivalent degree and are members of the following minority groups: African American, Hispanic, or Native American. They must be citizens of the United States and able to document financial need. Each school may nominate no more than 1 candidate for the fellowship. The application must include a 1-page statement written by the student describing the reasons for interest in city or regional planning, a letter of recommendation from the planning faculty, copies of all transcripts or previous academic work, copies of GRE scores or similar data, a complete statement documenting the student's financial need, and written verification from the university's financial officer or copies of a school publication indicating the average cost for 8 months of graduate school.

Financial data Awards range from $2,000 to $4,000 per year. The money may be applied to tuition and living expenses only. Payment will be to the university and divided by terms in the school year.

Duration 1 year; may reapply.

Special features The fellowship program started in 1970 as a Ford Foundation Minority Fellowship Program.

Number awarded 10 each year.

Deadline May of each year.

[679]
PODIATRIC PRIMARY CARE RESIDENCY TRAINING GRANTS

Health Resources and Services Administration
Attn: Bureau of Health Professions
Division of Medicine
Parklawn Building, Room 9A-27
5600 Fishers Lane
Rockville, MD 20857
(301) 443-3456   Fax: (301) 443-1945
E-mail: espirer@hrsa.ssw.dhhs.gov

Purpose To provide financial support for projects in primary care training for podiatric physicians.

Eligibility This program is open to accredited schools of podiatric medicine or private nonprofit hospitals. Funding is available for planning and implementing projects in primary care training for podiatric physicians in approved or provisionally approved residency programs, which shall provide financial assistance in the form of traineeships to residents who participate in such projects and who plan to specialize in primary care. Selection criteria include 1) the proposal includes a strategy and plan for recruiting and retaining minority and disadvantaged faculty, students, trainees, and/or residents (applicants are expected to reflect the diversity of the populations within their states); 2) the proposal includes clinically oriented, generalist-trained faculty who practice in community-based settings that include underserved populations; 3) the proposal includes a curriculum that emphasizes areas of study pertinent to the needs of special populations in urban, rural, and underserved areas (people with low incomes, members of racial and ethnic minority groups, people with disabilities, and at-risk population groups); 4) the proposal describes the actions taken by the institution that demonstrate faculty involvement with the curricular innovations that are beyond what is traditionally part of such a curriculum; and 5) the proposal includes data regarding the most recent 3-year average track record of a program in placing graduates in primary care training, primary care practice, or generalist faculty positions. Podiatric physicians interested in applying for traineeships through this program should contact the address above for a list of currently participating institutions.

Financial data The amounts of the awards vary; in recent year, the average institutional grant has been $90,357. The institutions that receive grants through this program determine the amounts they wish to devote to financial aid for students.

Duration 3 years.

Number awarded Varies each year.

Deadline January of each year.

[680]
POSTDOCTORAL FELLOWSHIP ON PEACE AND SECURITY IN A CHANGING WORLD

Social Science Research Council
810 Seventh Avenue
New York, NY 10019
(212) 377-2700   Fax: (212) 377-2727

Purpose To support postdoctoral research training on the implications for security issues of worldwide cultural, social, economic, military, and political changes.

Eligibility The competition is open to all scholars (in the first 10 years of their careers) whose competence for advanced research has been demonstrated by their previous work. In most cases, these scholars should already hold the doctoral degree (or its equivalent); however, possession of the degree is not a requirement for lawyers, public servants, journalists, or others who can demonstrate comparable research experience and an ability to contribute to the research literature. There are no citizenship, residency, or nationality requirements. Applicants must be working in the social/behavioral sciences (including history and foreign area studies), the humanities, or the physical and biological sciences, but must propose to undertake training that adds a new competence to the disciplinary skills that they already have. Minorities and women are particularly encouraged to apply.

Financial data The stipend, up to $37,500 per year, is appropriate for the fellow's current salary and the cost of living where the fellow will be working.

Duration In most cases, 2 years.

Special features The Social Science Research Council administers this program with funds provided by the John D. and Catherine T. MacArthur Foundation as part of its Program in International Peace and Security Studies. Training may occur in any setting of the recipient's choice, in any nation, and may consist of formal course work, tutorials, internships, senior apprenticeships, or supervised study with senior faculty.

Limitations The program requires and enables researchers to add to their present specialty a competence in a different area and to apply their newly-enhanced skills to specific research projects. The fellowships are not designed for and will not support research programs for which the applicant is already prepared by prior experience and training. Fellows must devote full time to the fellowship and are not permitted to be otherwise employed.

Number awarded Approximately 6 each year.

Deadline November of each year.

[681]
POSTDOCTORAL RESEARCH FELLOWSHIPS IN BIOSCIENCES RELATED TO THE ENVIRONMENT

National Science Foundation
Attn: Directorate for Biological Sciences
Division of Biological Infrastructure
4201 Wilson Boulevard, Room 615
Arlington, VA 22230
(703) 306-1469   E-mail: ckimsey@nsf.gov

Purpose To provide opportunities for junior doctoral-level scientists to engage in research training either in the United States or abroad on the fundamental mechanisms underlying the interactions between organisms and their environment.

Eligibility This program is open to persons who are citizens, nationals, or permanent residents of the United States at the time of application. Applicants must have earned a Ph.D. no earlier than 3 years preceding the deadline date and must be proposing to gain additional scientific training beyond the doctoral degree and to pursue innovation and imaginative research into the fundamental mechanisms underlying the interactions between organisms and their environment at the molecular, cellular, organismal, population, community, and or ecosystem level in any area of biology. Research training may be conducted at any appropriate nonprofit U.S. or foreign institution, including colleges and universities, government and national laboratories, and privately-sponsored nonprofit institutes and museums. Research plans oriented toward human, animal, or plant disease or toxicology and those with clinical or other applied objectives are ineligible. Applications are particularly encouraged from women, members of ethnic and racial minority groups, and persons with disabilities.

Financial data The fellowship provides a stipend of $28,000 and 2 special allowances: $8,000 to the fellow for research costs (scientific supplies, travel, publication expenses, and other research-related costs) and $4,000 to the institution as an administrative allowance for fringe benefits and expenses incurred in support of the fellow (space, equipment, and general-purpose supplies).

Duration 2 years; applicants who propose to spend at least 1 year at a foreign institution may request a third year of support to complete fellowship research and training at an appropriate U.S. institution.

Number awarded Approximately 40 each year.

Deadline October of each year.

[682]
PREDOCTORAL FELLOWSHIP AWARDS FOR MINORITY STUDENTS

National Institutes of Health
Attn: Office of Extramural Research
Extramural Outreach and Information Resources Office
6701 Rockledge Drive, Room 6207
MSC 7910
Bethesda, MD 20892-7910
(301) 435-0714   Fax: (301) 480-8443
E-mail: asknih@odrockm1.od.nih.gov

Purpose To encourage students from minority groups that are underrepresented in the biomedical and behavioral sciences to seek graduate degrees and thus increase the number of minority scientists who are prepared to pursue careers in biomedical and behavioral research.

Eligibility Applicants must be citizens, nationals, or permanent residents of the United States who are enrolled for research training leading to the Ph.D. or equivalent research degree, the combined M.D./Ph.D. degree, or other combined professional doctorate/research Ph.D. degrees in the biomedical or behavioral sciences. Support is not available for individuals enrolled in medical or other professional schools unless they are enrolled in a combined professional doctorate/Ph.D. degree program in biomedical or behavioral research. Underrepresented minority students are defined as individuals belonging to a particular ethnic or racial group which has been determined by the applicant's graduate institution to be underrepresented in biomedical or behavioral research in the United States; the program gives priority consideration to applications from African Americans, Hispanics, Native Americans, Alaskan Natives, and Pacific Islanders.

Financial data The fellowship provides an annual stipend of $10,008, a tuition and fee allowance, and an institutional allowance of $2,000 for travel to scientific meetings and for laboratory and other training expenses. Additional funds may be requested to make changes or adjustments in the academic or research environment to make it possible for the individual to perform the work necessary to meet the requirements of the degree program.

Duration Up to 5 years.

Special features These fellowships are offered by most components of the National Institutes of Health (NIH) as 1 of the F31 Awards. For a list of names and telephone numbers of contact persons at each component, contact the address above.

Number awarded Varies each year.

Deadline April and November of each year.

[683]
PROFESSIONAL NURSE TRAINEESHIPS

Health Resources and Services Administration
Attn: Bureau of Health Professions
Division of Nursing
Parklawn Building, Room 9-36
5600 Fishers Lane
Rockville, MD 20857
(301) 443-6193   Fax: (301) 443-8586

Purpose To provide grants to schools of nursing to meet the costs of traineeships for individuals in advanced degree nursing education programs.

Eligibility Public and private nonprofit schools of nursing may apply for these grants to provide traineeships to students who have completed basic nursing preparation in a master's of nursing program or are currently licensed as registered nurses. Trainees must be U.S. citizens, nationals, or permanent residents pursuing a master's or doctoral degree in nursing. Funding priority is given to programs which demonstrate either substantial progress over the last 3 years or a significant experience of 10 or more years in enrolling and graduating trainees from those minority populations identified as at risk of poor health outcomes. Applications for the traineeships provided through this program are submitted directly to schools which have received grants for that purpose; for a list of those schools, contact the address above.

Financial data Schools may award traineeships up to $8,800 per year; funds may be used only for tuition, fees, books, and reasonable living expenses.

Duration Up to 3 years.

Number awarded In recent years, 233 grants to institutions were made through this program annually, for a total of $15.6 million; the average grant has been $55,000.

Deadline December of each year.

[684]
PUBLIC POLICY AND INTERNATIONAL AFFAIRS GRADUATE FELLOWSHIPS

Woodrow Wilson National Fellowship Foundation
Attn: Program in Public Policy and International Affairs
5 Vaughn Drive, Suite 300
P.O. Box 2434
Princeton, NJ 08543-2434
(609) 452-7007   Fax: (609) 452-0066

Purpose To provide financial assistance to minority students who are enrolled in specified master's degree programs in public policy and international affairs.

Eligibility Minority students who successfully complete a Public Policy and International Affairs Junior Year Summer Institute are eligible to apply for these fellowships if they have been accepted into a master's degree program in public policy or international affairs at 1 of the 29 participating universities.

Financial data The funding package includes tuition and a stipend through a combination of awards, assistantships, and loan; the amount of the aid depends on the demonstrated financial need of the recipient.

Duration 2 years.

Special features Funding for this program is provided by the Ford Foundation, Rockefeller Foundation, Philip D. Clark Foundation, and Edna McConnell Clark Foundation. Degrees to which the program may lead include Master of Arts in International Affairs, Master of Public Policy, Master of Public Administration, and Master of Science in International Development Management.

Limitations Applications are submitted directly to the participating university; for a list, contact the address above.

Number awarded Varies each year.

Deadline Application deadlines are set by the participating universities.

[685]
PUBLIC POLICY AND INTERNATIONAL AFFAIRS SENIOR YEAR SUMMER PROGRAMS

Woodrow Wilson National Fellowship Foundation
Attn: Program in Public Policy and International Affairs
5 Vaughn Drive, Suite 300
P.O. Box 2434
Princeton, NJ 08543-2434
(609) 452-7007   Fax: (609) 452-0066

Purpose To enable minority students to participate in special programs during the summer following graduation to help prepare them for graduate work in public policy and international affairs.

Eligibility Minority students who successfully complete a Public Policy and International Affairs Junior Year Summer Institute may then participate in this program during the summer following graduation if they have been accepted into an approved graduate program in public policy or international affairs. The program may involve 1) internships with suitable public and nonprofit organizations and government agencies; 2) language institutes to study Chinese, Japanese, French, Spanish, German, or Russian at the Paul A. Nitze School of Advanced International Studies of Johns Hopkins University in Washington D.C., the Monterey Institute of International Studies in California, or Middlebury College in Vermont; 3) the Senior Institute for International Affairs in Washington, D.C.; or 4) additional course work required for graduate admission.

Financial data Students who perform internships receive an allowance toward living expenses; students who participate in language institutes or the Senior Institute for International Affairs receive a stipend and other support; students who take additional course work receive tuition support.

Duration Summer months, during the summer between completion of undergraduate study and the commencement of graduate work.

Special features Funding for this program is provided by the Ford Foundation, Rockefeller Foundation, Philip D. Clark Foundation, and Edna McConnell Clark Foundation.

Number awarded Varies each year.

[686]
RACIAL ETHNIC LEADERSHIP SUPPLEMENTAL GRANTS

Presbyterian Church (U.S.A.)
Attn: Office of Financial Aid for Studies
100 Witherspoon Street, Room M042
Louisville, KY 40202-1396
(502) 569-5776   Fax: (502) 569-5018

Purpose To provide financial assistance to minority students who are Presbyterian Church members interested in preparing for church occupations.

Eligibility Racial/ethnic graduate students (Asian American, African American, Hispanic American, Native American, or Alaska Native) who are members of the Presbyterian Church (U.S.A.) and preparing for professional church occupations are eligible to apply. They must be studying for the first professional degree, enrolled as an inquirer or candidate by a presbytery for a church occupation or planning to take a position within the Presbyterian Church (U.S.A.) or an ecumenical agency in which it participates, a U.S. citizen or permanent resident, enrolled at least half time in a prescribed program of study approved by the presbytery, in good academic standing, and in financial need.

Financial data The awards are intended to be supplementary and range from $500 to $1,000 per year.

Duration 1 year; nonrenewable.

Limitations These grants are not to replace traditional assistance from seminaries or other governing bodies; they may be applied for only after all other financial resources have been exhausted and documented need still exists.

Number awarded Varies each year.

Deadline Applicants may be submitted at any time.

[687]
RALPH W. ELLISON PRIZE

National Medical Fellowships, Inc.
Attn: Scholarships and Programs
110 West 32nd Street, 8th Floor
New York, NY 10001-3205
(212) 714-1007

Purpose To recognize and reward an outstanding graduating underrepresented medical student.

Eligibility This award is open to senior African American, Native American, Mexican American, and mainland Puerto Rican students enrolled in accredited U.S. medical schools. Candidates must be nominated by their medical schools during their senior year. Selection is based on academic achievement, leadership, community service, and potential to make significant contributions to medicine.

Financial data This honor includes a certificate of merit and a $500 stipend.

Duration 1 year; nonrenewable.

Special features This award was established in 1994 to honor Ralph W. Ellison, the novelist and author of *The Invisible Man* who co-chaired a fund-raising effort of National Medical Fellowships, Inc.

Number awarded 1 each year.

Deadline Nominations are requested in January of each year.

[688]
REAL ESTATE AND LAND USE INSTITUTE SCHOLARSHIPS FOR MINORITIES

Real Estate and Land Use Institute
Attn: Scholarship Selection Committee
7750 College Town Drive, Suite 102
Sacramento, CA 95826-2344
(916) 278-4823　　　　　　　Fax: (916) 278-4500

Purpose To provide financial assistance to minority and disadvantaged students in California who are interested in a career in real estate.

Eligibility Eligible to apply are minority and disadvantaged students at any of the 22 California State University campuses who are enrolled at least half-time or majoring in a program aimed at a career in real estate. Financial need must be demonstrated. Minority undergraduates must have a minimum grade point average of 2.25, non-minority undergraduates 2.5, and graduates 3.0.

Financial data A total of $60,300 in scholarships is offered each year; individual awards range from $375 to $600 per quarter or $603 to $935 per semester.

Duration 1 year; may be renewed.

Number awarded Varies; generally, at least 20 each year.

Deadline April of each year.

[689]
RESEARCH SUPPLEMENTS FOR UNDERREPRESENTED MINORITY INDIVIDUALS IN POSTDOCTORAL TRAINING

National Institutes of Health
Attn: Office of Extramural Research
Extramural Outreach and Information Resources Office
6701 Rockledge Drive, Room 6207
MSC 7910
Bethesda, MD 20892-7910
(301) 435-0714　　　　　　　Fax: (301) 480-8443
E-mail: asknih@odrockm1.od.nih.gov

Purpose To provide funding to minority individuals in the postdoctoral phase of their training to participate in ongoing research projects supported by the National Institutes of Health (NIH).

Eligibility This program is open to minority individuals (African Americans, Hispanics, Native Americans, Alaskan Natives, and Pacific Islanders) in postdoctoral training in either the applicant institution or any other institution. Only under extraordinary circumstances may applicants request to work with their former predoctoral mentor.

Financial data The sponsoring institute provides support for salary in addition to other necessary expenses (e.g. travel, supplies) to enable the minority individual to participate as a postdoctoral research assistant or associate on an institute-funded research project. The requested salary must be in accordance with the salary structure of the grantee institution and consistent with the level of effort. Additional funds, up to $6,000, may be requested for supplies and travel.

Duration 1 year or longer.

Special features Individuals interested in this type of postdoctoral support should make contact with the principal investigator on an eligible NIH research grant at their institution.

Limitations Support may not be used to purchase equipment.

Number awarded Varies each year.

[690]
RESEARCH TRAINING FELLOWSHIP FOR MINORITY NURSES

American Nurses Association
Attn: Minority Fellowship Programs
600 Maryland Avenue, S.W., Suite 100 West
Washington, DC 20024-2571
(202) 651-7244　　　　　　　Fax: (202) 789-1413

Purpose To provide financial support to nurses pursuing careers as research scientists on mental health issues related to minority populations.

Eligibility Applications are accepted from registered nurses who 1) are members of an ethnic or racial minority group, including but not limited to African Americans, Hispanics, American Indians, Asian Americans, and Pacific Islanders, and/or 2) can demonstrate a commitment to careers in behavioral science research related to ethnic minority mental health. Applicants must be U.S. citizens or permanent visa residents, registered nurses, members of the American Nurses Association (ANA), and holders of master's degrees pursuing a doctoral degree. Students specializing in the following areas of research are encouraged to apply: psychosocial processes and sociocultural factors which contribute to an understanding of mental health and illness; development and maintenance of personal networks and support systems as they affect individual and family functioning; and psychosocial stressors and coping mechanisms, particularly in populations at risk, such as children and adolescents, the elderly, the mentally ill, etc.

Financial data Awards include a stipend to defray the cost of living; the amounts of the awards depend on the availability of funding.

Duration Up to five years.

Special features Funding for this program is provided by the National Institute of Mental Health, a component of the National Institutes of Health.

Number awarded Varies each year.

Deadline January of each year.

[691]
RESEARCH TRAINING FELLOWSHIP IN PSYCHOLOGY

American Psychological Association
Attn: Minority Fellowship Program
750 First Street, N.E.
Washington, DC 20002-4242
(202) 336-6027   Fax: (202) 336-6012
TDD: (202) 336-6123   E-mail: mfp@apa.org

Purpose To increase the number of ethnic and racial minorities who complete doctoral programs in psychology.

Eligibility Applicants must be U.S. citizens or permanent residents, enrolled full time in an accredited doctoral program, committed to a career in psychology related to ethnic minority mental health, and members of an ethnic minority group, including but not limited to African Americans, Hispanics, American Indians, Asian Americans, Alaskan Natives, and Pacific Islanders. Students specializing in such research areas as developmental, physiological, experimental, social, industrial/organizational, quantitative, or educational psychology are encouraged to apply. Selection is based on research potential, scholarship, writing ability, ethnic minority identification, knowledge of broad issues in psychology, and professional commitment. Students of clinical and counseling psychology and students working on a master's degree only are ineligible.

Financial data The stipend is $834 per month. In some cases, the fellowship may pay for tuition, fees, and pre-selection travel.

Duration 1 academic or calendar year; may be renewed for up to 2 additional years.

Special features Funding is provided by the U.S. National Institute of Mental Health, a component of the National Institutes of Health.

Deadline January of each year.

[692]
RESIDENCY TRAINING IN GENERAL INTERNAL MEDICINE AND GENERAL PEDIATRICS GRANTS

Health Resources and Services Administration
Attn: Bureau of Health Professions
Division of Medicine
Parklawn Building, Room 9A-27
5600 Fishers Lane
Rockville, MD 20857
(301) 443-6821   Fax: (301) 443-1945
E-mail: bwilliam@hrsa.ssw.dhhs.gov

Purpose To provide financial support for programs to plan, develop, and operate or participate in approved graduate training programs in the fields of general internal medicine or general pediatrics.

Eligibility This program is open to accredited schools of medicine or osteopathic medicine, public or private nonprofit hospitals, or other public or private nonprofit entities. Applicants must request funding to plan, develop, and operate graduate training programs in the fields of general internal medicine or general pediatrics. Recipient institutions may also use this funding to support trainees in such programs who plan to specialize or work in the practice of general internal medicine or general pediatrics. Selection criteria include 1) the proposal includes a strategy and plan for recruiting and retaining minority and disadvantaged faculty, students, trainees, and/or residents (applicants are expected to reflect the diversity of the populations within their states); 2) the proposal includes clinically oriented, generalist-trained faculty who practice in community-based settings that include underserved populations; 3) the proposal includes a curriculum that emphasizes areas of study pertinent to the needs of special populations in urban, rural, and underserved areas (people with low incomes, members of racial and ethnic minority groups, people with disabilities, and at-risk population groups); 4) the proposal describes the actions taken by the institution that demonstrate faculty involvement with the curricular innovations that are beyond what is traditionally part of such a curriculum; and 5) the proposal includes data regarding the most recent 3-year average track record of a program in placing graduates in primary care training, primary care practice, or generalist faculty positions. Persons interested in applying for traineeships through this program should contact the address above to obtain a list of currently participating institutions.

Financial data The amounts of the awards vary; in recent years, the average grant has been $201,000 per year. The participating institutions determine the amounts they wish to award for traineeships.

Duration 3 years.

Special features Unlike residencies in internal medicine and pediatrics from which many physicians enter subspecialty training, programs supported by these grants are intended to emphasize continuity and ambulatory, preventive and psychosocial aspects of the practice of medicine. Grant funds may support the creation of new residency programs or facilitate the conversion of "traditional" programs to those in which the training emphasizes the provision of longitudinal, preventive, and comprehensive care.

Number awarded Varies each year.

Deadline November of each year.

[693]
ROCKY MOUNTAIN NASA SPACE GRANT CONSORTIUM GRADUATE RESEARCH FELLOWSHIPS

Rocky Mountain NASA Space Grant Consortium
c/o Utah State University
College of Engineering
EL Building Room 302
Logan, UT 84322-4140
(801) 797-1592   Fax: (801) 797-3382
E-mail: rmc@sdl.usu.edu

Purpose To provide financial support for research and study by graduate students in Utah in fields of interest to the National Aeronautics and Space Administration (NASA).

Eligibility This program is open to graduate students at member institutions of the Rocky Mountain NASA Space Grant Consortium (Utah State University, the University of Utah, Brigham

Young University, University of Denver, Weber State University, and Southern Utah University). U.S. citizenship is required. Selection is based on academic performance to date and potential for the future with emphasis on space-related research interests. This program is part of the NASA Space Grant program, which encourages participation by women, minorities, and persons with disabilities.

Financial data The amount of the awards depends on the availability of funds.

Special features This program is funded by NASA.

Number awarded Varies each year.

[694]
ROLLAN D. MELTON FELLOWSHIP

American Press Institute
Attn: Fellowship Program Coordinator
11690 Sunrise Valley Drive
Reston, VA 22091-1498
(703) 620-3611 Fax: (703) 620-5814
E-mail: vcju07a@prodigy.com

Purpose To provide financial support to college-level minority journalism educators who are interested in attending American Press Institute (API) seminars.

Eligibility Nominations are invited from all schools and departments of journalism and mass communications. Eligible to be nominated are college-level minority journalism educators who wish to attend API seminars. Each API seminar is designed for a particular specialty or problem.

Financial data The fellowship covers tuition, room, and board.

Special features This fellowship honors the former president of Speidel Newspapers (now merged with Gannett) and former member of the API board.

Number awarded 1 each year.

Deadline Nominations must be submitted by November of each year.

[695]
SAVANNAH RIVER SITE PROFESSIONAL INTERNSHIP PROGRAM

Oak Ridge Institute for Science and Education
Attn: Science/Engineering Education Division
P.O. Box 117
Oak Ridge, TN 37831-0117
(423) 576-3427 (423) 576-3426
(800) 569-7749 Fax: (423) 576-3643
E-mail: pipsrs@orau.gov E-mail: gpipsrs@orau.gov

Purpose To provide financial assistance for postsecondary study and practical research experience at the Savannah River Site in Aiken, South Carolina.

Eligibility This program is open to U.S. citizens or permanent residents at least 18 years of age who are currently enrolled in an accredited U.S. college or university in an academic program leading to an associate, baccalaureate, or graduate degree. High school juniors and seniors are also eligible. Students should be pursuing studies in chemistry, computer science, engineering, environmental sciences, geology, or physics. A cumulative grade point average of at least 2.5 is required. All programs operated by the Science/Engineering Education Division (SEED) of Oak Ridge Institute for Science and Education (ORISE) seek to broaden the participation of minorities, women, and persons with disabilities in science and engineering careers.

Financial data Participants receive tuition and fees for off-campus courses related to the research experience during the appointment period. Monthly stipends range from $800 to $1,300 for high school students and undergraduates or $1,300 to $1,400 for graduate students. Travel expenses for a single round trip from the student's campus to the research center are also reimbursed.

Duration 3 to 12 consecutive months.

Special features Interns are assigned individual research projects that relate to their academic majors, career goals, and the ongoing research and development missions of the Savannah River Site, which conducts research and development in support of the production of plutonium-239 and tritium for national defense purposes. Graduate students may utilize this program to conduct research for their theses or dissertations. This program is funded by the Savannah River Site and administered by ORISE/SEED.

Number awarded Varies each year.

Deadline February of each year for programs to begin in May or June; May of each year for programs to begin in August or September; September of each year for programs to begin in January.

[696]
SCHOLARSHIPS FOR DISADVANTAGED STUDENTS GRANTS

Health Resources and Services Administration
Attn: Bureau of Health Professions
Division of Student Assistance
Parklawn Building, Room 8-34
5600 Fishers Lane
Rockville, MD 20857
(301) 443-4776 Fax: (301) 443-0846

Purpose To provide financial support for full-time financially needy disadvantaged health professions students who are enrolled in accredited schools.

Eligibility Eligible to submit grant requests are accredited schools of medicine, nursing, osteopathic medicine, dentistry, pharmacy, podiatric medicine, optometry, veterinary medicine, public health, or allied health (baccalaureate and graduate degree programs of dental hygiene, medical laboratory technology, occupational therapy, physical therapy, and radiologic technology), and graduate programs in clinical psychology. They must be carrying out a program for recruiting and retaining students from disadvantaged backgrounds, including racial and ethnic minorities, and carrying out a program for recruiting and retaining minority faculty. Recipient institutions must use the funds received through this program to offer scholarships to students who are U.S. citizens, nationals, or permanent residents and who meet the definition of an individual from a disadvantaged background (either 1) individuals who come from an environment that has inhibited them from obtaining the knowledge, skill, and abilities required to enroll in and graduate from a health professions school, or from a program providing education or training in allied health professions, or 2) individuals who come from a family with low income, ranging from less than $10,200 for a family with 1 dependent to less than $26,700 for a family with 6 dependents). Applicant institutions must also have programs to 1) ensure that adequate instruction regarding minority health issues is provided for in the curricula of the school; 2) enter into agreements with 1 or more health clinics providing services to a significant number of individuals who are from disadvantaged backgrounds, including members of minority groups, for the purpose of providing students of the school with experience in providing clinical services to such individuals; 3) enter into arrangements with 1 or more public or nonprofit institutions of higher education (feeder schools) for the purpose of carrying out programs regarding the educational preparation of disadvantaged students, including minority students, into the health professions, and the recruitment of disadvantaged students, including minority students, into the health professions; and 4) establish a mentor program for assisting disadvantaged students, including minority students, regarding the completion of the educational requirements for degrees from the school. Students apply directly to their academic institution for support. For a list of schools participating in this program, contact the address above.

Financial data With these grants, schools award students funds to cover the costs of tuition and other reasonable educational expenses including fees, books, laboratory expenses and other costs of attending school. Scholarships cannot exceed a student's financial need. Of the funds available, 30 percent are set aside for schools that provide scholarships only for nurses.

Duration 1 year; may be renewed.

Number awarded Varies each year.

Deadline Deadline dates vary but are usually in June; check the *Federal Register* for the current schedule.

[697]
SCHOLARSHIPS FOR MINORITY ACCOUNTING STUDENTS

American Institute of Certified Public Accountants
1211 Avenue of the Americas
New York, NY 10036-8775
(212) 596-6270   Fax: (212) 596-6213

Purpose To provide financial assistance to underrepresented minority students interested in studying accounting.

Eligibility Undergraduate applicants must be minority students who are enrolled full time, have completed at least 30 semester hours of college work, are majoring in accounting with an overall grade point average of at least 3.0, and are U.S. citizens or permanent residents. Minority students who are interested in a graduate degree must be 1) in a 5-year accounting program; 2) an undergraduate accounting major currently accepted in a master's-level accounting, business administration, finance, or taxation program; or 3) any undergraduate major currently accepted in a master's-level accounting program. Selection is based primarily on merit (academic achievement); financial need is evaluated as a secondary criteria. For purposes of this program, the American Institute of Certified Public Accountants (AICPA) considers minority students as those of Black, Native American/Alaskan Native, or Pacific Island races, or of Hispanic ethnic origin.

Financial data Up to $5,000 per year.

Duration 1 year; may be renewed, if recipients are making satisfactory progress toward graduation.

Special features These scholarships are granted by the institute's Minority Educational Initiatives Committee.

Number awarded Up to 100 each year.

Deadline June of each year.

[698]
SHIRLEY CRAWFORD MINORITY SCHOLARSHIP

American Library Association
Attn: Office for Library Personnel Resources
50 East Huron Street
Chicago, IL 60611-2795
(312) 280-4281   (800) 545-2433, ext. 4281
TDD: (312) 944-7298   Fax: (312) 280-3256
E-mail: pjackson@ala.org

Purpose To encourage members of minority groups to train for a career in librarianship.

Eligibility The program is open to worthy American or Canadian students who are members of a principal minority group: American Indian or Alaska Native, Asian or Pacific Islander, African American, or Hispanic. The recipient must agree to enter a formal program of graduate study leading to a master's degree at a graduate library education program accredited by the American Library Association. Selection is based on academic excellence, leadership qualities, and evidence of a commitment to a career in librarianship.

Financial data The amount of the award is $3,000.

Duration 1 year.

Limitations Applicants cannot have already completed more than 12 semester hours toward a master's degree in library science.

Number awarded Varies, depending upon the total amount of contributed funds each year.

Deadline December of each year.

[699]
SHORT-TERM INSTITUTIONAL NATIONAL RESEARCH SERVICE AWARDS

National Institutes of Health
Attn: National Institute on Alcohol Abuse and Alcoholism
Office of Scientific Affairs
Willco Building, Suite 409
6000 Executive Boulevard MSC 7003
Bethesda, MD 20892-7003
(301) 443-2890   Fax: (301) 443-6077
E-mail: jv24p@nih.gov

Purpose To provide funding to eligible institutions to develop or enhance research training opportunities for individuals who are interested in careers in specific areas of biomedical and behavioral research.

Eligibility Eligible to apply are domestic nonprofit private or public institutions and professional organizations that have the staff and facilities to conduct the proposed research training in a suitable environment for performing high-quality work. Recipient institutions must develop a training program that provides opportunities for individual trainees with the primary objective of extending their skills and knowledge in preparation for a research career. Special attention should be given to the appointment of minorities and women. Trainee applicants must be U.S. citizens or permanent residents who are predoctoral students, medical students, postdoctoral students, residents interested in pursuing research careers, and research scientists. The program, however, is not intended, and may not be used, to support activities that would ordinarily be part of a research degree program; awards are not made for study leading to the M.D., D.O., D.D.S., or other similar professional degrees, nor do they support residency training. Predoctoral applicants must have received a baccalaureate degree and be enrolled in a doctoral degree program at the time of appointment. Postdoctoral individuals selected to receive these short-term traineeships must have received a Ph.D., Psy.D., M.D., D.D.S., D.S.W., Pharm.D., or equivalent degree. Students interested in applying for support should contact the address above to obtain a list of institutions that have received grants and are offering fellowships.

Financial data Postdoctoral fellows receive a stipend that is determined on the basis of the number of years of prior relevant postdoctoral experience; the annual rate ranges from $19,608 to $32,300. The stipend for predoctoral fellows is $834 per month. The institution may request up to $125 per month per predoctoral individual and $208 per month per postdoctoral individual to offset the cost of tuition, fees, supplies, certain types of travel for trainees, and other expenses; and actual indirect costs or 8 percent of allowable direct costs (whichever is less) to cover related institutional overhead.

Duration Awards to institutions are up to 5 years and are renewable. Short-term training for trainees is normally up to 3 months.

Special features This program is available through 3 components of the National Institutes of Health (NIH): the National Institute on Alcohol Abuse and Alcoholism (NIAAA), the National Institute on Drug Abuse (NIDA), and the National Institute of Mental Health (NIMH). For information on NIAAA activities, contact the address above; for the NIDA, information is available from the Office of Extramural Program Review, 5600 Fishers Lane, Room 10-42, Rockville, MD 20857, (301) 443-2755; information on the NIMH program is available from the Division of Extramural Activities, 5600 Fishers Lane, Room 9-105, Rockville, MD 20857, (301) 443-1596. The NIH designates this program as 1 of the T35 Awards.

Deadline January, May, or September of each year.

[700]
SOUTH CAROLINA SPACE GRANT CONSORTIUM GRADUATE FELLOWSHIPS

South Carolina Space Grant Consortium
c/o College of Charleston
Department of Geology
58 Coming Street
Charleston, SC 29424
(803) 953-5463   Fax: (803) 953-5446
E-mail: mcolgan@jove.cofc.edu

Purpose To provide financial assistance for space-related study to graduate students in South Carolina.

Eligibility This program is open to graduate students at member institutions of the South Carolina Space Grant Consortium (the University of Charleston, Clemson University, the University of South Carolina, South Carolina State University, and the University of the Virgin Islands). Applicants must be interested in space-related studies, although the program has accepted students with a interests ranging from remote sensing and engineering to astrophysics. U.S. citizenship is required. The South Carolina Space Grant Consortium is a component of the U.S. National Aeronautics and Space Administration (NASA) Space Grant program, which encourages the participation of women, minorities, and persons with disabilities.

Financial data The stipend is $3,000 per year.

Duration 1 year.

Special features This program is funded by NASA.

Number awarded Varies each year.

[701]
SOUTHERN CALIFORNIA CHEVRON MERIT AWARD

Independent Colleges of Southern California
411 West Fifth Street, Suite 1000
Los Angeles, CA 90013-1001
(213) 627-7091

Purpose To recognize and reward the outstanding classroom, school, and community achievements of high school seniors (or entering graduate school students) planning to major in business or the sciences at an independent college in southern California.

Eligibility Students who have an outstanding record of academic achievement, leadership, and participation in school and community activities and are interested in attending an independent college in southern California are invited to apply for these awards. Minorities and women are particularly encouraged to apply.

Financial data The stipend is $2,000 per year.

Duration 4 years for entering freshmen; 2 years for entering graduate students.

Special features Funding for this program is supplied by Chevron U.S.A. Inc.

Number awarded 8 each year. In even-numbered years, awards are for freshmen entering the following schools: Claremont McKenna College, Loyola Marymount University, Mount St. Mary's College, Occidental College, Scripps College, University of Redlands, Whittier College, and Claremont Graduate School (first-year graduate students). In odd-numbered years, the awards are for students entering: Chapman University, Harvey Mudd College, Pepperdine University, Pitzer College, Pomona College, University of La Verne, University of San Diego, Westmont College, and Claremont Graduate School (first-year graduate students).

Deadline February of each year.

[702]
SPECIAL LIBRARIES ASSOCIATION AFFIRMATIVE ACTION SCHOLARSHIP

Special Libraries Association
Attn: SLA Membership Department
1700 18th Street, N.W.
Washington, DC 20009-2508
(202) 234-4700   Fax: (202) 265-9317

Purpose To provide financial assistance to minority group members who are interested in pursuing a career in the fields of library or information science in the United States or Canada.

Eligibility To be eligible, applicants must be members of racial minority groups (Black, Hispanic, Asian or Pacific Islander, and American Indian or Alaskan native); enrolled or accepted for enrollment in a recognized school of library or information science; and in financial need. Preference is given to members of the Special Libraries Association and to persons who have worked in and for special libraries.

Financial data The stipend is $6,000.

Duration 2 quarters or 2 semesters.

Number awarded 1 each year.

Deadline October of each year.

[703]
SSRC—MELLON MINORITY FELLOWSHIP PROGRAM

Social Science Research Council
810 Seventh Avenue
New York, NY 10019
(212) 377-2700   Fax: (212) 377-2727

Purpose To provide financial assistance for graduate research and study to underrepresented minorities in designated fields at designated universities.

Eligibility This program is open to African Americans, Latinos, and Native Americans who participated in the Mellon Minority Undergraduate Fellowship (MMUF) program and who are currently enrolled or about to enroll in a Ph.D. program at designated universities. They must be studying American or English literature, foreign languages and literatures (including area studies), history, philosophy, classics, religion, art history, musicology, anthropology, demography, earth sciences, ecology, geology, mathematics, or physics.

Financial data The grant is $5,000.

Duration 1 academic year.

Special features This program is funded by the Andrew W. Mellon Foundation and administered by the Social Science Research Council (SSRC). In addition to the research and study grant, fellows are invited to participate in a summer conference which is designed to provide a forum for them to present their work, share their experiences in the academy, and initiate and expand professional networks with others who share similar conceptual, methodological, or policy concerns.

Deadline Application deadlines are established by the participating universities, which also select the recipients.

[704]
STAN BECK FELLOWSHIP

Entomological Society of America
Attn: Executive Director
9301 Annapolis Road
Lanham, MD 20706-3115
(301) 731-4535   Fax: (301) 731-4538

Purpose To assist "needy" students at any level of their science education.

Eligibility All society members are eligible to nominate candidates for this fellowship. Nominees must be "needy" students at any level of their science education. For the purposes of this program, need may be based on physical limitations, or economic, minority, or environmental conditions.

Financial data The fellowship is $4,000 per year.

Duration The award is presented annually.

Limitations Recipients are expected to be present at the society's annual meeting, where the award will be presented.

Number awarded 1 or more each year.

Deadline August of each year.

[705]
STAR GRADUATE ENVIRONMENTAL EDUCATION FELLOWSHIPS

Environmental Protection Agency
Attn: Office of Research and Development
National Center for Environmental Research and Quality
  Assurance
Waterside Mall, Room 2411
401 M Street, S.W.
Washington, DC 20460
(202) 260-3837   (800) 490-9194
Fax: (202) 260-2039

Purpose To provide financial support to graduate students planning to obtain advanced degrees and pursue careers in environmentally related fields.

Eligibility Applicants must be U.S. citizens or permanent residents enrolled or accepted for enrollment at a fully accredited U.S. college or university to pursue a master's or doctoral degree in an environmentally related field of specialization. Students who have been enrolled for more than 2 years in a master's program or 4 years in a doctoral program are not eligible. Eligible women, minorities, and students with disabilities are strongly encouraged to apply.

Financial data The total award is $34,000 per year, including a student stipend of $17,000, a student research expense allowance of $5,000, and an allowance of up to $12,000 for tuition and fees paid directly to the institution.

Duration Up to 2 years for master's students; up to 3 years for doctoral students.

Special features This program is the graduate student component of the Science to Achieve Results (STAR) program of the Environmental Protection Agency.

Limitations Fellows may conduct research outside the United States, but no additional funding is provided for foreign travel or other expenses.

Number awarded Between 50 and 100 each year.

Deadline January of each year.

[706]
STUDENT CEC/FEC ETHNIC DIVERSITY SCHOLARSHIP

Council for Exceptional Children
Attn: Coordinator of Student Activities
1920 Association Drive
Reston, VA 22091
(703) 620-3660   (800) 845-6232
Fax: (703) 264-9494   TDD: (703) 620-3660

Purpose To provide financial assistance to ethnic minority students who wish to pursue a career in special education.

Eligibility Eligible are student members of the Council for Exceptional Children (CEC), citizens of the United States or Canada, members of an ethnic minority group (African American or Black, American Indian, Alaska Native, Native Canadian, Hispanic, Asian, or Pacific Islander), and juniors, seniors, or graduate students enrolled in an accredited college or university majoring in special education with a grade point average of at least 2.5. Applications include documentation of financial need, a list of Student CEC and/or other activities relating to individuals with disabilities, and a brief biography explaining why the applicant chose special education as a career and plans for accomplishments as a special education teacher.

Financial data The stipend is $500.

Duration 1 year; nonrenewable.

Special features This program is administered by the Student CEC; the scholarship committee includes representatives of the Foundation for Exceptional Children (FEC) and the chair of the Student CEC Ethnic and Multicultural Concerns Committee.

Number awarded 1 each year.

Deadline December of each year.

[707]
SUBSTANCE ABUSE FELLOWSHIP

American Psychological Association
Attn: Minority Fellowship Program
750 First Street, N.E.
Washington, DC 20002-4242
(202) 336-6027   Fax: (202) 336-6012
TDD: (202) 336-6123   E-mail: mfp@apa.org

Purpose To provide financial assistance to minority students who are interested in completing a doctorate in psychology with an emphasis on substance abuse issues.

Eligibility Racial and ethnic minorities who are interested in earning a doctorate in psychology are eligible to apply. They must be American citizens or permanent visa residents, be enrolled full time in an accredited doctoral program, and be committed to a research career in mental health with an emphasis on substance abuse issues among minority populations.

Financial data The stipend is $834 per month. In some cases, the fellowship may pay for tuition, fees, and pre-selection travel.

Duration 1 year; may be renewed for up to 2 additional years.

Special features Funding is provided by the U.S. Substance Abuse and Mental Health Services Administration.

Limitations Students who receive a federally-funded grant from another source may not also accept funds from this program.

Number awarded 1 or more each year.

Deadline January of each year.

[708]
SUMMER INSTITUTE FOR BEHAVIORAL AND SOCIAL SCIENTISTS AND HUMANISTS

Center for Advanced Study in the Behavioral Sciences
Attn: Assistant to the Director
202 Junipero Serra Boulevard
Stanford, CA 94305
(415) 321-2052   Fax: (415) 321-1192

Purpose To help social scientists understand the links between research and policy in the field of education.

Eligibility All applicants must hold a doctoral degree. Preference is given to minority scholars, young scholars (under 35 years of age or earned the doctorate less than 7 years ago), and scholars affiliated with 4-year colleges, minority colleges and universities, or regional schools. In particular, the institute seeks younger scholars in traditional social science disciplines who might consider using educational settings and activities to continue their research programs.

Financial data The stipend is $4,500. Funds are to be used to cover transportation and the cost of living during the institute.

Duration 5 weeks during the summer.

Special features Participants exchange ideas through daily seminars and informal discussions; when the seminar is con-

ducted, it deals with a topic (last year: Research in Urban Education) that changes for each seminar.

Number awarded 20 every other year.

Deadline January of even-numbered years.

[709]
SUNY UNDERREPRESENTED GRADUATE FELLOWSHIP PROGRAM

State University of New York
Attn: Vice Chancellor
Diversity and Affirmative Action
SUNY Plaza
Albany, NY 12246
(518) 443-5676   Fax: (518) 443-5103

Purpose To provide financial assistance for graduate study at any of the campuses of the State University of New York (SUNY) to underrepresented minority students.

Eligibility This program is open to African Americans, Hispanic Americans, and Native Americans who are U.S. citizens or permanent residents and full-time graduate or professional students at any of the participating SUNY colleges.

Financial data Awards range from $7,500 to $10,000.

Duration 1 year; renewable.

Special features The participating institutions include the University Centers at Albany, Binghampton, Buffalo, and Stony Brook; the Health Science Centers at Brooklyn and Syracuse; the University Colleges of Arts and Sciences at Brockport, Buffalo, Cortland, Fredonia, Geneseo, New Paltz, Oneonta, Oswego, Plattsburgh, Potsdam, and Purchase; Empire State College; the College of Ceramics at Alfred University; the Institute of Technology at Utica/Rome; the College of Optometry; the Maritime College; the College of Environmental Science and Forestry; and the College of Agriculture and Life Sciences, the College of Human Ecology, the School of Industrial and Labor Relations, and the College of Veterinary Medicine at Cornell University.

Number awarded 500 each year.

[710]
SWS MINORITY SCHOLAR FUND

Sociologists for Women in Society
c/o Bernice McNair Barnett
Department of Educational Policy Studies
310 South Sixth Street, EPS 360
P.O. Box 1678
Champaign, IL 61820
(217) 333-7658   Fax: (217) 244-7064
E-mail: bmbarnet@uxicso.uiuc.edu

Purpose To provide financial assistance for graduate studies in sociology to minority women.

Eligibility Women minority graduate school students are eligible to apply if they are interested in preparing for a career in sociology.

Financial data The stipend is $2,500.

Duration 1 year.

Special features This program was established in 1986/87.

Number awarded 1 each year.

[711]
TEXAS SCHOLARSHIP PROGRAM FOR ETHNIC MINORITIES IN NURSING

Texas Higher Education Coordinating Board
Attn: Division of Student Services
P.O. Box 12788, Capitol Station
Austin, TX 78711-2788
(512) 483-6340   TDD: (800) 735-2988

Purpose To provide financial assistance for Texas minorities who are interested in preparing for a career in the nursing field.

Eligibility This program is open to minority undergraduate or graduate students who are residents of Texas and enrolled at least half time in a program leading to licensure as an L.V.N. (licensed vocational nurse) or in an associate, bachelor, or graduate degree program in professional nursing.

Financial data Up to $1,500 for L.V.N. students; up to $2,000 for A.D.N. (associate degree in nursing) students; up to $3,000 for B.S.N. (bachelor's degree in nursing) or graduate students.

Duration 1 academic year.

Special features This program was established in 1990.

Number awarded Varies; in a recent year, 20 of these scholarships were awarded to L.V.N. students and 53 to A.D.N., B.S.N., and graduate students.

Deadline Applicants should contact the financial aid director at the vocational or professional nursing school in which they plan to enroll for appropriate deadline dates.

[712]
TEXAS SPACE GRANT CONSORTIUM FELLOWSHIPS

Texas Space Grant Consortium
Attn: Public Service Programs
2901 North IH 35, Suite 200
Austin, TX 78722-2348
(512) 471-3583   Fax: (512) 471-3585
E-mail: fowler@utcsr.ae.utexas.edu

Purpose To provide financial assistance for graduate study at Texas universities in the fields of space science and engineering.

Eligibility Applicants must be U.S. citizens, be eligible for financial assistance, and be registered for full-time study in a graduate program at 1 or more of the following participating universities: Baylor University, Lamar University, Prairie View A&M University, Rice University, Southern Methodist University, Texas A&M University at Kingsville, Texas A&M University, Texas Christian University, Texas Southern University, Texas Tech University, University of Houston, University of Houston/Clear Lake, University of Houston/Downtown, University of Texas at Arlington, University of Texas at Austin, University of Texas at Dallas, University of Texas at El Paso, University of Texas at San Antonio, University of Texas Health Science Center at Houston, University of Texas Health Science Center at San Antonio, University of Texas Medical Branch at Galveston, University of Texas/Pan American, University of Texas Southwestern Medical Center, and West Texas A&M University. Students apply to their respective university representative; each representative then submits up to 3 candidates into the statewide selection process. Special attention is paid to applications submitted by persons with disabilities, women, and underrepresented minorities (African Americans, Hispanic Americans, Native Americans, and Pacific Islanders). Fellowships are awarded competitively, on the basis of grade point average, Graduate Record Examination scores, interest in space, and recommendations from the applicant's university.

Financial data The award is $5,000 and is to be used to supplement half-time graduate support (or a fellowship) offered by the home institution.

Duration 1 year; may be renewed for up to a maximum of 3 years.

Special features This program is funded by the National Aeronautics and Space Administration.

Number awarded 20 each year.

Deadline February of each year.

[713]
TEXAS STATE SCHOLARSHIP PROGRAM FOR ETHNIC RECRUITMENT

Texas Higher Education Coordinating Board
Attn: Division of Student Services
P.O. Box 12788, Capitol Station
Austin, TX 78711-2788
(512) 483-6340   TDD: (800) 735-2988

Purpose To provide financial assistance to educationally deprived students of a minority race in Texas who are capable of college-level work.

Eligibility To qualify, entering minority freshmen must be Texas residents, have attained an SAT score of at least 750 or an ACT score of at least 17; new transfer students must have a grade point average of at least 2.5 as undergraduates or 3.0 as graduate students. They must plan to enroll as a full-time graduate or undergraduate student in a Texas 4-year college or university and be a member of an ethnic group comprising less than 40 percent of that school's enrollment.

Financial data The maximum award is $2,000 per year.

Duration 1 academic year; may be renewed as long as undergraduates maintain a grade point average of 2.5 and graduate students 3.0.

Number awarded Varies; in a recent year, 556 of these scholarships were awarded.

Deadline Applicants should contact the financial aid director or minority recruitment officer at the public senior college in which they plan to enroll for appropriate deadline dates.

[714]
TRANSPORTATION PLANNING DIVISION SCHOLARSHIP

American Planning Association
Attn: Assistant for Divisions, Fellowships and Council Administration
1776 Massachusetts Avenue, N.W.
Washington, DC 20036-1904
(202) 872-0611   (800) 800-1589
Fax: (202) 872-0643

Purpose To provide financial assistance to minority undergraduate and graduate students specializing in transportation planning.

Eligibility This program is open to undergraduate and graduate students who are enrolled in an accredited planning program, are specializing in transportation planning, and are members of a minority group. Candidates must be nominated by their program chair.

Financial data The stipend is $2,500.

Duration 1 year.

Number awarded 1 or 2 each year.

Deadline May of each year.

[715]
UNIVERSITY OF MICHIGAN RESEARCH AND TRAINING PROGRAM ON POVERTY, THE UNDERCLASS AND PUBLIC POLICY

University of Michigan
Attn: Program on Poverty, the Underclass and Public Policy
540 East Liberty, Suite 202
Ann Arbor, MI 48104
(313) 998-8515   Fax: (313) 998-8516

Purpose To provide funding to minorities interested in conducting research and pursuing intensive training on poverty-related public policy issues.

Eligibility Applicants must be minority group members, U.S. citizens, postdoctorates (who received the degree within the past 5 years), and interested in conducting research and pursuing training on poverty and underclass issues at the University of Michigan.

Financial data The stipend is $37,000.

Duration 1 year.

Special features This program is funded by the Ford Foundation. Fellows spend the year participating in a seminar on poverty and public policy and conducting their own research.

Limitations Fellows must be in residence at the University of Michigan for the duration of the program.

Deadline January of each year.

[716]
VICTOR HORSLEY RESEARCH/CLINICAL TRAINING FELLOWSHIPS

Epilepsy Foundation of America
Attn: Department of Research and Professional Education
4351 Garden City Drive
Landover, MD 20785
(301) 459-3700   (800) EFA-1000
Fax: (301) 577-2684   TDD: (800) 332-2070
E-mail: postmaster@efa.org

Purpose To offer qualified individuals the opportunity to develop expertise in clinical epilepsy and epilepsy research.

Eligibility Applications are open to individuals who have received their M.D. degree and completed residency training. The proposed research may be either basic or clinical, but there must be an equal emphasis on clinical training and clinical epileptology. Special attention is given to applications submitted by women and minorities.

Financial data The stipend is $40,000.

Duration 1 year.

Limitations The fellowship must be carried out at a facility where there is an ongoing epilepsy research program. Research must be conducted in the United States.

Number awarded Varies each year.

Deadline August of each year.

[717]
VIRGIL HAWKINS FELLOWS SCHOLARSHIPS

Florida Department of Education
Attn: Office of Student Financial Assistance
State Programs—255 Collins
Tallahassee, FL 32399-0400
(904) 487-0049

Purpose To provide financial assistance to minorities in Florida who are interested in legal careers.

Eligibility First-year minority students who are attending law schools at accredited state universities in Florida (Florida State University and the University of Florida) are eligible to apply.

Financial data The stipend is $5,000 per year.

Duration 1 year; renewable up to 2 additional years.

Number awarded 10 each year.

[718]
VIRGINIA SPACE GRANT GRADUATE FELLOWSHIPS

Virginia Space Grant Consortium
c/o Old Dominion University Peninsula Center
2713-D Magruder Boulevard
Hampton, VA 23666-1563
(757) 865-0726   Fax: (757) 865-7965
E-mail: vsgc@pen.k12.va.us

Purpose To provide financial assistance for study and/or research in space-related fields to graduate students in Virginia.

Eligibility This program is open to graduate students who will be enrolled in a program of full-time study in aerospace-related graduate science or engineering at 1 of the Virginia Space Grant Colleges (College of William and Mary, Hampton University, Old Dominion University, the University of Virginia, and Virginia Polytechnic Institute and State University). Applicants must be U.S. citizens with a grade point average of at least 3.0. Selection of graduate students is based on their academic qualifications, the quality of their plan of study and/or proposed research, and their relevance to this program. Special consideration is given to members of underrepresented minority groups, females, and persons with disabilities who show aerospace promise.

Financial data The stipend is $5,000.

Duration 1 year; renewable.

Special features This program is funded by the U.S. National Aeronautics and Space Administration (NASA).

Limitations Students are required to certify through their academic department that basic research support of at least $5,000 is being provided before receipt of Space Grant funds.

Number awarded At least 5 each year.

Deadline January of each year.

[719]
VSGC GRADUATE RESEARCH ASSISTANTSHIPS

Vermont Space Grant Consortium
c/o University of Vermont
College of Engineering and Mathematics
119 Votey Building
Burlington, VT 05405-0156
(802) 656-1936   Fax: (802) 656-8802
E-mail: keller@emba.uvm.edu

Purpose To provide financial assistance for graduate study and research in space-related fields to students in Vermont.

Eligibility   Applicants for these assistantships must be currently enrolled as graduate students at institutions in Vermont. They must be planning to pursue a professional career that has direct relevance to the U.S. aerospace industry and the goal of the National Aeronautics and Space Administration (NASA), including mathematics, physics, engineering, and other basic sciences. The Vermont Space Grant Consortium (VSGC) is a component of the NASA Space Grant program, which encourages participation by women, minorities, and persons with disabilities.

Financial data   The program provides a stipend for a standard graduate student salary and the opportunity for the student to pay in-state tuition for graduate level course work and thesis research credit.

Duration   1 year, including a 10-week summer research period.

Special features   This program is funded by NASA.

Number awarded   4 each year.

Deadline   February of each year.

[720]
WILDER PENFIELD RESEARCH/CLINICAL TRAINING FELLOWSHIPS

Epilepsy Foundation of America
Attn: Department of Research and Professional Education
4351 Garden City Drive
Landover, MD 20785
(301) 459-3700   (800) EFA-1000
Fax: (301) 577-2684   TDD: (800) 332-2070
E-mail: postmaster@efa.org

Purpose   To offer qualified individuals the opportunity to develop expertise in clinical epilepsy and epilepsy research.

Eligibility   Applications are open to individuals who have received their M.D. degree and completed residency training. The proposed research may be either basic or clinical, but there must be an equal emphasis on clinical training and clinical epileptology. Special attention is given to applications submitted by women and minorities.

Financial data   The stipend is $40,000.

Duration   1 year.

Limitations   The fellowship must be carried out at a facility where there is an ongoing epilepsy research program. Research must be conducted in the United States.

Number awarded   Varies each year.

Deadline   August of each year.

[721]
WILLIAM AND CHARLOTTE CADBURY AWARD

National Medical Fellowships, Inc.
Attn: Scholarships and Programs
110 West 32nd Street, 8th Floor
New York, NY 10001-3205
(212) 714-1007

Purpose   To recognize and reward minority medical school students' outstanding academic achievement, leadership, and community service.

Eligibility   This award is open to minority students enrolled in their senior year at an accredited U.S. medical school. For the purposes of this program, "minority" is defined as African American, Native American, Mexican American, and mainland Puerto Rican students. Financial need is not a consideration. Candidates must be nominated by their medical school during the summer preceding their senior year.

Financial data   This honor includes a certificate of merit and a $2,000 stipend.

Duration   1 year; nonrenewable.

Special features   This award was established in 1977.

Number awarded   1 each year.

Deadline   Nominations are usually requested in June of each year.

[722]
WILLIAM G. LENNOX INTERNATIONAL CLINICAL RESEARCH FELLOWSHIPS

Epilepsy Foundation of America
Attn: Department of Research and Professional Education
4351 Garden City Drive
Landover, MD 20785
(301) 459-3700   (800) EFA-1000
Fax: (301) 577-2684   TDD: (800) 332-2070
E-mail: postmaster@efa.org

Purpose   To promote the exchange of medical and scientific information and expertise on epilepsy between the United States and other countries.

Eligibility   Individuals who have received their M.D. (or foreign equivalent) and have completed their residency training in neurology, neurosurgery, pediatrics, internal medicine, or psychiatry and desire additional postdoctoral clinical training may apply. The fellowships are designed for training purposes, not for individuals who have received faculty appointments at the level of assistant professor or higher. Applicants with previous research experience with seizure disorders are given preference. Americans may apply to train at a foreign institution, or foreigners may apply for an American research center. Although learning basic research tools is important in developing good clinical epileptologists, applicants should plan to spend a good deal of their time in clinical activities. Minorities and women are particularly encouraged to apply.

Financial data   Stipends are $30,000 per year.

Duration   1 year.

Special features   This fellowship is supported by Marion Merrell Dow Inc.

Number awarded   1 each year.

Deadline   August of each year.

[723]
WILLIAM GOWERS RESEARCH/CLINICAL TRAINING FELLOWSHIPS

Epilepsy Foundation of America
Attn: Department of Research and Professional Education
4351 Garden City Drive
Landover, MD 20785
(301) 459-3700   (800) EFA-1000
Fax: (301) 577-2684   TDD: (800) 332-2070
E-mail: postmaster@efa.org

Purpose   To offer qualified individuals the opportunity to develop expertise in clinical epilepsy and epilepsy research.

Eligibility   Applications are open to individuals who have received their M.D. degree and completed residency training. The proposed research may be either basic or clinical, but there must be an equal emphasis on clinical training and clinical epileptology. Special attention is given to applications submitted by women and minorities.

Financial data   The stipend is $40,000.

Duration 1 year.

Limitations The fellowship must be carried out at a facility where there is an ongoing epilepsy research program. Research must be conducted in the United States.

Number awarded Varies each year.

Deadline August of each year.

[724]
WILLIAM T. PORTER FELLOWSHIP AWARD

American Physiological Society
Attn: Executive Office
9650 Rockville Pike, Room 4403
Bethesda, MD 20814-3991
(301) 530-7118   Fax: (301) 571-8305

Purpose To provide fellowships in physiology to minority doctoral students, postdoctorates, and faculty members at predominantly Black schools.

Eligibility Applicants must wish to update their expertise in physiology.

Financial data This program provides fellows with a basic stipend (to cover tuition and expenses). An institutional allowance is given to the training department or laboratory where the recipient will work.

Duration 1 year.

Special features Funds are also available for lectureships and laboratory equipment to develop teaching consortia linking predominantly Black colleges with medical schools in the same area.

Number awarded Varies each year.

[725]
WISCONSIN SPACE GRANT CONSORTIUM GRADUATE FELLOWSHIPS

Wisconsin Space Grant Consortium
Attn: Program Office
333 Architecture and Urban Planning Building
2131 East Hartford Avenue
University of Wisconsin at Milwaukee
P.O. Box 413
Milwaukee, WI 53201-0413
(414) 229-3878   Fax: (414) 229-6976
E-mail: wsgc@csd.uwm.edu

Purpose To support graduate study and research in space and aerospace sciences at universities participating in the Wisconsin Space Grant Consortium.

Eligibility This program is open to graduate students enrolled at 1 of the universities participating in the Wisconsin Space Grant Consortium: University of Wisconsin at Milwaukee, University of Wisconsin at Madison, Marquette University, Carroll College, Lawrence University, Milwaukee School of Engineering, Northland College, Beloit College, Medical College of Wisconsin, St. Norbert College, University of Wisconsin at LaCrosse, University of Wisconsin at Green Bay, University of Wisconsin at Parkside, University of Wisconsin at Whitewater, or Ripon College. Applicants must be U.S. citizens; be enrolled full time in a master's or Ph.D. program related to space science, aerospace, or interdisciplinary space studies; have at least a 3.0 grade point average; and be interested in conducting space-related research. The consortium especially encourages applications from minorities, women, and the physically challenged. Selection is based on academic performance and potential for success.

Financial data Up to $3,500 per year.

Duration 1 academic year.

Special features Funding for this program is provided by the U.S. National Aeronautics and Space Administration.

Number awarded Varies; generally, at least 10 each year.

Deadline March of each year.

[726]
WOMEN AND MINORITIES IN ADMINISTRATION SCHOLARSHIP

Illinois Student Assistance Commission
Attn: Scholarship and Grant Services
1755 Lake Cook Road
Deerfield, IL 60015-5209
(708) 948-8550
(800) 899-ISAC (within IL, IA, IN, MO, and WI)

Purpose To provide financial aid to minorities and women in Illinois who are interested in preparing for a career in educational administration.

Eligibility Minorities (Blacks, Hispanics, Asian Americans, American Indians, and Alaskan Natives) and women who are residents of Illinois are eligible to apply for this program if they are college students or graduates and interested in enrolling in an approved administrative certification program in a senior institution in Illinois.

Financial data This program covers all tuition and fees (except revenue bond fees). Funds are paid directly to the participant's school (rather than directly to the participant).

Duration 1 semester or quarter; may be renewed.

Number awarded Varies; this program is awarded on a first-come, first-served basis, with priority to renewal applications, until all available funds are allocated.

Deadline July of each year for fall semester or quarter; November of each year for spring semester or winter quarter; February of each year for spring quarter; May of each year for summer term.

[727]
WOMEN OF COLOR SCHOLARS PROGRAM

United Methodist Church
Attn: Office of Loans and Scholarships
1001 19th Avenue South
P.O. Box 871
Nashville, TN 37202-0871
(615) 340-7344   Fax: (615) 340-7048

Purpose To provide financial assistance to minority women who are working on a graduate degree and are interested in preparing for a career in the United Methodist Church.

Eligibility This program is open to minority women (of African, Hispanic, Asian, or Native American descent) who have earned an M.Div. from a United Methodist Church seminary, have been members of the United Methodist Church for at least 3 years, and are working full time on a Ph.D. (in religious studies) or Th.D. degree. Applicants must wish to serve on the faculty or as an administrator at a United Methodist Church theological school.

Financial data The amount awarded varies, depending upon the needs of the recipient.

Duration 1 year; may be renewed.

Number awarded Up to 5 each year.

Deadline January of each year.

[728]
XEROX TECHNICAL MINORITY SCHOLARSHIP PROGRAM
Xerox Corporation
Attn: College Relations Manager
800 Phillips Road, 205-99E
Webster, NY 14580
(716) 422-7689

Purpose To provide financial assistance for minorities interested in postsecondary education in the sciences and/or engineering.

Eligibility Minorities enrolled full time in the following science and engineering degree programs at the baccalaureate level or above are eligible to apply: chemical engineering, computer engineering and science, electrical engineering, materials sciences, mechanical engineering, civil engineering, optical engineering, physics, and imaging.

Financial data The program provides annual tuition grants of up to $4,000 for undergraduates and $5,000 for graduate students.

Duration 1 or more years for the scholarship.

Deadline September of each year.

Loans

- *American Indians*
- *Native Alaskans*
- *Native Pacific Islanders*
- *Native Americans in General*

Described here are 59 programs open to Native Americans that provide money which must eventually be repaid—with or without interest. Of these listings, 13 are open specifically to American Indians, 4 to Native Alaskans, 2 to Native Pacific Islanders, and 40 to members of any of these groups (Native Americans in General). If you are looking for a particular program and don't find it in this section, be sure to check the Program Title Index to see if it is covered elsewhere in the directory.

American Indians

[729]
AISF LOANS

American Indian Scholarship Fund
c/o Native American Student Programs
University of California at Riverside
224 Costo Hall
Riverside, CA 92521
(909) 787-4143

Purpose To loan money to Native American college students in California on an emergency basis.

Eligibility Native American undergraduate and graduate students are eligible to apply if they are faced with a sudden financial emergency, can prove Indian blood (by tribal enrollment or birth certificate), and are currently enrolled in a college or university in California.

Financial data Loans are made up to $500 per application.

Number awarded Varies each year.

Deadline Applications may be submitted at any time.

[730]
HEALTH PROFESSIONS SCHOLARSHIP PROGRAM

Indian Health Service
Attn: Scholarship Program
Twinbrook Metro Plaza, Suite 100
12300 Twinbrook Parkway
Rockville, MD 20852
(301) 443-6197   Fax: (301) 443-6048

Purpose To provide financial support to students enrolled in health professions and allied health professions programs.

Eligibility Applicants must be at least high school graduates and be enrolled in a full-time study program leading to a degree in a health-related professions school within the United States. Even though non-Indian students may apply for this program, the Indian Health Care Improvement Act (P.L. 94-437) requires that priority for the awards be given to Indian and Native Alaskan applicants. Both the number of Indian applicants and the level of appropriations limit the availability of scholarship awards to non-Indians. Qualifying fields of study include associate degree nurse, chemical dependency counseling, clinical psychology (Ph.D. only), computer science (B.S.), dentistry, dietician (B.S.), civil engineering (B.S.), health education (master's only), health records, medical technology (B.S.), medical social work (master's only), allopathic and osteopathic medicine, nurse practitioner, nurse midwife, B.S. nurse, M.S. nurse, optometry, para-optometric, pharmacy (B.S.), physician assistant (B.S.), physical therapy, podiatry (D.P.M.), public health (M.P.H. only), public health nutrition (master's only), radiologic therapy (associate and B.S.), respiratory therapy (associate), and sonography.

Financial data Awards provide for payment of a monthly stipend to cover living expenses, including room and board, tuition and required fees, and all other reasonable educational expenses; the total award is approximately $18,000. In a recent year, approximately $6,300,000 was available for continuation awards and $1,860,751 for new awards.

Duration 1 year; may be renewed for up to 3 additional years.

Limitations Upon completion of their program of study, recipients are required to provide payback service of 1 year for each year of scholarship support at the Indian Health Service, 1 of 638 tribal health programs, an urban health program, or in private practice serving a substantial number of Indians.

Number awarded Varies; In a recent year, 350 continuing and 103 new awards were provided.

Deadline April of each year.

[731]
INDIAN FELLOWSHIP PROGRAM

Department of Education
Attn: Office of Elementary and Secondary Education
Office of Indian Education
Portals Building, Room 4300
600 Independence Avenue, S.W.
Washington, DC 20202-6335
(202) 260-1683   E-mail: Indian_Fellowships@ed.gov

Purpose To provide financial assistance to graduate students and selected undergraduate students who are Native Americans interested in preparing for careers in medicine, law, engineering, natural resources, business administration, education, psychology, and related fields.

Eligibility American Indian students who are attending or have been accepted for admission at an accredited institution of higher learning and working toward 1) a graduate degree in medicine, law, education, psychology, clinical psychology, or related fields or 2) a graduate or undergraduate degree in natural resources, business administration, engineering, or related fields may apply. All applicants must be U.S. citizens and Indians. By federal government definition, this means that applicants must be 1) a member of a tribe, band, or other organized group of Indians (including those tribes, bands, or groups terminated since 1940 and those recognized by the state in which they reside); 2) a descendant in the first or second degree of any individual described above; 3) considered by the Secretary of the Interior to be an Indian for any purpose or be an Eskimo, Aleut, or other Alaska Native; or 4) a member of an organized Indian group that received a grant under the Indian Education Act of 1988. Selection is based on academic record (60 points), letters of recommendation (15 points), and an essay on career goals, why the chosen field of study will benefit Indian people, life experiences and personal and family expectations that will enhance the applicant's anticipated career accomplishments, and anticipated commitment to providing service to Indian people (25 points).

Financial data Fellowships are intended to provide full financing for a student's educational expenses or to supplement other sources of financial aid.

Duration Up to 2 years for a master's degree; up to 4 years for an undergraduate or doctorate degree. Each year's renewal is dependent upon appropriations from Congress and satisfactory performance by the fellow.

Special features Up to 10 percent of the awards are to persons receiving training in guidance counseling with a specialty in the area of alcohol and substance abuse counseling and education.

Limitations Individuals receiving assistance under this program are required to perform work related to the training received and that benefits Indian people, or repay all or a prorated part of the assistance received. This payback must begin within 6 months from the date of the completion of the training and is equivalent to the total period of time for which training was actually received.

Number awarded   Varies; approximately 60 continuation and 550 new awards are made each year.

Deadline   January of each year.

[732]
INDIAN LOAN GUARANTY FUND

Bureau of Indian Affairs
Attn: Division of Financial Assistance
1849 C Street, N.W.
Washington, DC 20240
(202) 208-8427

Purpose   To finance Indian-owned, commercial, industrial, agricultural, or business activity organized for profit, provided that eligible Indian ownership constitutes not less than 51 percent of the business.

Eligibility   The applicant must be a federally recognized Indian tribe or Alaska Native group, a member of such a tribe or group, or an Indian-owned corporation, partnership, or cooperative association. The requested loan must benefit the economy of an Indian reservation.

Financial data   There are no limits on the amounts available for tribes or organizations, but there is a $500,000 limitation on guaranteed loans to individuals and non-tribal organizations. Up to 80 percent of the unpaid principal and interest due is guaranteed. Terms of the loan are determined by private lenders, but the maximum maturity is 30 years and the maximum variable interest rate is 2 3/4 percent above the New York Prime Rate for an 80 percent loan guarantee or 1 1/2 percent above the New York Prime Rate for a 90 percent loan guarantee.

Duration   Up to 30 years.

Special features   This program was established by the Indian Financing Act of 1974, as amended in 1984 and 1988.

Number awarded   Varies each year; currently, about $37 million is available for this program.

Deadline   Applications may be submitted at any time.

[733]
INDIAN PROFESSIONAL DEVELOPMENT GRANTS

Department of Education
Attn: Office of Elementary and Secondary Education
Office of Indian Education
Portals Building, Room 4300
600 Independence Avenue, S.W.
Washington, DC 20202-6335
(202) 260-3774   (800) 501-5795

Purpose   To provide financial assistance for development of programs for education of Indians.

Eligibility   Applications may be submitted by institutions of higher education, including Indian institutions of higher education; state or local educational agencies, in consortium with an institution of higher education; or an Indian tribe or organization in consortium with an institution of higher education. Funds must be used to develop programs that improve the skills of qualified Indian individuals; increase the number of qualified Indian individuals in professions that serve Indian persons; or support training programs for qualified Indian persons to become teachers, administrators, teacher aides, social workers, and ancillary educational personnel. Activities may include, but are not limited to, continuing programs, symposia, workshops, conferences, and

direct financial support. Grants for training educational personnel may be for preservice or inservice training. For individuals who are being trained to enter any field other than education, the training received must be in a program resulting in a graduate degree.

Financial data   Grants range from $75,000 to $275,000 and average approximately $200,000. For project participants receiving training, the stipend maximum is $1,000 per month for full-time students with a dependent allowance of $125 per month.

Duration   Up to 5 years.

Limitations   Individuals receiving assistance under this program are required to perform work related to the training received and that benefits Indian people, or repay all or a prorated part of the assistance received. This payback must begin within 6 months from the date of the completion of the training and is equivalent to the total period of time for which training was actually received.

Number awarded   Approximately 5 each year.

Deadline   August of each year.

[734]
INDIAN TRIBAL LOANS FOR PURCHASE OF LAND

Department of Agriculture
Attn: Farm Service Agency
Washington, DC 20250
(202) 720-4323

Purpose   To enable tribes and tribal corporations to mortgage lands as security for loans from the Farmers Home Administration to buy additional land within the reservation.

Eligibility   Funds are limited to any Indian tribe recognized by the Secretary of the Interior or tribal corporation established pursuant to the Indian Reorganization Act which does not have adequate uncommitted funds to acquire lands in the tribe's reservation or in a community in Alaska incorporated by the Secretary of the Interior pursuant to the Indian Reorganization Act. Tribal applicants must be unable to obtain adequate credit elsewhere and be able to show reasonable prospects of success.

Financial data   The loan assistance may equal the project cost, if the applicant is financially unable to contribute a part of the cost. Each loan must be adequately secured. Usually, an assignment of income is adequate, but in some cases a lien on the land may be required.

Duration   Loans may be for as long as 40 years; the interest rate is based on the cost of borrowing to the federal government and is subject to change if the cost of borrowing changes.

Special features   Loan funds may be used to buy lands, or acquire interest in lands, within an Indian reservation or an Alaska Native community. Examples of valid uses of the land include lease to tribal members for dwellings, grazing, or farming; use as a site for an enterprise beneficial to the tribe; addition to family-operated farms; or lease to a cooperative grazing association. The funds may also be used to pay expenses incidental to the purchase of land, including costs of appraisals, title and legal services, surveys, and loan closings.

Limitations   Loan funds may not be used for buildings, land development, equipment, or operating expenses. Land purchased with these funds must be for the benefit of the tribe's members and, for example, may be used in the following ways: leased to tribal members for dwellings, grazing, or farming; used as a site for an enterprise beneficial to the tribe; added to family-operated farms; or leased to a cooperative grazing association. The authorized tribal government body, the Bureau of Indian

Affairs, and the Farmers Home Administration must approve the plan for land use.

Number awarded Varies; approximately 6 each year.

Deadline Applications are accepted at any time. Applications should be submitted to the Farmers Home Administration county office serving the area in which the local tribe's reservation is located. If the local office is not known, applicants should contact the Farmers Home Administration at the address above.

[735]
LOAN GUARANTEES FOR INDIAN HOUSING

Department of Housing and Urban Development
Attn: Office of Native Amerian Programs
451 Seventh Street, S.W., Room B-133
Washington, DC 20410
(202) 755-0032   TDD: (800) 708-0850

Purpose To provide loan guarantees that will make private financing available to Native Americans in restricted areas where no source of funding is currently available.

Eligibility This program is open to Indians who plan to occupy a home for which they could not otherwise acquire financing because of the unique legal status of Indian trust land, and to Indian Housing Authorities. Loans, issued by conventional lending agencies but guaranteed under this program, may be used for the construction, acquisition, or rehabilitation of 1- to 4-family dwellings located on trust land or land located in an Indian area.

Financial data The maximum mortgage may not exceed 97 percent of the first $25,000 of the appraised value of the property and 95 percent of such value in excess of $25,000. The guarantee extends to 100 percent of the unpaid principal and interest of the underlying loan. Interest rates are set by the lender, but must be fixed. Borrowers must pay a guarantee fee of 1 percent of the principal obligation of the loan.

Duration The term of the loan may not exceed 30 years.

Limitations Adjustable rate loans are not permitted under this program.

Number awarded Varies each year.

[736]
NATIVE AMERICAN LEADERSHIP IN EDUCATION (NALE) PROGRAM

Native American Scholarship Fund
8200 Mountain Road, N.E., Suite 203
Albuquerque, NM 87110-7835
(505) 262-2351   Fax: (505) 262-0534

Purpose To provide financial assistance to American Indian paraprofessionals in the education field who wish to return to school.

Eligibility Paraprofessionals working in the schools are eligible to apply for this program if they 1) have at least a quarter Indian blood; 2) are members of a U.S. tribe that is either federally-recognized, state-recognized, or terminated; 3) are interested in returning to college to complete their undergraduate degrees and/or earn credentials as teachers, counselors, or administrators; 4) have been admitted to or are enrolled in college; 5) have grade point averages of at least 3.0 and scores on the SAT of at least 950 or ACT of at least 23; and 6) have applied for all other sources of funding for which they are eligible. They must attend an accredited 4-year college or university, but may be entering freshmen, undergraduate students, graduate students, or Ph.D. candidates. Awards are based on merit and the potential of the

applicant to improve the lives of Indian people; financial need is not a consideration. Students with no clear goals are discouraged from applying.

Financial data The amount awarded varies but is generally at least $500 in the form of grants, loans, or a combination of both.

Duration 1 year; may be renewed.

Number awarded Varies; generally, 15 or more each year.

Deadline April of each year for fall terms; September of each year for spring and winter terms; March of each year for summer school.

[737]
NAVAJO NATION VETERANS PERSONAL LOANS

Navajo Nation
Attn: Department of Veteran Affairs
P.O. Box 430
Window Rock, AZ 86515
(520) 871-6413

Purpose To loan money to Navajo veterans.

Eligibility This program is open to members of the Navajo Nation who served in the U.S. armed forces during any period and who were discharged under other than dishonorable conditions. Also eligible are Gold Star Mothers and surviving spouses who have shown ability to repay loans.

Financial data Loans range from $200 to $3,000; the interest rate is 9 percent with a maximum term of 36 months.

Special features Funds may be borrowed for any reason (e.g., consolidate bills, housing improvements, new vehicle purchase).

Number awarded Varies each year.

Deadline Applications may be submitted at any time.

[738]
NEW MEXICO MINORITY DOCTORAL ASSISTANCE STUDENT LOAN-FOR-SERVICE PROGRAM

New Mexico Commission on Higher Education
Attn: Financial Aid and Student Services
10668 Cerrillos Road
P.O. Box 15910
Santa Fe, NM 87506-5910
(505) 827-7383   (800) 279-9777 (within NM)
E-mail: highered@che.state.nm.us

Purpose To provide financial assistance to underrepresented minorities and women who reside in New Mexico and are interested in pursuing graduate study in selected fields.

Eligibility Eligible to apply for this program are ethnic minorities and women who have received a baccalaureate and/or master's degree from a state-supported 4-year higher education institution in New Mexico; wish to pursue a doctoral degree at an eligible sponsoring New Mexico institution in mathematics, engineering, the physical or life sciences, or any other academic discipline in which ethnic minorities and women are demonstrably underrepresented in New Mexico colleges and universities; and are willing after obtaining their degree to teach at an institution of higher education in the state. Applicants must be U.S. citizens and New Mexico residents.

Financial data This is a loan-for-service program in which the amount of the loan (up to $25,000 per year) may be wholly or partially forgiven upon completion of service as a college instructor in New Mexico.

Duration 1 year; may be renewed for up to 2 additional years for students who enter with a master's degree or up to 3 additional years for students who begin with a baccalaureate degree.
Special features Sponsoring institutions nominate candidates to the Commission on Higher Education for these awards.
Limitations Recipients must agree to teach at the college/university level in New Mexico upon completion of their doctoral degree. If the sponsoring institution where the recipient completes the degree is unable to provide a tenure-track position, it must arrange placement at another alternate and mutually-acceptable New Mexico public postsecondary instutition.
Number awarded Up to 12 each year.
Deadline March of each year.

[739]
ONEIDA TRIBE EMERGENCY PROGRAM

Oneida Nation of Wisconsin
Attn: Higher Education Office
P.O. Box 365
Oneida, WI 54155-0365
(414) 869-4333   (800) 236-2214, ext. 4333
Fax: (414) 869-4039
Purpose To provide emergency financial assistance to members of the Oneida Tribe of Wisconsin who are pursuing postsecondary education.
Eligibility Enrolled members of the Oneida Tribe of Wisconsin who are attending an accredited college or university may apply for this assistance if they are confronting an emergency financial situation that threatens to interrupt their educational goal or if their needs are not being met by the Oneida Tribe Higher Education or Adult Vocational Training Programs. Applicants may request either a grant or a loan; tribal officials will decide whether to award a grant or loan depending on applicants' financial hardship, nature of the emergency, and other information provided.
Financial data Up to $500.
Duration These are 1-time awards.
Number awarded Varies each year, depending upon the funds available and the number of applications.
Deadline Applications may be submitted at any time.

[740]
SOUTHEAST NEW MEXICO MINORITY AND HANDICAPPED TEACHERS' LOAN-FOR-SERVICE PROGRAM

New Mexico Commission on Higher Education
Attn: Financial Aid and Student Services
10668 Cerrillos Road
P.O. Box 15910
Santa Fe, NM 87506-5910
(505) 827-7383   (800) 279-9777 (within NM)
E-mail: highered@che.state.nm.us
Purpose To provide financial assistance to underrepresented minority and disabled residents of designated counties in southeastern New Mexico who are interested in becoming teachers in that area.
Eligibility Eligible to apply for this program are ethnic minorities and people with disabilities who are current or former residents of Lea, Otero, Eddy, Chaves, or Roosevelt Counties of New Mexico. Applicants must declare an intent to provide service at public schools in 1 of those counties and must be U.S. citizens or permanent residents.

Financial data This is a loan-for-service program in which the amount of the loan (up to $4,000 per year, depending on financial need) may be wholly or partially forgiven upon completion of service as an educator in the designated New Mexico counties.
Duration 1 year; may be renewed.
Number awarded Varies each year.

[741]
SUBSTANCE ABUSE FELLOWSHIP FOR MINORITY NURSES

American Nurses Association
Attn: Minority Fellowship Programs
600 Maryland Avenue, S.W., Suite 100 West
Washington, DC 20024-2571
(202) 651-7244   Fax: (202) 789-1413
Purpose To provide financial assistance for pre- and postdoctoral training to nurses pursuing careers in substance abuse prevention, intervention, or comorbidity in minority communities.
Eligibility Applications will be accepted from registered nurses who are members of an ethnic or racial minority group, including but not limited to African Americans, Hispanics, American Indians, Asian Americans, Pacific Islanders and/or others who can demonstrate a commitment to careers in psychiatric nursing, related to ethnic minority mental health. Applicants must be U.S. citizens or permanent residents, registered nurses, members of the American Nurses Association (ANA), and holders of master's degrees pursuing a doctoral degree or postdoctoral training. Students specializing in the following areas of research are encouraged to apply: psychosocial, behavioral, and psychological factors that contribute to alcohol, tobacco, and other drug use; development and testing of intervention strategies designed to improve clinical treatment outcomes for minority populations; and psychosocial and other coping mechanisms designed to prevent or ameliorate substance abuse.
Financial data Awards include a stipend to defray the cost of living; the amounts of awards depend on the availability of funds. This is a scholarship/loan program; recipients of these awards must agree to provide clinical services to underserved populations for a period of time equal to the length of support, within 2 years after termination of such support.
Duration Up to 3 years.
Special features Funds for this program are provided by the Substance Abuse and Mental Health Services Administration.
Deadline January of each year.

Native Alaskans

[742]
HEALTH PROFESSIONS SCHOLARSHIP PROGRAM

Indian Health Service
Attn: Scholarship Program
Twinbrook Metro Plaza, Suite 100
12300 Twinbrook Parkway
Rockville, MD 20852
(301) 443-6197   Fax: (301) 443-6048
Purpose To provide financial support to students enrolled in health professions and allied health professions programs.

Eligibility Applicants must be at least high school graduates and be enrolled in a full-time study program leading to a degree in a health-related professions school within the United States. Even though non-Indian students may apply for this program, the Indian Health Care Improvement Act (P.L. 94-437) requires that priority for the awards be given to Indian and Native Alaskan applicants. Both the number of Indian applicants and the level of appropriations limit the availability of scholarship awards to non-Indians. Qualifying fields of study include associate degree nurse, chemical dependency counseling, clinical psychology (Ph.D. only), computer science (B.S.), dentistry, dietician (B.S.), civil engineering (B.S.), health education (master's only), health records, medical technology (B.S.), medical social work (master's only), allopathic and osteopathic medicine, nurse practitioner, nurse midwife, B.S. nurse, M.S. nurse, optometry, para-optometric, pharmacy (B.S.), physician assistant (B.S.), physical therapy, podiatry (D.P.M.), public health (M.P.H. only), public health nutrition (master's only), radiologic therapy (associate and B.S.), respiratory therapy (associate), and sonography.

Financial data Awards provide for payment of a monthly stipend to cover living expenses, including room and board, tuition and required fees, and all other reasonable educational expenses; the total award is approximately $18,000. In a recent year, approximately $6,300,000 was available for continuation awards and $1,860,751 for new awards.

Duration 1 year; may be renewed for up to 3 additional years.

Limitations Upon completion of their program of study, recipients are required to provide payback service of 1 year for each year of scholarship support at the Indian Health Service, 1 of 638 tribal health programs, an urban health program, or in private practice serving a substantial number of Indians.

Number awarded Varies; In a recent year, 350 continuing and 103 new awards were provided.

Deadline April of each year.

[743]
INDIAN FELLOWSHIP PROGRAM

Department of Education
Attn: Office of Elementary and Secondary Education
Office of Indian Education
Portals Building, Room 4300
600 Independence Avenue, S.W.
Washington, DC 20202-6335
(202) 260-1683 E-mail: Indian_Fellowships@ed.gov

Purpose To provide financial assistance to graduate students and selected undergraduate students who are Native Americans interested in preparing for careers in medicine, law, engineering, natural resources, business administration, education, psychology, and related fields.

Eligibility American Indian students who are attending or have been accepted for admission at an accredited institution of higher learning and working toward 1) a graduate degree in medicine, law, education, psychology, clinical psychology, or related fields or 2) a graduate or undergraduate degree in natural resources, business administration, engineering, or related fields may apply. All applicants must be U.S. citizens and Indians. By federal government definition, this means that applicants must be 1) a member of a tribe, band, or other organized group of Indians (including those tribes, bands, or groups terminated since 1940 and those recognized by the state in which they reside); 2) a descendant in the first or second degree of any individual described above; 3) considered by the Secretary of the Interior to be an Indian for any

purpose or be an Eskimo, Aleut, or other Alaska Native; or 4) a member of an organized Indian group that received a grant under the Indian Education Act of 1988. Selection is based on academic record (60 points), letters of recommendation (15 points), and an essay on career goals, why the chosen field of study will benefit Indian people, life experiences and personal and family expectations that will enhance the applicant's anticipated career accomplishments, and anticipated commitment to providing service to Indian people (25 points).

Financial data Fellowships are intended to provide full financing for a student's educational expenses or to supplement other sources of financial aid.

Duration Up to 2 years for a master's degree; up to 4 years for an undergraduate or doctorate degree. Each year's renewal is dependent upon appropriations from Congress and satisfactory performance by the fellow.

Special features Up to 10 percent of the awards are to persons receiving training in guidance counseling with a specialty in the area of alcohol and substance abuse counseling and education.

Limitations Individuals receiving assistance under this program are required to perform work related to the training received and that benefits Indian people, or repay all or a prorated part of the assistance received. This payback must begin within 6 months from the date of the completion of the training and is equivalent to the total period of time for which training was actually received.

Number awarded Varies; approximately 60 continuation and 550 new awards are made each year.

Deadline January of each year.

[744]
INDIAN LOAN GUARANTY FUND

Bureau of Indian Affairs
Attn: Division of Financial Assistance
1849 C Street, N.W.
Washington, DC 20240
(202) 208-8427

Purpose To finance Indian-owned, commercial, industrial, agricultural, or business activity organized for profit, provided that eligible Indian ownership constitutes not less than 51 percent of the business.

Eligibility The applicant must be a federally recognized Indian tribe or Alaska Native group, a member of such a tribe or group, or an Indian-owned corporation, partnership, or cooperative association. The requested loan must benefit the economy of an Indian reservation.

Financial data There are no limits on the amounts available for tribes or organizations, but there is a $500,000 limitation on guaranteed loans to individuals and non-tribal organizations. Up to 80 percent of the unpaid principal and interest due is guaranteed. Terms of the loan are determined by private lenders, but the maximum maturity is 30 years and the maximum variable interest rate is 2 3/4 percent above the New York Prime Rate for an 80 percent loan guarantee or 1 1/2 percent above the New York Prime Rate for a 90 percent loan guarantee.

Duration Up to 30 years.

Special features This program was established by the Indian Financing Act of 1974, as amended in 1984 and 1988.

Number awarded Varies each year; currently, about $37 million is available for this program.

Deadline Applications may be submitted at any time.

[745]
INDIAN TRIBAL LOANS FOR PURCHASE OF LAND

Department of Agriculture
Attn: Farm Service Agency
Washington, DC 20250
(202) 720-4323

Purpose To enable tribes and tribal corporations to mortgage lands as security for loans from the Farmers Home Administration to buy additional land within the reservation.

Eligibility Funds are limited to any Indian tribe recognized by the Secretary of the Interior or tribal corporation established pursuant to the Indian Reorganization Act which does not have adequate uncommitted funds to acquire lands in the tribe's reservation or in a community in Alaska incorporated by the Secretary of the Interior pursuant to the Indian Reorganization Act. Tribal applicants must be unable to obtain adequate credit elsewhere and be able to show reasonable prospects of success.

Financial data The loan assistance may equal the project cost, if the applicant is financially unable to contribute a part of the cost. Each loan must be adequately secured. Usually, an assignment of income is adequate, but in some cases a lien on the land may be required.

Duration Loans may be for as long as 40 years; the interest rate is based on the cost of borrowing to the federal government and is subject to change if the cost of borrowing changes.

Special features Loan funds may be used to buy lands, or acquire interest in lands, within an Indian reservation or an Alaska Native community. Examples of valid uses of the land include lease to tribal members for dwellings, grazing, or farming; use as a site for an enterprise beneficial to the tribe; addition to family-operated farms; or lease to a cooperative grazing association. The funds may also be used to pay expenses incidental to the purchase of land, including costs of appraisals, title and legal services, surveys, and loan closings.

Limitations Loan funds may not be used for buildings, land development, equipment, or operating expenses. Land purchased with these funds must be for the benefit of the tribe's members and, for example, may be used in the following ways: leased to tribal members for dwellings, grazing, or farming; used as a site for an enterprise beneficial to the tribe; added to family-operated farms; or leased to a cooperative grazing association. The authorized tribal government body, the Bureau of Indian Affairs, and the Farmers Home Administration must approve the plan for land use.

Number awarded Varies; approximately 6 each year.

Deadline Applications are accepted at any time. Applications should be submitted to the Farmers Home Administration county office serving the area in which the local tribe's reservation is located. If the local office is not known, applicants should contact the Farmers Home Administration at the address above.

Native Pacific Islanders

[746]
NATIVE HAWAIIAN HEALTH SCHOLARSHIP PROGRAM

Health Resources and Services Administration
Attn: Bureau of Primary Health Care
Division of Scholarships and Loan Repayments
4350 East-West Highway, 10th Floor
Bethesda, MD 20814
(301) 594-4400   (800) 435-6464
(808) 842-8562   Fax: (301) 594-4981

Purpose To provide financial assistance to Native Hawaiians for training in health professions in exchange for service in a federally designated health professional shortage area (HPSA) in Hawaii.

Eligibility Applicants must be Native Hawaiians training in allopathic or osteopathic medicine, dentistry, clinical psychology, registered nursing, nurse midwifery, psychiatric nursing, public health/community nursing, social work, dental hygienist, physician assistant, or master of public health degree. Recipients must agree to serve in a federally designated HPSA in Hawaii on completion of training.

Financial data A stipend and other reasonable costs are paid directly to the scholar and full tuition is paid directly to the health professional school.

Duration 1 year; may be renewed for up to 3 additional years.

Limitations Participants are obligated to provide full-time clinical primary health care services to populations in federally-designated, high-priority HPSAs (these include Native Hawaiian health centers and medical facilities of the Federal Bureau of Prisons). Participants incur 1 year of obligated service in the National Health Service Corps for each full or partial year of support provided under this program. The minimum service obligation is 2 years.

Number awarded Varies each year, depending upon the funding available.

Deadline March of each year.

[747]
SUBSTANCE ABUSE FELLOWSHIP FOR MINORITY NURSES

American Nurses Association
Attn: Minority Fellowship Programs
600 Maryland Avenue, S.W., Suite 100 West
Washington, DC 20024-2571
(202) 651-7244   Fax: (202) 789-1413

Purpose To provide financial assistance for pre- and postdoctoral training to nurses pursuing careers in substance abuse prevention, intervention, or comorbidity in minority communities.

Eligibility Applications will be accepted from registered nurses who are members of an ethnic or racial minority group, including but not limited to African Americans, Hispanics, American Indians, Asian Americans, Pacific Islanders and/or others who can demonstrate a commitment to careers in psychiatric nursing, related to ethnic minority mental health. Applicants must be U.S.

citizens or permanent residents, registered nurses, members of the American Nurses Association (ANA), and holders of master's degrees pursuing a doctoral degree or postdoctoral training. Students specializing in the following areas of research are encouraged to apply: psychosocial, behavioral, and psychological factors that contribute to alcohol, tobacco, and other drug use; development and testing of intervention strategies designed to improve clinical treatment outcomes for minority populations; and psychosocial and other coping mechanisms designed to prevent or ameliorate substance abuse.

Financial data Awards include a stipend to defray the cost of living; the amounts of awards depend on the availability of funds. This is a scholarship/loan program; recipients of these awards must agree to provide clinical services to underserved populations for a period of time equal to the length of support, within 2 years after termination of such support.

Duration Up to 3 years.

Special features Funds for this program are provided by the Substance Abuse and Mental Health Services Administration.

Deadline January of each year.

Native Americans in General

[748]
ARTS IN EDUCATION PROGRAM OF THE NEW YORK STATE COUNCIL ON THE ARTS

New York State Council on the Arts
915 Broadway
New York, NY 10010
(212) 387-7000   (800) GET-ARTS

Purpose To provide financial support to cultural institutions in New York that from partnerships with schools to create programs that improve or enhance the study of the arts and environmental science.

Eligibility Nonprofit cultural and environmental organizations in New York may submit applications to form partnerships with schools in the state for the development of projects in all arts disciplines that focus on the creation, production, performance, and knowledge of the discipline; for interdisciplinary projects that use the arts to illuminate and enrich another area of the curriculum; for environmental projects that use the resources of arboreta, nature centers, and zoos; for local history projects; for staff development for artists and teachers; for program evaluation, research, or student assessment; or for services to the field. Special consideration is given to applications that address the needs of students in underserved or rural areas of the state; develop projects in new or emerging art forms, such as media arts or contemporary American music, or in areas traditionally undeveloped in the schools, such as folk arts, architecture, and design; address cultural diversity and promote a better understanding of the arts of different cultural traditions; or relate to the arts and culture of students who are African/Caribbean American, Latino/Hispanic, Asian/Pacific Islander, and Native American (priority is given to those programs utilizing artists or professionals who are representatives of the cultures being studied). Institutional support is available to organizations that have received general program support for the last 3 consecutive years, have arts in education

as a primary mission, have at least 1 paid full-time professional staff member. Project support is available to organizations for planning grants that enable them and their educational partners to assess needs, identify resources, develop an ongoing planning process, and explore program opportunities; implementation grants support the implementation of a wide range of projects for students and arts education practitioners; special project grants are incentive grants for institutional development.

Financial data Grants range from $60,000 per year (for general operating support), to $2,000-$7,000 (for planning grants), to $3,000-$25,000 (for implementation grants).

Duration Up to 3 years.

Number awarded Varies each year.

Deadline February of each year.

[749]
CAPITAL AID PROGRAM OF THE NEW YORK STATE COUNCIL ON THE ARTS

New York State Council on the Arts
915 Broadway
New York, NY 10010
(212) 387-7000   (800) GET-ARTS

Purpose To make funds available for the improvement, expansion, or rehabilitation of existing buildings owned or leased by nonprofit cultural institutions that receive programmatic funding from the New York State Council on the Arts (NYSCA).

Eligibility Nonprofit organizations in New York that have received funding from the NYSCA for the previous 3 years and either own their facility or hold a lease with an unexpired period of at least 5 years are eligible for these grants. Projects are limited to those that 1) improve, expand, or rehabilitate existing buildings to provide access for people with disabilities; 2) increase or assure public access to the arts; 3) address known health and safety deficiencies; 4) reduce an organization's operating costs; or 5) further cultural development in rural or minority communities. The NYSCA uses its best efforts to ensure that minority and women owned business enterprises, and the minority and female workforce, have the maximum practicable opportunity to participate in all Council funded construction projects.

Financial data The Council will support up to 50 percent of the costs of construction materials and labor, up to a maximum of $25,000. Grants must be matched on at least a 1-to-1 basis.

Special features Loans up to $100,000 are also available; the repayment period is 5 years and the interest rate is 5 percent below the prime rate (within a range of 3 percent to 10 percent).

Number awarded Varies each year.

Deadline February of each year.

[750]
CLINICAL TRAINING FELLOWSHIP FOR MINORITY NURSES

American Nurses Association
Attn: Minority Fellowship Programs
600 Maryland Avenue, S.W., Suite 100 West
Washington, DC 20024-2571
(202) 651-7244   Fax: (202) 789-1413

Purpose To provide financial assistance to nurses pursuing careers as psychiatric/mental health nurses who serve a minority population.

Eligibility Applications will be accepted from registered nurses who are members of an ethnic or racial minority group, including but not limited to African Americans, Hispanics, American Indians, Asian Americans, Pacific Islanders and/or who can demonstrate a commitment to careers in psychiatric nursing, related to ethnic minority mental health. Applicants must be U.S. citizens or permanent residents, registered nurses, members of the American Nurses Association (ANA), and holders of master's degrees pursuing a doctoral degree. Students specializing in the following areas of research are encouraged to apply: basic and clinical research on the nature, prevention, and treatment of mental disorders affecting ethnic/racial minority populations; clinical studies of ethnic/racial minority populations at high risk for clinical disorders; and cross-cultural, cross-ethnic and/or cross-racial studies in psychopathology, etc.

Financial data Awards include a stipend to defray the cost of living; the amounts of awards depend on the availability of funds. This is a scholarship/loan progam; recipients of these awards must agree to provide clinical services to underserved populations for a period of time equal to the length of support, within 2 years after termination of such support.

Duration Up to 3 years.

Special features Funds for this program are provided by the Substance Abuse and Mental Health Services Administration.

Deadline January of each year.

[751]
CSU FORGIVABLE LOAN/DOCTORAL INCENTIVE PROGRAM

California State University
c/o Office of the Chancellor
400 Golden Shore, Suite 222
Long Beach, CA 90802-4275
(310) 985-2692

Purpose To increase the number of minorities, women, and persons with disabilities with doctoral degrees in selected fields of study of particular interest and relevance to the California State University (CSU) system, and to increase the likelihood that those people will seek teaching careers within the CSU system.

Eligibility Applicants must be minorities, women, or persons with disabilities who are new or continuing full-time students enrolled in a doctoral program, whether affiliated with a CSU campus or not. Selection is based on: 1) potential for success—the applicant's potential to complete an approved doctoral program and compete successfully for a CSU tenure-track faculty position; considerations include the applicant's academic record, professional qualifications, and motivations to teach in the CSU, as well as the quality of the proposed doctoral field and the probable need for faculty in the candidate's field; this criterion is given greatest weight; 2) underrepresentation—the degree of underrepresentation in the national pool of doctoral recipients and in the CSU tenure-track faculty in the area of study proposed by the applicant; special consideration is given to applicants with backgrounds that are underrepresented in the natural sciences, engineering, computer science, and mathematics, although consideration is given to applicants in all fields where such underrepresentation exists; persons with disabilities are considered underrepresented in all fields; 3) faculty sponsor's plan of support—the plan submitted by a full-time tenured CSU faculty member who advises and supports the candidate throughout doctoral study.

Financial data Participants receive up to $10,000 per year. The loans are converted to fellowships at the rate of 20 percent of the total loan amount for each postdoctoral year that the program participant teaches, for up to 5 years. Thus, the entire loan will be forgiven after the recipient has taught full time for 5 years on a CSU campus. Recipients who do not teach on a CSU campus or who discontinue full-time studies will be required to repay the total loan amount within a 15-year period at the rate established for other student loans. The minimum repayment required for a $30,000 loan is approximately $300 per month to amortize the 8 percent per annum loan over a 15-year period. Waiver of loan obligations can be made in those exceptional cases where graduate work was discontinued for valid reasons and where repayment of the loan would cause an unnecessary or undue hardship.

Duration Up to 3 years.

Number awarded Varies each year.

Deadline February of each year.

[752]
DAVID A. DEBOLT TEACHER SHORTAGE SCHOLARSHIPS

Illinois Student Assistance Commission
Attn: Scholarship and Grant Services
1755 Lake Cook Road
Deerfield, IL 60015-5209
(708) 948-8550
(800) 899-ISAC (within IL, IA, IN, MO, and WI)

Purpose To provide financial assistance to students in Illinois who are interested in training or retraining for a teaching career in academic shortage areas.

Eligibility Eligible for support under this program are Illinois residents who are enrolled or planning to enroll in an Illinois institution of higher education to pursue careers as public preschool, elementary, and secondary school teachers in designated teacher shortage disciplines. Priority is given to minority students.

Financial data This programs pays tuition and fees, room and board, or a commuter allowance at academic institutions in Illinois, to a maximum of $5,000. Funds are paid directly to the school. This is a scholarship/loan program. Recipients must agree to take a teaching position in Illinois within 2 years of graduation and must remain in that position for at least 3 years. Recipients who fail to honor this work obligation must repay the award.

Duration 1 year; may be renewed.

Number awarded Varies each year.

Deadline April of each year.

[753]
DOCTORAL FELLOWSHIPS IN SOCIAL WORK FOR ETHNIC MINORITY STUDENTS PREPARING FOR LEADERSHIP ROLES IN MENTAL HEALTH AND/OR SUBSTANCE ABUSE

Council on Social Work Education
Attn: Minority Fellowship Program
1600 Duke Street, Suite 300
Alexandria, VA 22314-3421
(703) 683-8080

Purpose To increase the number of racial minority members in the mental health fields.

Eligibility Applicants must be American citizens or permanent residents who have been underrepresented in the field of social work. These include but are not limited to the following groups: American Indians/Alaskan Natives, Asian/Pacific Islanders (e.g. Chinese, East Indians and other South Asians, Filipinos, Hawaiians, Japanese, Koreans, and Samoans), Blacks, and Hispanics (e.g. Mexicans/Chicanos, Puerto Ricans, Cubans, Central or

South Americans). Selection is based upon potential for assuming leadership roles in mental health, a commitment to a career providing mental health and/or substance abuse services to ethnic minority clients and communities, and potential for success in doctoral studies. To be eligible for consideration, applicants must have already earned a master's degree in social work.

Financial data Awards provide a monthly stipend and some tuition support. A payback provision requires recipients to engage in clinical services in specific areas of need for a period of time equal to the length of support; such service could include teaching, consultation, research, or a combination of those.

Duration 1 academic year; renewable for 1 additional year if funds are available and the recipient achieves satisfactory progress toward the degree objectives.

Special features This program is funded by the Center for Mental Health Services of the Substance Abuse and Mental Health Services Administration.

Limitations The fellowship is to be used to pursue doctoral studies/research only.

Deadline February of each year.

[754]
DOT SHORT TERM LENDING PROGRAM

Department of Transportation
Attn: Office of Small and Disadvantaged Business Utilization
400 Seventh Street, S.W., Room 9410
Washington, DC 20590
(202) 366-2852   (800) 532-1169
Fax: (202) 366-7538

Purpose To provide short-term working capital for transportation-related projects to Disadvantaged Business Enterprises (DBE), Minority Business Enterprises (MBE), and Women-owned Business Enterprises (WBE).

Eligibility This program is open to small businesses (as defined by the Small Business Administration) that are also either an 8(a) firm certified by the Small Business Administration or a DBE/MBE/WBE certified by the Department of Transportation (DOT). Owners of DBEs are economically or socially disadvantaged individuals, defined as Black Americans; Hispanic Americans (Mexicans, Puerto Ricans, Cubans, Central or South Americans, or others of Spanish culture); Native Americans (American Indians, Eskimos, Aleuts, and native Hawaiians); Asia Pacific Americans (persons with origins from Japan, China, Taiwan, Korea, Vietnam, Laos, Cambodia, the Philippines, Samoa, Guam, Northern Mariana Islands, or the U.S. Trust Territory of the Pacific Islands); and Asian Indian Americans (persons with origins from India, Pakistan, and Bangladesh). Firms must possess a transportation-related contract which supports the application to finance accounts receivables.

Financial data The amount loaned varies, up to a maximum of $500,000; most loans have ranged from $100,00 to $200,000. Interest is charged at the current New York Prime Rate.

Duration Normally, loans are repayable in 1 year; in exceptional cases, a 2-year loan may be approved.

Special features This program is a public/private partnership, under which DOT provides up to 75 percent of the funding for each line-of-credit and 1 of 4 participating banks provides the balance of the financing and administers the line-of-credit. Currently, the 4 participating banks are Cathay Bank of Los Angeles, Hamilton Bank of Miami, First Texas Bank of Dallas, and NAB Bank of Chicago.

Number awarded Varies each year; recently, an annual total of $12.4 million in loans was approved through this program. Total annual program capacity is $20 million.

Deadline Applications may be submitted at any time.

[755]
EXTENDED OPPORTUNITY PROGRAMS AND SERVICES LOANS

California Community Colleges
Attn: EOPS Program Coordinator
1107 Ninth Street
Sacramento, CA 95814
(916) 445-8752

Purpose To provide emergency loans to meet unexpected or untimely costs for books, college supplies, transportation, or housing.

Eligibility To receive support under this program, students must be residents of California, be enrolled full time in a California community college, not have completed more than 70 units of course work in any combination of postsecondary institutions, be educationally disadvantaged, and be able to demonstrate financial need. Up to 10 percent of the EOPS students at each college may enroll for only 9 units; students with disabilities may enroll for fewer units, based on their disability. Educationally disadvantaged students include those who are not qualified to enroll in the minimum level English or mathematics course at their college, did not graduate from high school or obtain the GED, graduated from high school with a grade point below 2.5, previously enrolled in remedial education, or met other factors described in their college's plan, such as first generation college student, member of underrepresented group at the college, or English not the primary language.

Financial data Loans may not exceed $300 in a single academic year and must be repaid within the academic year in which the loan was made.

Duration 1 year.

Special features EOPS students are also eligible for other support in the form of counseling, tutoring, registration assistance, orientation, child care, transportation, and cultural activities.

Limitations Students apply to their community college, not to the sponsoring organization.

Number awarded Varies each year.

Deadline Varies by participating institution.

[756]
FACULTY DEVELOPMENT FELLOWSHIP PROGRAM

Department of Education
Attn: Office of Postsecondary Education
Division of Higher Education Incentive Programs
Portals Building, Suite C-80
600 Independence Avenue, S.W.
Washington, DC 20202-5329
(202) 260-3209

Purpose To provide grants to institutions of higher education to fund fellowships for individuals from underrepresented minority groups to enter or continue in the higher education professorate.

Eligibility Applications may be submitted by institutions of higher education, consortia of institutions, and consortia of institutions and nonprofit organizations if they have a demonstrated record of enhancing the access to graduate education of individuals from underrepresented minority groups. Funds must be used to award the following types of fellowships: 1) prospective faculty development fellowships, for talented baccalaureate degree recipients from underrepresented minority groups who wish to obtain a doctoral degree and enter the higher education professorate; 2) experienced faculty development fellowships, for talented faculty from underrepresented minority groups who wish to continue in the higher education professorate and obtain a doctoral degree; and 3) faculty professional development fellowships, for talented faculty from underrepresented minority groups who wish to participate in short-term professional development programs, including seminars, conferences, and workshops, specifically designed to enhance their skills and careers, but not for study leading to a doctoral degree. Preference is given to applications for projects that provide each fellow with a tuition waiver and a minimum $2,000 in support beyond the stipend received by each fellow. Institutions may award fellowships to underrepresented minorities who are U.S. citizens, nationals, or permanent residents, or residing in the United States for other than a temporary purpose and intending to become citizens or permanent residents.

Financial data　Grantee institutions may pay each fellow a level of support equal to the provided by the National Science Foundation graduate fellowships (currently $14,400 per year) or the fellow's demonstated level of financial need, whichever is less.

Duration　Prospective or experience faculty development fellowships: up to 5 years; faculty professional development fellowships: up to 3 years.

Special features　Recipients of prospective and experienced faculty development fellowships must enter into an agreement with the grantee in which they agree to teach full time, within 5 years after completing the doctoral degree for which the fellowship was awarded, for a period of not less than 1 year for each year for which financial assistance was received; experienced faculty development fellows must agree to teach in a public or private nonprofit institution of higher education that has a significant minority enrollment. Fellows who fail to comply with that agreement must repay the amount of the grant funds received, prorated according to the fraction of the teaching obligation not completed, with interest. Repayment of fellowship funds may be deferred while the recipient is serving in the armed forces (up to 3 years), temporarily and totally disabled (up to 3 years), providing care for an immediate member of the family who is disabled (up to 1 year), enrolled as a full-time doctoral student and making satisfactory progress toward a degree, serving as a Peace Corps volunteer, seeking and unable to find employment (up to 1 year), or engaged in full-time employment as an elementary or secondary school teacher. The obligation will be cancelled in case of the recipient's death or permanent and total disability.

Limitations　Prospective fellows must apply directly to recipient institutions, not to the Department of Education.

Number awarded　Varies each year.

Deadline　Application dates vary; for current information, check the *Federal Register*.

[757]

FARM OWNERSHIP LOANS FOR SOCIALLY DISADVANTAGED PERSONS

Department of Agriculture
Attn: Farm Service Agency
Washington, DC 20250
(202) 720-4323

Purpose　To set aside funds for farm ownership loans to eligible members of socially disadvantaged groups who operate family-size farms.

Eligibility　For the purposes of this program, a "socially disadvantaged group" is 1 whose members "have been subjected to racial or ethnic prejudice because of their identity as members of a group without regard to their individual qualities." Those groups are Black Americans, American Indians, Alaskan Natives, Hispanic Americans, and Asian or Pacific Islanders. Targeted farm ownership loan funds are set aside for states, for loans in designated counties (based on the percentage of socially disadvantaged persons in the rural population of the counties). In addition to belonging to a "socially disadvantaged group," borrowers must have a satisfactory history of meeting credit obligations, have 3 years of experience in operating a farm or ranch, be a U.S. citizen or legal resident, possess the legal capacity to incur the obligations of a loan or credit sale, be unable to obtain sufficient credit elsewhere at reasonable rates, and be the owner-operator of not larger than a family farm after the loan or credit sale is closed.

Financial data　A farm ownership loan cannot exceed the market value of the farm or other security. In any case, the maximum outstanding principal balance for a direct loan or credit sale is $200,000. Repayment terms and interest rates vary according to the type of loan made and the borrower's ability to repay a credit sale. The interest rate is set periodically, based on the cost of borrowing to the federal government. A lower interest rate is available for borrowers with limited resources.

Duration　The length of the loan varies but is generally 15 years, 30 years, or 40 years.

Special features　Funds from these loans can be used to construct, improve, or repair farm homes and farm service buildings; drill wells and otherwise improve onfarm water supplies; develop and improve farmland; establish and improve farm forests; provide drainage systems; and carry out basic land treatment practices and make other improvements. Regular credit assistance also may be used to provide facilities to produce fish under controlled conditions. This program is authorized by the Agricultural Credit Act of 1987.

Deadline　Applications may be submitted at any time.

[758]

FINANCIAL ASSISTANCE FOR DISADVANTAGED HEALTH PROFESSIONS STUDENTS GRANTS

Health Resources and Services Administration
Attn: Bureau of Health Professions
Division of Student Assistance
Parklawn Building, Room 8-34
5600 Fishers Lane
Rockville, MD 20857
(301) 443-4776　　　　　　　　　Fax: (301) 443-0846

Purpose　To provide financial support for disadvantaged health professions students who are enrolled in accredited medical schools.

Eligibility Eligible to submit grant requests are accredited schools (private or public) of medicine, osteopathic medicine, or dentistry. They must request funds for students at their institutions who are from a disadvantaged background and can demonstrate exceptional financial need; these students must be working on a degree in medicine, osteopathic medicine, or dentistry. Disadvantaged individuals are defined as those who 1) come from an environment that has inhibited the individual from obtaining the knowledge, skill, and abilities required to enroll in and graduate from a health professions school; or 2) come from a family with a low income, currently set at less than $10,200 for a family with 1 dependent, ranging to less than $26,700 for a family with 6 dependents. Applicant institutions must be carrying out programs to recruit and retain minority students and faculty.

Financial data With these grants, schools award students funds to cover the costs of tuition and other reasonable educational expenses including fees, books, laboratory expenses and other costs of attending school. In return for this support, students of medicine and osteopathic medicine must agree to enter and complete residency training in primary care and to practice in primary care for 5 years after completing a residency training program. Students of dentistry must agree to practice in general dentistry for 5 years after completing residency training.

Duration 1 year; may be renewed.

Special features Students apply directly to their academic institution for support. For a list of schools participating in this program, contact the address above.

Number awarded Varies each year.

Deadline Deadline dates vary but are usually in June; check the *Federal Register* for the current schedule.

[759]
GUARANTEED FARM OPERATING LOANS FOR SOCIALLY DISADVANTAGED PERSONS

Department of Agriculture
Attn: Farm Service Agency
Washington, DC 20250
(202) 720-4323

Purpose To guarantee farm operating loans made by other lenders to socially disadvantaged farmers and ranchers who operate family-size farms.

Eligibility For the purposes of this program, a "socially disadvantaged group" is 1 whose members "have been subjected to racial, ethnic, or gender prejudice because of their identity as members of a group without regard to their individual qualities." Those groups are women, African Americans, American Indians, Alaskan Natives, Hispanic Americans, and Asian or Pacific Islanders. In addition to belonging to a "socially disadvantaged group," applicants must have a satisfactory history of meeting credit obligations; have sufficient education, training, or at least 1 year of experience in managing or operating a farm or ranch within the last 5 years; be a U.S. citizen or legal resident; possess the legal capacity to incur the obligations of a loan; possess the industry and ability needed to succeed in farming; and be the owner or tenant operating not larger than a family farm after the loan is closed.

Financial data The size of the loan is agreed upon by the borrower and the lender, but total indebtedness in direct and guaranteed loans of the Farm Service Agency (FSA) may not exceed $400,000. Interest rates can be fixed or variable, as agreed upon by the borrower and the lender, but may not exceed the rate the lender charges its average farm customer. FSA guarantees up to 95 percent of the loan principal and interest against loss.

Duration Repayment terms are generally 1 year for loans used to pay annual operating expenses or up to 7 years for equipment and other operating loans.

Special features Funds from guaranteed loans may be used to pay for items needed for a successful operation, such as livestock, poultry, farm and home equipment, feed, seed, fuel, fertilizer, chemicals, hail and other crop insurance, food, clothing, medical care, and hired labor. Certain debts may be refinanced with this assistance. Funds may also be used to make minor improvements to buildings and real estate; to install or improve water systems for home, livestock, and irrigation use; to finance the purchase of equipment for producing and harvesting trees and other products; or for aquaculture operations.

Limitations Guaranteed operating loan funds cannot be used to purchase real estate or to make payments on real estate debts.

Deadline Applications may be submitted at any time.

[760]
INNER-CITY VENTURES FUND

National Trust for Historic Preservation
Attn: Office of Financial Services
1785 Massachusetts Avenue, N.W.
Washington, DC 20036
(202) 588-6054   Fax: (202) 588-6038

Purpose To provide funds to help revitalize historical neighborhoods for the benefit of low- and moderate-income residents, especially minorities.

Eligibility Neighborhood-based nonprofit incorporated organizations are eligible to apply for these funds. Eligible projects must include either the rehabilitation of a historic building in the United States or new construction on vacant land in a neighborhood that is already part of a historic district or in an area that is eligible to be listed in a historic district. Priority is given to projects that meet at least 1 of the following criteria: 1) will strengthen the capacity of a historic preservation group to engage in community development activities in partnership with community-based organizations; 2) is related to the emergence of a preservation group in a minority neighborhood; 3) is to finance the rehabilitation of a landmark related to historic contributions by minorities; or 4) demonstrates new local-state public policy which promotes the use of preservation as a community development strategy.

Financial data Maximum loan amounts are $150,000 for site specific projects and $200,000 for revolving funds. The interest rate is fixed at closing, and is generally based on the Wall Street Journal prime rate minus 1 point.

Duration Loan terms are up to 5 years.

Special features Loans may be used to defray any reasonable real estate development cost.

[761]
KANSAS ETHNIC MINORITY FELLOWSHIP

Kansas Board of Regents
700 S.W. Harrison Street, Suite 1410
Topeka, KS 66603-3760
(913) 296-3517

Purpose To encourage minorities to attend graduate school in Kansas.

Eligibility This program is open to Kansas residents. Applicants must be Asian American, African American, Hispanic American or Native American. They must be enrolled or accepted in a graduate school in Kansas. Financial need must be documented.

Financial data A minimum of $8,000 per year for full-time study. This is a scholarship/loan program; recipients must seek employment in a Kansas educational institution upon graduation, working 1 year for each year of support; if they fail to do so, they must repay the fellowship at 15 percent interest.

Duration 1 year; may be renewed.

Limitations Recipients must attend school on a full-time basis and may now work during enrollment.

Number awarded Varies each year.

[762]
KANSAS TEACHER SCHOLARSHIP

Kansas Board of Regents
700 S.W. Harrison Street, Suite 1410
Topeka, KS 66603-3760
(913) 296-3517

Purpose To provide financial assistance to high school seniors, high school graduates, and selected undergraduates who are interested in preparing for a career as a teacher in Kansas.

Eligibility This program is open to Kansas residents who plan to enter the teaching profession in specific curriculum areas, currently special education (85 percent of the awards), science (8 percent of the awards), and foreign language (7 percent of the awards). Minimum selection criteria include: 1) intention to enroll in 1 of the specified curricular areas of a teacher education program; 2) completion of the Regents Recommended Curriculum (4 years of English, 3 years of mathematics, 3 years of science, 3 years of social studies, and 2 years of foreign language); 3) ACT or SAT score; 4) high school grade point average; 5) high school class rank; 6) college transcript (for college-enrolled applicants); and 7) letter of recommendation from college or university official (for college-enrolled applicants). Special consideration is given to minority applicants because minorities continue to be underrepresented in the teaching profession in Kansas schools.

Financial data Participants receive $5,000 per year. This is a scholarship/loan program. Recipients must teach in Kansas 1 year for every year of funding received, or they must repay the amount received at 15 percent interest.

Duration 1 year; may be renewed for up to 3 additional years or up to 4 additional years for designated 5-year courses of study requiring graduate work.

Number awarded Approximately 100 each year.

Deadline March of each year.

[763]
LOANS FOR DISADVANTAGED STUDENTS PROGRAM GRANTS

Health Resources and Services Administration
Attn: Bureau of Health Professions
Division of Student Assistance
Parklawn Building, Room 8-34
5600 Fishers Lane
Rockville, MD 20857
(301) 443-4776   Fax: (301) 443-0846

Purpose To provide financial support for disadvantaged health professions students who are enrolled in accredited schools.

Eligibility Eligible to submit grant requests are accredited schools (private or public) of allopathic medicine, osteopathic

medicine, dentistry, optometry, pharmacy, podiatric medicine, or veterinary medicine. They must request funds to establish revolving loan funds for students at their institutions. Disadvantaged individuals are defined as those who 1) come from an environment that has inhibited the individual from obtaining the knowledge, skill, and abilities required to enroll in and graduate from a health professions school; or 2) come from a family with a low income, currently set at less than $10,200 for a family with 1 dependent, ranging to less than $26,700 for a family with 6 dependents. Applicant institutions must be carrying out programs to recruit and retain minority students and faculty.

Financial data With these grants, schools select recipients, make reasonable determinations of need, and provide loans which do not exceed tuition plus $2,500 for an academic year.

Duration 1 year; may be renewed.

Special features Students apply directly to their academic institution for support. For a list of schools participating in this program, contact the address above.

Number awarded Varies each year.

Deadline Deadline dates vary but are usually in June; check the *Federal Register* for the current schedule.

[764]
MESBEC PROGRAM

Native American Scholarship Fund
8200 Mountain Road, N.E., Suite 203
Albuquerque, NM 87110-7835
(505) 262-2351   Fax: (505) 262-0534

Purpose To provide financial assistance to Native American students interested in pursuing postsecondary education.

Eligibility Native American students (with at least a quarter Indian blood and members of a U.S. tribe that is federally-recognized, state-recognized, or terminated) are eligible to apply for this program if they are majoring in the 1 of the following fields: mathematics, engineering, science, business administration, education, or computer science. They should have a grade point average of at least 3.0 and scores on the SAT of at least 950 or ACT of at least 23 and must apply for all other sources of funding for which they are eligible. Applicants should demonstrate clear goals and plan to earn a 4-year or graduate degree. Awards are based on merit and the potential of the applicant to improve the lives of Indian people; financial need is not a consideration.

Financial data The amount awarded varies but is generally at least $500, in the form of grants, loans, or a combination of both.

Duration 1 year; may be renewed.

Special features MESBEC is an acronym that stands for the priority areas of this program: mathematics, engineering, science, business, education, and computers.

Number awarded Varies; generally, 30 to 35 each year.

Deadline April of each year for fall terms; September of each year for spring and winter terms; March of each year for summer school.

[765]
MHFA HOME MORTGAGE LOAN PROGRAM FOR MINORITY HOUSEHOLDS

Massachusetts Housing Finance Agency
One Beacon Street
Boston, MA 02108-4805
(617) 854-1020   TDD: (617) 854-1025

Purpose To provide low-interest loans for the purchase of homes by minority families in Massachusetts.

Eligibility Massachusetts residents may qualify for these loans if the borrower/coborrower is Black, Hispanic, Asian, Cape Verdean, or Native American Indian. Applicants must be first-time homebuyers (i.e., have had no ownership interest in a principal residence in the past 3 years), unless they are buying in Boston, Chelsea, Everett, Fall River, Lawrence, Lynn, North Adams, or Somerville. Depending on the area of the state where the applicant lives, the maximum family income for 1 or 2 persons is $46,000 to $50,000; for 3 or more persons, it is $52,000 to $57,000. A range of maximum purchase price restrictions also apply, depending upon the type of construction and market area within the state.

Financial data The Massachusetts Housing Finance Agency (MHFA) currently has $250 million in mortgage funds available, half of which are set aside for priority borrowers including lower-income households, veterans, minorities, and households in which a member has a permanent physical disability. Interest rates vary, but are 1 to 2 percentage points lower than on conventionally-financed loans.

Duration Up to 30 years.

Limitations Recipients who sell their homes within 10 years may have to pay back some or all of the savings they have received as a result of the lower interest rate mortgage.

Number awarded Up to 1,400 households.

Deadline Applications may be submitted at any time.

[766]
MINORITY BUSINESS DEVELOPMENT LOAN PROGRAM

Pennsylvania Minority Business Development Authority
Forum Building, Room 460
Harrisburg, PA 17120
(717) 783-1128

Purpose To assist existing and start up minority-owned businesses located and operating within Pennsylvania through long-term, low-interest loans.

Eligibility To be eligible for this program, applicants must be: residents of Pennsylvania or able to certify that such residency will be established on or before closing the loan; owners or executives of minority business enterprises (which are defined as businesses that are owned or controlled by 1 or more socially or economically disadvantaged person, including but not limited to African Americans, Native Americans, Latinos, Asian Americans); financially and legally responsible; sole proprietorships, partnerships, or corporations; committed to full-time management and control of the enterprise on a daily basis; and at least 18 years of age, if applicants are natural persons. In addition, applicants must have paid in full all national and state taxes; pledge and maintain real and personal property, as collateral, in the form and amount necessary to reasonably assure full payment of the loan in the event of default or bankruptcy; not be involved as a debtor in any bankruptcy proceeding; be current with respect to all amounts due under prior loans, if any; and demonstrate, through experience, training, or education that they are capable of performing their responsibilities in connection with the ownership, management, or control of the enterprise.

Financial data From $25,000 to $750,000 may be borrowed. The loan may represent up to 75 percent of the eligible costs; the remaining 25 percent must be obtained through owner's equity or through another lender. Loans are provided at interest rates determined by the board as long as such interest rates are not less than 4 percent or more than half the prevailing prime rate on the date of the loan approval.

Duration Varies.

Limitations All applicants are charged a non-refundable application fee. Funding is not provided for the acquisition, renovation, or alteration of a building or property for the principal purpose of real estate speculation or for the purpose of refinancing existing debts. If applicants are otherwise employed at the time of application, they must terminate such employment prior to or at the time of closing. Projects rejected by the selection board are not eligible to reapply for at least 1 year after the board decision, except by invitation of the board.

Number awarded Varies each year.

[767]
MINORITY FELLOWSHIP PROGRAM IN PSYCHIATRY

American Psychiatric Association
Attn: Office of Minority/National Affairs
1400 K Street, N.W.
Washington, DC 20005
(202) 682-6096   Fax: (202) 682-6352
E-mail: mking@psych.org

Purpose To provide educational enrichment to psychiatrists-in-training and stimulate their interest in providing quality and effective services to minorities and the underserved.

Eligibility Minority psychiatric residents who are in at least their second year of psychiatric training are eligible to apply. Fellows are selected on the basis of their commitment to serving minorities and underserved populations, demonstrated leadership abilities, and interest in the interrelationship between mental health/illness and transcultural factors.

Financial data A partial stipend is provided, usually lower than the normal salary paid by the training institution, which is then requested to pay the fellow the difference between the stipend and the usual salary. The institutions must use the remaining freed-up funds to institute or expand a teaching format within the resident's training program that focuses on culturally relevant issues in psychiatry. Fellows incur a payback obligation which they must fulfill by providing 1 year of service at a public inpatient mental institution, public or private nonprofit facility, or nursing home. At least 25 percent of the facility's patients must be 1 of the priority populations of the Center for Mental Health Services (CMHS)—racial/ethnic minorities, chronically mentally ill, rape victims, the elderly, physically handicapped, veterans, mentally retarded, criminal or delinquent populations, children and adolescents, poverty populations, migrants, members of the armed forces, and residents of any nursing home.

Duration 9 and a half months, beginning September 1.

Special features Funding for this program is provided by the CMHS, a component of the Substance Abuse and Mental Health Services Administration. Each fellow is appointed to a component of the organizational structure of the American Psychiatric Association (APA) and attends the association's annual meeting as an observer and active participant. This program is an outgrowth of the fellowships that were established in 1974 under a grant from the National Institute of Mental Health in answer to concerns about the underrepresentation of minorities in psychiatry.

Number awarded Varies; averages 10 each year.

Deadline March of each year.

[768]
MINORITY PREQUALIFICATION PILOT LOAN PROGRAM

Small Business Administration
Attn: Office of Minority Enterprise Development
409 Third Street, S..W.
Washington, DC 20416
(800) 8-ASK-SBA   Fax: (202) 205-7064
TDD: (202) 205-7333

Purpose To streamline the application process and provide a quick response to a nonprofit intermediary for loan requests of $250,000 or less to minority-owned and managed businesses.

Eligibility To be eligible, minority-owned businesses must meet the requirements of the regular Small Business Administration (SBA) 7(a) guaranty program (i.e., the average annual sales for the preceding 3 fiscal years must be less than $5 million and the average number of employees for the preceding 12 months must be less than 100 workers). Types of businesses not eligible for SBA loans are those engaged in speculation or investment in real estate or those organized as nonprofit. This pilot program is authorized for use in Baltimore, Maryland; Boston, Massachusetts; Columbia, South Carolina; Detroit, Michigan; Fargo, North Dakota; Helena, Montana; Houston, Texas; Kansas City, Missouri; Los Angeles, California; Miami, Florida; Milwaukee, Wisconsin; New York, New York; Phildelphia, Pennsylvania; St. Louis, Missouri; Santa Ana, California; and Seattle, Washington. Applications must be completed by a nonprofit or for-profit intermediary who has registered with the local SBA district office. Selection is based on character, credit, experience, and reliability. The primary considerations are: willingness to pay debts (as indicated by a good credit history), the likelihood that expected earnings will be sufficient to pay obligations; the likelihood that the business has a chance of succeeding. Business financial statements or tax returns and personal financial statements are required from all owners and guarantors. Owners of new businesses are also required to submit a business plan.

Financial data Up to $250,000 may be borrowed. The maximum interest rates lenders may charge are: Wall Street Journal Prime plus 2.5 percent for loans with maturity of under 7 years; prime plus 2.75 percent for loans with maturity over 7 years. The SBA guarantees up to 90 percent of the loan. Funds can be used for normal businesses operations, including working capital, debt payment, equipment and inventory purchases, construction, and purchasing existing real estate. Proceeds may not be used for distribution to principals or for payment of personal debt.

Duration The loan maturity is generally between 5 and 10 years for working capital; up to 10 years for machinery and equipment; and up to 25 years for real estate, construction, or the purchase of equipment with a useful life of 25 years. The actual maturity for each loan will be the shortest feasible term that the borrower is able to repay.

Special features A key feature of this pilot program is the use of nonprofit and for-profit organizations as intermediaries to assist prospective minority borrowers in developing a viable loan application package. That application can be submitted directly to the SBA for expedited consideration of a loan prequalification.

On approval, the intermediary can assist the applicant in locating a competitive lender. Intermediaries may charge a reasonable fee for loan packaging.

Number awarded Varies each year.

Deadline Loan applications may be submitted at any time.

[769]
MINORITY TEACHERS OF ILLINOIS SCHOLARSHIP PROGRAM

Illinois Student Assistance Commission
Attn: Scholarship and Grant Services
1755 Lake Cook Road
Deerfield, IL 60015-5209
(708) 948-8550
(800) 899-ISAC (within IL, IA, IN, MO, and WI)

Purpose To provide funding to minority students in Illinois who plan to become teachers at the preschool, elementary, or secondary level.

Eligibility Applicants must be Illinois residents, U.S. citizens or eligible noncitizens, members of a minority group (African American, Hispanic American, Asian American, or Native American), and high school graduates or holders of a General Educational Development (GED) certificate. They must be enrolled in college full time at the sophomore level or above, have at least a 2.5 grade point average, not be in default on any student loan, and be enrolled or accepted for enrollment in a teacher education program.

Financial data Up to $5,000 per year.

Duration 1 year.

Special features This is a scholarship/loan program. Recipients agree to teach full time 1 year for each year of support received. The teaching agreement may be fulfilled at a public, private, or parochial preschool, elementary school, or secondary school in Illinois; at least 30 percent of the student body at those schools must be minority.

Limitations If the teaching commitment is not fulfilled, the scholarship converts to a loan, and the student must repay the entire amount plus interest.

Number awarded Varies each year.

Deadline July of each year.

[770]
MISSOURI MINORITY TEACHER EDUCATION SCHOLARSHIP PROGRAM

Missouri Department of Elementary and Secondary
   Education
P.O. Box 480
Jefferson City, MO 65102-0480
(573) 751-1668

Purpose To provide financial assistance to minority high school graduates and college students in Missouri who are interested in preparing for a teaching career in mathematics or science.

Eligibility Applicants for this program must 1) be Missouri residents; 2) be African American, Asian American, Hispanic American, or Native American; 3) be high school graduates, college students, or individuals with a baccalaureate degree returning to an approved mathematics or science teacher education program; 4) rank in the top 25 percent of their high school class, or score at or above the 75th percentile on the ACT or SAT examination, or have 30 college hours with a grade point average of 3.0 or better; 5) enroll as full-time students in an approved mathematics or science teacher education program in Missouri; and 6) commit to teach mathematics or science in Missouri public schools for 5 years.

Financial data The stipend is $3,000 per year. This is a scholarship/loan program. The amount of the recipient's potential obligation is reduced by 20 percent for each year of teaching science or mathematics in the state. Recipients who fail to honor part or all of the 5-year teaching requirement must repay the balance.

Duration Up to 4 years.

Number awarded Varies each year.

[771]
MISSOURI TEACHER EDUCATION SCHOLARSHIP PROGRAM

Missouri Department of Elementary and Secondary
  Education
P.O. Box 480
Jefferson City, MO 65102-0480
(573) 751-1668

Purpose To provide financial assistance to high school seniors, high school graduates, and college students in Missouri who are interested in preparing for a teaching career.

Eligibility This program is open to graduating high school seniors, high school graduates, and lower-division college students who are Missouri residents, ranked in the top 15 percent of their high school class or scored in the top 15 percent on a national standardized test, and are entering or already enrolled at a teacher education program in a 4-year college or university in Missouri. Selection is based on class rank, ACT/SAT scores, school and community activities, leisure activities, leadership ability, employment experiences, essays, and recommendations. Special consideration is given to applicants who desire to teach in Missouri's urban areas or in certain "critical need" fields. Males, minorities, and nontraditional students are encouraged to apply. Each year, 15 percent of the scholarships are reserved for minority students.

Financial data The stipend is $2,000 (half of the award is paid by the state of Missouri and the other half is paid by the participating college or university). This is a scholarship/loan program. The amount of the recipient's potential obligation is reduced by 20 percent for each year of teaching in the state. Recipients who fail to honor part or all of the 5-year teaching requirement must repay the balance.

Duration 1 year; nonrenewable.

Number awarded Varies; generally, at least 200 each year.

Deadline February of each year.

[772]
NATIONAL HEALTH SERVICE CORPS SCHOLARSHIP PROGRAM

Health Resources and Services Administration
Attn: Bureau of Primary Health Care
National Health Service Corps Program
2070 Chain Bridge Road, Suite 450
Vienna, VA 22182-2536
(703) 821-8955   (800) 221-9393

Purpose To provide financial assistance to primary health care scholars willing to serve in a federally designated health professional shortage area on completion of training.

Eligibility The following requirements must be met by applicants to be eligible for these awards: U.S. citizenship or perma-

nent residency, full-time enrollment in an accredited school or program in the United States or its possessions, and a demonstrated potential for providing primary health care services, including allopathic and osteopathic medicine (with a specialty in family medicine, general pediatrics, general internal medicine, or obstetrics/gynecology), family nurse practitioner, nurse midwife, and physician assistant (either baccalaureate or master's level). Preference is given to applicants who have participated in the federal Scholarship Program for Students of Exceptional Financial Need at their medical schools, come from a disadvantaged background, and have characteristics that increase the probability they will continue to practice in a health professional shortage area (HPSA) after they have completed their service obligation.

Financial data The stipend is $817 per month. In addition, the program makes a direct payment to each participant's school for tuition and fees and a single additional payment toward other reasonable educational expenses (e.g., books, clinical supplies, laboratory expenses, uniforms, graduation fees, and clinical rotational travel). Participants incur 1 year of obligated service in the National Health Service Corps for each full or partial year of support provided under this program. The minimum service obligation is 2 years.

Duration 1 year; may be renewed for up to 3 additional years.

Special features This scholarship was first offered in 1978/9. It is the successor to the Public Health and National Health Service Corps Scholarship Training Program, which was in effect from 1973/4 to 1977/8.

Limitations Participants are obligated to provide full-time clinical primary health care services to populations in federally-designated, high-priority HPSAs (these include the Indian Health Service or medical facilities of the Federal Bureau of Prisons).

Number awarded Varies each year, depending upon the funding available. In a recent year, 220 scholarships were awarded.

Deadline March of each year.

[773]
NATIONAL RESEARCH SERVICE AWARD INDIVIDUAL FELLOWSHIPS IN HEALTH SERVICES RESEARCH

Agency for Health Care Policy and Research
Attn: NRSA Project Officer
Executive Office Center, Suite 501
2101 East Jefferson Street
Rockville, MD 20852
(301) 594-1362

Purpose To provide funding for academic training and supervised experience in applying quantitative research methods to the systematic analysis and evaluation of health services.

Eligibility Applicants must be U.S. citizens or permanent residents who have received a Ph.D., M.D., D.O., D.D.S., D.V.M., or equivalent doctoral degree from an accredited domestic or foreign institution. They must be proposing to pursue postdoctoral training at an appropriate institution under the guidance of a sponsor who is an established investigator active in health services research. The proposed training should provide a rigorous conceptual and methodological foundation for investigating such topics as determinants of successful health care market reform, including incentives for selection of efficient health plans by health care purchasers and effective management by health care providers; cost-effectiveness and cost-benefit analysis, including allocation of health care resources and its relationship to health status; analysis of service delivery, resource use, and costs of care for persons with HIV-related illnesses; evaluation of managed care and other approaches to organizing, financing, and reimbursing health care services; rural health issues, including primary care access, service delivery, technology diffusion, and supply of health professionals; and medical malpractice and liability. Applications are especially encouraged from women, minorities, and individuals with disabilities.

Financial data The award provides an annual stipend based on the number of years of postdoctoral experience, ranging from $19,608 for less than 1 year to $32,300 for 7 or more years. The initial 12 months of National Research Service Award postdoctoral support carries a service payback requirement, which can be fulfilled by continued training under the award or by engaging in other health-related research training, health-related research, or health-related teaching. Fellows who fail to fulfill the payback requirement of 1 month of acceptable service for each month of the initial 12 months of support received must repay all funds received with interest.

Duration Up to 3 years.

Number awarded Varies each year.

Deadline April, August, or December of each year.

[774]
NATIONAL RESEARCH SERVICE AWARD INSTITUTIONAL RESEARCH TRAINING GRANTS

National Institutes of Health
Attn: Office of Extramural Research
Extramural Outreach and Information Resources Office
6701 Rockledge Drive, Room 6207
MSC 7910
Bethesda, MD 20892-7910
(301) 435-0714   Fax: (301) 480-8443
E-mail: asknih@odrockm1.od.nih.gov

Purpose To provide funding to institutions to develop or enhance research training opportunities for individuals, selected by the institution, who are training for careers in specified areas of biomedical and behavioral research.

Eligibility This program is open to domestic, nonprofit, private or public institutions with the staff and facilities required for the proposed program of research training. The research training program director at the institution is responsible for the selection and appointment of trainees, who may be in 1 of 3 categories: 1) predoctoral, for trainees who have received a baccalaureate degree and are training at the postbaccalaureate level in a program leading to the Ph.D. in areas of basic biomedical and behavioral sciences or in an equivalent research doctoral degree program; 2) postdoctoral, for trainees who have received a Ph.D., M.D., or comparable doctoral degree and wish to pursue specialized training to meet national research priorities in the biomedical and behavioral sciences; or 3) short-term health professional, for health professional students who have completed at least 1 quarter in a program leading to a clinical doctorate and wish to engage in biomedical and/or behavioral research during the summer or other "off-quarter" periods. All candidates must be U.S. citizens or permanent citizens. Institutions must give particular attention to recruiting individuals from minority groups that are underrepresented nationally in biomedical and behavioral research (African Americans, Hispanics, Native Americans, Alaskan Natives, and Pacific Islanders).

Financial data For predoctoral trainees, the annual stipend is $10,008; health professional trainees receive the same stipend, prorated at $834 per month. For postdoctoral trainees, the award

provides an annual stipend based on the number of years of postdoctoral experience, ranging from $19,608 for less than 1 year to $32,300 for 7 or more years. Institutions may apply for training costs (such as staff salaries, consultant costs, equipment, research supplies, and staff travel) of up to $1,500 per year per predoctoral trainee or $2,500 per year per postdoctoral trainee; up to $125 per month to offset the cost of tuition, fees, travel, supplies, and other expenses for each short-term health professional research training position; and an indirect cost allowance of 8 percent of total allowable direct costs or actual indirect costs, whichever is less.

Duration Awards may be made for up to 5 years and are renewable. Predoctoral and postdoctoral trainee appointments are normally made in 12-month increments with support for additional years dependent on satisfactory progress and the continued availability of funds. Health professional traineeships are for 2 to 3 months.

Special features This award is offered by all funding Institutes and Centers of the National Institutes of Health (NIH) as part of the National Research Service Award (NRSA) program, originally established in 1974. The NIH designates this program as the T32 Awards.

Limitations The initial 12 months of NRSA postdoctoral support carries a service payback requirement, which can be fulfilled by continued training under the award or by engaging in other health-related research training, health-related research, or health-related teaching. Fellows who fail to fulfill the payback requirement of 1 month of acceptable service for each month of the initial 12 months of support received must repay all funds received with interest.

Number awarded Varies each year.

Deadline January, May, and September of each year; some Institutes accept applications only once each year; contact the address above for further information.

[775]
NATIONAL RESEARCH SERVICE AWARD SENIOR FELLOWSHIPS

National Institutes of Health
Attn: Office of Extramural Research
Extramural Outreach and Information Resources Office
6701 Rockledge Drive, Room 6207
MSC 7910
Bethesda, MD 20892-7910
(301) 435-0714   Fax: (301) 480-8443
E-mail: asknih@odrockm1.od.nih.gov

Purpose To provide mentored research training for experienced scientists who wish to make major changes in the direction of their research careers.

Eligibility Applications for this program may be submitted on behalf of the candidates by a sponsoring institution which may be private (profit or nonprofit) or public, including a federal laboratory. Individuals requesting foreign-site training must justify the particular suitability of the foreign site, based on the nature of the facilities and/or training opportunity, rather than a domestic institution. Only in cases where there are clear scientific advantages will foreign training be supported. Candidates must have received a Ph.D., D.D.S., D.M.D., or equivalent degree from an accredited domestic or foreign institution and must have had at least 7 subsequent years of relevant research experience. Applications from minorities and women are particularly encouraged.

Financial data Salaries are determined individually, based on the salary or remuneration which the individual would have received from the home institution, but may not exceed $32,300 per year. Institutional allowances for tuition, fees, individual health insurance, research supplies, equipment, travel to scientific meetings, and related items are up to $3,000 for nonfederal sponsoring institutions and $2,000 for federal laboratories. The initial 12 months of postdoctoral support carries a service payback requirement, which can be fulfilled by continued training under the award or by engaging in other health-related research training, health-related research, or health-related teaching. Fellows who fail to fulfill the payback requirement of 1 month of acceptable service for each month of the initial 12 months of support received must repay all funds received with interest.

Duration 5 years; nonrenewable.

Special features The National Institutes of Health (NIH) designates this program as the F33 Awards. It is offered by 8 components of the NIH: the National Institute on Aging, the National Institute on Alcohol Abuse and Alcoholism, the National Institute of Allergy and Infectious Diseases, the National Institute of Arthritis and Musculoskeletal and Skin Diseases, the National Cancer Institute, the National Institute of Child Health and Human Development, the National Institute on Deafness and Other Communication Disorders, and the National Institute of Dental Research.

Number awarded Varies each year.

Deadline April, August, and December of each year.

[776]
NATIONAL RESEARCH SERVICE AWARDS FOR INDIVIDUAL POSTDOCTORAL FELLOWS

National Institutes of Health
Attn: Office of Extramural Research
Extramural Outreach and Information Resources Office
6701 Rockledge Drive, Room 6207
MSC 7910
Bethesda, MD 20892-7910
(301) 435-0714   Fax: (301) 480-8443
E-mail: asknih@odrockm1.od.nih.gov

Purpose To provide funding for postdoctoral biomedical or behavioral research training.

Eligibility Applicants must 1) be U.S. citizens or permanent residents; 2) have received a Ph.D., M.D., D.O., D.D.S., D.V.M., or equivalent doctoral degree from an accredited domestic or foreign institution; 3) be interested in conducting biomedical or behavioral research; and 4) have arranged for appointment to an appropriate institution and acceptance by a sponsor who will supervise the training and research experience. The institution may be private (nonprofit or for-profit) or public, including a federal laboratory. If a foreign institution is selected as the research training site, applicants must explain the reasons for the choice. Applications are especially encouraged from women, minorities, individuals with disabilities, and clinicians who wish to become researchers.

Financial data The award provides an annual stipend based on the number of years of postdoctoral experience, ranging from $19,608 for less than 1 year to $32,300 for 7 or more years. For fellows sponsored by domestic non-federal institutions, the stipend is paid through the sponsoring institution; for fellows sponsored by federal or foreign institutions, the monthly stipend is paid directly to the fellow. Institutions also receive an allowance to help defray such awardee expenses as tuition and fees, self-only health insurance, research supplies, equipment, travel to sci-

entific meetings, and related items; the allowance is $3,000 per 12-month period for non-federal nonprofit institutions and $1,000 per 12-month period for federal laboratories and for-profit institutions. Awards for training at a foreign site include economy or coach round-trip airfare for the fellow only; no allowance is provided for dependents. The initial 12 months of National Research Service Award postdoctoral support carries a service payback requirement, which can be fulfilled by continued training under the award or by engaging in other health-related research training, health-related research, or health-related teaching. Fellows who fail to fulfill the payback requirement of 1 month of acceptable service for each month of the initial 12 months of support received must repay all funds received with interest.

Duration Up to 3 years.

Special features This award is offered by all funding Institutes and Centers of the National Institutes of Health (NIH) as part of the National Research Service Award (NRSA) program, originally established in 1974. The NIH designates this program as the F32 Awards.

Number awarded Varies; in a recent year, 793 awards were made through this program.

Deadline April, August, or December of each year.

[777]
NORTH CAROLINA TEACHING FELLOWS PROGRAM

North Carolina Teaching Fellows Commission
Koger Center, Cumberland Building
3739 National Drive, Suite 210
Raleigh, NC 27612
(919) 781-6833   Fax: (919) 781-6527

Purpose To provide financial assistance to high school seniors and graduates in North Carolina who wish to prepare for a career in teaching.

Eligibility Applicants must be North Carolina residents, interested in preparing for a career as a teacher, and accepted for enrollment at 1 of the following schools in North Carolina: Appalachian State University, East Carolina University, Elon College, Meredith College, North Carolina A&T University, University of North Carolina at Asheville, North Carolina Central University, North Carolina State University, Pembroke State University, University of North Carolina at Chapel Hill, University of North Carolina at Charlotte, University of North Carolina at Greensboro, University of North Carolina at Wilmington, or Western Carolina University. Selection is based on academic record, SAT scores, class standing, writing ability, community service, extracurricular activities, and recommendations. A particular goal of the program is to recruit and retain greater numbers of male and minority teacher education candidates in North Carolina.

Financial data The stipend is $5,000. This is a scholarship/loan program; 1 year of work as a teacher in North Carolina cancels 1 year of support under this program. Recipients who fail to honor the work obligation must repay the balance at 10 percent interest.

Duration 1 year; renewable for up to 3 additional years.

Number awarded Up to 400 each year.

[778]
OKLAHOMA FUTURE TEACHERS SCHOLARSHIP PROGRAM

Oklahoma State Regents for Higher Education
500 Education Building
State Capitol Complex
Oklahoma City, OK 73105-4503
(405) 524-9153   Fax: (405) 524-9230

Purpose To provide financial assistance to Oklahoma residents who are interested in teaching (particularly in teacher shortage fields) in Oklahoma.

Eligibility Candidates for this program are nominated by institutions of higher education in Oklahoma. Nominees must be high school seniors, high school graduates, or currently-enrolled undergraduate or graduate students. They must 1) rank in the top 15 percent of their high school graduating class; 2) place at least at the 85th percentile on the ACT or SAT either for their class as a whole or for a subdivision of Black Non-Hispanic, Hispanic, Native American, or Asian; 3) have been admitted into a professional education program at an accredited Oklahoma institution of higher education; or 4) have achieved an undergraduate record of outstanding success as defined by the institution. Recipients must agree to teach in critical shortage areas in the state upon graduation. These areas change periodically but in the past have included (for all applicants) special education, science, and foreign languages; (for graduate students) counseling, library/media specialist, and speech and language pathology; and (for renewal applicants) early childhood education and mathematics.

Financial data Full-time students receive up to $1,500 per year if they have completed 60 hours or more and up to $1,000 if they have completed fewer than 60 hours; part-time students receive up to $750 per year if they have completed 60 hours or more and up to $500 per year if they have completed fewer than 60 hours. Funds are paid directly to the institution on the student's behalf. This is a scholarship/loan program; recipients must agree to teach in Oklahoma public schools for 3 years following graduation and licensure.

Duration 1 year; may be renewable for up to 3 additional years as long as the recipient maintains a grade point average of at least 2.5.

Number awarded 100 or more each year.

Deadline Participating institutions set their own deadline dates, but must forward applications and prioritized nominations to the State Regents by June of each year.

[779]
OKLAHOMA MINORITY DOCTORAL STUDY GRANT PROGRAM

Oklahoma State Regents for Higher Education
500 Education Building
State Capitol Complex
Oklahoma City, OK 73105-4503
(405) 524-9143   Fax: (405) 524-9230

Purpose To increase the number of faculty and administrative staff from minority groups in the Oklahoma State System of Higher Education.

Eligibility This program is open to United States citizens who are of a disproportionately underrepresented minority group and are enrolled or accepted for enrollment as doctoral students at an Oklahoma institution of higher education. Candidates must be nominated by the dean of their instituiton.

Financial data The maximum stipend is $6,000 each year, paid directly to the student. This is a scholarship/loan program; recipients must agree to teach in a state system institution for a minimum of 1 year for each year of assistance received.

Duration 1 year; renewable.

Number awarded Varies each year.

Deadline May of each year.

[780]
OLD DOMINION UNIVERSITY PRESIDENT'S GRADUATE FELLOWSHIP

Old Dominion University
Attn: Office of Research, Economic Development and Graduate Studies
New Administration Building, Room 210
Norfolk, VA 23529-0013
(804) 683-3460   Fax: (804) 683-3004

Purpose To provide financial support to minorities and women working toward their terminal degree who are willing to serve in a tenure-track faculty position at Old Dominion University.

Eligibility This program is open to women and minorities who show strong potential for success in advanced graduate study and whose academic disciplines correspond to the programmatic needs of Old Dominion University. Candidates may be undergraduate or master's-level students. They must be enrolled in or accepted into a graduate program leading to a terminal degree (generally at a university other than Old Dominion). All applicants must be U.S. citizens. Fellowships are awarded on the basis of the individual's potential to contribute to their chosen discipline as a faculty member at Old Dominion.

Financial data Participants are given a non-tenure track faculty appointment with the appropriate academic department at Old Dominion University. Financial support will be negotiated but may include not only tuition and fees but also a stipend of up to one half of the non-tenured faculty salary, health coverage, and travel and research assistance. Every recipient is required to sign a program agreement with Old Dominion University which contains, among other items, an interest-bearing promissory note which will be cancelled upon successful completion of 3 years of employment with the University in a tenure-track faculty position. If a fellow fails to complete the degree within the program terms, or serves the University for fewer than 3 years because of unsatisfactory performance resulting in either involuntary or voluntary termination of employment, the portion of the note and interest which remains unfilled must be repaid.

Duration Up to 5 years.

Special features Upon completion of the terminal degree, fellows assume a tenure-track position in the designated department at Old Dominion University.

Deadline February of each year.

[781]
OREGON STATE BAR EXAM GRANTS

Oregon State Bar
Attn: Affirmative Action Program
5200 SW Meadows Road
P.O. Box 1689
Lake Oswego, OR 97035-0889
(503) 620-0222   (800) 452-8260 (within OR)
Fax: (503) 684-1366

Purpose To provide grants to minorities in Oregon who are preparing to take the state law bar examination.

Eligibility Applicants must be minorities who intend to practice in Oregon after the bar examination, are scheduled to take the next exam, and are in financial need (determined by subtracting the applicant's and spouse's available assets and the applicant's and spouse's income from the sum of their debts, current monthly expenses, and bar exam-related expenses for the 2 months preceding the bar exam).

Financial data The maximum amount of any grant will not exceed the combined costs of the bar exam application fee and the bar exam preparation course. The actual amount of the grant is determined by the amount of funds remaining in the budget for Bar Exam Grants, the number of other applicants, the applicant's financial need as compared to the need of other applicants, and the extent to which the financial need and other information on the application is complete, credible, and consistent. If the recipient withdraws from the bar exam, repayment in full is required within 1 month from the date of withdrawal.

Duration This is a 1-time grant.

Number awarded Varies each year.

[782]
SBA LOANS TO PARTICIPANTS IN THE 8(A) PROGRAM

Small Business Administration
Attn: Office of Minority Enterprise Development
409 Third Street, S.W.
Washington, DC 20416
(800) 8-ASK-SBA   Fax: (202) 205-7064
TDD: (202) 205-7333

Purpose To provide business development assistance to minority- and other disadvantaged-owned firms through direct and guaranteed loans.

Eligibility To be eligible for 8(a) program participation, a small business concern must be at least 51 percent owned, controlled, and operated by 1 or more socially or economically disadvantaged persons or by an economically disadvantaged Indian tribe, including an Alaska native corporation or an economically disadvantaged Hawaiian organization. "Socially disadvantaged individuals" are those who have been subjected to racial or ethnic prejudice or cultural bias because of their identification as members of certain groups. "Economically disadvantaged individuals" are those socially disadvantaged individuals whose ability to compete in the free enterprise system has been impaired due to diminished capital and credit opportunities. Black Americans, Native Americans, Hispanic Americans, Asian Pacific Americans, and Subcontinent Asian Americans have been officially designated socially disadvantaged. Members of other groups must show proof of social disadvantage. Economic disadvantage must be established for all applicants. The Small Business Administration (SBA) determines eligibility on a case-by-case basis.

Financial data The ceiling on direct loans from the SBA is $750,000. The SBA guarantees up to 80 percent of loans of $100,000 and less, and up to 75 percent of loans above $100,000, up to a maximum guaranty of $750,000. On guaranteed loans, the maximum interest rate is the prime rate plus 2.25 percent if the maturity is less than 7 years or prime plus 2.75 percent if the maturity is 7 years or more. For guaranteed loans of less than $25,000, the maximum interest rates are prime plus 4.25 and prime plus 4.75, respectively; for loans between $25,000 and $50,000, maximum rates must not exceed 3.25 percent and 3.75 percent, respectively. Interest rates on direct loans are 3 percent per year.

Duration Generally, maximum loan maturities are 25 years for real estate and equipment and 7 years for working capital.

Limitations Loans are not made for debt refinancing or to businesses engaged in speculation or investment in rental real estate.

Number awarded Varies each year.

Deadline Applications may be submitted at any time.

[783]
SBA MICROLOAN PROGRAM

Small Business Administration
Attn: Office of Women's Business Ownership
409 Third Street, S..W.
Washington, DC 20416
(800) 8-ASK-SBA   (202) 205-6673
Fax: (202) 205-7064   TDD: (202) 205-7333

Purpose To assist women, low income individuals, minority entrepreneurs, and other small businesses which need small amounts of financial assistance.

Eligibility The Small Business Administration (SBA) has made funds available to nonprofit organizations for the purpose of lending to small businesses that need small loans. Generally, the firm's average annual sales for the preceding 3 fiscal years must be less than $5 million and the average number of employees for the preceding 12 months must be less than 100 workers. Types of businesses not eligible for SBA loans are those engaged in speculation or investment in real estate or those organized as nonprofit. Money borrowed under this program can be used for the purchase of machinery and equipment, furniture and fixtures, inventory, supplies, and working capital. Applicants must demonstrate good character, enough management expertise and commitment for a successful operation, and show that there is a reasonable assurance that the loan will be repaid.

Financial data Loans range from less than $100 to a maximum of $25,000, and average about $10,000. The interest rate cannot be higher than 4 percent over the New York prime rate.

Duration Loan maturities must be as short as possible, but no longer than 6 years, depending on the earnings of the business.

Limitations Loans may not be used to pay existing debt.

Number awarded Varies each year.

Deadline Loan applications may be submitted at any time.

[784]
TENNESSEE MINORITY TEACHING FELLOWS PROGRAM

Tennessee Student Assistance Corporation
Parkway Towers
404 James Robertson Parkway, Suite 1950
Nashville, TN 37243-0820
(615) 741-1346   (800) 342-1663 (within TN)

Purpose To encourage talented minority Tennesseans to enter the teaching field.

Eligibility This program is open to minority residents of Tennessee who are entering college freshmen at a college in Tennessee. Applicants must be U.S. citizens with a 2.5 high school cumulative grade point average and a score of 18 on the ACT test, 850 on the SAT, or a ranking in the top 25 percent of their high school graduating class.

Financial data The stipend is $5,000 per year.

Duration 1 year; may be renewed for up to 3 additional years.

Limitations This is a scholarship/loan program; recipients incur an obligation to teach at the K-12 level in a Tennessee public school 1 year for each year the award is received.

Number awarded 19 each year.

Deadline May of each year.

[785]
UNC CAPITAL, LP

UNC Partners
711 Atlantic Avenue, 3rd Floor
Boston, MA 02111-2830
(617) 482-7070   Fax: (617) 482-9720

Purpose To provide financial assistance to businesses controlled by people of color.

Eligibility Businesses in which entrepreneurs of color (African Americans, Hispanics, Asian Americans, and Native Americans) exercise substantial ownership are eligible to apply. Investment is focused on the following industries: mass media and telecommunications, health and death services, and financial services.

Financial data Loans range between $500,000 and $1,500,000 per year. These loans are made from a revolving fund that contains nearly $30 million.

Duration 1 year or longer.

Special features This is the third fund raised by this organization; the first 2 were UNC Ventures, Inc., begun in 1971, and UNC Ventures II, LP, in 1982.

Limitations In exchange for the loan, this organization takes an equity position in the minority-controlled firm.

Number awarded Varies each year.

Deadline Applications may be submitted at any time.

[786]
UNDERGRADUATE SCHOLARSHIP PROGRAM FOR INDIVIDUALS FROM DISADVANTAGED BACKGROUNDS

National Institutes of Health
Attn: Loan Repayment and Scholarship Programs
Federal Building, Room 604
7550 Wisconsin Avenue MSC 9015
Bethesda, MD 20892-9015
(800) 528-7689   Fax: (301) 496-0840
TTY: (888) 352-3001   E-mail: kk10b@nih.gov

Purpose To provide financial assistance for undergraduate education in the life sciences to students from disadvantaged backgrounds.

Eligibility Eligible are U.S. citizens, nationals, and permanent residents who are enrolled or accepted for enrollment as full-time students at qualified accredited institutions of higher education and planning to pursue a career in biomedical research. Applicants must meet a definition of disadvantaged, that they either 1) come from an environment that inhibited (but did not prevent) them from obtaining the knowledge, skills, and ability required to enroll in an undergraduate institution; or 2) come from a family with an annual income below $10,200 for a 1-person family, ranging to below $26,700 for families of 6 or more. First priority is given to applicants who have demonstrated good academic performance, state a career goal of pursuing biomedical/biobehavioral research, and have characteristics which support the likelihood they will complete their service obligations. Second priority is given to individuals who are underrepresented in biomedical/biobehavioral research including women, individuals from minority groups, or persons with disabilities.

Financial data Stipends are available up to $20,000 per year, to be used for tuition, educational expenses such as books and lab fees, and qualified living expenses while attending a college or university. Recipients incur a service obligation to work as an employee of the National Institutes of Health (NIH) in Bethesda, Maryland for 10 consecutive weeks (during the summer) during the sponsored year and, upon graduation, for 12 months for each academic year of scholarship support. The NIH 12-month employment obligation may be deferred during enrollment in graduate or medical school.

Duration 1 year; may be renewed for up to 3 additional years.

Number awarded 15 each year.

[787]
VA HOME LOANS FOR NATIVE AMERICANS

Department of Veterans Affairs
810 Vermont Avenue, N.W.
Washington, DC 20420
(202) 418-4343   (800) 827-1000

Purpose To provide home loans to Native American veterans.

Eligibility Eligible Native American veterans may apply for these direct home loans if they wish to purchase, construct, or improve a home on Native American trust land.

Financial data Loans are limited to the cost of the home or $80,000, whichever is less. A funding fee is payable to VA; the fee is 1.25 percent for veterans, 2 percent for veterans who qualify based on service in the reserves or national guard that was not active duty, but waived for veterans receiving compensation for service-connected disability. The funding fee may be paid in cash or included in the loan; other closing costs may be included in the loan.

Number awarded Varies each year.
Deadline Applications may be submitted at any time.

Grants

American Indians ●
Native Alaskans ●
Native Pacific Islanders ●
Native Americans in General ●

Described here are 626 programs that provide funds to Native Americans for innovative efforts, travel, projects, creative activities, or research on any level (from undergraduate to postdoctorate and professional). In a number of cases, proposals may be submitted by institutions or organizations only; in others, individual Native Americans may submit proposals directly. Of the programs listed here, 43 are open specifically to American Indians, 19 to Native Alaskans, 9 to Native Pacific Islanders, and 555 to members of any of these specific groups (Native Americans in General). If you are looking for a particular program and don't find it in this section, be sure to check the Program Title Index to see if it is covered elsewhere in the directory.

American Indians

[788]
ADULT EDUCATION GRANTS FOR INDIAN EDUCATION

Department of Education
Attn: Office of Elementary and Secondary Education
Office of Indian Education
Portals Building, Room 4300
600 Independence Avenue, S.W.
Washington, DC 20202-6335
(202) 260-3774   (800) 501-5795

Purpose To provide financial support for the development and implementation of programs to improve educational opportunities for adult Indians.

Eligibility Only state and local educational agencies, Indian tribes, Indian institutions, and Indian organizations may apply; no funds are available for individuals. Funds may be used to 1) support planning, pilot, and demonstration projects designed to test and demonstrate the effectiveness or programs for improving employment and educational opportunities for Indian adults; or 2) assist in the establishment and operation of programs designed to stimulate basic literacy opportunities for all nonliterate Indian adults to qualify for a secondary school diploma, or its recognized equivalent, in the shortest period of time.

Financial data Grants range from $65,000 to $225,000; the average award is approximately $175,000. The total annual appropriation for this program is approximately $1.7 million.

Duration Up to 5 years.

Number awarded Varies; approximately 10 each year.

Deadline August of each year.

[789]
AMERICAN INDIAN MUSEUM STUDIES PROGRAM

Smithsonian Institution
Attn: Center for Museum Studies
Arts and Industries Building, Suite 2235
MRC 427
Washington, DC 20560
(202) 357-3101   Fax: (202) 357-3346
E-mail: ompem004@sivm.si.edu

Purpose To promote and assist Native Americans in the continuation and interpretation of tribal cultures as they define them.

Eligibility Native Americans working in tribal museums and American Indian cultural centers are eligible to participate in workshops and seminars conducted as part of this program.

Financial data Participants in the workshops and seminars receive a tuition waiver for the course and a scholarship to help defray travel and subsistence expenses.

Duration Most seminars last 3 to 5 days.

Special features This program also recruits American Indians and Alaska Natives who are currently enrolled in a higher education program or who are currently employed in a field related to museum work or cultural programming to participate in the Museum Intern Partnership Program of the Smithsonian's Center for Museum Studies. It also produces publications and technical assistance which provide additional resources not available else-

where for the enrichment of Native American museums and cultural centers.

Number awarded Varies each year.

Deadline The seminars and workshops, of which 4 or 5 are held each year at native communities throughout the United States and Canada, each set their own deadline dates.

[790]
AMERICAN INDIAN PROGRAM

National Museum of Natural History
Smithsonian Institution
10th Street and Constitution Avenue N.W.
NHB 112
Washington, DC 20560
(202) 357-4760   Fax: (202) 357-2208
E-mail: mnhan031@sivm.si.edu

Purpose To provide assistance for research, exhibitions, and public programming by and about Indian people.

Eligibility This program works with native individuals, communities, schools, and other cultural and educational institutions on a variety of collaborative projects. It encourages collection and archival research activities as well as exhibition and public program development. It also provides opportunities for museum training and supervised research projects in any aspect of Indian culture and history that is appropriate for the museum's holdings and staff expertise, including ethnology, archaeology, language, biological anthropology, and history. No educational requirements are imposed; prior fellows have come from age groups ranging from 16 to 82 and from all walks of life.

Financial data The amount of the award depends on the nature of the project.

Duration Project length varies.

Special features This program was established in 1986 to encourage participation of Native Americans in Smithsonian activities and to support collection research, exhibitions, and public programming as they relate to Native peoples. The program is particularly interested in collaborative projects with Indian-controlled museums, colleges, and other cultural and educational institutions, but welcomes inquiries about research, exhibitions, and other outreach activities from all interested parties.

Number awarded 3 to 5 each year.

Deadline Applications may be submitted at any time.

[791]
AMERICAN INDIAN STUDIES POSTDOCTORAL AND VISITING SCHOLARS FELLOWSHIP PROGRAM

American Indian Studies Center
Attn: Fellowship Coordinator
University of California at Los Angeles
3220 Campbell Hall
Box 951548
Los Angeles, CA 90095-1548
(310) 825-7315

Purpose To provide financial support for scholars to pursue research in Native American studies.

Eligibility Applicants must have completed a doctoral degree in Native American or related studies. UCLA faculty, students, and staff are not eligible.

Financial data Amounts vary, depending upon scholarly background and experience. In general, postdoctoral fellows receive $23,000 to $28,000 for the academic year; senior scholars' fellowship stipends are designed to supplement the sabbatical salary provided by their own institutions.

Duration 1 academic year; may be renewed.

Special features Fellows must teach or do research in the programs of the center. The award is offered in conjunction with UCLA's Institute of American Cultures.

Deadline December of each year.

[792]
AMERICAN PHILOSOPHICAL SOCIETY LIBRARY MELLON RESIDENT RESEARCH FELLOWSHIPS

American Philosophical Society
Attn: Library
105 South Fifth Street
Philadelphia, PA 19106-3386
(215) 440-3400   Fax: (215) 440-3436

Purpose To provide financial support for scholars, including doctoral candidates, who wish to conduct research at the American Philosophical Society Library.

Eligibility Eligible to apply are holders of the Ph.D. or the equivalent, Ph.D. candidates who have passed their preliminary exams, and independent scholars in any field of study relevant to the holdings of the American Philosophical Society Library. They may be foreign nationals or U.S. citizens who reside beyond a 75-mile radius of Philadelphia.

Financial data The stipend is $1,900 per month.

Duration 1 to 3 months.

Special features The library's holdings focus on the history of American science and technology and its European roots, as well as early American history and culture. Collections and subject areas include the papers of Benjamin Franklin; the American Revolution; 18th and 19th-century natural history; western scientific expeditions and travel including the journals of Lewis and Clark; polar exploration; American Indian languages; anthropology including the papers of Franz Boas; the papers of Charles Darwin and his forerunners, colleagues, critics, and successors; 20th-century medical research; and the history of physics, biophysics, biochemistry, physiology, genetics, eugenics, and evolution. These fellowships are funded by the Andrew W. Mellon Foundation.

Limitations Fellows are expected to be in residence in Philadelphia for at least 4 consecutive weeks during the period of their award.

Number awarded Varies each year.

Deadline February of each year.

[793]
BARBARA S. MOSBACHER FELLOWSHIP

John Carter Brown Library
Brown University
P.O. Box 1894
Providence, RI 02912
(401) 863-2725   E-mail: Karen_DeMaria@Brown.edu

Purpose To support scholars interested in conducting research at the John Carter Brown Library, which is renowned for its collection of historical sources pertaining to the Americas prior to 1830.

Eligibility This fellowship is open to Americans and foreign nationals who are engaged in pre- or postdoctoral or independent research. Graduate students must have passed their preliminary or general examinations at the time of application.

Financial data The stipend is $1,000 per month.

Duration From 2 to 4 months.

Special features Among the emphases of the library's holdings are works dealing with Native Americans in North and South America, colonial architecture books, economic history, maritime history, and works on the adaptation of religion and religious institutions to the New World.

Limitations Fellows are expected to be in regular residence at the library and to participate in the intellectual life of Brown University for the duration of the program.

Number awarded 1 each year.

Deadline January of each year.

[794]
BROOKHAVEN RESEARCH FELLOWSHIP IN PHYSICS

Brookhaven National Laboratory
Attn: Physics Department
Building 510A
Upton, NY 11973-5000
(516) 344-4063   E-mail: valli@bnl.gov

Purpose To increase the participation of underrepresented groups in the physics program at Brookhaven National Laboratory (BNL).

Eligibility This program is open to U.S. citizens who have recently completed (or will complete before taking up the fellowship) a Ph.D. in the 3 major areas represented in the physics department at BNL: high energy physics, nuclear physics, and condensed matter physics. Applicants must be members of groups underrepresented in physics—persons with disabilities, women, or American Indian, Black, or Hispanic ethnic groups.

Financial data The program provides a competitive salary and benefits package as well as an allowance for moving expenses and transportation for the fellow and family members. Short-term on-site housing is available.

Duration 2 years.

Special features The BNL facilities available to the fellow include the alternating gradient synchrotron, the high flux beam reactor, and the national synchrotron light source.

Deadline January of each year.

[795]
CHARLES H. WATTS MEMORIAL FELLOWSHIP

John Carter Brown Library
Brown University
P.O. Box 1894
Providence, RI 02912
(401) 863-2725   E-mail: Karen_DeMaria@Brown.edu

Purpose To support scholars interested in conducting research at the John Carter Brown Library, which is renowned for its collection of historical sources pertaining to the Americas prior to 1830.

Eligibility This fellowship is open to Americans and foreign nationals who are engaged in pre- or postdoctoral or independent research. Graduate students must have passed their preliminary or general examinations at the time of application.

Financial data The stipend is $1,000 per month.

Duration From 2 to 4 months.

Special features Among the emphases of the library's holdings are works dealing with Native Americans in North and South

America, colonial architecture books, economic history, maritime history, and works on the adaptation of religion and religious institutions to the New World.

Limitations Fellows are expected to be in regular residence at the library and to participate in the intellectual life of Brown University for the duration of the program.

Number awarded 1 each year.

Deadline January of each year.

[796]
D'ARCY MCNICKLE CENTER SUMMER INSTITUTE FOR SECONDARY AND TRIBAL COLLEGE TEACHERS

Newberry Library
Attn: D'Arcy McNickle Center for American Indian History
60 West Walton Street
Chicago, IL 60610-3380
(312) 255-3552

Purpose To enable teachers and administrators to participate in summer seminars at the D'Arcy McNickle Center for the History of the American Indian at the Newberry Library.

Eligibility This program is open to high school teachers of English, administrators actively involved in language arts curriculum at the secondary level, and teachers of English or Indian studies at American Indian tribal colleges. Applicants must desire to participate in a seminar on Native American literature at the Newberry Library in Chicago. Selection is based on the ability of the participants to make an impact on the teaching of Native American literature, demonstrated leadership record, and teaching excellence. Preference is given to those with at least 3 years' teaching experience.

Financial data The award provides a stipend of $1,500, room and board of $1,600, and round-trip travel to Chicago.

Duration 6 weeks.

Special features Funding for this program is provided by the National Endowment for the Humanities.

Number awarded 20 each year.

Deadline February of each year.

[797]
DEMONSTRATION GRANTS FOR INDIAN CHILDREN

Department of Education
Attn: Office of Elementary and Secondary Education
Office of Indian Education
Portals Building, Room 4300
600 Independence Avenue, S.W.
Washington, DC 20202-6335
(202) 260-3774   (800) 501-5795

Purpose To fund projects to develop, test, and demonstrate the effectiveness of services and programs that improve the educational opportunities for Indian students at the preschool, elementary, and secondary levels.

Eligibility Eligible applicants are state educational agencies, local educational agencies, Indian tribes, Indian organizations, and Indian institutions. Funds may be used for activities such as innovative programs related to the educational needs of educationally deprived children; educational services that are not available to such children in sufficient quantity or quality, including remedial instruction, to raise the achievement of Indian children in 1 or more of the core academic subjects of English, mathematics, science, foreign languages, art, history, and geography; bilin-

gual and bicultural programs and projects; special health and nutrition services, and other related activities, that address the special health, social, and psychological problems of Indian children; special compensatory and other programs and projects designed to assist and encourage Indian children to enter, remain in, or reenter school, and to increase the rate of secondary school graduation; comprehensive guidance, counseling, and testing services; early childhood and kindergarten programs, including family-based preschool programs that emphasize school readiness and parental skills, and the provision of services to Indian children with disabilities; partnership projects between local educational agencies and institutions of higher education that allow secondary school students to enroll in courses at the postsecondary level to aid those students in the transition from secondary school to college; partnership projects between schools and local businesses for school-to-work transition programs designed to provide Indian youth with the knowledge and skills the youth need to make an effective transition from school to a first job in a high-skill, high-wage career; or programs designed to encourage and assist Indian students to work toward, and gain entrance into, an institution of higher education.

Financial data Nearly $1.9 million has been allocated annually to support this program. Individual grants range from $75,000 to $225,000 and average $150,000.

Duration Up to 5 years.

Number awarded Approximately 12 each year.

Deadline August of each year.

[798]
EVEN START FAMILY LITERACY PROGRAM FOR FEDERALLY RECOGNIZED INDIAN TRIBES AND TRIBAL ORGANIZATIONS

Department of Education
Attn: Office of Elementary and Secondary Education
Compensatory Education Programs
Portals Building, Room 4400
600 Independence Avenue, S.W.
Washington, DC 20202-6132
(202) 260-0991

Purpose To provide financial assistance to Indian tribes and tribal organizations to integrate early childhood education, adult literacy or adult basic education, and parenting education into a unified family literacy program.

Eligibility Federally recognized Indian tribes and tribal organizations may apply for these grants if they wish to build on existing community resources to create a new range of services that establish a unified family literacy program. The parent or parents must be eligible for participation in an adult education program and the child or children must be younger than 8 years of age.

Financial data The total annual amount available for grants is approximately $1.2 million. Grants range from $75,000 to $200,000 and average $150,000. The federal share of the total project cost may not exceed 90 percent in the first year, 80 percent in the second year, 70 percent in the third year, 60 percent in the fourth year, and 50 percent in any subsequent year.

Duration Up to 4 years; may be renewed.

Number awarded Up to 8 each year.

Deadline June of each year.

[799]

FINANCIAL ASSISTANCE FOR THE MITIGATION OF ENVIRONMENTAL IMPACTS DUE TO DEPARTMENT OF DEFENSE ACTIVITIES

Department of Health and Human Services
Attn: Administration for Children and Families
Administration for Native Americans
Hubert H. Humphrey Building, Room 348F
200 Independence Avenue, S.W.
Washington, DC 20201-0001
(202) 690-5780

Purpose To provide funding to Native American organizations for addressing environmental problems and impacts from Department of Defense (DoD) activities to Indian lands.

Eligibility Applications may be submitted by federally recognized Indian tribes; incorporated non-federally and state recognized Indian tribes; Alaska Native villages and/or nonprofit village entities; nonprofit Alaska Native Regional Corporations/Associations in Alaska with village specific projects; and other tribal or village organizations or consortia of Indian tribes. Proposed activities may include training and technical assistance to tribes, related administrative support, the gathering of information, documenting of environmental damage, and developing a system for prioritizing of mitigation on Indian lands resulting from DoD activities.

Financial data Grants range from $100,000 to $1 million; grantees must provide at least 5 percent of the total approved cost of the project.

Duration Up to 3 years.

Number awarded Approximately 25 each year; $7 million was available for this program in a recent year.

Deadline March and November of each year.

[800]

FORMULA GRANTS TO LOCAL EDUCATIONAL AGENCIES FOR INDIAN EDUCATION

Department of Education
Attn: Office of Elementary and Secondary Education
Office of Indian Education
Portals Building, Room 4300
600 Independence Avenue, S.W.
Washington, DC 20202-6335
(202) 260-1683

Purpose To provide financial assistance to local educational agencies in their efforts to reform and improve elementary and secondary school programs that serve Indian students.

Eligibility This program is open to local educational agencies, certain schools funded by the U.S. Bureau of Indian Affairs, and Indian tribes under certain conditions. Applicants must propose programs that are based on challenging state content standards and state student performance standards used for all students, and that are designed to assist Indian students to meet those standards.

Financial data Grants range from $3,000 to $1.11 million and average $40,000; the total appropriation for this program is approximately $50 million.

Duration Up to 5 years.

Number awarded Varies; approximately 1,270 each year.

Deadline August of each year.

[801]

FRANCES C. ALLEN FELLOWSHIPS

Newberry Library
Attn: D'Arcy McNickle Center for American Indian History
60 West Walton Street
Chicago, IL 60610-3380
(312) 255-3564

Purpose To provide financial assistance to Native American women who wish to use the resources of the D'Arcy McNickle Center for the History of the American Indian at the Newberry Library.

Eligibility Only women college graduates of Indian heritage may apply for the grant to work at the Newberry Library. They must be enrolled in graduate school and be able to demonstrate the capacity to accomplish scholarly research. Applicants may be working in any graduate or pre-professional area, although preference is given to the humanities and social sciences.

Financial data Varies, depending upon financial need.

Duration Varies, from 1 month to 1 year.

Special features Funds are also provided for limited periods of field research and travel to archival collections. This program was established in 1983.

Limitations Recommendations are required. At least 2 must come from academic advisors or instructors who can comment on the significance of the proposed project of an applicant and explain how it will help in the achievement of professional goals. Fellows must spend a significant portion of their time at the library.

Deadline January of each year.

[802]

GRANTS TO COMBAT VIOLENT CRIMES AGAINST WOMEN

Department of Justice
Attn: Office of Justice Programs
Violence Against Women Program Office
633 Indiana Avenue, N.W., Fourth Floor
Washington, DC 20531
(202) 307-6026   (800) 421-6770

Purpose To provide financial assistance for programs to develop and strengthen effective law enforcement and prosecution strategies and victim services in cases involving violent crimes against women.

Eligibility State governments apply for and receive grants under this program; Indian tribal governments, units of local government, and nonprofit, nongovernmental victim service programs may receive subgrants from the respective states. Funds may be used to provide personnel, training, technical assistance, evaluation, data collection, and equipment for the more widespread apprehension, prosecution, and adjudication of persons committing violent crimes against women, including sexual assault and domestic violence. Eligible activities include developing, enlarging, or strengthening victim services programs; developing or improving delivery of victim services to racial, cultural, ethnic, and language minorities; providing specialized domestic violence court advocates in courts where a significant number of protection orders are granted; and developing, enlarging, or strengthening programs addressing the needs and circumstances of Indian tribes in dealing with violent crimes against women.

Financial data In a recent year, a total of $130 million was available for grants to states under this program. For most grants, the federal contribution may be no more than 75 percent of total project cost, with the remaining 25 percent coming from other nonfederal local funds. Nonprofit, nongovernmental victim services programs funded through subgrants are exempt from that matching requirement. Indian tribes that are subgrantees of a state may meet the 25 percent matching requirement by using funds appropriated by Congress for the activities of any agency of an Indian tribal government or for the activities of the Bureau of Indian Affairs performing law enforcement functions on any Indian lands. At least 4 percent of all funds available under this program must be allocated to Indian tribal governments.

Special features This program is also known as the Services Training Officers Prosecutors (STOP) Violence against Women Formula Grant Program.

Limitations To receive funding under this program, states must demonstrate how they plan to distribute their grant funds each year; at least 25 percent must be allocated to law enforcement, 25 percent to prosecution, and 25 percent to victim services programs.

Number awarded Each state is eligible to receive funding through this program; state agencies determine how many subgrants to award within their state.

[803]
GRANTS TO INDIAN TRIBAL ORGANIZATIONS FOR SUPPORTIVE AND NUTRITIONAL SERVICES FOR OLDER INDIANS

Department of Health and Human Services
Attn: Administration on Aging
Office for American Indian, Alaskan Native, and Native
    Hawaiian Programs
Wilbur J. Cohen Federal Building, Room 4257
330 Independence Avenue, S.W.
Washington, DC 20201
(202) 619-2713

Purpose To provide financial assistance to American Indian tribal organizations for the provision of nutritional and supportive services to elderly tribal members.

Eligibility Funding is provided to an Indian tribal organization if it represents at least 50 individuals who are 60 years of age or older and demonstrates the ability to deliver supportive services, including nutritional services.

Financial data Annual funding depends on the number of Indians over age 60 represented by the tribal organization, ranging from $49,000 for 50 to 100 individuals to $125,000 for 1,501 or more individuals.

Duration 3 years.

Special features Programs must include the provision of at least 1 hot meal a day for 5 days a week. Other supportive services may include legal assistance and transportation.

Number awarded Varies each year.

Deadline December of each year.

[804]
HELEN WATSON BUCKNER MEMORIAL FELLOWSHIP

John Carter Brown Library
Brown University
P.O. Box 1894
Providence, RI 02912
(401) 863-2725   E-mail: Karen_DeMaria@Brown.edu

Purpose To support scholars interested in conducting research at the John Carter Brown Library, which is renowned for its collection of historical sources pertaining to the Americas prior to 1830.

Eligibility This fellowship is open to Americans and foreign nationals who are engaged in pre- or postdoctoral or independent research. Graduate students must have passed their preliminary or general examinations at the time of application.

Financial data The stipend is $1,000 per month.

Duration From 2 to 4 months.

Special features Among the emphases of the library's holdings are works dealing with Native Americans in North and South America, colonial architecture books, economic history, maritime history, and works on the adaptation of religion and religious institutions to the New World.

Limitations Fellows are expected to be in regular residence at the library and to participate in the intellectual life of Brown University for the duration of the program.

Number awarded 1 each year.

Deadline January of each year.

[805]
IHS LOAN REPAYMENT PROGRAM

Indian Health Service
Attn: Scholarship Program
Twinbrook Metro Plaza, Suite 100
12300 Twinbrook Parkway
Rockville, MD 20852
(301) 443-3396   Fax: (301) 443-4815

Purpose To repay the health professional educational loans of Native American or other health professionals who are willing to work for 2 continuous years serving the health needs of American Indians.

Eligibility Applicants must have a degree in a health profession and 1) be eligible for, or hold, an appointment as a commissioned officer in the Regular or Reserve Corps of the Public Health Service (PHS); 2) be eligible for selection for civilian service in the Regular or Reserve Corps of the PHS; 3) meet the professional standards for civil service employment in the Indian Health Service (IHS); or 4) be employed in an Indian health program without service obligation. Eligible applicants include health professionals in postgraduate training or in their final year of health professions school. Health professions include family medicine, internal medicine, pediatrics, geriatric medicine, obstetrics and gynecology, podiatric medicine, nursing, public health nursing, dentistry, psychiatry, osteopathy, optometry, pharmacy, psychology, public health, social work, marriage and family therapy, chiropractic medicine, environmental health and engineering, and allied health professions. Current priorities for selection are given to allopathic physicians if they are board certified/eligible in anesthesiology, emergency room medicine, general surgery, opthalmalogy, obstetrics and gynecology, orthopedic surgery, otolaryngology and otorhinolaryngology, psychiatry, and radiology; mental health professionals; and nurse practitioners, registered nurses, and certified nurse midwives. In addition, sites are given scores based on a record of frequent staff turnover, current unmatched vacancies in a health profession discipine, and projected vacancies in a health profession discipline; sites that are provided high scores receive priority over sites that have lower scores. Consistent with those priorities, preference is given to American Indians, Alaska natives, and individuals recruited through the efforts of Indian tribes or tribal or Indian organizations.

Financial data Health professionals who have outstanding, qualified educational loans (undergraduate or graduate) receive up to $30,000 of repayment of those loans for each year of service in the IHS. In addition, the program pays up to 31 percent of federal taxes directly to the Internal Revenue Service.

Duration 2 years.

Number awarded Approximately 250 each year; at least 25 percent are provided to nurses, nurse practitioners, and nurse midwives, and at least 10 percent are provided to mental health professionals.

Deadline Applications may be submitted by the Friday of the second full week of each month.

[806]
INDIAN AND NATIVE AMERICAN EMPLOYMENT AND TRAINING PROGRAM

Department of Labor
Attn: Employment and Training Administration
Office of Special Targeted Programs
200 Constitution Avenue, N.W., Room N-4641
Washington, DC 20210
(202) 219-5500   Fax: (202) 219-6338

Purpose To reduce the economic disadvantages and advance the economic and social development of Indians and others of Native American descent.

Eligibility The priority order for these grants is: 1) Indian tribes, bands, or groups (including Alaska Native entities) on federal or state reservations; 2) Native American-controlled, community-based organizations (including tribes applying for geographic areas other than their own reservations); 3) organizations (private nonprofit or units of state or local governments) having significant Native American control; and 4) non-Native American-controlled organizations (but with a Native American advisory process).

Financial data Grants range from $50,000 to more than $7 million; the average award is $1 million. Funds are to be used for institutional training, on-the-job training, work experience, youth employment programs, day care, health care, and job placement. Only a limited amount of the grant may be used to cover administrative costs.

Duration 2 years; may be renewed on an annual basis.

Number awarded Approximately 200 new and recurring grants each year.

[807]
INDIAN CHILD WELFARE ACT GRANTS FOR OFF-RESERVATION INDIAN ORGANIZATIONS

Bureau of Indian Affairs
Attn: Office of Tribal Services
Division of Social Services
1849 C Street, N.W.
MS 4603-MIB
Washington, DC 20240
(202) 208-2721

Purpose To provide financial support to off-reservation Indian organizations for establishing and operating child and family service programs.

Eligibility This program is open to Indian organizations that are located off any reservation and propose to provide child and family services to prevent the breakup of Indian families and ensure that the permanent removal of an Indian child from the custody of his/her Indian parent or custodian is a last resort. Programs may include, but are not limited to, 1) a system for regulating, maintaining, and supporting Indian foster and adoptive homes, including a subsidy program under which Indian adoptive children may be provided support comparable to that for which they would be eligible as Indian foster children; 2) the operation and maintenance of facilities and services for the counseling and treatment of Indian families and Indian foster and adoptive children; 3) family assistance such as homemaker services and home counselors, protective day care and after school care, employment support services, recreational activities, and respite care; or 4) guidance, legal representation, and advice to Indian families involved in state child custody proceedings.

Financial data Grants depend on the population of the applicant's service area, ranging from a maximum of $10,000 for 500 to 1,500 individuals to a maximum of $72,166.66 for more than 200,001 individuals.

Duration 1 year.

Special features Applications must be submitted to the Area Director for the appropriate area within the Bureau of Indian Affairs (BIA); for a list of their names and addresses, contact the address above.

Number awarded In a recent year, a total of $866,000 was available for this program; that was divided among each of the 12 BIA area offices, so each office was allocated $72,166.66 to award within its area.

Deadline July of each year.

[808]
INDIAN ENVIRONMENTAL REGULATORY ENHANCEMENT PROJECTS

Department of Health and Human Services
Attn: Administration for Children and Families
Administration for Native Americans
Hubert H. Humphrey Building, Room 348F
200 Independence Avenue, S.W.
Washington, DC 20201-0001
(202) 690-5780

Purpose To provide funding for projects within Indian tribes in order to identify, plan, develop, and implement environmental programs in a manner that is consistent with tribal culture.

Eligibility Applications may be submitted by federally recognized Indian tribes; incorporated non-federally recognized Indian tribes; Alaska Native villages and/or nonprofit village consortia; nonprofit Alaska Native Regional Corporations/Associations in

Alaska with village specific projects; and other tribal or village organizations or consortia of Indian tribes. Some of the purposes for grants include: develop or enhance the tribal environmental regulatory infrastructure required to support a tribal environmental program; regulate and enforce environmental activities on Indian lands pursuant to federal and Indian law; develop regulations, ordinances, and laws to protect the environment; promote environmental training and education of tribal employees; and develop technical and program capability to meet tribal and federal regulatory requirements.

Financial data Grants up to $250,000 are available. Grantees must provide at least 20 percent of the total approved cost of the project.

Duration 1 year.

Number awarded Approximately 35 each year; $3 million was available for this program in a recent year.

Deadline March of each year.

[809]
INDIAN VOCATIONAL EDUCATION PROGRAM

Department of Education
Attn: Office of Vocational and Adult Education
Division of National Programs
Switzer Building, Room 4512
600 Independence Avenue, S.W.
Washington, DC 20202-7242
(202) 205-9270   E-mail: Gwen_Washington@ed.gov
E-mail: David_Jones@ed.gov

Purpose To provide assistance to Indian tribal organizations for vocational education.

Eligibility Applications may be submitted by a tribal organization of any Indian tribe or by a school funded by the Department of the Interior's Bureau of Indian Affairs (BIA) and offering a secondary education program. Consortia of eligible tribes or eligible BIA-funded schools may also apply. Grant funds must be used to plan, conduct, and administer vocational education and training projects.

Financial data Awards range from $250,000 to $500,000 and average $375,000. Last year, a total of $11,482,511 was available for this program.

Duration Up to 2 years.

Number awarded Up to 31 each year.

Deadline July of each year.

[810]
IRVINE MINORITY SCHOLARS

College of Arts and Sciences
Attn: Gerardo Marin
University of San Francisco
2130 Fulton Street
San Francisco, CA 94117-1080
(415) 422-5555

Purpose To offer ethnic minorities an opportunity to teach and conduct dissertation research at the University of San Francisco.

Eligibility Eligible to apply are U.S. citizens or permanent residents who have finished all course work leading to the Ph.D., are interested in considering a career in teaching, and are members of 1 of the following ethnic/racial groups: African American, Asian American, Hispanic/Latino, or American Indian. They must have specialized in 1 of the following areas: biology, chemistry, communication, computer science, economics, English, environmental science, exercise and sport science, fine and performing arts, history, mathematics, modern and classical languages, philosophy, physics, politics, psychology, sociology, or theology and religious studies.

Financial data The stipend is $24,000. Scholars also receive allowances for research costs, housing, and relocation expenses.

Duration 1 academic year.

Special features Scholars teach 1 course per semester in their discipline, serve as a resource person for faculty, students, and staff, receive office space, enjoy library privileges, and are given a mentor from among the senior faculty at the school.

Number awarded 3 each year.

Deadline February of each year.

[811]
JACOBS RESEARCH FUNDS SMALL GRANTS PROGRAM

Whatcom Museum
Attn: Jacobs Research Funds
121 Prospect Street
Bellingham, WA 98225
(360) 676-6981   Fax: (360) 738-7409

Purpose To provide funds for research in the field of social and cultural anthropology among living American native peoples.

Eligibility Research projects in the field of social and cultural anthropology among living American native peoples are eligible. Preference is given to the Pacific Northwest as an area of study, but other regions of North America (including Mexico) are eligible for consideration. Grants are given for work on problems in language, social organization, political organization, religion, mythology, music, other arts, psychology, and folk science.

Financial data Amount varies; generally, up to $1,200 is awarded. Funds may cover fees for consultants, supplies, transportation to and from the field, and lodging in the field.

Duration 1 year; renewable.

Special features This program was formerly known as the Melville and Elizabeth Jacobs Research Fund.

Limitations Funds are not supplied for salaries, ordinary living expenses, or major equipment. Projects that have as their goal only the application of anthropological knowledge, or which are for work in archaeology or biological anthropology are not considered; archival research is not supported. In addition, formal academic credentials are not required, but if the applicant has little or no academic research training or experience, research scholars must be found to act as sponsors.

Number awarded Varies each year.

Deadline February of each year.

[812]
JOHN CARTER BROWN LIBRARY ASSOCIATES FELLOWSHIP

John Carter Brown Library
Brown University
P.O. Box 1894
Providence, RI 02912
(401) 863-2725   E-mail: Karen_DeMaria@Brown.edu

Purpose To support scholars interested in conducting research at the John Carter Brown Library, which is renowned for its collection of historical sources pertaining to the Americas prior to 1830.

Eligibility This fellowship is open to Americans and foreign nationals who are engaged in pre- or postdoctoral or independent research. Graduate students must have passed their preliminary or general examinations at the time of application.

Financial data The stipend is $1,000 per month.

Duration From 2 to 4 months.

Special features Among the emphases of the library's holdings are works dealing with Native Americans in North and South America, colonial architecture books, economic history, maritime history, and works on the adaptation of religion and religious institutions to the New World.

Limitations Fellows are expected to be in regular residence at the library and to participate in the intellectual life of Brown University for the duration of the program.

Number awarded 1 each year.

Deadline January of each year.

[813]
JOHN CARTER BROWN LIBRARY LONG-TERM RESEARCH FELLOWSHIPS

John Carter Brown Library
Brown University
P.O. Box 1894
Providence, RI 02912
(401) 863-2725   E-mail: Karen_DeMaria@Brown.edu

Purpose To support scholars interested in conducting research at the John Carter Brown Library, which is renowned for its collection of historical sources pertaining to the Americas prior to 1830.

Eligibility Applicants must hold a doctorate and be American citizens or have been resident in the United States for 3 years immediately preceding the term of the fellowship. Selection is based on scholarly qualifications, the merits of the project, and the appropriateness of the inquiry to the holdings of the library.

Financial data Stipends are $13,375.

Duration 5 months.

Special features Among the emphases of the library's holdings are works dealing with Native Americans in North and South America, colonial architecture books, economic history, maritime history, and works on the adaptation of religion and religious institutions to the New World. These fellowships are funded by the National Endowment for the Humanities.

Limitations Fellows are expected to be in regular residence at the library and to participate in the intellectual life of Brown University for the duration of the program. Graduate students are not eligible for long-term fellowships.

Number awarded Up to 5 each year.

Deadline January of each year.

[814]
JOHN CARTER BROWN LIBRARY SHORT-TERM RESEARCH FELLOWSHIPS

John Carter Brown Library
Brown University
P.O. Box 1894
Providence, RI 02912
(401) 863-2725   E-mail: Karen_DeMaria@Brown.edu

Purpose To support scholars interested in conducting research at the John Carter Brown Library, which is renowned for its collection of historical sources pertaining to the Americas prior to 1830.

Eligibility These fellowships are open to Americans and foreign nationals who are engaged in pre- or postdoctoral or independent research. Graduate students must have passed their preliminary examinations at the time of application.

Financial data The stipend is $1,000 per month.

Duration From 2 to 4 months.

Special features Among the emphases of the library's holdings are works dealing with Native Americans in North and South America, colonial architecture books, economic history, maritime history, and works on the adaptation of religion and religious institutions to the New World.

Limitations Fellows are expected to be in regular residence at the library and to participate in the intellectual life of Brown University for the duration of the program.

Number awarded 15 to 17 each year.

Deadline January of each year.

[815]
LIBRARY SERVICES TO INDIAN TRIBES AND HAWAIIAN NATIVES PROGRAM SPECIAL PROJECTS GRANTS

Department of Education
Attn: Office of Educational Research and Improvement
Discretionary Library Programs Division
555 New Jersey Avenue, N.W., Room 300
Washington, DC 20208-5571
(202) 219-1670

Purpose To provide assistance to eligible Indian tribes and Alaska native villages for special library activities.

Eligibility Grant applications may be submitted by federally recognized Indian tribes and by Alaska native villages or regional or village corporations as defined in or established under the Alaska Native Claims Settlement Act. Preference is given to applications to 1) assess and plan for tribal library needs; 2) train or retrain Indians as library personnel; 3) utilize new information technologies to expand services to Indians in geographically isolated areas; or 4) conduct special library programs for Indians such as summer reading programs for children, outreach programs for elders, literacy tutoring, and training in computer use.

Financial data Grants range from $38,000 to $106,000 and average $68,000.

Duration 1 year.

Limitations All available funds for library services to Hawaiian natives are awarded through Library Services to Indian Tribes and Hawaiian Natives Program Basic Grants.

Number awarded Approximately 14 each year.

Deadline July of each year.

[816]
MAINE ARTS COMMISSION TRADITIONAL ARTS APPRENTICESHIP PROGRAM

Maine Arts Commission
55 Capitol Street
State House Station 25
Augusta, ME 04333-0025
(207) 287-2724   Fax: (207) 287-2335
TDD: (207) 287-5622

Purpose To provide an opportunity for Native American and other artists in Maine to share their skills with and train qualified apprentices.

Eligibility This program is open to master artists who are residents of Maine and practice a significant and/or endangered traditional art form in the state. Traditional arts are defined as artistic practices that reflect a community's share cultural heritage and are learned in an informal way, usually through example rather than through academic or institutional means. Special emphasis is given to artists who are members of the Native American and Acadian communities in Maine. Apprentices should be from the same ethnic, religious, occupational, or familial group as the master artist. Both master and apprentice must be legal Maine residents, be 18 years of age or older, and have resided in Maine for at least 183 of the past 365 days.

Financial data Funds are available for the master artist's teaching fee, apprentices' supplies and travel costs, and documentation of the apprenticeship.

Duration 1 year.

Special features Master artists and apprentices work together on a one-to-one basis. The work may be in crafts, dance, or music.

Number awarded Varies each year.

Deadline August of each year.

[817]
MINORITY BIOMEDICAL RESEARCH SUPPORT PROGRAM

National Institutes of Health
Attn: National Institute of General Medical Sciences
Division of Minority Opportunities in Research
Natcher Building, Suite 2AS37
45 Center Drive MSC 6200
Bethesda, MD 20892-6200
(301) 594-3900   Fax: (301) 480-2753
E-mail: em18v@nih.gov

Purpose To provide funding to educational institutions for support of programs that enhance health research career opportunities for their students.

Eligibility To be eligible for a grant under this program, an applicant must be 1) a public or private nonprofit university, 4-year college, or other institution offering undergraduate, graduate, or health professional degrees, with a traditionally high (more than 50 percent) minority student enrollment; or 2) a public or private nonprofit 2-year college, with a traditionally high (more than 50 percent) minority student enrollment; or 3) a public or private nonprofit university, 4-year college, or other institution offering undergraduate, graduate, or health professional degrees where a significant proportion of the student enrollment (but not necessarily more than 50 percent) is derived from ethnic minorities, provided the institution has a demonstrated commitment to the special encouragement of and assistance to ethnic minority faculty, students, and investigators; or 4) an American Indian tribe that

has a recognized governing body and that performs substantial governmental functions, or an Alaska Regional Corporation as defined in the Alaska Native Claims Settlement Act. Applicants must be located in the United States or its territories.

Financial data Grants range from $100,000 to $1.5 million per year. The average grant is $150,000. Funds may be used to pay academic year and summer salaries and wages for faculty, students, and support personnel needed to conduct a research project. Other cost categories include equipment, supplies, travel, and alterations and renovations.

Duration 3 to 5 years.

Special features A unique feature of the program is its emphasis on undergraduate participation in all aspects of biomedical research, including conceptualization of important research questions, design of experiments, review of the literature, collection and analysis of data, and interpretation and reporting of results at meetings and in scientific journals. The colleges select students to participate in the research projects of the faculty members and provide them with a salary. Students who wish to participate in this program should contact Minority Biomedical Research Support (MBRS) faculty at their institution; a list of participating institutions is available from the address above. The National Institutes of Health designates grants under this program as S06 Awards.

Number awarded Varies; approximately 80 each year.

Deadline January, May, or September of each year.

[818]
NATIONAL INSTITUTE ON THE EDUCATION OF AT-RISK STUDENTS

Department of Education
Attn: Office of Educational Research and Improvement
Field-Initiated Studies Program
555 New Jersey Avenue, N.W., Room 620
Washington, DC 20208-5531
(202) 219-2239   E-mail: bfine@inet.ed.gov

Purpose To expand research-based knowledge and strategies that will promote excellence and equity in the education of children and youth placed at risk of educational failure because of limited-English proficiency, poverty, race or ethnicity, or geographic location.

Eligibility Applications for these grants may be submitted by institutions of higher education; state and local education agencies; public and private organizations, institutions, and agencies; and individuals. The proposed research must relate to increasing academic achievement and reducing the dropout rates of American Indian and Alaska Native students; improving the success of students at-risk through coordinated school, community, and family programs, including programs designed to increase learning time; or improving student outcomes in schools where a majority of students live in poverty. Selection is based on national significance of the proposed research (30 points), quality of project design (30 points), quality and potential contributions of personnel (15 points), adequacy of resources (15 points), and quality of the management plan (10 points).

Financial data Recently, a total of $2,580,000 per year was available for these grants; awards ranged from $100,000 to $300,000 and averaged $250,000.

Duration 1 year or longer.

Number awarded 10 each year.

Deadline January of each year.

[819]
NIDDK AND NIAMS MINORITY TRAVEL AWARD PROGRAM

National Institutes of Health
Attn: National Institute of Diabetes and Digestive and Kidney Diseases
Minority Affairs Advisory Committee
Natcher Building, Room 6AS-49E
45 Center Drive MSC 6600
Bethesda, MD 20892-6600
(301) 594-8842   Fax: (301) 480-3504
E-mail: jg60d@nih.gov

Purpose To provide support for minority undergraduate and graduate students, minority individuals in postdoctoral training, and faculty members at minority institutions to accompany principal investigators of active regular research grants funded by the National Institute of Diabetes and Digestive and Kidney Diseases (NIDDK) and the National Institute of Arthritis and Musculoskeletal and Skin Diseases (NIAMS) to national scientific meetings.

Eligibility Principal investigators on NIDDK or NIAMS research grants are eligible to apply for administrative supplements so that minority students, minority individuals in postdoctoral training, or faculty members at minority institutions may attend national scientific meetings related to research interests of the institutes. For the purposes of this program, a minority institution is defined as a medical or nonmedical college, university, or equivalent school in which students of underrepresented minorities (including but not limited to Blacks, Hispanics, American Indians, and Pacific Islanders) comprise the majority or significant proportion of the school enrollment and which has a commitment to the special encouragement of minority faculty, students, and investigators.

Financial data Successful applications are funded as administrative supplements to the principal investigator's grant. Each minority student or faculty member may request up to $1,000 per year for travel expenses, which can be used for transportation, lodging, meals, and registration fees associated with the meeting.

Special features Minority students, minority individuals in postgraduate training, and faculty at minority institutions are encouraged to identify a principal investigator on a NIDDK or NIAMS research grant in order to participate in the Minority Travel Award Program. A list of all potential principal investigators is available from the above address. Information on the NIAMS program is available from Director, Women and Minority Health Issues, 45 Center Drive MSC 6500, Bethesda, MD 20892-6500, (301) 594-5052, Fax: (301) 480-4543, E-mail: Centers@ep.niams.nih.gov.

Deadline Applications may be submitted at any time.

[820]
OLD STURBRIDGE VILLAGE RESEARCH FELLOWSHIPS

Old Sturbridge Village
Attn: Research, Collections, and Library
1 Old Sturbridge Village Road
Sturbridge, MA 01566
(508) 347-3362, ext. 298

Purpose To provide funding to scholars interested in using the resources of Old Sturbridge Village (in Massachusetts) to conduct research on the social history and material culture of early rural New England.

Eligibility There are no rigid prerequisites, but candidates should give evidence of significant work and accomplishment in historical, archaeological, or material culture scholarship. Preference is given to candidates who are strongly committed to disseminating and publishing the results of their research. Applications should include a curriculum vitae, at least 2 letters of recommendation, a 3- to 5-page proposal, and a sample of scholarly work.

Financial data Up to $25,000.

Duration 6 to 12 weeks.

Special features The Village, a nonprofit educational institution, is an outdoor living history museum of national significance. Its recreated historical environment, collections, exhibits, and educational programs focus on rural society and culture in New England between 1790 and 1840.

Limitations This is a residential fellowship; fellows are expected to be in residence at Old Sturbridge Village for the duration of the program. Fellows are also expected to discuss their research in progress in informal colloquia and to give at least 1 public presentation to the museum staff.

Number awarded More than 1 each year. Funding may be available for a scholar whose project focuses on the life of African Americans and Native Americans in the region during the 18th and 19th centuries.

Deadline July of each year.

[821]
ONEIDA LICENSE, CERTIFICATE AND FEES PROGRAM

Oneida Nation of Wisconsin
Attn: Higher Education Office
P.O. Box 365
Oneida, WI 54155-0365
(414) 869-4333   (800) 236-2214, ext. 4333
Fax: (414) 869-4039

Purpose To provide financial assistance for obtaining a license or certificate to members of the Oneida Nation of Wisconsin.

Eligibility Applicants must be enrolled members of the Oneida Nation who have completed their education or training and need a license or certificate for their field of employment.

Financial data Up to $500 for direct costs may be granted.

Duration These are 1-time grants.

Number awarded Varies each year.

Deadline Applications may be submitted at any time, but at least 20 days prior to the exam/license/certificate application date.

[822]
PAUL CUFFE MEMORIAL FELLOWSHIPS

Mystic Seaport Museum
Attn: Munson Institute of American Maritime Studies
75 Greenmanville Avenue
P.O. Box 6000
Mystic, CT 06355-0990
(203) 572-5359   Fax: (203) 572-5329
E-mail: AnnaMSM@aol.com

Purpose To encourage research on the participation of African Americans and Native Americans in the maritime activities of southeastern New England.

Eligibility Research proposals are evaluated on the merits of the proposed study, the qualifications of the researchers to do the study, and the need for the researcher to use the resources of the Mystic Seaport Museum and other facilities in southeastern

New England. Any qualified researcher, with or without an academic affiliation, may apply.

Financial data The stipend is $2,400.

Special features These fellowships are named for Paul Cuffe, born in 1759 on Cuttyhunk Island, Massachusetts of a Wampanoag Indian mother and a former slave father. Before his death in 1817, he became a sea captain shipowner, landowner, and respected community leader of Westport, Massachusetts.

Limitations Fellows should be in residence at the museum during the fellowship period.

Number awarded 1 or more each year.

Deadline June of each year.

[823]
PHILLIPS FUND GRANTS FOR NATIVE AMERICAN RESEARCH

American Philosophical Society
104 South Fifth Street
Philadelphia, PA 19106-3387
(215) 440-3400   Fax: (215) 440-3436

Purpose To provide financial support for research in North American Indian anthropological linguistics and ethnohistory.

Eligibility Eligible to apply are scholars, preferably young scholars, working in the fields of linguistics and ethnohistory of Indians in the United States, the northwest coast, and Alaska. Graduate students may apply for research on master's or doctoral dissertations.

Financial data The grants average $1,200. These funds are intended for such extra costs as travel, tapes or films, and informants' fees.

Duration 1 year.

Limitations Grants are not made for projects in ethnography, archaeology, or psycholinguistics. Funds are not available for the preparation of pedagogical materials. Telephone requests for forms are not honored.

Number awarded Varies; the average number of grants is 17 per year.

Deadline February of each year.

[824]
PROGRAM FOR MINORITY RESEARCH TRAINING IN PSYCHIATRY

American Psychiatric Association
Attn: Office of Research
1400 K Street, N.W.
Washington, DC 20005
(202) 682-6225   (800) 852-1390

Purpose To provide financial assistance to minority medical students and residents interested in psychiatric research.

Eligibility This program is open to underrepresented minorities (American Indians, Blacks/African Americans, Hispanics, and Pacific Islanders) at 3 levels: medical students, residents, and graduates of residency programs. All candidates must be interested in training at research-intensive departments of psychiatry in major U.S. medical schools. Training sites with excellence as demonstrated by research facilities and resources, funded research, research faculty (including minority researchers), and successful training history are considered preferable.

Financial data Annual stipends are $10,008 for medical students, from $19,608 to $28,200 for residents, and up to $32,300

for post-residency fellows. Other benefits include travel funds to attend the annual meeting of the American Psychiatric Association (APA) or the American College of Neuropsychopharmacology, and limited tuition assistance for full-time trainees to attend specific courses that are required as part of their training.

Duration For medical students, 2 to 6 months, either during an elective period or as a summer experience; for residents, 3 to 6 months within or outside the home institution, although a year of full-time research training is also possible; for post-residency fellows, 2 years, although a third year is possible if appropriate to a trainee's career development.

Special features This program is funded by the National Institute of Mental Health and administered by the APA.

Number awarded Varies each year.

Deadline Medical students and residents seeking less than 1 year of training may apply at any time, but at least 3 months before the proposed training is to begin; medical students seeking summer training should apply by March of each year; residents seeking a year or more of training and post-residency fellows should apply by November of each year.

[825]
SACNAS CONFERENCE GRANTS

Society for Advancement of Chicanos and Native Americans in Science
1156 High Street
University of California at Santa Cruz
Santa Cruz, CA 95064
(408) 459-4272   Fax: (408) 459-3156
E-mail: sacnas@cats.ucsc.edu

Purpose To provide financial assistance to attend the annual conference of the Society for Advancement of Chicanos and Native Americans in Science (SACNAS).

Eligibility Chicano and Native American students and faculty who need financial assistance to attend SACNAS conferences are eligible to apply. Preference is given to undergraduate seniors who have not attended a previous conference but are presenting a poster to the current meeting; graduate students who have attended 3 previous conferences are not eligible for further support.

Financial data Funds are provided to cover conference attendance costs (i.e., travel, hotels, registration).

Duration These are 1-time grants.

Special features SACNAS was founded in 1972 by a group of American Indians and Mexican American scientists who recognized the need for collective efforts to increase the participation of Native Americans and Chicanos in science. Conferences and symposia are held by the association periodically.

Number awarded Varies each year, depending upon the funds available.

[826]
SCHOOL-TO-WORK OPPORTUNITIES ACT INDIAN PROGRAM GRANTS

Department of Labor
Attn: Employment and Training Administration
Division of Acquisition and Assistance
SGA/DAA 96-007
200 Constitution Avenue, N.W., Room S-4203
Washington, DC 20210
(202) 219-7300

Purpose To provide funding to partnerships involving local organizations and tribal organizations that propose to help prepare Indian youth for first jobs in high-skill, high-wage careers and further postsecondary education and training.

Eligibility This program is open to local partnerships involving tribal organizations responsible for economic development, employment, job training, and education; employers; representatives of schools funded by the Bureau of Indian Affairs (BIA) and local postsecondary vocations institutions; local educators; representatives of labor organizations or nonmanagerial employee representatives; and students and parents. Participation may be open to employer organizations, community-based organizations, national trade associations working at the local level, industrial extension centers, rehabilitation agencies and organizations, local vocational education entities, local government agencies, parent organizations, teacher organizations, vocational student organizations, and private industry councils. All partnerships must involve schools funded by the BIA. Proposals may be for either development or implementation grants, but must involve programs to help Indian youth acquire the knowledge, skills, abilities, and information about the labor market necessary to make an effective transition from school to career-oriented work.

Financial data Development grants are about $30,000 each and implementation grants range from $75,000 to $100,000 each.

Duration 1 year; may be renewed on an annual basis for 4 additional years.

Special features This program is operated jointly by the Employment and Training Administration of the Department of Labor and the Office of Vocational and Adult Education of the Department of Education.

Number awarded In a recent year, this program provided 7 development grants and 5 implementation grants.

Deadline July of each year.

[827]
TRIBAL DIVISION OF EDUCATION SCHOOL REFORM PROGRAM

Department of Education
Attn: Office of Elementary and Secondary Education
Office of Indian Education
Portals Building, Room 4300
600 Independence Avenue, S.W.
Washington, DC 20202-6335
(202) 260-1441

Purpose To provide financial assistance to tribal divisions of education in coordinating school reform plans developed for schools funded by the Bureau of Indian Affairs (BIA) and those plans developed for public schools.

Eligibility Eligible to apply for support under this program are the departments, agencies, boards, committees, or other institutions within tribes whose primary responsibility is planning, developing, and coordinating existing elementary and secondary education programs for the children of the tribe. A federally recognized tribe is any Indian tribe, band, nation, or other organized group or community that is recognized by the Secretary of the Interior. Tribal divisions of education must use funds from this program in building partnerships between public and BIA-funded schools, and could be used to support many types of coordination efforts, including activities such as improving consistency and compatibility of curricula among public and BIA-funded schools, assisting in the development of curricula that are culturally sensitive, creating mechanisms to increase communication among parents and the schools that their children attend, increasing tribal participation in the development and implementation of school improvement plans, and conducting professional development programs for local teachers.

Financial data Grants range from $50,000 to $75,000; the average award is approximately $62,500. The total annual appropriation for this program is approximately $500,000.

Duration Up to 4 years.

Number awarded Varies; approximately 8 each year.

Deadline July of each year.

[828]
TRIBALLY-CONTROLLED POSTSECONDARY VOCATIONAL INSTITUTIONS PROGRAM GRANTS

Department of Education
Attn: Office of Vocational and Adult Education
Division of National Programs
Switzer Building, Room 4523
600 Independence Avenue, S.W.
Washington, DC 20202-7242
(202) 205-5680   E-mail: Roberta_Lewis@ed.gov

Purpose To provide basic support for the education and training of Indian students.

Eligibility Tribally-controlled postsecondary vocational institutions apply directly to the Department of Education for grants under this program. Funds may be used to cover the costs of training, instruction, equipment, administration, and operation.

Financial data For the first year, awards range from $1,054,000 to $1,800,000, and average $1,459,500; funding for subsequent years depends on the availability of funds.

Duration 1 year; may be renewed up to 4 additional years.

Number awarded At least 2 each year.

Deadline April of each year.

[829]
VOCATIONAL REHABILITATION SERVICE PROJECTS FOR AMERICAN INDIANS WITH DISABILITIES

Department of Education
Attn: Office of Special Education and Rehabilitative Services
Rehabilitation Services Administration
Switzer Building, Room 3225
600 Independence Avenue, S.W.
Washington, DC 20202-2650
(202) 205-9544

Purpose To provide vocational rehabilitation services in order to prepare for suitable employment American Indians with disabilities who reside on federal or state reservations.

Eligibility Applications may be submitted by governing bodies of Indian tribes and consortia of those bodies located on federal or state reservations. Preference is given to applications for the continuation of tribal programs that have been funded previously under this program.

Financial data Grants range from $200,000 to $400,000 and average $285,000.

Number awarded Up to 11 each year.

Deadline June of each year.

[830]
W. LINCOLN HAWKINS UNDERGRADUATE RESEARCH FELLOWSHIP

National Action Council for Minorities in Engineering
3 West 35th Street
New York, NY 10001-2281
(212) 279-2626   Fax: (212) 629-5178

Purpose To provide financial assistance for a research project in chemical engineering by an underrepresented minority student.

Eligibility Engineering students who are African American, Latino, or American Indian are eligible for this award. They must be sophomores with a minimum grade point average of 3.0 proposing to conduct a research project in chemical engineering with a faculty mentor.

Financial data The stipend payable to the university is $10,000 per year, of which $5,000 per year is for the student award.

Duration 2 years.

Special features This program, which began in 1994, is named in honor of W. Lincoln Hawkins, the first African American scientist employed by AT&T's Bell Laboratories in the early 1940s. It is funded by personal contributions from his colleagues and a grant from the AT&T Foundation.

Number awarded 1 each year.

Native Alaskans

[831]
ALASKA STATE COUNCIL ON THE ARTS CAREER OPPORTUNITY GRANTS

Alaska State Council on the Arts
411 West Fourth Avenue, Suite 1E
Anchorage, AK 99501-2343
(907) 269-6610   Fax: (907) 269-6601
E-mail: asca@alaska.net

Purpose To provide cash awards to Alaskan artists to enable them to travel to events that will enhance their artistic skills or professional standing.

Eligibility Visual artists, writers, composers, choreographers, media artists, traditional Native artists, performing artists, and other artists who are residents of Alaska involved in the creation of new works may apply. Grants may be used to travel to in-state, regional, national, or international conferences, workshops, and seminars, or to travel to undertake projects directly related to the grantees' artistic careers.

Financial data Grants are awarded for up to two-thirds of travel costs by coach-class airfare or state mileage rates, whichever is less, up to a maximum of $1,000. Costs of tuition, workshop fees, per diem, or in-town surface transportation are not covered.

Limitations Full-time students are not eligible, and grants will not be awarded to an artist in consecutive years.

Number awarded Varies each year.

Deadline Applications may be submitted at any time, but they must be received at least 6 weeks prior to the requested departure date. Work must be completed within 6 months of official notification; the project must begin and end within the same state fiscal year (July 1 to June 30).

[832]
AMERICAN INDIAN MUSEUM STUDIES PROGRAM

Smithsonian Institution
Attn: Center for Museum Studies
Arts and Industries Building, Suite 2235
MRC 427
Washington, DC 20560
(202) 357-3101   Fax: (202) 357-3346
E-mail: ompem004@sivm.si.edu

Purpose To promote and assist Native Americans in the continuation and interpretation of tribal cultures as they define them.

Eligibility Native Americans working in tribal museums and American Indian cultural centers are eligible to participate in workshops and seminars conducted as part of this program.

Financial data Participants in the workshops and seminars receive a tuition waiver for the course and a scholarship to help defray travel and subsistence expenses.

Duration Most seminars last 3 to 5 days.

Special features This program also recruits American Indians and Alaska Natives who are currently enrolled in a higher education program or who are currently employed in a field related to museum work or cultural programming to participate in the Museum Intern Partnership Program of the Smithsonian's Center for Museum Studies. It also produces publications and technical assistance which provide additional resources not available elsewhere for the enrichment of Native American museums and cultural centers.

Number awarded Varies each year.

Deadline The seminars and workshops, of which 4 or 5 are held each year at native communities throughout the United States and Canada, each set their own deadline dates.

[833]
ARCTIC RESEARCH PROGRAM

National Science Foundation
Attn: Office of Polar Programs
4201 Wilson Boulevard
Arlington, VA 22230
(703) 306-1031   Fax: (703) 306-0139

Purpose To provide funding for research related to the Arctic.

Eligibility This program is open to investigators affiliated with U.S. universities, research institutions, or other organizations including local or state governments. Applicants must be proposing to conduct research in the 3 program areas of Arctic Natural Sciences (including atmospheric sciences, biological sciences, earth sciences, glaciology, and oceanography), Arctic Social Sciences (including archaeology; cultural, social, and physical anthropology; decision and risk management science; ethnology; history; geography; sociology; psychology; linguistics; political science; law; economics; and related subjects), and Arctic System Science (encompassing 5 components: the Greenland ice sheet program, paleoclimate of arctic lakes and estuaries, ocean/atmosphere/ice interactions, land/atmosphere/ice interactions, and synthesis, integration and modeling systems). Proposals should involve field studies in the arctic, although projects outside the arctic but directly related to arctic science and engineering are also considered as are related laboratory and theoretical studies. The program particularly encourages proposals from women, minorities, and persons with disabilities and welcomes proposals for research projects that include participation by undergraduates and high school students under guidelines established by cross-disciplinary programs of the National Science Foundation (NSF). Arctic research that addresses Native concerns and involves Native collaboration and training is particularly encouraged.

Financial data The amounts of the awards depend on the nature of the proposal and the availability of funds; recent funding provided approximately $40.5 million for arctic research, of which approximately $24.2 was provided by NSF and the remainder by other federal agencies.

Special features Other NSF activities that may be funded through the arctic progam include dissertation grants, research experiences for undergraduates, small grants for exploratory research, the small business innovation research program, and the small business technology transfer pilot program.

Number awarded Approximately 350 each year.

Deadline May and December of each year.

[834]
BARBARA S. MOSBACHER FELLOWSHIP

John Carter Brown Library
Brown University
P.O. Box 1894
Providence, RI 02912
(401) 863-2725   E-mail: Karen_DeMaria@Brown.edu

Purpose To support scholars interested in conducting research at the John Carter Brown Library, which is renowned for its collection of historical sources pertaining to the Americas prior to 1830.

Eligibility This fellowship is open to Americans and foreign nationals who are engaged in pre- or postdoctoral or independent research. Graduate students must have passed their preliminary or general examinations at the time of application.

Financial data The stipend is $1,000 per month.

Duration From 2 to 4 months.

Special features Among the emphases of the library's holdings are works dealing with Native Americans in North and South America, colonial architecture books, economic history, maritime history, and works on the adaptation of religion and religious institutions to the New World.

Limitations Fellows are expected to be in regular residence at the library and to participate in the intellectual life of Brown University for the duration of the program.

Number awarded 1 each year.

Deadline January of each year.

[835]
CHARLES H. WATTS MEMORIAL FELLOWSHIP

John Carter Brown Library
Brown University
P.O. Box 1894
Providence, RI 02912
(401) 863-2725   E-mail: Karen_DeMaria@Brown.edu

Purpose To support scholars interested in conducting research at the John Carter Brown Library, which is renowned for its collection of historical sources pertaining to the Americas prior to 1830.

Eligibility This fellowship is open to Americans and foreign nationals who are engaged in pre- or postdoctoral or independent research. Graduate students must have passed their preliminary or general examinations at the time of application.

Financial data The stipend is $1,000 per month.

Duration From 2 to 4 months.

Special features Among the emphases of the library's holdings are works dealing with Native Americans in North and South America, colonial architecture books, economic history, maritime history, and works on the adaptation of religion and religious institutions to the New World.

Limitations Fellows are expected to be in regular residence at the library and to participate in the intellectual life of Brown University for the duration of the program.

Number awarded 1 each year.

Deadline January of each year.

[836]
FINANCIAL ASSISTANCE FOR THE MITIGATION OF ENVIRONMENTAL IMPACTS DUE TO DEPARTMENT OF DEFENSE ACTIVITIES

Department of Health and Human Services
Attn: Administration for Children and Families
Administration for Native Americans
Hubert H. Humphrey Building, Room 348F
200 Independence Avenue, S.W.
Washington, DC 20201-0001
(202) 690-5780

Purpose To provide funding to Native American organizations for addressing environmental problems and impacts from Department of Defense (DoD) activities to Indian lands.

Eligibility Applications may be submitted by federally recognized Indian tribes; incorporated non-federally and state recognized Indian tribes; Alaska Native villages and/or nonprofit village entities; nonprofit Alaska Native Regional Corporations/Associations in Alaska with village specific projects; and other tribal or village organizations or consortia of Indian tribes. Proposed activities may include training and technical assistance to tribes, related administrative support, the gathering of information, documenting of environmental damage, and developing a system for prioritizing of mitigation on Indian lands resulting from DoD activities.

Financial data Grants range from $100,000 to $1 million; grantees must provide at least 5 percent of the total approved cost of the project.

Duration Up to 3 years.

Number awarded Approximately 25 each year; $7 million was available for this program in a recent year.

Deadline March and November of each year.

[837]
HELEN WATSON BUCKNER MEMORIAL FELLOWSHIP

John Carter Brown Library
Brown University
P.O. Box 1894
Providence, RI 02912
(401) 863-2725   E-mail: Karen_DeMaria@Brown.edu

Purpose   To support scholars interested in conducting research at the John Carter Brown Library, which is renowned for its collection of historical sources pertaining to the Americas prior to 1830.

Eligibility   This fellowship is open to Americans and foreign nationals who are engaged in pre- or postdoctoral or independent research. Graduate students must have passed their preliminary or general examinations at the time of application.

Financial data   The stipend is $1,000 per month.

Duration   From 2 to 4 months.

Special features   Among the emphases of the library's holdings are works dealing with Native Americans in North and South America, colonial architecture books, economic history, maritime history, and works on the adaptation of religion and religious institutions to the New World.

Limitations   Fellows are expected to be in regular residence at the library and to participate in the intellectual life of Brown University for the duration of the program.

Number awarded   1 each year.

Deadline   January of each year.

[838]
IHS LOAN REPAYMENT PROGRAM

Indian Health Service
Attn: Scholarship Program
Twinbrook Metro Plaza, Suite 100
12300 Twinbrook Parkway
Rockville, MD 20852
(301) 443-3396   Fax: (301) 443-4815

Purpose   To repay the health professional educational loans of Native American or other health professionals who are willing to work for 2 continuous years serving the health needs of American Indians.

Eligibility   Applicants must have a degree in a health profession and 1) be eligible for, or hold, an appointment as a commissioned officer in the Regular or Reserve Corps of the Public Health Service (PHS); 2) be eligible for selection for civilian service in the Regular or Reserve Corps of the PHS; 3) meet the professional standards for civil service employment in the Indian Health Service (IHS); or 4) be employed in an Indian health program without service obligation. Eligible applicants include health professionals in postgraduate training or in their final year of health professions school. Health professions include family medicine, internal medicine, pediatrics, geriatric medicine, obstetrics and gynecology, podiatric medicine, nursing, public health nursing, dentistry, psychiatry, osteopathy, optometry, pharmacy, psychology, public health, social work, marriage and family therapy, chiropractic medicine, environmental health and engineering, and allied health professions. Current priorities for selection are given to allopathic physicians if they are board certified/eligible in anesthesiology, emergency room medicine, general surgery, opthalmalogy, obstetrics and gynecology, orthopedic surgery, otolaryngology and otorhinolaryngology, psychiatry, and radiology; mental health professionals; and nurse practitioners, registered nurses, and cer-

tified nurse midwives. In addition, sites are given scores based on a record of frequent staff turnover, current unmatched vacancies in a health profession discipne, and projected vacancies in a health profession discipline; sites that are provided high scores receive priority over sites that have lower scores. Consistent with those priorities, preference is given to American Indians, Alaska natives, and individuals recruited through the efforts of Indian tribes or tribal or Indian organizations.

Financial data   Health professionals who have outstanding, qualified educational loans (undergraduate or graduate) receive up to $30,000 of repayment of those loans for each year of service in the IHS. In addition, the program pays up to 31 percent of federal taxes directly to the Internal Revenue Service.

Duration   2 years.

Number awarded   Approximately 250 each year; at least 25 percent are provided to nurses, nurse practitioners, and nurse midwives, and at least 10 percent are provided to mental health professionals.

Deadline   Applications may be submitted by the Friday of the second full week of each month.

[839]
INDIAN AND NATIVE AMERICAN EMPLOYMENT AND TRAINING PROGRAM

Department of Labor
Attn: Employment and Training Administration
Office of Special Targeted Programs
200 Constitution Avenue, N.W., Room N-4641
Washington, DC 20210
(202) 219-5500   Fax: (202) 219-6338

Purpose   To reduce the economic disadvantages and advance the economic and social development of Indians and others of Native American descent.

Eligibility   The priority order for these grants is: 1) Indian tribes, bands, or groups (including Alaska Native entities) on federal or state reservations; 2) Native American-controlled, community-based organizations (including tribes applying for geographic areas other than their own reservations); 3) organizations (private nonprofit or units of state or local governments) having significant Native American control; and 4) non-Native American-controlled organizations (but with a Native American advisory process).

Financial data   Grants range from $50,000 to more than $7 million; the average award is $1 million. Funds are to be used for institutional training, on-the-job training, work experience, youth employment programs, day care, health care, and job placement. Only a limited amount of the grant may be used to cover administrative costs.

Duration   2 years; may be renewed on an annual basis.

Number awarded   Approximately 200 new and recurring grants each year.

[840]
INDIAN ENVIRONMENTAL REGULATORY ENHANCEMENT PROJECTS

Department of Health and Human Services
Attn: Administration for Children and Families
Administration for Native Americans
Hubert H. Humphrey Building, Room 348F
200 Independence Avenue, S.W.
Washington, DC 20201-0001
(202) 690-5780

Purpose To provide funding for projects within Indian tribes in order to identify, plan, develop, and implement environmental programs in a manner that is consistent with tribal culture.

Eligibility Applications may be submitted by federally recognized Indian tribes; incorporated non-federally recognized Indian tribes; Alaska Native villages and/or nonprofit village consortia; nonprofit Alaska Native Regional Corporations/Associations in Alaska with village specific projects; and other tribal or village organizations or consortia of Indian tribes. Some of the purposes for grants include: develop or enhance the tribal environmental regulatory infrastructure required to support a tribal environmental program; regulate and enforce environmental activities on Indian lands pursuant to federal and Indian law; develop regulations, ordinances, and laws to protect the environment; promote environmental training and education of tribal employees; and develop technical and program capability to meet tribal and federal regulatory requirements.

Financial data Grants up to $250,000 are available. Grantees must provide at least 20 percent of the total approved cost of the project.

Duration 1 year.

Number awarded Approximately 35 each year; $3 million was available for this program in a recent year.

Deadline March of each year.

[841]
JACOBS RESEARCH FUNDS SMALL GRANTS PROGRAM

Whatcom Museum
Attn: Jacobs Research Funds
121 Prospect Street
Bellingham, WA 98225
(360) 676-6981   Fax: (360) 738-7409

Purpose To provide funds for research in the field of social and cultural anthropology among living American native peoples.

Eligibility Research projects in the field of social and cultural anthropology among living American native peoples are eligible. Preference is given to the Pacific Northwest as an area of study, but other regions of North America (including Mexico) are eligible for consideration. Grants are given for work on problems in language, social organization, political organization, religion, mythology, music, other arts, psychology, and folk science.

Financial data Amount varies; generally, up to $1,200 is awarded. Funds may cover fees for consultants, supplies, transportation to and from the field, and lodging in the field.

Duration 1 year; renewable.

Special features This program was formerly known as the Melville and Elizabeth Jacobs Research Fund.

Limitations Funds are not supplied for salaries, ordinary living expenses, or major equipment. Projects that have as their goal only the application of anthropological knowledge, or which are for work in archaeology or biological anthropology are not consid-

ered; archival research is not supported. In addition, formal academic credentials are not required, but if the applicant has little or no academic research training or experience, research scholars must be found to act as sponsors.

Number awarded Varies each year.

Deadline February of each year.

[842]
JOHN CARTER BROWN LIBRARY ASSOCIATES FELLOWSHIP

John Carter Brown Library
Brown University
P.O. Box 1894
Providence, RI 02912
(401) 863-2725   E-mail: Karen_DeMaria@Brown.edu

Purpose To support scholars interested in conducting research at the John Carter Brown Library, which is renowned for its collection of historical sources pertaining to the Americas prior to 1830.

Eligibility This fellowship is open to Americans and foreign nationals who are engaged in pre- or postdoctoral or independent research. Graduate students must have passed their preliminary or general examinations at the time of application.

Financial data The stipend is $1,000 per month.

Duration From 2 to 4 months.

Special features Among the emphases of the library's holdings are works dealing with Native Americans in North and South America, colonial architecture books, economic history, maritime history, and works on the adaptation of religion and religious institutions to the New World.

Limitations Fellows are expected to be in regular residence at the library and to participate in the intellectual life of Brown University for the duration of the program.

Number awarded 1 each year.

Deadline January of each year.

[843]
JOHN CARTER BROWN LIBRARY LONG-TERM RESEARCH FELLOWSHIPS

John Carter Brown Library
Brown University
P.O. Box 1894
Providence, RI 02912
(401) 863-2725   E-mail: Karen_DeMaria@Brown.edu

Purpose To support scholars interested in conducting research at the John Carter Brown Library, which is renowned for its collection of historical sources pertaining to the Americas prior to 1830.

Eligibility Applicants must hold a doctorate and be American citizens or have been resident in the United States for 3 years immediately preceding the term of the fellowship. Selection is based on scholarly qualifications, the merits of the project, and the appropriateness of the inquiry to the holdings of the library.

Financial data Stipends are $13,375.

Duration 5 months.

Special features Among the emphases of the library's holdings are works dealing with Native Americans in North and South America, colonial architecture books, economic history, maritime history, and works on the adaptation of religion and religious institutions to the New World. These fellowships are funded by the National Endowment for the Humanities.

Limitations Fellows are expected to be in regular residence at the library and to participate in the intellectual life of Brown University for the duration of the program. Graduate students are not eligible for long-term fellowships.

Number awarded Up to 5 each year.

Deadline January of each year.

[844]
JOHN CARTER BROWN LIBRARY SHORT-TERM RESEARCH FELLOWSHIPS

John Carter Brown Library
Brown University
P.O. Box 1894
Providence, RI 02912
(401) 863-2725   E-mail: Karen_DeMaria@Brown.edu

Purpose To support scholars interested in conducting research at the John Carter Brown Library, which is renowned for its collection of historical sources pertaining to the Americas prior to 1830.

Eligibility These fellowships are open to Americans and foreign nationals who are engaged in pre- or postdoctoral or independent research. Graduate students must have passed their preliminary examinations at the time of application.

Financial data The stipend is $1,000 per month.

Duration From 2 to 4 months.

Special features Among the emphases of the library's holdings are works dealing with Native Americans in North and South America, colonial architecture books, economic history, maritime history, and works on the adaptation of religion and religious institutions to the New World.

Limitations Fellows are expected to be in regular residence at the library and to participate in the intellectual life of Brown University for the duration of the program.

Number awarded 15 to 17 each year.

Deadline January of each year.

[845]
LIBRARY SERVICES TO INDIAN TRIBES AND HAWAIIAN NATIVES PROGRAM SPECIAL PROJECTS GRANTS

Department of Education
Attn: Office of Educational Research and Improvement
Discretionary Library Programs Division
555 New Jersey Avenue, N.W., Room 300
Washington, DC 20208-5571
(202) 219-1670

Purpose To provide assistance to eligible Indian tribes and Alaska native villages for special library activities.

Eligibility Grant applications may be submitted by federally recognized Indian tribes and by Alaska native villages or regional or village corporations as defined in or established under the Alaska Native Claims Settlement Act. Preference is given to applications to 1) assess and plan for tribal library needs; 2) train or retrain Indians as library personnel; 3) utilize new information technologies to expand services to Indians in geographically isolated areas; or 4) conduct special library programs for Indians such as summer reading programs for children, outreach programs for elders, literacy tutoring, and training in computer use.

Financial data Grants range from $38,000 to $106,000 and average $68,000.

Duration 1 year.

Limitations All available funds for library services to Hawaiian natives are awarded through Library Services to Indian Tribes and Hawaiian Natives Program Basic Grants.

Number awarded Approximately 14 each year.

Deadline July of each year.

[846]
MINORITY BIOMEDICAL RESEARCH SUPPORT PROGRAM

National Institutes of Health
Attn: National Institute of General Medical Sciences
Division of Minority Opportunities in Research
Natcher Building, Suite 2AS37
45 Center Drive MSC 6200
Bethesda, MD 20892-6200
(301) 594-3900   Fax: (301) 480-2753
E-mail: em18v@nih.gov

Purpose To provide funding to educational institutions for support of programs that enhance health research career opportunities for their students.

Eligibility To be eligible for a grant under this program, an applicant must be 1) a public or private nonprofit university, 4-year college, or other institution offering undergraduate, graduate, or health professional degrees, with a traditionally high (more than 50 percent) minority student enrollment; or 2) a public or private nonprofit 2-year college, with a traditionally high (more than 50 percent) minority student enrollment; or 3) a public or private nonprofit university, 4-year college, or other institution offering undergraduate, graduate, or health professional degrees where a significant proportion of the student enrollment (but not necessarily more than 50 percent) is derived from ethnic minorities, provided the institution has a demonstrated commitment to the special encouragement of and assistance to ethnic minority faculty, students, and investigators; or 4) an American Indian tribe that has a recognized governing body and that performs substantial governmental functions, or an Alaska Regional Corporation as defined in the Alaska Native Claims Settlement Act. Applicants must be located in the United States or its territories.

Financial data Grants range from $100,000 to $1.5 million per year. The average grant is $150,000. Funds may be used to pay academic year and summer salaries and wages for faculty, students, and support personnel needed to conduct a research project. Other cost categories include equipment, supplies, travel, and alterations and renovations.

Duration 3 to 5 years.

Special features A unique feature of the program is its emphasis on undergraduate participation in all aspects of biomedical research, including conceptualization of important research questions, design of experiments, review of the literature, collection and analysis of data, and interpretation and reporting of results at meetings and in scientific journals. The colleges select students to participate in the research projects of the faculty members and provide them with a salary. Students who wish to participate in this program should contact Minority Biomedical Research Support (MBRS) faculty at their institution; a list of participating institutions is available from the address above. The National Institutes of Health designates grants under this program as S06 Awards.

Number awarded Varies; approximately 80 each year.

Deadline January, May, or September of each year.

[847]
NATIONAL INSTITUTE ON THE EDUCATION OF AT-RISK STUDENTS

Department of Education
Attn: Office of Educational Research and Improvement
Field-Initiated Studies Program
555 New Jersey Avenue, N.W., Room 620
Washington, DC 20208-5531
(202) 219-2239　　　　　　E-mail: bfine@inet.ed.gov

Purpose To expand research-based knowledge and strategies that will promote excellence and equity in the education of children and youth placed at risk of educational failure because of limited-English proficiency, poverty, race or ethnicity, or geographic location.

Eligibility Applications for these grants may be submitted by institutions of higher education; state and local education agencies; public and private organizations, institutions, and agencies; and individuals. The proposed research must relate to increasing academic achievement and reducing the dropout rates of American Indian and Alaska Native students; improving the success of students at-risk through coordinated school, community, and family programs, including programs designed to increase learning time; or improving student outcomes in schools where a majority of students live in poverty. Selection is based on national significance of the proposed research (30 points), quality of project design (30 points), quality and potential contributions of personnel (15 points), adequacy of resources (15 points), and quality of the management plan (10 points).

Financial data Recently, a total of $2,580,000 per year was available for these grants; awards ranged from $100,000 to $300,000 and averaged $250,000.

Duration 1 year or longer.

Number awarded 10 each year.

Deadline January of each year.

[848]
NATIVE ALASKAN SOCIAL AND ECONOMIC DEVELOPMENT STRATEGIES PROJECTS

Department of Health and Human Services
Attn: Administration for Children and Families
Administration for Native Americans
Hubert H. Humphrey Building, Room 348F
200 Independence Avenue, S.W.
Washington, DC 20201-0001
(202) 690-5780

Purpose To provide funding for projects that attempt to promote the goal of social and economic self-sufficiency for Native Alaskans through locally developed social and economic development strategies.

Eligibility Applications may be submitted by federally recognized Indian tribes in Alaska; Alaska Native villages and/or nonprofit village consortia; incorporated nonprofit Alaska Native multi-purpose community-based organizations; nonprofit Alaska Native Regional Corporations/Associations in Alaska with village specific projects; and nonprofit Native organizations in Alaska with village specific projects. Proposals must enable the applicant organization to develop and implement community-based, long-term governance, social, and economic development strategies.

Financial data Grants for individual village projects are up to $100,000; grants for regional nonprofit and village consortia are up to $150,000. Grantees must provide at least 20 percent of the total approved cost of the project.

Duration 1 year.

Number awarded Approximately 15 to 18 each year; $1.5 million annually has been available for this program in recent years.

Deadline May of each year.

[849]
PHILLIPS FUND GRANTS FOR NATIVE AMERICAN RESEARCH

American Philosophical Society
104 South Fifth Street
Philadelphia, PA 19106-3387
(215) 440-3400　　　　　　Fax: (215) 440-3436

Purpose To provide financial support for research in North American Indian anthropological linguistics and ethnohistory.

Eligibility Eligible to apply are scholars, preferably young scholars, working in the fields of linguistics and ethnohistory of Indians in the United States, the northwest coast, and Alaska. Graduate students may apply for research on master's or doctoral dissertations.

Financial data The grants average $1,200. These funds are intended for such extra costs as travel, tapes or films, and informants' fees.

Duration 1 year.

Limitations Grants are not made for projects in ethnography, archaeology, or psycholinguistics. Funds are not available for the preparation of pedagogical materials. Telephone requests for forms are not honored.

Number awarded Varies; the average number of grants is 17 per year.

Deadline February of each year.

Native Pacific Islanders

[850]
NATIVE HAWAIIAN COMMUNITY-BASED EDUCATION LEARNING CENTERS PROGRAM

Department of Education
Attn: Office of Elementary and Secondary Education
School Improvement Program
Portals Building, Room 4500
600 Independence Avenue, S.W.
Washington, DC 20202-6140
(202) 260-2502　　　　　　Fax: (202) 205-0302

Purpose To provide financial assistance for collaborative efforts between community-based Native Hawaiian organizations and community colleges.

Eligibility Applications may be submitted by consortia of community-based Native Hawaiian organizations and community colleges. Grant funds must be used to develop, establish, and operate community-based education learning centers that meet the needs of families and communities through the coordination of such programs and services as preschool programs, after-school programs, and vocational and adult education programs.

Financial data A total of $800,000 is available for this program. Individual grants range from $267,000 to $800,000 and average $267,000.

Duration Up to 5 years.

Number awarded 1 to 3 each year.

Deadline May of each year.

[851]
NATIVE HAWAIIAN CURRICULUM DEVELOPMENT, TEACHER TRAINING AND RECRUITMENT PROGRAM

Department of Education
Attn: Office of Elementary and Secondary Education
School Improvement Program
Portals Building, Room 4500
600 Independence Avenue, S.W.
Washington, DC 20202-6140
(202) 260-2502　　　　　　Fax: (202) 205-0302

Purpose To provide financial support to operate programs of instruction conducted in the Hawaiian language.

Eligibility Applications may be submitted by Native Hawaiian educational organizations or educational entities with experience in developing or operating Native Hawaiian progams or programs of instruction conducted in the Native Hawaiian language. Grant funds may be used for 1) the development of curricula to address the needs of Native Hawaiian students, particularly elementary and secondary school students, which may include programs of instruction conducted in the Native Hawaiian language, and mathematics and science curricula incorporating the relevant application of Native Hawaiian culture and traditions; 2) the development and implementation of preteacher training programs in order to ensure that student teachers within the state of Hawaii, particularly student teachers who are likely to be employed in schools with a high concentration of Native Hawaiian students, are prepared to better address the unique needs of Native Hawaiian students, within the context of Native Hawaiian culture, language, and traditions; and 3) the development and implementation of inservice teacher training programs, in order to ensure that teachers, particularly teachers employed in schools with a high concentration of Native Hawaiian students, are prepared to better address the unique needs of Native Hawaiian students, within the context of Native Hawaiian culture, language, and traditions.

Financial data A total of $1,500,000 is available for this program. Individual grants range from $500,000 to $1,500,000 and average $500,000.

Duration Up to 5 years.

Number awarded 1 to 3 each year.

Deadline May of each year.

[852]
NATIVE HAWAIIAN FAMILY-BASED EDUCATION CENTERS PROGRAM

Department of Education
Attn: Office of Elementary and Secondary Education
School Improvement Program
Portals Building, Room 4500
600 Independence Avenue, S.W.
Washington, DC 20202-6140
(202) 260-2502　　　　　　Fax: (202) 205-0302

Purpose To provide financial support for projects that expand the operation of family-based education centers in Hawaii.

Eligibility Applications may be submitted by Native Hawaiian educational organizations or educational entities with experience in developing or operating Native Hawaiian progams or programs of instruction conducted in the Native Hawaiian language. Grant funds may be used for 1) parent-infant programs for prenatal through 3-year-olds; 2) preschool programs for 4- and 5-year-olds; 3) continued research and development; or 4) a long-term follow-up and assessment program, which may include educational support services for Native Hawaiian language immersion programs or transition to English-speaking programs.

Financial data A total of $5,600,000 is available for this program. Individual grants range from $1,500,000 to $5,600,000 and average $1,900,000.

Duration Up to 5 years.

Number awarded 1 to 3 each year.

Deadline May of each year.

[853]
NATIVE HAWAIIAN GIFTED AND TALENTED PROGRAM

Department of Education
Attn: Office of Elementary and Secondary Education
School Improvement Program
Portals Building, Room 4500
600 Independence Avenue, S.W.
Washington, DC 20202-6140
(202) 260-2502　　　　　　Fax: (202) 205-0302

Purpose To provide financial support for educational programs for gifted and talented Native Hawaiian elementary and secondary school students.

Eligibility Applications may be submitted by Native Hawaiian educational organizations or educational entities with experience in developing or operating Native Hawaiian progams or programs of instruction conducted in the Native Hawaiian language. Grant funds may be used to 1) address the special needs of Native Hawaiian elementary and secondary school students who are gifted and talented students; and 2) provide those support services to the families of such students that are needed to enable such students to benefit from the program.

Financial data A total of $1,200,000 is available for this program.

Duration Up to 5 years.

Number awarded 1 each year.

Deadline May of each year.

[854]
NATIVE HAWAIIAN SPECIAL EDUCATION PROGRAM

Department of Education
Attn: Office of Special Education and Rehabilitative Services
Division of Innovation and Development
Switzer Building, Room 3521
600 Independence Avenue, S.W.
Washington, DC 20202-2641
(202) 205-9099　　　　　　Fax: (202) 205-8105
E-mail: Linda_Glidewell@ed.gov

Purpose To provide financial support to projects that address the special education needs of Native Hawaiian students.

Eligibility Applications may be submitted by Native Hawaiian educational organizations or educational entities with experience in developing or operating Native Hawaiian progams or programs of instruction conducted in the Native Hawaiian language. Projects may include 1) the identification of Native Hawaiian students with disabilities or who are otherwise in need of special educational services; 2) the identification of the special educational needs of Native Hawaiian students, particularly with respect to the emotional and psychosocial needs of such students; 3) the provision of support services to the families of Native Hawaiian students that are needed to enable them to benefit from this program; 4) the conduct of educational activities which hold reasonable promise of resulting in substantial progress toward meeting the educational needs of such students; 5) the conduct of educational, psychosocial, and developmental activities which hold reasonable promise of resulting in substantial promise toward meeting the educational needs of such students, including demonstrating and exploring the use of the Native Hawaiian language and exposure to Native Hawaiian cultural traditions; and 6) appropriate research, evaluation, and related activities pertaining to the needs of such students.

Financial data A total of $1,200,000 is available for this program.

Duration Up to 5 years.

Number awarded 1 each year.

Deadline May of each year.

[855]
NATIVE HAWAIIAN VOCATIONAL EDUCATION PROGRAM

Department of Education
Attn: Office of Vocational and Adult Education
Division of National Programs
600 Independence Avenue, S.W.
Washington, DC 20202-7242
(202) 205-9650   E-mail: Paul_Geib@ed.gov

Purpose To provide assistance to plan, conduct, and administer programs or portions of programs that provide vocational training and related activities to native Hawaiians.

Eligibility Organizations that primarily serve and represent native Hawaiians and that are recognized by the governor of Hawaii are eligible to apply for grants under this program.

Financial data The amounts of the awards depend on the nature of the applications and the availability of funds.

Duration 1 year; renewable.

Number awarded Varies each year.

Deadline Deadline dates vary each year; check the latest edition of the *Federal Register* for the current application schedule.

[856]
NIDDK AND NIAMS MINORITY TRAVEL AWARD PROGRAM

National Institutes of Health
Attn: National Institute of Diabetes and Digestive and Kidney Diseases
Minority Affairs Advisory Committee
Natcher Building, Room 6AS-49E
45 Center Drive MSC 6600
Bethesda, MD 20892-6600
(301) 594-8842   Fax: (301) 480-3504
E-mail: jg60d@nih.gov

Purpose To provide support for minority undergraduate and graduate students, minority individuals in postdoctoral training, and faculty members at minority institutions to accompany principal investigators of active regular research grants funded by the National Institute of Diabetes and Digestive and Kidney Diseases (NIDDK) and the National Institute of Arthritis and Musculoskeletal and Skin Diseases (NIAMS) to national scientific meetings.

Eligibility Principal investigators on NIDDK or NIAMS research grants are eligible to apply for administrative supplements so that minority students, minority individuals in postdoctoral training, or faculty members at minority institutions may attend national scientific meetings related to research interests of the institutes. For the purposes of this program, a minority institution is defined as a medical or nonmedical college, university, or equivalent school in which students of underrepresented minorities (including but not limited to Blacks, Hispanics, American Indians, and Pacific Islanders) comprise the majority or significant proportion of the school enrollment and which has a commitment to the special encouragement of minority faculty, students, and investigators.

Financial data Successful applications are funded as administrative supplements to the principal investigator's grant. Each minority student or faculty member may request up to $1,000 per year for travel expenses, which can be used for transportation, lodging, meals, and registration fees associated with the meeting.

Special features Minority students, minority individuals in postgraduate training, and faculty at minority institutions are encouraged to identify a principal investigator on a NIDDK or NIAMS research grant in order to participate in the Minority Travel Award Program. A list of all potential principal investigators is available from the above address. Information on the NIAMS program is available from Director, Women and Minority Health Issues, 45 Center Drive MSC 6500, Bethesda, MD 20892-6500, (301) 594-5052, Fax: (301) 480-4543, E-mail: Centers@ep.niams.nih.gov.

Deadline Applications may be submitted at any time.

[857]
PROGRAM FOR MINORITY RESEARCH TRAINING IN PSYCHIATRY

American Psychiatric Association
Attn: Office of Research
1400 K Street, N.W.
Washington, DC 20005
(202) 682-6225   (800) 852-1390

Purpose To provide financial assistance to minority medical students and residents interested in psychiatric research.

Eligibility This program is open to underrepresented minorities (American Indians, Blacks/African Americans, Hispanics, and Pacific Islanders) at 3 levels: medical students, residents, and graduates of residency programs. All candidates must be interested in training at research-intensive departments of psychiatry in major U.S. medical schools. Training sites with excellence as demonstrated by research facilities and resources, funded research, research faculty (including minority researchers), and successful training history are considered preferable.

Financial data Annual stipends are $10,008 for medical students, from $19,608 to $28,200 for residents, and up to $32,300 for post-residency fellows. Other benefits include travel funds to attend the annual meeting of the American Psychiatric Association (APA) or the American College of Neuropsychopharmacology, and limited tuition assistance for full-time trainees to attend specific courses that are required as part of their training.

Duration For medical students, 2 to 6 months, either during an elective period or as a summer experience; for residents, 3 to 6 months within or outside the home institution, although a year of full-time research training is also possible; for post-residency fellows, 2 years, although a third year is possible if appropriate to a trainee's career development.

Special features This program is funded by the National Institute of Mental Health and administered by the APA.

Number awarded Varies each year.

Deadline Medical students and residents seeking less than 1 year of training may apply at any time, but at least 3 months before the proposed training is to begin; medical students seeking summer training should apply by March of each year; residents seeking a year or more of training and post-residency fellows should apply by November of each year.

[858]
SAFE AND DRUG-FREE SCHOOLS AND COMMUNITIES PROGRAM FOR NATIVE HAWAIIANS

Department of Education
Attn: Office of Elementary and Secondary Education
Safe and Drug-Free Schools Program
600 Independence Avenue, S.W.
Washington, DC 20202-6123
(202) 260-3954

Purpose To provide assistance to organizations that primarily serve and represent Hawaiian Natives for Drug and alcohol abuse education and prevention programs.

Eligibility Eligible to apply for grants under this program are organizations that primarily serve and represent Hawaiian natives and are recognized as such by the governor of Hawaii. Native Hawaiians are individuals, any of whose ancestors were natives, prior to 1778, of the area which now comprise the state of Hawaii.

Financial data Amounts of the grants depend on the merits of the application and the availability of funds.

Duration 1 year or longer; may be renewed.

Number awarded Varies each year.

Deadline Deadline dates vary; check the *Federal Register* for the current schedule.

Native Americans
in General

[859]
AAUW DISSERTATION FELLOWSHIPS

American Association of University Women
Attn: Educational Foundation
2201 North Dodge Street
Iowa City, IA 52243-4030
(319) 337-1716   Fax: (319) 337-1204

Purpose To provide financial assistance to women in the final year of writing their dissertation.

Eligibility Applicants must be citizens of the United States or hold permanent resident status and must intend to pursue their professional careers in the United States. They should have successfully completed all required course work, passed all preliminary examinations, and received written acceptance of their prospectus. Applicants may pursue research in any field except engineering (the Association offers Engineering Dissertation Fellow-

ships as a separate program). Women of color are strongly encouraged to apply.

Financial data Fellows receive $14,500.

Duration 1 year, beginning in July. Recipients may reapply for a second award.

Special features There are no restrictions on the applicant's age, field of study, or place of study.

Limitations It is expected that the fellowship would be used for the final year of doctoral work and that the degree would be received at the end of the fellowship year. The fellowship is not intended to fund extended field research. The recipient should be prepared to devote full time to the dissertation during the fellowship year.

Number awarded 50 each year.

Deadline November of each year.

[860]
AAUW SUMMER FELLOWSHIPS

American Association of University Women
Attn: Educational Foundation
2201 North Dodge Street
Iowa City, IA 52243-4030
(319) 337-1716   Fax: (319) 337-1204

Purpose To provide summer fellowships to women scholars for postdoctoral research.

Eligibility Tenured, nontenured, and adjunct women faculty at colleges and universities whose teaching loads limit active research may apply for these awards. Extra consideration goes to original research that enhances teaching and includes student participation. There are no restrictions on place of study, field of study, or age of applicant. Women of color are strongly encouraged to apply. Selection is based on scholarly excellence, teaching experience, and active commitment to helping women and girls through service in community, profession, or field of research.

Financial data Fellows receive $5,000.

Duration 8 weeks during the summer.

Limitations This program is not intended for scholars with strong publishing records.

Number awarded 6 each year.

Deadline November of each year.

[861]
ABE FELLOWSHIP PROGRAM

Social Science Research Council
810 Seventh Avenue
New York, NY 10019
(212) 377-2700   Fax: (212) 377-2727

Purpose To support postdoctoral research on contemporary policy-relevant affairs in Japan.

Eligibility This program is open to American and Japanese research professionals who have doctorate-equivalent or professional experience (other nationals affiliated with an American or Japanese institution are also eligible to apply). Applicants should be researchers interested in policy-relevant topics of long-range importance who are willing and able to become key members of a bilateral and global research network built around such topics. Previous language training is not a prerequisite for this fellowship. Minorities and women are particularly encouraged to apply.

Financial data The terms of the fellowship include a base award and supplementary research and travel expenses as necessary for completion of the research project.

Duration Up to 12 months (although fellowship tenure need not be continuous).

Special features Fellows are expected to affiliate with an American or Japanese institution appropriate to their research aims. In addition to receiving fellowship awards, fellows attend annual Abe Fellows Conferences, which promote the development of an international network of scholars concerned with research on contemporary policy issues. Funds are provided by the Japan Foundation's Center for Global Partnership.

Limitations Fellows should plan to spend at least one-third of their tenure abroad in Japan or the United States.

Deadline August of each year.

[862]
ACADEMIC CAREER AWARDS

National Institutes of Health
Attn: Office of Extramural Research
Extramural Outreach and Information Resources Office
6701 Rockledge Drive, Room 6207
MSC 7910
Bethesda, MD 20892-7910
(301) 435-0714   Fax: (301) 480-8443
E-mail: asknih@odrockm1.od.nih.gov

Purpose To provide financial support to individuals interested in introducing or improving curriculum in a particular scientific field as a means of enhancing the educational or research capacity at the grantee institution.

Eligibility Candidates for these awards must have a clinical or research doctoral degree. The program is open both to junior investigators who are interested in developing an academic and research expertise in a particular field and to senior scientists with acknowledged scientific expertise and leadership skills who are interested in improving the curricula and enhancing the research capacity within the academic institution. Junior candidates should propose a plan of teaching, curriculum building, research, and leadership development, under the guidance of a mentor who is an expert in the research field of interest and has a record of providing the type of supervision required by this award; these candidates must be able to devote at least 75 percent of full-time professional effort to the research and development programs required for academic development. Senior candidates must have sufficient clinical training, research, or teaching experience to implement a program of curriculum development within the applicant institution; must have an academic appointment at a level sufficient to exert an influence on the coordination of research, teaching, and clinical practice in an emerging field; and must be able to devote at least 25 percent effort to the program. Applications may be submitted on behalf of candidates by domestic, non-federal organizations, public or private, such as medical, dental, or nursing schools or other institutions of higher education. Minorities and women are particularly encouraged to apply. Candidates must be U.S. citizens or permanent residents.

Financial data This program provides salary and fringe benefits for the candidate only; each component establishes its own salary limits on career awards. Indirect costs are reimbursed at 8 percent of modified total direct costs, or at the actual indirect cost rate, whichever is less.

Duration 5 years for junior awards; 2 to 5 years for senior awards.

Special features Awards under this program are available from 6 agencies of the National Institutes of Health (NIH): the National Institute on Aging, the National Institute on Alcohol Abuse and Alcoholism, the National Institute of Arthritis and Musculoskeletal and Skin Diseases, the National Cancer Institute, the National Institute of Environmental Health Sciences, and the National Institute of Mental Health. The names and addresses of staff people at each agency are available from the address above. The NIH designates this program as the K07 Awards.

Number awarded Varies each year.

Deadline January, May, or September of each year.

[863]
ACADEMIC EXCELLENCE AWARDS IN BILINGUAL EDUCATION

Department of Education
Attn: Office of Bilingual Education and Minority Languages
  Affairs
Switzer Building, Room 5609
600 Independence Avenue, S.W.
Washington, DC 20202-6510
(202) 205-8728

Purpose To provide financial assistance for programs of bilingual education, special alternative instruction, and professional development that demonstrate promise of assisting children and youth of limited English proficiency to meet challenging state standards.

Eligibility State education agencies (SEAs) may apply for these grants if they have programs that have been implemented already at 1 or more sites. Local education agencies, institutions of higher education, or private nonprofit organizations may also apply upon nomination by the appropriate SEA. Selection is based on evidence of effectiveness (25 points), sound research (15 points), potential for adoption (20 points), management plan (20 points), evaluation plan (15 points), key personnel (10 points), and coordination of activities (10 points).

Financial data The amounts of the awards depend on the nature of the applications and the availability of funds.

Duration 1 year or longer.

Number awarded Varies each year.

Deadline Deadline dates vary each year; check the latest edition of the *Federal Register* for the current application schedule.

[864]
ACADEMIC RESEARCH ENHANCEMENT AWARD

National Institutes of Health
Attn: Office of Extramural Research
Extramural Outreach and Information Resources Office
6701 Rockledge Drive, Room 6207
MSC 7910
Bethesda, MD 20892-7910
(301) 435-0714   Fax: (301) 480-8443
E-mail: asknih@odrockm1.od.nih.gov

Purpose To stimulate research in educational institutions (particularly minority and women's institutions) that provide baccalaureate training for a significant number of American research scientists but that have not been major participants in National Institutes of Health (NIH) programs.

Eligibility This grant program is offered to researchers at domestic institutions that offer baccalaureate or advanced degrees in the sciences related to health, except those that have received research grants and cooperative agreements from the National Institutes of Health (NIH) totaling more than $2 million per year in each of the preceding 4 or more years. Health professional schools (e.g., schools of medicine, dentistry, nursing, osteopathy, pharmacy, veterinary medicine, public health, allied health, and optometry) are eligible, as are officially discrete campuses of a university. Investigators eligible for the program are those who will not have active research grant support from the NIH at the time of application. Scientists working in eligible minority and women's educational institutions are particularly encouraged to submit an application.

Financial data Up to $75,000 in direct costs, plus applicable indirect costs, for a 36-month period. No more than $35,000 may be requested for direct costs for any 1 year.

Duration Up to 36 months.

Special features The NIH designates this program as the R15 awards.

Limitations Investigators applying for this program may not submit a separate grant application for essentially the same project to the NIH. Principal investigators are expected to conduct the majority of their research at their own institution, although limited access to special facilities or equipment at another institution is permitted.

Number awarded Approximately 140 each year. A total of approximately $14 million per year has been available for this program.

Deadline June of each year.

---

[865]
ACE FELLOWS PROGRAM

American Council on Education
Attn: Office of Minorities in Higher Education
One Dupont Circle, N.W.
Washington, DC 20036-1193
(202) 939-9420   Fax: (202) 833-4760

Purpose To identify and train administrators, especially women and minorities, for higher education.

Eligibility Faculty members and junior administrators may be nominated by the president/senior officer of an American academic institution. Nominees must have at least 5 years of teaching or administrative experience and demonstrate an ability for academic administration. Minorities and women are strongly urged to apply.

Financial data The nominating institution continues to pay the Fellow's full salary and benefits; the host institution is responsible for paying the Fellow's travel and meeting attendance costs of approximately $10,000 per year and for paying a program fee of $3,000 to the American Council on Education; grants between $10,000 and $12,000 are available to the nominating institution to help offset the expense of replacing the Fellow.

Duration 1 academic year.

Special features Fellows work with a mentor at policy and routine levels at the host college or university. In addition, they attend national and regional seminars and meetings.

Number awarded 30 each year.

Deadline October of each year.

[866]
ACLS FELLOWSHIPS

American Council of Learned Societies
228 East 45th Street
New York, NY 10017-3398
(212) 697-1505   Fax: (212) 949-8058
E-mail: grants@acls.org

Purpose To provide financial assistance for postdoctoral research in all disciplines of the humanities and the humanities-related social sciences.

Eligibility Applicants must be U.S. citizens or permanent residents who received a Ph.D. degree at least 2 years prior to the date of application and who have not held supported research leave time for at least 5 years prior to the start of the proposed research. Scholars at all stages of their careers, both institutionally-affiliated and independent, are eligible. Especially encouraged are scholars, both tenured and untenured, whose teaching loads restrict time for research, whose normal places of work are remote from repositories of research materials, and who have no institutional support for their research and writing. Applications are particularly invited from women and members of minority groups.

Financial data Stipends up to $20,000 are available. Normally, fellowships are intended as salary replacement and may be held concurrently with other fellowships and grants and any sabbatical pay, up to an amount equal to the candidate's current academic year salary.

Duration 6 to 12 months.

Special features This program is supported in part by funding from the Ford Foundation, the Andrew W. Mellon Foundation, the National Endowment for the Humanities, and the Rockefeller Foundation.

Number awarded Varies each year.

Deadline September of each year.

[867]
ADHF/AGA STUDENT RESEARCH FELLOWSHIPS

American Digestive Health Foundation
7910 Woodmont Avenue, Suite 700
Bethesda, MD 20814-3015
(301) 654-2635   Fax: (301) 654-5920

Purpose To provide funding for research on digestive diseases or nutrition to students at any level.

Eligibility This program is open to high school, undergraduate, graduate, or medical students in North America who are not yet engaged in thesis research. They must be interested in conducting research on digestive diseases or nutrition. Candidates must not hold similar salary support awards from other agencies (e.g., American Liver Foundation, Crohn's and Colitis Foundation). Women and minority students are strongly encouraged to apply. Selection is based on novelty, feasibility and significance of the proposal, attributes of the candidate, record of the sponsor, institutional commitment, and laboratory environment.

Financial data The grant is at least $2,500. No indirect costs are allowed. The award is paid directly to the student and is to be used as a stipend.

Duration 10 to 12 weeks. The work may take place at any time during the year.

Special features In an effort to attract and encourage minorities, 7 of the awards are set aside specifically for underrepresented minority students (African Americans, Hispanic Americans, Native Americans, Alaskan Natives, and Pacific Islanders).

This award is administered by the American Digestive Health Foundation (ADHF) and sponsored by the American Gastroenterological Association (AGA).

Limitations Funds may not be used to support thesis research.

Number awarded Up to 35 each year (7 of which are set aside specifically for underrepresented minorities).

Deadline January of each year.

[868]
ADOPTION OPPORTUNITIES PROGRAM GRANTS

Department of Health and Human Services
Attn: Administration for Children and Families
Administration on Children, Youth and Families
Children's Bureau
370 L'Enfant Promenade, S.W.
Washington, DC 20447
(800) 351-2293

Purpose To provide financial assistance to public agencies involved with adoption services for special needs children.

Eligibility Currently, 6 priority areas have been identified for grants: 1) achieving increased adoptive placement of children in foster care; 2) innovations increasing adoptive placements of minority children; 3) strategic collaboration for completing and sustaining adoptions of children with developmental disabilities; 4) expanding options for permanency; 5) developing resource materials for foster and adoptive parents to meet the needs of children of a different race, color, or national origin; and 6) operation of a national adoption information exchange system. Eligibility requirements vary for each priority area, but generally extend to states, local government entities, public or private nonprofit licensed child welfare or adoption agencies, and adoption exchanges and community-based organizations, especially those with experience in working with minority populations.

Financial data The maximum annual federal share of project costs is $100,000 ($75,000 for developing resource materials for foster and adoptive parents, $500,000 for operation of a national adoption information exchange system). The applicant share of project costs is 10 percent of total project costs (25 percent for operation of a national adoption information exchange system).

Duration Up to 3 years, depending on the priority area.

Number awarded The number of awards varies according to priority area; recently, available funding allowed for 2 projects for achieving increased adoptive placement of children in foster care, 4 projects for increasing adoptive placements of minority children, 2 projects for completing and sustaining adoptions of children with developmental disabilities, 2 projects for expanding options for permanency, 2 projects for developing resource materials, and 1 project for operation of a national adoption information exchange system.

Deadline August of each year.

[869]
ADVANCED NURSE EDUCATION GRANTS

Health Resources and Services Administration
Attn: Bureau of Health Professions
Division of Nursing
Parklawn Building, Room 9-36
5600 Fishers Lane
Rockville, MD 20857
(301) 443-6333   Fax: (301) 443-8586

Purpose To provide grants to collegiate schools of nursing to increase the number of registered nurses prepared as nurse educators, public health nurses, or other clinical nurse specialists.

Eligibility Public and private nonprofit collegiate schools of nursing may apply for these grants to 1) plan, develop, and operate, or 2) significantly expand programs at the master's or doctoral level to prepare professional nurses to serve as nurse educators, public health nurses, or in clinical nurse specialities that require advanced education. Selection is based on the need for the proposed project; the need for nurses in the proposed specialty in the state in which the education program is located, as compared with the need for these nurses in other states; the potential effectiveness of the proposed project in carrying out the educational purposes; the capability of the applicant to carry out the proposed project; the soundness of the fiscal plan; the potential of the project to continue on a self-sustaining basis after the period of grant support; and the degree to which the applicant proposes to attract, retain, and graduate minority and financially needy students.

Financial data Recently, $11.9 million per year in grants was provided through this program; the average grant was $189,700.

Duration 1 year; may be renewed.

Number awarded Approximately 60 each year.

Deadline February of each year.

[870]
ADVANCED TECHNOLOGICAL EDUCATION PROGRAM

National Science Foundation
Attn: Directorate for Education and Human Resources
Division of Undergraduate Education
4201 Wilson Boulevard, Room 835
Arlington, VA 22230
(703) 306-1668   E-mail: undergrad@nsf.gov

Purpose To provide funding for programs that seek to improve advanced technological education.

Eligibility Proposals are invited from 2-year colleges, other associate degree granting institutions, 2-year college systems, and consortia of 2-year colleges as well as consortia of 2-year colleges with other appropriate organizations and institutions such as 4-year colleges and universities, secondary schools, professional societies, industry, and nonprofit, educational research and development groups. The proposals may be for 1) projects, including those for curriculum and instructional materials, teacher and faculty development, technical experiences for students, or laboratory development; 2) national/regional centers of excellence for advanced technological education, to promote curriculum development and program improvement; 3) workshops, conferences, seminars, studies, and other special projects. The National Science Foundation (NSF) particularly encourages proposals that strengthen undergraduate education by increasing the participation of women, underrepresented minorities, and persons with disabilities, especially if the projects present models for increasing the numbers who successfully pursue careers in science, mathematics, engineering, and technology. Underrepresented minorities are defined as African Americans, Alaskan Natives (Eskimos and Aleuts), Hispanics, Native Americans, and Native Pacific Islanders (Micronesians and Polynesians).

Financial data Planning grants for centers may be funded for up to $50,000; implementation grants for centers may receive up to $1 million per year; curriculum and instructional materials projects may receive from $50,000 to $500,000 per year; teacher and faculty development grants normally range from $25,000 to $500,000 per year; the maximum NSF request for instrumentation and laboratory improvement is $100,000, which must be matched by an equal or greater amount of non-federal dollars.

Duration Awards for centers are 3 to 5 years; curriculum and instructional materials projects extend from 1 to 4 years; teacher and faculty development projects are from 1 to 3 years.

Special features This program is jointly managed by 2 divisions within the NSF Directorate for Education and Human Resources: Undergraduate Education (at the address and telephone number above), and Elementary, Secondary, and Informal Education, at (703) 306-1614.

Number awarded The number of awards granted depends on the quality of the proposals received and the availability of funds for the program; in a recent year, this program provided 39 new and 15 continuing awards.

Deadline Preliminary proposals must be submitted by June of each year; formal proposals are due by December.

[871]
AGENCY FOR TOXIC SUBSTANCES AND DISEASE REGISTRY CLINICAL FELLOWSHIPS IN ENVIRONMENTAL MEDICINE

Oak Ridge Institute for Science and Education
Attn: Science/Engineering Education Division
P.O. Box 117
Oak Ridge, TN 37831-0117
(423) 576-8503   (423) 576-2875
(800) 569-7749   Fax: (423) 576-3643
E-mail: atsdrcfe@orau.gov

Purpose To provide support for applied, environmentally-related clinical research that helps prevent or mitigate the adverse human health effects and diminished quality of life that may result from exposure to hazardous substances in the non-workplace environment.

Eligibility This program is open to persons who have completed a medical degree and are board eligible in a clinical specialty with 1 or more years of additional training in occupational medicine and/or clinical (environmental) toxicology. All programs operated by the Science/Engineering Education Division (SEED) of Oak Ridge Institute for Science and Education (ORISE) seek to broaden the participation of minorities, women, and persons with disabilities in science and engineering careers.

Financial data Participants receive an annual stipend of $26,000, equivalent to half-time service.

Duration 1 year; renewable.

Special features Recipients of these fellowships engage in research at facilities (hospitals, clinics, or medical schools) recognized by the Association of Occupational and Environmental Health. The Agency for Toxic Substances and Disease Registry (ATSDR) was established by Superfund legislation in 1980; its mission is to prevent or mitigate adverse human health effects and diminished quality of life resulting from exposure to hazard-

ous substances in the environment. This program is funded by an interagency agreement between the U.S. Department of Energy and ATSDR (part of the U.S. Public Health Service) and administered by ORISE/SEED.

Number awarded Varies each year.

Deadline January of each year.

[872]
AGENCY FOR TOXIC SUBSTANCES AND DISEASE REGISTRY FACULTY RESEARCH PARTICIPATION PROGRAM

Oak Ridge Institute for Science and Education
Attn: Science/Engineering Education Division
P.O. Box 117
Oak Ridge, TN 37831-0117
(423) 576-8807   (423) 576-8158
(800) 569-7749   Fax: (423) 576-3643
E-mail: frppatsd@orau.gov

Purpose To support faculty research in exposure and disease registries, health investigations, public health assessments, toxicological profiles, emergency response, and health education at the Agency for Toxic Substances and Disease Registry (ATSDR) in Atlanta, Georgia.

Eligibility This program is open to college or university full-time faculty members in toxicology, epidemiology, environmental or public health, medicine, pharmacology, or related disciplines in the biological, medical, or physical sciences. All programs operated by the Science/Engineering Education Division (SEED) of Oak Ridge Institute for Science and Education (ORISE) seek to broaden the participation of minorities, women, and persons with disabilities in science and engineering careers.

Financial data Participants receive a negotiable stipend based on their regular salary and reimbursement for travel.

Duration 10 weeks to 3 months.

Special features Some sabbatical appointments are available. ATSDR was established by Superfund legislation in 1980; its mission is to prevent or mitigate adverse human health effects and diminished quality of life resulting from exposure to hazardous substances in the environment. This program is funded by an interagency agreement between the U.S. Department of Energy and ATSDR (part of the U.S. Public Health Service) and administered by ORISE/SEED.

Number awarded Varies each year.

Deadline Applications may be submitted at any time.

[873]
AGENCY FOR TOXIC SUBSTANCES AND DISEASE REGISTRY POSTGRADUATE RESEARCH PROGRAM

Oak Ridge Institute for Science and Education
Attn: Science/Engineering Education Division
P.O. Box 117
Oak Ridge, TN 37831-0117
(423) 576-8503   (423) 576-2875
(800) 569-7749   Fax: (423) 576-3643
E-mail: prpatsdr@orau.gov

Purpose To support research in exposure and disease registries, health investigations, public health assessments, toxicological profiles, emergency response, and health education at the Agency for Toxic Substances and Disease Registry (ATSDR) in Atlanta, Georgia.

Eligibility This program is open to persons who have completed a graduate degree within the past 3 years; other applicants are considered on a case-by-case basis. Candidates should have earned a degree in toxicology, epidemiology, environmental or public health, medicine, pharmacology, or related scientific disciplines. All programs operated by the Science/Engineering Education Division (SEED) of Oak Ridge Institute for Science and Education (ORISE) seek to broaden the participation of minorities, women, and persons with disabilities in science and engineering careers.

Financial data Participants receive a monthly stipend based on research area and degree; limited reimbursement for inbound travel and moving are also provided.

Duration 1 year; renewable.

Special features ATSDR was established by Superfund legislation in 1980; its mission is to prevent or mitigate adverse human health effects and diminished quality of life resulting from exposure to hazardous substances in the environment. This program is funded by an interagency agreement between the U.S. Department of Energy and ATSDR (part of the U.S. Public Health Service) and administered by ORISE/SEED.

Number awarded Varies each year.

Deadline Applications may be submitted at any time.

[874]
AHCPR SMALL PROJECT GRANT PROGRAM

Agency for Health Care Policy and Research
Attn: Office of Planning and Evaluation
Executive Office Center, Suite 603
2101 East Jefferson Street
Rockville, MD 20852-4908
(301) 594-1455   Fax: (301) 594-2157

Purpose To provide funding for small research projects designed to improve the quality, appropriateness, and effectiveness of health care services and access to those services.

Eligibility This program is open to investigators at domestic, nonprofit, public and private organizations, including universities, clinics, units of state and local governments, nonprofit firms, and nonprofit foundations. Applicants must be proposing projects for promoting improvements in clinical practice and in the organization, financing, and delivery of health care services. Proposals may be for research, evaluation, demonstrations, or pilot studies. The Agency for Health Care Policy and Research (AHCPR) especially encourages women, members of minority groups, persons with disabilities, and new investigators to apply as principal investigator.

Financial data Total direct costs may not exceed $50,000.

Duration Up to 2 years.

Limitations Funding from this program may not be used for dissertation research.

Number awarded Varies each year.

Deadline Applications may be submitted at any time.

[875]
AIR FORCE OFFICE OF SCIENTIFIC RESEARCH BROAD AGENCY ANNOUNCEMENT

Air Force Office of Scientific Research
Attn: Directorate of Academic and International Affairs
110 Duncan Avenue, Room B115
Bolling Air Force Base, DC 20332-8080
(202) 767-4969   Fax: (202) 767-5012
E-mail: jan.cerveny@afosr.af.mil

Purpose To provide funding for scientific research of interest to the U.S. Air Force.

Eligibility This program is open to investigators qualified to perform research in designated scientific and technical areas. The general fields of interest include aerospace and materials sciences, physics and electronics, chemistry and life sciences, and mathematics and geosciences. Assistance includes grants to university scientists, support for academic institutions, contracts for industry research, cooperative agreements, and support for basic research in Air Force laboratories. Because the Air Force encourages the sharing and transfer of technology, it welcomes proposals that envision cooperation among 2 or more partners from academia, industry, and Air Force organizations. It particularly encourages proposals from Historically Black Colleges and Universities (HBCUs), other Minority Institutions (MIs), and minority researchers.

Financial data The amounts of the awards depend on the nature of the proposals and the availability of funds. Recently, a total of $239.9 million per year has been available for this program; the average award has been approximately $150,000. Each year, a percentage of total funding is set aside for HBCUs and MIs.

Duration Grants are normally for up to 5 years.

Special features Contact the address above for details on particular program areas of interest. Outstanding principal investigators on grants issued through this program are nominated to receive Presidential Early Career Awards for Scientists and Engineers.

Number awarded Varies; approximately 1,600 grants and contracts are awarded to about 400 academic institutions and industrial firms each year.

Deadline Each program area specifies deadline dates.

[876]
ALABAMA SPACE GRANT CONSORTIUM GRADUATE FELLOWSHIP PROGRAM

Alabama Space Grant Consortium
c/o University of Alabama in Huntsville
Materials Science Building, Room 205
Huntsville, AL 35899
(205) 890-6028   Fax: (205) 890-6061
E-mail: jcgregory@matsci.uah.edu
E-mail: jfreasoner@matsci.uah.edu

Purpose To provide financial assistance for graduate study or research related to the space sciences at universities participating in the Alabama Space Grant Consortium.

Eligibility This program is open to graduate students enrolled at 1 of the 6 universities participating in the Alabama Space Grant Consortium: University of Alabama in Huntsville, Alabama A&M University, University of Alabama, University of Alabama at Birmingham, University of South Alabama, and Auburn University. Applicants must be studying in a field related to space, including the physical, natural, and biological sciences, engineering, education, economics, business, sociology, behavioral sciences, computer science, communications, law, international affairs, and public administration. They must be U.S. citizens. Individuals from underrepresented groups—specifically African Americans, Hispanics, American Indians, Pacific Islanders, Asian Americans, people with disabilities, and women of all races—are encouraged to apply. Interested students should submit a completed application form, description of the proposed research, a schedule, a budget, a list of references, a vitae, and undergraduate and graduate transcripts. Selection is based on 1) academic qualifications, 2) quality of the proposed research program and its relevance to the aerospace science and technology program of the National Aeronautics and Space Administration (NASA), 3) quality of the proposed interdisciplinary approach, 4) merit of the proposed utilization of a NASA center to carry out the objectives of the program, 5) prospects for completing the project within the allotted time, and 6) applicant's motivation for a career in aerospace.

Financial data The award for 12 months includes $16,000 for a student stipend and up to $4,000 for a tuition/student research allowance.

Duration Up to 36 months.

Number awarded Varies; generally, 10 to 12 each year.

Deadline February of each year.

[877]
ALEXANDER HOLLAENDER DISTINGUISHED POSTDOCTORAL FELLOWSHIP PROGRAM

Oak Ridge Institute for Science and Education
Attn: Science/Engineering Education Division
P.O. Box 117
Oak Ridge, TN 37831-0117
(423) 576-9975   (423) 576-3192
(800) 569-7749   Fax: (423) 576-3643
E-mail: alexpgm@orau.gov

Purpose To provide financial assistance for postdoctoral research and training in energy-related life, biomedical, and environmental sciences.

Eligibility Applicants must have completed a doctoral degree within the past 2 years and be proposing a program of research and training in biomedical sciences, life sciences, environmental sciences, and other scientific disciplines related to energy. Awards are tenable at laboratories in the United States that are affiliated with or supported by the U.S. Department of Energy; for a list of those, contact the address above. All programs operated by the Science/Engineering Education Division (SEED) of Oak Ridge Institute for Science and Education (ORISE) seek to broaden the participation of minorities, women, and persons with disabilities in science and engineering careers.

Financial data The stipend is $37,500 per year for the first year and $40,500 for the second year; reimbursement for inbound travel, moving, and medical insurance are also provided.

Duration 1 year; renewable for 1 additional year.

Special features This program is funded by the DOE Office and Health and Environmental Research within the Office of Energy Research and administered by ORISE/SEED.

Number awarded Varies each year.

Deadline January of each year.

[878]
ALEXANDER SISSON AWARD

Geological Society of America
Attn: Research Grants Administrator
3300 Penrose Place
P.O. Box 9140
Boulder, CO 80301-9140
(303) 447-2020, ext. 137   Fax: (303) 447-1133
E-mail: jforstro@geosociety.org

Purpose To provide partial support for geological research by graduate students.

Eligibility This program is open to graduate students in geology at the master's or doctoral level. Both members and non-members of the society are eligible. Special consideration is given to students pursuing studies in Alaska and the Caribbean. Applications from women, minorities, and persons with disabilities are strongly encouraged.

Financial data Grants range up to $2,500; the average grant recently was $1,604.

Duration 1 year.

Number awarded 1 or more each year.

Deadline February of each year.

[879]
ALLAN V. COX AWARD

Geological Society of America
Attn: Research Grants Administrator
3300 Penrose Place
P.O. Box 9140
Boulder, CO 80301-9140
(303) 447-2020, ext. 137   Fax: (303) 447-1133
E-mail: jforstro@geosociety.org

Purpose To provide partial support for geological research by graduate students at universities in the United States, Canada, Mexico, and Central America.

Eligibility This program is open to graduate students in geology at the master's or doctoral level. Both members and non-members of the society are eligible. Special consideration may be given to students who propose research on 1 or more aspects of geophysics. Applications from women, minorities, and persons with disabilities are strongly encouraged.

Financial data Grants range up to $2,500; the average grant recently was $1,604.

Duration 1 year.

Special features This program is sponsored by the Geological Society of America's Geophysics Division.

Number awarded 1 or more each year.

Deadline February of each year.

[880]
ALLIANCES FOR MINORITY PARTICIPATION GRANTS

National Science Foundation
Attn: Directorate for Education and Human Resources
Division of Human Resource Development
4201 Wilson Boulevard, Room 815
Arlington, VA 22230
(703) 306-1632   E-mail: hrdamp@nsf.gov

Purpose To support programs designed to increase the quality and quantity of undergraduate students in science and engineering fields, especially minority students and others who are currently underrepresented.

Eligibility Organizations eligible to apply are limited to academic institutions that have exemplary records over several years of enrolling and retaining significant numbers of undergraduate students who are underrepresented in science, mathematics, engineering, and technology (SMET) fields (minorities, women and girls, and persons with disabilities) and who earn baccalaureate degrees in those fields. The eligible institution must apply as part of a coalition involving community colleges, colleges and universities, state/local governments, industry, private foundations, SMET professional organizations, and other federal agencies. Applicants must be proposing programs for undergraduate education, including student enrichment activities, academic enrichment and curricular improvement activities, enhancement of student participation at institutions with significant SMET enrollment, and direct student support to enable students to attend summer enrichment activities.

Financial data Grants are made up to $1 million per year.

Duration Up to 5 years.

Special features Undergraduate students interested in participating in this program should contact the address above to obtain a list of participating institutions.

Number awarded Approximately 5 each year.

Deadline October of each year.

[881]
ALZHEIMER'S ASSOCIATION INVESTIGATOR-INITIATED RESEARCH GRANTS

Alzheimer's Association
Attn: Medical and Scientific Affairs
919 North Michigan Avenue, Suite 1000
Chicago, IL 60611-1676
(312) 335-8700

Purpose To provide funding for research on Alzheimer's Disease.

Eligibility Qualified investigators with at least 3 years postdoctoral experience who are working in nonprofit institutions may submit research proposals. Grants are intended to pursue the following objectives: 1) finding the cause(s) of Alzheimer's disease by seeking its biological underpinnings; 2) preventing the disease by discovering selective risk factors and their interactions with genetic and epigenetic factors; 3) developing safe and effective treatments using pharmacological and behavioral approaches that would delay institutionalization by 5 to 10 years; 4) developing effective care and management strategies using behavioral approaches aimed at prolonging independent functioning; 5) investigating the impact of behavioral, social, cultural, economic, and environmental factors on the clinical course of the disease; and 6) discovering methods for preventing disruptive behaviors and delaying the onset of symptoms that increase the burden of care by determining the interactions between behavioral, social, environmental, and biological risk factors. Investigators at a formative point in their careers, women, minorities, and persons with disabilities are strongly encouraged to apply.

Financial data Up to $50,000 per year, including direct expenses and up to 10 percent for overhead costs.

Duration From 1 to 3 years.

Special features This program operates under the auspices of the Ronald and Nancy Reagan Research Institute.

Number awarded Up to 15 each year.

Deadline February of each year.

[882]
AMERICAN HEART ASSOCIATION ESTABLISHED INVESTIGATOR GRANT

American Heart Association
Attn: Division of Research Administration
7272 Greenville Avenue
Dallas, TX 75231-4596
(214) 706-1453   Fax: (214) 706-1341
E-mail: ncrp@amhrt.org

Purpose To support the career development of highly promising clinician-scientists who have recently acquired independent status to ensure their continued success as cardiovascular investigators.

Eligibility Applicants must be citizens or permanent residents of the United States who hold an M.D., Ph.D., D.O., or equivalent degree at the time of application. They must be full-time members of a department or unit within an academic or research institution, usually with the rank of assistant professor; customarily, they should be 4 to 9 years past their first faculty appointment. The proposed research project must have received no previous financial support from other graning agencies. Applicants representative of a divergent population in regard to gender and racial/ethnic composition are encouraged.

Financial data The annual award of $75,000 includes salary, fringe benefits, indirect costs, and project costs (at least $40,000 for project support).

Duration 4 years.

Deadline June of each year.

Number awarded 50 each year.

[883]
AMERICAN HEART ASSOCIATION GRANT-IN-AID

American Heart Association
Attn: Division of Research Administration
7272 Greenville Avenue
Dallas, TX 75231-4596
(214) 706-1453   Fax: (214) 706-1341
E-mail: ncrp@amhrt.org

Purpose To encourage development of well-defined research proposals by independent beginning investigators and by established investigators pursuing new areas of research broadly related to cardiovascular function and disease, stroke, basic science, clinical, or public health problems.

Eligibility Proposals may be submitted by junior independent investigators or established investigators pursuing new areas of research. Applicants must have earned a doctoral degree, be on the staff of nonprofit institutions, and be U.S. citizens, permanent residents, or foreign nationals holding H1, H1B, or J1 immigrant status. The proposed research must be clearly distinct from ongoing research activities. Participation by applicants representative of a divergent population in regard to gender and racial/ethnic composition is encouraged.

Financial data Up to $55,000 per year (including 10 percent overhead).

Duration Up to 3 years.

Number awarded 100 each year.

Deadline June of each year.

[884]

AMERICAN HEART ASSOCIATION SCIENTIST DEVELOPMENT GRANT

American Heart Association
Attn: Division of Research Administration
7272 Greenville Avenue
Dallas, TX 75231-4596
(214) 706-1453   Fax: (214) 706-1341
E-mail: ncrp@amhrt.org

Purpose To assist promising beginning scientists to develop independent research programs by supporting a program that bridges the gap between completion of research training and readiness for competition as an independent investigator.

Eligibility Applicants must be citizens or permanent residents of the United States who hold an M.D., Ph.D, D.O., or equivalent degree and who are in the final year of a postdoctoral research fellowship or in the initial years of first faculty appointment. They cannot hold or have held any other national award. Applicants representative of a divergent population in regard to gender and racial/ethnic composition are encouraged.

Financial data The award includes $65,000 annually for salary, fringe benefits, indirect costs, and project costs (at least $35,000 for project support).

Duration 4 years.

Number awarded 70 each year.

Deadline June of each year.

[885]

AMERICAN INDIAN, ALASKA NATIVE, AND NATIVE HAWAIIAN MENTAL HEALTH RESEARCH GRANTS

National Institutes of Health
Attn: National Institute of Mental Health
Division of Epidemiology and Services Research
Parklawn Building, Room 10C-06
5600 Fishers Lane
Rockville, MD 20857
(301) 443-3364   Fax: (301) 443-4045
E-mail: ah21k@nih.gov

Purpose To encourage research that seeks to improve the care and quality of life of American Indians, Alaska Natives, and Native Hawaiians who suffer from mental illnesses.

Eligibility Applications may be submitted by researchers at any domestic public or private nonprofit or for-profit organization, including units of state and local governments, universities, colleges, hospitals, laboratories, tribal governments and organizations, and eligible agencies of the federal government. Proposals should involve research and research demonstration studies among American Indian, Alaska Native, and Native Hawaiian populations of the epidemiology and prevention of mental disorders, co-occurring substance abuse disorders, and suicide; family and individual coping styles and resiliency; family violence; and mental health service use and quality of care. Women and minority investigators are especially encouraged to apply.

Financial data Approximately $15 million per year is available for grants under this program.

Duration Up to 5 years.

Limitations Grant funds may not be used to operate a treatment, rehabilitation, or other service program, except in the case of a research demonstration grant.

Deadline January, May, or September of each year.

[886]

AMERICAN LIBRARY ASSOCIATION MINORITY FELLOWSHIP PROGRAM

American Library Association
Attn: Office for Literacy and Outreach Services
50 East Huron Street
Chicago, IL 60611-2795
(312) 280-4294   (800) 545-2433, ext. 4294
TDD: (312) 944-7298   Fax: (312) 280-3257

Purpose To provide an opportunity for underrepresented ethnic librarians to participate fully in the profession by working in the offices of the American Library Association (ALA).

Eligibility Fellowship applicants must be underrepresented ethnic professional librarians interested in acquiring association management experience and in analyzing current library issues. Underrepresented ethnicities are American Indians and Alaskan Natives, Asians and Pacific Islanders, African Americans, and Latinos. They must hold a master's degree from an accredited library school (or from a program that meets the ALA/AASL curriculum guidelines within a unit accredited by the National Council for the Accreditation of Teacher Education), have a minimum of 3 years and a maximum of 5 years of post-M.L.S. professional work experience in a library or information science environment, and be a member of the American Library Association at the start of the fellowship.

Financial data The stipend is $31,000, plus medical, dental, life insurance, and disability benefits as well as relocation assistance to Chicago.

Duration 1 year.

Special features Fellows are invited to indicate the division(s) in which they wish to work as part of the fellowship program; these include American Association of School Librarians/Young Adult Library Services Association, American Library Trustee Association, Association for Library Collections and Technical Services, Association for Library Service to Children, Association for College and Research Libraries, Association of Specialized and Cooperative Library Agencies, Library Administration and Management Association, Library and Information Technology Association, Public Library Association, Reference and User Services Division, Office for Intellectual Freedom, Office for Literacy and Outreach Services, and Office for Library Personnel Resources.

Number awarded 1 or more each year.

Deadline July of each year.

[887]

AMERICAN SOCIETY FOR MICROBIOLOGY FACULTY FELLOWSHIP PROGRAM

American Society for Microbiology
Attn: Office of Education and Training
1325 Massachusetts Avenue, N.W.
Washington, DC 20005-4171
(202) 942-9295   Fax: (202) 942-9329
E-mail: beidemiller@asmusa.org

Purpose To provide underrepresented minority faculty who are members of the American Society for Microbiology (ASM) with support for research.

Eligibility Applicants must be full-time faculty at accredited institutions teaching undergraduate students in the microbiological sciences or closely related fields, members of an underrepresented group in the biological sciences (African American, Hispanic American, Native American or Pacific Islander) or faculty members at an institution with enrollment predominantly from those groups, members of the Society, and U.S. citizens or permanent residents. They must be proposing a short-term program of research in the microbiological sciences. Applicants may not have received funding from the National Institutes of Health, National Science Foundation, or the Society within the past 5 years.

Financial data   Awards up to $4,000 are available.

Duration   1 to 2 months.

Special features   Usually the program involves a sustained summer experience in a formal course or relationship with a host scientist at another institution or facility.

Number awarded   Varies each year.

Deadline   January of each year.

[888]
ANDREW W. MELLON POSTDOCTORAL FELLOWSHIPS IN THE HUMANITIES AT BRYN MAWR COLLEGE

Graduate School of Arts and Sciences
Attn: Dean
Bryn Mawr College
101 North Merion Avenue
Bryn Mawr, PA 19010-2899
(610) 526-5074   E-mail: sbernhar@brynmawr.edu

Purpose   To provide funding for postdoctoral research in the humanities at Bryn Mawr College.

Eligibility   This program is open to postdoctorates interested in conducting research at Bryn Mawr College. The 2 positions are for 1) a specialist in Latino(a) literature and culture, who is expected to teach 1 course per semester in the area of expertise and to pursue his or her own research interests; and 2) a qualified scholar interested in the transnational flows of people, ideas, and artifacts both within and/or between East Asia and Southeast Asia (priority is given to researchers whose work focuses on social and intellectual histories, religion and/or gender concerns, and/or the intersections of language, identity, and politics relevant to those transnational flows). Applicants must have earned their doctorate prior to the commencement of the fellowship. Minority and women candidates are particularly encouraged to apply.

Financial data   The stipend is $30,000.

Duration   1 year.

Number awarded   2 each year.

Deadline   January of each year for the Latino(a) literature and culture fellowship; February of each year for the Asian transnational studies fellowship.

[889]
ANL LABORATORY–GRADUATE RESEARCH APPOINTMENTS

Argonne National Laboratory
Attn: Division of Educational Programs
Graduate Student Program Office
9700 South Cass Avenue
Argonne, IL 60439-4845
(630) 252-3371   Fax: (630) 252-3193
E-mail: ettinger@dep.anl.gov

Purpose   To offer opportunities for qualified graduate students to carry out their master's or doctoral thesis research at the Argonne National Laboratory.

Eligibility   Appointments are available for graduate students at U.S. universities who wish to carry out their thesis research under the co-sponsorship of a Laboratory staff member and a faculty member. Research may be conducted in the basic physical and life sciences, mathematics, computer science, and engineering, as well as in a variety of applied areas relating to conservation, environment, fission and fusion energy, and other energy technologies. Applicants must be U.S. citizens or permanent residents. The Laboratory encourages applications from all qualified persons, especially women and members of underrepresented minority groups.

Financial data   Support consists of a stipend, tuition payments up to $5,000 per year, and certain travel expenses. In addition, the student's faculty sponsor may receive payment for limited travel expenses.

Duration   1 year; may be renewed.

Special features   This program, which is also referred to as the Lab–Grad Program, is sponsored by the U.S. Department of Energy. In certain cases, students may be awarded support for pre-thesis studies on campus, provided they intend to carry out their thesis research at Argonne. Mutual interest in an area of research by the student and the Argonne staff sponsor is essential for the successful arrangement of a Lab-Grad appointment. To help the parties gauge their mutual interest, a limited number of temporary appointments are available for qualified graduate students, so they may work with an Argonne staff member and become familiar with his/her research program. These temporary appointments have a tenure of 3 months and support consists of a per diem payment to help defray the cost of living away from home, plus travel expenses.

Number awarded   Varies each year.

Deadline   Applications may be submitted at any time, but a complete application should be submitted at least 2 months prior to any proposed starting date.

[890]
ANTARCTIC RESEARCH PROGRAM

National Science Foundation
Attn: Office of Polar Programs
4201 Wilson Boulevard
Arlington, VA 22230
(703) 306-1033   Fax: (703) 306-0139

Purpose   To provide funding for research related to Antarctica.

Eligibility   This program is open to investigators at U.S. institutions, primarily universities and, to a lesser extent, federal agencies and other organizations. Applicants must be proposing to conduct research in the areas of astrophysics, atmospheric sciences, earth sciences, environmental sciences, glaciology, instrumentation, marine biology, marine geology and geophysics, medical sciences, physical and chemical oceanography, terrestrial biology, and upper atmosphere physics. Proposals must involve research in Antarctica or related research and data analysis in the United States. The program particularly encourages proposals from women and minorities and welcomes proposals for research projects that include participation by undergraduates and high school students under guidelines established by cross-disciplinary programs of the National Science Foundation (NSF).

Financial data   The amounts of the awards depend on the nature of the proposal and the availability of funds; a recent year's funding provided approximately $29 million as awards to institutions for research, $42 million as direct support of research projects, and $125 as operational support.

Special features The NSF operates 3 year-round research stations, additional research facilities and camps, airplanes, helicopters, various types of surface vehicles, and ships.

Number awarded Approximately 130 each year.

Deadline May of each year.

[891]
ANTOINETTE LIERMAN MEDLIN SCHOLARSHIP AWARD

Geological Society of America
Attn: Research Grants Administrator
3300 Penrose Place
P.O. Box 9140
Boulder, CO 80301-9140
(303) 447-2020, ext. 137   Fax: (303) 447-1133
E-mail: jforstro@geosociety.org

Purpose To provide partial support for geological research by undergraduate or graduate students at universities in the United States, Canada, Mexico, and Central America.

Eligibility This program is open to undergraduate and graduate students (at the master's or doctoral level) in geology. Both members and nonmembers of the society are eligible. Special consideration may be given to students who propose research on 1 or more aspects of coal geology. Applications from women, minorities, and persons with disabilities are strongly encouraged.

Financial data Grants range up to $2,500; the average grant recently was $1,604.

Duration 1 year.

Special features This program is sponsored by the Geological Society of America's Coal Geology Division. Applications are also available from the Division Secretary, Cortland F. Eble, Kentucky Geological Survey, 228 Mining and Minerals Resources Building, University of Kentucky, Lexington, KY 40506-0107.

Number awarded 1 or more each year.

Deadline February of each year.

[892]
ARCHAEOLOGICAL CONSERVATION POSTGRADUATE FELLOWSHIP

Smithsonian Institution
Attn: Conservation Analytical Laboratory
Education and Training, MSC
MRC 534
Washington, DC 20560
(301) 238-3700   Fax: (301) 238-3709
E-mail: cal.etp@cal.si.edu

Purpose To enable postgraduates interested in archaeological conservation to conduct research at the Smithsonian Institution's Conservation Analytical Laboratory (CAL).

Eligibility This program is open to recent graduates of recognized conservation training programs or persons with comparable training and experience. Recipients spend approximately half the year at archaeological sites with which CAL is associated; in the past, CAL conservators have worked with excavation teams at Harappa (Pakistan), Cerén (El Salvador), and Copán (Honduras). For the remainder of the time, fellows work in the Objects Conservation Laboratory at CAL, where they treat archaeological artifacts or carry out research. Minorities are particularly encouraged to apply.

Financial data The stipend is $20,000, plus a travel and research allowance of $2,000. Health insurance is provided for fellows without personal coverage.

Duration 1 year.

Number awarded 1 each year.

Deadline January of each year.

[893]
ARCHIVES PRESERVATION POSTGRADUATE FELLOWSHIPS

Smithsonian Institution
Attn: Conservation Analytical Laboratory
Education and Training, MSC
MRC 534
Washington, DC 20560
(301) 238-3700   Fax: (301) 238-3709
E-mail: cal.etp@cal.si.edu

Purpose To provide specialized training in preservation of archival materials to postgraduate fellows at the Conservation Analytical Laboratory (CAL) of the Smithsonian Institution.

Eligibility This program is open to all recent graduates of recognized conservation training programs, or persons of comparable training and experience. Recipients work at CAL and with collections of the Smithsonian Institution, which has many archives, library, and research holdings including a full range of paper materials (manuscripts, documents, prints, drawings, and papers), as well as parchment and photographic materials. Minorities are particularly encouraged to apply.

Financial data The stipend is $20,000, plus a travel and research allowance of $2,000. Health insurance is provided for fellows without personal coverage.

Duration 1 year.

Special features Fellows undertake surveys, design and carry out rehousing projects, participate in and learn to organize training workshops, and initiate training projects for collections managers. Fellows may also treat selected archive-related artifacts and materials, and carry out research, making use of well-equipped scientific laboratories. This program is jointly administered by CAL and the Smithsonian's Office of Fellowships and Grants.

Number awarded 1 each year.

Deadline January of each year.

[894]
ARCO FOUNDATION HIGHER EDUCATION GRANTS

ARCO Foundation
515 South Flower Street
Los Angeles, CA 90071
(213) 486-3342

Purpose To enhance minority student achievement and retention by increasing the number of minority students who major in, and successfully complete, undergraduate degrees in disciplines of interest to the energy industry.

Eligibility Colleges and universities, state associations of private colleges where ARCO has business interests, and national scholarship organizations may apply for grants to support minority student retention or financial aid programs. Grants should be used to increase the number of minority students who receive undergraduate degrees in such disciplines as engineering, chemistry, and the geosciences.

Financial data Grants range from less than $1,000 to more than $100,000. Total support of education, including both pre-college and higher education programs, exceeds $4 million each year.

Duration Some grants are 1-year awards; others are longer-term commitments.

Limitations The Foundation does not consider support of unrestricted annual grants for specific colleges or universities or awards to individuals, including support for specific students, researchers, or specific research projects.

Number awarded Varies each year.

Deadline Applications may be submitted at any time.

[895]
ARMY RESEARCH LABORATORY BROAD AGENCY ANNOUNCEMENT

Army Research Laboratory
Attn: AMSRL-CS-PR
2800 Powder Mill Road
Adelphi, MD 20783-1197
(301) 394-3690   Fax: (301) 394-3887
E-mail: kwishnow@arl.mil

Purpose To provide funding for scientific research of interest to the U.S. Army.

Eligibility This program is open to investigators qualified to perform research in designated scientific and technical areas. Topics currently of interest to the Army Research Laboratory include corporate information and computing, human research and engineering, information science and technology, sensors and electron devices, survivability/lethality analysis, technology transfer, vehicle technology, and weapons and materials research. At least 28 percent of all funds awarded to institutions of higher education are set aside for the Historically Black Colleges and Universities and other Minority Institutions (HBCU/MI) program.

Financial data The amounts of the awards depend on the nature of the proposal and the availability of funds.

Duration Up to 2 years.

Special features Information on the HBCU/MI program is available from its Program Manager, AMSRL-SP, (301) 394-3014, E-mail: birby@arl.mil.

Number awarded Varies each year.

Deadline Applications may be submitted at any time.

[896]
ARMY RESEARCH OFFICE BROAD AGENCY ANNOUNCEMENT

U.S. Army Research Office
Attn: AMXRO-ICA
4300 South Miami Boulevard
P.O. Box 12211
Research Triangle Park, NC 27709-2211
(919) 549-4375

Purpose To provide funding for scientific research of interest to the U.S. Army.

Eligibility This program is open to investigators qualified to perform research in designated scientific and technical areas. The general fields of interest include biosciences, chemistry, electronics, engineering sciences, environmental sciences, materials science, mathematical and computer sciences, and physics. Appli-

cations are especially encouraged from Historically Black Colleges and Universities (HBCUs) and Minority Institutions (MIs).

Financial data The amounts of the awards depend on the nature of the proposal and the availability of funds.

Duration 3 years.

Limitations Although the Army Research Office intends to award a fair proportion of its acquisitions to HBCUs and MIs, it does not set aside a specified percentage due to the impracticality of reserving discrete or severable areas of the research for exclusive competition among the entities.

Number awarded Varies each year.

Deadline Applications may be submitted at any time.

[897]
ARTHRITIS AND SKIN DISEASES IN MINORITY POPULATIONS

National Institutes of Health
Attn: National Institute of Arthritis and Musculoskeletal and Skin Diseases
Natcher Building, Room 5AN44A
45 Center Drive MSC 4500
Bethesda, MD 20892-4500
(301) 594-5014   Fax: (301) 402-2406
E-mail: rl27b@nih.gov

Purpose To provide funding for research on the etiology, treatment, and prevention of arthritis, musculoskeletal, and skin diseases in minority populations and other populations at special risk.

Eligibility This program is open to investigators at domestic and foreign for-profit and nonprofit, public and private organizations, such as universities, colleges, laboratories, units of state and local government, and eligible agencies of the federal government. Applicants must be proposing to conduct epidemiologic research in minority groups and other populations at special disease risk as related to arthritis, musculoskeletal, and skin diseases. Women and members of minority groups are particularly encouraged to apply as principal investigators.

Financial data The amount of the awards depends on the nature of the proposal and the availability of funds.

Duration 3 to 5 years.

Number awarded Varies each year.

Deadline January, May, and September of each year.

[898]
ARTHUR D. HOWARD RESEARCH GRANTS

Geological Society of America
Attn: Research Grants Administrator
3300 Penrose Place
P.O. Box 9140
Boulder, CO 80301-9140
(303) 447-2020, ext. 137   Fax: (303) 447-1133
E-mail: jforstro@geosociety.org

Purpose To provide partial support for geological research by graduate students at universities in the United States, Canada, Mexico, and Central America.

Eligibility This program is open to graduate students (at the master's or doctoral level) in geology. Both members and non-members of the society are eligible. Applicants must propose research on Quaternary geology or geomorphology. Applications from minorities, women, and persons with disabilities are strongly encouraged.

Financial data Grants range up to $2,500; the average grant recently was $1,604.
Duration 1 year.
Special features This program is sponsored by the Geological Society of America's Quaternary Geology and Geomorphology Division. Applications are also available from J. Steven Kite, Department of Geology and Geography, West Virginia University, P.O. Box 6300, Morgantown, WV 26505-6300.
Number awarded 1 or more each year.
Deadline February of each year.

[899]
ARTHUR M. OKUN MEMORIAL FELLOWSHIP

Brookings Institution
1775 Massachusetts Avenue, N.W.
Washington, D.C. 20036-2188
(202) 797-6127   Fax: (202) 797-6181
E-mail: brookinfo@brook.edu

Purpose To support predoctoral policy-oriented research in economics at the Brookings Institution.
Eligibility Candidates cannot apply; they must be nominated by their graduate department. Nominees must meet the following criteria: doctoral students who have completed their preliminary examinations, have selected a dissertation topic that directly relates to public policy issues and the major research issues of the Institution (economic growth, international economics, human resources, industrial organization, regulation, public finance, monetary economics, and economic stabilization), and be able to benefit from access to the resources and personnel at the Institution. The Institution particularly encourages the nomination of women and minority candidates.
Financial data Fellows receive a stipend of $15,000 for the academic year, supplementary assistance for copying and other essential research requirements up to $600, reimbursement for research-related travel up to $500, health insurance, and access to computer/library facilities.
Duration 1 year.
Special features Fellows participate in seminars, conferences, and meetings at the institution. Outstanding dissertations may be published by the institution.
Limitations Fellows are expected to pursue their research at the Brookings Institution.
Number awarded 1 each year.
Deadline Nominations must be submitted by mid-December and applications by mid-February.

[900]
ARTISTS' BOOK PRODUCTION GRANTS

Women's Studio Workshop
P.O. Box 489
Rosendale, NY 12472
(914) 658-9133

Purpose To assist artists working in their own studios with the publication of smaller scale book works.
Eligibility Applications should include a 1-page description of the proposed project, the medium used to print the book, the number of pages, page size, edition number, a structural dummy, a materials budget, a resume, and 6 to 10 slides. Applications are reviewed by past grant recipients and a Women's Studio Workshop staff artist. Women of color are particularly encouraged to apply.

Financial data Up to $750 to cover the production costs of new book works.
Duration From 1 to 2 months.
Special features Funds are given to artists working off site.
Limitations These grants are not intended for reissuing already published material or as partial funding for a larger project.
Number awarded Varies each year.
Deadline November of each year.

[901]
ARTISTS' BOOK RESIDENCY GRANTS

Women's Studio Workshop
P.O. Box 489
Rosendale, NY 12472
(914) 658-9133

Purpose To provide financial assistance and a residency to women book artists.
Eligibility Artists should submit proposals for new books that are in an edition of at least 100. Applications should include a 1-page description of the proposed project; specify the medium used to print the book, number of pages, page size, and edition number; and provide a dummy, a materials budget, and a resume. Women of color are particularly encouraged to apply.
Financial data The program provides a stipend of $1,800, a $450 materials grant, and housing while in residence.
Duration 6 weeks.
Special features This program provides an opportunity for book artists to come and work in residency at the studio. Selected artists are involved in all aspects of the design and production of their new books. The studio provides technical advice and, when possible, help with editing. Assistance with marketing is also available.
Limitations No residencies are available during the summer.
Number awarded Varies each year.
Deadline November of each year.

[902]
ARTS ADVANCEMENT AND EXPANSION GRANTS

Tennessee Arts Commission
Attn: Arts Access Director
400 Charlotte Avenue
Nashville, TN 37243-0780
(615) 741-1701

Purpose To provide funds for direct support for arts projects and/or technical assistance to arts organizations of color in Tennessee.
Eligibility Nonprofit organizations of color providing art programs and services in Tennessee are eligible to apply. At least 51 percent of an applicant organization's board must reflect the culture of the population being targeted. Advancement grants are for technical assistance from consultants who will help raise the capabilities of the applicant in such areas as staff development, governance, marketing, financial systems management, and long-range fiscal and program planning. Expansion grants focus on a new or significantly expanded arts-oriented project that will have artistic significance in relation to the cultural standards of the participating communities and will expand the artistry of the applicant organization.
Financial data Grants range from $500 to $5,000; recipient organizations must provide a 1:1 cash match (although the matching may not be required for certain advancement grants).

Duration 1 year.

Special features Funding for this program is provided in part under a special grant from the National Endowment for the Arts.

Number awarded Varies each year; in recent years, a total of $40,000 has been available for this program annually.

Deadline February of each year.

[903]
ARTS IN EDUCATION PROGRAM OF THE NEW YORK STATE COUNCIL ON THE ARTS

New York State Council on the Arts
915 Broadway
New York, NY 10010
(212) 387-7000 (800) GET-ARTS

Purpose To provide financial support to cultural institutions in New York that from partnerships with schools to create programs that improve or enhance the study of the arts and environmental science.

Eligibility Nonprofit cultural and environmental organizations in New York may submit applications to form partnerships with schools in the state for the development of projects in all arts disciplines that focus on the creation, production, performance, and knowledge of the discipline; for interdisciplinary projects that use the arts to illuminate and enrich another area of the curriculum; for environmental projects that use the resources of arboreta, nature centers, and zoos; for local history projects; for staff development for artists and teachers; for program evaluation, research, or student assessment; or for services to the field. Special consideration is given to applications that address the needs of students in underserved or rural areas of the state; develop projects in new or emerging art forms, such as media arts or contemporary American music, or in areas traditionally undeveloped in the schools, such as folk arts, architecture, and design; address cultural diversity and promote a better understanding of the arts of different cultural traditions; or relate to the arts and culture of students who are African/Caribbean American, Latino/Hispanic, Asian/Pacific Islander, and Native American (priority is given to those programs utilizing artists or professionals who are representatives of the cultures being studied). Institutional support is available to organizations that have received general program support for the last 3 consecutive years, have arts in education as a primary mission, have at least 1 paid full-time professional staff member. Project support is available to organizations for planning grants that enable them and their educational partners to assess needs, identify resources, develop an ongoing planning process, and explore program opportunities; implementation grants support the implementation of a wide range of projects for students and arts education practitioners; special project grants are incentive grants for institutional development.

Financial data Grants range from $60,000 per year (for general operating support), to $2,000-$7,000 (for planning grants), to $3,000-$25,000 (for implementation grants).

Duration Up to 3 years.

Number awarded Varies each year.

Deadline February of each year.

[904]
ASIAN, BLACK, HISPANIC, AND NATIVE AMERICAN UNITED METHODIST HISTORY RESEARCH AWARDS

United Methodist Church
General Commission on Archives and History
Attn: Assistant General Secretary
36 Madison Avenue
P.O. Box 127
Madison, NJ 07940
(201) 408-3189 Fax: (201) 408-3909

Purpose To provide support for research on the history of ethnic groups in the United Methodist Church or its antecedents.

Eligibility Proposed research must deal with the history of Asian, Black, Hispanic, or Native American groups in the United Methodist Church or its antecedents.

Financial data The grant is either $1,500 or $3,000.

Duration These grants are given annually.

Number awarded 1 (of $3,000) or 2 (of $1,500) each year.

Deadline December of each year.

[905]
ASM/NIGMS MINORITY UNDERGRADUATE RESEARCH FELLOWSHIP

American Society for Microbiology
Attn: Office of Education and Training
1325 Massachusetts Avenue, N.W.
Washington, DC 20005-4171
(202) 942-9295 Fax: (202) 942-9329
E-mail: Fellowships-CareerInformation@asmusa.org

Purpose To provide underrepresented minority college students with the opportunity to conduct research in microbiology.

Eligibility Eligible are African Americans, Hispanic Americans, Native Americans, or Pacific Islanders who are enrolled as full-time matriculating undergraduate students, entering their junior or senior year, majoring in the microbiological or related sciences, involved in a research project at their institution, and U.S. citizens or permanent residents. Applicants must desire to undertake a summer research project at 1 of 60 participating institutions. Selection is based on relevant career goals and objectives, academic achievement, leadership and potential for professional growth.

Financial data Students receive up to $2,500 as a stipend, round-trip travel and housing at the site of summer research, 1-year student membership in the American Society for Microbiology (ASM), and travel support if they present the results of the research project at the ASM general meeting the following year.

Duration 8 to 10 weeks, during the summer.

Special features This program is sponsored by ASM and the National Institute of General Medical Sciences.

Number awarded Varies each year.

Deadline January of each year.

[906]
ASPEN INSTITUTE NONPROFIT SECTOR RESEARCH FUND

Aspen Institute
1333 New Hampshire Avenue, N.W., Suite 1070
Washington, DC 20036
(202) 736-5800   Fax: (202) 467-0790
E-mail: nsrfund1@aol.com

Purpose To support research by scholars and practitioners on nonprofit activities, including philanthropy and its underlying values.

Eligibility Grants are awarded to institutions and individuals. In addition to supporting scholars who are already working in the nonprofit sector field, the fund encourages applications from scholars new to the field, researchers working in nonprofit organizations, doctoral candidates (there is a special category for doctoral research), women, and minorities. The fund is particularly interested in supporting studies that investigate basic propositions about the role and value of nonprofits and the tradition or philanthropy both in the United States and in other countries. Priority is given to proposals dealing with any of the following topics: the capacity, effectiveness, or impact of specific types of nonprofit organizations and philanthropies; the implications of various proposed tax reforms on charitable giving and on nonprofit revenues; the impact of imposing taxes on nonprofits; the extent and effects of lobbying and advocacy by nonprofits; the impacts on nonprofits of different types of lobbying regulations; the relationships of nonprofits with governments at all levels; impacts on nonprofits of different types of block grants; and the extent and implications or nonprofit commercial activities for competition between nonprofits and businesses. Research proposals should be double spaced, not exceed 10 pages, and include: 1) a 1-page summary of the proposal; 2) an explicit statement of the questions to be examined; 3) a description and justification of the methodology, data collection, and data analysis; 4) a statement of the project's relevance to people and institutions interested in the field; 5) a time frame and schedule for completing the project; 6) a detailed budget and narrative description; 7) a review of relevant literature; and 8) a dissemination plan. Applications also must include: 1) a self-addressed stamped postcard to acknowledge receipt of proposal; 2) the current application form; 3) a curriculum vitae of the principal researchers; 4) a description of the researchers' institutions (if applicable); 5) 1 brief sample of analytic writing (up to 5 pages); and 6) names and telephone numbers of 3 references. Doctoral applicants should also include a letter from the appropriate university official verifying their doctoral status and approval of their dissertation topic.

Financial data Grants are awarded in 2 categories: 1) up to $20,000 to support doctoral dissertation research; and 2) up to $50,000 to support research by any eligible applicant.

Duration 1 year.

Number awarded Varies each year.

Deadline May or December of each year.

[907]
ASTRAEA GENERAL GRANTMAKING PROGRAM

Astraea National Lesbian Action Foundation
Attn: Program Director
116 East 16th Street, Seventh Floor
New York, NY 10003
(212) 529-8021   Fax: (212) 982-3321
E-mail: anlaf@aol.com

Purpose To provide economic and social support to projects that empower the lives of lesbians and other women and girls.

Eligibility Nonprofit local, regional, and national organizations that focus on organizing, advocacy, and empowerment services may apply for these grants. Funding priorities include: organizations directed by and targeted to lesbians of color; multicultural/multiracial lesbian organizations; women's organizations, or lesbian and gay organizations that have lesbians in leadership roles, include lesbian issues as an integral part of their work, and are seeking funding for a project that specifically addresses heterosexism and homophobia; projects, focusing on community building and coalition work among lesbian organizations and between constituencies for the purpose of promoting a mutual social change agenda; lesbian projects focusing on particular constituencies such as low-income people, older people, lesbian and gay youth, and people with disabilities; and projects in rural communities and other geographic areas where isolation and various factors may present barriers to lesbian visibility and community/organization building.

Financial data Grants range from $500 to $5,000.

Duration Grants are awarded twice each year.

Special features In 1990, the sponsoring organization changed its name from Astraea Foundation to Astraea National Lesbian Action Foundation.

Number awarded Varies each year.

Deadline February and September of each year.

[908]
ATHENS ENVIRONMENTAL RESEARCH LABORATORY POSTGRADUATE RESEARCH PARTICIPATION PROGRAM

Oak Ridge Institute for Science and Education
Attn: Science/Engineering Education Division
P.O. Box 117
Oak Ridge, TN 37831-0117
(423) 576-8503   (423) 241-2875
(800) 569-7749   Fax: (423) 576-3643
E-mail: prppaer@orau.gov

Purpose To provide funding to postgraduates who wish to participate in environmental research at the Athens Environmental Research Laboratory of the Environmental Protection Agency (EPA).

Eligibility Applicants should have completed a baccalaureate or graduate degree within the past 3 years; others are considered on a case-by-case basis. Their field of study should have been environmental sciences, engineering, physical sciences, life sciences, or other related scientific disciplines. They must propose to conduct research at EPA's Athens Environmental Research Laboratory in Athens, Georgia. All programs operated by the Science/Engineering Education Division (SEED) of Oak Ridge Institute for Science and Education (ORISE) seek to broaden the participation of minorities, women, and persons with disabilities in science and engineering careers.

Financial data The stipend is based on research area and degree; a limited reimbursement for inbound travel and moving is also provided.

Duration 1 year; renewable.

Special features This program is funded by an interagency agreement between the U.S. Department of Energy and EPA and administered by ORISE/SEED.

Number awarded Varies each year.

Deadline Applications may be submitted at any time.

[909]
ATLANTA WOMEN'S FUND GRANTS

Atlanta Women's Fund
Hurt Building, Suite 449
Atlanta, GA 30303
(404) 688-5525   Fax: (404) 688-3060

Purpose To fund programs that help women and girls overcome racial, economic, political, sexual, and social barriers in the Atlanta, Georgia area.

Eligibility Support is offered to programs that are led by women, serve primarily women and girls, respond to women's needs and interests (especially in low-income and women of color communities), create leadership opportunities for women, have limited access to other funding, and have budgets that are lean and show evidence of good management and planning. Applicants must be nonprofit, tax-exempt organizations in the 19-county Metropolitan Atlanta area. Proposals are not accepted for individual efforts, including educational scholarships or research; endowment campaigns; debt reduction; projects that are normally the funding responsibility of federal, state, or local governments; projects that discriminate on the basis of sexual orientation, age, ethnicity, race, or disability; or projects of a sectarian nature, or that require religious participation as a condition for receiving services.

Financial data Grants range from $2,500 to $25,000.

Duration 1 year; may be renewed.

Special features This program began in 1993.

Number awarded Varies; generally, at least 12 each year.

[910]
AVIATION RESEARCH GRANTS PROGRAM

Department of Transportation
Attn: Federal Aviation Administration
Office of Research and Technology Applications
William J. Hughes Technical Center
Building 270, Room B115
Atlantic City International Airport, NJ 08405
(609) 485-5777   Fax: (609) 485-6509
E-mail: snyderf@admin.tc.faa.gov

Purpose To provide funding for research required for the long-term growth of civil aviation.

Eligibility This program is open to qualified investigators at colleges and universities; at other nonprofit organizations (such as independent museums; observatories; research laboratories; hospitals; stock centers; consortia; professional, scientific, and educational associations or societies; and similar organizations); and at other appropriate research institutions, facilities, and for-profit organizations with demonstrated ability to conduct research. Applicants must be proposing research projects in the areas of capacity and air traffic control technology; communications, navigation, and surveillance; aviation weather; airports; air-

port safety technology; system security technology; human factors and aviation medicine; environment and energy; and systems science and operations research. The Federal Aviation Administration (FAA) is seeking to ensure an equitable geographic distribution of grant funds and the inclusion of Historically Black Colleges and Universities (HBCUs) and other minority institutions for funding consideration.

Financial data The amounts of the awards depend on the nature of the proposal and the availability of funds.

Duration 1 year; may be renewed provided funds are available and the results achieved warrant further support.

Special features Applications for this program are automatically considered for 2 related programs: the Catastrophic Failure Prevention Research Grants Program (for research that encourages the development of technologies and methods that can assess risk and prevent the defects that can cause the catastrophic failure of aircraft) and the Aviation Security Research Grant Program (for research on the development and implementation of technologies, procedures, and equipment to counteract terrorist acts against aviation).

Number awarded Varies each year.

Deadline Applications may be submitted at any time, but preferably by August of each year.

[911]
BEHAVIORAL SCIENCES RESEARCH TRAINING
FELLOWSHIPS

Epilepsy Foundation of America
Attn: Department of Research and Professional Education
4351 Garden City Drive
Landover, MD 20785
(301) 459-3700   (800) EFA-1000
Fax: (301) 577-2684   TDD: (800) 332-2070
E-mail: postmaster@efa.org

Purpose To offer qualified individuals an opportunity to develop expertise in the area of epilepsy research related to the behavioral sciences through training and involvement in an epilepsy research project.

Eligibility Individuals who have received their doctoral degree in a field of the behavioral sciences by the time the fellowship begins and desire additional postdoctoral research experience in epilepsy may apply. Appropriate fields of study for applications in the behavioral sciences include sociology, social work, psychology, anthropology, nursing, political science, and others relevant to epilepsy research and practice. Special attention is given to applications submitted by women and minorities.

Financial data Up to $30,000 per year, depending upon the experience and qualifications of the applicant and the scope and duration of the proposed project.

Duration 1 year.

Limitations The project must be carried out at an approved facility. Research must be conducted in the United States.

Number awarded Varies each year.

Deadline February of each year.

[912]
BILINGUAL EDUCATION CAREER LADDER PROGRAM GRANTS

Department of Education
Attn: Office of Bilingual Education and Minority Languages
   Affairs
Switzer Building, Room 5090
600 Independence Avenue, S.W.
Washington, DC 20202-6510
(202) 205-8842

Purpose To upgrade the qualifications and skills of existing educational personnel to meet high professional standards including certification and licensure as bilingual education teachers and other educational personnel serving limited English proficient students.

Eligibility Institutions of higher education are eligible to apply in consortia with 1 or more local educational agencies (LEAs) or 1 or more state educational agencies (SEAs); consortia may include community-based organizations or professional educational organizations. Funds may be used to 1) upgrade the qualifications and skills of noncertified educational personnel—especially educational paraprofessionals—to meet high professional standards, including certification and licensure as bilingual education teachers and other educational personnel who serve limited English proficient (LEP) students; and 2) help recruit and train secondary school students as bilingual education teachers and other educational personnel to serve LEP students.

Financial data Grants range from $140,000 to $200,000 and average $170,000.

Duration Up to 5 years.

Number awarded Approximately 46 each year.

Deadline January of each year.

[913]
BILINGUAL EDUCATION PROGRAM DEVELOPMENT AND IMPLEMENTATION GRANTS

Department of Education
Attn: Office of Bilingual Education and Minority Languages
   Affairs
Switzer Building, Room 5090
600 Independence Avenue, S.W.
Washington, DC 20202-6510
(202) 205-8766

Purpose To provide financial support to develop and implement new bilingual education or special alternative instruction education, the gifted and talented, and preschool children.

Eligibility Eligible to submit proposals are local educational agencies, institutions of higher education, and private nonprofit organizations applying separately or jointly.

Financial data Grants range from $100,000 to $175,000 and average $150,000.

Duration 1 year or longer.

Special features These grants are intended to be preparatory or supplementary to projects assisted or funded under other bilingual education programs.

Number awarded Approximately 100 each year.

Deadline January of each year.

[914]
BILINGUAL EDUCATION PROGRAM ENHANCEMENT PROJECTS

Department of Education
Attn: Office of Bilingual Education and Minority Languages
   Affairs
Switzer Building, Room 5090
600 Independence Avenue, S.W.
Washington, DC 20202-6510
(202) 205-8766

Purpose To provide financial assistance for projects to expand or refine existing bilingual education for linguistically and culturally diverse students.

Eligibility Applications are accepted from 1 or more local education agencies applying alone or in collaboration with an institution of higher education, community-based organization, local educational agency, or state educational agency. They must be proposing to carry out highly focused, innovative, locally designed projects to expand or enhance an existing bilingual education program or a special alternative instructional program for limited English proficient students.

Financial data The amounts of the awards depend on the nature of the applications and the availability of funds.

Duration Up to 2 years.

Number awarded Varies each year.

Deadline Deadline dates vary each year; check the latest edition of the *Federal Register* for the current application schedule.

[915]
BILINGUAL EDUCATION TEACHERS AND PERSONNEL GRANTS

Department of Education
Attn: Office of Bilingual Education and Minority Languages
   Affairs
Switzer Building, Room 5090
600 Independence Avenue, S.W.
Washington, DC 20202-6510
(202) 205-8842

Purpose To provide financial assistance for programs that support professional development of bilingual education personnel.

Eligibility Applications may be submitted by institutions of higher education which have consortia arrangements with local or state educational agencies. They must be proposing to provide preservice and inservice professional development for bilingual teachers, administrators, pupil services personnel, and other education personnel who are either involved in, or preparing to be involved in, the provision of education services for limited English proficient students.

Financial data The amounts of the awards depend on the nature of the applications and the availability of funds.

Duration Up to 5 years.

Number awarded Varies each year.

Deadline Deadline dates vary each year; check the latest edition of the *Federal Register* for the current application schedule.

[916]
BILINGUAL VOCATIONAL INSTRUCTOR TRAINING PROGRAM

Department of Education
Attn: Office of Vocational and Adult Education
Division of National Programs
600 Independence Avenue, S.W.
Washington, DC 20202-7242
(202) 205-5864   E-mail: Cynthia_Towsner@ed.gov

Purpose To fund programs that provide training for personnel participating or preparing to participate in bilingual vocational training programs for persons with limited English proficiency (LEP).

Eligibility This program is open to local education agencies and nonprofit organizations planning projects to provide pre-service or in-service training for bilingual instructors, aides, counselors, and other support personnel participating or preparing to participate in bilingual vocational training programs for LEP individuals.

Financial data The amounts of the awards depend on the nature of the applications and the availability of funds.

Duration 1 year; renewable.

Limitations Applications for this program are not currently being solicited; its future depends on the availability of funds.

Number awarded Varies each year.

Deadline Deadline dates vary each year; check the latest edition of the *Federal Register* for the current application schedule.

[917]
BILINGUAL VOCATIONAL MATERIALS, METHODS, AND TECHNIQUES PROGRAM

Department of Education
Attn: Office of Vocational and Adult Education
Division of National Programs
600 Independence Avenue, S.W.
Washington, DC 20202-7242
(202) 205-5864   E-mail: Cynthia_Towsner@ed.gov

Purpose To fund programs that produce and disseminate materials supportive of bilingual vocational education programs.

Eligibility This program is open to local education agencies and nonprofit organizations planning projects to develop instructional and curriculum materials, methods, or techniques for bilingual vocational training programs for persons with limited English proficiency.

Financial data The amounts of the awards depend on the nature of the applications and the availability of funds.

Duration 1 year; renewable.

Limitations Applications for this program are not currently being solicited; its future depends on the availability of funds.

Number awarded Varies each year.

Deadline Deadline dates vary each year; check the latest edition of the *Federal Register* for the current application schedule.

[918]
BILINGUAL VOCATIONAL TRAINING PROGRAM

Department of Education
Attn: Office of Vocational and Adult Education
Division of National Programs
600 Independence Avenue, S.W.
Washington, DC 20202-7242
(202) 205-5864   E-mail: Cynthia_Towsner@ed.gov

Purpose To fund programs that provide bilingual vocational education and training and English-language instruction to persons with limited English proficiency (LEP) and to prepare those persons for employment.

Eligibility This program is open to local education agencies and nonprofit organizations planning projects that provide both occupational skills training and job-related ESL to LEP adults. Applicants must intend to teach language and skills training in an integrated manner so students are ready for jobs in recognized (including new and emerging) occupations after a relatively short training period.

Financial data The amounts of the awards depend on the nature of the applications and the availability of funds.

Duration 1 year; renewable.

Limitations Applications for this program are not currently being solicited; its future depends on the availability of funds.

Number awarded Varies each year.

Deadline Deadline dates vary each year; check the latest edition of the *Federal Register* for the current application schedule.

[919]
BOSTON WOMEN'S FUND GRANT PROGRAM

Boston Women's Fund
14 Beacon Street, Suite 805
Boston, MA 02108
(617) 725-0035   Fax: (617) 725-0277

Purpose To provide grants to women's organizations within the greater Boston area that are involved in organizing women for social and economic change.

Eligibility Eligible to apply are grassroots organizations and agencies in the Boston area that have been established to serve women. Special emphasis is given to 1) projects that strive to transcend the barriers of race, age, physical abilities, and social class, and encourage women of diverse backgrounds to work together; and 2) community organizing projects and direct service projects that empower women who are the most vulnerable and have the least access to resources (e.g. low-income women, women of color, older women, single mothers, teens, lesbians, differently-able women). Priority is given to organizations that have budgets under $150,000.

Financial data Grants range from $1,500 to $5,000.

Duration 1 year; may be extended.

Special features This organization was founded in 1983, as a 501(c) fund for women's programs.

Number awarded Varies; at least 15 each year.

Deadline March and September of each year.

[920]
BRODY ARTS FUND AWARDS

California Community Foundation
606 South Olive Street, Suite 2400
Los Angeles, CA 90014-1526
(213) 413-4042   Fax: (213) 383-2046

Purpose To provide funds to emerging artists and small to mid-sized organizations working "to recognize the cultural richness of Southern California and to foster broad artistic excellence."

Eligibility Small arts organizations (with operating budgets no larger than $150,000) in residence in Los Angeles County for at least 1 year are eligible to apply. Special consideration is given to organizations "rooted in and reflective of the diverse multicultural communities of Los Angeles County." Applications are accepted within all disciplines and for a variety of organizational needs. Individual awards are made in literature (to poets, screenwriters, playwrights, etc.), in media (for video, film, etc.), in performing arts, and in visual arts; the specific art form varies from year to year.

Financial data Grant amounts for single agency requests do not exceed $5,000. Amounts for collaborative efforts are considered on a case-by-case basis. Awards to individuals are $2,500.

Duration 1 year; may be renewed.

Number awarded Varies; recently, 5 individuals and 16 organizations received support annually.

Deadline March of each year.

[921]
BRUCE L. "BIFF" REED AWARD

Geological Society of America
Attn: Research Grants Administrator
3300 Penrose Place
P.O. Box 9140
Boulder, CO 80301-9140
(303) 447-2020, ext. 137   Fax: (303) 447-1133
E-mail: jforstro@geosociety.org

Purpose To provide partial support for geological research by graduate students.

Eligibility This program is open to graduate students in geology at the master's or doctoral level. Both members and nonmembers of the society are eligible. Special consideration is given to students with the best application in the field of tectonic and magmatic evolution of Alaska and its mineral deposits. Applications from women, minorities, and persons with disabilities are strongly encouraged.

Financial data Grants range up to $2,500; the average grant recently was $1,604.

Duration 1 year.

Number awarded 1 or more each year.

Deadline February of each year.

[922]
BUREAU OF ENGRAVING AND PRINTING FACULTY RESEARCH PARTICIPATION PROGRAM

Oak Ridge Institute for Science and Education
Attn: Science/Engineering Education Division
P.O. Box 117
Oak Ridge, TN 37831-0117
(423) 576-8807   (423) 576-8158
(800) 569-7749   Fax: (423) 576-3643
E-mail: frppbep@orau.gov

Purpose To provide an opportunity to scholars who wish to conduct collaborative research at the Bureau of Engraving and Printing (BEP) or other laboratories carrying out BEP research.

Eligibility This program is open to college and university full-time faculty members in physical sciences, graphic arts, artificial intelligence, computer sciences, or engineering who are interested in participating in research at the Bureau of Engraving and Printing or other laboratories that is aimed at improving the quality of products, reducing manufacturing costs, and strengthening deterrents to counterfeiting. All programs operated by the Science/Engineering Education Division (SEED) of Oak Ridge Institute for Science and Education (ORISE) seek to broaden the participation of minorities, women, and persons with disabilities in science and engineering careers.

Financial data A stipend is awarded; the amount is based on the recipient's regular salary. Reimbursement for travel is also provided.

Duration 10 weeks to 3 months; some sabbatical appointments are also available.

Special features This program is funded through an interagency agreement between the U.S. Department of Energy and the U.S. Department of the Treasury and administered by ORISE/SEED.

Number awarded Varies each year.

Deadline Applications may be submitted at any time.

[923]
BUREAU OF ENGRAVING AND PRINTING POSTGRADUATE RESEARCH PROGRAM

Oak Ridge Institute for Science and Education
Attn: Science/Engineering Education Division
P.O. Box 117
Oak Ridge, TN 37831-0117
(423) 576-8503   (423) 241-2875
(800) 569-7749   Fax: (423) 576-3643
E-mail: prpbep@orau.gov

Purpose To provide funding to postgraduates who wish to conduct collaborative research at the Bureau of Engraving and Printing (BEP) or other laboratories carrying out BEP research.

Eligibility This program is open to scholars who completed a graduate degree within the last 3 years in physical sciences, graphic arts, artificial intelligence, computer sciences, or engineering. They must be interested in participating in research at the Bureau of Engraving and Printing or other laboratories that is aimed at improving the quality of products, reducing manufacturing costs, and strengthening deterrents to counterfeiting. All programs operated by the Science/Engineering Education Division (SEED) of Oak Ridge Institute for Science and Education (ORISE) seek to broaden the participation of minorities, women, and persons with disabilities in science and engineering careers.

Financial data A stipend is awarded; the amount is based on research area and degree. Limited reimbursement for inbound travel and moving is provided.

Duration 1 year; may be renewed.

Special features This program is funded through an interagency agreement between the U.S. Department of Energy and the U.S. Department of the Treasury and administered by ORISE/SEED.

Number awarded Varies each year.

Deadline Applications may be submitted at any time.

[924]
BYRON HANKE FELLOWSHIP FOR GRADUATE RESEARCH ON COMMUNITY ASSOCIATIONS

Community Associations Institute Research Foundation
1630 Duke Street
Alexandria, VA 22314
(703) 548-8600   Fax: (703) 684-1581

Purpose To provide funding to graduate students interested in working on research related to community associations.

Eligibility Applicants must be enrolled in an accredited master's, doctoral, or law program. They may be working in any subject area, but their proposed research must relate to community associations. Community associations govern common-interest communities of any kind—condominiums, cooperatives, townhouse developments, planned unit developments, and other developments where homeowners support an association with mandatory financial assessments and are subject to use and aesthetic restrictions. Proposed projects may address management, institution, organization and administration, public policy, architecture, as well as political, economic, social, and intellectual trends in community association housing. Academic disciplines include law, economics, sociology, and urban planning. The foundation is especially interested in substantive papers from the social sciences which place community association housing within political or economic organizational models. In all cases, the topic must have the approval of the graduate student's general academic advisor or of another full-time faculty member who will supervise the project. Minority applicants are particularly encouraged to apply. Selection is based on academic achievement, faculty recommendations, demonstrated research and writing ability, and the nature of the proposed topic and its benefit to the study and understanding of community associations.

Financial data The grant is $2,500. Funds are paid in 2 equal installments and may be used for tuition, books, or other educational expenses.

Duration 1 year.

Special features The foundation may publish the final project.

Limitations Recipients must provide the foundation with a copy of their final project.

Deadline Applications may be submitted at any time.

[925]
CALIFORNIA ARTS COUNCIL MULTI-CULTURAL ADVANCEMENT GRANT

California Arts Council
1300 I Street, Suite 930
Sacramento, CA 95814
(916) 322-6555   Fax: (916) 322-6575
TDD: (916) 322-6569

Purpose To assist multi-cultural organizations in California achieve stability and advancement towards institutional status.

Eligibility Applicant organizations must be based within a multi-cultural (defined as being deeply rooted in and reflective of an ethnic community, such as African American, Asian, Chicano/Latino, Native American/Alaskan Native, or Pacific Islander) community, with an annual operating budget between $50,000 and $750,000, and a recipient of an Arts Council Organizational Support Program grant during the preceding 3 years.

Financial data Grants range up to $50,000 per organization each year for 3 years; the recipient organization must provide matching funds of 25 percent of the grant in the second year and 50 percent in the third year.

Duration 3 years.

Limitations Funding is not provided for out-of-state activities, private organizations with a for-profit format, capital expenditures, hospitality or food costs, expenses incurred before the grant's starting date, or projects that are part of an academic curricula.

Number awarded Approximately 10 grants are awarded each year.

Deadline A letter of interest is due by June and a proposal by August.

[926]
CALIFORNIA ARTS COUNCIL MULTI-CULTURAL ENTRY GRANT

California Arts Council
1300 I Street, Suite 930
Sacramento, CA 95814
(916) 322-6555   Fax: (916) 322-6575
TDD: (916) 322-6569

Purpose To provide funding to small multi-cultural arts groups in California that need developmental assistance.

Eligibility Eligible are multi-cultural (defined as being deeply rooted in and reflective of an ethnic community such as Asian, African American, Chicano/Latino, Native American/Alaskan Native, or Pacific Islander) community music groups, theater groups, dance companies, artists' collectives, film and video groups, and literary groups that have been doing arts programming in California for at least 1 year.

Financial data $2,000 is awarded each year, but in the second year must be matched by $500 and in the third year by $1,000.

Duration 3 years.

Limitations Funding is not provided for out-of-state activities, private organizations with a for-profit format, capital expenditures, hospitality or food costs, expenses incurred before the grant's starting date, or projects that are part of an academic curricula.

Number awarded Varies each year.

Deadline October of each year.

[927]
CALIFORNIA COMMUNITY FOUNDATION GRANTS

California Community Foundation
606 South Olive Street, Suite 2400
Los Angeles, CA 90014-1526
(213) 413-4042   Fax: (213) 383-2046

Purpose To provide support for organizations that help to meet basic human needs, celebrate cultural diversity, encourage cooperation among groups and communities, develop leadership, strengthen pluralism, and improve the quality of life and access to opportunity for all the residents of the Los Angeles region.

Eligibility Organizations with IRS tax-exempt status rendering direct services to individuals in Los Angeles or western San Bernardino counties on a nonsectarian basis are eligible to submit proposals. Proposals should meet the needs of clients or communities with limited access to resources or services, including but not limited to ethnic communities, women, youth, the economically disadvantaged, immigrants and refugees, and people with disabilities. Areas in which the Foundation awards grants include civic affairs, community development, community education, community health and medicine, animal welfare, human services, environment, and children, youth, and families.

Financial data The amount granted varies, depending upon the specific needs and nature of the request. Recent grants have ranged from $3,500 to $60,000.

Duration 1 year; renewable.

Limitations No grants are made to individuals or for annual campaigns or special fundraising events, building campaigns, endowments, existing obligations, equipment, routine operating expenses, sectarian purposes, or programs that will regrant the funds to others.

Deadline Application dates vary with the type of activity: May and November of each year for civic affairs, community education, and community health and medicine; February and August of each year for human services, community development, environment, animal welfare, and children, youth, and families.

[928]
CALIFORNIA COUNCIL FOR THE HUMANITIES FILM & SPEAKER MINIGRANTS

California Council for the Humanities
312 Sutter Street, Suite 601
San Francisco, CA 94108
(415) 391-1474

Purpose To provide funding for nonprofit organizations in California that wish to show and create programs around the ethnic or women's films distributed by the California Council for the Humanities (CCH).

Eligibility Nonprofit organizations located in California are eligible for a minigrant if they are interested in renting an ethnic or women's film distributed by the CCH and bringing an academic speaker to the program. The speaker must have a doctorate or master's degree in a humanities discipline related to the subject of the film, be interested in meeting with adult audiences outside the classroom and in leading a discussion, and live or work in the general vicinity of the sponsoring organization. Priority is given to non-academic organizations that reach such underserved audiences as African Americans, Latinos, and senior citizens. The films available for distribution in this program include, on African Americans, Flyers in Search of a Dream, Routes of Rhythm with Harry Belafonte, Black Is..Black Ain't, Color Adjustment, and Ethnic Notions; on Asian Americans, The Color of Honor: The Japanese American Soldier in WWII, American Chinatown, Rebuilding the Temple: Cambodians in America, When They All Still Lived, Moving Mountains: The Story of the Yiu Mien, In No One's Shadow, and The New Puritans: The Sikhs of Yuba City; on Hispanic Americans, Chicano Park, The Trail North, La Ofrenda: The Days of the Dead, and The Lemon Grove Incident; on Native Americans, The Probable Passing of Elk Creek, Of Land and Life: People of the Klamath Part I, and Preserving a Way of Life: People of the Klamath Part II; on women, Acting Our Age, Cowgirls, Miss...or Myth?, Stories of Change, and The Flapper Story.

Financial data The minigrant is $500. All of these grants must be matched, dollar for dollar. The minigrant includes provision of an honorarium of $150 for the speaker and travel expenses of 24 cents a mile.

Duration Any eligible organization can receive a maximum of 2 of these minigrants within a 12 month period.

Deadline Applications may be submitted at any time; organizations should allow at least 2 months for a response.

[929]
CALIFORNIA COUNCIL FOR THE HUMANITIES GRANTS

California Council for the Humanities
312 Sutter Street, Suite 601
San Francisco, CA 94108
(415) 391-1474

Purpose To provide funding for nonprofit organizations in California for projects in the humanities.

Eligibility Nonprofit organizations located in California are eligible to apply for support of activities that foster multicultural understanding and strengthen community life throughout the state. Grants are awarded for public programs, exhibits, lecture/discussions, reading and discussions, performance and discussions, symposia and conferences, media scripts, and media production.

Financial data Grants range from $3,000 to $30,000; many require matching by the recipient organizations.

Deadline The council awards nearly $600,000 in grants each year.

[930]
CALIFORNIA DOMESTIC VIOLENCE ASSISTANCE PROGRAM

Office of Criminal Justice Planning
Attn: Sexual Assault/Domestic Violence Branch
1130 K Street, Suite 300
Sacramento, CA 95814
(916) 324-9120   Fax: (916) 324-9167

Purpose To provide financial and technical assistance to domestic violence centers in California.

Eligibility Application may be made by a local unit of government or a nonprofit organization in California that is interested in providing comprehensive services to domestic violence victims and their children, including crisis intervention, counseling, safe homes or shelters, emergency food and clothing, emergency transportation, and law enforcement advocacy and assistance. Special attention is paid to proposals to establish a targeted program for the development of services in currently unserved or underserved populations, such as those in rural areas, non-English speaking groups, minorities, and geographical areas currently without services.

Financial data The amount awarded varies, depending upon the scope of the proposed program.
Duration 1 year; may be renewed for up to 2 additional years.

[931]
CAPACITY BUILDING FOR TRADITIONALLY UNDERSERVED POPULATIONS

Department of Education
Attn: Office of Special Education and Rehabilitative Services
Rehabilitation Services Administration
Switzer Building, Room 3038
600 Independence Avenue, S.W.
Washington, DC 20202-2575
(202) 205-8292

Purpose To assist organizations that serve traditionally underserved individuals to enhance their competitiveness for grants under the Rehabilitation Act.
Eligibility Applications may be submitted by states, other public and nonprofit agencies and organizations, and for-profit agencies and organizations that propose to provide outreach services and other related activities to: 1) Historically Black Colleges and Universities, Hispanic-serving institutions of higher education, and other institutions of higher education whose minority student enrollment is at least 51 percent; 2) nonprofit and for-profit agencies at least 51 percent owned or controlled by 1 or more minority individuals; or 3) underrepresented populations. Funds must be used to enhance their capacity and increase their participation in competitions for grants, contracts, and cooperative agreements under Titles I through VIII of the Rehabilitation Act.
Financial data Grants range from $80,000 to $120,000 and average $100,000.
Number awarded Up to 14 each year.
Deadline February of each year.

[932]
CAPITAL AID PROGRAM OF THE NEW YORK STATE COUNCIL ON THE ARTS

New York State Council on the Arts
915 Broadway
New York, NY 10010
(212) 387-7000   (800) GET-ARTS

Purpose To make funds available for the improvement, expansion, or rehabilitation of existing buildings owned or leased by nonprofit cultural institutions that receive programmatic funding from the New York State Council on the Arts (NYSCA).
Eligibility Nonprofit organizations in New York that have received funding from the NYSCA for the previous 3 years and either own their facility or hold a lease with an unexpired period of at least 5 years are eligible for these grants. Projects are limited to those that 1) improve, expand, or rehabilitate existing buildings to provide access for people with disabilities; 2) increase or assure public access to the arts; 3) address known health and safety deficiencies; 4) reduce an organization's operating costs; or 5) further cultural development in rural or minority communities. The NYSCA uses its best efforts to ensure that minority and women owned business enterprises, and the minority and female workforce, have the maximum practicable opportunity to participate in all Council funded construction projects.
Financial data The Council will support up to 50 percent of the costs of construction materials and labor, up to a maximum of $25,000. Grants must be matched on at least a 1-to-1 basis.

Special features Loans up to $100,000 are also available; the repayment period is 5 years and the interest rate is 5 percent below the prime rate (within a range of 3 percent to 10 percent).
Number awarded Varies each year.
Deadline February of each year.

[933]
CAREER ADVANCEMENT AWARDS FOR MINORITY SCIENTISTS AND ENGINEERS

National Science Foundation
Attn: Directorate for Education and Human Resources
Senior Staff Associate for Cross Directorate Programs
4201 Wilson Boulevard, Room 805
Arlington, VA 22230
(703) 306-1603

Purpose To enable minority researchers whose science/engineering careers are still evolving (or who are changing research direction, or who have had a significant research career interruption) to progress in their research activities.
Eligibility The applicant should have had some prior experience as a principal investigator or research project leader, hold a faculty or research-related position at a U.S. institution, be an underrepresented minority (Native American, African American, Hispanic, Native Alaskan, or Native Pacific Islander), and be a U.S. citizen or national. Normally, candidates are at least 5 years beyond any postdoctoral appointment and are applying for funding to: 1) help acquire expertise in new areas to enhance research capability; 2) support the development of innovative research methods in collaboration with investigators at the applicant's home institution or at another appropriate institution (including 1 in a foreign country); 3) assist the conduct of exploratory or pilot work to determine the feasibility of a new line of inquiry; or 4) make it possible for those who have had a significant career interruption to acquire updating for reentry into their respective fields.
Financial data Awards of up to $50,000 are available; an additional amount of up to $10,000 may be requested for equipment. Funds are provided for salary, professional travel, consultant fees, research assistants, and other research-related expenses.
Duration 1 year; these are 1-time, nonrenewable awards.
Special features This program is offered through the various disciplinary divisions of the National Science Foundation (NSF); for the telephone numbers of the participating divisions, contact the address above.
Limitations These awards are not substitutes for regular research grants, and they are not intended to provide start-up funds to establish a laboratory.
Deadline Each of the participating NSF disciplinary divisions sets its own deadline.

[934]
CARNEGIE INSTITUTION OF WASHINGTON POSTDOCTORAL FELLOWSHIPS

Carnegie Institution of Washington
1530 P Street, N.W.
Washington, DC 20005-1910
(202) 387-6400

Purpose To encourage the development of researchers in the fields of astronomy, geophysics, physics and related subjects, plant biology, and embryology.
Eligibility Qualified scientists who have obtained the doctoral degree are eligible. Candidates are evaluated on the basis of aca-

demic record, recommendations of professors and associates, and growth potential. Special efforts are made to recruit qualified minorities and women.

Financial data Stipends average approximately $15,000 each year; in addition to financial support, fellows receive the use of the institution's laboratory and observational facilities, including special equipment when needed. Some travel funds are provided.

Duration 1 to 2 years.

Special features Facilities of the Carnegie Institution include the Department of Embryology in Baltimore, Maryland, the Department of Plant Biology in Stanford, California, the Geophysical Laboratory and the Department of Terrestrial Magnetism in Washington, D.C., and the Observatories in Pasadena, California and Las Campanas, Chile.

Limitations Fellowships are tenable at the institution's facilities only.

Number awarded More than 70 each year.

Deadline Applications should be submitted at least 1 year in advance.

[935]
CARNEGIE INSTITUTION OF WASHINGTON PREDOCTORAL FELLOWSHIPS

Carnegie Institution of Washington
1530 P Street, N.W.
Washington, DC 20005-1910
(202) 387-6400

Purpose To fund doctoral thesis research in the sciences.

Eligibility Doctoral students from universities situated near Carnegie departments or other major universities may apply for funding to carry out their thesis research using Carnegie Institution facilities if they are working in the following areas: embryology, plant biology, or astronomy. Applications should be supported by a current curriculum vitae and 3 letters of recommendation. Special consideration is given to applications submitted by women and minorities.

Financial data The amount awarded varies, depending upon the scope of the funded research.

Duration 1 academic year, generally starting in July.

Special features The relevant Carnegie facilities are the Department of Embryology on the grounds of The Johns Hopkins University (Baltimore, Maryland), the Department of Plant Biology on the Stanford University campus (Stanford, California), and the Observatories situated near the California Institute of Technology (Pasadena, California).

Number awarded Varies each year.

Deadline December of each year.

[936]
CAROLINA MINORITY POSTDOCTORAL SCHOLARS PROGRAM

Office of the Vice Provost for Graduate Studies and
    Research
University of North Carolina at Chapel Hill
CB# 4000, South Building
Chapel Hill, NC 27599-4000
(919) 962-1319   Fax: (919) 962-1476
E-mail: Sharon_Windsor@unc.edu

Purpose To support minority scholars who are interested in teaching and research.

Eligibility Minorities who have completed their doctoral degrees within the past 4 years are eligible to apply. Preference is given to U.S. citizens and permanent residents. The program is open to underrepresented minorities, with an emphasis on Afro-Americans and Native Americans. Selection is based on the evidence of scholarship potential and ability to compete for tenure tract appointments in research universities.

Financial data Fellows receive $33,500 per year, plus an allowance for research and travel.

Duration Up to 2 years.

Special features Fellows must be in residence at the Chapel Hill campus for the duration of the program. They teach 1 course per year and spend the rest of the time in research. This program began in 1983.

Number awarded 5 or 6 each year.

Deadline January of each year.

[937]
CENTER FOR BIOLOGICS EVALUATION AND RESEARCH POSTGRADUATE RESEARCH PROGRAM

Oak Ridge Institute for Science and Education
Attn: Science/Engineering Education Division
P.O. Box 117
Oak Ridge, TN 37831-0117
(423) 576-8503   (423) 241-2875
(800) 569-7749   Fax: (423) 576-3643
E-mail: prpcber@orau.gov

Purpose To provide opportunities and support for biologics research at the Center for Biologics Evaluation and Research in Rockville, Maryland.

Eligibility Applicants must have completed their master's or doctoral degree in life sciences, physical sciences, medical sciences, bioengineering, biostatistics, or other related scientific disciplines within the past 3 years. Other candidates are considered on a case-by-case basis. All programs operated by the Science/Engineering Education Division (SEED) of Oak Ridge Institute for Science and Education (ORISE) seek to broaden the participation of minorities, women, and persons with disabilities in science and engineering careers.

Financial data A stipend is awarded, based on research area and highest degree earned. Reimbursement is also provided for inbound travel and moving.

Duration 1 year; may be renewed.

Special features Participants work at the Center for Biologics Evaluation and Research of the U.S. Food and Drug Administration in Rockville, Maryland. This program is funded through an interagency agreement between the U.S. Department of Energy and the U.S. Food and Drug Administration and administered by ORISE/SEED.

Number awarded The number awarded varies each year.

Deadline Applications may be submitted at any time.

[938]
CENTER FOR DEVICES AND RADIOLOGICAL HEALTH POSTGRADUATE RESEARCH PROGRAM

Oak Ridge Institute for Science and Education
Attn: Science/Engineering Education Division
P.O. Box 117
Oak Ridge, TN 37831-0117
(423) 576-8503   (423) 241-2875
(800) 569-7749   Fax: (423) 576-3643
E-mail: prpcdrh@orau.gov

Purpose To provide funding for postgraduate research on medical devices and radiation emissions from electronic products at the Center for Devices and Radiological Health in Maryland.

Eligibility Applicants should have completed a master's or doctoral degree within the past 3 years; others are considered on a case-by-case basis. Their field of study should have been life sciences, physics, materials sciences and engineering, medical electronics, medical imaging and computer applications, human epidemiology, biostatistics, or other related scientific disciplines. They must propose to conduct research at the Center for Devices and Radiological Health in Rockville, Maryland. All programs operated by the Science/Engineering Education Division (SEED) of Oak Ridge Institute for Science and Education (ORISE) seek to broaden the participation of minorities, women, and persons with disabilities in science and engineering careers.

Financial data The stipend is based on research area and degree; a limited reimbursement for inbound travel and moving is also provided.

Duration 1 year; renewable.

Special features This program is funded by an interagency agreement between the U.S. Department of Energy and the U.S. Food and Drug Administration and administered by ORISE/SEED.

Number awarded Varies each year.

Deadline Applications may be submitted at any time.

[939]
CENTER FOR THE STUDY OF AMERICAN RELIGION POSTDOCTORAL FELLOWSHIPS

Center for the Study of American Religion
Princeton University
1879 Hall
Princeton, NJ 08544-1006
(609) 258-5545   Fax: (609) 258-2346
E-mail: askline@princeton.edu

Purpose To provide financial support to postdoctoral scholars who wish to conduct research at the Center for the Study of American Religion at Princeton University.

Eligibility This program is open to young postdoctoral scholars interested in conducting research on religion in North America in its historical legacy and contemporary dynamics. Because the Center is committed to noting the interaction among varied American perspectives, it urges participation by minority scholars with a focus that includes minority points of view.

Financial data Scholars receive salary support equivalent to a second-year assistant professor at Princeton, access to libraries, and computer support.

Special features The Center was established in 1991. It is funded by the Lilly Endowment and the Pew Charitable Trusts.

Number awarded 2 each year.

[940]
CENTERS OF EXCELLENCE IN MINORITY HEALTH PROFESSIONS EDUCATION GRANTS

Health Resources and Services Administration
Attn: Bureau of Health Professions
Division of Disadvantaged Assistance
Parklawn Building, Room 8A09
5600 Fishers Lane
Rockville, MD 20857
(301) 443-4493   Fax: (301) 443-6343
E-mail: bbrooks@hrsa.ssw.dhhs.gov

Purpose To provide financial assistance to health professions schools to support programs of health education for minority individuals.

Eligibility This program is open to 1) certain Historically Black Colleges and Universities; 2) medical, osteopathic medicine, and dental schools with at least 25 enrolled Hispanic students, and schools of pharmacy with at least 20 enrolled Hispanic students; 3) medical and dental schools with at least 8 enrolled Native American students, and schools of pharmacy and osteopathic medicine with at least 5 enrolled Native American students; and 4) other health professions schools with above the national average of underrepresented minorities (medicine 13 percent, osteopathic medicine 8 percent, dentistry 15 percent, or pharmacy 11 percent) enrolled in the school. Applicants must present evidence that any particular subgroup of Asian individuals is underrepresented in a particular discipline. Funding must be used to establish, strengthen, or expand programs to enhance the academic performance of minority students attending the school; establish, strengthen, or expand programs to increase the number and quality of minority applicants to the school; improve the capacity of such schools to train, recruit, and retain minority faculty; to carry out activities to improve the information resources and curricula of the school and clinical education at the school with respect to minority health issues; and to facilitate faculty and student research on minority health issues.

Financial data The amount of the awards depends on the availability of funds and the nature of the applications. Of the amount appropriated for any fiscal year, the first $12 million is allocated to certain Historically Black Colleges and Universities; of the remaining balance, 60 percent must be allocated to Hispanic and Native American Centers of Excellence, and 40 percent must be allocated to the other Centers of Excellence. Annual grants for each center must be at least $500,000.

Duration Up to 3 years.

Number awarded Varies each year, depending on the availability of funds.

Deadline February of each year.

[941]
CENTERS OF RESEARCH EXCELLENCE IN SCIENCE AND TECHNOLOGY

National Science Foundation
Attn: Directorate for Education and Human Resources
Division of Human Resource Development
4201 Wilson Boulevard, Room 815
Arlington, VA 22230
(703) 306-1634   E-mail: hrdmrce@nsf.gov

Purpose To support the enhancement of research and education activities at the most productive minority institutions in fields supported by the National Science Foundation (NSF).

Eligibility Institutions eligible to submit proposals under this program are those that have 1) enrollments of 50 percent of more of minority groups that are underrepresented in advanced levels of science and engineering (Alaskan Native, American Indian, African American, Mexican American, Native Pacific Islander, or Puerto Rican); 2) graduate programs in NSF-supported fields of science or programs (undergraduate or graduate) in engineering; 3) demonstrated strengths in NSF-related fields; 4) a willingness and capacity to serve as a regional resource center; 5) demonstrated commitment and track record in enrolling and graduating minority scientists and engineers; and 6) strong alliances with universities or laboratories operating centers focused in the same research area(s). Grants are designed to implement a comprehensive research and training improvement plan. Activities may include exploratory research projects; acquisition of materials, supplies, research equipment, and instrumentation; hiring nationally competitive scientists and engineers as short- or long-term consultants; faculty attendance at professional meetings and seminars; faculty sabbaticals and exchange programs; undergraduate and graduate research activities; development of outreach and other enhancement programs with neighboring institutions; and strengthening technical support personnel.

Financial data Up to $1 million per year.

Duration Up to 5 years.

Special features This program was formerly known as Minority Research Centers of Excellence.

Number awarded Up to 4 each year.

Deadline November of each year.

[942]
CHALLENGE GRANTS FOR TECHNOLOGY IN EDUCATION

Department of Education
Attn: Office of Educational Research and Improvement
Interagency Technology Task Force
Washington, DC 20202-5544
(202) 708-6001   Fax: (202) 708-6003
E-mail: ito_staff1@ed.gov

Purpose To provide funding to consortia of educational agencies for the development and innovative use of technology.

Eligibility Only consortia may receive grants under this program; at least 1 member of the consortium must be a local educational agency (LEA) with a high percentage or number of children living below the poverty level; other members may be other LEAs, state educational agencies, institutions of higher education, businesses, academic content experts, software designers, museums, libraries, and other appropriate entities. Applicants must be proposing to improve and expand new applications of technology to strengthen the school reform effort, improve student achievement, and provide sustained professional development of teachers, administrators, and school library media personnel. Each project should clearly focus on integrating innovative learning technologies into the curriculum to improve learning productivity in the community.

Financial data In a recent year, a total of $23,000,000 was available through this program; the annual level of individual grants ranged from $500,000 to $2,000,000 and averaged $1,000,000.

Duration Up to 4 years.

Number awarded Up to 23 each year.

Deadline June of each year.

[943]
CHARLES A. EASTMAN DISSERTATION FELLOWSHIP FOR NATIVE AMERICAN SCHOLARS

Dartmouth College
Attn: Assistant Dean of Graduate Studies
6062 Wentworth, Room 305
Hanover, NH 03755-3526
(603) 646-2107

Purpose To provide funding to Native American doctoral students who are interested in working on their dissertation at Dartmouth College.

Eligibility This program is open to U.S. citizens of Native American descent who are planning a career in college or university teaching. They must have completed all other Ph.D. requirements and be interested in working on their dissertation at Dartmouth College.

Financial data The stipend is $25,000. In addition, fellows receive office space, library privileges, and a $2,500 research allowance.

Duration 1 year, beginning in September.

Special features The fellows are affiliated with a department or program at Dartmouth College.

Limitations Fellows are expected to be in residence at Dartmouth College for the duration of the program and to complete their dissertation during that time. They are also expected to teach a course, either as the primary instructor or as part of a team.

Number awarded 1 each year.

Deadline March of each year.

[944]
CHICAGO FOUNDATION FOR WOMEN GRANT PROGRAM

Chicago Foundation for Women
Attn: Allocations Committee Chair
230 West Superior Street, Suite 400
Chicago, IL 60610-3536
(312) 266-1176   Fax: (312) 266-0990
TDD: (312) 266-2983

Purpose To fund programs in the Chicago area that create solutions to the overwhelming range of problems facing women.

Eligibility Eligible to apply are organizations and agencies in the Chicago area (Cook, Lake, DuPage, McHenry, Will, and Kane counties) that have been established to serve women and girls, especially in low income and/or minority communities. They must have little or no access to other funding resources, be led by women and intended to respond to women's needs and interests, facilitate women of diverse backgrounds in working together, have a board and staff that reflect the diversity of the communities they serve, and show evidence of good management and planning.

Financial data In total, more than $500,000 each year is awarded. Individual grants range from $500 to $7,500.

Duration 1 year; may be extended.

Special features This program was established in 1984. It is intended to augment funding resources for programs and to increase—not replace—existing sources of support for women's programs in the Chicago area. There are many special programs that help to generate these grants, including the Sophia Fund for Advocacy (for programs focusing on social change advocacy in the areas of reproductive rights, economic justice, violence against women, public awareness of women's issues, and expanding philanthropy for women), the Jane Whitman Women in the Workplace Fund (for work issues facing women), the Eleanor Fund (established in 1992 for the advancement of women), the Fay Clayton Fund (established in 1990 for a variety of programs for women and girls), the Women's Health Initiative (in partnership with the John D. and Catherine T. MacArthur Foundation to build and strengthen women's health projects within women's and community organizations), the Women's Housing Fund (for housing for women and girls), and the Roslyn Fund for the Arts (for projects related to women and girls in the arts).

Limitations Funding is not provided to projects with budgets over $250,000, government agencies, individual scholarships or individual efforts, religious organizations for religious purposes, endowments, general support for individual dary care center operations, capital drives, campaigns to elect candidates to office, more than 1 proposal per year from any 1 organization, organizations that are not pro-choice in regards to women's reproductive health, or public or private schools or universities.

Number awarded Varies; approximately 25 each year.

Deadline Letters of intent are due in February or August of each year; full proposals are due in September or March of each year.

[945]
CIRES VISITING FACULTY AND POSTDOCTORAL FELLOWSHIPS

Cooperative Institute for Research in Environmental
    Sciences
Attn: Dr. Howard P. Hanson
University of Colorado at Boulder
Campus Box 216
Boulder, CO 80309-0216

Purpose To provide an opportunity for scholars to conduct research in the sciences at the Cooperative Institute for Research in Environmental Sciences (CIRES) at the University of Colorado.

Eligibility This program is open to scientists with research interests in the following areas: physics, chemistry, and dynamics of the earth system; global and regional environmental change; climate system monitoring, diagnostics, and modeling; and development and application of remote sensing and measurement techniques for the earth and its atmosphere, cryosphere, ecosystems, and oceans. The program is open to Ph.D. scientists at all levels and from any country. Faculty planning sabbatical leave and recent Ph.D. recipients are especially encouraged to apply. Applications are particularly solicited from women, ethnic minorities, persons with disabilities, and veterans.

Financial data The amount awarded varies, depending upon the scope of the research program.

Duration 1 year; the program may begin at anytime during the year.

Special features This program is sponsored jointly by the University of Colorado and the National Oceanic and Atmospheric Administration (with support from other public and private sources).

Number awarded Varies each year.

Deadline December of each year.

[946]
CISE MINORITY INSTITUTIONS INFRASTRUCTURE PROGRAM

National Science Foundation
Attn: Directorate for Computer and Information Science and
    Engineering
Office of Cross-Disciplinary Activities
Research Infrastructure Program
4201 Wilson Boulevard
Arlington, VA 22230
(703) 306-1980   E-mail: rrodrigu@nsf.gov

Purpose To provide support for efforts to increase minority participation in academic and research activities in computer and information science and engineering.

Eligibility This program is open to U.S. institutions and consortia of institutions which have: 1) student enrollments of more than 50 percent from the following minority groups which are underrepresented in advanced levels of science and engineering: African Americans, Alaskan Natives, Hispanics, Native Americans, and Native Pacific Islanders (Micronesian or Polynesian), or at least 20 percent from 1 of the preceding groups; and 2) a presence (such as curricula or degree programs) in disciplinary areas of computer and information science and engineering. Proposers may seek support for infrastructure which enhances or makes possible a variety of activities, including but not limited to research programs involving minority students, curriculum development projects, mentoring, and outreach. Continuing grants are to aid in the establishment, enhancement, and operation of facilities to support research activities and educational programs in any of the computer and information science and engineering. Planning grants are intended to strengthen the proposal writing and planning capabilities for developing projects eligible for continuing grants.

Financial data Continuing grants provide from $800,000 to $1,500,000 over the full period of the award. Planning grants up to $50,000 are available.

Duration Continuing grants are for 5 years; planning grants are for 1 year.

Number awarded Each year, 3 or 4 continuing grants and 1 to 5 planning grants are awarded.

Deadline February of each year.

[947]
CISE POSTDOCTORAL RESEARCH ASSOCIATES IN COMPUTATIONAL SCIENCE AND ENGINEERING

National Science Foundation
Attn: Directorate for Computer and Information Science and
    Engineering
Division of Advanced Scientific Computing
New Technologies Program
4201 Wilson Boulevard
Arlington, VA 22230
(703) 306-1970   E-mail: ntpd@nsf.gov

Purpose To provide funding to academic institutions interested in increasing the number of faculty (especially women, minorities, and persons with disabilities) who can work on research in an area of interest to the Computer and Information Science and Engineering (CISE) Directorate of the National Science Foundation (NSF).

Eligibility Applications must be submitted by U.S. universities, colleges, and other research institutions that provide access, either on site or by network, to high performance, scalable parallel computing systems. The proposal must identify a researcher who received a doctoral degree less than 3 years before the proposed deadline (or will do so before taking up the project) in computational science and engineering, computer science and engineering, or a closely-related discipline, and who is eligible to be appointed as a research associate or research assistant professor. The application must include a research and training plan for the proposed research associate that utilizes the institution's computing systems for research in an area of interest to the CISE Directorate. Designation of women, minorities, and persons with disabilities as research associates is strongly encouraged.

Financial data Awards include a stipend (salary and benefits) of $25,000 to $38,000; a research expense allowance of $4,000, expendable at the associate's discretion for travel, publication expenses, and other research-related costs; and an allowance of $4,200 to the sponsoring institution, in lieu of indirect costs, as partial reimbursement for expenses incurred in support of the research. Those payments are for the full term of the grant; the institution must match the NSF award on a dollar-for-dollar basis excluding the $4,200 granted in lieu of indirect costs.

Duration 2 years.

Number awarded 15 each year.

Deadline October of each year.

[948]
CISE POSTDOCTORAL RESEARCH ASSOCIATES IN EXPERIMENTAL COMPUTER SCIENCE

National Science Foundation
Attn: Directorate for Computer and Information Science and
    Engineering
Office of Cross-Disciplinary Activities
Postdoctoral Program Director
4201 Wilson Boulevard
Arlington, VA 22230
(703) 306-1980   E-mail: espd@nsf.gov

Purpose To provide funding to academic institutions interested in increasing the number of researchers (especially women, minorities, and persons with disabilities) who can work on research in an area of interest to the Computer and Information Science and Engineering (CISE) Directorate of the National Science Foundation (NSF).

Eligibility Applications must be submitted by U.S. universities, colleges, and other research institutions with an established laboratory performing research in experimental areas of interest to the CISE Directorate. The proposal must identify a researcher who received a doctoral degree less than 3 years before the proposed deadline (or will do so before taking up the project) in computational science and engineering, computer science and engineering, or a closely-related discipline, and who is eligible to be appointed as a research associate or research assistant professor. The application must include a research and training plan in experimental research supported by the CISE Directorate. Designation of women, minorities, and persons with disabilities as research associates is strongly encouraged.

Financial data Awards include a stipend (salary and benefits) of $25,000 to $38,000; a research expense allowance of $4,000, expendable at the associate's discretion for travel, publication expenses, and other research-related costs; and an allowance of $4,200 to the sponsoring institution, in lieu of indirect costs, as partial reimbursement for expenses incurred in support of the research. Those payments are for the full term of the grant; the institution must match the NSF award on a dollar-for-dollar basis excluding the $4,200 granted in lieu of indirect costs.

Duration 2 years.

Number awarded 15 each year.

Deadline October of each year.

[949]
CISE RESEARCH INFRASTRUCTURE PROGRAM

National Science Foundation
Attn: Directorate for Computer and Information Science and
    Engineering
Office of Cross-Disciplinary Activities
Research Infrastructure Program
4201 Wilson Boulevard
Arlington, VA 22230
(703) 306-1981   E-mail: jchernia@nsf.gov
E-mail: tfeng@nsf.gov

Purpose To provide support to institutions to aid in the establishment, enhancement, and operation of major experimental facilities planned to support activities in computer and information science and engineering.

Eligibility This program is open to research groups associated with U.S. institutions with Ph.D. degree-granting departments that have research programs in any area of computer and information science and engineering research. The proposing research group should have an existing core of active researchers and research projects. The program provides support for acquisition of experimental facilities not normally available under individual research grants. The program encourages proposers to address the full participation of women, minorities, and persons with disabilities in research activities. Examples of activities appropriate to the program are: a departmental effort to recruit female graduate students, a research collaboration with a minority institution, or a project that is focused on designing a system to provide systems access to persons with a visual disorder.

Financial data Budget requests may include costs of equipment, software, maintenance, and appropriate technical support. Students, research assistants, postdoctoral research associates, secretarial, and clerical personnel are not eligible project costs. Faculty salaries are eligible project costs only in the case of the project director when 1 month per year of salary and associated indirect costs may be allowable if the requested experimental facilities are sufficiently complex and appropriate justification is presented. Awards generally range from $800,000 to $2,000,000 over the full period of the grant.

Duration Up to 5 years.

Number awarded Varies each year.

Deadline October of each year.

[950]
COLLABORATIVE NEUROLOGICAL SCIENCES AWARD

National Institutes of Health
Attn: National Institute of Neurological Disorders and Stroke
Division of Extramural Activities
Federal Building, Room 1016
7550 Wisconsin Avenue MSC 9190
Bethesda, MD 20892-9190
(301) 496-4188   Fax: (301) 402-4370
E-mail: ed25b@nih.gov

Purpose To develop and promote competitive neurological science research programs at predominantly minority institutions.

Eligibility This program is open to predominantly minority institutions that wish to establish collaborative investigations with grantees from research-intensive institutions that have grant support to conduct neurological science research from the National Institutes of Health (NIH). The nature of the collaborations includes joint research efforts, specialized training in research techniques, and participation in research seminars. Both institutions must be a non-federal, public or private nonprofit institution located in the United States. The applicant investigator must have a doctoral degree in a basic or clinical science area, and should have completed 1 or more years of postdoctoral research experience. The collaborating investigator must be a grantee from a research-intensive institution who has current NIH support to conduct neurological science.

Financial data Awards range from $150,000 to $200,000 per year in direct costs.

Duration Up to 5 years.

Number awarded Varies each year.

[951]
COLLABORATIVES FOR EXCELLENCE IN TEACHING PREPARATION PROGRAM

National Science Foundation
Attn: Directorate for Education and Human Resources
Division of Undergraduate Education
4201 Wilson Boulevard, Room 835
Arlington, VA 22230
(703) 306-1669   E-mail: undergrad@nsf.gov

Purpose To support design and implementation of teacher preparation programs that will produce K-12 teachers who demonstrate the latest thinking on the teaching and learning of mathematics and science.

Eligibility Proposals are invited from collaboratives that typically involve cooperative efforts including science, mathematics, and education faculty and their departments, K-12 teachers, and university and school district administrators. The institutions may include comprehensive and research universities, 2-year and 4-year colleges, schools and/or school districts, community organizations, and the private sector. Appropriate activities of a collaborative include, but are not limited to, redesign of courses and curricula, workshops for faculty and mentor teachers to explore and design new methodologies and technologies, extensive field experiences for students, mentor support for students, a support system for novice teachers, and comprehensive assessment and dissemination programs. The National Science Foundation (NSF) particularly encourages proposals that strengthen undergraduate education by increasing the participation of women, underrepresented minorities, and persons with disabilities, especially if the projects present models for increasing the numbers who suc-

cessfully pursue careers in science, mathematics, engineering, and technology. Underrepresented minorities are defined as African Americans, Alaskan Natives (Eskimos and Aleuts), Hispanics, Native Americans, and Native Pacific Islanders (Micronesians and Polynesians).

Financial data Projects are funded at levels between $200,000 and $1 million per year.

Duration Up to 5 years.

Number awarded The number of awards granted depends on the quality of the proposals received and the availability of funds for the program; in a recent year, this program supported 44 new and 3 continuing awards.

Deadline Preliminary proposals must be submitted by March of each year; final proposals are due by September.

[952]
COMMUNITY ACTION GRANTS

American Association of University Women
Attn: Educational Foundation
2201 North Dodge Street
Iowa City, IA 52243-4030
(319) 337-1716   Fax: (319) 337-1204

Purpose To provide seed money to branches or divisions of the American Association of University Women or to individual women for projects or nondegree research that promotes education and equity for women and girls.

Eligibility Projects funded in the past include math/science camps for girls, mentoring programs for girls and women, career days, parenting/family education programs, adolescent pregnancy prevention campaigns, women's history month events, and conferences on women's issues. Grant projects may not seek to influence new or pending legislation or favor a particular political candidate or party. Project directors must be U.S. citizens or permanent residents and hold a baccalaureate degree. The proposed activity must have direct and demonstrated community or public impact. Applicants may apply up to 2 times for the same proposed grant project. Women of color are strongly encouraged to apply.

Financial data Grants range from $500 to $5,000. Funds are to be used for such project-related costs as office and mailing expenses, promotional materials, honoraria, and transportation costs. Funds cannot cover salaries for project directors or regular, ongoing overhead costs for any organization.

Duration 1 year.

Number awarded Varies; approximately 45 each year.

Deadline January or August of each year.

[953]
COMMUNITY BRIDGES GRANTS

California Community Foundation
606 South Olive Street, Suite 2400
Los Angeles, CA 90014-1526
(213) 413-4042   Fax: (213) 383-2046

Purpose To provide support to organizations in the Los Angeles area in the areas of conflict resolution, neighborhood organizing, and youth leadership development.

Eligibility Grants are available to nonprofit, grassroots, community-based, constituent-led organizations in the Los Angeles area. Applicants must be proposing initiatives to improve relations between and among the many ethnic and racial groups in Los Angeles County.

Financial data The amount granted varies, depending upon the specific needs and nature of the request. Recently, grants ranged from $11,000 to $25,000.

Duration 1 year; renewable.

Special features This program began in 1992; partial funding is provided by the Ford, William Randolph Hearst, Greenville, and Pacific Mutual Foundations.

Number awarded Varies; in a recent year, 4 grants were made for conflict resolution, 3 for neighborhood organizing, and 5 for youth leadership development.

Deadline May of each year.

[954]
COMMUNITY FOUNDATION FOR PALM BEACH AND MARTIN COUNTIES HUMAN AND RACE RELATIONS GRANTS

Community Foundation for Palm Beach and Martin Counties
324 Datura Street, Suite 340
West Palm Beach, FL 33401-5431
(561) 659-6800   Fax: (561) 832-6542

Purpose To support organizations in Florida that work to reduce or heal racial, ethnic, or religious tensions and misunderstandings.

Eligibility Eligible are nonprofit tax-exempt organizations in Palm Beach or Martin Counties that encourage cooperation and understanding between racial and ethnic groups in the fields of economic development, finance, and employment opportunity. Programs should bring together racially and divergent groups that have little or no history of working together.

Financial data Grants are $5,000 or $10,000 per year.

Special features This program is funded by a grant from the Ford Foundation.

Number awarded 6 each year.

[955]
COMMUNITY ISSUES GRANTS

Horizons Foundation
870 Market Street, Suite 718
San Francisco, CA 94102
(415) 398-2333

Purpose To provide support to organizations addressing the needs and issues of lesbians and gay men in the San Francisco Bay area.

Eligibility To be considered for the project grants, an organization must 1) be a nonprofit, 501(c)3 organization or sponsored under a 501(c)3 fiscal agent umbrella; 2) benefit lesbians and gay men; and 3) have a project service area within the 9-county Bay area. Projects may be for social and human services, health, public education and awareness, civil rights, or arts and culture. Programs that benefit gays and lesbians of color are especially encouraged.

Financial data Grants range from $500 to $5,000.

Number awarded Varies each year.

Deadline May of each year.

[956]
COMMUNITY-BASED HUMAN IMMUNODEFICIENCY VIRUS (HIV) PREVENTION PROJECTS

Centers for Disease Control and Prevention
Attn: National Center for HIV, STD, and TB Prevention
1600 Clifton Road
MS D-21
Atlanta, GA 30333
(404) 639-0902

Purpose To provide financial support for HIV prevention projects to minority and other community-based organizations (CBOs).

Eligibility This program is organizations applying either as minority CBOs or CBOs serving other high-risk populations. Minority CBOs are defined as having 1) a governing board composed of more than 50 percent racial or ethnic minority members (African Americans, Alaskan Natives, American Indians, Asian Americans, Latinos/Hispanics, and Pacific Islanders); 2) a significant number of minority individuals in key program positions; and 3) an established record of service to a racial or ethnic minority community or communities. Whether qualifying as a minority CBO or not, organizations must apply as either a high prevalence Metropolitan Statistical Area (MSA) or a lower prevalence MSA; high prevalence MSAs are those with more than 500 reported AIDS cases in racial or ethnic minorities. All applicants must qualify as nonprofit, tax-exempt organizations proposing to develop and implement effective community-based HIV prevention programs, and to promote collaboration and coordination of HIV prevention efforts among CBOs and the local activities of HIV prevention service agencies, public agencies, substance abuse agencies, educational agencies, criminal justice systems, and affiliates of national and regional organizations.

Financial data Within high prevalence MSAs, awards range from $75,000 to $300,000, and average $200,000; within lower prevalence MSAs, awards average $100,000.

Number awarded Varies; in a recent year, approximately 80 awards were presented, for a total expenditure of $17 million; of total grants, approximately $16 million was granted to organizations within high prevalence MSAs ($12 million to minority CBOs and $4 million to CBOs serving other high-risk populations) and $1 million was provided to lower prevalence MSAs ($750,000 to minority CBOs and $250,000 to CBOs serving other high-risk populations).

Deadline October of each year.

[957]
COMPACT FOR FACULTY DIVERSITY

New England Board of Higher Education
45 Temple Place
Boston, MA 02111
(617) 357-9620   Fax: (617) 338-1577
E-mail: aburton@mecn.mass.edu

Purpose To provide financial assistance to African American, Hispanic American, and Native American doctoral students in science, mathematics, and engineering at universities in New England.

Eligibility This program is open to African American, Hispanic American, and Native American students who wish to begin doctoral study in order to pursue a career in college teaching. Applicants must contact 1 of the participating departments: molecular and cell biology at the University of Connecticut, biological sciences at the University of Rhode Island, chemistry at the University of New Hampshire, chemistry at Wesleyan University, mathematics and statistics at the University of Massachusetts at Amherst, geological sciences at Brown University, physics at the University of Maine, chemical engineering at Northeastern University, or electrical and systems engineering at the University of Connecticut.

Financial data The program provides tuition and fee forgiveness, a fellowship with no teaching duties for the first year, graduate assistantships for the second year and beyond, and a travel budget so scholars can attend a national teaching institute and professional conferences.

Duration Up to 5 years.

Special features Other benefits of this program include faculty mentoring within the doctoral department, peer support by clustering 4 to 6 participating scholars within each graduate department, and networking events where scholars can build community with other graduate students and faculty of color in New England.

Limitations Candidates should contact the participating doctoral department for applications and further information.

Number awarded Varies each year.

[958]
COMPREHENSIVE PARTNERSHIPS FOR MATHEMATICS AND SCIENCE ACHIEVEMENT

National Science Foundation
Attn: Directorate for Education and Human Resources
Division of Human Resource Development
4201 Wilson Boulevard, Room 815
Arlington, VA 22230
(703) 306-1633   E-mail: hrdpmsa@nsf.gov

Purpose To provide funding to city school systems to link with other organizations to enhance the achievement of participating precollege students in order to increase their enrollment and success in science and mathematics undergraduate programs.

Eligibility Proposals may be submitted by city school systems that 1) have large numbers of school age children (ages 5-17) living in economic poverty; 2) are not eligible to participate in the Urban Systemic Initiatives (USI) program; and 3) have not received a Local Systemic Change (LSC) program award. Applicants must form alliances with institutions of higher education, business and industry, professional organizations, community-based organizations, and other educational organizations. The primary focus of proposed efforts must be science and mathematics education. Priority is given to proposals that seek systematically and comprehensively to increase the number of precollege students in science and mathematics and influence the quality of mathematics and science education from K-12. Activities may include curriculum reform, curriculum enhancement, teacher enhancement, strategic use of resources, student enrichment activities, and summer enrichment activities.

Financial data The maximum award for the first year is normally $200,000; for subsequent years, awards range from $200,000 to $800,000 per year. Allowable costs include staff salaries, materials, instrumentation, equipment and supplies for classroom and laboratory activities, teacher stipends, and relevant travel.

Duration Up to 5 years.

Special features This program was formerly known as Comprehensive Partnerships for Minority Student Achievement.

Number awarded Approximately 5 each year.

Deadline October of each year.

[959]
COMPREHENSIVE SCHOOL GRANTS IN BILINGUAL EDUCATION

Department of Education
Attn: Office of Bilingual Education and Minority Languages Affairs
Switzer Building, Room 5090
600 Independence Avenue, S.W.
Washington, DC 20202-6510
(202) 205-5530

Purpose To provide financial assistance for the implementation of schoolwide bilingual education programs or special alternative instructional programs within schools that serve all (or virtually all) children and youth of limited English proficiency (LEP).

Eligibility Applications may be submitted by local educational agencies (LEAs) either separately or in collaboration with institutions of higher education, community-based organizations, other LEAs, or state educational agencies. They must be proposing instructional programs for reforming, restructuring, and upgrading all relevant programs and operations within an individual school with all or nearly all LEP children and youth.

Financial data Awards range from $150,000 to $350,000 and average $250,000; the total funding for this program in a recent year was $10 million.

Duration Up to 5 years.

Number awarded Up to 40 each year.

Deadline May of each year.

[960]
CONGRESSIONAL SCIENCE AND ENGINEERING FELLOWSHIPS

American Association for the Advancement of Science
Attn: Science and Engineering Fellowship Programs
1200 New York Avenue, N.W.
Washington, DC 20005-3920
(202) 326-6600   Fax: (202) 289-4950
E-mail: science_policy@aaas.org

Purpose To provide postdoctoral and midcareer scientists and engineers an opportunity to work as special legislative assistants on the staffs of members of Congress or congressional committees.

Eligibility Applicants must have a Ph.D. or equivalent doctoral level degree at the time of application in any physical, biological, or social science or any field of engineering; persons with a master's degree in engineering and at least 3 years of post-degree experience may apply. All applicants must be U.S. citizens. Federal employees are not eligible. Minorities and persons with disabilities are especially encouraged to apply.

Financial data The stipend is $43,000, plus an allowance for relocation and travel expenses.

Duration 1 year, beginning in September.

Special features The program includes an orientation on congressional and executive branch operations and a year-long seminar program on issues involving science and public policy.

Number awarded 2 each year.

Deadline January of each year.

[961]
CONNECTICUT SPACE GRANT COLLEGE CONSORTIUM TRAVEL GRANTS

Connecticut Space Grant College Consortium
c/o College of Engineering
United Technology Hall, Room 317
200 Bloomfield Avenue
West Hartford, CT 06117
(860) 768-4813   Fax: (860) 768-5073
E-mail: ctspgrant@uhavax.hartford.edu

Purpose To provide funding for travel to faculty members at member institutions of the Connecticut Space Grant College Consortium.

Eligibility This program is open to faculty members at the University of Connecticut, University of Hartford, University of New Haven, or Trinity College. Applicants must be proposing to collaborate with researchers of the U.S. National Aeronautics and Space Administration (NASA), to present their aerospace-related research at conferences, or to visit NASA centers to establish research contacts. Travel is normally limited to within the United States. The program actively encourages women, minorities, and those with disabilities to apply.

Financial data Grants cover expenses up to $1,000 per trip.

Special features This program is funded by NASA.

Number awarded Varies each year.

Deadline September of each year.

[962]
CONNECTICUT SPACE GRANT COLLEGE CONSORTIUM UNDERGRADUATE AND GRADUATE STUDENT FELLOWSHIPS

Connecticut Space Grant College Consortium
c/o College of Engineering
United Technology Hall, Room 317
200 Bloomfield Avenue
West Hartford, CT 06117
(860) 768-4813   Fax: (860) 768-5073
E-mail: ctspgrant@uhavax.hartford.edu

Purpose To enable students at member institutions of the Connecticut Space Grant College Consortium to work on space-related projects under the guidance of a faculty member.

Eligibility This program is open to graduate and undergraduate students at the University of Connecticut, University of Hartford, University of New Haven, or Trinity College. Applicants must be proposing to conduct research in aerospace science and engineering in areas normally funded by the U.S. National Aeronautics and Space Administration (NASA). U.S. citizenship is required. The program actively encourages women, minorities, and those with disabilities to apply.

Financial data Stipends are $2,000 for undergraduates and $5,000 for graduate students.

Duration 1 year.

Special features This program is funded by NASA.

Number awarded Varies each year.

Deadline September of each year.

[963]
CONTEMPLATIVE PRACTICE FELLOWSHIPS

American Council of Learned Societies
228 East 45th Street
New York, NY 10017-3398
(212) 697-1505   Fax: (212) 949-8058
E-mail: grants@acls.org

Purpose To provide financial assistance for the development of courses and teaching materials that explore contemplative practice from a variety of disciplinary and interdisciplinary perspectives.

Eligibility This program is open to faculty members at academic institutions in the United States who wish to develop curricula during a summer or non-teaching semester in contemplative practices. Fellowships are available in all fields, including the arts and humanities, sciences, social sciences, and the professions. There are no citizenship requirements and prior experience with contemplative practice is helpful but not required. Applications are particularly invited from women and members of minority groups.

Financial data Stipends up to $20,000 are available.

Duration Summer months, for development of courses to be taught the following academic year.

Special features This program is supported by funding from the Nathan Cummings Foundation. It is intended to support the study of contemplation not just as a category of religious practice but as an intentional focusing of the mind. Such practice and the qualities and values associated with it could be explored in any field, from the architecture of sacred space to the poetry of Rilke or the painting of Mondrian; from the relationship between contemplative practice and medical practice to the study of the nature of contemplative learning itself. They might include the history of contemplative practice in 19th century America or the relationship of contemplative practice to scientific creativity.

Number awarded Varies each year.

Deadline October of each year.

[964]
COR HONORS HIGH SCHOOL RESEARCH EDUCATION GRANTS

National Institutes of Health
Attn: National Institute of Mental Health
Career Opportunities in Research Education and Training
Parklawn Building, Room 17C-14
5600 Fishers Lane MSC 8030
Rockville, MD 20857-8030
(301) 443-3641   Fax: (301) 443-8552
E-mail: rc30x@nih.gov

Purpose To assist institutions of higher education with substantial enrollment of racial/ethnic minority students to provide special research training programs for high school students.

Eligibility Eligible to apply for the Career Opportunities in Research Education and Training (COR) Program are 4-year colleges and universities with at least 55 percent racial-ethnic minority student enrollment. Such institutions may apply for funding to provide a program of summer and year-round involvement in research experiences at the college or university to minority high school students. The selected students should work with faculty or scientists at the applicant institution on research in the biomedical and behavioral sciences, emphasizing mental health. Trainees, who are selected by the institution, must be U.S. citizens in their third or fourth year of high school maintaining a minimum grade point average of 3.0.

Financial data   Institutions may request up to $2,000 per student. Grants to institutions range from $4,000 to $35,000 per year, and average $15,000.

Duration   The maximum period of grant support to an institution is 5 years. The maximum period of support a trainee may receive is 2 years. The training must be for a minimum of 3 months during any single year, including a mixture of full-time summer experience and part-time experience during the school year.

Special features   The National Institute of Mental Health (NIMH) operates this program as part of the R25 program. Students interested in the program should contact the address above to obtain a current list of participating institutions.

Number awarded   Each institution may serve up to 6 minority high school students each year.

Deadline   May of each year.

[965]
COR HONORS UNDERGRADUATE RESEARCH TRAINING GRANTS

National Institutes of Health
Attn: National Institute of Mental Health
Career Opportunities in Research Education and Training
Parklawn Building, Room 17C-14
5600 Fishers Lane MSC 8030
Rockville, MD 20857-8030
(301) 443-3641   Fax: (301) 443-8552
E-mail: rc30x@nih.gov

Purpose   To assist institutions with substantial enrollment of racial/ethnic minority students to train greater numbers of scientists as teachers and researchers related to research in mental health.

Eligibility   Eligible to apply for the Career Opportunities in Research Education and Training (COR) Program are 4-year colleges and universities with at least 55 percent racial-ethnic minority student enrollment. Trainees, who are selected by the institution, must be U.S. citizens in their third or fourth year at the institution, maintaining a minimum grade point average of 3.0.

Financial data   Awards to institutions range from $100,000 to $200,000 per year, and average $150,000. Trainees receive an annual stipend of $7,656.

Duration   The maximum period of grant support to an institution is 5 years. The maximum period of support a trainee may receive is 2 years.

Special features   The National Institute of Mental Health (NIMH) operates this program as part of the T34 program. Students interested in the program should contact the address above to obtain a current list of participating institutions.

Deadline   May of each year.

[966]
COURSE AND CURRICULUM DEVELOPMENT PROGRAM

National Science Foundation
Attn: Directorate for Education and Human Resources
Division of Undergraduate Education
4201 Wilson Boulevard, Room 835
Arlington, VA 22230
(703) 306-1681   E-mail: undergrad@nsf.gov

Purpose   To provide funding to academic institutions and organizations interested in revitalizing the content, conduct, and quality of undergraduate education in science, mathematics, engineering, and technology.

Eligibility   Proposals are invited from organizations in the United States and its territories: 2-year colleges; 4-year colleges; universities; professional societies; consortia of institutions; nonprofit, non-academic institutions that are directly associated with educational or research activities; and, under certain circumstances, for-profit organizations. The target for all programs is undergraduates enrolled in science, mathematics, engineering, and technology courses, especially future teachers at the elementary and secondary school level. The National Science Foundation (NSF) particularly encourages proposals that strengthen undergraduate education by increasing the participation of women, underrepresented minorities, and persons with disabilities, especially if the projects present models for increasing the numbers who successfully pursue careers in science, mathematics, engineering, and technology. Underrepresented minorities are defined as African Americans, Alaskan Natives (Eskimos and Aleuts), Hispanics, Native Americans, and Native Pacific Islanders (Micronesians and Polynesians).

Financial data   The amount awarded varies, depending upon the scope of the proposed project and the availability of funding. Recently, grants ranged from $30,000 to $800,000 and averaged $130,000.

Duration   Up to 5 years.

Special features   Basic Course and Curriculum Development Projects (CCD) emphasize introductory-level courses, curricula, and laboratories—those that enroll primarily first- and second-year college students—especially those that are interdisciplinary and those that address the needs of future teachers. In some cases, the program will consider proposals that address courses for upper-level students. In addition to the basic CCD projects, this program includes 3 special programs: 1) Systemic Changes in the Undergraduate Chemistry Curriculum (CCD-CHEM), to make fundamental changes in the role of chemistry within the institution; 2) Mathematical Sciences and their Applications throughout the Curriculum (CCD-MATH), to promote broad and significant improvements in undergraduate education that lead to increased student appreciation of and ability to use mathematics; 3) Institution-Wide Reform of Undergraduate Education in Science, Mathematics, Engineering, and Technology (IR); and 4) Integrating Undergraduate Education in Science and Humanities (CCD-S&H), to fund proposals that meaningfully link the study of science and the humanities. The latter project is jointly funded by NSF, the Department of Education, and the National Endowment for the Humanities (NEH); formal proposals may be submitted to NEH, although because of funding restrictions NEH is not currently accepting applications for the program.

Number awarded   The number of awards granted depends on the quality of the proposals received and the availability of funds for the program. In a recent year, this program supported 98 new and 25 continuing awards in the basic CCD program, 7 new and

0 continuing awards in the CCD-CHEM program, 3 new and 2 continuing awards in the CCD-MATH program, and 10 new and 0 continuing awards in the CCD-S&H program; the IR program began in 1996.

Deadline For the CCD, CCD-CHEM, and CCD-MATH programs: June of each year. For the IR program, letters of intent are due in April and final applications in June.

[967]
CREATION AND PRESENTATION GRANTS TO ORGANIZATIONS

National Endowment for the Arts
Attn: Heritage and Preservation
Nancy Hanks Center
1100 Pennsylvania Avenue, N.W.
Washington, DC 20506-0001
(202) 682-5452   TTY: (202) 682-5496

Purpose To provide funding to organizations for the creation of new works of art or presentation of existing works.

Eligibility Nonprofit tax-exempt organizations of demonstrated artistic excellence may apply if they have a 4-year history of programming, have professional staff, compensate all professional performers and related or supporting professional personnel, assure that no part of any supported project will be performed or engaged in under unsanitary or hazardous conditions, and comply with other federal regulations. Applicants may be arts institutions, local arts agencies, arts service organizations, tribal communities and Indian tribes, official units of city governments, and other organizations that can further the goals of the National Endowment for the Arts (NEA). They should be proposing projects involving the creation/development of specific works, commissions, residencies, rehearsals, workshops, performances, exhibitions, festivals, literary publishing, design charettes, touring, new technologies that assist in the creation and/or presentation of work, or production and/or broadcast of creative film video, and audio works. Projects should recognize the role of both individuals and organizations in sustaining and making available to the American public our rich cultural legacy and artistic creativity in all their forms. Selection is based on artistic excellence and artistic merit of the proposed project and the applicant organization, impact of the project, and ability to carry out the project.

Financial data Grants generally range from $5,000 to $200,000 and require a match of at least 1 to 1.

Duration Up to 2 years.

Special features The NEA remains committed to supporting equitable opportunity for all and investing in as diverse a reflection of our society as possible.

Limitations Funding is not provided for general operating support; seasonal support; construction or renovation of facilities; marketing expenses that are not directly related to the proposed project; commercial enterprises or activities; fundraising or development; debt and deficit reduction; cash reserves and endowments; social activities, entertainment costs, receptions, etc.; lobbying expenses; individuals directly; elementary and secondary schools directly; avocational or student groups; professional training in degree-granting institutions; work toward academic degrees; literary projects, programming, or publishing that does not focus primarily on contemporary literature and/or writers; research that is directed primarily to academic purposes or scholarly projects; publication of books or exhibition of works by the applicant organization's staff, board members, faculty, or trustees; exhibitions of, and other projects involving, single, privately owned collections; purchase of major equipment; subgranting or regranting, except for state arts agencies and regional arts organizations.

Deadline April of each year.

[968]
CSWS VISITING SCHOLAR PROGRAM

Center for the Study of Women in Society
Attn: Director
340 Hendricks Hall
1201 University of Oregon
Eugene, OR 97403-1201
(541) 346-5015

Purpose To establish a visiting scholar pool for the University of Oregon.

Eligibility Scholars working in the field of women's studies (or a related area) are eligible to apply if they have earned a doctorate or have equivalent experience. The center is particularly interested in receiving applications from scholars whose work focuses on the experiences and concerns of women of color.

Financial data Stipends are ordinarily intended to supplement other income; the amount awarded is competitive and may be negotiated.

Duration Length of time in residence is negotiable. Generally, at least 1 academic quarter is required.

Special features Fellows may be asked to teach an upper-division course, to participate in a faculty seminar, and/or to give a public lecture.

Limitations This program has been suspended temporarily, pending a review of the status of the Center.

Number awarded 1 or more each year.

Deadline February of each year.

[969]
DEPARTMENT OF DEFENSE AUGMENTATION AWARDS FOR SCIENCE AND ENGINEERING RESEARCH TRAINING

Air Force Office of Scientific Research
Attn: Directorate of Academic and International Affairs
110 Duncan Avenue, Room B115
Bolling Air Force Base, DC 20332-8080
(202) 767-4969   Fax: (202) 767-5012
E-mail: jan.cerveny@afosr.af.mil

Purpose To provide supplemental funding to recipients of research grants from the Department of Defense (DoD) so they can include students as research assistants on their projects.

Eligibility This program is open to investigators operating under ongoing DoD research grants. They may apply for this additional funding to provide support for graduate students to serve as research assistants on their projects, and to involve undergraduate and precollege students in their work. Students must be U.S. citizens or nationals whose research is directly related to the investigator's DoD-sponsored research and who are in addition to students normally accommodated by the parent grant. Graduate students normally are supported for the third through fifth year of education, following 1 to 2 years of required course work and the successful completion of a qualifying examination. Proposals are encouraged from Historically Black Colleges and Universities and other Minority Institutions, as defined by federal regulations. All proposers are encouraged to use funding from this program to recruit students from groups underrepresented among U.S. citizens holding advanced degrees in science and engineering, including ethnic minorities (Black, Hispanic, American Indian, Alaskan Eskimo/Aleut, or American Samoan, Micronesian, Guamian, and Northern Marianian), women, and persons with disabilities. Increased funding allowances for persons with disabilities are considered to offset special education expenses.

Financial data The program provides graduate students' tuition and fees (at the normal research assistant rate), salary, and the cost of research training required for the advanced degree; research training costs vary greatly depending on the institution, discipline, and nature of the research. For undergraduate and precollege students, awards cover salary and research operating costs associated with the students' participation but do not cover tuition or fees.

Duration Grants are for 3 years.

Special features This program is also available through the Office of Naval Research, 800 North Quincy Street, Arlington, VA 22217-5660; the Army Research Office, 4300 South Miami Boulevard, P.O. Box 12211, Research Triangle Park, NC 27709-2211; and the Ballistic Missile Defense Organization, 7100 Defense, BMDO-TRI, The Pentagon: Mail Room 1E117, Washington, DC 20310-7100. Students interested in this program should contact 1 of the sponsoring agencies to obtain a list of principal investigators currently holding appropriate grants.

Number awarded Varies; a total of approximately $45 million is available through this program each year, distributed through the Air Force Office of Scientific Research ($12 million), Army Research Office ($11 million), Ballistic Missile Defense Organization ($5 million), and Office of Naval Research ($17 million).

Deadline November of each year.

[970]
DEPARTMENT OF DEFENSE INFRASTRUCTURE SUPPORT PROGRAM FOR HISTORICALLY BLACK COLLEGES AND UNIVERSITIES AND MINORITY INSTITUTIONS

Air Force Office of Scientific Research
Attn: Directorate of Academic and International Affairs
110 Duncan Avenue, Room B115
Bolling Air Force Base, DC 20332-8080
(202) 767-4970   Fax: (202) 767-5012
E-mail: jerome.franck@afosr.af.mil

Purpose To provide funding to Historically Black Colleges and Universities (HBCUs) and other Minority Institutions (MIs) to build their capacity to participate in defense research activities.

Eligibility This program is open to federally-designated HBCUs and MIs. Applicants must be proposing the acquisition of science and technology equipment/instrumentation for educational and/or research use to enhance their ability to increase the number of underrepresented minority graduates in the fields of science, engineering, and mathematics, and to conduct research of interest to the Department of Defense.

Financial data Awards range from $40,000 to $400,000.

Special features This program is also available through the Office of Naval Research, 800 North Quincy Street, Arlington, VA 22217-5660, and the Army Research Office, Attn: AMXRO-AAA, 4300 South Miami Boulevard, P.O. Box 12211, Research Triangle Park, NC 27709-2211.

Number awarded Varies; a total of approximately $8 million is available through the participating Department of Defense agencies each year.

Deadline October of each year.

[971]
DEPARTMENT OF DEFENSE SMALL BUSINESS INNOVATION RESEARCH GRANTS

Department of Defense
Attn: SBIR Program Manager
OSD/SADBU
The Pentagon, Room 2A338
Washington, DC 20301-3061
(800) 382-4634   Fax: (800) 462-4128
E-mail: SBIRHELP@us.teltech.com

Purpose To support small businesses that have the technological experience to contribute to the research and development mission of various agencies within the Department of Defense.

Eligibility For the purposes of this program, a "small business" is defined as any organization that is independently owned and operated for profit, not dominant in the field in which it is operating, and meets the size standard of 500 employees or less. The primary employment of the principal investigator must be with the firm at the time of award and during the conduct of the proposed project. Preference is given to women-owned small business concerns and to socially and economically disadvantaged small business concerns. Women-owned small business concerns are those which are at least 51 percent owned by a woman or women who also control and operate it. Socially and economically disadvantaged small business concerns are at least 51 percent owned by an Indian tribe, a native Hawaiian organization, or 1 or more socially and economically disadvantaged individuals (Black Americans, Hispanic Americans, Native Americans, Asian-Pacific Americans, or subcontinent Asian Americans). The project must be performed in the United States. Agencies that have Department of Defense Small Business Innovation Research (SBIR) programs are the Department of the Navy, Department of the Air Force, Defense Advanced Research Projects Agency, Defense Special Weapons Agency, Special Operations Command, and Ballistic Missile Defense Organization.

Financial data Grants are offered in 2 phases. In phase 1, awards normally may not exceed $100,000 (for both direct and indirect costs); in phase 2, awards normally may not exceed $750,000 (including both direct and indirect costs).

Duration Phase 1: up to 6 months; phase 2: up to 2 years.

Number awarded Varies; in a recent year, the Department of Defense awarded approximately $500 million in SBIR grants.

Deadline January and July of each year.

[972]
DEPARTMENT OF DEFENSE SMALL BUSINESS TECHNOLOGY TRANSFER GRANTS

Department of Defense
Attn: STTR Program Manager
OSD/SADBU
The Pentagon, Room 2A338
Washington, DC 20301-3061
(703) 697-1481   (800) 382-4634
Fax: (800) 462-4128   E-mail: SBIRHELP@us.teltech.com

Purpose To provide financial support to cooperative research and development projects carried out between small business concerns and research institutions in areas of interest to various agencies within the Department of Defense.

Eligibility For the purposes of this program, a "small business" is defined as any organization that is independently owned and operated for profit, not dominant in the field in which it is operating, and meets the size standard of 500 employees or less. Unlike the Department of Defense Small Business Innovation Research Grants, the primary employment of the principal investigator does not need to be with the business concern. This program, however, requires that the small business apply in collaboration with a nonprofit research institution for conduct of a project that has potential for commercialization. At least 40 percent of the work must be performed by the small business and at least 30 percent of the work must be performed by the research institution. The principal investigator may have his/her primary employment with an organization other than the small business concern, including the research institution. Preference is given to women-owned small business concerns and to socially and economically disadvantaged small business concerns. Women-owned small business concerns are those which are at least 51 percent owned by a woman or women who also control and operate it. Socially and economically disadvantaged small business concerns are at least 51 percent owned by an Indian tribe, a native Hawaiian organization, or 1 or more socially and economically disadvantaged individuals (Black Americans, Hispanic Americans, Native Americans, Asian-Pacific Americans, or subcontinent Asian Americans). The project must be performed in the United States. Agencies of the Department of Defense currently participating in this program are the Department of the Army, Department of the Navy, Department of the Air Force, Defense Advanced Research Projects Agency, and the Ballistic Missile Defense Organization.

Financial data In the first phase, annual awards may not exceed $100,000 for direct costs, indirect costs, and negotiated fixed fees. In the second phase, awards up to $500,000 are available.

Duration Normally 1 year for the first phase and 2 years for the second phase.

Special features Grants in the first phase are to determine the scientific, technical, and commercial merit and feasibility of the proposed cooperative effort and the quality of performance of the small business concern. In the second phase, the research and development efforts continue, depending on the results of the first phase.

Number awarded Varies; the Department of Defense awards approximately $36 million through this program each year.

Deadline April of each year.

[973]
DEPARTMENT OF EDUCATION SMALL BUSINESS INNOVATION RESEARCH GRANTS

Department of Education
Attn: Office of Educational Research and Improvement
MS 5530
555 New Jersey Avenue, N.W., Room 602D
Washington, DC 20208
(202) 219-2050

Purpose To support small businesses that have the technological experience to contribute to the research and development mission of the Department of Education.

Eligibility For the purposes of this program, a "small business" is defined as any organization that is independently owned and operated for profit, not dominant in the field in which it is operating, and meets the size standard of 500 employees or less. The primary employment of the principal investigator must be with the

firm at the time of award and during the conduct of the proposed project. Preference is given to women-owned small business concerns and to socially and economically disadvantaged small business concerns. Women-owned small business concerns are those which are at least 51 percent owned by a woman or women who also control and operate it. Socially and economically disadvantaged small business concerns are at least 51 percent owned by an Indian tribe, a native Hawaiian organization, or 1 or more socially and economically disadvantaged individuals (Black Americans, Hispanic Americans, Native Americans, Asian-Pacific Americans, or subcontinent Asian Americans). The project must be performed in the United States. Firms with strong research capabilities in science, engineering, or educational technology in any of the topic areas are encourage to participate. Recently, the topic areas were: 1) development or adaptation of assistive devices, mechanisms, technologies, or techniques for individuals with disabilities; 2) development or adaptation of devices, mechanisms, or techniques for individuals with hearing disabilities; 3) innovative technologies to enhance self-determination, job development, job modification, job opportunities, or transition from school to work for individuals with disabilities; 4) development or adaptation of telecommunications, electronics networks, multimedia, or management information systems and software to meet the needs of individuals with disabilities, their families, and professionals in rehabilitation and special education; 5) development or adaptation of innovative technologies to enhance learning and development of children with disabilities; 6) development or adaptation of technologies to foster the inclusion and facilitate the successful integration of children and youth with disabilities into regular school settings; and 7) development or adaptation of devices or technologies to assist children, youth, and adults with disabilities in the arts, recreation, or leisure-time activities.

Financial data Grants are offered in 2 phases. In phase 1, awards normally may not exceed $40,000 (for both direct and indirect costs); in phase 2, awards normally may not exceed $250,000 (including both direct and indirect costs).

Duration Phase 1: up to 6 months; phase 2: up to 2 years.

Number awarded Varies each year.

Deadline March of each year.

[974]
DEPARTMENT OF ENERGY DISTINGUISHED POSTDOCTORAL RESEARCH PROGRAM

Oak Ridge Institute for Science and Education
Attn: Science/Engineering Education Division
P.O. Box 117
Oak Ridge, TN 37831-0117
(423) 576-9934   (423) 576-3192
(800) 569-7749   Fax: (423) 576-3643
E-mail: doedprp@orau.gov

Purpose To provide financial assistance for postdoctoral research and training in energy-related engineering, physical sciences, and computer sciences.

Eligibility Applicants must have completed a doctoral degree within the past 3 years and be proposing a program of research and training in computer sciences, physical sciences, engineering, and other scientific disciplines related to energy. Awards are tenable at laboratories in the United States that are affiliated with or supported by the U.S. Department of Energy (DOE); for a list of those, contact the address above. All programs operated by the Science/Engineering Education Division (SEED) of Oak Ridge Institute for Science and Education (ORISE) seek to broaden the participation of minorities, women, and persons with disabilities in science and engineering careers.

Financial data   The stipend is $52,800 per year; reimbursement for inbound travel, moving, travel to 2 domestic scientific meetings per year, and medical insurance are also provided.

Duration   1 year; renewable.

Special features   This program is funded by the DOE Office of Science Education Programs and administered by ORISE/SEED.

Number awarded   Varies each year.

Deadline   December of each year.

[975]
DEPARTMENT OF ENERGY FACULTY RESEARCH PARTICIPATION PROGRAM

Oak Ridge Institute for Science and Education
Attn: Science/Engineering Education Division
P.O. Box 117
Oak Ridge, TN 37831-0117
(423) 576-8807   (423) 576-8158
(800) 569-7749   Fax: (423) 576-3643
E-mail: facrshpt@orau.gov

Purpose   To provide funding for cooperative participation by faculty members who wish to engage in ongoing energy research at specified facilities of the U.S. Department of Energy (DOE).

Eligibility   College and university full-time faculty members in engineering, physical and natural sciences, mathematics, or computer science may apply for this program. They must propose to conduct research at 1 of the following DOE facilities: Atmospheric Turbulence and Diffusion Division, Oak Ridge, Tennessee; Continuous Electron Beam Accelerator Facility, Newport News, Virginia; Oak Ridge Institute for Science and Education, Oak Ridge, Tennessee; Oak Ridge National Laboratory, Oak Ridge, Tennessee; Savannah River Ecology Laboratory, Savannah River Site, and Savannah River Archaeological Research Program, Aiken, South Carolina; or Triangle Universities Nuclear Laboratory, Research Triangle Park, North Carolina. All programs operated by the Science/Engineering Education Division (SEED) of Oak Ridge Institute for Science and Education (ORISE) seek to broaden the participation of minorities, women, and persons with disabilities in science and engineering careers.

Financial data   The stipend is negotiable, but based on the recipient's regular university salary; some reimbursement for travel is available.

Duration   10 weeks to 3 months; some sabbatical appointments up to 12 months may be available.

Special features   This program is funded by DOE and administered by ORISE/SEED.

Number awarded   Varies each year.

Deadline   January of each year.

[976]
DEPARTMENT OF ENERGY GRADUATE STUDENT RESEARCH PARTICIPATION PROGRAM

Oak Ridge Institute for Science and Education
Attn: Science/Engineering Education Division
P.O. Box 117
Oak Ridge, TN 37831-0117
(423) 576-1083   (423) 576-3426
(800) 569-7749   Fax: (423) 576-3643
E-mail: gradsrpp@orau.gov

Purpose   To provide funding for graduate research in advanced energy technologies and procedures at selected energy research facilities.

Eligibility   This program is open to students currently working on a graduate degree in the life sciences, physical sciences, social sciences, mathematics, or engineering. All programs operated by the Science/Engineering Education Division (SEED) of Oak Ridge Institute for Science and Education (ORISE) seek to broaden the participation of minorities, women, and persons with disabilities in science and engineering careers.

Financial data   Participants are paid a monthly stipend of $1,600 to $1,700. They also receive a travel reimbursement.

Duration   From 1 to 12 months, depending upon the center at which they conduct their research.

Special features   Participants may conduct research at the following locations: Atmospheric Turbulence and Diffusion Division in Oak Ridge, Tennessee; Continuous Electron Beam Accelerator Facility in Newport News, Virginia; Lockheed Martin Energy Systems in Oak Ridge, Tennessee; Oak Ridge Institute for Science and Education in Oak Ridge, Tennessee; Oak Ridge National Laboratory in Oak Ridge, Tennessee; Pittsburgh Energy Technology Center in Pittsburgh, Pennsylvania; Pittsburgh Research Center at the U.S. Bureau of Mines in Pittsburgh, Pennsylvania; Savannah River Archaeological Research Program, Savannah River Ecology Laboratory, and Savannah River Site in Aiken, South Carolina. This program is funded by the Office of Energy Research and the Office of Fossil Energy of the U.S. Department of Energy (DOE) and administered by ORISE/SEED.

Number awarded   Varies; generally, approximately 30 each year.

Deadline   Applications may be submitted at any time.

[977]
DEPARTMENT OF ENERGY LABORATORY COOPERATIVE POSTGRADUATE RESEARCH TRAINING PROGRAM

Oak Ridge Institute for Science and Education
Attn: Science/Engineering Education Division
P.O. Box 117
Oak Ridge, TN 37831-0117
(423) 576-3456   (423) 576-3192
(800) 569-7749   Fax: (423) 576-3643
E-mail: lbcooppr@orau.gov

Purpose   To provide funding for postgraduate research and training in a broad range of energy research and engineering activities at research facilities of the U.S. Department of Energy (DOE).

Eligibility   This program is open to postgraduates who completed a graduate degree within the last 3 years in the life sciences, earth sciences, physical sciences, computer sciences, mathematics, engineering, environmental sciences, or other scientific disciplines. All programs operated by the Science/Engineering Education Division (SEED) of Oak Ridge Institute for Science and Education (ORISE) seek to broaden the participation of minorities, women, and persons with disabilities in science and engineering careers.

Financial data Stipends depend on research area and degree; inbound travel and moving expenses are reimbursed.

Duration 1 year; renewable.

Special features Participants engage in research or training at 1 of the following participating laboratories: Atmospheric Turbulence and Diffusion Division in Oak Ridge, Tennessee; Oak Ridge Institute for Science and Education or Oak Ridge National Laboratory in Oak Ridge, Tennessee; Savannah River Ecology Laboratory or Savannah River Technology Center in Aiken, South Carolina. This program is funded by DOE and the host laboratories and administered by ORISE/SEED.

Number awarded Varies each year.

Deadline Applications may be submitted at any time.

[978]
DEPARTMENT OF ENERGY LABORATORY GRADUATE PARTICIPATION PROGRAM

Oak Ridge Institute for Science and Education
Attn: Science/Engineering Education Division
P.O. Box 117
Oak Ridge, TN 37831-0117
(423) 576-3427   (423) 576-3426
(800) 569-7749   Fax: (423) 576-3643
E-mail: labgpp@orau.gov

Purpose To provide funding for graduate thesis or dissertation research at selected U.S. Department of Energy (DOE) research laboratories.

Eligibility This program is open to graduate students in the life sciences, physical sciences, social sciences, mathematics, and engineering who have completed all degree requirements except their thesis or dissertation research. All programs operated by the Science/Engineering Education Division (SEED) of Oak Ridge Institute for Science and Education (ORISE) seek to broaden the participation of minorities, women, and persons with disabilities in science and engineering careers.

Financial data Annual stipends range from $12,000 to $14,400. An allowance for dependents is available. Tuition and fees up to $3,500 per year are paid.

Duration From 6 to 12 months; may be renewed.

Special features Participants conduct thesis or dissertation research under the joint direction of their major professor and a DOE staff member at 1 of the following participating laboratories: Atmospheric Turbulence and Diffusion Division in Oak Ridge, Tennessee; Continuous Beam Accelerator Facility in Newport News, Virginia; Oak Ridge Institute for Science and Education or Oak Ridge National Laboratory in Oak Ridge, Tennessee; Pittsburgh Energy Technology Center in Pittsburgh, Pennsylvania; Savannah River Ecology Laboratory, Savannah River Technology Center, or Savannah River Archaeological Research Program in Aiken, South Carolina. This program is funded by DOE's Office of Energy Research and Office of Fossil Energy and administered by ORISE/SEED.

Limitations Students must participate in this research program on a full-time basis.

Number awarded Varies; generally, approximately 15 each year.

Deadline Applications may be submitted at any time.

[979]
DEPARTMENT OF ENERGY MINORITY INSTITUTION RESEARCH TRAVEL GRANTS

Department of Energy
Attn: Office of Economic Impact and Diversity
Forrestal Building, Room 5B-110, ED-2
1000 Independence Avenue, S.W.
Washington, DC 20585
(202) 586-5876

Purpose To provide travel support to faculty members and graduate students at minority colleges and universities.

Eligibility Regular full-time faculty members and accompanying graduate students at minority postsecondary educational institutions are eligible to apply for support for travel to government research laboratories, research institutes, academic institutions, and industrial organizations for the acquisition of new and improved scientific and technical skills.

Financial data The maximum per diem is $175; the maximum grant is $2,000.

Duration 1 to 5 days.

Special features This program is administered by the National Association for Equal Opportunity in Higher Education (NAFEO). Applications are first submitted to it at NAFEO Lovejoy Building, MIRT Program, 400 12th Street, N.E., Washington, D.C. 20002, (202) 543-9111.

Number awarded Varies each year.

Deadline Applications may be submitted at any time.

[980]
DEPARTMENT OF ENERGY RESEARCH TRAVEL CONTRACTS

Oak Ridge Institute for Science and Education
Attn: Science/Engineering Education Division
P.O. Box 117
Oak Ridge, TN 37831-0117
(423) 576-3425   (423) 576-2358
(800) 569-7749   Fax: (423) 576-3643
E-mail: rshtrav@orau.gov

Purpose To provide funding for short, collaborative research visits to Department of Energy (DOE) research and development facilities.

Eligibility This program is open to college or university faculty members and graduate students in the following disciplines: natural sciences, physical sciences, environmental sciences, and other energy-related areas of study. All programs operated by the Science/Engineering Education Division (SEED) of Oak Ridge Institute for Science and Education (ORISE) seek to broaden the participation of minorities, women, and persons with disabilities in science and engineering careers.

Financial data Grants provide travel support and living expenses while conducting research at the laboratory.

Duration From 1 to 14 days.

Special features This program is funded by DOE's Office of Science Education Programs and administered by ORISE/SEED.

Number awarded Varies; generally, approximately 225 each year.

Deadline Applications may be submitted at any time.

[981]
DEPARTMENT OF TRANSPORTATION SMALL BUSINESS INNOVATION RESEARCH GRANTS

Department of Transportation
Attn: Research and Special Programs Administration
John A. Volpe National Transportation Systems Center
55 Broadway, Kendall Square
Cambridge, MA 02142-1093
(617) 494-2756   Fax: (617) 494-2497
E-mail: Kovatch@volpel.dot.gov

Purpose To support small businesses that have the technological experience to contribute to the research and development mission of the Department of Transportation and other related agencies.

Eligibility For the purposes of this program, a "small business" is defined as any organization that is independently owned and operated for profit, not dominant in the field in which it is operating, and meets the size standard of 500 employees or less. The primary employment of the principal investigator must be with the firm at the time of award and during the conduct of the proposed project. Preference is given to women-owned small business concerns and to socially and economically disadvantaged small business concerns. Women-owned small business concerns are those which are at least 51 percent owned by a woman or women who also control and operate it. Socially and economically disadvantaged small business concerns are at least 51 percent owned by an Indian tribe, a native Hawaiian organization, or 1 or more socially and economically disadvantaged individuals (Black Americans, Hispanic Americans, Native Americans, Asian-Pacific Americans, or subcontinent Asian Americans). The project must be performed in the United States.

Financial data Support is offered in 2 phases. In phase 1, awards normally may not exceed $50,000 (for both direct and indirect costs); in phase 2, awards normally may not exceed $250,000 (including both direct and indirect costs).

Duration Phase 1: up to 6 months; phase 2: up to 2 years.

Number awarded Varies each year.

Deadline April of each year.

[982]
DEVELOPMENTAL GRANTS FOR MINORITY COLLABORATIVE PROJECTS

National Institutes of Health
Attn: National Institute on Alcohol Abuse and Alcoholism
Division of Basic Research
Willco Building, Suite 402
6000 Executive Boulevard MSC 7003
Rockville, MD 20892-7003
(301) 443-2530   Fax: (301) 594-0673
E-mail: wl10q@nih.gov

Purpose To provide financial assistance for collaborative research projects between established alcohol research scientists and scientists in minority and/or predominantly minority institutions.

Eligibility This program is open to investigators at domestic nonprofit and for-profit, public and private institutions, such as universities, colleges, hospitals, laboratories, units of state and local government, and eligible agencies of the federal government. The principal investigator must apply with a colleague from a laboratory or research site in the collaborating institution. The proposal should encourage exploratory/developmental studies that complement and enhance existing alcohol research efforts.

Racial/ethnic minority individuals, women, and persons with disabilities are encouraged to apply as principal investigators.

Financial data Awards may be up to $70,000 in direct costs per year, but most are expected to be smaller.

Duration Up to 2 years.

Number awarded Up to 4 each year, depending on the availability of funds.

Deadline January, April, or August of each year.

[983]
DIRECTORATE OF ENVIRONMENT-FORT MCCLELLAN RESEARCH PARTICIPATION PROGRAM

Oak Ridge Institute for Science and Education
Attn: Science/Engineering Education Division
P.O. Box 117
Oak Ridge, TN 37831-0117
(423) 576-8503   (423) 241-2875
(800) 569-7749   Fax: (423) 576-3643
E-mail: rppdefm@orau.gov

Purpose To provide funding to postgraduates interested in conducting research in environmental fields, cultural resources, natural resources, and geographical information systems at Fort McClellan in Alabama.

Eligibility Applicants should have completed a baccalaureate or graduate degree within the past 3 years; others are considered on a case-by-case basis. Their field of study should have been environmental sciences, engineering, physical sciences, life sciences, or other related scientific disciplines. They must propose to conduct research at the Directorate of Environment at Fort McClellan, Alabama. All programs operated by the Science/Engineering Education Division (SEED) of Oak Ridge Institute for Science and Education (ORISE) seek to broaden the participation of minorities, women, and persons with disabilities in science and engineering careers.

Financial data The stipend is based on research area and degree; a limited reimbursement for inbound travel and moving is also provided.

Duration 1 year; renewable.

Special features This program is funded by an interagency agreement between the U.S. Department of Energy and the Directorate of Environment-Fort McClellan, U.S. Army, and administered by ORISE/SEED.

Number awarded Varies each year.

Deadline Applications may be submitted at any time.

[984]
DISADVANTAGED FACULTY LOAN REPAYMENT PROGRAM

Health Resources and Services Administration
Attn: Bureau of Health Professions
Division of Disadvantaged Assistance
Parklawn Building, Room 8A09
5600 Fishers Lane
Rockville, MD 20857
(301) 443-3680   Fax: (301) 443-5242

Purpose To repay the educational loans of faculty from disadvantaged backgrounds in health professional schools.

Eligibility Applicants for this assistance must be from a disadvantaged background, defined as individuals who either 1) come from an environment that has inhibited them from obtaining the knowledge, skill, and abilities required to enroll in and graduate from a health professions school, or from a program providing education or training in an allied health profession; or 2) come from a low income family, with an income ranging from less than $10,200 for a family with 1 dependent to $26,700 for a family with 6 dependents. They must have a degree from a school of medicine, osteopathic medicine, podiatric medicine, veterinary medicine, dentistry, pharmacy, optometry, nursing, or public health, or from a school offering graduate programs in clinical psychology; must not have been a member of the faculty of any school at any time during the preceding 18 months; and must have entered into an eligible health professions school to serve as a full-time faculty member for a minimum of 2 years.

Financial data This program provides, for each year of service, as much as $20,000 of the outstanding principal and interest on the recipient's educational loans. The employing school must agree to pay a sum (in addition to faculty salary) equal to that paid by this program.

Duration Service must be for a minimum of 2 years.

Number awarded Varies each year.

Deadline June of each year.

[985]
DISSERTATION FELLOWSHIP ON PEACE AND SECURITY IN A CHANGING WORLD

Social Science Research Council
810 Seventh Avenue
New York, NY 10019
(212) 377-2700   Fax: (212) 377-2727

Purpose To support doctoral research and training on the implications for security issues of worldwide cultural, social, economic, military, and political changes.

Eligibility The competition is open to researchers who are finishing course work, examinations, or similar requirements for the doctoral degree (Ph.D. or its equivalent), but desire to undertake training that adds a new competence to the disciplinary skills that they already have. Applicants should be nearing completion of all requirements for the Ph.D. except the dissertation at the time of application. They must propose to make substantial revisions in their dissertation plans during the course of this fellowship. There are no citizenship, residency, or nationality requirements. Applicants must be working in the social/behavioral sciences (including history and foreign area studies), the humanities, or the physical and biological sciences. Minorities and women are particularly encouraged to apply.

Financial data The stipend, up to $17,500, is appropriate for the cost of living where the fellow will be working.

Duration In most cases, 2 years.

Special features The Social Science Research Council administers this program with funds provided by the John D. and Catherine T. MacArthur Foundation as part of its Program in International Peace and Security Studies. Training may occur in any setting of the recipient's choice, in any nation, and may consist of formal course work, tutorials, internships, senior apprenticeships, or supervised study with senior faculty.

Limitations The program requires and enables researchers to add to their present specialty a competence in a different area and to apply their newly-enhanced skills to specific research projects. The fellowships are not designed for and will not support programs for which the applicant is already prepared by prior experience and training. Fellows must devote full time to the fellowship and are not permitted to be otherwise employed.

Number awarded Approximately 7 each year.

Deadline November of each year.

[986]
DISSERTATION FELLOWSHIPS FOR GRADUATE STUDENTS OF COLOR IN HUMANITIES AND SOCIAL SCIENCES

New England Board of Higher Education
45 Temple Place
Boston, MA 02111
(617) 357-9620   Fax: (617) 338-1577
E-mail: aburton@mecn.mass.edu

Purpose To encourage African American, Hispanic American, and Native American students to pursue college and university teaching in New England.

Eligibility This program is open to African American, Hispanic American, and Native American graduate students who are U.S. citizens, have completed all doctoral work except the dissertation, and are interested in preparing for a college teaching career in New England. They should be in a strong position to complete their dissertation within a year. Applicants must submit 1) a full curriculum vitae; 2) a copy of the dissertation prospectus; 3) a graduate school transcript; 4) a statement of scholarship and teaching goals; and 5) 3 letters or recommendation (1 of which must be from the dissertation advisor at the home campus).

Financial data The stipend is $21,000 per year.

Duration 1 year.

Special features Successful applicants spend a year completing their dissertation at 1 of the following host campuses: University of Vermont, University of Maine System, Bridgewater State College, University of New Hampshire, or Boston College. The host campuses select their fellows. Office space and library privileges are provided. These fellowships are offered under the auspices of the newly-launched "Compact for Faculty Diversity."

Limitations Recipients are expected to present their work-in-progress at campus forums and to participate in several discussions with undergraduates on "how to succeed in graduate school." There are no formal teaching assignments during the fellowship year.

Number awarded 5 each year: 1 at each participating school.

Deadline February of each year.

[987]
DISSERTATION FELLOWSHIPS IN EAST EUROPEAN STUDIES

American Council of Learned Societies
228 East 45th Street
New York, NY 10017-3398
(212) 697-1505   Fax: (212) 949-8058
E-mail: grants@acls.org

Purpose To provide financial assistance to doctoral candidates to conduct doctoral research or writing in the social sciences and humanities relating to eastern Europe.

Eligibility Applicants must be citizens or permanent legal residents of the United States who are doctoral candidates desiring to engage in dissertation research or writing in the social sciences or humanities relating to Albania, Bulgaria, the Czech Republic, Hungary, Poland, Romania, Slovakia, or the successor states of Yugoslavia. The research or writing may be undertaken at any university or institution in any country, except those in eastern Europe. Proposals dealing with Albania, Bulgaria, Romania, and the former Yugoslavia are particularly encouraged. Applications are specifically invited from women and members of minority groups.

Financial data The maximum stipend is $15,000 plus expenses per year.

Duration 1 year; may be renewed for 1 additional year.

Special features In awarding these grants, consideration is given to the scholarly merit of the proposal, its importance to the development of eastern European studies, and the scholarly potential, accomplishments, and financial need of the applicant. All proposals should be for scholarly work, the product of which is to be disseminated in English. This program is sponsored jointly by the American Council of Learned Societies (ACLS) and the Social Science Research Council, funded by the U.S. Department of State but administered by ACLS.

Limitations This program is not intended to support research within eastern Europe.

Number awarded Varies each year.

Deadline October of each year.

[988]
DIVERSITY ACTION GRANTS

American Society of Mechanical Engineers
Attn: Board on Minorities and Women
1828 L Street, N.W., Suite 906
Washington, DC 20036-5104
(202) 785-3756   Fax: (202) 429-9417
E-mail: engles@asme.org

Purpose To provide funding to student sections of the American Society of Mechanical Engineers (ASME) for increasing the participation of minority and women students in student section activities.

Eligibility Any ASME student section member who is interested in promoting diversity in the section and fostering the career development of minority and women engineers may apply. Proposals must 1) be potentially applicable to other schools; 2) be innovative; 3) include realistic methodology; 4) have an evaluation plan and anticipated benefits; 5) encourage costsharing from local industry, universities, or the local ASME section; and 6) have a realistic budget and cost-effectiveness.

Financial data Grants range from $500 to $1,500.

Duration 1 academic year.

Limitations Any funds that remain unused at the end of the year must be returned to the ASME.

Number awarded Varies each year.

Deadline October of each year.

[989]
DOCTORAL DISSERTATION FELLOWSHIPS IN LAW AND SOCIAL SCIENCE

American Bar Foundation
Attn: Assistant Director
750 North Lake Shore Drive
Chicago, IL 60611
(312) 988-6500

Purpose To encourage original and significant research on law, the legal profession, and legal institutions.

Eligibility Applications are invited from outstanding students who are candidates for the Ph.D. degree in the social sciences. They must have completed all doctoral requirements except the dissertation. Proposed research must be in the general area of sociolegal studies or in social scientific approaches to law, the legal profession, or legal institutions. The dissertation must address critical issues in the field and show promise of making a major contribution to social scientific understanding of law and legal processes. Applications must include 1) transcripts of graduate work; 2) 2 letters of recommendation; 3) a curriculum vitae; and 4) a dissertation prospectus or proposal with an outline of the substance and methodology of the intended research. Minority students are especially encouraged to apply.

Financial data The stipend is $14,000 per year. Fellows also may request up to $1,000 each fellowship year to reimburse expenses associated with dissertation research, travel to meet with dissertation advisors, and travel to conferences at which papers are presented. Moving expenses of up to $1,000 may be reimbursed on application.

Duration 1 year; may be renewed for 1 additional year.

Special features Fellows are offered access to the computing and word processing facilities of the American Bar Foundation and the libraries of Northwestern University and the University of Chicago.

Limitations Fellowships must be held in residence at the American Bar Foundation. Appointments to the fellowship are full time; fellows are not permitted to undertake other work.

Number awarded 2 each year.

Deadline January of each year.

[990]
DOCTORAL DISSERTATION IMPROVEMENT GRANTS IN THE DIRECTORATE FOR BIOLOGICAL SCIENCES

National Science Foundation
Attn: Directorate for Biological Sciences
Division of Environmental Biology
4201 Wilson Boulevard
Arlington, VA 22230
(703) 306-1483   E-mail: ebehrens@nsf.gov

Purpose To provide partial support for dissertation research in selected areas of the biological sciences.

Eligibility Applications may be submitted through regular university channels by dissertation advisors on behalf of graduate students who have advanced to candidacy and have begun or are about to begin dissertation research. Students must be enrolled at U.S. institutions but need not be U.S. citizens. Proposals should focus on the ecology, ecosystems, systematics, or population biology programs in the Division of Environmental Biology, or the animal behavior or ecological and evolutionary physiology programs in the Division of Integrative Biology and Neuroscience. Women, minorities, and persons with disabilities are strongly encouraged to apply.

Financial data Awards range from $3,000 to $10,000; funds may be used for travel to specialized facilities or field research locations, use of specialized research equipment, purchase of supplies and services not otherwise available, fees for computerized or other forms of data, and rental of environmental chambers or other research facilities.

Duration Normally 2 years.

Special features Information on programs in the Division of Environmental Biology is available at the address and telephone number above; information from the Division of Integrative Biology and Neuroscience is available at (703) 306-1421.

Limitations Funding is not provided for stipends, tuition, textbooks, journals, allowances for dependents, travel to scientific meetings, publication costs, dissertation preparation or reproduction, or indirect costs.

Number awarded Varies; approximately $750,000 is available for this program each year.

Deadline October of each year.

[991]
DOE SMALL BUSINESS INNOVATION RESEARCH GRANTS

Department of Energy
Attn: Office of Energy Research
SBIR Program Manager
19901 Germantown Road
Germantown, MD 20874-1290
(301) 903-5707   Fax: (301) 903-6067
E-mail: sbir-sttr@oer.doe.gov

Purpose To support small businesses (especially those owned by minorities and women) that have the technological expertise to contribute to the research and development mission of the Department of Energy.

Eligibility For the purposes of this program, a "small business" is defined as any organization that is independently owned and operated for profit, is not dominant in the field in which it is operating, and meets the size standard of 500 employees or less. The primary employment of the principal investigator must be with the firm at the time of award and during the conduct of the proposed project. Preference is given to women-owned small business concerns and socially and economically disadvantaged small business concerns. Women-owned small business concerns are those which are at least 51 percent owned by a woman or women who also control and operate it. Socially and economically disadvantaged small business concerns are at least 51 percent owned by an Indian tribe, a native Hawaiian organization, or 1 or more socially and economically disadvantaged individuals (Black Americans, Hispanic Americans, Native Americans, Asian-Pacific Americans, or subcontinent Asian Americans). The project must be performed in the United States. Some of the research topics which have received support recently include remediation of subsurface contaminants, characterization technologies for environmental remediation and waste management, efficient separations processes, advanced environmental monitoring technology, atmospheric measurement and sampling technology, medical applications, occupational exposure assessment, biologically-based catalysis for energy applications, computational geosciences, materials joining, processing for surface hardness, and metal forming.

Financial data Support is offered in 2 phases: in phase 1, awards normally may not exceed $75,000 (for both direct and indirect costs); in phase 2, awards normally may not exceed $750,000 (including both direct and indirect costs).

Duration Phase 1: up to 6 months; phase 2: up to 2 years.

Special features The objectives of this program include increasing private sector commercialization of technology developed through research and development supported by the Department of Energy, stimulating technological innovation in the private sector, strengthening the role of small business in meeting federal research and development needs, and improving the return on investment from federally funded research for economic and social benefits to the nation.

Number awarded Approximately 200 each year.

Deadline March of each year.

[992]
DOE SMALL BUSINESS TECHNOLOGY TRANSFER GRANTS

Department of Energy
Attn: Office of Energy Research
STTR Program Manager
19901 Germantown Road
Germantown, MD 20874-1290
(301) 903-5707   Fax: (301) 903-5488
E-mail: sbir-sttr@oer.doe.gov

Purpose To provide financial support to cooperative research and development projects carried out between small business concerns and research institutions in areas of interest to the Department of Energy.

Eligibility For the purposes of this program, a "small business" is defined as any organization that is independently owned and operated for profit, not dominant in the field in which it is operating, and meets the size standard of 500 employees or less. Unlike the Department of Energy Small Business Innovation Research Grants, the primary employment of the principal investigator does not need to be with the business concern. This program, however, requires that the small business apply in collaboration with a nonprofit research institution for conduct of a project that has potential for commercialization. At least 40 percent of the work must be performed by the small business and at least 30 percent of the work must be performed by the research institution. The principal investigator may have his/her primary employment with an organization other than the small business concern, including the research institution. Preference is given to women-owned small business concerns and to socially and economically disadvantaged small business concerns. Women-owned small business concerns are those which are at least 51 percent owned by a woman or women who also control and operate it. Socially and economically disadvantaged small business concerns are at least 51 percent owned by an Indian tribe, a native Hawaiian organization, or 1 or more socially and economically disadvantaged individuals (Black Americans, Hispanic Americans, Native Americans, Asian-Pacific Americans, or subcontinent Asian Americans). The project must be performed in the United States.

Financial data In the first phase, annual awards may not exceed $100,000 for direct costs, indirect costs, and negotiated fixed fees. In the second phase, awards up to $500,000 are available.

Duration Normally 9 months for the first phase and 2 years for the second phase.

Special features Grants in the first phase are to determine the scientific, technical, and commercial merit and feasibility of the proposed cooperative effort and the quality of performance of the small business concern. In the second phase, the research and development efforts continue, depending on the results of the first phase.

Number awarded In a recent year, the Department of Energy awarded 15 grants through this program.

Deadline December of each year.

[993]
DOROTHY DANFORTH COMPTON FELLOWSHIPS

Institute for the Study of World Politics
1755 Massachusetts Avenue, N.W.
Washington, DC 20036

Purpose To provide funding to underrepresented minority students interested in preparing for a career in world affairs.

Eligibility This program is open to African American, Hispanic American, and Native American students pursuing a master's or doctoral degree in preparation for a career in world affairs (as scholars or practitioners). Applicants should be U.S. citizens pursuing degrees from U.S. institutions. Ph.D. candidates who have completed their course work and are engaged in dissertation research should submit an application and cover letter. Students pursuing a master's degree or a Ph.D. degree (but are not yet at the dissertation stage) should submit an application form, a curriculum vitae, a statement of plans for a career in world affairs, standardized test scores, and letters of recommendation.

Financial data The amount awarded varies, depending upon the status and needs of the recipient.

Duration 1 year.

Special features The Institute for the Study of World Politics (ISWP) awards fellowships to students of political science, economics, international relations, and history as long as the work relates to political, economic, and social issues that affect the security, well-being, and dignity of peoples of the world. Dissertation level doctoral student applicants are also considered for ISWP Doctoral Dissertation Fellowships.

Limitations Telephone inquiries are not accepted.

Number awarded Varies each year.

Deadline February of each year for applicants engaged in dissertation research; March of each year for applicants engaged in work at the master's or pre-dissertation Ph.D. level.

[994]
DRUG ABUSE PREVENTION INTERVENTION FOR WOMEN AND MINORITIES

National Institutes of Health
Attn: National Institute on Drug Abuse
Division of Epidemiology and Prevention Research
Parklawn Building, Room 9A-53
5600 Fishers Lane
Rockville, MD 20857
(301) 443-1514   Fax: (301) 443-2636
E-mail: rn29e@nih.gov

Purpose To advance research to develop, refine, and test the efficacy and effectiveness of theory-based, universal, selective, and indicated drug abuse prevention interventions for minorities and women.

Eligibility Eligible to apply are public, nonprofit, or for-profit institutions (including universities, colleges, hospitals, community agencies) and local, state, or federal government agencies. Proposals should seek to identify risk and protective factors that may be associated with core cultural and/or gender value systems and life experiences in order to design and test under controlled conditions comprehensive, theory-based preventive interventions that are sensitive to cultural and/or gender norms or needs. Women, racial/ethnic minority individuals, and persons with disabilities are particularly encouraged to apply as principal investigators. Selection is based on quality of the proposed project as determined by peer review, availability of funds, and program priority.

Financial data The amount awarded varies, depending upon the funds available and the scope of the programs supported.

Duration 1 year or longer.

Special features This program is jointly sponsored by the National Institute on Drug Abuse (NIDA) and the National Institute of Mental Health (NIMH). Information is also available from the NIMH, Office on AIDS, 5600 Fishers Lane, Room 10-75, Rockville,

MD 20857, (301) 443-6100, Fax: (301) 443-9719, E-mail wpequegn@aoamh2.ssw.dhhs.gov.

Number awarded Varies each year.

Deadline January, May, or September of each year.

[995]
DRUG AND ALCOHOL USE AND ABUSE IN RURAL AMERICA

National Institutes of Health
Attn: National Institute on Drug Abuse
Division of Epidemiology and Prevention Research
Parklawn Building, Room 9A-53
5600 Fishers Lane
Rockville, MD 20857
(301) 443-6720   Fax: (301) 443-2636
E-mail: ph45z@nih.gov

Purpose To encourage research on drug and alcohol use and abuse behaviors in rural America.

Eligibility This program is open to principal investigators at foreign and domestic, for-profit and nonprofit organizations, public or private, such as universities, colleges, hospitals, laboratories, units of state or local governments, and eligible agencies of the federal government. Racial/ethnic minority individuals, women, and persons with disabilities are especially encouraged to apply as principal investigators. Applicants must be proposing to conduct research on drug and alcohol use and abuse behaviors in rural America, the consequences of such use and abuse, and the delivery of appropriate prevention and treatment services. Studies that deal with underserved groups in the rural setting are especially encouraged; such groups include Native Americans, migrant workers, Hispanics, and African Americans.

Financial data The amounts of the awards depend on the nature of the proposal and the availability of funds.

Duration Up to 5 years; may be renewed.

Special features This program is jointly administered by the National Institute on Drug Abuse (at the address above), the National Institute on Alcohol Abuse and Alcoholism (at 6000 Executive Boulevard, Suite 505, Bethesda, MD 20892-7003, (301) 443-8766), and the Agricultural Research Service of the Department of Agriculture (at Unit No. 83, Riverdale, MD 20737, (301) 734-8596).

Number awarded Varies each year.

Deadline January, May, or September of each year.

[996]
DRUG USE AND ABUSE IN MINORITY AND UNDERSERVED POPULATIONS GRANTS

National Institutes of Health
Attn: National Institute on Drug Abuse
Division of Epidemiology and Prevention Research
Parklawn Building, Room 9A-53
5600 Fishers Lane
Rockville, MD 20857
(301) 443-6720   Fax: (301) 443-2636
E-mail: mr93q@nih.gov

Purpose To encourage research on the extent and nature of drug use and abuse among ethnic/racial minority groups and other underserved populations.

Eligibility This program is open to principal investigators at public or private nonprofit or profit-making organizations, such as universities, colleges, hospitals, laboratories, units of state or local governments, and eligible agencies of the federal government. Women and minority investigators are especially encouraged to apply. Minority populations to be served include American Indians and Alaskan Natives, Asian Americans and Pacific Islanders, African Americans, and Hispanics. Underserved populations include, but are not limited to, school dropouts, gang members, the homeless, migrant workers, prostitutes, children of drug users, recent immigrant groups, the unemployed or working poor, the elderly, veterans, incarcerated adults and juveniles, the mentally ill, or other vulnerable groups.

Financial data The amounts of the awards depend on the nature of the proposal and the availability of funds.

Duration Up to 5 years; may be renewed.

Number awarded Varies each year.

Deadline May of each year.

[997]
EARTH SCIENCES POSTDOCTORAL RESEARCH FELLOWSHIPS

National Science Foundation
Attn: Directorate for Geosciences
Division of Earth Sciences
4201 Wilson Boulevard, Room 785
Arlington, VA 22230
(703) 306-1557

Purpose To provide opportunities for junior postdoctoral scientists to conduct research either in the United States or abroad in geology.

Eligibility This program is open to persons who are citizens, nationals, or permanent residents of the United States at the time of application. Applicants must have earned a Ph.D. no earlier than 3 years preceding the deadline date. Research may be conducted at any appropriate nonprofit U.S. or foreign institution, including colleges and universities, government and national laboratories, and privately-sponsored nonprofit institutes. Research should involve any of the geological sciences supported by the Division of Earth Sciences of the National Science Foundation (NSF). Preference is given to new researchers who wish to pursue independent research goals in a new environment that includes the opportunity to learn appropriate new intellectual and technical skills. Proposals are welcomed from all qualified scientists; applications from women, minorities, and persons with disabilities is strongly encouraged.

Financial data The fellowship provides a stipend of $2,500 per month and an additional allowance of $3,500 per year to help defray the costs of research (travel, publication costs, and other research-related items). The host institution receives an allowance of $5,000 as partial reimbursement for expenses incurred in support of the research (space, secretarial assistance, equipment, and general-purpose supplies).

Duration 2 years; a 1-year no-cost extension may be granted in certain cases.

Number awarded Approximately 10 each year.

Limitations This program is not designed as an alternative for conventional research grant support, nor as a device for maintaining postdoctoral research associates in the candidate's doctoral institution. Its purpose is not to support extensions of dissertation research, not provide first jobs for new Ph.D.s, nor maintain experienced postdoctoral fellows in yet another cycle of research.

Deadline November of each year.

[998]
ECONOMIC JUSTICE FOR WOMEN GRANTS

Rockefeller Family Fund
1290 Avenue of the Americas
New York, NY 10104
(212) 373-4252   E-mail: rff@mcimail.com

Purpose To provide funding for projects that support the economic aspects of women's rights.

Eligibility The fund supports projects designed to promote economic justice for women. In particular, the program seeks to provide women with equitable employment opportunities and to improve their work lives. Examples of past grants that fit these guidelines include support to help women gain entry into nontraditional jobs; a national advocacy, research, and public education effort aimed at achieving pay equity; a campaign focusing on the need for equitable part-time employment options; and litigation to upgrade the job status and salaries of women of color confronting race and sex discrimination. Eligible to apply for these grants are tax-exempt organizations engaged in educational and charitable activities of national significance. The fund does not make grants to support individuals, scholarships, profit-making businesses, construction or restoration projects, international programs, domestic programs dealing with international issues, or efforts to reduce an organization's debt.

Financial data Grants range from $15,000 to more than $30,000.

Duration 1 year.

Number awarded Varies; generally, at least 15 each year.

Deadline Proposals may be submitted at any time.

[999]
EDUCATION AND ACCESS GRANTS TO ORGANIZATIONS

National Endowment for the Arts
Attn: Heritage and Preservation
Nancy Hanks Center
1100 Pennsylvania Avenue, N.W.
Washington, DC 20506-0001
(202) 682-5438   TTY: (202) 682-5496

Purpose To provide funding to organizations that broaden and deepen educational experiences for Americans of all ages and that make the arts available to those Americans who lack adequate opportunities to participate in the arts.

Eligibility Nonprofit tax-exempt organizations of demonstrated artistic excellence may apply if they have a 4-year history of programming, have professional staff, compensate all professional performers and related or supporting professional personnel, assure that no part of any supported project will be performed or engaged in under unsanitary or hazardous conditions, and comply with other federal regulations. Applicants may be arts institutions, local arts agencies, arts service organizations, tribal communities and Indian tribes, official units of city governments, and other organizations that can further the goals of the National Endowment for the Arts (NEA). They should be proposing projects in such areas as touring performances and exhibitions and other activities that are designed to reach populations which ordinarily would not have the opportunity to participate in such events; curriculum-based arts instruction for students in grades pre-K through 12 that provides substantive and sequential learning in the arts; instruction (not for academic credit) that is offered by arts organizations or artists that provides sequential learning in the arts over an extended period of time; activities, such as the distribution of publications, that provide access to underexposed art forms; activities which extend the work of older, disabled, and/or ethnically diverse artists to the general public; master classes, workshops, and apprenticeship programs; lecture series and symposia that are not a part of the regular curriculum of colleges and universities; curriculum development, including interdisciplinary or integrated instructional programs; training and development for artists and/or teachers that enhances their skills relating to arts education; program evaluation and/or assessment of student learning; outreach projects which engage diverse communities in partnerships; activities that build coalitions to support the arts as an integral part of education reform; national broadcast of significant television or radio programs on the arts; or innovative uses of technologies to improve teaching and learning in the arts or to make the arts more widely available. Works may be in any art form: visual, performing, design, media, literature, etc. Selection is based on artistic excellence and artistic merit of the proposed project and the applicant organization, impact of the project, and ability to carry out the project.

Financial data Grants generally range from $5,000 to $200,000 and require a match of at least 1 to 1.

Duration Up to 2 years.

Special features The NEA remains committed to supporting equitable opportunity for all and investing in as diverse a reflection of our society as possible.

Limitations Funding is not provided for general operating support; seasonal support; construction or renovation of facilities; marketing expenses that are not directly related to the proposed project; commercial enterprises or activities; fundraising or development; debt and deficit reduction; cash reserves and endowments; social activities, entertainment costs, receptions, etc.; lobbying expenses; individuals directly; elementary and secondary schools directly; avocational or student groups; professional training in degree-granting institutions; work toward academic degrees; literary projects, programming, or publishing that does not focus primarily on contemporary literature and/or writers; research that is directed primarily to academic purposes or scholarly projects; publication of books or exhibition of works by the applicant organization's staff, board members, faculty, or trustees; exhibitions of, and other projects involving, single, privately owned collections; purchase of major equipment; subgranting or regranting, except for state arts agencies and regional arts organizations.

Deadline March of each year.

[1000]
EDUCATION OF DISADVANTAGED CHILDREN GRANTS

Department of Education
Attn: Office of Elementary and Secondary Education
Compensatory Education Programs
Portals Building, Room 4400
600 Independence Avenue, S.W.
Washington, DC 20202-6132
(202) 260-0826

Purpose To provide financial assistance to local educational agencies to meet the special educational needs of educationally deprived children at the preschool, elementary, and secondary school levels.

Eligibility Local educational agencies (private or public, on the elementary or secondary school level) must apply to appropriate state educational agencies; states apply directly to the federal

government. Formula grants are provided to schools in areas with high concentrations of children from low-income families to help the children gains the skills and confidence necessary to be prepared to succeed in their present environment and with later responsibilities in school and life.

Financial data Grants range from $700,000 to more than $300 million; the average grant is $52 million.

Duration 3 years or longer; may be renewed.

Special features Funds are to be used to provide compensatory instructional activities and to deliver support services not available from other sources. These services are intended to supplement, not to replace, those that are normally provided. Programs may include supplemental instruction in basic and more advanced skills during the school day, before and after school programs, summer school programs, schoolwide programs in high poverty schools, staff development, coordination of the curriculum with the regular instructional program, coordination with other programs addressing the needs of educationally deprived children, regular evaluation of performance and program improvement based on results, and parent and community involvement. This program was formerly known as the Chapter 1 Program but is currently referred to as Title I.

Number awarded Varies each year.

Deadline Deadlines vary annually; check the *Federal Register* for the current schedule.

[1001]
EDUCATIONAL OPPORTUNITY CENTERS PROGRAM GRANTS

Department of Education
Attn: Office of Postsecondary Education
Division of Student Services
Portals Building, Suite 600D
600 Independence Avenue, S.W.
Washington, DC 20202-5249
(202) 708-7270   Fax: (202) 401-6132
E-mail: trio@ed.gov

Purpose To provide support for programs that offer counseling and information on college admissions to qualified adults who want to enter or continue a program of postsecondary education.

Eligibility Proposals may be submitted by colleges and universities, public and private agencies and organizations and, under special circumstances, secondary schools. They must be proposing to establish and operate an Educational Opportunity Center to increase the number of adult participants who enroll in postsecondary education institutions and successfully complete degree programs. At least two-thirds of the students must be first-generation, low-income persons and at least 19 years of age.

Financial data Recently, an annual total of $24,650,489 was awarded through this program; the minimum grant was $180,000 and the average was $333,115. The average cost per participant was $157.

Duration Competitions for funding are held every fourth or fifth year.

Special features Program services may include academic advice, personal counseling, career workshops, information on postsecondary educational opportunities, information on student financial assistance, help in completing applications for college admissions and financial aid, coordination with nearby postsecondary institutions, and media activities designed to acquaint the community with higher education opportunities.

Number awarded In the most recent year, 74 awards were made by this program; the average number of participants per institution was 2,117.

Deadline The next closing date for receipt of applications is scheduled for fall of 1997; check the *Federal Register* for the current schedule.

[1002]
ELEANOR ROOSEVELT TEACHER FELLOWSHIPS

American Association of University Women
Attn: Educational Foundation
2201 North Dodge Street
Iowa City, IA 52243-4030
(319) 337-1716   Fax: (319) 337-1204

Purpose To increase the effectiveness of women teachers who are responsible for mathematics and science courses or at-risk girls.

Eligibility Women public school teachers with at least 3 consecutive years of full-time teaching experience in grades K through 12 are eligible to apply if they are responsible for mathematics, science, or technology courses for at-risk girls and are committed to creating gender equity in schools. Applicants must be U.S. citizens or permanent residents. This fellowship is designed for those who will return to teaching for at least 3 years after the fellowship year. Women of color are strongly encouraged to apply.

Financial data The amount awarded varies from $1,000 to $10,000, depending upon the recipient's proposed sabbatical program. Funds can be used by the recipients to pay for graduate study, thesis research, or course work that will improve their expertise.

Duration 1 year, beginning in July.

Special features This program was established in 1990. It is part of the foundation's Eleanor Roosevelt Fund for Women and Girls.

Number awarded 15 each year.

Deadline January of each year.

[1003]
ELSEVIER RESEARCH INITIATIVE AWARDS

American Digestive Health Foundation
7910 Woodmont Avenue, Suite 700
Bethesda, MD 20814-3015
(301) 654-2635   Fax: (301) 654-5920

Purpose To provide funding to new or established investigators to support pilot research projects in gastroenterology-related areas.

Eligibility Applicants must hold an M.D. or Ph.D. degree (or the equivalent) and a faculty position at an accredited North American institution. They may not hold awards on a similar topic from other agencies. Women and minority investigators are strongly encouraged to apply. Selection is based on novelty, importance, feasibility, environment, commitment of the institution, and overall likelihood that the projects will lead to more substantial grant applications.

Financial data The grant is $25,000 per year. Funds may be used for salary, supplies, or equipment. Indirect costs are not allowed.

Duration The award is granted annually.

Special features This award is administered by the American Digestive Health Foundation (ADHF) and sponsored by the American Gastroenterological Association (AGA).

Number awarded 1 or more each year.

Deadline January of each year.

[1004]
ENGINEERING DISSERTATION FELLOWSHIPS

American Association of University Women
Attn: Educational Foundation
2201 North Dodge Street
Iowa City, IA 52243-4030
(319) 337-1716   Fax: (319) 337-1204

Purpose To provide financial assistance to women who are working on their doctoral dissertations in engineering.

Eligibility This program is open to women who have completed all required course work and passed all preliminary examinations for the doctorate in engineering. Students holding any fellowship for the writing of their dissertation in the prior year are not eligible to apply for this program. Applicants must be U.S. citizens or permanent residents. Special consideration is given to applicants who show professional promise in innovative or neglected areas of research and/or practice in public interest concerns. Women of color are strongly encouraged to apply.

Financial data The stipend is $14,500. These funds may not be used to cover tuition for additional course work.

Duration 1 year, beginning in July.

Limitations Fellows are expected to devote full time to writing their dissertation and to receive their degree at the end of the fellowship year.

Deadline November of each year.

[1005]
ENGINEERING EDUCATION COALITIONS

National Science Foundation
Attn: Directorate for Engineering
Division of Engineering Education and Centers
4201 Wilson Boulevard, Room 585
Arlington, VA 22230
(703) 306-1380

Purpose To provide support to coalitions of engineering educational institutions for development of new models for undergraduate engineering education.

Eligibility This program is open to coalitions of at least 4 U.S. institutions and organizations offering baccalaureate engineering programs or engineering-related undergraduate programs, including research universities, primarily undergraduate institutions, minority institutions, 2-year colleges, and others, as appropriate. Applicants must be proposing to 1) design and implement comprehensive, systematic, and structural reform of undergraduate engineering education; 2) provide tested alternative curricula and new instructional delivery systems that improve the quality of undergraduate engineering education; 3) create substantive resource linkages among engineering baccalaureate-producing and precollege institutions; and 4) increase the number of baccalaureate engineering degrees awarded, especially to women, underrepresented minorities, and persons with disabilities.

Financial data Support is provided at a level of approximately $2 to $3 million.

Duration Up to 5 years.

Number awarded Varies; the National Science Foundation plans to award grants to 2 coalitions each year, but its plans depend upon the availability of funds.

[1006]
ENGINEERING GEOLOGY DIVISION GRANTS

Geological Society of America
Attn: Research Grants Administrator
3300 Penrose Place
P.O. Box 9140
Boulder, CO 80301-9140
(303) 447-2020, ext. 137   Fax: (303) 447-1133
E-mail: jforstro@geosociety.org

Purpose To provide partial support for geological research by graduate students at universities in the United States, Canada, Mexico, and Central America.

Eligibility This program is open to graduate students in geology at the master's or doctoral level. Both members and nonmembers of the society are eligible. Special consideration may be given to students who propose research on 1 or more aspects of engineering geology. Applications from minorities, women, and persons with disabilities are strongly encouraged.

Financial data Grants range up to $2,500; the average grant recently was $1,604.

Duration 1 year.

Special features This program is sponsored by the Geological Society of America's Engineering Geology Division.

Number awarded 1 or more each year.

Deadline February of each year.

[1007]
ENVIRONMENTAL MANAGEMENT RESEARCH PARTICIPATION PROGRAM FOR THE U.S. ARMY ENVIRONMENTAL CENTER

Oak Ridge Institute for Science and Education
Attn: Science/Engineering Education Division
P.O. Box 117
Oak Ridge, TN 37831-0117
(423) 576-3456   (423) 241-2875
(800) 569-7749   Fax: (423) 576-3643
E-mail: emrppaec@orau.gov

Purpose To provide funding for postgraduate research in environmental programs at the U.S. Army Environmental Center in Maryland.

Eligibility Applicants should have completed a baccalaureate or graduate degree within the past 3 years; others are considered on a case-by-case basis. Their field of study should have been environmental sciences, engineering, physical sciences, life sciences, health sciences, or other related scientific disciplines. They must propose to conduct research at the U.S. Army Environmental Center in Aberdeen Proving Ground, Maryland that involves restoration, compliance, conservation, pollution prevention, validation, demonstration, transfer, quality assurance and quality control, training, information management and reporting, and related resource management and planning programming. All programs operated by the Science/Engineering Education Division (SEED) of Oak Ridge Institute for Science and Education (ORISE) seek to broaden the participation of minorities, women, and persons with disabilities in science and engineering careers.

Financial data The stipend is based on research area and degree; a limited reimbursement for inbound travel and moving is also provided.

Duration 1 year; renewable.

Special features This program is funded by an interagency agreement between the U.S. Department of Energy and the U.S. Army Environmental Center and administered by ORISE/SEED.

Number awarded Varies each year.

Deadline Applications may be submitted at any time.

[1008]
ENVIRONMENTAL MONITORING SYSTEMS LABORATORY RESEARCH PARTICIPATION PROGRAM

Oak Ridge Institute for Science and Education
Attn: Science/Engineering Education Division
P.O. Box 117
Oak Ridge, TN 37831-0117
(423) 576-8503   (423) 241-2875
(800) 569-7749   Fax: (423) 576-3643
E-mail: rppemsl@orau.gov

Purpose To provide opportunities and support for research on environmental monitoring systems at the Environmental Monitoring Systems Laboratory in Cincinnati, Ohio.

Eligibility Applicants must have completed their bachelor's, master's, or doctoral degree in environmental sciences, engineering, physical sciences, or other related scientific disciplines within the past 3 years; others are considered on a case-by-case basis. Participants work at the Environmental Monitoring Systems Laboratory (EMSL) of the U.S. Environmental Protection Agency (EPA) in Cincinnati, Ohio. All programs operated by the Science/Engineering Education Division (SEED) of Oak Ridge Institute for Science and Education (ORISE) seek to broaden the participation of minorities, women, and persons with disabilities in science and engineering careers.

Financial data The stipends depend on research area and highest degree earned, but begin at $28,860 for applicants with doctoral degrees, $22,200 for master's degrees, or $18,500 for baccalaureate degrees. Reimbursement is also provided for inbound travel and moving.

Duration 1 year; may be renewed.

Special features This program is funded by an interagency agreement between EPA and the U.S. Department of Energy but operated and managed by ORISE/SEED. Information is also available from EMSL at (513) 569-7334.

Number awarded The number awarded varies each year.

Deadline Applications may be submitted at any time.

[1009]
ENVIRONMENTAL SCIENCE AND ENGINEERING FELLOWSHIPS

American Association for the Advancement of Science
Attn: Directorate for Science and Policy Programs
1200 New York Avenue, N.W.
Washington, DC 20005-3920
(202) 326-6600   Fax: (202) 289-4950
E-mail: science_policy@aaas.org

Purpose To provide postdoctoral and midcareer scientists and engineers an opportunity to observe how the U.S. Environmental Protection Agency (EPA) formulates environmental policy.

Eligibility Prospective fellows must have a Ph.D. at the time of application and must show exceptional competence in some area of science or engineering related to environmental science; have a good scientific and technical background; and have a strong interest and some experience in applying scientific or other professional knowledge toward the identification and assessment of future environmental problems. Applications are invited from individuals in any physical, biological, or social science, any field of engineering, or any relevant interdisciplinary field. Persons with a master's degree in engineering and at least 3 years of post-degree experience may apply. U.S. citizenship is required; federal employees are not eligible. Minorities and persons with disabilities are especially encouraged to apply.

Financial data The stipend is $950 per week.

Duration 10 weeks in the summer.

Special features Fellows work at the EPA in Washington, D.C. on a variety of research projects.

Number awarded 10 each year.

Deadline January of each year.

[1010]
ENVIRONMENTAL SCIENCE AND MANAGEMENT FELLOWS PROGRAM

National Urban Fellows, Inc.
55 West 44th Street, Suite 600
New York, NY 10036
(212) 921-9400　　　　　　　　Fax: (212) 921-9572

Purpose To provide mid-career executives and scientists who are women, minorities, or members of socially disadvantaged groups with an opportunity to enhance their skills through a program of academic study and professional experience in the administrative, technical, and scientific realms of environmental protection and management.

Eligibility Eligible to apply are U.S. citizens who have a bachelor's degree, have 3 years of full-time work experience in an administrative or managerial capacity, have demonstrated exceptional ability and leadership potential, meet academic admission requirements, have a high standard of integrity and work ethic, and are willing to relocate for the duration of the fellowship year.

Financial data The fellowship provides a stipend, tuition, and other program-related expenses.

Duration 2 years.

Special features The program begins with an academic year of study in environmental sciences at Duke University in Durham, North Carolina. Following this, fellows spend 12 months in mentorship assignments as special assistants to key executives and scientists in the environmental protection and conservation community. A summer session at Duke following the mentorship concludes the program. Fellows who successfully complete all requirements are granted a master of science degree from Tufts.

Number awarded Varies; approximately 15 each year.

Deadline February of each year.

[1011]
EPA SMALL BUSINESS INNOVATION RESEARCH GRANTS

Environmental Protection Agency
Attn: Office of Research and Development
National Center for Environmental Research and Quality
　　Assurance
Contracts Management Division (MD-33)
79 T.W. Alexander Drive
Research Triangle Park, NC 27711
(919) 541-5293　　　　E-mail: peele.kathryn@epamail.epa.gov

Purpose To support small businesses that have the technological experience to contribute to the research and development mission of the Environmental Protection Agency (EPA).

Eligibility For the purposes of this program, a "small business" is defined as any organization that is independently owned and operated for profit, not dominant in the field in which it is operating, and meets the size standard of 500 employees or less. The primary employment of the principal investigator must be with the firm at the time of award and during the conduct of the proposed project. Preference is given to women-owned small business concerns and to socially and economically disadvantaged small business concerns. Women-owned small business concerns are those which are at least 51 percent owned by a woman or women who also control and operate it. Socially and economically disadvantaged small business concerns are at least 51 percent owned by an Indian tribe, a native Hawaiian organization, or 1 or more socially and economically disadvantaged individuals (Black Americans, Hispanic Americans, Native Americans, Asian-Pacific Americans, or subcontinent Asian Americans). The project must be performed in the United States. Current priority areas of research include: drinking water treatment; technologies for prevention and control of NOx, VOCs, SO2, and toxic air emissions; waste reduction and pollution prevention; solid and hazardous waste disposal; technologies for treatment of hazardous waste at superfund sites; municipal and industrial wastewater treatment and pollution control; and technologies for continuous monitoring of processes for compliance and control effectivity determination.

Financial data Grants are offered in 2 phases. In phase 1, awards normally may not exceed $70,000 (for both direct and indirect costs); in phase 2, awards normally may not exceed $225,000 (including both direct and indirect costs).

Duration Phase 1: up to 6 months; phase 2: up to 2 years.

Number awarded EPA plans to grant approximately 30 phase 1 and from 10 to 20 phase 2 awards each year.

Deadline January of each year.

[1012]
EPIDEMIOLOGIC RESEARCH STUDIES OF ACQUIRED IMMUNODEFICIENCY SYNDROME (AIDS) AND HUMAN IMMUNODEFICIENCY VIRUS (HIV) INFECTION IN SELECTED POPULATION GROUPS

Centers for Disease Control and Prevention
Attn: National Center for Infectious Diseases
Division of HIV/AIDS
1600 Clifton Road
MS E-45
Atlanta, GA 30333
(404) 639-6130

Purpose To provide funding for research on epidemiologic issues concerning AIDS and HIV infection amoung minority populations.

Eligibility   This program is open to investigators in state and local government agencies and other public and private nonprofit organizations. Applicants must be proposing to conduct research of important HIV-related epidemiologic issues concerning risks of transmission, development and evaluation of behavioral recommendations for reducing AIDS and HIV infection, and the natural history and transmission of the disease in certain populations, especially African Americans, Asian/Pacific Islanders, Latino/Hispanics, and Native Americans.

Financial data   Grants include funds for direct costs (such as personnel, travel, equipment, and supplies) necessary to carry out an approved project as well as funds for the reimbursement of applicable indirect costs.

Number awarded   Varies each year, depending on the availability of funds.

[1013]
EPILEPSY FOUNDATION HEALTH SCIENCES STUDENT FELLOWSHIPS

Epilepsy Foundation of America
Attn: Department of Research and Professional Education
4351 Garden City Drive
Landover, MD 20785
(301) 459-3700   (800) EFA-1000
Fax: (301) 577-2684   TDD: (800) 332-2070
E-mail: postmaster@efa.org

Purpose   To provide financial assistance for medical and health science students to work on an epilepsy study project.

Eligibility   Medical and health science students may apply for these fellowships to carry out a project at a U.S. institution where there are ongoing programs of research, training, or service in epilepsy. A preceptor must accept responsibility for supervision of the student and the project. Applications from women and minorities are especially encouraged.

Financial data   Stipends are $2,000.

Duration   3 months.

Number awarded   Varies each year.

Deadline   February of each year.

[1014]
EPILEPSY FOUNDATION OF AMERICA JUNIOR INVESTIGATOR RESEARCH GRANTS

Epilepsy Foundation of America
Attn: Department of Research and Professional Education
4351 Garden City Drive
Landover, MD 20785
(301) 459-3700   (800) EFA-1000
Fax: (301) 577-2684   TDD: (800) 332-2070
E-mail: postmaster@efa.org

Purpose   To support basic and clinical research in the biological, behavioral, and social sciences that will advance the understanding, treatment, and prevention of epilepsy.

Eligibility   Priority is given to beginning investigators just entering the field of epilepsy research, to new or innovative projects, and to investigators whose research is relevant to developmental or pediatric aspects of epilepsy. Applications in the behavioral sciences are encouraged. Applications from established investigators with other sources of support are discouraged. Research grants are not intended to provide support for postdoctoral fel-

lows. Special attention is given to applications from women and minorities.

Financial data   Support is limited to $40,000.

Duration   Up to 1 year.

Limitations   Research must be conducted in the United States.

Number awarded   Approximately 15 each year.

Deadline   August of each year.

[1015]
EPILEPSY FOUNDATION OF AMERICA RESEARCH TRAINING FELLOWSHIPS

Epilepsy Foundation of America
Attn: Department of Research and Professional Education
4351 Garden City Drive
Landover, MD 20785
(301) 459-3700   (800) EFA-1000
Fax: (301) 577-2684   TDD: (800) 332-2070
E-mail: postmaster@efa.org

Purpose   To offer qualified individuals the opportunity to develop expertise in epilepsy research through training and involvement in an epilepsy research project.

Eligibility   Application is open to physicians or Ph.D. neuroscientists who are interested in a postdoctoral research experience. The proposed research may be either basic or clinical but must address a question of fundamental importance. A clinical training component is not required. Preference is given to applicants whose proposals have a pediatric or developmental emphasis. Special attention is given to applications from minorities and women.

Financial data   The stipend is $40,000.

Duration   1 year.

Limitations   The fellowship must be carried out at a facility where there is an ongoing epilepsy research program. Research must be conducted in the United States.

Number awarded   Approximately 3 each year.

Deadline   August of each year.

[1016]
EPILEPSY FOUNDATION OF AMERICA RESEARCH/CLINICAL TRAINING FELLOWSHIPS

Epilepsy Foundation of America
Attn: Department of Research and Professional Education
4351 Garden City Drive
Landover, MD 20785
(301) 459-3700   (800) EFA-1000
Fax: (301) 577-2684   TDD: (800) 332-2070
E-mail: postmaster@efa.org

Purpose   To offer qualified individuals the opportunity to develop expertise in clinical epilepsy and epilepsy research through training experience and involvement in an epilepsy research project.

Eligibility   Applications are open to individuals who have received their M.D. degree and completed residency training. The proposed research may be either basic or clinical, but there must be a substantial clinical training component of the program. Emphasis is placed on individuals who will be trained in research in epilepsy rather than use epilepsy as a tool in their research in other fields. Special attention is given to applications submitted by women and minorities.

Financial data   The stipend is $40,000.

Duration 1 year.

Limitations The fellowship must be carried out at a facility where there is an ongoing epilepsy research program. Research must be conducted in the United States.

Number awarded Approximately 7 each year.

Deadline August of each year.

[1017]
ESTABLISHMENT OF DEPARTMENTS OF FAMILY MEDICINE GRANTS

Health Resources and Services Administration
Attn: Bureau of Health Professions
Division of Medicine
Parklawn Building, Room 9A-27
5600 Fishers Lane
Rockville, MD 20857
(301) 443-3615   Fax: (301) 443-1945
E-mail: sbiedenk@hrsa.ssw.dhhs.gov

Purpose To provide financial support for programs to establish, maintain, or improve family medicine academic administrative units.

Eligibility This program is open to accredited public or private nonprofit schools of medicine or osteopathic medicine. Applicants must request funding to 1) plan and develop model educational predoctoral, faculty development, and graduate medical education programs in family medicine; and 2) support academic and clinical activities relevant to the field of family medicine. Selection criteria include 1) the proposal includes a strategy and plan for recruiting and retaining minority and disadvantaged faculty, students, trainees, and/or residents (applicants are expected to reflect the diversity of the populations within their states); 2) the proposal includes clinically oriented, generalist-trained faculty who practice in community-based settings that include underserved populations; 3) the proposal includes a curriculum that emphasizes areas of study pertinent to the needs of special populations in urban, rural, and underserved areas (people with low incomes, members of racial and ethnic minority groups, people with disabilities, and at-risk population groups); 4) the proposal describes the actions taken by the institution that demonstrate faculty involvement with the curricular innovations that are beyond what is traditionally part of such a curriculum; and 5) the proposal includes data regarding the most recent 3-year average track record of a program in placing graduates in primary care training, primary care practice, or generalist faculty positions.

Financial data The amounts of the awards vary; recently, the average grant was $161,000.

Duration 3 years.

Special features The program may also assist schools to strengthen the administrative base and structure that is responsible for the planning, direction, organization, coordination, and evaluation of all undergraduate and graduate family medicine activities.

Limitations Funds are to complement rather than duplicate programmatic activities for actual operation of family medicine training programs.

Number awarded Varies each year.

Deadline February of each year.

[1018]
ETA RESEARCH AND DEMONSTRATION GRANTS

Department of Labor
Attn: Employment and Training Administration
Division of Research and Demonstration
200 Constitution Avenue, N.W., Room N-5637
Washington, DC 20210
(202) 219-5677   Fax: (202) 219-5455

Purpose To sponsor research on such topics as labor market processes, the factors contributing to unemployment and underemployment, the results of technological change, the causes of disadvantagement, and the needs of at-risk populations.

Eligibility Organizations, individuals, colleges, universities, state and local government units, and public, private, and other entities having research and development capabilities in the employment and training area may submit applications. Proposals commonly focus on the needs of specific target groups: older workers, dislocated workers, veterans, youth, individuals with disabilities, minority group members, offenders, and women.

Financial data Approximately $40 to $50 million per year is available for this program; the amounts of the individual grants depends on the nature and merit of the proposed projects.

Limitations Very few unsolicited proposals obtain funding; the vast majority of grants are awarded on a competitive basis through Requests for Proposals (RFPs) announced in the *Commerce Business Daily* or Solicitations for Grant Applications (SGAs) announced in the *Federal Register*.

Number awarded Varies each year.

[1019]
ETS POSTDOCTORAL FELLOWSHIP PROGRAM

Educational Testing Service
Mail Stop 16-T
Princeton, NJ 08541-0001
(609) 734-1806   E-mail: ldelauro@ets.org

Purpose To provide financial assistance to postdoctorates who wish to conduct research at the Educational Testing Service (ETS).

Eligibility Applicants must hold a doctorate in a relevant discipline and be able to provide evidence of prior research. They must be interested in conducting research at the Educational Testing Service in 1 of the following areas: minority issues; testing issues, including alternate forms of assessment for special populations; psychometrics; educational, occupational, or vocational testing; educational technology; statistics; psychology; computer science; testing issues associated with new forms of assessment; sociology of education; linguistics; policy research; or education. An explicit goal of the program is to increase the number of women and minority professionals in educational measurement and related fields.

Financial data The stipend is $35,000; fellows and their families also receive limited reimbursement for relocation expenses.

Duration 1 year; beginning in September.

Special features Fellows work with senior staff at the Educational Testing Service in Princeton, New Jersey.

Number awarded Up to 3 each year.

Deadline January of each year.

[1020]
FACULTY AWARDS FOR RESEARCH

National Aeronautics and Space Administration
Attn: Office of Equal Opportunity Programs
Minority University Research and Education Division
Code EU
Washington, DC 20546-0001
(202) 358-0948　　　　　　　Fax: (202) 358-3745
E-mail: john.malone@hq.nasa.gov

Purpose To provide funding for space-related research to faculty at Historically Black Colleges and Universities (HBCUs) and at Other Minority Universities (OMUs).

Eligibility This program is open to tenure-track faculty holding Ph.D.s in relevant engineering, mathematics, or science disciplines and employed at eligible HBCUs and OMUs (which include tribal colleges and universities, designated Hispanic-Serving Institutions, and other accredited colleges or universities with enrollment of a single underrepresented minority group or combination of underrepresented minority groups that exceeds 50 percent of the total student enrollment). The university must offer degrees in engineering, mathematics, or science. Applicants must be proposing to conduct research at their university or at any institution or facility engaged in substantial research for the National Aeronautics and Space Administration (NASA). U.S. citizenship is required. The field of study may relate to 1 or more of the 4 NASA Strategic Enterprises described in the NASA Strategic Plan: mission to planet Earth, aeronautics, human exploration and development of space, and space science. Faculty members who received more than $250,000 in NASA research grants during the last 5 years are not eligible.

Financial data Up to $100,000 per year. Research funding may include support of research assistants, undergraduate student researchers, professional travel, research supplies and equipment, principal investigator summer salary, and release time for conducting research.

Duration Up to 3 years.

Special features Students interested in working on a project should contact the address above for a list of current recipients and the sites where they are conducting research.

Limitations Principal investigators must involve socially and economically disadvantaged and/or disabled graduate and undergraduate students who are U.S. citizens in their research. At least 25 percent of the funds each year must go to support for U.S. citizen graduate and undergraduate students involved with the research project.

Number awarded Approximately 20 each year: 10 for faculty at HBCUs and 10 for faculty at OMUs.

Deadline January of each year.

[1021]
FACULTY DEVELOPMENT IN FAMILY MEDICINE GRANTS

Health Resources and Services Administration
Attn: Bureau of Health Professions
Division of Medicine
Parklawn Building, Room 9A-27
5600 Fishers Lane
Rockville, MD 20857
(301) 443-6822　　　　　　　Fax: (301) 443-1945
E-mail: equinone@hrsa.ssw.dhhs.gov

Purpose To provide financial support for programs for the training of physicians who plan to teach in family medicine training programs.

Eligibility This program is open to accredited schools of medicine or osteopathic medicine, public or private nonprofit hospitals, or other public or private nonprofit entities. Applicants must request funding to promote the development of faculty skills in physicians who are currently teaching or who plan teaching careers in family medicine training programs. These grants also provide financial assistance in meeting the cost of supporting physicians who are trainees in such programs. Selection criteria include 1) the proposal includes a strategy and plan for recruiting and retaining minority and disadvantaged faculty, students, trainees, and/or residents (applicants are expected to reflect the diversity of the populations within their states); 2) the proposal includes clinically oriented, generalist-trained faculty who practice in community-based settings that include underserved populations; 3) the proposal includes a curriculum that emphasizes areas of study pertinent to the needs of special populations in urban, rural, and underserved areas (people with low incomes, members of racial and ethnic minority groups, people with disabilities, and at-risk population groups); 4) the proposal describes the actions taken by the institution that demonstrate faculty involvement with the curricular innovations that are beyond what is traditionally part of such a curriculum; and 5) the proposal includes data regarding the most recent 3-year average track record of a program in placing graduates in primary care training, primary care practice, or generalist faculty positions.

Financial data The amounts of the awards vary; recently, average grants were $142,000 per year.

Duration 3 years.

Number awarded Varies each year.

Deadline December of each year.

[1022]
FACULTY DEVELOPMENT IN GENERAL INTERNAL MEDICINE AND GENERAL PEDIATRICS GRANTS

Health Resources and Services Administration
Attn: Bureau of Health Professions
Division of Medicine
Parklawn Building, Room 9A-27
5600 Fishers Lane
Rockville, MD 20857
(301) 443-6822　　　　　　　Fax: (301) 443-1945
E-mail: equinone@hrsa.ssw.dhhs.gov

Purpose To provide financial support for programs to plan, develop, and operate programs for the training of physicians who plan to teach in general internal medicine or general pediatrics training programs.

Eligibility This program is open to accredited schools of medicine or osteopathic medicine, public or private nonprofit hospitals, or other public or private nonprofit entities. Applicants must request funding to promote the development of faculty skills in physicians who are currently teaching or who plan teaching careers in internal medicine or general pediatrics. Proposals may also provide financial assistance in meeting the cost of supporting physicians who are trainees in such programs. Selection criteria include 1) the proposal includes a strategy and plan for recruiting and retaining minority and disadvantaged faculty, students, trainees, and/or residents (applicants are expected to reflect the diversity of the populations within their states); 2) the proposal includes clinically oriented, generalist-trained faculty who practice in community-based settings that include underserved populations; 3) the proposal includes a curriculum that emphasizes areas of study pertinent to the needs of special populations in urban, rural, and underserved areas (people with low incomes, members of racial and ethnic minority groups, people with disabilities, and at-risk population groups); 4) the proposal describes the actions taken by the institution that demonstrate faculty involvement with the curricular innovations that are beyond what is traditionally part of such a curriculum; and 5) the proposal includes data regarding the most recent 3-year average track record of a program in placing graduates in primary care training, primary care practice, or generalist faculty positions.

Financial data The amounts of the awards vary; recently, the average grant was $157,000.

Duration 3 years.

Number awarded Varies each year.

Deadline December of each year.

[1023]
FACULTY EARLY CAREER DEVELOPMENT PROGRAM

National Science Foundation
Attn: Directorate for Education and Human Resources
Senior Staff Associate for Cross Directorate Programs
4201 Wilson Boulevard, Room 805
Arlington, VA 22230
(703) 306-1603

Purpose To provide support for science and engineering research to outstanding new faculty who intend to develop academic careers involving both research and education.

Eligibility This program, identified as the CAREER program, is open to faculty members who meet all of the following requirements: 1) be employed at an institution in the United States, its territories or possessions, or the Commonwealth of Puerto Rico, which awards a baccalaureate or advanced degree in a field supported by the National Science Foundation (NSF); 2) be in their first or second full-time tenure-track or equivalent appointment at any institution and have begun the first appointment within the preceding 5 years; 3) not hold or have held tenure; and 4) not be a current or former recipient of a Presidential or NSF Young Investigator, Presidential Faculty Fellow, or CAREER award. In addition, other faculty may be eligible if they can document a reason for an exemption from the above requirements; the possible exceptions include 1) individuals who are engaged in significant education and research activities at 2-year colleges or nonprofit or non-academic institutions such as museums, observatories, and research laboratories; and 2) non-tenured faculty whose initial full-time tenure-track appointment was more than 5 years ago but who have interrupted their careers for substantive reasons such as family leave or serious health problems. Proposals may be for any area of research supported by the National Science Foundation (NSF). Proposals from women, underrepresented minorities, and persons with disabilities are especially encouraged. Plans for international collaborations are also encouraged.

Financial data The total grant ranges from $200,000 to $500,000 over the full period of the award.

Duration 4 to 5 years.

Special features This program is operated by various disciplinary divisions within the NSF; for a list of the participating divisions and their telephone numbers, contact the address above. Outstanding recipients of these grants are nominated for the NSF component of the Presidential Early Career Awards for Scientists

and Engineers, which are awarded to 30 recipients (15 scientists and 15 engineers) of these grants.

Number awarded Approximately 350 each year.

Deadline October of each year.

[1024]
FACULTY RESEARCH ENHANCEMENT SUPPORT PROGRAM

National Institutes of Health
Attn: Extramural Associates Program
Rockledge II, Room 6187A
6701 Rockledge Drive MSC 7910
Bethesda, MD 20892-7910
(301) 435-2692   Fax: (301) 480-0393
E-mail: mk51q@nih.gov

Purpose To improve opportunities for minorities and women to participate in and contribute to biomedical research by enabling faculty or administrators to participate in a program at the National Institutes of Health (NIH) in Bethesda, Maryland.

Eligibility Academic institutions that have a significant enrollment of minorities, or are women's colleges, may nominate 1 scientific faculty member or academic administrator. In addition to the qualifications and interests of the nominee, selection is based on the demonstrated contribution of the institution to the advancement of ethnic minorities and/or women, its readiness to improve health research or research training, and its plan to utilize the associate's expertise after participating in the program. This program is intended for nominees from institutions that do not award degrees in health-related sciences higher than the baccalaureate and have little or no research funding.

Financial data Salaries are comparable to those being received by the associate at the time of selection. Cost-sharing is required, depending on the institution's resources. Travel, housing, and subsistence expenses while at NIH, and any costs incurred that are directly related to the training, are reimbursed by the NIH.

Duration 10 weeks, during the summer.

Special features During their tenure at the NIH, associates acquire a thorough knowledge of the NIH, the support mechanisms through which research is being accomplished, and the policies and procedures which govern the awarding of grants and contracts. Associates also obtain information about other federal health-related programs; grant and contract activities; legislative, budgetary and similar processes; and administrative procedures, including participation in staff meetings, review meetings, site visits, workshops, and conferences. Following completion of the program, associates return to their institutions with an Extramural Associates Research Development Award (EARDA) which provides developmental funds to the associate's institution for a period of 3 years, with a possible extension to 6 years. The EARDA program is designated as G11 Awards.

Number awarded Varies each year.

[1025]
FAMILY PLANNING SERVICES GRANTS

Department of Health and Human Services
Attn: Office of Population Affairs
Office of Family Planning
West Tower, Suite 200
4350 East-West Highway
Bethesda, MD 20814
(301) 594-4008   Fax: (301) 594-5980
E-mail: EEckard@osophs.dhhs.gov

Purpose To assist in the establishment and operation of voluntary family planning projects which offer a broad range of acceptable and effective family planning methods and services (including natural family planning methods, infertility services, and services for adolescents).

Eligibility Public and nonprofit private agencies are eligible to apply. Projects consist of the educational, comprehensive, medical, and social services necessary to aid individuals to determine freely the number and spacing of their children. Current priorities include: 1) increasing outreach to individuals not likely to seek services, such as males, homeless persons, people with disabilities, substance abusers, and adolescents; 2) expanding the comprehensiveness of reproductive health services; 3) serving adolescents; 4) eliminating disincentives to providing long-acting, highly effective contraceptives; and 5) emphasizing training and retention of women's health nurse practitioners, particularly minority nurse practitioners and nurse practitioners serving disadvantaged and medically underserved communities.

Financial data In a recent year, grants ranged from $481,247 to $6,771,384.

Duration 3 to 5 years.

Limitations Projects may not promote, encourage, or advocate the use of abortion as a method of family planning or provide referral or counseling for abortion as a method of family planning.

Number awarded Varies each year; recently, a total of 23 awards were made annually with total funding of nearly $70 million.

Deadline Deadline dates are established by each regional office of the Department of Health and Human Services (DHHS).

[1026]
FAMILY PLANNING SERVICES TRAINING GRANTS

Department of Health and Human Services
Attn: Office of Population Affairs
Office of Family Planning
West Tower, Suite 200
4350 East-West Highway
Bethesda, MD 20814
(301) 594-4008   Fax: (301) 594-5980
E-mail: EEckard@osophs.dhhs.gov

Purpose To provide training for personnel to improve the delivery of family planning services.

Eligibility Public or nonprofit private agencies are eligible to apply. Grants are to be used to establish regional training centers with an emphasis on 1) expansion of current clinic sites and development of new clinics in high need areas; 2) outreach to low-income women, adolescents, and persons at high risk of unintended pregnancy or infection with sexually transmitted diseases (including HIV) not now receiving family planning services; 3) increased emphasis on services to adolescents, including enhanced counseling as well as new service arrangements for providing services to teens; 4) increased focus on quality and comprehensiveness of services, including treatment of sexually transmitted diseases, screening for cervical cancer and prevention of breast cancer, substance abuse counseling, and counseling on avoidance of high risk behavior; and 5) increased emphasis on training and retention of family planning nurse practitioners, particularly minority nurse practitioners and those working in clinics serving high risk populations.

Financial data The amount available varies in different regions of the Department of Health and Human Services (DHHS), from $168,400 to $348,600.

Duration Up to 5 years.

Limitations No portion of the federal funds may be used to train personnel for programs where abortion is a method of family planning or to provide professional training to any student as part of education in pursuit of an academic degree.

Number awarded Varies each year, depending on the availability of funds; recently, funding was available for 3 awards: 1 in region I (Connecticut, Maine, Massachusetts, New Hampshire, Rhode Island, and Vermont), 1 in region V (Illinois, Indiana, Michigan, Minnesota, Ohio, and Wisconsin), and 1 in region VII (Iowa, Kansas, Missouri, and Nebraska); in future years, grants will be available in different regions. Approximately 250 new family planning nurse practitioners receive training through this program each year.

Deadline May of each year.

[1027]
FANNIE LOU HAMER AWARD

Money for Women/Barbara Deming Memorial Fund, Inc.
P.O. Box 40-1043
Brooklyn, NY 11240-1043

Purpose To provide financial support to individual women in the arts who are working to combat racism.

Eligibility Eligible to apply are women whose proposed work will combat racism or celebrate women of color through an educational or artistic project. Artists include musicians, writers, poets, and photographers.

Financial data The grant is $1,000.

Duration The grants are awarded annually.

Special features The grant is named for the civil rights activist from Mississippi who worked for voter registration in the 1960s.

Limitations The Fund does not give educational assistance, monies for personal study or loans, monies for dissertation or research projects, grants for group projects, business ventures, or emergency funds for hardships.

Number awarded 1 each year.

Deadline December and June of each year.

[1028]
FEDERAL TRANSIT ADMINISTRATION HUMAN RESOURCES PROGRAM

Department of Transportation
Attn: Federal Transit Administration
Office of Research, Demonstration and Innovation
400 Seventh Street, S.W., Room 6429
Washington, DC 20590
(202) 366-0816   Fax: (202) 366-3475

Purpose To provide funding for projects that address human resource needs in public transit.

Eligibility This program is open to transit systems, state and local governments, universities, nonprofit organizations, and private businesses. Applicants must be proposing projects designed to develop and enhance the skills and talents of minorities, women, and other disadvantaged persons in mass transit.

Financial data The amounts of the awards depend on the availability of funds and the nature of the proposal. Recent grants have ranged from $25,000 to $490,118.

Number awarded Varies; in a recent year, 13 projects were funded through this program.

Deadline Initial proposals may be submitted at any time.

[1029]
FELLOWSHIPS FOR POSTDOCTORAL RESEARCH IN EAST EUROPEAN STUDIES

American Council of Learned Societies
228 East 45th Street
New York, NY 10017-3398
(212) 697-1505   Fax: (212) 949-8058
E-mail: grants@acls.org

Purpose To provide financial assistance for original research in the social sciences and humanities relating to eastern Europe.

Eligibility Applicants must be citizens or permanent legal residents of the United States who have received a Ph.D. or equivalent degree at least 3 years prior to the date of application and who have not held a supported research leave during the prior 3 years. Their field of study must be in the social sciences or humanities relating to Albania, Bulgaria, the Czech Republic, Hungary, Poland, Romania, Slovakia, or the successor states of Yugoslavia. Normally, fellowships are intended as salary replacement to provide established faculty members time free for research; the funds may be used to supplement sabbatical salaries or awards from other sources if they will intensify or extend the contemplated research. In special circumstances, untenured scholars or younger independent scholars without an academic appointment may apply. The research may be undertaken at universities or institutions in any country, except those in eastern Europe. Proposals dealing with Albania, Bulgaria, Romania, or the former Yugoslavia are especially encouraged. Applications are particularly invited from women and members of minority groups.

Financial data Up to $30,000 is provided as a stipend.

Duration 6 to 12 months.

Special features In awarding these grants, consideration is given to the scholarly merit of the proposal, its importance to the development of eastern European studies, and the scholarly potential, accomplishments, and financial need of the applicant. All proposals should be for scholarly work, the product of which is to be disseminated in English. This program is sponsored jointly by the American Council of Learned Societies (ACLS) and the Social Science Research Council, funded by the U.S. Department of State but administered by ACLS.

Limitations This program is not intended to support research within eastern Europe.

Number awarded Varies each year.

Deadline October of each year.

[1030]
FIELD-INITIATED RESEARCH IN BILINGUAL EDUCATION

Department of Education
Attn: Office of Bilingual Education and Minority Languages
   Affairs
Switzer Building
600 Independence Avenue, S.W.
Washington, DC 20202-6510
(202) 205-8722   (202) 205-9723
(202) 205-9700

Purpose To provide funding for research in bilingual education.

Eligibility Current or recent recipients of Title VII grants in bilingual education may apply for these grants. The proposed research should provide for longitudinal studies of students or teachers in bilingual education, monitoring the education of students from entry in bilingual education through secondary school completion.

Financial data The amounts of the awards depend on the nature of the applications and the availability of funds.

Duration 1 year or longer.

Number awarded Varies each year.

Deadline Deadlines vary annually; check the *Federal Register* for the current schedule.

[1031]
FINE ARTS WORK CENTER FELLOWSHIPS

Fine Arts Work Center in Provincetown
24 Pearl Street
Provincetown, MA 02657
(508) 487-9960   Fax: (508) 487-8873

Purpose To provide funding and a residency at the Fine Arts Work Center in Provincetown, Massachusetts to emerging writers and artists.

Eligibility This program is open to visual artists (painters, installation artists, sculptors, printmakers, photographers) or writers (fiction, poetry) of outstanding promise who have completed their formal training and are now working on their own. They must be at least 18 years of age. Minority candidates are particularly encouraged to apply.

Financial data The residency provides living space, studio space, a $375 monthly stipend, and a $75 monthly materials allowance.

Duration 7 months, beginning in October.

Limitations Fellows must be in residence at the Fine Arts Work Center for the duration of the program. There is a $25 application fee.

Number awarded 20 each year: 10 visual artists and 10 writers (4 poets, 4 fiction writers, and 2 returning fellows).

Deadline January of each year.

[1032]
FIRST INDEPENDENT RESEARCH SUPPORT AND TRANSITION (FIRST) AWARDS

National Institutes of Health
Attn: Office of Extramural Research
Extramural Outreach and Information Resources Office
6701 Rockledge Drive, Room 6207
MSC 7910
Bethesda, MD 20892-7910
(301) 435-0714   Fax: (301) 480-8443
E-mail: asknih@odrockm1.od.nih.gov

Purpose To provide research support for newly independent, biomedical and behavioral science investigators to initiate their own research and demonstrate the merit of their own research ideas.

Eligibility To be eligible for an award through this program, the proposed principal investigator must be genuinely independent of a mentor, yet be at the beginning stages of his or her research career, with no more than 5 years of research experience since completing postdoctoral research training or , its equivalent. Research must be conducted at nonprofit or for-profit, public or private organizations, such as universities, colleges, hospitals, laboratories, units of state and local governments, and eligible agencies of the federal government. Applications are accepted for health-related research and development in all areas within the scope of NIH's mission and by all Institutes and Centers that comprise the NIH. Specific subjects of research are announced periodically either as Program Announcements (PAs) for ongoing research or as Requests for Applications (RFAs) for specific 1-time research projects. Research must be conducted within the United States. For all projects, racial/ethnic minority individuals, women, and persons with disabilities are particularly encouraged to apply as principal investigators.

Financial data The level of funding depends on the scope of the proposed research. Total costs may not exceed $350,000, or $100,000 in any budget year.

Duration 5 years; nonrenewable.

Special features This award is offered by all NIH components; grants are designated as R29 Awards. The most meritorious recipients of these awards are nominated for the Presidential Early Career Awards for Scientists and Engineers.

Deadline January, May, or September of each year.

[1033]
FIVE COLLEGE FELLOWSHIP PROGRAM FOR MINORITY SCHOLARS

Five Colleges, Incorporated
Attn: Coordinator
97 Spring Street
Amherst, MA 01002-2324
(413) 256-8316   Fax: (413) 256-0249

Purpose To provide funding to minority graduate students who have completed all the requirements for the Ph.D. except the dissertation and enable them to engage in teaching at 5 colleges in Massachusetts.

Eligibility Fellows are chosen by the host department in each of the 5 campuses (Amherst, Hampshire, Mount Holyoke, Smith, and the University of Massachusetts). Applicants must be minority graduate students who have completed all requirements except the dissertation and are interested in devoting full time to the completion of the dissertation.

Financial data The stipend is $25,000, plus office space, library privileges, and housing assistance.

Duration 9 months, beginning in September.

Special features Although the primary goal is completion of the dissertation, each fellow also has many opportunities to experience working with students and faculty colleagues on the host campus as well as with those at the other colleges. The fellows are also given an opportunity to teach (generally as a team teacher, in a section of a core course, or in a component within a course). Fellows meet monthly with each other to share their experiences. At Smith College, this program is named Mendenhall Fellowships for Minority Scholars.

Number awarded Approximately 4 to 6 each year.

Deadline January of each year.

[1034]
FLORIDA ARTS ORGANIZATIONS GRANTS—FOLK ARTS

Florida Arts Council
c/o Division of Cultural Affairs
Florida Department of State
The Capitol
Tallahassee, FL 32399-0250
(904) 487-2980   Fax: (904) 922-5259

Purpose To provide funding for organizations that preserve the arts and crafts traditionally associated with ethnic, regional, occupational, geographical, or familial groups located in Florida.

Eligibility Nonprofit, tax-exempt cultural organizations, media centers, vocational/educational institutions, local arts agencies, and tribal groups are eligible to apply. Proposals should encourage public awareness of and appreciation for the arts and crafts that have characterized Florida throughout its history; these folk arts include crafts, music, dance, song, poetry, stories, and rituals.

Financial data The amount awarded varies, up to a maximum of $50,000 per year for general program support or $25,000 for a specific project.

Duration 1 year; may be renewed.

Special features Examples of funded projects include: local/regional festivals, exhibits, workshops, community celebrations, and residencies.

Limitations In the past, panels have rejected proposals for research for scholarly purposes only; historical presentations or re-creations; exhibits limited to historical objects; highly choreographed or orchestrated interpretations of traditional folk or ethnic dance or music; contemporary studio crafts or reproductions; and competitive events such as pow wows or fiddle contests.

Number awarded Varies each year.

Deadline February of each year.

[1035]
FLORIDA SPACE GRANT CONSORTIUM UNDERGRADUATE SPACE RESEARCH PARTICIPATION PROGRAM

Florida Space Grant Consortium
c/o University of Florida
Department of Astronomy
405 Space Sciences Research Building
Gainesville, FL 32611-2055
(352) 392-6750   Fax: (352) 392-3456
E-mail: fsgc@astro.ufl.edu

Purpose To provide research opportunities to undergraduate students enrolled in universities participating in the Florida Space Grant Consortium.

Eligibility This program is open to undergraduate students enrolled in universities participating in the Florida Space Grant Consortium: Embry-Riddle Aeronautical University, Florida State University, University of Miami, Florida Atlantic University, Florida A&M University, University of North Florida, Florida Institute of Technology, University of Central Florida, University of South Florida, Florida International University, University of Florida, and University of West Florida. Applicants must be proposing to conduct a space-related research project under faculty mentorship. U.S. citizenship is required. The Florida Space Grant Consortium is a component of the U.S. National Aeronautics and Space Administration (NASA) Space Grant program, which encourages participation by women, minorities, and persons with disabilities.

Financial data Stipends are provided.

Duration 10 weeks, during the summer.

Special features This program is funded by NASA.

Number awarded Up to 30 each year.

[1036]
FLORIDA STATEWIDE ARTS GRANT PROGRAM

Florida Arts Council
c/o Division of Cultural Affairs
Florida Department of State
The Capitol
Tallahassee, FL 32399-0250
(904) 487-2980   Fax: (904) 922-5259

Purpose To fund arts programs or projects sponsored by non-profit organizations in Florida.

Eligibility Applications are evaluated on the following: artistic quality, creativity, potential public exposure and benefit, grant request, and administrative ability. In addition to these criteria, the council gives special attention to those projects that make the arts accessible to special constituencies such as persons with disabilities, elderly people, culturally and economically deprived people, as well as African American, Hispanic, and other ethnic minorities.

Financial data The amount awarded varies but ranges up to up $50,000 in general program support for arts organizations or up to $25,000 for a specific project by a non-arts organization, depending upon the scope of the funded project.

Duration 1 year or longer; may be renewed.

Number awarded Varies each year.

Deadline February of each year.

[1037]
FOLK ARTS PROGRAM OF THE NEW YORK STATE COUNCIL ON THE ARTS

New York State Council on the Arts
915 Broadway
New York, NY 10010
(212) 387-7000   (800) GET-ARTS

Purpose To support organizations that present, preserve, and perpetuate the folk arts in New York.

Eligibility This program focuses on folk traditions practiced by ethnic and other identified groups, including performing traditions in music, dance and drama, traditional storytelling and other verbal arts, festivals, traditional crafts, visual arts, architecture, the adornment and transformation of the built environment, and other forms of material folk culture. Applicants are strongly encouraged to develop appropriate methods of presentation, both for activities presented to general audiences and for programming within a community where a tradition has originated. Theater, orchestral, choral, or dance companies that dramatize, stylize or choreograph folk dance and music in a way that alters traditions to a significant extent are ineligible for support from this program. General operating support is available to organizations that have as their primary purpose folk arts programming or the providing of services to the folk arts field, have received funding from this program for at least 3 consecutive years, and have a year-round administrator, paid or voluntary. Project support is available for presentations, exhibitions, apprenticeships, publications, recordings, film and electronic media production, presentation of folk arts for broadcast on radio and television, institutional development, staff folklorist positions, services to the field, and planning and development.

Financial data The amount awarded varies, depending upon the scope of the funded project.

Duration 1 or more years; may be renewed.

Number awarded Varies each year.

Deadline February of each year.

[1038]
FOLLOW THROUGH GRANTS

Department of Education
Attn: Office of Elementary and Secondary Education
Compensatory Education Programs
Portals Building, Room 4400
600 Independence Avenue, S.W.
Washington, DC 20202-6132
(202) 260-0991

Purpose To provide comprehensive services to children from low-income families who are in kindergarten and primary grades and who have had Head Start or similar preschool experience.

Eligibility Local educational agencies or other public and non-profit private agencies, organizations and institutions are eligible to submit proposals. Grants are provided for financial assistance to 1) local educational agencies for comprehensive programs including instruction and related services for children of low-income families enrolled in kindergarten through third grade; 2) public and private agencies, organizations, and institutions (sponsors) for the development, implementation, evaluation, and dissemination of innovative instructional approaches to early childhood education; and 3) public and nonprofit agencies, institutions, or organizations to conduct research directly related to the program.

Financial data Grants for local projects range from $180,000 to more than $220,000; the average grant is $200,000. Grants for sponsors range from $150,000 to $200,000 and average $180,000 each.

Duration 1 year or longer.

Limitations Because of Congressional action, applications are not currently being accepted for this program.

Number awarded Varies each year.

Deadline Deadline date varies, although it is usually in April; check the latest *Federal Register* for the current schedule.

[1039]
FORD FOUNDATION DISSERTATION FELLOWSHIP PROGRAM FOR MINORITIES

National Research Council
Attn: Fellowship Office
2101 Constitution Avenue
Washington, DC 20418
(202) 334-2872   Fax: (202) 334-3419
E-mail: infofell@nas.edu

Purpose To increase minority presence in the arts and sciences on college and university faculties.

Eligibility Black/African American, Puerto Rican, Mexican American/Chicano, Native American Indian, Native Alaskan (Eskimo or Aleut), and Native Pacific Islander (Micronesian or Polynesian) graduate students who have completed all the requirements for the doctorate except the dissertation are eligible to apply. They must be American citizens or nationals of the United States at the time of application. Awards are given to applicants who have demonstrated superior scholarship and show greatest promise for future achievement as scholars, researchers, and teachers in institutions of higher education.

Financial data The stipend is $18,000 per year; stipend payments are made through fellowship institutions.

Duration 9 to 12 months.

Special features Awards are made for dissertation work in research-based doctoral programs in the behavioral and social sciences, humanities, engineering, mathematics, physical sciences, and biological sciences, or for interdisciplinary programs comprised of 2 or more eligible disciplines. The fellowships are tenable at any accredited nonprofit institution of higher education in the United States that offers Ph.D.s or Sc.D.s in the fields eligible for support. The competition for this program is conducted by the National Research Council on behalf of the Ford Foundation. Applicants who merit receiving the fellowship but to whom awards cannot be made because of insufficient funds will be given Honorable Mentions; this recognition does not carry with it a monetary award but honors applicants who have demonstrated substantial academic achievement. The National Research Council will publish a list of those Honorable Mentions who wish their names publicized.

Limitations Awards are not made in such areas as business administration and management, public health, health sciences, home economics, library science, personnel and guidance, social work, speech pathology and audiology, fine arts and performing arts, or education. In addition, awards are not made for work leading to terminal master's degrees, doctorates in education, Doctor of Fine Arts degrees, joint degrees such as M.D./Ph.D. or M.F.A./Ph.D., or professional degrees in such areas as medicine, law, or business. Fellows may not accept remuneration from another fellowship or similar external award while on this program; however, supplementation from institutional funds, educa-

tional benefits from the Veterans Administration, or educational incentive funds may be received concurrently with Ford Foundation support. Dissertation fellows are required to submit an interim progress report 6 months after the start of the fellowship and a final report at the end of the 12 month tenure.

Number awarded Approximately 20 each year.

Deadline November of each year.

[1040]
FORD FOUNDATION POSTDOCTORAL FELLOWSHIPS FOR MINORITIES

National Research Council
Attn: Fellowship Office
2101 Constitution Avenue
Washington, DC 20418
(202) 334-2860   Fax: (202) 334-3419
E-mail: infofell@nas.edu

Purpose To help members of minority groups already engaged in college or university teaching to develop as scholars in their respective fields and to acquire the professional associations that will make them more effective and productive when they resume academic employment.

Eligibility Applicants must be citizens or nationals of the United States by the application deadline date; be members of 1 of the following ethnic minority groups: Black/African Americans, Mexican Americans/Chicanos, Native Pacific Islanders (Micronesians or Polynesians), Puerto Ricans, Alaskan Natives (Eskimo or Aleut), or Native American Indians; and have earned within the preceding 7 years a Ph.D. or Sc.D. degree in 1 of the eligible fields (behavioral and social sciences, humanities, engineering, mathematics, physical sciences, life sciences, and interdisciplinary programs). Awards are not made to candidates in professional fields, including medicine, law, social work, library science, business administration, management, fine arts, performing arts, speech pathology, audiology, health sciences, personnel and guidance, public health, home economics, and education. Selection is based on achievement and ability as evidenced by academic records and quality of proposed plan of study or research.

Financial data The stipend is $25,000; in addition, fellows receive a travel and relocation allowance up to $3,000. Most institutions receive a $2,000 cost-of-research allowance to provide partial support for the fellow's study and research program. The allowance is prorated for tenure less than 12 months. Finally, each fellow's employing institution is given a $2,500 grant-in-aid for the fellow's use once the fellowship tenure is completed. The employing institution is expected to match the grant. These funds are designated to be used for the fellow's research expenditures.

Duration Up to 12 months. Tenable at any appropriate nonprofit U.S. institution, including a research university, government laboratory, privately-sponsored nonprofit institute, or center for advanced study (such as the Woodrow Wilson Center for Scholars, the Institute for Advanced Study, the Center for Advanced Study in the Behavioral Sciences, the Newberry Library, or the University of Wisconsin's Institute for Research on Poverty), as long as it is an institution other than that from which the candidate applies.

Limitations Fellows may not accept another major fellowship while they are being supported by this program. Applicants who wish to affiliate with institutions outside the United States must provide evidence of the particular benefits that would accrue from affiliation with a foreign center.

Number awarded Varies; approximately 25 each year.

Deadline January of each year.

[1041]
FOSSIL ENERGY FACULTY RESEARCH PARTICIPATION PROGRAM

Oak Ridge Institute for Science and Education
Attn: Science/Engineering Education Division
P.O. Box 117
Oak Ridge, TN 37831-0117
(423) 576-8807   (423) 576-8158
(800) 569-7749   Fax: (423) 576-3643
E-mail: fosenfrp@orau.gov

Purpose To provide funding to faculty members for cooperative participation in ongoing fossil energy research and development at the Pittsburgh Energy Technology Center or the Morgantown Energy Technology Center.

Eligibility This program is open to college or university full-time faculty members in computer sciences, engineering, natural sciences, mathematics, or physical sciences. They must be interested in conducting fossil energy-related research at the Pittsburgh Energy Technology Center (in Pennsylvania) or the Morgantown Energy Technology Center (in West Virginia). All programs operated by the Science/Engineering Education Division (SEED) of Oak Ridge Institute for Science and Education (ORISE) seek to broaden the participation of minorities, women, and persons with disabilities in science and engineering careers.

Financial data Participants receive a negotiable stipend based on regular salary plus reimbursement for travel.

Duration Regular appointments are for 10 weeks to 3 months; also available are sabbatical appointments and part-time appointments of up to 2 days a week.

Special features This program is funded by the U.S. Department of Energy's Office of Fossil Energy but operated and managed by ORISE/SEED. Further information on the Morgantown program is available at (615) 241-2875; further information on the Pittsburgh program is available at (412) 892-4638.

Number awarded Varies each year.

Deadline Applications may be submitted at any time.

[1042]
FOSSIL ENERGY POSTGRADUATE RESEARCH TRAINING PROGRAM

Oak Ridge Institute for Science and Education
Attn: Science/Engineering Education Division
P.O. Box 117
Oak Ridge, TN 37831-0117
(423) 576-8503   (423) 241-2875
(800) 569-7749   Fax: (423) 576-3643
E-mail: feprtp@orau.gov

Purpose To provide funding to postgraduates who are interested in fossil energy-related research and training at the Pittsburgh Energy Technology Center or the Morgantown Energy Technology Center.

Eligibility This program is open to anyone who completed a graduate degree within the past 3 years in computer sciences, engineering, earth sciences, mathematics, or physical sciences. Applicants must be interested in conducting fossil energy-related research at the Pittsburgh Energy Technology Center (in Pennsylvania) or the Morgantown Energy Technology Center (in West Virginia). All programs operated by the Science/Engineering Education Division (SEED) of Oak Ridge Institute for Science and Edu-

cation (ORISE) seek to broaden the participation of minorities, women, and persons with disabilities in science and engineering careers.

Financial data Participants receive a monthly stipend that depends on research area and degree plus limited reimbursement for inbound travel and moving.

Duration 1 year; renewable.

Special features This program is funded by the U.S. Department of Energy's Office of Fossil Energy but operated and managed by ORISE/SEED. Further information on the Morgantown program is available at (615) 241-2875; further information on the Pittsburgh program is available at (412) 892-4638.

Number awarded Varies each year.

Deadline Applications may be submitted at any time.

[1043]
FOSSIL ENERGY RESEARCH AND EDUCATION PROGRAM FOR HISTORICALLY BLACK COLLEGES AND UNIVERSITIES AND OTHER MINORITY INSTITUTIONS

Department of Energy
Attn: Office of Fossil Energy
Pittsburgh Energy Technology Center
P.O. Box 10940
MS 921-143
Pittsburgh, PA 15236-0940
(412) 892-6219   Fax: (412) 892-6216
E-mail: columbia@petc.doe.gov

Purpose To provide support to Historically Black Colleges and Universities (HBCUs) and other minority institutions for research projects on advanced coal, oil, and natural gas concepts.

Eligibility Applications are solicited from federally-recognized HBCUs and other minority institutions to conduct research projects on fossil energy. Proposals must involve collaboration with an industrial partner, and each research team must include a teaching professor and at least 1 student registered at the institution, who receives compensation from the federal grant. Core program applications may be for research on 1 of 6 technical topics: advanced environmental control technology for coal, advanced coal utilization, coal liquefaction technology, heavy oil upgrading and processing, advanced environmental and recovery technologies for oil, and natural gas supply; a seventh area is faculty/student exploratory grants.

Financial data Maximum awards for core program technical grants are $80,000 for 1 year, $140,000 for 2 years, or $200,000 for 3 years; the maximum faculty/student exploratory grant is $10,000.

Duration Up to 3 years.

Special features Recent recipients included Clark Atlanta University (Atlanta, Georgia), Fort Valley State College (Fort Valley, Georgia), Hampton University (Hampton, Virginia), Morgan State University (Baltimore, Maryland), Prairie View A&M University (Prairie View, Texas), and Southern University (Baton Rouge, Louisiana). For a list of other recent recipients and information on opportunities for student participation, contact the address above.

Number awarded Current plans call for 4 to 6 research and development grants on technical topics and 2 to 4 faculty/student exploratory grants each year; total funding is approximately $780,000 per year.

[1044]
FRAMELINE FILM/VIDEO COMPLETION FUND

Frameline
346 Ninth Street
San Francisco, CA 94103
(415) 703-8650   Fax: (415) 861-1404

Purpose To provide funding to lesbian and gay film/video artists.

Eligibility This program is open to lesbian and gay artists who are in the last stages of the production of documentary, dramatic, educational, animated, or experimental projects about or of interest to lesbians and gay men and their communities. Applicants must be interested in completion or post-production work, including subtitling or conversion from video to film (or vice versa). In particular, women and people of color are encouraged to apply. Selection is based on financial need, the contribution the grant will make to completing the project, the viability of the project, and the statement the project makes about lesbians and gay men.

Financial data Up to $2,000.

Limitations Grants are not awarded for script development, research, or pre-production work.

Number awarded Up to 6 each year.

Deadline December of each year.

[1045]
FUND FOR THE DEVELOPMENT OF HUMAN RESOURCES

Women of the Evangelical Lutheran Church in America
Attn: Fund for the Development of Human Resources
8765 West Higgins Road
Chicago, IL 60631-4189
(312) 380-2730   (800) 638-3522, ext. 2730
Fax: (312) 380-2419   E-mail: womnelca@elca.org

Purpose To provide financial assistance to organizations associated with the Evangelical Lutheran Church of America (ELCA) that enhance the development of human resources, especially among women.

Eligibility These grants are available for projects or programs associated with the ELCA and/or Women of the ELCA that supplement available resources and assist individuals or groups for whom use of the grant will have an expanding or multiplying effect; that serve those most in need; that involve women, not only as clients, but also in the planning, decision-making, and evaluation of the project; and that meet needs in the community that are not currently being met by other agencies or services in the area. Priority is given to proposals which have the least access to other funding sources, contribute to self-determination and empowerment rather than dependency, demonstrate creativity and fiscal responsibility, recognize the interrelationship between economic and spiritual needs of communities, and involve women of color or whose language is other than English. Grants are not made for rental or purchase of land or buildings.

Financial data The awards depend on the nature of the proposal and the availability of funds.

Duration 1 year; may be renewed but for no more than 3 grants in a 10-year period.

Number awarded Varies each year, depending upon the funds available.

Deadline February of each year.

[1046]
FUND FOR THE IMPROVEMENT OF POSTSECONDARY EDUCATION COMPREHENSIVE PROGRAMS

Department of Education
Attn: Office of Postsecondary Education
Fund for the Improvement of Postsecondary Education
Regional Office Building 3, Room 3100
Seventh and D Streets, S.W.
Washington, DC 20202-5175
(202) 708-5750   E-mail: FIPSE@ed.gov

Purpose To improve postsecondary educational opportunities by providing financial assistance to educational institutions and agencies.

Eligibility Educational institutions and agencies interested in developing programs that reform and improve postsecondary education are eligible to apply; these include 2- and 4-year colleges, universities, community organizations, libraries, museums, consortia, student groups, local governmental agencies, nonprofit corporations, and associations. Priority is given to projects that: 1) support new ways of ensuring equal access to postsecondary education and that improve rates of retention and program completion, especially for low income and underrepresented minority students; 2) create programs to prepare students for entering the workforce and serve the continuing education and retraining needs of workers; 3) improve the campus climate by creating an environment that is safe, welcoming, and conducive to learning for all students; 4) transform programs and teaching to promote more student learning relative to institutional resources expended; 5) promote cooperation between colleges and universities and elementary and secondary schools; 6) support innovative reforms of undergraduate, graduate, and professional curricula that improve not only what students learn but how they learn; 7) support the development of faculty as professionals; and 8) disseminate to other institutions innovative postsecondary educational programs that have been locally developed and implemented.

Financial data Grants range from $15,000 to $150,000; the average grant is $75,000.

Duration Up to 3 years.

Number awarded Approximately 70 each year.

Deadline October of each year for preapplications; March of each year for final proposals.

[1047]
FUSION ENERGY POSTDOCTORAL RESEARCH PROGRAM

Oak Ridge Institute for Science and Education
Attn: Science/Engineering Education Division
P.O. Box 117
Oak Ridge, TN 37831-0117
(423) 576-8503   (423) 241-2875
(800) 569-7749   Fax: (423) 576-3643
E-mail: feprp@orau.gov

Purpose To provide financial assistance for postdoctoral research in fusion energy research and development programs.

Eligibility Applicants must have completed a doctoral degree within the past 3 years in an appropriate science or engineering discipline and be proposing a program of research in fusion energy research and development programs. Awards are tenable at laboratories in the United States that are supported by the Office of Fusion Energy of the U.S. Department of Energy (DOE) or contractor sites; for a list of those, contact the address above. All programs operated by the Science/Engineering Education Division (SEED) of Oak Ridge Institute for Science and Education (ORISE) seek to broaden the participation of minorities, women, and persons with disabilities in science and engineering careers.

Financial data The stipend is $37,000 per year; reimbursement for inbound travel, moving, and partial medical insurance are also provided.

Duration 1 year; renewable.

Special features This program is funded by the DOE Office of Fusion Energy and administered by ORISE/SEED.

Number awarded Varies each year.

Deadline January of each year.

[1048]
GAIUS CHARLES BOLIN FELLOWSHIPS FOR MINORITY GRADUATE STUDENTS

Dean of the Faculty
Williams College
Hopkins Hall
Williamstown, MA 01267

Purpose To encourage minority doctoral students to pursue careers in college teaching.

Eligibility Applicants must be minority graduate students, have completed all doctoral work except for the dissertation, be U.S. citizens, and be pursuing degrees in the humanities or the natural, social, or behavioral sciences.

Financial data Fellows receive $25,000 for the academic year, plus housing support and an allowance of up to $2,500 to cover research expenses.

Duration 1 academic year, beginning in September.

Special features Bolin fellows are assigned a faculty advisor in the appropriate department.

Limitations Fellows are expected to teach a 1-semester course. They must be in residence at Williams College for the duration of the fellowship.

Number awarded 2 each year.

Deadline January of each year.

[1049]
GEOLOGICAL SOCIETY OF AMERICA GENERAL RESEARCH GRANTS PROGRAM

Geological Society of America
Attn: Research Grants Administrator
3300 Penrose Place
P.O. Box 9140
Boulder, CO 80301-9140
(303) 447-2020, ext. 137   Fax: (303) 447-1133
E-mail: jforstro@geosociety.org

Purpose To provide partial support for geological research by graduate students at universities in the United States, Canada, Mexico, and Central America.

Eligibility This program is open to graduate students in geology at the master's or doctoral level. Both members and non-members of the society are eligible. Applications from minorities, women, and persons with disabilities are strongly encouraged.

Financial data Grants range up to $2,500; the average grant recently was $1,604.

Duration 1 year.

Number awarded Varies; generally, at least 200 each year.

Deadline February of each year.

[1050]
GEORGES LURCY RESEARCH FELLOWSHIP IN ECONOMICS

Brookings Institution
1775 Massachusetts Avenue, N.W.
Washington, D.C. 20036-2188
(202) 797-6127   Fax: (202) 797-6181
E-mail: brookinfo@brook.edu

Purpose To support predoctoral policy-oriented research in economics at the Brookings Institution.

Eligibility Candidates cannot apply; they must be nominated by their graduate department. Nominees must meet the following criteria: doctoral students who have completed their preliminary examinations, have selected a dissertation topic that directly relates to public policy issues and the major research issues of the Institution (economic growth, international economics, human resources, industrial organization, regulation, public finance, monetary economics, and economic stabilization), and be able to benefit from access to the resources and personnel at the Institution. The Institution particularly encourages the nomination of women and minority candidates.

Financial data Fellows receive a stipend of $15,000 for the academic year, supplementary assistance for copying and other essential research requirements up to $600, reimbursement for research-related travel up to $500, health insurance, and access to computer/library facilities.

Duration 1 year.

Special features Fellows participate in seminars, conferences, and meetings at the institution. Outstanding dissertations may be published by the institution.

Limitations Fellows are expected to pursue their research at the Brookings Institution.

Number awarded 1 each year.

Deadline Nominations must be submitted by mid-December and applications by mid-February.

[1051]
GERIATRIC EDUCATION CENTERS GRANTS

Health Resources and Services Administration
Attn: Bureau of Health Professions
Division of Associated, Dental and Public Health Professions
Parklawn Building, Room 8-101
5600 Fishers Lane
Rockville, MD 20857
(301) 443-6889   Fax: (301) 443-1164

Purpose To provide funding to support the development of collaborative arrangements involving several health professions schools and health care facilities to offer training in geriatrics.

Eligibility This program is open to accredited health professions schools, programs for the training of physician assistants, schools of allied health, or schools of nursing located in the United States or its possessions. Applicants must be proposing to offer training involving 4 or more health professions: 1 must be allopathic or osteopathic medicine and the others may be drawn from dentists, optometrists, podiatrists, pharmacists, nurses, nurse practitioners, physician assistants, chiropractors, clinical psychologists, health administrators, and allied health professionals. Projects must address 1 or more of the following purposes: 1) improve the training of health professionals in geriatrics; 2) develop and disseminate curricula relating to the treatment of the health problems of elderly people; 3) expand and strengthen instruction in methods of such treatment; 4) support the training and retraining of faculty to provide such instruction; 5) support continuing education of health professional and allied health professionals who provide such treatment; or 6) establish new affiliations with nursing homes, chronic and acute disease hospitals, ambulatory care centers, and senior centers in order to provide students with clinical training in geriatric medicine. Selection criteria include the potential of the project to recruit and/or retain minority faculty members and trainees for participation in long-term and/or short-term training experiences.

Financial data   Recently, $5,778,000 per year was available for this program, including $3,720,000 for continuation support and $1,853,000 for new competing awards; the average competing grant was $145,000.

Duration   Up to 3 years; may be extended for an additional 3 years.

Number awarded   Varies each year; in recent years, 12 new competing grants have been awarded annually.

Deadline   January of each year.

[1052]
GIRLS SPORTS TRAVEL FUND

Women's Sports Foundation
Eisenhower Park
1899 Hempstead Turnpike, Suite 400
East Meadow, NY 11554-1000
(516) 542-4700   (800) 227-3988
Fax: (516) 542-4716   E-mail: wosport@aol.com

Purpose   To provide financial support to local community and club girls sports teams that advance to state or national competitions.

Eligibility   Eligible to apply for these grants are local community or club girls sports teams that advance to state or national competition and need funding to travel.

Financial data   Grants up to $1,000 are available.

Number awarded   Up to 5 each year.

Deadline   Applications may be submitted at any time.

[1053]
GRADUATE TRAINING IN FAMILY MEDICINE GRANTS

Health Resources and Services Administration
Attn: Bureau of Health Professions
Division of Medicine
Parklawn Building, Room 9A-27
5600 Fishers Lane
Rockville, MD 20857
(301) 443-3456   Fax: (301) 443-1945
E-mail: espirer@hrsa.ssw.dhhs.gov

Purpose   To provide financial support for programs to plan, develop, and operate or participate in approved graduate training programs in the field of family medicine.

Eligibility   This program is open to accredited schools of medicine or osteopathic medicine, public or private nonprofit hospitals, or other public or private nonprofit entities. Applicants must request funding to plan, develop, and operate graduate training programs in the field of family medicine. Recipient institutions may also use this funding to support trainees in such programs who plan to specialize or work in the practice of family medicine.

Selection criteria include 1) the proposal includes a strategy and plan for recruiting and retaining minority and disadvantaged faculty, students, trainees, and/or residents (applicants are expected to reflect the diversity of the populations within their states); 2) the proposal includes clinically oriented, generalist-trained faculty who practice in community-based settings that include underserved populations; 3) the proposal includes a curriculum that emphasizes areas of study pertinent to the needs of special populations in urban, rural, and underserved areas (people with low incomes, members of racial and ethnic minority groups, people with disabilities, and at-risk population groups); 4) the proposal describes the actions taken by the institution that demonstrate faculty involvement with the curricular innovations that are beyond what is traditionally part of such a curriculum; and 5) the proposal includes data regarding the most recent 3-year average track record of a program in placing graduates in primary care training, primary care practice, or generalist faculty positions.

Financial data   The amounts of the awards vary; in recent years, the average grant has been $107,000.

Duration   3 years.

Number awarded   Varies each year.

Deadline   November of each year.

[1054]
GRANTS FOR HEALTH SERVICES DISSERTATION RESEARCH

Agency for Health Care Policy and Research
Attn: Office of Scientific Affairs
Executive Office Center, Suite 400
2101 East Jefferson Street
Rockville, MD 20852-4908
(301) 594-1449   E-mail: small@po7.ahcpr.gov

Purpose   To provide financial assistance to doctoral candidates engaged in research for a dissertation that examines some aspect of the health care system.

Eligibility   Eligible for these grants are registered doctoral candidates who have completed all requirements for the doctoral degree other than the dissertation. The dissertation topic must relate to some aspect of the health care system; the Agency for Health Care Policy and Research (AHCPR) determines if the dissertation topic falls within its mandate. Applications from women, members of minority groups, and persons with disabilities are especially encouraged. U.S. citizenship is not required, but candidates who are neither U.S. citizens nor permanent residents must apply through their institution. Applications from students enrolled in foreign institutions are accepted if the application is in English and the candidate applies through the institution.

Financial data   Total direct costs may not exceed $30,000.

Duration   Up to 2 years.

Number awarded   Varies each year.

Deadline   April and November of each year.

[1055]
GRANTS FOR IMPROVING DOCTORAL DISSERTATION RESEARCH

National Science Foundation
Attn: Directorate for Social, Behavioral, and Economic Sciences
Division of Social, Behavioral, and Economic Research
4201 Wilson Boulevard
Arlington, VA 22230
(703) 306-1733

Purpose To provide partial support for dissertation research in selected areas of the social, behavioral, and economic sciences.

Eligibility Applications may be submitted through regular university channels by dissertation advisors on behalf of graduate students who have advanced to candidacy and have begun or are about to begin dissertation research. Students must be enrolled at U.S. institutions but need not be U.S. citizens. Programs that have been most active in supporting dissertation research include anthropology; decision, risk, and management science; geography and regional science; linguistics; law and social science; political science; sociology; and studies in science, technology, and society (including ethics and values studies). Budget requests may be submitted for such dissertation research related expenses as data collection and sample survey costs, microfilms and other forms of specialized data, payments to subjects or informants, specialized research equipment, analysis and services not otherwise available, supplies and travel to specialized facilities or field research locations, and partial living expenses for conducting necessary research away from the student's university. Women, minorities, and persons with disabilities are strongly encouraged to apply.

Financial data Grants have the limited purpose of providing funds to enhance the quality of dissertation research. They are to be used exclusively for necessary expenses incurred in the actual conduct of the dissertation research.

Duration Up to 2 years.

Limitations Funding is not provided for stipends, tuition, textbooks, journals, allowances for dependents, travel to scientific meetings, publication costs, dissertation preparation or reproduction, or indirect costs.

Number awarded Varies each year, depending on the availability of funds.

Deadline Deadline dates for the submission of dissertation improvement grant proposals differ by program within the Division of Social, Behavioral, and Economic Research; applicants should obtain information regarding target dates for proposals from the relevant program.

[1056]
GRANTS FOR STATE LOAN REPAYMENT PROGRAMS

Health Resources and Services Administration
Attn: Bureau of Primary Health Care
Division of Scholarships and Loan Repayments
4350 East-West Highway, 10th Floor
Bethesda, MD 20814
(301) 594-4400   (800) 435-6464
Fax: (301) 594-4981

Purpose To provide funding to states for operation of programs for repayment of the undergraduate and graduate loans of health professionals.

Eligibility This program is open to state agencies which use the funding to operate state-level programs of payment of all or part of the qualifying educational loans of health professionals agreeing to provide primary health services in federally designated health professional shortage areas (HPSAs). Each state agency must establish state priorities for the selection of health professionals consistent with federal guidelines; currently, priority is given to programs for physicians (M.D.s or D.O.s) in speciality areas of family practice, obstetrics/gynecology, internal medicine, and pediatrics; nurse practitioners; physician assistants; certified nurse-midwives; and dentists. Selection of states for participation in this program is based on the extent of the state's need for health professionals specified by the program; the extent to which special consideration will be extended to federally designated HPSAs with large minority populations; the number and type of providers the state proposes to support through this program; the appropriateness of the proposed placements of recipients; the appropriateness of the qualifications, the administrative and managerial ability of the staff to implement the proposed project; the suitability of the state's approach and the degree to which the plan of a state is coordinated with federal, state, and other programs for meeting the state's health professional needs and resources; the source and plans for the use of the state match; and the adequacy and appropriateness of the proposed budget.

Financial data Participating state agencies may repay up to $35,000 per year of the educational loans (including interest, principal, and related expenses) of qualified health professionals. In operating the program, states must match federal funds received on a 1:1 basis.

Duration The minimum service obligation is 2 years; extensions may be arranged.

Special features Contact the address above for a list of the state agencies currently participating in this program.

Limitations Participants are obligated to provide full-time clinical primary health care services to populations in federally-designated, high-priority HPSAs (these include the Indian Health Service or medical facilities of the Federal Bureau of Prisons).

Number awarded Varies each year, depending upon the funding available. At the present time, 29 states participate in this program.

Deadline State agencies must submit grant applications by April of each year; each state agency sets a deadline date for applications from health professionals in its state.

[1057]
GRASSROOTS ARTS PROGRAM

North Carolina Arts Council
Attn: Department of Cultural Resources
Cambridge House
407 North Person Street
Raleigh, NC 27601-2807
(919) 733-7897, ext. 25

Purpose To support arts organizations in North Carolina and to assist them in diversifying their activities in order to provide opportunities for every North Carolinian to experience the arts.

Eligibility Eligible to apply are nonprofit, tax-exempt established arts organizations in North Carolina. In 81 of the state's 100 counties, Local Distributing Agents (LDAs) receive funding from the North Carolina Arts Council and distribute it to organizations within their county; the LDAs determine what organizations are eligible to apply within their respective counties. Organizations in counties without an LDA apply directly to the Council, which requires that a representative portion of these funds be distributed for arts programming that reflects the racial and ethnic diversity of the county; therefore, priority is given to applications from African American, Native American, Asian American, and Latino organizations and for programs which represent the cultures of those populations. Other selection criteria include responsiveness to community needs, artistic and program merit, strong community support, cooperation among existing arts and community organizations, involvement of traditionally underserved audiences, and organizational strength.

Financial data Funds are distributed on a per capita basis to each county of the state; award amounts depend on the size of the county allotment and the number of organizations requesting funds.

Duration 1 year.

Number awarded Varies each year.

Deadline LDAs must submit county spending plans by January of each year and set local deadlines for subgrant applications within their respective counties; applications from organizations in counties without LDAs must be submitted by February of each year.

[1058]
GRETCHEN L. BLECHSCHMIDT AWARD

Geological Society of America
Attn: Research Grants Administrator
3300 Penrose Place
P.O. Box 9140
Boulder, CO 80301-9140
(303) 447-2020, ext. 137   Fax: (303) 447-1133
E-mail: jforstro@geosociety.org

Purpose To provide funding for research conducted by women working on a Ph.D. in geology.

Eligibility This program is open to women interested in achieving a Ph.D. in the geological sciences and a career in academic research. Special consideration may be given to women 1) whose proposals are in the fields of biostratigraphy and/or paleoceanography and 2) who have an interest in sequence stratigraphy analysis, particularly in conjunction with research into deep-sea sedimentology. Disabled and minority women are particularly encouraged to submit research proposals.

Financial data Grants range up to $2,500; the average grant recently was $1,604.

Duration 1 year.

Number awarded 1 each year.

Deadline February of each year.

[1059]
HAROLD T. STEARNS FELLOWSHIP AWARD

Geological Society of America
Attn: Research Grants Administrator
3300 Penrose Place
P.O. Box 9140
Boulder, CO 80301-9140
(303) 447-2020, ext. 137   Fax: (303) 447-1133
E-mail: jforstro@geosociety.org

Purpose To provide partial support for Pacific Islands geological research by graduate students at universities in the United States, Canada, Mexico, and Central America.

Eligibility This program is open to graduate students in geology at the master's or doctoral level. Both members and non-

members of the society are eligible. Special consideration may be given to students who propose research on 1 or more aspects of the geology of the Pacific Islands and of the circum-Pacific region. Applications from minorities, women, and persons with disabilities are strongly encouraged.

Financial data Grants range up to $2,500; the average grant recently was $1,604.

Duration 1 year.

Number awarded 1 or more each year.

Deadline February of each year.

[1060]
HAWAI'I SPACE GRANT CONSORTIUM GRADUATE FELLOWSHIP PROGRAM

Hawai'i Space Grant Consortium
Attn: Director
2525 Correa Road
Honolulu, HI 96822
(808) 956-3955   Fax: (808) 956-6322
E-mail: spacegr@kahana.pgd.hawaii.edu

Purpose To provide financial assistance for graduate research in space-related fields to students at member institutions of the Hawai'i Space Grant Consortium.

Eligibility This program is open to graduate students at the University of Hawaii at Manoa involved in fields of study (including astronomy, geology, meteorology, oceanography, mathematics, physics, engineering, computer sciences, or life sciences) that are concerned with the understanding, utilization, or exploration of space, or concerned with the investigation of the earth from the perspective of space. A faculty member who is willing to act as the student's advisor during the period of the award must sponsor the applicant. U.S. citizenship and full-time enrollment are required. As a component of the U.S. National Aeronautics and Space Administration (NASA) Space Grant program, the Hawai'i Space Grant Consortium encourages women, underrepresented minorities (Native Hawaiians, Filipinos, other Pacific Islanders, Native Americans, Blacks, and Hispanics), and persons with disabilities to apply.

Financial data Grants are $12,000 per year and up to $1,000 for supplies or travel.

Duration 9 months; may be renewed for another 9-month period.

Special features This program is funded by NASA.

Limitations Fellows are expected to spend 10 to 15 hours per week on their projects.

Number awarded 2 each year.

Deadline June of each year for fall semester; November of each year for spring semester.

[1061]
HAWAI'I SPACE GRANT CONSORTIUM UNDERGRADUATE FELLOWSHIP PROGRAM

Hawai'i Space Grant Consortium
Attn: Director
2525 Correa Road
Honolulu, HI 96822
(808) 956-3138   Fax: (808) 956-6322
E-mail: spacegr@kahana.pgd.hawaii.edu

Purpose To provide financial assistance for undergraduate research in space-related fields to students at member institutions of the Hawai'i Space Grant Consortium.

Eligibility This program is open to undergraduate students at the University of Hawaii at Manoa, the University of Hawaii at Hilo, Leeward Community College, Maui Community College, and Windward Community College. Applicants must be proposing to conduct a research project in astronomy, geology, meteorology, oceanography, mathematics, physics, engineering, computer sciences, or life sciences in ways that are concerned with the understanding, utilization, or exploration of space. A faculty member who is willing to act as the student's advisor during the period of the award must sponsor the applicant. U.S. citizenship is required. As a component of the U.S. National Aeronautics and Space Administration (NASA) Space Grant program, the Hawai'i Space Grant Consortium encourages women, underrepresented minorities (Native Hawaiians, Filipinos, other Pacific Islanders, Native Americans, Blacks, and Hispanics), and persons with disabilities to apply.

Financial data Grants are up to $1,750 per semester and up to $500 for supplies or travel.

Duration 2 semesters.

Special features This program is funded by NASA.

Limitations Fellows are expected to spend 10 to 15 hours per week on their projects.

Number awarded Up to 20 each year.

Deadline June of each year for fall semester; November of each year for spring semester.

[1062]
HCFA DISSERTATION FELLOWSHIPS

Department of Health and Human Services
Attn: Health Care Financing Administration
Office of Research and Demonstrations
Office of Operations Support
Division of Program Support
C-3-11-17
7500 Security Boulevard
Baltimore, MD 21244-1850
(410) 786-6644   E-mail: CHackerman@hcfa.gov

Purpose To provide financial assistance to doctoral candidates writing dissertations in various social science disciplines investigating health care financing and delivery issues.

Eligibility Students enrolled in an accredited doctoral degree program in social, management, or health sciences may apply for these research grants if they are sponsored by their universities and conducting or intending to conduct research on issues related to the delivery or financing of health care services. Topics of special interest to the Health Care Financing Administration (HCFA) include monitoring and evaluating health system performance, improving health care financing and delivery mechanisms, meeting the needs of vulnerable populations, and information to improve consumer choice and health status. Applicants must have completed all course work and academic requirements for the doctoral degree, other than the research and dissertation. Applications from minority and women researchers are specifically encouraged.

Financial data The budget for direct costs (investigator's salary, travel, data processing and supplies) may be up to $20,000; the sponsoring university may receive indirect costs of up to 8 percent of direct costs.

Limitations Applications must be submitted jointly by the student and the university, but funds are dispensed only to the university.

Number awarded 10 to 15 each year.

Deadline October of each year.

[1063]
HEALTH PHYSICS FACULTY RESEARCH AWARD PROGRAM

Oak Ridge Institute for Science and Education
Attn: Science/Engineering Education Division
P.O. Box 117
Oak Ridge, TN 37831-0117
(423) 576-1078   (423) 576-1716
(800) 569-7749   Fax: (423) 576-3643
E-mail: hpfrap@orau.gov

Purpose To provide funding to faculty members who wish to engage in research or educational activities at their institutions in the areas of health physics and radiation protection.

Eligibility Full-time faculty at accredited U.S. colleges or universities may apply for these grants to support research or education activities in applied health physics-related technical areas that are supportive of the mission of the U.S. Department of Energy (DOE). Proposals may involve radiation dosimetry (e.g. equipment; protocols; and internal, external, whole-body, and specific organs), risk assessment and ALARA (As Low as Reasonably Achievable) concepts, radiological emergency management, radiation protection standards and regulation, environmental monitoring and assessment, and air monitoring and sampling. All programs operated by the Science/Engineering Education Division (SEED) of Oak Ridge Institute for Science and Education (ORISE) seek to broaden the participation of minorities, women, and persons with disabilities in science and engineering careers.

Financial data Awards up to $50,000 are available.

Duration 1 year; may be renewed up to 2 additional years.

Special features This program is funded by DOE's Office of Environment, Safety and Health and administered by ORISE/SEED.

Number awarded Varies each year.

Deadline February of each year.

[1064]
HEALTH POLICY RESEARCH INSTITUTE FOR MINORITY NURSES

American Nurses Association
Attn: Minority Fellowship Programs
600 Maryland Avenue, S.W., Suite 100 West
Washington, DC 20024-2571
(202) 651-7244   Fax: (202) 789-1413

Purpose To provide funding to promote research conducted in the areas of health services and policy for ethnic/racial minority populations.

Eligibility Applications are accepted from doctorally prepared registered nurses who are teaching in an academic setting or practicing in a service delivery area and can demonstrate an interest in health policy research regarding minority populations or issues.

Financial data Awards cover a health policy conference and support for research development and technical assistance in preparing a grant proposal.

Duration 2 years: 1 year for the health policy conference and 1 year for preparation of a grant proposal.

Special features Funds for this program are provided by the Agency for Health Care Policy and Research.

Limitations Recipients of these awards are expected to submit their final grant proposal for funding through available sources.
Deadline November of each year.

[1065]
HENRY LUCE FOUNDATION/ACLS DISSERTATION FELLOWSHIP PROGRAM IN AMERICAN ART

American Council of Learned Societies
228 East 45th Street
New York, NY 10017-3398
(212) 697-1505　　　　　　　　　　Fax: (212) 949-8058
E-mail: grants@acls.org

Purpose To provide financial assistance for dissertation research on the history of American art.
Eligibility Eligible to apply are Ph.D. candidates in departments of art history whose dissertations are focused on a topic in the history of the visual arts of the United States. Interdisciplinary and interdepartmental projects are eligible only if the degree is to be granted in art history. U.S. citizenship or permanent resident status is required. Students who previously received grants of $5,000 or more from the Henry Luce Program administered through university departments of art history are not eligible. Applications are particularly invited from women and members of minority groups.
Financial data The grant is $18,500.
Duration 1 year; nonrenewable.
Special features This program is funded by the Henry Luce Foundation and administered by the American Council of Learned Societies (ACLS).
Limitations Fellowship funds may not be used to defray tuition costs.
Number awarded Varies each year.
Deadline November of each year.

[1066]
HERITAGE AND PRESERVATION GRANTS TO ORGANIZATIONS

National Endowment for the Arts
Attn: Heritage and Preservation
Nancy Hanks Center
1100 Pennsylvania Avenue, N.W.
Washington, DC 20506-0001
(202) 682-5428　　　　　　　　　　TTY: (202) 682-5496

Purpose To provide funding to organizations that preserve significant artistic accomplishments for future generations, conserve important works of art, and assist artists reflective of the many cultural groups that make up the nation.
Eligibility Nonprofit tax-exempt organizations of demonstrated artistic excellence may apply if they have a 4-year history of programming, have professional staff, compensate all professional performers and related or supporting professional personnel, assure that no part of any supported project will be performed or engaged in under unsanitary or hazardous conditions, and comply with other federal regulations. Applicants may be arts institutions, local arts agencies, arts service organizations, tribal communities and Indian tribes, official units of city governments, and other organizations that can further the goals of the National Endowment for the Arts (NEA). They should be proposing projects in such areas as the documentation and/or presentation to the public of artists and art forms that reflect our diverse cultural traditions; projects that pass artistic repertoire, techniques, aes-

thetic principles, and oral traditions on to future generations through apprenticeships or other forms of instruction; the documentation and preservation of significant artistic works, styles, techniques, and aesthetic/cultural perspectives; projects that provide technical assistance to traditional/folk artists; publications that document and/or disseminate artistic works, models of preservation, or other material that is aimed at strengthening our artistic heritage; the conservation treatment of highly significant works of art, artifacts, and collections wholly owned by the applicant; or innovative uses of modern technology as a means of preserving and strengthening our artistic heritage. Selection is based on artistic excellence and artistic merit of the proposed project and the applicant organization, impact of the project, and ability to carry out the project.
Financial data Grants generally range from $5,000 to $200,000 and require a match of at least 1 to 1.
Duration Up to 2 years.
Special features The NEA remains committed to supporting equitable opportunity for all and investing in as diverse a reflection of our society as possible.
Limitations Funding is not provided for general operating support; seasonal support; construction or renovation of facilities; marketing expenses that are not directly related to the proposed project; commercial enterprises or activities; fundraising or development; debt and deficit reduction; cash reserves and endowments; social activities, entertainment costs, receptions, etc.; lobbying expenses; individuals directly; elementary and secondary schools directly; avocational or student groups; professional training in degree-granting institutions; work toward academic degrees; literary projects, programming, or publishing that does not focus primarily on contemporary literature and/or writers; research that is directed primarily to academic purposes or scholarly projects; publication of books or exhibition of works by the applicant organization's staff, board members, faculty, or trustees; exhibitions of, and other projects involving, single, privately owned collections; purchase of major equipment; subgranting or regranting, except for state arts agencies and regional arts organizations.
Deadline March of each year.

[1067]
HHMI RESEARCH TRAINING FELLOWSHIPS FOR MEDICAL STUDENTS PROGRAM

Howard Hughes Medical Institute
Attn: Office of Grants and Special Programs
4000 Jones Bridge Road
Chevy Chase, MD 20815-6789
(301) 215-8889　　　　　　　　　　Fax: (301) 215-8888
E-mail: fellows@hq.hhmi.org

Purpose To increase the proportion of physicians who are involved in research by providing financial assistance for medical students to receive research training.
Eligibility Applicants must be enrolled in a medical school in the United States, although they may be citizens of any country. They must describe a proposed research project to be conducted at an academic or nonprofit research institution in the United States, other than a facility of the National Institutes of Health in Bethesda, Maryland. Research proposals should reflect the interests of the Howard Hughes Medical Institute (HHMI), especially in biochemistry, biophysics, biostatistics, cell biology, developmental biology, epidemiology, genetics, immunology, mathematical and computational biology, microbiology, molecular biology,

neuroscience, pharmacology, physiology, structural biology, and virology. Applications from women and minorities underrepresented in the sciences (Blacks, Hispanics, Native Americans, Native Alaskans, and Native Pacific Islanders) are especially encouraged. Selection is based on letters of reference, the research plan, and a mentor's plans for training the student.

Financial data Fellows receive a stipend of $15,000 per year; their institution receives an institutional allowance of $5,500 and a research allowance of $5,500. Research Training Fellows who are chosen to receive support to complete their studies toward the M.D. degree are given an annual stipend of $15,000 and a $15,000 annual allowance toward tuition and other education-related expenses.

Duration 1 year; may be renewed for a second year of research. A small number of Fellows may be allowed to return to medical school and continue receiving support for 2 additional years.

Special features This program complements the HHMI-NIH Research Scholars Program; students may not apply to both programs in the same year.

Limitations Fellows may not be enrolled in an M.D./Ph.D. program.

Number awarded Up to 60 each year.

Deadline December of each year.

[1068]
HHMI-NIH RESEARCH SCHOLARS PROGRAM

Howard Hughes Medical Institute
1 Cloister Court
Bethesda, MD 20814-1460
(301) 951-6770   (800) 424-9924
Fax: (30) 951-6776   E-mail: gpub@hhmi.od.nih.gov

Purpose To give outstanding students at U.S. medical schools the opportunity to receive research training at the National Institutes of Health (NIH), in Bethesda, Maryland.

Eligibility To apply, students must be in good standing at a medical school in the United States or Puerto Rico. The applicants must also be U.S. citizens or permanent residents. Those who are enrolled in an M.D./Ph.D. program or who already have an M.D. or a Ph.D. in a natural science are not eligible. After the conclusion of the program year, a small number of outstanding Research Scholars are selected to receive continued support for up to 2 years while completing studies toward the M.D. degree. To be eligible for this support, Research Scholars must be returning directly to medical school at the conclusion of their participation in the Research Scholars Program, and they may not be enrolled in an M.D./Ph.D., Ph.D., or Sc.D. degree program. These awards are based on demonstrated research abilities, potential for future achievement in biomedical research, and career intentions (including any plans for additional research training upon completion of medical school). Students' financial indebtedness resulting from school loans may also be considered as a secondary factor. Women and members of minority groups are encouraged to apply.

Financial data Research Scholars receive an monthly salary of $1,400 for rent, food, and other living expenses. Scholars are also eligible for medical, life, and accidental death and dismemberment insurance. Students are reimbursed for round-trip moving expenses for personal belongings (not furniture) for themselves and their dependents from and back to medical school. In addition, tuition is paid for Research Scholars who wish to take courses from the Foundation for Advanced Education in the Sci-

ences (FAES). They also receive allowances for the purchase of textbooks and scientific journals related to their area of research and for travel to scientific meetings. Research Scholars who are chosen to receive support to complete their studies toward the M.D. degree are given an annual stipend of $15,000 and a $15,000 annual allowance toward tuition and other education-related expenses.

Duration 1 year, beginning in July or August; may be extended for 1 additional year.

Special features Research Scholars work as part of a research team in a laboratory at the NIH's main campus in Bethesda, conducting basic research under the mentorship of an NIH senior investigator or preceptor. They learn the latest laboratory techniques and experience the creative thinking involved in at least 1 of the following biomedical areas: biochemistry, biophysics, biostatistics, cell biology, developmental biology, epidemiology, genetics, immunology, mathematical and computational biology, microbiology, molecular biology, neuroscience, pharmacology, physiology, structural biology, and virology. This program is unique in that it does not require students to propose a research project or select a laboratory at the NIH as part of the application process. Instead, Research Scholars are encouraged to take their first couple of weeks in the program to interview investigators and explore different laboratories at the NIH before making a selection. This program is jointly sponsored by the Howard Hughes Medical Institute and the National Institutes of Health—the largest private and public biomedical research institutions in the United States. It complements the HHMI Research Training Fellowships for Medical Students Program; students may not apply to both programs in the same year.

Number awarded 40 each year.

Deadline January of each year.

[1069]
HIGH TEMPERATURE MATERIALS LABORATORY FACULTY FELLOWSHIP PROGRAM

Oak Ridge Institute for Science and Education
Attn: Science/Engineering Education Division
P.O. Box 117
Oak Ridge, TN 37831-0117
(423) 576-3425   (423) 576-2358
(800) 569-7749   Fax: (423) 576-3643
E-mail: htmlfpp@orau.gov

Purpose To provide funding to university faculty members who wish to engage in research at the High Temperature Materials Laboratory (HTML) in Oak Ridge, Tennessee.

Eligibility Full-time academic staff members of an ABET-approved university department in advanced materials may apply for this program. They must proposed to conduct research at the HTML. All programs operated by the Science/Engineering Education Division (SEED) of Oak Ridge Institute for Science and Education (ORISE) seek to broaden the participation of minorities, women, and persons with disabilities in science and engineering careers.

Financial data The stipend is negotiable, but based on the recipient's regular university salary; round-trip for travel and some moving expenses are reimbursed.

Duration 1 month to 1 year.

Special features This program is funded by the Office of Transportation Technologies of the U.S. Department of Energy and administered by ORISE/SEED.

Number awarded Varies each year.

Deadline Applications may be submitted at any time.

[1070]
HIGH TEMPERATURE MATERIALS LABORATORY GRADUATE STUDENT FELLOWSHIPS

Oak Ridge Institute for Science and Education
Attn: Science/Engineering Education Division
P.O. Box 117
Oak Ridge, TN 37831-0117
(423) 576-3425   (423) 576-2358
(800) 569-7749   Fax: (423) 576-3643
E-mail: htmlgsf@orau.gov

Purpose To provide financial assistance to doctoral candidates who wish to conduct research at the High Temperature Materials Laboratory (HTML) in Oak Ridge, Tennessee.

Eligibility Doctoral candidates who have an approved dissertation topic related to advanced technical materials areas of the U.S. Department of Energy may apply for this program. They must proposed to conduct research at the HTML. All programs operated by the Science/Engineering Education Division (SEED) of Oak Ridge Institute for Science and Education (ORISE) seek to broaden the participation of minorities, women, and persons with disabilities in science and engineering careers.

Financial data The program provides reimbursement of tuition and fees up to a maximum of $5,000 per year, a monthly stipend of $2,104, and reimbursement for inbound travel and moving.

Duration 1 year; may be renewed up to 3 additional years.

Special features This program is funded by Oak Ridge National Laboratory and administered by ORISE/SEED.

Number awarded Approximately 4 each year.

Deadline Applications may be submitted at any time.

[1071]
HOWARD HUGHES MEDICAL INSTITUTE PRECOLLEGE AND PUBLIC SCIENCE EDUCATION PROGRAM

Howard Hughes Medical Institute
Attn: Office of Grants and Special Programs
4000 Jones Bridge Road
Chevy Chase, MD 20815-6789
(301) 215-8873   Fax: (301) 215-8888
E-mail: grantvpr@hq.hhmi.org

Purpose To provide financial support to institutions involved in precollege science education, especially for women and minority students.

Eligibility Eligible to apply for these grants are scientific institutions such as museums, natural history museums, science and technology centers, aquaria, botanical gardens, zoos, medical schools, academic health centers, and independent research laboratories. Applicants must be proposing to conduct programs to encourage precollege students, especially girls and minorities underrepresented in the sciences, to choose scientific careers, to provide teachers with research opportunities and new teaching tools, and to address national concerns about the low level of scientific knowledge and interest in the general population.

Financial data The amount awarded varies. Since this program began, a total of $21 million has been disbursed in grants, of which 47 percent went to precollege science education programs focusing on students, 46 percent for teachers and curriculum, and 7 percent for families and community groups.

Duration Up to 5 years.

Special features This program began in 1991.

Number awarded Varies; since 1991, grants have been made to 93 institutions.

[1072]
HOWARD HUGHES MEDICAL INSTITUTE UNDERGRADUATE BIOLOGICAL SCIENCES EDUCATION INITIATIVE

Howard Hughes Medical Institute
Attn: Office of Grants and Special Programs
4000 Jones Bridge Road
Chevy Chase, MD 20815-6789
(301) 215-8872   Fax: (301) 215-8888
E-mail: barkanic@hq.hhmi.org

Purpose To strengthen undergraduate biological science education, especially for women and minority students.

Eligibility Academic institutions with demonstrable records of pursuing the objectives of the initiative are eligible for these grants. The areas of interest of the Howard Hughes Medical Institute include 1) student research and broadening access to science, especially for women and minority students underrepresented in the sciences; 2) equipment and laboratories in response to the needs of science departments to upgrade their undergraduate teaching infrastructure; 3) faculty and curriculum, with support for newly appointed faculty, opportunities for existing faculty to broaden their scientific expertise and increase their involvement in undergraduate education, and recruitment of women and underrepresented minorities to faculties; and 4) precollege and outreach programs to strengthen science and mathematics education, especially for groups underrepresented in the sciences, through partnerships between the academic institutions and elementary and secondary schools and 2-year colleges. Selected institutions may apply for grants to support any or all of those 4 purposes.

Financial data The amount awarded varies. In a recent year, grants ranged from $600,000 to $1,600,000 and totaled approximately $43 million.

Duration Up to 4 years.

Limitations The program does not provide support for post-baccalaureate, graduate, or postdoctoral students as teaching fellows, laboratory or teaching assistants, and other positions, nor does it support training students in those roles.

Number awarded Varies; since 1988, grants have been made to 213 public and private colleges and universities, including 15 Historically Black Colleges and Universities, 10 other schools enrolling substantial numbers of undergraduate minority students, 7 women's colleges, and 3 universities in Puerto Rico.

[1073]
HOWARD HUGHES POSTDOCTORAL RESEARCH FELLOWSHIPS FOR PHYSICIANS

Howard Hughes Medical Institute
Attn: Office of Grants and Special Programs
4000 Jones Bridge Road
Chevy Chase, MD 20815-6789
(301) 215-8889   Fax: (301) 215-8888
E-mail: fellows@hq.hhmi.org

Purpose To provide funding for biological research at academic or research institutions in any country.

Eligibility Eligible to apply are postdoctorates (M.D., D.O., or M.D./Ph.D. degrees) from any country who are interested in conducting biological research in the United States or abroad. They must have received their first medical degree no more than 10 years prior to application but must have at least 2 years of postgraduate clinical training. They may not be enrolled in a graduate degree program and may have no more than 2 years of postdoctoral research training. Applicable specialities include biochemistry, biophysics, biostatistics, cell biology, developmental biology, epidemiology, genetics, immunology, mathematical and computational biology, microbiology, molecular biology, neuroscience, pharmacology, physiology, structural biology, and virology. The program is open to applicants who are citizens or nationals of the United States or who are foreign citizens or nationals. Applications are specifically encouraged from women and members of minority groups underrepresented in the sciences (Blacks, Hispanics, Native Alaskans, Native Americans, and Native Pacific Islanders).

Financial data The total award ranges from $69,000 to $89,000 per year, including a stipend of $40,000 to $60,000 (rising annually in the second and third years), a $16,000 research allowance payable to the institution, and a $13,000 institutional allowance.

Duration 3 years.

Limitations Fellows are expected to spend full time on their funded research.

Number awarded 30 each year.

Deadline December of each year.

[1074]
HYDROGEOLOGY DIVISION GRANT

Geological Society of America
Attn: Research Grants Administrator
3300 Penrose Place
P.O. Box 9140
Boulder, CO 80301-9140
(303) 447-2020, ext. 137   Fax: (303) 447-1133
E-mail: jforstro@geosociety.org

Purpose To provide partial support for geological research by graduate students at universities in the United States, Canada, Mexico, and Central America.

Eligibility This program is open to graduate students in geology at the master's or doctoral level. Both members and nonmembers of the society are eligible. Special consideration may be given to students who propose research on 1 or more aspects of hydrogeology. Applications from minorities, women, and persons with disabilities are strongly encouraged.

Financial data Grants range up to $2,500; the average grant recently was $1,604.

Duration 1 year.

Special features This program is sponsored by the Geological Society of America's Hydrogeology Division.

Number awarded 1 or more each year.

Deadline February of each year.

[1075]
IDAHO SPACE GRANT CONSORTIUM HIGHER EDUCATION AND RESEARCH PROGRAM

Idaho Space Grant Consortium
c/o University of Idaho
College of Engineering
Mechanical Engineering
Moscow, ID 83844-1011
(208) 885-7018   Fax: (208) 885-6645
E-mail: rgill@uidaho.edu

Purpose To provide financial assistance for study and research in space-related fields to students and faculty at member institutions of the Idaho Space Grant Consortium.

Eligibility This program is open to students and faculty at the University of Idaho, Boise State University, Idaho State University, and other member institutions of the Idaho Space Grant Consortium. Faculty members may apply for funding to travel to facilities of the U.S. National Aeronautics and Space Administration (NASA) or other aerospace related agencies/industries to obtain research funding. Students may apply for scholarships, assistantships, or fellowships for space related programs. U.S. citizenship is required. As a component of the NASA Space Grant program, the Idaho Space Grant Consortium encourages participation by women, minorities, and persons with disabilities.

Financial data The amounts of the awards depend on the availability of funds and the nature of the proposal.

Duration Depends on the nature of the proposal.

Special features This program is funded by NASA.

Number awarded Varies each year. Since it began in 1991, this program has awarded 33 faculty research initiation awards, 21 scholarships, and 6 fellowships.

[1076]
INDEPENDENT SCIENTIST AWARDS

National Institutes of Health
Attn: Office of Extramural Research
Extramural Outreach and Information Resources Office
6701 Rockledge Drive, Room 6207
MSC 7910
Bethesda, MD 20892-7910
(301) 435-0714   Fax: (301) 480-8443
E-mail: asknih@odrockm1.od.nih.gov

Purpose To provide financial support to newly independent scientists who can demonstrate the need for a period of intensive research focus as a means of enhancing their research careers.

Eligibility This program is open to candidates who have a doctoral degree and peer-reviewed, independent research support at the time the award is made. They must be willing to spend a minimum of 75 percent of full-time professional effort conducting research and research career development activities for the period of the award. Candidates must demonstrate that the requested period of research focus will foster their career as highly productive scientists in the indicated field of research. Applications may be submitted on behalf of candidates by domestic, non-federal organizations, public or private, such as medical, dental, or nursing schools or other institutions of higher education. Minorities and women are particularly encouraged to apply. Candidates must be U.S. citizens or permanent residents.

Financial data This program provides salary and fringe benefits for the candidate only; each component establishes its own salary limits on career awards. Indirect costs are reimbursed at

8 percent of modified total direct costs, or at the actual indirect cost rate, whichever is less.

Duration   5 consecutive 12-month appointments.

Special features   Awards under this program are available from 12 agencies of the National Institues of Health (NIH): the National Institute on Aging, the National Institute on Alcohol Abuse and Alcoholism, the National Institute of Allergy and Infectious Diseases, the National Institute of Arthritis and Musculoskeletal and Skin Diseases, the National Institute of Child Health and Human Development, the National Institute on Deafness and Other Communication Disorders, the National Institute of Dental Research, the National Institute of Diabetes and Digestive and Kidney Diseases, the National Institute on Drug Abuse, the National Institute of Environmental Health Sciences, the National Heart, Lung, and Blood Institute, and the National Institute of Mental Health. The names and addresses of staff people at each agency are available from the address above. The NIH designates this program as the K02 Awards.

Number awarded   Varies each year.

Deadline   January, May, or September of each year.

[1077]
INDIANA SPACE GRANT CONSORTIUM RESEARCH GRANTS

Indiana Space Grant Consortium
c/o Purdue University
School of Aeronautics and Astronautics
1282 Grissom Hall
West Lafayette, IN 47907-1282
(317) 494-5135   Fax: (317) 494-0307
E-mail: andrisan@ecn.purdue.edu

Purpose   To provide financial support to space-related related research at institutions in Indiana.

Eligibility   This program is open to researchers affiliated with Indiana University, Purdue University, or the University of Notre Dame. U.S. citizenship is required. The Indiana Space Grant Consortium is a component of the U.S. National Aeronautical and Space Administration (NASA) Space Grant program, which encourages participation by women, minorities, and persons with disabilities.

Financial data   A total of $100,000 is available through this program each year; funds are distributed by a formula of $25,000 to Indiana University, $25,000 to the University of Notre Dame, and $50,000 to the Calumet and West Lafayette campuses of Purdue University.

Special features   This program is funded by NASA.

Number awarded   Each participating university determines how to allocate its funds.

Deadline   Deadline dates are established by the participating universities; contact the address above for information on the programs at each institution.

[1078]
INDUSTRY RESEARCH SCHOLAR AWARDS

American Digestive Health Foundation
7910 Woodmont Avenue, Suite 700
Bethesda, MD 20814-3015
(301) 654-2635   Fax: (301) 654-5920

Purpose   To provide salary support for young investigators working in any area of gastroenterology, hepatology, or related fields.

Eligibility   Applicants must hold full-time faculty positions at North American universities or professional institutes at the time of application. Applicants should be early in their careers (established investigators are not appropriate candidates). Those who have been at the assistant professor level for more than 5 years are not eligible. The primary intent of this award is to support physician-investigators who have the potential to develop independent, productive research careers in gastroenterology and hepatology. However, nonphysician candidates with a Ph.D. will also be considered. Selection is based on novelty, feasibility and significance of the proposal, attributes of the candidate, evidence of institutional commitment, and the laboratory environment. Women and minority investigators are strongly encouraged to apply. To increase the number of underrepresented minority scientists participating in gastroenterology research, the association has reserved 1 of these awards specifically for an applicant who is African American, Hispanic American, Native American, Alaska Native, or Pacific Islander.

Financial data   The award consists of $50,000 per year. Funds are to be used for salary support. Indirect costs are not allowed.

Duration   3 years.

Special features   This award is administered by the American Digestive Health Foundation (ADHF) and sponsored by the American Gastroenterological Association (AGA).

Limitations   At least 70 percent of the recipient's research effort should relate to the gastrointestinal tract or liver. Recipients cannot hold or have held a R01, R29, K121, K08, VA Research Award, or any award with similar objectives from nonfederal sources.

Number awarded   6 each year; 1 of the awards is specifically set aside for an underrepresented minority recipient.

Deadline   September of each year.

[1079]
INDUSTRY-BASED GRADUATE RESEARCH ASSISTANTSHIPS AND COOPERATIVE FELLOWSHIPS IN THE MATHEMATICAL SCIENCES

National Science Foundation
Attn: Directorate for Mathematical and Physical Sciences
Division of Mathematical Sciences
4201 Wilson Boulevard, Room 1025
Arlington, VA 22230
(703) 306-1870   Fax: (703) 306-0555
E-mail: uicrp@nsf.gov

Purpose   To provide financial assistance to graduate students in mathematics who wish to gain experience in industrial settings.

Eligibility   This program is open to graduate students in mathematics who are U.S. citizens, nationals, or permanent residents. Applicants may propose either 1) a research assistantship, in which they conduct research for a master's thesis or doctoral dissertation under the joint supervision of a university faculty member and an industrial scientist, spending part-time at the industrial site on a regular basis and the remainder in the classroom or in other campus-based activities; or 2) a cooperative fellowship, in which they work full-time as an intern in an industrial setting. Applications are especially encouraged from women, underrepresented minorities, and persons with disabilities.

Financial data   The program provides up to 50 percent (with an upper limit of $20,000) of the total support for each student. The university faculty member involved in the joint supervision of such students may request up to $6,000 as a faculty research allowance.

Duration Up to 1 year.

Number awarded Varies each year.

Deadline November of each year.

[1080]
INFORMAL SCIENCE EDUCATION PROGRAM

National Science Foundation
Attn: Directorate for Education and Human Resources
Division of Elementary, Secondary and Informal Education
4201 Wilson Boulevard, Room 885
Arlington, VA 22230
(703) 306-1616 Fax: (703) 306-0412

Purpose To support projects that promote public understanding of science, mathematics, and technology outside of formal school settings.

Eligibility Organizations with a scientific or educational mission may submit a proposal. These include colleges and universities, state and local education agencies, professional societies, museums, research laboratories, print or electronic media producers, private foundations, private industries, publishers, and other public and private organizations, whether for profit or nonprofit. NSF especially welcomes proposals that involve the collaboration or individuals or organizations from more than 1 of those areas, that increase the involvement of parents in science and mathematics education, and that increase participation of minorities, girls/women, and youth from economically disadvantaged areas in those disciplines.

Financial data The amount awarded depends on the nature of the proposal and the availability of funds; in recent years, grants have ranged from $25,000 to $3,000,000.

Duration 1 to 5 years.

Number awarded Approximately 44 each year.

Deadline Preliminary proposals must be submitted by February and August of each year; full proposals are due by May and November of each year.

[1081]
INITIATIVE FOR MINORITY STUDENT DEVELOPMENT

National Institutes of Health
Attn: National Institute of General Medical Sciences
Division of Minority Opportunities in Research
Natcher Building, Suite 2AS37H
45 Center Drive MSC 6200
Bethesda, MD 20892-6200
(301) 594-3900 Fax: (301) 480-2753
E-mail: em18v@nih.gov

Purpose To promote the initiation and development of new programs, as well as the expansion and enhancement of existing programs, that motivate and foster the development of underrepresented minority students in biomedical research careers.

Eligibility Applications may be submitted by domestic private and public educational institutions. The application may be directed toward the development of underrepresented minority scientists who are in any phase of their career development, from the undergraduate level through the Ph.D. The fields of study may be any of the mathematical, natural, physical, or behavioral sciences relevant to biomedical research. Applications proposing to develop the competitive research skills of recent clinical doctorates are also eligible. Underrepresented minorities are defined as

African Americans, Hispanic Americans, Native Americans, and natives of the U.S. Pacific Islands.

Financial data Students may receive salary/wages and/or other forms of compensation in lieu of wages. Tuition remission is allowable for graduate students. Institutions may receive up to $500,000 per year in total direct costs and up to 8 percent of direct costs as indirect costs. Unallowable costs include undergraduate tuition, housing, food, recruitment expenses, and support for faculty research.

Duration Up to 4 years.

Special features Some of the activities which institutions may provide as part of this program include research opportunities for undergraduate, graduate, medical, or post-clinical doctoral students (for which students may receive compensation); research-oriented technical training courses or workshops for students; strengthening the research capabilities of faculty who are uniquely successful in the development of underrepresented minority students or who are critical to the development of an environment supportive of minority students; activities to improve technical skills of students such as writing; student travel for presentation of research at scientific meetings; and mentoring activities.

Number awarded Varies each year.

Deadline January of each year.

[1082]
INITIATIVE FOR MINORITY STUDENTS: BRIDGES TO THE BACCALAUREATE DEGREE PROGRAM

National Institutes of Health
Attn: National Institute of General Medical Sciences
Natcher Building, Suite 2AS13H
45 Center Drive MSC 6200
Bethesda, MD 20892-6200
(301) 594-0533 Fax: (301) 480-2004
E-mail: ar25f@nih.gov

Purpose To facilitate partnerships between 2-year and 4-year institutions in areas relevant to the biomedical sciences.

Eligibility Applications must include a partnership between a 2-year institution that offers the associate degree as the only undergraduate degree in the sciences within the participating departments and has a significant enrollment of underrepresented minorities (African Americans, Hispanic Americans, Native Americans, and Pacific Islanders), and a college or university offering baccalaureate degrees in science relevant to biomedical research disciplines.

Financial data Students may receive salary/wages and/or other forms of compensation such as tuition remission. Grants to institutions are limited to $320,000 for the 2-year period for direct costs and indirect costs of 8 percent of direct costs.

Duration 1 year; may be renewed.

Special features Students interested in this program should contact their college; for a list of currently participating institutions, write to the address above.

Number awarded 20 to 40 each year.

[1083]
INITIATIVE FOR MINORITY STUDENTS: BRIDGES TO THE DOCTORAL DEGREE PROGRAM

National Institutes of Health
Attn: National Institute of General Medical Sciences
Natcher Building, Suite 2AS13H
45 Center Drive MSC 6200
Bethesda, MD 20892-6200
(301) 594-0533   Fax: (301) 480-2004
E-mail: ar25f@nih.gov

Purpose To encourage the development of new and innovative programs and the expansion of existing programs to improve the academic competitiveness of underrepresented minority students and facilitate their transition to careers in biomedical research.

Eligibility Applications must include a partnership between an institution that offers the M.S. degree as the only postgraduate degree in the sciences within the participating departments and has a significant enrollment of underrepresented minorities (African Americans, Hispanic Americans, Native Americans, and Pacific Islanders), and a research university providing Ph.D. degree programs in areas relevant to the biomedical sciences.

Financial data Students may receive salary/wages and/or other forms of compensation such as tuition remission. Stipends, housing, tuition, and fees are not allowable costs. Grants to institutions are limited to $320,000 for direct costs for the 2-year period and indirect costs of 8 percent of direct costs.

Duration 1 year; may be renewed.

Special features Students interested in this program should contact their university; for a list of currently participating institutions, write to the address above.

Number awarded 20 to 40 each year.

[1084]
INSTITUTE OF EARLY AMERICAN HISTORY AND CULTURE POSTDOCTORAL FELLOWSHIP

Institute of Early American History and Culture
Attn: Director
P.O. Box 8781
Williamsburg, VA 23187-8781

Purpose To provide funding to postdoctorates who are interested in conducting research in any area of early American studies at the Institute of Early American History and Culture in Williamsburg, Virginia.

Eligibility This program is open to individuals who have completed their doctorate. A significant portion of the dissertation or other research project must be submitted at the time of application; scholars who have already attained the Ph.D. and begun careers are also eligible. Applications may be submitted by eligible U.S. citizens or permanent residents. Applications also may be submitted by foreign nationals, if they have lived in the United States for at least 3 years immediately preceding the date of the fellowship award. None of the applicants may have previously published a book. The principal criterion for selection is that the candidate's dissertation or other research project has significant potential for publication as a distinguished, book-length contribution to scholarship. Members of underrepresented groups (including people of color, persons with disabilities, Vietnam veterans, and women) are specifically encouraged to apply.

Financial data The stipend is $30,000 per year. In addition, the fellow receives an office, research and computer facilities, and funds for travel to conferences and other research centers.

Duration 2 years.

Special features Fellows hold concurrent appointment as assistant professor in the appropriate department at the College of William and Mary and teach a total of 6 semester hours during the 2-year term. Fellows have the option of spending a summer at the Huntington Library on a full grant within 5 years of their residency in Williamsburg. Interests of the Institute include all aspects of the lives of North America's indigenous and immigrant peoples during the colonial, Revolutionary, and early national periods of the United States and the related histories of Canada, the Caribbean, Latin America, the British Isles, Europe, and Africa, from the 16th century to approximately 1815. Funding is currently provided by the National Endowment for the Humanities.

Limitations Fellows must devote most of their time during the fellowship to research and teaching. They must work closely with members of the editorial staff and participate in colloquia and other scholarly activities at the institute. The institute has first claim on publishing the fellow's completed manuscript.

Number awarded 1 each year.

Deadline October of each year.

[1085]
INSTITUTIONAL DENTIST SCIENTIST AWARDS

National Institutes of Health
Attn: National Institute of Dental Research
Division of Extramural Research
Natcher Building, Room 4AN-18J
45 Center Drive MSC 6402
Bethesda, MD 20892-6402
(301) 594-2618   Fax: (301) 480-8318
E-mail: jl46d@nih.gov

Purpose To provide dentists with advanced clinical training to prepare them to become researchers.

Eligibility Dental institutions may obtain funding under this program in order to provide support to dentists who wish to pursue career development experiences leading to research independence. Program directors at the institutions select candidates who have already attained a D.D.S., D.M.D., or equivalent degree but who normally have not started postgraduate clinical training. Candidates must intend to pursue a program that includes didactic and supervised basic, clinical, or behavioral research experiences which result in the Ph.D. degree, and advanced clinical training in either a recognized clinical specialty or equivalent dental clinical discipline. The program strongly encourages the recruitment and retention of women and underrepresented minorities for this program.

Financial data Starting salaries are based on relevant experience, ranging from $26,500 for no experience to a maximum of $39,226 with 10 or more years of experience. In addition, the institute allows $15,000 per year for research development support such as tuition, fees, and books related to career development; research expenses for supplies, equipment, and technical personnel; travel to research meetings or training; and statistical services including personnel and computer time.

Duration 5 years.

Special features Currently, 9 institutions are participating in this program: the University of Alabama at Birmingham, the University of California at San Francisco, the University of Connecticut Health Center, the University of Iowa, the Harvard School of Dental Medicine, the University of Minnesota, the State University of New York at Buffalo, the University of Rochester, and the University of Washington. The National Institutes of Health (NIH) designates this program as the K16 Awards.

Number awarded   18 each year: 2 at each of the 9 participating schools of dentistry.

Deadline   Application deadlines are established by each dental school participating in the program.

[1086]
INSTITUTIONAL DEVELOPMENT AWARDS

National Institutes of Health
Attn: National Center for Research Resources
Research Infrastructure Area
One Rockledge Center, Suite 6030
6705 Rockledge Drive MSC 7965
Bethesda, MD 20892-7965
(301) 435-0766   Fax: (301) 480-3770
E-mail: cc10d@nih.gov

Purpose   To enhance the competitiveness of research institutions in states with historically low success rates of funding from the National Institutes of Health (NIH).

Eligibility   This program is open to domestic, for-profit and nonprofit, public and private organizations, such as universities, colleges, hospitals, laboratories, and research foundations in the following states: Alaska, Arkansas, Delaware, Idaho, Kansas, Kentucky, Mississippi, Montana, Nebraska, New Mexico, North Dakota, Oklahoma, South Dakota, West Virginia, and Wyoming (states in which the ratio of NIH funds awarded vs. funds requested was less than 20 percent for the period of 1982-1994). In each state, 1 institution may apply for funding for research or research training activities in the biomedical or behavioral sciences. Applications from institutions with significant minority enrollments are especially encouraged.

Financial data   Direct costs up to $200,000, along with appropriate indirect costs, are available.

Duration   Up to 3 years; nonrenewable.

Number awarded   Up to 10 each year.

Deadline   January of each year.

[1087]
INSTRUCTIONAL MATERIALS DEVELOPMENT PROGRAM

National Science Foundation
Attn: Directorate for Education and Human Resources
Division of Elementary, Secondary and Informal Education
4201 Wilson Boulevard, Room 885
Arlington, VA 22230
(703) 306-1614   Fax: (703) 306-0412

Purpose   To provide support for development of curricula and materials that promote improvement of science, mathematics, and technology education at K-12 levels.

Eligibility   Organizations with a scientific or educational mission may submit a proposal. These include colleges and universities, state and local education agencies, professional societies, museums, research laboratories, print or electronic media producers, private foundations, private industries, publishers, and other public and private organizations, whether for profit or nonprofit. Products should be designed to ensure the success of all students, regardless of background or ability; they should promote students' positive attitudes toward science, mathematics, and technology, as well as positive perceptions of themselves as learners. Although demonstration models may be funded, projects are expected to be national in scope and significance so that upon completion, materials are ready for utilization by teachers and

students across the nation. Projects should establish mechanisms for documenting changes in student learning outcomes; increases in female and minority student performance; and modifications in instructional approaches that are prompted by the new instructional materials.

Financial data   The amount awarded depends on the nature of the proposal and the availability of funds; in a recent year, grants ranged from $10,000 to $2,794,000.

Duration   1 to 4 years.

Number awarded   Approximately 42 each year.

Deadline   Preliminary proposals must be submitted by April of each year; full proposals are due by August.

[1088]
INSTRUMENTATION AND LABORATORY IMPROVEMENT PROGRAM

National Science Foundation
Attn: Directorate for Education and Human Resources
Division of Undergraduate Education
4201 Wilson Boulevard, Room 835
Arlington, VA 22230
(703) 306-1667   E-mail: undergrad@nsf.gov

Purpose   To encourage and support development of experiments and laboratory curricula that improve the education of undergraduate students, both majors and non majors, in science, mathematics, engineering, and technology, including pre-service teachers.

Eligibility   Proposals are invited from organizations in the United States and its territories: 2-year colleges; 4-year colleges; universities; professional societies; consortia of institutions; nonprofit, non-academic institutions that are directly associated with educational or research activities; and, under certain circumstances, for-profit organizations. The target for all programs is undergraduates enrolled in science, mathematics, engineering, and technology courses, especially future teachers at the elementary and secondary school level. The National Science Foundation (NSF) particularly encourages proposals that strengthen undergraduate education by increasing the participation of women, underrepresented minorities, and persons with disabilities, especially if the projects present models for increasing the numbers who successfully pursue careers in science, mathematics, engineering, and technology. Underrepresented minorities are defined as African Americans, Alaskan Natives (Eskimos and Aleuts), Hispanics, Native Americans, and Native Pacific Islanders (Micronesians and Polynesians).

Financial data   Within the Instrumentation and Laboratory Improvement Program, the range of awards for Instrumentation Projects (ILI-IP) is from $5,000 to $100,000; the range of awards for Leadership in Laboratory Development Projects (ILI-LLD) is from $30,000 to $200,000. Both subprograms require matching by the grantee institution of an amount equal to or greater than the award from NSF.

Duration   Up to 2 years for ILI-IP projects; from 1 to 3 years for ILI-LLD

Special features   The ILI-IP component of this program aims to improve the quality of undergraduate instruction by supporting the acquisition of instruments for laboratory courses in science, mathematics, engineering, and technology. The ILI-LLD component supports national models for undergraduate laboratory instruction which undertake fundamental reform and improvement, including content, methods, modes of operation, new technology, or the contexts for science, mathematics, engineering, and technology education at any level in any discipline or combination of disciplines ordinarily supported by NSF.

Number awarded The number of awards granted depends on the quality of the proposals received and the availability of funds for the program; in a recent year, this program provided 484 new and 3 continuing ILI-IP awards and 10 new ILI-LLD awards.

Deadline November of each year.

[1089]
INTERNATIONAL MIGRATION DISSERTATION FELLOWSHIPS

Social Science Research Council
810 Seventh Avenue
New York, NY 10019
(212) 377-2700   Fax: (212) 377-2727

Purpose To provide financial assistance for doctoral dissertation research that advances theoretical understanding of immigration to the United States, the processes of settlement, and the outcomes for both immigrants and Americans.

Eligibility Eligible are U.S. citizens, permanent residents, and foreign students matriculated in social science doctoral programs (including history) at U.S. institutions. Applicants must have their proposals approved by their dissertation committees and must complete all course work and exams before the fellowship begins. The proposed research should focus on international migration to the United States and its economic, sociocultural, and political contexts. Applications from women and from members of minority racial, ethnic, and nationality groups are especially encouraged.

Financial data The fellowships provide a stipend of $12,000 and up to $3,000 in research expenses.

Duration 1 academic year; applicants who do not intend to finish their research by the end of the 1-year fellowship must explain how they plan to complete the unfunded portion of their research.

Special features Funding for this program is provided by the Andrew W. Mellon Foundation.

Number awarded 7 each year.

Deadline January of each year.

[1090]
INTERNATIONAL MIGRATION MINORITY SUMMER DISSERTATION WORKSHOP

Social Science Research Council
810 Seventh Avenue
New York, NY 10019
(212) 377-2700   Fax: (212) 377-2727

Purpose To assist minority graduate students develop research proposals for doctoral dissertations that advance theoretical understanding of immigration to the United States, the processes of settlement, and the outcomes for both immigrants and Americans.

Eligibility Eligible are U.S. citizens or permanent residents who are of African, Latino, Asian, Pacific Island, or Native American ancestry and are matriculated in social science doctoral programs (including history) at U.S. institutions. Applicants must have taken course work related to international migration, be completing their first year of graduate study, and have developed a preliminary research focus for their dissertations. They must desire to participate in a workshop to undergo training on refining research topics, designing research methods, and preparing proposals for funding.

Financial data The fellowships provide transportation, room and board, other participation costs, and a stipend for workshop participants.

Duration 2 weeks in June and 1 week in August.

Special features Funding for this program is provided by the Andrew W. Mellon Foundation.

Number awarded 10 to 15 each year.

Deadline January of each year.

[1091]
INTERNATIONAL MIGRATION POSTDOCTORAL FELLOWSHIPS

Social Science Research Council
810 Seventh Avenue
New York, NY 10019
(212) 377-2700   Fax: (212) 377-2727

Purpose To provide financial assistance for original research that advances theoretical understanding of immigration to the United States, the processes of settlement, and the outcomes for both immigrants and Americans.

Eligibility Applicants must be citizens or permanent residents of the United States who hold a Ph.D. or equivalent in any of the social sciences (including history) or in a related professional field. Foreign scholars are eligible if they are affiliated with a U.S. academic or research institution during the time of the award. The proposed research should focus on international migration to the United States and its economic, sociocultural, and political contexts. Applications from women and from members of minority racial, ethnic, and nationality groups are especially encouraged.

Financial data The stipend is up to $20,000.

Duration 1 academic year; applicants who do not intend to finish their research by the end of the 1-year fellowship must explain how they plan to complete the unfunded portion of their research.

Special features Funding for this program is provided by the Andrew W. Mellon Foundation.

Number awarded 6 each year.

Deadline January of each year.

[1092]
INTERNATIONAL MIGRATION RESEARCH PLANNING GRANTS

Social Science Research Council
810 Seventh Avenue
New York, NY 10019
(212) 377-2700   Fax: (212) 377-2727

Purpose To foster interdisciplinary collaboration in preparing research proposals that advance theoretical understanding of immigration to the United States, the processes of settlement, and the outcomes for both immigrants and Americans.

Eligibility Eligible are U.S. citizens, permanent residents, and foreign scholars affiliated with a U.S. academic or research institution. Applications are accepted from teams of 2 or more scholars from at least 2 different disciplines who hold a Ph.D. or equivalent in 1 of the social sciences (including history) or in an allied professional field. They must propose funding to support meetings, preliminary investigations, and other activities needed to prepare interdisciplinary research proposals. The proposed research should focus on international migration to the United States and its economic, sociocultural, and political contexts. Applications from women and from members of minority racial, ethnic, and nationality groups are especially encouraged.

Financial data Grants are approximately $5,000.
Special features Funding for this program is provided by the Andrew W. Mellon Foundation.
Number awarded Up to 8 each year.
Deadline January of each year.

[1093]
INTERNATIONAL SECURITY AND ARMS CONTROL POSTDOCTORAL FELLOWSHIPS

Center for International Security and Arms Control
Attn: Director of Fellowship Programs
Stanford University
320 Galvez Street
Stanford, CA 94305-6165
(415) 723-9626   Fax: (415) 723-0089
E-mail: barbara.platt@stanford.edu

Purpose To provide funding for postdoctorates who are interested in conducting research on arms control and international security at Stanford University's Center for International Security and Arms Control.

Eligibility Postdoctorates interested in studying or researching international security and arms control issues at the Center are eligible to apply. Topics suitable for support might include security relationships in Europe and Asia; U.S.-Russian strategic relations; peacekeeping; prevention of deadly conflicts; U.S. defense and arms control policies; proliferation of nuclear, chemical, and biological weapons; the commercialization of national defense technologies; and ethnic and civil conflict. Applications are welcome from military officers or civilian members of the U.S. government, members of military or diplomatic services from other countries, and journalists interested in arms control and international security issues. The center is especially interested in applications from minorities and women.

Financial data The stipend is $28,000. Additional funds may be available for dependents and travel.
Duration 9 months.
Number awarded Varies; generally, 2 each year.
Deadline February of each year.

[1094]
INTERNATIONAL SECURITY AND ARMS CONTROL PREDOCTORAL FELLOWSHIPS

Center for International Security and Arms Control
Attn: Director of Fellowship Programs
Stanford University
320 Galvez Street
Stanford, CA 94305-6165
(415) 723-9626   Fax: (415) 723-0089
E-mail: barbara.platt@stanford.edu

Purpose To provide funding for doctoral students who are interested in writing a dissertation on the problems of arms control and international security at Stanford University's Center for International Security and Arms Control.

Eligibility Students currently enrolled in doctoral programs (particularly those that involve U.S.-Soviet security relations and East Asian security issues) at academic institutions in the United States who would benefit from access to the facilities offered by the Center are eligible to apply. Topics suitable for support might include security relationships in Europe and Asia; U.S.-Russian strategic relations; peacekeeping; prevention of deadly conflicts; U.S. defense and arms control policies; proliferation of nuclear,

chemical, and biological weapons; the commercialization of national defense technologies; and ethnic and civil conflict. The center is especially interested in receiving applications from minorities and women.

Financial data The stipend is $16,000. Additional funds may be available for dependents and travel.
Duration 9 months.
Number awarded Varies; generally, 4 each year.
Deadline February of each year.

[1095]
INTERNATIONAL SECURITY AND ARMS CONTROL SCIENCE FELLOWS PROGRAM

Center for International Security and Arms Control
Attn: Director of Fellowship Programs
Stanford University
320 Galvez Street
Stanford, CA 94305-6165
(415) 723-9626   Fax: (415) 723-0089
E-mail: barbara.platt@stanford.edu

Purpose To provide funding to mid-career scholars who are interested in conducting research on international security or arms control issues at Stanford University's Center for International Security and Arms Control.

Eligibility Mid-career scientists who have strong technical backgrounds and an interest in conducting research on international security or arms control at the Center are eligible to apply. At the time of application, they should be employed in academic or research institutions, government agencies, or private sector enterprises. The center is particularly interested in receiving applications from minorities or women.

Financial data The amount awarded varies, depending upon the current salary, background, and experience of each year recipient. A typical stipend is $50,000. Health insurance is provided, and funds are available for travel and other research-related expenses.

Duration Up to 1 year.
Special features Science fellows pursue research, audit courses, and work with the center's faculty and research staff. They have the opportunity to interact with specialists in arms control, politics, and military affairs.
Number awarded 3 each year.
Deadline February of each year.

[1096]
INTRODUCTION TO BIOMEDICAL RESEARCH PROGRAM

National Institutes of Health
Attn: National Institute of Allergy and Infectious Diseases
Solar Building, Room 4B-03
6003 Executive Boulevard MSC 7630
Bethesda, MD 20892-7630
(301) 496-8697   Fax: (301) 496-8729
E-mail: jw25v@nih.gov

Purpose To inform academically talented students from underrepresented minority groups of career opportunities in the broad field of biomedical research.

Eligibility Deans and faculty from colleges and universities in the United States, Puerto Rico, the Virgin Islands, and Guam may recommend college juniors, seniors, first-year medical students, and first-year graduate students for this program. Nominees must be members of underrepresented minority groups (American Indians, Alaska Natives, Asians, Pacific Islanders, Blacks, or Hispanics), be U.S. citizens or permanent residents, and have a grade point average of 3.0 or better.

Financial data Undergraduates receive per diem expenses and round-trip transportation from the student's academic institution to the National Institutes of Health (NIH) in Bethesda, Maryland. Graduate students also receive a salary.

Duration 5 days, in February.

Special features The program consists of a series of scientific lectures, interviews, and tours of the NIH facilities. Students have the opportunity to discuss current research initiatives and advances and career concerns with staff scientists as well as summer positions in the NIH Summer Internship Program in Biomedical Research.

Number awarded Approximately 60 each year.

Deadline November of each year.

[1097]
IRVINE MINORITY SCHOLARS

College of Arts and Sciences
Attn: Gerardo Marin
University of San Francisco
2130 Fulton Street
San Francisco, CA 94117-1080
(415) 422-5555

Purpose To offer ethnic minorities an opportunity to teach and conduct dissertation research at the University of San Francisco.

Eligibility Eligible to apply are U.S. citizens or permanent residents who have finished all course work leading to the Ph.D., are interested in considering a career in teaching, and are members of 1 of the following ethnic/racial groups: African American, Asian American, Hispanic/Latino, or American Indian. They must have specialized in 1 of the following areas: biology, chemistry, communication, computer science, economics, English, environmental science, exercise and sport science, fine and performing arts, history, mathematics, modern and classical languages, philosophy, physics, politics, psychology, sociology, or theology and religious studies.

Financial data The stipend is $24,000. Scholars also receive allowances for research costs, housing, and relocation expenses.

Duration 1 academic year.

Special features Scholars teach 1 course per semester in their discipline, serve as a resource person for faculty, students, and staff, receive office space, enjoy library privileges, and are given a mentor from among the senior faculty at the school.

Number awarded 3 each year.

Deadline February of each year.

[1098]
J. HOOVER MACKIN RESEARCH GRANTS

Geological Society of America
Attn: Research Grants Administrator
3300 Penrose Place
P.O. Box 9140
Boulder, CO 80301-9140
(303) 447-2020, ext. 137   Fax: (303) 447-1133
E-mail: jforstro@geosociety.org

Purpose To provide partial support for geological research by graduate students at universities in the United States, Canada, Mexico, and Central America.

Eligibility This program is open to graduate students (at the master's or doctoral level) in geology. Both members and non-members of the society are eligible. Applicants must propose research on Quaternary geology or geomorphology. Applications from minorities, women, and persons with disabilities are strongly encouraged.

Financial data Grants range up to $2,500; the average grant recently was $1,604.

Duration 1 year.

Special features This program is sponsored by the Geological Society of America's Quaternary Geology and Geomorphology Division. Applications are also available from J. Steven Kite, Department of Geology and Geography, West Virginia University, P.O. Box 6300, Morgantown, WV 26505-6300.

Number awarded 1 or more each year.

Deadline February of each year.

[1099]
J. PAUL GETTY TRUST FUND FOR THE VISUAL ARTS

California Community Foundation
606 South Olive Street, Suite 2400
Los Angeles, CA 90014-1526
(213) 413-4042   Fax: (213) 383-2046

Purpose To provide funds to accomplished artists and mid-sized arts organizations in Los Angeles County.

Eligibility Mid-sized arts organizations in Los Angeles County may apply for institutional development or project support. Individual visual artists are also eligible. Priority is given to projects which encourage and support cultural diversity or collaboration and resource sharing among arts organizations.

Financial data Grant amounts for single agency requests range from $2,500 to $15,000. Individual fellowships are $15,000.

Duration 1 year; may be renewed.

Special features Recent individual recipients were in the fields of sculpture, mixed media-collage, installation, photography, and video/installation.

Number awarded Varies; in a recent year, 5 individuals and 14 organizations received support.

Deadline September of each year.

[1100]
J. ROBERT OPPENHEIMER FELLOWS PROGRAM

Los Alamos National Laboratory
Attn: Human Resource Division
Special Programs and Services
Mail Stop P290
P.O. Box 1663
Los Alamos, NM 87545
(505) 667-0872   Fax: (505) 665-4562
E-mail: postdoc-info@lanl.gov

Purpose To provide an opportunity for outstanding postdoctoral scholars to pursue independent research at the Los Alamos National Laboratory (LANL).

Eligibility This program is open to scholars who received a doctoral degree within the past 5 years in astrophysics, bioscience, biotechnology, chemistry, computer science, earth sciences, engineering, environmental sciences, materials science, mathematics, metallurgy, optics, physics, or space sciences. Applicants must display exceptional ability in scientific research and must be proposing to pursue independent research on a topic of their own choice at the Laboratory. The program encourages a culturally diverse workforce.

Financial data The annual stipend ranges from $67,400 to $69,800, depending on the date of completion of the Ph.D. A comprehensive benefits package includes incoming relocation reimbursement.

Duration 3 years.

Number awarded Up to 2 each year.

[1101]
JACOB K. JAVITS GIFTED AND TALENTED STUDENTS EDUCATION PROGRAM

Department of Education
Attn: Office of Educational Research and Improvement
Development and Demonstration Division
555 New Jersey Avenue, N.W., Room 502
Washington, DC 20208-5645
(202) 219-1674   Fax: (202) 219-2053

Purpose To provide grants to elementary and secondary schools to meet the special educational needs of gifted and talented students.

Eligibility Applications may be submitted by state educational agencies, local educational agencies, institutions of higher education, and other public and private agencies and organizations, including Indian tribes and organizations and Native Hawaiian organizations. At least half of the grants in any given year must serve students who are economically disadvantaged, are limited English proficient, or have disabilities.

Financial data Recently, a total of $1,765,000 per year has been available through this program; individual grants ranged from $100,000 to $275,000 and averaged $250,000.

Duration Up to 3 years.

Number awarded Up to 7 each year.

Deadline June of each year.

[1102]
JAPAN ADVANCED RESEARCH GRANTS

Social Science Research Council
810 Seventh Avenue
New York, NY 10019
(212) 377-2700   Fax: (212) 377-2727

Purpose To provide financial assistance for advanced research on Japan in all areas of the social sciences and humanities.

Eligibility Eligible to apply are scholars who are U.S. citizens and have either a Ph.D. or equivalent research or analytical experience. The program encourages innovative research in the social sciences that is comparative and contemporary in nature, and has long-range applied policy implications, or that engages Japan in wide regional and global debates. Minorities and women are particularly encouraged to apply.

Financial data The amount awarded varies. Support is disbursed in dollars and/or yen, depending on the location of the research.

Duration 2 months to 1 year.

Special features Depending on the nature of the proposed project, the research may be carried out in Japan, the United States, and/or other countries. Scholars may apply for support to conduct research in collaboration with Japanese scholars who have other support.

Limitations These grants are not for training and candidates for academic degrees are not eligible. If travel is planned, applicants must try to arrange for affiliation with an American or foreign university or research institute.

Number awarded Varies each year.

Deadline November of each year.

[1103]
JAPAN STUDIES DISSERTATION WORKSHOP

Social Science Research Council
810 Seventh Avenue
New York, NY 10019
(212) 377-2700   Fax: (212) 377-2727

Purpose To enable graduate students in Japanese studies to participate in a workshop with faculty members where they can obtain critical feedback prior to and following dissertation field work.

Eligibility Applications are accepted from full-time advanced graduate students, regardless of citizenship, working at a U.S. university toward a Ph.D. in the social sciences or humanities on a topic related to Japan. They may be at any stage in the dissertation process except the final write-up phase and must have an approved dissertation prospectus. A narrative description of the dissertation topic and a letter of reference from the student's advisor are required as part of the application. Minorities and women are especially encouraged to apply.

Financial data The award covers participants' travel, lodging, and meals for the duration of the workshop.

Duration 1 week.

Special features Student participants are asked to write a 10-page paper analyzing and linking the research projects of all the participants for circulation prior to the workshop. Dissertation proposals or dissertations-in-progress are discussed and critiqued. This program is funded by the Japan Foundation.

Number awarded 10 to 12 students and 4 to 5 faculty members each year.

Deadline September of each year.

[1104]
JOHN HUGHLINGS JACKSON RESEARCH/CLINICAL TRAINING FELLOWSHIPS

Epilepsy Foundation of America
Attn: Department of Research and Professional Education
4351 Garden City Drive
Landover, MD 20785
(301) 459-3700   (800) EFA-1000
Fax: (301) 577-2684   TDD: (800) 332-2070
E-mail: postmaster@efa.org

Purpose To offer qualified individuals the opportunity to develop expertise in clinical epilepsy and epilepsy research through training experience and involvement in an epilepsy research project.

Eligibility Applications are open to individuals who have received their M.D. degree and completed residency training. The proposed research may be either basic or clinical, but there must be an equal emphasis on clinical training and clinical epileptology. Special attention is given to applications submitted by women and minorities.

Financial data The stipend is $30,000.

Duration 1 year.

Limitations The fellowship must be carried out at a facility where there is an ongoing epilepsy research program. Research must be conducted in the United States.

Number awarded Varies each year.

Deadline August of each year.

[1105]
JOHN M. OLIN POSTDOCTORAL FELLOWSHIPS IN U.S. MILITARY HISTORY AND INTERNATIONAL SECURITY

International Security Studies
Yale University
Attn: Administrator
P.O. Box 208206
New Haven, CT 06520-8206

Purpose To provide funding to postdoctorates interested in conducting research in the fields of U.S. military history or international security at Yale University.

Eligibility This program is open to younger scholars whose research interests focus on how military and international security issues (and their histories) bear upon the United States. Applicants should have received their doctorate by the time they would begin this program. Interested candidates should submit their vitae, a research proposal, their transcripts, a short (up to 50 pages) writing sample, and 3 references. Females, minorities, and candidates with disabilities, as well as veterans of the Vietnam era, are encouraged to apply.

Financial data The stipend is $29,000 per year.

Duration 2 years.

Limitations This is a residential fellowship; fellows are expected to be in residence at Yale University for the duration of the program.

Number awarded 1 each year.

Deadline March of each year.

[1106]
JOHN T. DILLON ALASKA RESEARCH AWARD

Geological Society of America
Attn: Research Grants Administrator
3300 Penrose Place
P.O. Box 9140
Boulder, CO 80301-9140
(303) 447-2020, ext. 137   Fax: (303) 447-1133
E-mail: jforstro@geosociety.org

Purpose To provide partial support for Alaskan geological research by graduate students.

Eligibility This program is open to graduate students in geology at the master's or doctoral level. Both members and non-members of the society are eligible. Special consideration may be given to students whose proposals are 1) field-based studies dealing with the structural and tectonic development of Alaska and 2) studies that include some aspect of geochronology (either paleontologic or radiometric) to provide new age control for significant rock units in Alaska. Candidates with other objectives in Alaskan earth science research are also considered. Applications from minorities, women, and persons with disabilities are strongly encouraged.

Financial data Grants range up to $2,500; the average grant recently was $1,604.

Duration 1 year.

Number awarded 1 or more each year.

Deadline February of each year.

[1107]
JOINTLY SPONSORED NIH PREDOCTORAL TRAINING PROGRAM IN THE NEUROSCIENCES

National Institutes of Health
Attn: National Institute of Neurological Disorders and Stroke
Division of Fundamental Neurosciences and Developmental Disorders
Federal Building, Room 916
7550 Wisconsin Avenue MSC 9170
Bethesda, MD 20892-9170
(301) 496-5745   Fax: (301) 402-1501
E-mail: rb175y@nih.gov

Purpose To provide support to institutions for programs of predoctoral training in the neurosciences.

Eligibility This program is open to domestic, nonprofit, private or public institutions with the staff and facilities required for the proposed program of research training. The research training program director at the institution is responsible for the selection and appointment of trainees, who must have received a baccalaureate degree and be training at the postbaccalaureate level in a program leading to a Ph.D. in the neurosciences. All candidates must be U.S. citizens or permanent citizens. Institutions must give particular attention to recruiting individuals from minority groups that are underrepresented nationally in biomedical and behavioral research (African Americans, Hispanics, Native Americans, Alaskan Natives, and Pacific Islanders).

Financial data For trainees, the annual stipend is $10,008. Institutions may apply for training costs (such as staff salaries, consultant costs, equipment, research supplies, and staff travel) of up to $1,500 per year per trainee; up to $125 per month to offset the cost of tuition, fees, travel, supplies, and other expenses for each short-term health professional research training position; and an indirect cost allowance of 8 percent of total allowable direct costs or actual indirect costs, whichever is less.

Duration 5 years; may be renewed.

Special features This program is jointly administered by 8 components of the National Institutes of Health (NIH): the National Institute on Aging, the National Institute of Child Health and Human Development, the National Institute on Deafness and Other Communication Disorders, the National Institute of Dental Research, the National Institute of General Medical Sciences, the National Institute of Mental Health, the National Institute of Neurological Disorders and Stroke, and the National Institute of Nursing Research. The NIH administers this program as part of its National Research Service Award Institutional Research Training Grants (T32).

Number awarded Varies each year.

Deadline Letters of intent must be submitted by February of each year and applications are due by May.

[1108]
JOSEPH E. MURRAY AWARD

National Kidney Foundation of Massachusetts and Rhode Island
105 Eastern Avenue, Suite 211
P.O. Box 9103
Dedham, MA 02027-9103

Purpose To encourage research that will have significant impact on our understanding and treatment of kidney and urological diseases.

Eligibility This program is open to junior scientists in Massachusetts and Rhode Island who are planning independent research careers or to more senior investigators who have experienced temporary loss of research funding. Applicants should have a serious commitment to a career in research. There is no age limitation for the applicants. Awards are not made to individuals whose work will be concurrently supported by NIH K, RO1, R29 awards or their equivalent. Applications are encouraged in all areas of research related to adult and pediatric kidney and urological diseases, including hypertension and transplantation. Both clinical and basic research proposals are considered. Applications from women and members of underrepresented minority groups are encouraged as are applications dealing with diseases that are prevalent in minority communities.

Financial data The grant is $35,000.

Duration 1 year.

Number awarded 1 each year.

Deadline March of each year.

[1109]
JOSEPH L. FISHER DISSERTATION FELLOWSHIPS

Resources for the Future
1616 P Street, N.W.
Washington, DC 20036-1400
(202) 328-5067   Fax: (202) 939-3460

Purpose To support doctoral dissertation research in economics on issues related to the environment, natural resources, or energy.

Eligibility This fellowship is intended to support graduate students in the final year of their dissertation research. The sponsor particularly encourages women and minority group members to apply. Applicants must submit the following: a brief letter of application and a curriculum vitae, a graduate transcript, a 1-page abstract of the dissertation, a technical summary of the dissertation (up to 2,500 words), a letter from the student's department chair, and 2 letters of recommendation from faculty members on the student's dissertation committee. The technical summary should describe clearly the aim of the dissertation, its significance in relation to the existing literature, and the research methods to be used.

Financial data The stipend is $12,000 per year.

Duration 1 academic year.

Limitations It is expected that recipients will not hold other employment during the fellowship period. Recipients must notify Resources for the Future of any financial assistance they receive from any other source for support of doctoral work.

Deadline February of each year.

[1110]
JOSEPH SHANKMAN AWARD

National Kidney Foundation of Massachusetts and Rhode Island
105 Eastern Avenue, Suite 211
P.O. Box 9103
Dedham, MA 02027-9103

Purpose To encourage research that will have significant impact on our understanding and treatment of kidney and urological diseases.

Eligibility This program is open to junior scientists in Massachusetts and Rhode Island who are planning independent research careers or to more senior investigators who have experienced temporary loss of research funding. Applicants should have a serious commitment to a career in research. There is no

age limitation for the applicants. Awards are not made to individuals whose work will be concurrently supported by NIH K, RO1, R29 awards or their equivalent. Applications are encouraged in all areas of research related to adult and pediatric kidney and urological diseases, including hypertension and transplantation. Both clinical and basic research proposals are considered. Applications from women and members of underrepresented minority groups are encouraged as are applications dealing with diseases that are prevalent in minority communities.

Financial data The grant is $35,000.

Duration 1 year.

Number awarded 1 each year.

Deadline March of each year.

[1111]
KATRIN H. LAMON FELLOWSHIP

School of American Research
Attn: Resident Scholar Program
P.O. Box 2188
Santa Fe, NM 87504-2188
(505) 982-2919

Purpose To provide funding for Native American scholars who would benefit from a residency at the School of American Research in Santa Fe, New Mexico.

Eligibility Eligible to apply are Native Americans who are interested in conducting research from the perspective of anthropology or from anthropologically informed perspectives in allied fields such as history, sociology, art, law, and philosophy. They may be postdoctoral scholars, retired scholars, or Ph.D. candidates who are working on their dissertation. Preference is given to candidates who have completed their research and need time to write up their findings. Selection is based on overall excellence and significance of the proposed project, in addition to such factors as clarity of presentation and the applicant's record of academic accomplishments.

Financial data Fellowships provide apartments and offices on the campus of the School of American Research, stipends, library assistance, and other benefits.

Duration 9 months, beginning in September.

Special features Participants are given an opportunity to interact with scholars, visiting anthropologists, and staff at the School of American Research. Funding for this program is provided by the Katrin H. Lamon Endowment for Native American Art and Education.

Limitations Participants must spend their 9-month residency at the school in New Mexico.

Number awarded 1 each year.

Deadline November of each year.

[1112]
KENTUCKY FOUNDATION FOR WOMEN ORGANIZATIONAL GRANTS

Kentucky Foundation for Women
Heyburn Building
332 West Broadway, Suite 1215
Louisville, KY 40202-2184
(502) 562-0045

Purpose To support women's organizations in the arts and humanities in Kentucky.

Eligibility Eligible to apply for these funds are nonprofit organizations that wish to create new programs and projects that fulfill the goals of the Kentucky Foundation for Women–to use the arts for social change, specifically for equality for all women regardless of class, age, sexual preference, or color. Proposals should be for programs that are innovative and uniquely feminist, that promote the philosophies of feminism, that are on the cutting edge of feminist expression, and that directly affect the lives of women in Kentucky.

Financial data Grants up to $15,000 are available.

Duration Up to 1 year.

Special features The foundation was established in 1985.

Number awarded Varies each year.

Deadline September of each year.

[1113]
KENTUCKY SPACE GRANT CONSORTIUM RESEARCH GRANTS

Kentucky Space Grant Consortium
c/o Western Kentucky University
Department of Physics and Astronomy, TCCW 246
Hardin Planetarium and Astrophysical Observatory
1 Big Red Way
Bowling Green, KY 42101-3576
(502) 745-4156   Fax: (502) 745-6471
E-mail: ksgc@wkuvx1.wku.edu

Purpose To provide financial assistance for space-related research by faculty members of designated institutions in Kentucky.

Eligibility This program is open to faculty members at member institutions of the Kentucky Space Grant Consortium (Centre College, Eastern Kentucky University, Kentucky State University, Morehead State University, Murray State University, Northern Kentucky University, Thomas More College, Transylvania University, University of Kentucky, University of Louisville, and Western Kentucky University). Applicants must be requesting research "seed money" to enhance their competitiveness for future funding. Preference is given to proposals that involve students in the research. Investigators are encouraged to develop projects related to strategic enterprises of the U.S. National Aeronautics and Space Administration (NASA), to collaborate with NASA field centers, or to utilize NASA data. The Kentucky Space Grant Consortium is a component of the NASA Space Grant program, which encourages participation by women, minorities, and persons with disabilities.

Financial data Awards up to $5,000 require a 1:1 institutional match; awards up to $10,000 require a 2:1 match.

Duration 1 year; may be renewed.

Special features This program is funded by NASA.

Limitations The institution must provide adequate faculty time and any indirect costs.

Number awarded Varies each year.

Deadline March of each year.

[1114]
KENTUCKY SPACE GRANT CONSORTIUM SUPPORT FOR TEACHER WORKSHOPS

Kentucky Space Grant Consortium
c/o Western Kentucky University
Department of Physics and Astronomy, TCCW 246
Hardin Planetarium and Astrophysical Observatory
1 Big Red Way
Bowling Green, KY 42101-3576
(502) 745-4156   Fax: (502) 745-6471
E-mail: ksgc@wkuvx1.wku.edu

Purpose To provide funding for workshops for teachers in Kentucky that will develop expertise for relating space activities to the teaching of science and mathematics.

Eligibility The principal investigator on applications for these grants must be a faculty member at a member institution of the Kentucky Space Grant Consortium (Centre College, Eastern Kentucky University, Kentucky State University, Morehead State University, Murray State University, Northern Kentucky University, Thomas More College, Transylvania University, University of Kentucky, University of Louisville, and Western Kentucky University). The proposal must be for a workshop to develop or enhance the capabilities of college or pre-college teachers in the teaching of space-related subjects. The Kentucky Space Grant Consortium is a component of the U.S. National Aeronautics and Space Administration (NASA), which encourages participation by women, minorities, and persons with disabilities.

Financial data Awards up to $8,000 are available. At least 50 percent of the grant must be matched by the investigator's institution.

Special features This program is funded by NASA.

Limitations The institution must provide any indirect costs.

Number awarded Varies each year.

Deadline March of each year.

[1115]
LANL POSTDOCTORAL RESEARCH ASSOCIATES PROGRAM

Los Alamos National Laboratory
Attn: Human Resource Division
Special Programs and Services
Mail Stop P290
P.O. Box 1663
Los Alamos, NM 87545
(505) 667-0872   Fax: (505) 665-4562
E-mail: postdoc-info@lanl.gov

Purpose To provide an opportunity for postdoctoral scholars to pursue research on programs of the Los Alamos National Laboratory (LANL).

Eligibility This program is open to scholars who received a doctoral degree within the past 3 years in areas of competency of the Laboratory. Candidates must be nominated and sponsored by a member of the technical staff. Selection is based on academic qualifications and research excellence. The program encourages a culturally diverse workforce.

Financial data The annual stipend ranges from $44,020 to $47,570, depending on the date of completion of the Ph.D. A comprehensive benefits package includes incoming relocation reimbursement.

Duration 2 years; may be renewed for 1 additional year.

Special features Core competencies of LANL include theory, modeling, and high-performance computing; complex experimentation and measurement; nuclear and advanced materials; nuclear weapons science and technology; analysis and assessment; earth and environmental systems; bioscience and biotechnology; and nuclear science, plasmas, and beams.

Number awarded A limited number of appointments is provided.

Deadline Applications may be submitted at any time; appointments are made 4 times yearly.

[1116]
LASPACE RESEARCH ENHANCEMENT AWARDS PROGRAM

Louisiana Space Consortium
c/o Louisiana State University
Physics and Astronomy
277 Nicholson Hall
Baton Rouge, LA 70803-4001
(504) 388-8697   Fax: (504) 388-1222
E-mail: wefel@phepds.dnet.nasa.gov

Purpose To provide financial assistance for programs in Louisiana that will help build a research infrastructure in aerospace related fields.

Eligibility This program is open to students and faculty at Louisiana Space Consortium (LaSPACE) member schools: Dillard University, Grambling State University L.S.U. Agricultural Center, Louisiana State University and A&M College, Louisiana Tech University, Loyola University, McNeese State University, Northwestern State University of Louisiana, Northeast Louisiana University, Southern University and A&M College, Southern University at New Orleans, Southern University at Shreveport, Tulane University, University of New Orleans, University of Southwestern Louisiana, Xavier University of Louisiana. Applicants may be proposing projects in 1 of 4 subprogram areas: 1) research facilitation/initiation awards, to provide faculty with research support for aerospace-related activities, such as travel to a field center, support to develop a new research project among scientists at several LaSPACE campuses, or faculty summer support; 2) training grants, to encourage students by supporting their work in aerospace-related laboratories and research institutes; 3) visiting researchers, to bring outside researchers to LaSPACE campuses for extended visits; and 4) travel awards, to provide funds for faculty and students to make short trips to present results at scientific meetings or to visit research facilities. LaSPACE is a component of the U.S. National Aeronautics and Space Administration (NASA) Space Grant program, which encourages participation by women, minorities, and persons with disabilities.

Financial data The amounts of the awards depends on the availability of funds and the nature of the proposal.

Duration Depends on the nature of the proposal.

Special features Funding for this program is provided by NASA.

Number awarded Varies; a total of $60,000 is available for this program each year.

[1117]
LEADERSHIP ENRICHMENT FUND GRANTS

Ms. Foundation for Women
120 Wall Street, 33rd Floor
New York, NY 10005
(212) 742-2300

Purpose To fund local and national women's organizations that are grassroots, activist, and creative.

Eligibility Eligible to apply are women's organizations that previously received Ms. Foundation General Grants. These grants are especially targeted to programs that break down barriers faced by women of color, low-income women, older women, lesbians, and women with disabilities.

Financial data Up to $2,000. The funds are to be used to pay for technical assistance to the organization.

Duration Up to 1 year.

Number awarded Varies each year.

Deadline Applications may be submitted at any time.

[1118]
LEO MODEL FELLOWSHIP

Brookings Institution
1775 Massachusetts Avenue, N.W.
Washington, D.C. 20036-2188
(202) 797-6127   Fax: (202) 797-6181
E-mail: brookinfo@brook.edu

Purpose To support predoctoral policy-oriented research in economics at the Brookings Institution.

Eligibility Candidates cannot apply; they must be nominated by their graduate department. Nominees must meet the following criteria: doctoral students who have completed their preliminary examinations, have selected a dissertation topic that directly relates to public policy issues and the major research issues of the Institution (economic growth, international economics, human resources, industrial organization, regulation, public finance, monetary economics, and economic stabilization), and be able to benefit from access to the resources and personnel at the Institution. The Institution particularly encourages the nomination of women and minority candidates.

Financial data Fellows receive a stipend of $15,000 for the academic year, supplementary assistance for copying and other essential research requirements up to $600, reimbursement for research-related travel up to $500, health insurance, and access to computer/library facilities.

Duration 1 year.

Special features Fellows participate in seminars, conferences, and meetings at the institution. Outstanding dissertations may be published by the institution.

Limitations Fellows are expected to pursue their research at the Brookings Institution.

Number awarded 1 each year.

Deadline Nominations must be submitted by mid-December and applications by mid-February.

[1119]
LESBIAN AND GAY COMMUNITY FUND

California Community Foundation
606 South Olive Street, Suite 2400
Los Angeles, CA 90014-1526
(213) 413-4042   Fax: (213) 383-2046

Purpose To provide support to organizations in the Los Angeles area that serve the gay and lesbian community.

Eligibility Grants are available to nonprofit organizations in Los Angeles County serving the gay and lesbian community. Preference is given to programs serving youth, the elderly, persons of color, and women.

Financial data The amount granted varies, depending upon the specific needs and nature of the request. A total of $43,000 is currently available for this program, but the foundation has pledged to triple the amount.

Duration 1 year; renewable.

Special features This program began in 1995 with a grant from the National Gay and Lesbian Community Funding Partnership, a collaborative initiative designed to put lesbian and gay issues on the agenda of the philanthropic community.

[1120]
LESBIAN NATURAL RESOURCES APPRENTICESHIP PROGRAM

Lesbian Natural Resources
P.O. Box 8742
Minneapolis, MN 55408-0742

Purpose To pay lesbians living on the land to act as mentors to other lesbians interested in developing rural skills and self-sufficiency.

Eligibility This program is open to experienced land lesbians who are willing to take a lesbian apprentice and teach her rural self-sufficiency and/or rural trade skills.

Financial data The sponsor receives $1,500 to cover the costs of food, housing, tools, transportation related to work, learning materials, and other community expenses incurred related to the apprenticeship. Priority is given to apprenticeships that share skills with lesbians underrepresented in the lesbian community, especially elderly lesbians and those of color, with disabilities, and from poverty.

Duration At least 3 months.

Number awarded Varies each year.

[1121]
LIBRARY SERVICES TO INDIAN TRIBES AND HAWAIIAN NATIVES PROGRAM BASIC GRANTS

Department of Education
Attn: Office of Educational Research and Improvement
Discretionary Library Programs Division
555 New Jersey Avenue, N.W., Room 300
Washington, DC 20208-5571
(202) 219-1670

Purpose To provide assistance to eligible Indian tribes, Alaska native villages, and Hawaiian native organizations to establish or improve public library service.

Eligibility Grant applications may be submitted by federally recognized Indian tribes, by Alaska native villages or regional or village corporations as defined in or established under the Alaska Native Claims Settlement Act, and by Hawaiian native organizations that are recognized by the governor of Hawaii as serving or representing Hawaiian natives.

Financial data Grants average $4,524.

Duration 1 year.

Number awarded Approximately 210 each year.

Deadline July of each year.

[1122]
LIPMAN RESEARCH AWARD

Geological Society of America
Attn: Research Grants Administrator
3300 Penrose Place
P.O. Box 9140
Boulder, CO 80301-9140
(303) 447-2020, ext. 137   Fax: (303) 447-1133
E-mail: jforstro@geosociety.org

Purpose To provide partial support for geological research by graduate students.

Eligibility This program is open to graduate students in geology at the master's or doctoral level. Both members and non-members of the society are eligible. Special consideration may be given to students with the best application in the field of volcanology and petrology in the western United States and Alaska. Applications from women, minorities, and persons with disabilities are strongly encouraged.

Financial data Grants range up to $2,500; the average grant recently was $1,604.

Duration 1 year.

Number awarded 1 or more each year.

Deadline February of each year.

[1123]
LITERATURE PROGRAM OF THE NEW YORK STATE COUNCIL ON THE ARTS

New York State Council on the Arts
915 Broadway
New York, NY 10010
(212) 387-7000   (800) GET-ARTS

Purpose To support organizations in New York that promote the creation, publication, and distribution of important writing and that encourage the appreciation of literature by the general public.

Eligibility Funding is available for the following purposes: general operating support (for literary organizations that have been funded by this program for the past 3 years and that have a paid professional staff), technical assistance and professional consultants, book publication, literary magazine publication, public programs, translation, writers-in-residence programs, and signing for the deaf. All applicants are strongly urged to provide opportunities for writers historically excluded from the mainstream: minorities, women, and persons with disabilities.

Financial data Grants vary, but include up to $2,500 (for signing for the deaf) or $2,500 per month (for writers-in-residence programs).

Duration Up to 3 years.

Number awarded Varies each year.

Deadline February of each year.

[1124]
LOAN REPAYMENT PROGRAM FOR CLINICAL RESEARCHERS FROM DISADVANTAGED BACKGROUNDS

National Institutes of Health
Attn: Loan Repayment and Scholarship Programs
Federal Building, Room 604
7550 Wisconsin Avenue MSC 9015
Bethesda, MD 20892-9015
(800) 528-7689   Fax: (301) 402-8098
TTY: (888) 352-3001   E-mail: mh18h@nih.gov

Purpose To recruit health professionals from disadvantaged backgrounds who are willing to exchange loan repayment benefits for service at the National Institutes of Health (NIH).

Eligibility Eligible are U.S. citizens, nationals, and permanent residents who hold an M.D., D.O., D.D.S., D.M.D., A.D.N./B.S.N., or equivalent degree, are willing to become NIH employees, and have qualifying educational debt in excess of 20 percent of their annual salary. Applicants must meet a definition of disadvantaged, that they either 1) come from an environment that inhibited (but did not prevent) them from obtaining the knowledge, skills, and ability required to enroll in a medical or graduate institution; or 2) come from a family with an annual income below $10,200 for a 1-person family, ranging to below $26,700 for families of 6 or more. First priority is given to applicants who have demonstrated good academic performance, state a career goal of pursuing biomedical/biobehavioral research, and have characteristics which support the likelihood they will complete their service obligations. Second priority is given to individuals who are underrepresented in biomedical/biobehavioral research, including women, individuals from minority groups, and persons with disabilities.

Financial data The program pays a maximum of $20,000 per year directly to the recipients' lenders for qualifying educational debt. Actual loan repayments are based on funding availability and the proportion of the participants' qualifying debt relative to their NIH salary.

Duration At least 2 years.

Special features During their service tenure at the NIH facilities in Bethesda, Maryland, recipients engage in research on biomedical and behavioral studies of etiology, epidemiology, prevention (and prevention strategies), diagnosis, or treatment of diseases, disorders, or conditions, including but not limited to clinical trials.

Number awarded Varies each year.

[1125]
LOCAL ARTS AGENCIES PROJECT GRANTS

North Carolina Arts Council
Attn: Department of Cultural Resources
Cambridge House
407 North Person Street
Raleigh, NC 27601-2807
(919) 733-7897, ext. 17

Purpose To provide financial assistance to local arts agencies in North Carolina.

Eligibility This program is open to North Carolina local arts agencies, which may be a nonprofit organization or local government agency involved in activities in 2 or more art forms and that exists to provide programs, planning, financial support, or services for arts organizations, individual artists, and the community as a whole. Project grants are intended to assist local arts agen-

cies in complying with the Americans with Disabilities Act, increase access to information technology, or provide arts programs to 1) people in rural areas or inner cities; 2) people with disabilities, older adults, and people in hospitals and assisted living care facilities; and 3) African American, Asian American, Latino, and Native American populations. Selection is based on artistic and program merit of the proposed project, appropriate payment to artists, selection process in hiring artists, involvement of racially and culturally diverse participants as appropriate to the project, management and financial accountability of the applicant organization, responsiveness to community and constituency needs, evidence of commitment from proposed collaborators, and economic need.

Financial data Grants up to $5,000 are provided to individual local arts agencies and up to $15,000 for a regional consortium

Duration 1 year.

Number awarded Varies each year.

Deadline February of each year.

[1126]
LONG-TERM MINORITY INVESTIGATOR RESEARCH SUPPLEMENT

National Institutes of Health
Attn: Office of Extramural Research
Extramural Outreach and Information Resources Office
6701 Rockledge Drive, Room 6207
MSC 7910
Bethesda, MD 20892-7910
(301) 435-0714   Fax: (301) 480-8443
E-mail: asknih@odrockm1.od.nih.gov

Purpose To supply long-term research support to underrepresented minority faculty members who are seeking to enhance their research skills in areas of interest to the National Institutes of Health (NIH).

Eligibility The minority investigator may be affiliated with either the applicant institution or any other institution. The investigator must have a doctoral degree, be beyond the level of a research trainee, and be a member of the faculty with at least 1 year of postdoctoral experience. Individuals who have received previous funding from a component institute or center as an independent principal investigator on regular research grants, program project grants, or research career program awards are not eligible. The institutes consider African Americans, Hispanic Americans, Native Americans, Alaskan Natives, and Pacific Islanders as underrepresented minority investigators.

Financial data The minority faculty supplemental award is for a maximum of $50,000 in direct costs per year. A maximum of $40,000 may be requested for salary and fringe benefits; additional funds totaling $10,000 may be requested for supplies and travel. Equipment may not be purchased except in unusual circumstances.

Duration At least 30 percent time during each 12-month period, for up to 4 years.

Number awarded Varies each year.

[1127]
LOS ALAMOS NATIONAL LABORATORY POSTDOCTORAL FELLOWS PROGRAM

Los Alamos National Laboratory
Attn: Human Resource Division
Special Programs and Services
Mail Stop P290
P.O. Box 1663
Los Alamos, NM 87545
(505) 667-0872   Fax: (505) 665-4562
E-mail: postdoc-info@lanl.gov

Purpose To provide an opportunity for postdoctoral scholars to pursue independent research at the Los Alamos National Laboratory (LANL).

Eligibility This program is open to scholars who received a doctoral degree within the past 3 years in astrophysics, bioscience, biotechnology, chemistry, computer science, earth sciences, engineering, environmental sciences, materials science, mathematics, metallurgy, optics, physics, or space sciences. Applicants must be proposing to pursue independent research on a topic of their own choice at the Laboratory. The program encourages a culturally diverse workforce.

Financial data The annual stipend ranges from $44,020 to $47,570, depending on the date of completion of the Ph.D. A comprehensive benefits package includes incoming relocation reimbursement.

Duration 2 years; may be renewed for 1 additional year.

Number awarded A limited number of appointments is provided.

[1128]
MANAGEMENT AND TECHNICAL ASSISTANCE 7(J) PROGRAM GRANTS

Small Business Administration
Attn: Office of Minority Enterprise Development
409 Third Street, S.W.
Washington, DC 20416
(800) 8-ASK-SBA   (202) 205-6420
Fax: (202) 205-7064   TDD: (202) 205-7333

Purpose To provide grants to individuals and organizations that propose to assist economically and disadvantaged business persons achieve competitive viability in the marketplace.

Eligibility This program is open to individuals and organizations (nonprofit and for-profit), including small business concerns, minority educational institutions, and other educational institutions, that wish to operate management and technical assistance programs for businesses that qualify under Section 7(j) of the Small Business Act. To be eligible for 7(j) program participation, a small business concern must be at least 51 percent owned, controlled, and operated by 1 or more socially or economically disadvantaged persons or by an economically disadvantaged Indian tribe, including an Alaska native corporation or an economically disadvantaged Hawaiian organization. "Socially disadvantaged individuals" are those who have been subjected to racial or ethnic prejudice or cultural bias because of their identification as members of certain groups. "Economically disadvantaged individuals" are those socially disadvantaged individuals whose ability to compete in the free enterprise system has been impaired due to diminished capital and credit opportunities. Black Americans, Native Americans, Hispanic Americans, Asian Pacific Americans, and Subcontinent Asian Americans have been officially designated socially disadvantaged. Members of other groups

must show proof of social disadvantage. Economic disadvantage must be established for all applicants. The Small Business Administration (SBA) determines eligibility on a case-by-case basis. Grantees under this program provide assistance to firms eligible for 7(j) assistance in 4 areas: accounting, marketing, proposal/bid preparation, and industry-specific technical assistance.

Financial data The amount of the awards depends on the nature of the proposal and the availability of funds.

Duration 1 year or longer.

Number awarded Varies each year.

Deadline Applications may be submitted at any time, but awards are made only after SBA has considered proposals made in response to program announcements.

[1129]
MANHATTAN COMMUNITY ARTS FUND REGRANT PROGRAM

Manhattan Community Arts Fund
c/o Lower Manhattan Cultural Council
1 World Trade Center, Suite 1717
New York, NY 10048-0202
(212) 269-0320

Purpose To develop arts projects of interest and relevance to the local community and to increase support to community-based arts organizations in Manhattan, New York by providing them with government funds.

Eligibility Individual artists are not eligible to apply. Nonprofit organizations are eligible if they are Manhattan-based; propose an arts project to be located in Manhattan (in dance, music, theatre, opera, visual arts, design, media, photography, literature, or inter-arts); and have a demonstrated record of achievement in the arts. Selection is based on community benefit to be derived from the proposed project, artistic merit, purpose of the project, lack of existing services for the public in the program area, and demonstrated need for support.

Financial data The total amount of funds available is $49,000. The maximum amount of a single grant is $3,000, even though the project itself may exceed that amount. However, the average award recently was $871.

Duration Up to 8 months. Projects may not begin prior to April and must end by December.

Special features The Manhattan Community Arts Fund is a consortium composed of the Association of Hispanic Arts, the Chinese American Arts Council, and the Lower Manhattan Cultural Council.

Limitations Organizations that have received funding from the New York State Council on the Arts or the National Endowment for the Arts the year prior to application or are currently receiving institutional support or program support from the New York City Department of Cultural Affairs are ineligible to apply. In addition, schools, libraries, branches of city or state government, and individuals are not eligible for funding. Finally, funding is not available for general operating support; projects that serve only an organization's membership and/or exclude public participation; proposals from educational, health or welfare institutions unless they can demonstrate a history of providing arts services; or deficit budgets, capital improvements, equipment, fundraising events, or administrative expenses not related to the specific project for which funds are requested. Late applications are not accepted under any circumstances.

Number awarded Varies; generally, 60 or more each year.

Deadline January of each year.

[1130]
MANHATTAN THEATRE CLUB PLAYWRITING FELLOWSHIPS

Manhattan Theatre Club
Attn: Literary Assistant
453 West 16th Street
New York, NY 10011
(212) 645-5590, ext. 161   Fax: (212) 691-9106

Purpose To provide funding to emerging playwrights (at the beginning of their careers) who are interested in developing their craft, identifying their career goals, and learning about the tools needed to realize those goals.

Eligibility To be eligible, writers must be 35 years of age or under. They must have completed their formal education (either undergraduate or graduate) by the time the fellowship begins. Applicants must submit 1 writing sample (full-length dramatic works are preferred), a resume, a statement of purpose, and 1 letter of recommendation. Preference is given to New York-based writers from diverse cultural and minority backgrounds who can demonstrate financial need. Selection is based on quality of work, financial need (must be documented), dedication to theater, and potential for growth as artists and professionals as the result of this program.

Financial data Each fellowship consists of: a commission of $5,000 for a new play, a production assistantship with a stipend of $1,500, and $3,500 for living and other expenses.

Duration 1 year, beginning in September.

Special features Fellows observe rehearsals for plays presented at the club each season, receive professional guidance from the club's script department staff, and are given access to the resources available through the club and its network of theater professionals.

Number awarded 2 each year.

Deadline February of each year.

[1131]
MANUFACTURING OPPORTUNITIES THROUGH SCIENCE AND TECHNOLOGY

Oak Ridge Institute for Science and Education
Attn: Science/Engineering Education Division
P.O. Box 117
Oak Ridge, TN 37831-0117
(423) 576-6226   (800) 569-7749
Fax: (423) 576-3643   E-mail: mftopp@orau.gov

Purpose To provide high school staff members with an opportunity to expand content knowledge and career awareness, enhance teaching skills, and develop teaching materials in the area of manufacturing technology.

Eligibility This program is open to high school teachers, guidance counselors, curriculum directors, and administrators involved in mathematics, science, technology, and vocational education activities. All programs operated by the Science/Engineering Education Division (SEED) of Oak Ridge Institute for Science and Education (ORISE) seek to broaden the participation of minorities, women, and persons with disabilities in science and engineering careers.

Financial data Participants receive a biweekly stipend, travel, lodging, and tuition reimbursement for graduate credit.

Duration 4 weeks during the summer; some academic-year activities are also available.

Special features Activities take place at ORISE and the Centers for Manufacturing Technology, both in Tennessee. This pro-

gram is funded by the U.S. Department of Energy but operated and administered by ORISE/SEED.

Number awarded 30 each year.

Deadline March of each year.

[1132]
MANY VOICES MULTICULTURAL COLLABORATION GRANTS

Playwrights' Center
2301 Franklin Avenue East
Minneapolis, MN 55406-1099
(612) 332-7481

Purpose To provide funding for culturally diverse teams to collaborate on the creation and development of new theater pieces.

Eligibility This program is open to teams of Minnesota or national artists of differing cultural backgrounds led by a Minnesota playwright of color. Applicants must be proposing to create new theater pieces for performance in the Twin Cities.

Financial data Grants up to $1,500 are available.

Duration Grants are awarded annually.

Number awarded 4 each year.

[1133]
MANY VOICES RESIDENCIES

Playwrights' Center
2301 Franklin Avenue East
Minneapolis, MN 55406-1099
(612) 332-7481

Purpose To provide funding for Minneosta playwrights of color so they can spend a year in residence at the Playwrights' Center in Minneapolis.

Eligibility This program is open to Minnesota playwrights of color interested in playwriting and creating theater in a supportive artists' community.

Financial data The program provides stipends of $1,000; mentorships; classes; script workshops and readings with professional actors, directors, and dramaturgs; and a membership in the Playwrights' Center.

Duration 1 year.

Limitations Fellows must be in residence at the Playwrights' Center for the duration of the program.

Number awarded 8 each year.

[1134]
MARION WRIGHT EDELMAN SCHOLARSHIP

Lisle Fellowship
433 West Sterns Road
Temperance, MI 48182
(313) 847-7126   (800) 477-1538
Fax: (419) 530-1245   E-mail: mkinney@utnet.utoledo.edu

Purpose To enable a person of racial or cultural diversity to participate in a Lisle Fellowship International Program.

Eligibility People of racial or cultural diversity may apply for this scholarship if they desire to participate in a seminar sponsored by the Lisle Fellowship, Inc. Selection is based on the candidate's history of commitment to the creation of a just and peaceful world, ability to follow through with projects that work with and toward world community, and concrete evidence that others will benefit from the experience of the scholarship winner.

Financial data The scholarship is $1,000, to be used for partial payment of tuition for a seminar.

Duration 2 to 6 weeks.

Special features Seminars are held in the United States and around the world. Recent programs included Life in the Ahupua'a: Exploring the Practices and Values of Ancient Hawaiian Society; Into Africa: Models of Development for Uganda and the World; Bali: Tools for Community Harmony; Japan: Fostering Community in an Age of Individualism; Costa Rica: Ecotourism and People Centered Development for a Sustainable Future; and Native Americans and Oklahoma: Exploring the Circles of Life.

Number awarded 1 each year.

Deadline March of each year.

[1135]
MARTIN LUTHER KING, JR., CESAR CHAVEZ, ROSA PARKS VISITING PROFESSORS PROGRAM

Office of the Vice Provost for Academic and Multicultural Affairs
University of Michigan
503 Thompson Street
3084 Fleming Administration Building
Ann Arbor, MI 48109-1340
(313) 764-3982   Fax: (313) 764-4546

Purpose To provide funds for minority scholars to visit and lecture/teach at the University of Michigan.

Eligibility Outstanding minority (African American, Asian American, Latino/a (Hispanic) American, and Native American) post-doctorates or scholars/practitioners are eligible to be nominated by department chairs or deans at the University. Nominations that include collaborations with other universities are of high priority.

Financial data Visiting Professors receive round-trip transportation and an appropriate honorarium.

Duration Visits range from 1 to 5 days.

Special features This program was established in 1986.

Limitations Visiting Professors are expected to lecture or teach at the university, offer at least 1 event open to the general public, and meet with minority campus/community groups including local K-12 schools.

Number awarded Varies each year.

Deadline January for the summer term; March for the fall term; August for the winter term; and November for the spring term.

[1136]
MARY LITTY MEMORIAL FELLOWSHIP

Epilepsy Foundation of America
Attn: Department of Research and Professional Education
4351 Garden City Drive
Landover, MD 20785
(301) 459-3700   (800) EFA-1000
Fax: (301) 577-2684   TDD: (800) 332-2070
E-mail: postmaster@efa.org

Purpose To provide financial assistance for vocational rehabilitation students to work on an epilepsy study project.

Eligibility Vocational rehabilitation or rehabilitation counseling students may apply for these fellowships to carry out a project at a U.S. institution where there are ongoing programs of study or training in epilepsy. A preceptor must accept responsibility for supervision of the student and the project. Applications from women and minorities are especially encouraged.

Financial data Stipends are $2,000.

Duration 3 months.

Special features These fellowships are also known as the Behavior Sciences Student Fellowships.

Number awarded Varies each year.

Deadline February of each year.

[1137]
MARY'S PENCE GRANT PROGRAM

Mary's Pence
P.O. Box 29078
Chicago, IL 60629-9078
(708) 499-3771

Purpose To provide funding for projects in the Americas that empower Catholic women.

Eligibility Eligible to apply are Catholic women in the United States who are working toward societal or ecclesial structures that improve or empower the lives of women. Eligible programs include 1) direct service with women that in some way brings self-empowerment and change to their lives; 2) promotion of ecclesial and societal change of oppressive structures; 3) theological studies that promote pastoral alternatives or influence change; or 4) studies in other disciplines that directly impact the lives of women. Special priority is given to requests that focus on the needs of economically disadvantaged women as well as ministries created and managed by women of color. Grants are restricted to projects, programs, or courses of study for ministry in the Americas.

Financial data Grants are provided up to $3,000 for direct service and up to $1,500 for study.

Duration These are 1-time grants; the funds are distributed in October.

Special features The program (which began in 1987) is named for the 3 Marys in scripture.

Number awarded Varies, depending on the availability of funds.

Deadline June of each year.

[1138]
MASGC UNDERGRADUATE RESEARCH OPPORTUNITY PROGRAM

Massachusetts Space Grant Consortium
c/o MIT
Building 33, Room 208
77 Massachusetts Avenue
Cambridge, MA 02139
(617) 258-5546   Fax: (617) 253-0823
E-mail: halaris@mit.edu

Purpose To provide funding for undergraduate research in space science or engineering by students in Massachusetts.

Eligibility This program is open to undergraduate students at institutions that are members of the Massachusetts Space Grant Consortium (MASGC). Applicants must be proposing to conduct research projects related to space science and/or space engineering with faculty or at nearby laboratories. U.S. citizenship is required. MASGC is a component of the U.S. National Aeronautics and Space Administration (NASA) Space Grant program, which encourages participation by women, minorities, and persons with disabilities.

Financial data The amount of the award depends on the availability of funding and the nature of the proposal.

Duration 1 semester.

Special features This program is funded by NASA.
Number awarded Varies each year.
Deadline December of each year.

[1139]
MATHEMATICAL SCIENCES POSTDOCTORAL RESEARCH FELLOWSHIPS

National Science Foundation
Attn: Directorate for Mathematical and Physical Sciences
Division of Mathematical Sciences
4201 Wilson Boulevard, Room 1025
Arlington, VA 22230
(703) 306-1870   Fax: (703) 306-0555
E-mail: msprf@nsf.gov

Purpose To provide financial assistance for postdoctoral research training in mathematics.

Eligibility To become fellows, candidates must 1) be U.S. citizens, nationals, or permanent residents; 2) have earned a Ph.D. in a mathematical science or have had research training and experience equivalent to that represented by such a Ph.D.; 3) have held the Ph.D. for no more than 5 years; and 4) not have previously held any other postdoctoral fellowship from the National Science Foundation (NSF). They must be proposing to conduct a program of postdoctoral research training at an appropriate nonprofit U.S. institution, including government laboratories, national laboratories, and privately sponsored nonprofit institutes, as well as institutions of higher education. A senior scientist at the institution must indicate availability for consultation and agreement to work with the fellow. Women, underrepresented minorities, and persons with disabilities are strongly encouraged to apply.

Financial data The stipend is $2,750 per full-time month or $1,375 per half-time month, for a total of $66,000. In addition, the fellow receives an allowance of $4,500 to defray research costs (travel, publication costs, and other research-related items) and the institution receives an allowance of $4,500 as partial reimbursement for expenses incurred in support of the research (space, supplies, equipment, secretarial assistance, etc.).

Duration The program provides support for 2 9-month academic years and 6 summer months, for a total of 24 months of support. Fellows have 2 options for the academic years' stipend: full-time support for any 18 academic-year months in a 3-year period, in intervals not shorter than 3 consecutive months, or a combination of full-time and half-time support over a period of 3 academic years, usually 1 academic year full-time and 2 academic years half-time. Not more than 2 summer months' support may be received in any calendar year.

Special features Under certain circumstances, it may be desirable for portions of the work to be done at foreign institutions. Approval to do so must be obtained in advance from both the sponsoring senior scientist and the NSF.

Number awarded 30 to 40 each year.

Deadline October of each year.

[1140]
MATHEMATICAL SCIENCES UNIVERSITY–INDUSTRY POSTDOCTORAL RESEARCH FELLOWSHIPS

National Science Foundation
Attn: Directorate for Mathematical and Physical Sciences
Division of Mathematical Sciences
4201 Wilson Boulevard, Room 1025
Arlington, VA 22230
(703) 306-1870   Fax: (703) 306-0555
E-mail: uicrp@nsf.gov

Purpose To provide financial assistance to recent doctoral recipients in mathematics who wish to broaden their knowledge, experience, and research perspectives by exposure to industrial environments.

Eligibility Candidates to become fellows must 1) be U.S. citizens, nationals, or permanent residents; 2) be eligible to be appointed as a research associate or assistant professor at the institution submitting the proposal; 3) have earned a Ph.D. in a mathematical science or have had research training and experience equivalent to that represented by such a Ph.D.; 4) have held the Ph.D. for no more than 7 years; 5) not hold a tenured position at any academic institution; and 6) not have previously held any other postdoctoral fellowship from the National Science Foundation (NSF). Applications must be submitted by a university principal investigator who will serve as scientific mentor to a fellow with an industrial sponsor. The proposal may either identify the prospective postdoctoral fellow or present a plan for recruiting the fellows. Principal investigators are encouraged to submit proposals that include women, underrepresented minorities, and persons with disabilities as postdoctoral fellows, or whose recruitment plans include strategies for identifying highly qualified postdoctoral fellows from those groups. Selection is based on the quality of the proposed research to be conducted at both the academic and industrial sites, the qualifications of and commitment by both the faculty mentor and the industrial sponsor, the appropriateness of the academic/industrial interaction, and the impact of the proposed training on the professional development of the postdoctoral fellow.

Financial data The total award is $111,000, of which $71,000 is provided by the National Science Foundation and $40,000 by the industrial sponsor. The award includes a stipend allowance for the fellow of $80,000 ($40,000 per year) plus a fringe benefit allowance of $16,000 ($8,000 per year), an allowance of $4,500 for the sponsoring institution in lieu of indirect costs, a research allowance of $4,500 for the fellow to be used for travel, publication costs, and other research-related expenses, and an allowance of $6,000 for the faculty mentor for research expenses related to the industrial partnership.

Duration 2 years.

Number awarded Varies each year.

Deadline November of each year.

[1141]
MATHEMATICAL SCIENCES UNIVERSITY–INDUSTRY SENIOR RESEARCH FELLOWSHIPS

National Science Foundation
Attn: Directorate for Mathematical and Physical Sciences
Division of Mathematical Sciences
4201 Wilson Boulevard, Room 1025
Arlington, VA 22230
(703) 306-1870   Fax: (703) 306-0555
E-mail: uicrp@nsf.gov

Purpose To provide financial assistance to senior scholars in mathematics who wish to broaden their knowledge, experience, and research perspectives by exposure to industrial environments, and to industrial researchers who wish to experience and participate in the full range of university research environments.

Eligibility This program is open to faculty members and industrial scientists who are U.S. citizens, nationals, or permanent residents and who have earned a Ph.D. in a mathematical science or have had research training and experience equivalent to that represented by such a Ph.D. Faculty members must be proposing to conduct research in an industrial setting, and industrial scientists must be proposing to conduct research in a university environment. All applicants must make a commitment to return to the home institution for a minimum of 1 year following the fellowship tenure. Applications are especially encouraged from women, underrepresented minorities, and persons with disabilities.

Financial data The program provides a salary equivalent to the fellow's regular 6-month full-time salary (to a maximum of $50,000, or $60,000 including fringe benefits), a research allowance of $10,000, and an institutional allowance, in lieu of indirect costs, of $10,000.

Duration Normally 12 months.

Special features Faculty fellows are usually expected to participate in this program during a sabbatical leave.

Number awarded Varies each year.

Deadline November of each year.

[1142]
MCCORMICK TRIBUNE MINORITY FELLOWSHIP IN URBAN JOURNALISM AT THE CHICAGO REPORTER

Chicago Reporter
Attn: Editor
332 South Michigan Avenue, Suite 500
Chicago, IL 60604
(312) 427-4830   Fax: (312) 427-6130

Purpose To provide opportunities for minority journalists to work on projects at the *Chicago Reporter.*

Eligibility Experienced minority journalists with a baccalaureate degree and 2 to 3 years of print reporting experience are eligible to apply for this fellowship. Interested candidates must submit a resume and 5 clips.

Financial data The position pays a competitive salary and benefits.

Duration 1 year.

Special features Fellows work at the *Chicago Reporter,* a monthly newspaper known for its coverage of the role minorities play in newspapers. Recipients may take courses at Northwestern University's Medill School of Journalism.

Number awarded 1 each year.

[1143]
MCKNIGHT JUNIOR FACULTY DEVELOPMENT FELLOWSHIP PROGRAM

Florida Education Fund
201 East Kennedy Boulevard, Suite 1525
Tampa, FL 33602
(813) 272-2772   Fax: (813) 272-2784

Purpose To provide minority and women junior faculty at colleges and universities in Florida with an opportunity to earn a graduate degree or conduct independent research.

Eligibility This program is open to minorities (especially African Americans) and women in underrepresented fields. Applicants should have between 2 and 6 years of service as faculty members in a Florida public or private university, 4-year college, or community college and should not have obtained tenure (the non-tenure requirement does not apply to community college faculty). They must desire to spend a year away from their teaching duties in order to pursue graduate course work, work on a doctoral dissertation, or conduct independent research. Faculty in all fields of study are eligible, but applications are especially encouraged in agriculture, biology, business administration, chemistry, computer science, engineering, marine biology, mathematics, physics, and psychology.

Financial data The recipient's institution receives $15,000 to cover the necessary teaching replacement cost. The recipient continues to receive full pay and benefits.

Duration 1 year.

Number awarded 20 each year.

Deadline January of each year.

[1144]
MEDICARE AND MEDICAID SMALL BUSINESS INNOVATION RESEARCH GRANTS

Department of Health and Human Services
Attn: Health Care Financing Administration
Office of Research and Demonstrations
Office of Operations Support
Division of Program Support
C-3-11-17
7500 Security Boulevard
Baltimore, MD 21244-1850
(410) 786-6644   E-mail: CHackerman@hcfa.gov

Purpose To support small businesses that have the technological experience to contribute to the research and development mission of the Health Care Financing Administration, which operates the Medicare and Medicaid programs.

Eligibility For the purposes of this program, a "small business" is defined as any organization that is independently owned and operated for profit, not dominant in the field in which it is operating, and meets the size standard of 500 employees or less. The primary employment of the principal investigator must be with the firm at the time of award and during the conduct of the proposed project. Preference is given to women-owned small business concerns and to socially and economically disadvantaged small business concerns. Women-owned small business concerns are those which are at least 51 percent owned by a woman or women who also control and operate it. Socially and economically disadvantaged small business concerns are at least 51 percent owned by an Indian tribe, a native Hawaiian organization, or 1 or more socially and economically disadvantaged individuals (Black Americans, Hispanic Americans, Native Americans, Asian-Pacific Americans, or subcontinent Asian Americans). The project must be performed in the United States. Previous research topics have included high quality and effective care, management of ambulatory services, beneficiary information and assistance, and program efficiencies and improvement.

Financial data Support is offered in 2 phases. In phase 1, awards range up to $50,000 (for both direct and indirect costs); in phase 2, awards are generally approximately $100,000 (including both direct and indirect costs).

Duration Phase 1: up to 12 months; phase 2: up to 2 years.

Number awarded In a recent year, funding provided for 10 to 15 awards in both phases.

Deadline March of odd-numbered years for Phase 1 applications; March of even-numbered years for Phase 2 applications.

[1145]
MENTORED CLINICAL SCIENTIST DEVELOPMENT AWARDS

National Institutes of Health
Attn: Office of Extramural Research
Extramural Outreach and Information Resources Office
6701 Rockledge Drive, Room 6207
MSC 7910
Bethesda, MD 20892-7910
(301) 435-0714   Fax: (301) 480-8443
E-mail: asknih@odrockm1.od.nih.gov

Purpose To provide financial support for specialized study to clinically trained professionals who are committed to a career in research and have the potential to develop into independent investigators.

Eligibility This program is open to candidates who 1) have a clinical degree or its equivalent; 2) can identify a mentor with extensive research experience; and 3) are willing to spend a minimum of 75 percent of full-time professional effort conducting research and research career development activities for the period of the award. Applications may be submitted on behalf of candidates by domestic, non-federal organizations, public or private, such as medical, dental, or nursing schools or other institutions of higher education. Minorities and women are particularly encouraged to apply. Candidates must be U.S. citizens or permanent residents.

Financial data This program provides salary and fringe benefits for the candidate only; each component establishes its own salary limits on career awards. Each appointee is allowed up to $20,000 per year for tuition, fees, and books related to career development; research expenses, such as supplies, equipment, and technical personnel; travel to research meetings or training; and statistical services including personnel and computer time. Indirect costs are reimbursed at 8 percent of modified total direct costs, or at the actual indirect cost rate, whichever is less.

Duration 3 to 5 years.

Special features Awards under this progam are available from 15 agencies of the National Institutes of Health (NIH): the National Institute on Aging, the National Institute on Alcohol Abuse and Alcoholism, the National Institute of Allergy and Infectious Diseases, the National Institute of Arthritis and Musculoskeletal and Skin Diseases, the National Cancer Institute, the National Institute of Child Health and Human Development, the National Institute on Deafness and Other Communication Disorders, the National Institute of Dental Research, the National Institute of Diabetes and Digestive and Kidney Diseases, the National Institute on Drug Abuse, the National Institute of Environmental Health Sciences, the National Eye Institute, the National Heart, Lung, and Blood

Institute, the National Institute of Mental Health, and the National Institute of Neurological Disorders and Stroke. The names and addresses of staff people at each agency are available from the address above. The NIH designates this program as the K08 Awards.

Number awarded Varies each year.

Deadline January, May, or September of each year.

[1146]
MENTORED CLINICAL SCIENTIST DEVELOPMENT PROGRAM AWARDS

National Institutes of Health
Attn: Office of Extramural Research
Extramural Outreach and Information Resources Office
6701 Rockledge Drive, Room 6207
MSC 7910
Bethesda, MD 20892-7910
(301) 435-0714   Fax: (301) 480-8443
E-mail: asknih@odrockm1.od.nih.gov

Purpose To provide financial support to clinicians who wish to become independent researchers.

Eligibility Individuals participating in this program must be recruited and selected by departments or divisions from domestic, non-federal organizations such as medical, dental, or nursing schools, or from comparable institutions of higher education that have strong, well-established research and training programs. Candidates must be U.S. citizens or permanent residents who have a clinical degree or its equivalent, have initiated internship and residency training (or its equivalent), and are provided with a mentor who has extensive research experience and a record of providing the type of training required. The candidate must also be willing to spend a minimum of 75 percent of full-time professional effort conducting research, career development, and/or research related activities. Minorities and women are particularly encouraged to apply.

Financial data This progam provides salary and fringe benefits for the candidate only; each component establishes its own salary limits on career awards. Each appointee is allowed up to $20,000 per year for tuition, fees, and books related to career development; research expenses, such as supplies, equipment, and technical personnel; travel to research meetings or training; and statistical services including personnel and computer time. Indirect costs are reimbursed at 8 percent of modified total direct costs, or at the actual indirect cost rate, whichever is less.

Duration 3 to 5 years.

Special features Awards under this program are available from 2 agencies of the National Institutes of Health (NIH): the National Institute on Aging and the National Institute of Dental Research. The names and addresses of staff people at each agency are available from the address above. The NIH designates this program as the K12 Awards.

Number awarded Varies each year.

Deadline January, May, or September of each year.

[1147]
MENTORED RESEARCH SCIENTIST DEVELOPMENT AWARDS

National Institutes of Health
Attn: Office of Extramural Research
Extramural Outreach and Information Resources Office
6701 Rockledge Drive, Room 6207
MSC 7910
Bethesda, MD 20892-7910
(301) 435-0714   Fax: (301) 480-8443
E-mail: asknih@odrockm1.od.nih.gov

Purpose To provide financial support to research scientists who need an additional period of sponsored research experience as a way to gain expertise in a research area new to the candidate or in an area that would demonstrably enhance the candidate's scientific career.

Eligibility This program is open to candidates who have a research or a health-professional doctorate or its equivalent and who have demonstrated the capacity or potential for highly productive independent research in the period after the doctorate. The candidate must identify a mentor with extensive research experience, and must be willing to spend a minimum of 75 percent of full-time professional effort conducting research and research career development activities for the period of the award. Applications may be submitted on behalf of candidates by domestic, non-federal organizations, public or private, such as medical, dental, or nursing schools or other institutions of higher education. Minorities and women are particularly encouraged to apply. Candidates must be U.S. citizens or permanent residents.

Financial data This program provides salary and fringe benefits for the candidate only; each component establishes its own salary limits on career awards. Each appointee is allowed up to $20,000 per year for tuition, fees, and books related to career development; research expenses, such as supplies, equipment, and technical personnel; travel to research meetings or training; and statistical services including personnel and computer time. Indirect costs are reimbursed at 8 percent of modified total direct costs, or at the actual indirect cost rate, whichever is less.

Duration 3 to 5 years.

Special features Awards under this program are available from 10 agencies of the National Institutes of Health (NIH): the National Institute on Aging, the National Institute on Alcohol Abuse and Alcoholism, the National Institute of Arthritis and Musculoskeletal and Skin Diseases, the National Cancer Institute, the National Institute of Environmental Health Sciences, the National Institute of Mental Health, the National Institute of Neurological Disorders and Stroke, the National Institute of Nursing Research, the National Center for Human Genome Research, and the National Center for Research Resources. The names and addresses of staff people at each agency are available from the address above. The NIH designates this program as the K01 Awards.

Number awarded Varies each year.

Deadline January, May, or September of each year.

[1148]
MERRITT-PUTNAM INTERNATIONAL VISITING PROFESSORSHIP

Epilepsy Foundation of America
Attn: Department of Research and Professional Education
4351 Garden City Drive
Landover, MD 20785
(301) 459-3700   (800) EFA-1000
Fax: (301) 577-2684   TDD: (800) 332-2070
E-mail: postmaster@efa.org

Purpose To promote the exchange of medical and scientific information and expertise on epilepsy between the United States and other countries.

Eligibility Interested countries or institutions within the country are asked to define their specific needs and interests and submit them to the Epilepsy Foundation of America. The foundation selects 1 nominee to be a visiting professor. At least 1 party in the exchange must be from the United States. Applications from minorities and women are particularly encouraged.

Financial data The foundation covers the visiting professor's transportation and incidental expenses. The host institution assumes the responsibility for paying the living and subsistence costs of the visiting professor.

Duration 3 to 6 weeks.

Special features The program is supported in part by Parke-Davis, Division of Warner-Lambert Company.

Number awarded Approximately 10 each year.

Deadline Applications may be submitted at any time.

[1149]
MERRITT-PUTNAM RESEARCH/CLINICAL TRAINING FELLOWSHIPS

Epilepsy Foundation of America
Attn: Department of Research and Professional Education
4351 Garden City Drive
Landover, MD 20785
(301) 459-3700   (800) EFA-1000
Fax: (301) 577-2684   TDD: (800) 332-2070
E-mail: postmaster@efa.org

Purpose To offer qualified individuals the opportunity to develop expertise in clinical epilepsy and epilepsy research through training experience and involvement in an epilepsy research project.

Eligibility Applications are open to individuals who have received their M.D. degree and completed residency training. The proposed research may be either basic or clinical, but there must be an equal emphasis on clinical training and clinical epileptology. Special attention is given to applications submitted by women and minorities.

Financial data The stipend is $40,000.

Duration 1 year.

Limitations The fellowship must be carried out at a facility where there is an ongoing epilepsy research program. Research must be conducted in the United States.

Number awarded Varies each year.

Deadline August of each year.

[1150]
MFT MINORITY SUPERVISION STIPEND PROGRAM

American Association for Marriage and Family Therapy
Attn: Research and Education Foundation
1133 15th Street, N.W., Suite 300
Washington, DC 20005-2710
(202) 452-0109   Fax: (202) 223-2329

Purpose To support the recruitment, training, and retention of minorities as supervisors in the field of marriage and family therapy.

Eligibility Eligible to apply are minority individuals (including African Americans, Hispanics, Native Americans, Asian Americans, and Pacific Islanders) engaged in a program to become marriage and family therapy supervisors approved by the American Association for Marriage and Family Therapy (AAMFT). Applicants must be U.S. or Canadian citizens or permanent visa residents and hold a graduate degree in marriage and family therapy or a related discipline. Information on financial need is not required but is a significant factor considered in the review process.

Financial data Awardees receive up to $1,000 and waiver of the processing fee.

Duration 1 year.

Special features This program began in 1990.

Number awarded 1 each year.

Deadline April of each year.

[1151]
MICHELE CLARK FELLOWSHIP

Radio and Television News Directors Foundation
1000 Connecticut Avenue, N.W, Suite 615
Washington, DC 20036
(202) 659-6510   Fax: (202) 223-4007
E-mail: gwenl@rtndf.org

Purpose To provide financial assistance for an educational purpose to minority journalists employed in electronic news.

Eligibility Applicants must be minority journalists employed in electronic news who have 1 to 5 years of full-time experience.

Financial data The award is $1,000, plus an expense-paid trip to the International Convention of the Radio-Television News Directors Association held that year.

Duration The award is presented annually.

Special features The grant, named for CBS journalist Michele Clark, may be used in any way to improve the craft and enhance the excellence of the recipient's news operation.

Limitations Applications must include samples of the journalist's work done as the member of a news staff, with a script and tape (audio or video) up to 15 minutes.

Number awarded 1 each year.

Deadline February of each year.

[1152]
MICHIGAN SPACE GRANT CONSORTIUM FELLOWSHIPS

Michigan Space Grant Consortium
c/o University of Michigan
College of Engineering
2106 Space Research Building
2455 Hayward Avenue
Ann Arbor, MI 48109-2143
(313) 747-3430   Fax: (313) 763-0437
E-mail: rmjohnson@engin.umich.edu

Purpose To provide financial assistance to students in Michigan who wish to conduct space-related research.

Eligibility This program is open to undergraduate and graduate students at affiliates of the Michigan Space Grant Consortium (Eastern Michigan University, Grand Valley State University, Hope College, Michigan State University, Michigan Technological University, Oakland University, Saginaw Valley State University, University of Michigan, Wayne State University, and Western Michigan University). Applicants must be proposing to conduct research in aerospace, space science, mathematics, and other science of engineering related fields, as well as educational research topics in mathematics, science, or technology. U.S. citizenship is required. The Michigan Space Grant Consortium is a component of the U.S. National Aeronautics and Space Administration (NASA) Space Grant program, which encourages participation by women, minorities, and persons with disabilities.

Financial data The amounts of the awards depend on the availability of funds and the nature of the proposal.

Special features This program is funded by NASA.

Number awarded Varies each year.

[1153]
MICHIGAN SPACE GRANT CONSORTIUM HIGHER EDUCATION INCENTIVE PROGRAM

Michigan Space Grant Consortium
c/o University of Michigan
College of Engineering
2106 Space Research Building
2455 Hayward Avenue
Ann Arbor, MI 48109-2143
(313) 747-3430   Fax: (313) 763-0437
E-mail: rmjohnson@engin.umich.edu

Purpose To provide supplementary grants for innovative higher education interdisciplinary course development, conference, and workshop support for students or teachers in space-related programs in Michigan.

Eligibility This program is open to faculty and researchers at affiliates of the Michigan Space Grant Consortium (Eastern Michigan University, Grand Valley State University, Hope College, Michigan State University, Michigan Technological University, Oakland University, Saginaw Valley State University, University of Michigan, Wayne State University, and Western Michigan University). The program encourages the development and the dissemination of software, problem sets, videos, courses in mathematics, science, technology, and space or aerospace related topics. The Michigan Space Grant Consortium is a component of the U.S. National Aeronautics and Space Administration (NASA) Space Grant program, which encourages participation by women, minorities, and persons with disabilities.

Financial data The amounts of the awards depend on the availability of funds and the nature of the proposal.

Special features This program is funded by NASA.
Number awarded Varies; a total of $30,000 is available through this program each year.

[1154]
MICHIGAN SPACE GRANT CONSORTIUM K-12 EDUCATOR INCENTIVE PROGRAM GRANTS

Michigan Space Grant Consortium
c/o University of Michigan
College of Engineering
2106 Space Research Building
2455 Hayward Avenue
Ann Arbor, MI 48109-2143
(313) 747-3430   Fax: (313) 763-0437
E-mail: rmjohnson@engin.umich.edu

Purpose To provide funding to teachers in Michigan for travel in support of space-related activities.
Eligibility Teachers in Michigan may apply for these grants to attend conferences on space-related mathematics, science, and technology, or to engage in educational enhancement activities in mathematics, science, and technology. The Michigan Space Grant Consortium is a component of the U.S. National Aeronautics and Space Administration (NASA) Space Grant program, which encourages participation by women, minorities, and persons with disabilities.
Financial data The amounts of the awards depend on the availability of funds and the nature of the proposal.
Special features This program is funded by NASA.
Number awarded Varies; a total of $5,000 is available through this program each year.

[1155]
MICHIGAN SPACE GRANT CONSORTIUM PRE-COLLEGE OUTREACH PROGRAM GRANTS

Michigan Space Grant Consortium
c/o University of Michigan
College of Engineering
2106 Space Research Building
2455 Hayward Avenue
Ann Arbor, MI 48109-2143
(313) 747-3430   Fax: (313) 763-0437
E-mail: rmjohnson@engin.umich.edu

Purpose To provide funding for programs and projects that encourage and enrich the study of mathematics, science, or technology in general space science, aerospace, and aeronautics for K-12 students.
Eligibility Teachers in Michigan may apply for these grants to fund programs or projects for the development, implementation, and/or testing of innovative enhanced curricula or curriculum resources that meet state or national standards for science education. The Michigan Space Grant Consortium is a component of the U.S. National Aeronautics and Space Administration (NASA) Space Grant program, which encourages participation by women, minorities, and persons with disabilities.
Financial data The amounts of the awards depend on the availability of funds and the nature of the proposal.
Special features This program is funded by NASA.
Number awarded Varies; a total of $35,000 is available through this program each year.

[1156]
MICHIGAN WOMEN'S FOUNDATION GRANTS

Michigan Women's Foundation
Attn: Grants Distribution Committee
119 Pere Marquette, Suite 2A
Lansing, MI 48912-1213
(517) 374-7270

Purpose To provide funding to organizations in Michigan that are committed to advancing the cause of women.
Eligibility Nonprofit organizations in Michigan are eligible to apply for these grants if they are involved in projects designed to improve women's role and status in society. In particular, the foundation is looking for proposals that serve low-income and/or minority women and girls, are women-run, have little or no access to other funding resources, and are serving within the state of Michigan. Funding is provided in the categories of advocacy, domestic violence/sexual assault, employment/economic development, leadership development, and management assistance.
Financial data Grants range from $1,000 to $10,000.
Duration Up to 1 year; nonrenewable.
Limitations Funding is not available to support scholarships for individuals, for conference attendance by nonprofit organization members, to organizations with budgets over $500,000, for campaigns to elect candidates to office, to government agencies, for endowments, or to organizations headquartered outside of Michigan.
Number awarded Varies; generally, 10 each year.
Deadline February of each year.

[1157]
MIGRANT AND SEASONAL FARMWORKERS EMPLOYMENT AND TRAINING PROGRAM

Department of Labor
Attn: Employment and Training Administration
Office of Special Targeted Programs
200 Constitution Avenue, N.W., Room N-4641
Washington, DC 20210
(202) 219-5500   Fax: (202) 219-6338

Purpose To provide the employment, training, and supportive services needed by migrant and seasonal farmworkers and their families to find economically viable alternatives to seasonal agricultural work for those who remain in the agricultural labor market.
Eligibility Eligible to submit program proposals are: public agencies and private nonprofit organizations authorized by charter or articles of incorporation to provide employment and training. Persons eligible to participate in the programs must have been employed as seasonal farmworkers or migrant farmworkers during any consecutive 12-month period within the 24-month period preceding their application for enrollment, must have received at least half their total earned income or been employed at least half of their total work time in farmwork, and must have been identified as a member of a family which receives public assistance or whose annual family income does not exceed the higher of either the poverty level or 70 percent of the lower living standard income level. Dependents of such individuals are also eligible.
Financial data Grants range from $120,000 to more than $4 million. Funds may be used to provide classroom and occupational training, on-the-job training, work experience, job development, job placement, relocation assistance, health services, day care, legal aid, housing, and other supportive services.

Duration 1 to 2 years; may be renewed 1 additional year.

Limitations Unsolicited proposals are not considered for funding. Announcements of Solicitations for Grant Applications (SGAs) are published in the *Federal Register*.

Number awarded Approximately 50,000 persons are served by the program each year.

Deadline The deadline is established annually and is reported in the *Federal Register*.

[1158]
MIGRANT HEALTH SERVICES GRANTS

Health Resources and Services Administration
Attn: Bureau of Primary Health Care
Division of Community and Migrant Health
4350 East-West Highway
Rockville, MD 20857
(301) 594-4303

Purpose To provide comprehensive primary care services to address the unique health care needs of migrant and seasonal farmworkers and their families.

Eligibility Any public or nonprofit private entity is eligible to apply. Grants may be used for planning and developing migrant health centers, operating migrant health centers, operating migrant health entities, planning and developing migrant health programs, operating migrant health programs, or technical assistance.

Financial data Annual appropriations for this program are approximately $56 million. The amount of individual grants depends on the amount necessary for direct project costs plus an additional amount for indirect costs.

Special features Services include primary care, preventive care, outreach, transportation, dental, and environmental and are provided by physicians, nurse practitioners, and physician assistants.

Number awarded More than 100 community based migrant health centers and programs receive grants and provide services at 364 sites in 35 states and Puerto Rico.

Deadline Deadline dates vary; check the *Federal Register* for the current schedule.

[1159]
MINNESOTA HISTORICAL SOCIETY RESEARCH GRANTS

Minnesota Historical Society
Attn: Research Department
345 Kellogg Boulevard West
St. Paul, MN 55102-1906
(612) 297-4464

Purpose To support original research and interpretive writing on the history of Minnesota.

Eligibility Eligible to apply for this support are academicians, independent scholars, and professional or nonprofessional writers. Preference is given to projects that will produce article- or book-length manuscripts that could be considered for publication in *Minnesota History* (the Society's quarterly) or by the Minnesota Historical Society Press. Especially encouraged are projects that add a multicultural dimension to the area's history and that cover subjects not now well represented in the published record (e.g., agriculture, workers and work, historic preservation, sports). Projects that focus on the history of women continue to be of particular interest. Grant applications should include: a description of the

project (up to 4 pages), budget, timetable, prior work on this topic, and a statement of the applicant's qualifications.

Financial data Up to $1,500 for research to result in an annotated article and up to $5,000 for a book-length study. Funds may not be used to purchase computers or other equipment.

Duration 1 year.

Special features Before submitting their application, applicants are encouraged to consult with the society's research department.

Limitations Grants are not awarded to support work on a dissertation or thesis.

Number awarded Varies each year.

Deadline February, September, or December of each year.

[1160]
MINORITIES IN MEDICAL ONCOLOGY PROGRAM GRANTS

National Institutes of Health
Attn: National Cancer Institute
Division of Extramural Activities
Executive Plaza North, Room 620
6130 Executive Boulevard MSC 7405
Bethesda, MD 20892-7405
(301) 496-7344   Fax: (301) 402-4551
E-mail: ss165i@nih.gov

Purpose To provide funding to underrepresented minority physicians for research in medical oncology.

Eligibility This program is open to individuals with an M.D. or D.O. degree who are members of an ethnic or racial group that is underrepresented in biomedical and behavioral research, i.e., African Americans, Latinos (Mexican Americans, Cubans, Puerto Ricans, and Central Americans), Native Americans, and non-Asian Pacific Islanders. Applicants must be proposing a program of intensive, supervised research in medical oncology, including subjects such as the development and application of biomarkers for assessing cancer risk in minority populations, cancer treatment or prevention clinical trials targeting minority populations, or psychosocial aspects of cancer prevention and control in defined populations. Candidates must be nominated by domestic nonprofit and for-profit, public and private organizations, such as universities, colleges, hospitals, laboratories, units of state or local government, and eligible agencies of the federal government. Women and persons with disabilities are encouraged to apply as principal investigators.

Financial data The amount of the award depends on the candidate's training, experience, and accomplishments, to a maximum of $50,000 per year for salary and a total of $15,000 per year for supplies, travel, equipment, fringe benefits, and other allowable expenses.

Duration Up to 4 years.

Special features This program is sponsored by the Comprehensive Minority Biomedical Program within the National Cancer Institute.

Number awarded Varies each year, depending on the availability of funds.

Deadline January, May, and September of each year.

[1161]
MINORITY ACCESS TO RESEARCH CAREERS (MARC) SENIOR FACULTY FELLOWSHIPS

National Institutes of Health
Attn: National Institute of General Medical Sciences
Director, Minority Access to Research Careers Program
Natcher Building, Suite 2AS43C
45 Center Drive MSC 6200
Bethesda, MD 20892-6200
(301) 594-3900   Fax: (301) 480-2753
E-mail: at21z@nih.gov

Purpose   To provide opportunities for advanced research training for selected faculty members at 4-year academic institutions serving predominantly minority students.

Eligibility   Colleges, universities, and health professional schools with substantial enrollments of underrepresented minorities may nominate for these fellowships full-time, permanent faculty members in biomedically-related science or mathematics who have held that position for at least 3 years and who received the Ph.D. or equivalent at least 7 years before the date of the application. Underrepresented minorities include African Americans, Hispanic Americans, Native Americans, and Pacific Islanders. The candidate must demonstrate a commitment to research and teaching in a minority institution and be a U.S. citizen, national, or permanent resident. Fellows must pursue a program of postdoctoral studies and research training in the biomedical sciences, and are expected to return to their home institutions after completion of their fellowships.

Financial data   Annual stipends up to $32,300 are provided. An institutional allowance of up to $3,000 may also be requested to help defray costs directly related to the candidate's training.

Duration   1 to 2 years.

Special features   The National Institutes of Health (NIH) designates these fellowships as part of the F34 program.

Limitations   Fellows may train at any nonprofit private or public institution in the United States with suitable facilities.

Number awarded   Varies each year.

Deadline   April of December of each year.

[1162]
MINORITY ACCESS TO RESEARCH CAREERS (MARC) VISITING SCIENTIST FELLOWSHIPS

National Institutes of Health
Attn: National Institute of General Medical Sciences
Director, Minority Access to Research Careers Program
Natcher Building, Suite 2AS43C
45 Center Drive MSC 6200
Bethesda, MD 20892-6200
(301) 594-3900   Fax: (301) 480-2753
E-mail: at21z@nih.gov

Purpose   To strengthen research and training in the biomedical sciences for the benefit of the students and faculty at minority institutions by drawing upon the special talents of scientists from other, primarily majority, institutions.

Eligibility   Individuals nominated as visiting scientists in this program should be recognized scientists-scholars in such biomedical science fields as cellular and molecular biology, genetics, pharmacology, toxicology, biomedical engineering, physiological sciences, and/or clinical research areas. They must be sponsored by a university, 4-year college, or health professional school with a substantial minority student enrollment.

Financial data   Stipends are determined on an individual basis according to the nominee's current salary. Any expected concurrent sabbatical or any other salary support for the proposed period in residence is taken into account. A travel allowance equivalent to round-trip coach airfare between the visiting scientist's home institution and the sponsoring institution is provided. The sponsoring institution may receive up to $3,000 as an allowance for costs of supplies, supporting services, and demonstration costs related to activities proposed for the visiting scientist.

Duration   Up to 1 year.

Special features   The National Institutes of Health designates this program as the F36 Awards.

Number awarded   Varies each year.

Deadline   April or December of each year.

[1163]
MINORITY CLINICAL ASSOCIATE PHYSICIAN PROGRAM

National Institutes of Health
Attn: National Center for Research Resources
General Clinical Research Centers Program
One Rockledge Center, Room 6030
6705 Rockledge Drive MSC 7965
Bethesda, MD 20892-7965
(301) 435-0790   Fax: (301) 480-3660
E-mail: hg15k@nih.gov

Purpose   To provide an opportunity for young underrepresented minority physicians and dentists to develop into independent clinical investigators in a General Clinical Research Center (GCRC) environment.

Eligibility   Applications for this program are submitted as supplemental grant applications from a funded GCRC grant supported by the National Center for Research Resources. Candidates may be either a physician or dentist who has completed residency; completion of subspecialty training for 2 years is preferred but not required. U.S. citizenship or permanent residency is required. Candidates may not be the principal investigator on an independent peer-reviewed, grant-supported research project/grant prior to or concurrently with funding of the application. The candidate should work closely with an appropriate mentor who is a clinical investigator supported by peer-reviewed grants. The mentor must work with the candidate in selecting appropriate course work to complement laboratory and patient-oriented clinical research.

Financial data   Salary support up to $42,500 with associated fringe benefits is provided. Funds for supplies, domestic travel to scientific meetings, and other expenses may be requested to a total of $5,000 per year. Applicable indirect costs are provided.

Duration   Candidates are supported for 1 year of course work and research activities.

Special features   Approximately 73 research institutions hold GCRC grants; for a list, contact the address above.

Number awarded   5 to 6 each year.

Deadline   September of each year.

[1164]
MINORITY DISSERTATION RESEARCH GRANTS IN AGING

National Institutes of Health
Attn: National Institute on Aging
Office of Extramural Affairs
Gateway Building, Room 2C-218
7201 Wisconsin Avenue MSC 9205
Bethesda, MD 20892-9205
(301) 496-9322 Fax: (301) 402-2945
E-mail: rb42h@nih.gov

Purpose To encourage minority doctoral students to conduct research on aging.

Eligibility This program is open to minority graduate students enrolled in an accredited doctoral program in the biomedical, social, or behavioral sciences. The National Institute on Aging (NIA) defines underrepresented minorities as African Americans, Hispanics, Native Americans, Alaskan Natives, and Pacific Islanders. Applicants must have completed all requirements for the doctoral degree except the dissertation and have had their dissertation proposal approved. Their research must deal with some aspect of aging. Grants are administered by the applicant's institution, which must be within the United States, although the performance site may be foreign or domestic.

Financial data Direct costs may not exceed $30,000 in total or $25,000 in any 1 year. The institution may receive up to 8 percent of direct costs as indirect costs in any 1 year. Salary for the investigator, included in direct costs, may not exceed $12,000 for 12 months.

Duration Up to 2 years.

Special features The National Institutes of Health (NIH) administers this program as part of its small grants program, designated as R03.

Number awarded From 10 to 12 each year.

Deadline January of each year.

[1165]
MINORITY DISSERTATION RESEARCH GRANTS IN MENTAL HEALTH

National Institutes of Health
Attn: National Institute of Mental Health
Division of Epidemiology and Services Research
Parklawn Building, Room 10C-06
5600 Fishers Lane
Rockville, MD 20857
(301) 443-3364 Fax: (301) 443-4045
E-mail: ah21k.nih.gov

Purpose To provide financial support to minority doctoral candidates planning to pursue research careers in any area relevant to mental health and/or mental disorders.

Eligibility Applicants must be African Americans, Hispanic Americans, American Indians, Alaskan Natives, or Asian and Pacific Islanders enrolled in an accredited doctoral degree program in the behavioral, biomedical, or social sciences. Their dissertation topic, which must have been approved by their academic committee, must focus on a significant problem in mental health/mental disorders.

Financial data The maximum award is $25,000 per year; that includes investigator's salary (up to $14,000 per 12 months of full-time effort) and direct research project expenses, such as data processing, payments to subjects, supplies, and printing and binding of the dissertation. Travel funds up to $750 may be requested to attend 1 scientific meeting. No funding is provided for tuition, alterations/renovations, contracting costs, or space rental.

Duration 1 year; may be renewed 1 additional year.

Special features Inquiries on programs of prevention, clinical services and service systems research, epidemiology, psychopathology, violence and traumatic stress, assessment, classification, law and mental health, and health and behavior, with special attention to minority and other populations, should be directed to the Division of Epidemiology and Services Research, (301) 443-3373; questions involving behavioral and social sciences, cognitive sciences, and neurosciences, including neuroimaging, neurophysiology, neuropsychopharmacology, and cellular and molecular neurobiology, with special attention to minority and other special populations, should be addressed to the Division of Neuroscience and Behavioral Science, (301) 443-4347; for further information on psychopathology, classification, assessment, etiology, genetics, clinical course, outcome, and treatment of mental disorders with emphasis on schizophrenic disorders, affective and anxiety disorders, and mental disorders of children and adolescents, the elderly, minorities, and other special populations, contact the Division of Clinical and Treatment Research, (301) 443-3264; for research that focuses on mental health issues for persons with AIDS, persons who are HIV positive, or persons who are at risk of contracting the virus, contact the Office on Aids, (301) 443-6100.

Number awarded Up to 25 each year.

Deadline April, August, or December of each year.

[1166]
MINORITY FELLOWSHIP PROGRAM IN GENERAL SOCIOLOGY

American Sociological Association
Attn: Minority Affairs Program
1722 N Street, N.W.
Washington, DC 20036-2981
(202) 833-3410, ext. 322/321 Fax: (202) 785-0146
TDD: (202) 872-0486 E-mail: minority.affairs@asanet.org

Purpose To provide financial assistance to minority doctoral candidates in sociology.

Eligibility These fellowships are available to American citizens or permanent residents who are Blacks/African Americans, Latinos (e.g., Chicanos, Puerto Ricans, Cubans), American Indians or Alaskan Natives, Asian Americans (e.g., Southeast Asian, Japanese, Chinese, Korean), or Pacific Islanders (e.g., Filipino, Samoan, Hawaiian, Guamanian). The competition is open to students beginning or continuing study in sociology at the doctoral level. Selection is based on commitment to research, academic achievement, scholarship, writing ability, research potential, and financial need.

Financial data The stipend is $10,008 per year; candidates who have completed all course work and who have been advanced to degree candidacy may receive a dissertation grant of up to $5,000.

Duration 1 year; renewable for 5 additional years.

Number awarded 1 or 2 each year.

Deadline December of each year.

[1167]
MINORITY FELLOWSHIP PROGRAM IN MENTAL HEALTH

American Sociological Association
Attn: Minority Affairs Program
1722 N Street, N.W.
Washington, DC 20036-2981
(202) 833-3410, ext. 322/321   Fax: (202) 785-0146
TDD: (202) 872-0486   E-mail: minority.affairs@asanet.org

Purpose To provide financial assistance to minority doctoral candidates in sociology who are interested in conducting research on mental health issues relating to minority groups.

Eligibility These fellowships are available to American citizens or permanent residents who are Blacks/African Americans, Latinos (e.g., Chicanos, Puerto Ricans, Cubans), American Indians or Alaskan Natives, Asian Americans (e.g., Southeast Asian, Japanese, Chinese, Korean), or Pacific Islanders (e.g., Filipino, Samoan, Hawaiian, Guamanian). The competition is open to students beginning or continuing study in sociology at the doctoral level. Selection is based on commitment to research in mental health and mental illness, scholarship, writing ability, research potential, and financial need.

Financial data The stipend is $10,008 per year; candidates who have completed all course work and who have been advanced to degree candidacy may receive a dissertation grant of up to $5,000.

Duration 1 year; renewable for 5 additional years.

Special features This program is funded by a grant from the U.S. National Institute of Mental Health, a component of the National Institutes of Health.

Limitations Upon completion of their studies, recipients are expected to engage in mental health and mental illness research and/or teaching for a period equal to the period of support beyond 12 months.

Number awarded 10 each year.

Deadline December of each year.

[1168]
MINORITY FELLOWSHIPS IN TRANSPLANTATION

National Institutes of Health
Attn: National Institute of Allergy and Infectious Diseases
Division of Allergy, Immunology and Transplantation
Solar Building, Room 4A-14
6003 Executive Boulevard MSC 7640
Bethesda, MD 20892-7640
(301) 496-5598   Fax: (301) 402-2571
E-mail: sr8j@nih.gov

Purpose To provide funding to racial/ethnic minority individuals, women, and persons with disabilities who are interested in research training on the etiology, pathogenesis, diagnosis, and/or treatment and prevention of transplant rejection.

Eligibility This program is open to racial/ethnic minority individuals, women, and persons with disabilities who are U.S. citizens, nationals, or permanent residents and who hold a Ph.D., M.D., D.O., D.D.S., O.D., D.P.M., Sc.D., Eng.D., or equivalent degree. Applicants must be proposing a program of research training on the rejection of transplanted organs or tissues.

Financial data The amounts of the awards depend on the availability of funds.

Duration Individuals may receive up to 3 years of aggregate support at the postdoctoral level, including any combination of support from institutional training grants and individual fellowship awards.

Special features The program is jointly sponsored by the National Institute of Allergy and Infectious Diseases (NIAID) within the National Institutes of Health (NIH) and the American Society of Transplant Physicians (ASTP). The NIH administers this program as 1 of its National Research Service Awards for Individual Postdoctoral Fellows (F32 Awards).

Number awarded 2 each year.

Deadline April, August, and December of each year.

[1169]
MINORITY INSTITUTION GRANTS FOR PERSONNEL TRAINING FOR THE EDUCATION OF INDIVIDUALS WITH DISABILITIES

Department of Education
Attn: Office of Special Education and Rehabilitative Services
Division of Personnel Preparation
Switzer Building, Room 3513
600 Independence Avenue, S.W.
Washington, DC 20202-2651
(202) 205-8687   Fax: (202) 205-9070
E-mail: Victoria_Mims@ed.gov

Purpose To provide grants to minority educational institutions to increase the quantity and improve the quality of personnel available to serve infants, toddlers, children, and youth with disabilities.

Eligibility Applications are accepted from Historically Black Colleges and Universities and other institutions of higher education whose minority student enrollment is at least 25 percent. Awards must be designed to increase the capabilities of the institution to provide training of personnel to serve young people with disabilities.

Financial data Grants range from $190,000 to $200,000 and average $195,000.

Duration Up to 4 years.

Number awarded Up to 18 each year.

Deadline December of each year.

[1170]
MINORITY JOURNALISM EDUCATORS FELLOWSHIP

American Press Institute
Attn: Fellowship Program Coordinator
11690 Sunrise Valley Drive
Reston, VA 22091-1498
(703) 620-3611   Fax: (703) 620-5814
E-mail: vcju07a@prodigy.com

Purpose To provide financial support to minority college-level journalism educators who are interested in attending American Press Institute (API) seminars.

Eligibility Nominations are invited from all schools and departments of journalism and mass communications. Eligible to be nominated are college-level minority journalism educators who wish to attend API seminars. Each API seminar is designed for a particular specialty or problem.

Financial data The fellowship covers tuition, room, and meals.

Special features The program includes a 10-day seminar followed by a 1-month internship in a newspaper or broadcast newsroom.

Number awarded 1 each year.

Deadline Nominations must be submitted by November of each year.

[1171]
MINORITY MEDICAL FACULTY DEVELOPMENT PROGRAM

Robert Wood Johnson Foundation
College Road East and U.S. Route 1
P.O. Box 2316
Princeton, NJ 08543-2316
(609) 452-8701

Purpose To provide financial support and continued training for minority physicians who are interested in academic careers in biomedical research, clinical investigation, or health services research.

Eligibility African American, Mexican American, Native American, and mainland Puerto Rican physicians residing in the United States are eligible to apply if they have completed or will have completed formal clinical training. Applicants must be U.S. citizens with outstanding academic backgrounds and a commitment to academic medicine. Preference is given to physicians who have recently completed their clinical training and are seeking advanced research training.

Financial data The stipend is $50,000 per year, plus a $25,000 annual research allowance.

Duration 2 years; renewable for an additional 2 years.

Special features Fellows study and conduct research under the supervision of a senior faculty member located at any academic center in the United States that is noted for the training of young faculty and that offers research opportunities of interest to the fellow.

Limitations An interview is required.

Number awarded Up to 12 each year.

Deadline March of each year.

[1172]
MINORITY POSTDOCTORAL RESEARCH FELLOWSHIPS

National Science Foundation
Attn: Directorate for Biological Sciences
Division of Biological Infrastructure
4201 Wilson Boulevard, Room 615
Arlington, VA 22230
(703) 306-1469   E-mail: ckimsey@nsf.gov

Purpose To provide financial assistance for postdoctoral research training to minority scientists in the biological, social, economic, and behavioral sciences.

Eligibility Eligible to apply are underrepresented minorities (African Americans, Hispanics, Native Pacific Islanders, and Native Americans) who are American citizens or permanent residents and will complete their doctorate within a year or have completed it within the previous 4 years but have not completed more than 2 years of postdoctoral support. They must be proposing research training that falls within the program areas of the National Science Foundation (NSF) Directorate for Biological Sciences or the Directorate for Social, Behavioral, and Economic Sciences to be conducted at any appropriate nonprofit U.S. or foreign institution (government laboratory, institution of higher education, national laboratory, or public or private research institute), but not at the same institution where the doctorate was obtained.

Financial data The program provides a stipend of $28,000 per year, an institutional allowance of $4,000 for partial reimbursement of indirect research costs (space, equipment, general purpose supplies, and fringe benefits), and a special allowance of $8,000 for direct research costs (scientific supplies, research-related travel, publication expenses, and other research-related costs).

Duration 2 years; applicants who propose to spend their 2-year tenure at a foreign institution may apply for a third year of support at an appropriate U.S. institution.

Special features Information on the programs from the Directorate for Social, Behavioral, and Economic Sciences is available at (703) 306-1733.

Number awarded Approximately 12 each year.

Deadline November of each year.

[1173]
MINORITY RESEARCH INFRASTRUCTURE SUPPORT PROGRAM GRANTS

National Institutes of Health
Attn: National Institute of Mental Health
Office for Special Populations
Parklawn Building, Room 17C-14
5600 Fishers Lane MSC 8030
Rockville, MD 20857-8030
(301) 443-3641   Fax: (301) 443-8552
E-mail: rc30x@nih.gov

Purpose To provide financial assistance to minority institutions to develop and/or expand existing capacities for conducting behavioral and neuroscience research in all fields related to mental health.

Eligibility Eligible to apply for these grants are domestic public and private universities, 4-year colleges, nonprofit and for-profit domestic organizations such as hospitals, laboratories, units of public agencies of state or local governments, eligible agencies of the federal government, or other institutions conducting research in mental health related fields. Applicants must also be 1) an academic institution with at least 55 percent minority student enrollment; 2) an institution with more than 30 percent minority student enrollment in each of the past 3 years that can provide evidence of efforts to recruit members of ethnic or racial groups into scientific careers; or 3) an Indian tribe applying in conjunction with 1 or more institutions of higher learning that offer undergraduate and graduate degrees in mental health-related fields. Support may be requested for, but is not limited to, partial salary support for persons engaged in the project; research training for junior investigators; scientific and statistical consultation, including expenses incurred by a scientific advisory committee; biostatistical and data management services; research technicians and assistants; research instruments; small, project-specific equipment; pilot and feasibility studies; research subject costs; and data acquisition costs. Proposals may involve either institutional research development support (as for laboratory development, support of collaborative linkages with senior scientists in other institutions, and provision of resources for data management and statistical analyses) or individual investigator research projects for 2 or more faculty members. Racial/ethnic minority individuals, women, and persons with disabilities are particularly encouraged to apply as principal investigators.

Financial data Grants average $300,000 per year plus negotiated indirect costs. The infrastructure core component averages

$50,000 per year in direct costs; individual investigator projects average $50,000 per year in direct costs.

Duration First-time awards are limited to 3 years; the core infrastructure component is renewable for intervals of up to 5 years; individual investigators are limited to a total of 6 years of support.

Deadline May of each year.

[1174]
MINORITY SCHOLAR AWARDS

American Association for Cancer Research
Public Ledger Building
150 South Independence Mall West, Suite 816
Philadelphia, PA 19106-3483
(215) 440-9300   Fax: (215) 440-9313
E-mail: jahmaacr@aol.com

Purpose To provide financial assistance to minority scientists who wish to attend meetings of the American Association for Cancer Research (AACR).

Eligibility Eligible to apply for this assistance are medical and graduate students, physicians in training, and postdoctoral fellows who are members of minority groups underrepresented in cancer research. They must be planning to attend the annual meeting or a special conference of the AACR. Eligible minorities are African Americans, Hispanic Americans, Native Americans, Native Pacific Islanders, and Alaskan Americans.

Financial data Awards are available for payment of costs of accommodations and travel.

Special features Funding for this program is provided by the Comprehensive Minority Biomedical Program of the National Cancer Institute.

Number awarded Varies each year.

[1175]
MINORITY SCHOLAR-IN-RESIDENCE PROGRAM

Consortium for a Strong Minority Presence at Liberal Arts
    Colleges
c/o Vice-President for Human Resources and Special
    Projects
Grinnell College
P.O. Box 805
Grinnell, IA 50112-0810
(515) 269-3000

Purpose To make available the facilities of liberal arts colleges to minority scholars (African American, Asian American, Hispanic American, and Native American) who are working on their dissertation or who have recently received their doctoral/advanced degree.

Eligibility There are 2 types of fellowships supported under this program: dissertation fellowships, open to minority scholars who have completed all the requirements for the doctorate (in the liberal arts or engineering) except the dissertation; and postdoctoral fellowships, open to minority scholars who have received the Ph.D. or M.F.A. degree within the past 5 years. None of the applicants should have more than 5 years of teaching or relevant work experience.

Financial data Dissertation fellows receive a stipend equivalent to the average salary paid to instructors at the participating colleges; postdoctoral fellows receive a stipend equivalent to the average salary paid to beginning assistant professors there.

Start-up funds (between $3,000 and $5,000) are also available to finance the fellow's proposed research.

Duration 1 year.

Special features The following schools are participating in the program: Bates, Bowdoin, Bryn Mawr, Colby, Colorado, Davidson, Franklin and Marshall, Grinnell, Haverford, Macalester, Oberlin, Occidental, Pomona, Reed, Swarthmore, Vassar, and Wellesley Colleges.

Limitations Fellows are expected to teach at least 1 course, participate in departmental seminars, and interact with students.

Number awarded 1 to 2 at each participating school.

Deadline November of each year.

[1176]
MINORITY SCIENCE IMPROVEMENT PROGRAM

Department of Education
Attn: Office of Postsecondary Education
Division of Higher Education Incentive Programs
Portals Building, Suite C-80
600 Independence Avenue, S.W.
Washington, DC 20202-5329
(202) 260-3261   Fax: (202) 260-7615
E-mail: argelia_velez_rodriguez@ed.gov

Purpose To provide grants to effect long-range improvement in science education at predominantly minority institutions and to increase the flow of underrepresented ethnic minorities, particularly minority women, into careers in the sciences and engineering.

Eligibility Public or private accredited colleges and universities that have 50 percent or more minority enrollment are eligible to apply. Nonprofit organizations and scientific societies are also eligible to apply for awards if they render a needed service to eligible minority institutions or if they provide in-service training for project directors, scientists, or engineers from eligible minority institutions. Applications may request grants in 4 categories: 1) design projects, to provide assistance in developing long-range science improvement plans; 2) institutional projects for implementing a comprehensive science improvement plan; 3) cooperative projects to assist groups of institutions to work together to conduct a science improvement project; and 4) special projects to support activities to improve quality training in the sciences and engineering and enhance the minority institutions' general scientific research capabilities.

Financial data Design project grants range from $16,000 to $20,000 and average $18,000; institutional grants range from $100,000 to $300,000 and average $120,000; cooperative grants range from $200,000 to $500,000 and average $293,000; and special project grants range from $20,000 to $150,000 and average $25,000.

Duration Varies by program: design project grants are for 1 year; institutional grants are up to 36 months; cooperative grants are for no longer than 36 months; special project grants are for a maximum of 24 months.

Number awarded Approximately 29 each year: 2 design project, 15 institutional projects, 2 cooperative projects, and 10 special projects.

Deadline December of each year.

[1177]
MINORITY TRAVEL FELLOWSHIP PROGRAM

American College of Neuropsychopharmacology
320 Centre Building
2014 Broadway
Nashville, TN 37203
(615) 322-2075   Fax: (615) 343-0662

Purpose To provide funding to underrepresented minority postdoctorates who are interested in attending an annual conference on neuropsychopharmacology.

Eligibility Eligible to apply are American citizens or permanent residents who have received their Ph.D. or M.D. within the past 5 years and who have indicated an interest in neuropsychopharmacology. Preference is given to candidates who can demonstrate evidence of continuing and future involvement in the field. Applicants must be members of an ethnic minority group underrepresented in biomedical areas, including but not limited to Blacks and Hispanics living in the Continental United States. Previous awardees are not eligible.

Financial data Fellows receive paid registration at an annual conference of the American College of Neuropsychopharmacology (ACNP), round-trip transportation, up to 7 nights lodging in a meeting hotel, $50 per day for meals and incidental expenses, a ground transportation allowance of $100, and paid registration for the next 4 annual conferences.

Duration The conference is held annually.

Special features This program is funded by a grant from the National Institute of Mental Health of the National Institutes of Health.

Number awarded Up to 5 each year.

Deadline May of each year.

[1178]
MONTANA SPACE GRANT CONSORTIUM RESEARCH INITIATION GRANTS

Montana Space Grant Consortium
c/o Montana State University
Physics Department
AJM Johnson Hall
Bozeman, MT 59717-0350
(406) 994-4223   Fax: (406) 994-4452
E-mail: msgc@orion.physics.montana.edu

Purpose To provide seed money for research related to space sciences and engineering.

Eligibility This program is open to individuals in Montana (most of the awards go to graduate students) who need support to conduct research related to space sciences and/or engineering. This program is part of the U.S. National Aeronautics and Space Administration (NASA) Space Grant program, which encourages participation by women, minorities, and persons with disabilities.

Financial data These grants provide "seed money" only.

Duration 1 year; generally nonrenewable.

Limitations Awardees are required to submit a follow-on proposal to NASA for regular research funding during the year of the grant.

[1179]
MORE FACULTY DEVELOPMENT AWARDS

National Institutes of Health
Attn: National Institute of General Medical Sciences
Director, Minority Access to Research Careers Program
Natcher Building, Suite 2AS43C
45 Center Drive MSC 6200
Bethesda, MD 20892-6200
(301) 594-3900   Fax: (301) 480-2753
E-mail: at21z@nih.gov

Purpose To enable faculty at minority institutions to sharpen their research skills by spending intervals conducting full-time research in a research-intensive laboratory.

Eligibility Candidates for this program must have been full-time permanent faculty in a biomedically-related science, including behavioral science, or mathematics at the home institution for at least 3 years; have received the Ph.D. or equivalent at least 5 years before the date of the application; intend to remain at the home institution at the end of the training period; demonstrate a commitment to research and teaching in a minority institution; plan to conduct research in a science (including mathematics) related to biomedical or behavioral research; and be a citizen or permanent resident of the United States. The home institution must be a domestic private or public educational institution with a significant enrollment of underrepresented minorities, defined as African Americans, Hispanic Americans, Native Americans, and Pacific Islanders, that offers at least the baccalaureate degree in the biomedical or behavioral sciences or mathematics. The research institution is the university or other institution at which the candidate conducts full-time research and takes courses; the research institution may not be the same as the home institution.

Financial data Candidates may request a salary equal to their actual annual salary and appropriate fringe benefits prorated for the time during which they are engaged in full-time research (salary support is not provided for the time candidates are enrolled in academic courses); up to $3,000 per year for supplies, equipment, travel, and other costs directly related to their full-time research experience; and funds to pay tuition and fees for 1 course per academic term to be taken at the research institution. nominee's current salary. Any expected concurrent sabbatical or any other salary support for the proposed period in residence is taken into account. A travel allowance equivalent to round-trip coach airfare between the visiting scientist's home institution and the sponsoring institution is provided. The sponsoring institution may receive up to $3,000 as an allowance for costs of supplies, supporting services, and demonstration costs related to activities proposed for the visiting scientist.

Duration Up to 1 year.

Special features The National Institute of General Medical Sciences, a component of the National Institutes of Health (NIH), operates this program as part of its Minority Opportunities for Research (MORE) Division.

Number awarded Varies each year.

Deadline January, May, and September of each year.

[1180]
MORE MINORITIES IN THE HEALTH PROFESSIONS GRANTS

Henry J. Kaiser Family Foundation
2400 Sand Hill Road
Menlo Park, CA 94025
(415) 854-9400

Purpose To fund demonstration and evaluation projects that are concerned with preparing increased numbers of low-income, minority students for careers in the health professions.
Eligibility Colleges, health science centers, and public school systems in selected communities are given an opportunity to work with this program. Unsolicited proposals for support are not accepted.
Financial data Up to $4 million will be spent on this program.
Duration The pilot projects each run for 3 years.
Special features This program began in 1987 and will continue through 1997.

[1181]
MS. FOUNDATION COLLABORATIVE GRANTS

Ms. Foundation for Women
120 Wall Street, 33rd Floor
New York, NY 10005
(212) 742-2300

Purpose To provide funding to women's organizations in collaboration with other funders.
Eligibility Nonprofit, tax-exempt women's organizations are eligible for these grants. The foundation funds and assists women's self-help organizing efforts to pursue changes in public consciousness, law, philanthropy, and social policy; it is especially interested in breaking down barriers faced by women of color, low-income women, older women, lesbians, and women with disabilities. These grants are available only in response to a Request for Proposals or other special solicitation.
Financial data The grants are from special funds in collaborations with other funders to address specific issues.
Duration Up to 3 years.
Limitations The foundation does not fund cultural or media groups, individuals, research projects, colleges, or other institutions of higher learning.
Number awarded Varies each year.
Deadline Applications may be submitted at any time.

[1182]
MS. FOUNDATION GENERAL GRANTS

Ms. Foundation for Women
120 Wall Street, 33rd Floor
New York, NY 10005
(212) 742-2300

Purpose To foster and strengthen the women's movement by providing financial support to organizations interested in working to break down barriers faced by women of color, low income women, older women, lesbians, and women with disabilities.
Eligibility All grants are to tax-exempt organizations to work on issues of concern to women. No grants are made to individuals, publications, cultural or media projects, research, school-sponsored programs, university projects, state agencies, or religious organizations. Special consideration is given to organizations that are actively building coalitions across race, ethnicity,

class, and sexual orientation and that bridge timely and important progressive concerns. The areas of concern that the foundation funds are: 1) economic justice, focusing on workplace organizing and labor rights for women workers, rural and urban poverty, welfare organizing, nontraditional employment, and economic development; 2) safety, addressing the root causes and prevention of all types of violence against women and girls, including domestic violence, sexual assault, incest, lesbian battering, and hate crimes against women; and 3) girls, including activities that challenge gender stereotyping of girls, address the increasing incidence of violence in girls' lives, and sustain the self-confidence and vitality of adolescent girls, aged 9 to 15.
Financial data Awards range from $5,000 to $25,000.
Duration 1 year; some awards are renewable.
Special features Since its inception in 1972, this foundation has supported the efforts of grassroots women to fight discrimination and violence, protect children and develop healthy families, achieve economic and social empowerment, launch nonsexist, multiracial curriculum programs, and safeguard reproductive rights.
Number awarded Varies each year.

[1183]
MSGC RESEARCH ACCELERATION GRANT PROGRAM

Maine Space Grant Consortium
c/o Maine Science and Technology Foundation
87 Winthrop Street
Augusta, ME 04330
(207) 621-6350   Fax: (207) 621-6369
E-mail: Mahmood@mstf.org

Purpose To provide funding for research projects in Maine that will accelerate researchers in becoming nationally competitive in aerospace-related research.
Eligibility Proposals may be submitted by individuals in the public and private sectors in Maine. Collaborations with other Maine institutions and with scientists at research centers of the U.S. National Aeronautics and Space Administration (NASA) are encouraged but not required. Funds may be used for new projects or to supplement or complement ongoing research. The Maine Space Grant Consortium (MSGC) is a component of the NASA Space Grant program, which encourages participation by women, minorities, and persons with disabilities.
Financial data Grants up to $22,000 are available. A match of 1 dollar for every 2 dollars requested is required.
Duration 1 year or less.
Special features This program is funded by NASA.
Number awarded Up to 3 each year.
Deadline Letters of intent must be submitted by October of each year; final proposals are due by December.

[1184]
MSGC TRAVEL GRANT PROGRAM

Maine Space Grant Consortium
c/o Maine Science and Technology Foundation
87 Winthrop Street
Augusta, ME 04330
(207) 621-6350   Fax: (207) 621-6369
E-mail: Mahmood@mstf.org

Purpose To provide funding for research-related travel to investigators in Maine involved in space-oriented activities.

Eligibility Proposals may be submitted by faculty members and researchers at public or private colleges and universities and not-for-profit research institutions in Maine. Applicants must be requesting funding to present research papers at professional conferences, make contacts and establish research relationships with out-of-state researchers and with scientists at research centers of the U.S. National Aeronautics and Space Administration (NASA), or to make peer contacts for enhancing their research programs. The Maine Space Grant Consortium (MSGC) is a component of the NASA Space Grant program, which encourages participation by women, minorities, and persons with disabilities.

Financial data Awards up to $500 are available.

Special features This program is funded by NASA.

Limitations For overseas travel, a strong case must be made that the proposed travel is for a project of interest to NASA and will enhance specific areas of research pursued by NASA or its affiliates.

Number awarded Varies each year.

Deadline Applications may be submitted at any time, but at least 30 days prior to the proposed travel.

[1185]
MULTICULTURAL ORGANIZATION DEVELOPMENT PROGRAM

North Carolina Arts Council
Attn: Department of Cultural Resources
Cambridge House
407 North Person Street
Raleigh, NC 27601-2807
(919) 733-7897, ext. 16

Purpose To provide funds that will support the organizational development of multicultural organizations in North Carolina and to strengthen their arts programs.

Eligibility Eligible to apply are North Carolina nonprofit African American, Asian American, Latino, or Native American organizations with strong arts programs that are seeking funds to support their administrative and artistic development. Selection is based on the artistic merit of the organization's programs, the organization's contribution to the artistic and cultural growth of its community, management capabilities and financial accountability, and ability to share information and expertise with other organizations.

Financial data Grants range from $5,000 to $15,000 per year, but must be matched dollar for dollar from the organization's own budget. Funds may be used for artistic and administrative expenses including salaries, artist fees, travel, promotion, production costs, printing, postage, telephone, and facility operation.

Duration 1 year.

Special features Funded organizations participate in the council's management/technical assistance component of the program, which provides arts consultants to work with the emerging organizations (for up to 9 months) to strengthen their artistic programs.

Number awarded Varies each year.

Deadline February of each year.

[1186]
NAA FOUNDATION MINORITY FELLOWSHIP PROGRAM

Newspaper Association of America Foundation
The Newspaper Center
Attn: Diversity Department
11600 Sunrise Valley Drive
Reston, VA 22091-1499
(703) 648-1131   Fax: (703) 620-1265

Purpose To provide financial assistance to minority journalists to attend newspaper-related training conferences and seminars and help minorities move into management positions.

Eligibility Candidates must be nominated in order to be considered for this program. They may nominate themselves (with a supervisor's recommendation) or be recommended by newspaper executives or by journalism school administrators. Minority journalists currently at newspapers or members of journalism faculties are eligible for consideration. Preference is given to candidates who demonstrate managerial potential.

Financial data The fellowship includes funds for travel, lodging, meals, and training fees to newspaper-related training conferences and seminars.

Special features This program began in 1981. Funding may be used to attend newspaper-related seminars offered by the American Press Institute, Poynter Institute for Media Studies, the Newspaper Management Center, Northwestern University, or other academic and media organizations.

Limitations Students are not eligible for this program.

Number awarded Varies; approximately 40 per year.

Deadline March of each year for spring; September of each year for fall.

[1187]
NAPT PUBLIC TELEVISION PRODUCTION FUND

Native American Public Telecommunications, Inc.
1800 North 33rd Street
P.O. Box 83111
Lincoln, NE 68501-3111
(402) 472-3522   Fax: (402) 472-8675

Purpose To provide funding for the creation of Native American theme programs for broadcast to public television audiences.

Eligibility This program invites producers to submit competitive proposals for the research and development, scripting, or completion of culture-specific programs that originate from the Native American experience and are intended for national public television audiences. All subjects and themes are invited, but the consortium is particularly interested in projects that examine and illuminate the contemporary stories and realities of Native American diversity, identity, spirituality, and lifestyles. The consortium gives the highest consideration to projects that have Native American participation in 4 of the following 6 categories: executive producer, producer, director, writer, subject, and cinematographer/editor. If proposals are submitted from an independent production team, the producer or director must be Native American. Station-based productions must ensure Native American participation. All program categories are eligible, except industrial films and videos, student productions, and similar nonbroadcast programs. Applicants must be U.S. citizens or legal residents. Only 1 proposal per applicant will be accepted. All proposals are evaluated on the following criteria: Native Americans in key positions; visualization and clarity of the written proposal; demonstrated ability of the applicant to complete the work; demonstrated fiscal management; relevance of the subject matter to the national Native American community; adaptability of the subject matter to the television medium; opportunities for internship/training for Native American personnel on the project. All Native American applicants and project participants should be clearly identified on the proposal form.

Financial data Program grants can range from $3,000 to $30,000; funds may be used for research and development, script development, and/or completion/post production.

Duration Up to 1 year.

Special features This program is underwritten by the Corporation for Public Broadcasting.

Number awarded Varies each year.

Deadline August of each year.

[1188]
NASA GRADUATE STUDENT RESEARCHERS PROGRAM

National Aeronautics and Space Administration
Attn: Office of Human Resources and Education
Code FE
Headquarters Room 4D45
Washington, DC 20546-0001
(202) 358-1517   Fax: (202) 358-4068
E-mail: anurrid@hq.nasa.gov

Purpose To support graduate research in aeronautics, space science, space applications, and space technology.

Eligibility Full-time students enrolled or planning to enroll in an accredited graduate program at a U.S. college or university are eligible for these awards. They must be citizens of the United States, sponsored by a faculty advisor or department chair, and interested in conducting research in space sciences at their home university, individual field centers of the National Aeronautics and Space Administration (NASA), or the Jet Propulsion Laboratory. Selection is based on academic qualifications, quality of the proposed research and its relevance to NASA's program, the student's proposed utilization of center research facilities (except for NASA headquarters), and ability of the student to accomplish the defined research. Students from traditionally underrepresented groups (African Americans, Native Americans, Alaskan Natives, Mexican Americans, Puerto Ricans, Native Pacific Islanders, women, and persons with disabilities) are strongly urged to apply.

Financial data In addition to a $16,000 student stipend, an allowance of $6,000 ($3,000 for the student and $3,000 for the university) may be requested to cover tuition costs or to provide a per diem and travel allowance for the student and faculty advisor.

Duration 1 year; may be renewed for up to 2 additional years.

Special features This program was established in 1980. Awards for NASA Headquarters are sponsored by the Office of Space Science (OSS), the Office of Life and Microgravity Sciences and Applications (OLMSA), and the Office of Mission to Planet Earth (MTPE). The areas of interest include structure/evolution of the universe, origins/planetary systems, solar system exploration, sun-earth connection, information systems, microgravity science and applications, life sciences, and earth sciences. Fellows selected by NASA Headquarters conduct research at their respective universities. Other awards are distributed through NASA field centers, each of which has its own research agenda and facilities. These centers include Ames Research Center (Moffett Field, California), Hugh L. Dryden Flight Research Facility (Edwards, California), Goddard Space Flight Center (Greenbelt, Maryland), Jet Propulsion Laboratory (Pasadena, California), Lyndon B. Johnson Space Center (Houston, Texas), John F. Kennedy Space Center (Cape Canaveral, Florida), Langley Research Center (Hampton, Virginia), Lewis Research Center (Cleveland, Ohio), George C. Marshall Space Flight Center (Huntsville, Alabama), and John C. Stennis Space Center (Stennis Space Center, Mississippi). Fellows spend some period of time in residence at the center, taking advantage of the unique research facilities of the installation and working with center personnel. To date, more than 1,200 students have been supported under this program. Travel outside the United States is allowed if it is essential to the research effort and charged to a grant.

Number awarded 150 new awards each year; approximately 60 of the awards are administered through NASA Headquarters and the remainder are distributed through NASA's field centers.

Deadline January of each year.

[1189]
NASA SMALL BUSINESS INNOVATION RESEARCH GRANTS

National Aeronautics and Space Administration
Attn: SBIR Program Manager
Goddard Space Flight Center
Code 705
Greenbelt, MD 20771
(301) 286-8888   E-mail: nasasbir@alliedtech.com

Purpose To support small businesses that have the technological experience to contribute to the research and development mission of the National Aeronautics and Space Administration (NASA).

Eligibility For the purposes of this program, a "small business" is defined as any organization that is independently owned and operated for profit, not dominant in the field in which it is operating, and meets the size standard of 500 employees or less. The primary employment of the principal investigator must be with the firm at the time of award and during the conduct of the proposed project. Preference is given to women-owned small business concerns and to socially and economically disadvantaged small business concerns. Women-owned small business concerns are those which are at least 51 percent owned by a woman or women who also control and operate it. Socially and economically disadvantaged small business concerns are at least 51 percent owned by an Indian tribe, a native Hawaiian organization, or 1 or more socially and economically disadvantaged individuals (Black Americans, Hispanic Americans, Native Americans, Asian-Pacific Americans, or subcontinent Asian Americans). The project must be performed in the United States. Recent technical topics included aeronautics technologies; general aviation; supersonic transport technologies; materials and structures; teleoperators and robotics; mission operations and on-board autonomy; spacecraft and sensor platforms; satellite and space systems communications; multi-spacecraft systems; interferometry missions technology; large aperture space telescopes; earth remote sensing; instrumentation, sensors, and optics; space transportation and propulsion; fuels and space propellants for reusable launch vehicles; technologies for human exploration of space; and space applications and micro-gravity sciences.

Financial data Grants are offered in 2 phases. In phase 1, awards normally may not exceed $70,000 (for both direct and indirect costs); in phase 2, awards normally may not exceed $600,000 (including both direct and indirect costs).

Duration Phase 1: up to 6 months; phase 2: up to 2 years.

Number awarded Varies each year.

Deadline July of each year.

[1190]
NASA SMALL BUSINESS TECHNOLOGY TRANSFER GRANTS

National Aeronautics and Space Administration
Attn: STTR Program Manager
Goddard Space Flight Center
Code 705
Greenbelt, MD 20771
(301) 286-8888   E-mail: nasasbir@alliedtech.com

Purpose To provide financial support to cooperative research and development projects carried out between small business concerns and research institutions in areas of interest to the National Aeronautics and Space Administration (NASA).

Eligibility For the purposes of this program, a "small business" is defined as any organization that is independently owned and operated for profit, not dominant in the field in which it is operating, and meets the size standard of 500 employees or less. Unlike the NASA Small Business Innovation Research Grants, the primary employment of the principal investigator does not need to be with the business concern. This program, however, requires that the small business apply in collaboration with a nonprofit research institution for conduct of a project that has potential for commercialization. At least 40 percent of the work must be performed by the small business and at least 30 percent of the work must be performed by the research institution. The principal investigator may have his/her primary employment with an organization other than the small business concern, including the research institution. Preference is given to women-owned small business concerns and to socially and economically disadvantaged small business concerns. Women-owned small business concerns are those which are at least 51 percent owned by a woman or women who also control and operate it. Socially and economically disadvantaged small business concerns are at least 51 percent owned by an Indian tribe, a native Hawaiian organization, or 1 or more socially and economically disadvantaged individuals (Black Americans, Hispanic Americans, Native Americans, Asian-Pacific Americans, or subcontinent Asian Americans). The project must be performed in the United States. Recent research topics included general aviation, access to space, advanced technology for space science, and human exploration and development of space.

Financial data In the first phase, annual awards may not exceed $100,000 for direct costs, indirect costs, and negotiated fixed fees. In the second phase, awards up to $500,000 are available.

Duration Normally 1 year for the first phase and 2 years for the second phase.

Special features Grants in the first phase are to determine the scientific, technical, and commercial merit and feasibility of the proposed cooperative effort and the quality of performance of the small business concern. In the second phase, the research and development efforts continue, depending on the results of the first phase.

Number awarded In a recent year, NASA issued 33 phase 1 awards.

Deadline January of each year.

[1191]
NASA/DESGC UNDERGRADUATE SUMMER SCHOLARSHIPS

Delaware Space Grant Consortium
c/o University of Delaware
Bartol Research Institute
217 Sharp Laboratory
Newark, DE 19716-4793
(302) 831-8116   Fax: (302) 831-1843
E-mail: sherry@brivs2.bartol.udel.edu

Purpose To provide financial support to undergraduate students in Delaware for summer research on space-related subjects.

Eligibility This program is open to undergraduate students at member or affiliate colleges and universities of the Delaware Space Grant Consortium (DESGC). Applicants must have a proven interest and aptitude for space-related studies and be proposing a summer research project. U.S. citizenship is required. The DESGC is a component of the U.S. National Aeronautics and Space Administration (NASA) Space Grant program, which encourages applications from women, minorities, and persons with disabilities.

Financial data A stipend is provided.

Duration Summer months.

Special features This program is funded by NASA.

Number awarded Varoes each year.

Deadline March of each year.

[1192]
NATIONAL ASSESSMENT OF EDUCATIONAL PROGRESS (NAEP) VISITING SCHOLAR PROGRAM

Educational Testing Service
Mail Stop 16-T
Princeton, NJ 08541-0001
(609) 734-1806   E-mail: ldelauro@ets.org

Purpose To provide financial assistance to postdoctoral scholars who wish to conduct research on education for minorities at the Educational Testing Service.

Eligibility Applicants must have earned a doctorate in a relevant discipline. They must be prepared to conduct research on some aspect of education using the database of the National Assessment of Educational Progress (NAEP). Studies focused on issues concerning the education of minority students are especially encouraged. An explicit goal of the program is to increase the number of women and minority professionals in educational measurement and related fields.

Financial data The stipend is set in relation to compensation at the home institution. Scholars and their families also receive reimbursement for relocation expenses.

Duration 10 months, from September through June of the following year.

Special features Fellows work with senior staff at the Educational Testing Service in Princeton, New Jersey and have access to senior NAEP research staff.

Number awarded 1 each year.

Deadline November of each year.

[1193]
NATIONAL CANCER INSTITUTE MINORITY ENHANCEMENT AWARD

National Institutes of Health
Attn: National Cancer Institute
Division of Extramural Activities
Executive Plaza North, Room 620
6130 Executive Boulevard MSC 7405
Bethesda, MD 20892-7405
(301) 496-7344   Fax: (301) 402-4551
E-mail: pg36f@nih.gov

Purpose To expand minority involvement in cancer control research.

Eligibility Applications are accepted from institutions capable of accessing large minority populations on a regular basis. They may apply to broaden the institution's operational base to facilitate the expansion of cancer control efforts in early detection, prevention, screening, pretreatment evaluation, treatment, continuation care, rehabilitation, and the increased involvement of primary care providers to the minority population. Also eligible are efforts that promote the participation of minorities in clinical treatment research.

Financial data Funding is made in accordance with the usual National Institutes of Health policy.

Duration Awards are issued on an annual basis, with continued support dependent on approval of a satisfactory annual progress report and proposed budget.

Special features General research objectives include, but are not limited to, smoking behavior in minority youth; studies of communication strategies for presenting information to minorities about cancer and its prevention; investigations of patient perspectives of cancer risks; the design and evaluation of interventions to minimize and prevent distress of minority patients with cancer; the development of pilot studies for minority clinical prevention trials; and psychosocial studies and perception of cancer risks in minorities.

Number awarded Varies each year.

[1194]
NATIONAL CANCER INSTITUTE MINORITY HEALTH PROFESSIONAL TRAINING INITIATIVE

National Institutes of Health
Attn: National Cancer Institute
Division of Extramural Activities
Executive Plaza North, Room 620
6130 Executive Boulevard MSC 7405
Bethesda, MD 20892-7405
(301) 496-7344   Fax: (301) 402-4551
E-mail: pg36f@nih.gov

Purpose To address the problem of low numbers of minority clinicians, clinical researchers, and other health professionals engaged in research in oncology or with training in subspecialities related to cancer.

Eligibility Minority investigators, defined as U.S. citizens or nationals from an underrepresented ethnic American nationality (Black, Hispanic, Native American, Asian, or Pacific Islander), may apply for support through this initiative. The program encompasses 3 awards: 1) Minority Oncology Leadership Award, for faculty as minority health professional schools to free up research time, improve the curriculum and research opportunities, and pay 1 additional professional to do research; 2) Clinical Investigator Award for Research on Special Populations, to encourage newly trained clinicians to develop research interests and skills in the basic and applied sciences relevant to cancers and risks for cancers that may have a high prevalence or incidence in special populations that may be underserved by limited access to current knowledge and medical care; and 3) Minority School Faculty Development Awards, to encourage the development of faculty investigators at minority schools and to enhance their research capabilities in specified health and health-related areas.

Financial data The amount of the awards depends on the nature of the proposals and the availability of funds.

Duration 4 years; may be renewed for an additional 3 years.

Number awarded Varies each year.

[1195]
NATIONAL CENTER FOR ATMOSPHERIC RESEARCH POSTDOCTORAL PROGRAM

National Center for Atmospheric Research
Attn: Advanced Study Program
P.O. Box 3000
Boulder, CO 80307-3000
(303) 497-1650   Fax: (303) 497-1400
E-mail: barbm@asp2.ucar.edu

Purpose To provide an opportunity for talented atmospheric scientists who have recently received their Ph.D.s to continue to pursue their research interests and to develop expertise in new areas.

Eligibility Eligible are physicists, chemists, applied mathematicians, engineers, and specialists from other natural scientific disciplines who are just receiving their Ph.D. or received it within the past 4 years and who wish to apply their training to research in the atmospheric sciences. Applications from minorities and women are particularly encouraged. Selection is based on the applicant's scientific capability and potential, originality and independence, and the ability to take advantage of the research opportunities at the National Center for Atmospheric Research (NCAR).

Financial data Successful applicants with recent Ph.D.s receive a stipend of $33,415 per year. Those with more than 1 year's experience receive a stipend of $34,645 per year. All appointees are eligible for life and health insurance. Travel expenses are reimbursed for the fellow and family, normally up to a maximum of $800. Fellows living abroad have round-trip travel for themselves and their families paid, up to a maximum of $2,500. A small allowance for moving and storing personal belongings is provided. Scientific travel for the fellow up to $1,050 per year is normally available.

Duration Up to 1 year, beginning between June and October. If fellows wish to stay longer at the center, they may apply for a second term of up to 1 year.

Special features Fellows are free to choose their own research projects but are encouraged to select studies that take maximum advantage of the opportunities available at the center. In order to give fellows a broad introduction to research being done at the center, a series of seminars are offered periodically. It is expected that all fellows will give 1 or more scientific seminars either with the center or for other divisions before completing their tenure there. NCAR is operated by the University Corporation for Atmospheric Research (a consortium of 61 universities) and sponsored by the National Science Foundation.

Number awarded Varies; currently, 8 to 10 each year. At least 50 percent of these are reappointed.

Deadline January of each year.

[1196]
NATIONAL CENTER FOR TOXICOLOGICAL RESEARCH FACULTY RESEARCH PARTICIPATION PROGRAM

Oak Ridge Institute for Science and Education
Attn: Science/Engineering Education Division
P.O. Box 117
Oak Ridge, TN 37831-0117
(423) 576-8807   (423) 576-8158
(800) 569-7749   Fax: (423) 576-3643
E-mail: frppnctr@orau.gov

Purpose To provide funding to faculty members who wish to participate in research activities on biological effects of potentially toxic chemicals at the National Center for Toxicological Research in Arkansas.

Eligibility College and university full-time faculty members in toxicology, pharmacology, biological sciences, mathematics, chemistry, medicine, computer science, or other related scientific disciplines may apply for this program. They must propose to conduct research at the National Center for Toxicological Research in Jefferson, Arkansas. All programs operated by the Science/Engineering Education Division (SEED) of Oak Ridge Institute for Science and Education (ORISE) seek to broaden the participation of minorities, women, and persons with disabilities in science and engineering careers.

Financial data The stipend is negotiable, but based on the recipient's regular university salary; some reimbursement for travel and moving is available.

Duration 10 weeks to 3 months; some sabbatical appointments up to 12 months may be available.

Special features This program is funded by an interagency agreement between the U.S. Department of Energy and the U.S. Food and Drug Administration and administered by ORISE/SEED.

Number awarded Varies each year.

Deadline Applications may be submitted at any time.

[1197]
NATIONAL CENTER FOR TOXICOLOGICAL RESEARCH POSTGRADUATE RESEARCH PROGRAM

Oak Ridge Institute for Science and Education
Attn: Science/Engineering Education Division
P.O. Box 117
Oak Ridge, TN 37831-0117
(423) 576-3190   (423) 241-2875
(800) 569-7749   Fax: (423) 576-3643
E-mail: prpnctr@orau.gov

Purpose To provide funding to postgraduates who wish to participate in research on the biological effects of potentially toxic chemicals at the National Center for Toxicological Research in Arkansas.

Eligibility Applicants should have completed a graduate degree within the past 3 years; others are considered on a case-by-case basis. Their field of study should have been toxicology, pharmacology, biological sciences, mathematics, chemistry, medicine, computer science, or other related scientific disciplines. They must propose to conduct research at the National Center for Toxicological Research in Jefferson, Arkansas. All programs operated by the Science/Engineering Education Division (SEED) of Oak Ridge Institute for Science and Education (ORISE) seek to broaden the participation of minorities, women, and persons with disabilities in science and engineering careers.

Financial data The stipend is based on research area and degree.

Duration 1 year; renewable.

Special features This program is funded by an interagency agreement between the U.S. Department of Energy and the U.S. Food and Drug Administration and administered by ORISE/SEED.

Number awarded Varies each year.

Deadline Applications may be submitted at any time.

[1198]
NATIONAL COUNCIL OF TEACHERS OF ENGLISH REGULAR GRANTS-IN-AID

National Council of Teachers of English
Attn: Research Foundation
1111 West Kenyon Road
Urbana, IL 61801-1096
(217) 328-3870   Fax: (217) 328-0977

Purpose To provide financial assistance to graduate students who are members of the National Council of Teachers.

Eligibility Applicants must be working on dissertations that have significance for the teaching or learning of English, language arts, or related fields. Especially encouraged are proposals focusing on underrepresented populations.

Financial data Up to $12,500. Funding is awarded in 3 phases: 70 percent of the award is given upon approval of the proposal, 15 percent upon submission of the interim report, and 15 percent upon approval of the final report and budget summary.

Duration 1 year.

Limitations Recipients cannot hold concurrent awards, but they are eligible to apply for another grant after they have filed their final report.

Number awarded Varies each year.

Deadline February of each year.

[1199]
NATIONAL FOUNDATION FOR THE IMPROVEMENT OF EDUCATION STUDENT SUCCESS PROGRAM

National Foundation for the Improvement of Education
Attn: Director of Programs
1201 16th Street, N.W.
Washington, D.C. 20036-3207
(202) 822-7840   Fax: (202) 822-7779
E-mail: cedwards00@aol.com

Purpose To provide financial assistance to school faculties interested in helping at-risk students.

Eligibility Teams of K-12 teachers who are interested in helping at-risk students or students from groups that have been underrepresented in fields that require advanced knowledge in math and science are eligible to apply. Teachers must demonstrate how they will use the grants to assess their academic knowledge across the curriculum and to create and implement a professional development plan that will strengthen educators' content knowledge.

Financial data The award is a maximum of $5,000 the first year and $10,000 the second year.

Duration 2 years.

Special features The National Education Association established the National Foundation for the Improvement of Education in 1969 as a nonprofit, tax-exempt foundation to help teachers, education support personnel, and higher education faculty and staff acquire the knowledge and expertise to serve students from every background and of every ability.

Number awarded 10 each year.

Deadline February of each year.

[1200]
NATIONAL HEALTH SERVICE CORPS LOAN REPAYMENT PROGRAM

Health Resources and Services Administration
Attn: Bureau of Primary Health Care
National Health Service Corps Program
2070 Chain Bridge Road, Suite 450
Vienna, VA 22182-2536
(703) 821-8955   (800) 221-9393

Purpose To provide funding to trained health professionals for repayment of undergraduate and graduate loans in exchange for the participant's serving in a federally designated health professional shortage area (HPSA).

Eligibility Eligible to apply for this program are individuals who are 1) fully trained allopathic (M.D.) or osteopathic (D.O.) physicians specializing in family practice, obstetrics/gynecology, internal medicine, or pediatrics; 2) certified as a nurse midwife, nurse practitioner, or physician assistant; 3) other medical health professionals, in clinical psychology, clinical social work, or dental hygiene; 4) dentists; 5) enrolled in an approved graduate training program in allopathic or osteopathic medicine, dentistry, or other health profession; or 6) enrolled as full-time students at an accredited school in the final year of a course of study or program leading to a degree in allopathic or osteopathic medicine, dentistry, or other health profession. Preference is given to applicants whose health profession or specialty is most needed by the program; who has and whose spouse, if any, has characteristics that increase the probability of continuing to serve in a HPSA upon completion of his or her service obligation; and who is from a disadvantaged background.

Financial data For the first 2 years of full-time service at an approved site in a federally designated HPSA, the program repays up to $25,000 per year of the educational loans of participants; for subsequent years of full-time service, the program repays up to $35,000 per years. In addition, the program makes payments to the individual in an amount equal to 39 percent of the total amount of loans repayments made for the taxable year involved.

Duration The minimum service obligation is 2 years; extensions may be arranged.

Limitations Participants are obligated to provide full-time clinical primary health care services to populations in federally-designated, high-priority HPSAs (these include the Indian Health Service or medical facilities of the Federal Bureau of Prisons).

Number awarded Varies each year, depending upon the funding available.

Deadline June of each year.

[1201]
NATIONAL HEART, LUNG, AND BLOOD INSTITUTE RESEARCH DEVELOPMENT AWARD FOR MINORITY FACULTY

National Institutes of Health
Attn: National Heart, Lung, and Blood Institute
Division of Lung Diseases
Two Rockledge Center, Room 10112
6701 Rockledge Drive MSC 7952
Bethesda, MD 20892-7952
(301) 435-0222   Fax: (301) 480-1046
E-mail: mr50w@nih.gov

Purpose To develop the research capabilities of minority faculty investigators in areas relevant to cardiovascular, pulmonary, and hematologic diseases and resources, and to increase the number of minority individuals involved in research endeavors.

Eligibility Awards in this program are made to domestic institutions or organizations on behalf of awardees. Individuals must possess a doctoral degree (M.D., Ph.D., D.V.M., D.O., or equivalent), have a faculty appointment at an accredited college or university, be U.S. citizens, noncitizen nationals, or permanent residents at the time of application, and be members of a minority ethnic group.

Financial data The awardee receives salary support of up to $50,000 per year plus fringe benefits. Support for up to 5 percent of the sponsor's salary may also be requested. In addition, up to $30,000 per year will be provided for research support. These research funds may be used for equipment, supplies, travel, tuition and fees, and other related costs (e.g., personnel, publication costs, computer costs).

Duration 3 to 5 years.

Special features Support is also available through the Division of Heart and Vascular Diseases and the Division of Blood Diseases and Resources.

Number awarded Varies each year.

Deadline August of each year.

[1202]
NATIONAL INSTITUTE OF DIABETES AND DIGESTIVE AND KIDNEY DISEASES RESEARCH TRAINING OF UNDERREPRESENTED MINORITIES

National Institutes of Health
Attn: National Institute of Diabetes and Digestive and Kidney Diseases
Division of Extramural Activities
Natcher Building, Room 6AS-49E
45 Center Drive MSC 6600
Bethesda, MD 20892-6600
(301) 594-8842   Fax: (301) 480-3504
E-mail: jg60d@nih.gov

Purpose To facilitate the recruitment of underrepresented minority graduate and postdoctoral students into existing research training grants of the National Institute of Diabetes and Digestive and Kidney Diseases (NIDDK).

Eligibility Principal investigators on institute research grants are eligible to apply for administrative supplements so that minority graduate and postdoctoral students can receive research training as part of the grant. Students must be U.S. citizens, nationals, or permanent residents who have received a baccalaureate or doctoral degree as of the date of appointment and who are pursuing careers in biomedical science. These awards do not support clinical residency training or training directed towards a career in clinical practice.

Financial data Successful applications are funded as administrative supplements to the principal investigator's grant. Supplements provide a stipend of $10,008 per year for graduate students; postdoctoral candidates receive an annual stipend that ranges from $19,608 to $32,300, depending on the number of years of postdoctoral experience. All trainees also receive travel expenses to scientific meetings, an institutional allowance, trainee tuition, and medical insurance.

Duration Predoctoral trainees receive up to 5 years of support; postdoctoral trainees receive up to 3 years of support.

Special features Students should identify and contact an NIDDK training program director at his or her institution. The NIDDK administers this program as part of the T32 Awards program.

Limitations The initial 12 months of postdoctoral support carries a service payback requirement, which can be fulfilled by continued training under the award or by engaging in other health-related research training, health-related research, or health-related teaching. Fellows who fail to fulfill the payback requirement of 1 month of acceptable service for each month of the initial 12 months of support received must repay all funds received with interest.

Deadline Applications may be submitted at any time.

[1203]
NATIONAL INSTITUTE OF DIABETES AND DIGESTIVE AND KIDNEY DISEASES SUMMER RESEARCH TRAINING PROGRAM FOR UNDERGRADUATE MINORITY STUDENTS

National Institutes of Health
Attn: National Institute of Diabetes and Digestive and Kidney Diseases
Building 31, Room 9A18
31 Center Drive
Bethesda, MD 20892
(301) 486-3670				E-mail: rp86d@nih.gov

Purpose To provide minority undergraduate students with an opportunity to conduct research in the laboratory of a National Institute of Diabetes and Digestive and Kidney Diseases (NIDDK) intramural scientist.

Eligibility Graduating seniors who have participated in the Minority Access to Research Careers (MARC) Student Training in Academic Research (U-STAR) Program are eligible to participate in this program. They must wish to conduct experiments, co-author scientific papers, and present results of their research at scientific meetings.

Financial data In addition to their MARC stipend, students receive $300 per week, round-trip airfare to Bethesda, Maryland, and $50 for ground transportation.

Duration 10 weeks, during the summer.

[1204]
NATIONAL INSTITUTE OF STANDARDS AND TECHNOLOGY SMALL BUSINESS INNOVATION RESEARCH GRANTS

Department of Commerce
Attn: National Institute of Standards and Technology
SBIR Program Manager
Building 820, Room 306
Gaithersburg, MD 20899
(301) 975-4517				Fax: (301) 548-0624
E-mail: Norman.Taylor@nist.gov

Purpose To support small businesses that have the technological experience to contribute to the research and development mission of the National Institute of Standards and Technology (NIST).

Eligibility For the purposes of this program, a "small business" is defined as any organization that is independently owned and operated for profit, not dominant in the field in which it is operating, and meets the size standard of 500 employees or less. The primary employment of the principal investigator must be with the firm at the time of award and during the conduct of the proposed project. Preference is given to women-owned small business concerns and to socially and economically disadvantaged small business concerns. Women-owned small business concerns are those which are at least 51 percent owned by a woman or women who also control and operate it. Socially and economically disadvantaged small business concerns are at least 51 percent owned by an Indian tribe, a native Hawaiian organization, or 1 or more socially and economically disadvantaged individuals (Black Americans, Hispanic Americans, Native Americans, Asian-Pacific Americans, or subcontinent Asian Americans). The project must be performed in the United States. Current priority areas of research include: quality assurance, electronics and electrical engineering, manufacturing engineering, chemical science and technology, physics, materials science and engineering, building and fire research, and computer systems.

Financial data Grants are offered in 2 phases. In phase 1, awards normally may not exceed $50,000 (for both direct and indirect costs); in phase 2, awards normally may not exceed $200,000 (including both direct and indirect costs).

Duration Phase 1: up to 6 months; phase 2: up to 2 years.

Number awarded Varies; in recent years, NIST has planned to award 35 Phase 1 contracts.

Deadline January of each year.

[1205]
NATIONAL INSTITUTE ON AGING RESEARCH TRAINING OF UNDERREPRESENTED MINORITIES

National Institutes of Health
Attn: National Institute on Aging
Office of Extramural Affairs
Gateway Building, Room 2C-218
7201 Wisconsin Avenue MSC 9205
Bethesda, MD 20892-9205
(301) 496-9322				Fax: (301) 402-2945
E-mail: rb42h@nih.gov

Purpose To facilitate the recruitment of underrepresented minority graduate and postdoctoral students into existing research training grants of the National Institute on Aging (NIA).

Eligibility Principal investigators on NIA research grants are eligible to apply for administrative supplements so that minority graduate and postdoctoral students can receive research training as part of the grant. Students must be U.S. citizens, nationals, or permanent residents who have received a baccalaureate or doctoral degree as of the date of appointment and who are pursuing careers in biomedical science. These awards do not support clinical residency training or training directed towards a career in clinical practice.

Financial data   Successful applications are funded as administrative supplements to the principal investigator's grant. Supplements provide a stipend of $10,008 per year for graduate students; postdoctoral candidates receive an annual stipend that ranges from $19,608 to $32,300, depending on the number of years of postdoctoral experience. All trainees also receive travel expenses to scientific meetings, an institutional allowance, trainee tuition, and medical insurance.

Duration   Predoctoral trainees receive up to 5 years of support; postdoctoral trainees receive up to 3 years of support.

Special features   Students should identify and contact an NIA training program director at his or her institution. The NIA administers this program as part of the T32 Awards program.

Limitations   The initial 12 months of postdoctoral support carries a service payback requirement, which can be fulfilled by continued training under the award or by engaging in other health-related research training, health-related research, or health-related teaching. Fellows who fail to fulfill the payback requirement of 1 month of acceptable service for each month of the initial 12 months of support received must repay all funds received with interest.

Deadline   Applications may be submitted at any time.

[1206]
NATIONAL INSTITUTES OF HEALTH INDIVIDUAL RESEARCH PROJECT GRANTS

National Institutes of Health
Attn: Office of Extramural Research
Extramural Outreach and Information Resources Office
6701 Rockledge Drive, Room 6207
MSC 7910
Bethesda, MD 20892-7910
(301) 435-0714   Fax: (301) 480-8443
E-mail: asknih@odrockm1.od.nih.gov

Purpose   To support biomedical and behavioral research that will improve human health in areas of interest to the National Institutes of Health (NIH).

Eligibility   Investigators at nonprofit and for-profit, public and private organizations, such as universities, colleges, hospitals, laboratories, units of state and local governments, and eligible agencies of the federal government, may apply for these research grants. Applications are accepted for health-related research and development in all areas within the scope of the institues' mission and by all component Institutes and Centers. Specific subjects of research are announced periodically either as Program Announcements (PAs) for ongoing research or as Requests for Applications (RFAs) for specific 1-time research projects. Usually, the research is to be conducted within the United States, but research projects conducted at foreign sites may be proposed if they meet the following conditions: 1) have specific relevance to the institutes and have the potential for significantly advancing the health sciences in the United States; 2) present special opportunities for further research through the use of unusual talents, resources, populations, or environmental conditions; and 3) have a rating that falls within the normally established payline. For all projects, racial/ethnic minority individuals, women, and persons with disabilities are particularly encouraged to apply as principal investigators.

Financial data   The level of funding depends on the scope of the proposed research. Funds may be used for supplies, equipment, personnel, and travel. Foreign institutions do not receive support for administrative costs associated with the research.

Duration   1 year or longer.

Special features   This award is offered by 15 of NIH's component institutes; grants are designated as R01 Awards. The most meritorious first-time recipients of these awards who are new investigators (with no more than five years of research experience since completion of postdoctoral training) are also nominated to receive Presidential Early Career Awards for Scientists and Engineers.

Deadline   January, May, or September of each year.

[1207]
NATIONAL INSTITUTES OF HEALTH SMALL BUSINESS TECHNOLOGY TRANSFER GRANTS

National Institutes of Health
Attn: Office of Extramural Research
Extramural Outreach and Information Resources Office
6701 Rockledge Drive, Room 6207
MSC 7910
Bethesda, MD 20892-7910
(301) 435-0714   Fax: (301) 480-8443
E-mail: asknih@odrockm1.od.nih.gov

Purpose   To support cooperative research and development activities between small business concerns and research institutions in areas of interest to the National Institutes of Health (NIH).

Eligibility   For the purposes of this program, a "small business" is defined as any organization that is independently owned and operated for profit, not dominant in the field in which it is operating, and meets the size standard of 500 employees or less. Unlike Public Health Service Small Business Innovation Research Grants, the primary employment of the principal investigator does not need to be with the business concern. This program, however, requires that the small business apply in collaboration with a nonprofit research institution for conduct of a project that has potential for commercialization. The principal investigator may have his/her primary employment with an organization other than the small business concern, including the research institution. Preference is given to women-owned small business concerns and to socially and economically disadvantaged small business concerns. Women-owned small business concerns are those which are at least 51 percent owned by a woman or women who also control and operate it. Socially and economically disadvantaged small business concerns are at least 51 percent owned by an Indian tribe, a native Hawaiian organization, or 1 or more socially and economically disadvantaged individuals (Black Americans, Hispanic Americans, Native Americans, Asian-Pacific Americans, or subcontinent Asian Americans). The project must be performed in the United States.

Financial data   In the first phase, annual awards may not exceed $100,000 for direct costs, indirect costs, and negotiated fixed fees. In the second phase, awards up to $500,000 are available.

Duration   Normally 1 year for the first phase and 2 years for the second phase.

Special features   Grants in the first phase are to determine the scientific, technical, and commercial merit and feasibility of the proposed cooperative effort and the quality of performance of the small business concern. In the second phase, the research and development efforts continue, depending on the results of the first phase. The NIH designates phase I grants as R41 Awards and phase II grants as R42 Awards. All institutes and centers that comprise the NIH participate in this program; for a list of the names and addresses of the contact people in the various NIH components, write to the address above. Further information is available from those people, but actual program solicitations are available only from the SBIR/STTR Solicitation Office, 13687 Baltimore Avenue, Laurel, MD 20707-5096, (301) 206-9385, Fax: (301) 206-9722, E-Mail: a2y@cu.nih.gov.

Deadline March, July, and November of each year.

[1208]
NATIONAL INSTITUTES OF HEALTH SMALL GRANT PROGRAM

National Institutes of Health
Attn: Office of Extramural Research
Extramural Outreach and Information Resources Office
6701 Rockledge Drive, Room 6207
MSC 7910
Bethesda, MD 20892-7910
(301) 435-0714   Fax: (301) 480-8443
E-mail: asknih@odrockm1.od.nih.gov

Purpose To support pilot projects conducted by new and minority investigators, and other scientists, who would benefit from assistance to position themselves to compete successfully for research project grant support.

Eligibility This program is open to investigators changing areas of research, investigators whose research careers were interrupted and are intended to be resumed, established investigators needing quick support for a pilot project, minority and women investigators, those located at institutions not traditionally associated with health research, and recently trained or less experienced investigators. The awards are available to applicants at both nonprofit and for-profit organizations. The research may deal with relevant biomedical or behavioral science.

Financial data Applicants may request up to $50,000 (direct costs) for supplies, travel, small items of equipment, and salary for technical personnel; no more than $35,000 may be awarded for any 1 year.

Duration Up to 24 months.

Special features These grants are offered by all component Institutes and Centers within the National Institutes of Health (NIH), which designated these as the R03 Awards.

Number awarded Varies each year.

Deadline April, August, and December of each year.

[1209]
NATIONAL RESEARCH SERVICE AWARD INDIVIDUAL FELLOWSHIPS IN HEALTH SERVICES RESEARCH

Agency for Health Care Policy and Research
Attn: NRSA Project Officer
Executive Office Center, Suite 501
2101 East Jefferson Street
Rockville, MD 20852
(301) 594-1362

Purpose To provide funding for academic training and supervised experience in applying quantitative research methods to the systematic analysis and evaluation of health services.

Eligibility Applicants must be U.S. citizens or permanent residents who have received a Ph.D., M.D., D.O., D.D.S., D.V.M., or equivalent doctoral degree from an accredited domestic or foreign institution. They must be proposing to pursue postdoctoral training at an appropriate institution under the guidance of a sponsor who is an established investigator active in health services research. The proposed training should provide a rigorous conceptual and methodological foundation for investigating such topics as determinants of successful health care market reform, including incentives for selection of efficient health plans by health care purchasers and effective management by health care providers; cost-effectiveness and cost-benefit analysis, including allocation of health care resources and its relationship to health status; analysis of service delivery, resource use, and costs of care for persons with HIV-related illnesses; evaluation of managed care and other approaches to organizing, financing, and reimbursing health care services; rural health issues, including primary care access, service delivery, technology diffusion, and supply of health professionals; and medical malpractice and liability. Applications are especially encouraged from women, minorities, and individuals with disabilities.

Financial data The award provides an annual stipend based on the number of years of postdoctoral experience, ranging from $19,608 for less than 1 year to $32,300 for 7 or more years. The initial 12 months of National Research Service Award postdoctoral support carries a service payback requirement, which can be fulfilled by continued training under the award or by engaging in other health-related research training, health-related research, or health-related teaching. Fellows who fail to fulfill the payback requirement of 1 month of acceptable service for each month of the initial 12 months of support received must repay all funds received with interest.

Duration Up to 3 years.

Number awarded Varies each year.

Deadline April, August, or December of each year.

[1210]
NATIONAL RESEARCH SERVICE AWARDS FOR INDIVIDUAL POSTDOCTORAL FELLOWS

National Institutes of Health
Attn: Office of Extramural Research
Extramural Outreach and Information Resources Office
6701 Rockledge Drive, Room 6207
MSC 7910
Bethesda, MD 20892-7910
(301) 435-0714   Fax: (301) 480-8443
E-mail: asknih@odrockm1.od.nih.gov

Purpose To provide funding for postdoctoral biomedical or behavioral research training.

Eligibility Applicants must 1) be U.S. citizens or permanent residents; 2) have received a Ph.D., M.D., D.O., D.D.S., D.V.M., or equivalent doctoral degree from an accredited domestic or foreign institution; 3) be interested in conducting biomedical or behavioral research; and 4) have arranged for appointment to an appropriate institution and acceptance by a sponsor who will supervise the training and research experience. The institution may be private (nonprofit or for-profit) or public, including a federal laboratory. If a foreign institution is selected as the research training site, applicants must explain the reasons for the choice. Applications are especially encouraged from women, minorities, individuals with disabilities, and clinicians who wish to become researchers.

Financial data The award provides an annual stipend based on the number of years of postdoctoral experience, ranging from $19,608 for less than 1 year to $32,300 for 7 or more years. For fellows sponsored by domestic non-federal institutions, the stipend is paid through the sponsoring institution; for fellows sponsored by federal or foreign institutions, the monthly stipend is paid directly to the fellow. Institutions also receive an allowance to help defray such awardee expenses as tuition and fees, self-only health insurance, research supplies, equipment, travel to scientific meetings, and related items; the allowance is $3,000 per 12-month period for non-federal nonprofit institutions and $1,000 per 12-month period for federal laboratories and for-profit institutions. Awards for training at a foreign site include economy or coach round-trip airfare for the fellow only; no allowance is provided for dependents. The initial 12 months of National Research Service Award postdoctoral support carries a service payback requirement, which can be fulfilled by continued training under the award or by engaging in other health-related research training, health-related research, or health-related teaching. Fellows who fail to fulfill the payback requirement of 1 month of acceptable service for each month of the initial 12 months of support received must repay all funds received with interest.

Duration Up to 3 years.

Special features This award is offered by all funding Institutes and Centers of the National Institutes of Health (NIH) as part of the National Research Service Award (NRSA) program, originally established in 1974. The NIH designates this program as the F32 Awards.

Number awarded Varies; in a recent year, 793 awards were made through this program.

Deadline April, August, or December of each year.

[1211]
NATIONAL URBAN/RURAL FELLOWS PROGRAM

National Urban Fellows, Inc.
55 West 44th Street, Suite 600
New York, NY 10036
(212) 921-9400   Fax: (212) 921-9572

Purpose To provide mid-career minority and women public sector professionals an opportunity to strengthen leadership skills through an academic program coupled with a mentorship.

Eligibility Eligible to apply are U.S. citizens who have a bachelor's degree, have 3 years of full-time work experience in an administrative or managerial capacity, have demonstrated exceptional ability and leadership potential, meet academic admission requirements, have a high standard of integrity and work ethic, and are willing to relocate for the duration of the fellowship year.

Financial data The stipend is up to $20,000. The program also provides full payment of tuition fees, a relocation allowance of $500, and reimbursement for program related travel.

Duration 14 months.

Special features The program begins with a semester of study at Bernard M. Baruch College of the City University of New York. Following this, fellows spend 9 months in mentorship assignments as special assistants to governors, mayors, city managers, or county administrators of urban and rural organizations. Fellows who successfully complete all requirements are granted a master's of public administration from Bernard M. Baruch College.

Number awarded Varies; approximately 20 each year.

Deadline February of each year.

[1212]
NATIVE AMERICAN COMMUNITY SCHOLAR AWARDS

Smithsonian Institution
Attn: Office of Fellowships and Grants
955 L'Enfant Plaza, Suite 7000
MRC 902
Washington, DC 20560
(202) 287-3271   Fax: (202) 287-3691
E-mail: siofg@sivm.si.edu

Purpose To provide opportunities for Native Americans to pursue projects related to Native American topics at the Smithsonian Institution.

Eligibility Native Americans who are formally or informally related to a Native American community are eligible to apply. Applicants may be students at any level or independent scholars, but they must undertake a project that is related to a Native American topic and requires the use of Native American resources at the Smithsonian Institution.

Financial data Subsistence of $75 per day and travel allowances are provided.

Duration Up to 12 weeks.

Special features Projects are carried out in association with the Smithsonian's research staff.

Limitations Fellows are required to be in residence at the Smithsonian for the duration of the fellowship.

Number awarded Varies each year.

Deadline Applications are accepted year-round, but it is advisable to submit a completed application at least 3 months prior to the proposed date of appointment.

[1213]
NATIVE AMERICAN LANGUAGES PRESERVATION AND ENHANCEMENT PROJECTS

Department of Health and Human Services
Attn: Administration for Children and Families
Administration for Native Americans
Hubert H. Humphrey Building, Room 348F
200 Independence Avenue, S.W.
Washington, DC 20201-0001
(202) 690-7843

Purpose To provide funding for projects which assist Native Americans to ensure the survival and continuing vitality of their languages.

Eligibility Applications may be submitted by federally recognized Indian tribes; consortia of Indian tribes; incorporated non-federally recognized tribes; incorporated nonprofit multi-purpose community-based Indian organizations; urban Indian centers; national or regional incorporated nonprofit Native American organizations with Native American community-specific objectives; Alaska Native villages and/or nonprofit village consortia; incorporated nonprofit Alaska Native multi-purpose community-based organizations; nonprofit Alaska Native Regional Corporations/Associations in Alaska with village specific projects; nonprofit Native organizations in Alaska with village specific projects; public and nonprofit private agencies serving Native Hawaiians; public and nonprofit private agencies serving native peoples from Guam, American Samoa, Palau, or the Commonwealth of the Northern Mariana Islands; and tribally controlled community colleges, tribally controlled postsecondary vocational institutions, and colleges and universities in Hawaii, Guam, American Samoa, Palau, or the Commonwealth of the Northern Mariana Islands which serve Native American Pacific Islanders. Proposals may be either for planning grants or for design and/or implementation grants. Planning grants must enable the applicant organization to conduct an assessment and to develop the plan needed to describe the current status of the language(s) to be addressed and to establish community long-range goals to ensure its survival. Design and/or implementation grants enable a tribe or community to design and/or implement a language program to achieve the community's long-range language goal(s).

Financial data Planning grants up to $50,000 and design/implementation grants up to $125,000 are available. Grantees must provide at least 20 percent of the total approved cost of the project.

Duration 1 year.

Number awarded Varies; in a recent year, approximately $1 million was available for this program.

Deadline March of each year.

[1214]
NAVAL AIR WARFARE CENTER TRAINING SYSTEMS DIVISION FACULTY RESEARCH PARTICIPATION PROGRAM

Oak Ridge Institute for Science and Education
Attn: Science/Engineering Education Division
P.O. Box 117
Oak Ridge, TN 37831-0117
(423) 576-8807   (423) 576-8158
(800) 569-7749   Fax: (423) 576-3643
E-mail: frppnawc@orau.gov

Purpose To provide funding to faculty members who wish to participate in research on advanced simulation and training systems technology at the Naval Air Warfare Center Training Systems Division in Orlando, Florida.

Eligibility Applicants must be full-time college or university faculty members in behavioral sciences, computer science, or engineering. All programs operated by the Science/Engineering Education Division (SEED) of Oak Ridge Institute for Science and Education (ORISE) seek to broaden the participation of minorities, women, and persons with disabilities in science and engineering careers.

Financial data A stipend is awarded, based on the recipient's university salary. Reimbursement for inbound and outbound travel is also provided.

Duration 3 months to 1 year.

Special features Participants work at the Naval Air Warfare Center Training Systems Division in Orlando, Florida. This program is funded through an interagency agreement between the U.S. Department of Energy and the Naval Air Warfare Center Training Systems Division of the U.S. Navy.

Number awarded The number awarded varies each year.

Deadline Applications may be submitted at any time.

[1215]
NAVAL AIR WARFARE CENTER TRAINING SYSTEMS DIVISION POSTGRADUATE RESEARCH PARTICIPATION PROGRAM

Oak Ridge Institute for Science and Education
Attn: Science/Engineering Education Division
P.O. Box 117
Oak Ridge, TN 37831-0117
(423) 576-8503   (423) 576-2875
(800) 569-7749   Fax: (423) 576-3643
E-mail: prpnawct@orau.gov

Purpose To provide funding to postgraduates who wish to participate in research on advanced simulation and training systems technology at the Naval Air Warfare Center Training Systems Division in Orlando, Florida.

Eligibility Applicants must have completed their master's or doctoral degrees in behavioral sciences, computer science, or engineering within the past 3 years. All programs operated by the Science/Engineering Education Division (SEED) of Oak Ridge Institute for Science and Education (ORISE) seek to broaden the participation of minorities, women, and persons with disabilities in science and engineering careers.

Financial data A stipend is awarded, based on research area and highest degree earned. Reimbursement for inbound travel and moving is also provided.

Duration 1 year; may be renewed.

Special features Participants work at the Naval Air Warfare Center Training Systems Division in Orlando, Florida. This program is funded through an interagency agreement between the U.S. Department of Energy and the Naval Air Warfare Center Training Systems Division of the U.S. Navy.

Number awarded The number awarded varies each year.

Deadline Applications may be submitted at any time.

[1216]
NAVAL RESEARCH LABORATORY BROAD AGENCY ANNOUNCEMENT

Naval Research Laboratory
455 Overlook Avenue, S.W.
Washington, DC 20375-5320
Fax: (202) 767-6197   E-mail: patricia.schaefer@nrl.navy.mil

Purpose To provide funding for scientific research of interest to the U.S. Navy.

Eligibility This program is open to investigators qualified to perform research in designated scientific and technical areas. Topics cover a wide range of technical and scientific areas; recent programs included radar technology, artificial intelligence technologies, software engineering, surface chemistry sciences, ceramic materials, structural acoustics, and seafloor sciences. The Naval Research Laboratory (NRL) encourages industry, educational institutions, small businesses, small disadvantaged business concerns, Historically Black Colleges and Universities, and Minority Institutions to submit proposals.

Financial data The typical range of funding is from $100,000 to $2,000,000.

Duration 1 year.

Special features The Naval Research Laboratory conducts most of its research in its own facilities in Washington, D.C., Stennis Space Center, Mississippi, and Monterey, California, but also funds some related research.

Number awarded Varies each year.

Deadline Each program establishes its own application deadline; for a complete list of all the programs including their deadlines, contact the address above.

[1217]
NCHGR MINORITY INSTITUTION TRAVEL AWARD PROGRAM

National Institutes of Health
Attn: National Center for Human Genome Research
Chief, Mapping Technology Branch
Building 38A, Room 613
Bethesda, MD 20892
(301) 496-7531   Fax: (301) 480-2770
E-mail: bg30t@nih.gov

Purpose To provide support for students (both undergraduate and graduate) and faculty at minority institutions to attend scientific meeting, courses, and workshops relevant to the Human Genome Project.

Eligibility Principal investigators on research grants of the National Center for Human Genome Research (NCHGR) are eligible to apply for administrative supplements so that students and faculty members at minority institutions may attend scientific meetings, courses, and workshops relevant to the Human Genome Project. For the purposes of this program, a minority institution is defined as a medical or nonmedical college, university, or equivalent school in which students of underrepresented minorities (including but not limited to Blacks, Hispanics, Native Americans, and Asian or Pacific Islanders) comprise the majority or significant proportion of the school enrollment and which has a commitment to the special encouragement of minority faculty, students, and investigators. Students may be at the undergraduate, graduate, predoctoral, or postdoctoral level.

Financial data Allowable expenses include cost of transportation, lodging, meals, registration or tuition fees associated with the meeting, workshop, or course.

Special features Students and faculty at minority institutions are encouraged to identify a principal investigator on a NCHGR research grant (write to the above for a list) or a Research Centers in Minority Institutions grant in order to participate in the Minority Institution Travel Award Program.

Deadline Applications may be submitted at any time, but at least 3 months prior to date of meeting, course, or workshop

[1218]
NCHGR VISITING INVESTIGATOR PROGRAM

National Institutes of Health
Attn: National Center for Human Genome Research
Director, Visiting Investigator Program
Building 9, Room 1E106
9000 Rockville Pike MSC 0950
Bethesda, MD 20892-0950
(301) 402-2012   Fax: (301) 402-2440
E-mail: bw47i@nih.gov

Purpose To enable faculty members to spend a period of time engaging in study or research in the laboratories of the National Center for Human Genome Research (NCHGR).

Eligibility Applicants must be independent faculty investigators with potential or demonstrated excellence in a clinical or research discipline. They must be proposing to use NCHGR laboratories to learn new technologies, develop research collaborations, or pursue sabbatical research projects. Basic, clinical, and social

scientists may access the center's laboratories, core facilities, and training programs for study in any area of human genetic disease, including the ethical, legal, and social implications of genetic research. U.S. citizenship or permanent resident status is required. Women and minority candidates are strongly encouraged to apply.

Financial data Stipends provide up to 50 percent of current salary support. Funding for research related expenses and limited travel support are also available.

Deadline Applications may be submitted at any time.

[1219]
NCRR MINORITY INITIATIVE FOR K-12 TEACHERS AND HIGH SCHOOL STUDENTS

National Institutes of Health
Attn: National Center for Research Resources
Research Infrastructure Area
One Rockledge Center, Suite 6030
6705 Rockledge Drive MSC 7965
Bethesda, MD 20892-7965
(301) 435-0769   Fax: (301) 480-3770
E-mail: mb73m@nih.gov

Purpose To provide structured science research experiences for both teachers and underrepresented minority high school students in the laboratories, and under the direction, of active biomedical and/or behavioral researchers.

Eligibility This program is open to domestic, for-profit and nonprofit, public and private organizations, such as universities, colleges, hospitals, laboratories, units of state and local government, and eligible agencies of the federal government. Racial/ethnic minority individuals, women, and persons with disabilities are encouraged to apply as program directors. Applicant institutions must be proposing to offer programs to the following members of minority groups underrepresented in biomedical and/or behavioral research (Black Americans, Hispanic Americans, Native Americans, and Pacific Islanders): 1) students who are currently in high school or who have just graduated from high school; 2) elementary, middle, junior, and senior high school science teachers who are either members of an underrepresented minority group or teach a significant number of underrepresented minority students; 3) preservice teachers who have expressed an interest in teaching life sciences at the K-12 level with a focus on underrepresented minority students. Applications must request support for both students and teachers, with a minimum of 8 students per year.

Financial data Applicant organizations must establish the rate of salary and fringe benefit compensation to be provided for students and teachers employed on the grant activity, to a maximum of $2,000 per student, $3,000 per preservice teacher, and $5,000 per inservice teacher. Institutions may also apply for up to $250 per participant as a lump sum to defray costs such as supplies required for their research experiences.

Duration Student activities are 6 to 8 weeks in the summer; activities for teachers are 4 weeks or more.

Special features High school students, no more than 2 students to 1 mentor, work in an active research laboratory; teachers engage in mentored laboratory research experiences.

Number awarded Varies each year.

Deadline January and May of each year.

[1220]
NCSGC FELLOWSHIPS AND SCHOLARSHIPS

North Carolina Space Grant Consortium
c/o North Carolina State University
Mechanical and Aerospace Engineering
Box 7515
1009 Capability Drive, Room 216E
Raleigh, NC 27695-7515
(919) 515-4240   Fax: (919) 515-5934
E-mail: dejar@eos.ncsu.edu

Purpose To provide funding for space-related research proposals by students at member institutions of the North Carolina Space Grant Consortium (NCSGC).

Eligibility This program is open to undergraduate and graduate students at North Carolina State University, North Carolina A&T State University, Duke University, North Carolina Central University, the University of North Carolina at Charlotte, the University of North Carolina at Chapel Hill, and Winston-Salem State University. Applicants must be pursuing degrees in engineering or science disciplines of interest to the U.S. National Aeronautics and Space Administration (NASA). Selection is based on the quality of the research proposal, relevance to space, and academic achievement. U.S. citizenship is required. The NCSGC is a component of the NASA Space Grant program, which encourages participation by women, minorities, and persons with disabilities.

Financial data The amounts of the awards depend on the nature of the proposal and the availability of funds.

Special features This program is funded by NASA.

Number awarded At least 5 graduate fellowships and 10 undergraduate scholarships are awarded each year.

[1221]
NEBRASKA SPACE GRANT RESEARCH AWARDS

Nebraska Space Grant Consortium
c/o UNO Aviation Institute
Allwine Hall 422
University of Nebraska at Omaha
Omaha, NE 68182-0508
(402) 554-3772   (800) 858-8648
Fax: (402) 554-3781   E-mail: nasa@cwis.unomaha.edu

Purpose To fund aerospace-related research on the undergraduate and graduate school level for students in Nebraska.

Eligibility This program is open to all eligible undergraduate and graduate students at the following schools in Nebraska: University of Nebraska at Omaha, University of Nebraska at Lincoln, University of Nebraska at Kearney, University of Nebraska Medical Center, Creighton University, and Chadron State College. Applicants must be U.S. citizens and interested in conducting research in an aerospace-related area under the supervision of a faculty mentor. Special attention is given to applications submitted by women, underrepresented minorities, and individuals with disabilities.

Financial data The amount of the award depnds on the scope of the proposal and the qualifications of the applicant.

Duration Academic awards are 1 year; summer awards are for the summer months. Both awards are renewable.

Special features Recipients conduct research in an aerospace-related area and receive at least 3 semester credits for that activity during the year of the award. Funding for this program is provided by the National Aeronautics and Space Administration.

Limitations Recipients must submit a progress report each semester on the aerospace project to their designated faculty monitor. Failure to provide that report disqualifies the student from reapplying for a renewal fellowship.

[1222]
NEW HAMPSHIRE SPACE GRANT CONSORTIUM RESEARCH INFRASTRUCTURE GRANTS

New Hampshire Space Grant Consortium
c/o University of New Hampshire
Institute for the Study of Earth, Oceans, and Space
Morse Hall
Durham, NH 03824-3525
(603) 862-0094   Fax: (603) 862-1915
E-mail: nhspacegrant@unh.edu

Purpose To provide funding to organizations in New Hampshire that are interested in conducting space-related research.

Eligibility Institutions in New Hampshire may apply for these grants for funding of space-related research infrastructure activities, including seed money for research, release time for proposal writing, the use of facilities, the establishment of research collaboration, computer services, equipment acquisition, and research-related graduate and undergraduate student support exclusive of fellowship and scholarship awards. The New Hampshire Space Grant Consortium is a component of the U.S. National Aeronautics and Space Administration (NASA) Space Grant program, which encourages participation by women, minorities, and persons with disabilities.

Financial data The amounts of the awards depend on the nature of the proposal and the availability of funds.

Special features This program is funded by NASA.

Number awarded Varies each year.

[1223]
NEW JERSEY SPACE GRANT CONSORTIUM INDUSTRY/UNIVERSITY COOPERATIVE RESEARCH GRANTS

New Jersey Space Grant Consortium
c/o Stevens Institute of Technology
Department of Mechanical Engineering
Castle Point on the Hudson
Hoboken, NJ 07030
(201) 216-8964   Fax: (201) 216-8929
E-mail: sthangam@stevens-tech.edu

Purpose To provide funding for space-related research at institutions in New Jersey.

Eligibility This program is open to researchers at member institutions of the New Jersey Space Grant Consortium (David Sarnoff Research Center, New Jersey Institute of Technology, Princeton University, Rutgers, Seton Hall University, Stevens Institute of Technology, and the University of Medicine and Dentistry of New Jersey). Applicants must be proposing a program of space-related research in collaboration with industrial partners. U.S. citizenship is required. The New Jersey Space Grant Consortium is a component of the U.S. National Aeronautics and Space Administration (NASA) Space Grant program, which encourages participation by women, minorities, and people with disabilities.

Financial data Awards up to $25,000 are available, with a matching requirement for the industrial partner.

Duration Varies.

Special features This program is funded by NASA.

Number awarded 4 or 5 each year.

[1224]
NEW YORK WOMEN'S FOUNDATION GRANTS

New York Women's Foundation
Attn: Program Director
120 Wooster Street, 4th Floor
New York, NY 10012
(212) 226-2220   Fax: (212) 226-3854

Purpose To provide funding to organizations in New York City for projects that encourage and enhance the self-sufficiency of low-income women and girls.

Eligibility Nonprofit organizations located in New York City are eligible to apply if they are involved in projects aimed at New York women. Funding is provided to programs and organizations that are for low-income women and/or girls; are for women and/or girls of color; work with women and/or girls who are newcomers to the United States; are grassroots and community-based; are led by women on both board and staff; include women who are recognized leaders of their communities; reflect input from the women and/or girls affected by the problems addressed; have limited access to ongoing traditional funding sources, such as private individuals, foundations, or government; address the root causes of poverty and work toward social change through direct services, advocacy, or both; serve the employment, education, child care, housing, or health care needs of women and/or girls; and practice a philosophy of women helping women.

Financial data Grants range from $7,500 to $30,000.

Duration 1 year; may be renewed.

Limitations Funding is not provided for individuals, capital fund drives, endowments, fund-raising events, feasibility studies, real estate purchases, large CBOs, campaigns to elect candidates to public office, programs to promote religious activities, programs which are primarily artistic or cultural, programs located outside the 5 boroughs of New York City, or programs that do not comply with equal employment opportunity statutes.

Number awarded Varies; in a recent year, a total of approximately $500,000 was available for grant-making.

Deadline November of each year.

[1225]
NHLBI/MARC SUMMER RESEARCH TRAINING PROGRAM

National Institutes of Health
Attn: National Heart, Lung, and Blood Institute
Office of Special Concerns
Building 31, Room 4A28
31 Center Drive MSC 2490
Bethesda, MD 20892-2490
(301) 496-1763   Fax: (301) 402-2322
E-mail: ms85c@nih.gov

Purpose To encourage students participating in the Minority Access to Research Centers (MARC) Student Training in Academic Research (U-STAR) Program to continue their training in the areas of heart, blood vessel, lung, and blood diseases and transfusion medicine.

Eligibility Any student participating in the U-STAR is eligible to participate in this program. They must be recommended by their MARC program director, but final selection is made by scientists at the National Heart, Lung, and Blood Institute (NHLBI). Participants receive a summer research training experience in the NHLBI intramural laboratories in Bethesda, Maryland.

Financial data Students receive an allowance of $3,500, that includes $500 for round-trip transportation to Bethesda.

Duration 10 weeks, in the summer.

Deadline January of each year.

[1226]
NIAID/MODELL MINORITY FELLOWSHIPS IN PRIMARY IMMUNE DEFICIENCY

National Institutes of Health
Attn: National Institute of Allergy and Infectious Diseases
Division of Allergy, Immunology and Transplantation
Solar Building, Room 4A-19
6003 Executive Boulevard MSC 7640
Bethesda, MD 20892-7640
(301) 496-7104   Fax: (301) 402-2571
E-mail: hd7e@nih.gov

Purpose To provide funding to racial/ethnic minority individuals, women, and persons with disabilities who are interested in conducting research on the etiology, pathogenesis, diagnosis, and/or treatment of primary immune deficiency diseases.

Eligibility This program is open to minority, women, and disabled investigators who hold a Ph.D., M.D., or equivalent doctoral degree from an accredited domestic or foreign institution. They must be proposing to conduct research on the immune system and diseases that result from abnormalities of this system. Applicants must be proposing to conduct research into the basic mechanisms by which sex hormones or non-hormonal gender differences affect the immune response and protect from or contribute to a break in self tolerance.

Financial data For the first year of the award, a total of $32,300 is available for direct and indirect costs for each grant awarded.

Duration Up to 3 years.

Special features This program is administered by the National Institute of Allergy and Infectious Diseases (NIAID), a component of the National Institutes of Health (NIH), with funding provided by the Jeffrey Modell Foundation, established by Vicki and Fred Modell in memory of their son, Jeffrey, who died in 1986, at the age of 15, of an inherited immune deficiency.

Number awarded 2 each year.

[1227]
NIDDK AND NIAMS MINORITY INVESTIGATOR RESEARCH ENHANCEMENT AWARD

National Institutes of Health
Attn: National Institute of Diabetes and Digestive and Kidney Diseases
Minority Affairs Advisory Committee
Natcher Building, Room 6AS-49E
45 Center Drive MSC 6600
Bethesda, MD 20892-6600
(301) 594-8842   Fax: (301) 480-3504
E-mail: jg60d@nih.gov

Purpose To provide support for minority faculty members at minority institutions to allow them to collaborate with principal investigators of active regular research grants funded by the National Institute of Diabetes and Digestive and Kidney Diseases (NIDDK) and the National Institute of Arthritis and Musculoskeletal and Skin Diseases (NIAMS).

Eligibility For the purposes of this program, a minority institution is defined as a medical or nonmedical college, university, or equivalent school in which students of underrepresented minorities (including but not limited to Blacks, Hispanics, American Indians, and Pacific Islanders) comprise the majority or significant proportion of the school enrollment and which has a commitment to the special encouragement of minority faculty, students, and investigators. A minority investigator is defined in this program as a faculty member of a minority institution who is engaged in biomedical research. Minority investigators must be citizens of the United States or permanent residents, have a doctoral degree or equivalent in a biomedical or behavioral science, and have the background to benefit from this program. They should not have spent an extended period of time in the applicant laboratory and should not have been a principal investigator on any traditional grant mechanism from the National Institutes of Health.

Financial data Successful applications are funded as administrative supplements to the investigator's grant. The maximum award is $50,000 in total direct costs, including up to $40,000 for salary and fringe benefits and up to $10,000 for supplies and travel.

Duration Up to 4 years.

Special features Minority investigators are encouraged to identify a principal investigator on a NIDDK or NIAMS research grant in order to participate in this program. A list of all potential principal investigators is available from the above address. Information on the NIAMS program is available from Director, Women and Minority Health Issues, 45 Center Drive MSC 6500, Bethesda, MD 20892-6500, (301) 594-5052, Fax: (301) 480-4543, E-mail: Centers@ep.niams.nih.gov.

Limitations The program is not intended to pay stipends for student trainees or support candidates without previous research backgrounds.

Deadline Applications may be submitted at any time.

[1228]
NLM FELLOWSHIP IN APPLIED INFORMATICS

National Institutes of Health
Attn: National Library of Medicine
Division of Extramural Programs
Building 38A, Suite 5S-518
Bethesda, MD 20894
(301) 496-4221   Fax: (301) 402-0421
E-mail: pc49n@nih.gov

Purpose To provide financial assistance to health professionals and students who wish to pursue additional training on the use of computers and telecommunications to manage health information.

Eligibility Physicians, nurses, health science librarians, researchers, administrators, and others involved in health care activities are eligible. They must be nominated by domestic, nonprofit, public or private organizations, such as universities, colleges, hospitals, laboratories, units of state and local government, and eligible agencies of the federal government. Candidates must hold a baccalaureate, master's, or doctoral degree in a field related to health care, or be enrolled in a program leading to such a degree. They may, but need not, utilize the training for credit leading to a degree or certification in an educational program. Both mid-career professionals and junior applicants are eligible. Applications from minority individuals and women are strongly encouraged.

Financial data Stipends are based on the salary or remuneration that the individual would have been paid by the home institution, to a maximum of $58,000 per year. The applicant's institution may request an institutional allowance up to $3,000 per year

for support of supplies, equipment, travel, tuition, fees, insurance, and other training-related costs.

Duration 1 or 2 years.

Special features These awards are intended for health science professionals whose primary interest is not in research but in learning how to put informatics into practice, develop modern information systems in traditional organizations, use the new information techniques in a specific field, and help disseminate promising programs and systems. The National Library of Medicine (NLM), a component of the National Institutes of Health, designates these grants as F38 Awards.

Number awarded Varies each year.

Deadline April, August, and December of each year.

[1229]
NMSGC EDUCATION SCHOLARSHIPS

New Mexico Space Grant Consortium
c/o New Mexico State University
College of Engineering
Wells Hall, Bay 4
Wells and Locust
Las Cruces, NM 88003
(505) 646-6414   Fax: (505) 646-7791
E-mail: nmsgc@pathfinder.nmsu.edu

Purpose To provide funding to education students in New Mexico who wish to develop mathematics or science materials as part of their student teaching assignment.

Eligibility This program is open to full-time undergraduate students at colleges and universities that are affiliated with the New Mexico Space Grant Consortium (NMSGC) as education majors. Applicants must have a minimum cumulative grade point average of 3.0 and must be U.S. citizens. Proposals must describe how the applicants propose to develop space science and mathematics classroom materials for their student teaching experience. The NMSGC is a component of the U.S. National Aeronautics and Space Administration (NASA) Space Grant program, which encourages participation by women, minorities, and persons with disabilities.

Financial data Stipends are $2,000.

Duration 1 semester.

Special features This program is funded by NASA.

Limitations Students are required to spend 8 hours in the NASA/FAA Regional Teacher Resource Center on the campus of New Mexico State University developing lesson plans and to submit those plans to the NMSGC program office at the end of their semester.

Number awarded Varies each year.

Deadline October of each year.

[1230]
NOAA SMALL BUSINESS INNOVATION RESEARCH GRANTS

Department of Commerce
Attn: National Oceanic and Atmospheric Administration
Office of Research and Technology Applications
Silver Spring Metro Center Building 3, Room 15342
1325 East-West Highway
Silver Spring, MD 20910
(301) 713-3565   Fax: (301) 713-4100
E-mail: jmbishop@rdc.noaa.gov

Purpose To support small businesses that have the technological experience to contribute to the research and development mission of the National Oceanic and Atmospheric Administration (NOAA).

Eligibility For the purposes of this program, a "small business" is defined as any organization that is independently owned and operated for profit, not dominant in the field in which it is operating, and meets the size standard of 500 employees or less. The primary employment of the principal investigator must be with the firm at the time of award and during the conduct of the proposed project. Preference is given to women-owned small business concerns and to socially and economically disadvantaged small business concerns. Women-owned small business concerns are those which are at least 51 percent owned by a woman or women who also control and operate it. Socially and economically disadvantaged small business concerns are at least 51 percent owned by an Indian tribe, a native Hawaiian organization, or 1 or more socially and economically disadvantaged individuals (Black Americans, Hispanic Americans, Native Americans, Asian-Pacific Americans, or subcontinent Asian Americans). The project must be performed in the United States. Current priority areas of research include: atmospheric and hydrological sciences, ocean observation systems, living marine resources, ocean science, and cartography and photogrammetry.

Financial data Grants are offered in 2 phases. In phase 1, awards normally may not exceed $50,000 (for both direct and indirect costs); in phase 2, awards normally may not exceed $200,000 (including both direct and indirect costs).

Duration Phase 1: up to 6 months; phase 2: up to 2 years.

Number awarded Varies; for a recent year, NOAA planned to award 12 Phase 1 contracts.

Deadline January of each year.

[1231]
NONPROLIFERATION TEACHER INSTITUTE

Oak Ridge Institute for Science and Education
Attn: Science/Engineering Education Division
P.O. Box 117
Oak Ridge, TN 37831-0117
(423) 241-2874   (423) 576-5660
(800) 569-7749   Fax: (423) 576-3643
E-mail: nonptins@orau.gov

Purpose To provide funding to elementary and secondary school teachers who wish to engage in hands-on activities, research, and curriculum development to create innovative mechanisms to produce student awareness of global nuclear proliferation issues and nonproliferation efforts.

Eligibility This program is open to K-12 teachers with at least 1 year of experience in any academic discipline. All programs operated by the Science/Engineering Education Division (SEED) of Oak Ridge Institute for Science and Education (ORISE) seek

to broaden the participation of minorities, women, and persons with disabilities in science and engineering careers.

Financial data Participants receive a weekly stipend and tuition reimbursement for graduate credit.

Duration 8 weeks during the summer.

Special features Activities take place at ORISE. This program is funded by the U.S. Department of Energy but operated and administered by ORISE/SEED.

Number awarded 4 to 6 each year.

Deadline February of each year.

[1232]
NORTH CAROLINA ARTS COUNCIL OUTREACH PROJECTS

North Carolina Arts Council
Attn: Department of Cultural Resources
Cambridge House
407 North Person Street
Raleigh, NC 27601-2807
(919) 733-7897, ext. 16

Purpose To provide financial support to organizations in North Carolina that present arts programs to minority populations, people with disabilities, older adults, or people in hospitals and assisted care facilities.

Eligibility This program is open to 1) nonprofit African American, Asian American, Latino, or Native American organizations that present arts programs, and 2) nonprofit organizations that present arts programs for people with disabilities, older adults, and people in hospitals and assisted living care facilities. Selection is based on the artistic and program merit of the proposed project, involvement of professional artists, potential effectiveness of the proposed project, plan for engaging audiences/participants for the project, and the management and financial accountability of the applicant organization.

Financial data Grants range up to $5,000 per year, but must be matched dollar for dollar from the organization's own budget.

Duration 1 year; projects may extend over more than 1 year, but must be reapplied for annually.

Number awarded Varies each year.

Deadline February of each year.

[1233]
NORTH DAKOTA SPACE GRANT PROGRAM SCIENCE TEACHING ENHANCEMENT GRANTS

North Dakota Space Grant Program
c/o University of North Dakota
Center for Aerospace Studies
Department of Space Studes
Box 9008
University Avenue and Tulane
Grand Forks, ND 58202-9008
(701) 777-3167   Fax: (701) 777-3177
E-mail: cwood@badlands.nodak.edu

Purpose To provide funding to K-12 teachers in North Dakota who wish to improve their teaching of science.

Eligibility This program is open to North Dakota teachers at the K-12 level who are proposing projects to improve their teaching of science, especially as it relates to space. The North Dakota Space Grant Program is a component of the U.S. National Aeronautics and Space Administration (NASA) Space Grant program, which encourages the participation of women, minorities, and persons with disabilities.

Financial data Awards are $250.

Special features This program is funded by NASA.

Number awarded Varies; since the program began, 168 grants have been awarded to teachers in 50 of the 52 counties in North Dakota.

[1234]
NORTH DAKOTA SPACE GRANT PROGRAM STUDENT RESEARCH GRANTS

North Dakota Space Grant Program
c/o University of North Dakota
Center for Aerospace Studies
Department of Space Studes
Box 9008
University Avenue and Tulane
Grand Forks, ND 58202-9008
(701) 777-3167   Fax: (701) 777-3177
E-mail: cwood@badlands.nodak.edu

Purpose To provide funding for space-related research to students in North Dakota.

Eligibility This program is open to students at North Dakota colleges and universities who are proposing to conduct space-related research. U.S. citizenship is required. The North Dakota Space Grant Program is a component of the U.S. National Aeronautics and Space Administration (NASA) Space Grant program, which encourages the participation of women, minorities, and persons with disabilities.

Financial data The amounts of the awards depend on the nature of the proposals and the availability of funding.

Special features This program is funded by NASA.

Number awarded Varies; last semester, 18 student research projects received funding through this program.

[1235]
NORTH-CENTRAL SECTION UNDERGRADUATE GRANTS

Geological Society of America
Attn: Research Grants Administrator
3300 Penrose Place
P.O. Box 9140
Boulder, CO 80301-9140
(303) 447-2020, ext. 137   Fax: (303) 447-1133
E-mail: jforstro@geosociety.org

Purpose To provide partial support for geological research by undergraduate students at universities in the north central states.

Eligibility This program is open to undergraduate students who are majoring in geology at universities located within the geographic area of the North-Central Section of the Geological Society of America. Both members and nonmembers of the society are eligible. Applications from women, minorities, and persons with disabilities are strongly encouraged.

Financial data Grants range up to $2,500; the average grant recently was $1,604.

Duration 1 year.

Special features This program is sponsored by the Geological Society of America's North-Central Section. Applications are also available from George R. Hallberg, University of Iowa Hygienic Laboratory, 102 Oakdale Campus, H101 OH, Iowa City, IA 52242-5002.

Number awarded 1 or more each year.

Deadline February of each year.

[1236]
NORTHEASTERN SECTION STUDENT RESEARCH GRANTS

Geological Society of America
Attn: Research Grants Administrator
3300 Penrose Place
P.O. Box 9140
Boulder, CO 80301-9140
(303) 447-2020, ext. 137   Fax: (303) 447-1133
E-mail: jforstro@geosociety.org

Purpose To provide partial support for geological research by undergraduate students at universities in the northeastern part of the United States.

Eligibility This program is open to undergraduate students who are majoring in geology at universities located within the geographic area of the Northeastern Section. Applicants must be Student Associates of the Geological Society of America. Applications from women, minorities, and persons with disabilities are strongly encouraged.

Financial data Grants range up to $2,500; the average grant recently was $1,604.

Duration 1 year.

Special features This program is sponsored by the Geological Society of America's Northeastern Section. Applications are also available from Kenneth N. Weaver, Maryland Geological Survey, 2300 St. Paul Street, Baltimore, MD 21218.

Number awarded 1 or more each year.

Deadline February of each year.

[1237]
NPN CREATION FUND

National Performance Network
219 West 19th Street
New York, NY 10011-4079
(212) 645-6200   Fax: (212) 645-6317
E-mail: dtwnpn@artswire.com

Purpose To promote the performing arts by funding commissioning of new works.

Eligibility Any arts and/or community organization in collaboration with 2 or more Primary Sponsor organizations of the National Performance Network (NPN) may apply for funding to commission a work by an artist of their choice. A particular goal of the program is to engage diverse publics in substantive interactive relationships with artists.

Financial data Up to $4,500 is available for each grant. The co-commissioners must provide at least $2,000 toward the commissioning fee.

Special features Funding for this program is provided by Philip Morris Companies.

Number awarded Varies; in a recent year, 6 grants were offered through this program.

Deadline Applications may be submitted at any time.

[1238]
NPN SPECIAL UNDERWRITING, RESEARCH AND FRONTIER FUND

National Performance Network
219 West 19th Street
New York, NY 10011-4079
(212) 645-6200   Fax: (212) 645-6317
E-mail: dtwnpn@artswire.com

Purpose To promote the performing arts by funding community cultural development projects that deepen the interactive relationship between artist and community.

Eligibility Any arts and/or community organization in collaboration with a Primary Sponsor organization of the National Performance Network (NPN) may apply for funding for education projects, enhanced and long-term residencies, diversification projects, satellite engagements in the surrounding region, special promotion and production projects, or other speical projects. A particular goal of the program is to engage diverse publics in substantive interactive relationships with artists.

Financial data Up to $10,000 is available for each grant.

Special features Funding for this program is provided by the Rockefeller Foundation.

Number awarded Varies; in a recent year, 18 organizations received grants through this program.

Deadline July and November of each year.

[1239]
NSF JOINT SEMINARS AND WORKSHOPS

National Science Foundation
Attn: Directorate for Social, Behavioral, and Economic
    Sciences
Division of International Programs
4201 Wilson Boulevard
Arlington, VA 22230
(703) 306-1710   (800) 437-7408
Fax: (703) 306-0474   E-mail: intpubs@nsf.gov

Purpose To allow U.S. and foreign counterpart investigators to identify common priorities in specific science and engineering research areas and to begin preparation of cooperative research proposals.

Eligibility U.S. scientists and engineers may organize a seminar or workshop in cooperation with a foreign scholar, to be held either in the United States or overseas. Applications for funding should describe the seminar or workshop topic and explain its importance for the respective field of science or engineering, for science and engineering education, or for international science policy-relevant research. Up to 30 participants may be invited, but usually the seminar or workshop includes 10 U.S. and 10 foreign participants, with no more than 2 U.S. participants from any 1 institution. Foreign participants may come from more than 1 country. Meetings must be organized in cooperation with appropriate foreign institutions, including universities or equivalent organizations, professional societies, or multilateral organizations.

Financial data In general, grants are available to provide economy airfare and per diem for up to 12 U.S. participants to travel to the site of the seminar or workshop, whether held in the United States or abroad; transportation from point of entry in the United States to the site of the seminar or workshop, lodging, health insurance, and subsistence at prevailing U.S. government per diem rates for up to 10 foreign participants; up to $2,000 for publication and dissemination of workshop proceedings; and organizational expenses for the U.S. coordinator of up to $1,000 for seminars or workshops held in the United States or up to $500 for seminars or workshops held overseas.

Special features Organizers of joint seminars and conferences should ensure that women and minority scientists and engineers are adequately represented in the participant list. Upon request from the principal investigator, the National Science Foundation (NSF) will assist in identifying appropriate women and minority scientists and engineers.

Deadline Proposals may be submitted at any time, but at least 10 months prior to the scheduled workshop or seminar.

[1240]
NSF SMALL BUSINESS INNOVATION RESEARCH GRANTS

National Science Foundation
Attn: Directorate for Engineering
Division of Design, Manufacture, and Industrial Innovation
4201 Wilson Boulevard, Room 590
Arlington, VA 22230
(703) 306-1391   Fax: (703) 306-0337

Purpose To provide support to small and creative engineering-, science-, education-, and technology-related firms to conduct innovative, high-risk research on scientific and technical problems.

Eligibility For the purposes of this program, a "small business" is any organization that is independently owned and operated for profit, not dominant in the field in which it is operating, and meets the size standard of 500 employees or less. The primary employment of the principal investigator must be with the firm at the time of award and during the conduct of the proposed project. Members of minority racial and ethnic groups, women, and persons with disabilities are particularly encouraged to apply as principal investigators. Preference is given to women-owned small business concerns and to socially and economically disadvantaged small business concerns. Women-owned small business concerns are at least 51 percent owned by a woman or women who also control and operate it. Socially and economically disadvantaged small business concerns are at least 51 percent owned by an Indian tribe, native Hawaiian organization, or 1 or more socially and economically disadvantaged individuals (Black Americans, Hispanic Americans, Native Americans, Asian-Pacific Americans, or subcontinent Asian Americans). The project must be performed in the United States. Current priorities for critical technology areas of national importance include applied molecular biology; distributed computing and telecommunications; integrated, flexible manufacturing; materials synthesis and processing; microelectronics and optoelectronics; pollution minimization and remediation; software; and transportation.

Financial data Support is offered in 2 phases. In phase 1, awards normally may not exceed $75,000 (for both direct and indirect costs); in phase 2, awards normally may not exceed $300,000 (including both direct and indirect costs).

Duration Phase 1: up to 6 months; phase 2: up to 2 years.

Number awarded Depends on the availability of funds; the National Science Foundation (NSF) plans to award 250 to 300 phase 1 grants each year.

Deadline June of each year.

[1241]
NSF SMALL BUSINESS TECHNOLOGY TRANSFER GRANTS

National Science Foundation
Attn: Directorate for Engineering
Division of Design, Manufacture, and Industrial Innovation
4201 Wilson Boulevard, Room 590
Arlington, VA 22230
(703) 306-1391   Fax: (703) 306-0337
E-mail: dgorman@nsf.gov

Purpose To provide financial support to cooperative research and development projects carried out between small business concerns and research institutions in areas of concern to the National Science Foundation (NSF).

Eligibility For the purposes of this program, a "small business" is defined as any organization that is independently owned and operated for profit, not dominant in the field in which it is operating, and meets the size standard of 500 employees or less. Unlike the NSF Small Business Innovation Research Grants, the primary employment of the principal investigator does not need to be with the business concern. This program, however, requires that the small business apply in collaboration with a nonprofit research institution for conduct of a project that has potential for commercialization. At least 40 percent of the work must be performed by the small business and at least 30 percent of the work must be performed by the research institution. The principal investigator may have his/her primary employment with an organization other than the small business concern, including the research institution. Preference is given to women-owned small business concerns and to socially and economically disadvantaged small business concerns. Women-owned small business concerns are those which are at least 51 percent owned by a woman or women who also control and operate it. Socially and economically disadvantaged small business concerns are at least 51 percent owned by an Indian tribe, a native Hawaiian organization, or 1 or more socially and economically disadvantaged individuals (Black Americans, Hispanic Americans, Native Americans, Asian-Pacific Americans, or subcontinent Asian Americans). The project must be performed in the United States.

Financial data In the first phase, annual awards may not exceed $100,000 for direct costs, indirect costs, and negotiated fixed fees. In the second phase, awards up to $350,000 are available.

Duration Normally 12 months for the first phase and 2 years for the second phase.

Special features Grants in the first phase are to determine the scientific, technical, and commercial merit and feasibility of the proposed cooperative effort and the quality of performance of the small business concern. In the second phase, the research and development efforts continue, depending on the results of the first phase.

Limitations Currently, the NSF is making Small Business Technology Transfer Grants only in the field of novel materials for flat panel displays.

Number awarded 10 to 15 each year.

Deadline January of each year.

[1242]
NSF STANDARD AND CONTINUING GRANTS

National Science Foundation
4201 Wilson Boulevard
Arlington, VA 22230
(703) 306-1234   TDD: (703) 306-0090
E-mail: info@nsf.gov

Purpose To provide financial support for research in broad areas of science and engineering.

Eligibility The National Science Foundation (NSF) supports research through its Directorates of Biological Sciences; Computer and Information Science and Engineering; Education and Human Resources; Engineering; Geosciences; Mathematical and Physical Sciences; and Social, Behavioral, and Economic Sciences. Within those general areas of science and engineering, NSF awards 2 types of grants: 1) standard grants, in which NSF agrees to provide a specific level of support for a specified period of time with no statement of NSF intent to provide additional future support without submission of another proposal; and 2) continuing grants, in which NSF agrees to provide a specific level of support for an initial specified period of time with a statement of intent to provide additional support of the project for additional periods, provided funds are available and the results achieved warrant further support. Although NSF often solicits proposals for support of targeted areas through issuance of specific program solicitations, it also accepts unsolicited proposals. Scientists, engineers, and educators usually act as the principal investigator and initiate proposals that are officially submitted by their employing organization. Most employing organizations are universities, colleges, and nonprofit nonacademic organizations (such as museums, observatories, research laboratories, and professional societies). Certain programs are open to for-profit organizations, state and local governments, or unaffiliated individuals. Principal investigators usually must be U.S. citizens, nationals, or permanent residents. NSF particularly encourages members of racial and ethnic minority groups, women, and persons with disabilities to apply as principal investigators.

Financial data Funding levels vary, depending on the nature of the project and the availability of funds. Awards resulting from unsolicited research proposals are subject to statutory cost-sharing.

Duration Standard grants specify the period of time, usually up to 1 year; continuing grants normally specify 1 year as the initial period of time, with support to continue for additional periods.

Special features Researchers interested in support from NSF should contact the address above to obtain further information on areas of support and programs operating within the respective directorates. They should consult with a program officer before submitting an application. Information on programs is available on the NSF home page at http://www.nsf.gov.

Limitations NSF does not normally support technical assistance, pilot plant efforts, research requiring security classification, the development of products for commercial marketing, or market research for a particular project or invention. Bioscience research with disease-related goals, including work on the etiology, diagnosis, or treatment of physical or mental disease, abnormality, or malfunction in human beings or animals, is normally not supported.

Number awarded Approximately 10,000 new awards are issued each year.

Deadline Many programs accept proposals at any time. Other programs establish target dates or deadlines; those target dates and deadlines are published in the *NSF Bulletin* and in specific program announcements/solicitations.

[1243]
NURSE ANESTHETIST EDUCATION PROGRAMS

Health Resources and Services Administration
Attn: Bureau of Health Professions
Division of Nursing
Parklawn Building, Room 9-36
5600 Fishers Lane
Rockville, MD 20857
(301) 443-6193   Fax: (301) 443-8586

Purpose To provide grants to schools of nursing to meet the costs of projects for the education of nurse anesthetists.

Eligibility Public and private nonprofit schools of nursing may apply for these grants to develop and operate, or maintain or expand programs designed to qualify registered nurses to become certified registered nurse anesthetists. Funding priority is given to programs which demonstrate either substantial progress over the last 3 years or a significant experience of 10 or more years in enrolling and graduating trainees from those minority populations identified as at risk of poor health outcomes.

Financial data In recent years, grants totaling $1.8 million have been awarded under this program annually; the average grant has been $153,900.

Number awarded Recently, 12 grants to institutions have been made through this program annually.

Deadline January of each year.

[1244]
NURSE PRACTITIONER AND NURSE MIDWIFERY GRANTS

Health Resources and Services Administration
Attn: Bureau of Health Professions
Division of Nursing
Parklawn Building, Room 9-36
5600 Fishers Lane
Rockville, MD 20857
(301) 443-6333   Fax: (301) 443-8586

Purpose To provide grants to schools of nursing to meet the costs of projects to educate nurse practitioners and nurse midwives.

Eligibility Public and private nonprofit schools of nursing may apply for these grants to 1) plan, develop, and operate, or 2) maintain or significantly expand programs for the education of nurse practitioners and nurse midwives so they will be qualified to provide effective primary health care in settings such as homes, ambulatory care facilities, and other health care institutions. Programs must be at least 1 academic year in length; curricula must include a combination of clinical practice and at least 4 months of didactic instruction; enrollment must total no fewer than 6 full-time equivalent students per class. Funding priority is given to applicant institutions that demonstrate either substantial progress over the last 3 years or a significant experience of 10 or more years in enrolling and graduating trainees from those minority or low-income populations identified as at risk of poor health outcomes.

Financial data Recently, $16.9 million in grants per year have been provided through this program; the average grant has been $243,600.

Duration 1 year; may be renewed.

Number awarded Approximately 69 each year.
Deadline December of each year.

[1245]
NUTRITION ACTION FELLOWSHIP

Center for Science in the Public Interest
Attn: Executive Director
1875 Connecticut Avenue, N.W., Suite 300
Washington, DC 20009-5728
(202) 332-9110   Fax: (202) 265-4954

Purpose To provide funding to professionals or postdoctorates interested in serving as a nutrition advocate at the Center for Science in the Public Interest.

Eligibility This program is open to recent graduates with a Ph.D., M.D., M.P.H., M.S., or other advanced degree. Applicants should have demonstrated interest in public interest advocacy and nutrition science, food safety, or health policy. They should also be able to demonstrate academic achievement and writing ability. Minorities, women, and persons with disabilities are particularly encouraged to apply.

Financial data The stipend is $30,000.

Duration 1 year, generally starting in June.

Special features Fellows work in the center's Washington office on nutrition science policy and/or food safety issues.

Number awarded 1 each year.

Deadline Applications may be submitted at any time.

[1246]
OAK RIDGE NATIONAL LABORATORY POSTDOCTORAL RESEARCH ASSOCIATES PROGRAM

Oak Ridge Institute for Science and Education
Attn: Science/Engineering Education Division
P.O. Box 117
Oak Ridge, TN 37831-0117
(423) 241-2877   (423) 576-4805
(800) 569-7749   Fax: (423) 576-3643
E-mail: ornlprap@orau.gov

Purpose To provide financial assistance for postdoctoral research and training in a broad range of science and engineering activities related to basic sciences, energy, and environment.

Eligibility Applicants must have completed a doctoral degree within the past 5 years in engineering, life sciences, physical sciences, earth sciences, environmental sciences, mathematics, computer sciences, or other scientific disciplines. Awards are tenable at Oak Ridge National Laboratory in Tennessee. All programs operated by the Science/Engineering Education Division (SEED) of Oak Ridge Institute for Science and Education (ORISE) seek to broaden the participation of minorities, women, and persons with disabilities in science and engineering careers.

Financial data The stipend is based on research area and degree; reimbursement for inbound travel and moving are also provided.

Duration 1 year; renewable.

Special features This program is funded by Oak Ridge National Laboratory and administered by ORISE/SEED.

Number awarded Varies each year.

Deadline Applications may be submitted at any time.

[1247]
OFFICE OF GROUND WATER AND DRINKING WATER POSTGRADUATE INTERNSHIP PROGRAM

Oak Ridge Institute for Science and Education
Attn: Science/Engineering Education Division
P.O. Box 117
Oak Ridge, TN 37831-0117
(423) 576-8503   (423) 241-2875
(800) 569-7749   Fax: (423) 576-3643
E-mail: pipogwdw@orau.gov

Purpose To provide funding to postgraduates for research on drinking water regulations for the Office of Ground Water and Drinking Water of the Environmental Protection Agency (EPA).

Eligibility Applicants should have completed a baccalaureate, master's, or doctoral degree within the past 3 years; others are considered on a case-by-case basis. Their field of study should have been environmental sciences, engineering, physical sciences, or other related scientific disciplines. They must propose to conduct research at EPA's Office of Ground Water and Drinking Water in Cincinnati, Ohio. All programs operated by the Science/Engineering Education Division (SEED) of Oak Ridge Institute for Science and Education (ORISE) seek to broaden the participation of minorities, women, and persons with disabilities in science and engineering careers.

Financial data The stipend is based on research area and degree; a limited reimbursement for inbound travel and moving is also provided.

Duration 1 year; renewable.

Special features This program is funded by an interagency agreement between the U.S. Department of Energy and EPA and administered by ORISE/SEED.

Number awarded Varies each year.

Deadline Applications may be submitted at any time.

[1248]
OFFICE OF NAVAL RESEARCH LONG-RANGE SCIENTIFIC PROJECTS

Office of Naval Research
Attn: Code 353
800 North Quincy Street
Arlington, VA 22217-5660
(703) 696-4111   E-mail: hughesd@onr.navy.mil

Purpose To provide funding for long-range research projects which offer potential for advancement and improvement of naval operations.

Eligibility This program is open to qualified investigators in specified scientific and technical areas. The exact research topics vary annually; some of the recent program areas included materials and structures databases for use in naval aircraft, engineered lumber for waterfront construction technology development, submarine force security/survivability, mobile offshore bases, and human information management and advanced training technology. Historically Black Colleges and Universities, minority institutions, and small and disadvantaged businesses are encouraged to apply. Selection is based on 1) overall scientific, technical, or socio-economic merits of the proposal; 2) potential naval relevance and contributions of the effort to the agency's specific mission; 3) the offeror's capabilities, related experience, facilities, techniques, or unique combinations of these which are integral factors for achieving the proposal objectives; 4) the qualifications, capabilities, and experience of the proposed principal investigator, team leader, or key personnel who are critical in achieving

the proposal objectives; and 5) realism of the proposed cost and availability of funds. For awards made as contracts, the socio-economics merits of each proposal are evaluated based on the commitment to provide meaningful subcontracting opportunities for small business, small disadvantaged business, woman-owned small business concerns, Historically Black Colleges and Universities, and Minority Institutions.

Financial data Amounts of the awards depend on the nature of the proposal and the availability of funds.

Duration Up to 3 years.

Number awarded Varies each year.

Deadline Each specific research program establishes its own application deadline; for complete information on all the programs including their deadlines, contact the address above.

[1249]
ONCOLOGY NURSING FOUNDATION ETHNIC MINORITY RESEARCHER AND MENTORSHIP GRANTS

Oncology Nursing Foundation
501 Holiday Drive
Pittsburgh, PA 15220-2749
(412) 921-7373   Fax: (412) 921-6565
E-mail: onsmain@nauticom.net

Purpose To fund oncology nursing research conducted by ethnic minorities.

Eligibility Principal investigators must be ethnic minority researchers (Native American, African American, Asian American, Pacific Islander, Hispanic/Latino, or other ethnic minority background). Beginning or novice researchers must utilize a research mentor for consultive services in research design and statistical analyses.

Financial data The grant is $5,000 ($4,000 for the conduct of the research project and $1,000 for the research mentor or consultant).

Special features Every effort is made to find an ethnic minority mentor; however, the primary criteria for matching the investigator and mentor is the substantive area of the research and the expertise of the mentor.

Number awarded 2 each year.

Deadline October of each year.

[1250]
OPERATION PATHFINDER

Department of Commerce
Attn: National Oceanic and Atmospheric Administration
Office of Oceanic and Atmospheric Research
Silver Spring Metro Center Building 3, 11th Floor
1315 East-West Highway
Silver Spring, MD 20910
(301) 713-2448, ext. 142   Fax: (301) 713-0799
E-mail: Dale.Ingmanson@noaa.gov

Purpose To enable elementary and middle school teachers to participate in a program that introduces them to oceanographic and coastal processes.

Eligibility This program is open to elementary and middle school teachers with an interest in marine sciences. Participants attend seminars at 6 regional campuses and marine laboratories affiliated with the National Sea Grant College Program. Topics include deep ocean discoveries and technologies, marine and aquatic resources, marine and aquatic habitat, marine and estuarine pollution, physical processes, and plate tectonics. The program attempts to recruit minority teachers, teachers of minority students, and teachers of students from economically disadvantaged backgrounds.

Financial data Participants receive a stipend, food and lodging, and round-trip travel to host institutions.

Duration 12 days, during the summer.

Special features For a list of the dates and locations of the programs, contact the address above. The program is sponsored by the National Sea Grant Program and the National Environmental Satellite, Data, and Information Service within the National Oceanic and Atmospheric Administration; the Office of Naval Research and the Naval Oceanography and Meteorology Command with the U.S. Navy, and the Office of Insular Affairs within the Department of Interior.

Number awarded Varies each year.

Deadline April of each year.

[1251]
OREGON STATE BAR EXAM GRANTS

Oregon State Bar
Attn: Affirmative Action Program
5200 SW Meadows Road
P.O. Box 1689
Lake Oswego, OR 97035-0889
(503) 620-0222   (800) 452-8260 (within OR)
Fax: (503) 684-1366

Purpose To provide grants to minorities in Oregon who are preparing to take the state law bar examination.

Eligibility Applicants must be minorities who intend to practice in Oregon after the bar examination, are scheduled to take the next exam, and are in financial need (determined by subtracting the applicant's and spouse's available assets and the applicant's and spouse's income from the sum of their debts, current monthly expenses, and bar exam-related expenses for the 2 months preceding the bar exam).

Financial data The maximum amount of any grant will not exceed the combined costs of the bar exam application fee and the bar exam preparation course. The actual amount of the grant is determined by the amount of funds remaining in the budget for Bar Exam Grants, the number of other applicants, the applicant's financial need as compared to the need of other applicants, and the extent to which the financial need and other information on the application is complete, credible, and consistent. If the recipient withdraws from the bar exam, repayment in full is required within 1 month from the date of withdrawal.

Duration This is a 1-time grant.

Number awarded Varies each year.

[1252]
OSGC RESEARCH PROGRAM

Oklahoma Space Grant Consortium
c/o University of Oklahoma
College of Geosciences
Oklahoma Climatological Survey
100 East Boyd, Suite 1210
Norman, Oklahoma 73019-0628
(405) 325-1240   Fax: (405) 325-2550
E-mail: vduca@geoadm.gen.uoknor.edu

Purpose To provide funding for research activities in Oklahoma

that are related to the mission of the U.S. National Aeronautics and Space Administration (NASA).

Eligibility This program provides support for space-related research activities at member and affiliate institutions of the Oklahoma Space Grant Consortium (OSGC)—Oklahoma State University, the University of Oklahoma, Cameron University, and Langston University. Proposals may be submitted by faculty and staff of those institutions 1) to foster multi-disciplinary and multi-university research through special conferences, programs, and correspondence; and 2) to enhance the support infrastructure for faculty to facilitate the pursuit of NASA-related research to include both administrative support and marginal funds for travel and critical equipment or supplies. The OSGC is a component of the NASA Space Grant program, which encourages participation by women, minorities, and persons with disabilities.

Financial data Financing depends on the availability of funds.

Special features This program is funded by NASA.

[1253]
OUTCOMES RESEARCH TRAINING AWARDS

American Digestive Health Foundation
7910 Woodmont Avenue, Suite 700
Bethesda, MD 20814-3015
(301) 654-2635   Fax: (301) 654-5920

Purpose To provide financial support to individuals trained in gastroenterology to obtain advanced training in outcomes research.

Eligibility This program is open to M.D.s who are committed to academic careers and who have completed the clinical training necessary for board eligibility. They must be sponsored by an individual member of any member organization of the American Digestive Health Foundation (ADHF) who directs a gastroenterology-related unit that is engaged in research training in a North American medical school-affiliated teaching hospital or research institute. Applicants must demonstrate a coherent plan to obtain formal training in outcomes research disciplines; the plan must include a preceptor who is committed to the training and development of the awardee. Women and minorities are particularly encouraged to apply. Selection is based on past training and experience, the record and commitment of the sponsor and preceptor, the institutional environment, and the proposed curriculum.

Financial data The award is $50,000 per year; that includes $36,000 for salary and $14,000 for tuition and training-related expenses.

Duration 2 years.

Special features This award is administered by ADHF sponsored by the American Gastroenterological Association (AGA).

Number awarded 1 or 2 each year.

Deadline September of each year.

[1254]

PACIFIC NORTHWEST COASTAL ECOSYSTEM REGIONAL STUDY (PNCERS) PROGRAM

Department of Commerce
Attn: National Oceanic and Atmospheric Administration
Coastal Ocean Program
Silver Spring Metro Center Building 3, Room 9608
1315 East-West Highway
Silver Spring, MD 20910
(301) 713-3338

Purpose To provide funding for regional ecosystem studies in the Pacific Northwest.

Eligibility This programs is open to teams comprised of individuals from all academic, federal, state and local government, and private institutions. Applicants must be proposing a research project on the coastal waters of the Pacific Northwest from the continental shelf break through the estuaries, between Vancouver Island and Cape Mendocino, with the atmosphere, open ocean, and riverine environments acting as key influences. The program strongly encourages women, minorities, and persons with disabilities to compete fully in the research.

Financial data Expected funding is up to $850,000 for the first year, up to $1,000,000 per year for years 2 through 4, and up to $700,000 for the fifth year.

Duration 5 years.

Special features This program is administered by a project management team of representatives from the Oregon Coastal Management Program, Washington Sea Grant Program, Oregon Sea Grant Program, and the National Marine Fisheries Service's Northwest Fisheries Science Center. Further information is also available from the PNCERS Program Office, Department of Environmental Quality, 811 SW Sixth Avenue, Portland, OR 97204-1390, (503) 229-6978, Fax: (503) 229-6124, E-mail: gregory.mcmurray@state.or.us.

Number awarded Varies each year.

Deadline Proposals are due in January and full proposals must be submitted by March.

[1255]

PAUL P. VOURAS DISSERTATION RESEARCH GRANT

Association of American Geographers
1710 16th Street, N.W.
Washington, DC 20009-3198
(202) 234-1450   Fax: (202) 234-2744
E-mail: gaia@aag.org

Purpose To provide financial assistance to graduate students preparing dissertations in geography.

Eligibility Graduate students currently working on Ph.D.s in geography are eligible to apply if they have completed all of the requirements except the dissertation and have been members of the Association of American Geographers for at least 1 year prior to submitting an application. Preference is given to minority applicants.

Financial data The amount awarded varies, up to a maximum of $500.

Duration 1 year.

Limitations Funds must be used for direct research expenses only and may not be used to cover overhead costs.

Number awarded 1 each year.

Deadline December of each year.

[1256]

PAUL W. MCQUILLEN MEMORIAL FELLOWSHIP

John Carter Brown Library
Brown University
P.O. Box 1894
Providence, RI 02912
(401) 863-2725   E-mail: Karen_DeMaria@Brown.edu

Purpose To support scholars interested in conducting research at the John Carter Brown Library, which is renowned for its collection of historical sources pertaining to the Americas prior to 1830.

Eligibility This fellowship is open to Americans and foreign nationals who are engaged in pre- or postdoctoral or independent research. Graduate students must have passed their preliminary or general examinations at the time of application.

Financial data The stipend is $1,000 per month.

Duration From 2 to 4 months.

Special features Among the emphases of the library's holdings are works dealing with Native Americans in North and South America, colonial architecture books, economic history, maritime history, and works on the adaptation of religion and religious institutions to the New World.

Limitations Fellows are expected to be in regular residence at the library and to participate in the intellectual life of Brown University for the duration of the program.

Number awarded 1 each year.

Deadline January of each year.

[1257]

PEMBROKE CENTER POSTDOCTORAL FELLOWSHIP

Pembroke Center for Teaching and Research on Women
Brown University
Box 1958
Providence, RI 02912
(401) 863-2643   Fax: (401) 863-1298

Purpose To provide research support for scholars interested in conducting research on the cross-cultural study of gender.

Eligibility Fellowships are open to anyone in the humanities, social sciences, or sciences who does not hold a tenured position at an American college or university. Applicants must be willing to spend a year in residence at the Pembroke Center and participate in a research project related to gender on a theme that changes annually. A recent theme was "The Future of Gender." The center encourages minority and Third World scholars to apply.

Financial data The stipend is $25,000.

Duration 1 year.

Special features Postdoctoral fellows in residence participate in weekly seminars and present at least 1 public paper during the year, as well as pursue an individual research project. Supplementary funds are available for assistance with travel expenses from abroad.

Number awarded 4 each year: 2 to scholars in the humanities/social sciences and 2 to minority/Third World scholars.

Deadline December of each year.

[1258]
PERGAMON—NWSA GRADUATE SCHOLARSHIP IN WOMEN'S STUDIES

National Women's Studies Association
7100 Baltimore Avenue, Suite 301
College Park, MD 20740
(301) 403-0525   Fax: (301) 403-4137
E-mail: nwsa@umail.umd.edu

Purpose To provide financial assistance for graduate research in women's studies.

Eligibility Applicants must be doing research for or writing a master's thesis or Ph.D. dissertation in the interdisciplinary field of women's studies. Preference is given to nominees who are members of the National Women's Studies Association (NWSA) and whose research project addresses issues relevant to women of color or class.

Financial data Scholarships are $500 and $1,000.

Duration 1 year.

Special features The $1,000 award is funded by Pergamon Press and the $500 scholarship is sponsored by the NWSA.

Number awarded 2 each year: 1 of $500 and 1 of $1,000.

Deadline February of each year.

[1259]
PEW EVANGELICAL SCHOLARS PROGRAM

University of Notre Dame
G123 Hesburgh Library
Notre Dame, IN 46556
(219) 631-8347   Fax: (219) 631-8721

Purpose To fund research and writing projects designed to bring Christian voice to important scholarly problems in the humanities, social sciences, and theological disciplines.

Eligibility This program is open to Christian scholars who are Canadian or American citizens and from Christian scholars who are foreign nationals with long-term appointments to North American institutions. Applicants must have earned a doctorate; scholars who are currently active candidates for an advanced degree are not eligible. Women and minority candidates are especially encouraged to apply. Proposals on both non-religious and religious topics in the humanities, social sciences, and theological disciplines are invited. Proposals that proceed from demonstrably Christian perspective are particularly encouraged. Proposals should address important critical issues in their discipline. Projects should be designed to produce a book-length work or the equivalent, should be publishable by a major academic press, and should target scholarly audiences (not students, practitioners, or the general public). Proposals to revise dissertations for publication or for improving teaching methods will not be considered. Proposal are evaluated in 4 areas: quality of scholarship, potential of the applicant, scholarly significance of the project, and the impact of Christian thinking on the project's conception, perspective, interpretive strategy, or methodology.

Financial data The stipend is $35,000. Funds are awarded to the fellow's institution (other arrangements are worked out for independent scholars). Fellows are free to spend their fellowship tenure at any location conducive to their work.

Duration 1 year, including summer seminars.

Special features Funds for this program come from the Pew Charitable Trusts. A fellow may hold other grants and fellowships, but only if the total grant funds received for the academic year do not exceed the fellow's normal salary. The program convenes annual summer seminars at which the fellows discuss their research. The program funds travel, lodging, and dining expenses for these seminars.

Limitations Fellows are expected to devote their time solely to research and writing during the fellowship.

Number awarded 14 each year.

Deadline November of each year.

[1260]
PHYSICIAN ASSISTANT TRAINING GRANTS

Health Resources and Services Administration
Attn: Bureau of Health Professions
Division of Medicine
Parklawn Building, Room 9A-27
5600 Fishers Lane
Rockville, MD 20857
(301) 443-3456   Fax: (301) 443-1945
E-mail: espirer@hrsa.ssw.dhhs.gov

Purpose To provide financial support for programs for training physician assistants.

Eligibility This program is open to accredited schools of medicine or osteopathic medicine or other public or private nonprofit entities. Eligible physician assistant programs are those which are either accredited by the American Medical Association's Committee on Allied Health Education and Accreditation or its successor organization, the Commission on Accreditation of Allied Health Education Programs. Funding may be used for planning, developing, and operating or maintaining programs for the training of physician assistants and for training faculty to teach in such programs. Selection criteria include 1) the proposal includes a strategy and plan for recruiting and retaining minority and disadvantaged faculty, students, trainees, and/or residents (applicants are expected to reflect the diversity of the populations within their states); 2) the proposal includes clinically oriented, generalist-trained faculty who practice in community-based settings that include underserved populations; 3) the proposal includes a curriculum that emphasizes areas of study pertinent to the needs of special populations in urban, rural, and underserved areas (people with low incomes, members of racial and ethnic minority groups, people with disabilities, and at-risk population groups); 4) the proposal describes the actions taken by the institution that demonstrate faculty involvement with the curricular innovations that are beyond what is traditionally part of such a curriculum; and 5) the proposal includes data regarding the most recent 3-year average track record of a program in placing graduates in primary care training, primary care practice, or generalist faculty positions.

Financial data The amounts of the awards vary; recently, the average grant has been $135,000.

Duration 3 years.

Number awarded Varies each year.

Deadline January of each year.

[1261]
PLANNING AND STABILIZATION GRANTS TO ORGANIZATIONS

National Endowment for the Arts
Attn: Heritage and Preservation
Nancy Hanks Center
1100 Pennsylvania Avenue, N.W.
Washington, DC 20506-0001
(202) 682-5429   TTY: (202) 682-5496

Purpose To provide funding to organizations to enable them to focus on strategies for building partnerships and resources with related organizations, or to assess carefully their organizational strengths, weaknesses, and financial health.

Eligibility Nonprofit tax-exempt organizations of demonstrated artistic excellence may apply if they have a 4-year history of programming, have professional staff, compensate all professional performers and related or supporting professional personnel, assure that no part of any supported project will be performed or engaged in under unsanitary or hazardous conditions, and comply with other federal regulations. Applicants may be arts institutions, local arts agencies, arts service organizations, tribal communities and Indian tribes, official units of city governments, and other organizations that can further the goals of the National Endowment for the Arts (NEA). Applicants for stabilization grants must have a minimum annual operating expenditure level of $200,000; there is no minimum annual operating expenditure level for organizations applying for planning support only, except orchestras and opera companies, which must have an annual operating expenditure level of $100,000. All applicants should be proposing projects involving technical assistance to develop long-range plans, improve the skills of staff members, or otherwise strengthen their capabilities or those of their fields; enhance earned income through the creation or development of products and/or services; efforts to identify and target potential audiences, and to streamline box office operations, through an improved use of technology; other income- or capacity-building projects that contribute to organizational strengthening; community planning to examine the feasibility of a new or enhanced performing/presenting venue that would serve arts organizations and audiences throughout the community; development of a consortium or other alliance of organizations that come together to share expertise and resources; collection and dissemination, in computer-accessible form, of information on the range of arts resources and programming available throughout the community; development, by a national service or other appropriate organization, of a model computer program for ticket sales, scheduling, or marketing purposes that could be made available to arts groups; or the acquisition of term endowment or term cash reserve funds. Selection is based on artistic excellence and artistic merit of the proposed project and the applicant organization, impact of the project, and ability to carry out the project.

Financial data Grants generally range from $15,000 to $500,000 for planning projects and from $40,000 to $500,000 for stabilization projects. All grants of $100,000 or less require a match of at least 1 to 1; grants between $100,001 and $250,000 require a match of at least 3 to 1; grants between $250,001 and $500,000 require a match of at least 5 to 1.

Duration Up to 2 years.

Special features The NEA remains committed to supporting equitable opportunity for all and investing in as diverse a reflection of our society as possible.

Limitations Funding is not provided for general operating support; seasonal support; construction or renovation of facilities; marketing expenses that are not directly related to the proposed project; commercial enterprises or activities; fundraising or development; debt and deficit reduction; cash reserves and endowments; social activities, entertainment costs, receptions, etc.; lobbying expenses; individuals directly; elementary and secondary schools directly; avocational or student groups; professional training in degree-granting institutions; work toward academic degrees; literary projects, programming, or publishing that does not focus primarily on contemporary literature and/or writers; research that is directed primarily to academic purposes or scholarly projects; publication of books or exhibition of works by the applicant organization's staff, board members, faculty, or trustees; exhibitions of, and other projects involving, single, privately owned collections; purchase of major equipment; subgranting or regranting, except for state arts agencies and regional arts organizations.

Deadline April of each year.

[1262]
PLAYWORKS FESTIVAL AT UTEP

Department of Theatre Arts
Attn: Head of Playwriting and Directing
University of Texas at El Paso
Fox Fine Arts Center
El Paso, TX 79968-0549
(915) 747-7854   Fax: (915) 747-5438
E-mail: mwright@utep.edu

Purpose To offer students the opportunity to write new plays from scratch in residence at the University of Texas at El Paso (UTEP).

Eligibility This program is open only to student playwrights. Applicants must be currently enrolled at a college or university in the continental United States. Submissions from Latino/Hispanic/Chicano and Native American students are especially encouraged. To apply, submit sample work (full-length or 1-act play) plus a proposal for a new play to be written in residence.

Financial data Participants receive a stipend (the amount depends on the funding available), travel, room, and board.

Duration 3 weeks in the early summer.

Special features This program started in 1992. The winning entrants must be in residence at UTEP during the summer to write new plays from scratch, have them developed in class, and present public readings.

Number awarded Several each year.

Deadline January of each year.

[1263]
POSTDOCTORAL FELLOWSHIP ON PEACE AND SECURITY IN A CHANGING WORLD

Social Science Research Council
810 Seventh Avenue
New York, NY 10019
(212) 377-2700   Fax: (212) 377-2727

Purpose To support postdoctoral research training on the implications for security issues of worldwide cultural, social, economic, military, and political changes.

Eligibility The competition is open to all scholars (in the first 10 years of their careers) whose competence for advanced research has been demonstrated by their previous work. In most cases, these scholars should already hold the doctoral degree (or its equivalent); however, possession of the degree is not a requirement for lawyers, public servants, journalists, or others who can demonstrate comparable research experience and an ability to contribute to the research literature. There are no citizenship, residency, or nationality requirements. Applicants must be working in the social/behavioral sciences (including history and foreign area studies), the humanities, or the physical and biological sciences, but must propose to undertake training that adds a new competence to the disciplinary skills that they already have. Minorities and women are particularly encouraged to apply.

Financial data   The stipend, up to $37,500 per year, is appropriate for the fellow's current salary and the cost of living where the fellow will be working.

Duration   In most cases, 2 years.

Special features   The Social Science Research Council administers this program with funds provided by the John D. and Catherine T. MacArthur Foundation as part of its Program in International Peace and Security Studies. Training may occur in any setting of the recipient's choice, in any nation, and may consist of formal course work, tutorials, internships, senior apprenticeships, or supervised study with senior faculty.

Limitations   The program requires and enables researchers to add to their present specialty a competence in a different area and to apply their newly-enhanced skills to specific research projects. The fellowships are not designed for and will not support research programs for which the applicant is already prepared by prior experience and training. Fellows must devote full time to the fellowship and are not permitted to be otherwise employed.

Number awarded   Approximately 6 each year.

Deadline   November of each year.

[1264]
POSTDOCTORAL RESEARCH FELLOWSHIPS IN BIOSCIENCES RELATED TO THE ENVIRONMENT

National Science Foundation
Attn: Directorate for Biological Sciences
Division of Biological Infrastructure
4201 Wilson Boulevard, Room 615
Arlington, VA 22230
(703) 306-1469   E-mail: ckimsey@nsf.gov

Purpose   To provide opportunities for junior doctoral-level scientists to engage in research training either in the United States or abroad on the fundamental mechanisms underlying the interactions between organisms and their environment.

Eligibility   This program is open to persons who are citizens, nationals, or permanent residents of the United States at the time of application. Applicants must have earned a Ph.D. no earlier than 3 years preceding the deadline date and must be proposing to gain additional scientific training beyond the doctoral degree and to pursue innovation and imaginative research into the fundamental mechanisms underlying the interactions between organisms and their environment at the molecular, cellular, organismal, population, community, and or ecosystem level in any area of biology. Research training may be conducted at any appropriate nonprofit U.S. or foreign institution, including colleges and universities, government and national laboratories, and privately-sponsored nonprofit institutes and museums. Research plans oriented toward human, animal, or plant disease or toxicology and those with clinical or other applied objectives are ineligible. Applications are particularly encouraged from women, members of ethnic and racial minority groups, and persons with disabilities.

Financial data   The fellowship provides a stipend of $28,000 and 2 special allowances: $8,000 to the fellow for research costs (scientific supplies, travel, publication expenses, and other research-related costs) and $4,000 to the institution as an administrative allowance for fringe benefits and expenses incurred in support of the fellow (space, equipment, and general-purpose supplies).

Duration   2 years; applicants who propose to spend at least 1 year at a foreign institution may request a third year of support to complete fellowship research and training at an appropriate U.S. institution.

Number awarded   Approximately 40 each year.

Deadline   October of each year.

[1265]
POSTDOCTORAL/FACULTY LEAVE FELLOWSHIPS

American Association of University Women
Attn: Educational Foundation
2201 North Dodge Street
Iowa City, IA 52243-4030
(319) 337-1716   Fax: (319) 337-1204

Purpose   To enable American women scholars who have achieved distinction or promise of distinction in their fields of scholarly work to engage in additional research.

Eligibility   Women of outstanding scholarly achievement who are working on postdoctoral research in any field and are U.S. citizens or permanent residents are eligible to apply; 1 award is set aside specifically for an underrepresented minority woman. Applicants must have achieved the doctorate by the time the application is submitted. Selection is based on scholarly excellence, teaching experience, and active commitment to helping women and girls through service in community, profession, or field of research.

Financial data   The stipend ranges from $20,000 to $25,000.

Duration   1 year, beginning in July.

Special features   There are no restrictions on the applicant's age, academic field, or place of study.

Limitations   Postdoctoral fellowships normally will not be awarded to women who have received the doctorate within the past 3 years or for revision of the dissertation. Recipients are expected to spend the fellowship year in full-time research. The award may be not be used to cover the costs of research equipment, research assistants, publication, travel to professional meetings or seminars, tuition for additional course work, or repayment of loans or other personal obligations. Applications should be made 1 year in advance of the academic year for which funding is sought.

Number awarded   10 each year: 3 in the arts and humanities, 3 in the social sciences, 3 in the natural sciences, and 1 allocated to an underrepresented minority woman.

Deadline   November of each year.

[1266]
POYNTER INSTITUTE WRITERS CAMP FOR GRADE K-8 TEACHERS AND ELEMENTARY AND MIDDLE SCHOOL STUDENTS

Poynter Institute for Media Studies
831 Third Street South
St. Petersburg, FL 33701
(813) 821-9494   Fax: (813) 821-0583
E-mail: info@poynter.org

Purpose To enhance the journalistic skills of elementary school teachers and students in Florida.

Eligibility Public and private school reading and language arts teachers, grades K-8, who have been teaching in Pinellas County schools for at least 2 years are eligible to participate in this program. Students in grades 4-8 with an interest and talent may also participate. Applications from minority students are strongly encouraged.

Financial data Participants receive a $600 stipend.

Duration 3 weeks, in the summer.

Special features All programs are conducted at the Poynter Institute for Media Studies in St. Petersburg, Florida. The programs enable participating teachers to write every day and share their writing with each other and with students, exchange their best teaching techniques and develop new ones, work each day with a team of visiting writers and editors to put theory into practice, and gain a deeper insight into the writing process by conferring with professional journalists.

Deadline March of each year.

[1267]
POYNTER INSTITUTE WRITERS CAMP FOR HIGH SCHOOL STUDENTS

Poynter Institute for Media Studies
831 Third Street South
St. Petersburg, FL 33701
(813) 821-9494   Fax: (813) 821-0583
E-mail: info@poynter.org

Purpose To enhance the journalistic skills of high school students in Florida.

Eligibility High school students in Pinellas County, Florida who are interested in journalism and writing may apply to participate in this camp. The program emphasizes minority recruiting and training, but includes students of all races.

Financial data Participants receive a $500 stipend.

Duration 4 weeks, in the summer.

Special features All programs are conducted at the Poynter Institute for Media Studies in St. Petersburg, Florida. The programs teach the essentials of journalism to high school students interested in working on their school newspapers and to students aiming for writing careers. Students hear lectures by visiting professionals, discuss journalistic issues, and write and publish their own work.

Number awarded 24 to 30 each year.

Deadline March of each year.

[1268]
PREDOCTORAL RESEARCH FELLOWSHIPS IN ECONOMIC STUDIES

Brookings Institution
1775 Massachusetts Avenue, N.W.
Washington, DC 20036-2188
(202) 797-6127   Fax: (202) 797-6181
E-mail: brookinfo@brook.edu

Purpose To support predoctoral policy-oriented research in economics at the Brookings Institution.

Eligibility Candidates cannot apply; they must be nominated by their graduate department. Nominees must meet the following criteria: doctoral students who have completed their preliminary examinations, have selected a dissertation topic that directly relates to public policy issues and the major research issues of the Institution (economic growth, international economics, human resources, industrial organization, regulation, public finance, monetary economics, and economic stabilization), and be able to benefit from access to the resources and personnel at the Institution. The Institution particularly encourages the nomination of women and minority candidates.

Financial data Fellows receive a stipend of $15,000 for the academic year, supplementary assistance for copying and other essential research requirements up to $600, reimbursement for research-related travel up to $500, health insurance, and access to computer/library facilities.

Duration 1 year.

Special features Fellows participate in seminars, conferences, and meetings at the institution. Outstanding dissertations may be published by the institution.

Limitations Fellows are expected to pursue their research at the Brookings Institution.

Number awarded Up to 5 each year.

Deadline Nominations must be submitted by mid-December and applications by mid-February.

[1269]
PREDOCTORAL RESEARCH FELLOWSHIPS IN FOREIGN POLICY STUDIES

Brookings Institution
1775 Massachusetts Avenue, N.W.
Washington, DC 20036-2188
(202) 797-6036   Fax: (202) 797-6004
E-mail: brookinfo@brook.edu

Purpose To support predoctoral policy-oriented research in U.S. foreign policy and international relations at the Brookings Institution.

Eligibility Candidates cannot apply; they must be nominated by their graduate department. Nominees must meet the following criteria: doctoral students who have completed their preliminary examinations, have selected a dissertation topic that directly relates to public policy issues and the major research issues of the Institution (security policy and international economics issues, focusing primarily on the regions of East Asia, the former Soviet Union, eastern Europe, Germany, Africa, Latin America, and the Middle East), and be able to benefit from access to the resources and personnel at the Institution. The Institution particularly encourages the nomination of women and minority candidates.

Financial data Fellows receive a stipend of $15,000 for the academic year, supplementary assistance for copying and other essential research requirements up to $600, reimbursement for research-related travel up to $500, health insurance, and access to computer/library facilities.

Duration 1 year.

Special features Fellows participate in seminars, conferences, and meetings at the institution. Outstanding dissertations may be published by the institution.

Limitations Fellows are expected to pursue their research at the Brookings Institution.

Number awarded Up to 5 each year.

Deadline Nominations must be submitted by mid-December and applications by mid-February.

[1270]
PREDOCTORAL RESEARCH FELLOWSHIPS IN GOVERNMENTAL STUDIES

Brookings Institution
1775 Massachusetts Avenue, N.W.
Washington, DC 20036-2188
(202) 797-6054   Fax: (202) 797-6144
E-mail: brookinfo@brook.edu

Purpose To support predoctoral policy-oriented research in governmental studies at the Brookings Institution.

Eligibility Candidates cannot apply; they must be nominated by their graduate department. Nominees must meet the following criteria: doctoral students who have completed their preliminary examinations, have selected a dissertation topic that directly relates to public policy issues and the major research issues of the Institution (American political institutions and politics, economic and social policy, and governmental regulations), and be able to benefit from access to the resources and personnel at the Institution. The Institution particularly encourages the nomination of women and minority candidates.

Financial data Fellows receive a stipend of $15,000 for the academic year, supplementary assistance for copying and other essential research requirements up to $600, reimbursement for research-related travel up to $500, health insurance, and access to computer/library facilities.

Duration 1 year.

Special features Fellows participate in seminars, conferences, and meetings at the institution. Outstanding dissertations may be published by the institution.

Limitations Fellows are expected to pursue their research at the Brookings Institution.

Number awarded Up to 5 each year.

Deadline Nominations must be submitted by mid-December and applications by mid-February.

[1271]
PREDOCTORAL TRAINING IN FAMILY MEDICINE GRANTS

Health Resources and Services Administration
Attn: Bureau of Health Professions
Division of Medicine
Parklawn Building, Room 9A-27
5600 Fishers Lane
Rockville, MD 20857
(301) 443-3616   Fax: (301) 443-1945
E-mail: bball@hrsa.ssw.dhhs.gov

Purpose To provide financial support for predoctoral training programs in the field of family medicine.

Eligibility This program is open to public or private nonprofit accredited schools of medicine or osteopathic medicine. Applicants must request funding for planning, developing and operating, or participating in approved predoctoral training programs in the field of family medicine. Grants may include support for the program only or support for both the program and the trainees. Selection criteria include 1) the proposal includes a strategy and plan for recruiting and retaining minority and disadvantaged faculty, students, trainees, and/or residents (applicants are expected to reflect the diversity of the populations within their states); 2) the proposal includes clinically oriented, generalist-trained faculty who practice in community-based settings that include underserved populations; 3) the proposal includes a curriculum that emphasizes areas of study pertinent to the needs of special populations in urban, rural, and underserved areas (people with low incomes, members of racial and ethnic minority groups, people with disabilities, and at-risk population groups); 4) the proposal describes the actions taken by the institution that demonstrate faculty involvement with the curricular innovations that are beyond what is traditionally part of such a curriculum; and 5) the proposal includes data regarding the most recent 3-year average track record of a program in placing graduates in primary care training, primary care practice, or generalist faculty positions.

Financial data The amounts of the awards vary; recently, the average institutional grant has been $115,000.

Duration 3 years.

Special features Persons interested in applying for traineeships through this program should contact the address above to obtain a list of currently participating institutions.

Number awarded Varies each year.

Deadline December of each year.

[1272]
PRESENTING PROGRAM OF THE NEW YORK STATE COUNCIL ON THE ARTS

New York State Council on the Arts
915 Broadway
New York, NY 10010
(212) 387-7000   (800) GET-ARTS

Purpose To help make possible culturally diverse performances of high professional standards and artistic excellence for the people of New York State by supporting both established and developing organizations that engage, present, pay, and promote performing artists in music, dance, theatre, mime, and performance art for public appearances.

Eligibility Nonprofit organizations in New York that have been presenting under stable administrative direction for at least 2 years, present outside Manhattan a minimum of 3 performances by 3 different artists (or present within Manhattan 6 performances by 4 different artists), have had presentations evaluated by Council staff within the preceding 12 months, and are committed to paying artists a guaranteed specified dollar amount as a fee are eligible for these grants. Priority is given to organizations that 1) demonstrate a clear artistic vision with balanced programming; 2) incorporate into their seasons residency activity, including the presentation of lesser known artists, minority artists, contemporary work, and work by living American artists; 3) present unique programming concepts; 4) present performances and undertake residency activity to minority communities and underserved audiences; or 5) undertake interpretive efforts to enhance the public's knowledge, understanding, and appreciation of the presentations through effective education, interpretation, or orientation components.

Financial data The Council will support up to 30 percent of an organization's general operating expenses, up to 50 percent of project costs, and up to $5,000 for special new presenter development grants.

Duration Up to 3 years for general operating support; up to 2 years for project support.

Number awarded Varies each year.

Deadline February of each year.

[1273]
PRESIDENTIAL EARLY CAREER AWARDS FOR SCIENTISTS AND ENGINEERS

National Science and Technology Council
Attn: Office of Science and Technology Policy
Executive Office of the President
Washington, DC 20502
(202) 456-6020   Fax: (202) 456-6026
E-mail: jhall@ostp.eop.gov

Purpose To recognize and reward the nation's most outstanding young science and engineering faculty members by providing them with additional research funding.

Eligibility Eligible for these awards are U.S. citizens, nationals, and permanent residents who have been selected to receive research grants from other departments of the U.S. government. Recipients of designated research grant programs are automatically considered for these Presidential Early Career Awards for Scientists and Engineers (PECASE). Most of the participating programs encourage applications from racial/ethnic minority individuals, women, and persons with disabilities.

Financial data Awards carry a grant of $100,000 per year.

Duration 5 years.

Special features The departments with research programs that nominate candidates for the PECASE program are: 1) the National Aeronautics and Space Administration, which selects recipients of Early Career Awards based on exceptionally meritorious proposals funded through the traditional research grant process or the unsolicited proposal process; 2) the Department of Veterans Affairs, which nominates the most meritorious recipients of Veterans Health Administration Investigator Initiated/Career Development Research Awards; 3) the National Institutes of Health, which nominates the most meritorious investigators funded through its First Independent Research Support and Transition (FIRST) Awards and NIH Individual Research Project Grants (R01) programs; 4) the Department of Energy, which nominates staff members of the national laboratories and the most meritorious recipients of the Office of Defense Programs Young Scientist and Engineer Awards; 5) the Department of Defense, which nominates outstanding recipients of the Office of Naval Research Young Investigator Program, the Air Force Office of Scientific Research Broad Agency Program, and the Army Research Office Young Investigator Program; 6) the Department of Agriculture, which nominates staff scientists from the Agricultural Research Service, the most meritorious investigators funded through the Agricultural Research Enhancement Awards (AREA) New Investigator Awards, and staff scientists of the Forest Service; 7) the Department of Commerce, which nominates outstanding staff members of the National Oceanic and Atmospheric Administration and the National Institute of Standards and Technology; and 8) the National Science Foundation, which selects its nominees from the most meritorious investigators funded through the Faculty Early Career Development (CAREER) Program. For a list of the names, addresses, and telephone numbers of contact persons at each of the participating agencies, write to the address above.

Number awarded Varies; each of the participating agencies is allocated a specified number of awards. For instance, the National Science Foundation presents 30 each year: 15 in the sciences and 15 in engineering; the Department of Energy Office of Defense Programs grants 12 Young Scientist and Engineer Awards, of whom 6 are nominated for the Presidential Early Career Award for Scientists and Engineers.

[1274]
PREVENTING ALCOHOL-RELATED PROBLEMS AMONG ETHNIC MINORITIES

National Institutes of Health
Attn: National Institute on Alcohol Abuse and Alcoholism
Prevention Research Branch
Willco Building, Suite 505
6000 Executive Boulevard MSC 7003
Bethesda, MD 20892-7003
(301) 443-8820   Fax: (301) 443-8774
E-mail: kb57c@nih.gov

Purpose To encourage research related to the prevention of alcohol-related problems among ethnic minority groups of African Americans, Hispanic Americans, Native American, Asian Americans, and Pacific Islanders.

Eligibility Applicants must be affiliated with public or private nonprofit or for-profit organizations (including colleges, universities, laboratories, hospitals, and governmental units). Research may focus on the culturally-appropriate development or adaptation of interventions within minority settings, or how ethnic minority identity relates to prevention research outcomes. In particular, minority and women investigators are encouraged to apply.

Financial data The average direct cost per year for regular research grants is $220,000; for small grants, up to $50,000 per year is available; applicants may also use the First Independent Research Support and Transition (FIRST) mechanism, for which grants may not exceed a total of $350,000 or $100,000 in any 1 year.

Duration Regular and FIRST grants are up to 5 years; small grants are up to 2 years; regular grants may be renewed but FIRST and small grants may not.

Number awarded Varies each year.

Deadline January, May, or September of each year.

[1275]
PROFESSIONAL ASSOCIATES PROGRAM FOR MINORITIES AND WOMEN AT BROOKHAVEN NATIONAL LABORATORY

Brookhaven National Laboratory
Attn: Diversity Office, Human Resources Division
Building 185A
P.O. Box 5000
Upton, New York 11973-5000
(516) 344-3709   Fax: (516) 344-2476
E-mail: ligon1@bnl.gov

Purpose To provide professional experience in scientific areas at Brookhaven National Laboratory (BNL) to underrepresented minorities and women.

Eligibility This program is open to underrepresented minorities (African Americans, Hispanics, Native Americans, or Pacific Islanders) and women who have earned a baccalaureate degree or equivalent. Applicants must be seeking professional experience in such fields as biology, chemistry, computer science, engineering, health physics, medical research, and physics.

Financial data Participants receive a competitive salary.

Duration 1 year.

Special features Interns work in a goal-oriented on-the-job training program under the supervision of employees who are experienced in their areas of interest.

Number awarded Varies each year.

Deadline Applications may be submitted at any time.

[1276]
PROGRAMS AND SHELTERS FOR BATTERED WOMEN

Chicago Resource Center
104 South Michigan Avenue, Suite 1220
Chicago, IL 60603
(312) 759-8700

Purpose To provide funding for programs and shelters for battered women.

Eligibility Programs in rural areas, programs serving women of color, new organizations, state coalitions, and model projects (those projects that have broad application within the battered women's movement and that may be replicated) are eligible to apply. Preference is given to smaller programs with limited funding resources and to organizations that focus exclusively on domestic violence.

Financial data Grants range from $1,000 to $4,000.

Duration 1 year.

Limitations The center does not fund programs for children, programs for men who batter, multi-service agencies, film or video projects, or direct service organizations with budgets over $100,000. Programs previously funded may apply again in subsequent years. However, requests from funded organizations will not be considered prior to the 1 year anniversary of the previous award.

Number awarded Varies each year.

Deadline March, June, and September of each year.

[1277]
PROGRAMS TO ENCOURAGE MINORITY STUDENTS TO BECOME TEACHERS

Department of Education
Attn: Office of Postsecondary Education
Division of Higher Education Incentive Programs
Portals Building, Suite C-80
600 Independence Avenue, S.W.
Washington, DC 20202-5329
(202) 260-3291   Fax: (202) 260-7615

Purpose To support projects to develop new minority teaching programs to increase the number of minorities in the teaching profession.

Eligibility Proposals may be submitted by accredited academic institutions either as partnership grants (between 1 or more institutions of higher education with a demonstrated record in carrying out the purposes of this program and 1 or more local educational agencies, a state educational agency, or 1 or more community-based organizations) or as teacher placement grants

(to institutions of higher education that have schools or departments of education). Funds must be used to improve recruitment and teaching opportunities in education for minority individuals, including language minority individuals; to increase the number of minority teachers, including language minority teachers, in elementary and secondary schools; and to identify and encourage minority students in the 7th through 12th grades to aspire to, and to prepare for, careers in elementary and secondary school teaching.

Financial data Grants range from $120,000 to $300,000 and average $210,000.

Duration Up to 3 years.

Number awarded Approximately 4 each year.

Deadline November of each year.

[1278]
PUBLIC HEALTH SERVICE SMALL BUSINESS INNOVATION RESEARCH PROGRAM

Public Health Service
Attn: SBIR/STTR Solicitation Office
13687 Baltimore Avenue
Laurel, MD 20707-5096
(301) 206-9385   Fax: (301) 206-9722
E-mail: a2y@cu.nih.gov

Purpose To emphasize increased private sector commercialization of technology developed through federal research and development, to increase small business participation in federal research and development, and to foster and encourage participation of socially and economically disadvantaged small business concerns and women-owned small business concerns.

Eligibility For the purposes of this program, a "small business" is any organization that is independently owned and operated for profit, not dominant in the field in which it is operating, and meets the size standard of 500 employees or less. The primary employment of the principal investigator must be with the firm at the time of award and during the conduct of the proposed project. Preference is given to women-owned small business concerns and to socially and economically disadvantaged small business concerns. Women-owned small business concerns are at least 51 percent owned by a woman or women who also control and operate it. Socially and economically disadvantaged small business concerns are at least 51 percent owned by an Indian tribe, native Hawaiian organization, or 1 or more socially and economically disadvantaged individuals (Black Americans, Hispanic Americans, Native Americans, Asian-Pacific Americans, or subcontinent Asian Americans). The project must be performed in the United States.

Financial data Support is offered in 2 phases. In phase 1, awards normally may not exceed $100,000 (for both direct and indirect costs); in phase 2, awards normally may not exceed $750,000 (including both direct and indirect costs).

Duration Phase 1: up to 6 months; phase 2: up to 2 years.

Special features Grants are offered by 3 components of the Public Health Service (PHS): National Institutes of Health (NIH), Centers for Disease Control and Prevention (CDC), and Food and Drug Administration (FDA). For information on the research interests of each of those components and their various agencies, contact the address above. Actual solicitations are available only from the address above.

Number awarded Each year, approximately 700 awards are made by NIH, 10 by CDC, and 2 by FDA.

Deadline April, August, and December of each year for NIH awards; December of each year for CDC and FDA awards.

[1279]
PUBLIC HEALTH SPECIAL PROJECT GRANTS

Health Resources and Services Administration
Attn: Bureau of Health Professions
Division of Associated, Dental and Public Health Professions
Parklawn Building, Room 8-101
5600 Fishers Lane
Rockville, MD 20857
(301) 443-6896   Fax: (301) 443-1164

Purpose To provide funding to schools of public health to plan, develop, demonstrate, operate, and evaluate projects.

Eligibility This program is open to accredited schools of public health. Funding may be used for 1) establishing and strengthening community-academic partnerships, including linkages with state and local health agencies, community-based organizations, health care facilities, industry, schools, and other education and training programs; 2) developing strategies to make public health education more relevant to practice and more available to employed public health practitioners; 3) improving methods to recruit minority and disadvantaged individuals into careers in public health; or 4) improving access and quality in health care for vulnerable populations and the public at large.

Financial data In recent years, $3,000,000 annually has been available for this program, including $500,000 for continuation support and $2,500,000 for new competing awards; the average competing grant has been $150,000.

Duration Up to 3 years; may be extended for an additional 2 years.

Number awarded Varies; recently, 11 new competing grants have been awarded each year.

Deadline January of each year.

[1280]
PUBLIC TELECOMMUNICATIONS FACILITIES PROGRAM GRANTS

Department of Commerce
Attn: National Telecommunications and Information Administration
Public Broadcasting Division
1401 Constitution Avenue, N.W., Room H-4625
Washington, DC 20230
(202) 482-5802   Fax: (202) 482-2156
E-mail: dconnors@ntia.doc.gov

Purpose To provide assistance to noncommercial entities for planning and construction of telecommunications facilities and services available to, operated by, and owned by minorities and women.

Eligibility Eligible to submit proposals are: public or noncommercial educational broadcast stations; noncommerical telecommunications entities; systems of public telecommunications entities; nonprofit corporations, institutions, foundations, or associations; and state or local governmental agencies. The priority order for grants is 1) proposals to bring public telecommunications services to geographic areas that are presently unserved; 2) replacement of basic equipment of existing essential broadcast stations; 3) establishment of a first local origination capacity in a geographic area; and 4) improvement of public broadcasting services. Special consideration is given to applications that foster ownership (or control) of public telecommunications entities by women and minorities, or that feature programming designed specifically for women and minorities.

Financial data The amounts of the awards depend on the nature of the proposals and the availability of funds. In general, the program provides 75 percent of the funds necessary for the planning of a public telecommunications construction project, although 100 percent funding is available in cases of extraordinary need; for actual construction, the federal share normally is 75 percent for projects to activate stations or extend service, 50 percent for the replacement, improvement, or augmentation of equipment. In a recent year, a total of $13.4 was awarded through this program; individual grants ranged from $3,592 to $791,727.

Duration 1 year or longer.

Number awarded Varies; in a recent year, 96 projects received funding.

Deadline February of each year.

[1281]
R. ROBERT & SALLY D. FUNDERBURG RESEARCH SCHOLAR AWARD IN GASTRIC BIOLOGY RELATED TO CANCER

American Digestive Health Foundation
7910 Woodmont Avenue, Suite 700
Bethesda, MD 20814-3015
(301) 654-2635   Fax: (301) 654-5920

Purpose To provide funding to an established investigator who is working on research that enhances fundamental understanding of gastric cancer pathobiology.

Eligibility Candidates must hold a faculty position at an accredited institution. They must have established themselves as independent investigators in the field of gastric biology, pursuing novel approaches to gastric mucosal cell biology, regeneration and regulation of cell growth, inflammation as precancerous lesions, genetics of gastric carcinoma, oncogenes in gastric epithelial malignancies, epidemiology of gastric cancer, etiology of gastric epithelial malignancies, or clinical research in diagnosis or treatment of gastric carcinoma. Women and minority investigators are strongly encouraged to apply. Selection is based on the novelty, feasibility, and significance of the proposal; attributes of the candidate; and the likelihood that support will lead the applicant toward a research career in the field of gastric cancer biology. Preference is given to novel approaches, especially for initiation of projects by young investigators or established investigators new to the field.

Financial data The award is $25,000 per year. Funds are to be used for the salary of the investigator. Indirect costs are not allowed.

Duration 2 years.

Special features This award is administered by the American Digestive Health Foundation (ADHF) and sponsored by the American Gastroenterological Association (AGA).

Number awarded 1 each year.

Deadline September of each year.

[1282]
REPRODUCTIVE RIGHTS COALITION FUND GRANTS

Ms. Foundation for Women
120 Wall Street, 33rd Floor
New York, NY 10005
(212) 742-2300

Purpose To provide funding to organizations involved in supporting reproductive rights.

Eligibility Organizations and statewide coalitions concerned with the support of reproductive rights are eligible to apply. Funds may be used to support the development and growth of statewide coalitions, women of color organizing efforts, and other constituency-based coalitions organizing around reproductive rights and health issues in targeted states around the country.

Financial data Grants range between $10,000 and $15,000. Smaller grants are also available for technical assistance or emergencies.

Duration 1 year; may be renewed upon reapplication.

Special features Grants are to be used to pay for technical assistance, organizational internships, and special opportunities or emergencies.

Number awarded Varies each year.

Deadline Applications may be submitted at any time.

[1283]
RESEARCH ASSISTANTSHIPS FOR MINORITY HIGH SCHOOL STUDENTS

National Science Foundation
Attn: Directorate for Education and Human Resources
Senior Staff Associate for Cross Directorate Programs
4201 Wilson Boulevard, Room 805
Arlington, VA 22230
(703) 306-1603

Purpose To encourage principal investigators to provide research opportunities to talented and promising underrepresented minority students at the high school level.

Eligibility Investigators who submit proposals to the National Science Foundation (NSF) may request supplemental funding for student stipends and associated research costs (supplies, computer time, etc.). Students eligible for this type of support must be 1) members of underrepresented minority groups (Native American, African American, Hispanic, Alaskan Native, or Native Pacific Islander) and 2) citizens or nationals of the United States. There are 2 options for investigators to use to apply for support: 1) request for funding may be included in the initial proposal submitted to the NSF; 2) current NSF grantees may request special supplemental funding from this program to add to their existing grant.

Financial data Student stipends for summer projects are expected to be at least $1,000, with academic year students comparable on a pro rata basis. The amount of total indirect costs allowed is limited to 25 percent of the student stipends. The total costs for the year may not exceed $3,000 per student.

Duration Academic year or summer months.

Special features The students are given the opportunity to be involved with the principal investigator in meaningful and challenging experiences.

Limitations Each student research assistant in this program is required at the end of the support period to submit a statement

(1 page in length) summarizing the nature and results of participation in the project.

Number awarded Normally, no more than 2 students per project will be funded, but exceptions may be considered for additional minority, physically disabled, and women students.

[1284]
RESEARCH CENTERS IN MINORITY INSTITUTIONS AWARDS

National Institutes of Health
Attn: National Center for Research Resources
Research Infrastructure Area
One Rockledge Center, Suite 6030
6705 Rockledge Drive MSC 7965
Bethesda, MD 20892-7965
(301) 435-0760   Fax: (301) 480-3770
E-mail: rh50b@nih.gov

Purpose To enable predominantly minority health professional schools and graduate institutions to become more competitive in obtaining support for the conduct of biomedical and/or behavioral research relevant to the mission of the U.S. Public Health Service.

Eligibility Eligible to apply is any institution that has more than 50 percent minority enrollment and that awards doctoral degrees in the health professions (M.D., D.D.S., D.V.M., etc.) or Ph.D. degrees in science fields related to health.

Financial data Up to $1,000,000 per year is available per institution.

Duration 3 to 5 years.

Special features Funding is provided for faculty expansion and development; research support personnel; renovation of laboratories, animal quarters, and other facilities; acquisition of state-of-the-art instrumentation; enhancement of grants management and research development offices; biostatistical and computer resources; conduct of symposia and technology tansfer workshops; and other institutional biomedical research and research-related infrastructure activities and components. The National Institutes of Health designates this program as the G12 Awards.

Number awarded Varies; generally, 5 each year.

Deadline January, May, and September of each year.

[1285]
RESEARCH EXPERIENCES FOR UNDERGRADUATES SITES PROGRAM

National Science Foundation
Attn: Directorate for Education and Human Resources
Senior Staff Associate for Cross Directorate Programs
4201 Wilson Boulevard, Room 805
Arlington, VA 22230
(703) 306-1603   E-mail: reu.coord@nsf.gov

Purpose To enable universities to provide research opportunities to talented and promising undergraduate students.

Eligibility Any U.S. academic institution conducting research in the disciplines supported by the National Science Foundation (NSF) may apply for these grants to utilize undergraduate students in the research programs of the host institution. Students eligible to participate must be citizens or permanent residents of the United States enrolled in a degree program leading to a bachelor's degree. High school graduates who have not yet enrolled and students who have received their baccalaureate degrees and are no longer enrolled as undergraduates generally are ineligible.

Project directors are particularly encouraged to involve women, members of underrepresented minority groups (Native American, African American, Hispanic, Alaskan Native, or Native Pacific Islander), and persons with disabilities in the proposed projects. Grants are awarded to proposals to initiate and conduct undergraduate research participation projects for a number of students appropriate to the discipline and the setting. Most projects are expected to be within the scope of a single discipline and/or single academic department. Interdisciplinary proposals and proposals with an ethics-in-science component are also encouraged, but multiple discipline or multiple department proposals without a common project focus are discouraged.

Financial data Student stipends for summer projects are expected to be at least $250 per week. Normal total project costs are expected to be approximately $5,000 per participating student. In addition, if the proposal involves an ethics component, an additional $4,000 may be requested.

Special features Funding may be requested from any of the disciplinary research directorates of the National Science Foundation; for telephone numbers and E-mail addresses of each of the respective directorates, contact the address above. Undergraduate students may also contact the address above to obtain a list of current grantees offering projects through this program.

Number awarded Approximately 100 of these awards are made each year. Each institution normally hosts at least 6 undergraduates, about half of whom should come from an institution different from the host.

Deadline September of each year.

[1286]
RESEARCH EXPERIENCES FOR
UNDERGRADUATES SUPPLEMENTS PROGRAM

National Science Foundation
Attn: Directorate for Education and Human Resources
Senior Staff Associate for Cross Directorate Programs
4201 Wilson Boulevard, Room 805
Arlington, VA 22230
(703) 306-1603   E-mail: reu.coord@nsf.gov

Purpose To enable principal investigators to provide research opportunities to talented and promising undergraduate students.

Eligibility Principal investigators with awards from the National Science Foundation (NSF) may apply for supplemental funding to permit the association with their projects of 1 or 2 undergraduate student research assistants. Students eligible for this type of support must be citizens or permanent residents of the United States enrolled in a degree program leading to a bachelor's degree. Investigators are particularly encouraged to involve women, members of underrepresented minority groups (Native Americans, African Americans, Hispanics, Alaskan Natives, or Native Pacific Islanders), and persons with disabilities in their proposals.

Financial data Student stipends for summer projects are expected to be at least $1,000 per month, with academic year students paid comparably on a pro rata basis. Normal total project costs are expected to be approximately $5,000 per student participant.

Duration Most awards are for summer support, but arrangements may sometimes be made for the academic year.

Special features Undergraduate students who wish to participate in this program should contact the address above to obtain a list of the investigators who currently hold supplementary grants.

Number awarded Depends on the number of grant applications that seek the use of an undergraduate researcher.

Deadline Supplemental requests may be submitted at any time, but principal investigators are encouraged to contact their cognizant NSF program officer as early as possible in the fiscal year, which begins October 1 of each year.

[1287]
RESEARCH INFRASTRUCTURE IN MINORITY
INSTITUTIONS AWARDS

National Institutes of Health
Attn: National Center for Research Resources
Research Infrastructure Area
One Rockledge Center, Suite 6030
6705 Rockledge Drive MSC 7965
Bethesda, MD 20892-7965
(301) 435-0760   Fax: (301) 480-3770
E-mail: rh50b@nih.gov

Purpose To enable predominantly minority institutions to enhance their capacity to conduct biomedical and behavioral research by developing and strengthening formal, collaborative agreements with research-intensive, doctoral degree-granting institutions.

Eligibility This program is open to domestic academic institutions with more than 50 percent minority enrollment that offer 1 or more baccalaureate and/or master's degrees in the sciences related to health. Minority institutions that award an M.D., D.D.S., Pharm.D., D.V.M., or other doctoral degree in the health professions, and/or a Ph.D. in the sciences related to health are not eligible. Applicant institutions must have formal collaborative agreements with 1 or more research-intensive universities offering doctoral degrees in the health-related sciences. These collaborations must encourage and facilitate research between faculty in the participating institutions. They should also facilitate the participation of students from the undergraduate institution in the doctoral degree programs.

Financial data Up to $600,000 per year in direct costs is available per institution.

Duration Up to 5 years.

Number awarded Awards are granted when funds are available.

Deadline January in years when awards are offered.

[1288]
RESEARCH ON THE MENTAL HEALTH OF
MINORITY POPULATIONS

National Institutes of Health
Attn: National Institute of Mental Health
Division of Epidemiology and Services Research
Parklawn Building, Room 10C-06
5600 Fishers Lane
Rockville, MD 20857
(301) 443-3364   Fax: (301) 443-4045
E-mail: ah21k.nih.gov

Purpose To provide financial support for the development, conduct, and maintenance of research program projects focusing on the mental health of minority populations (American Indians, Asian Americans, Alaskan Natives, African Americans, Hispanics, Native Hawaiians, and Pacific Islanders).

Eligibility Eligible applicant institutions include domestic non-profit or for-profit, public or private organizations, such as universities, colleges, hospitals, laboratories, units of state and local government, and eligible agencies of the federal government. They must be proposing a research program project (RPP) that may include the understanding and improvement of mental health and the prevention and treatment of mental illness among the specific minority group(s) selected. It must consist of at least 3 research subprojects. Racial/ethnic minority individuals, women, and persons with disabilities are encouraged to apply as principal investigators.

Financial data The maximum award is $600,000 in direct costs per year, plus negotiated indirect costs.

Duration Up to 5 years.

Special features Inquiries on programs of prevention, clinical services and service systems research, epidemiology, psychopathology, violence and traumatic stress, assessment, classification, law and mental health, and health and behavior, with special attention to minority and other populations, should be directed to the Division of Epidemiology and Services Research, (301) 443-3364; questions involving behavioral and social sciences, cognitive sciences, and neurosciences, including neuroimaging, neurophysiology, neuropsychopharmacology, and cellular and molecular neurobiology, with special attention to minority and other special populations, should be addressed to the Division of Neuroscience and Behavioral Science, (301) 443-8033; for further information on psychopathology, classification, assessment, etiology, genetics, clinical course, outcome, and treatment of mental disorders with emphasis on schizophrenic disorders, affective and anxiety disorders, and mental disorders of children and adolescents, the elderly, minorities, and other special populations, contact the Division of Clinical and Treatment Research, (301) 443-4527; for research that focuses on mental health issues for persons with AIDS, persons who are HIV positive, or persons who are at risk of contracting the virus, contact the Office on Aids, (301) 443-7281.

Number awarded Varies each year.

Deadline May of each year.

[1289]
RESEARCH OPPORTUNITY AWARDS

National Science Foundation
Attn: Directorate for Education and Human Resources
Senior Staff Associate for Cross Directorate Programs
4201 Wilson Boulevard, Room 805
Arlington, VA 22230
(703) 306-1603

Purpose To enable faculty members at predominantly undergraduate institutions to work with investigators who already hold or are applying for a grant from the National Science Foundation (NSF).

Eligibility Participants must be citizens or nationals of the United States, faculty members employed in U.S. academic institutions, working in any NSF-supported field, but lacking the resources for research at their own institutions. In addition, science teachers who teach middle and high school levels and who have a keen interest in research may also take part. Individuals interested in becoming visiting researchers make their own contacts with investigators who currently have or are applying for NSF research grants. A principal investigator may also initiate the collaboration. Applications may be submitted as part of a new NSF proposal, as a supplement to an ongoing NSF award, or by rearranging the project budget in an ongoing award without requesting supplemental funding from NSF. The NSF strongly encourages women, minorities, and persons with disabilities to participate in this program.

Financial data Faculty summer support may not exceed two-ninths of the academic year salary. Indirect costs are limited to 25 percent of the stipends. Most NSF programs limit support to moderate amounts ($10,000 to $15,000).

Duration Support is available for a summer, or, if funding is available, for part-time activities during the academic year.

Special features This program operates through the various disciplinary divisions within the NSF; for a list of the respective telephone numbers, contact the address above.

Number awarded Depends on the number of grant applications that seek the use of a visiting researcher.

Deadline If the request is part of a new proposal to the NSF, deadlines are the same as for the grant application. Requests generally should be submitted by the end of January in order to be considered for that summer or the following academic year.

[1290]
RESEARCH PLANNING GRANTS FOR MINORITY SCIENTISTS AND ENGINEERS

National Science Foundation
Attn: Directorate for Education and Human Resources
Senior Staff Associate for Cross Directorate Programs
4201 Wilson Boulevard, Room 805
Arlington, VA 22230
(703) 306-1603

Purpose To enable minority scientists to conduct preliminary studies and other activities to facilitate the development of more competitive National Science Foundation (NSF) research proposals.

Eligibility This program is open to members of certain ethnic groups (African Americans, Native Americans, Hispanics, Alaskan Natives, and Native Pacific Islanders) who are U.S. citizens or nationals; hold faculty or research-related positions in U.S. colleges, universities, or other nonprofit institutions; and have not previously served as principal investigators on independent federal awards for scientific or engineering research. Tenure or tenure-track status is not an eligibility factor. A co-investigator is not appropriate for this program, although use of senior researchers is encouraged.

Financial data Up to $18,000.

Duration Up to 12 months; not renewable.

Special features This program is offered through the various disciplinary divisions of the National Science Foundation (NSF); for the telephone numbers of the participating divisions, contact the address above.

Limitations Recipients are expected to submit a research proposal to the NSF regular research program after completion of the planning grant.

Deadline Each of the participating NSF disciplinary divisions sets its own deadline.

[1291]
RESEARCH PROPOSAL DEVELOPMENT PROGRAM FOR MINORITY NURSES

American Nurses Association
Attn: Minority Fellowship Programs
600 Maryland Avenue, S.W., Suite 100 West
Washington, DC 20024-2571
(202) 651-7244   Fax: (202) 789-1413

Purpose To assist nurses in the preparation of research proposals on minority issues in mental health, substance abuse, or behavioral science.

Eligibility Applications are accepted from nurses who completed 1 of the ethnic/racial minority fellowship programs of the American Nurses Association (ANA) and received their doctoral degree within the past 5 years. They must be interested in conducting research on minority issues in mental health, substance abuse, or behavioral science.

Financial data The program provides a stipend of $2,000 to aid in developing a research proposal.

Limitations Recipients of these awards are expected to seek and obtain funding from public and/or private sources.

Deadline March of each year.

[1292]
RESEARCH SUPPLEMENTS FOR UNDERREPRESENTED MINORITY INDIVIDUALS IN POSTDOCTORAL TRAINING

National Institutes of Health
Attn: Office of Extramural Research
Extramural Outreach and Information Resources Office
6701 Rockledge Drive, Room 6207
MSC 7910
Bethesda, MD 20892-7910
(301) 435-0714   Fax: (301) 480-8443
E-mail: asknih@odrockm1.od.nih.gov

Purpose To provide funding to minority individuals in the postdoctoral phase of their training to participate in ongoing research projects supported by the National Institutes of Health (NIH).

Eligibility This program is open to minority individuals (African Americans, Hispanics, Native Americans, Alaskan Natives, and Pacific Islanders) in postdoctoral training in either the applicant institution or any other institution. Only under extraordinary circumstances may applicants request to work with their former predoctoral mentor.

Financial data The sponsoring institute provides support for salary in addition to other necessary expenses (e.g. travel, supplies) to enable the minority individual to participate as a postdoctoral research assistant or associate on an institute-funded research project. The requested salary must be in accordance with the salary structure of the grantee institution and consistent with the level of effort. Additional funds, up to $6,000, may be requested for supplies and travel.

Duration 1 year or longer.

Special features Individuals interested in this type of postdoctoral support should make contact with the principal investigator on an eligible NIH research grant at their institution.

Limitations Support may not be used to purchase equipment.

Number awarded Varies each year.

[1293]
RIDGE INITIATIVE POSTDOCTORAL FELLOWSHIPS

National Science Foundation
Attn: Directorate for Geosciences
Division of Ocean Sciences
4201 Wilson Boulevard, Room 725
Arlington, VA 22230
(703) 306-1586   E-mail: depp@nsf.gov

Purpose To provide opportunities for young scientists to conduct geological research on the mid-ocean ridge system as part of the Ridge Inter-Disciplinary Global Experiments (RIDGE) Initiative.

Eligibility Eligible are U.S. citizens, nationals, or permanent resident aliens who will have earned a doctoral degree within 1 year of taking up the award and who have arranged to conduct research under a senior scientist at an appropriate U.S. nonprofit institution (government laboratory, privately-sponsored nonprofit institution, national laboratory, or institution of higher education). The proposed research must attempt to understand the geophysical, geochemical, and geobiological causes and consequences of the energy transfer within the global rift system through time. The program has identified 4 areas of the world for study: the Arctic Ridge, the Southwest and Southeast Indian Ridges, the Pacific-Antarctic Ridge, and the southern East Pacific Ridge. Selection is based on the suitability and availability of the sponsoring senior scientist and other associated colleagues, suitability of the host institution for the proposed research, likely impact on the future scientific development of the applicant, scientific quality of the research likely to emerge, and the potential impact of the research on the RIDGE Initiative. Women, minorities, and persons with disabilities are particularly encouraged to apply.

Financial data The fellow receives a stipend of $35,000 per year and a special allowance of $5,000 per year for scientific equipment and supplies, travel, publication expenses, other research-related costs, and medical insurance; the host institution receives $300 per month for expenses incurred in support of the research, in lieu of indirect costs.

Duration 2 years.

Special features Additional information is available from the RIDGE office, University of New Hampshire, Room 142 Morse Hall, Durham, NH 03824-3525, (603) 862-4051, Fax: (603) 862-0083, E-mail: ridge@unh.edu.

Limitations Because the RIDGE Initiative is intended to foster cross-disciplinary approaches, the research institution must be different from that where the applicant received the doctoral degree and the senior scientist must have a field of expertise different from that of the applicant. Fellows must devote full time to the proposed research.

Number awarded Up to 2 each year.

Deadline February and August of each year.

[1294]
RISK ASSESSMENT SCIENCE AND ENGINEERING FELLOWSHIPS

American Association for the Advancement of Science
Attn: Directorate for Science and Policy Programs
1200 New York Avenue, N.W.
Washington, DC 20005-3920
(202) 326-6600   Fax: (202) 289-4950
E-mail: science_policy@aaas.org

Purpose To provide postdoctoral and midcareer scientists and engineers an opportunity to provide scientific and technical input on issues of human health and/or environmental risk assessment.

Eligibility Prospective fellows must have a Ph.D. or equivalent doctoral level degree in any physical, biological, or social science, any field of engineering, or any interdisciplinary field as long as their work relates to risk assessment; persons with a master's degree in engineering and at least 3 years of post-degree experience may apply. Candidates must demonstrate exceptional competence in some area of science or engineering related to environmental or public health science; have a good scientific and technical background; and have a strong interest and some experience in applying scientific or other professional knowledge toward the identification and assessment of public health or environmental problems. U.S. citizenship is required; federal employees are not eligible. Fellows provide scientific and technical input on issues relating to human health and/or environmental risk assessment in areas of relevance to the U.S. Environmental Protection Agency (EPA) or U.S. Department of Agriculture (USDA). Minorities and persons with disabilities are especially encouraged to apply.

Financial data The stipend is $41,000.

Duration 1 year, beginning in September.

Special features Fellows work at the EPA's National Center for Environmental Assessment or USDA's Office of Risk Assessment and Cost-Benefit Analysis.

Number awarded Each year, 5 fellows are selected to work with EPA and 1 or more with USDA.

Deadline January of each year.

[1295]
RISK REDUCTION ENGINEERING RESEARCH LABORATORY RESEARCH PARTICIPATION PROGRAM

Oak Ridge Institute for Science and Education
Attn: Science/Engineering Education Division
P.O. Box 117
Oak Ridge, TN 37831-0117
(423) 576-8503   (423) 241-2875
(800) 569-7749   Fax: (423) 576-3643
E-mail: rpprrerl@orau.gov

Purpose To provide funding for postgraduate research on environmental and physical sciences for the Risk Reduction Engineering Research Laboratory of the Environmental Protection Agency (EPA).

Eligibility Applicants should have completed a baccalaureate, master's, or doctoral degree within the past 3 years; others are considered on a case-by-case basis. Their field of study should have been environmental sciences, engineering, physical sciences, or other related scientific disciplines. They must propose to conduct research at EPA's Risk Reduction Engineering Research Laboratory in Cincinnati, Ohio. All programs operated by the Science/Engineering Education Division (SEED) of Oak Ridge Institute for Science and Education (ORISE) seek to broaden the participation of minorities, women, and persons with disabilities in science and engineering careers.

Financial data The stipend is based on research area and degree; a limited reimbursement for inbound travel and moving is also provided.

Duration 1 year; renewable.

Special features This program is funded by an interagency agreement between the U.S. Department of Energy and EPA and administered by ORISE/SEED.

Number awarded Varies each year.

Deadline Applications may be submitted at any time.

[1296]
ROBERT D. WATKINS MINORITY GRADUATE FELLOWSHIP

American Society for Microbiology
Attn: Office of Education and Training
1325 Massachusetts Avenue, N.W.
Washington, DC 20005-4171
(202) 942-9295   Fax: (202) 942-9329
E-mail: Fellowships-CareerInformation@asmusa.org

Purpose To provide minority doctoral students with the opportunity to conduct research in microbiology.

Eligibility Eligible are African Americans, Hispanic Americans, Native Americans, or Native Pacific Islanders, enrolled as full-time graduate students who have completed their first year of doctoral study and who are members of the American Society for Microbiology (ASM). They must propose a joint research plan in collaboration with an ASM-member scientist. U.S. citizenship or permanent resident status is required. Individuals with a medical or veterinarian degree are not eligible to apply. Selection is based on academic achievement, evidence of a successful research plan developed in collaboration with a research advisor/mentor, and relevant career goals in the microbiological sciences.

Financial data Students receive up to $12,000 per year as a stipend; funds should not be used for tuition or fees.

Duration 2 years.

Number awarded Varies each year.

Deadline April of each year.

[1297]
ROBERT K. FAHNESTOCK MEMORIAL AWARD

Geological Society of America
Attn: Research Grants Administrator
3300 Penrose Place
P.O. Box 9140
Boulder, CO 80301-9140
(303) 447-2020, ext. 137   Fax: (303) 447-1133
E-mail: jforstro@geosociety.org

Purpose To provide partial support for geological research by graduate students at universities in the United States, Canada, Mexico, and Central America.

Eligibility This program is open to graduate students in geology at the master's or doctoral level. Both members and nonmembers of the society are eligible. Special consideration may be given to students with the best application in the field of sediment transport or related aspects of fluvial geomorphology. Applications from women, minorities, and persons with disabilities are strongly encouraged.

Financial data Grants range up to $2,500; the average grant recently was $1,604.

Duration 1 year.

Number awarded 1 or more each year.

Deadline February of each year.

[1298]
ROBERT W. HARTLEY MEMORIAL FELLOWSHIP

Brookings Institution
1775 Massachusetts Avenue, N.W.
Washington, D.C. 20036-2188
(202) 797-6054   Fax: (202) 797-6144
E-mail: brookinfo@brook.edu

Purpose To support predoctoral policy-oriented research in governmental studies at the Brookings Institution.

Eligibility Candidates cannot apply; they must be nominated by their graduate department. Nominees must meet the following criteria: doctoral students who have completed their preliminary examinations, have selected a dissertation topic that directly relates to public policy issues and the major research issues of the Institution (American political institutions and politics, economic and social policy, and government regulations), and be able to benefit from access to the resources and personnel at the Institution. The Institution particularly encourages the nomination of women and minority candidates.

Financial data Fellows receive a stipend of $15,000 for the academic year, supplementary assistance for copying and other essential research requirements up to $600, reimbursement for research-related travel up to $500, health insurance, and access to computer/library facilities.

Duration 1 year.

Special features Fellows participate in seminars, conferences, and meetings at the institution. Outstanding dissertations may be published by the institution.

Limitations Fellows are expected to pursue their research at the Brookings Institution.

Number awarded 1 each year.

Deadline Nominations must be submitted by mid-December and applications by mid-February.

[1299]
ROLLAN D. MELTON FELLOWSHIP

American Press Institute
Attn: Fellowship Program Coordinator
11690 Sunrise Valley Drive
Reston, VA 22091-1498
(703) 620-3611   Fax: (703) 620-5814
E-mail: vcju07a@prodigy.com

Purpose To provide financial support to college-level minority journalism educators who are interested in attending American Press Institute (API) seminars.

Eligibility Nominations are invited from all schools and departments of journalism and mass communications. Eligible to be nominated are college-level minority journalism educators who wish to attend API seminars. Each API seminar is designed for a particular specialty or problem.

Financial data The fellowship covers tuition, room, and board.

Special features This fellowship honors the former president of Speidel Newspapers (now merged with Gannett) and former member of the API board.

Number awarded 1 each year.

Deadline Nominations must be submitted by November of each year.

[1300]
RONALD E. MCNAIR POSTBACCALAUREATE ACHIEVEMENT PROGRAM GRANTS

Department of Education
Attn: Office of Postsecondary Education
Division of Student Services
Portals Building, Suite 600D
600 Independence Avenue, S.W.
Washington, DC 20202-5249
(202) 708-4804   Fax: (202) 401-6132
E-mail: trio@ed.gov

Purpose To provide grants to institutions of higher education to enable them to prepare low-income, first-generation college students, and students from groups underrepresented in graduate education for doctoral study.

Eligibility Accredited institutions of higher learning are eligible to apply. Recipient institutions must use these funds to assist their students in securing admission and financial assistance for graduate education, provide opportunities for summer internships and participation in seminars, provide research opportunities with stipends, and provide such academic support services as tutoring, counseling, and mentoring. For all projects, at least two-thirds of the participants must be low-income, first-generation college students; the remaining participants must be from groups that are underrepresented in graduate education.

Financial data In the last cycle of awards for this program, more than $19 million was distributed; the minimum grant was $190,000 and the average was $194,716. The average cost per participant was $7,754.

Duration Grants are awarded in a 4-year cycle.

Special features Program services may include research opportunities for participants who have completed their sophomore year of college, mentoring, seminars and other scholarly activities designed to prepare students for doctoral studies, summer internships, tutoring, academic counseling, assistance in obtaining student financial aid, and assistance in securing admission and financial aid for enrollment in graduate programs.

Limitations This is not a fellowship program and only institutions of higher education may apply. Students must apply directly to the institution; for a list of participating universities, contact the address above.

Number awarded In the last 4-year cycle, 98 awards were made. The average number of participants per institution was 25.

Deadline The next closing date for receipt of applications under this program will be fall of 1998.

[1301]
RUI FACULTY RESEARCH PROJECTS

National Science Foundation
Attn: Directorate for Education and Human Resources
Senior Staff Associate for Cross Directorate Programs
4201 Wilson Boulevard, Room 805
Arlington, VA 22230
(703) 306-1603

Purpose To provide support to faculty at predominantly undergraduate institutions for science or engineering research.

Eligibility This program is open to faculty members in all fields of science and engineering supported by the National Science Foundation (NSF) who are teaching at predominantly undergraduate institutions, defined as U.S. 2-year, 4-year, masters-level, and small doctoral colleges and universities (those that awarded no more than 20 Ph.D.s or D.Sc.s during the 2 academic years preceding proposal submission). If the institution offers doctoral degrees, the applicant must be teaching in a nondoctoral department. Proposals may be for research at the home institution (including work in the field) and/or away from the home institution at a research university or a government or industrial laboratory. Applications are especially encouraged from women, minorities, and persons with disabilities.

Financial data Awards range from $5,000 to more than $250,000. Funding may cover salaries and wages, research assistantships (focused upon undergraduate students), fringe benefits, travel, materials and supplies, publication costs and page charges, consultant services, equipment needed for individual research projects with a single research focus, field work, research at other institutions, and indirect costs.

Duration 1 to 3 years.

Special features This program is part of the NSF Research in Undergraduate Institutions (RUI) program; it is operated by various disciplinary divisions within the NSF; for a list of the participating divisions and their telephone numbers, contact the address above.

Deadline Deadlines are established by the respective participating NSF disciplinary divisions.

[1302]
RUI RESEARCH INSTRUMENTATION GRANTS

National Science Foundation
Attn: Directorate for Education and Human Resources
Senior Staff Associate for Cross Directorate Programs
4201 Wilson Boulevard, Room 805
Arlington, VA 22230
(703) 306-1603

Purpose To provide funding for the acquisition of research equipment to multi-investigator/user teams at predominantly undergraduate institutions.

Eligibility This program is open to teams of 2 or more co-investigators who are faculty members in all fields of science and engineering supported by the National Science Foundation (NSF) teaching at predominantly undergraduate institutions, defined as U.S. 2-year, 4-year, masters-level, and small doctoral colleges and universities (those that awarded no more than 20 Ph.D.s or D.Sc.s during the 2 academic years preceding proposal submission). If the institution offers doctoral degrees, the applicants must be teaching in nondoctoral departments. Proposals may be for 1) purchasing or upgrading instrumentation or equipment needed for conducting the proposed faculty research, or 2) developing new instrumentation that will extend current capability in terms of sensitivity or resolution, or that will provide new or alternative techniques for detection and observation. Requests may be for single items or multi-component systems. Applications are especially encouraged from women, minorities, and persons with disabilities.

Financial data Awards range from $5,000 to more than $250,000. This program requires cost-sharing; matching requirements differ by program, but may range up to half of the total cost.

Special features This program is part of the NSF Research in Undergraduate Institutions (RUI) program; it is operated by various disciplinary divisions within the NSF; for a list of the participating divisions and their telephone numbers, contact the address above.

Deadline Deadlines are established by the respective participating NSF disciplinary divisions.

[1303]
RURAL ARTS PROJECTS SUPPORT GRANTS

Tennessee Arts Commission
Attn: Arts Access Director
400 Charlotte Avenue
Nashville, TN 37243-0780
(615) 741-1701

Purpose To provide funds for direct support for arts projects to organizations located in rural areas of Tennessee.

Eligibility Nonprofit tax-exempt organizations providing art programs and services are eligible to apply if they are chartered in Tennessee and located in a county that is not part of a Metropolitan Statistical Area. A wide range of activities may be supported, including improved program accessibility for special constituencies such as children, people living in rural-based and/or isolated settings, people with disabilities, people of color, and aging people. Selection criteria include a demonstration that the diverse cultural, ethnic, and artistic plurality of its community are represented in the planning, execution, and evaluation of its program and services.

Financial data Grants range from $500 to $4,000 and must be matched dollar for dollar.

Duration 1 year.

Number awarded Varies each year.

Deadline February of each year.

[1304]
SALTONSTALL-KENNEDY FISHERIES RESEARCH AND DEVELOPMENT GRANTS

Department of Commerce
Attn: National Oceanic and Atmospheric Administration
National Marine Fisheries Service
1335 East-West Highway
Silver Spring, MD 20910
(301) 713-2358

Purpose To foster the development and to stimulate the growth of the fishing industry in the United States, especially by comprehensive funding projects.

Eligibility Universities, state and local governments, fisheries development foundations, industry associations, private firms, and individuals are eligible to submit proposals. Potential topics include fisheries utilization, fisheries management, bycatch, aquaculture, and product quality and safety. Women and minorities are particularly encouraged to apply as principal investigators.

Financial data Grants range from $5,000 to more than $2 million per year. The average grant is $100,000.

Duration Grants up to 18 months are available, but most are for 1 year.

Number awarded Varies each year.

Deadline May of each year.

[1305]
SARA JACKSON AWARD

Western History Association
University of New Mexico
1080 Mesa Vista Hall
Albuquerque, NM 87131-1181
(505) 277-5234   Fax: (505) 277-6023

Purpose To support graduate research on western American history.

Eligibility This program is open to graduate students (master's or doctorate) interested in conducting research in the field of western history. Preference is given to African American or other minority applicants. Interested students should send a letter of application, a vitae, and a description of the proposed research project plus a letter of support from their faculty adviser.

Financial data The grant is $500.

Duration 1 year.

Number awarded 1 each year.

Deadline June of each year.

[1306]
SCHOOL, COLLEGE AND UNIVERSITY PARTNERSHIP GRANTS

Department of Education
Attn: Office of Postsecondary Education
Division of Student Services
Portals Building, Suite 600D
600 Independence Avenue, S.W.
Washington, DC 20202-5249
(202) 708-4804   Fax: (202) 401-6132
E-mail: trio@ed.gov

Purpose To encourage partnerships between institutions of higher education and secondary schools serving students from disadvantaged backgrounds.

Eligibility Applications are accepted from institutions of higher education, or from state higher education agencies in partnership with a local education agency. They must be proposing programs for low-income, at-risk students by helping them develop the skills they will need to succeed in higher education or in the job market. Proposals may include tutoring, basic academic skills instruction, preparation for employment after high school graduation, preparation for postsecondary education, and community service and learning activities.

Financial data In a recent year, a total of $3,893,000 was awarded through this program; the minimum award was $250,000 per year, and the average was $353,909. Recipients must provide a non-federal costsharing of 30, 40, and 50 percent of total project costs for the first, second, third, and subsequent years of the project, respectively.

Duration 1 year; may be renewed for a total of 5 years.

Number awarded Varies; in a recent year, 11 awards were made through this program.

Deadline January of each year.

[1307]
SCHOOL-TO-WORK OPPORTUNITIES ACT URBAN/RURAL PROGRAM GRANTS

Department of Labor
Attn: Employment and Training Administration
Division of Acquisition and Assistance
SGA/DAA 96-007
200 Constitution Avenue, N.W., Room S-4203
Washington, DC 20210
(202) 219-7300

Purpose To provide funding to partnerships involving local organizations that serve high poverty areas and that propose to help prepare young people in such communities for first jobs in high-skill, high-wage careers and further postsecondary education and training.

Eligibility This program is open to local partnerships involving employers, representatives of local educational agencies and local postsecondary educational institutions (including representatives of area vocational education schools, where applicable), local educators, representatives of labor organizations or non-managerial employee representatives; and students. Applicants are also required to meet the definition of "high poverty area." Proposals must identify and address a great variety of needs of youth residing or attending school in the area, with an ability to coordinate its strategies for serving in-school and out-of-school youth, to assess and address the multiple needs of high poverty area youth, and to link effectively with both schoolwide reform efforts and with the state's plan for a comprehensive School-to-Work Opportunities system.

Financial data Grants range from $200,000 to $650,000 per year.

Duration 1 year; may be renewed on an annual basis for 4 additional years.

Special features This program is operated jointly by the Employment and Training Administration of the Department of Labor and the Office of Vocational and Adult Education of the Department of Education.

Number awarded 25 to 35 each year; in a recent year, a total of $15 million was available for this program

Deadline January of each year.

[1308]
SCIENCE, ENGINEERING, AND DIPLOMACY FELLOWSHIPS

American Association for the Advancement of Science
Attn: Science and Engineering Fellowship Programs
1200 New York Avenue, N.W.
Washington, DC 20005-3920
(202) 326-6600   Fax: (202) 289-4950
E-mail: science_policy@aaas.org

Purpose To provide postdoctoral and midcareer scientists and engineers an opportunity to demonstrate the value of science and technology in dealing with foreign affairs and international development programs of the U.S. Agency for International Development (USAID) or the Bureau of Oceans and International Environmental and Scientific Affairs of the U.S. Department of State.

Eligibility Prospective fellows may have a Ph.D. or equivalent doctoral level degree in any physical, biological, or social science, any field of engineering, or any relevant interdisciplinary field; persons with a master's degree in engineering and at least 3 years of post-degree experience may apply. Candidates must demonstrate exceptional competence in some area of science or engineering; be cognizant of the ways in which science and technology affect a broad range of international development and foreign policy issues; communicate and work effectively with decision-makers and others outside of the scientific and engineering communities; exhibit willingness and flexibility to tackle problems in a number of nonscientific areas; demonstrate sensitivity toward political, economic, and social issues; and have some experience and/or strong interest in applying knowledge toward the solution of problems in the area of foreign affairs or international development. Applicants must be U.S. citizens and must obtain a security clearance; federal employees are not eligible. Minorities and persons with disabilities are especially encouraged to apply.

Financial data Stipends depend on education and experience, but begin at approximately $46,000.

Duration 1 year, beginning in September; may be renewed for 1 additional year.

Special features Fellows assigned to USAID work on matters related to sustainable development, especially in economic growth, the environment, population and health, and democratization. Fellows assigned to the State Department assist in foreign policy development and implementation in the areas of biodiversity, conservation, and transboundary environmental issues. Both fellowship assignments provide international travel opportunities. Fellows assigned to the State Department are employees of that agency; that program is known as the Parker-Gentry Biodiversity Fellowship, in honor of 2 biologists, Theodore A. Parker and Alwyn Gentry, who died in Ecuador in August 1993. Fellows assigned to USAID receive stipends from the American Association for the Advancement of Science.

Number awarded 12 each year for USAID and 1 each year for the State Department.

Deadline January of each year.

[1309]
SCIENTIST DEVELOPMENT AWARD FOR NEW MINORITY FACULTY

National Institutes of Health
Attn: National Institute of Mental Health
Office for Special Populations
Parklawn Building, Room 17C-14
5600 Fishers Lane MSC 8030
Rockville, MD 20857-8030
(301) 443-3641　　　　　　　　Fax: (301) 443-8552
E-mail: rc30x@nih.gov

Purpose To provide financial support to new minority faculty members to initiate a program of research and to help them to become outstanding independent investigators in mental health research.

Eligibility This program is open to non-tenured faculty members at domestic, nonprofit, public and private universities, colleges, and professional schools engaged in mental health research who are U.S. citizens and members of minority groups (American Indians, Alaskan Natives, Asian/Pacific Islanders, Blacks, and Hispanics). Applicants must have earned a doctorate (Ph.D., M.D., D.Sc., etc.) by the time the award is made and must be proposing to devote at least 75 percent of professional time to career development activities, research, or other research-related activities relevant to their career goals.

Financial data Salary support depends on the established structure for full-time, 12-month staff appointments at the grantee institution. The awards through this program are 100 percent of base for salaries up to $45,000, $45,000 for base salaries of $45,001 to $60,000, or 75 percent of base for salaries over $60,001, to a maximum of $75,000.

Duration 5 years; nonrenewable.

Special features Applications must designate a mentor to work with the candidate. The proposed mentor must be a recognized, well-established, active investigator in the candidate's proposed research area who has not served in this role during the candidate's pre- or postdoctoral training.

Deadline January, May, and September of each year.

[1310]
SCSU SUMMER MINORITY TEACHING FELLOWS

St. Cloud State University
Attn: Academic Affairs Office
209 Administrative Services Building
720 4th Avenue, South
St. Cloud, MN 56301-4498

Purpose To provide teaching experience at St. Cloud State University to minorities interested in preparing for an academic career.

Eligibility This program is open to minority graduate students who are completing their terminal degree. Preference is given to students who are within 1 year of completing their degree. Candidates must be interested in teaching summer school at the university.

Financial data The stipend is $3,500.

Duration Summer months.

Special features This program was established in 1989. All colleges and departments at the university are eligible to have a fellow. A number of participants have later been hired to join the faculty at the university.

Limitations This program has been discontinued pending an evaluation and review for possible restructuring; the date of its resumption has not been established.

Number awarded 10 each year.

[1311]
SECRETARY OF NAVY DOCTORAL RESEARCH FELLOWSHIPS FOR NAVAL READINESS

Office of Naval Research
ONR 353/NR
800 North Quincy Street
Arlington, VA 22217-5660
(703) 696-4111　　　　　　　E-mail: hughesd@onr.navy.mil

Purpose To provide financial assistance for doctoral research in the social sciences to candidates whose dissertations will contribute to improved understanding of determinants of the readiness of U.S. naval forces.

Eligibility Applicants must be U.S. citizens currently engaged in doctoral research who are within 2 years of formally submitting dissertations to their institutions of higher education. Appropriate fields of study include, but are not limited to, economics, operations research, statistics, management science, psychology, sociology, and social anthropology. Preference is given to dissertations involving the analyses of actual naval readiness data. Dissertation work must involve interaction with an academic, Navy, or Marine Corps researcher actively engaged in research on some aspect of the naval readiness problem. Applications are specifically encouraged from women, minorities (American Indians, Blacks, Hispanics, Native Alaskans, or Native Pacific Islanders), and persons with disabilities.

Financial data The fellowships provide payment of tuition, an annual stipend of $15,000, up to $5,000 to cover dissertation-related research, and up to $15,000 for costs related to the required interaction with the mentor researcher. Persons with disabilities may qualify for additional allowances to offset special education expenses.

Duration Up to 2 years.

Special features For a list of naval facilities where aspects of naval readiness are explored and appropriate academic researchers, contact the address above.

Number awarded Up to 4 each year.

Deadline January of each year.

[1312]
SEDIMENTARY GEOLOGY DIVISION GRANT

Geological Society of America
Attn: Research Grants Administrator
3300 Penrose Place
P.O. Box 9140
Boulder, CO 80301-9140
(303) 447-2020, ext. 137   Fax: (303) 447-1133
E-mail: jforstro@geosociety.org

Purpose To provide partial support for geological research by graduate students at universities in the United States, Canada, Mexico, and Central America.

Eligibility This program is open to graduate students in geology at the master's or doctoral level. Both members and non-members of the society are eligible. Special consideration may be given to students who propose research on 1 or more aspects of sedimentary geology. Applications from women, minorities, and persons with disabilities are strongly encouraged.

Financial data Grants range up to $2,500; the average grant recently was $1,604.

Duration 1 year.

Special features This program is sponsored by the Geological Society of America's Sedimentary Geology Division.

Number awarded 1 or more each year.

Deadline February of each year.

[1313]
SENIOR SCIENTIST AWARDS

National Institutes of Health
Attn: Office of Extramural Research
Extramural Outreach and Information Resources Office
6701 Rockledge Drive, Room 6207
MSC 7910
Bethesda, MD 20892-7910
(301) 435-0714   Fax: (301) 480-8443
E-mail: asknih@odrockm1.od.nih.gov

Purpose To provide financial support to outstanding scientists who have already demonstrated a sustained, high level of productivity in research.

Eligibility This program is open to senior scientists who have a distinguished record of original research contributions, long-term support from a funding institute or center, and peer-reviewed grant support at the time of the award. Applications may be submitted on behalf of candidates by domestic, non-federal organizations, public or private, such as medical, dental, or nursing schools or other institutions of higher education. Minorities and women are particularly encouraged to apply. Candidates must be U.S. citizens or permanent residents.

Financial data This program provides salary and fringe benefits for the candidate only; each component establishes its own salary limits on career awards. Indirect costs are reimbursed at 8 percent of modified total direct costs, or at the actual indirect cost rate, whichever is less.

Duration 5 years.

Special features Awards under this program are available from 3 agencies of the National Institutes of Health (NIH): the National Institute on Alcohol Abuse and Alcoholism, the National Institute on Drug Abuse, and the National Institute of Mental Health. The names and addresses of staff people at each agency are available from the address above. The NIH designates this program as the K05 Awards.

Number awarded Varies each year.

Deadline January, May, or September of each year.

[1314]
SEVENTH GENERATION FUND GENERAL SUPPORT GRANTS

Seventh Generation Fund
P.O. Box 4569
Arcata, CA 95518
(707) 825-7640   Fax: (707) 825-7639

Purpose To support Native American initiated and controlled efforts to maintain and promote the uniqueness of Native people and nations by offering small grants.

Eligibility The fund provides grants for projects whose purpose, design, and implementation strategy originate from the Indigenous people it will serve; whose leadership and decision-making authority are vested in the people it will impact; that promotes and enhances the culture, traditional institutions, language, values, and way of life of its constituents; that impacts the largest number of people and broadest segments of their society; and that does not promote or perpetuate racism, sexism, oppression, or exploitation of other humans or the natural environment.

Financial data Grants up to $5,000 are provided to cover administrative and operating costs of a project.

Duration 1 year; may be renewed for 2 additional years.

Special features The Seventh Generation Fund is the first national Native American community foundation. Its name is derived from the Great Law of the Haudenosaunee (Six Nations Iroquois Confederacy) that "in our every deliberation we must consider the impact on the seventh generation."

Number awarded Varies each year.

Deadline Applications may be submitted at any time.

[1315]
SEXUALITY RESEARCH PROGRAM DISSERTATION FELLOWSHIPS

Social Science Research Council
810 Seventh Avenue
New York, NY 10019
(212) 377-2700   Fax: (212) 377-2727

Purpose To provide financial support for dissertation research on sexuality topics.

Eligibility Students should have completed all requirements for the Ph.D. except the dissertation and be matriculating in a full-time graduate program in the United States leading to the Ph.D. in a social or behavioral science. Students enrolled in a public health department or division of an accredited U.S. college or university are also eligible. Applications are invited from a wide range of disciplines, including but not limited to anthropology, demography, economics, education, ethics, history, cultural and women's studies, political science, psychology, and sociology; applications from other fields, such as the nursing, law, and clinical/social work fields, are welcome as long as they are grounded in social science theory and methodology. The research proposals should seek to investigate a wide range of sexuality topics as conceptualized by the respective disciplines and conducted within the United States, including but not limited to: sexual/gender role socialization within the context of society and culture; historical, comparative, and/or cross-cultural analyses of sexuality; social construction analysis of sexuality; the diversity and distribution of sexual values, beliefs, and behaviors within different populations and their meanings for individuals; the link between sexuality and gender relations; sexual orientation; sexual coercion; the impact of economic change or of other institutional influences, such as religion or the media, on sexuality; and the formation of social policy based on cultural norms regarding sexuality. Women and members of minority groups are especially encouraged to apply. There are no citizenship, residency, or nationality requirements.

Financial data The stipend of $28,000 covers direct research costs, matriculation fees, and living expenses. An additional $3,000 is awarded to the fellow's host institution and $3,000 to the fellow's research advisor or associate to defray expenses associated with the fellow's training, including direct research.

Duration Up to 12 months.

Special features Funding for this program is provided by the Ford Foundation.

Number awarded 10 each year.

Deadline December of each year.

[1316]
SEXUALITY RESEARCH PROGRAM POSTDOCTORAL FELLOWSHIPS

Social Science Research Council
810 Seventh Avenue
New York, NY 10019
(212) 377-2700   Fax: (212) 377-2727

Purpose To provide financial support for postdoctoral research on sexuality topics.

Eligibility Applicants must hold the Ph.D. or its equivalent in a social or behavioral science from an accredited university in the United States, or an equivalent Ph.D. degree from an accredited foreign university. Applications are invited from a wide range of disciplines, including but not limited to anthropology, demography, economics, education, ethics, history, cultural and women's studies, political science, psychology, and sociology; applications from other fields, such as the nursing, law, and clinical/social work fields, are welcome as long as they are grounded in social science theory and methodology. The applicant may be a recent recipient of the doctorate or well advanced in the postdoctoral research process. Fellows may already have conducted research in the field of human sexuality or may be newly committing themselves to using their more general training to address sexuality issues. Postdoctoral candidates who have conducted research on sexuality for more than 8 years are not considered. The research proposals should seek to investigate a wide range of sexuality topics as conceptualized by the respective disciplines and conducted within the United States, including but not limited to: sexual/gender role socialization within the context of society and culture; historical, comparative, and/or cross-cultural analyses of sexuality; social construction analysis of sexuality; the

diversity and distribution of sexual values, beliefs, and behaviors within different populations and their meanings for individuals; the link between sexuality and gender relations; sexual orientation; sexual coercion; the impact of economic change or of other institutional influences, such as religion or the media, on sexuality; and the formation of social policy based on cultural norms regarding sexuality. Women and members of minority groups are especially encouraged to apply. There are no citizenship, residency, or nationality requirements.

Financial data The stipend is $38,000 per year, to cover research costs and living expenses.

Duration Up to 2 years; continuation of the grant for more than 12 months requires submission and satisfactory review of a progress report to the fellowship program.

Special features Funding for this program is provided by the Ford Foundation.

Limitations This program does not support curriculum development or evaluation, direct service provision, public/community education, or the creation and maintenance of organizations.

Number awarded 4 each year.

Deadline December of each year.

[1317]
SHARED RESEARCH EQUIPMENT PROGRAM

Oak Ridge Institute for Science and Education
Attn: Science/Engineering Education Division
P.O. Box 117
Oak Ridge, TN 37831-0117
(423) 576-3425   (423) 576-2358
(800) 569-7749   Fax: (423) 576-3643
E-mail: sharrsh@orau.gov

Purpose To provide funding for research using sophisticated microanalytical facilities in the areas of electron microscopy (transmission, scanning, analytical), atom probe field ion microscopy, and mechanical properties microanalysis at the Oak Ridge National Laboratory in Tennessee.

Eligibility This program is open to faculty members, postdoctoral fellows, industrial participants, and graduate students interested in conducting basic or applied research on energy-related materials. All programs operated by the Science/Engineering Education Division (SEED) of Oak Ridge Institute for Science and Education (ORISE) seek to broaden the participation of minorities, women, and persons with disabilities in science and engineering careers.

Financial data The program covers travel and living expenses while participants use the research facilities at the Oak Ridge National Laboratory.

Duration Only short-term visits are supported.

Special features This program is funded by the Office of Energy Research of the U.S. Department of Energy and administered by ORISE/SEED.

Number awarded Varies; approximately 25 each year.

Deadline September of each year.

[1318]
SHELL INCENTIVE FUNDS

Shell Oil Company Foundation
Two Shell Plaza
P.O. Box 2099
Houston, TX 77252
(713) 241-3616   Fax: (713) 241-3329

Purpose To provide funds to academic institutions that are interested in encouraging minority students to pursue a bachelor's degree in business or technical fields.

Eligibility Academic institutions are eligible to apply to provide support for tuition and fees, stipends for living expenses, and unrestricted grants to the institutions in which the students are enrolled.

Financial data Since 1971, when the program was initiated, more than $2 million has been expended. In a recent year, a total of $260,000 was available through this program.

Duration 1 year; may be renewed.

Number awarded Varies; in a recent year, 23 institutions received support through this program.

[1319]
SHIELDS-GILLESPIE SCHOLARSHIP

American Orff-Schulwerk Association
Attn: Executive Secretary
P.O. Box 391089
Cleveland, OH 44139
(216) 543-5366

Purpose To provide financial aid to teachers of preschool and kindergarten children from minority and low-income populations who recognize the important role music can play in early childhood education.

Eligibility Applicants must be members of the American Orff-Schulwerk Association and actively involved in preschool or kindergarten education programs for minority and low-income populations. Applicants must demonstrate strong motivation to study and use music, particularly the Orff-Schulwerk process, in early childhood education. Applicants must demonstrate real financial need and must be citizens of or have resided in the United States for the past 5 years.

Financial data The amount awarded varies, depending upon the funds available and the needs of the recipient; in a recent year, grants for $330 and $500 were approved.

Duration 1 year.

Number awarded 1 or 2 each year.

Deadline December of each year.

[1320]
SHORT-TERM MINORITY INVESTIGATOR
RESEARCH SUPPLEMENT

National Institutes of Health
Attn: Office of Extramural Research
Extramural Outreach and Information Resources Office
6701 Rockledge Drive, Room 6207
MSC 7910
Bethesda, MD 20892-7910
(301) 435-0714   Fax: (301) 480-8443
E-mail: asknih@odrockm1.od.nih.gov

Purpose To supply short-term research support to underrepresented minority faculty members who are seeking to enhance their research skills leading to an independent research career in fields supported by the National Institutes of Health.

Eligibility The minority investigator may be affiliated with either the applicant institution or any other institution. The investigator must have a doctoral degree, be beyond the level of a research trainee, and be a member of the faculty with at least 1 year of postdoctoral experience. Individuals who have received previous funding from a component institute or center as an independent principal investigator on regular research grants, program project grants, or research career program awards are not eligible. The institutes consider African Americans, Hispanic Americans, Native Americans, Alaskan Natives, or Pacific Islanders as underrepresented minority investigators.

Financial data The minority faculty supplemental award is for a maximum of $50,000 in direct costs per year. A maximum of $40,000 may be requested for salary and fringe benefits; additional funds totaling $10,000 may be requested for supplies and travel. Equipment may not be purchased except in unusual circumstances.

Duration 3 to 5 months, full time, for up to 4 years.

Number awarded Varies each year.

[1321]
SISTER FUND GRANTS

Sister Fund
Attn: Director
116 East 16th Street, 7th Floor
New York, NY 10003
(212) 260-4446   Fax: (212) 260-4633
E-mail: SisterFund@aol.com

Purpose To fund organizational programs (primarily in the New York City area) that foster women's economic, social, political, and spiritual empowerment.

Eligibility This program is open only to public charity organizations; grants are not given to individuals. Primary consideration is given to proposals from organizations that both serve and are led by women and girls affected by economic, social, mental, and physical oppression—especially women of color, lesbians, the economically disadvantaged, the aged, and/or women with disabilities. Potential grantees are invited to submit a brief proposal (5 to 10 pages) that outlines the project for which funds are sought. Only 1 proposal from an organization may be submitted each year. Approximately 50 percent of the grants focus on New York City and 50 percent support national and international efforts.

Financial data Annually, more than $500,000 is distributed. Individual grants range from $5,000 to $30,000.

Duration Grants are awarded 3 times a year.

Special features This fund was established in 1992.

Number awarded Varies; generally, 50 or more each year.

Deadline March, July, or December of each year.

[1322]
SISTER-TO-SISTER GRANT PROGRAM

Holding Our Own, Inc.
79 Central Avenue
Albany, NY 12206
(518) 462-2871

Purpose To provide funding to women's groups, organizations, and projects in the area of Albany, New York.

Eligibility To be eligible, the women's groups, organizations, or projects must be located in Albany, Rensselaer, Saratoga, and Schenectady Counties, New York. Preference is given to proposals that focus on projects that build and strengthen women's communities, enhance the ability of lesbians of all races to live more open lives, promote the leadership and interests of women of color of all sexualities, and serve the needs of all women who have limited access to traditional sources of funding. Most grants involve coalitions of 2 or more groups working together on a project which serves predominantly women or girls.

Financial data The maximum amount granted is $2,000; generally, grants are at least $200. Since it was founded in 1982, Holding Our Own has awarded more than $250,000 in grants through this program.

Duration 1 year; recipients may reapply.

Number awarded Varies; generally around 15 each year.

Deadline July of each year.

[1323]
SMALL GRANT PROGRAM FOR CONFERENCE SUPPORT

Agency for Health Care Policy and Research
Attn: Center for Health Information Dissemination
Executive Office Center, Suite 501
2101 East Jefferson Street
Rockville, MD 20852-4908
(301) 594-1360, ext. 145   Fax: (301) 594-2286

Purpose To provide funding for conferences on issues relevant to health services research.

Eligibility Any nonprofit organization is eligible to submit an application to the Agency for Health Care Policy and Research (AHCPR) for a small grant to support a conference. Eligible organizations include: academic institutions, agencies of state and local government, and private research and service organizations and foundations. Profit making organizations are not eligible. Types of eligible conferences include research development conferences which define issues or problems in the delivery of health services and develop a research agenda or strategy for studying them; design and methodology conferences which address methodological and technical issues of major importance in the field of health services research; and dissemination conferences which provide research information to organizations and individuals involved in formulating or evaluating health policy, managing health care programs, and purchasing or using health services. AHCPR encourages women and members of minority groups to submit applications.

Financial data Total direct costs may not exceed $50,000. Direct cost expenditures may include equipment, travel, supplies, conference services, publication costs, registration fees, entertainment and personal expenses, honoraria, and meals.

Number awarded Varies each year.

Deadline April and November of each year.

[1324]
SMITHSONIAN AWARDS FOR MUSEUM LEADERSHIP

Smithsonian Institution
Attn: Center for Museum Studies
Arts and Industries Building, Suite 2235
MRC 427
Washington, DC 20560
(202) 357-3101   Fax: (202) 357-3346
E-mail: ompem017@sivm.si.edu

Purpose To provide training to minority professionals who work in museums or related institutions.

Eligibility Eligible to apply for this training program are minorities (African Americans, Alaska Natives, American Indians, Asian Americans, Latinos, Native Hawaiians, and Pacific Islanders) who are in the early years of their museum careers (3 to 8 years after completion of formal education) and who are currently working in museums or related institutions. Selection is based upon oral and written communication skills, ability to relate to others, potential to effect change, knowledge of and commitment to the museum field, openness to new ideas, and ability to think creatively and critically.

Financial data The selected professionals receive an allowance for travel and living expenses.

Duration The training lasts 5 days, in March.

Special features The participants receive training at the Smithsonian Institution; the training is provided by the Center for Museum Studies.

Number awarded 15 each year.

Deadline January of each year.

[1325]
SMITHSONIAN FELLOWSHIPS IN MUSEUM PRACTICE

Smithsonian Institution
Attn: Center for Museum Studies
Arts and Industries Building, Suite 2235
MRC 427
Washington, DC 20560
(202) 357-3101   Fax: (202) 357-3346
E-mail: ompem002@sivm.si.edu

Purpose To enable museum professionals to undertake original research in museum theory and operations, using resources and facilities at the Smithsonian Institution.

Eligibility Mid- or senior level staff who work in museums or allied cultural and educational institutions are eligible to apply for these grants. Proposals from small, minority, emerging, or rural institutions are strongly encouraged. Selection is based on the quality of scholarship, clarity of problem to be explored and rationale of approach, feasibility, relevance to the aims of the program, importance of access to Smithsonian resources, evidence of the applicant's ability to perform the project, and the degree to which the project promotes closer ties between the applicant's institution and the Smithsonian.

Financial data The award includes travel costs and a stipend to help defray expenses incurred during residency in Washington, D.C. Stipends are computed on the basis of $500 per week; the maximum amount that can be provided is $4,000.

Duration 2 to 12 months.

Number awarded Varies each year.

Deadline February of each year.

[1326]
SOCIAL AND ECONOMIC DEVELOPMENT STRATEGIES PROJECTS FOR NATIVE AMERICANS

Department of Health and Human Services
Attn: Administration for Children and Families
Administration for Native Americans
Hubert H. Humphrey Building, Room 348F
200 Independence Avenue, S.W.
Washington, DC 20201-0001
(202) 690-5780

Purpose To provide funding for projects that attempt to promote the goal of social and economic self-sufficiency for Native Americans through locally developed social and economic development strategies.

Eligibility Applications may be submitted by federally recognized Indian tribes; consortia of Indian tribes; incorporated non-federally recognized tribes; incorporated nonprofit multi-purpose community-based Indian organizations; urban Indian centers; national or regional incorporated nonprofit Native American organizations with Native American community-specific objectives; Alaska Native villages and/or nonprofit village consortia; incorporated nonprofit Alaska Native multi-purpose community-based organizations; nonprofit Alaska Native Regional Corporations/Associations in Alaska with village specific projects; nonprofit Native organizations in Alaska with village specific projects; public and nonprofit private agencies serving Native Hawaiians; public and nonprofit private agencies serving native peoples from Guam, American Samoa, Palau, or the Commonwealth of the Northern Mariana Islands; and tribally controlled community colleges, tribally controlled postsecondary vocational institutions, and colleges and universities in Hawaii, Guam, American Samoa, Palau, or the Commonwealth of the Northern Mariana Islands which serve Native American Pacific Islanders. Proposals must enable the applicant organization to develop and implement community-based, long-term governance, social, and economic development strategies.

Financial data Grants range from $30,000 to $1,000,000. Grantees must provide at least 20 percent of the total approved cost of the project.

Duration 1 year.

Number awarded Approximately 120 each year; $14 million was available for this program in a recent year.

Deadline October, February, and May of each year.

[1327]
SOUTH CAROLINA ARTS COMMISSION MULTICULTURAL GRANTS FOR ETHNIC ARTISTS

South Carolina Arts Commission
1800 Gervais Street
Columbia, SC 29201-3585
(803) 734-8696   Fax: (803) 734-8526

Purpose To provide assistance to ethnic artists in South Carolina.

Eligibility Ethnic artists, defined as African Americans, Asian Americans, Spanish Americans, and American Indians, are eligible for these grants for 1 specific arts activity for career advancement or professional development. Applicants must be at least 18 years of age and have maintained a permanent residence address in South Carolina for at least 6 months prior to the date of application and throughout the grant period. Degree-seeking, full-time undergraduate students and students who will earn academic credit as a result of the proposed project are ineligible.

Selection is based on appropriateness and feasibility of the proposed culturally diverse project, extent to which the project will contribute to the professional development or career advancement of the applicant, artistic quality of the work samples submitted, qualifications of the applicant to undertake the proposed project, and appropriateness and feasibility of the proposed budget.

Financial data The maximum award is $1,000; most grants are funded for less. Matching of 50 percent by the recipient is required, although up to half of the cash match may be accounted for by the cash value of the artist's time.

Duration 1 year; may be renewed for 1 additional year.

Special features Funds may be used for such projects as: the creation of art that reflects the culture of an ethnic or tribal community; professional development; development of marketing, promotion, and documentation; performances, exhibitions, or readings; or training subsidies to attend workshops, conferences, etc.

Number awarded Varies each year; within the guidelines, funds are distributed on a first-come, first-served basis.

Deadline For projects starting from July through September, May of each year; for projects starting from October through December, August of each year; for projects starting from January through March, November of each year; for projects starting from April through June, February of each year.

[1328]
SOUTH CAROLINA ARTS COMMISSION MULTICULTURAL GRANTS FOR ETHNIC ORGANIZATIONS

South Carolina Arts Commission
1800 Gervais Street
Columbia, SC 29201-3585
(803) 734-8696   Fax: (803) 734-8526

Purpose To provide assistance to arts organizations in South Carolina that celebrate, recognize, and support cultural diversity.

Eligibility Nonprofit ethnic arts organizations or tribal communities in South Carolina may apply for these grants. For the purpose of this program, "ethnic organization" refers to organizations that represent and provide programs or services that reflect the ethnic culture of African Americans, Hispanic Americans, Asian Americans, and American Indians; "tribal communities" are characterized by their American Indian traditions and are geographically and culturally distinguished by their customs, religion, social tradition, creative expression, and their oral and written histories. All applicants must be chartered in South Carolina as a nonprofit organization or governmental agency and be exempt from federal taxation. Selection is based on evidence that the applicant plans to develop issues, events, and themes from a multicultural perspective; the extent to which the multicultural community's need for the project and the importance of the project are demonstrated; the significance of the proposed objectives and the extent to which objectives are appropriate and responsive to needs; evidence that the applicant is artistically and administratively qualified to undertake the proposed project; evidence that program and planning are inclusive of the whole community; appropriateness and feasibility of the proposed project activities; and quality of the application materials.

Financial data The maximum award is $2,000; most grants are funded for less. Matching by the recipient is required.

Duration 1 year; may be renewed for 1 additional year.

Special features Funds may be used for such projects as: the creation, development, and enhancement of art that reflects the culture of an ethnic or tribal community; development of marketing, promotion, and documentation that would assist the organization in attracting new or broader audiences; administrative internships to enhance leadership and administrative skills of the organization's staff; projects that relate to organizational development; projects that provide opportunities for cosponsorships and regional networking; professionally directed performances or exhibitions designed to provide access to quality art of all types to a community that does not usually have such access; and training subsidies to attend workshops, conferences, etc.

Number awarded Varies each year; within the guidelines, funds are distributed on a first-come, first-served basis.

Deadline For projects starting from July through September, May of each year; for projects starting from October through December, August of each year; for projects starting from January through March, November of each year; for projects starting from April through June, February of each year.

[1329]
SOUTH CAROLINA ARTS COMMISSION MULTICULTURAL GRANTS FOR NON-ETHNIC ARTS AND NON-ARTS ORGANIZATIONS

South Carolina Arts Commission
1800 Gervais Street
Columbia, SC 29201-3585
(803) 734-8696   Fax: (803) 734-8526

Purpose To provide assistance to organizations in South Carolina that wish to encourage cultural diversity.

Eligibility Nonprofit organizations in South Carolina whose staffs, boards, or constituencies are not 50 percent or more ethnic in their composition may apply for these grants. They must wish to develop innovative planning strategies for underserved ethnic (African American, Hispanic American, or Asian American) or tribal (American Indian) populations. All applicants must be chartered in South Carolina as a nonprofit organization or governmental agency and be exempt from federal taxation. Selection is based on evidence that the applicant plans to develop issues, events, and themes from a multicultural perspective; the extent to which the multicultural community's need for the project and the importance of the project are demonstrated; the significance of the proposed objectives and the extent to which objectives are appropriate and responsive to needs; evidence that the applicant is artistically and administratively qualified to undertake the proposed project; evidence that program and planning are inclusive of the whole community; appropriateness and feasibility of the proposed project activities; and quality of the application materials.

Financial data The maximum award is $2,000; most grants are funded for less. Matching by the recipient is required.

Duration 1 year; may be renewed for 1 additional year.

Special features Funds may be used for planning strategies such as assessing the community's multicultural needs, establishing a multicultural task force, or identifying community leaders and issues relating to multicultural development.

Number awarded Varies each year; within the guidelines, funds are distributed on a first-come, first-served basis.

Deadline For projects starting from July through September, May of each year; for projects starting from October through December, August of each year; for projects starting from January through March, November of each year; for projects starting from April through June, February of each year.

[1330]
SOUTH-CENTRAL SECTION GRADUATE STUDENT GRANTS

Geological Society of America
Attn: Research Grants Administrator
3300 Penrose Place
P.O. Box 9140
Boulder, CO 80301-9140
(303) 447-2020, ext. 137   Fax: (303) 447-1133
E-mail: jforstro@geosociety.org

Purpose To provide partial support for geological research by graduate students at universities in the south central states.

Eligibility This program is open to graduate students (at the master's or doctoral level) who are studying geology at universities located within the geographic area of the South-Central Section. Both members and nonmembers of the society are eligible. Applications from women, minorities, and persons with disabilities are strongly encouraged.

Financial data Grants range up to $2,500; the average grant recently was $1,604.

Duration 1 year.

Special features This program is sponsored by the Geological Society of America's South-Central Section.

Number awarded 1 or more each year.

Deadline February of each year.

[1331]
SOUTH-CENTRAL SECTION UNDERGRADUATE STUDENT GRANTS

Geological Society of America
Attn: Research Grants Administrator
3300 Penrose Place
P.O. Box 9140
Boulder, CO 80301-9140
(303) 447-2020, ext. 137   Fax: (303) 447-1133
E-mail: jforstro@geosociety.org

Purpose To provide partial support for geological research by undergraduate students at universities in the south central states.

Eligibility This program is open to undergraduate students who are majoring in geology at universities located within the geographic area of the South-Central Section. Both members and nonmembers of the society are eligible. Applications from women, minorities, and persons with disabilities are strongly encouraged.

Financial data Grants range up to $2,500; the average grant recently was $1,604.

Duration 1 year.

Special features This program is sponsored by the Geological Society of America's South-Central Section. Applications are also available from Rena M. Bonem, Department of Geology, Baylor University, Waco, TX 76798-7354.

Number awarded 1 or more each year.

Deadline October of each year.

[1332]
SOUTHEASTERN SECTION STUDENT RESEARCH GRANTS

Geological Society of America
Attn: Research Grants Administrator
3300 Penrose Place
P.O. Box 9140
Boulder, CO 80301-9140
(303) 447-2020, ext. 137 Fax: (303) 447-1133
E-mail: jforstro@geosociety.org

Purpose To provide partial support for geological research by undergraduate and graduate students at universities in the southeastern part of the United States.

Eligibility This program is open to undergraduate and graduate students who are majoring in geology at universities located within the geographic area of the Southeastern Section. Applicants must be Student Associates or Student Members of the Geological Society of America. Applications from women, minorities, and persons with disabilities are strongly encouraged.

Financial data Grants range up to $2,500; the average grant recently was $1,604.

Duration 1 year.

Special features This program is sponsored by the Geological Society of America's Southeastern Section. Applications are also available from Harold H. Stowell, Department of Geology, Box 870338, University of Alabama, Tuscaloosa, AL 35487-0338.

Number awarded 1 or more each year.

Deadline February of each year.

[1333]
SOVIET UNION AND ITS SUCCESSOR STATES DISSERTATION FELLOWSHIPS

Social Science Research Council
810 Seventh Avenue
New York, NY 10019
(212) 377-2700 Fax: (212) 377-2727

Purpose To provide funding for graduate students working on a dissertation dealing with the Soviet Union and/or its successor states.

Eligibility This program is open to students who have completed research for their doctoral dissertation and who expect to complete the writing of their dissertation during the next academic year. Applicants must be U.S. citizens and specializing in a discipline of the social sciences or humanities that deals with the Soviet Union and/or its successor states. Minorities and women are particularly encouraged to apply.

Financial data Up to $15,000.

Duration Up to 1 year.

Deadline November of each year.

[1334]
SOVIET UNION AND ITS SUCCESSOR STATES POSTDOCTORAL FELLOWSHIPS

Social Science Research Council
810 Seventh Avenue
New York, NY 10019
(212) 377-2700 Fax: (212) 377-2727

Purpose To improve the academic employment and tenure opportunities of scholars who recently received a Ph.D. in the study of the Soviet Union and/or its successor states.

Eligibility This program is open to U.S. citizens who have received a Ph.D. after 1990 but who are untenured. Their work may be in any discipline of the social sciences and humanities in the study of the Soviet Union and its successor states. Women and members of minority groups are especially encouraged to apply.

Financial data The stipend is $27,000.

Duration 3 years of summer support plus 1 semester free of teaching.

Deadline November of each year.

[1335]
SPECIAL ARTS SERVICES PROGRAM OF THE NEW YORK STATE COUNCIL ON THE ARTS

New York State Council on the Arts
915 Broadway
New York, NY 10010
(212) 387-7000 (800) GET-ARTS

Purpose To provide financial support for programs that strengthen the pluralism of New York's cultural life.

Eligibility Support is extended to both established institutions and groups in early stages of development (with strong growth potential), if they represent professional arts activities within the African/Caribbean, Latino/Hispanic, Asian/Pacific Islander, Native American/Indian, and other distinct cultural communities. Only entities in New York are eligible to apply for the grants. Selection is based on, in order of importance, artistic quality, viability of programming and future goals, evidence of community participation at the staff and board of directors level, and proven commitment to programs serving communities of color and those with distinct ethnic traditions. Priority is given to organizations that pay artists' and curators' fees.

Financial data The amount granted varies, depending upon the needs and nature of the program. Generally, first-time support ranges from $1,000 to $5,000.

Special features Funds are available to support general operations and programs, administrative salaries, exhibitions, professional performances, and instruction and training (both professional and preprofessional).

Deadline February of each year.

[1336]
SPONSORED RESEARCH INFRASTRUCTURE PROGRAM

National Institutes of Health
Attn: Extramural Associates Program
Rockledge II, Room 6187A
6701 Rockledge Drive MSC 7910
Bethesda, MD 20892-7910
(301) 435-2692 Fax: (301) 480-0393
E-mail: mk51q@nih.gov

Purpose To improve opportunities for minorities and women to participate in and contribute to biomedical research by enabling faculty or administrators to participate in a program at the National Institutes of Health (NIH) in Bethesda, Maryland.

Eligibility Academic institutions that have a significant enrollment of minorities, or are women's colleges, may nominate 1 scientific faculty member or academic administrator. In addition to the qualifications and interests of the nominee, selection is based on the demonstrated contribution of the institution to the advancement of ethnic minorities and/or women, its readiness to improve health research or research training, and its plan to utilize the associate's expertise after participating in the program. This program is intended for nominees from institutions which award master's, Ph.D.s, and professional degrees such as the M.D., D.D.S., D.V.M., and Pharm.D.

Financial data Salaries are comparable to those being received by the associate at the time of selection. Cost-sharing is required, depending on the institution's resources. Travel, housing, and subsistence expenses while at NIH, and any costs incurred that are directly related to the training, are reimbursed by the NIH.

Duration 5 months.

Special features During their tenure at the NIH, associates acquire a thorough knowledge of the NIH, the support mechanisms through which research is being accomplished, and the policies and procedures which govern the awarding of grants and contracts. Associates also obtain information about other federal health-related programs; grant and contract activities; legislative, budgetary and similar processes; and administrative procedures, including participation in staff meetings, review meetings, site visits, workshops, and conferences. Following completion of the program, associates return to their institutions with an Extramural Associates Research Development Award (EARDA) which provides developmental funds to the associate's institution for a period of 3 years, with a possible extension to 6 years. The EARDA program is designated as G11 Awards.

Number awarded Varies each year.

[1337]
SPONSORED RESEARCH SYMPOSIA AWARDS

American Digestive Health Foundation
7910 Woodmont Avenue, Suite 700
Bethesda, MD 20814-3015
(301) 654-2635   Fax: (301) 654-5920

Purpose To provide travel support for young investigators and selected established investigators to participate in symposia on gastrointestinal-related topics.

Eligibility This program is open to directors of symposia who are established investigators at North American institutions and members of the American Gastroenterological Association (AGA). Women and minority investigators and encouraged to apply. Symposium speakers may be 1) junior investigators, who are less than 40 years old, and are at or below the rank of assistance professor, and 2) established investigators who are invited speakers, with preference given to individuals whose expertise is outside mainstream gastroenterology-related areas and/or investigators who have been infrequent participants at previous AGA-sponsored symposia. Women, minorities, and junior investigators should be included in the symposium program; their lack of representation should be explained. Symposia are selected on the basis of scientific program, timeliness, quality of organizers and invitees, relationship to gastroenterology, mix of basic scientists and clinicians, selection process for junior investigators, meeting site, and the extent to which women, minorities, and junior investigators are represented on the symposium faculty.

Financial data The amounts of the awards vary, but average $10,000 per symposium. Indirect costs are not allowed.

Special features This program is administered by the American Digestive Health Foundation (ADHF) and sponsored by the AGA.

Number awarded Varies each year.

Deadline Applications may be submitted at any time, but at least 6 months prior to the symposium date.

[1338]
ST. LOUIS DISTRICT, U.S. ARMY CORPS OF ENGINEERS RESEARCH PARTICIPATION PROGRAM

Oak Ridge Institute for Science and Education
Attn: Science/Engineering Education Division
P.O. Box 117
Oak Ridge, TN 37831-0117
(423) 576-8503   (423) 241-2875
(800) 569-7749   Fax: (423) 576-3643
E-mail: rppusace@orau.gov

Purpose To provide funding for postgraduate research in applied anthropology at the U.S. Army Corps of Engineers in St. Louis, Missouri.

Eligibility Applicants should have completed a baccalaureate or graduate degree within the past 3 years; others are considered on a case-by-case basis. Their field of study should have been environmental sciences, engineering, physical sciences, life sciences, or other related scientific disciplines. They must propose to conduct research for the St. Louis District, U.S. Army Corps of Engineers concerning federal legislation and American archaeology; the history and status of collections curation at the national, regional, and Army installation levels; and the developing role of Native Americans, Hawaiians, and Alaskans in federal legislation. All programs operated by the Science/Engineering Education Division (SEED) of Oak Ridge Institute for Science and Education (ORISE) seek to broaden the participation of minorities, women, and persons with disabilities in science and engineering careers.

Financial data The stipend is based on research area and degree; a limited reimbursement for inbound travel and moving is also provided.

Duration 1 year; renewable.

Special features This program is funded by an interagency agreement between the U.S. Department of Energy and the St. Louis District, U.S. Army Corps of Engineers, and administered by ORISE/SEED.

Number awarded Varies each year.

Deadline Applications may be submitted at any time.

[1339]
STANFORD HUMANITIES CENTER EXTERNAL FACULTY FELLOWSHIPS

Stanford Humanities Center
Mariposa House
Stanford, CA 94305-8630
(415) 723-3052   Fax: (415) 723-1895

Purpose To offer scholars an opportunity to conduct research and teach at Stanford University.

Eligibility External fellowships fall into 2 categories: 1) senior fellowships for well-established scholars, and 2) junior fellowships for scholars who at the time of application are at least 3 years beyond receipt of the Ph.D. but normally no more than 10. Applications from scholars of color are encouraged. Applications are judged on 1) the promise of the specific research project being proposed; 2) the originality and intellectual distinction of the candidate's previous work; 3) the research project's potential interest to scholars in different fields of the humanities; and 4) the applicant's ability to engage in collegial interaction.

Financial data The annual stipend is up to $25,000 for junior Fellows and up to $40,000 for senior Fellows. In addition, a housing/travel subsidy of up to $10,000, depending on size of family, is offered.

Duration 1 academic year.

Special features In addition to these External Fellowships, the Humanities Center offers 6 Internal Fellowships to Stanford faculty each year. All Fellows are expected to make an intellectual contribution not only within the Center but to humanistic studies in general at Stanford. Normally, this requirement is fulfilled by teaching an undergraduate or graduate course or seminar for 1 quarter within a particular department or program.

Limitations Fellows should live within the immediate area of Stanford University. Regular attendance at Center events is expected and Fellows are expected to be present during the fall, winter, and spring quarters and to attend weekday lunches on a regular basis.

Number awarded 6 each year.

Deadline November of each year.

[1340]
STARTER RESEARCH GRANTS

National Science Foundation
Attn: Directorate for Biological Sciences
Division of Biological Infrastructure
4201 Wilson Boulevard, Room 615
Arlington, VA 22230
(703) 306-1469   E-mail: ckimsey@nsf.gov

Purpose To assist minority scientists to establish an independent research program in the biological, social, economic, and behavioral sciences.

Eligibility Eligible to apply are underrepresented minorities (African Americans, Hispanics, Native Pacific Islanders, and Native Americans) who received a Minority Postdoctoral Research Fellowship from the National Science Foundation (NSF) and have accepted a tenure-track position at a U.S. institution. Their field of study must fall within the program areas of the NSF Directorate for Biological Sciences or Directorate for Social, Behavioral, and Economic Sciences.

Financial data Grants up to $35,000 are available; the recipient's institution must provide matching funds on a 2:1 basis.

Duration 1 year; nonrenewable.

Special features Information on the programs from the Directorate for Social, Behavioral, and Economic Sciences is available at (703) 306-1733.

Number awarded Varies each year.

Deadline Applications may be submitted at any time.

[1341]
STATE GRANT PROGRAM IN BILINGUAL EDUCATION

Department of Education
Attn: Office of Bilingual Education and Minority Languages
    Affairs
Switzer Building, Room 5090
600 Independence Avenue, S.W.
Washington, DC 20202-6510
(202) 205-9907

Purpose To support state programs in bilingual education.

Eligibility State education agencies may apply for these grants. Funds may be used to 1) collect data on the state's limited

English proficient (LEP) population and the educational programs and services available to that population; 2) assist local educational agencies (LEAs) in the state with program design, capacity building, assessment of student performance, and program evaluation; and 3) train state personnel in educational issues affecting LEP children and youth.

Financial data The amounts of the awards depend on the nature of the applications and the availability of funds.

Duration Up to 36 months.

Number awarded Approximately 7 each year.

Deadline January of each year.

[1342]
STROKE IN BLACKS, OTHER MINORITIES, AND WOMEN RESEARCH GRANTS

National Institutes of Health
Attn: National Institute of Neurological Disorders and Stroke
Division of Stroke and Trauma
Federal Building, Room 8A13
7550 Wisconsin Avenue
Bethesda, MD 20892
(301) 496-4226

Purpose To provide financial support for research that will increase knowledge and understanding of cerebrovascular disease in Blacks, other minorities, and women.

Eligibility This program is open to investigators at domestic and foreign public and private nonprofit and for-profit organizations such as universities, colleges, hospitals, laboratories, units of state and local government, and eligible agencies of the federal government. Applicants must be proposing to conduct basic, applied, and clinical studies related, in the broadest sense, to the etiology, prevention, early diagnosis, and treatment of stroke, including rehabilitation, as these may related to Blacks, other minorities, and women. Minorities and women are particularly encouraged to apply as principal investigators.

Financial data The amount of the awards depends on the nature of the proposal and the availability of funds.

Duration 3 to 5 years.

Number awarded Varies each year.

Deadline January, May, or September of each year.

[1343]
STRUCTURAL GEOLOGY AND TECTONICS DIVISION GRANT

Geological Society of America
Attn: Research Grants Administrator
3300 Penrose Place
P.O. Box 9140
Boulder, CO 80301-9140
(303) 447-2020, ext. 137   Fax: (303) 447-1133
E-mail: jforstro@geosociety.org

Purpose To provide partial support for geological research by graduate students at universities in the United States, Canada, Mexico, and Central America.

Eligibility This program is open to graduate students in geology at the master's or doctoral level. Both members and nonmembers of the society are eligible. Special consideration may be given to students who propose research on 1 or more aspects of structural geology or tectonics. Applications from women, minorities, and persons with disabilities are strongly encouraged.

Financial data　Grants range up to $2,500; the average grant recently was $1,604.

Duration　1 year.

Special features　This program is sponsored by the Geological Society of America's Structural Geology and Tectonics Division.

Number awarded　1 or more each year.

Deadline　February of each year.

[1344]
STUDENT INTERDISCIPLINARY RESEARCH TRAINING PROGRAM

Argonne National Laboratory
Attn: Division of Educational Programs
Cross Division Programs
9700 South Cass Avenue
Argonne, IL 60439-4845
(630) 252-1751　　　　　　　E-mail: washington@dep.anl.gov

Purpose　To give minority undergraduate students an opportunity to conduct research at Argonne National Laboratory.

Eligibility　Applicants must be 1) members of ethnic/racial groups underrepresented in science, technology, and engineering professions (African Americans, Hispanic Americans, and Native Americans); 2) enrolled as a freshman or sophomore student in an accredited U.S. college or university, community college, or technical institute; 3) in good academic standing; 4) highly motivated and interested in pursuing a career in science, information technology, or engineering; and 5) a U.S. citizen or permanent resident. The program is a hands-on educational training experience encompassing short courses, workshops, seminars, field trips, laboratory work, and attendance at national scientific symposia.

Financial data　Participants receive a stipend of $225 per week and complementary housing or a housing allowance. Transportation expenses are reimbursed if the round-trip distance is greater than 100 miles.

Duration　8 to 10 weeks, beginning during the last week of May.

Number awarded　Varies each year, depending on the availability of funding.

Deadline　February of each year.

[1345]
STUDENT SUPPORT SERVICES GRANTS

Department of Education
Attn: Office of Postsecondary Education
Division of Student Services
Portals Building, Suite 600D
600 Independence Avenue, S.W.
Washington, DC 20202-5249
(202) 708-4804　　　　　　　Fax: (202) 401-6132
E-mail: trio@ed.gov

Purpose　To enable institutions of higher education to provide support services to students with special needs in order to increase their retention and graduation rates.

Eligibility　Institutions of higher education or consortia of institutions of higher education are eligible to submit project proposals if they wish to establish support services for first-generation college students, low-income students, and students with disabilities evidencing academic need. Two-thirds of the participants must be either disabled or first-generation students from low-income families; one-third of the disabled participants must be low-income students. Institutions must assure that all participants

will be offered financial aid packages sufficient to meet their full financial needs.

Financial data　Recently, the annual total awarded for this program was $143,543,694; the minimum grant was $170,000 and the average was $203,320. The average cost per participating student was $867.

Duration　1 year; renewable.

Special features　Program services may include instruction in basic study skills, tutorial services, assistance in securing admission and financial aid for enrollment in 4-year institutions or in graduate and professional programs, information about career options, mentoring, and special services for students with limited English proficiency.

Number awarded　In a recent year, 706 institutions received these awards; the average number of participants per institution was 235.

Deadline　Competitions are held every 4 or 5 years; check the *Federal Register* for the current schedule.

[1346]
SUMMER RESEARCH TRAINING FOR MINORITY AND WOMEN STUDENTS IN DENTAL SCHOOL

National Institutes of Health
Attn: National Institute of Dental Research
Division of Extramural Research
Natcher Building, Room 4AN-18J
45 Center Drive MSC 6402
Bethesda, MD 20892-6402
(301) 594-2618　　　　　　　Fax: (301) 480-8318
E-mail: jl46d@nih.gov

Purpose　To provide minority and women dental students with an opportunity to engage in research training in the dental sciences.

Eligibility　Applicants for this program must be women or members of an ethnic or racial group underrepresented in biomedical or behavioral research nationally (Blacks, Hispanics, Native Americans, or Pacific Islanders). They must be U.S. citizens or nationals who have successfully completed at least 1 semester in a dental school in the United States or Puerto Rico.

Financial data　Grants provide a stipend of $834 per month.

Duration　2 months during the summer.

Special features　At their dental school, recipients engage in a program to prepare for a career in basic and clinical oral health research. For a list of the participating institutions, contact the address above. The National Institutes of Health (NIH) designates this program as part of its T35 Awards.

Number awarded　Varies each year.

Deadline　Application deadlines are established by each dental school participating in the program, but are usually in the spring of each year.

[1347]
SUMMER STUDY IN GEOPHYSICAL FLUID DYNAMICS

Woods Hole Oceanographic Institution
Attn: Fellowship Committee
Education Office
Clark Laboratory
Woods Hole, MA 02543-1541
(508) 457-2000, ext. 2219   Fax: (508) 457-2188
E-mail: lcampbell@whoi.edu

Purpose To provide research and study opportunities at Woods Hole Oceanographic Institution to pre- and postdoctoral scholars interested in geophysical fluid dynamics.

Eligibility This program is open to pre- and postdoctorates who are interested in geophysical fluid dynamics. Applications are particularly encouraged from women and members of underrepresented racial and ethnic groups.

Financial data The stipend is $3,900.

Duration 10 weeks, during the summer. An allowance is also available for travel expenses within the United States.

Special features Each year, the program revolves around a central theme. A recent theme was multicomponent diffusion; the program brought together researchers with backgrounds in theory, experimentation, and observation. The main components of the summer program are a series of principal lectures, a set of supplementary research seminars, and research projects conducted by the student fellows with the active support of the staff.

Number awarded Up to 10 each year.

Deadline February of each year.

[1348]
SUPPLEMENTAL FUNDING FOR SUPPORT OF WOMEN, MINORITY, AND DISABLED ENGINEERING RESEARCH ASSISTANTS

National Science Foundation
Attn: Directorate for Engineering
Division of Engineering Education and Centers
4201 Wilson Boulevard, Room 585
Arlington, VA 22230
(703) 306-1380

Purpose To encourage principal investigators on projects funded by the National Science Foundation (NSF) to include in their research projects high school and/or undergraduate engineering research assistants who are members of groups underrepresented in the advanced levels of U.S. science and engineering.

Eligibility The supplemental funding is expected to support students from underrepresented groups who will contribute to the NSF project with meaningful research work under the supervision of the principal investigator. For the purposes of this program, "underrepresented groups" include 1) minority groups (i.e., Native American, African American, Hispanic, Alaskan Native, or Native Pacific Islander); 2) women; and 3) persons with disabilities. Students must be citizens or nationals of the United States at the time of proposal submission.

Financial data Supplemental funding of up to $5,000, including indirect costs, may be requested for each student to be added to the project. Funds provided by this program are limited to 2 students per grant. Up to 10 percent of this amount may be used for supplies and services. Additional funds in excess of $5,000 may be requested, if necessary, to provide special equipment, modify equipment, or provide other services required specifically for participation of physically handicapped individuals.

Duration The support may be used for a summer, quarter, or academic year.

Special features Support may be requested in 2 ways: 1) requests for supplemental funding may be included in the initial proposal submission; or 2) current grantees may request supplemental funding of existing grants to add up to 2 students to the grant. Students interested in participating in this program should contact the address above to obtain a list of principal investigators in their area who have research grants from the Directorate for Engineering.

Limitations The students are expected to be involved in an interesting and challenging aspect of the research, and the principal investigator should be available to participate in the research experience with the student.

Number awarded Varies each year.

[1349]
SUSAN JANG YOUTH LEADERSHIP FUND

Women's Foundation
340 Pine Street, Suite 302
San Francisco, CA 94104
(415) 837-1113   Fax: (415) 837-1144
E-mail: womensfoun@igc.apc.org

Purpose To provide money to organizations that will provide work experience to girls of color at risk in the San Francisco area.

Eligibility The foundation gives money to organizations in the San Francisco area; these, in turn, select the participants for the program: minority girls who are at risk but have leadership potential.

Financial data All participants receive a stipend. A few—the most outstanding participants—receive a monetary award at the end of the program.

Special features Participants go through a training program and work with nonprofit organizations.

Limitations This program is still building its financial base.

Number awarded 30 to 50 participants; 2 to 3 awards each year.

[1350]
SYSTEMWIDE IMPROVEMENT GRANTS IN BILINGUAL EDUCATION

Department of Education
Attn: Office of Bilingual Education and Minority Languages Affairs
Switzer Building, Room 5090
600 Independence Avenue, S.W.
Washington, DC 20202-6510
(202) 205-5530

Purpose To provide financial assistance to local educational agencies (LEAs) to implement districtwide bilingual education programs or special alternative instructional programs that will serve a significant number of limited English proficient (LEP) children and youth.

Eligibility Applications may be submitted by LEAs either separately or in collaboration with institutions of higher education, community-based organizations, other LEAs, or state educational agencies. They must be proposing to implement districtwide bilingual education programs or special alternative instructional programs to improve, reform, and upgrade relevant programs and operations. The project must serve only LEAs in which the number of LEP students is at least 1,000 or at least 25 percent of the total student enrollment.

Financial data The amounts of the awards depend on the nature of the applications and the availability of funds.

Duration Up to 5 years.

Number awarded Varies each year.

Deadline Deadlines vary annually; check the *Federal Register* for the current schedule.

[1351]
TALENT SEARCH GRANTS

Department of Education
Attn: Office of Postsecondary Education
Division of Student Services
Portals Building, Suite 600D
600 Independence Avenue, S.W.
Washington, DC 20202-5249
(202) 708-4804   Fax: (202) 401-6132
E-mail: trio@ed.gov

Purpose To provide financial support for programs that increase the number of youths (aged 11 to 27 years) from disadvantaged backgrounds who complete high school and enroll in the postsecondary education institution of their choice.

Eligibility Eligible to submit program proposals are institutions of higher education, public and private agencies and organizations, and, in exceptional cases, secondary schools. Proposed programs must be geared toward secondary school students from disadvantaged backgrounds with an exceptional potential for postsecondary education; these students may include high school and college dropouts and high school graduates who have not gone on to college. The program provides academic, career, and financial counseling to its participants and encourages them to graduate from high school and continue on to the postsecondary school of their choice, or to reenter the educational system and complete their education. Two-thirds of the students reached by the program must be potential first-generation college students from low-income families.

Financial data Recently, an annual total of $78,838,888 was awarded through this program; the minimum grant size was $180,000 and the average was $247,144. The average cost per participating student was $263.

Duration The grants are awarded every 4 years.

Special features Program services may include career exploration and aptitude assessment, tutorial services, information on postsecondary education, exposure to college campuses, information on student financial assistance, mentoring programs, assistance in completing college admissions and financial aid applications, assistance in preparing for college entrance exams, and workshops for the parents of participants.

Number awarded Varies; in recent years, 319 awards have been made by this program annually; the average number of participants per institution has been 940.

Deadline The next closing date for receipt of competitive applications under this program is planned for the fall of 1997; check the *Federal Register* for the actual schedule.

[1352]
TAMPAX GRANTS FOR GIRLS SPORTS

Women's Sports Foundation
Eisenhower Park
1899 Hempstead Turnpike, Suite 400
East Meadow, NY 11554-1000
(516) 542-4700   (800) 227-3988
Fax: (516) 542-4716   E-mail: wosport@aol.com

Purpose To provide financial support for sports and fitness programs that serve young girls.

Eligibility Eligible to apply for these grants are organizations that provide new or existing sports programs for girls aged 9 to 14.

Financial data Grants up to $500 are available.

Limitations Funds may not be used for staffing or travel to competitions.

Number awarded Up to 70 each year.

Deadline December of each year.

[1353]
TEACHER ENHANCEMENT PROGRAM

National Science Foundation
Attn: Directorate for Education and Human Resources
Division of Elementary, Secondary and Informal Education
4201 Wilson Boulevard, Room 885
Arlington, VA 22230
(703) 306-1613   Fax: (703) 306-0412

Purpose To support the development of effective approaches and creative materials for the continuing education of elementary, middle, and secondary school mathematics and science teachers.

Eligibility Any organization with a scientific or educational mission may submit a proposal. These include colleges and universities, state and local education agencies, professional societies, museums, research laboratories, print or electronic media producers, private foundations, private industries, publishers, and other public and private organizations, whether for profit or nonprofit. Proposals are solicited in 5 categories: 1) local systemic change projects focused on science, mathematics, and technology, grades K-8, and on mathematics, grades 7-12; 2) teaching enhancement; 3) replication and infrastructure; 4) professional development materials; and 5) professional support for the teaching workforce. Proposals are especially encouraged that focus on areas of greatest education need (e.g., geographic areas with high percentages of disadvantaged and underserved populations).

Financial data The amount awarded depends on the nature of the proposal and the availability of funds; recent grants have ranged from $19,000 to $5,999,000 annually.

Duration 1 to 5 years.

Number awarded Approximately 92 each year.

Deadline Preliminary proposals must be submitted by March of each year; full proposals are due by August.

[1354]
TEACHER OPPORTUNITIES TO PROMOTE SCIENCE (TOPS)

Sandia National Laboratories
Attn: Education Outreach
MS 1351, Organization 3020
P.O. Box 5800
Albuquerque, NM 87185-1350
(505) 889-2325   Fax: (505) 889-2331

Purpose To enhance the skills of science/mathematics teachers working in areas with predominately Hispanic and Native American populations.

Eligibility This program is open to middle school science and mathematics teachers who work in the rural areas of New Mexico that have large Hispanic and Native American populations. Applicants must be interested in enhancing math and science teaching skills, integrating math and science concepts thoughout the curricula, and remaining with his or her school district for a minimum of 3 years and serving as a role model and mentor for colleagues.

Financial data Participants are paid a stipend following completion of each summer institute; housing and travel reimbursements are provided for both the summer institutes and academic-year workshops at Los Alamos or Sandia National Laboratories and to conduct research at those laboratories.

Duration 3 weeks in the summer; 3 follow-up workshops during each successive academic year.

Special features The program also involves academic-year activities and classroom visits. Participants may also choose to establish a student-parent science enrichment program at their school.

Limitations This program is not currently operating, pending the securing of sponsors.

Number awarded 25 teachers participate at each of the sponsoring national laboratories, Sandia and Los Alamos.

[1355]
TEACHER RESEARCH ASSOCIATES PROGRAM

Department of Energy
Attn: Office of Energy Research
University and Science Education Programs
1000 Independence Avenue, S.W., Room GP-180
Mail Stop ER-7
Washington, DC 20585
(202) 586-0987   E-mail:cindy.musick@hq.doe.gov

Purpose To provide middle and high school science, mathematics, and technology teachers with professional scientific and engineering experiences through summer research at national laboratories.

Eligibility This program is open to teachers of science, mathematics, and technology at grade levels 7 through 12. Applicants must be interested in conducting research under the guidance of a mentor at designated national laboratories of the U.S. Department of Energy (DOE). Teachers from groups underrepresented in science and mathematics and teachers of students in those groups are especially encouraged to apply.

Financial data The stipend is $550 per week. Round-trip travel to the facility and a housing allowance up to $1,000 are also provided. Teachers who wish to earn graduate credit for the experience receive an allowance of $200 toward the cost of the academic credit.

Duration 8 weeks, in the summer.

Special features Participating DOE facilities are Argonne National Laboratory (Argonne, Illinois), Brookhaven National Laboratory (Upton, New York), Thomas Jefferson National Accelerator Laboratory (Newport News, Virginia), Fermilab (Batavia, Illinois), Idaho National Engineering Laboratory (Idaho Falls, Idaho), Lawrence Berkeley National Laboratory (Berkeley, California), Oak Ridge National Laboratory (Oak Ridge, Tennessee), Pacific Northwest National Laboratory (Richland, Washington), and Princeton Plasma Physics Laboratory (Princeton, New Jersey). The names, addresses, and telephone numbers of contact persons at each facility are available from the above address or from Associated Western Universities, 4190 South Highland Drive, Suite 211, Salt Lake City, UT 84124, (801) 273-8931. This program is also known as the TRAC Program.

Number awarded Varies; approximately 70 at each laboratory each year.

Deadline October of each year.

[1356]
TECHNOLOGY POLICY SCIENCE AND ENGINEERING FELLOWSHIPS

American Association for the Advancement of Science
Attn: Science and Engineering Fellowship Programs
1200 New York Avenue, N.W.
Washington, DC 20005-3920
(202) 326-6600   Fax: (202) 289-4950
E-mail: science_policy@aaas.org

Purpose To provide postdoctoral and midcareer scientists and engineers an opportunity to gain experience in scientific and technical policy issues related to industry by working at the RAND Critical Technologies Institute (CTI) in Washington, D.C.

Eligibility Prospective fellows must have a Ph.D. or equivalent doctoral level degree at the time of application; persons with a master's degree in engineering and at least 3 years of post-degree experience may apply. Applicants should have significant hands-on industrial experience; demonstrate exceptional competence in some area of science or engineering; be cognizant of many matters in nontechnical areas; demonstrate sensitivity toward political and social issues; and have a strong interest and some experience in applying technical knowledge toward formulating policies that enhance U.S. technological and industrial effectivenss. U.S. citizenship is required. Minorities and persons with disabilities are especially encouraged to apply.

Financial data Stipends, health coverage, and moving allowances are negotiable.

Duration 1 year, beginning in September; may be renewed for 1 additional year.

Special features The program includes an orientation on congressional and executive branch operations and a year-long seminar program on issues involving science, technology, and public policy. CTI is a federally-funded research and development center, established in 1992 within RAND, a nonprofit institution that seeks to improve public policy through research and analysis.

Number awarded 1 or more each year.

Deadline January of each year.

[1357]
TELECOMMUNICATIONS AND INFORMATION INFRASTRUCTURE ASSISTANCE PROGRAM GRANTS

Department of Commerce
Attn: National Telecommunications and Information
   Administration
1401 Constitution Avenue, N.W., Room 4092
Washington, DC 20230
(202) 482-2048   Fax: (202) 501-5136
E-mail: tiiap@ntia.doc.gov

Purpose To provide grants to state and local governmental agencies as well as nonprofit organizations to promote the development and widespread availability of advanced telecommunications and information technologies to serve the public interest.
Eligibility Eligible to submit proposals are: state, local, and Indian tribal governments; colleges and universities; and other nonprofit entities. Grants are to be used to fund projects that contribute to the development of an advanced national information infrastructure by providing innovative examples of how telecommunications and information technologies can be used to provide valuable services to communities and by extending those opportunities to underserved Americans (individuals and communities that are subject to barriers that limit or prevent their access to the benefits of information infrastructure technologies and services; those barriers may be technological, geographic, economic, physical, linguistic, or cultural). Funding is not provided for replacement or upgrade of exisiting facilities, 1-way networks (all services and networks must be interactive), content development projects, hardware or software development projects, single-organization projects, or training projects. Proposals must be for projects in 5 areas: community-wide networking; education, culture, and lifelong learning; health; public and community services; and public safety.
Financial data Approximately $18.5 million per year is available for this program; the amounts of the individual grants depend on the nature and merit of the proposed projects. Grants provide up to 50 percent of the total project cost, although extraordinary circumstances may warrant a grant of up to 75 percent. The average award has been $300,000, although applicants may request up to $750,000 in federal support.
Duration 12 to 36 months.
Number awarded Varies; in a recent year, the program awarded 67 grants.
Deadline March of each year.

[1358]
TENNESSEE ARTS COMMISSION ARTS PROJECTS SUPPORT GRANTS

Tennessee Arts Commission
Attn: Arts Access Director
400 Charlotte Avenue
Nashville, TN 37243-0780
(615) 741-1701

Purpose To provide funds for direct support for arts projects to organizations located in metropolitan areas of Tennessee.
Eligibility Nonprofit tax-exempt organizations providing art programs and services are eligible to apply if they are chartered in Tennessee and located in a county that is part of a Metropolitan Statistical Area. Statewide organizations are service or single-discipline arts organizations whose board of directors geographically represent the state and whose statewide mission can be

legally demonstrated in the language of their by-laws. A wide range of activities may be supported, including improved program accessibility for special constituencies such as children, people living in rural-based and/or isolated settings, people with disabilities, people of color, and aging people. Selection criteria include a demonstration that the diverse cultural, ethnic, and artistic plurality of its community are represented in the planning, execution, and evaluation of its program and services.
Financial data Grants range from $500 to $5,000 for statewide organizations or from $500 to $4,000 for other organizations.
Duration 1 year.
Number awarded Varies each year.
Deadline February of each year.

[1359]
TENNESSEE VALLEY AUTHORITY RESEARCH PARTICIPATION PROGRAM

Oak Ridge Institute for Science and Education
Attn: Science/Engineering Education Division
P.O. Box 117
Oak Ridge, TN 37831-0117
(423) 576-8503   (423) 241-2875
(800) 569-7749   Fax: (423) 576-3643
E-mail: rpptva@orau.gov

Purpose To provide funding for postgraduate research on environmental issues for the Tennessee Valley Authority (TVA).
Eligibility Applicants must have completed a graduate degree within the past 3 years in environmental sciences, engineering, physical sciences, or related disciplines. They must be proposing to conduct research at various TVA sites; for a listing of those sites, contact the address above. All programs operated by the Science/Engineering Education Division (SEED) of Oak Ridge Institute for Science and Education (ORISE) seek to broaden the participation of minorities, women, and persons with disabilities in science and engineering careers.
Financial data The stipend is based on research area and degree; a limited reimbursement for inbound travel and moving is also provided.
Duration 1 year; renewable.
Special features This program is funded by an interagency agreement between the U.S. Department of Energy and TVA and administered by ORISE/SEED.
Number awarded Varies each year.
Deadline Applications may be submitted at any time.

[1360]
TESOL LEADERSHIP MENTORING PROGRAM

Teachers of English to Speakers of Other Languages, Inc.
1600 Cameron Street, Suite 300
Alexandria, VA 22314-2751
(703) 836-0774   Fax: (703) 836-7864
E-mail: tesol@tesol.edu

Purpose To enable underrepresented groups within Teachers of English to Speakers of Other Languages (TESOL) to become more involved in the work of the organization.
Eligibility This program is open to members of TESOL who are nonnative speakers of English, employed in settings other than universities, and/or racial minorities in the United States. Candidates must be nominated by TESOL members who provide a 500-word statement explaining the candidate's potential as a future leader of TESOL, including past involvement at the affiliate

level, experience in leadership positions, and professional contributions (such as workshops, conference presentations, or published articles). Candidates then submit a statement of support from their employers and a 500-word explanation of why they want to participate in the program, what they hope to gain from it, and what they can contribute to TESOL.

Financial data   The program provides basic registration to the TESOL annual meeting, a cash award of $300 for lodging expenses during the convention, a mentoring relationship with a TESOL leader, and the opportunity to volunteer for a TESOL activity of the candidate's choice during the convention and throughout the year.

Duration   Candidates are asked to volunteer at least 10 hours of service to a TESOL committee, interest section, or the local committee during the convention, attend organizational meetings during the convention, serve on a standing committee, interest section, or task force of their choice for at least 1 year, maintain regular contact with a mentor, submit an article for possible inclusion in *TESOL Matters* or *TESOL Journal,* and provide TESOL with a written assessment of their experiences.

Number awarded   Varies each year.

Deadline   October of each year.

[1361]
THANK OFFERING GRANTS OF CREATIVE MINISTRIES OF PRESBYTERIAN WOMEN

Presbyterian Church (U.S.A.)
Attn: Presbyterian Women
100 Witherspoon Street
Louisville, KY 40202-1396
(502) 569-5402

Purpose   To provide financial assistance for programs that meet a crucial need for persons who are hurting or are judged of critical importance in accordance with mission concerns and policies of the Presbyterian Church (U.S.A.).

Eligibility   Presbyterian organizations may apply for assistance for projects that provide aid directly related to the persons served, are new programs or new thrusts of an existing program, and that work for women, children, and racial ethnic persons to improve conditions of life for them. Written endorsement of the Presbyterian synod or presbytery is required; for projects outside the United States, written endorsement of the indigenous church is required. At least 40 percent of the grants are for health ministries, including annual grants to overseas hospitals.

Financial data   Grants range from $1,000 to $30,000.

Duration   These are 1-time grants, although the project may not necessarily be completed in a single year.

Special features   Funds for these grants are provided from the Thank Offering that began in the late 1800s when Eliza Clokey of Springfield, Ohio suggested that each woman in what was then the United Presbyterian Church of North America give a special gift to the Women's General Missionary Society. Currently the offering is given in the fall in congregations of the Presbyterian Church (U.S.A.).

Number awarded   Varies; in a recent year, 85 projects received support from this fund. An additional 44 annual grants were made to overseas hospitals.

Deadline   September of each year.

[1362]
THEATRE PROGRAM OF THE NEW YORK STATE COUNCIL ON THE ARTS

New York State Council on the Arts
915 Broadway
New York, NY 10010
(212) 387-7000   (800) GET-ARTS

Purpose   To preserve and advance theater in New York in its many forms: contemporary, classical, alternative, music theater, and theater for young audiences; and to widen opportunities in theater for the inclusion of persons of color and persons with disabilities in programmatic and administrative activities and as audience members.

Eligibility   General operating support is available to theatrical organizations that have received support for the 3 years prior to application, offer no fewer than 24 performances of 2 productions annually, have been audited at least twice in the previous 2 years, and have a full-time administrator. Project support is available in several categories, including professional performances, services to the field, new theater advancement, new works for public performance, and shared resources. Not eligible for support are classes, training, student productions, popular entertainment and events (e.g., carnivals, circuses, sideshows, parades, cabaret activities, and variety shows), support of commercial productions, or theater groups that collect fees from company members.

Financial data   Grants range from $50,000 per year (professional performances) to $1,500 (for performance art initiatives).

Duration   Up to 3 years.

Number awarded   Varies each year.

Deadline   February of each year.

[1363]
TRAINING AND TECHNICAL ASSISTANCE GRANT PROGRAM

Seventh Generation Fund
P.O. Box 4569
Arcata, CA 95518
(707) 825-7640   Fax: (707) 825-7639

Purpose   To provide funding to important Native American community change initiatives.

Eligibility   This program supports project-specific and culturally appropriate training and technical assistance programs proposed by Native American groups. Grants are also made to enable projects to participate in regional and national workshops, special convenings, and conferences.

Financial data   Grants range from $2,000 to $4,000.

Duration   1 year; may be renewed.

Special features   This grant may be awarded independently or in conjunction with Seventh Generation Fund General Support Grants.

Number awarded   Varies each year.

Deadline   Applications may be submitted at any time.

[1364]
TRAINING FOR ALL TEACHERS IN BILINGUAL EDUCATION PROGRAM GRANTS

Department of Education
Attn: Office of Bilingual Education and Minority Languages
Affairs
Switzer Building
600 Independence Avenue, S.W.
Washington, DC 20202-6510
(202) 205-8722   (202) 205-9723
(202) 205-9700

Purpose To provide financial assistance for the incorporation of courses and curricula on bilingual education into mainstream preparation programs for all education personnel.

Eligibility Applications may be submitted by institutions of higher education, local educational agencies, state educational agencies, or nonprofit organizations that have consortia arrangements with 1 of those institutions or agencies. They must be proposing to provide for the incorporation of courses and curricula on appropriate and effective instructional and assessment methodologies, strategies, and resources specific to limited English proficient students into preservice and inservice professional development programs for teachers, pupil services personnel, administrators, and other education personnel in order to prepare individual to provide effective services to limited English proficient students.

Financial data The amounts of the awards depend on the nature of the applications and the availability of funds.

Duration Up to 5 years.

Number awarded Varies each year.

Deadline Deadlines vary annually; check the *Federal Register* for the current schedule.

[1365]
TRAINING PROGRAM FOR FEDERAL TRIO PROGRAMS

Department of Education
Attn: Office of Postsecondary Education
Division of Student Services
Portals Building, Suite 600D
600 Independence Avenue, S.W.
Washington, DC 20202-5249
(202) 708-4804   Fax: (202) 401-6132
E-mail: trio@ed.gov

Purpose To provide funds for the training of staff and leadership personnel employed in (or preparing for employment in) programs supported under the U.S. Department of Education's TRIO Programs.

Eligibility Public agencies, nonprofit organizations, and institutions of higher education are eligible to apply if they wish to enhance the skills and expertise of project directors and staff employed in the Federal TRIO Programs (Ronald E. McNair Post-baccalaureate Achievement, Student Support Services, Upward Bound, Talent Search Program, Educational Opportunity Centers, and School, College and University Partnerships). Training projects may include conferences, seminars, internships, workshops, or publication of manuals.

Financial data In a recent year, a total of $2,016,203 was awarded through this program; the average grant was $168,016. The average cost per participant was $263.

Duration 1 year; may be renewed.

Special features The training program provides training and information on improving student retention, counseling services, student testing, working with specific TRIO populations, legislative and regulatory requirements, program evaluation, assisting students in securing adequate financial aid, the design and operation of model TRIO projects, and new director training.

Number awarded Varies each year; in a recent year, 12 awards were made; the average number of participants per program was 168.

Deadline Competitions are held in even-numbered year; check the *Federal Register* for the current schedule.

[1366]
TRANSLATIONAL RESEARCH PROGRAM

Leukemia Society of America
Attn: Director of Research Administration
600 Third Avenue
New York, NY 10016
(212) 573-8484   Fax: (212) 856-9686
E-mail: blermand@aol.com

Purpose To encourage and provide early-stage support for clinical research on leukemia and its related cancers, emphasizing novel approaches and strategies.

Eligibility Applications are sought from individuals working in domestic or foreign nonprofit organizations (e.g., universities, colleges, hospitals, laboratories, units of state and local governments, or eligible federal agencies), if these applications propose novel approaches related to the management of leukemia and lymphoma. Proposals must be conceptually innovative and rationally based on molecular, cellular or integrated systems findings. Examples of research areas that proposals might focus on include (but are not limited to): regulation of apoptosis, gene-directed therapies, cell adhesion factors, angiogenesis, tumor targeting, differentiating agents, signal transduction regulators, and novel cytotoxic agents. Applications from minority and women investigators are particularly encouraged.

Financial data Up to $100,000 annually in direct costs and 8 percent in overhead.

Duration 2 years; funding for a third year may be provided.

Special features This program has been developed in consultation with the National Cancer Institute.

Deadline February of each year.

[1367]
TRAVEL AWARDS FOR MINORITY GRADUATE STUDENTS

National Science Foundation
Attn: Directorate for Biological Sciences
Division of Biological Infrastructure
4201 Wilson Boulevard, Room 615
Arlington, VA 22230
(703) 306-1469   E-mail: ckimsey@nsf.gov

Purpose To enable minority graduate students to travel to assist in the selection of a postdoctoral mentor and to apply for postdoctoral fellowships.

Eligibility Eligible to apply are underrepresented minorities (African Americans, Hispanics, Native Pacific Islanders, and Native Americans) who are American citizens or permanent residents and are within 18 months of earning their Ph.D. degrees. Their field of study must fall within the program areas of the Directorate for Biological Sciences or the Directorate for Social, Behavioral, and Economic Sciences of the National Science Foundation (NSF). Awards are intended to allow them to travel within the United States or abroad to select a postdoctoral mentor or to develop an application for an NSF Minority Postdoctoral Research Fellowship.

Financial data Awards up to $3,000 are provided for airfare and living expenses while visiting the host scientist's institution.

Duration Up to 3 visits may be supported.

Special features Information on the programs from the Directorate for Social, Behavioral, and Economic Sciences is available at (703) 306-1733.

Number awarded Varies each year.

Deadline Applications may be submitted at any time, but at least 3 months prior to the planned travel.

[1368]
TRAVEL FELLOWSHIPS FOR MINORITY STUDENTS IN PHYSIOLOGY

American Physiological Society
Attn: Education Office
9650 Rockville Pike, Room 4301
Bethesda, MD 20814-3991
(301) 530-7132   Fax: (301) 571-8305
E-mail: mmatyas@aps.faseb.org

Purpose To provide funds to underrepresented minority students, faculty, and teachers interested in attending conferences sponsored by the American Physiological Society (APS).

Eligibility Members of minority groups may apply for these grants if they fall into 1 of 4 categories: 1) students who wish to attend the fall conferences of the APS; 2) students who wish to attend the annual spring meeting on experimental biology; 3) faculty members at institutions participating in the Minority Access to Research Career (MARC) or Minority Biomedical Research Support (MBRS) programs of the National Institutes of Health who wish to attend either the APS fall conference or the spring meeting on experimental biology; or 4) high school or middle school science teachers participating in the APS Science Teachers Summer Research in Physiology Program. Underrepresented minority groups include African Americans, Hispanics, Native Americans, and Pacific Islanders.

Financial data Awards provide funds for travel and per diem.

Duration The fall conferences range from 3 to 5 days; the spring meeting on experimental biology is 5 days.

Special features This program is supported by a grant from the National Institute of Diabetes and Digestive and Kidney Diseases (NIDDK) of the National Institutes of Health.

Number awarded Varies each year.

[1369]
TRAVEL FELLOWSHIPS FOR UNDERREPRESENTED MINORITY STUDENTS IN COMMUNICATION SCIENCES AND DISORDERS

National Institutes of Health
Attn: National Institute on Deafness and Other
    Communication Disorders
Division of Human Communication
Executive Plaza South, Room 400C
6120 Executive Boulevard MSC 7180
Bethesda, MD 20892-7180
(301) 496-5061   Fax: (301) 402-6251
E-mail: jc148m@nih.gov

Purpose To encourage participation of underrepresented minority students in scientific meetings and research forums related to communication sciences and disorders.

Eligibility Organizations planning to submit conference grant applications to the National Institute on Deafness and Other Communication Disorders (NIDCD) may include requests to support travel by minority students to those meetings. In addition, conference grant applications limited to support for minority student travel are encouraged from the sponsoring organizers of scientific meetings and conferences. The NIDCD defines underrepresented minority students as African Americans, Hispanic Americans, Native Americans, and Pacific Islanders. Students may be at the undergraduate, graduate, or postdoctoral level.

Financial data Applicants may request support for transportation, meals, lodging, conference fees, and other travel expenses.

Number awarded Varies each year.

Deadline Applications may be submitted at any time.

[1370]
TRAVEL GRANTS FOR MINORITY SPEAKERS PROGRAM

American Physical Society
Attn: Tara McLoughlin
One Physics Ellipse
College Park, MD 20740-3844
(301) 209-3231   Fax: (301) 209-0865
E-mail: tara@aps.org

Purpose To encourage the invitation of minority physics colloquium speakers and to defray part of their travel expenses.

Eligibility All physics and/or science departments in the United States are eligible to apply if they plan to invite minority speakers to participate in a colloquium or seminar in physics or a closely related field; the scientists may be African American, Native American, or Hispanic. Speakers must currently reside in the United States.

Financial data Grants provide up to $500 for travel and lodging expenses; honoraria, local meals, or extraneous expenses are not reimbursed.

Duration An institution may submit 1 request each year.

Deadline Applications may be submitted at any time.

[1371]
UNDERGRADUATE FACULTY ENHANCEMENT PROGRAM

National Science Foundation
Attn: Directorate for Education and Human Resources
Division of Undergraduate Education
4201 Wilson Boulevard, Room 835
Arlington, VA 22230
(703) 306-1669   E-mail: undergrad@nsf.gov

Purpose To provide support for activities that help faculty members who are primarily engaged in the instruction of undergraduates to gain experience with recent advances in their fields, new experimental techniques, effective teaching methods, and ways of incorporating those into undergraduate instruction.

Eligibility Proposals are invited from organizations in the United States and its territories: 2-year colleges; 4-year colleges; universities; professional societies; consortia of institutions; non-profit, non-academic institutions that are directly associated with educational or research activities; and, under certain circumstances, for-profit organizations. Preference is given to projects in 2 areas: 1) assisting faculty just beginning their academic careers in gaining experience and knowledge about instructional strategies for effective undergraduate science, engineering, mathematics, and technology education; and 2) enabling faculty to gain experience with successful programs for preparing graduate students for roles in undergraduate education, such as teaching assistants, discussion section leaders, readers, student mentors, and, in some cases, as future faculty. The National Science Foundation (NSF) particularly encourages proposals that strengthen undergraduate education by increasing the participation of women, underrepresented minorities, and persons with disabilities, especially if the projects present models for increasing the numbers who successfully pursue careers in science, mathematics, engineering, and technology. Underrepresented minorities are defined as African Americans, Alaskan Natives (Eskimos and Aleuts), Hispanics, Native Americans, and Native Pacific Islanders (Micronesians and Polynesians).

Financial data Projects are funded at levels between $180 and $350 per participant-day. Recently, annual grants ranged from $18,000 to $204,000.

Duration Up to 3 years; in most cases, the second and third years of support are contingent upon successful completion of the first- and second-year's activities

Special features The types of projects supported by this program include workshops, short courses, conferences, a series of such activities, or learning activities of novel design. They must be regional or national in scope. Grantee institutions conduct those activities for groups of faculty members in the sciences, mathematics, engineering, and technology.

Number awarded The number of awards granted depends on the quality of the proposals received and the availability of funds for the program; in a recent year, this program supported 50 new and 6 continuing awards.

Deadline June of each year.

[1372]
UNDERREPRESENTED MINORITY INVESTIGATORS IN ASTHMA AND ALLERGY RESEARCH AWARDS

American Academy of Allergy, Asthma & Immunology
611 East Wells Street
Milwaukee, WI 53202-3889
(414) 272-6071   Fax: (414) 276-3349
E-mail: info@aaaai.org

Purpose To provide financial assistance for research in asthma and allergy to underrepresented minority postdoctoral scientists.

Eligibility Applicants must be African Americans, Hispanics, Native Americans, Pacific Islanders, or other racial group members who have been found to be underrepresented in biomedical or behavioral research nationally. For the component of this program operated by the American Academy of Allergy, Asthma & Immunology (AAAAI), an M.D. degree is required; for the component administered by 2 of the institutes within the National Institutes of Health (NIH)—the National Institute of Allergy and Infectious Diseases and the National Heart, Lung, and Blood Institute—candidates may hold either an M.D. or a Ph.D. All applicants must be U.S. citizens or permanent residents and postdoctoral scientists in NIH and non-NIH funded programs of asthma or allergy research.

Financial data For the AAAAI component, the stipend is $30,000 per year plus supplies and travel; the participating institution may not charge any overhead allowances. For the NIH component, the awards provide up to $50,000 per year in salary, plus supplies, travel, and indirect costs.

Duration 2 years.

Special features Funding for the AAAAI program is provided by Abbott Laboratories.

Number awarded 4 each year: 2 from AAAAI and 2 from NIH.

Deadline March of each year.

[1373]
UNIVERSITY FELLOWSHIP PROGRAM AT THE UNIVERSITY OF VERMONT

Graduate College
Attn: Dean Delcie Durham
University of Vermont
335 Waterman Building
Burlington, VT 05405-0160
(802) 656-3160   Fax: (802) 656-0519

Purpose To provide funding to minority postdoctorates and predoctorates who are interested in developing the strong credentials that would be needed to assume a faculty position at the University of Vermont or another institution of higher education.

Eligibility This program is open to African Americans, Hispanic Americans, and Native Americans; postdoctorates must have completed their doctoral degree within the past 3 years; predoctorates must have completed all degree requirements except the dissertation; all candidates must be interested in conducting research and doing some teaching at the University of Vermont. Fellowship applications must include 1) a full curriculum vitae, 2) a copy of the dissertation prospectus, 3) a statement of scholarship and teaching goals, 4) a graduate school transcript, and 5) 3 letters of recommendation.

Financial data The stipend is $21,000.

Duration 1 to 2 years.

Special features Fellows may be asked to do some teaching. They are given office or laboratory space and access to equipment. Predoctorates complete the dissertation with support from a University of Vermont mentor; postdoctorates conduct significant scholarship with support of a faculty mentor.

Limitations All fellows are expected to present their work-in-progress at campus forums and to participate in several discussions with undergraduates on "how to succeed in graduate school."

Number awarded 1 or more each year.

Deadline February of each year

[1374]
UNIVERSITY OF CALIFORNIA PRESIDENT'S POSTDOCTORAL FELLOWSHIP PROGRAM

University of California
Attn: Office of the President
300 Lakeside Drive, 18th Floor
Oakland, CA 94612-3550
(510) 987-9500

Purpose To provide financial assistance to American minorities and women who are committed to careers in university teaching and research, and to increase representation of minorities and women on the faculty of the 9 University of California campuses.

Eligibility Applicants must be U.S. citizens or permanent residents and must hold a Ph.D. from an accredited university. Preference is given to minority and women candidates historically underrepresented in their disciplines in higher education. For the purposes of this program, "minority" is defined as American Indian, African American, Filipino American, Latino, Mexican American, Asian American, and Puerto Rican. Women are considered underrepresented in physical sciences, mathematics, computer science, and engineering. Selection is based on ability as evidenced by scholarly achievements and publications; letters of recommendation; quality and significance of the proposed research; and commitment of the applicant's faculty mentor to the goals of the program.

Financial data The stipend is $27,000 to $29,000, depending on the field represented and the level of experience documented. The program also offers health benefits and up to $4,000 for supplemental and research-related expenses.

Duration Appointments are for 1 academic year, with possible renewal for a second year.

Special features Research may be conducted on any of the University of California's 9 campuses or 3 laboratories. The program provides mentoring and guidance in preparing for an academic career.

Number awarded Approximately 20 to 25 appointments each year.

Deadline November of each year.

[1375]
UNIVERSITY OF MICHIGAN RESEARCH AND TRAINING PROGRAM ON POVERTY, THE UNDERCLASS AND PUBLIC POLICY

University of Michigan
Attn: Program on Poverty, the Underclass and Public Policy
540 East Liberty, Suite 202
Ann Arbor, MI 48104
(313) 998-8515   Fax: (313) 998-8516

Purpose To provide funding to minorities interested in conducting research and pursuing intensive training on poverty-related public policy issues.

Eligibility Applicants must be minority group members, U.S. citizens, postdoctorates (who received the degree within the past 5 years), and interested in conducting research and pursuing training on poverty and underclass issues at the University of Michigan.

Financial data The stipend is $37,000.

Duration 1 year.

Special features This program is funded by the Ford Foundation. Fellows spend the year participating in a seminar on poverty and public policy and conducting their own research.

Limitations Fellows must be in residence at the University of Michigan for the duration of the program.

Deadline January of each year.

[1376]
UNIVERSITY OF WISCONSIN VISITING MINORITY SCHOLAR LECTURE PROGRAM

Wisconsin Center for Education Research
1025 West Johnson Street
Madison, WI 53706
(608) 263-4200   Fax: (608) 263-6448

Purpose To make minority scholars and their work in education more visible on the University of Wisconsin campus.

Eligibility Minority scholars on the faculty of other universities are invited to present lectures on topics related to minorities and education at the University of Wisconsin.

Financial data Lecturers receive travel expenses and an honorarium.

Duration Each visit lasts for 2 days.

Special features The visiting scholar makes a general presentation open to the University of Wisconsin's community and meets with a group of minority students at the university to discuss the scholar's work. This program is cosponsored by the University of Wisconsin's School of Education and the Wisconsin Center for Education Research.

Number awarded 6 each year.

[1377]
UNIVERSITY POSTDOCTORAL FELLOWSHIP PROGRAM

Ohio State University
Attn: Dean of the Graduate School
250 University Hall
230 North Oval Mall
Columbus, OH 43210-1366
(614) 292-6031   Fax: (614) 292-3656

Purpose To provide an opportunity for postdoctorates to pursue research at Ohio State University.

Eligibility Nominations may be submitted by the Ohio State University's graduate faculty members who would like to coordinate a fellow's research. Faculty sponsors can host only 1 University Postdoctoral Fellow at a time. Eligible to be nominated are individuals who have held a doctorate for 5 years or less. Nomination of minority and women candidates is particularly encouraged. Certain categories of persons are ineligible to be nominated: persons with doctoral degrees from Ohio State University, persons currently on appointment at Ohio State University (or who have held a postdoctoral appointment there), senior faculty (associate or full professors) from other institutions, and individuals who received a Ph.D. more than 5 years ago.

Financial data The stipend is $24,000, plus a $500 moving allowance and a $500 travel allowance (to attend professional meetings).

Duration From 9 to 12 months; nonrenewable.

Number awarded Varies each year.

Deadline January of each year.

[1378]
UNIVERSITY RESEARCH EXPEDITIONS PROGRAM TEACHER RESEARCH PARTICIPATION PROGRAM

University Research Expeditions Program
University of California at Berkeley
Berkeley, CA 94720-7050
(510) 642-6586   Fax: (510) 642-6791
E-mail: urep@uclink.berkeley.edu

Purpose To provide research grants to school teachers in the natural or social sciences who are interested in participating in the University Research Expeditions Program (UREP).

Eligibility Elementary, junior high, and secondary school teachers in the natural and social sciences are eligible to apply. Top priority is given to California teachers of grades 6 through 12. Teachers of color are especially encouraged to apply.

Financial data The grants cover a portion of the expedition costs and in some cases also a portion of the airfare to the project area. The exact amount of each award is determined on a sliding scale basis. In addition, participants receive a $300 stipend upon completion of all program requirements.

Duration Varies; generally from 2 to 4 weeks.

Special features Since its inception, UREP has sponsored hundreds of field teams in over 50 countries worldwide. These grants support investigations into issues of importance in the health and biological sciences, the arts and humanities, environmental studies, and the social sciences. The Teacher Research Participation Program is supported in part by grants from the National Science Foundation, the Brownlee Foundation, and individual donors. The program provides hands-on research experience to teachers who return to their classrooms with a better understanding of the scientific process and of the cultures and environments in which the expeditions take place. Curriculum development workshops provided by the program before and after the expeditions help teachers translate their field experiences into classroom projects and activities. Some of the recent projects include food chains in the rain forest in Costa Rica, medieval churches of Aran in Ireland, and foxes of the Channel Islands in California.

Number awarded To date, more than 100 teachers have received funding.

Deadline March of each year.

[1379]
UPWARD BOUND GRANTS

Department of Education
Attn: Office of Postsecondary Education
Division of Student Services
Portals Building, Suite 600D
600 Independence Avenue, S.W.
Washington, DC 20202-5249
(202) 708-4804   Fax: (202) 401-6132
E-mail: trio@ed.gov

Purpose To support precollege programs for high school students from low-income families so participants will enroll in and graduate from institutions of postsecondary education.

Eligibility Program proposals may be submitted by institutions of higher education, public and private agencies, and, in exceptional cases, secondary schools. Proposed programs must provide academic support for high school students from families in which neither parent holds a baccalaureate degree, and low-income, first generation military veterans who are preparing to enter postsecondary education. Students must have completed the 8th grade, be between the ages of 13 and 19 (except veterans) and have a need for academic support in order to pursue a program of postsecondary education. Two-thirds of the participants in a program must be both low-income and first-generation college students.

Financial data Recently, a total of $171,579,797 per granting cycle was awarded through this program; the minimum grant was $190,000 and the average was $285,967. The average cost per participant was $3,838.

Duration Funding competitions are held every fourth or fifth year.

Special features Program services may include exposure to academic programs and cultural events, tutorial services, information on postsecondary education opportunities, assistance in completing college entrance and financial aid applications, assistance in preparing for college entrance exams, and academic, financial, or personal counseling.

Limitations All Upward Bound projects must provide instruction in math, laboratory science, composition, literature, and foreign language.

Number awarded In recent years, 600 awards have been made by this program in each granting cycle; the average number of participating students per institution has been 75.

Deadline The next closing date is scheduled for the fall of 1998; check the *Federal Register* for the current schedule.

[1380]
UPWARD BOUND MATH/SCIENCE GRANTS

Department of Education
Attn: Office of Postsecondary Education
Division of Student Services
Portals Building, Suite 600D
600 Independence Avenue, S.W.
Washington, DC 20202-5249
(202) 708-4804   Fax: (202) 401-6132
E-mail: trio@ed.gov

Purpose To fund math and science centers that will assist high school students from low-income families to recognize and develop their potential to excel in the fields of math and science and encourage them to pursue postsecondary degrees in math and science.

Eligibility Program proposals may be submitted by institutions of higher education, public and private agencies, and, in exceptional cases, secondary schools. Proposed programs must provide academic support for high school students eligible to participate in the Upward Bound Program, i.e. they must be from families in which neither parent holds a baccalaureate degree, or low-income, first generation military veterans who are preparing to enter postsecondary education. Students must have completed the 9th grade, although they do not necessarily have to be participating in a regular Upward Bound Program.

Financial data Recently, a total of $18,983,672 was awarded per granting cycle through this program; the minimum grant was

$190,000 and the average was $234,366. The average cost per participant was $5,114.

Duration Funding competitions are held every fourth or fifth year.

Special features Program services may include summer programs of intensive math and science training, year-round counseling and advisement, exposure to university faculty who do research in math and science, computer training, and participant-conducted scientific research under the guidance of a faculty member or graduate student serving as the participant's mentor.

Number awarded In recent years, 81 awards have been made by this program in each granting cycle; the average number of participating students per institution has been 46.

Deadline The next closing date is scheduled for the fall of 1998; check the *Federal Register* for the current schedule.

[1381]
URBAN AND RURAL SCHOOL IMPROVEMENT PROGRAM

Department of Education
Attn: Office of Elementary and Secondary Education
Goals 2000 Program
Portals Building, Room 4000
600 Independence Avenue, S.W.
Washington, DC 20202-2110
(202) 401-0039   Fax: (202) 205-0303

Purpose To provide financial assistance to urban and rural local educational agencies (LEAs) with large numbers or concentrations of students who are economically disadvantaged or who have limited English proficiency.

Eligibility Applications may be submitted by urban and rural LEAs with large numbers or concentrations of students who are economically disadvantaged or who have limited English proficiency. Preference is given to proposals from LEAs with at least 1 of the following conditions: 1) the number of economically disadvantaged students is at least 35,000; 2) the number of economically disadvantaged students is at least 70 percent of the total number of students; 3) the number of students who have limited English proficiency is at least 10,000; or 4) the number of students who have limited English proficiency is at least 25 percent of the total number of students. As part of the application, the LEA should explain how its proposed process for developing and implementing a local improvement plan would help all students, especially economically disadvantaged and limited English proficient students, reach challenging academic standards.

Financial data For large urban LEAs (those with a total enrollment of 100,000 or more elementary and secondary school students), grants range from $200,000 to $1,000,000; for mid-sized urban LEAs (those with total enrollment of at least 50,000 but less than 100,000), grants range from $150,000 to $750,000; for small urban LEAs (those with total enrollment of less than 50,000), grants range from $100,000 to $500,000; for rural LEAs, grants range from $25,000 to $250,000. Current total funding for this program is approximately $10.1 million.

Duration Up to 4 years.

Number awarded Approximately 40 each year.

Deadline July of each year.

[1382]
U.S. ARMY CENTER FOR HEALTH PROMOTION AND PREVENTIVE MEDICINE POSTGRADUATE INTERNSHIP PROGRAM

Oak Ridge Institute for Science and Education
Attn: Science/Engineering Education Division
P.O. Box 117
Oak Ridge, TN 37831-0117
(423) 576-3456   (423) 241-2875
(800) 569-7749   Fax: (423) 576-3643

Purpose To provide funding to postgraduates interested in applied clinical research and training activities of concern to the U.S. Army Center for Health Promotion and Preventive Medicine (USACHPPM) in Maryland.

Eligibility Applicants must have completed their bachelor's, master's, or doctoral degrees in an appropriate science or engineering discipline within the past 3 years; other candidates are considered on a case-by-case basis. The USACHPPM conducts research and training activities in environmental health engineering, entomology, ionizing and nonionizing radiation, occupational and environmental health, industrial hygiene and worksite hazards, environmental sanitation and hygiene, and laboratory services. All programs operated by the Science/Engineering Education Division (SEED) of Oak Ridge Institute for Science and Education (ORISE) seek to broaden the participation of minorities, women, and persons with disabilities in science and engineering careers.

Financial data A stipend is awarded, based on research area and highest degree earned. Reimbursement for inbound travel and moving is also provided.

Duration 1 year; may be renewed.

Special features Participants work at the USACHPPM in Aberdeen Proving Ground, Maryland. This program is funded by an interagency agreement between the U.S. Department of Energy and the USACHPPM of the U.S. Army, and administered by ORISE/SEED.

Number awarded The number awarded varies each year.

Deadline Applications may be submitted at any time.

[1383]
U.S. ARMY CONSTRUCTION ENGINEERING RESEARCH LABORATORY RESEARCH PARTICIPATION PROGRAM

Oak Ridge Institute for Science and Education
Attn: Science/Engineering Education Division
P.O. Box 117
Oak Ridge, TN 37831-0117
(423) 576-8503   (423) 241-2875
(800) 569-7749   Fax: (423) 576-3643
E-mail: rppacerl@orau.gov

Purpose To provide funding for postgraduate research and training related to the military construction efforts, environmental issues, and related activities at the U.S. Army Construction Engineering Research Laboratory in Champaign, Illinois.

Eligibility Applicants should have completed a baccalaureate, master's, or doctoral degree within the past 3 years; others are considered on a case-by-case basis. Their field of study should have been an appropriate science or engineering discipline. All programs operated by the Science/Engineering Education Division (SEED) of Oak Ridge Institute for Science and Education (ORISE) seek to broaden the participation of minorities, women, and persons with disabilities in science and engineering careers.

Financial data The stipend is based on research area and degree; a limited reimbursement for inbound travel and moving is also provided.

Duration 1 year; renewable.

Special features This program is funded by an interagency agreement between the U.S. Department of Energy and the U.S. Army Construction Engineering Research Laboratory and administered by ORISE/SEED.

Number awarded Varies each year.

Deadline Applications may be submitted at any time.

[1384]
U.S. NAVY–ASEE SABBATICAL LEAVE PROGRAM

American Society for Engineering Education
Attn: Projects Department
1818 N Street, N.W., Suite 600
Washington, DC 20036-2479
(202) 331-3525   Fax: (202) 265-8504
E-mail: projects@asee.org

Purpose To provide support to faculty members in engineering and science who wish to conduct research at selected Navy facilities while on sabbatical leave.

Eligibility This program is open to U.S. citizens with teaching or research appointments in engineering and science at U.S. universities or colleges. Applicants must intend to conduct research while in residence at selected facilites of the U.S. Navy. Faculty from Historically Black Colleges and Universities and other minority institutions are especially encouraged to apply.

Financial data Fellows receive a stipend equivalent to the difference between their regular salary and the sabbatical leave pay from their home institution. Fellows who must relocate their residence receive a relocation allowance and all fellows receive a travel allowance.

Duration Appointments are for a minimum of 1 semester and a maximum of 1 year.

Special features Participating facilities include the Naval Air Warfare Center, Aircraft Division (Patuxent River, Maryland); Naval Air Warfare Center, Training Systems Division (Orlando, Florida); Naval Air Warfare Center, Weapons Division (China Lake, California); Naval Command, Control and Ocean Surveillance Center, RDT&E Division (San Diego, California); Naval Facilities Engineering Service Center (Port Hueneme, California); Naval Research Laboratories (Washington, D.C.; Stennis Space Center, Mississippi; and Monterey, California); Naval Surface Warfare Centers (Carderock, Maryland; Annapolis, Maryland; Dahlgren, Virginia; and Panama City, Florida); Naval Undersea Warfare Center (Newport, Rhode Island); Defense Equal Opportunity Management Institute (Cocoa Beach, Florida); Navy Personnel Research and Development Center (San Diego, California); Naval Aerospace Medical Research Laboratory (Pensacola, Florida); Naval Health Research Center (San Diego, California); Naval Medical Research Institute (Bethesda, Maryland); and Naval Submarine Medical Research Laboratory (Groton, Connecticut). This program is funded by the U.S. Navy but administered by the American Society for Engineering Education.

Number awarded Varies each year.

Deadline March, June, September, and December of each year.

[1385]
U.S. NAVY–ASEE SUMMER FACULTY RESEARCH PROGRAM

American Society for Engineering Education
Attn: Projects Department
1818 N Street, N.W., Suite 600
Washington, DC 20036-2479
(202) 331-3525   Fax: (202) 265-8504
E-mail: projects@asee.org

Purpose To provide support to faculty members in engineering and science who wish to conduct summer research at selected Navy facilities.

Eligibility This program is open to U.S. citizens with teaching or research appointments in engineering and science at U.S. universities or colleges. In addition to appointments as Summer Faculty Fellows, positions as Senior Summer Faculty Fellows are available to applicants who have at least 5 years of research experience in their field of expertise since earning a Ph.D. or equivalent field and a substantial, significant record of research accomplishments and publications. A limited number of appointments are also available as Distinguished Summer Faculty Fellows to faculty members who are pre-eminent in their field of research, with a senior appointment at a leading research university and international recognition for their research accomplishments. Faculty from Historically Black Colleges and Universities and other minority institutions are especially encouraged to apply.

Financial data The weekly stipend is $1,230 at the Summer Faculty Fellow level, $1,480 at the Senior Summer Faculty Fellow level, and $1,730 at the Distinguished Summer Faculty Fellow level. Fellows who must relocate their residence receive a relocation allowance and all fellows receive a travel allowance.

Duration 10 weeks, during the summer; fellows may reapply in subsequent years.

Special features Participating facilities include the Naval Air Warfare Center, Aircraft Division (Patuxent River, Maryland); Naval Air Warfare Center, Training Systems Division (Orlando, Florida); Naval Air Warfare Center, Weapons Division (China Lake, California); Naval Command, Control and Ocean Surveillance Center, RDT&E Division (San Diego, California); Naval Facilities Engineering Service Center (Port Hueneme, California); Naval Research Laboratories (Washington, D.C.; Stennis Space Center, Mississippi; and Monterey, California); Naval Surface Warfare Centers (Carderock, Maryland; Annapolis, Maryland; Dahlgren, Virginia; and Panama City, Florida); Naval Undersea Warfare Center (Newport, Rhode Island); Defense Equal Opportunity Management Institute (Cocoa Beach, Florida); Navy Personnel Research and Development Center (San Diego, California); Naval Aerospace Medical Research Laboratory (Pensacola, Florida); Naval Health Research Center (San Diego, California); Naval Medical Research Institute (Bethesda, Maryland); and Naval Submarine Medical Research Laboratory (Groton, Connecticut). This program is funded by the U.S. Navy's Office of Naval Research but administered by the American Society for Engineering Education.

Number awarded Varies each year.

Deadline January of each year.

[1386]
USDA SMALL BUSINESS INNOVATION RESEARCH PROGRAM

Department of Agriculture
Attn: Cooperative State Research, Education, and Extension Service
Director, SBIR Program
Stop 2243
1400 Independence Avenue, S.W.
Washington, DC 20250-2243
(202) 401-4002   Fax: (202) 205-3641
E-mail: ccleland@reeusda.gov

Purpose To stimulate technological innovation related to agriculture in the private sector by small business firms owned by women or members of socially and economically disadvantaged groups.

Eligibility For the purposes of this program, a "small business" is any organization that is independently owned and operated for the size standard of 500 employees or less. The primary employment of the principal investigator must be with the firm at the time of award and during the conduct of the proposed project. Preference is given to socially and economically disadvantaged small business concerns and to women-owned small business concerns. A socially and economically disadvantaged small business concern is at least 51 percent owned by either 1) an Indian tribe or a native Hawaiian organization, or 2) 1 or more socially disadvantaged individuals (Black Americans, Hispanic Americans, Native Americans, Asian-Pacific Americans, or Subcontinent Asian Americans). A woman-owned small business concern is at least 51 percent owned by a woman or women who also control and operate it. The project must be performed in the United States, its territories or possessions.

Financial data Support is offered in 2 phases. In phase 1, awards normally may not exceed $55,000 (for both direct and indirect costs); in phase 2, awards normally may not exceed $250,000 (including both direct and indirect costs).

Duration Phase 1: up to 6 months; phase 2: up to 2 years.

Special features Phase 1 is to determine the scientific or technical feasibility of ideas submitted by the applicants on research topic areas. Phase 2 awards are made to firms with approaches that appear sufficiently promising as a result of phase 1 studies.

Number awarded Approximately 60 phase 1 awards each year; the number of phase 2 awards varies.

Deadline September of each year.

[1387]
VICTOR HORSLEY RESEARCH/CLINICAL TRAINING FELLOWSHIPS

Epilepsy Foundation of America
Attn: Department of Research and Professional Education
4351 Garden City Drive
Landover, MD 20785
(301) 459-3700   (800) EFA-1000
Fax: (301) 577-2684   TDD: (800) 332-2070
E-mail: postmaster@efa.org

Purpose To offer qualified individuals the opportunity to develop expertise in clinical epilepsy and epilepsy research.

Eligibility Applications are open to individuals who have received their M.D. degree and completed residency training. The proposed research may be either basic or clinical, but there must be an equal emphasis on clinical training and clinical epileptology.

Special attention is given to applications submitted by women and minorities.

Financial data The stipend is $40,000.

Duration 1 year.

Limitations The fellowship must be carried out at a facility where there is an ongoing epilepsy research program. Research must be conducted in the United States.

Number awarded Varies each year.

Deadline August of each year.

[1388]
VIOLENCE AND TRAUMATIC STRESS RESEARCH GRANTS

National Institutes of Health
Attn: National Institute of Mental Health
Violence and Traumatic Stress Research Branch
Parklawn Building, Room 10C-24
5600 Fishers Lane
Rockville, MD 20857
(301) 443-3728   Fax: (301) 443-1726
E-mail: ss75f@nih.gov

Purpose To fund research that deals with the prevention and treatment of problems associated with antisocial behavior, particularly rape and other sexual assaults.

Eligibility Individuals and organizations/institutions are eligible to apply. Proposals may deal with 1) victims of interpersonal violence, including rape, sexual assault, child abuse, incest, family violence, and criminal violence; 2) victims major traumatic events, including natural and technological disaster, combat and war, refugee trauma and relocation, and torture; and 3) perpetrators of youth violence, serious adult crime, sexual offenses (adult and juvenile), and intimate partners assaults. Racial/ethnic minority individuals, women, and persons with disabilities are encouraged to apply as principal investigators.

Financial data Recently, approximately $3,500,000 per year was available for grants through this program; the average grant was approximately $175,000.

Duration Up to 5 years.

Limitations Before preparing a formal proposal, applicants are encouraged to consult with center staff.

Number awarded 20 each year.

Deadline Applications may be submitted by January, May, or September of each year.

[1389]
VIRGINIA SPACE GRANT GRADUATE FELLOWSHIPS

Virginia Space Grant Consortium
c/o Old Dominion University Peninsula Center
2713-D Magruder Boulevard
Hampton, VA 23666-1563
(757) 865-0726   Fax: (757) 865-7965
E-mail: vsgc@pen.k12.va.us

Purpose To provide financial assistance for study and/or research in space-related fields to graduate students in Virginia.

Eligibility This program is open to graduate students who will be enrolled in a program of full-time study in aerospace-related graduate science or engineering at 1 of the Virginia Space Grant Colleges (College of William and Mary, Hampton University, Old Dominion University, the University of Virginia, and Virginia Polytechnic Institute and State University). Applicants must be U.S. citizens with a grade point average of at least 3.0. Selection of graduate students is based on their academic qualifications, the quality of their plan of study and/or proposed research, and their relevance to this program. Special consideration is given to members of underrepresented minority groups, females, and persons with disabilities who show aerospace promise.

Financial data The stipend is $5,000.

Duration 1 year; renewable.

Special features This program is funded by the U.S. National Aeronautics and Space Administration (NASA).

Limitations Students are required to certify through their academic department that basic research support of at least $5,000 is being provided before receipt of Space Grant funds.

Number awarded At least 5 each year.

Deadline January of each year.

[1390]
VISITING PROFESSORSHIPS FOR WOMEN

National Science Foundation
Attn: Directorate for Education and Human Resources
Division of Human Resource Development
Programs for Women and Girls
4201 Wilson Boulevard, Room 815
Arlington, VA 22230
(703) 306-1637   Fax: (703) 306-0423
E-mail: vpw@nsf.gov

Purpose To enable doctoral women scientists and engineers to undertake research and teaching at host institutions so they can advance their careers and provide guidance and encouragement to young women seeking to pursue research careers.

Eligibility To be eligible, an applicant should hold a doctorate in a field of research supported by NSF or have equivalent experience; have independent research experience in academia, industry, or the public sector; be currently or recently affiliated with an institution in the United States or 1 of its possessions or territories; be a U.S. citizen, national, or permanent resident; and not have a salaried position or the promise of a position at the host institution. Applicants may undertake international collaborative research projects, including planning visits, cooperative research, and joint seminars and workshops. Minority women and women with disabilities are especially encouraged to submit proposals.

Financial data Funds may be requested to defray such normally allowable project costs as salary (based on the salary at the home institution), travel, and research support. Indirect costs may be requested. Funds for equipment will not normally be provided.

Duration From 6 to 15 months (the maximum award tenure provide support for 1 academic year and 2 summers).

Special features The primary task of the visiting professors will be to carry out research in a university or 4-year college having the facilities necessary for the proposed research. The visitors will also be expected to teach and to serve as advisors, counselors, and mentors. Approximately 70 percent of the award period should be spent on research and 30 percent on teaching.

Number awarded Varies; approximately 15 each year.

Deadline November of each year.

[1391]
VISUAL ARTS PROGRAM OF THE NEW YORK STATE COUNCIL ON THE ARTS

New York State Council on the Arts
915 Broadway
New York, NY 10010
(212) 387-7000   (800) GET-ARTS

Purpose To support traditional modes of contemporary visual arts expression and to seek out high quality contemporary projects that expand traditional parameters, transcend disciplinary constraints, and reflect the diverse ethno-cultural profile of the state of New York.

Eligibility Nonprofit organizations in New York may submit proposals for projects that expand the range of contemporary art. Especially welcome are programs/projects that are adventurous, risk taking, interdisciplinary, performance oriented, experimental, or different from the commonly-held notions of contemporary art. Institutional support is available to organizations that have received general program support for the last 3 consecutive years, have broad artists' representation on the policy-making board, have at least 1 paid full-time professional staff member, and receive funds from a variety of sources. Project support is available to organizations that provide participating artists with fees in addition to other traditional services and that have artists involved in programmatic decisions and policy development. Support is also available for special projects, artists-in-residence, and single exhibitions. Funds are not available for the following: educational projects, workshops, general audience instruction programs, cooperative galleries, start-up costs for new periodicals, commercial publications, exhibitions that primarily include nonprofessional participants, juror's fees, fundraising events, reception costs, capital expenditures, surveys, short-term demonstrations, or slide registries. Special attention will be paid to proposals that promote equal participating opportunities for: women artists, artists of diverse racial and ethnic backgrounds, artists with disabilities, or mid-career artists.

Financial data Grants range from $60,000 per year (for general operating support) to $3,000 (for technical assistance).

Duration Up to 3 years.

Number awarded Varies each year.

Deadline February of each year.

[1392]
VOCATIONAL REHABILITATION SERVICE PROJECTS FOR MIGRATORY AGRICULTURAL AND SEASONAL FARMWORKERS WITH DISABILITIES

Department of Education
Attn: Office of Special Education and Rehabilitative Services
Rehabilitation Services Administration
Switzer Building, Room 3330
600 Independence Avenue, S.W.
Washington, DC 20202-2740
(202) 205-9297

Purpose To provide grants for vocational rehabilitation services for migratory agricultural workers or seasonal farmworkers with disabilities.

Eligibility Applications may be submitted by state vocational rehabilitation agencies (SVRAs), nonprofit agencies working in collaboration with the SVRAs, local agencies administering vocational rehabilitation programs under written agreements with SVRAs, and SVRAs that enter into agreements with the SVRAs of 1 or more other states to develop cooperative programs for the provision of vocational rehabilitation services. Funds must be used to support projects and demonstrations for the rehabilitation of migratory agricultural workers and seasonal farmworkers with disabilities.

Financial data Grants range from $150,000 to $175,000 and average $162,500.

Duration Up to 5 years.

Number awarded Up to 3 each year.

Deadline January of each year.

[1393]
VOLUNTEER/DONOR AWARD

National Kidney Foundation of Massachusetts and Rhode Island
105 Eastern Avenue, Suite 211
P.O. Box 9103
Dedham, MA 02027-9103

Purpose To encourage research that will have significant impact on our understanding and treatment of kidney and urological diseases.

Eligibility This program is open to junior scientists in Massachusetts and Rhode Island who are planning independent research careers or to more senior investigators who have experienced temporary loss of research funding. Applicants should have a serious commitment to a career in research. There is no age limitation for the applicants. Awards are not made to individuals whose work will be concurrently supported by NIH K, RO1, R29 awards or their equivalent. Applications are encouraged in all areas of research related to adult and pediatric kidney and urological diseases, including hypertension and transplantation. Both clinical and basic research proposals are considered. Applications from women and members of underrepresented minority groups are encouraged as are applications dealing with diseases that are prevalent in minority communities.

Financial data The grant is $35,000.

Duration 1 year.

Number awarded 1 each year.

Deadline March of each year.

[1394]
VSGC GRADUATE RESEARCH ASSISTANTSHIPS

Vermont Space Grant Consortium
c/o University of Vermont
College of Engineering and Mathematics
119 Votey Building
Burlington, VT 05405-0156
(802) 656-1936   Fax: (802) 656-8802
E-mail: keller@emba.uvm.edu

Purpose To provide financial assistance for graduate study and research in space-related fields to students in Vermont.

Eligibility Applicants for these assistantships must be currently enrolled as graduate students at institutions in Vermont. They must be planning to pursue a professional career that has direct relevance to the U.S. aerospace industry and the goal of the National Aeronautics and Space Administration (NASA), including mathematics, physics, engineering, and other basic sciences. The Vermont Space Grant Consortium (VSGC) is a component of the NASA Space Grant program, which encourages participation by women, minorities, and persons with disabilities.

Financial data The program provides a stipend for a standard graduate student salary and the opportunity for the student to pay in-state tuition for graduate level course work and thesis research credit.

Duration 1 year, including a 10-week summer research period.

Special features This program is funded by NASA.

Number awarded 4 each year.

Deadline February of each year.

[1395]
WILDER PENFIELD RESEARCH/CLINICAL TRAINING FELLOWSHIPS

Epilepsy Foundation of America
Attn: Department of Research and Professional Education
4351 Garden City Drive
Landover, MD 20785
(301) 459-3700   (800) EFA-1000
Fax: (301) 577-2684   TDD: (800) 332-2070
E-mail: postmaster@efa.org

Purpose To offer qualified individuals the opportunity to develop expertise in clinical epilepsy and epilepsy research.

Eligibility Applications are open to individuals who have received their M.D. degree and completed residency training. The proposed research may be either basic or clinical, but there must be an equal emphasis on clinical training and clinical epileptology. Special attention is given to applications submitted by women and minorities.

Financial data The stipend is $40,000.

Duration 1 year.

Limitations The fellowship must be carried out at a facility where there is an ongoing epilepsy research program. Research must be conducted in the United States.

Number awarded Varies each year.

Deadline August of each year.

[1396]
WILLIAM AND FLORA HEWLETT FOUNDATION GRANTS

William and Flora Hewlett Foundation
525 Middlefield Road, Suite 200
Menlo Park, CA 94025-3495
(415) 329-1070

Purpose To provide funding to organizations in the areas of education, performing arts, population, environment, conflict resolution, and family and community development.

Eligibility The foundation makes grants to nonprofit organizations nationally, but earmarks a proportion of its disbursable funds for projects in the San Francisco area. In the area of education, it invites applications from liberal arts colleges and research universities for support of programs that promote the twin goals of pluralism and unity. It also supports, in partnership with the Bush Foundation, an ongoing program of grants for capital needs and faculty development at private Black colleges and universities.

Financial data The amount awarded varies.

Duration 1 year or longer.

Limitations The foundation does not fund proposals for basic research; capital construction funds; grants in the medical or health-related fields; general fund-raising drives; grants or loans to individuals; or grants intended directly or indirectly to support candidates for political office or to influence legislation.

Number awarded Varies each year.

Deadline   Applications may be submitted at any time.

[1397]
WILLIAM GOWERS RESEARCH/CLINICAL TRAINING FELLOWSHIPS

Epilepsy Foundation of America
Attn: Department of Research and Professional Education
4351 Garden City Drive
Landover, MD 20785
(301) 459-3700   (800) EFA-1000
Fax: (301) 577-2684   TDD: (800) 332-2070
E-mail: postmaster@efa.org

Purpose   To offer qualified individuals the opportunity to develop expertise in clinical epilepsy and epilepsy research.

Eligibility   Applications are open to individuals who have received their M.D. degree and completed residency training. The proposed research may be either basic or clinical, but there must be an equal emphasis on clinical training and clinical epileptology. Special attention is given to applications submitted by women and minorities.

Financial data   The stipend is $40,000.

Duration   1 year.

Limitations   The fellowship must be carried out at a facility where there is an ongoing epilepsy research program. Research must be conducted in the United States.

Number awarded   Varies each year.

Deadline   August of each year.

[1398]
WILLIAM T. GRANT FOUNDATION FACULTY SCHOLARS PROGRAM

William T. Grant Foundation
Attn: Faculty Scholars Program
515 Madison Avenue
New York, NY 10022-5403
(212) 752-0071

Purpose   To provide funding for research on child development or mental health.

Eligibility   Eligible for this program are young scholars interested in conducting research in social and behavioral sciences, such as anthropology, economics, education, political science, history, and sociology, as well as in those fields traditionally concerned with child development and mental health, such as pediatrics, psychology, psychiatry, and social work. Research that is interdisciplinary and addresses multiple issues or problems within the same program is of particular interest. Applicants must be on the faculty of a university or nonprofit research institute either in the United States or abroad. Preference is given to postdoctorates who recently received their degree and to minority investigators. Awards are not intended for established investigators. Candidates must be nominated by their home institution.

Financial data   Awards are made to the applicant's institution to provide support for up to $50,000 per year, including an indirect cost allowance of 7.5 percent. The money may be used only for the research efforts of the investigator, with no more than half of the faculty member's salary met by the grant, which must not replace current university support.

Duration   Up to 5 years.

Special features   Fellows may conduct research at an institution in any country and in any discipline.

Limitations   Fellows must spend at least 50 percent of their time in research on areas of interest to the foundation.

Number awarded   Up to 5 investigators per year are supported.

Deadline   June of each year.

[1399]
WILLIAM TOWNSEND PORTER FELLOWSHIP FOR MINORITY INVESTIGATORS

Woods Hole Marine Biological Laboratory
Attn: Office of Research Administration & Education
Woods Hole, MA 02543
(508) 548-3705   Fax: (508) 457-1924

Purpose   To encourage and assist young, underrepresented minority physiologists in the United States.

Eligibility   This program is open to young scientists (undergraduates, senior graduate students, and postdoctoral trainees) who are from an underrepresented minority group (African Americans, Hispanics, or Native Americans), are U.S. citizens or permanent residents, and are interested in conducting research in the field of physiology with senior investigators at the Marine Biological Laboratory in Woods Hole, Massachusetts.

Financial data   Participants receive a stipend and a travel allowance.

Duration   Summer months.

Special features   This fellowship was first awarded in 1921. Funding is provided by the Harvard Apparatus Foundation.

Number awarded   Varies each year.

[1400]
WISCONSIN SPACE GRANT CONSORTIUM GRADUATE FELLOWSHIPS

Wisconsin Space Grant Consortium
Attn: Program Office
333 Architecture and Urban Planning Building
2131 East Hartford Avenue
University of Wisconsin at Milwaukee
P.O. Box 413
Milwaukee, WI 53201-0413
(414) 229-3878   Fax: (414) 229-6976
E-mail: wsgc@csd.uwm.edu

Purpose   To support graduate study and research in space and aerospace sciences at universities participating in the Wisconsin Space Grant Consortium.

Eligibility   This program is open to graduate students enrolled at 1 of the universities participating in the Wisconsin Space Grant Consortium: University of Wisconsin at Milwaukee, University of Wisconsin at Madison, Marquette University, Carroll College, Lawrence University, Milwaukee School of Engineering, Northland College, Beloit College, Medical College of Wisconsin, St. Norbert College, University of Wisconsin at LaCrosse, University of Wisconsin at Green Bay, University of Wisconsin at Parkside, University of Wisconsin at Whitewater, or Ripon College. Applicants must be U.S. citizens; be enrolled full time in a master's or Ph.D. program related to space science, aerospace, or interdisciplinary space studies; have at least a 3.0 grade point average; and be interested in conducting space-related research. The consortium especially encourages applications from minorities, women, and the physically challenged. Selection is based on academic performance and potential for success.

Financial data   Up to $3,500 per year.

Duration 1 academic year.

Special features Funding for this program is provided by the U.S. National Aeronautics and Space Administration.

Number awarded Varies; generally, at least 10 each year.

Deadline March of each year.

[1401]
WISCONSIN SPACE GRANT CONSORTIUM SPECIAL INITIATIVES PROGRAM

Wisconsin Space Grant Consortium
Attn: Program Office
333 Architecture and Urban Planning Building
2131 East Hartford Avenue
University of Wisconsin at Milwaukee
P.O. Box 413
Milwaukee, WI 53201-0413
(414) 229-3878   Fax: (414) 229-6976
E-mail: wsgc@csd.uwm.edu

Purpose To support efforts of organizations in Wisconsin to encourage participation by underrepresented groups in space-related pursuits.

Eligibility This program is open to organizations in Wisconsin, including but not limited to, schools (K-12 and higher education), aerospace industries, government agencies, and nonprofit aerospace associations. Applicants must be seeking planning grants and program supplement grants for on-going or new programs which have aerospace content and are intended to encourage, attract, and retain underrepresented groups, especially women, minorities, and the developmentally challenged.

Financial data Awards up to $2,000 are available. Recipient organizations must provide 25 percent matching funding.

Duration 1 year, beginning in June.

Number awarded Varies each year.

Deadline March of each year.

[1402]
WISCONSIN SPACE GRANT CONSORTIUM UNDERGRADUATE RESEARCH AWARDS

Wisconsin Space Grant Consortium
Attn: Program Office
333 Architecture and Urban Planning Building
2131 East Hartford Avenue
University of Wisconsin at Milwaukee
P.O. Box 413
Milwaukee, WI 53201-0413
(414) 229-3878   Fax: (414) 229-6976
E-mail: wsgc@csd.uwm.edu

Purpose To enable undergraduate students at colleges and universities participating in the Wisconsin Space Grant Consortium to conduct space-related research.

Eligibility This program is open to undergraduate students enrolled at 1 of the institutions participating in the Wisconsin Space Grant Consortium: Alverno College, University of Wisconsin at Milwaukee, University of Wisconsin at Madison, College of the Menominee Nation, Marquette University, Carroll College, Lawrence University, Milwaukee School of Engineering, Northland College, Beloit College, Medical College of Wisconsin, St. Norbert College, University of Wisconsin at LaCrosse, University of Wisconsin at Green Bay, University of Wisconsin at Parkside, University of Wisconsin at Whitewater, or Ripon College. Applicants must be U.S. citizens; be enrolled full time in a baccalaureate pro-

gram related to space science, aerospace, or interdisciplinary space studies; and have at least a 3.0 grade point average. They must be proposing to create and implement a small research project of their own design as academic year, summer, or part-time employment that is directly related to their interests and career objectives in space science, aerospace, or space-related studies. The student requests a faculty or research staff member on their campus to act as an advisor; the consortium locates a scientist or enginner from 1 of the research-intensive universities to serve as a second mentor for successful applicants. The consortium especially encourages applications from students at small colleges and universities, students in departments with newly developing space research infrastructure, minorities, women, and the physically challenged.

Financial data Stipends up to $2,500 per year or summer session are available.

Duration 1 academic year or summer.

Special features Funding for this program is provided by the U.S. National Aeronautics and Space Administration.

Number awarded Varies each year.

Deadline March of each year.

[1403]
WOMEN IN UNITED METHODIST HISTORY RESEARCH GRANT

United Methodist Church
General Commission on Archives and History
Attn: Assistant General Secretary
36 Madison Avenue
P.O. Box 127
Madison, NJ 07940
(201) 408-3189   Fax: (201) 408-3909

Purpose To support research related to the history of women in the United Methodist Church.

Eligibility Proposed research projects must deal specifically with the history of women in the United Methodist Church or its antecedents. Proposals on women of color and on history at the grassroots level are especially encouraged.

Financial data This grant provides seed money only. Grants are either $500 or $1,000.

Duration These grants are awarded annually.

Limitations Grant funds are not to be used for equipment, publication costs, or researcher's salary.

Number awarded 1 (of $1,000) or 2 (of $500) each year.

Deadline December of each year

[1404]
WOMEN'S COMMUNITY FOUNDATION GRANTS

Women's Community Foundation
12200 Fairhill Road
Cleveland, OH 44120
(216) 229-5001   Fax: (216) 229-2030

Purpose To provide funding to organizations in the Cleveland area that encourage the independence and self reliance of women and girls (particularly those of color).

Eligibility Nonprofit organizations in Cuyahoga County are eligible to apply if they are interested in working on projects that improve the lives of girls and women. A major concern of the foundation are organizations that support women with the least access to resources because of discrimination based on age, poverty, race, sexual orientation, or disability. Preference is given to programs working for social change, community organizing, and education using advocacy as a method. Requests for funding may be made for a specific project, for general support, or for start-up costs. Grants will not be made for endowments, religious organizations for religious purposes, campaigns to elect candidates to public office, individuals who are looking for scholarship support, capital for small businesses, or any personal gain. No program is too small or too new to be considered for funding.

Financial data The amount awarded varies, from $500 to $5,000 each.

Duration 1 year.

Special features The foundation was formed in 1984 and began making grants in 1986.

Limitations Proposals cannot be submitted for endowments, religious activities, election campaigns, or individual scholarships.

Number awarded Varies; generally, up to 20 each year.

Deadline January of each year.

[1405]
WOMEN'S FOUNDATION GRANTS

Women's Foundation
340 Pine Street, Suite 302
San Francisco, CA 94104
(415) 837-1113   Fax: (415) 837-1144
E-mail: womensfoun@igc.apc.org

Purpose To fund organizations in northern California that empower women and girls and contribute to their self determination, self reliance, and independence.

Eligibility Only organizations in northern California are eligible to apply. For the purposes of this program, northern California is defined as encompassing the area from the Oregon border to the southern borders of San Luis Obispo, Kern, and Inyo counties. The foundation funds organizations whose efforts are aimed at low income women and girls. Specifically, the foundation has identified a number of target population groups as priorities: women and girls of color, older women, immigrant and refugee women, women and girls with disabilities, lesbians, and single mothers. Only organizations serving low income women and girls in these target populations are eligible to apply. Preference is given to organizations in which the members of these target populations are involved in planning and decision making and to organizations with budgets under $500,000. Grants must be used for activities that develop and/or strengthen an organization's stability, sustainability, self-sufficiency, and/or income base.

Financial data The maximum grant awarded by the foundation is $10,000. The average grant ranges from $5,000 to $7,000. Funds may not be used to cover general operating costs, individual scholarships, capital improvements, endowments, loans, research, or literary publications. Since its beginning, in 1981, the foundation has given more than $1.5 million to nearly 300 programs.

Duration 1 year.

Special features Interviews are scheduled after an application has qualified for consideration.

Number awarded Varies each year.

Deadline January of each year.

[1406]
WOMEN'S FUND OF GREATER OMAHA GRANTS

Women's Fund of Greater Omaha
Omaha Community Foundation
Two Central Park Plaza
222 South 15th Street
Omaha, NE 68102
(402) 342-3458

Purpose To assist programs that encourage the economic, educational, physical, emotional, social, and personal growth of women and girls in the Omaha area.

Eligibility Eligible to apply for these grants are formal, nonprofit organizations in the Omaha area, informal groups of women in the Omaha area who have come together for a specific project that is charitable in nature, and emerging, grass roots groups or organizations in the Omaha area that have come together for a specific project that is charitable in nature. Grants are not made to individuals. Except under unusual circumstances, the fund does not make grants for endowments or deficit funding. The fund supports programs that 1) advocate policy and system changes that work to reverse social trends and conditions that have a negative effect on women and girls, and 2) enable women and organizations serving women and girls to achieve economic self sufficiency. High priority is given to groups in which women are the primary decision makers. Special consideration is given to projects that address the needs of low income and underserved women and girls, especially women and girls of color. As a general policy, the fund gives less consideration to applications from tax-supported institutions, individual churches and similar religious groups, veteran and labor organizations, social clubs, and fraternal organizations.

Financial data The amount awarded varies; a total of $25,000 is distributed each year.

Number awarded Varies each year.

Deadline October of each year.

[1407]
WOMEN'S FUNDING ALLIANCE COMMUNITY FUND

Women's Funding Alliance
Attn: Executive Director
603 Stewart Street, Suite 207
Seattle, WA 98101-1229
(206) 467-6733   Fax: (206) 467-7537

Purpose To provide funding to nonprofit programs and agencies that are not currently members of the Women's Funding Alliance and that do not have access to traditional funding sources.

Eligibility This program is open to community-based organizations in the Seattle area that have a grass roots orientation, 501(c)(3) status, an annual budget less than $300,000, and a history or mission of providing solid programming serving women and/or girls. The alliance is interested in funding grant requests that have women in leadership positions. The proposed programs should provide advocacy, support, and empowerment services for older women, women and girls of color, women and girls who are HIV positive or have AIDS, young women, and/or lesbians. Eligible organizations are different from the Women's Funding Alliance members: the Center for the Prevention of Sexual and Domestic Violence, Domestic Abuse Women's Network, Feminist Women's Health Center, Harborview Sexual Assault Center, King County Sexual Assault Resource Center, Lesbian Resource Center, Northwest Women's Law Center, Seattle Rape Relief, Solo

Parenting Alliance, Washington State NARAL Foundation, and Welfare Rights Organizing Coalition.

Financial data Grants range from $500 to $1,000. Approximately $8,000 is distributed each year.

Duration Grants are awarded annually.

Special features Examples of grant recipients include: Refugee Women's Alliance, Teen Pregnancy Action Coalition, Asian Pacific Island Family Safety Center, Seattle Lesbian Cancer Project, and Counterpoint's Senior Filipino Women's Program.

Limitations Faxed proposals are not accepted.

Number awarded Up to 15 each year.

Deadline May of each year.

[1408]
WOMEN'S HEALTH FUNDING INITIATIVE

Michigan Women's Foundation
Attn: Grants Distribution Committee
119 Pere Marquette, Suite 2A
Lansing, MI 48912-1213
(517) 374-7270

Purpose To provide funding to organizations in Michigan for efforts targeted at improving women's and girls' economic well-being by addressing related health barriers.

Eligibility Nonprofit organizations in Michigan are eligible to apply for these grants if they are seeking funding for collaborative programs that improve access to services and encourage substantive systematic change to enable women and girls to participate fully in the economic life of their communities by addressing barriers to good health. This program encourages collaborative efforts, but at least 1 of the partners involved in the effort should be a woman-run organizations. Special emphasis is placed on efforts that serve the needs of women and girls from diverse and/or disadvantaged backgrounds.

Financial data Average grant size is approximately $50,000.

Duration Up to 1 year.

Limitations Funding is not available to support scholarships for individuals, for conference attendance by nonprofit organization members, for building campaigns, for research, for endowments, or to organizations headquartered outside of Michigan.

Number awarded 2 or 3 each year.

Deadline December of each year.

[1409]
WOMEN'S HEALTH OVER THE LIFECOURSE: SOCIAL AND BEHAVIORAL ASPECTS GRANTS

National Institutes of Health
Attn: National Institute on Aging
Behavioral and Social Research Program
Gateway Building, Suite 2C231
7201 Wisconsin Avenue MSC 9205
Bethesda, MD 20892-9205
(301) 496-3136   Fax: (301) 402-0010
E-mail: mo12x@nih.gov

Purpose To support research on the social and behavioral aspects of women's health during adulthood.

Eligibility Applications are accepted from investigators at public or private, nonprofit or for-profit organizations, such as universities, colleges, hospitals, or laboratories. Research should focus on such topics as improved healthy life expectancy, psychological adjustment, and quality of life; women's health behaviors, especially in the context of family, work, and community; labor

force participation over the lifespan and its relationship to women's well-being, health, and mortality; multiple roles, stress, stress buffers (such as social support), and physical, psychological, and social consequences for women; and minorities, special populations, and cross-national research. Women and minority investigators are particularly encouraged to apply.

Financial data The amount awarded varies.

Duration 1 year; may be renewed.

Special features The National Institute on Aging sponsors this research in cooperation with 2 other agencies within the National Institutes of Health (NIH): the National Institute of Child Health and Human Development (for further information, call (301) 496-1174) and the National Institute of Mental Health (call (301) 443-3942).

Number awarded Varies each year.

Deadline January, May, and September of each year.

[1410]
WOMEN'S MENTAL HEALTH RESEARCH GRANTS

National Institutes of Health
Attn: National Institute of Mental Health
Office for Special Populations
Parklawn Building, Room 17C-14
5600 Fishers Lane MSC 8030
Rockville, MD 20857-8030
(301) 443-2847   Fax: (301) 443-8552
E-mail: dp23a@nih.gov

Purpose To provide financial assistance for research on mental disorders, symptoms, and behavioral, cognitive, and social concerns in women across the lifespan.

Eligibility This program is open to investigators at foreign and domestic, for-profit and nonprofit, public and private organizations, such as universities, colleges, hospitals, laboratories, units of state and local government, and eligible agencies of the federal government. The proposed research may deal with such issues as gender differences in age of onset of mental disorders, knowledge about ethnic minority women's mental health, comorbidity with physical illness, and the genetics of mental disorders. Racial/ethnic minority individuals, women, and persons with disabilities are encouraged to apply as principal investigators.

Financial data The amounts of the awards depends on the nature of the proposal and the availability of funds.

Duration 1 year or longer; may be renewed.

Number awarded Varies each year.

Deadline January, May, and September of each year.

[1411]
WOMEN'S STUDIES DISSERTATION FELLOWSHIP

Women's Studies Program
University of California at Santa Barbara
Santa Barbara, CA 93106-7110
(805) 893-4330   Fax: (805) 893-3597

Purpose To provide funding for women's studies dissertations.

Eligibility This program is open to graduate students at any university in the United States who are U.S. citizens, have advanced to candidacy in the humanities or social sciences, demonstrate strong research and teaching interests, are working on a dissertation in women's studies, and would benefit from a residency at the University of California at Santa Barbara. To apply, send a curriculum vitae, a brief description of the dissertation project, a writing sample (up to 25 pages), and 3 letters of reference. Applications are particularly encouraged from minority women.

Financial data The stipend is $18,000.

Duration 9 months.

Special features Recipients teach 1 undergraduate course while in residence.

Limitations Recipients are expected to complete their dissertation during the residency.

Number awarded 2 each year.

Deadline February of each year.

[1412]
WOODS HOLE OCEANOGRAPHIC INSTITUTION SUMMER STUDENT FELLOWSHIP PROGRAM

Woods Hole Oceanographic Institution
Attn: Fellowship Committee
Education Office
Clark Laboratory
Woods Hole, MA 02543-1541
(508) 457-2000, ext. 2219　　　　Fax: (508) 457-2188
E-mail: education@whoi.edu

Purpose To provide funding for undergraduate and graduate research at the Woods Hole Oceanographic Institution.

Eligibility This program is open to upper-division undergraduates (i.e., completed the junior year) and beginning graduate students studying at colleges or universities in biology, chemistry, engineering, geology, geophysics, mathematics, physics, oceanography, or marine policy. Applicants must submit 3 letters of recommendation, complete college and university transcripts, and a statement on research interests, future education, career plans, and reasons for applying to the program. Women and minorities are particularly encouraged to apply. Selection is based on previous academic and scientific achievements and promise as future ocean scientists or ocean engineers.

Financial data The stipend is $3,900. Additional support may be provided for travel.

Duration 12 weeks, during the summer.

Special features Fellows pursue independent research projects under the guidance of a member of the institution's research staff. They are not required to take any prescribed courses nor are they required to provide any services to the institution in return for the grant.

Limitations Fellows are expected to give an oral report on their research.

Deadline February of each year.

[1413]
YOUNG SCHOLARS PROGRAM

National Science Foundation
Attn: Directorate for Education and Human Resources
Division of Elementary, Secondary and Informal Education
4201 Wilson Boulevard, Room 885
Arlington, VA 22230
(703) 306-1616　　　　Fax: (703) 306-0412

Purpose To provide funding to organizations for programs that encourage students entering grades 7 through 12 to investigate and pursue careers in science, mathematics, and technology.

Eligibility Proposals may be submitted by 4-year colleges or universities, their associations or consortia, scientific or professional societies whose members are primarily university faculty or researchers, and for-profit industries or other organizations that are engaged in significant advanced research efforts and have experience interacting with students. Schools, school districts, and other organizations with programs focused on secondary education are not eligible. Participants should be students (U.S. citizens or permanent residents) entering grades 7 through 12 who have demonstrated high ability and/or high potential, as well as a strong interest in science, mathematics, engineering, and technology. Projects are expected to serve at least 15 students. Recruitment mechanisms to ensure the broad-based and geographically representative participation of students must be described. Excessive representation from any single school is strongly discouraged; whenever possible, projects should attract students on a regional or national basis. While projects must be open to all eligible students in a targeted geographic area, they may contain special features that encourage participation of group(s) underrepresented in science, mathematics, or technology.

Financial data The amount awarded depends on the nature of the proposal and the availability of funds; in a recent year, grants ranged from $53,000 to $488,000.

Duration 1 to 2 years.

Number awarded Preliminary proposals must be submitted by September of each year; full proposals are due by December

Deadline May of each year.

Awards

American Indians ●
Native Alaskans ●
Native Americans in General ●

Described in this section are 76 competitions, prizes, and honoraria open to Native Americans in recognition or support of creative work and public service. Excluded are prizes received solely as the result of entering contests. Of the programs listed here, 48 are open to all Native Americans equally, and the remainder are set aside for American Indians and Native Alaskans. If you are looking for a particular program and don't find it in this section, be sure to check the Program Title Index to see if it is covered elsewhere in the directory.

American Indians

[1414]
ALLAN & JOYCE NIEDERMAN AWARD

Red Cloud Indian Art Show
Heritage Center, Inc.
Box 100
Pine Ridge, SD 57770
(605) 867-5491

Purpose To recognize and reward the best traditional art work submitted to the annual Red Cloud Indian Art Show.

Eligibility Young Native American tribal members 18 years of age or older who submit traditional artistic works to the Red Cloud Indian Art Show are considered for the award. Their work must be available for sale, not be done in felt pen, not weight more than 100 pounds if a 3-dimensional work, and be an original produced by a living artist within the past 2 years.

Financial data The award is $100.

Duration The award is presented annually.

Number awarded 1 each year.

Deadline May of each year.

[1415]
APLAN AWARD

Red Cloud Indian Art Show
Heritage Center, Inc.
Box 100
Pine Ridge, SD 57770
(605) 867-5491

Purpose To recognize and reward Native American artists submitting outstanding works to the Red Cloud Indian Art Show.

Eligibility Young Native American tribal members 18 years of age or older who submit outstanding artistic works to the Red Cloud Indian Art Show are considered for the award. Their work must be available for sale, not be done in felt pen, not weigh more than 100 pounds if a 3-dimensional work, and be an original produced by a living artist within the past 2 years.

Financial data The award is $100.

Duration The award is presented annually.

Number awarded At least 1 each year.

Deadline May of each year.

[1416]
BENNETT COUNTY BOOSTER AWARD

Red Cloud Indian Art Show
Heritage Center, Inc.
Box 100
Pine Ridge, SD 57770
(605) 867-5491

Purpose To recognize and reward the most innovative art work submitted to the annual Red Cloud Indian Art Show.

Eligibility Young Native American tribal members 18 years of age or older who submit innovative artistic works to the Red Cloud Indian Art Show are considered for the award. Their work must be available for sale, not be done in felt pen, not weigh more than 100 pounds if a 3-dimension work, and be an original produced by a living artist within the past 2 years.

Financial data The award is $100.

Duration The award is presented annually.

Number awarded At least 1 each year.

Deadline May of each year.

[1417]
BILL AND SUE HENSLER AWARD

Red Cloud Indian Art Show
Heritage Center, Inc.
Box 100
Pine Ridge, SD 57770
(605) 867-5491

Purpose To recognize and reward Native American sculptors who submit works to the Red Cloud Indian Art Show.

Eligibility Native Americans tribal members 18 years of age or older who submit sculpture to the annual Red Cloud Indian Art Show are considered for the award. Their work must be a traditional representation, be available for sale, not weigh more than 100 pounds, and be an original produced by a living artist within the past 2 years.

Financial data The award is $50.

Duration The award is presented annually.

Number awarded 1 each year.

Deadline May of each year.

[1418]
BLACKFEET TRIBAL GRADUATION GRANT

Blackfeet Nation
P.O. Box 850
Browning, MT 59417
(406) 338-7539   Fax: (406) 338-7530

Purpose To recognize and reward Blackfeet Indians who complete their high school requirements.

Eligibility Enrolled members of the Blackfeet Tribe who receive their high school diploma or equivalency diploma (GED) are eligible to receive this grant (whether they attended Browning Public High School, attended an off-reservation school, or earned a GED certificate).

Financial data The award is $50.

Duration The award is distributed annually, at the end of the school year.

Limitations The names of eligible recipients are submitted automatically by Browning Public High School; eligible students who attended an off-reservation school or received a GED degree must provide the tribal office with a copy of their high school diploma or GED certificate within 1 year of graduation.

Deadline Notification may be sent to the education department (address above) any time within 1 year of graduation.

[1419]
BONNIE ERICKSON AWARD

Red Cloud Indian Art Show
Heritage Center, Inc.
Box 100
Pine Ridge, SD 57770
(605) 867-5491

Purpose To recognize and reward the best art work representing children submitted to the annual Red Cloud Indian Art Show.

Eligibility Young Native American tribal members 18 years of age or older who submit artistic works representing Indian children to the Red Cloud Indian Art Show are considered for the award. Their work must be available for sale, not be done in felt pen, not weigh more than 100 pounds if a 3-dimensional work, and be an original produced by a living artist within the past 2 years.

Financial data The award is $150.

Duration The award is presented annually.

Number awarded 1 each year.

Deadline May of each year.

[1420]
DIANE DECORAH MEMORIAL AWARD

Greenfield Review Literary Center
Attn: Native Authors First Book Awards
Two Middle Grove Road
P.O. Box 308
Greenfield Center, NY 12833
(518) 584-1728

Purpose To recognize and reward outstanding unpublished book-length poetry.

Eligibility This award is open to Native Americans of American Indian, Aleut, Inuit, or Metis ancestry who have not yet published a book of poetry. They may submit a book-length poetry manuscript (between 48 and 100 pages).

Financial data The prize is $500.

Duration The prize is given annually.

Special features The winning manuscript may be published by Greenfield Review Press (a sponsor of the award).

Number awarded 1 each year.

Deadline April of each year.

[1421]
DIEDERICH AWARD

Red Cloud Indian Art Show
Heritage Center, Inc.
Box 100
Pine Ridge, SD 57770
(605) 867-5491

Purpose To recognize and reward the artist at the annual Red Cloud Indian Art Show who submits the best depiction of a traditional Sioux Indian.

Eligibility Young Native American tribal members (18 years of age or older) who submit paintings of traditional Sioux Indians to the Red Cloud Indian Art Show are considered for this award. Their work must be available for sale, not be done in felt pen, not weigh more than 100 pounds if a 3-dimensional work, and be an original produced by a living artist within the past 2 years.

Financial data The award is $250.

Duration The award is presented annually.

Number awarded 1 each year.

Deadline May of each year.

[1422]
DIEDERICH IMPROVEMENT AWARD

Red Cloud Indian Art Show
Heritage Center, Inc.
Box 100
Pine Ridge, SD 57770
(605) 867-5491

Purpose To recognize and reward the most improved Native American artist at the annual Red Cloud Indian Art Show.

Eligibility Young Native American tribal members (18 years of age or older) who submit abstract paintings to the Red Cloud Indian Art Show are considered for this award. Their work must be available for sale, not be done in felt pen, not weigh more than 100 pounds if a 3-dimensional work, and be an original produced by a living artist within the past 2 years. The artist at the show whose work shows the greatest improvement is selected for this award.

Financial data The award is $250.

Duration The award is presented annually.

Number awarded 1 each year.

Deadline May of each year.

[1423]
DIEDERICH LANDSCAPE AWARDS

Red Cloud Indian Art Show
Heritage Center, Inc.
Box 100
Pine Ridge, SD 57770
(605) 867-5491

Purpose To recognize and reward the outstanding landscape paintings by Native American artists at the annual Red Cloud Indian Art Show.

Eligibility Young Native American tribal members (18 years of age or older) who submit landscape paintings to the Red Cloud Indian Art Show are considered for this award. Their work must be available for sale, not be done in felt pen, not weigh more than 100 pounds if a 3-dimensional work, and be an original produced by a living artist within the past 2 years. The works should include no human figures.

Financial data Each award is $250.

Duration The awards are presented annually.

Number awarded 2 each year: 1 for Black Hills/Badlands, 1 for lakes, mountains, or prairies.

Deadline May of each year.

[1424]
DR. AND MRS. JIM GILLIHAN AWARD

Red Cloud Indian Art Show
Heritage Center, Inc.
Box 100
Pine Ridge, SD 57770
(605) 867-5491

Purpose To recognize and reward the best artistic representation of an American Indian on horseback submitted to the annual Red Cloud Indian Art Show.

Eligibility Young Native American tribal members 18 years of age or older who submit artistic works representing Indians on horseback to the Red Cloud Indian Art Show are considered for the award. Their work must be available for sale, not be done in felt pen, not weigh more than 100 pounds if a 3-dimensional work, and be an original produced by a living artist within the past 2 years.

Financial data The award is $100.

Duration The award is presented annually.

Number awarded 1 each year.

Deadline May of each year.

[1425]
GREAT PLAINS FILM FESTIVAL AWARDS

Great Plains Film Festival
Mary Riepma Ross Film Theater
University of Nebraska
College of Fine and Peforming Arts
Lincoln, NE 68588-0302
(402) 472-5353   Fax: (402) 472-9185

Purpose To recognize and reward outstanding films and video-tapes, particularly those that deal with the Great Plains.

Eligibility Priority is given to films and videotapes that contribute to the understanding of the diverse ethnic heritage of the Great Plains: Colorado, Iowa, Kansas, Minnesota, Missouri, Montana, Nebraska, New Mexico, North Dakota, Oklahoma, South Dakota, Texas, Wyoming, Alberta, Manitoba, and Saskatchewan. Particularly encouraged to compete are Native American film and video artists. Entries may be submitted on 1/2 inch and 3/4 inch video or 16mm and 35mm film. They are judged in the following categories: dramatic feature, documentary feature, dramatic short, documentary short, film or video by Native Americans.

Financial data A total of $10,000 in prize money is distributed each year.

Duration The competition is held annually.

Limitations There is a $15 entry for shorts and a $25 entry fee for feature length submissions.

[1426]
IRON CLOUD FAMILY AWARD

Red Cloud Indian Art Show
Heritage Center, Inc.
Box 100
Pine Ridge, SD 57770
(605) 867-5491

Purpose To recognize and reward the artist at the annual Red Cloud Indian Art Show who submits artwork depicting the best sense of humor.

Eligibility Young Native American tribal members (18 years of age or older) who submit artwork (paintings, water colors, graphics, mixed media, or 3-dimensional works) to the Red Cloud Indian Art Show are considered for this award. Their work must be available for sale, not be done in felt pen, not weigh more than 100 pounds if a 3-dimensional work, and be an original produced by a living artist within the past 2 years.

Financial data The award is $150.

Duration The award is presented annually.

Number awarded 1 each year.

Deadline May of each year.

[1427]
LOUIS LITTLECOON OLIVER MEMORIAL AWARD

Greenfield Review Literary Center
Attn: Native Authors First Book Awards
Two Middle Grove Road
P.O. Box 308
Greenfield Center, NY 12833
(518) 584-1728

Purpose To recognize and reward outstanding unpublished works of fiction.

Eligibility This award is open to Native Americans of American Indian, Aleut, Inuit, or Metis ancestry who have not yet published a work of fiction. They may submit between 120 and 230 pages of short stories, a novella, or a novel.

Financial data The prize is $500.

Duration The prize is given annually.

Special features The winning manuscript may be published by Greenfield Review Press (a sponsor of the award).

Number awarded 1 each year.

Deadline April of each year.

[1428]
MISS INDIAN USA SCHOLARSHIP PROGRAM

American Indian Heritage Foundation
6051 Arlington Boulevard
Falls Church, VA 22044-2788
(202) INDIANS   (703) 237-7500
Fax: (703) 532-1921

Purpose To recognize and reward the most beautiful and talented Native American women.

Eligibility Native American women aged 18 to 26 are eligible to enter this national contest if they are high school graduates and have never been married, cohabited with the opposite sex, been pregnant, or had children.

Financial data The National Miss Indian USA and her Court Members receive $12,000 in scholarships.

Duration This competition is held annually.

Special features The program involves a week long competition in the Washington, D.C. metropolitan area that includes seminars, interviews, cultural presentations, and many public appearances.

Limitations An application fee of $25 is required.

Deadline February of each year.

[1429]
M.L. WOODARD AWARD

Red Cloud Indian Art Show
Heritage Center, Inc.
Box 100
Pine Ridge, SD 57770
(605) 867-5491

Purpose To recognize and reward Native American artists at the Red Cloud Indian Art Show whose work depicts Indian themes.

Eligibility Native American tribal members, 18 years of age or older who submit paintings, drawings, or sketches depicting Indian themes to the annual Red Cloud Indian Art Show are considered for the award. Their work must be available for sale, be an original, be matted and framed, and be produced by a living artist within the past 2 years.

Financial data The award is $50.
Duration The award is presented annually.
Number awarded At least 1 each year.
Deadline May of each year.

[1430]
NICOLAUS ROSTKOWSKI AWARD

Red Cloud Indian Art Show
Heritage Center, Inc.
Box 100
Pine Ridge, SD 57770
(605) 867-5491

Purpose To recognize and reward the best abstract painting submitted to the annual Red Cloud Indian Art Show.
Eligibility Young Native American tribal members (18 years of age or older) who submit abstract paintings to the Red Cloud Indian Art Show are considered for this award. Their work must be available for sale, not be done in felt pen, not weigh more than 100 pounds if a 3-dimensional work, and be an original produced by a living artist within the past 2 years.
Financial data The award is $100.
Duration The award is presented annually.
Number awarded 1 each year.
Deadline May of each year.

[1431]
OSCAR HOWE MEMORIAL AWARD

Red Cloud Indian Art Show
Heritage Center, Inc.
Box 100
Pine Ridge, SD 57770
(605) 867-5491

Purpose To recognize and reward the best cubist painting by an artist at the annual Red Cloud Indian Art Show.
Eligibility Young Native American tribal members (18 years of age or older) who submit cubist paintings to the annual Red Cloud Indian Art Show are considered for this award. Their work must be available for sale, not be done in felt pen, not weigh more than 100 pounds if a 3-dimensional work, and be an original produced by a living artist within the past 2 years.
Financial data The award is $100.
Duration The award is presented annually.
Number awarded 1 each year.
Deadline May of each year.

[1432]
POSTER SESSION AWARDS

Society for Advancement of Chicanos and Native Americans
    in Science
1156 High Street
University of California at Santa Cruz
Santa Cruz, CA 95064
(408) 459-4272   Fax: (408) 459-3156
E-mail: sacnas@cats.ucsc.edu

Purpose To recognize and reward outstanding biomedical research posters presented at the annual conference of the Society for Advancement of Chicanos and Native Americans in Science (SACNAS).

Eligibility Chicano and Native American students who present biomedical research posters at the Society's annual conference are eligible for these awards.
Financial data The stipend is $250.
Duration The competition is held annually.
Number awarded 3 each year: 2 in basic research and 1 in clinical research.

[1433]
POWERS AWARD

Red Cloud Indian Art Show
Heritage Center, Inc.
Box 100
Pine Ridge, SD 57770
(605) 867-5491

Purpose To recognize and reward Native American artists whose works at the Red Cloud Indian Art Show depict Indian women.
Eligibility Young Native American tribal members 18 years of age or older who submit artistic works depicting Indian women to the Red Cloud Indian Art Show are considered for the award. Their work must be available for sale, not be done in felt pen, not weigh more than 100 pounds if a 3-dimensional work, and be an original produced by a living artist within the past 2 years.
Financial data The award is $100.
Duration The award is presented annually.
Number awarded At least 1 each year.
Deadline May of each year.

[1434]
RED CLOUD INDIAN ART SHOW AWARDS

Red Cloud Indian Art Show
Heritage Center, Inc.
Box 100
Pine Ridge, SD 57770
(605) 867-4391

Purpose To recognize and reward Native American artists who submit works to the Red Cloud Indian Art Show.
Eligibility Any Native American tribal member who is 18 years of age or older is eligible to submit works in the following categories: 1) oil, tempera, casein, encaustic, polymer, and acrylic paintings; 2) water color paintings; 3) pencil, pen and ink, cray-pas, pastel, crayon, wash, and charcoal graphics; 4) mixed media; and 5) 3-dimensional media. All works submitted to the show must be for sale.
Financial data $300 merit awards are available for each of the 5 artistic categories.
Duration The show is held annually.
Limitations Artists may enter only 3 pieces in any of the first 4 categories; 2 pieces in the 3-dimensional media category. Works done in felt pen are not accepted. There is a 100 pound limit for 3-dimensional works. All submissions in the first 4 categories must be matted and framed. All works must remain on exhibit until the end of the show. All works must be originals produced by living artists within the past 2 years.
Deadline May of each year.

[1435]
TECHFORCE PREENGINEERING PRIZE
National Action Council for Minorities in Engineering
3 West 35th Street
New York, NY 10001-2281
(212) 279-2626   Fax: (212) 629-5178

Purpose To recognize and reward outstanding underrepresented minority high school seniors who are planning to pursue a career in engineering.

Eligibility This program is open to African American, Latino, and American Indian high school seniors who have demonstrated academic excellence, leadership skills, and commitment to engineering as a career.

Financial data Semifinalists receive $500 per year, primary finalists receive $1,000 per year, and top scholars receive the 3M Engineering Award of an additional $2,500 per year.

Duration Semifinalists: 1 year; primary finalists: 4 years; 3M Engineering Award recipients: 4 years.

Number awarded 10 semifinalists, 10 primary finalists, and 2 3M Engineering Award recipients each year.

[1436]
THUNDERBIRD FOUNDATION SCHOLARSHIP
Red Cloud Indian Art Show
Heritage Center, Inc.
Box 100
Pine Ridge, SD 57770
(605) 867-5491

Purpose To provide financial assistance for the education of Native American artists.

Eligibility Young Native American tribal members (18 years of age or older) who submit artistic works to the Red Cloud Indian Art Show are considered for this award.

Financial data A total of $5,000 in art scholarships is awarded, at the discretion of the Red Cloud Indian Art Show judges, to show participants.

Duration The award is presented annually.

Number awarded Varies each year.

Deadline May of each year.

[1437]
TONY BEGAY MEMORIAL AWARD
Red Cloud Indian Art Show
Heritage Center, Inc.
Box 100
Pine Ridge, SD 57770
(605) 867-5491

Purpose To recognize and reward Native American artists whose works at the Red Cloud Indian Art Show depict Indian themes.

Eligibility Young Native American tribal members 18 years of age or older who submit artistic works depicting Indian themes to the Red Cloud Indian Art Show are considered for the award. Their work must be available for sale, not be done in felt pen, not weigh more than 100 pounds if a 3-dimensional work, and be an original produced by a living artist within the past 2 years.

Financial data The award is $50.

Duration The award is presented annually.

Number awarded At least 1 each year.

Deadline May of each year.

[1438]
VIGIL AWARDS
Society for Advancement of Chicanos and Native Americans in Science
1156 High Street
University of California at Santa Cruz
Santa Cruz, CA 95064
(408) 459-4272   Fax: (408) 459-3156
E-mail: sacnas@cats.ucsc.edu

Purpose To recognize and reward outstanding undergraduate research posters presented at the annual conference of the Society for Advancement of Chicanos and Native Americans in Science (SACNAS).

Eligibility Chicano and Native American undergraduate students who present research posters in biological and physical sciences at the Society's annual conference are eligible for these awards.

Financial data The stipend is $500.

Duration The competition is held annually.

Number awarded 4 each year.

[1439]
YAKAMA INCENTIVE AWARDS PROGRAM
Yakama Indian Nation
Attn: Higher Education Programs
Department of Human Services
P.O. Box 151
Toppenish, WA 98948
(509) 865-5121   (800) 543-2802
Fax: (509) 865-6994

Purpose To recognize and reward the outstanding academic achievement of Yakama Indians.

Eligibility Yakama Indian college students who maintain excellent academic and attendance performance during the year are eligible to apply.

Financial data Monetary awards are presented to college students based on cumulative grade point average, course level, and class level.

Duration The awards are presented annually.

Number awarded Varies each year.

Native Alaskans

[1440]
DIANE DECORAH MEMORIAL AWARD
Greenfield Review Literary Center
Attn: Native Authors First Book Awards
Two Middle Grove Road
P.O. Box 308
Greenfield Center, NY 12833
(518) 584-1728

Purpose To recognize and reward outstanding unpublished book-length poetry.

Eligibility This award is open to Native Americans of American Indian, Aleut, Inuit, or Metis ancestry who have not yet published a book of poetry. They may submit a book-length poetry manuscript (between 48 and 100 pages).

Financial data The prize is $500.
Duration The prize is given annually.
Special features The winning manuscript may be published by Greenfield Review Press (a sponsor of the award).
Number awarded 1 each year.
Deadline April of each year.

[1441]
LOUIS LITTLECOON OLIVER MEMORIAL AWARD

Greenfield Review Literary Center
Attn: Native Authors First Book Awards
Two Middle Grove Road
P.O. Box 308
Greenfield Center, NY 12833
(518) 584-1728

Purpose To recognize and reward outstanding unpublished works of fiction.
Eligibility This award is open to Native Americans of American Indian, Aleut, Inuit, or Metis ancestry who have not yet published a work of fiction. They may submit between 120 and 230 pages of short stories, a novella, or a novel.
Financial data The prize is $500.
Duration The prize is given annually.
Special features The winning manuscript may be published by Greenfield Review Press (a sponsor of the award).
Number awarded 1 each year.
Deadline April of each year.

Native Americans in General

[1442]
AAUW FOUNDERS DISTINGUISHED SENIOR SCHOLAR AWARD

American Association of University Women
Attn: Educational Foundation
2201 North Dodge Street
Iowa City, IA 52243-4030
(319) 337-1716   Fax: (319) 337-1204

Purpose To recognize and reward outstanding women scholars.
Eligibility Eligible for nomination for this award are women scholars in any field at the pinnacle of their careers. Applications may be submitted by the scholar herself or by a colleague or a member of the American Association of University Women (AAUW). Women of color are especially encouraged to apply.
Financial data The award is $1,000.
Duration The award is presented annually.
Number awarded 1 each year.
Deadline November of each year.

[1443]
ANISFIELD-WOLF BOOK AWARD IN RACE RELATIONS

Cleveland Foundation
1400 Hanna Building
1422 Euclid Avenue
Cleveland, OH 44115-2001
(216) 861-3810

Purpose To recognize and reward recent books that have contributed to understanding of racism or appreciation of the rich diversity of human cultures.
Eligibility Published works in any field that contribute to the betterment of race relations are eligible to be considered if they fall into 1 of these 2 categories: scholarly books published in the field of race relations; books concerned with racial problems in the field of creative literature (fiction, drama, poetry, biography, autobiography). Plays and screenplays are not eligible, nor are works in progress.
Financial data The prize is $10,000 per book.
Duration The awards are presented annually.
Number awarded 3 each year.
Deadline January of each year.

[1444]
ANNUAL WOMEN OF COLOR PSYCHOLOGIES AWARD

Association for Women in Psychology
c/o Angela R. Gillem
Beaver College
450 South Easton Road
Glenside, PA 19038-3295
(215) 572-2184   Fax: (215) 572-0240
E-mail: gillem@castle.beaver.edu

Purpose To recognize and reward papers that contribute to the understanding of the psychology of women of color.
Eligibility Single and jointly authored manuscripts, approximately journal length, by and about women of color may be submitted. Papers that have been submitted for publication or presented as a professional meeting are eligible, along with papers that have been previously published or accepted for publication. Selection is based on creativity, sound methodology, clarity of style, and relevance to the greater understanding of the psychology of women of color.
Financial data A prize of up to $250 for travel to the Association for Women in Psychology conference is awarded.
Duration The award is presented annually.
Number awarded 1 each year.
Deadline March of each year.

[1445]
ARTS DANCE COMPETITION SCHOLARSHIPS

National Foundation for Advancement in the Arts
800 Brickell Avenue, Suite 500
Miami, FL 33131
(305) 377-1148   (800) 970-ARTS
E-mail: nfaa@artbank.com

Purpose To recognize and reward outstanding high school student dancers or choreographers.
Eligibility Applicants must be U.S. citizens or permanent residents who are graduating high school seniors or, if not enrolled

in high school, are 17 or 18 years old. Dancers should have several years of concentrated study and choreographers should have a record of serious interest and production extending over at least 1 year. Acceptable categories are ballet, choreography, jazz, modern, tap, and additional (such as African, East Indian, Native American, Irish Step, and Spanish); applicants may enter 1 or more of the categories. Applicants submit videotapes showing up to 2 minutes of technique, up to 2 minutes of solo performance, and a brief full-face shot, half-body shot, and full-body shot at the end of the tape. Selection is based on presence, technique, musicality and phrasing, and artistry. On the basis of the tapes, judges invite award winners to Miami for the final competitions. An Affirmative Action Panel works with other panels to ensure minority and special needs applicants are equitably evaluated, and special arrangements are made to permit full participation by applicants with special needs.

Financial data First-level awards are $3,000 each, second level $1,500, third level $1,000, fourth level $500, and fifth level $100; honorable mentions receive $100 awards but are not invited to Miami.

Duration The competition is held annually.

Special features ARTS (Arts Recognition and Talent Search) is sponsored by the National Foundation for Advancement in the Arts, which is funded by many corporations, foundations, and individuals. The names of all ARTS applicants are provided to 100 participating colleges, universities, and professional institutions that have $3 million in scholarships available for ARTS applicants.

Limitations The application fee is $25 for early applications and $35 for regular applications.

Number awarded Up to 20 award candidates compete in Miami; an unlimited number of honorable mention awards are made to candidates who are not invited to Miami.

Deadline Early applications must be submitted by May of each year; regular applications are due by September of each year.

[1446]
ARTS JAZZ COMPETITION SCHOLARSHIPS

National Foundation for Advancement in the Arts
800 Brickell Avenue, Suite 500
Miami, FL 33131
(305) 377-1148 (800) 970-ARTS
E-mail: nfaa@artbank.com

Purpose To recognize and reward outstanding high school student jazz musicians.

Eligibility Applicants must be graduating high school seniors (including both U.S. and foreign citizens) or, if not enrolled in high school, are 17 or 18 years old. Candidates submit an audiotape of 20 to 30 minutes (15 to 30 minutes for vocalists) in 1 or more of the categories of keyboard, violin, viola, cello, double bass, guitar, flute, oboe, clarinet, saxophone, trumpet, trombone, percussion, vocalist, or composer. Selection is based on improvisation, tone production, technique, diction, rhythm, intonation, interpretation, and phrasing. On the basis of the audiotapes, judges select award winners to come to Miami for the final competitions. An Affirmative Action Panel works with other panels to ensure minority and special needs applicants are equitably evaluated, and special arrangements are made to permit full participation by applicants with special needs.

Financial data First-level awards are $3,000 each, second level $1,500, third level $1,000, fourth level $500, and fifth level $100; honorable mentions receive $100 awards but are not invited to Miami.

Duration The competition is held annually.

Special features ARTS (Arts Recognition and Talent Search) is sponsored by the National Foundation for Advancement in the Arts and the International Association of Jazz Educators (IAJE); funding is provided by many corporations, foundations, and individuals. Candidates who are invited to participate in ARTS Week are named Clifford Brown/Stan Getz Fellows and also attend and perform at the annual convention of IAJE. The names of all ARTS applicants are provided to 100 participating colleges, universities, and professional institutions that have $3 million in scholarships available for ARTS applicants.

Limitations The application fee is $25 for early applications and $35 for regular applications.

Number awarded Up to 5 award candidates compete in Miami; an unlimited number of honorable mention awards are made to candidates who are not invited to Miami.

Deadline Early applications must be submitted by May of each year; regular applications are due by September of each year.

[1447]
ARTS MUSIC COMPETITION SCHOLARSHIPS

National Foundation for Advancement in the Arts
800 Brickell Avenue, Suite 500
Miami, FL 33131
(305) 377-1148 (800) 970-ARTS
E-mail: nfaa@artbank.com

Purpose To recognize and reward outstanding high school student musicians.

Eligibility Applicants must be U.S. citizens or permanent residents who are graduating high school seniors or, if not enrolled in high school, are 17 or 18 years old. They may compete in the following categories: classical instruments (each instrument is a separate category), popular piano, and composition. Selection in the performance categories is based on tone production, technique, rhythm, intonation, interpretation, and phrasing; selection in the composition category is based on musical ideas, musical structure, and control of medium. Applicants submit audiotapes for each category entered, and judges select award winners to come to Miami for the final competitions. An Affirmative Action Panel works with other panels to ensure minority and special needs applicants are equitably evaluated, and special arrangements are made to permit full participation by applicants with special needs.

Financial data First-level awards are $3,000 each, second level $1,500, third level $1,000, fourth level $500, and fifth level $100; honorable mentions receive $100 awards but are not invited to Miami.

Duration The competition is held annually.

Special features ARTS (Arts Recognition and Talent Search) is sponsored by the National Foundation for Advancement in the Arts which is funded by many corporations, foundations, and individuals. The names of all ARTS applicants are provided to 100 participating colleges, universities, and professional institutions that have $3 million in scholarships available for ARTS applicants.

Limitations The application fee is $25 for early applications and $35 for regular applications.

Number awarded Up to 20 award candidates compete in Miami; an unlimited number of honorable mention awards are made to candidates who are not invited to Miami.

Deadline Early applications must be submitted by May of each year; regular applications are due by September of each year.

[1448]
ARTS PHOTOGRAPHY COMPETITION SCHOLARSHIPS

National Foundation for Advancement in the Arts
800 Brickell Avenue, Suite 500
Miami, FL 33131
(305) 377-1148   (800) 970-ARTS
E-mail: nfaa@artbank.com

Purpose To recognize and reward outstanding high school student photographers.

Eligibility Applicants must be U.S. citizens or permanent residents who are graduating high school seniors, or, if not enrolled in high school, are 17 or 18 years old. Competitors may submit any form of photography, including color, black-and-white, mixed media, non-silver processes, documentary, etc. Entries consist of a portfolio of 10 slides, 5 of which tell a story or are thematically related. Selection criteria include original thinking, an artistic commitment, and a willingness to take creative risks. On the basis of the portfolios, judges select award recipients to come to Miami for the final competitions. An Affirmative Action Panel works with other panels to ensure minority and special needs applicants are equitably evaluated, and special arrangements are made to permit full participation by applicants with special needs.

Financial data First-level awards are $3,000 each, second level $1,500, third level $1,000, fourth level $500, and fifth level $100; honorable mentions receive $100 awards but are not invited to Miami.

Duration The competition is held annually.

Special features ARTS (Arts Recognition and Talent Search) is sponsored by the National Foundation for Advancement in the Arts which is funded by many corporations, foundations, and individuals. This photography category is sponsored by photographer Nancy Ellison and her husband, William D. Rollnick. The names of all ARTS applicants are provided to 100 participating colleges, universities, and professional institutions that have $3 million in scholarships available for ARTS applicants.

Limitations The application fee is $25 for early applications and $35 for regular applications.

Number awarded Up to 10 award candidates compete in Miami; an unlimited number of honorable mention awards are made to candidates who are not invited to Miami.

Deadline Early applications must be submitted by May of each year; regular applications are due by September of each year.

[1449]
ARTS THEATER COMPETITION SCHOLARSHIPS

National Foundation for Advancement in the Arts
800 Brickell Avenue, Suite 500
Miami, FL 33131
(305) 377-1148   (800) 970-ARTS
E-mail: nfaa@artbank.com

Purpose To recognize and reward outstanding high school student actors.

Eligibility Applicants must be U.S. citizens or permanent residents who are graduating high school seniors, or, if not enrolled in high school, are 17 or 18 years old. Competition is in either spoken acting only or in spoken and musical theater acting. Applicants submit a videotape containing 2 auditions, each 2 minutes in length: 1 from a play published before 1910 and 1 from a play published in or after 1910. The 2 auditions should represent a maximum contrast (such as comedy/serious, verse/prose, representational/naturalistic, etc.) and, for candidates in musical

theater acting, 1 must be spoken and 1 may be a selection from a musical play. Selection is based on the actor's ability to demonstrate concentration, control of material, flexibility and versatility of voice, movement, and expression. On the basis of the videotapes, judges select award recipients to come to Miami for the final competitions. An Affirmative Action Panel works with other panels to ensure minority and special needs applicants are equitably evaluated, and special arrangements are made to permit full participation by applicants with special needs.

Financial data First-level awards are $3,000 each, second level $1,500, third level $1,000, fourth level $500, and fifth level $100; honorable mentions receive $100 awards but are not invited to Miami.

Duration The competition is held annually.

Special features ARTS (Arts Recognition and Talent Search) is sponsored by the National Foundation for Advancement in the Arts which is funded by many corporations, foundations, and individuals. The names of all ARTS applicants are provided to 100 participating colleges, universities, and professional institutions that have $3 million in scholarships available for ARTS applicants.

Limitations The application fee is $25 for early applications and $35 for regular applications.

Number awarded Up to 20 award candidates compete in Miami; an unlimited number of honorable mention awards are made to candidates who are not invited to Miami.

Deadline Early applications must be submitted by May of each year; regular applications are due by September of each year.

[1450]
ARTS VISUAL ARTS COMPETITION SCHOLARSHIPS

National Foundation for Advancement in the Arts
800 Brickell Avenue, Suite 500
Miami, FL 33131
(305) 377-1148   (800) 970-ARTS
E-mail: nfaa@artbank.com

Purpose To recognize and reward outstanding high school student artists.

Eligibility Applicants must be U.S. citizens or permanent residents who are graduating high school seniors or, if not enrolled in high school, are 17 or 18 years old. There are 2 categories of competition; in the first, which includes ceramics, costume design, drawing, graphic design, jewelry making, painting, printmaking, sculpture, textile and fiber design, and theater set design, candidates submit 10 slides, illustrating a minimum of 5 of their original works; in the other category, applicants submit a VHS cassette videotape of up to 10 minutes for which they had primary creative responsibility; the work may have been produced on film but must be transferred to videotape. Selection in both categories is based on imagination, competence, and the skillful use of materials. On the basis of the slides or videotapes, judges select award winners to come to Miami for the final competitions. An Affirmative Action Panel works with other panels to ensure minority and special needs applicants are equitably evaluated, and special arrangements are made to permit full participation by applicants with special needs.

Financial data First-level awards are $3,000 each, second level $1,500, third level $1,000, fourth level $500, and fifth level $100; honorable mentions receive $100 awards but are not invited to Miami.

Duration The competition is held annually.

Special features ARTS (Arts Recognition and Talent Search) is sponsored by the National Foundation for Advancement in the

Arts which is funded by many corporations, foundations, and individuals. The names of all ARTS applicants are provided to 100 participating colleges, universities, and professional institutions that have $3 million in scholarships available for ARTS applicants.

Limitations The application fee is $25 for early applications and $35 for regular applications.

Number awarded Up to 20 award candidates compete in Miami; an unlimited number of honorable mention awards are made to candidates who are not invited to Miami.

Deadline Early applications must be submitted by May of each year; regular applications are due by September of each year.

[1451]
ARTS VOICE COMPETITION SCHOLARSHIPS

National Foundation for Advancement in the Arts
800 Brickell Avenue, Suite 500
Miami, FL 33131
(305) 377-1148   (800) 970-ARTS
E-mail: nfaa@artbank.com

Purpose To recognize and reward outstanding high school student singers.

Eligibility Applicants must be U.S. citizens or permanent residents who are graduating high school seniors or, if not enrolled in high school, are 17 or 18 years old. They must compete in either classical voice (soprano, mezzo soprano, contralto, tenor, baritone, bass) or popular music vocals. Selection is based on tone production, technique, diction, rhythm, intonation, interpretation, and phrasing. Applicants submit audiotapes for each category entered, and judges select award winners to come to Miami for the final competitions. An Affirmative Action Panel works with other panels to ensure minority and special needs applicants are equitably evaluated, and special arrangements are made to permit full participation by applicants with special needs.

Financial data First-level awards are $3,000 each, second level $1,500, third level $1,000, fourth level $500, and fifth level $100; honorable mentions receive $100 awards but are not invited to Miami.

Duration The competition is held annually.

Special features ARTS (Arts Recognition and Talent Search) is sponsored by the National Foundation for Advancement in the Arts which is funded by many corporations, foundations, and individuals. The names of all ARTS applicants are provided to 100 participating colleges, universities, and professional institutions that have $3 million in scholarships available for ARTS applicants.

Limitations The application fee is $25 for early applications and $35 for regular applications.

Number awarded Up to 5 award candidates compete in Miami; an unlimited number of honorable mention awards are made to candidates who are not invited to Miami.

Deadline Early applications must be submitted by May of each year; regular applications are due by September of each year.

[1452]
ARTS WRITING COMPETITION SCHOLARSHIPS

National Foundation for Advancement in the Arts
800 Brickell Avenue, Suite 500
Miami, FL 33131
(305) 377-1148   (800) 970-ARTS
E-mail: nfaa@artbank.com

Purpose To recognize and reward outstanding high school student writers.

Eligibility Applicants must be U.S. citizens or permanent residents who are graduating high school seniors, or, if not enrolled in high school, are 17 or 18 years old. Competitors may enter portfolios in 1 or more of these categories: poetry (up to 6 poems in up to 10 pages), short story—fiction (up to 3 stories in up to 16 pages), play or script for film or television (up to 3 scripts for dramatic performance in any medium in up to 20 pages), selection from a novel (up to 20 pages, preceded by a description of the complete work and how the excerpt fits into it), or expository (up to 3 essays in up to 16 pages). Selection is based on language, originality, imagination, and overall excellence. On the basis of the portfolios, award winners are invited to Miami for the final competitions. An Affirmative Action Panel works with other panels to ensure minority and special needs applicants are equitably evaluated, and special arrangements are made to permit full participation by applicants with special needs.

Financial data First-level awards are $3,000 each, second level $1,500, third level $1,000, fourth level $500, and fifth level $100; honorable mention recipients receive $100 awards but are not invited to Miami.

Duration The competition is held annually.

Special features ARTS (Arts Recognition and Talent Search) is sponsored by the National Foundation for Advancement in the Arts which is funded by many corporations, foundations, and individuals. The names of all ARTS applicants are provided to 100 participating colleges, universities, and professional institutions that have $3 million in scholarships available for ARTS applicants.

Limitations The application fee is $25 for early applications and $35 for regular applications.

Number awarded Up to 20 award candidates compete in Miami; an unlimited number of honorable mention awards are made to candidates who are not invited to Miami.

Deadline Early applications must be submitted by May of each year; regular applications are due by September of each year.

[1453]
ASEE MINORITIES IN ENGINEERING AWARD

American Society for Engineering Education
1818 N Street, N.W., Suite 600
Washington, DC 20036-2479
(202) 331-3550   Fax: (202) 265-8504

Purpose To recognize and reward outstanding achievements by an engineering educator to increase participation of women and/or minority students in engineering curricula.

Eligibility Eligible for nomination are engineering educators who, as part of their education activity, either assume or are charged with the responsibility of motivating female and/or minority candidate students to enter and continue in engineering curricula at the college or university level, graduate or undergraduate. Nominees from previous years will be eligible for the award provided they have been renominated in a letter from the original nominator that includes updated material. Renominated candidates will be considered on the same basis as new nominees.

Financial data The award consists of $1,500, a certificate, and a grant of $500 for travel expenses to the ASEE annual conference.

Duration The award is granted annually.

Number awarded 1 each year.

[1454]
AUDRE LORDE MEMORIAL PROSE PRIZE

National Women's Studies Association
7100 Baltimore Avenue, Suite 301
College Park, MD 20740
(301) 403-0525   Fax: (301) 403-4137
E-mail: nwsa@umail.umd.edu

Purpose To recognize and reward feminist fiction or prose.
Eligibility The contest is open to all feminist authors who write fiction or prose. The work submitted should take up a topic of discourse found in the work of Audre Lorde (1934-1992), an African-Caribbean feminist poet and writer, or seek to illustrate a condition, idea, or ideal inherent in her fiction or prose. Fiction and nonfiction submissions are to be original, unpublished, and from 500 to 7,000 words in length.
Financial data Each prize is $250.
Duration The competition is held annually.
Special features Funding for this award has been provided by Woman in the Moon Publications, a Black-owned, woman-owned book publisher. This prize honors Audre Lorde and her effort to reach women of color.
Limitations A submissions fee of $20 is required.
Number awarded 2 each year: 1 for fiction and 1 for nonfiction.
Deadline November of each year.

[1455]
AWARD FOR ENCOURAGING DISADVANTAGED STUDENTS INTO CAREERS IN THE CHEMICAL SCIENCES

American Chemical Society
Attn: Awards Office
1155 16th Street, N.W.
Washington, DC 20036
(202) 872-4481

Purpose To recognize and reward individuals who have significantly stimulated or fostered the interests of students—especially minority and/or economically disadvantaged students—in chemistry.
Eligibility Only nominations may be submitted. Nominees for the award may come from any professional setting: academia, industry, government, or other independent facility in the United States. The award is given without regard to the age or nationality of the recipient.
Financial data The award consists of $5,000, a certificate, and a $1,500 expense allowance for travel to the meeting at which the award will be presented. In addition, a grant of $10,000 is made to an academic institution, designated by the recipient, to strengthen its activities in meeting the objectives of this award.
Duration The award is presented annually.
Special features The award was established in 1993 and has been funded since then by the Camille and Henry Dreyfus Foundation, Inc.
Number awarded 1 each year.
Deadline Nominations must be submitted by the end of January of each year.

[1456]
BORDER PLAYWRIGHTS PROJECT

Borderlands Theater
P.O. Box 2791
Tucson, AZ 85702
(520) 882-8607

Purpose To recognize and reward unproduced, full-length playscripts by playwrights who work reflects the cultural diversity of the Border region and the Border as a metaphor.
Eligibility Eligible plays must be unproduced (except in workshops or as readings) and unpublished. English, Spanish, or bilingual scripts are acceptable. Special consideration is given to Latino, Native American, African American, and Asian American playwrights.
Financial data The winning playwrights receive an honorarium, plus travel to and lodging in Tucson.
Duration The competition is held annually.
Special features Borderlands Theater is a multicultural arts organization in Tucson, Arizona. Winning plays are produced by Borderlands.
Limitations This program has been suspended temporarily; it will be resumed when funding is arranged.
Number awarded 1 or more each year.
Deadline March of each year.

[1457]
CHARLES H. AND N. MILDRED NILON EXCELLENCE IN MINORITY FICTION AWARD

Department of English
Attn: Publications Center
University of Colorado at Boulder
Campus Box 494
Boulder, CO 80309-0494
(303) 492-8938

Purpose To recognize and reward outstanding fiction written by American minorities.
Eligibility The contest is open to the following U.S. racial and ethnic minorities: Asians, Pacific Islanders, African Americans, Hispanics, and Native Americans (including Alaskan Natives). To be eligible, the writing must be in the English language and must be of book length: novels, novellas, or short story collections.
Financial data The winner receives $1,000, plus publication of the winning entry.
Duration The competition is held annually.
Special features The competition is cosponsored by the University of Colorado at Boulder and the Fiction Collective Two.
Number awarded 1 each year.
Deadline November of each year.

[1458]
CHICAGO SPIRIT AWARD

Sara Lee Foundation
Three First National Plaza
Chicago, IL 60602-4260
(312) 726-2600

Purpose To recognize and reward outstanding organizations in the Chicago area that have made contributions to the minority community.
Eligibility This program annually rewards a Chicago-based nonprofit organization that has demonstrated exceptional leader-

ship in helping disadvantaged people make a lasting change for the better. Selection is based on innovation, sound management, and the organization's ability to inspire community and volunteer participation.

Financial data The award is $50,000.

Duration The award is presented annually.

Number awarded 1 each year.

[1459]
C.R. BARD FOUNDATION PRIZE

National Medical Fellowships, Inc.
Attn: Scholarships and Programs
110 West 32nd Street, 8th Floor
New York, NY 10001-3205
(212) 714-1007

Purpose To recognize and reward the outstanding talents and future potential of a graduating underrepresented medical student who intends to practice in the field of cardiology or urology.

Eligibility This award is open to senior African American, Native American, Mexican American, and mainland Puerto Rican students enrolled in accredited U.S. medical schools and planning to pursue careers in cardiology or urology. Candidates must be nominated by their medical schools during their senior year. Selection is based on academic achievement, leadership, and potential to make significant contributions in their field.

Financial data This honor includes a certificate of merit and a $5,000 stipend.

Duration 1 year; nonrenewable.

Special features This award was established in 1996 by C.R. Bard, Inc., a developer, manufacturer, and marketer of cardiovascular, urological, and surgical products.

Number awarded 1 each year.

Deadline Nominations are requested in January of each year.

[1460]
C.S. KILNER LEADERSHIP AWARD

A Better Chance, Inc.
Attn: Vice President for Administration and Development
419 Boylston Street
Boston, MA 02116
(617) 421-0950   Fax: (617) 421-0965

Purpose To recognize and reward outstanding minority high school students.

Eligibility This award is presented to the ABC (A Better Chance) senior who has best displayed leadership qualities throughout his or her secondary school career. Only nominations are accepted.

Financial data The award is $1,000.

Duration The competition is held annually.

Special features A Better Chance, Inc. (ABC) is a national, nonprofit organization serving junior and senior high school minority students and member schools. ABC seeks qualified minority students, from all economic backgrounds and every part of the country, and provides them with access to college preparatory educations at outstanding independent and public schools. Students are admitted to ABC on the basis of academic merit, personal motivation, and promise. As a general rule, applicants are in the top 10 percent of their class and have good academic and personal recommendations. The great majority of students apply to ABC while in the eighth or ninth grade and begin their ABC experience at the ninth or tenth grade level.

Number awarded 1 each year.

Deadline March of each year.

[1461]
DAMON WALSH MEMORIAL AWARD

A Better Chance, Inc.
Attn: Vice President for Administration and Development
419 Boylston Street
Boston, MA 02116
(617) 421-0950   Fax: (617) 421-0965

Purpose To recognize and reward outstanding minority high school students.

Eligibility This award is presented to the ABC (A Better Chance) student who, during his or her first year in the program, best demonstrated courage, tenacity, and perseverance to a purpose or ideal in the face of great obstacles. Only nominations are accepted.

Financial data The award is $500.

Duration The award is presented annually.

Special features A Better Chance, Inc. (ABC) is a national, nonprofit organization serving junior and senior high school minority students and member schools. ABC seeks qualified minority students, from all economic backgrounds and every part of the country and provides them with access to college preparatory educations at outstanding independent and public schools. Students are admitted to ABC on the basis of academic merit, personal motivation, and promise. As a general rule, applicants are in the top 10 percent of their class. The great majority of students apply to ABC while in the eighth or ninth grade and begin their ABC experience at the ninth or tenth grade level.

Number awarded 1 each year.

Deadline October of each year.

[1462]
DENALI PRESS AWARD

American Library Association
Attn: Reference and User Services Association
50 East Huron Street
Chicago, IL 60611-2795
(312) 280-4398   (800) 545-2433, ext. 4398
TDD: (312) 944-7298   Fax: (312) 944-8085
E-mail: rusa@ala.org

Purpose To recognize and reward the creation of outstanding reference works that provide information specifically about ethnic and minority groups in the United States.

Eligibility Any reference work published in the preceding 2 years is eligible to be nominated if it focuses on ethnic and minority groups in the United States. Selection is based on accuracy, scope, usefulness, format, special features, access, and the gap in the literature filled by the work.

Financial data The award is $500.

Duration The award is presented annually.

Special features Funding for this award is provided by Denali Press.

Number awarded 1 each year.

Deadline January of each year.

[1463]
ELLIOTT RUDWICK PRIZE

Organization of American Historians
Attn: Award and Prize Committee Coordinator
112 North Bryan Street
Bloomington, IN 47408-4199
(812) 855-7311   Fax: (812) 855-0696
E-mail: oah@indiana.edu

Purpose To recognize and reward outstanding books on the minority experience in America.

Eligibility Considered for this prize are books dealing with racial and ethnic minority experiences in the United States. Books on interactions between 2 or more minority groups, or comparing the experience of 2 or more minority groups, are especially welcomed. No book that has won the James A. Rawley Prize is eligible to be considered for this award.

Financial data The prize is $2,000.

Duration The competition is held biennially, in odd-numbered years.

Special features This award was established in 1991 in memory of Elliott Rudwick, professor of history and sociology at Kent State University.

Limitations This prize will be awarded only until 2001.

Number awarded 1 every other year.

Deadline August of even-numbered years.

[1464]
EMIERT/GALE RESEARCH MULTICULTURAL AWARD

American Library Association
Attn: Ethnic Materials Information Exchange Round Table
50 East Huron Street
Chicago, IL 60611-2795
(312) 280-4294   (800) 545-2433, ext. 4294
TDD: (312) 944-7298   Fax: (312) 280-3257
E-mail: sgraves@ala.org

Purpose To recognize and reward significant accomplishments in library service that result in improving, spreading, and promoting multicultural librarianship.

Eligibility Persons in the library world are eligible to be considered for this award if their record demonstrates outstanding achievement and leadership in serving the multicultural community. The emphasis here is multicultural/multiethnic, rather than multilingual (as in the Leonard Wertheimer Multilingual Award).

Financial data The award is $1,000 and a citation.

Duration The competition is held annually, although if no suitable candidate is judged to merit the award in a given year, the award is not presented.

Special features This award was created in 1993. Funds for it are provided by Gale Research Company; selection of recipients is made by the Ethnic Materials Information Exchange Round Table (EMIERT) of the American Library Association. Further information is available from David Cohen at Queens College, NSF 316, Flushing, NY 11367, (718) 997-3626.

Number awarded 1 each year.

Deadline November of each year.

[1465]
EQUALITY AWARD

American Library Association
Attn: Member Programs and Services
50 East Huron Street
Chicago, IL 60611-2795
(312) 280-3247   (800) 545-2433, ext. 3247
TDD: (312) 944-7298   Fax: (312) 280-3256
E-mail: awards@ala.org

Purpose To recognize and reward the person or group that best promotes equality in librarianship.

Eligibility Eligible to be nominated for this award are groups or individuals who have contributed significantly to correcting the inequality that has existed in librarianship, especially between men and women. Nominators are asked to indicate the category that best represents the area in which the nominee has contributed to equality; these include minority concerns, sexual discrimination in librarianship, and comparable worth/pay equity.

Financial data The award is $500 and a certificate.

Duration The award is presented annually.

Special features The award is funded by Scarecrow Press and administered by the American Library Association.

Number awarded 1 each year.

Deadline November of each year.

[1466]
FLORINA LASKER CIVIL LIBERTIES AWARD

New York Civil Liberties Union
132 West 43rd Street
New York, NY 10036
(212) 382-0557   Fax: (212) 354-2583

Purpose To recognize and reward an individual, organization, or group displaying consistent and outstanding courage and integrity in the defense of civil liberties.

Eligibility To be considered for the award, an individual, organization, or group must have demonstrated courage and integrity during the past year in defending civil liberties and, in the process, have made a constructive and significant contribution to the status of civil liberties.

Financial data The award is $1,000.

Duration The award is presented annually.

Number awarded 1 or more each year.

[1467]
FRANKLIN C. MCLEAN AWARD

National Medical Fellowships, Inc.
Attn: Scholarships and Programs
110 West 32nd Street, 8th Floor
New York, NY 10001-3205
(212) 714-1007

Purpose To recognize and reward the outstanding academic achievement, leadership, and community service of senior medical school minority students.

Eligibility This award is open to senior African American, Native American, Mexican American, and mainland Puerto Rican students enrolled in accredited U.S. medical schools. Financial need is not a consideration. Candidates must be nominated by their medical schools during the summer preceding their senior year.

Financial data This honor includes a certificate of merit and a $3,000 award.

Duration 1 year; nonrenewable.

Special features This award, the first award offered by the National Medical Fellowship, was established in 1968 in memory of the Chicago bone physiologist who founded the organization.

Number awarded 1 each year.

Deadline June of each year.

[1468]
GERBER PRIZE FOR EXCELLENCE IN PEDIATRICS

National Medical Fellowships, Inc.
Attn: Scholarships and Programs
110 West 32nd Street, 8th Floor
New York, NY 10001-3205
(212) 714-1007

Purpose To recognize and reward an underrepresented minority medical student who will pursue a career in pediatric medicine.

Eligibility Candidates must be African Americans, Mexican Americans, Native Americans, or mainland Puerto Ricans who are seniors at 1 of the following allopathic medical schools in Michigan: University of Michigan Medical School, Michigan State University School of Human Medicine, Michigan State University College of Osteopathic Medicine, or Wayne State University School of Medicine. They must be nominated by the medical school dean and chair of the department of pediatrics at the medical school in which they are enrolled, be able to demonstrate academic achievement, plan to pursue a career in pediatric medicine, and meet the requirements of pediatric residence programs.

Financial data The award is $2,000.

Duration The competition is held annually.

Special features This award was established in 1990.

Number awarded 1 each year.

Deadline Nominations are due in January of each year.

[1469]
IRENE RYAN ACTING SCHOLARSHIPS

Kennedy Center American College Theater Festival
Attn: Producing Director
Education Department
Kennedy Center
Washington, DC 20566
(202) 416-8857   Fax: (202) 416-8802
E-mail: skshaffer@mail.kennedy-center.org

Purpose To recognize and reward outstanding college performers with scholarships for their continuing education.

Eligibility Eligible are students enrolled in any accredited junior or senior college in the United States or in countries contiguous to the continental United States. Participants must appear as actors in plays produced by their college and entered in 1 of the 8 regional festivals of the Kennedy Center American College Theater Festival (KC/ACTF). From each of the regional festivals, 2 winners and their acting partners are invited to the national festival at the John F. Kennedy Center for the Performing Arts in Washington, D.C. to participate in an "Evening of Scenes." Scholarships are awarded to outstanding student performers at each regional festival and from the "Evening of Scenes."

Financial data Regional winners receive $500 scholarships; national winners receive $2,500 scholarships; the best partner receives a special award. All scholarship monies are paid directly to the institutions designated by the recipients and may be used for any field of study.

Duration The competition is held annually.

Special features These awards have been presented since 1972 by the Irene Ryan Foundation of Encino, California. The national finalists are eligible to receive a fellowship to participate in the National Stage Combat Workshop conducted by the Society of American Fight Directors and to receive a Classical Acting Award of Excellence. Minority national finalists are eligible to receive an apprenticeship to participate in an 11-week workshop at the Williamstown Theatre Festival in the Berkshire Hills of northwestern Massachusetts.

Limitations The sponsoring college or university must pay a registration fee of $250 for each production.

Number awarded The number of regional winners varies each year; at the national festival "Evening of Scenes," 2 performers and 1 best partner receive awards.

Deadline The regional festivals are held in January and February of each year; the national festival is held in April of each year. Application deadlines are set within each region.

[1470]
IRVING GRAEF MEMORIAL SCHOLARSHIP

National Medical Fellowships, Inc.
Attn: Scholarships and Programs
110 West 32nd Street, 8th Floor
New York, NY 10001-3205
(212) 714-1007

Purpose To recognize and reward third-year minority medical school students' outstanding academic achievement, leadership, and community service.

Eligibility This competition is open only to third-year minority medical school students who received financial assistance from National Medical Fellowships during their second year. For the purposes of this program, "minority" is defined as African American, Native American, Mexican American, and mainland Puerto Rican students. Candidates must be able to demonstrate outstanding academic achievement and leadership. They must be nominated by their medical schools in the summer before the students' third year. The Graef family reviews candidates' dossiers and selects the student most deserving of the award.

Financial data This honor includes a certificate of merit and an annual stipend of $2,000.

Duration 1 year; renewable in the fourth year of medical school, if the recipient continues in good academic standing.

Special features This program is named in honor of an active National Medical Fellowship board member who was also an associate professor of clinical medicine at New York University's School of Medicine. It was established in 1978.

Number awarded 1 each year.

Deadline Nominations are usually requested in July of each year.

[1471]
JAMES A. RAWLEY PRIZE

Organization of American Historians
Attn: Award and Prize Committee Coordinator
112 North Bryan Street
Bloomington, IN 47408-4199
(812) 855-7311   Fax: (812) 855-0696
E-mail: oah@indiana.edu

Purpose To recognize and reward outstanding books dealing with race relations in the United States.

Eligibility Books on race relations in America that were published 1 year before the award presentation date are eligible to be considered. A copy of the book must be sent to each member of the selection committee by October (or page proofs, for books published between October and December 31 of that year).

Financial data The award is $750.

Duration The award is presented annually.

Special features The award was established in 1990 in honor of James A. Rawley, Carl Adolph Happold Professor of History-Emeritus at the University of Nebraska-Lincoln.

Number awarded 1 each year.

Deadline September of each year.

[1472]
JAMES H. ROBINSON MEMORIAL PRIZE IN SURGERY

National Medical Fellowships, Inc.
Attn: Scholarships and Programs
110 West 32nd Street, 8th Floor
New York, NY 10001-3205
(212) 714-1007

Purpose To recognize and reward the outstanding performance in surgery of underrepresented minority medical students enrolled in their senior year at accredited medical schools.

Eligibility Only nominations are accepted; students may not apply directly. Nominees must be underrepresented minority students (African American, Native American, Mexican American, or mainland Puerto Rican) attending accredited medical schools in the United States who are graduating during the academic year in which the awards are available. Awards are given for outstanding performance in the surgical disciplines and for overall good academic standing.

Financial data The honor includes a certificate of merit and a $500 award.

Duration The awards are presented annually; they are nonrenewable.

Special features These awards were established in 1986 to honor the memory of James H. Robinson, who was clinical professor of surgery and associate dean of student affairs at Jefferson Medical College of Thomas Jefferson University in Philadelphia.

Number awarded 1 each year.

Deadline Nominations should be submitted in December of each year.

[1473]
JOANNE KATHERINE JOHNSON AWARD FOR UNUSUAL ACHIEVEMENT IN MATHEMATICS OR SCIENCE

A Better Chance, Inc.
Attn: Vice President for Administration and Development
419 Boylston Street
Boston, MA 02116
(617) 421-0950   Fax: (617) 421-0965

Purpose To recognize and reward minority high school students who have excelled in mathematics or science.

Eligibility This award is presented to the ABC (A Better Chance) high school junior who has best demonstrated his or her accomplishment in mathematics or sciences. Only nominations are accepted.

Financial data The award is $500.

Duration The competition is held annually.

Special features A Better Chance, Inc. (ABC) is a national, nonprofit organization serving junior and senior high school minority students and member schools. ABC seeks qualified minority students, from all economic backgrounds and every part of the country, and provides them with access to college preparatory educations at outstanding independent and public schools. Students are admitted to ABC on the basis of academic merit, personal motivation, and promise. As a general rule, nominees are in the top 10 percent of their class and have good academic and personal recommendations. The great majority of students apply to ABC while in the eighth or ninth grade and begin their ABC experience in the ninth or tenth grade.

Number awarded 1 each year.

Deadline March of each year.

[1474]
LEONARD WERTHEIMER MULTILINGUAL AWARD

American Library Association
Attn: Public Library Association
50 East Huron Street
Chicago, IL 60611-2795
(312) 280-5027   (800) 545-2433, ext. 5027
TDD: (312) 944-7298   Fax: (312) 280-3257
E-mail: dwood@ala.org

Purpose To recognize and reward work that enhances, improves, and promotes multilingual public library service.

Eligibility Persons, groups, or organizations may be nominated for this award. The nominee's achievements should represent an outstanding contribution in the area of publications, lectures, programs, or other projects that have been presented in a public library setting and have encouraged the development of multilingual service on a national or international scale.

Financial data The award consists of $1,000 and a plaque.

Duration The award is presented annually.

Special features Funding for this award is provided by the NTC Publishing Group.

Number awarded 1 each year.

Deadline November of each year.

[1475]
LOS ANGELES PHILHARMONIC FELLOWSHIPS FOR EXCELLENCE IN DIVERSITY

Los Angeles Philharmonic
Attn: Education Department
135 North Grand Avenue
Los Angeles, CA 90012
(213) 972-0703

Purpose To identify, nurture, and support talented minority instrumentalists in the southern California area.

Eligibility Applicants must reside (or have parents who reside) in southern California, be between the ages of 16 and 30, and be musicians from historically underrepresented communities: African American, Asian American, Native American, or Latino. Live auditions are required. Applications must include all of the following materials: federal tax form, letter of recommendation from a noted musical authority, a recent photograph, and a brief biographical statement (including career goals).

Financial data Fellowships range from $500 to $2,000; individual awards are determined on the basis of talent and financial circumstances. Funds are to be used to underwrite specific 1-time costs, such as tuition at an accredited institution, travel expenses for audition or solo appearances, instrument purchase, or participation in a summer music festival.

Duration The competition is held annually.

Special features Previous applicants and fellowship winners may reapply.

Number awarded Varies each year.

Deadline April of each year.

[1476]
MARIE F. PETERS ETHNIC MINORITIES OUTSTANDING ACHIEVEMENT AWARD

National Council on Family Relations
3989 Central Avenue, N.E., Suite 550
Minneapolis, MN 55421
(612) 781-9331   Fax: (612) 781-9348

Purpose To recognize and reward minorities who have made significant contributions to the research on ethnic minority families.

Eligibility Members of the National Council on Family Relations (NCFR) who have demonstrated excellence in the area of ethnic minority families are eligible for this award. Selection is based on leadership, scholarship, research, publication, teaching and community service, contribution to the ethnic minorities section, and contribution to the NCFR.

Financial data The award is $500.

Duration The award is granted biennially, in even-numbered years.

Special features This award, which was established in 1984, is named after a prominent Black researcher and family sociologist who served in many leadership roles in NCFR. It is sponsored by the Ethnic Minorities Section of NCFR.

Number awarded 1 every other year.

Deadline April of even-numbered years.

[1477]
METROPOLITAN LIFE FOUNDATION AWARDS PROGRAM FOR ACADEMIC EXCELLENCE IN MEDICINE

National Medical Fellowships, Inc.
Attn: Scholarships and Programs
110 West 32nd Street, 8th Floor
New York, NY 10001-3205
(212) 714-1007

Purpose To provide financial assistance to underrepresented minority medical students.

Eligibility Students must be nominated by their medical school deans. They must be 1) African American, mainland Puerto Rican, Mexican American, or Native American medical students in their second or third year, 2) enrolled in medical schools located in (or residents of) the following cities only: Phoenix, Arizona; San Francisco, California; Los Angeles, California; Denver, Colorado; Washington, D.C.; Miami, Florida; Tampa/St. Petersburg, Florida; Atlanta, Georgia; Aurora/Chicago, Illinois; Wichita, Kansas; Boston, Massachusetts; St. Louis, Missouri; Metropolitan New York, New York (including northern New Jersey and lower Connecticut); Tulsa, Oklahoma; Philadelphia, Pennsylvania; Pittsburgh, Pennsylvania; Scranton, Pennsylvania; Warwick/Providence, Rhode Island; Greenville, South Carolina; Austin, Texas; Dallas/Fort Worth, Texas; or Houston, Texas; and 3) able to demonstrate financial need, outstanding academic achievement, leadership, and potential for distinguished contributions to medicine.

Financial data The stipend is $3,500.

Duration 1 year; nonrenewable.

Special features The funding for this program is provided by the Metropolitan Life Foundation of New York, New York.

Number awarded Up to 14 each year.

Deadline Nominations are requested in August of each year.

[1478]
MISSOURI LIFESTYLE AWARDS FOR REPORTING

Missouri School of Journalism
Ninth and Elm
281 Gannett
Columbia, MO 65211
(573) 882-7771   Fax: (573) 882-9002

Purpose To recognize and reward the most outstanding reporting in features journalism.

Eligibility Newspaper reporters (staff or local freelance) may enter this competition in the categories of single story, series or special section, arts and entertainment, short feature, consumer affairs, fashion and design, food and nutrition, health and fitness, or multicultural journalism. Entries may not exceed 1,000 words and must have been published during the preceding contest year. Reporters may enter more than 1 category or more than 1 article in any category. Entries may come from any section of the paper, but the emphasis is on feature reporting and writing. Selection is based on thoroughness of research, organization, readability, style, news value, impact, and service to the reader.

Financial data The prizes are $1,000.

Duration The awards are presented annually.

Limitations Submissions must include a $20 entry fee for each entry ($30 for series/special sections).

Number awarded 9 each year: 1 for each category.

Deadline January of each year.

[1479]
NATIONAL ASSOCIATION FOR BILINGUAL EDUCATION OUTSTANDING DISSERTATIONS OF THE YEAR COMPETITION

National Association for Bilingual Education
Attn: Chair, Outstanding Dissertations Competition
Maricopa Community Colleges
2411 West 14th Street
Tempe, AZ 85281-6941
(602) 731-8101 Fax: (602) 731-8111

Purpose To recognize and reward dissertations that make significant contributions to knowledge in the bilingual education field.

Eligibility The competition is open to those who have completed doctoral dissertations in the field of bilingual education up to 3 years prior to submission. Studies using any research approach (historical, experimental, survey, etc.) are eligible for consideration. Selection is based on the appropriateness of the research approach used, the scholarly quality of the dissertation, and the significance of its contribution to knowledge in the bilingual education field.

Financial data Semifinalists receive certificates of recognition and finalists receive travel expenses and per diem to the annual convention, at which they are honored.

Duration The award is presented annually.

Number awarded There are 2 types of winners: 1) 7 to 10 semifinalists who are the writers of the top abstracts from which the 3 finalists are selected; 2) 3 finalists, who are the writers of the dissertations and placed as first, second, or third place winners.

Deadline September of each year.

[1480]
NELSON MANDELA AWARD FOR HEALTH AND HUMAN RIGHTS

Henry J. Kaiser Family Foundation
2400 Sand Hill Road
Menlo Park, CA 94025
(415) 854-9400 Fax: (415) 854-4800

Purpose To recognize and reward extraordinary accomplishments in improving the health of disadvantaged people in the United States and South Africa.

Eligibility Individuals in the United States and in South Africa may be nominated for this award if they have contributed to improving the health care of disadvantaged people in the 2 countries.

Financial data The award of a trophy bearing a likeness of President Mandela, a grant of up to $10,000 to be used to fund organizations committed to the goals of the award, and support for a program of travel and technical exchange between the 2 countries.

Special features The first of these awards was presented in 1993. In recent years, the award ceremonies have been held in Cape Town, South Africa, and President Mandela himself has presented the awards.

Number awarded 2 each year: 1 to a citizen of the United States and 1 to a South African.

[1481]
NORTH AMERICAN NATIVE AUTHORS FIRST BOOK AWARDS

Greenfield Review Literary Center
2 Middle Grove Road
P.O. Box 308
Greenfield Center, NY 12833
(518) 884-1728

Purpose To recognize and reward outstanding new Native American writers.

Eligibility This award is given to Native Americans (American Indian, Aleut, Inuit, or Metis ancestry) who have not yet published a book. Candidates are invited to submit between 48 and 100 pages of poetry or between 120 and 240 pages of prose (including nonfiction, essays, autobiography, historical writing, short stories, a novella, or a single unified work of creative fiction). Writers may be from any part of North America, including Mexico and Central America.

Financial data Each award is $500. The winning author's manuscript is published by Greenfield Review Press.

Duration The award is granted annually.

Number awarded 2 each year: 1 for prose and 1 for poetry.

Deadline April of each year.

[1482]
PAUL TOBENKIN MEMORIAL AWARD

Columbia University
Attn: Graduate School of Journalism
2950 Broadway
New York, NY 10027-7004
(212) 854-5984

Purpose To recognize and reward outstanding newspaper writing that reflects the spirit of Paul Tobenkin, who fought all his life against racial and religious hatred, bigotry, bias, intolerance, and discrimination.

Eligibility Materials reflecting the spirit of Paul Tobenkin may be submitted by newspaper reporters in the United States, editors of their publications, or interested third parties. The items submitted must have been published during the previous calendar year in a weekly or daily newspaper.

Financial data The award is $250, plus a certificate.

Duration The award is granted annually.

Number awarded 1 to 3 each year.

Deadline February of each year.

[1483]
RALPH J. BUNCHE AWARD

American Political Science Association
1527 New Hampshire Avenue, N.W.
Washington, DC 20036
(202) 483-2512 Fax: (207) 483-2657
E-mail: incem023@sivm.si.edu

Purpose To recognize and reward an outstanding scholarly work on ethnic/cultural pluralism.

Eligibility Eligible to be nominated (by publishers or individuals) are scholarly books issued the previous year that explore issues of ethnic and/or cultural pluralism.

Financial data The award is $500.

Duration The competition is held annually.

Number awarded 1 each year.

Deadline February of each year.

[1484]
RALPH W. ELLISON PRIZE

National Medical Fellowships, Inc.
Attn: Scholarships and Programs
110 West 32nd Street, 8th Floor
New York, NY 10001-3205
(212) 714-1007

Purpose To recognize and reward an outstanding graduating underrepresented medical student.

Eligibility This award is open to senior African American, Native American, Mexican American, and mainland Puerto Rican students enrolled in accredited U.S. medical schools. Candidates must be nominated by their medical schools during their senior year. Selection is based on academic achievement, leadership, community service, and potential to make significant contributions to medicine.

Financial data This honor includes a certificate of merit and a $500 stipend.

Duration 1 year; nonrenewable.

Special features This award was established in 1994 to honor Ralph W. Ellison, the novelist and author of *The Invisible Man* who co-chaired a fund-raising effort of National Medical Fellowships, Inc.

Number awarded 1 each year.

Deadline Nominations are requested in January of each year.

[1485]
ROBERT F. KENNEDY BOOK AWARDS

Robert F. Kennedy Memorial
1206 30th Street, N.W.
Washington, DC 20007
(202) 333-1880, ext. 229   Fax: (202) 333-4903
E-mail: rfkmem@igc.apc.org

Purpose To recognize and reward the best book of fiction or nonfiction that most faithfully reflects Robert Kennedy's purposes.

Eligibility Works of fiction and nonfiction written during the past year may be submitted for consideration if they address Kennedy's concern for the poor and the powerless, his struggle for honest and even-handed justice, his conviction that a decent society must assure all young people a fair chance, and his faith that a free democracy can act to remedy disparities of power and opportunity. There is no limit to the number of entries submitted by a publishing house or an individual.

Financial data The award is $2,500.

Duration The award is presented annually.

Limitations Each book must be submitted in quadruplicate. Each entry must be accompanied by a $25 handling fee. A descriptive cover letter or press release must also accompany each book.

Number awarded 1 each year.

Deadline December of each year.

[1486]
ROBERT F. KENNEDY JOURNALISM AWARDS

Robert F. Kennedy Memorial
1206 30th Street, N.W.
Washington, DC 20007
(202) 333-1880   Fax: (202) 333-4903
E-mail: rfkmem@igc.apc.org

Purpose To recognize and reward works of journalism and photojournalism that best reflect Robert F. Kennedy's concern for the disadvantaged.

Eligibility To be eligible, entries must have been published or broadcast in the United States for the first time during the year preceding the award. They must address the life styles, handicaps or potentialities of the disadvantaged in the United States; provide insights into the causes, conditions, or remedies of their plight; or present critical analyses of public policies, programs, attitudes, or private endeavors relevant to their lives. Entries may be submitted either by individuals or by appropriate media organizations. Awards are made in 6 professional categories of journalistic coverage: print (newspaper, magazine), cartoons, television, radio, photojournalism, and international; a separate student competition for college undergraduates only is open to print, broadcast, and photojournalism students.

Financial data A cash prize of $1,000 may be awarded to the entry judged most outstanding in each category. A grand prize of $2,000 may be awarded to the most outstanding of the 6 category winners.

Duration The awards are presented annually.

Limitations An entry fee of $20 is required for professional categories; no entry fee for students is required.

Number awarded Varies; up to 6 category awards and 1 grand prize each year.

Deadline January of each year.

[1487]
SIDNEY HILLMAN FOUNDATION PRIZE AWARDS

Sidney Hillman Foundation
1710 Broadway
New York, NY 10019
(212) 265-7000, ext. 365

Purpose To recognize and reward outstanding contributions dealing with themes relating to the ideals that Sidney Hillman held throughout his life and expressed in his works.

Eligibility Contributions in the fields of daily or periodical journalism, nonfiction, radio, or television will be considered if the works deal with at least 1 of the following themes: improved race relations, protection of individual civil liberties, a strengthened labor movement, the advancement of social welfare and economic security, or greater world understanding. Radio and television contributions must have been produced under professional auspices in the previous calendar year. No unpublished manuscripts are eligible for consideration. Material may be submitted by the author, the publisher, or anyone else connected with it.

Financial data The award is $1,000.

Duration The prize is awarded annually.

Number awarded Varies; generally up to 7 each year.

Deadline January of each year.

[1488]
TEACHER INCENTIVE AWARDS

Anti-Defamation League
Attn: A World of Difference Institute
126 High Street
Boston, MA 02110
(617) 457-8800   Fax: (617) 988-6244

Purpose To recognize and reward teachers in New England who develop exemplary programs to heighten awareness and appreciation of diversity.

Eligibility These awards are presented to current employees of school systems in New England who are involved in addressing issues of multiculturalism and diversity in a school setting and are willing to share their teaching strategies with others. Applicants may be either self-nominated or nominated by others. Their programs or creative strategies should establish a learning environment in which 1) human diversity is acknowledged and made an integral part of the learning process; 2) students and staff interact cooperatively to gain a greater understanding of a diverse world; 3) intergroup understanding and harmony are valued and visible goals; and 4) all students are enabled to reach their potential successfully.

Financial data The award is $500 and an engraved medallion.

Duration The awards are presented annually.

Special features This program began in 1985 during a time of racial, religious, and ethnic tensions in Boston.

Number awarded 10 each year.

Deadline December of each year.

[1489]
WILLIAM AND CHARLOTTE CADBURY AWARD

National Medical Fellowships, Inc.
Attn: Scholarships and Programs
110 West 32nd Street, 8th Floor
New York, NY 10001-3205
(212) 714-1007

Purpose To recognize and reward minority medical school students' outstanding academic achievement, leadership, and community service.

Eligibility This award is open to minority students enrolled in their senior year at an accredited U.S. medical school. For the purposes of this program, "minority" is defined as African American, Native American, Mexican American, and mainland Puerto Rican students. Financial need is not a consideration. Candidates must be nominated by their medical school during the summer preceding their senior year.

Financial data This honor includes a certificate of merit and a $2,000 stipend.

Duration 1 year; nonrenewable.

Special features This award was established in 1977.

Number awarded 1 each year.

Deadline Nominations are usually requested in June of each year.

Internships

American Indians ●
Native Alaskans ●
Native Americans in General ●

Described here are 287 work experience programs open to undergraduate, graduate, or postgraduate Native Americans. Only salaried positions are covered. Of the programs listed here, 258 are open to all Native Americans equally, and the remainder are set aside for American Indians and Native Alaskans. If you are looking for a particular program and don't find it in this section, be sure to check the Program Title Index to see if it is covered elsewhere in the directory.

American Indians

[1490]
ALL INDIAN PUEBLO COUNCIL JOBS TRAINING PARTNERSHIP ACT

All Indian Pueblo Council, Inc.
Attn: JTPA Department
3939 San Pedro NE, Suite D
P.O. Box 3256
Albuquerque, NM 87190
(505) 884-3820   Fax: (505) 883-7682

Purpose To provide employment and training to selected Pueblo Indians.

Eligibility Eligible to apply are enrolled and verified members of the Isleta and San Felipe Pueblos who are unemployed, underemployed, or economically disadvantaged.

Financial data Tuition and other services are offered to recipients.

Duration Up to 1 year.

Special features This program provides short-term employment within the pueblo work force for eligible individuals, as well as vocational training.

[1491]
ALL INDIAN PUEBLO COUNCIL SUMMER YOUTH EMPLOYMENT PROGRAM

All Indian Pueblo Council, Inc.
Attn: JTPA Department
3939 San Pedro NE, Suite D
P.O. Box 3256
Albuquerque, NM 87190
(505) 884-3820   Fax: (505) 883-7682

Purpose To provide summer employment to Pueblo Indian youth.

Eligibility Eligible to apply are disadvantaged youth aged 14 through 21 who are members of the Isleta or San Felipe Pueblos. Applicants must meet an income criteria set by the U.S. Department of Labor.

Financial data Paid employment on the pueblos is provided.

Duration 1 summer.

[1492]
AMERICAN INDIAN MUSEUM STUDIES PROGRAM

Smithsonian Institution
Attn: Center for Museum Studies
Arts and Industries Building, Suite 2235
MRC 427
Washington, DC 20560
(202) 357-3101   Fax: (202) 357-3346
E-mail: ompem004@sivm.si.edu

Purpose To promote and assist Native Americans in the continuation and interpretation of tribal cultures as they define them.

Eligibility Native Americans working in tribal museums and American Indian cultural centers are eligible to participate in workshops and seminars conducted as part of this program.

Financial data Participants in the workshops and seminars receive a tuition waiver for the course and a scholarship to help defray travel and subsistence expenses.

Duration Most seminars last 3 to 5 days.

Special features This program also recruits American Indians and Alaska Natives who are currently enrolled in a higher education program or who are currently employed in a field related to museum work or cultural programming to participate in the Museum Intern Partnership Program of the Smithsonian's Center for Museum Studies. It also produces publications and technical assistance which provide additional resources not available elsewhere for the enrichment of Native American museums and cultural centers.

Number awarded Varies each year.

Deadline The seminars and workshops, of which 4 or 5 are held each year at native communities throughout the United States and Canada, each set their own deadline dates.

[1493]
BECHTEL UNDERGRADUATE FELLOWSHIP AWARD

National Action Council for Minorities in Engineering
3 West 35th Street
New York, NY 10001-2281
(212) 279-2626   Fax: (212) 629-5178

Purpose To provide financial assistance for education in construction engineering to underrepresented minority students.

Eligibility Engineering students who are African American, Latino, or American Indian are eligible for this award. Candidates must be sophomores with a minimum grade point average of 3.0 nominated by their deans. Selection is based on high academic achievement and interest in a corporate career in construction engineering.

Financial data The stipend is $5,000 per year.

Duration 2 years.

Special features Funding for this program is provided by the Bechtel Foundation. Fellows also receive an internship and a mentor.

Number awarded 1 each year.

[1494]
CERT SUMMER TRIBAL INTERNSHIP PROGRAM

Council of Energy Resource Tribes
Attn: Student Services Coordinator
1999 Broadway, Suite 2600
Denver, CO 80202-5726
(303) 297-2378   Fax: (303) 296-5690

Purpose To offer work opportunities to Native American college students who are interested in the scientific, technical, or policy areas.

Eligibility This program is open to Native American undergraduate or graduate students who are interested in working with senior Council of Energy Resource Tribes (CERT) staff, tribal leaders, and host companies on technical and scientific issues, policies, and projects (in such areas as energy and natural resource development, environmental protection, and economic development).

Financial data The internship provides round-trip transportation, housing, and a salary of $10 an hour.

Duration 10 weeks in the summer; may be renewed for subsequent summers.

Special features As project team members, interns have an opportunity to become acquainted with the range of issues that impact tribes. The internship emphasizes the interplay between science, technology, policy, tribal governance, and the preservation of cultural integrity in every aspect of work being conducted. In the past, intern projects have included work on water pollution source analysis, tribal/state solid waste management systems, tribal water quality studies, U.S. Department of Defense environmental analysis systems research, integrated pest management systems, tribal air quality management and regulatory issues, hazardous waste operations training, biodiversity, and hazardous waste transportation routes in Indian Country. Interns divide their time between CERT headquarters and a sponsoring organization.
Deadline March of each year.

[1495]
CERT YEAR-LONG INTERNSHIP

Council of Energy Resource Tribes
Attn: Student Services Coordinator
1999 Broadway, Suite 2600
Denver, CO 80202-5726
(303) 297-2378 Fax: (303) 296-5690

Purpose To provide work experience to Indian undergraduate and graduate students at the offices of the Council of Energy Resource Tribes (CERT).

Eligibility Former participants in the CERT Summer Tribal Intern Program as well as other Indian undergraduate and graduate students may apply for these internships. Students are encouraged to continue their respective academic pursuits at the same time they are working as interns.

Financial data Interns receive a salary of $10 per hour for 30 hours a week.

Duration 1 year.

Special features Interns work along side CERT technical staff in Denver to broaden their technical training in a professional environment. Prior intern projects have focused on tribal/state solid waste management systems, tribal water quality studies, renewable energy resources, integrated pest management systems, hazardous waste management, and construction of natural gas compressors.

[1496]
CULTURALLY DIVERSE INSTITUTIONS UNDERGRADUATE STUDENT FELLOWSHIPS

Environmental Protection Agency
Attn: Office of Research and Development
National Center for Environmental Research and Quality
  Assurance
401 M Street, S.W.
Washington, DC 20460
(800) 490-9194

Purpose To provide financial assistance to students in culturally diverse 4-year colleges who are interested in majoring in fields related to the environment.

Eligibility Applicants for this program must be U.S. citizens or permanent residents who are enrolled full time with a minimum grade point average of 3.0 in a 4-year accredited institution that meets the definition of the Environmental Protection Agency (EPA) as a culturally diverse institution: Historically Black Colleges and Universities (HBCUs), members of the Hispanic Association of Colleges and Universities (HACU), and members of the Ameri-

can Indian Consortium for Higher Education (AICHE). Students must be majoring in environmental science, physical sciences, biological sciences, computer science, environmental health, social sciences, mathematics, or engineering. They must be available to work as interns at an EPA facility during the summer between their junior and senior years.

Financial data The fellowship provides payment of tuition and fees, an annual book allowance of $250, and an annual stipend of $1,125. During the summer internship, students receive up to $600 in relocation support and up to $5,000 as a stipend to cover living expenses.

Duration 2 years: the final 2 years of baccalaureate study, including 12 weeks during the summer between those years.

Special features This program began in 1982.

Number awarded Approximately 25 each year.

Deadline February of each year.

[1497]
GEM M.S. ENGINEERING FELLOWSHIP PROGRAM

National Consortium for Graduate Degrees for Minorities in
  Engineering and Science (GEM)
P.O. Box 537
Notre Dame, IN 46556
(219) 631-7778 Fax: (219) 287-1486
E-mail: GEM.1@nd.edu

Purpose To provide financial assistance to minority graduate students in engineering with fellowships and paid summer internships.

Eligibility Criteria for selection are: American citizenship; specific ethnicity—those ethnic minorities underrepresented in the engineering profession: American Indians, Black Americans, Mexican Americans, Puerto Ricans, and other Hispanic Americans; enrolled as at least a junior in an accredited engineering discipline with a minimum grade point average of 2.8; and an academic record that indicates the ability to pursue graduate studies in engineering. Recipients must attend 1 of the 75 GEM member universities that offer a master's degree.

Financial data The fellowship pays tuition and fees and a stipend of $6,000 per academic year. In addition, each participant receives a salary during the summer work assignment as a GEM Summer Intern, making the value of the total award between $20,000 and $40,000. Employer members reimburse GEM participants for travel expenses to and from the summer work site.

Duration Up to 3 semesters or 4 quarters, plus a summer work internship lasting 10 to 14 weeks for up to 3 summers, depending on whether the student applies as a junior, senior, or college graduate; recipients begin their internship upon acceptance into the program and work each summer until completion of their master's degree.

Special features During the summer internship, each fellow is assigned an engineering project in a research setting. Each project is based on the fellow's interest and background and is carried out under the supervision of an experienced engineer. At the conclusion of the internship, each fellow writes a project report.

Limitations Recipients must seek the master's degree in the same engineering discipline as their baccalaureate degree.

Number awarded More than 200 each year.

Deadline November of each year.

[1498]
GEM PH.D. SCIENCE FELLOWSHIP PROGRAM

National Consortium for Graduate Degrees for Minorities in
 Engineering and Science (GEM)
P.O. Box 537
Notre Dame, IN 46556
(219) 631-7778   Fax: (219) 287-1486
E-mail: GEM.1@nd.edu

Purpose To provide opportunities for minority students to
obtain a Ph.D. degree in the natural sciences (chemistry, physics,
earth sciences, mathematics, biological sciences, and computer
sciences).

Eligibility Criteria for selection include: American citizenship;
specific ethnicity underrepresented in the natural sciences—American Indians, Black Americans, Mexican Americans,
Puerto Ricans, and other Hispanic Americans; enrolled as at least
a junior in an accredited science discipline with a minimum grade
point average of 3.0; and an academic record that indicates the
ability to pursue doctoral studies in the natural sciences.

Financial data The stipend is $12,000 per year, plus tuition
and fees. In addition, there is a summer internship program that
provides a salary and reimbursement for travel expenses to and
from the summer work site. The total value of the award is
between $60,000 and $100,000, depending upon academic status at time of application, summer employer, and graduate school
attended.

Duration 3 to 5 years for the fellowship; 12 weeks for at least
1 summer for the internship. Fellows selected as juniors or
seniors intern each summer until entrance to graduate school; fellows selected after college graduation intern at least 1 summer.

Special features This program is valid only at 1 of 53 participating GEM member universities; for a list, write to the address
above. The fellowship award is designed to support the student
in the first year of the doctoral program without working. Subsequent years are subsidized by the respective university and will
usually include either a teaching or research assistantship.

Limitations Recipients must participate in the GEM summer
internship; failure to agree to accept the internship cancels the
fellowship. Recipients must enroll in the same scientific discipline
as their undergraduate major.

Number awarded Varies; approximately 30 each year.

Deadline November of each year.

[1499]
HEADLANDS INDIAN HEALTH CAREERS COUNSELOR GRANTS

University of Oklahoma Health Sciences Center
Basic Sciences Education Building, Room 200
P.O. Box 26901
Oklahoma City, OK 73190-3040
(405) 271-2250   Fax: (405) 271-2254

Purpose To provide experience as tutors in a program
designed to enhance the science and mathematics background
and communication skills of Native American students interested
in preparing for careers as health professionals.

Eligibility The Headlands Indian Health Careers program is an
intensive academic enrichment and reinforcement program consisting of mini-block courses in biology, chemistry, physics, calculus, writing, and other communication skills. Courses are
designed to increase the students' background and skills so they
are better prepared for required college-level math and science
course work in pre-health programs. Counselors for the program

should be upperclassmen majoring in language arts, mathematics, science, or health-related careers or be health professional
students. They should have maintained a 3.0 grade point average
and be able to tutor in at least 1 of the following subjects: beginning calculus, biology, chemistry, physics, or writing skills. Indian
applicants indicate their tribal affiliation; other applicants are also
considered.

Financial data Each counselor is provided with free room and
board during the program, as well as round-trip airfare and a stipend of $1,600.

Duration 8 weeks during the summer.

Special features The Headlands program is held on the campus of the University of Oklahoma in Norman.

Number awarded Varies each year.

Deadline March of each year.

[1500]
MAINE ARTS COMMISSION TRADITIONAL ARTS APPRENTICESHIP PROGRAM

Maine Arts Commission
55 Capitol Street
State House Station 25
Augusta, ME 04333-0025
(207) 287-2724   Fax: (207) 287-2335
TDD: (207) 287-5622

Purpose To provide an opportunity for Native American and
other artists in Maine to share their skills with and train qualified
apprentices.

Eligibility This program is open to master artists who are residents of Maine and practice a significant and/or endangered traditional art form in the state. Traditional arts are defined as artistic
practices that reflect a community's share cultural heritage and
are learned in an informal way, usually through example rather
than through academic or institutional means. Special emphasis
is given to artists who are members of the Native American and
Acadian communities in Maine. Apprentices should be from the
same ethnic, religious, occupational, or familial group as the master artist. Both master and apprentice must be legal Maine residents, be 18 years of age or older, and have resided in Maine for
at least 183 of the past 365 days.

Financial data Funds are available for the master artist's
teaching fee, apprentices' supplies and travel costs, and documentation of the apprenticeship.

Duration 1 year.

Special features Master artists and apprentices work together
on a one-to-one basis. The work may be in crafts, dance, or
music.

Number awarded Varies each year.

Deadline August of each year.

[1501]
MIT LINCOLN LABORATORY SUMMER MINORITY INTERNSHIP PROGRAM

Massachusetts Institute of Technology
Lincoln Laboratory
Attn: Paul F. Hezel
244 Wood Street
Lexington, MA 02173-9108
(617) 981-7048

Purpose To offer graduate and undergraduate minority students the opportunity to improve their engineering and scientific

skills, supplement their academic course work, and gain unique hands-on work experience.

Eligibility To be eligible, applicants must have completed their sophomore year in college; be majoring in electrical engineering, computer science, or applied physics; be interested in a research career; be able to demonstrate excellent academic performance; and be American citizens. This program is specifically for minorities underrepresented in engineering and science careers, i.e., African Americans, American Indians, Mexican Americans, and Puerto Ricans.

Financial data Program participants receive weekly salaries, housing on the MIT campus, round-trip travel to the Boston area, and daily round-trip transportation between the MIT campus and the laboratory.

Duration 10 weeks during the summer, from early June through mid-August. Students who receive successful work and course evaluations, maintain excellent academic averages at their home institutions, and continue to pursue a degree in electrical engineering, computer science, or physics will be reappointed for successive summers.

Special features The program was established in 1975. Participants have access to the extensive athletic facilities on the MIT campus. Participants who are admitted to MIT after college are eligible to receive substantial support for their graduate education.

Deadline February of each year.

[1502]
MUSEUM INTERN PARTNERSHIP PROGRAM

Smithsonian Institution
Attn: Center for Museum Studies
Arts and Industries Building, Suite 2235
MRC 427
Washington, DC 20560
(202) 357-3101   Fax: (202) 357-3346
E-mail: ompem004@sivm.si.edu

Purpose To promote the professional growth and development of students from culturally diverse backgrounds who are interested in pursuing museum careers.

Eligibility Students and current employees in a field related to museum work or cultural programming are eligible to apply for these internships. The Vincent Wilkinson Endowment Fund recruits students from traditionally Black colleges, as well as colleges and universities close to African American museums and historical sites. The American Indian Museum Studies program (also part of the Smithsonian's Center for Museum Programs) recruits students and museum employees, who are nominated by their tribes to work on a project that is mutually beneficial to both the Smithsonian and the tribe. Selection of interns is based on a demonstrated interest in pursuing a career in a museum or community-based cultural institution; appropriateness of the project to the applicant's stated career goals; evidence that the candidate will contribute to the work of the hosting museums; and evidence of lack of access to training or other internship programs.

Financial data Interns receive round-trip transportation to the hosting museums and a weekly stipend of $350.

Duration 4 months.

Special features Interns selected to participate in this program work at both the Smithsonian and at smaller, African American and Native American community-focused museums around the country.

Number awarded Varies each year.
Deadline February of each year.

[1503]
NACME CORPORATE SCHOLARS PROGRAM

National Action Council for Minorities in Engineering
3 West 35th Street
New York, NY 10001-2281
(212) 279-2626   Fax: (212) 629-5178

Purpose To support exceptional underrepresented minority students in preparing for careers at the frontier of engineering technology.

Eligibility This program is open to African Americans, Latinos, and American Indians who are currently enrolled full time in an undergraduate engineering program, are U.S. citizens or permanent residents, and have demonstrated engineering leadership potential.

Financial data This program provides students with scholarships of up to $5,000 per year, depending on their financial need, and paid internships.

Duration 1 year; may be renewed if recipients maintain at least a 2.5 grade point average.

Special features This program also offers R&D work experience, academic and career mentoring, summer internships, and professional development opportunities. The National Action Council for Minorities in Engineering (NACME) supports corporate mentors with a broad range of appropriate training. Recipients attend a leadership development seminar, the cost of which is underwritten by sponsoring companies. The program was started in 1991.

Number awarded Varies; generally, more than 60 each year.

[1504]
NMAI CONSERVATION INTERNSHIPS

National Museum of the American Indian
Smithsonian Institution
Attn: Chief Conservator, Research Branch
3401 Bruckner Boulevard
Bronx, NY 10461
(212) 825-4496

Purpose To provide an educational opportunity for Native American students in the area of conservation at the Research Branch of the National Museum of the American Indian (NMAI).

Eligibility These internships are intended primarily for American Indian and Alaska Native graduate students currently enrolled in a program in conservation or undergraduates planning to go on to a graduate program in conservation. Applicants must be interested in working in the Research Branch of the NMAI in the Bronx, New York.

Financial data These are stipended positions.

Duration 12 months.

Number awarded 2 each year: 1 graduate student and 1 undergraduate.

[1505]
NMAI INTERNSHIP PROGRAM

National Museum of the American Indian
Smithsonian Institution
Attn: Intern Coordinator
470 L'Enfant Plaza, Suite 7103
MRC 934
Washington, DC 20560
(202) 287-2020   E-mail: alyce@ic.si.edu

Purpose To provide an educational opportunity for Native American students in the area of museum practice and related programming through guided work and/or research experience at the National Museum of the American Indian (NMAI).

Eligibility These internships are intended primarily for American Indian and Alaska Native students currently enrolled in undergraduate or graduate academic programs, although recent college graduates are also eligible. Applicants must be prepared to work either in Washington D.C. (at the executive and staff offices of the National Museum of the American Indian or at other Smithsonian Institution facilities) or in New York (at the George Gustav Heye Center in Manhattan or the research branch of the National Museum of the American Indian in the Bronx). Completed applications include a statement by the students indicating their interest in the museum field, why they wish to intern at the National Museum of the American Indian, and how the internship will contribute to their academic goals or professional development. Selection is based on potential to make a contribution to the museum, potential for education or career to benefit from an internship, and strong interest in the museum field.

Financial data The total stipend is $3,000; round-trip travel and housing may also be provided.

Duration 8 to 10 weeks, during the summer.

Special features Museum departments assign projects that interns are expected to complete. The average work week is 40 hours.

Number awarded 6 each year.

Deadline February of each year.

[1506]
ONEIDA INTERNSHIP

Oneida Nation of Wisconsin
Attn: Higher Education Office
P.O. Box 365
Oneida, WI 54155-0365
(414) 869-4333   (800) 236-2214, ext. 4333
Fax: (414) 869-4039

Purpose To provide work experience to members of the Oneida Tribe of Wisconsin.

Eligibility Applicants must be enrolled members of the Oneida Tribe of Wisconsin who are attending accredited colleges or universities as full-time students with a minimum grade point average of 2.0. Participants work for the Oneida Nation of Wisconsin in a capacity that is consistent with their interests and career goals. Applicants are accepted on a first come priority as long as funds are available.

Financial data The wage is determined by the Human Resource Department and the Education Department based upon the job description.

Duration Up to 400 hours.

Special features Interns may obtain credit by arrangement with their college.

Number awarded Varies each year.

Deadline Applications may be submitted at any time.

[1507]
ONEIDA TRIBE/RADISSON INN SCHOLARSHIP

Oneida Nation of Wisconsin
Attn: Higher Education Office
P.O. Box 365
Oneida, WI 54155-0365
(414) 869-4333   (800) 236-2214, ext. 4333
Fax: (414) 869-4039

Purpose To provide financial assistance to members of the Oneida Tribe who are enrolled in an accredited hospitality management program.

Eligibility Applicants must enrolled members of the Oneida Tribe of Wisconsin who are attending a 4-year college or university in a hotel/restaurant management program.

Financial data The stipend is $1,000.

Duration 1 year.

Special features Funds for this program are provided by the Radisson Inn.

Limitations An internship is required as part of the program.

Number awarded 5 each year.

Deadline July of each year for fall term; October of each year for spring term.

[1508]
PHILIP D. REED UNDERGRADUATE FELLOWSHIP IN ENVIRONMENTAL ENGINEERING

National Action Council for Minorities in Engineering
3 West 35th Street
New York, NY 10001-2281
(212) 279-2626   Fax: (212) 629-5178

Purpose To provide financial assistance for education in environmental engineering to underrepresented minority students.

Eligibility Engineering sophomores who are African American, Latino, or American Indian are eligible to be nominated by their deans for this award. Selection is based on high academic achievement and interest in environmental engineering.

Financial data The stipend is $5,000 per year.

Duration 1 year; may be renewed for 1 additional year if the recipient maintains a minimum grade point average of 3.0.

Special features Funding for this program, which began in 1996, is provided by the Philip D. Reed Foundation. The program may include internships, mentors, and undergraduate research.

Number awarded 1 or 2 each year.

[1509]
QEM NETWORK INTERNSHIPS

Quality Education for Minorities (QEM) Network
1818 N Street, N.W., Suite 350
Washington, DC 20036
(202) 659-1818   Fax: (202) 659-5408
E-mail: qemnetwork@qem.org

Purpose To provide underrepresented minority students with an opportunity to work at Quality Education for Minorities (QEM) to further develop their leadership potential and to enhance their awareness of major issues related to the education of minorities.

Eligibility This program is open to African Americans, Alaska Natives, American Indians, Mexican Americans, and Puerto

Ricans who have successfully completed at least the sophomore year in an accredited, degree-granting institution. Applicants must be interested in 1) pursuing a post-baccalaureate degree; 2) assuming a leadership role at their college/university; and 3) participating in community activities to influence national state, or local policy as it relates to the education of minorities. Students are eligible if they are studying any area, but preference is given to majors in business administration, computer science, economics, education, engineering, life or physical sciences, political science, or public policy.

Financial data The stipend is $3,000 for undergraduates and $4,000 for graduate students. Other benefits include round-trip fare between home or school and Washington, D.C. and housing for all interns who are not from the Washington, D.C. metropolitan area.

Duration 10 weeks, during the summer.

Special features Assignments may involve areas such as community outreach, program planning and evaluation, education policy analysis, data collection and analysis, network communications, and the preparation of background papers on major education issues and their implications for the education of minorities.

Limitations Interns are also expected to become involved in an academic year project at their home institutions. Each intern must identify a faculty advisor and define a specific project that provides quality educational experiences for low-income, minority students; interns prepare a written description of the follow-up project, an interim progress report, and a final report on the outcome of the project.

Number awarded Varies each year.

Deadline February of each year.

[1510]
QEM SCIENCE STUDENT INTERNSHIPS

Quality Education for Minorities (QEM) Network
1818 N Street, N.W., Suite 350
Washington, DC 20036
(202) 659-1818   Fax: (202) 659-5408
E-mail: qemnetwork@qem.org

Purpose To provide underrepresented minority students with an opportunity to work with agencies and organizations involved in making science policy.

Eligibility This program is open to African Americans, Alaska Natives, American Indians, Mexican Americans, and Puerto Ricans who have successfully completed at least the sophomore year in an accredited, degree-granting institution. Applicants must be 1) pursuing a graduate or undergraduate degree in a mathematics, science (life or physical sciences, political science, or computer science), or engineering field; 2) interested in increasing and affecting the public's understanding of mathematics, science, and engineering issues; and 3) concerned about influencing science-oriented public policy at the national, state, and local levels. U.S. citizenship is required.

Financial data The stipend is $3,000 for undergraduates and $4,000 for graduate students. Other benefits include round-trip fare between home or school and Washington, D.C. and housing for all interns who are not from the Washington, D.C. metropolitan area.

Duration 10 weeks, during the summer.

Special features Past assignments have included work in the National Science Foundation, the National Aeronautics and Space Administration, the Smithsonian Institution, the Environ-

mental Protection Agency, and the mathematics, science, and engineering component of the Quality Education for Minorities (QEM) Network.

Limitations Interns are also expected to become involved in an academic year project at their home institutions. Each intern must identify a faculty advisor and define a specific project that provides quality educational experiences for low-income, minority students; interns prepare a written description of the follow-up project, an interim progress report, and a final report on the outcome of the project.

Number awarded Varies each year.

Deadline February of each year.

[1511]
SHARP PLUS PROGRAM

Quality Education for Minorities (QEM) Network
1818 N Street, N.W., Suite 350
Washington, DC 20036
(202) 659-1818   Fax: (202) 659-5408
E-mail: sharpplus@qem.org

Purpose To enable underrepresented minority high school students to work with mathematics, science, and engineering researchers at industrial sites or in research laboratories at academic institutions.

Eligibility This program is open to African Americans, Alaska Natives, American Indians, Mexican Americans, and Puerto Ricans who are at least 16 years of age; have completed at least the 10th grade by the start of the program; will return to high school in the fall as a junior or senior; have completed at least 1 semester of algebra and geometry and at least 1 year of biology, chemistry, or physics with a grade of B or better in each course; and speak and write English at a level that does not require significant assistance. Applicants must be interested in continuing their education in mathematics, science, or engineering at the college or university level.

Financial data Interns receive room and board on a university campus and a salary of $4.75 per hour for a 40-hour work week.

Duration 8 weeks, usually beginning around mid-June.

Special features This program is funded by the National Aeronautics and Space Administration (NASA) as an adjunct to its Summer High School Apprenticeship Research (SHARP) program. In that program, students live at home and commute to NASA field centers; in this SHARP Plus program, students live at research institutions in 1 of the 8 states in which there are NASA field centers (Alabama, California, Florida, Maryland, Mississippi, Ohio, Texas, and Virginia) and work with researchers/mentors at nearby industrial sites or in research laboratories at the institutions.

Number awarded 300 each year: 20 at each participating site.

Deadline February of each year.

[1512]
SOUTH DAKOTA SPACE GRANT CONSORTIUM FELLOWSHIPS AND ASSISTANTSHIPS

South Dakota Space Grant Consortium
c/o South Dakota School of Mines and Technology
Graduate Education and Research Office
501 East St. Joseph Street
Rapid City, SD 57701-3995
(605) 394-2291   Fax: (605) 394-6061
E-mail: psmith@nimbus.ias.sdsmt.edu

Purpose To provide support for space-related activities in South Dakota.

Eligibility This program is open to faculty, graduate students, and undergraduate students at member institutions of the South Dakota Space Grant Consortium (South Dakota School of Mines and Technology and South Dakota State University). Activities include summer faculty fellowships at the EROS Data Center in Sioux Falls, graduate fellowships, and undergraduate assistantships. Participants must be U.S. citizens. Underrepresented groups, primarily Native Americans and women, are especially encouraged to participate.

Financial data Approximately $70,000 per year is available to support the program.

Special features This program is funded by the U.S. National Aeronautics and Space Administration (NASA).

Number awarded Varies each year.

[1513]
SUMMER RESEARCH PROGRAM FOR MINORITIES AND WOMEN

AT&T Bell Laboratories
Attn: SRP Manager
600 Mountain Avenue, Room 3D-303
Murray Hill, NJ 07974-0636
(908) 949-3728

Purpose To provide work experience to women or members of underrepresented minority groups interested in technical employment.

Eligibility Male candidates must be members of an underrepresented ethnic minority group (Black, Hispanic, Native American Indian). Women candidates may be from any racial or ethnic group. All applicants are expected to have completed their junior year in college and to be able to demonstrate an interest in scientific fields (physics, chemistry, computer science, ceramic engineering, chemical engineering, communications science, computer engineering, electrical engineering, information science, materials science, mathematics, mechanical engineering, operations research, or statistics). Selection is based on academic achievement, personal motivation, and compatibility of student interests with current Bell Laboratories' activities.

Financial data Salaries are commensurate with those of regular AT&T Bell Laboratories' employees who have comparable education and work experience (approximately $500 per week). Trainees are reimbursed for their travel to and from New Jersey. Assistance in locating housing is offered.

Duration The minimum traineeship is 10 weeks during the summer.

Special features Trainees work in AT&T Bell Laboratories located in Crawford Hill, Holmdel, Murray Hill, Shippany, South Plainfield, Short Hills, or West Long Branch, New Jersey.

Number awarded 60 to 100 each year.

Deadline November of each year.

Native Alaskans

[1514]
AMERICAN INDIAN MUSEUM STUDIES PROGRAM

Smithsonian Institution
Attn: Center for Museum Studies
Arts and Industries Building, Suite 2235
MRC 427
Washington, DC 20560
(202) 357-3101   Fax: (202) 357-3346
E-mail: ompem004@sivm.si.edu

Purpose To promote and assist Native Americans in the continuation and interpretation of tribal cultures as they define them.

Eligibility Native Americans working in tribal museums and American Indian cultural centers are eligible to participate in workshops and seminars conducted as part of this program.

Financial data Participants in the workshops and seminars receive a tuition waiver for the course and a scholarship to help defray travel and subsistence expenses.

Duration Most seminars last 3 to 5 days.

Special features This program also recruits American Indians and Alaska Natives who are currently enrolled in a higher education program or who are currently employed in a field related to museum work or cultural programming to participate in the Museum Intern Partnership Program of the Smithsonian's Center for Museum Studies. It also produces publications and technical assistance which provide additional resources not available elsewhere for the enrichment of Native American museums and cultural centers.

Number awarded Varies each year.

Deadline The seminars and workshops, of which 4 or 5 are held each year at native communities throughout the United States and Canada, each set their own deadline dates.

[1515]
MASTER ARTIST AND APPRENTICE GRANTS IN TRADITIONAL NATIVE ARTS

Alaska State Council on the Arts
411 West Fourth Avenue, Suite 1E
Anchorage, AK 99501-2343
(907) 269-6610   Fax: (907) 269-6601
E-mail: asca@alaska.net

Purpose To support and encourage the maintenance and development of the traditional arts of Alaska's native people.

Eligibility The apprentice applicants must be residents of Alaska, have demonstrated experience in the art form in which they are interested, and have identified and located a master artist willing to accept apprentices. Priority is given to apprentices who wish to study an art form within his/her own cultural tradition.

Financial data The amount of the grant is $2,000. The funds are to be used to pay the fees of the master artist and to cover essential expenses of the apprenticeship (primarily materials and, in rare cases, travel).

Special features Apprenticeships may be in any traditional Alaska native art form. Grants have been awarded in carving, basketry, storytelling, dance, skin sewing, weaving, tanning, and beadwork. Apprenticeships are planned jointly by the apprentice and the master artist.

Limitations The master artist must be able to demonstrate excellence in the form to be taught.

Number awarded Varies each year.

Deadline April and September of each year.

[1516]
NMAI CONSERVATION INTERNSHIPS

National Museum of the American Indian
Smithsonian Institution
Attn: Chief Conservator, Research Branch
3401 Bruckner Boulevard
Bronx, NY 10461
(212) 825-4496

Purpose To provide an educational opportunity for Native American students in the area of conservation at the Research Branch of the National Museum of the American Indian (NMAI).

Eligibility These internships are intended primarily for American Indian and Alaska Native graduate students currently enrolled in a program in conservation or undergraduates planning to go on to a graduate program in conservation. Applicants must be interested in working in the Research Branch of the NMAI in the Bronx, New York.

Financial data These are stipended positions.

Duration 12 months.

Number awarded 2 each year: 1 graduate student and 1 undergraduate.

[1517]
NMAI INTERNSHIP PROGRAM

National Museum of the American Indian
Smithsonian Institution
Attn: Intern Coordinator
470 L'Enfant Plaza, Suite 7103
MRC 934
Washington, DC 20560
(202) 287-2020   E-mail: alyce@ic.si.edu

Purpose To provide an educational opportunity for Native American students in the area of museum practice and related programming through guided work and/or research experience at the National Museum of the American Indian (NMAI).

Eligibility These internships are intended primarily for American Indian and Alaska Native students currently enrolled in undergraduate or graduate academic programs, although recent college graduates are also eligible. Applicants must be prepared to work either in Washington D.C. (at the executive and staff offices of the National Museum of the American Indian or at other Smithsonian Institution facilities) or in New York (at the George Gustav Heye Center in Manhattan or the research branch of the National Museum of the American Indian in the Bronx). Completed applications include a statement by the students indicating their interest in the museum field, why they wish to intern at the National Museum of the American Indian, and how the internship will contribute to their academic goals or professional development. Selection is based on potential to make a contribution to the museum, potential for education or career to benefit from an internship, and strong interest in the museum field.

Financial data The total stipend is $3,000; round-trip travel and housing may also be provided.

Duration 8 to 10 weeks, during the summer.

Special features Museum departments assign projects that interns are expected to complete. The average work week is 40 hours.

Number awarded 6 each year.

Deadline February of each year.

[1518]
QEM NETWORK INTERNSHIPS

Quality Education for Minorities (QEM) Network
1818 N Street, N.W., Suite 350
Washington, DC 20036
(202) 659-1818   Fax: (202) 659-5408
E-mail: qemnetwork@qem.org

Purpose To provide underrepresented minority students with an opportunity to work at Quality Education for Minorities (QEM) to further develop their leadership potential and to enhance their awareness of major issues related to the education of minorities.

Eligibility This program is open to African Americans, Alaska Natives, American Indians, Mexican Americans, and Puerto Ricans who have successfully completed at least the sophomore year in an accredited, degree-granting institution. Applicants must be interested in 1) pursuing a post-baccalaureate degree; 2) assuming a leadership role at their college/university; and 3) participating in community activities to influence national state, or local policy as it relates to the education of minorities. Students are eligible if they are studying any area, but preference is given to majors in business administration, computer science, economics, education, engineering, life or physical sciences, political science, or public policy.

Financial data The stipend is $3,000 for undergraduates and $4,000 for graduate students. Other benefits include round-trip fare between home or school and Washington, D.C. and housing for all interns who are not from the Washington, D.C. metropolitan area.

Duration 10 weeks, during the summer.

Special features Assignments may involve areas such as community outreach, program planning and evaluation, education policy analysis, data collection and analysis, network communications, and the preparation of background papers on major education issues and their implications for the education of minorities.

Limitations Interns are also expected to become involved in an academic year project at their home institutions. Each intern must identify a faculty advisor and define a specific project that provides quality educational experiences for low-income, minority students; interns prepare a written description of the follow-up project, an interim progress report, and a final report on the outcome of the project.

Number awarded Varies each year.

Deadline February of each year.

[1519]
QEM SCIENCE STUDENT INTERNSHIPS

Quality Education for Minorities (QEM) Network
1818 N Street, N.W., Suite 350
Washington, DC 20036
(202) 659-1818   Fax: (202) 659-5408
E-mail: qemnetwork@qem.org

Purpose To provide underrepresented minority students with an opportunity to work with agencies and organizations involved in making science policy.

Eligibility This program is open to African Americans, Alaska Natives, American Indians, Mexican Americans, and Puerto Ricans who have successfully completed at least the sophomore year in an accredited, degree-granting institution. Applicants must be 1) pursuing a graduate or undergraduate degree in a mathematics, science (life or physical sciences, political science, or computer science), or engineering field; 2) interested in increasing and affecting the public's understanding of mathematics, science, and engineering issues; and 3) concerned about influencing science-oriented public policy at the national, state, and local levels. U.S. citizenship is required.

Financial data The stipend is $3,000 for undergraduates and $4,000 for graduate students. Other benefits include round-trip fare between home or school and Washington, D.C. and housing for all interns who are not from the Washington, D.C. metropolitan area.

Duration 10 weeks, during the summer.

Special features Past assignments have included work in the National Science Foundation, the National Aeronautics and Space Administration, the Smithsonian Institution, the Environmental Protection Agency, and the mathematics, science, and engineering component of the Quality Education for Minorities (QEM) Network.

Limitations Interns are also expected to become involved in an academic year project at their home institutions. Each intern must identify a faculty advisor and define a specific project that provides quality educational experiences for low-income, minority students; interns prepare a written description of the follow-up project, an interim progress report, and a final report on the outcome of the project.

Number awarded Varies each year.

Deadline February of each year.

[1520]
SHARP PLUS PROGRAM

Quality Education for Minorities (QEM) Network
1818 N Street, N.W., Suite 350
Washington, DC 20036
(202) 659-1818   Fax: (202) 659-5408
E-mail: sharpplus@qem.org

Purpose To enable underrepresented minority high school students to work with mathematics, science, and engineering researchers at industrial sites or in research laboratories at academic institutions.

Eligibility This program is open to African Americans, Alaska Natives, American Indians, Mexican Americans, and Puerto Ricans who are at least 16 years of age; have completed at least the 10th grade by the start of the program; will return to high school in the fall as a junior or senior; have completed at least 1 semester of algebra and geometry and at least 1 year of biology, chemistry, or physics with a grade of B or better in each course; and speak and write English at a level that does not require significant assistance. Applicants must be interested in continuing their education in mathematics, science, or engineering at the college or university level.

Financial data Interns receive room and board on a university campus and a salary of $4.75 per hour for a 40-hour work week.

Duration 8 weeks, usually beginning around mid-June.

Special features This program is funded by the National Aeronautics and Space Administration (NASA) as an adjunct to its Summer High School Apprenticeship Research (SHARP) program. In that program, students live at home and commute to

NASA field centers; in this SHARP Plus program, students live at research institutions in 1 of the 8 states in which there are NASA field centers (Alabama, California, Florida, Maryland, Mississippi, Ohio, Texas, and Virginia) and work with researchers/mentors at nearby industrial sites or in research laboratories at the institutions.

Number awarded 300 each year: 20 at each participating site.

Deadline February of each year.

Native Americans in General

[1521]
ABC NEWSPAPER INTERNSHIP PROGRAM

ABC Newspaper Internship Program
Attn: Director
7 Upper Church Street, Suite 206
West Springfield, MA 01089
(413) 731-7478

Purpose To strengthen the minority reporting, editing, photojournalism, and graphic arts ranks within the journalism profession.

Eligibility Recent college graduates who majored in journalism or communications are eligible to apply. They must submit a resume, 3 to 5 samples of their writing, at least 4 references, and a letter detailing their qualifications and interest in the program. This program is oriented toward minorities.

Financial data Interns earn a weekly salary. Other benefits include medical insurance, a rent-free, fully furnished apartment at each location, subsidized utilities, and a moving stipend for each change of location.

Duration Interns work 4 months at 3 different newspapers, for a total of 1 year.

Special features The newspapers participating in this program are the 6 newspapers owned by ABC (a division of the Walt Disney Company). *The Kansas City Star* (Kansas City, Missouri); *Albany Democrat-Herald* (Albany, Oregon); *The Oakland Press* (Pontiac, Michigan); *Fort Worth Star-Telegram* (Fort Worth, Texas); *The Times Leader* (Wilkes-Barre, Pennsylvania); and *Belleville News-Democrat* (Belleville, Illinois).

Limitations Interns must provide their own car.

Number awarded 10 each year.

Deadline January of each year.

[1522]
ADVANCED INDUSTRIAL CONCEPTS MATERIALS SCIENCE PROGRAM

Oak Ridge Institute for Science and Education
Attn: Science/Engineering Education Division
P.O. Box 117
Oak Ridge, TN 37831-0117
(423) 576-9279   (423) 576-2194
(800) 569-7749   Fax: (423) 576-3643
E-mail: aicmsp@orau.gov

Purpose To provide financial assistance to selected minorities for graduate study and work experience in materials science and related disciplines.

Eligibility This program is open to African American or Native American graduating seniors and graduate students who have not completed their first year. They must be enrolled or planning to enroll in an accredited U.S. institution with a major in materials science, materials engineering, metallurgical engineering, polymer science and engineering, ceramic engineering, chemical engineering, or chemistry.

Financial data Participants receive a monthly stipend of $1,200, a dislocation allowance of $300 during the research appointment, and payment of tuition and fees up to $6,000 per year.

Duration 12 months; renewable to 24 months.

Special features The program includes a research appointment at Oak Ridge National Laboratory (ORNL) in Tennessee. This program is funded by ORNL and administered by the Science/Engineering Education Division (SEED) of Oak Ridge Institute for Science and Education (ORISE).

Number awarded Varies each year.

Deadline February of each year.

[1523]
AGENCY FOR TOXIC SUBSTANCES AND DISEASE REGISTRY STUDENT INTERNSHIP PROGRAM

Oak Ridge Institute for Science and Education
Attn: Science/Engineering Education Division
P.O. Box 117
Oak Ridge, TN 37831-0117
(423) 576-1083   (423) 576-3426
(800) 569-7749   Fax: (423) 576-3643
E-mail: sipatsdr@orau.gov

Purpose To support student research in exposure and disease registries, health investigations, public health assessments, toxicological profiles, emergency response, and health education at the Agency for Toxic Substances and Disease Registry (ATSDR) in Atlanta, Georgia.

Eligibility This program is open to students who are working on a baccalaureate, master's, or doctoral degree in toxicology, epidemiology, environmental or public health, medicine, pharmacology, or related disciplines in the biological, medical, or physical sciences. All programs operated by the Science/Engineering Education Division (SEED) of Oak Ridge Institute for Science and Education (ORISE) seek to broaden the participation of minorities, women, and persons with disabilities in science and engineering careers.

Financial data Participants receive a monthly stipend of $1,350 to $1,650 (undergraduate student) or $1,650 to $2,150 (graduate students); the exact amount depends on academic status and research area. They also receive limited travel funds. The off-campus tuition and fees required by their home institution are paid by the program.

Duration 10 weeks to 12 months.

Special features Both full- and part-time appointments are available. ATSDR was established by Superfund legislation in 1980; its mission is to prevent or mitigate adverse human health effects and diminished quality of life resulting from exposure to hazardous substances in the environment. This program is funded by an interagency agreement between the U.S. Department of Energy and ATSDR (part of the U.S. Public Health Service) and administered by ORISE/SEED.

Number awarded Varies each year.

Deadline Applications may be submitted at any time.

[1524]
ALBUQUERQUE JOURNAL PUBLISHERS' SCHOLARSHIP FUND FOR MINORITIES

Albuquerque Journal
7777 Jefferson Street, N.E.
Albuquerque, NM 87109-4360
(505) 823-7777

Purpose To provide financial assistance and work experience to minority students in journalism at universities in New Mexico.

Eligibility This program is open to minority students majoring or minoring in journalism at 1 of 4 universities in New Mexico: University of New Mexico, New Mexico State University, Eastern New Mexico University, or New Mexico Highlands University.

Financial data The scholarship is $2,000; the recipient also receives a paid internship and moving expenses.

Duration 1 year.

Special features This program is funded by the *Albuquerque Journal*, where the internship takes place, but applications are submitted through the 4 universities.

Number awarded 1 each year.

Deadline February of each year.

[1525]
ALEXANDER THWEATT SALES INTERNSHIP PROGRAM

Merck U.S. Human Health Division
Attn: Coordinator, Recruiting and Selection
Building 39-243
West Point, PA 19486
(215) 652-5000

Purpose To provide an opportunity for participants to learn about pharmaceutical industry sales and marketing and to enable Merck to identify talented individuals who have the potential to make a positive contribution to the organization's success.

Eligibility This program is open to college students who are interested in pharmaceutical sales and marketing. All majors and all degrees are considered, but the internship is dedicated to students of color (Black, Hispanic, Asian, and Native American). Selection is based on a strong work ethic, excellent interpersonal skills, creativity, flexibility, and exceptional academic performance at the undergraduate and/or graduate level.

Financial data Interns receive a stipend and other benefits.

Duration Summer months.

Special features This program was originally called the Merck Sharp & Dohme Minority Summer Internship Program. In 1991, the program was renamed the Alexander Thweatt Minority Internship Program, in memory of a late senior regional sales director.

Number awarded Varies each year.

[1526]
AMERICAN ECONOMIC ASSOCIATION/FEDERAL RESERVE SYSTEM MINORITY FELLOWSHIP PROGRAM

American Economic Association
Attn: Committee on the Status of Minority Groups in the Economics Profession
c/o The Brookings Institution
1775 Massachusetts Avenue, N.W.
Washington, DC 20036-2188
(202) 797-6000   Fax: (202) 797-6004

Purpose To provide financial assistance to underrepresented minority economics doctoral students who are about to begin their dissertation research.

Eligibility Applicants must be U.S. citizens who are Black, Hispanic, or Native American and are enrolled in an accredited doctoral program in economics in the United States where they have completed their comprehensive examinations and are about to begin their dissertation research. Preference is given to applicants whose areas of concentration are of special interest to the Federal Reserve System (e.g., financial markets and monetary policy, nonfinancial macroeconomics, forecasting, banking markets and financial structure, regional studies, the external sector of the U.S. economy, the economics of other countries, foreign exchange markets, and international banking and financial markets). Selection is based on academic performance.

Financial data The stipend is $900 per month during the academic year. Institutions nominating candidates must agree to provide a tuition waiver without requiring research or teaching assistantship.

Special features Recipients are assigned an advisor from the Federal Reserve System and given the opportunity to complete an internship at the Federal Reserve Board or a Federal Reserve Bank.

Limitations Because of uncertainty about the legal status of affirmative action programs, new applications are not currently being solicited for this program.

Deadline February of each year.

[1527]
AMERICAN HEART ASSOCIATION STUDENT RESEARCH PROGRAM

American Heart Association—California Affiliate
Attn: Research Department
1710 Gilbreth Road
Burlingame, CA 94010-1317
(415) 259-6700

Purpose To encourage gifted students from all disciplines to consider careers in cardiovascular and cerebrovascular research.

Eligibility This program is open to students who are enrolled full time at an accredited academic institution at the junior or senior level. They must be either California residents or attending a college/university in California. Applicants must have completed the following (or equivalent) courses: 4 semesters (or 6 quarters) of biological sciences, physics, or chemistry; and 1 quarter of calculus, statistics, computational methods, or computer science. Selection is based on an assessment of the student's application, academic record (preference is given to students with superior academic standing), and faculty recommendations. Women and minorities are particularly encouraged to apply.

Financial data Participants receive a $2,500 stipend.

Duration 10 weeks, during the summer.

Special features Participants are assigned to laboratories in California to work under the direction and supervision of experienced scientists.

Deadline Applications must be requested by December of each year and submitted by January of each year.

[1528]
AMERICAN METEOROLOGICAL SOCIETY INDUSTRY GRADUATE FELLOWSHIPS

American Meteorological Society
Attn: Fellowship/Scholarship Coordinator
45 Beacon Street
Boston, MA 02108-3693
(617) 227-2426, ext. 235   E-mail: sarmstrg@ametsoc.org

Purpose To encourage students entering their first year of graduate school to pursue an advanced degree in the atmospheric and related oceanic and hydrologic sciences.

Eligibility Students in the following fields are encouraged to apply: atmospheric sciences, oceanography, hydrology, chemistry, computer sciences, engineering, environmental sciences, mathematics, and physics. Applicants must be in the first year of graduate school, pursuing a full-time course of study in the atmospheric, oceanic, or hydrologic sciences, and a U.S. citizen or permanent resident. The Society encourages applications from women, minorities, and students with disabilities. Awards are based on academic performance and plans to pursue a career in meteorology or a related science.

Financial data The stipend is $15,000 per academic year.

Duration 9 months.

Special features This program was initiated in 1991. Corporations who have supported the program include: Cray Research, Inc., PRC Inc., Hughes Information Technology Company, Unisys Corporation, Government Systems Group, ITT Aerospace Communications Division, Space Systems/Loral, Martin Marietta Astro Space, GTE's Federal Systems Division, and NOAA's Office of Global Programs. Most industry-sponsored fellowship recipients have the opportunity to work at the corporation that granted their award during the summer following the academic year of their award. The summer employment opportunities are coordinated by AMS.

Limitations Requests for an application must be accompanied by a self-addressed stamped envelope.

Number awarded Varies; approximately 8 each year.

Deadline February of each year.

[1529]
AMERICAN SOCIETY OF MECHANICAL ENGINEERS MINORITY LEADERSHIP PROGRAM

American Society of Mechanical Engineers
Attn: Board on Minorities and Women
1828 L Street, N.W., Suite 906
Washington, DC 20036-5104
(202) 785-3756   Fax: (202) 429-9417
E-mail: engles@asme.org

Purpose To familiarize minority members of the American Society of Mechanical Engineers (ASME) with the workings of the Society.

Eligibility Underrepresented minority members who have attained a minimum of associate member status in the Society are eligible for this program. Applicants must desire to participate at the operating board/committee level by engaging in the activities of selected or sponsoring groups. Their employers must agree to provide sufficient time away from the office to support their activities.

Financial data While on Society business, interns are eligible for reimbursement of lodging and meal expenses up to $80 per day.

Duration 1 year, during which interns attend at least 2 out-of-town meetings of 2 to 3 days' duration each.

Number awarded 5 each year.

Deadline May of each year.

[1530]
ANCHORAGE DAILY NEWS INTERNSHIP

Anchorage Daily News
Attn: Human Resources
P.O. Box 149001
Anchorage, AK 99514-9001
(907) 257-4200   (800) 478-4200

Purpose To provide work experience at the *Anchorage Daily News* to college students interested in journalism as a career.

Eligibility College students are eligible to apply for this internship if they have published work in school or other publications, and have been trained in the basics of journalism. Internships are available for general assignment reporters, as well as in photography, art, and copy editing. Members of minority groups and women are particularly encouraged to apply.

Financial data The salary is approximately $9.35 per hour for 40 hours per week.

Duration 12 weeks in the summer.

Special features Interns work on newspaper layout/design.

Number awarded 3 to 4 each year.

Deadline November of each year.

[1531]
ANL LABORATORY–GRADUATE RESEARCH APPOINTMENTS

Argonne National Laboratory
Attn: Division of Educational Programs
Graduate Student Program Office
9700 South Cass Avenue
Argonne, IL 60439-4845
(630) 252-3371   Fax: (630) 252-3193
E-mail: ettinger@dep.anl.gov

Purpose To offer opportunities for qualified graduate students to carry out their master's or doctoral thesis research at the Argonne National Laboratory.

Eligibility Appointments are available for graduate students at U.S. universities who wish to carry out their thesis research under the co-sponsorship of a Laboratory staff member and a faculty member. Research may be conducted in the basic physical and life sciences, mathematics, computer science, and engineering, as well as in a variety of applied areas relating to conservation, environment, fission and fusion energy, and other energy technologies. Applicants must be U.S. citizens or permanent residents. The Laboratory encourages applications from all qualified persons, especially women and members of underrepresented minority groups.

Financial data Support consists of a stipend, tuition payments up to $5,000 per year, and certain travel expenses. In addition, the student's faculty sponsor may receive payment for limited travel expenses.

Duration 1 year; may be renewed.

Special features This program, which is also referred to as the Lab–Grad Program, is sponsored by the U.S. Department of Energy. In certain cases, students may be awarded support for pre-thesis studies on campus, provided they intend to carry out their thesis research at Argonne. Mutual interest in an area of research by the student and the Argonne staff sponsor is essential for the successful arrangement of a Lab-Grad appointment. To help the parties gauge their mutual interest, a limited number of temporary appointments are available for qualified graduate students, so they may work with an Argonne staff member and become familiar with his/her research program. These temporary appointments have a tenure of 3 months and support consists of a per diem payment to help defray the cost of living away from home, plus travel expenses.

Number awarded Varies each year.

Deadline Applications may be submitted at any time, but a complete application should be submitted at least 2 months prior to any proposed starting date.

[1532]
APA/GLAXO WELLCOME FELLOWSHIP PROGRAM

American Psychiatric Association
Attn: Office of Minority/National Affairs
1400 K Street, N.W.
Washington, DC 20005
(202) 682-6097   Fax: (202) 682-6352

Purpose To provide psychiatric residents an opportunity to work closely within the American Psychiatric Association (APA).

Eligibility This program is open to PGY II residents who are APA members and have passed a national or state board examination. Applicants must be interested in a program to acquaint them with the work of the APA and with national issues affecting psychiatry, and to give the APA the benefit of ideas and perspectives of future leaders in psychiatry. Each accredited psychiatric residency training program is invited to nominate 1 resident for the fellowship. Selection is based on clinical acumen, leadership performance, educational performance, teaching, and research/publication. The APA encourages nomination of residents from minority groups.

Financial data A salary is provided.

Duration 2 years, beginning September 1.

Special features This program was established in 1968 as the Falk Fellowship Program, to recognize its sponsorship by the Maurice Falk Medical Fund. In 1984, financial responsibility was assumed by the Burroughs Wellcome Company. Following acquisition of that company by Glaxo, the program took its present name in 1996. Fellows work with assigned APA components, representing the resident's point of view in the discussion of policy and issues in psychiatry.

Number awarded 10 each year.

Deadline March of each year.

[1533]
APPLIED HEALTH PHYSICS FELLOWSHIP PROGRAM

Oak Ridge Institute for Science and Education
Attn: Science/Engineering Education Division
P.O. Box 117
Oak Ridge, TN 37831-0117
(423) 576-9279   (423) 576-2194
(800) 569-7749   Fax: (423) 576-3643
E-mail: ahpfp@orau.gov

Purpose To provide funding for graduate study and work experience in applied health physics (radiation protection).

Eligibility This program is open to students working on a master's degree in applied health physics at universities participating in this program (for a list of participating schools, write to the address above). Applicants must be U.S. citizens or permanent residents with a baccalaureate degree in either the life or physical sciences, engineering, or mathematics. All programs operated by the Science/Engineering Education Division (SEED) of Oak Ridge Institute for Science and Education (ORISE) seek to broaden the participation of minorities, women, and persons with disabilities in science and engineering careers.

Financial data Fellows receive full payment of tuition and fees and a stipend of $14,400 per year. An additional $300 per month is paid during the practicum period. A $1,000 annual allowance is paid to the recipient's university.

Duration Up to 24 months.

Special features Participants perform a research practicum as interns at various U.S. Department of Energy (DOE) research facilities for 3 months during the summer between the 2 years of the program. This program is funded by DOE and administered by ORISE/SEED.

Number awarded Varies each year.

Deadline January of each year.

[1534]
ARCHAEOLOGICAL CONSERVATION GRADUATE INTERNSHIP

Smithsonian Institution
Attn: Conservation Analytical Laboratory
Education and Training, MSC
MRC 534
Washington, DC 20560
(301) 238-3700   Fax: (301) 238-3709
E-mail: cal.etp@cal.si.edu

Purpose To provide training at the Smithsonian Institution's Conservation Analytical Laboratory (CAL) to graduate students interested in archaeological conservation.

Eligibility This program is open to graduate students entering the internship year in a conservation training program or the equivalent. Recipients spend approximately half the year at archaeological sites with which CAL is associated; in the past, CAL conservators have worked with excavation teams at Harappa (Pakistan), Cerén (El Salvador), and Copán (Honduras). For the remainder of the time, interns work in the Objects Conservation Laboratory at CAL, where they treat archaeological artifacts or carry out research. Minorities are particularly encouraged to apply.

Financial data Travel costs and living expenses at the archaeological site are provided; supplemental funding up to $14,000 may also be available.

Duration 1 year.

Number awarded 1 each year.

Deadline January of each year.

[1535]
ARCHIVES PRESERVATION INTERNSHIPS

Smithsonian Institution
Attn: Conservation Analytical Laboratory
Education and Training, MSC
MRC 534
Washington, DC 20560
(301) 238-3700   Fax: (301) 238-3709
E-mail: cal.etp@cal.si.edu

Purpose To provide specialized training in preservation of archival materials to postgraduate fellows at the Conservation Analytical Laboratory (CAL) of the Smithsonian Institution.

Eligibility This program is open to students entering the internship year in a graduate conservation training program or the equivalent. Recipients work at CAL and with collections of the Smithsonian Institution, which has many archives, library, and research holdings including a full range of paper materials (manuscripts, documents, prints, drawings, and papers), as well as parchment and photographic materials. Minorities are particularly encouraged to apply.

Financial data Supplemental funding up to $14,000 may be available.

Duration 1 year.

Special features Interns undertake surveys, design and carry out rehousing projects, participate in and learn to organize training workshops, and initiate training projects for collections managers. Interns may also treat selected archive-related artifacts and materials, and carry out research, making use of well-equipped scientific laboratories. This program is jointly administered by CAL and the Smithsonian's Office of Fellowships and Grants.

Number awarded 1 each year.

Deadline January of each year.

[1536]
ART PETERS EDITING PROGRAM

Philadelphia Inquirer
Attn: Assistant Managing Editor
400 North Broad Street
P.O. Box 8263
Philadelphia, PA 19101
(215) 854-4671

Purpose To provide copy editing experience to minority college students interested in careers in journalism.

Eligibility Minority college students entering their sophomore, junior, or senior year in college are eligible to apply if they are interested in the practical work of copy editing. Selection is based on experience, potential, academic record, and extracurricular activities.

Financial data Interns' wages are based on the newspaper's contract with the Newspaper Guild.

Duration 10 weeks beginning in June.

Special features After 1 week of intensive instruction, interns are assigned to 1 of 6 copy desks at the *Philadelphia Inquirer*: metro, neighbors, foreign, national, business news, or features. Assistance is given to interns interested in finding full-time employment after graduation.

Number awarded 4 each year.

Deadline   December of each year.

[1537]
ARTS MIDWEST MINORITY ARTS ADMINISTRATION FELLOWSHIPS

Arts Midwest
528 Hennepin Avenue, Suite 310
Minneapolis, MN 55403-1899
(612) 341-0755   Fax: (612) 341-0902
TDD: (612) 341-0901

Purpose   To provide work experience to minorities interested in arts administration.

Eligibility   High school graduates or people with substantial experience are eligible to apply if they are members of a minority group (African American, Asian American, Latino, or Native American), residents of 1 of Arts Midwest's 9 states (Illinois, Indiana, Iowa, Michigan, Minnesota, North Dakota, Ohio, South Dakota, Wisconsin), willing to relocate, and interested in preparing for a career in arts administration. Students currently enrolled in a degree-granting institution are not eligible.

Financial data   Fellows receive a stipend of $22,000 plus travel and professional development awards of $3,500.

Duration   10 months, from February to November.

Special features   After a 2-day orientation in Minneapolis, Fellows are placed with 2 host organizations for a period of 5 months each. A variety of work sites participate in the program, including art museums, public radio stations, arts foundations, and performance theaters. Fellows are given experience in a number of aspects of art administration, including development, marketing, management, planning, and public relations.

Limitations   This program currently lacks funding; its renewal depends on the availability of future financing.

Number awarded   4 to 6 each year.

Deadline   October of each year.

[1538]
ASBURY PARK PRESS SCHOLARSHIP IN THE MEDIA FOR MINORITY STUDENTS

Asbury Park Press
Attn: Scholarship Committee
3601 Highway 66
P.O. Box 1550
Neptune, NJ 07754-1551
(908) 922-6000, ext. 4262   Fax: (908) 922-4818

Purpose   To provide financial assistance to minority students from selected counties in New Jersey who are interested in postsecondary education in the field of communications.

Eligibility   Graduating minority high school students from Monmouth County, New Jersey and Ocean County, New Jersey are eligible to apply if they are seeking a career in the field of communications, including reporting, broadcasting, marketing, and advertising. Also eligible are college students entering their junior year with a demonstrated commitment to a newspaper reporting or editing career; preference is given to students from New Jersey or attending New Jersey colleges.

Financial data   The award is $2,000.

Duration   1 year; may be renewed for 1 additional year (with continued satisfactory work).

Special features   Recipients are offered an internship at the Asbury Park Press for 1 summer.

Number awarded   3 each year: 1 to a high school senior from Monmouth County, 1 to a high school senior from Ocean County, and 1 to a current college student entering the junior year.

Deadline   April of each year.

[1539]
ASSOCIATED PRESS MINORITY INTERNSHIP

Associated Press
Attn: Director of Recruiting
50 Rockefeller Plaza
New York, NY 10020-1666
(212) 621-1500

Purpose   To provide journalistic work experience to minority undergraduate and graduate students.

Eligibility   Black, Hispanic, Asian American, and Native American college juniors, seniors, and graduate students are eligible to apply. Applicants must demonstrate an interest in a career in journalism.

Financial data   Amount varies.

Duration   13 weeks in the summer.

Special features   Interns work in 1 of the Associated Press' domestic bureaus in print editorial, broadcast, photo, and graphics work. Interns who successfully complete the program may be offered a full-time job with the Associated Press after graduation.

Limitations   Applications are not mailed out. Candidates must write to the nearest Associated Press bureau or designated test site and schedule a date to apply in person.

Number awarded   Approximately 17 each year.

Deadline   February of each year.

[1540]
ATLANTA HISTORY CENTER MUSEUM FELLOWS PROGRAM FOR MINORITY STUDENTS

Atlanta History Center
130 West Paces Ferry Road, N.W.
Atlanta, GA 30305-1366
(404) 814-4000

Purpose   To provide museum training to minority students in the Atlanta area.

Eligibility   Academic institutions with a 4-year undergraduate liberal arts program in the metropolitan Atlanta area may nominate minority undergraduate students interested in preparing for a museum career. Nominees must be full-time juniors or seniors in the following academic year with a declared major in a liberal arts discipline. Minority students (African American, Asian American, Latino American, Native American, or any other ethnic group underrepresented in the museum profession) are encouraged to seek nomination from their major professors.

Financial data   The stipend is $6,000.

Duration   12 months.

Special features   This program began in 1994. Funding is provided by the Coca-Cola Foundation. During the academic year, fellows attend 26 weekly seminars at the Atlanta History Center, where they conduct research and receive hands-on experience in curation, collections care, exhibitions development, interpretive programming, education, development and fundraising, public relations and marketing, and library/archives management. During the summer, fellows perform a 12-week apprenticeship at the Atlanta History Center that includes travel to the Smithsonian Institution and other museums throughout the United States.

Number awarded   4 or more each year.

[1541]
ATLANTA JOURNAL AND CONSTITUTION INTERNSHIP

Atlanta Journal and Constitution
Attn: News Personnel Manager
72 Marietta Street, N.W.
Atlanta, GA 30303
(404) 526-5325

Purpose To provide work experience on newspapers in Atlanta, Georgia to college students who are interested in preparing for a career in journalism.

Eligibility This program is open to full-time juniors, seniors, or graduate students who have worked on their campus newspaper or other publications and have experience in previous internships. People who have graduated within 6 months of the start of the internship are also eligible. Applicants must be interested in working as an intern on the *Journal* or the *Constitution* and must submit a 500-word essay explaining why they want to be a journalist and how the internship will help them pursue their goals; copies of 5 to 10 news clips or samples of photos, graphics, or headlines; a resume; and references. Special consideration is given to applications from minorities.

Financial data Interns are paid $350 to $400 per week.

Duration 10 weeks during the summer, beginning in June.

Special features Interns are offered work opportunities as a reporter, copy editor, graphic artist, or news librarian.

Number awarded 10 each year.

Deadline December of each year.

[1542]
ATLANTIC COAST CONFERENCE INTERNSHIP

Atlantic Coast Conference
P.O. Box ACC
Greensboro, NC 27419-6999
(919) 854-8787

Purpose To provide work experience to women or minorities interested in college sports.

Eligibility This program is open to recent college graduates interested in college sports. Women and minorities are particularly encouraged to apply.

Financial data The stipend is $1,200 per month.

Duration 12 months.

Special features Interns work as media relations assistant for the Atlantic Coast Conference, in Greensboro, North Carolina.

Number awarded 2 each year.

[1543]
AT&T COOPERATIVE RESEARCH FELLOWSHIP PROGRAM

AT&T Bell Laboratories
Attn: CRFP Manager
101 Crawfords Corner Road
P.O. Box 3030
Holmdel, NJ 07733-3030
(908) 949-2943

Purpose To develop scientific and engineering ability among members of minority groups currently underrepresented in the sciences.

Eligibility Outstanding Blacks, Hispanics, and Native American Indians who are college seniors and interested in pursuing a Ph.D. degree in chemistry, chemical engineering, electrical engineering, information science, materials sciences, mathematics, mechanical engineering, physics, or statistics are eligible to apply.

Financial data This program covers tuition and fees, a textbook allowance, a $13,200 annual stipend, and conference travel. Recipients also participate in a summer internship at AT&T and receive housing, a salary, and transportation during that time.

Duration 1 academic year plus a summer internship; may be renewed.

Special features During the summer preceding graduate work, fellowship recipients are employed at AT&T Bell Laboratories and are assigned an appropriate research mentor.

Number awarded 9 to 12 each year.

Deadline January of each year.

[1544]
AUSTIN AMERICAN-STATESMAN MARKETING INTERNSHIPS

Austin American-Statesman
Attn: Assistant Director of Marketing
305 South Congress Avenue
P.O. Box 670
Austin, TX 78767
(512) 445-3526

Purpose To provide work experience at the *Austin American-Statesman* in Texas to college students interested in careers in newspaper marketing.

Eligibility This program is open to students from any state, with a preference for seniors. Applicants must be interested in working in the marketing department of a newspaper. Minorities are especially encouraged to apply.

Financial data The salary is $5.50 per hour.

Duration Approximately 8 weeks, during the summer.

Number awarded 2 each year.

Deadline Applications should be submitted early in the spring of each year.

[1545]
BEACON JOURNAL MINORITY INTERNSHIP

Akron Beacon Journal
Attn: Michelle LeComte
44 East Exchange Street
P.O. Box 640
Akron, OH 44309-0640
(330) 996-3569

Purpose To provide work experience on the *Beacon Journal* in Akron, Ohio to minority college students interested in journalism as a career.

Eligibility Minority college students are eligible to apply for this internship, if they are majoring in graphic arts or a related field.

Financial data The stipend is approximately $300 per week.

Duration Summer months.

Special features Interns work on newspaper layout/design or information graphics.

Number awarded 3 each year: 2 for layout/design and 1 for information graphics.

Deadline December of each year.

[1546]
BLETHEN FAMILY NEWSPAPER INTERNSHIP PROGRAM FOR MINORITIES

Seattle Times
Attn: Blethen Family Internship
1120 John Street
P.O. Box 70
Seattle, WA 98111-0070
(206) 464-3274

Purpose To provide work experience to minority college graduates who are interested in careers in journalism.

Eligibility Eligible are African American, Asian American, Latino, Native American, and Pacific Islander college graduates committed to working as print journalists. Applicants should have a strong desire to pursue their career in the Pacific Northwest.

Financial data Housing, medical coverage, and a salary ranging from $260 to $320 per week are provided.

Duration 1 year.

Special features Interns spend 4 months in training at the *Walla Walla Union-Bulletin,* then 4 months at the *Yakima Herald-Republic,* and the final 4 months at *The Seattle Times.* Internships are available to reporters, copy editors, photographers, and graphic artists.

Deadline March, July, and November of each year.

[1547]
BOSTON GLOBE MINORITY DEVELOPMENT PROGRAM

Boston Globe
Attn: Assistant Managing Editor
135 Morrissey Boulevard
P.O. Box 2378
Boston, MA 02107-2378
(617) 929-3120

Purpose To provide work experience at the *Boston Globe* to minority college graduates interested in journalism as a career.

Eligibility Minority newspaper reporters, copy editors, photographers, and graphic designers with a minimum of 6 months of full-time newspaper experience are eligible to apply.

Financial data Interns are paid competitive salaries.

Duration 12 months.

Special features About 70 percent of those completing the program are offered staff positions.

Number awarded Approximately 2 each year.

[1548]
BRADENTON HERALD INTERNSHIPS

Bradenton Herald
Attn: Executive Editor
102 Manatee Avenue West
Bradenton, FL 34205
(941) 748-0411

Purpose To provide work experience to college students who are interested in preparing for a career in journalism.

Eligibility This program is open to college students who are interested in working as journalists or photographers in the newspaper industry. Applicants may be from any state. Minorities are particularly encouraged to apply. Preference is given to rising seniors.

Financial data The stipend is $250 per week.

Duration 10 weeks, during the summer.

Special features Interns work in the news/editorial department or as photographers for the paper.

Number awarded 3 each summer: 2 news/editorial and 1 photography.

Deadline January of each year.

[1549]
BROOKHAVEN NATIONAL LABORATORY COMMUNITY COLLEGE HONORS PROGRAM

Brookhaven National Laboratory
Attn: Educational Programs
Science Education Center, Building 438
P.O. Box 5000
Upton, New York 11973-5000
(516) 344-3316   Fax: (516) 344-5832
E-mail: flack@bnl.gov

Purpose To provide a summer science research or technical experience to underrepresented minority students from designated northeastern community colleges.

Eligibility This program is open to underrepresented minority (African American/Black, Hispanic, Native American, or Pacific Islander) students at Bronx Community College (Bronx, New York), LaGuardia Community College (Long Island City, New York), Monroe Community College (Rochester, New York), Nassau Community College (Garden City, New York), North Shore Community College (Lynn, Massachusetts), and Suffolk Community College (Selden, New York). Applicants must 1) be U.S. citizens or permanent residents; 2) be at least 18 years of age; 3) have a grade point average of at least 3.0; and 4) be referred by the science enrichment program coordinator at their college.

Financial data Participants receive a weekly stipend, round-trip travel expenses at the lowest rate, and single room dormitory housing.

Duration 10 weeks, during the summer.

Special features Students work with members of the scientific, technical, and professional staff of Brookhaven National Laboratory (BNL) who provide experience in modern science and technology.

Deadline March of each year.

[1550]
BUILDING TECHNOLOGY SUMMER RESEARCH PARTICIPATION PROGRAM AT HISTORICALLY BLACK COLLEGES AND UNIVERSITIES

Oak Ridge Institute for Science and Education
Attn: Science/Engineering Education Division
P.O. Box 117
Oak Ridge, TN 37831-0117
(423) 576-5300   (423) 576-4813
(800) 569-7749   Fax: (423) 576-3643
E-mail: hbcubcth@orau.gov   E-mail: hbcuubts@orau.gov

Purpose To provide opportunities for students at Historically Black Colleges and Universities (HBCUs) to engage in collaborative research in the building technology area that relates to the mission of the U.S. Department of Energy (DOE).

Eligibility Juniors, seniors, and graduate students enrolled in a program of chemical engineering, mechanical engineering, environmental engineering, architectural engineering, or applied physics may apply if they are U.S. citizens or permanent residents. Applicants must be enrolled at HBCUs, although the program is open to all qualified persons without regard to race, age, gender, religion, color, national origin, mental or physical disability, or veteran status. All eligible applicants are considered, but African Americans and Native American Indians receive special consideration because of their underrepresentation in the workplace as scientists and engineers.

Financial data The monthly stipend is $1,100 for juniors, $1,200 for seniors, and $1,600 for graduate students. Transportation expenses are reimbursed for 1 round trip between the facility and the participant's home or university if the distance exceeds 50 miles.

Duration 10 to 12 weeks during the summer.

Special features Internships are conducted at the Efficiency and Renewables Research Section of the Energy Division of Oak Ridge National Laboratory (ORNL). Students work on mentor projects with mentor guidance. This program is funded by ORNL and administered by the Science/Engineering Education Division (SEED) of Oak Ridge Institute for Science and Education (ORISE).

Deadline February of each year.

[1551]
BUSH LEADERSHIP FELLOWS PROGRAM

Bush Foundation
E-900 First National Bank Building
332 Minnesota Street
St. Paul, MN 55101-1387
(612) 227-0891   Fax: (612) 297-6485

Purpose To provide educational and/or internship experiences to strongly motivated individuals in midcareer to prepare them for higher-level responsibilities.

Eligibility Men and women in mid-career who are between the ages of 28 and 54 and are deemed likely to advance to leading positions in architecture, business, engineering, farming, forestry, government, journalism, law, law enforcement, social work, theology, trade unionism, and in the administration of arts, education, health, or scientific organizations are eligible to apply. Applicants must have substantial standing in their fields, at least 5 years of work experience, residency in Minnesota, North Dakota, South Dakota, or the 26 northern and western Wisconsin counties that fall within the Ninth Federal Reserve District, and American citizenship or permanent resident status. The application may be either for a long term, involving a policy-level internship experience and often leading to an academic degree, or for a short term, to enroll in university programs to enhance managerial skills on a non-degree basis. Members of minority groups are particularly encouraged to apply.

Financial data Long-term fellows receive monthly stipends and short-term fellows receive weekly stipends; the amount of the stipends is intended to cover basic living expenses. In addition, all fellows receive reimbursement for 50 percent of their tuition charges up to $8,000 plus 80 percent of tuition charges over $8,000.

Duration From 4 to 18 months for long-term awards; from 3 to 10 weeks for short-term awards.

Special features Awards are for full-time study and internships anywhere in the United States. This program began in 1965; the shorter awards were added in 1973.

Limitations Fellowships are not awarded for applicants who are already enrolled as full-time students, part-time study combined with full- or part-time employment, academic research, publications, or design and development of service programs or projects. Fellowships are unlikely to be awarded for unstructured

internships, full-time study plans built on academic programs designed primarily for part-time students, programs intended to meet the coninuing education requirements for professional certification, completion of basic educational requirements for non-administrative jobs or professions, segments of degree programs that cannot be completed within or near the end of the fellowship period, or projects that might more properly be the subjects of grant proposals from organizations.

Number awarded Approximately 35 each year.

Deadline November of each year for long-term fellowships; February of each year for short-term fellowships.

[1552]
CALIFORNIA STATE LIBRARY MULTI-ETHNIC RECRUITMENT SCHOLARSHIPS

California State Library
Attn: Library Development Services
900 N Street
P.O. Box 942837
Sacramento, CA 94237-0001
(916) 653-6822   (800) 654-0183
E-mail: klow@library.ca.gov

Purpose To provide financial assistance to minorities in California who are interested in pursuing a degree or gaining greater work experience in public librarianship.

Eligibility Applicants must be members of an ethnic minority group underrepresented in the library profession (Asian/Pacific Islander, Black/African American, Hispanic, and American Indian) seeking a master's degree in library and information science at an accredited graduate library school in California. Selection is based on an essay (75 percent) and previous experience in working with an ethnic community (25 percent). Candidates must be nominated by a public library, academic library, cooperative library system, or accredited graduate library school in California.

Financial data Up to $6,000 each year. Funds are awarded to the sponsoring library or library school, which may charge up to 10 percent of the scholarship monies for administrative overhead.

Duration 1 year; may be renewed for 1 additional year, although first priority is given to first time applicants.

Special features Recipients are assigned an internship in a public library that serves a predominately ethnic community or conduct research in an area of public librarianship that makes a contribution toward the improvement of library services to ethnic minority populations in California.

Number awarded Up to 8 each year.

Deadline Students must submit their applications to the sponsoring graduate library school, library, or library system by March of each year; the library system or library submits the application packets to the library school the student will be attending by April of each year; the library school submits the formal application to the State Library by May of each year.

[1553]
CAPITOL HILL NEWS INTERNSHIPS

Radio and Television News Directors Foundation
1000 Connecticut Avenue, N.W., Suite 615
Washington, DC 20036
(202) 659-6510   Fax: (202) 223-4007

Purpose To provide work experience to recent graduates in electronic journalism who are interested in covering congressional activities in Washington, D.C.

Eligibility Eligible are recent (within 1 year) college graduates of a program in electronic journalism; preference is given to minority students. Applications include an essay explaining why the candidate is interested in this program and how it will help meet career goals. Excellent writing skills are essential. The Radio and Television News Directors Foundation (RTNDF) recognizes African Americans, Asian Americans, Hispanic Americans, and Native Americans as minorities.

Financial data The stipend is $1,000 per month. Interns are responsible for their own housing and living expenses.

Duration 3 months; the spring program begins in March and the summer program begins in June.

Special features Interns cover newsworthy congressional activities and help coordinate broadcast coverage of those activities; they obtain hands-on experience in the House and Senate radio-TV galleries, working side by side with the Washington press and congressional staff to cover the political process.

Number awarded 2 in the spring and 2 in the summer of each year.

Deadline January for the spring program; February for the summer program.

[1554]
CARNEGIE MUSEUM OF NATURAL HISTORY NATIVE AMERICAN STUDENT INTERNSHIP

Carnegie Museum of Natural History
Edward O'Neill Research Center
5800 Baum Boulevard
Pittsburgh, PA 15206
Fax: (412) 665-2751

Purpose To provide work experience at the Carnegie Museum to Native American undergraduates or graduate students.

Eligibility This program is open to Native American students enrolled in undergraduate or graduate programs. Preference is given to those with an interest in museum studies or studio art or design.

Financial data The stipend is $1,000 per month, plus a travel allowance.

Duration 2 to 3 months, beginning in either the summer or the fall.

Special features Interns assist staff at the museum in the divisions of anthropology, exhibit design, and education on projects related to the development of the Alcoa Foundation Hall of Native Americans (which is scheduled to open in 1997).

Limitations This program did not operate in 1996. Its resumption is currently uncertain.

Number awarded 1 or more each year.

Deadline March of each year.

[1555]
CHALLENGE PROGRAM IN SCIENCE AND ENGINEERING

Oak Ridge Institute for Science and Education
Attn: Science/Engineering Education Division
P.O. Box 117
Oak Ridge, TN 37831-0117
(423) 576-5300   (423) 576-4813
(800) 569-7749   Fax: (423) 576-3643
E-mail: chalnge@orau.gov

Purpose To provide minority secondary school students in designated Tennessee counties with an opportunity to participate in a structured program of summer and academic-year activities in science and engineering.

Eligibility This program is open to seventh through twelfth grade students in Anderson, Blount, Knox, Loudon, and Roane counties who are American Indians, Blacks, Hispanics, Native Alaskans, and Native Pacific Islanders and interested in studying science, engineering, or mathematics. The program includes a mentoring system, a summer science camp, seminars, field trips, and enrichment activities during the academic year at various facilities in Oak Ridge, Tennessee.

Financial data Participants receive a stipend during summer camp and internships.

Duration 1 year; renewable.

Special features This program is funded by the U.S. Department of Energy, Lockheed Martin Energy Systems, Inc. (operator of Oak Ridge National Laboratory), and Oak Ridge Associated Universities, but operated and administered by the Science/Engineering Education Division (SEED) of Oak Ridge Institute for Science and Education (ORISE).

Number awarded Varies each year.

Deadline Applications for the academic year program are accepted at any time; applications for the summer science camp must be submitted by February of each year.

[1556]
CHARLOTTE OBSERVER INTERNSHIPS

Charlotte Observer
Attn: Regional Editor
600 South Tryon Street
P.O. Box 32188
Charlotte, NC 28232-2188
(704) 358-5020

Purpose To provide work experience at the *Charlotte Observer* in North Carolina to college students interested in careers in journalism.

Eligibility This program is open to students from any state, with a preference for juniors or seniors. Applicants must be planning to pursue careers in newspaper reporting or editing. Minorities are especially encouraged to apply.

Financial data The salary is approximately $500 per week.

Duration 12 weeks, during the summer.

Number awarded 4 each year.

Deadline November of each year.

[1557]
CHICAGO SUN-TIMES MINORITY SCHOLARSHIP AND INTERNSHIP PROGRAM

Chicago Sun-Times
Attn: Assistant to the Executive Editor
401 North Wabash Avenue
Chicago, IL 60611
(312) 321-3000

Purpose To provide financial assistance to minority college students in the Chicago area who are interested in preparing for a career in print journalism.

Eligibility Minority students are eligible to apply if they are entering their junior year in college, graduated from a Chicago-area high school or have lived in the Chicago metropolitan area for at least 5 years, and have demonstrated an interest in print journalism.

Financial data Students selected for this program receive a $1,500 scholarship plus a paid internship.

Duration The program provides a scholarship in the junior year, a paid internship during the summer between the junior and senior years, and a renewal of the scholarship in the senior year if the recipient maintains a 3.0 grade point average.

Special features The Chicago metropolitan area includes Cook, DuPage, Kane, Lake, McHenry, and Will counties in Illinois and Lake and Porter counties in Indiana. Recipients may use the scholarship at any school of their choosing. For the summer internships, assignments are available in reporting, editing, graphics, or photography.

Number awarded 1 or more each year.

Deadline March of each year.

[1558]
CHIPS QUINN SCHOLARS PROGRAM

Freedom Forum
Attn: Journalism Scholarships Committee
1101 Wilson Boulevard
Arlington, VA 22209
(703) 528-0800   Fax: (703) 528-7766

Purpose To provide work experience, career mentoring, and scholarship support to minority college students who are majoring in journalism.

Eligibility Deans of all journalism schools in the country are each invited to nominate 1 junior-year journalism student for this program. Students must also apply for an internship for the summer following their junior year.

Financial data Students chosen for this program receive a travel stipend to attend a spring workshop at the Freedom Forum in Arlington, Virginia and, upon completion of the internship, a $1,000 scholarship.

Duration 1 year, including the summer internship.

Special features Students are invited to the workshop at the Freedom Forum at the end of their junior year and then work as an intern during the summer at a newspaper where they are linked with a mentor editor. This program was established in 1990 in memory of the late John D. Quinn Jr., managing editor of the *Poughkeepsie Journal*. Funding is provided by the Freedom Forum, formerly the Gannett Foundation.

Number awarded Varies each year; in a recent year, 36 scholarships were awarded through this program.

Deadline January of each year.

[1559]
CIA MINORITY UNDERGRADUATE SCHOLAR PROGRAM

Central Intelligence Agency
Attn: Personnel Representative
P.O. Box 12727
Arlington, VA 22209-8727
(703) 351-2028   (800) JOBS CIA

Purpose To provide summer work experience to minority or disabled undergraduates who are interested in employment with the Central Intelligence Agency (CIA).

Eligibility Undergraduate students, particularly minorities and people with disabilities, are eligible for this program if they will have completed 1 or 2 years of college or university study; are at least 17 1/2 years of age at the time of application; are U.S. citizens; have and maintain a minimum grade point average of 2.75; are majoring in computer science, economics, electrical engineering, foreign affairs, geography, international studies, languages, mathematics, physical science, or political science; and meet the same employment standards as permanent CIA employees. They must be available to work in metropolitan Washington, D.C. for at least 90 calendar days each summer following their sophomore year.

Financial data Interns receive salaries ranging from the GS-3 to GS-7 level, depending on the number of credit hours completed. Travel to Washington D.C. and a housing allowance while there are also provided. Recipients are also eligible to apply for the CIA Tuition Assistance Program.

Duration Up to 3 summers.

Special features During their summer employment, interns are evaluated by the CIA as potential future permanent employees.

Number awarded Varies each year.

Deadline September of each year.

[1560]
CIA SUMMER INTERNSHIP PROGRAM

Central Intelligence Agency
Attn: Personnel Representative
P.O. Box 12727
Arlington, VA 22209-8727
(703) 351-2028   (800) JOBS CIA

Purpose To give promising undergraduate students (particularly minorities and persons with disabilities) an opportunity to gain practical summer work experience at the Central Intelligence Agency.

Eligibility To qualify for this program, students must have completed their sophomore year, be U.S. citizens, have and maintain at least a 2.75 grade point average, and meet the same employment standards as permanent employees. Applicants should be studying computer science, economics, electrical engineering, foreign affairs, geography, international studies, languages, mathematics, physical sciences, or political science. Particularly encouraged to apply are minorities and people with disabilities.

Financial data Salaries range from GS-5 to GS-7, depending upon the number of credit hours completed.

Duration Summer months.

Special features Interns receive many of the same benefits as permanent employees and are eligible to apply for the agency's tuition assistance program. They are given the opportunity to work with highly skilled professionals and see first hand the role the CIA plays in supporting U.S. officials who make our country's foreign policy.

Limitations Applicants should be prepared to spend 1 to 3 days in Washington D.C. at government expense for interviews and other administrative requirements. Students are required to work at least 90 calendar days each summer.

Number awarded Several each year.

Deadline October of each year.

[1561]
CIA UNDERGRADUATE SCHOLAR PROGRAM

Central Intelligence Agency
Attn: Personnel Representative
P.O. Box 12727
Arlington, VA 22209-8727
(703) 351-2028 (800) JOBS CIA

Purpose To provide financial assistance to minority or disabled undergraduates who are interested in completing their postsecondary education and gaining work experience at the Central Intelligence Agency (CIA).

Eligibility Graduating high school seniors, particularly minorities from inner city neighborhoods and people with disabilities, are eligible for this program. They must be U.S. citizens, be 18 years of age by May 1 of their senior year, achieve a score of at least 1,000 on the SAT or 21 on the ACT, have a high school grade point average of 2.75 or higher, demonstrate financial need, and meet the same employment standards as permanent CIA employees. Recipients must attend an accredited college or university as full-time students in a 4- or 5-year program, majoring in computer science, engineering, economics, foreign languages (non-romance), or foreign area studies.

Financial data The scholarships provide a yearly salary at the GS-2 to GS-5 levels and up to $15,000 per school year for tuition, fees, books, and supplies. Travel to Washington D.C. and a housing allowance while there are also provided.

Duration Up to 5 years of study; up to 4 years of summer internships.

Special features During the summer, recipients work for the CIA in the Washington, D.C. metropolitan area.

Limitations After graduation, participants are eligible for promotion to a general professional entry grade level as a CIA employee (GS-7 level). They must work for the agency for a period of 1 1/2 times the length of their college career.

Number awarded Varies each year.

Deadline Applications must be submitted by the end of the first semester of senior year in high school or, for students who do not meet the age requirement, by the end of the first semester as a college freshman (usually December of each year).

[1562]
CIVILIAN RADIOACTIVE WASTE MANAGEMENT FELLOWSHIP PROGRAM

Oak Ridge Institute for Science and Education
Attn: Science/Engineering Education Division
P.O. Box 117
Oak Ridge, TN 37831-0117
(423) 241-2890 (423) 576-2600
(800) 569-7749 Fax: (423) 576-3643
E-mail: crwmfp@orau.gov

Purpose To provide graduate study and research opportunities in fields related to the management of spent nuclear fuel and high-level radioactive wastes.

Eligibility This program is open to graduate students who are working on a master's or doctoral degree in earth sciences, engineering, materials sciences, or radiation sciences at participating schools (for a list of these schools, write to the address above). Application should be made before or during the first year of graduate school. All programs operated by the Science/Engineering Education Division (SEED) of Oak Ridge Institute for Science and Education (ORISE) seek to broaden the participation of minorities, women, and persons with disabilities in science and engineering careers.

Financial data Participants receive an annual stipend of $14,400, plus an additional $300 per month during their practicum. Participants are also paid for some of their travel and tuition and fees up to $8,000 per year.

Duration 1 year; may be renewed for up to 4 additional years.

Special features Participants intern at various U.S. Department of Energy (DOE) research facilities. This program is funded by the DOE's Office of Civilian Radioactive Waste Management and administered by ORISE/SEED.

Number awarded Varies each year.

Deadline January of each year.

[1563]
CLARKSVILLE LEAF-CHRONICLE INTERNSHIPS

Clarksville Leaf-Chronicle
Attn: Editor
P.O. Box 829
Clarksville, TN 37041-0829
(615) 552-1808

Purpose To provide work experience at the *Clarksville Leaf-Chronicle* in Tennessee to college students interested in careers in journalism.

Eligibility This program is open to students from any state, with a preference for juniors and seniors. Applicants must be planning to pursue careers in newspaper reporting or editing. Minorities are especially encouraged to apply.

Financial data The salary is $280 per week.

Duration 12 weeks, during the summer.

Number awarded 2 each year.

Deadline February of each year.

[1564]
CLINICAL TRAINING FELLOWSHIP PROGRAM FOR MINORITY MEDICAL STUDENTS IN SUBSTANCE ABUSE RESEARCH AND TREATMENT

National Medical Fellowships, Inc.
Attn: Scholarships and Programs
110 West 32nd Street, 8th Floor
New York, NY 10001-3205
(212) 714-1007

Purpose To encourage academically outstanding underrepresented minority medical school students to participate in substance abuse research, treatment, and policy studies.

Eligibility Only nominations are accepted; students may not apply directly. Nominees must be underrepresented minority (African American, Native American, Mexican American, and mainland Puerto Rican) second- and third-year students attending accredited medical schools in the United States. Selection is based on academic excellence, potential for significant contributions to medicine, and leadership.

Financial data The internship stipend is $5,000.

Duration 3 months; nonrenewable.

Special features Fellows participate in a 3-day orientation sponsored by the Center on Addiction and Substance Abuse (CASA) of Columbia University in New York where they receive basic information on the effects and costs of substance abuse to the American health care system, and are introduced to the policy implications of treatment and research. They then go to

Philadelphia for a training program at the Center for Studies of Addiction (CSA) of the University of Pennsylvania School of Medicine where they receive clinical and research training in current behavioral, psychological, and pharmacological substance abuse treatment techniques. This program was created in 1994 with a grant from Pew Charitable Trusts; it is jointly administered by CASA, CSA, and National Medical Fellowships, Inc.

Number awarded 10 each year.

Deadline Nominations are requested from medical schools in September of each year.

[1565]
COLLEGE ART ASSOCIATION PROFESSIONAL PLACEMENTS

College Art Association of America
Attn: Fellowship Coordinator
275 Seventh Avenue
New York, NY 10001
(212) 691-1051, ext. 209   Fax: (212) 627-2381

Purpose To provide internships at institutions with collections or programs in American art.

Eligibility This program arranges internships at participating institutions (colleges, universities, museums, art centers, etc.) with collections or programs in American art, located anywhere in the world. Applicants must be U.S. citizens or permanent residents, whether living in the United States or abroad. Artists and art historians of color and from other culturally diverse or economically disadvantaged backgrounds are encouraged to apply. Selection is based on financial need.

Financial data Interns receive stipends.

Duration 1 to 2 years.

Number awarded Up to 10 each year.

Deadline January of each year.

[1566]
COLLEGE SUMMER EMPLOYMENT PROGRAM OF THE NATIONAL SECURITY AGENCY

National Security Agency
Attn: Coordinator, Summer Employment Program
M3221
Fort Meade, Maryland 20755-6000
(410) 859-4590   (800) 962-9398

Purpose To provide students with an opportunity to participate in the work of the National Security Agency (NSA) during a summer internship.

Eligibility This program is open to U.S. citizens who are majoring in electrical, electronic, or computer engineering, computer science, applied mathematics, statistics, or a Slavic (except Russian), Middle Eastern, or Asian language. Applicants must have a 3.0 grade point average in engineering, computer science, or languages (or a 3.5 grade point average in mathematics) and be eligible for a high-level security clearance. Students usually work during the summer following their junior year, although summer employment is also available to students pursuing graduate degrees. NSA is firmly committed to affirmative action policies for members of minority groups, women, veterans, and the disabled.

Financial data For undergraduate, a stipend is paid at the annual rate of $22,554; for graduate students, the stipend depends on education and experience.

Duration 12 weeks, during the summer.

Number awarded Varies each year.

Deadline November of each year.

[1567]
COLUMBUS LEDGER-ENQUIRER INTERNSHIPS

Columbus Ledger-Enquirer
Attn: Managing Editor
17 West 12th Street
P.O. Box 711
Columbus, GA 31901-2413
(706) 571-8582

Purpose To provide work experience at the *Columbus Ledger-Enquirer* in Georgia to college students interested in careers in journalism.

Eligibility This program is open to college students from any state, with a preference for juniors or seniors. Applicants must be planning to pursue careers in newspaper journalism or photography. Minorities are especially encouraged to apply.

Financial data The salary is $300 per week; some unpaid internships are also available.

Duration Internships usually extend for 12 weeks; they are tenable at various times of the year.

Number awarded The number of news/editorial internships varies each year; photography internships are offered only occasionally.

Deadline Applications may be submitted at any time.

[1568]
COMMUNITY COLLEGES AND TECHNICAL INSTITUTES INITIATIVE

Argonne National Laboratory
Attn: Division of Educational Programs
Community Colleges and Technical Institutes Initiative
9700 South Cass Avenue
Argonne, IL 60439-4845
(630) 252-3371   E-mail: washington@dep.anl.gov

Purpose To provide underrepresented minority students at community colleges in the Chicago area with educational and employment opportunities at Argonne National Laboratory.

Eligibility This program is open to U.S. citizens and permanent residents who are enrolled in community colleges and technical institutes in Chicago and the surrounding suburbs with at least 1 trimester of study concluded. Applicants must be seeking a program of research training and other enrichment activities at the Laboratory in electronics and computing technology, science education, electronic publishing, analytical chemistry, biotechnology, biology, decision information sciences, office automation technology, electronics and engineering technology, physical and life sciences, mathematics, computer science and engineering, and applied research programs relating to coal, conservation, environmental impact and technology, fission, and fusion technology.

Financial data Wages are calculated at an hourly rate based on academic year standing.

Duration These are short-term appointments.

Number awarded Varies each year, depending on the availability of funding.

Deadline Applications may be submitted at any time.

[1569]
CONSORTIUM FOR GRADUATE STUDY IN MANAGEMENT FELLOWSHIPS

Consortium for Graduate Study in Management
200 South Hanley Road, Suite 1102
St. Louis, MO 63105-3415
(314) 935-5614   E-mail: cgsm@wuolin.wustl.edu

Purpose To accelerate the entry of racial minorities into managerial positions in business.

Eligibility Eligible to apply are African Americans, Hispanic Americans (Chicanos, Cubans, Dominicans, and Puerto Ricans), and Native Americans who have graduated from college and are interested in a career in business. An undergraduate degree in business or economics is not required. Applicants must be U.S. citizens and planning to pursue a Master's of Business Administration degree at 1 of the Consortium's schools: University of California at Berkeley, Indiana University, University of Michigan, New York University, University of North Carolina at Chapel Hill, University of Rochester, University of Southern California, University of Texas at Austin, University of Virginia, Washington University, or University of Wisconsin at Madison. Preference is given to applicants under 31 years of age.

Financial data The fellowship provides full tuition and required fees. Summer internships with the consortium's cooperative sponsors, providing paid practical experience, are also offered.

Duration Up to 4 semesters.

Limitations Fellowships are tenable at member schools only.

Number awarded Varies; approximately 180 each year.

Deadline January of each year.

[1570]
COOPERATIVE EDUCATION INTERNSHIPS

Seattle Personnel Department
Attn: Special Employment Programs Office
710 Second Avenue
Dexter Horton Building, 12th Floor
Seattle, WA 98104-1793
(206) 684-7996   TDD: (206) 684-7888

Purpose To provide work experience in Seattle municipal government to college students.

Eligibility Full-time college students, in 4-year, community, or vocational colleges, are eligible for these internships. Women, minorities, and persons with disabilities are encouraged to apply.

Financial data The salary is $11.03 per hour.

Duration Up to 6 months of full-time work if special arrangements are made with the college, or 9 to 12 months of part-time work.

Special features Assignments are in paraprofessional, technical, or service work situations.

Number awarded Depends on the availability of openings.

[1571]
CORNELL–SACNAS SUMMER PROGRAM FOR LATINOS AND NATIVE AMERICANS

Cornell University
Attn: Mathematical and Theoretical Biology Institute
Biometrics Unit
435 Warren Hall
Ithaca, NY 14853
(607) 255-8103   Fax: (607) 255-4698
E-mail: mtbi@cornell.edu

Purpose To enable Chicano, Latino, and Native American students to participate in a summer institute on mathematical biology at Cornell University.

Eligibility Chicano, Latino, and Native American undergraduates completing their sophomore or junior year with a major in mathematics, biology, or related fields, and who have completed a year of calculus, are eligible to apply. They must wish to participate in an institute at the University on mathematical biology.

Financial data Participants receive a stipend of $2,000, round-trip transportation to Ithaca, New York, and room and board.

Duration 7 weeks, during the summer.

Special features This program began in 1996. It is sponsored by the Society for Advancement of Chicanos and Native Americans in Science (SACNAS), 1156 High Street, University of California at Santa Cruz, Santa Cruz, CA 95064, (408) 459-4272, Fax: (408) 459-3156, E-mail: sacnas@cats.ucsc.edu. Funding is provided by the National Security Agency, the National Science Foundation, and, at Cornell University, the Office of the Provost, the College of Agriculture and Life Sciences, and the Biometrics Unit.

Number awarded 30 each year.

Deadline February of each year.

[1572]
CORPORATE-SPONSORED SCHOLARSHIPS FOR MINORITY UNDERGRADUATE STUDENTS WHO MAJOR IN PHYSICS

American Physical Society
One Physics Ellipse
College Park, MD 20740-3844
(301) 209-3200   Fax: (301) 209-0865

Purpose To provide financial assistance to minority group students interested in studying physics on the undergraduate level.

Eligibility Any African American, Hispanic American, or Native American U.S. citizen who plans to major in physics and who is a high school senior or college freshman or sophomore may apply. A selection committee recommended by the association's Committee on Minorities in Physics and appointed by the association's president selects the scholarship recipients and the host institutions. The selection committee also arranges for a physicist to provide appropriate mentor guidance for each scholarship recipient. The scholarships are awarded in 2 modes: institutionally attached scholarships and portable scholarships. The institutionally attached scholarships are assigned to institutions with historically or predominantly Black, Hispanic, or Native American enrollment. The portable scholarships allow recipients to enroll in programs of their choice. It is anticipated that in any award year, half of the scholarships will be institutionally attached and half will be portable.

Financial data Each scholarship consists of $2,000 awarded to the student for tuition, room, and board, and $500 awarded to the host department. The scholarships may be supplemented in some cases by a work-study program arranged by the corporate sponsor with the scholarship recipient and with the concurrence of the association's selection committee.

Duration 1 year; renewable for 1 additional year with the approval of the APS selection committee.

Special features APS conducts the scholarship program in conjunction with the Corporate Associates of the American Institute of Physics. Each scholarship is sponsored by a corporation, which is normally designated as the sponsor. A corporation generally sponsors from 1 to 10 scholarships, depending upon its size and the utilization of physics in the business.

Number awarded Varies; generally, 6 new and 11 renewed scholarships each year.

Deadline February of each year.

[1573]
COX MINORITY JOURNALISM SCHOLARSHIP PROGRAM

Cox Enterprises, Inc.
Attn: Scholarship Administrator
P.O. Box 4689
Atlanta, GA 30302
(404) 526-5151

Purpose To provide work experience and financial assistance to minority high school graduates in areas served by Cox Enterprises newspapers.

Eligibility Applicants must be financially needy racial minorities who are enrolled as seniors in public high schools in the city selected for the particular year and who plan to attend college in the same city. They must have at least a 3.0 grade point average and an interest in journalism. Applications include an essay of 500 words or more on "Why I Want a Career in the Newspaper Industry."

Financial data All educational expenses are paid for 4 years of college, including room, board, books, and tuition. A variety of part-time newspaper work experiences will be offered while the student attends college and (full time) during the summer. The approximate total value of the award is $40,000.

Duration The scholarship is awarded for 4 years. The recipient is expected to intern for approximately 20 hours weekly throughout the 4 years of college.

Special features Employment at 1 of Cox Enterprises, Inc. newspapers is offered upon successful completion of the program. The scholarship rotates on an annual basis among the different cities where Cox Enterprises owns and operates newspapers; headquarters of the corporation are in Atlanta.

Number awarded 1 each year.

Deadline April of each year.

[1574]
THE DAY SCHOLARSHIP FOR MINORITY JOURNALISTS

The Day Publishing Company
47 Eugene O'Neill Drive
P.O. Box 1231
New London, CT 06320-1231
(203) 442-2200, ext. 238

Purpose To provide financial assistance and work experience in journalism for minorities who live or attend college in eastern Connecticut.

Eligibility Minorities (African Americans, Latinos, Asian Americans, or Native Americans) who live or attend school in eastern Connecticut may apply if they are interested in journalism as a career. Applicants may be 1) high school seniors who will enroll as college freshmen in the fall following application or 2) current college students. A minimum high school or college grade point average of 2.5 is required.

Financial data Recipients receive up to $10,000 in scholarship money and paid internships during school breaks.

Duration 4 years.

Special features During the internship periods, which may begin as early as the summer after high school graduation, students participate in the newsroom training program, receive special attention from editors and a mentor, and undergo a formal evaluation regularly. Upon graduation from college, recipients are offered an entry-level job and are expected to work at The Day for 2 years.

Number awarded Varies each year.

Deadline February of each year.

[1575]
DEPARTMENT OF ENERGY STUDENT RESEARCH PARTICIPATION PROGRAM

Oak Ridge Institute for Science and Education
Attn: Science/Engineering Education Division
P.O. Box 117
Oak Ridge, TN 37831-0117
(423) 576-1083   (423) 576-3426
(800) 569-7749   Fax: (423) 576-3643
E-mail: studrpp@orau.gov

Purpose To provide funding to undergraduate students interested in conducting research on energy production, use, and conservation under the guidance of staff members of the U.S. Department of Energy (DOE).

Eligibility College juniors and seniors in social sciences, engineering, physical sciences, life sciences, or mathematics may apply for this program. They must propose to conduct research at 1 of the following DOE facilities: Atmospheric Turbulence and Diffusion Division, Oak Ridge, Tennessee; Continuous Electron Beam Accelerator Facility, Newport News, Virginia; Oak Ridge Institute for Science and Education, Oak Ridge, Tennessee; Oak Ridge National Laboratory, Oak Ridge, Tennessee; Savannah River Ecology Laboratory, Savannah River Site, and Savannah River Archaeological Research Program, Aiken, South Carolina; Lockheed Martin Energy Systems, Inc., Oak Ridge, Tennessee; Pittsburgh Energy Technology Center; or the Triangle Universities Research Laboratory, Durham, North Carolina. All programs operated by the Science/Engineering Education Division (SEED) of Oak Ridge Institute for Science and Education (ORISE) seek to broaden the participation of minorities, women, and persons with disabilities in science and engineering careers.

Financial data The weekly stipend ranges from $225 to $250; some reimbursement for travel is available.

Duration 10 weeks in the summer; some academic-year appointments may be available.

Special features This program is funded by DOE's Office of Energy Research and administered by ORISE/SEED.

Number awarded Approximately 50 each year.

Deadline January of each year.

[1576]

DETROIT FREE PRESS MINORITY JOURNALISM SCHOLARSHIP

Detroit Free Press
Attn: Publishers Office
321 West Lafayette Boulevard
Detroit, MI 48226
(313) 222-6400   (800) 678-6400
Fax: (313) 222-8874

Purpose   To encourage outstanding minority high school seniors in the circulation area of the *Detroit Free Press* to prepare for a newspaper career.

Eligibility   This program is open to minority high school seniors in the newspaper's circulation area who plan to become writers, editors, or photojournalists. They must have earned at least a 3.0 grade point average and plan to major in journalism in college. Selection is based on academic record, journalism-related extra-curricular activities, recommendations, and a 5-page essay on why the applicant wants to become a journalist.

Financial data   The first-place winner receives $1,000 and the second-place winner receives $750.

Duration   1 year.

Special features   The first-place winner is automatically considered for the 4-year Knight-Ridder Minority Scholarship Program.

Number awarded   At least 3 each year.

Deadline   January of each year.

[1577]

DOW JONES NEWSPAPER FUND BUSINESS REPORTING PROGRAM

Dow Jones Newspaper Fund
P.O. Box 300
Princeton, NJ 08543-0300
(609) 452-2820   (800) DOWFUND
Fax: (609) 520-5804
E-mail: newsfund@wsf.dowjones.com

Purpose   To provide work experience and financial assistance to minority college students who are interested in careers in journalism.

Eligibility   Minority college sophomores and juniors who are U.S. citizens are eligible to apply if they are interested in careers in journalism and summer internships at daily newspapers as business reporters.

Financial data   Interns receive regular wages from the newspapers for which they work and a $1,000 scholarship at the successful completion of the summer of work.

Duration   3 months for the summer internship; 1 year for the scholarship.

Number awarded   Up to 12 each year.

Deadline   November of each year.

[1578]

DURACELL—NATIONAL URBAN LEAGUE SCHOLARSHIP AND INTERN PROGRAM

National Urban League
Attn: Scholarship Coordinator
500 East 62nd Street, 10th Floor
New York, NY 10021-8379
(212) 310-9212

Purpose   To assist and encourage outstanding minority students who are interested in completing their college education in the areas of engineering, sales, marketing, manufacturing operations, finance, or business administration.

Eligibility   Eligible to apply are minority students who are pursuing full-time studies leading to a bachelor's degree at an accredited institution of higher learning. They must be juniors or third-year students at the time the scholarship award begins, rank within the top 25 percent of their class when the application is submitted, and be majoring in the areas of engineering, sales, marketing, manufacturing operations, finance, or business administration. Applications must be submitted to a local Urban League office. These applications are screened and sent to the appropriate National Urban League regional office. Each regional office may nominate up to 4 potential scholarship recipients who meet the competition criteria. The National Urban League interviews each of the semifinalists to select the 10 finalists. In the final step of the selection process, Duracell and the National Urban League review the 10 finalists and select the 5 winners.

Financial data   The $10,000 scholarships are divided equally between the junior and senior years of the winners (in amounts of $5,000 per school year).

Duration   2 years.

Special features   During the summer between the junior and senior years, scholarship recipients work as interns at a Duracell USA facility; many recipients have accepted employment opportunities at Duracell.

Limitations   The stipends are sent directly to the recipient's college or university; the school is custodian of the funds and disburses the money consistent with the purposes of the program.

Number awarded   5 each year.

Deadline   Applications must be submitted to local Urban League offices by April of each year.

[1579]

DURHAM HERALD-SUN INTERNSHIPS

Durham Herald-Sun
Attn: Managing Editor
2828 Pickett Road
P.O. Box 2092
Durham, NC 27702
(919) 419-6635

Purpose   To provide work experience at the *Durham Herald-Sun* in North Carolina to college students interested in careers in journalism.

Eligibility   This program is open to students from any state, with a preference for juniors. Applicants must be planning to pursue careers in newspaper reporting, editing, or photography. Minorities are especially encouraged to apply.

Financial data   The salary is $300 per week.

Duration   13 weeks, during the summer.

Number awarded   2 or 3 in news/editorial and 1 in photography each year.

Deadline December of each year.

[1580]
EQUAL RIGHTS ADVOCATES LAW CLERKSHIPS

Equal Rights Advocates, Inc.
1663 Mission Street, Suite 550
San Francisco, CA 94103
(415) 621-0672   Fax: (415) 621-6744

Purpose To provide work experience for law students who are interested in working for the equal rights of women.

Eligibility Applicants should be entering second- or third-year law students who are committed to improving the condition of women and women of color. Selection criteria include demonstrated involvement in issues of public concern, legal skills, public speaking skills, ability to work with diverse communities, critical thinking, ability to write well, and a sense of humor; the ability to speak Spanish is preferred.

Financial data These are paid internships.

Duration 1 semester or summer.

Special features Equal Rights Advocates (ERA) is a nonprofit, public interest law firm that litigates impact cases, authors amicus briefs, and works on public policy issues. It focuses on employment discrimination, sexual harassment in education, women and immigration, women and health, and other related issues concerning women of color and poor working women.

Number awarded 3 each semester or summer.

Deadline November of each year for summer; any time for semester internships.

[1581]
ETS SUMMER INTERNSHIPS IN PROGRAM DIRECTION

Educational Testing Service
Mail Stop 16-T
Princeton, NJ 08541-0001
(609) 734-1806   E-mail: ldelauro@ets.org

Purpose To provide summer work experience at Educational Testing Service's (ETS) headquarters near Princeton, New Jersey, especially for women and minority professionals.

Eligibility Candidates must have completed a master's degree program; particularly welcome are applications from individuals working on a doctoral degree, especially in the areas of psychology, teaching/administration in secondary or higher education, or business management. Selection is based on academic record and the match of courses and experiences with ETS program and development areas. Consideration is given to representation from various areas of the country and to candidates' ethnic origin and gender.

Financial data Each participant receives $2,500 for the program, plus a supplemental living allowance for a spouse or child ($350) or for a spouse and children ($500). Participants are also reimbursed for travel to and from Princeton.

Duration 8 weeks during the summer, starting in June.

Special features The program is modelled after the ETS Summer Program in Research for Graduate Students and gives participants the opportunity to work closely with ETS professional staff who manage the development and operation of ETS's testing programs. Interns are invited to participate in a series of seminars on aspects of management, development, and research.

Deadline January of each year.

[1582]
ETS SUMMER PROGRAM IN RESEARCH FOR GRADUATE STUDENTS

Educational Testing Service
Mail Stop 16-T
Princeton, NJ 08541-0001
(609) 734-1806   E-mail: ldelauro@ets.org

Purpose To provide work experience to minority and women graduate students in educational measurement and related fields.

Eligibility Graduate students who have completed 40 or more credits in a doctoral program emphasizing psychometrics; psychology; educational technology; statistics; computer science; linguistics; education; educational, occupational, or vocational testing; education of the deaf; minority issues; sociology of education; testing issues, including alternate forms of assessment for special populations; new forms of assessment; or policy research are eligible to apply. An explicit goal of the program is to increase the number of women and minority professionals in educational measurement and related fields.

Financial data The stipend is $2,500, plus a supplemental living allowance for participants who bring a spouse ($350) or children ($500). In addition, participants and their families are reimbursed for travel expenses from their universities to ETS (in Princeton) and back.

Duration 8 weeks during the summer.

Special features Participants work under the supervision of ETS staff members.

Number awarded Up to 12 each year.

Deadline January of each year.

[1583]
FAIRCHILD MINORITY ACCESS PROGRAM

Fairchild Publications
Attn: Human Resources
7 West 34th Street
New York, NY 10001-8191
(212) 630-4291

Purpose To provide work experience to minority college graduates interested in publishing.

Eligibility Minorities who have just graduated from college are eligible to apply for this program. Applicants for editorial trainee should have a bachelor's degree in English or journalism and previous reporting or editing experience through an internship or the school yearbook or newspaper. Applicants for sales trainee should have a bachelor's degree in a related area of study and previous exposure to sales.

Financial data Successful candidates receive competitive entry-level salaries.

Duration 6 months to 1 year.

Special features Fairchild Publications is engaged in gathering and publishing news and ideas for 13 trade and consumer publications. Each publication has its own advertising and editorial staffs. Training is available in either the sales or editorial departments of 1 of the publications.

Number awarded 2 each year.

Deadline The starting date depends on job availability.

[1584]
FAYETTEVILLE OBSERVER-TIMES INTERNSHIPS

Fayetteville Observer-Times
Attn: Managing Editor
458 Whitfield Street
P.O. Box 849
Fayetteville, NC 28302
(910) 323-4848

Purpose To provide work experience at the *Fayetteville Observer-Times* in North Carolina to college students interested in careers in journalism.

Eligibility This program is open to students from any state, with a preference for rising seniors. Applicants must be planning to pursue careers in newspaper reporting, editing, or photography. Minorities are especially encouraged to apply.

Financial data The salary is $290 per week.

Duration 12 weeks, during the summer.

Number awarded 5 in news/editorial and 1 in photography each year.

Deadline January of each year.

[1585]
FELLOWSHIP PROGRAM IN ACADEMIC MEDICINE FOR MINORITY STUDENTS

National Medical Fellowships, Inc.
Attn: Scholarships and Programs
110 West 32nd Street, 8th Floor
New York, NY 10001-3205
(212) 714-1007

Purpose To encourage academically outstanding underrepresented minority medical school students to pursue careers in biomedical research and academic medicine by offering them a research internship in the summer.

Eligibility Only nominations are accepted; students may not apply directly. Nominees must be underrepresented minority (African American, Native American, Mexican American, and mainland Puerto Rican) second- and third-year students attending accredited medical schools in the United States. Selection of finalists is based on academic performance, potential for a successful career in academic medicine, leadership ability, and a firm commitment from a senior scientist-mentor. From a list of finalists, fellows are chosen by lottery. U.S. citizenship is required.

Financial data The internship stipend is $6,000.

Duration From 8 to 12 weeks; nonrenewable.

Special features Interns work in a major research laboratory under the tutelage of a well-known biomedical scientist. The program was created in 1983 with grant support from The Commonwealth Fund of New York to foster mentor relationships between students and prominent scientists. Bristol-Myers Squibb Company joined as a cosponsor in 1990 and assumed sole sponsorship in 1993.

Number awarded 35 each year.

Deadline Nominations are requested from medical schools in October of each year.

[1586]
FERMILAB SUMMER INTERNSHIPS IN SCIENCE AND TECHNOLOGY FOR MINORITY STUDENTS

Fermi National Accelerator Laboratory
Attn: Manager, Equal Opportunity Office
MS 117
P.O. Box 500
Batavia, IL 60510
(708) 840-4633   E-mail: sist@fnal.gov

Purpose To provide work experience at Fermi National Accelerator Laboratory (Fermilab) to underrepresented minority students.

Eligibility Historically underrepresented minorities in the sciences (Hispanics, African Americans, and Native Americans) are eligible to apply if they are undergraduate or graduate students in science.

Financial data Weekly stipends are $400 for freshmen, $428 for sophomores, $460 for juniors, $505 for seniors, and $538 for graduate students. In addition, the program provides round-trip airfare to the laboratory, housing at partial cost to the interns, and transportation between housing and the laboratory.

Duration 11 weeks, beginning in late May.

Special features Interns join selected staff members on research projects, attend academic lectures, and prepare a final report.

Number awarded Approximately 20 each year.

Deadline February of each year.

[1587]
FLEET SCHOLARS WORK/STUDY SCHOLARSHIP PROGRAM

Fleet Bank of Maine
Attn: Education Finance Manager
P.O. Box 1280
Portland, ME 04104
(207) 874-5102

Purpose To provide financial assistance to minority high school students in Maine who are interested in working on a college degree.

Eligibility This program is open to minority high school seniors graduating from public, private or parochial high schools in Maine. Selection is based on academic record and financial need.

Financial data The stipend is $1,000 per year.

Duration 1 year; may be renewed for up to 3 additional years as long as the recipient maintains a minimum grade point average of 3.0.

Special features During the summer, recipients are encouraged to work (full- or part-time), but employment at Fleet Bank is not mandatory. Upon graduation from college, they are eligible to enroll in Fleet Bank's management training program.

Number awarded 4 each year.

Deadline March of each year.

[1588]
FLORENCE TIMESDAILY INTERNSHIPS

Florence TimesDaily
Attn: Executive Editor
219 West Tennessee Street
Florence, AL 35630
(205) 766-3434

Purpose To provide work experience at the *Florence Times-Daily* in Alabama to college students interested in careers in journalism.

Eligibility This program is open to students from any state, with a preference for seniors. Applicants must be planning to pursue careers in newspaper reporting or editing. Minorities are especially encouraged to apply.

Financial data The salary is $300 per week.

Duration 10 weeks, during the summer.

Number awarded 1 each year.

Deadline January of each year.

[1589]
FLORIDA SPACE GRANT CONSORTIUM FELLOWSHIP PROGRAM

Florida Space Grant Consortium
c/o University of Florida
Department of Astronomy
405 Space Sciences Research Building
Gainesville, FL 32611-2055
(352) 392-6750   Fax: (352) 392-3456
E-mail: fsgc@astro.ufl.edu

Purpose To provide financial assistance for graduate space studies at universities participating in the Florida Space Grant Consortium.

Eligibility Eligible to be nominated for this program are U.S. citizens who are enrolled in aerospace-related doctoral studies at universities participating in the Florida Space Grant Consortium: Embry-Riddle Aeronautical University, Florida State University, University of Miami, Florida Atlantic University, Florida A&M University, University of North Florida, Florida Institute of Technology, University of Central Florida, University of South Florida, Florida International University, University of Florida, and University of West Florida. The Florida Space Grant Consortium is a component of the U.S. National Aeronautics and Space Administration (NASA) Space Grant program, which encourages participation by women, minorities, and persons with disabilities.

Financial data Each fellow receives a $12,000 stipend and a supplementary summer traineeship stipend from a participating industry, government, or private laboratory.

Duration Up to 3 years.

Special features Fellows work during the summer in a government, industry, or private laboratory. This program is funded by NASA.

Number awarded 6 each year.

Deadline February of each year.

[1590]
FLORIDA TODAY INTERNSHIPS

Florida Today
Attn: Managing Editor
P.O. Box 419000
Melbourne, FL 32941-9000
(407) 242-3898

Purpose To provide work experience at *Florida Today* in Melbourne, Florida to students interested in a career in journalism.

Eligibility This program is open to students from any state with a career interest in journalism. Positions are available in news/editorial, advertising, or production. Minorities are especially encouraged to apply.

Financial data Weekly salaries are $375 for news/editorial, $270 to $325 for advertising, and $400 for production.

Duration 12 weeks, during the summer.

Number awarded 4 in news/editorial, 2 in advertising, and 1 in production each year.

Deadline January of each year for advertising; February of each year for news/editorial and production.

[1591]
FOREIGN AFFAIRS FELLOWSHIP PROGRAM

Woodrow Wilson National Fellowship Foundation
Attn: Foreign Affairs Fellowship Program
5 Vaughn Drive, Suite 300
P.O. Box 2437
Princeton, NJ 08543-2437
(609) 452-7007   Fax: (609) 452-0066

Purpose To provide financial assistance for the education of students interested in pursuing a career with the Foreign Service of the Department of State.

Eligibility Applicants must be U.S. citizens in the sophomore year of undergraduate study at an accredited 4-year college or university with a cumulative grade point average of at least 3.2. They must plan to pursue graduate study in the field of international affairs and a career in the Foreign Service. Selection is based on general qualifications, academic performance, interest in a career in the Foreign Service, financial need, and potential for success in the program. Special emphasis is given to promoting knowledge, awareness of, and interest in employment with the Foreign Service among minority students. Children of State Department employees are not eligible.

Financial data Fellows receive support for college tuition, fees, room, board, and books during the final 2 years of undergraduate study and the first year of graduate work. Their graduate institution provides similar support during the second year of graduate study, depending upon financial need. For the summer institute and the internships, travel expenses and stipends are paid. The overseas internship includes medical insurance. Married fellows receive additional funding for university room and board, but are themselves responsible for travel and accommodations for their spouse and family during the institute and the internships.

Duration 4 years: the final 2 years of undergraduate study and the first 2 years of graduate work (provided the student maintains a minimum 3.2 grade point average).

Special features Each May, the fellows participate in orientation and training sessions in Washington, D.C. to help prepare them for Foreign Service careers. During the summer between their junior and senior years, they attend a 6- to 8-week summer institute in a graduate school of public policy and international affairs, with courses in international relations, public policy, policy analysis, policy modules, economics, calculus, and communication skills. During the summer following graduation, they are assigned to an internship at an overseas post of the State Department. Between the first and second year of graduate school, they serve a summer internship in the Department of State in Washington, D.C. This program is funded by the State Department and administered by the Woodrow Wilson National Fellowship Foundation.

Limitations Fellows must commit to a minimum of 4 and a half years of service in an appointment as a Foreign Service Officer following the second year of graduate study. Candidates who do not successfully complete the program and Foreign Service entry requirements must reimburse the Department of State for expenses paid under the fellowship.

Number awarded Approximately 10 each year.

Deadline February of each year.

[1592]
FORT LAUDERDALE SUN-SENTINEL ADVERTISING INTERNSHIPS

Fort Lauderdale Sun-Sentinel
Attn: Manager of Display Advertising
200 East Las Olas Boulevard
Fort Lauderdale, FL 33301-2293
(954) 356-4536

Purpose To provide work experience to college students who are interested in preparing for a career in newspaper advertising.

Eligibility This program is open to college students, preferably juniors or seniors, who are interested in gaining work experience in newspaper advertising. Minority students are especially encouraged to apply.

Financial data The stipend is $435 per week.

Duration 10 to 13 weeks, during the summer.

Number awarded 2 each year.

Deadline May of each year.

[1593]
FORT LAUDERDALE SUN-SENTINEL MINORITY STUDENT JOURNALISM PROGRAM

Fort Lauderdale Sun-Sentinel
Attn: Recruitment Coordinator
200 East Las Olas Boulevard
Fort Lauderdale, FL 33301-2293
(954) 356-4604

Purpose To provide work experience to minority students in Florida who are interested in training to become a journalist.

Eligibility This program is open to high school students (including graduating seniors) who are minorities, residents of Broward and Palm Beach counties, and interested in preparing for a career as a journalist.

Financial data The stipend is $200 per week.

Duration 6 weeks, beginning in June.

Special features At the mid-point of the program, participants begin writing for the *Fort Lauderdale Sun-Sentinel*. Interns work with experienced reporters, photographers and artists, producing news stories, photographs, and graphics.

Number awarded 8 each year.

Deadline March of each year.

[1594]
FORT WAYNE NEWS-SENTINEL MINORITY INTERNSHIP

Fort Wayne News-Sentinel
Attn: Assistant Managing Editor
600 West Main Street
P.O. Box 102
Fort Wayne, IN 46801
(219) 461-8417

Purpose To provide work experience to minority college students interested in journalism as a career.

Eligibility Minority college students are eligible to apply for this internship, if they are majoring in journalism or a related field.

Financial data The salary is $325 per week.

Duration 10 weeks during the summer.

Special features Interns work in various departments of the newspaper.

Number awarded 6 each year: 1 each as metro reporter, features reporter, neighbors reporter, copy editor, page designer, and photographer.

[1595]
FORT WORTH STAR-TELEGRAM INTERNSHIPS

Fort Worth Star-Telegram
Attn: Human Resources Generalist
400 West Seventh Street
P.O. Box 1870
Fort Worth, TX 76101
(817) 551-2178

Purpose To provide work experience at the *Fort Worth Star-Telegram* in Texas to college students interested in careers in journalism.

Eligibility This program is open to students from any state, with a preference for juniors and seniors. Applicants must be planning to pursue careers in newspaper reporting, editing, or advertising. Minorities are especially encouraged to apply.

Financial data Salaries vary, depending on the interns' educational level and housing need.

Duration Approximately 12 weeks, during the summer.

Number awarded Varies each year.

Deadline February of each year.

[1596]
FOSSIL ENERGY TECHNOLOGY INTERNSHIP PROGRAM

Oak Ridge Institute for Science and Education
Attn: Science/Engineering Education Division
P.O. Box 117
Oak Ridge, TN 37831-0117
(423) 576-1083   (423) 576-3426
(800) 569-7749   Fax: (423) 576-3643
E-mail: fetip@orau.gov

Purpose To provide research experience in fossil energy at the Pittsburgh Energy Technology Center to associate degree candidates.

Eligibility This program is open to associate degree candidates in chemistry, physics, engineering, mathematics, computer sciences, or safety and health aspects of fossil energy. They must be interested in conducting fossil energy-related research at the Pittsburgh Energy Technology Center in Pennsylvania. All programs operated by the Science/Engineering Education Division (SEED) of Oak Ridge Institute for Science and Education (ORISE) seek to broaden the participation of minorities, women, and persons with disabilities in science and engineering careers.

Financial data The full-time stipend is $1,000 per month; part-time assignments are prorated appropriately. Also provided are transportation to the center and any normal tuition and fees required by the recipient's home institution for an off-campus program.

Duration 6 consecutive months or 2 segments of 3 months each. Both full-time and part-time assignments are available.

Special features This program is funded by the U.S. Department of Energy's Office of Fossil Energy but operated and managed by ORISE/SEED.

Number awarded Approximately 5 each year.

Deadline Applications may be submitted at any time.

[1597]
FOUR DIRECTIONS SUMMER RESEARCH PROGRAM

Harvard Medical School
Attn: Admissions Office
Division of Medical Sciences
260 Longwood Avenue
Boston, MA 02115
(617) 432-4980   (800) 367-9019
Fax: (617) 432-2644

Purpose To provide an opportunity for Native American students to engage in research at Harvard Medical School.

Eligibility This program is open to Native American college students who have had at least 1 summer (or equivalent) of laboratory research.

Financial data The program provides a stipend of approximately $1,800, transportation, and lodging expenses.

Duration 8 weeks, during the summer.

Number awarded Varies each year.

Deadline March of each year.

[1598]
FREE LANCE-STAR INTERNSHIP

Free Lance-Star
Attn: Human Resources
616 Amelia Street
Fredericksburg, VA 22401-3887
(540) 374-5453

Purpose To provide work experience at the *Free Lance-Star* in Fredericksburg, Virginia to college students who are interested in preparing for a career in journalism.

Eligibility Students who are studying journalism are eligible to apply. Preference is given to rising juniors, seniors, or graduating seniors. Applicants may be from any state. Minorities are particularly encouraged to apply.

Financial data This is a paid internship.

Duration 10 weeks, during the summer months.

Special features Interns work either as editors or as reporters.

Number awarded 1 each summer.

Deadline February of each year.

[1599]
FRESNO BEE SUMMER JOURNALISM INTERNSHIP

Fresno Bee
Attn: Rich Marshall
1626 E Street
Fresno, CA 93786-0001
(209) 441-6443   (800) 877-7300

Purpose To provide work experience at the *Fresno Bee* to minority and other students interested in preparing for newspaper careers.

Eligibility College juniors, seniors, or graduates are eligible to apply if they have majored in journalism or have prepared for a career in newspapers. The newspaper is looking for interns who are able to "step in and do entry-level quality work" as reporters, copy editors, and photographers. Minorities are particularly encouraged to apply.

Financial data Interns earn $350 per week.

Duration 12 weeks, during the summer.

Number awarded 3 each year.

Deadline December of each year.

[1600]
FRIENDS OF THE NATIONAL ZOO INTERNSHIPS

National Zoological Park
Smithsonian Institution
Attn: Human Resource Office
3001 Connecticut Avenue, N.W.
Washington, DC 20008
(202) 673-4639

Purpose To provide work experience at the National Zoological Park of the Smithsonian Institution to undergraduate and graduate students.

Eligibility Selection is based on the applicant's statement of interest (up to 1,000 words), scholastic achievement, relevant experience, and letters of reference. Preference is given to juniors and seniors in college and recent graduates. Minority and women students are encouraged to apply.

Financial data Although many internships are on a voluntary basis, some stipends are paid.

Duration 12 weeks, at a time determined mutually by the trainee and the supervisor.

Special features Internships may be offered in some or all of the following areas: accounting, arts and graphics, development services, membership, food operations, visitor services and operations, public relations, special events, and human resources. All programs are at the National Zoological Park in Washington, D.C.

Number awarded Varies each year.

Deadline December of each year.

[1601]
GETTY GRANT PROGRAM MULTICULTURAL INTERNSHIPS

Getty Grant Program
1200 Getty Center Drive, Suite 800
Los Angeles, CA 90049-1685
(310) 440-7320   Fax: (310) 440-7703

Purpose To enable museums and visual arts organizations in Los Angeles County to provide multicultural undergraduate summer internships.

Eligibility Museums and visual arts organizations in Los Angeles County may apply for this funding if they wish to offer summer internships to multicultural undergraduate students.

Financial data The amount awarded varies, but ranges from $3,000 to $3,300 per internship supported.

Duration Grants are for 1 year; internships are for summer months.

Special features For a list of institutions offering internships, contact the address above.

Number awarded In a recent year, 50 organizations received support to offer a total of 95 internships.

Deadline October of each year.

[1602]
GLOBAL CHANGE GRADUATE FELLOWSHIPS

Oak Ridge Institute for Science and Education
Attn: Science/Engineering Education Division
P.O. Box 117
Oak Ridge, TN 37831-0117
(423) 576-9655   (423) 576-7009
(800) 569-7749   Fax: (423) 576-3643
E-mail: gfglobal@orau.gov

Purpose To provide funding for graduate study and work experience in various aspects of global change.

Eligibility This program is open to graduate students in atmospheric sciences, meteorology, ecology, ocean sciences, biology, and other scientific disciplines related to global change. Applicants must be enrolled in master's or doctoral programs at universities participating in this program (for a list of participating schools, write to the address above). All programs operated by the Science/Engineering Education Division (SEED) of Oak Ridge Institute for Science and Education (ORISE) seek to broaden the participation of minorities, women, and persons with disabilities in science and engineering careers.

Financial data Fellows receive full payment of tuition and fees and a stipend of $14,400 per year. An additional $300 per month is paid during the research experience. A $1,000 annual allowance is paid to the recipient's university.

Duration 1 year; renewable.

Special features Participants perform a required collaborative research experience as interns at either a U.S. Department of Energy (DOE) or other government agency global change research facility. This program is funded by DOE's Office of Energy Research, Environmental Sciences Division, Office of Health and Environmental Research, and administered by ORISE/SEED.

Number awarded Varies each year.

Deadline January of each year.

[1603]
GREENSBORO NEWS & RECORD SUMMER INTERNSHIPS

Greensboro News & Record
Attn: Features Editor
200 East Market Street
P.O. Box 20848
Greensboro, NC 27420
(910) 373-7000

Purpose To provide work experience at the *Greensboro News & Record* in North Carolina to college students interested in careers in journalism.

Eligibility This program is open to students from any state, with a preference for juniors, seniors, graduate students, and recent graduates. Applicants must be planning to pursue careers in newspaper reporting, editing, or photography. Minorities are especially encouraged to apply.

Financial data The salary is $325 per week.

Duration 12 weeks, during the summer.

Number awarded 6 in news/editorial (including sports and features), 2 in copy editing, and 1 in photography each year.

Deadline November of each year.

[1604]
HARTFORD COURANT MINORITY INTERNSHIPS

Hartford Courant
Attn: Jeff Rivers, Associate Editor
285 Broad Street
Hartford, CT 06115
(860) 241-6481   (800) 524-4242, ext. 6481

Purpose To provide on-the-job training at the *Hartford Courant* for minorities interested in careers in journalism.

Eligibility Candidates should no longer be in school and need not hold a degree but must have a strong interest in pursuing a career in newspapers. Applicants from Connecticut are strongly preferred. Selection is based on personal interviews, clips or writing samples, letters of recommendation, and writing tests.

Financial data Interns receive $400 per week. Expenses for on-the-job transportation, interviewing, and telephoning are reimbursed.

Duration Varies; generally, 1 to 2 years.

Special features Interns receive regular guidance and critiques of their work and written formal progress reviews every 3 months.

Number awarded 1 each year.

Deadline March of each year.

[1605]
HATTIESBURG AMERICAN INTERNSHIP

Hattiesburg American
Attn: Managing Editor
825 North Main Street
P.O. Box 1111
Hattiesburg, MS 39401-3433
(601) 584-3125

Purpose To provide work experience at the *Hattiesburg American* in Mississippi to college students who are interested in preparing for a career in journalism.

Eligibility College students (particularly seniors) from any state who are interested in working on a daily newspaper are invited to apply. Preference is given to women and minorities.

Financial data The stipend is $300 per week for full-time interns or $7.50 per hour for part-time interns.

Duration 13 weeks during the summer.

Special features Interns are offered work opportunities in news/editorial.

Number awarded 2 each year: 1 full-time and 1 part-time.

Deadline March of each year.

[1606]
HEARST BROADCAST NEWS FELLOWSHIP

WCVB-TV
Attn: Human Resources Department
5 TV Place
Needham Heights, MA 02194-2303
(617) 433-4062   Fax: (617) 449-0260

Purpose To provide training and on-the-job experience in the area of news writing and producing to minorities, the disadvantaged, or those who have encountered substantial difficulty in gaining access to broadcast careers.

Eligibility Applicants must have at least a bachelor's degree and a proven interest in broadcast journalism (as demonstrated by past positions or extracurricular activities). They must live in or attend colleges in 1 of the 6 Hearst Television communities: Boston, Pittsburgh, Milwaukee, Baltimore, Kansas City, or Dayton, but the internship is conducted at WCVB-TV in Boston.

Financial data The intern receives a competitive salary and is eligible for standard company benefits.

Duration 9 months, beginning in September.

Special features The program focuses on writing skills and on the fundamentals of newscast producing. Upon completing the program, the interns are assisted in looking for a position in broadcast news.

Limitations Finalists must be interviewed in Boston. Opportunities for employment within WCVB-TV or Hearst Broadcasting upon completion of the program are not guaranteed.

Number awarded 1 each year.

Deadline April of each year.

[1607]
HERCULES MINORITY ENGINEERS DEVELOPMENT PROGRAM

Hercules Incorporated
Attn: Human Resources Department
Hercules Plaza
1313 North Market Street
Wilmington, DE 19894-0001
(302) 594-5000

Purpose To provide financial assistance for minority students interested in pursuing careers in engineering.

Eligibility Eligible are minority group members who have completed at least 1 semester of university study before applying, are interested in careers in engineering, have earned a 3.0 grade point average, and attend 1 of the 5 schools participating in the program (Georgia Institute of Technology, University of Michigan, North Carolina State University, University of Virginia, and University of Utah).

Financial data The scholarship stipend is $4,000 per year.

Duration 1 year; renewable for up to 3 additional years.

Special features Recipients are eligible to work as interns during the summer months throughout their undergraduate years. Information about the scholarship/internship program can be obtained by writing to Hercules Incorporated or contacting the participating university.

Limitations Candidates must be nominated by their Dean of Engineering.

Deadline Varies from school to school.

[1608]
HEWLETT-PACKARD SEED PROGRAM

Hewlett-Packard Company
Attn: Corporate College Relations
3000 Hanover Street
MS: 20AK
Palo Alto, CA 94304-1181
(408) 773-6200

Purpose To provide work experience in engineering and business to undergraduate and graduate students.

Eligibility Undergraduate students who have completed at least their freshman year in college and graduate students are eligible to apply if they are studying electrical engineering, computer science, computer engineering, mechanical engineering, industrial engineering, information technology, finance, or business administration. Minorities, women, and people with disabilities are especially encouraged to apply. Applicants must be U.S. citizens, nationals, permanent residents, temporary residents, or refugees; non-immigrants such as F-1, H-1, or J-1 visa holders are not eligible.

Financial data Included are a salary, medical insurance, round-trip transportation, and an allowance to help cover initial relocation costs.

Duration 10 weeks, either in the summer or during the school year through a co-op program if the intern's school offers such a program.

Special features Students work at 1 of many Hewlett-Packard facilities in the country as part of this Student Employment and Educational Development (SEED) program. Available assignments include work in research and development, manufacturing, marketing, quality, materials, facilities, information technology, finance, or personnel.

Limitations Applicants may sign up at their campus placement center for an interview during Hewlett-Packard recruitment dates or they may write to the address above.

Number awarded Varies each year.

Deadline April of each year for summer employment; any time for co-op positions.

[1609]
HUNTINGTON HERALD-DISPATCH INTERNSHIPS

Huntington Herald-Dispatch
Attn: Executive Editor
946 Fifth Avenue
Huntington, WV 25701
(304) 526-2749

Purpose To provide work experience at the *Huntington Herald-Dispatch* in West Virginia to college students interested in careers in journalism.

Eligibility This program is open to students from any state with preference for juniors and seniors. Applicants must be planning to pursue careers in newspaper reporting, editing, or advertising. Minorities are especially encouraged to apply.

Financial data These are paid internships.

Duration 3 to 6 months.

Number awarded Varies each year.

Deadline Applications may be submitted at any time.

[1610]
INDIANAPOLIS STAR MINORITY INTERNSHIP

Indianapolis Star
Attn: Jon Schwantes
P.O. Box 145
Indianapolis, IN 46206-9197
(317) 633-9087

Purpose To provide work experience at the *Indianapolis Star* to minority college students interested in journalism as a career.

Eligibility Minority college students are eligible to apply for this internship, if they are majoring in graphic arts or a related field.

Financial data This is a paid internship.

Duration 1 academic term or longer.

Special features Interns work in the newsroom.

Number awarded 1 each quarter.

[1611]
INDUSTRIAL HYGIENE GRADUATE FELLOWSHIP PROGRAM

Oak Ridge Institute for Science and Education
Attn: Science/Engineering Education Division
P.O. Box 117
Oak Ridge, TN 37831-0117
(423) 576-9655   (423) 576-7009
(800) 569-7749   Fax: (423) 576-3643
E-mail: indhyggf@orau.gov

Purpose To provide financial assistance for graduate study and work experience in the area of industrial hygiene.

Eligibility This program is open to students at designated participating universities (write to the address above for a list of these) who are working on a master's degree in industrial hygiene. All programs operated by the Science/Engineering Education Division (SEED) of Oak Ridge Institute for Science and Education (ORISE) seek to broaden the participation of minorities, women, and persons with disabilities in science and engineering careers.

Financial data Participants receive a monthly stipend of $1,300 plus $400 per month during the practicum period. In addition, there is an annual $1,500 academic allowance.

Duration 2 years.

Special features Participants intern at a U.S. Department of Energy (DOE) research facility. This program is funded by DOE's Office of Health, Industrial Hygiene Programs Division and administered by ORISE/SEED.

Number awarded Varies each year.

Deadline January of each year.

[1612]
INDUSTRY-BASED GRADUATE RESEARCH ASSISTANTSHIPS AND COOPERATIVE FELLOWSHIPS IN THE MATHEMATICAL SCIENCES

National Science Foundation
Attn: Directorate for Mathematical and Physical Sciences
Division of Mathematical Sciences
4201 Wilson Boulevard, Room 1025
Arlington, VA 22230
(703) 306-1870   Fax: (703) 306-0555
E-mail: uicrp@nsf.gov

Purpose To provide financial assistance to graduate students in mathematics who wish to gain experience in industrial settings.

Eligibility This program is open to graduate students in mathematics who are U.S. citizens, nationals, or permanent residents. Applicants may propose either 1) a research assistantship, in which they conduct research for a master's thesis or doctoral dissertation under the joint supervision of a university faculty member and an industrial scientist, spending part-time at the industrial site on a regular basis and the remainder in the classroom or in other campus-based activities; or 2) a cooperative fellowship, in which they work full-time as an intern in an industrial setting. Applications are especially encouraged from women, underrepresented minorities, and persons with disabilities.

Financial data The program provides up to 50 percent (with an upper limit of $20,000) of the total support for each student. The university faculty member involved in the joint supervision of such students may request up to $6,000 as a faculty research allowance.

Duration Up to 1 year.

Number awarded Varies each year.

Deadline November of each year.

[1613]
INROADS/COLLEGE INTERNSHIP

INROADS, Inc.
10 South Broadway, Suite 700
St. Louis, MO 63102
(314) 241-7488   Fax: (314) 241-9325

Purpose To identify, train, and develop talented minority youth for responsible positions of leadership in corporate America.

Eligibility Eligible to apply are African Americans, Hispanics, and Native Americans who reside in the areas served by INROADS and wish to pursue careers in business, computer science, or engineering. Applicants must be high school seniors or college freshmen or sophomores. Preference goes to students who have a scholastic average of 3.0 or better, an ACT composite score of 20 or better, an SAT combined score of 800 or better, or a ranking within the top 10 percent of their high school class.

Financial data Salaries vary, depending upon the specific internship assigned; the range is from $170 to $750 per week.

Duration Summer employment, for up to 4 years.

Special features INROADS places interns in local companies, where training focuses of management competencies such as business sophistication and effective communication, as well as academic and technical skills and community service. The INROADS organization offers internship opportunities through 46 local affiliates.

Number awarded More than 6,000 high school and college students are currently working for nearly 900 corporate sponsors nationwide.

Deadline December of each year.

[1614]
INSTITUTE FOR WOMEN'S POLICY RESEARCH FELLOWSHIPS

Institute for Women's Policy Research
1400 20th Street, N.W., Suite 104
Washington, DC 20036
(202) 785-5100

Purpose To assist in the professional development of college graduates and graduate students who are interested in economic justice for women.

Eligibility Applicants should have a minimum of a bachelor's degree in a social science, statistics, or women's policy issues and intend to attend graduate school in the social sciences to study women's policy issues. Those currently enrolled in graduate school and interested in taking a year off are also encouraged to apply. Applicants should have basic quantitative and library research skills and excellent communication skills, both oral and written. Knowledge of women's issues is also essential, and computer programming skills are preferred. Women of color are especially encouraged to apply.

Financial data The stipend is $1,200 per month and includes health insurance.

Duration 9 months, beginning in September.

Special features The institute is a nonprofit, scientific research organization that works primarily on issues related to equal opportunity and economic and social justice for women. Of the fellowships currently available, 1 is assigned to work on all aspects of planning for the Women's Policy Research Conference; 1 is to work as a general research assistant on a variety of research and research-dissemination projects, including reviewing literature, collecting, checking and analyzing data, gathering information, and preparing reports and report graphics; 1 is to serve as the development fellow, assisting the director of development in all aspects of fundraising. All fellows are responsible for some amount of general office work, including such tasks as responding to information requests and assisting in maintaining the library.

Number awarded 3 each year.

Deadline June of each year.

[1615]
INTERNSHIPS FOR DIVERSITY IN THE MUSEUM PROFESSION

National Gallery of Art
Attn: Education Division
Office of Academic Programs
Washington, DC 20565
(202) 842-6182   Fax: (202) 842-6935

Purpose To provide work experience to underrepresented minorities who are interested in preparing for a museum career.

Eligibility U.S. citizens who have completed at least an undergraduate degree by September of the internship year may apply. Preference is given to applicants with relevant museum experience, those currently enrolled in a university program leading to a graduate degree in art history or another field related to the internship, or to those who have recently completed a relevant graduate degree. The program encourages applications from African Americans, Alaskan Natives, American Indians, Asian Americans, Hispanics, and Pacific Islanders.

Financial data The stipend is $14,000.

Duration 9 months.

Special features Interns participate in the ongoing work of the department to which they are assigned and are treated as staff members. Responsibilities are determined by the intern's educational background and work experience and the department's needs. Interns are expected to complete a project or some discrete portion of a major project.

Number awarded 3 each year.

Deadline April of each year.

[1616]
IVY LEAGUE-PUBLIC INFORMATION INTERNSHIP

Council of Ivy Group Presidents
120 Alexander Street
Princeton, NJ 08544
(609) 258-6426   Fax: (609) 258-1690

Purpose To provide work experience for college graduates interested in preparing for a career in collegiate sports.

Eligibility Recent college graduates interested in a career in college athletics are eligible to apply. They should have sports information experience. Women and minorities are particularly encouraged to apply.

Financial data The stipend is $12,100 per year.

Duration 10 months.

Special features Interns are involved in publicizing conference events. Academic credit may be arranged.

Number awarded 1 each year.

Deadline April of each year.

[1617]
JACKIE JOYNER KERSEE/RAY BAN MINORITY INTERNSHIP

Women's Sports Foundation
Eisenhower Park
1899 Hempstead Turnpike, Suite 400
East Meadow, NY 11554-1000
(516) 542-4700   (800) 227-3988
Fax: (516) 542-4716   E-mail: wosport@aol.com

Purpose To provide women of color an opportunity to get a start in a sports-related career.

Eligibility Eligible to apply for these internships are women of color who are undergraduate students, college graduates, graduate students, or women in career change. The internships are conducted in the offices of the Women's Sports Foundation on Long Island, New York.

Financial data The salary is $5,000.

Duration 6 months.

Number awarded 2 each year.

Deadline Applications may be submitted at any time.

[1618]
JAMES COMER MINORITY RESEARCH FELLOWSHIP FOR MEDICAL STUDENTS

American Academy of Child & Adolescent Psychiatry
Attn: Office of Research
3615 Wisconsin Avenue, N.W.
Washington, DC 20016
(202) 966-7300   Fax: (202) 966-2891

Purpose To provide funding to minority medical students who are interested in working with a child and adolescent psychiatric researcher during the summer.

Eligibility Applications are accepted from African American, Asian American, Native American, Alaska Native, Mexican American, Hispanic, and Pacific Islander students in accredited U.S. medical schools. If an applicant is interested in applying for the fellowship but is not linked with a child and adolescent psychiatrist, the academy will match the student with an appropriate mentor who will work with the student to prepare the final proposal. Applications from them should include the following: a 2-page statement outlining the student's background, interests, career goals, and specific clinical interest for this fellowship; the student's resume; and a letter verifying the student's good standing in medical school. If the applicant has an established link with a child and adolescent psychiatrist who will work with the student throughout the summer, the mentor should submit the proposal. Applications, in that case, should include the following: the mentor's outline of the clinical experience with a description of the student's involvement in the project; a 2-page statement outlining the student's background, clinical interests, and career goals; the student' resume; and a letter verifying the student's good standing in medical school.

Financial data The award provides $2,500 to pay for the fellow's work with a child and adolescent psychiatrist investigator-mentor during the summer.

Duration Summer months.

Special features Upon completion of the training program, the student is required to submit a brief paper summarizing the research experience. The fellowship pays expenses for the fellow to attend the academy's annual meeting and present this paper.

Number awarded 5 each year.

Deadline Students without links: February of each year; students with links: March of each year.

[1619]
JAMES E. WEBB INTERNSHIPS

Smithsonian Institution
Attn: Office of Equal Employment and Minority Affairs
905 L'Enfant Plaza, S.W.
Washington, DC 20560
(202) 287-3508   TDD: (202) 287-3494

Purpose To provide internship opportunities throughout the Smithsonian Institution for minority students in business or public administration.

Eligibility This program is open to U.S. minority undergraduate and graduate students majoring in areas of business or public administration (finance, human resource management, accounting, or general business administration). Applicants must seek placement in offices, museums, and research institutes throughout the Smithsonian Institution.

Financial data Interns receive a stipend and housing.

Duration 10 weeks, starting in June.

Number awarded Varies each year.

Deadline February of each year.

[1620]
JEANNE SPURLOCK MINORITY MEDICAL STUDENT CLINICAL FELLOWSHIP IN CHILD AND ADOLESCENT PSYCHIATRY

American Academy of Child & Adolescent Psychiatry
Attn: Office of Research
3615 Wisconsin Avenue, N.W.
Washington, DC 20016
(202) 966-7300   Fax: (202) 966-2891

Purpose To provide funding to minority medical students who are interested in working with a child and adolescent psychiatrist during the summer.

Eligibility Applications are accepted from African American, Asian American, Native American, Alaska Native, Mexican American, Hispanic, and Pacific Islander students in accredited U.S. medical schools. If an applicant is interested in applying for the fellowship but is not linked with a child and adolescent psychia-

trist, the academy will match the student with an appropriate mentor who will work with the student to prepare the final proposal. Applications from them should include the following: a 2-page statement outlining the student's background, interests, career goals, and specific clinical interest for this fellowship; the student's resume; and a letter verifying the student's good standing in medical school. If the applicant has an established link with a child and adolescent psychiatrist who will work with the student throughout the summer, the mentor should submit the proposal. Applications, in that case, should include the following: the mentor's outline of the clinical experience with a description of the student's involvement in the project; a 2-page statement outlining the student's background, clinical interests, and career goals; the student' resume; and a letter verifying the student's good standing in medical school.

Financial data The award provides $2,500 to pay for the fellow's work with a child and adolescent psychiatrist mentor during the summer.

Duration Summer months.

Special features Upon completion of the training program, the student is required to submit a brief paper summarizing the clinical experience. The fellowship pays expenses for the fellow to attend the academy's annual meeting and present this paper.

Number awarded 5 each year.

Deadline Students without links: March of each year; students with links: April of each year.

[1621]
JEANNE SPURLOCK RESEARCH FELLOWSHIP IN DRUG ABUSE AND ADDICTION FOR MINORITY MEDICAL STUDENTS

American Academy of Child & Adolescent Psychiatry
Attn: Office of Research
3615 Wisconsin Avenue, N.W.
Washington, DC 20016
(202) 966-7300   Fax: (202) 966-2891

Purpose To provide funding to minority medical students who are interested in working with a child and adolescent psychiatrist research-mentor during the summer.

Eligibility Applications are accepted from African American, Asian American, Native American, Alaska Native, Mexican American, Hispanic, and Pacific Islander students in accredited U.S. medical schools. All applications must relate to substance abuse research. If an applicant is interested in applying for the fellowship but is not linked with a child and adolescent psychiatric investigator, the academy will match the student with an appropriate mentor who will work with the student to prepare the final proposal. Applications from them should include the following: a 2-page statement outlining the student's background, interests, career goals, and specific clinical interest for this fellowship; the student's resume; and a letter verifying the student's good standing in medical school. If the applicant has an established link with a child and adolescent psychiatrist investigator-mentor who will work with the student throughout the summer, the mentor should submit the proposal. The research proposal should include a rationale for this study within the context of enhancing the scientific knowledge of drug abuse and addiction treatment, prevention, and/or intervention. Applications, in that case, should include the following: the mentor's outline of the clinical experience with a description of the student's involvement in the project; a 2-page statement outlining the student's background, clinical interests, and career goals; the student' resume; and a letter verifying the student's good standing in medical school.

Financial data The award provides $2,500 to pay for the fellow's work with a child and adolescent psychiatrist mentor during the summer.

Duration Summer months.

Special features Upon completion of the training program, the student is required to submit a brief paper summarizing the research experience. The fellowship pays expenses for the fellow to attend the academy's annual meeting and present this paper.

Number awarded 5 each year.

Deadline Students without links: February of each year; students with links: March of each year.

[1622]
KAISER MEDIA INTERNSHIPS IN URBAN HEALTH REPORTING

Henry J. Kaiser Family Foundation
2400 Sand Hill Road
Menlo Park, CA 94025
(415) 854-9400   Fax: (415) 854-4800

Purpose To provide work experience to minority college or graduate students who want to specialize in urban health reporting.

Eligibility Minority college or graduate students studying journalism or a related field may apply for this program if their career goals are to be reporters on urban health matters.

Financial data This program provides a stipend of $500 per week, all travel expenses, and a grant of $1,000 to participants who complete the program.

Duration 12 weeks in the summer.

Special features The Henry J. Kaiser Family Foundation sponsors this program which began in 1994. The newspapers that served as hosts for it during its first year of operation were *Newsday* (of New York), *Detroit Free Press, Dallas Morning News, Milwaukee Journal, Philadelphia Inquirer,* and *Portland Oregonian.* The program begins with a 1-week orientation program at the Washington Journalism Center in June and concludes with a 2-day wrap-up in Atlanta at the end of the summer. In between, interns report and write urban health stories at their host papers.

[1623]
KNIGHT-RIDDER MINORITY SCHOLARSHIP PROGRAM

Knight-Ridder, Inc.
One Herald Plaza
Miami, FL 33132-1609
(305) 376-3800

Purpose To provide financial assistance to minority students who are interested in going to college to prepare for a career in journalism.

Eligibility Graduating minority high school seniors are eligible to apply if they are attending a school in an area served by Knight-Ridder and are interested in majoring in journalism in college. Candidates first apply to their local Knight-Ridder newspaper and compete for local scholarships; selected winners are then nominated for this award.

Financial data The stipend is $5,000.

Duration 1 year; may be renewed for up to 3 additional years, based on the recipient's academic performance.

Special features Scholarship recipients are offered an internship opportunity at a Knight-Ridder newspaper during the summer.

Limitations At the end of the program, recipients must work at a Knight-Ridder newspaper for 1 year.

Number awarded 4 each year.

[1624]
KNIGHT-RIDDER MINORITY SPECIALTY DEVELOPMENT PROGRAM

Knight-Ridder, Inc.
c/o Philadelphia Inquirer
Attn: Arlene Morgan, Senior Editor
400 North Broad Street
P.O. Box 8263
Philadelphia, PA 19101
(215) 854-2419

Purpose To offer a unique training program for young minority journalists who would like to concentrate in a speciality beat or department.

Eligibility Minorities who recently graduated from college with a major in journalism are eligible to apply if they interested in working in a speciality beat or department (e.g., investigative/legal affairs, medical/science, business, critical writing/features, graphic arts, and news editing). Finalists must be interviewed.

Financial data Salaries are determined by the scale of the participating newspapers.

Duration 2 years.

Special features The first year of training takes place at 1 of the larger circulation Knight-Ridder papers, either the *Philadelphia Inquirer* or the *Detroit Free Press.* The second year is spent using that training at 1 of the following mid-size Knight-Ridder papers: *Charlotte Observer, Akron Beacon-Journal, St. Paul Pioneer Press, Long Beach Press-Telegram, Wichita Eagle-Beacon,* or *Gary Post Tribune.*

Number awarded 4 each year.

Deadline December of each year.

[1625]
KNIGHT-RIDDER SCHOLARSHIP FOR NATIVE AMERICAN JOURNALISTS

Knight-Ridder, Inc.
c/o Linda Fullerton
St. Paul Pioneer Press
345 Cedar Street
St. Paul, MN 55101-1057
(612) 228-5465   (800) 950-9080

Purpose To provide financial assistance to Native American students who are interested in going to college to prepare for a career in journalism.

Eligibility This program is open to Native American students interested in pursuing a newspaper journalism career. The recipient is required to work as a paid intern during the summer at a Knight-Ridder newspaper, and is eligible to apply for other Knight-Ridder scholarships.

Financial data The stipend is $5,000.

Duration 1 year.

Number awarded 1 each year.

Deadline March of each year.

[1626]
KNTV MINORITY SCHOLARSHIP

KNTV Television
Attn: Janet Neill
645 Park Avenue
San Jose, CA 95110
(408) 286-1111   Fax: (408) 295-5461

Purpose To provide financial assistance for postsecondary education to minority students in selected areas of California who are interested in preparing for a career in television.

Eligibility This program is open to minority students who are residents of Monterey, San Benito, Santa Clara, and Santa Cruz counties. Applicants should be high school seniors or college freshmen, sophomores, or juniors. They should be majoring (or planning to major) in television production, journalism, or a related field (e.g., marketing, public relations, advertising, or graphics), able to demonstrate financial need, and planning to attend college in California on a full-time basis (at least 12 semester units). Selection is based on interest in television, financial need, involvement in the community, academic achievement, and career aspirations.

Financial data The stipend is $1,000.

Duration 1 year.

Special features Recipients have the option of 8 weeks of paid summer employment at KNTV in San Jose.

Number awarded 2 each year.

Deadline April of each year.

[1627]
LANDMARK COMMUNICATIONS MINORITY INTERNSHIPS

Landmark Communications, Inc.
Attn: Minority Recruitment Director
150 West Brambleton Avenue
Norfolk, VA 23510
(804) 446-2538

Purpose To provide work experience to minority college graduates who are interested in preparing for a career in journalism.

Eligibility Minorities who have completed their undergraduate education are eligible to apply if they are interested in becoming journalists. Selection is based on SAT or ACT scores, academic achievement, and writing background. Applicants must send samples of their work as part of the application process.

Financial data The interns are paid $17,900. Between the second and third moves they also receive a moving allowance of $300.

Duration 1 year.

Special features The program is designed to train participants for full-time employment at 1 of Landmark's newspapers. Interns spend 4 months at 3 different mid-sized dailies, in Norfolk, Virginia; Roanoke, Virginia; and Greensboro, North Carolina; assignments are also made to smaller community newspapers in Elizabethtown, Kentucky; Westminster, Maryland; and Inverness, Florida. During the internship, participants receive the same benefits as other employees (e.g., hospitalization, life insurance, and vacation). Positions are available for news and sports reporters, copy editors, and photographers.

Number awarded 8 each year.

[1628]
LAW AND SOCIAL SCIENCE SUMMER RESEARCH FELLOWSHIPS FOR MINORITY UNDERGRADUATES

American Bar Foundation
Attn: Assistant Director
750 North Lake Shore Drive
Chicago, IL 60611
(312) 988-6500

Purpose To provide work experience to underrepresented minority undergraduates who might be considering a legal career.

Eligibility Undergraduate students who are African American, Mexican, Puerto Rican, or Native American are eligible to apply if they are sophomores or juniors in college, have earned at least a 3.0 grade point average, are working on a major in the social sciences or humanities, and are willing to consider a legal career.

Financial data Participants receive a stipend of $3,500.

Duration 35 hours per week for 10 weeks during the summer.

Special features Students are assigned to an American Bar Foundation Research Fellow who involves the student in the design and conduct of the fellow's research project and who acts as mentor during the student's tenure.

Number awarded 4 each year.

Deadline February of each year.

[1629]
LAWRENCE WADE JOURNALISM FELLOWSHIP

Heritage Foundation
Attn: Selection Committee
214 Massachusetts Avenue, N.E.
Washington, DC 20002
(202) 546-4400

Purpose To provide financial assistance and work experience to college students who are interested in a career in journalism.

Eligibility This program is open to undergraduate or graduate students who are currently enrolled full time and are interested in a career as a journalist upon graduation. Applicants need not be majoring in journalism, but they must submit writing samples of published news stories, editorial commentaries, or broadcast scripts. Preference is given to candidates who are Asian Americans, African Americans, Hispanic Americans, or Native Americans.

Financial data The winner receives a $1,000 scholarship and participates in a 10-week salaried internship at the Foundation.

Number awarded 1 each year.

Deadline February of each year.

[1630]
LEO L. BERANEK FELLOWSHIP

WCVB-TV
Attn: Human Resources Department
5 TV Place
Needham Heights, MA 02194-2303
(617) 433-4062   Fax: (617) 449-0260

Purpose To provide on-the-job training in broadcast journalism for those who are minority or disadvantaged and who encounter substantial difficulty in gaining access to broadcast careers as a result.

Eligibility Ethnic minorities and others who have experienced social or economic disadvantages are eligible to apply if they have a proven interest in broadcast journalism. Applicants must have at least a B.A. or B.S. degree in communications or journalism; they should be able to provide other evidence of interest in broadcast journalism such as prior employment and extracurricular activities.

Financial data The fellow receives a competitive weekly salary. By agreement with the Boston local of the American Federation of Television and Radio Artists, AFTRA waives initiation fees and dues for the participant for the duration of the training period.

Duration 9 months.

Special features WCVB-TV is an ABC affiliate (on channel 5) in Boston. Fellows are involved in writing, editing, producing, and reporting.

Number awarded 1 each year.

Deadline March of each year.

[1631]
LIBRARY OF CONGRESS JUNIOR FELLOWS PROGRAM

Library of Congress
Collections Services
Attn: Junior Fellows Program Coordinator
LM-642
Washington, DC 20540-4700
(202) 707-8253   E-mail: jrfell@loc.gov

Purpose To provide work experience at the Library of Congress to upper-division and graduate students.

Eligibility The Library of Congress is looking for applicants with subject expertise in the following areas: American history and literature, cataloging, history of graphic arts, history of photography, film, television and radio, sound recordings, music, rare books and book arts, American popular culture, librarianship, preservation, and area studies (particularly Asian, African, Middle Eastern, European, and Hispanic studies). Applicants must 1) be juniors or seniors at an accredited college or university, 2) be at the graduate school level, or 3) have completed their degree in the past year. Applications from women and minorities are particularly encouraged. Applications must include the following materials: cover letter, Application for Federal Employment (SF 171) or a resume, letter of recommendation, and official transcript. Telephone interviews are conducted with the most promising applicants.

Financial data Fellows are paid a taxable stipend of $300 per week.

Duration 2 to 3 months, beginning in either May or June. Fellows work a 40-hour week.

Special features Fellows work with primary source materials and assist selected divisions at the Library of Congress in the organization and documentation of archival collections, production of finding aids and bibliographic records, preparation of materials for preservation and service, and completion of bibliographical research.

Number awarded Varies each year.

Deadline February of each year.

[1632]
LOS ALAMOS NATIONAL LABORATORY GRADUATE STUDENT PROGRAM

Los Alamos National Laboratory
Attn: Human Resource Division
Special Programs and Services
Mail Stop P290
P.O. Box 1663
Los Alamos, NM 87545
(505) 667-5919   Fax: (505) 665-1079
E-mail: eduprogs@lanl.gov

Purpose To provide work experience throughout the year at the Los Alamos National Laboratory (LANL) to interested graduate students.

Eligibility Eligibility is limited to students who have completed their bachelor's degree and who intend to continue with graduate studies. The majority of the appointments are in the technical and scientific disciplines (chemistry, computer science, earth and space science, economics, engineering, health and environmental sciences, life sciences, materials sciences/metallurgy, mathematics, optics and electro-optics, physics, and astrophysics), but a few are made in other disciplines, such as business, law, and human resources. In some cases, students can arrange to conduct master's or doctoral thesis research at the Laboratory. Women, minorities, individuals with disabilities, and veterans are particularly encouraged to apply.

Financial data Participants receive an hourly wage, based on the number of credit hours or semesters they have completed and the type of work; the current wage structure ranges from $10.99 per hour for students with a bachelor's degree but no graduate credit to $16.45 per hour for students who have completed 6 or more semesters of graduate school. For students conducting thesis research, the scale is from $7.16 per hour with 3 semesters of graduate school to $9.87 per hour with 6 or more semesters. Benefits are available, based on length of appointment.

Duration From 90 days to 1 year; appointments may be renewed.

Special features Limited housing is available, on a first-come, first-served basis.

Number awarded Varies each year.

Deadline January of each year.

[1633]
LOS ALAMOS NATIONAL LABORATORY UNDERGRADUATE STUDENT PROGRAM

Los Alamos National Laboratory
Attn: Human Resource Division
Special Programs and Services
Mail Stop P290
P.O. Box 1663
Los Alamos, NM 87545
(505) 667-0870   Fax: (505) 665-1079
E-mail: eduprogs@lanl.gov

Purpose To provide work experience during the summer to undergraduate students interested in working at the Los Alamos National Laboratory.

Eligibility Eligibility is limited to students who have completed high school and are enrolled in an undergraduate program. A cumulative grade point average of 2.0 is required for freshmen applicants and 2.5 for sophomore, junior, and senior applicants.

Women, minorities, individuals with disabilities, and veterans are particularly encouraged to apply.

Financial data Participants receive an hourly wage, based on the number of credit hours or semesters they have completed and the type of work; the current wage structure ranges from $5.10 per hour for recent high school graduates to $11.33 for college seniors. Benefits are available, based on length of appointment.

Duration 90 days during the summer.

Special features Limited housing is available, on a first-come, first-served basis. Participants can work in a variety of technical disciplines: chemistry; computer science, earth and space science, economics, engineering, health and environmental sciences, life sciences, materials sciences/metallurgy, mathematics, optics and electro-optics, physics, and astrophysics. Limited opportunities are available in the administrative fields.

Number awarded Varies each year.

Deadline January of each year.

[1634]
LUBBOCK AVALANCHE-JOURNAL INTERNSHIP

Lubbock Avalanche-Journal
Attn: Assistant Managing Editor
710 Avenue J
P.O. Box 491
Lubbock, TX 79408
(806) 762-8844

Purpose To provide experience to college students who are interested in working for the *Lubbock Avalanche-Journal* as preparation for a career in journalism.

Eligibility College students from any state who are interested in working on a daily newspaper are invited to apply to work as an intern on the newspaper. Applicants must have completed the sophomore year with a major in journalism. Minorities are especially encouraged to apply.

Financial data Interns are paid $275 per week.

Duration 12 weeks during the summer.

Number awarded 3 each year.

Deadline March of each year.

[1635]
MACON TELEGRAPH INTERNSHIPS

Macon Telegraph
Attn: Managing Editor
P.O. Box 4167
Macon, GA 31213
(912) 744-4200

Purpose To provide work experience at the *Macon Telegraph* in Georgia to college students interested in careers in journalism.

Eligibility This program is open to college students from any state, with a preference for juniors or seniors. Applicants must be planning to pursue careers in newspaper journalism or advertising. Minorities are especially encouraged to apply.

Financial data The salary is $250 per week.

Duration 12 weeks; news/editorial internships are tenable at any time of the year; advertising internships are provided during the summer.

Number awarded 4 news/editorial and 2 advertising internships each year.

Deadline January of each year for news/editorial; March of each year for advertising.

[1636]
MAERC STUDENT FELLOWSHIPS

Associated Western Universities
Attn: MAERC Program
4190 South Highland Drive, Suite 211
Salt Lake City, UT 84124
(801) 273-8904   Fax: (801) 277-5632

Purpose To identify, encourage, and support outstanding college students in California and Texas who are enrolled in science or engineering programs.

Eligibility This program is open to students who are enrolled in science or engineering programs at the Los Angeles, Northridge, or San Diego campuses of the California State University system or at the University of Texas at Austin. Applicants must have junior standing by the start date of the fellowship, a grade point average of 2.5 or better, and U.S. citizenship. Selection is based on academic program and performance, promise of success in the program, demonstrated leadership qualities, career interests and goals, extracurricular activities, and compatibility of applicant's research interests with those of the host facilities. Underrepresented minorities, women, and the physically challenged are especially encouraged to apply.

Financial data The stipend is $400 per month during the academic year and $1,000 per month during the summer. Other benefits during the academic year are tuition and fees up to $1,500 per year and research assistance up to $1,000 per year; during the summer the program provides round-trip travel to the U.S. Department of Energy (DOE) facility and a relocation allowance of $200 per month ($380 in California).

Duration Initially, 12 months (9 months during the academic year and 10 weeks in the summer); renewable to a maximum of 24 months depending on year in school and satisfactory performance.

Special features The Minority Access to Energy-Related Research Careers (MAERC) program is sponsored by DOE and administered by Associated Western Universities. Participants spend the academic year at their home campus and the summer in a research practicum appointment at 1 of the participating DOE facilities: Idaho National Engineering Laboratory (Idaho Falls, Idaho); Lawrence Berkeley Laboratory (Berkeley, California); Los Alamos National Laboratory (Los Alamos, New Mexico); or National Renewable Energy Laboratory (Golden, Colorado).

Deadline March of each year.

[1637]
MAGNETIC FUSION ENERGY TECHNOLOGY FELLOWSHIP PROGRAM

Oak Ridge Institute for Science and Education
Attn: Science/Engineering Education Division
P.O. Box 117
Oak Ridge, TN 37831-0117
(423) 576-9558   (423) 576-2600
(800) 569-7749   Fax: (423) 576-3643
E-mail: mfetfp@orau.gov

Purpose To provide funding for graduate study and work experience in magnetic fusion energy technology.

Eligibility Applications are generally submitted before the student has received a bachelor's degree or during the first year of graduate school. Applicants should be working or planning to work on a doctorate in the physical sciences, mathematics, or engineering at participating universities (for a list of these schools, write to the address above). All programs operated by the Science/Engineering Education Division (SEED) of Oak Ridge Institute for Science and Education (ORISE) seek to broaden the participation of minorities, women, and persons with disabilities in science and engineering careers.

Financial data The stipend is $15,600 per year. An additional $200 per month is paid during the practicum period. Tuition and fees are covered. Some travel money is available.

Duration 1 year; may be renewed for up to 4 additional years.

Special features Participants intern at various research facilities of the U.S. Department of Energy (DOE). This program is funded by DOE's Office of Fusion Energy and administered by ORISE/SEED.

Number awarded Varies each year.

Deadline January of each year.

[1638]
MAGNETIC FUSION SCIENCE FELLOWSHIP PROGRAM

Oak Ridge Institute for Science and Education
Attn: Science/Engineering Education Division
P.O. Box 117
Oak Ridge, TN 37831-0117
(423) 576-9558   (423) 576-2600
(800) 569-7749   Fax: (423) 576-3643
E-mail: magfsfp@orau.gov

Purpose To provide funding for graduate study and work experience in magnetic fusion science.

Eligibility Applications are generally submitted before or during the first year of graduate school. Applicants should be working or planning to work on a doctorate in the physical sciences, mathematics, or engineering at participating universities (for a list of these schools, write to the address above). All programs operated by the Science/Engineering Education Division (SEED) of Oak Ridge Institute for Science and Education (ORISE) seek to broaden the participation of minorities, women, and persons with disabilities in science and engineering careers.

Financial data The stipend is $15,600 per year. An additional $200 per month is paid during the practicum period. Tuition and fees are covered. Some travel money is available.

Duration 1 year; may be renewed for up to 3 additional years.

Special features Participants intern at various research facilities of the U.S. Department of Energy (DOE). This program is funded by DOE's Office of Fusion Energy and administered by ORISE/SEED.

Number awarded Varies each year.

Deadline January of each year.

[1639]
MARILYN LLOYD FELLOWSHIP PROGRAM

Oak Ridge Institute for Science and Education
Attn: Science/Engineering Education Division
P.O. Box 117
Oak Ridge, TN 37831-0117
(423) 576-9279   (423) 576-2194
(800) 569-7749   Fax: (423) 576-3643
E-mail: mlloydfl@orau.gov

Purpose To provide financial assistance for graduate study and work experience in areas of interest to the U.S. Department of Energy (DOE).

Eligibility This program is open to students at designated participating universities (write to the address above for a list of these) who are working on a master's degree with a major in science or engineering and a minor in risk assessment, political science, public policy, economics, law, or business administration. All programs operated by the Science/Engineering Education Division (SEED) of Oak Ridge Institute for Science and Education (ORISE) seek to broaden the participation of minorities, women, and persons with disabilities in science and engineering careers.

Financial data Participants receive a monthly stipend of $1,200 and payment of tuition and fees.

Duration The program provides tuition support for 2 years with a 3-month summer practicum.

Special features Participants intern at DOE headquarters or operations offices. This program is funded by DOE and administered by ORISE/SEED.

Number awarded Varies each year.

Deadline May of each year.

[1640]
MARILYN LLOYD SCHOLARSHIP PROGRAM

Oak Ridge Institute for Science and Education
Attn: Science/Engineering Education Division
P.O. Box 117
Oak Ridge, TN 37831-0117
(423) 576-0128   (423) 576-9272
(800) 569-7749   Fax: (423) 576-3643
E-mail: mlloydsp@orau.gov

Purpose To provide financial assistance for undergraduate study and work experience in areas of interest to the U.S. Department of Energy (DOE).

Eligibility This program is open to students at designated participating universities (write to the address above for a list of these) who are working on an associates's or bachelor's degree with a major in science or engineering and a minor in risk assessment, political science, public policy, economics, law, or business administration. All programs operated by the Science/Engineering Education Division (SEED) of Oak Ridge Institute for Science and Education (ORISE) seek to broaden the participation of minorities, women, and persons with disabilities in science and engineering careers.

Financial data Participants receive a monthly stipend of $600 and payment of tuition and fees.

Duration The program provides tuition support for 2 years with a 3-month summer practicum.

Special features Participants intern at DOE headquarters or operations offices. This program is funded by DOE and administered by ORISE/SEED.

Number awarded Varies each year.

Deadline   May of each year.

[1641]
MASGC SUMMER JOBS PROGRAM

Massachusetts Space Grant Consortium
c/o MIT
Building 33, Room 208
77 Massachusetts Avenue
Cambridge, MA 02139
(617) 258-5546   Fax: (617) 253-0823
E-mail: halaris@mit.edu

Purpose   To provide work experience at space-related firms to undergraduate students in Massachusetts.

Eligibility   This program is open to undergraduate students at institutions that are members of the Massachusetts Space Grant Consortium (MASGC). Applicants must be interested in employment at participating companies involved in space science and/or space engineering. U.S. citizenship is required. MASGC is a component of the U.S. National Aeronautics and Space Administration (NASA) Space Grant program, which encourages participation by women, minorities, and persons with disabilities.

Financial data   Stipends are provided.

Duration   Summer months.

Special features   In a recent year, the participating companies included The Aerospace Corporation, Hughes, Lockheed Martin, MIT Lincoln Laboratory, NASA Goddard Space Flight Center, Jet Propulsion Laboratory, Orbital Sciences Corporation, Space Systems Loral, Rockwell International, TRW, United Technologies, and Trimble Navigation.

Number awarded   Varies each year.

Deadline   December of each year.

[1642]
MASS MEDIA SCIENCE AND ENGINEERING FELLOWS PROGRAM

American Association for the Advancement of Science
Attn: Directorate for Education and Human Resources
1200 New York Avenue, N.W.
Washington, DC 20005-3920
(202) 326-6760   Fax: (202) 371-9849
E-mail: aking@aaas.org

Purpose   To provide internships in print and broadcast journalism for coverage of topics related to science.

Eligibility   The program is designed primarily to support advanced graduate students in the natural/social sciences and engineering. Applications may also be submitted by outstanding undergraduate and postdoctoral students. Students from underrepresented communities, including Black, Hispanic, Native American, and those with disabilities, are encouraged to apply.

Financial data   Fellows receive a stipend that depends on the site assignment and travel expenses.

Duration   10 weeks in the summer; may be extended, depending upon the interest of the media site.

Special features   Interns work as reporters, researchers, or production assistants in a variety of media. They may be assigned to work for newspapers, magazines, television, or radio. This program began in 1973.

Limitations   Students majoring in English, journalism, or other nontechnical fields are not eligible to apply.

Number awarded   Varies; generally, 20 each year.

Deadline   January of each year.

[1643]
MAT INTERNSHIPS

Minority Advertising Training Program
6404 Wilshire Boulevard, Suite 1111
Los Angeles, CA 90048
(213) 655-1951   Fax: (213) 655-8627

Purpose   To provide education and training opportunities to minority individuals in southern California interested in a career in advertising.

Eligibility   Applicants must be juniors, seniors, or recent graduates of colleges and universities in southern California. They must be minority individuals interested in an internship at selected advertising agencies or broadcast outlets in the region.

Financial data   The salary is $200 per week for a 30-hour week.

Duration   Interns work 13 weeks for 20 to 30 hours per week.

Special features   The Minority Advertising Training Program (MAT) is a coalition of the Western States Advertising Agencies Association, the Advertising Club of Los Angeles, and Chiat/Day/Mojo.

Number awarded   Varies each year.

Deadline   December of each year for spring internships; April for other times.

[1644]
MAYNARD INSTITUTE EDITING PROGRAM FOR MINORITY JOURNALISTS

Robert C. Maynard Institute for Journalism Education
1211 Preservation Park Way
Oakland, CA 94612
(510) 891-9202   Fax: (510) 891-9565

Purpose   To provide assistance to journalists who want to excel as copy editors or assignment editors.

Eligibility   Applicants must have at least 1 year of experience in print media. Although the program emphasizes significant nonwhite representation, participation is also open to white journalists. Each applicant must complete the program application and submit a 1,000-word autobiographical essay and an 800-word critique of the daily newspaper the candidate works for or reads regularly. Semifinalists are invited for testing and interviewing by a selection panel of experienced daily newspaper editors and officers of the Robert C. Maynard Institute for Journalism Education.

Financial data   Successful candidates receive transportation to the University of Arizona in Tucson, tuition, and housing. Transportation and expenses for interviews are also covered. Candidates not receiving salaries from sponsoring newspapers receive a $200-a-week stipend. Sponsoring newspapers cover transportation from Tucson to the city in which the newspaper is located. The program does not pay for: required books, meals, or other incidental expenses; transportation from Tucson to the participant's home city at the end of the program; or transportation of family or relocation of belongings.

Duration   8 weeks, beginning in June.

Special features   During the 8-week program, participants work as editors on the program's newspaper and on the copy desks of the Tucson newspapers. Participants work under the guidance of veteran daily newspaper editors. They use video display terminals and learn the basics and fine points of copy editing, headline writing, newspaper layout and design, city desk operations, photo editing, libel law, and newspaper production. Management training is also provided during the session; instruction includes assessment of management and leadership skills, group discussions, problem-solving exercises in newsroom management, and information on newsroom finances. After completing the session, participants go on to copy desk jobs at sponsoring daily newspapers. Those not sponsored by a newspaper are matched to newspapers and sent on 1 or more interviews before the program begins. The Robert C. Maynard Institute for Journalism Education was incorporated in 1977 as the Institute for Journalism Education; it was renamed in 1993 in honor of the late *Oakland Tribune* owner who co-founded the nonprofit corporation.

Limitations Newspapers wishing to guarantee a copy desk job for a selected candidate are asked to pay a fee of $2,500. During the 8-week session, participants are required to live in apartments provided by the program. Family members may not accompany them.

Number awarded 10 to 12 each session.

Deadline February of each year.

[1645]
MEMPHIS COMMERCIAL APPEAL INTERNSHIP PROGRAM

Memphis Commercial Appeal
Attn: Deputy Managing Editor
495 Union Avenue
Memphis, TN 38103
(901) 529-2447

Purpose To provide work experience at the *Memphis Commercial Appeal* to students who are interested in preparing for a career in journalism.

Eligibility College students majoring in journalism are eligible to apply. Preference is given to juniors, seniors, and graduate students. Applications from minority students are especially encouraged.

Financial data The salary is $356 per week.

Duration 12 weeks, in the summer or fall.

Number awarded 12 each year in news and editorial; 1 to 2 each year in photography.

Deadline January of each year.

[1646]
MENTORED COLLABORATIVE RESEARCH PROJECT AT LANL

Los Alamos National Laboratory
Attn: Science and Technology Base Directorate
University Programs
Mail Stop F673
P.O. Box 1663
Los Alamos, NM 87545
(505) 667-1230   E-mail: abad@lanl.gov

Purpose To provide research experience on specific target projects to student and faculty teams at the Los Alamos National Laboratory (LANL).

Eligibility This program is open to teams of students who are pursuing postsecondary education at several levels (associate, baccalaureate, and graduate) as well as faculty members. The student/faculty teams work alongside Laboratory researchers on a project of direct relevant to its core defense missions. Teams may include participants from different disciplines in science, engineering, and technology. The program focuses on students and faculty from New Mexico and regional universities, with an emphasis on diversity. U.S. citizenship or permanent resident status is required.

Financial data A stipend is paid, based on the academic level of the participant.

Duration Summer months.

Special features A recent project was microstructures and properties of erbium oxide. Other potential projects include dynamic behavior of materials, including fracture; energetic materials; aging and corrosion of materials; fabrication, machining, forming, casting, and joining; and intelligent controls.

Number awarded Varies each year.

[1647]
METPRO/EDITING PROGRAM

Newsday
Attn: METPRO/Editing Director
235 Pinelawn Road
Melville, NY 11747-4250
(516) 843-3087   (800) NEWSDAY, ext. 3087

Purpose To increase the number of minorities trained for editing positions on daily metropolitan newspapers.

Eligibility Applicants should be college graduates with excellent writing skills and an interest in a newspaper career. Selection is based on academic record and potential. Previous professional editing experience is not required.

Financial data Trainees receive a weekly stipend, a monthly housing allowance, and medical benefits for the first year. During the second year, trainees receive compensation and benefits applicable at the newspaper where they are working.

Duration 2 years.

Special features Participants in this program (Minority Editorial Training Program) receive intensive training in editing at Newsday during the first year, including a 2-week orientation, 3 weeks or reporting in Queens and on Long Island, 10 weeks of full-time classroom instruction, and 31 weeks of work as editors on Newsday copy desks. During the second year, they work for 1 of the Times Mirror newspapers (in Stamford, Connecticut; Baltimore, Maryland; Hartford, Connecticut; Los Angeles, California; Allentown, Pennsylvania; or Melville, New York).

Number awarded 10 each year.

Deadline December of each year.

[1648]
METPRO/REPORTING PROGRAM

Los Angeles Times
Attn: METPRO/Reporting Director
Times Mirror Square
Los Angeles, CA 90053
(800) 223-NEWS, ext. 74487

Purpose To increase the number of minorities trained for reporting or photography positions on daily metropolitan newspapers.

Eligibility Applicants should be college graduates with excellent writing skills and an interest in a newspaper career. Selection is based on essays, a review of written work or photographs, college transcripts, recommendations, writing tests, and personal interviews. Previous professional reporting experience is not required.

Financial data Trainees receive a regular stipend for the first year and are furnished housing, utilities, and medical insurance while in the program. During the second year, trainees receive compensation and benefits applicable at the newspaper where they are working.

Duration 2 years.

Special features Participants in this program (Minority Editorial Training Program) spend the first 9 months at the *Los Angeles Times,* beginning with a full-time classroom instruction phase that includes reporting and writing techniques, interviewing, researching, and beat coverage; then several weeks covering a police beat; then full-time reporting assignments in the Times newsroom, frequently tailored to trainee interests; concluding with work at 1 of the Times regional editions. During the second year, they work for 1 of the Times Mirror newspapers in Stamford, Connecticut; Baltimore, Maryland; Greenwich, Connecticut; Hartford, Connecticut; Los Angeles, California; Allentown, Pennsylvania; or Melville, New York.

Number awarded 10 each year.

Deadline November of each year.

[1649]
METROPOLITAN MUSEUM OF ART 6-MONTH INTERNSHIPS

Metropolitan Museum of Art
Attn: Internship Programs
1000 Fifth Avenue
New York, NY 10028-0198
(212) 879-5500

Purpose To provide museum work experience to minority undergraduate and graduate students.

Eligibility Applicants must be Black, Hispanic, or other minority students who are graduating college seniors, college graduates, master's candidates, or doctoral candidates in art history or related fields. Selection is based on academic achievement and work/educational experience.

Financial data The stipend is $8,000.

Duration 6 months, beginning in June.

Special features This program is funded in part by the National Endowment for the Arts. Interns work at the Metropolitan Museum for 35 hours a week.

Number awarded 2 each year.

Deadline February of each year.

[1650]
METROPOLITAN MUSEUM OF ART 9-MONTH INTERNSHIPS

Metropolitan Museum of Art
Attn: Internship Programs
1000 Fifth Avenue
New York, NY 10028-0198
(212) 879-5500

Purpose To provide museum work experience to minorities from New York.

Eligibility This program is open to disadvantaged (especially minority) New Yorkers who are graduating college seniors, recent college graduates, or graduate students in art history, art administration, conservation, or art education. An interview is required.

Financial data The honorarium is $12,000.

Duration 9 months, beginning in September.

Special features Interns are assigned to 1 or more of the Metropolitan Museum of Art's departments, where they work on projects that match their academic background, professional skills, and career goals.

Limitations This program was not funded for 1997. Its continuation depends on the availability of future funding.

Number awarded 3 each year.

Deadline February of each year.

[1651]
MIAMI HERALD INTERNSHIP

Miami Herald
Attn: Assistant Managing Editor/Staff Development
One Herald Plaza
Miami, FL 33132
(305) 376-3592

Purpose To provide work experience at the *Miami Herald* to minority and other college students interested in journalism as a career.

Eligibility College juniors, seniors, or graduate students are eligible to apply for this internship, if they are interested in reporting, copy-editing, photography, advertising, information systems, or graphics. Special attention is given to applications submitted by local and minority candidates.

Financial data The stipend is $520 per week for news/editorial and photography; interns in advertising, information systems, and graphics earn approximately $10 per hour.

Duration 12 weeks, in spring, summer, or fall.

Number awarded 12 each year in news/editorial, 1 to 3 each year in photography, 3 to 4 each year in advertising, 3 to 4 each year in information systems, 1 each year in graphic art.

Deadline October of each year.

[1652]
MID-AMERICAN ATHLETIC CONFERENCE INTERNSHIPS

Mid-American Athletic Conference
Four SeaGate, Suite 102
Toledo, OH 43604
(419) 249-7177   Fax: (419) 249-7199

Purpose To provide work experience to minorities or women interested in college sports.

Eligibility Minorities and women who have graduated from college, have worked in an athletic department, have some computer skills, and are interested in working with college sports are eligible to apply.

Financial data The stipend is $1,000 per month, plus a $100 monthly living expense allowance.

Duration 9 months.

Special features Interns work in marketing, sports information, compliance, TV and radio, and sports management.

Number awarded 1 each year.

Deadline June of each year.

[1653]
MINORITY ADVERTISING INTERN PROGRAM

American Association of Advertising Agencies
405 Lexington Avenue
New York, NY 10174-1801
(212) 682-2500   (800) 676-9333
Fax: (212) 682-8391

Purpose To provide racial minority students with job experience in advertising agencies and to present them with an overview of the agency business.

Eligibility Eligible to apply are full-time students from any racial minority group who will be seniors or graduate students in the fall following the internship and who are majoring in advertising, communications, liberal arts, marketing, or a related area with a minimum grade point average of 2.7. Applicants must be U.S. citizens or permanent residents committed to a career in the advertising world.

Financial data Interns are paid approximately $300 per week. Interns who are relocating receive 60 percent of the costs of transportation and housing.

Duration 10 weeks during the summer.

Special features Interns may be assigned duties in 4 career areas of advertising: account management, media, research, and creative (art direction or copywriting).

Number awarded Varies each year; in recent years, 52 students have been placed in 38 member advertising agency offices in Atlanta, Boston, Chicago, Detroit, Los Angeles, New York, Pittsburgh, and San Francisco.

Deadline January of each year.

[1654]
MINORITY FACULTY FELLOWSHIP PROGRAM

Indiana University
Attn: Minority Faculty Fellowship Program
Memorial Hall West 111
Bloomington, IN 47405-6701
(812) 855-0543   Fax: (812) 855-4869
E-mail: torchins@ucs.indiana.edu

Purpose To aid in recruiting outstanding minority faculty to the Indiana University campus; to identify minority scholars who might be available for longer-term positions.

Eligibility African American, Hispanic American, and Native American scholars who either are nearing completion of the doctorate or have completed the doctorate within the last 4 years are encouraged to apply. The program seeks candidates who have demonstrated a strong commitment to scholarly research and creative teaching. U.S. citizenship or permanent resident status is required.

Financial data The fellowship package includes a salary equivalent to that ordinarily paid to an Indiana University faculty member of the same rank, plus a $3,000 stipend for research and living expenses.

Duration Summer months or academic year.

Number awarded Varies each year.

Special features The program was established in 1986. Summer fellows teach 1 or 2 courses. Academic-year fellows teach in the fall and spring terms.

Deadline October of each year for summer fellows; November of each year for academic-year appointments.

[1655]
MINORITY FELLOWSHIP PROGRAM IN PSYCHIATRY

American Psychiatric Association
Attn: Office of Minority/National Affairs
1400 K Street, N.W.
Washington, DC 20005
(202) 682-6096   Fax: (202) 682-6352
E-mail: mking@psych.org

Purpose To provide educational enrichment to psychiatrists-in-training and stimulate their interest in providing quality and effective services to minorities and the underserved.

Eligibility Minority psychiatric residents who are in at least their second year of psychiatric training are eligible to apply. Fellows are selected on the basis of their commitment to serving minorities and underserved populations, demonstrated leadership abilities, and interest in the interrelationship between mental health/illness and transcultural factors.

Financial data A partial stipend is provided, usually lower than the normal salary paid by the training institution, which is then requested to pay the fellow the difference between the stipend and the usual salary. The institutions must use the remaining freed-up funds to institute or expand a teaching format within the resident's training program that focuses on culturally relevant issues in psychiatry. Fellows incur a payback obligation which they must fulfill by providing 1 year of service at a public inpatient mental institution, public or private nonprofit facility, or nursing home. At least 25 percent of the facility's patients must be 1 of the priority populations of the Center for Mental Health Services (CMHS)—racial/ethnic minorities, chronically mentally ill, rape victims, the elderly, physically handicapped, veterans, mentally retarded, criminal or delinquent populations, children and adolescents, poverty populations, migrants, members of the armed forces, and residents of any nursing home.

Duration 9 and a half months, beginning September 1.

Special features Funding for this program is provided by the CMHS, a component of the Substance Abuse and Mental Health Services Administration. Each fellow is appointed to a component of the organizational structure of the American Psychiatric Association (APA) and attends the association's annual meeting as an observer and active participant. This program is an outgrowth of the fellowships that were established in 1974 under a grant from the National Institute of Mental Health in answer to concerns about the underrepresentation of minorities in psychiatry.

Number awarded Varies; averages 10 each year.

Deadline March of each year.

[1656]
MISSISSIPPI PSYCHOLOGY APPRENTICESHIP PROGRAM

Mississippi Office of State Student Financial Aid
3825 Ridgewood Road
Jackson, MS 39211-6453
(601) 982-6589   (800) 327-2980 (within MS)

Purpose To provide work experience in the field of psychology to students in Mississippi.

Eligibility Current legal Mississippi residents who are enrolled as full-time undergraduate or graduate students majoring in psychology at a Mississippi accredited college or university with a minimum grade point average of 3.0 are eligible for this program. Participants engage in research and training in the professional practice of psychology at the Mississippi Department of Veterans Affairs Medical Center in Biloxi. Special consideration is given to economically disadvantaged, educationally disadvantaged, and/or socially disadvantaged applicants.

Financial data Stipends are $1,000 per month for graduate students and $500 per month for undergraduates.

Duration 3 months, during the summer.

Deadline March of each year.

[1657]
MISSOURI SPACE GRANT CONSORTIUM SUMMER HIGH SCHOOL INTERNSHIPS

Missouri Space Grant Consortium
c/o University of Missouri at Rolla
College of Engineering
Mechanical and Aerospace Engineering and Engineering
  Mechanics
101 Mechanical Engineering Building
Rolla, Mo 65401-0249
(314) 341-4671   Fax: (314) 341-4607
E-mail: bpaul@umr.edu

Purpose To provide work experience during the summer to high school students in Missouri interested in a career in an aerospace field.

Eligibility This program is open to Missouri high school students who have just completed their junior or senior year. Applicants must be proposing a specific research or education project in a research laboratory, a computing facility, or the galleries of the St. Louis Science Center. U.S. citizenship is required. The Missouri Space Grant Consortium is a component of the U.S. National Aeronautics and Space Administration (NASA), which encourages participation by women, minorities, and persons with disabilities.

Financial data The maximum funding is $2,000.

Duration Summer months.

Special features This program is funded by NASA.

Number awarded Approximately 10 each year.

[1658]
MISSOURI SPACE GRANT CONSORTIUM UNDERGRADUATE INTERNSHIPS

Missouri Space Grant Consortium
c/o University of Missouri at Rolla
College of Engineering
Mechanical and Aerospace Engineering and Engineering
  Mechanics
101 Mechanical Engineering Building
Rolla, Mo 65401-0249
(314) 341-4671   Fax: (314) 341-4607
E-mail: bpaul@umr.edu

Purpose To provide work experience during the summer to undergraduate students in Missouri pursuing a degree in an aerospace field.

Eligibility This program is open to undergraduate students studying engineering, physics, astronomy, or planetary sciences at member institutions of the Missouri Space Grant Consortium (Southwest Missouri State University, University of Missouri at Columbia, University of Missouri at Rolla, University of Missouri at St. Louis, or Washington University). Applicants must be proposing a specific research or education project in a research laboratory, a computing facility, or the galleries of the St. Louis Science Center. U.S. citizenship is required. The Missouri Space Grant Consortium is a component of the U.S. National Aeronau-

tics and Space Administration (NASA), which encourages participation by women, minorities, and persons with disabilities.

Financial data The maximum funding is $3,000.

Duration Both summer and academic year appointments are available.

Special features This program is funded by NASA.

Number awarded 10 or more each year in the summer; 10 or more each year during the academic year.

[1659]
MISSOURI VALLEY CONFERENCE ADMINISTRATIVE INTERNSHIP

Missouri Valley Conference
1000 Union Station, Suite 333
St. Louis, MO 63103
(314) 421-0339   Fax: (314) 421-3505

Purpose To provide work experience to minorities and women interested in college sports.

Eligibility Applicants should have collegiate athletic experience, particularly the sports information field, and possess a baccalaureate degree. Strong organizational and interpersonal skills, particularly in the areas of writing, editing, and publications design, are necessary qualifications. Desk-top publishing experience is required. Minorities and women are particularly encouraged to apply.

Financial data A monetary stipend is provided.

Duration 11 months.

Special features A major focus of this position is to assist the conference office staff in annual publications.

Number awarded 1 each year.

Deadline May of each year.

[1660]
MODESTO BEE MINORITY INTERN PROGRAM

Modesto Bee
Attn: Executive Editor
1325 H Street
P.O. Box 5256
Modesto, CA 95352
(209) 578-2000

Purpose To provide work experience at the *Modesto Bee* in California to minorities who are interested in a career in journalism.

Eligibility Applicants must be minorities who have completed at least their junior year in college; they should have majored in journalism or have newspaper experience. Both students still in school and recent graduates are eligible.

Financial data The stipend is $375 per week.

Duration 10 to 12 weeks, in the spring, summer, fall, or winter.

Deadline Applications may be submitted at any time but should be received at least 1 semester before the internship is to start.

[1661]
MUNICIPAL GOVERNMENT INTERNSHIPS
Seattle Personnel Department
Attn: Special Employment Programs Office
710 Second Avenue
Dexter Horton Building, 12th Floor
Seattle, WA 98104-1793
(206) 684-7996   TDD: (206) 684-7888

Purpose To provide work experience in Seattle municipal government to college students.

Eligibility Full-time college students, especially those enrolled in graduate programs, are eligible to apply. Preference is given to applications from minorities, women, and persons with disabilities.

Financial data The salary is $11.03 per hour.

Duration 6 to 18 months.

Special features The emphasis is on management training assignments.

Number awarded Depends on the availability of openings.

[1662]
MUSKOGEE DAILY PHOENIX INTERNSHIPS
Muskogee Daily Phoenix
Attn: Executive Editor
214 Wall Street
P.O. Box 1968
Muskogee, OK 74402-1968
(918) 684-2900

Purpose To provide work experience at the *Muskogee Daily Phoenix* in Oklahoma to college students interested in careers in journalism.

Eligibility This program is open to students from any state, with a preference for juniors and seniors. Applicants must be planning to pursue careers in newspaper reporting, editing, or photography. Minorities are especially encouraged to apply.

Financial data The salary is competitive.

Duration Summer months.

Number awarded 2 each year: 1 in news/editorial and 1 in photography.

Deadline April of each year.

[1663]
MYRTLE BEACH SUN NEWS INTERNSHIPS
Myrtle Beach Sun News
Attn: Deputy Managing Editor
P.O. Box 406
Myrtle Beach, SC 29578-0406
(803) 626-0300   Fax: (803) 626-0356

Purpose To provide experience to minority and other college students who are interested in working for the *Myrtle Beach Sun News* in South Carolina as preparation for a career in journalism.

Eligibility College students (particularly seniors) from any state who are interested in working on a daily newspaper are invited to apply to work as an intern on the newspaper. Special consideration is given to applications from minorities. Applicants should submit a resume, samples of their work, and a letter indicating why they are interested in working at the newspaper.

Financial data Interns are paid $300 per week.

Duration 10 weeks during the summer.

Special features Interns are offered work opportunities in news/editorial or photography.

Number awarded 3 each year.

Deadline January of each year.

[1664]
NAPLES DAILY NEWS INTERNSHIPS
Naples Daily News
Attn: Managing Editor
1075 Central Avenue
Naples, FL 34102-6295
(941) 263-4777

Purpose To provide work experience at the *Naples Daily News* in Florida to students interested in careers in journalism.

Eligibility This program is open to college students from any state, with a preference for seniors. Applicants must be planning to pursue careers in newspaper journalism or photography. Minorities are especially encouraged to apply.

Financial data The salary is $9 per hour.

Duration News/editorial internships are for 13 weeks; photography internships are for 26 weeks; all positions are available throughout the year.

Number awarded 1 to 2 each year in both news/editorial and photography.

Deadline Applications may be submitted at any time.

[1665]
NARAL INTERNSHIP PROGRAM
National Abortion and Reproductive Rights Action League
Attn: Human Resources Department
1156 15th Street, N.W., Suite 700
Washington, DC 20005
(202) 973-3049   Fax: (202) 973-3096

Purpose To offer opportunities to work as an intern in any of the departments (executive, communications, field organization, finance and administration, legal/research, and legislative/political) of the National Abortion and Reproductive Rights Action League (NARAL).

Eligibility All internships require some knowledge of reproductive rights issues and support of the pro-choice movement. Specific internships have particular requirements based on the responsibilities of that department. People of color are strongly urged to apply.

Financial data Interns may receive limited compensation (e.g., reimbursement for travel expenses to and from work) or a stipend; most appointments are voluntary in nature.

Duration Internship periods vary.

Special features Interns may receive college credit for their work with the organization. NARAL is a 750,000 member political organization working to keep abortion legal.

Number awarded Varies each year.

Deadline Applications are accepted at any time.

[1666]
NASA ACADEMIES

National Aeronautics and Space Administration
Attn: Office of University Programs
Goddard Space Flight Center
Code 160
Greenbelt, MD 20771
(301) 286-9690   Fax: (301) 286-1660
E-mail: gsoffen@pop100.gsfc.nasa.gov

Purpose To provide opportunities to selected students to work on research projects at specified field centers of the National Aeronautics and Space Administration (NASA).

Eligibility Applicants for this program must 1) be enrolled as juniors, seniors, or first-year graduate students; 2) maintain a minimum grade point average of 3.0; 3) major in engineering, science, mathematics, computer science, or other area of interest to the space program; 4) be U.S. citizens or permanent residents; and 5) be interested in a program at a NASA field center in which they work at a NASA field center under the direction of NASA scientists and engineers. NASA is strongly committed to increasing cultural diversity among its pool of future leaders; underrepresented minority and female students are encouraged to apply.

Financial data Stipends range from $3,000 to $4,000; round-trip travel to the center, housing, and local transportation are also provided.

Duration 10 weeks, during the summer.

Special features The flagship for this program is NASA's Goddard Space Flight Center in Greenbelt, Maryland; other NASA field centers that have participated include Dryden Flight Research Center (Edwards, California), Marshall Space Flight Center (Huntsville, Alabama), and Ames Research Center (Moffett Field, California). Applications are also available from the Space Grant Consortium office in each state; for a list of those, contact the address above.

Number awarded Approximately 4 students participate at each of the participating NASA field centers.

Deadline January of each year.

[1667]
NASHVILLE BANNER INTERNSHIPS

Nashville Banner
Attn: Managing Editor
1100 Broadway
Nashville, TN 37203
(615) 259-8800

Purpose To provide work experience at the *Nashville Banner* in Tennessee to college students interested in careers in journalism.

Eligibility This program is open to students from any state, with a preference for juniors and seniors. Applicants must be planning to pursue careers in newspaper reporting, editing, or photography. Minorities are especially encouraged to apply.

Financial data Salaries range from $280 to $320 per week.

Duration 10 to 12 weeks, during the summer.

Limitations Interested students are requested not to inquire by telephone.

Number awarded 4 to 6 each year in news/editorial; 1 each year in photography.

Deadline February of each year.

[1668]
NATIONAL ASSOCIATION FOR GIRLS AND WOMEN IN SPORT INTERNSHIP

National Association for Girls and Women in Sport
1900 Association Drive
Reston, VA 22091
(703) 476-3450   Fax: (703) 476-9527

Purpose To provide work experience to minorities and others interested in college sports.

Eligibility This program is open to upper-division undergraduate and graduate students interested in college sports. They should be able to work independently and to assimilate new information. Minorities and women are particularly encouraged to apply.

Financial data The stipend is $100 per month; interns are responsible for their own housing, transportation, board, travel, and other expenses.

Duration 1 academic term.

Special features Interns work 7 and a half hours a day, 5 days a week on such projects as promotional brochures, newsletters, information requests, grant writing, National Coaches Institute, and National Girls and Women in Sports Day. Academic credit can be arranged.

Number awarded 2 each term.

Deadline February for the summer session; April for the fall term; October for the spring term.

[1669]
NATIONAL CENTER FOR TOXICOLOGICAL RESEARCH GRADUATE STUDENT RESEARCH PARTICIPATION PROGRAM

Oak Ridge Institute for Science and Education
Attn: Science/Engineering Education Division
P.O. Box 117
Oak Ridge, TN 37831-0117
(423) 576-1083   (423) 576-3426
(800) 569-7749   Fax: (423) 576-3643
E-mail: gsrpnctr@orau.gov

Purpose To provide funding to graduate students who wish to participate in research on biological effects of potentially toxic chemicals at the National Center for Toxicological Research in Arkansas.

Eligibility Students currently enrolled in graduate degree programs in toxicology, pharmacology, biological sciences, mathematics, chemistry, medicine, computer science, or other related scientific disciplines may apply for this program. They must propose to participate in research activities at the National Center for Toxicological Research in Jefferson, Arkansas. All programs operated by the Science/Engineering Education Division (SEED) of Oak Ridge Institute for Science and Education (ORISE) seek to broaden the participation of minorities, women, and persons with disabilities in science and engineering careers.

Financial data The stipend is based on research areas and academic classification.

Duration 3 months to 1 year; both full-time and part-time appointments are available.

Special features This program is funded by an interagency agreement between the U.S. Department of Energy and the U.S. Food and Drug Administration and administered by ORISE/SEED.

Number awarded Varies each year.

Deadline Applications may be submitted at any time.

[1670]
NATIONAL CENTER FOR TOXICOLOGICAL RESEARCH UNDERGRADUATE PROGRAM

Oak Ridge Institute for Science and Education
Attn: Science/Engineering Education Division
P.O. Box 117
Oak Ridge, TN 37831-0117
(423) 576-1083   (423) 576-3426
(800) 569-7749   Fax: (423) 576-3643
E-mail: undnctr@orau.gov

Purpose To provide funding to undergraduates who wish to participate in research on biological effects of potentially toxic chemicals at the National Center for Toxicological Research in Arkansas.

Eligibility Applicants must be undergraduates studying toxicology, pharmacology, biological sciences, mathematics, chemistry, medicine, computer science, or other related scientific disciplines may apply for this program. They must propose to conduct research at the National Center for Toxicological Research in Jefferson, Arkansas. All programs operated by the Science/Engineering Education Division (SEED) of Oak Ridge Institute for Science and Education (ORISE) seek to broaden the participation of minorities, women, and persons with disabilities in science and engineering careers.

Financial data The stipend is based on research areas and academic classification.

Duration 3 months to 1 year; full- and part-time appointments are available.

Special features This program is funded by an interagency agreement between the U.S. Department of Energy and the U.S. Food and Drug Administration and administered by ORISE/SEED.

Number awarded Varies each year.

Deadline Applications may be submitted at any time.

[1671]
NATIONAL COMMITTEE ON PAY EQUITY INTERNSHIP PROGRAM

National Committee on Pay Equity
1126 16th Street, N.W., Suite 411
Washington, DC 20036
(202) 331-7343   Fax: (202) 331-7406

Purpose To provide work experience to students interested in the pay equity issue.

Eligibility College students who are interested in the areas of public policy or development and are seeking a challenging internship opportunity in Washington, D.C. are eligible to apply for this program. The committee is a small, nonprofit membership coalition of women's, civil rights, and labor organizations (as well as individuals) committed to eliminating sex- and race-based wage discrimination by conducting advocacy research, providing information materials, and supplying technical assistance on all aspects of pay equity.

Financial data The semester stipend is $800 for full-time work, $400 for half-time work.

Duration 15 weeks.

Number awarded 1 or more during the year.

Deadline Applications may be submitted at any time, but priority is given to students who apply by the end of October for the spring term, the end of February for the summer session, and the end of July for the fall term.

[1672]
NATIONAL LAWYERS GUILD SUMMER PROJECTS

National Lawyers Guild
126 University Place, Fourth Floor
New York, NY 10013
(212) 627-2656   Fax: (212) 627-2404
E-mail: nlgno@igc.apc.org

Purpose To provide law students with direct experience in progressive legal work, encouraging careers in fields of law dedicated to using the legal system in the service of justice.

Eligibility This program is open to law students, legal workers, and lawyers interested in working with civil rights and poverty law groups. Women and ethnic minorities are particularly encouraged to apply.

Financial data Interns receive a $2,000 stipend. Recipients are encouraged to seek other funding sources, including law school work-study and fellowship programs.

Duration 10 weeks during the summer; renewable the following year.

Special features Summer Project programs are located throughout the country, in rural and urban areas. Interns have the opportunity to work on issues concerning Central American and Haitian refugees, farm worker rights, union democracy, opposition to the death penalty and inhumane prison conditions, women's economic and reproductive rights, unemployment rights, Philippine solidarity work, the farm crisis, voting rights, Native American treaty rights, Asian American housing and job rights, and workplace health and safety. Among the participating agencies are: Association of Community Organizations for Reform Now, Asian Law Caucus, California Center for Law and the Deaf, Michigan Migrant Legal Assistance Project, and the Native American Rights Fund.

Number awarded Approximately 20 each year.

Deadline February of each year.

[1673]
NATIONAL ZOOLOGICAL PARK RESEARCH TRAINEESHIPS

National Zoological Park
Smithsonian Institution
Attn: Human Resource Office
3001 Connecticut Avenue, N.W.
Washington, DC 20008
(202) 673-4639

Purpose To provide work experience in zoological activities at the Smithsonian Institution's National Zoological Park to undergraduate and graduate students.

Eligibility Selection is based on the applicant's statement of interest (up to 1,000 words), scholastic achievement, relevant experience, and letters of reference. Preference is given to advanced undergraduates, recent graduates, and graduate students. Minority and women students are encouraged to apply.

Financial data The stipend is $2,400.

Duration 12 weeks, at a time determined mutually by the trainee and the sponsor.

Special features Research traineeships are offered in some or all of the following areas: animal behavior, reproductive physiology, nutrition, genetics, husbandry/exhibit interpretation, zoo animal medicine, veterinary pathology. Responsibilities may include animal observation and handling, data recording, laboratory analysis, data processing, and report writing. All programs are at the National Zoological Park in Washington, D.C.

Number awarded 10 each year.
Deadline December of each year.

[1674]
NATIONAL ZOOLOGICAL PARK TRAINEESHIPS IN EXHIBIT INTERPRETATION, PUBLIC AFFAIRS, VIDEO PRODUCTION, HORTICULTURE, AND COMMUNICATIONS

National Zoological Park
Smithsonian Institution
Attn: Human Resource Office
3001 Connecticut Avenue, N.W.
Washington, DC 20008
(202) 673-4639

Purpose To provide work experience in exhibit interpretation, public affairs, horticulture, video production, and communications at the Smithsonian Institution's National Zoological Park to undergraduate and graduate students.
Eligibility Selection is based on the applicant's statement of interest (up to 1,000 words), scholastic achievement, relevant experience, and letters of reference. Preference is given to advanced undergraduates and recent graduates. Minority and women students are encouraged to apply.
Financial data The stipend is $2,400.
Duration 12 weeks, at a time determined mutually by the trainee and the sponsor.
Special features Traineeships may be offered in some or all of the following areas: exhibit interpretation, public affairs, horticulture, video production, and communications. All programs are at the National Zoological Park in Washington, D.C.
Number awarded Varies each year.
Deadline December of each year.

[1675]
NATIVE AMERICAN JOURNALISTS ASSOCIATION INTERNSHIPS

Native American Journalists Association
Attn: College Scholarships
1433 East Franklin Avenue, Suite 11
Minneapolis, MN 55404-2135
(612) 874-8833   Fax: (612) 874-9007

Purpose To provide work experience to Native American undergraduates who are interested in majoring in journalism in college.
Eligibility Native American students pursuing a degree in journalism or a related field are eligible. Applications include proof of enrollment in a federal or state recognized tribe, work samples (including printed works and photographs), grade transcripts showing an above average grade point average, a personal statement that demonstrates financial need and the student's reasons for pursuing a career in journalism, and a letter of recommendation from an academic advisor or a member of the community that attests to the applicant's ability to complete the desired education.
Financial data Stipends are provided.
Duration Most assignments are in the summer.
Special features Internships are arranged by the Native American Journalists Association (NAJA), with placements in Native and mainstream media organizations.
Number awarded Varies each year.

[1676]
NATIVE AMERICAN RIGHTS FUND SUMMER CLERKSHIP

Native American Rights Fund
1506 Broadway
Boulder, CO 80302-6296
(303) 447-8760   Fax: (303) 443-7776

Purpose To provide work experience to law students with an interest in Native American law.
Eligibility This program is open to second-year law students who are experienced in Indian law or have a background in Native American affairs.
Financial data Salaries are competitive with those of the federal government and nonprofit law firms.
Duration 10 weeks during the summer.
Special features Positions are available at Native American Rights Fund offices in the following cities: Boulder, Anchorage, and Washington, D.C. Legal activities fall into 5 main areas: protection of tribal natural resources, promotion of Native American human rights, accountability of governments to Native Americans, preservation of tribal existence, and development of Indian law.
Number awarded 1 or more each year.
Deadline November of each year.

[1677]
NAVAL AIR WARFARE CENTER TRAINING SYSTEMS DIVISION GRADUATE RESEARCH PARTICIPATION PROGRAM

Oak Ridge Institute for Science and Education
Attn: Science/Engineering Education Division
P.O. Box 117
Oak Ridge, TN 37831-0117
(423) 576-1083   (423) 576-3426
(800) 569-7749   Fax: (423) 576-3643
E-mail: grppawct@orau.gov

Purpose To provide funding to graduate students who wish to participate in research on advanced simulation and training systems technology at the Naval Air Warfare Center Training Systems Division in Orlando, Florida.
Eligibility This program is open to currently-enrolled master's and doctoral students who are working on a degree in behavioral sciences, computer science, or engineering. They must be interested in research participation in advanced simulation and training systems technology. All programs operated by the Science/Engineering Education Division (SEED) of Oak Ridge Institute for Science and Education (ORISE) seek to broaden the participation of minorities, women, and persons with disabilities in science and engineering careers.
Financial data A stipend is awarded; the amount is based on research areas and academic classification.
Duration 3 to 12 months.
Special features Students may participate on a full-time or part-time basis. This program is funded through an interagency agreement between the U.S. Department of Energy and the Naval Air Warfare Center Training Systems Division of the U.S. Navy.
Number awarded Varies each year.
Deadline Applications may be submitted at any time.

[1678]
NAVAL AIR WARFARE CENTER TRAINING SYSTEMS DIVISION UNDERGRADUATE RESEARCH PARTICIPATION PROGRAM

Oak Ridge Institute for Science and Education
Attn: Science/Engineering Education Division
P.O. Box 117
Oak Ridge, TN 37831-0117
(423) 576-1083   (423) 576-3426
(800) 569-7749   Fax: (423) 576-3643
E-mail: urrpnawc@orau.gov

Purpose To provide funding to undergraduates who wish to participate in research on advanced simulation and training systems technology at the Naval Air Warfare Center Training Systems Division in Orlando, Florida.

Eligibility This program is open to currently-enrolled undergraduate students who are working on a degree in behavioral sciences, computer science, or engineering. They must be interested in research participation in advanced simulation and training systems technology. All programs operated by the Science/Engineering Education Division (SEED) of Oak Ridge Institute for Science and Education (ORISE) seek to broaden the participation of minorities, women, and persons with disabilities in science and engineering careers.

Financial data A stipend is awarded; the amount is based on research areas and academic classification.

Duration 3 to 12 months.

Special features Students may participate on a full-time or part-time basis. This program is funded through an interagency agreement between the U.S. Department of Energy and the Naval Air Warfare Center Training Systems Division of the U.S. Navy.

Number awarded Varies each year.

Deadline Applications may be submitted at any time.

[1679]
NCAA ETHNIC MINORITY AND WOMEN'S INTERNSHIP PROGRAMS

National Collegiate Athletic Association
Attn: Director of Professional Development
6201 College Boulevard
Overland Park, KS 66211-2422
(913) 339-1906

Purpose To provide work experience at the National Collegiate Athletic Association (NCAA) office to college graduates.

Eligibility Candidates must be women or ethnic minorities who have completed the requirements for an undergraduate degree. They must have demonstrated a commitment to pursuing a career in intercollegiate athletics and the ability to succeed in such a career.

Financial data Interns receive up to $1,400 per month; this includes a $200 monthly housing allowance.

Duration 1 year.

Special features Interns work at the NCAA national office.

Number awarded Several each year.

Deadline February of each year.

[1680]
NEW JERSEY SPACE GRANT CONSORTIUM STUDENT FELLOWSHIPS

New Jersey Space Grant Consortium
c/o Stevens Institute of Technology
Department of Mechanical Engineering
Castle Point on the Hudson
Hoboken, NJ 07030
(201) 216-8964   Fax: (201) 216-8929
E-mail: sthangam@stevens-tech.edu

Purpose To provide financial assistance for summer research experiences in space-related fields to students in New Jersey.

Eligibility This program is open to undergraduate students at member institutions of the New Jersey Space Grant Consortium (New Jersey Institute of Technology, Princeton University, Rutgers, Seton Hall University, and Stevens Institute of Technology). Applicants must be proposing a program of space-related research in industry or at universities and their affiliated research laboratories. U.S. citizenship is required. The New Jersey Space Grant Consortium is a component of the U.S. National Aeronautics and Space Administration (NASA) Space Grant program, which encourages participation by women, minorities, and people with disabilities.

Financial data The stipend is $400 per week, with an additional $500 per student available for laboratory supplies.

Duration 10 weeks, during the summer.

Special features This program is funded by NASA.

Number awarded Approximately 13 each year.

[1681]
NEW YORK SPACE GRANT CONSORTIUM UNDERGRADUATE SUMMER INTERNSHIPS

New York Space Grant Consortium
c/o Cornell University
Astronomy Department
512 Space Sciences Building
Ithaca, NY 14853-6801
(607) 255-4935   Fax: (607) 255-9817
E-mail: terzian@astrosun.tn.cornell.edu

Purpose To provide funding for undergraduate students in New York who wish to work as student assistants on space-related research projects.

Eligibility This program is open to undergraduate students at member institutions of the New York Space Grant Consortium (Cornell University, City College of the City University of New York, Clarkson University, Columbia University, SUNY Buffalo, and Syracuse University). Applicants must be seeking appointments as interns on ongoing research projects sponsored by the U.S. National Aeronautics and Space Administration (NASA). U.S. citizenship is required. The New York Space Grant Consortium is a component of the NASA Space Grant program, which encourages participation by women, minorities, and persons with disabilities.

Financial data The amounts of the awards depends on the availability of funding.

Duration 8 weeks, during the summer.

Special features This program is funded by NASA. Most internships are at Cornell, but others are at City College, Clarkson, Columbia, Grumman Aircraft Ithaca, and the NASA Goddard Space Flight Center.

Number awarded 24 each year.

[1682]
NEW YORK STATE SENATE UNDERGRADUATE SESSION ASSISTANTS PROGRAM

New York State Senate
Attn: Director, Senate Student Programs
90 South Swan Street, Room 401
Albany, NY 12247
(518) 455-2611   Fax: (518) 432-5470

Purpose To provide undergraduate students an opportunity to work for the New York State Senate as assistants.

Eligibility Applicants must be currently enrolled full-time undergraduate students with a minimum grade point average of 3.0 in an accredited campus in New York State, residents of New York, and citizens of the United States. The program is intended and designed for college juniors and seniors; exceptional sophomores may be selected but freshmen are ineligible. Applicants must be able to arrange to earn campus credit for working 1 semester in the New York State Senate; most schools award 15 hours of credit. The Senate seeks and expects a significant proportion of qualified applicants from underrepresented populations. Selection is based on overall ability (grades, other academic and non-academic performance and considerations, demonstrated communications skills, letters of recommendation, and endorsement by a campus liaison officer), evidence that the applicant is well-suited for participation in the assistantship, and consideration of balancing factors (broader geographic and demographic representation sensitive to minority populations, and a representative sampling of academic affiliations). The Senate welcomes majors in all accredited disciplines; training in the history, politics, or government of New York is not a prerequisite.

Financial data The stipend is $2,500, payable biweekly.

Duration 4 months (January through April).

Limitations Assistants are responsible for arranging their own housing in Albany.

Number awarded Up to 61 each year.

Deadline October of each year.

[1683]
NEWPORT NEWS DAILY PRESS SUMMER INTERNSHIPS

Newport News Daily Press
Attn: Staff Development Editor
7505 Warwick Boulevard
Newport News, VA 23607
(757) 247-4776   Fax: (757) 245-8618
E-mail: DPFelmas@aol.com

Purpose To provide work experience at the *Newport News Daily Press* to college students or recent graduates who are interested in preparing for a career in journalism.

Eligibility College students (particularly juniors and seniors) and recent graduates from any state who are interested in working on a daily newspaper are invited to apply. Selection is based on experience (college newspaper and professional internships), clips, transcripts, references, an essay, and interviews. Women and minorities are encouraged to apply.

Financial data The stipend is $360 per week; no benefits are included.

Duration 10 weeks during the summer.

Special features Interns are offered work opportunities in local news, sports, business, features, copy desk, photo, or graphics.

Number awarded 4 each year.

Deadline December of each year.

[1684]
NEWPORT NEWS DAILY PRESS 1-YEAR INTERNSHIP

Newport News Daily Press
Attn: Staff Development Editor
7505 Warwick Boulevard
Newport News, VA 23607
(757) 247-4776   Fax: (757) 245-8618
E-mail: DPFelmas@aol.com

Purpose To provide work experience at the *Newport News Daily Press* to recent college graduates who are interested in preparing for a career in journalism.

Eligibility Recent graduates from any state who are interested in working on a daily newspaper are invited to apply. Selection is based on experience (college newspaper and professional internships), transcripts, references, an essay, and interviews. Women and minorities are encouraged to apply.

Financial data The stipend is $400 per week, plus full benefits.

Duration 1 year, beginning in the summer.

Special features Interns are offered work opportunities in local news, sports, business, features, copy desk, photo, or graphics. They are teamed with other staff members for coaching, and their supervising editor conducts quarterly performance evaluations.

Number awarded 1 each year.

Deadline December of each year.

[1685]
NMSGC FACULTY RESEARCH STUDENT SUPPORT PROGRAM

New Mexico Space Grant Consortium
c/o New Mexico State University
College of Engineering
Wells Hall, Bay 4
Wells and Locust
Las Cruces, NM 88003
(505) 646-6414   Fax: (505) 646-7791
E-mail: nmsgc@pathfinder.nmsu.edu

Purpose To award scholarships to undergraduate and graduate students in New Mexico who are interested in working with faculty on funded space-related research.

Eligibility This program is open to full-time undergraduate and graduate students at colleges and universities that are affiliated with the New Mexico Space Grant Consortium (NMSGC). Undergraduates must have completed 60 semester hours with a minimum cumulative grade point average of 3.0; all applicants must be U.S. citizens. Faculty members select students to apply for NMSGC funding to work on their ongoing space-related research as student assistants. The NMSGC is a component of the U.S. National Aeronautics and Space Administration (NASA) Space Grant program, which encourages participation by women, minorities, and persons with disabilities.

Financial data Stipends are $2,000 for undergraduates and $4,000 for graduate students. Funds are paid directly to the students.

Duration 1 calendar year.

Special features This program is funded by NASA.

Number awarded Varies; a maximum of 3 students may be funded for 1 space or aerospace research project.

Deadline October of each year.

[1686]
NOW LEGAL DEFENSE AND EDUCATION FUND ACADEMIC YEAR INTERNSHIP

NOW Legal Defense and Education Fund
99 Hudson Street, 12th Floor
New York, NY 10013-2871
(212) 925-6635   Fax: (212) 226-1066

Purpose To provide law students with the opportunity to perform a broad range of legal and educational services in support of women's efforts to eliminate sex-based discrimination and secure equal rights.

Eligibility The internship is open to second- or third-year law students. Both full-time and part-time internships are available. Applications are welcome from students willing to volunteer their time as well as from students who need to be paid. Applications are encouraged from people of color, lesbians and gays, and differently abled individuals.

Financial data The stipend is approximately $10 per hour.

Duration 1 or more semesters; the minimum time commitment is 10 hours per week.

Special features Interns participate in litigation and other projects, performing such duties as research and drafting legal memoranda and briefs, preparing Congressional testimony, drafting model legislation, screening potential cases for Legal Defense and Education Fund involvement, and drafting information pamphlets on legal topics. Interns should expect most of their work to involve legal research and writing. The Legal Defense and Education Fund collaborates with the National Organization for Women (NOW) on many projects but is a separate entity.

Deadline Applications may be submitted at any time.

[1687]
NOW LEGAL DEFENSE AND EDUCATION FUND SUMMER INTERNSHIP

NOW Legal Defense and Education Fund
99 Hudson Street, 12th Floor
New York, NY 10013-2871
(212) 925-6635   Fax: (212) 226-1066

Purpose To provide law students with the opportunity to perform a broad range of legal and educational services in support of women's efforts to eliminate sex-based discrimination and secure equal rights.

Eligibility The internship is open to first- or second-year law students. Applications are encouraged from people of color, lesbians and gays, and differently abled individuals.

Financial data Interns receive a weekly stipend of approximately $350.

Duration Summer months.

Special features Interns participate in litigation and other projects, performing such duties as research and drafting legal memoranda and briefs, preparing Congressional testimony, drafting model legislation, screening potential cases for Legal Defense and Education Fund involvement, and drafting information pamphlets on legal topics. In addition, interns are invited to participate in regular meetings with the legal staff and other groups.

Limitations Interviews are required and are not held on campus.

Number awarded 4 each year.

Deadline Application deadlines are: December for second-year students; January for first-year students.

[1688]
NOW LEGAL DEFENSE AND EDUCATION FUND UNDERGRADUATE INTERN PROGRAM

NOW Legal Defense and Education Fund
99 Hudson Street, 12th Floor
New York, NY 10013-2871
(212) 925-6635   Fax: (212) 226-1066

Purpose To provide work experience to students who have a demonstrated interest in women's issues, the law, education, and/or public policy.

Eligibility The internship is open to undergraduate students from a variety of educational backgrounds. Applications are encouraged from people of color, persons with disabilities, and individuals of minority sexual orientation who are comfortable with feminist advocacy.

Financial data Stipends in the summer are $165 per week; stipends are available during the academic year only if the budget permits.

Duration Internships are available at all times of the year. During the summer, a 20 hour weekly minimum commitment is preferred; during the school year, scheduling is flexible and may be arranged on an individual basis.

Special features Interns work in various issue areas including employment discrimination, sexual harassment, family law, reproductive freedom, and educational equity. Internships may also be available to assist the fundraising department with public relations, marketing, development of written materials, and general fundraising activities, and assisting the communications department with media-related activities. The Legal Defense and Education Fund collaborates with the National Organization for Women (NOW) on many projects but is a separate entity.

Number awarded 2 per semester or session.

Deadline March, for summer internships; for semester, quarter, or intersession internships, applications should be submitted 1 month prior to the desired starting date.

[1689]
NPSC GRADUATE FELLOWSHIPS

National Physical Science Consortium
c/o Ms. L. Nan Snow, Executive Director
New Mexico State University
O'Loughlin House on University Boulevard
Box 30001, Department 3NPS
Las Cruces, NM 88003-8001
(505) 646-6038   (800) 952-4118
Fax: (505) 646-6097   E-mail: npsc@nmsu.edu

Purpose To provide financial assistance to underrepresented minorities and women interested in pursuing graduate study in astronomy, chemistry, computer science, geology, materials sciences, mathematics, or physics.

Eligibility To be eligible, applicants must be either 1) an African American, Hispanic, American Indian, Eskimo, Aleut, or Polynesian or 2) a female. In addition, they must be a U.S. citizen; have earned at least a 3.0 cumulative grade point average through the senior year in college; and be able to pursue doctoral study at a participating member university of the National Physical Science Consortium (NPSC). For a list of participating universities, write to the address above. Students who are completing a master's degree at an institution that does not offer a Ph.D. in their discipline are also eligible, but students currently enrolled in a master's or Ph.D. program at an institution that offers the Ph.D. in the student's field are not eligible.

Financial data The fellowship pays tuition and fees plus an annual stipend of $12,500 during the first 4 years and $15,000 during the fifth and sixth years. It also provides on-site paid summer employment to enhance technical experience. The exact value of the fellowship depends on academic standing, summer employment, and graduate school attended.

Duration Up to 6 years.

Special features Among the employers in the internship part of the program are: Argonne, Lawrence Berkeley, Lawrence Livermore, Los Alamos, and Sandia National Laboratories; National Security Agency; Ford Motor Company; Department of Energy; Jet Propulsion Laboratory; IBM; Polaroid; Xerox Corporation; the National Aeronautics and Space Administration and its Ames, Goddard Space, Johnson Space, Kennedy Space, Langley Research, Lewis Research, Marshall Space, and Stennis Space centers; Navajo Nation; Clorox Corporation; and the National Institute of Standards and Technology.

Number awarded Varies each year.

Deadline November of each year.

[1690]
NUCLEAR ENGINEERING AND HEALTH PHYSICS FELLOWSHIP PROGRAM

Oak Ridge Institute for Science and Education
Attn: Science/Engineering Education Division
P.O. Box 117
Oak Ridge, TN 37831-0117
(423) 576-9558   (423) 576-2600
(800) 569-7749   Fax: (423) 576-3643
E-mail: nehpfp@orau.gov

Purpose To provide funding for graduate study and research experience in nuclear science and engineering or health physics.

Eligibility This program is open to highly capable students who are interested in working on a master's or doctoral degree in nuclear science, nuclear engineering, or health physics at a participating university (for a list of participating schools, write to the address above). Applications are usually submitted during the senior year of undergraduate school. Applicants may not be enrolled in or have been previously enrolled in a full-time graduate program at the time of application. All programs operated by the Science/Engineering Education Division (SEED) of Oak Ridge Institute for Science and Education (ORISE) seek to broaden the participation of minorities, women, and persons with disabilities in science and engineering careers.

Financial data The stipend is $14,400 per year. An additional $300 per month is paid during the practicum period. Tuition and fees are covered. Some travel money is available.

Duration 1 year; may be renewed for up to 4 additional years.

Special features Participants intern at various research facilities of the U.S. Department of Energy (DOE). This program is funded by DOE's Office of Nuclear Energy and administered by ORISE/SEED.

Number awarded Varies each year.

Deadline January of each year.

[1691]
OAK RIDGE NATIONAL LABORATORY LAW INTERNSHIP PROGRAM

Oak Ridge Institute for Science and Education
Attn: Science/Engineering Education Division
P.O. Box 117
Oak Ridge, TN 37831-0117
(423) 576-3427   (423) 576-3426
(800) 569-7749   Fax: (423) 576-3643
E-mail: lawintrn@orau.gov

Purpose To provide work experience in energy-related issues to second- or third-year law students.

Eligibility This program is open to currently-enrolled law students who have completed the first year of law school with an emphasis on environmental and patent law. They must be interested in conducting research at the Savannah River Site or Oak Ridge National Laboratory on the legal aspects of energy-related techniques and procedures, national energy-related problems, and efforts related to their solutions. All programs operated by the Science/Engineering Education Division (SEED) of Oak Ridge Institute for Science and Education (ORISE) seek to broaden the participation of minorities, women, and persons with disabilities in science and engineering careers.

Financial data The stipend is $2,000 per month. A travel reimbursement is also provided.

Duration 3 months during the summer.

Special features Sometimes, appointments are available during the regular academic year. This program is funded by Oak Ridge National Laboratory and Savannah River Site but administered by ORISE/SEED.

Number awarded Varies each year.

Deadline February of each year.

[1692]
OHIO LEGISLATIVE INTERNSHIP PROGRAM

Ohio Legislative Service Commission
Attn: Intern Coordinator
77 South High Street, Ninth Floor
Columbus, OH 43266-0342
(614) 466-3615

Purpose To provide recent college graduates with an opportunity to work as aides for the Ohio legislature.

Eligibility Applicants must hold at least a baccalaureate degree with a strong academic record (usually at least a 3.0 grade point average) and excellent communication and interpersonal skills. They must be interested in a full-time internship that includes researching various subjects of interest to members of the state legislature, assisting members in their constituent work, attending committee hearings, and compiling information for speeches or press releases. Applications from minorities are especially encouraged.

Financial data The salary is $19,200 per year.

Duration 13 months, beginning in December.

Number awarded 22 each year.

Deadline April of each year.

[1693]
OHIO STATE UNIVERSITY LIBRARIES MINORITY INTERNSHIP

Ohio State University Libraries
Attn: Personnel Librarian
1858 Neil Avenue Mall
Columbus, OH 43210-1286
(614) 292-6151   Fax: (614) 292-7859

Purpose   To increase the representation of minority librarians at Ohio State and to further the growth and development of minority librarians within the profession.

Eligibility   Eligible to apply are recent library school graduates who are interested in working in a university/research library. Members of minority groups underrepresented at Ohio State are the focus of this program (African Americans, Hispanic Americans, and Native Americans).

Financial data   The interns earn $25,080 to $27,500 each year, plus benefits.

Duration   2 years.

Special features   The first year of the internship includes introduction/orientation to the various departments and operations within the library; the second year emphasizes 1 or more areas of special interest to the interns.

Number awarded   1 each year.

Deadline   April of each year (or until the internship is filled).

[1694]
OREGON STATE BAR FIRST-YEAR MINORITY HONORS PROGRAM

Oregon State Bar
Attn: Affirmative Action Program
5200 SW Meadows Road
P.O. Box 1689
Lake Oswego, OR 97035-0889
(503) 620-0222   (800) 452-8260 (within OR)
Fax: (503) 684-1366

Purpose   To prepare minority law students for work in law firms in Oregon.

Eligibility   Qualified minority law students are identified by faculty selection committees at Oregon's 3 law schools (Willamette, University of Oregon, and Lewis and Clark) after the completion of their first year of law school. Selection is based on academic achievement, leadership skills, and community service. Participating employers select summer law clerks to work at their firms from this pool.

Financial data   Participants work at law firms in Oregon and receive a stipend.

Duration   Summer months between the recipient's first and second year at law school.

Special features   Participants are placed with large, prestigious legal firms in Oregon. Summer clerks receive employment orientations and are offered mentoring relationships.

Number awarded   Varies each year.

[1695]
OREGON STATE BAR MINORITY CLERKSHIP

Oregon State Bar
Attn: Affirmative Action Program
5200 SW Meadows Road
P.O. Box 1689
Lake Oswego, OR 97035-0889
(503) 620-0222   (800) 452-8260 (within OR)
Fax: (503) 684-1366

Purpose   To provide job opportunities for minority law students in Oregon and to provide an incentive to prospective employers to hire minority law students in the state.

Eligibility   Applicants must be minority law students (African Americans, Asian Americans, Native Americans, or Hispanic Americans) with financial need. They are not required to be enrolled at 1 of the 3 law schools in Oregon, but they must demonstrate a commitment to practice in the state. Selection is based on academic record, work experience, and community involvement.

Financial data   This program pays a stipend of $5.00 per hour; the employer must then at least match that stipend.

Duration   1 academic year or summer months.

Special features   The selected student is responsible for finding work under this program. The job should be in Oregon, although exceptions will be made if the job offers the student special experience not available within Oregon.

Number awarded   No law firm may employ more than 1 student for school-year clerkships or 2 students for summer clerkships.

[1696]
THE OREGONIAN MINORITY INTERNSHIP PROGRAM

The Oregonian
Attn: Recruiting Director
1320 S.W. Broadway
Portland, OR 97201
(503) 221-8039

Purpose   To provide work experience at *The Oregonian* in Portland to minority recent college graduates who are interested in a career in journalism.

Eligibility   Minority journalists with a commitment to a career in newspapers are eligible to apply for this internship that combines practical experience with professional mentoring in specialized areas.

Financial data   A competitive salary is paid.

Duration   2 years.

Special features   Midway through the second year, interns may apply for any position open on the staff of *The Oregonian;* if no opening is available, assistance is provided in finding another job.

Number awarded   1 each year.

Deadline   April of each year.

[1697]
ORISE MINORITY STUDENT ADMINISTRATIVE SUMMER INTERNSHIP PROGRAM

Oak Ridge Institute for Science and Education
Attn: Science/Engineering Education Division
P.O. Box 117
Oak Ridge, TN 37831-0117
(423) 576-3165   (423) 576-3164
(800) 569-7749   Fax: (423) 576-3643
E-mail: msasip@orau.gov

Purpose To provide summer internships to minority students in administrative and business areas at Oak Ridge Institute for Science and Education (ORISE).

Eligibility This program is open to minority students who have a minimum grade point average of 3.0; have completed their junior or senior years in college or their first year of graduate school; are studying business administration, management, finance, accounting, human resources, training, economics, public administration, computer science, or instructional technology; and are interested in an internship at ORISE in Tennessee.

Financial data The salary is based on educational level completed, but ranges from $335 to $420 per week; travel expenses are reimbursed.

Duration 10 to 12 weeks in the summer.

Special features This program is funded by the U.S. Department of Energy and administered by the Science/Engineering Education Division (SEED) of ORISE.

Number awarded Varies each year.

Deadline February of each year.

[1698]
ORNL PROFESSIONAL INTERNSHIP PROGRAM

Oak Ridge Institute for Science and Education
Attn: Science/Engineering Education Division
P.O. Box 117
Oak Ridge, TN 37831-0117
(423) 576-3427   (423) 576-3426
(800) 569-7749   Fax: (423) 576-3643
E-mail: piporni@orau.gov   E-mail: gpiporni@orau.gov

Purpose To provide financial assistance for postsecondary study and practical research experience at Oak Ridge National Laboratory (ORNL).

Eligibility This program is open to U.S. citizens or permanent residents at least 18 years of age who are currently enrolled in an accredited U.S. college or university in an academic program leading to an associate, baccalaureate, or graduate degree. High school seniors are eligible if they have been accepted in an associate or baccalaureate program. Students should be pursuing studies in chemistry, computer science, civil engineering, environmental engineering, hydrogeology, mechanical engineering, environmental science, geology, or hydrology. A cumulative grade point average of at least 2.5 is required. All programs operated by the Science/Engineering Education Division (SEED) of Oak Ridge Institute for Science and Education (ORISE) seek to broaden the participation of minorities, women, and persons with disabilities in science and engineering careers.

Financial data Participants receive tuition and fees for off-campus courses related to the research experience during the appointment period. Monthly stipends range from $1,000 to $1,300 for undergraduates or $1,300 to $1,400 for graduate students. Travel expenses for a single round trip from the student's campus to the research center are also reimbursed.

Duration 3 to 12 consecutive months.

Special features Interns are assigned individual research projects that relate to their academic majors, career goals, and the ongoing research and development missions of ORNL: to carry out applied research and engineering development in energy production and conservation technologies as well as experimental and theoretical research in the physical and life sciences to advance fundamental knowledge and to lay the foundation for technology development. A secondary mission is to address other nationally important issues, such as environmental protection and waste management and non-nuclear defense technologies, when such work is closely related to the primary mission. This program is funded by Oak Ridge National Laboratory but managed and operated by ORISE/SEED.

Number awarded Varies each year.

Deadline February of each year for programs to begin in May or June; May of each year for programs to begin in August or September; September of each year for programs to begin in January.

[1699]
ORNL TECHNOLOGY INTERNSHIP PROGRAM

Oak Ridge Institute for Science and Education
Attn: Science/Engineering Education Division
P.O. Box 117
Oak Ridge, TN 37831-0117
(423) 576-1083   (423) 576-3426
(800) 569-7749   Fax: (423) 576-3643
E-mail: tiporni@orau.gov

Purpose To provide associate degree students with an opportunity to work with technical and administrative staff members engaged in energy research at Oak Ridge National Laboratory (ORNL).

Eligibility This program is open to associate degree students majoring in chemical engineering, electrical engineering, health physics, or mechanical engineering technology. Assignments are available at ORNL and sites of the Hazardous Waste Remedial Actions Program. All programs operated by the Science/Engineering Education Division (SEED) of Oak Ridge Institute for Science and Education (ORISE) seek to broaden the participation of minorities, women, and persons with disabilities in science and engineering careers.

Financial data The monthly stipend is $1,000, prorated for part-time assignments.

Duration 1 to 12 months; both full- and part-time assignments are available.

Special features Interns are assigned individual research projects that relate to their academic goals. This program is funded by ORNL but managed and operated by ORISE/SEED.

Number awarded Approximately 10 each year.

Deadline Applications are accepted at any time.

[1700]
PACIFIC 10 CONFERENCE ADMINISTRATIVE FELLOWSHIPS

Pacific 10 Conference
Attn: Chris Hoyles
800 South Broadway, Suite 400
Walnut Creek, CA 94596
(510) 932-4411

Purpose To provide work experience to minorities and women interested in college sports.

Eligibility This program is open to recent college graduates who have experience as collegiate athletes. Preference is given to women and minorities who have graduated from a university in the Pac 10 conference.

Financial data A stipend is offered. The exact amount is negotiable.

Duration 10 months.

Number awarded 1 each year.

Deadline April of each year.

[1701]
PADUCAH SUN INTERNSHIPS

Paducah Sun
Attn: Executive Editor
P.O. Box 2300
Paducah, KY 42002-2300
(502) 443-1771

Purpose To provide work experience at the *Paducah Sun* in Kentucky to college students interested in careers in journalism.

Eligibility This program is open to students from any state, with a preference for juniors. Applicants must be planning to pursue careers in newspaper reporting or editing. Minorities from nearby colleges are especially encouraged to apply.

Financial data The salary is $240 per week.

Duration 12 weeks, during the summer.

Number awarded 3 each year.

Deadline December of each year.

[1702]
PALM BEACH POST INTERNSHIP

Palm Beach Post
Attn: Director of Administration/Newsroom
2751 South Dixie Highway
P.O. Box 24700
West Palm Beach, FL 33416-4700
(561) 820-4439   Fax: (561) 820-4340

Purpose To provide on-the-job experience at the *Palm Beach Post* in Florida to college students who are interested in newspaper careers.

Eligibility To qualify, applicants must be college freshmen, sophomores, or juniors (seniors are rarely accepted) who are interested in careers in journalism, have acquired basic newspaper skills, and have good grammar and spelling. Preference is given to journalism majors. Minority candidates are desired.

Financial data Interns earn $400 per week.

Duration 10 to 12 weeks in the summer or 16 weeks in spring or fall.

Special features Interns work in general reporting, copy editing, photojournalism, or library work under the guidance of the newspaper's editors.

Limitations Photography internships require previous experience as an intern.

Number awarded Varies; generally, 3 each fall, 3 each spring, and 6 each summer.

Deadline August of each year for spring; November of each year for summer; March of each year for fall.

[1703]
PAULINE A. YOUNG RESIDENCY

University of Delaware Library
Attn: Assistant Director for Library Administrative Services
Newark, DE 19717-5267
(302) 831-2231   Fax: (302) 831-1046

Purpose To provide full-time professional work experience in a large academic library to minority and other graduates of accredited library schools.

Eligibility Individuals who have recently completed master's degree programs at library schools accredited by the American Library Association are eligible if they have an interest in academic librarianship and a desire for professional growth. Women and members of underrepresented racial and ethnic groups are encouraged to apply.

Financial data Compensation is at the level of assistant librarian (currently $27,211 per year); benefits include health coverage, dental insurance, course fee waiver, and relocation assistance.

Duration 2 years; nonrenewable.

Special features In the first year, residents gain professional experience by rotating through several different areas of the library. In the second year, they concentrate in 1 area to further specific professional goals. In addition, they are offered opportunities for committee service, specialized training, and professional workshops. Residents are eligible to apply for continuing positions at the library.

Number awarded 1 each year.

Deadline April of each year.

[1704]
PENSACOLA NEWS JOURNAL INTERNSHIPS

Pensacola News Journal
Attn: Deputy Managing Editor
101 East Romana Street
P.O. Box 12710
Pensacola, FL 32571
(904) 435-8600

Purpose To provide work experience at the *Pensacola News Journal* in Florida to college students interested in careers in journalism.

Eligibility This program is open to college students from any state, with a preference for seniors. Applicants must be planning to pursue careers in newspaper journalism or photography. Minorities are especially encouraged to apply.

Financial data Interns receive scholarships equivalent to $5 per hour.

Duration 8 to 12 weeks, tenable any time of the year.

Number awarded Varies each year.

Deadline Applications may be submitted at any time.

[1705]
PHILADELPHIA DAILY NEWS INTERNSHIP

Philadelphia Daily News
Attn: Assistant Managing Editor
400 North Broad Street
P.O. Box 7788
Philadelphia, PA 19101
(215) 854-2000

Purpose To provide work experience at the *Philadelphia Daily News* to minority college students interested in journalism as a career.

Eligibility Minority college students are eligible to apply for these internships if they have good academic records and some journalism experience. Internships are available as artists, copy editors in news or sports, and reporters in news, features, sports, and business.

Financial data The salary is $493 per week.
Duration Summer months.
Number awarded Varies each year.
Deadline November of each year.

[1706]
PHILADELPHIA INQUIRER MINORITY PHOTOJOURNALISM INTERNSHIP

Philadelphia Inquirer
Attn: Director of Photography
400 North Broad Street
P.O. Box 8263
Philadelphia, PA 19101
(215) 854-2620

Purpose To provide work experience at the *Philadelphia Inquirer* to minority college students who are interested in preparing for a career in photojournalism.

Eligibility Minorities who are fully matriculated undergraduate or graduate students with at least 1 prior internship are eligible to apply if they are interested in gaining work experience in photojournalism. Applicants must submit a portfolio with up to 2 pages of slide dupes showing creativity in news, general features, sports, and environmental portraiture. At least 1 photo essay should be included.

Financial data A weekly stipend is paid.
Duration 10 weeks, during the summer.
Special features A complete set of Nikon equipment is available for use during the internship.
Number awarded 1 or more each year.
Deadline January of each year.

[1707]
PHILADELPHIA INQUIRER SUMMER INTERNSHIP

Philadelphia Inquirer
Attn: Director of Training
400 North Broad Street
P.O. Box 8263
Philadelphia, PA 19101
(215) 854-2206

Purpose To provide reporting experience at the *Philadelphia Inquirer* to college students interested in preparing for a career in journalism.

Eligibility Students who have experience on a college newspaper or as a prior professional newspaper intern are eligible to apply if they are interested in gaining work experience. Strong interest in a print journalism career is required. Among the positions available are a reporting internship for minorities interested in a medical/health specialty (candidates must be juniors or seniors) and a minority copy editing program for a candidate entering the sophomore year.

Financial data The stipend is approximately $480 per week.
Duration 10 weeks, during the summer.
Number awarded 1 or more each year.
Deadline January of each year.

[1708]
PITTSBURGH ENERGY TECHNOLOGY CENTER PROFESSIONAL INTERNSHIP PROGRAM

Oak Ridge Institute for Science and Education
Attn: Science/Engineering Education Division
P.O. Box 117
Oak Ridge, TN 37831-0117
(423) 576-3427   (423) 576-3426
(800) 569-7749   Fax: (423) 576-3643
E-mail: pippetc@orau.gov   E-mail: gpippetc@orau.gov

Purpose To provide financial assistance for postsecondary study and practical research experience at the Pittsburgh Energy Technology Center.

Eligibility This program is open to U.S. citizens or permanent residents at least 18 years of age who are currently enrolled in an accredited U.S. college or university in an academic program leading to an associate, baccalaureate, or graduate degree. High school seniors are eligible if they have been accepted to an associate or baccalaureate program. Students should be pursuing studies in chemistry, computer science, engineering, environmental sciences, mathematics, statistics, geology, or physics. A cumulative grade point average of at least 2.5 is required. All programs operated by the Science/Engineering Education Division (SEED) of Oak Ridge Institute for Science and Education (ORISE) seek to broaden the participation of minorities, women, and persons with disabilities in science and engineering careers.

Financial data Participants receive tuition and fees for off-campus courses related to the research experience during the appointment period. Monthly stipends range from $1,000 to $1,300 for undergraduates or $1,300 to $1,400 for graduate students. Travel expenses for a single round trip from the student's campus to the research center are also reimbursed.

Duration 3 to 12 consecutive months.

Special features Interns are assigned individual research projects that relate to their academic majors, career goals, and the ongoing research and development missions of the Pittsburgh Energy Technology Center in multidisciplinary coal-related research and development. This program is funded by the Office of Fossil Energy of the U.S. Department of Energy and administered by ORISE/SEED.

Number awarded Varies each year.

Deadline February of each year for programs to begin in May or June; May of each year for programs to begin in August or September; September of each year for programs to begin in January.

[1709]
PNL STUDENT RESEARCH APPRENTICESHIP PROGRAM

Pacific Northwest National Laboratory
Attn: University and Science Education Program
P.O. Box 999, MISN K1-12
Richland, WA 99352
(509) 375-6929   E-mail: re aikin@pnl.gov

Purpose To provide an opportunity for high school students from under-utilized ethnic groups in the Yakima Valley of Washington to conduct research at Pacific Northwest National Laboratory (PNL).

Eligibility This program is open to Yakima Valley students in the 10th, 11th, and 12th grades from ethnic groups traditionally under-utilized in mathematics, science, and engineering (Hispanics, African Americans, Native Americans, and Pacific Islanders). Applicants must have a background in science and mathematics and an interest in and potential for a career in science and mathematics.

Financial data The stipend is $1,400 for the first year, $1,600 for the second year, $1,800 for the third year, and $2,000 for first-year college students.

Duration 8 weeks, during the summer. Apprentices may participate for up to 3 summers as high school students and for 1 summer after the first year of college.

Special features Students work 4 days each week in the laboratory and spend the fifth day participating in education enrichment activities, which are guided by a science education center staff member and a teacher/counselor.

Number awarded 20 to 25 each year.

Deadline January of each year.

[1710]
POST COLLEGE APPOINTMENT PROGRAM

Lawrence Livermore National Laboratory
Attn: Employment Programs Manager
Affirmative Action and Diversity Program
P.O. Box 808, L-716
Livermore, CA 94551-9900
(510) 422-1770   Fax: (510) 422-9679

Purpose To provide work experience to college graduates who have completed the academic requirements of their profession but who lack sufficient experience to compete successfully for current professional career positions in the sciences and/or engineering.

Eligibility Individuals who have completed or are close to completing a B.S., M.S., or Ph.D. degree are eligible to apply. Relevant fields include engineering, physics, chemistry, materials science, biology and biotechnology, computer science, environmental science, human resources, and administration. Preference is given to applications from minorities, women, veterans, and persons with disabilities.

Financial data Salaries paid to interns are competitive.

Duration Participants work full time for 1 to 2 years.

Special features Successful completion of the assignment and the existence of an appropriate opening can lead to career employment at Lawrence Livermore National Laboratory.

Number awarded Varies each year.

Deadline Applications may be submitted at any time.

[1711]
PROCTER & GAMBLE GRADUATE R&D SUMMER PROGRAM

Procter & Gamble Company
Miami Valley Laboratories
P.O. Box 538707
Cincinnati, OH 45253-8707
(513) 627-1035

Purpose To provide work experience to graduate students who are interested in chemical or biological careers.

Eligibility Applicants must be currently enrolled in graduate school or in the senior year of undergraduate study planning to enter graduate school in the fall to pursue a Ph.D. in chemistry, life sciences, or chemical engineering. U.S. citizenship or permanent resident status is required. Postitions are also available to students currently studying for or planning to study for a Pharm.D., M.D., D.V.M., or D.D.S. degree. These internships are intended for students who intend to pursue careers as research associates in research and product development. Special consideration is given to applications from underrepresented minority (African American, Hispanic/Latino, Native American) students.

Financial data Interns receive competitive salaries, depending of their year in school and field of study. Procter & Gamble pays round-trip airfare between school or home and Cincinnati as well as local transportation between university housing and the work site.

Duration 10 to 12 weeks each summer.

Special features Interns engage in full-time research at 1 of Procter & Gamble's 4 corporate technical centers in Cincinnati.

Number awarded 15 to 20 each year.

Deadline February of each year.

[1712]
PROCTER & GAMBLE R&D SUMMER PROGRAM FOR ENGINEERS

Procter & Gamble Company
Attn: US Recruiting—R&D
P.O. Box 599 TN-4
Cincinnati, OH 45201-0599
(513) 983-3732

Purpose To provide work experience to engineering students who are interested in chemical or biological careers.

Eligibility Applicants must be enrolled in an upper division undergraduate or a master's degree program; preference is given to students of chemical engineering although candidates in other engineering specialties (as mechanical and packaging), chemistry, biology, statistics, and other scientific disciplines are also considered. U.S. citizenship or permanent resident status is required. These internships are intended for students who intend to pursue careers as research associates in research and product development. Special consideration is given to applications from underrepresented minority (African American, Hispanic/Latino, Native American) students.

Financial data Interns receive competitive salaries, depending of their year in school and field of study. Procter & Gamble pays round-trip airfare between school or home and Cincinnati as well as local transportation between university housing and the work site.

Duration 10 to 12 weeks each summer.

Special features Interns engage in full-time research at 1 of Procter & Gamble's 4 corporate technical centers in Cincinnati.

Limitations Nearly all interns are selected through direct on-campus recruiting; check with your school's placement office for information on Procter & Gamble interview schedules.

Number awarded 60 to 80 each year.

Deadline February of each year.

[1713]
PROCTER & GAMBLE UNDERGRADUATE R&D SUMMER PROGRAM

Procter & Gamble Company
Attn: US Recruiting—R&D
P.O. Box 599 TN-4
Cincinnati, OH 45201-0599
(513) 983-3732

Purpose To provide work experience to undergraduate students who are interested in chemical or biological careers.

Eligibility Applicants must have completed the first year of an associate or baccalaureate degree with a major in any discipline within chemistry, mathematics, or the biological sciences. U.S. citizenship or permanent resident status is required. These internships are intended for students who intend to pursue careers as research associates in research and product development. Special consideration is given to applications from underrepresented minority (African American, Hispanic/Latino, Native American) students.

Financial data Interns receive competitive salaries, depending of their year in school. Procter & Gamble pays round-trip airfare between school or home and Cincinnati as well as local transportation between university housing and the work site.

Duration 10 to 12 weeks each summer.

Special features Interns engage in full-time research at 1 of Procter & Gamble's 4 corporate technical centers in Cincinnati.

Number awarded 15 to 20 each year.

Deadline February of each year.

[1714]
PROJECT SEED: SUMMER EDUCATIONAL EXPERIENCE FOR THE DISADVANTAGED

American Chemical Society
Attn: Education Division
1155 16th Street, N.W.
Washington, DC 20036
(202) 872-4380

Purpose To provide economically disadvantaged high school students with an opportunity to work during the summer in an academic, industrial, or governmental research laboratory under the supervision of a researcher or research assistant.

Eligibility Interested institutions apply to the American Chemical Society (ACS) Committee on Project SEED for funding at the beginning of each year. Priority for funding is given to those institutions with matching supplemental funds from local sources or ACS local sections. The funded institutions recruit their own students to participate in the program. Students are selected on the basis of grade point average, standardized test scores, and teacher recommendations. All students must have completed the junior or senior year in high school, live within commuting distance of the institution, have completed a course in high school chemistry, and come from an economically disadvantaged family. The standards for economic disadvantage follow federal poverty guidelines for family size, but the maximum family income is $27,000 except in cases where other factors are present that may

deter a student from considering a career in science; family income may be up to $34,000 if the student is a member of an underrepresented ethnic group (Black, Hispanic, Native American), if the parents have not attended college, or if the family is single-parent or very large. Students who have matriculated in college are not eligible. Laboratory facilities must permit full participation by students with physical disabilities.

Financial data Students receive a stipend of $1,500 for their first summer (after their junior year); students who participate for a second summer (after their senior year) receive a stipend of $1,700 and a travel grant of up to $100.

Duration 8 to 10 weeks during the summer.

Special features SEED does not try to create scientists; rather, the program attempts to overcome some of the obstacles—social, institutional, attitudinal, and educational—that have traditionally excluded the disadvantaged from preparation for and entrance into professional careers.

Number awarded Varies; averages 100 per year. Since Project SEED began in 1968, more than 4,000 high school students and 200 institutions have participated in the program.

[1715]
RACINE EDUCATION COUNCIL AWARDS

Racine Education Council
310 Fifth Street, Room 101
Racine, WI 53403
(414) 634-9200   Fax: (414) 631-5606

Purpose To provide financial assistance for postsecondary education to minority and low-income youths living in Racine, Wisconsin.

Eligibility Only minority group members and low-income youths who are residents of Racine (for at least 1 year) and/or graduates of a local high school are eligible to apply.

Financial data Stipend amounts vary, depending upon the needs of each student. All grants are made to the students through their respective schools.

Duration The awards are granted annually.

Special features To date, more than 3,700 students have participated in this program: 75 percent Black, 12 percent Spanish, and 13 percent nonminority students. Priority is given to grant recipients for Racine's Summer Employment Program, which assists economically disadvantaged youths (between the ages of 17 and 21) in obtaining summer jobs within the city's industrial or business community.

Number awarded Approximately 125 per year.

Deadline June and October of each year.

[1716]
RESEARCH AND ENGINEERING APPRENTICESHIP PROGRAM (REAP) FOR HIGH SCHOOL STUDENTS

Academy of Applied Science
98 Washington Street
Concord, NH 03301
(603) 225-2072   Fax: (603) 228-0210

Purpose To motivate students (particularly minority students) to choose mathematics, science, or technology as a career.

Eligibility Applicants must be minority and disadvantaged juniors or seniors in high school who have an interest in mathematics, science, or technology. Recipients are selected on the basis of previously demonstrated abilities and interest in science, mathematics, and technology; potential for a successful career in the field as indicated from overall scholastic achievement, aptitude, and interest areas; recommendations of high school teachers and administrators; and through the interview process.

Financial data Interns receive a stipend of $1,250; an equal amount is given to the professor "mentor."

Duration Summer months.

Special features The program provides intensive summer training for high school students in the laboratories of scientists. The program is funded by a grant from the U.S. Army.

Limitations Students must live at home while they participate in the program and must live in the area where an approved professor lives. The program does not exist in every state.

Number awarded Varies; generally, at least 100 each year.

Deadline February of each year.

[1717]
RESEARCH SUPPLEMENTS FOR UNDERREPRESENTED MINORITY GRADUATE RESEARCH ASSISTANTS

National Institutes of Health
Attn: Office of Extramural Research
Extramural Outreach and Information Resources Office
6701 Rockledge Drive, Room 6207
MSC 7910
Bethesda, MD 20892-7910
(301) 435-0714   Fax: (301) 480-8443
E-mail: asknih@odrockm1.od.nih.gov

Purpose To provide funding to minority graduate students in the biomedical and behavioral sciences of concern to the National Institutes of Health (NIH) for development of their research capabilities more completely.

Eligibility Any underrepresented minority (African American, Hispanic, Native American, Alaskan Native, or Pacific Islander) graduate student who is actively pursuing a doctoral degree in 1 of the biomedical or behavioral sciences is eligible for consideration. Students enrolled in a master's degree program in nursing sciences or social work may also be eligible. The student must be affiliated with the applicant institution.

Financial data The sponsoring institute provides support for a salary in addition to other necessary expenses to enable the minority individual to participate as a graduate research assistant in research projects funded by the institute. The requested salary must be in accordance with the salary structure of the grantee institution. Tuition remission is allowable as a form of compensation in lieu of wages. Additional funds, up to $3,000 per year, may be requested for supplies and travel.

Duration 3 months during the summer or academic year.

Special features Students should contact their office of sponsored research to identify eligible principal investigators on NIH projects who are willing to apply for supplemental support.

Limitations Support may not be used to purchase equipment.

Number awarded Varies each year.

[1718]
RESEARCH SUPPLEMENTS FOR UNDERREPRESENTED MINORITY HIGH SCHOOL STUDENTS

National Institutes of Health
Attn: Office of Extramural Research
Extramural Outreach and Information Resources Office
6701 Rockledge Drive, Room 6207
MSC 7910
Bethesda, MD 20892-7910
(301) 435-0714   Fax: (301) 480-8443
E-mail: asknih@odrockm1.od.nih.gov

Purpose To enable underrepresented minority high school students to obtain a meaningful experience in various aspects of health-related research to stimulate their interest in careers in the biomedical or behavioral sciences of interest to the National Institutes of Health (NIH).

Eligibility Principal investigators in research programs sponsored by the institutes identify appropriate high school students; the students must currently be enrolled and in good standing at their high school and be interested in biomedical or behavioral research. Underrepresented minority students are defined as African Americans, Hispanics, Native Americans, Alaskan Natives, and Pacific Islanders.

Financial data Up to $2,000 per student.

Duration 3 months: full time during the summer; part time during the academic year.

Special features Students interested in this program should identify an eligible principal investigator on an NIH-funded project.

Limitations Support may not be used to purchase equipment.

Number awarded Varies each year.

[1719]
RESEARCH SUPPLEMENTS FOR UNDERREPRESENTED MINORITY UNDERGRADUATE STUDENTS

National Institutes of Health
Attn: Office of Extramural Research
Extramural Outreach and Information Resources Office
6701 Rockledge Drive, Room 6207
MSC 7910
Bethesda, MD 20892-7910
(301) 435-0714   Fax: (301) 480-8443
E-mail: asknih@odrockm1.od.nih.gov

Purpose To enable minority undergraduate students interested in biomedical or behavioral research to participate in a research project funded by the National Institutes of Health (NIH) during the summer months or during the school year.

Eligibility Principal investigators of institutes-funded research may be eligible to submit a request for an administrative supplement to support a minority (African American, Hispanic, Native American, Alaskan Native, or Pacific Islander) undergraduate student. Participating students may be affiliated with either the applicant institution or any other academic institution. Any undergraduate minority student interested in biomedical or behavioral research is encouraged to participate in this program.

Financial data Up to $6 per hour for salary plus $125 per month for supplies and travel.

Duration Support should be for a minimum of 3 months during any 1 year, but is expected to last over a period of at least 2 years.

Special features Students interested in obtaining support under this program should identify eligible principal investigators on NIH-funded research projects by contacting the office of sponsored programs at their institution.

Limitations Support may not be used to purchase equipment. Students are expected to devote full time to the research project and related activities during the period of support.

Number awarded Varies each year.

[1720]
RFF SUMMER INTERNSHIPS

Resources for the Future
1616 P Street, N.W.
Washington, DC 20036-1400
(202) 328-5067   Fax: (202) 939-3460

Purpose To provide summer internships to graduate students interested in working on research projects in public policy.

Eligibility Candidates must be in their first or second year of graduate training, with skills in microeconomics, quantitative methods, or occasionally other social and natural sciences. Outstanding undergraduates may also be considered. They must be interested in spending an internship in Washington, D.C. in 1 of the divisions of Resources for the Future (RFF): Center for Risk Management, Energy and Natural Resources, or Quality of the Environment. Applicants must be able to work without supervision in a careful and conscientious manner. Women and minority candidates are strongly encouraged to apply.

Financial data Stipends depend upon experience and length of stay.

Duration Summer months; beginning and ending dates can be adjusted to meet particular student needs.

Special features Interns assist in research projects in complex public policy problems amenable to interdisciplinary analysis, often drawing heavily on economics. Further information on the Center for Risk Management is available from Marilyn Vogt at (202) 328-5077; on Energy and Natural Resources from Pauline Wiggins at (202) 328-5045; on Quality of the Environment from Sue Lewis at (202) 328-5088.

Deadline March of each year.

[1721]
ROCK HILL HERALD INTERNSHIPS

Rock Hill Herald
Attn: Managing Editor
132 West Main Street
P.O. Box 11707
Rock Hill, SC 29731
(803) 329-4000

Purpose To provide work experience at the *Rock Hill Herald* in South Carolina to college students interested in careers in journalism.

Eligibility This program is open to students from any state, with a preference for juniors and seniors. Applicants must be planning to pursue careers in newspaper reporting or editing. Minorities are especially encouraged to apply.

Financial data The salary is $250 per week.

Duration 12 weeks, during the summer.

Number awarded 1 each year.

Deadline March of each year.

[1722]
RTNDF ENTRY LEVEL INTERNSHIPS

Radio and Television News Directors Foundation
1000 Connecticut Avenue, N.W., Suite 615
Washington, DC 20036
(202) 659-6510   Fax: (202) 223-4007

Purpose To provide work experience to recent minority graduates in electronic journalism.

Eligibility Eligible are recent (within 1 year) minority graduates of a program in electronic journalism at an accredited university. Applications include an essay explaining why the candidate seeks a career in radio or television news management and a letter of endorsement from a faculty sponsor that verifies the applicant's intention to pursue a career in news management. The Radio and Television News Directors Foundation (RTNDF) recognizes African Americans, Asian Americans, Hispanic Americans, and Native Americans as minorities.

Financial data The stipend is $1,300 per month.

Duration 6 months, beginning in June.

Special features Interns receive hands-on experience in a management related capacity, such as administration, production, or the assignment desk.

Limitations The RTNDF reserves the sole right to determine placement of interns.

Number awarded 3 each year.

Deadline February of each year.

[1723]
RTNDF SUMMER INTERNSHIPS

Radio and Television News Directors Foundation
1000 Connecticut Avenue, N.W., Suite 615
Washington, DC 20036
(202) 659-6510   Fax: (202) 223-4007

Purpose To provide work experience to minority students enrolled in electronic journalism.

Eligibility Eligible are junior or more advanced undergraduate or graduate students enrolled in an electronic journalism sequence at an accredited or nationally recognized college or university. Applications include an essay explaining why the candidate seeks a career in radio or television news management and a letter of endorsement from a faculty sponsor that verifies the applicant's intention to pursue a career in news management. The Radio and Television News Directors Foundation (RTNDF) recognizes African Americans, Asian Americans, Hispanic Americans, and Native Americans as minorities.

Financial data The stipend is $1,000 per month. Interns are responsible for their own housing and living expenses.

Duration 3 months, in the summer.

Special features Interns are assigned to a supervisor in management, production, or the assignment desk and receive hands-on experience in the day to day management of electronic news.

Limitations The RTNDF reserves the sole right to determine placement of interns.

Number awarded Varies each year.

Deadline February of each year.

[1724]
RUTH CHANCE LAW FELLOWSHIP

Equal Rights Advocates, Inc.
1663 Mission Street, Suite 550
San Francisco, CA 94103
(415) 621-0672 Fax: (415) 621-6744

Purpose To provide work experience for graduates of law school who are interested in working for the equal rights of women.

Eligibility Applicants should be third-year law students or recent graduates who are committed to improving the condition of women and women of color. Selection is based on knowledge of and commitment to women's rights and legal issues affecting women, knowledge of and commitment to civil rights and legal issues affecting people of color, ability to work independently, demonstrated commitment and involvement with community concerns, oral and written communication skills, ability to juggle many and varied tasks, and expertise relevant to the described responsibilities.

Financial data The annual salary is $30,000; benefits are also provided.

Duration 1 year, beginning in September.

Special features Equal Rights Advocates (ERA) is a nonprofit, public interest law firm that is dedicated to combatting the disenfranchisement of women, particulary low-income and minority women. The responsibilities of the fellow include overseeing and coordinating an advice and counseling program, assisting staff attorneys with ongoing litigation, and participating in the firm's public policy and education activities.

Number awarded 1 each year.

Deadline October of each year.

[1725]
SAN ANGELO STANDARD-TIMES INTERNSHIP

San Angelo Standard-Times
Attn: Editor
34 West Harris
P.O. Box 5111
San Angelo, TX 76902
(915) 653-1221

Purpose To provide work experience at the *San Angelo Standard-Times* in Texas to students who are interested in preparing for a career in journalism.

Eligibility College students who are majoring in journalism are eligible to apply. Preference is given to rising juniors or seniors. Applicants may be from any state. Applications from minority students are encouraged.

Financial data The stipend is $250 per week.

Duration 10 weeks, during the summer.

Special features Interns work in news/editorial.

Number awarded 2 to 3 each year.

Deadline January of each year.

[1726]
SAN JOSE MERCURY NEWS MINORITY SCHOLARSHIP

San Jose Mercury News
Attn: Human Resources Department
750 Ridder Park Drive
San Jose, CA 95190
(408) 271-3689

Purpose To provide financial assistance to minority students interested in pursuing careers in journalism and newspaper management.

Eligibility Minority high school seniors in the San Francisco/San Jose area are eligible to apply if they are interested in majoring in journalism or communications in college. They must have professional experience or high school newspaper/yearbook experience, be nominated by their journalism advisor or teacher, send up to 5 samples of their work, and submit a 500-word essay on why they want to pursue a career in journalism or newspaper management.

Financial data The stipend is $500.

Duration 1 year; may be renewed for up to 3 additional years.

Special features The *Mercury News* selects its winners by February of each year and submits their applications to the Knight-Ridder Minority Scholarship Program. These winners are given the chance to compete for a 4-year Knight-Ridder scholarship/internship and the promise of a job in journalism upon graduation. The internship takes place at a Knight-Ridder paper in the recipient's community; interns work each year, during the summer.

Number awarded 2 each year.

Deadline December of each year.

[1727]
SAVANNAH MORNING NEWS INTERNSHIPS

Savannah Morning News
Attn: State Editor
111 West Bay Street
P.O. Box 1088
Savannah, GA 31402-1088
(912) 652-0323

Purpose To provide work experience at the *Savannah Morning News* in Georgia to college students interested in careers in journalism.

Eligibility This program is open to college students from any state, with a preference for juniors, seniors, or graduate students. Applicants must be planning to pursue careers in newspaper journalism, photography, or design. Minorities are especially encouraged to apply.

Financial data The salary is $325 per week.

Duration 13 weeks, during the summer.

Number awarded 3 news/editorial, 1 photography, and 1 newspaper design internships are offered each year.

Deadline December of each year.

[1728]
SAVANNAH RIVER SITE PROFESSIONAL INTERNSHIP PROGRAM

Oak Ridge Institute for Science and Education
Attn: Science/Engineering Education Division
P.O. Box 117
Oak Ridge, TN 37831-0117
(423) 576-3427   (423) 576-3426
(800) 569-7749   Fax: (423) 576-3643
E-mail: pipsrs@orau.gov   E-mail: gpipsrs@orau.gov

Purpose To provide financial assistance for postsecondary study and practical research experience at the Savannah River Site in Aiken, South Carolina.

Eligibility This program is open to U.S. citizens or permanent residents at least 18 years of age who are currently enrolled in an accredited U.S. college or university in an academic program leading to an associate, baccalaureate, or graduate degree. High school juniors and seniors are also eligible. Students should be pursuing studies in chemistry, computer science, engineering, environmental sciences, geology, or physics. A cumulative grade point average of at least 2.5 is required. All programs operated by the Science/Engineering Education Division (SEED) of Oak Ridge Institute for Science and Education (ORISE) seek to broaden the participation of minorities, women, and persons with disabilities in science and engineering careers.

Financial data Participants receive tuition and fees for off-campus courses related to the research experience during the appointment period. Monthly stipends range from $800 to $1,300 for high school students and undergraduates or $1,300 to $1,400 for graduate students. Travel expenses for a single round trip from the student's campus to the research center are also reimbursed.

Duration 3 to 12 consecutive months.

Special features Interns are assigned individual research projects that relate to their academic majors, career goals, and the ongoing research and development missions of the Savannah River Site, which conducts research and development in support of the production of plutonium-239 and tritium for national defense purposes. Graduate students may utilize this program to conduct research for their theses or dissertations. This program is funded by the Savannah River Site and administered by ORISE/SEED.

Number awarded Varies each year.

Deadline February of each year for programs to begin in May or June; May of each year for programs to begin in August or September; September of each year for programs to begin in January.

[1729]
SCIENCE AND ENGINEERING OPPORTUNITY PROGRAM FOR MINORITIES AND WOMEN AT BROOKHAVEN NATIONAL LABORATORY

Brookhaven National Laboratory
Attn: Diversity Office, Human Resources Division
Building 185A
P.O. Box 5000
Upton, New York 11973-5000
(516) 344-3709   Fax: (516) 344-2476
E-mail: ligon1@bnl.gov

Purpose To provide on-the-job training in scientific areas at Brookhaven National Laboratory (BNL) to underrepresented minority and women students.

Eligibility This program is open to underrepresented minority (African American/Black, Hispanic, Native American, or Pacific Islander) students and women who have completed their freshman, sophomore, or junior year of college. Applicants must be U.S. citizens or permanent residents, at least 18 years of age, and majoring in applied mathematics, engineering, physical and life sciences, or scientific journalism. Since no transportation or housing allowance is provided, preference is given to students who reside in the BNL area.

Financial data Participants receive a competitive stipend.

Duration 12 weeks, during the summer.

Special features Students work with members of the scientific, technical, and professional staff of BNL in an educational training program developed to give research experience in areas of applied mathematics, biology, chemistry, engineering, high and low energy particle accelerators, nuclear medicine, physics, and science writing.

Number awarded Approximately 9 each year.

Deadline March of each year.

[1730]
SCIENCE AND TECHNOLOGY ALLIANCE SUMMER STUDENT PROGRAM

Los Alamos National Laboratory
Attn: Science and Technology Base Directorate
University Programs
Mail Stop F673
P.O. Box 1663
Los Alamos, NM 87545
(505) 667-1230   E-mail: abad@lanl.gov

Purpose To provide research experience during the summer at designated national laboratories to underrepresented minority students from participating institutions.

Eligibility The Science and Technology Alliance is comprised of North Carolina A&T State University, New Mexico Highlands University, the Ana G. Mendez Educational Foundation in Puerto Rico, the Montana Consortium of American Indian Tribal Colleges, Sandia National Laboratory, Oak Ridge National Laboratory, and Los Alamos National Laboratories. Students at any of the 4 institutional members may participate in summer research internships at any of the 3 national laboratory members provided they 1) have completed their freshman year in college; 2) have a minimum cumulative grade point average of 3.0; 3) plan to pursue a career in engineering, physics, mathematics, computer science, life science, or other disciplines of interest to the national laboratories; 4) are U.S. citizens; and 5) can obtain a security clearance (if applicable).

Financial data A stipend is paid, based on the number of semesters of university study completed.

Duration Summer months.

Special features At the laboratories, students work with mentors who assign them specific research projects. Results are presented in final papers and oral presentations, and participants also attend professional development seminars. For information on the Los Alamos program, contact the address above; for Oak Ridge, contact Science Education and External Relations, 105 Mitchell Road, P.O. Box 2008, Oak Ridge, TN 37831-6496, (423) 574-7717, E-mail: eab@ornl.gov; for Sandia, contact the S&T Alliance Project Manager, P.O. Box 5800, Division 3613/MS-1351, Albuquerque, NM 87185-1351, (505) 271-7841, E-mail: keholle@sandia.gov.

Number awarded Approximately 30 each year at each laboratory.

[1731]
SIGNIFICANT OPPORTUNITIES IN ATMOSPHERIC RESEARCH AND SCIENCE (SOARS) PROGRAM

University Corporation for Atmospheric Research
Attn: SOARS Program Manager
P.O. Box 3000
Boulder, CO 80307-3000
(303) 497-8717   (303) 497-8702
E-mail: nnorris@ncar.ucar.edu

Purpose To provide work experience to underrepresented minority undergraduate or graduate students who are interested in pursuing a career in atmospheric or a related science.

Eligibility Student applicants must 1) be U.S. citizens or permanent residents; 2) be Hispanic, Native American, or African American; 3) have completed their sophomore year of college by the time the internship begins; 4) be majoring in an atmospheric science such as meteorology, or a related field such as chemistry, mathematics, physics, biology, social science, environmental science, oceanography, engineering, or computer science; 5) have a minimum grade point average of 3.0; and 6) plan to pursue a career in the field of atmospheric or a related science.

Financial data Participants receive a competitive stipend and a housing allowance. Round-trip travel between Boulder and any 1 location within the continental United States is also provided. Students who are accepted into a graduate-level program receive full scholarships (with SOARS and the participating universities each sharing the costs).

Duration 10 weeks, during the summer. Students are encouraged to continue for 4 subsequent summers.

Special features This program began in 1996 and is scheduled to run through 2001. Students are assigned positions with a research project. They are exposed to the research facilities at the National Center for Atmospheric Research (NCAR), including computers, libraries, laboratories, and aircraft. NCAR is operated by the University Corporation for Atmospheric Research (a consortium of 61 universities) and sponsored by the National Science Foundation. Before completing their senior years, students are encouraged to apply to a master's or doctoral degree program at 1 of the participating universities. By 2001, approximately 60 students will have participated in the SOARS program; the goal is that at least 32 of those students will receive master's and, preferably, doctoral degrees.

Number awarded At least 12 each year.

Deadline March of each year.

[1732]
SMITHSONIAN ENVIRONMENTAL RESEARCH CENTER WORK/LEARN PROGRAM

Smithsonian Environmental Research Center
P.O. Box 28
Edgewater, MD 21037
(410) 798-4424

Purpose To enable students to conduct individual projects in environmental studies under the supervision of professional staff members of the Smithsonian Environmental Research Center (SERC).

Eligibility Undergraduate and graduate students may apply to this program to conduct projects involving terrestrial or estuarine

environmental research within the disciplines of mathematics, chemistry, microbiology, botany, and zoology. Ethnic and racial minorities are encouraged to apply for internships at SERC, created to promote cultural diversity in environmental science professions.

Financial data Internships provide a stipend of $190 per week and living accommodations in the SERC dormitory. Minority graduate students receive a stipend of $240 per week and living accommodations. Minority students are eligible for a travel allowance, based on place of residence.

Duration The starting date and duration of the projects are arranged between the student and the supervisor; normally, projects are 40 hours per week, from 12 weeks to 1 year.

Special features Research is conducted at the SERC facilities in Edgewater, Maryland.

Number awarded Varies each year.

Deadline October of each year for projects beginning between January and May; February of each year for projects between May and August.

[1733]
SMITHSONIAN MINORITY STUDENT INTERNSHIP

Smithsonian Institution
Attn: Office of Fellowships and Grants
955 L'Enfant Plaza, Suite 7000
MRC 902
Washington, DC 20560
(202) 287-3271   Fax: (202) 287-3691
E-mail: siofg@sivm.si.edu

Purpose To provide minority undergraduate or graduate students the opportunity to work on research or museum procedure projects in specific areas of history, art, or science at the Smithsonian Institution.

Eligibility Internships are offered to minority students who are actively engaged in graduate study at any level or in upper-division undergraduate study. An overall grade point average of 3.0 is generally expected.

Financial data The program provides a stipend of $250 per week for undergraduates and $300 per week for graduate students. Interns receive assistance in locating inexpensive housing, especially for summer appointments, and travel allowances.

Duration 10 weeks during the summer or academic year.

Number awarded Varies each year.

Deadline February of each year.

[1734]
SMITHSONIAN NATIVE AMERICAN STUDENT INTERNSHIP

Smithsonian Institution
Attn: Office of Fellowships and Grants
955 L'Enfant Plaza, Suite 7000
MRC 902
Washington, DC 20560
(202) 287-3271   Fax: (202) 287-3691
E-mail: siofg@sivm.si.edu

Purpose To support Native American students interested in pursuing projects related to Native American topics that require the use of Native American resources at the Smithsonian Institution.

Eligibility Applicants must be Native American students who are actively engaged in graduate or undergraduate study, are interested in studying Native American topics at the Smithsonian Institution, and have an overall grade point average of at least 3.0.

Financial data The stipend is $250 per week for undergraduates, $300 per week for graduate students, and a travel allowance for both groups.

Duration Up to 12 weeks.

Limitations Recipients must be in residence at the Smithsonian Institution for the duration of the program.

Number awarded Varies each year.

Deadline February for summer residency; June for fall residency; October for winter/spring residency.

[1735]
SNPA MINORITY INTERNSHIP PROGRAM

Southern Newspaper Publishers Association
Attn: Foundation
P.O. Box 28875
Atlanta, GA 30358
(404) 256-0444

Purpose To provide funding to member newspapers of the Southern Newspaper Publishers Association (SNPA) that wish to employ minority students as summer interns.

Eligibility Newspapers that are members of the Association may apply for funding to establish summer internships for students who are racial minorities. Candidates for the program should have completed their sophomore year by the current spring quarter and should be potential candidates for full-time employment at the newspaper following graduation from an accredited college or university. Students do not have to be journalism majors, but they should intend to pursue a career at a newspaper. Selection criteria include financial need, clips, letters of reference, and grade point average. Students interested in this program should contact their local newspaper; for a list of members of the Association, write to the address above.

Financial data Newspapers receive $2,500 to be used for the salary of the intern; any expenses in excess of that amount are to be incurred by the newspaper.

Duration 9 weeks, during the summer.

Limitations Applications are not accepted directly from students or colleges.

Number awarded 2 newspapers receive funding each year.

Deadline Nominations must be submitted by March of each year.

[1736]
SOUTHERN CONFERENCE INTERNSHIP

Southern Conference
One West Pack Square, Suite 1508
Ashville, NC 28801
(704) 255-7872

Purpose To provide work experience to minorities, women, and others interested in college sports.

Eligibility This program is open to college graduates who are interested in working with college athletics. Applications from minorities and women are specifically encouraged.

Financial data The stipend is $1,000 per month.

Duration 10 months.

Special features Interns work at the Southern Conference, in Ashville, North Carolina.

Limitations Internships are not currently being offered; the program may be resumed in the near future.

Number awarded 1 each year.

Deadline June of each year.

[1737]
SOUTHWEST EDUCATIONAL DEVELOPMENT LABORATORY MINORITY INTERNSHIP PROGRAM

Southwest Educational Development Laboratory
Attn: Vice President, Resources for School Improvement
211 East Seventh Street
Austin, TX 78701-3281
(512) 476-6861   Fax: (512) 476-2286

Purpose To offer minority graduate students an opportunity to intern at the Southwest Educational Development Laboratory (SEDL).

Eligibility This program is open to graduate (doctoral level) students. Applicants should be American citizens and members of 1 of the following minority groups: African American, American Pacific Island, Asian American, Hispanic American, or Native American Indian. Applicants should be currently enrolled in a doctoral program in 1 of these fields: education, social work, educational policy, or a related area (e.g., psychology). They should have completed 24 semester hours of course work toward the doctoral degree. In addition, they should be able to demonstrate interest in an educational research and development field.

Duration Internships may be 3, 6, 9, or 12 months.

Special features Interns participate in a wide range of SEDL activities, including developing research-based products, providing training and technical assistance activities in the field, planning and conducting evaluations, documenting and reporting program activities, and participating in state or national conferences.

Number awarded 4 each year.

Deadline January of each year.

[1738]
ST. PAUL PIONEER PRESS MINORITY INTERNSHIP

St. Paul Pioneer Press
Attn: Ruben Rosario
345 Cedar Street
St. Paul, MN 55101
(612) 228-5490

Purpose To provide work experience at the *St. Paul Pioneer Press* to minority college students interested in journalism as a career.

Eligibility Minority college students are eligible to apply for this internship, if they are majoring in graphic arts or a related field. Previous intern experience is preferred, but potential, creativity, and a passion for journalism are essential.

Financial data Interns receive a salary of approximately $500 per week and assistance in finding a place to live.

Duration 12 weeks in the summer.

Special features Interns work in copy editing, reporting, computer-assisted reporting, photography, and graphic design.

Number awarded 4 each year.

Deadline January of each year.

[1739]
STAR PUBLICATIONS MINORITY INTERNSHIP

Star Publications
Attn: Human Resources
1526 Otto Boulevard
P.O. Box 157
Chicago Heights, IL 60411
(708) 755-6161

Purpose To provide work experience to minority students who are interested in careers in journalism.

Eligibility Minority students who have completed their junior year in college with a major or minor concentration in print journalism or photojournalism are eligible to apply. They must have completed basic courses in reporting and interviewing.

Financial data Interns are paid $6.50 per hour.

Duration Up to 3 months for up to 37.5 hours per week.

Special features The internship includes supervised training and experience in a variety of reporting skills. Star Publications publishes 20 twice-weekly newspapers in the south and southwest suburbs of Chicago.

Number awarded 1 each semester or quarter.

Deadline Applications may be submitted at any time.

[1740]
STATE FARM SUMMER MINORITY INTERN PROGRAM

State Farm Insurance Companies
Attn: Human Relations Department
One State Farm Plaza, South K1
Bloomington, IL 61710
(309) 763-2827

Purpose To allow minority college students to explore insurance as a career and acquire some work experience that could help them get a job after graduation.

Eligibility This program is open to minorities who are currently completing their junior year in college and are interested in actuarial sciences as a career. Selection is based on credentials, interests, and available openings.

Financial data Interns are paid a stipend and receive travel expenses to and from Bloomington, Illinois. Housing is provided for interns working in Bloomington, but those in other areas are responsible for their own housing.

Duration 10 weeks from June through August of each year.

Special features Interns work in designated departments within State Farm's corporate headquarters in Bloomington, in other Bloomington offices, or in 1 of several claims offices outside of Bloomington. They receive an intensified orientation to the insurance industry as a whole and State Farm Insurance Companies in particular. They are often assigned projects that allow them to become familiar with their department and its role in the company. Students may apply through college placement directors and faculty members, by interviewing during State Farm's regular campus recruiting sessions, or by applying directly to the address above.

Number awarded Varies; averages 20 per year.

[1741]
STUDENT TECHNOLOGY EXPERIENCE PROGRAM

Lawrence Livermore National Laboratory
Attn: Employment Programs Manager
Affirmative Action and Diversity Program
P.O. Box 808, L-716
Livermore, CA 94551-9900
(510) 422-1770   Fax: (510) 422-9679

Purpose To provide minority and women high school and college students with an opportunity to obtain work experience in the sciences and engineering.

Eligibility Minority and women high school and college students in northern California are eligible to apply if they are interested in obtaining work experience at Lawrence Livermore National Laboratory. Work assignments include, but are not limited to, engineering, physics, chemistry, materials science, biology and biotechnology, computer science, environmental science, human resources, and administration. Selection is based on academic proficiency, career objectives, and disciplinary interests, as well as the availability of an appropriate Laboratory assignment.

Financial data Salaries paid to interns are competitive.

Duration Interns work full time during the summer and up to 16 hours per week during the academic year.

Number awarded Varies each year.

Deadline Applications may be submitted at any time.

[1742]
STUDIO ARTS INTERNSHIPS

Women's Studio Workshop
P.O. Box 489
Rosendale, NY 12472
(914) 658-9133

Purpose To provide internship opportunities to all people interested in the arts.

Eligibility All people interested in internships at the Women's Studio Workshop (WSW) are eligible, although the WSW is especially interested in young women art students and recent college graduates. Applications from women of color are especially encouraged. Applicants should send a resume, 10 to 20 slides, 3 letters of reference, and a letter of interest.

Financial data Interns receive off-site housing and a stipend of $75 per month.

Duration Fall internships run from September through December and spring internships are from February through June.

Special features Tasks include but are not limited to preparing studios for and assisting artist/teachers with young people in an Art-in-Education program; designing, printing, and distributing catalogs, brochures, and posters; assisting in all aspects of exhibition program, including spackling and painting, installation, press releases, etc.; answering phones and conducting studio tours; and preparing upstairs apartment for visiting artists.

Number awarded 2 each semester

Deadline July of each year for fall and November of each year for spring.

[1743]
SUMMER ARTS INSTITUTE INTERNSHIPS

Women's Studio Workshop
P.O. Box 489
Rosendale, NY 12472
(914) 658-9133

Purpose To provide internship opportunities to all people interested in the arts.

Eligibility All people interested in internships at the Women's Studio Workshop (WSW) are eligible, although the WSW is especially interested in young women art students and recent college graduates. Applications from women of color are especially encouraged. Applicants should send a resume, 10 to 20 slides, 3 letters of reference, and a letter of interest.

Financial data Interns receive off-site housing.

Duration 3 months, from June through the end of August.

Special features Interns spend half of their summer taking workshops at no charge and the rest of the time working at such tasks as organizing studios for specific workshops, preparing the upstairs apartment for visiting instructors, setting up for evening programs, managing the set up and break down of lunch each day, and assisting with preparations for the annual fund raising auction.

Number awarded 3 each year.

Deadline March of each year.

[1744]
SUMMER HIGH SCHOOL APPRENTICESHIP RESEARCH PROGRAM

National Aeronautics and Space Administration
Attn: Lewis Research Center
Office of Educational Programs
Mail Stop 7-4
21000 Brookpark Road
Cleveland, OH 44135
(206) 433-5580   E-mail: judith.a.budd@lerc.nasa.gov

Purpose To provide an opportunity for underrepresented minority high school students in the Cleveland area to participate in research projects at the Lewis Research Center of the National Aeronautics and Space Administration (NASA).

Eligibility This program is open to underrepresented minority students who are currently high school sophomores or juniors, are highly recommended by their science or mathematics teacher, are in good academic standing, and demonstrate a strong interest in and aptitude for a career in mathematics, engineering, and/or science. Students must be permanent residents of the greater Cleveland commuting area interested in participating in a summer research program at NASA's Lewis Research Center.

Financial data Students receive a stipend at the GS-1 level, approximately $4.65 an hour.

Duration 8 weeks, during the summer.

Number awarded 25 each year.

Deadline February of each year.

[1745]
SUMMER HONORS UNDERGRADUATE RESEARCH PROGRAM

Harvard Medical School
Attn: Admissions Office
Division of Medical Sciences
260 Longwood Avenue
Boston, MA 02115
(617) 432-4980   (800) 367-9019
Fax: (617) 432-2644

Purpose To provide an opportunity for underrepresented minority students to engage in research at Harvard Medical School.

Eligibility This program is open to underrepresented minority college students who have had at least 1 summer (or equivalent) of laboratory research.

Financial data The program provides a stipend of approximately $1,800, transportation, and lodging expenses.

Duration 8 weeks, during the summer.

Number awarded Varies each year.

Deadline January of each year.

[1746]
SUMMER INTERNSHIP PROGRAM IN BIOMEDICAL RESEARCH

National Institutes of Health
Attn: Office of Student Programs
Office of Education
Building 10, Room 1C129
10 Center Drive MSC 1158
Bethesda, MD 20892-1158
(301) 496-2427   Fax: (301) 402-0483
E-mail: dc26a@nih.gov

Purpose To enable students to receive training and participate in ongoing research studies in a variety of laboratory and clinically related disciplines at the National Institutes of Health (NIH).

Eligibility Applicants must be enrolled at least half time in degree-granting programs as third or fourth year undergraduates, graduate students, or professional program students, and interested in or studying disciplines related to biomedical research, including the biological, chemical, physical, behavioral, and computer sciences and biomedical engineering. They must be at least 18 years of age and U.S. citizens or permanent residents.

Financial data For undergraduate students, the salary is $1,200 per month; for graduate students with less than 1 year of study completed, the monthly salary is $1,400; with 1 year, $1,600; with 2 years, $1,800; with 3 or more years, $2,000.

Duration 10 weeks, in the summer.

Special features Minority students who participate in the NIAID Introduction to Biomedical Research Program may apply for this internship program, but other students are also eligible regardless of ethnic status. Laboratories are located in Bethesda and Rockville, Maryland and in Hamilton, Montana.

Number awarded Varies each year.

Deadline January of each year.

[1747]
SUMMER RESEARCH OPPORTUNITIES PROGRAM (SROP)

Committee on Institutional Cooperation
302 East John Street, Suite 1705
Champaign, IL 61820-5698
(217) 333-8475   Fax: (217) 244-7127
E-mail: vschutz@uiuc.edu

Purpose To provide work experience to minority undergraduates who are interested in obtaining research experience.

Eligibility Applicants must be African American, Mexican American, Native American, or Puerto Rican sophomores, or students with at least 2 semesters remaining before graduation. They must be interested in conducting a research program at 1 of the institutions affiliated with the Committee on Institutional Cooperation (CIC): University of Chicago, University of Illinois at Urbana-Champaign, University of Illinois at Chicago, University of Iowa, University of Michigan, University of Minnesota, University of Wisconsin at Madison, University of Wisconsin at Milwaukee, Indiana University, Michigan State University, Northwestern University, Ohio State University, Indiana University/Purdue University at Indianapolis, Pennsylvania State University, and Purdue University.

Financial data Participants are paid a stipend of $2,500, plus up to $1,100 toward room and board and travel to and from the host institution. Faculty mentors receive a $500 research allowance for the cost of materials.

Duration 8 to 10 weeks, during the summer.

Special features Participants work directly with faculty mentors at the institution of their choice and also engage in other enrichment activities, such as workshops and social gatherings. In July, all participants come together at 1 of the CIC campuses for the annual SROP conference.

Limitations Students are required to write a paper and an abstract describing their projects and to present the results of their work at a campus symposium.

Deadline January of each year.

[1748]
SUMMER RESEARCH PROGRAM

Procter & Gamble Company
Miami Valley Laboratories
P.O. Box 538707
Cincinnati, OH 45253-8707
(513) 627-1035

Purpose To provide work experience to graduate students who are interested in chemical or biological careers.

Eligibility Applicants must be currently enrolled in graduate school or in the senior year of undergraduate study planning to enter graduate school in the fall to pursue a Ph.D. in chemistry, life sciences, or chemical engineering. U.S. citizenship or permanent resident status is required. Postitions are also available to students currently studying for or planning to study for a Pharm.D., M.D., D.V.M., or D.D.S. degree. These internships are intended for students who intend to pursue careers as research associates in research and product development. Special consideration is given to applications from underrepresented minority (African American, Hispanic/Latino, Native American) students.

Financial data Interns receive competitive salaries, depending of their year in school and field of study. Procter & Gamble pays round-trip airfare between school or home and Cincinnati as well as local transportation between university housing and the work site.

Duration 10 to 12 weeks each summer.

Special features Interns engage in full-time research at 1 of Procter & Gamble's 4 corporate technical centers in Cincinnati.

Number awarded 15 to 20 each year.

Deadline February of each year.

[1749]
TEACH FOR AMERICA FELLOWSHIPS

Teach for America
20 Exchange Place, 8th Floor
New York, NY 10005
(212) 425-9039   (800) 832-1230
Fax: (212) 425-9347

Purpose To boost the number of ethnic teachers in America's rural and urban public school classrooms.

Eligibility This program recruits students or graduates of top colleges for 2-year appointments in school districts with severe teacher shortages. Priority is given to people of color, bilingual speakers, and mathematics, science, and foreign language majors. No previous education course work is required.

Financial data This program covers major expenses for the summer institute, including room and board and academic materials. It also covers room and board during a regional induction. Corps members are responsible for the cost of transportation to the summer institute, and from the summer institute to their placement site. They are also responsible for their own moving expenses, testing fees, and any necessary credits and district fees. Teach for America then places recruits in jobs paying $17,000 to $30,000.

Duration 2 years.

Special features Once selected for this program, participants attend a 5-week summer institute where they receive additional professional development and support. They then travel to their assigned regions for a 1- to 2-week induction, which helps orient them to the schools, school districts, and communities where they will be teaching.

Number awarded Varies; generally, 500 each year.

Deadline January of each year.

[1750]
TEACHER OPPORTUNITIES TO PROMOTE SCIENCE (TOPS)

Sandia National Laboratories
Attn: Education Outreach
MS 1351, Organization 3020
P.O. Box 5800
Albuquerque, NM 87185-1350
(505) 889-2325   Fax: (505) 889-2331

Purpose To enhance the skills of science/mathematics teachers working in areas with predominately Hispanic and Native American populations.

Eligibility This program is open to middle school science and mathematics teachers who work in the rural areas of New Mexico that have large Hispanic and Native American populations. Applicants must be interested in enhancing math and science teaching skills, integrating math and science concepts thoughout the curricula, and remaining with his or her school district for a minimum of 3 years and serving as a role model and mentor for colleagues.

Financial data Participants are paid a stipend following completion of each summer institute; housing and travel reimbursements are provided for both the summer institutes and academic-year workshops at Los Alamos or Sandia National Laboratories and to conduct research at those laboratories.

Duration 3 weeks in the summer; 3 follow-up workshops during each successive academic year.

Special features The program also involves academic-year activities and classroom visits. Participants may also choose to establish a student-parent science enrichment program at their school.

Limitations This program is not currently operating, pending the securing of sponsors.

Number awarded 25 teachers participate at each of the sponsoring national laboratories, Sandia and Los Alamos.

[1751]
TECHNICAL TRAINING PROGRAM FOR MINORITIES AND WOMEN AT BROOKHAVEN NATIONAL LABORATORY

Brookhaven National Laboratory
Attn: Diversity Office, Human Resources Division
Building 185A
P.O. Box 5000
Upton, New York 11973-5000
(516) 344-3709   Fax: (516) 344-2476
E-mail: ligon1@bnl.gov

Purpose To provide on-the-job training for underrepresented minorities and women who are pursuing a career in the field of mechanical technology.

Eligibility This program is open to underrepresented minority (African American/Black, Hispanic, Native American, or Pacific Islander) students and women who are able and willing to participate in an associate (A.A.S.) or baccalaureate (B.S.E.T.) degree program in mechanical technology while working at Brookhaven National Laboratory (BNL). Applicants should have previous educational or life experiences such as trade school or the military.

Financial data Participants receive a competitive salary.

Duration 1 year.

Special features Trainees are involved in large and intricate mechanical assembly procedures, the use of machine shop tools, basic electricity, and vacuum procedures. Duties include fabrication of mechanical assemblies, installation of mechanical instruments, and servicing of the instrumentation assemblies.

Number awarded Varies each year.

Deadline Applications may be submitted at any time.

[1752]
TIMES RECORD NEWS INTERNSHIPS

Times Record News
Attn: Editor
1301 Lamar Street
P.O. Box 120
Wichita Falls, TX 76307
(817) 767-8341

Purpose To provide work experience at the *Times Record News* in Wichita Falls, Texas to college students interested in careers in journalism.

Eligibility This program is open to students from any state at any academic level. Applicants must be planning to pursue careers in newspaper reporting or editing. Minorities are especially encouraged to apply.

Financial data Some internships provide a salary of $100 per week; others are unpaid.

Duration The length of time depends on the requirements of the school.

Number awarded Approximately 2 each year.

Deadline Applications should be submitted during the school's spring break.

[1753]
TIMES-PICAYUNE SUMMER INTERNSHIPS

Times-Picayune
Attn: Personnel Department
3800 Howard Avenue
New Orleans, LA 70140-1002
(504) 826-3422

Purpose To provide work experience on the *New Orleans Times-Picayune* to college students interested in journalism as a career.

Eligibility College students are eligible to apply for internships in reporting, copy editing, photography, and graphic arts. Previous intern experience or work on a daily college newspaper is helpful. Minorities are encouraged to apply.

Financial data Competitive wages are paid.

Duration 12 weeks, during the summer.

Special features Students who live in the New Orleans area may obtain an application in the *Times-Picayune* main lobby during regular business hours; students who live more than 100 miles away from New Orleans may write for an application.

Number awarded 6 each year.

Deadline December of each year.

[1754]
TRAINEESHIPS IN OCEANOGRAPHY FOR MINORITY UNDERGRADUATES

Woods Hole Oceanographic Institution
Attn: Fellowship Committee
Education Office
Clark Laboratory
Woods Hole, MA 02543-1541
(508) 457-2000, ext. 2200   Fax: (508) 457-2188
E-mail: education@whoi.edu

Purpose To provide work experience to minority group members who are interested in pursuing careers in the physical or natural sciences, mathematics, or engineering.

Eligibility Eligible to apply are ethnic minority undergraduates enrolled in U.S. colleges or universities who have completed at least 2 semesters of study and who are interested in the physical or natural sciences, mathematics, or engineering.

Financial data Interns receive the same salary as that paid other employees of the Woods Hole Oceanographic Institution with similar experience.

Duration 10 to 12 weeks during the summer or 1 semester during the academic year; renewable.

Special features Trainees are assigned advisors who supervise their research programs and supplementary study activities. Some traineeships involve field work or research cruises.

Number awarded 4 to 5 each year.

Deadline For a summer appointment, applications must be submitted in March of each year. For the remaining portion of the year, applications may be submitted at any time, but they must be submitted at least 2 months before the anticipated starting date.

[1755]
TRAINING PROGRAM FOR MINORITY MEDICAL STUDENTS AND MEDICAL RESIDENTS

National Medical Fellowships, Inc.
Attn: Scholarships and Programs
110 West 32nd Street, 8th Floor
New York, NY 10001-3205
(212) 714-1007

Purpose To introduce underrepresented minority medical school students and residents to the role and applications of telecommunications technology in medicine and public health practices.

Eligibility This program is open to underrepresented minority (African American, Native American, Mexican American, and mainland Puerto Rican) medical students and medical residents. Candidates must either be enrolled full time in medical schools or in residency programs at hospitals located in 4 designated cities (Basking Ridge, New Jersey; Atlanta, Georgia; Washington, D.C.; or Los Angeles, California). Applicants must have experience in using computers and express interest in technology and its applications to medicine.

Financial data The internship stipend is $400.

Duration The program includes 2 1-day training sessions.

Special features The training sessions, conducted in the 4 participating cities, introduce participants to state-of-the-art equipment and technology, including telemedicine, wireless communication, and computer telephony integration. This program was created in 1996 with support from AT&T Foundation and Lucent Technologies.

Number awarded 45 each year.

Deadline Applications are available at medical schools or through the offices of directors of residency programs in the spring.

[1756]
UCSB LIBRARY MINORITY FELLOWSHIP PROGRAM

University of California at Santa Barbara
Library
Attn: Assistant University Librarian, Personnel
Santa Barbara, CA 93106
(805) 961-2741

Purpose To encourage the growth and development of minority librarians in academic research libraries.

Eligibility Minority students who are about to graduate or who recently graduated from a library school accredited by the American Library Association are eligible to apply. They must have a knowledge of and interest in academic librarianship and a strong desire for professional growth.

Financial data Fellows are regular (but temporary) employees of the university and receive the same salary and benefits as other librarians at the same rank.

Duration 2 years.

Special features The program began in 1985. Fellows spend time in at least 2 different departments in the library, serve on library committees, attend professional meetings, receive travel support for 2 major conferences, and participate in the Librarians' Association of the University of California.

Number awarded 1 each year.

Deadline February of each year.

[1757]
UNDERREPRESENTED MINORITY AND FEMALE PROGRAM AT LANL

Los Alamos National Laboratory
Attn: Science and Technology Base Directorate
University Programs
Mail Stop F673
P.O. Box 1663
Los Alamos, NM 87545
(505) 667-1230   E-mail: abad@lanl.gov

Purpose To provide research experience during the summer to women and underrepresented minorities at the Los Alamos National Laboratory (LANL).

Eligibility This program is open to women and underrepresented minorities (especially Hispanics and Native Americans) from Arizona, California, Colorado, New Mexico, and Texas who are interested in careers in science, mathematics, engineering, and technology. University and graduating high school students come to the Laboratory for research internships under the direction of a mentor. U.S. citizenship or permanent resident status is required.

Financial data A stipend is paid, based on the number of semesters of university study completed.

Duration Summer months.

Special features Under this initiative, LANL has other programs to encourage women and underrepresented minorities choose careers in science, mathematics, engineering and technology. LANL staff members work with minority institutions to improve research and teaching capabilities; high school students enroll in a summer program conducted by LANL and the University of New Mexico at Los Alamos; and students in transition from 2-year to 4-year institutions participate in the Alliance for Minority Participation at New Mexico State University work in laboratories at the university with assistance from LANL scientists.

Number awarded 30 each year.

[1758]
UNITED METHODIST PUBLISHING HOUSE MERIT SCHOLARSHIP PROGRAM

United Methodist Church
Attn: Office of Loans and Scholarships
1001 19th Avenue South
P.O. Box 871
Nashville, TN 37202-0871
(615) 340-7344   Fax: (615) 340-7048

Purpose To recognize and support superior academic effort by ethnic minorities who are interested in professional lay employment with the United Methodist Church and with the United Methodist Publishing House.

Eligibility Ethnic minority students who are enrolled in full-time undergraduate study are eligible to apply if they are planning on pursuing a career with the United Methodist Church (and particularly the Publishing House) upon graduation. They must be U.S. citizens enrolled as sophomores, juniors, or seniors at a college or university related to the United Methodist Church with a grade point average of at least 2.7.

Financial data Up to $5,000 per year.
Duration 1 year; may be renewed.
Special features Recipients also work as interns at the United Methodist Publishing House.
Deadline March of each year.

[1759]
UNITED STATES DEPARTMENT OF STATE STUDENT INTERN PROGRAM

Department of State
Attn: Recruitment Division
P.O. Box 9317, Rosslyn Station
Arlington, VA 22219
(703) 875-7490   (800) JOB-OVERSEAS

Purpose To provide a work/study opportunity for undergraduate and graduate students interested in foreign service.
Eligibility Currently enrolled undergraduate students (with at least two years of study completed) and graduate students are eligible to apply if they are U.S. citizens, have completed some academic studies relevant to the type of work they wish to perform for the State Department, and are in good academic standing in an accredited institution. The State Department particularly encourages eligible women and minority students with an interest in foreign affairs to apply.
Financial data College juniors are placed at the GS-4 level with an annual salary of $18,085; college seniors and first-year graduate students are placed at the GS-5 level with an annual salary of $20,233; second-year graduate students are placed at the GS-7 level with an annual salary of $25,061. Interns placed abroad may also receive housing, medical insurance, a travel allowance, and a dependents' allowance.
Duration Paid internships are available only for 10 weeks during the summer. Unpaid internships are available for 1 semester or quarter during the academic year, or for 10 weeks during the summer.
Special features Interns can be placed at 1 of 230 embassies and consulates abroad or in Washington, D.C. Depending upon the needs of the department, interns are assigned junior-level professional duties, which may include research, preparing reports, drafting replies to correspondence, working in computer science, analyzing international issues, financial management, intelligence, security, or assisting in cases related to domestic and international law.
Limitations Interns must agree to return to their schooling immediately upon completion of their internships.
Number awarded Varies each year.
Deadline February for fall internship; June for spring internship; October for summer internship.

[1760]
UNIVERSITY COAL RESEARCH INTERNSHIP PROGRAM

Oak Ridge Institute for Science and Education
Attn: Science/Engineering Education Division
P.O. Box 117
Oak Ridge, TN 37831-0117
(423) 576-2492   (423) 576-3426
(800) 569-7749   Fax: (423) 576-3643
E-mail: ucrip@orau.gov

Purpose To provide summer internships to undergraduate students interested in coal-related research.

Eligibility This program is open to college juniors and seniors majoring in biology, chemistry, engineering, environmental science, geology, physics, and other disciplines and technologies related to coal. Assignments are at host universities under the guidance of a principal investigator who has an active university coal research grant from the U.S. Department of Energy (DOE) Pittsburgh Energy Technology Center. All programs operated by the Science/Engineering Education Division (SEED) of Oak Ridge Institute for Science and Education (ORISE) seek to broaden the participation of minorities, women, and persons with disabilities in science and engineering careers.
Financial data Participants receive a weekly stipend of $200, travel reimbursement, and housing.
Duration 10 weeks, during the summer.
Special features This program is funded by DOE's Office of Fossil Energy and administered by ORISE/SEED.
Number awarded Approximately 25 each year.
Deadline February of each year.

[1761]
UNIVERSITY OF MINNESOTA AFFIRMATIVE ACTION RESIDENCY PROGRAM

University of Minnesota Twin Cities
University Libraries
Attn: Human Resources and Organizational Development
    Officer
453 Wilson Library
309 19th Avenue South
Minneapolis, MN 55455
(612) 625-0822   Fax: (612) 626-9353

Purpose To provide work experience to underrepresented minority graduates of accredited library schools.
Eligibility Applicants must be recent graduates from an accredited library school with a Master's in Library and Information Science, be interested in working in an academic library, have some online experience, and be members of minority groups underrepresented at the University of Minnesota and in academic librarianship (African Americans, American Indians, Asians, and Hispanics). Selection is based on experience and potential.
Financial data Interns receive a salary equivalent to that awarded to beginning assistant librarians.
Duration 2 years.
Special features During the first year, the intern receives an introduction and orientation to the various departments and operations; in the second year, the intern focuses on 1 area of personal interest. This program began in 1990.
Number awarded Up to 2 per year.

[1762]
UPJOHN MINORITY SUMMER FELLOW PROGRAM

American College of Neuropsychopharmacology
320 Centre Building
2014 Broadway
Nashville, TN 37203
(615) 322-2075   Fax: (615) 343-0662

Purpose To promote and enhance the interest of minority graduate students and residents in careers in psychopharmacology and the neurosciences.
Eligibility Minority graduate students and residents interested in preparing for a career in psychopharmacology or the neuro-

sciences are eligible to apply. Selection is based on academic record and research/laboratory experience.

Financial data The grant provides enough to cover room and board, a stipend that ranges from $1,000 to $2,000, transportation to and from the laboratory site, and funds to allow the trainee to attend the American College of Neuropsychopharmacology's (ACNP) annual conference. Just how the funds are distributed to each recipient is somewhat negotiable and depends in part on the trainee's projected costs for living and travel.

Duration 6 to 8 weeks during the summer.

Special features Recipients carry out a research project in the laboratory of ACNP's immediate past president.

Number awarded 1 each year.

Deadline March of each year.

[1763]
U.S. ARMY CENTER FOR HEALTH PROMOTION AND PREVENTIVE MEDICINE GRADUATE INTERNSHIP PROGRAM

Oak Ridge Institute for Science and Education
Attn: Science/Engineering Education Division
P.O. Box 117
Oak Ridge, TN 37831-0117
(423) 576-1083   (423) 576-3426
(800) 569-7749   Fax: (423) 576-3643
E-mail: chppmgip@orau.gov

Purpose To provide funding to graduate students interested in applied clinical research and training activities in areas of concern to the U.S. Army Center for Health Promotion and Preventive Medicine (USACHPPM) in Maryland.

Eligibility Applicants must be graduate students currently enrolled in computer sciences, physical sciences, biological sciences, medical sciences, engineering, or supporting disciplines. The USACHPPM conducts research and training activities in environmental health engineering, entomology, ionizing and nonionizing radiation, occupational and environmental health, industrial hygiene and worksite hazards, environmental sanitation and hygiene, and laboratory services. All programs operated by the Science/Engineering Education Division (SEED) of Oak Ridge Institute for Science and Education (ORISE) seek to broaden the participation of minorities, women, and persons with disabilities in science and engineering careers.

Financial data The monthly stipend ranges from $1,350 to $1,750, depending on research areas and academic classification.

Duration 3 months to 1 year.

Special features Both full-time and part-time appointments are available. Participants work at the USACHPPM in Aberdeen Proving Ground, Maryland. This program is funded by an interagency agreement between the U.S. Department of Energy and the USACHPPM of the U.S. Army, and administered by ORISE/SEED.

Number awarded The number awarded varies each year.

Deadline Applications may be submitted at any time.

[1764]
U.S. ARMY CENTER FOR HEALTH PROMOTION AND PREVENTIVE MEDICINE UNDERGRADUATE INTERNSHIP PROGRAM

Oak Ridge Institute for Science and Education
Attn: Science/Engineering Education Division
P.O. Box 117
Oak Ridge, TN 37831-0117
(423) 576-1083   (423) 576-3426
(800) 569-7749   Fax: (423) 576-3643
E-mail: chppmuip@orau.gov

Purpose To provide funding to undergraduates interested in applied clinical research and training activities in areas of concern to the U.S. Army Center for Health Promotion and Preventive Medicine (USACHPPM) in Maryland.

Eligibility Applicants must be undergraduate students currently enrolled in computer sciences, physical sciences, biological sciences, medical sciences, engineering, or supporting disciplines for an associate or baccalaureate degree. The USACHPPM conducts research and training activities in environmental health engineering, entomology, ionizing and nonionizing radiation, occupational and environmental health, industrial hygiene and worksite hazards, environmental sanitation and hygiene, and laboratory services. All programs operated by the Science/Engineering Education Division (SEED) of Oak Ridge Institute for Science and Education (ORISE) seek to broaden the participation of minorities, women, and persons with disabilities in science and engineering careers.

Financial data The stipend depends on research areas and academic classification.

Duration 3 months to 1 year.

Special features Both full-time and part-time appointments are available. Participants work at the USACHPPM in Aberdeen Proving Ground, Maryland. This program is funded by an interagency agreement between the U.S. Department of Energy and the USACHPPM of the U.S. Army, and administered by ORISE/SEED.

Number awarded The number awarded varies each year.

Deadline Applications may be submitted at any time.

[1765]
USAID INTERN INVESTMENT PROGRAM

Agency for International Development
Attn: Recruitment Branch
2401 E Street, N.W., Room 1026 SA-1
Washington, DC 20523-0116
(703) 302-4128   Fax: (703) 875-1879

Purpose To prepare and encourage qualified students to enter a Foreign Service career through professional and academic preparation as interns for the United States Agency for International Development (USAID).

Eligibility Students in their sophomore year of college with a minimum grade point average of 3.0 are recruited for this program. Minorities and women are targeted. Candidates must express an interest in international development and living abroad, with an intention to attend graduate school in health, environment, public administration or policy, international development or management, business administration, economics, sociology, finance/accounting, agricultural sciences, anthropology, demography, natural resources, law, commerce/trade, or other fields. U.S. citizenship is required.

Financial data Interns receive a salary at the GS-04 level, or approximately $17,086 per year on the current rate. They are required to pay their own housing and transportation costs.

Duration 10 weeks during summers; at least 2 summers of internships are provided, with the possibility of additional work.

Special features Initially, interns spend the 2 summers following their sophomore and junior years working in USAID offices in Washington, D.C. They are evaluated on their work during those 2 summers, and those with the highest marks and accepted to graduate school participate in internships with USAID overseas missions between their college graduation and their first year in graduate school. Evaluations continue, and selected students are offered 1-year internships overseas following graduate school. A final evaluation is made to determine the students' ability to serve as junior Foreign Service Officers.

Number awarded Varies each year.

Deadline Interviews are conducted at participating colleges and universities from September through November of each year.

[1766]
USDA RESEARCH APPRENTICESHIP PROGRAM FOR MINORITY HIGH SCHOOL STUDENTS

Department of Agriculture
Attn: Cooperative State Research, Education, and Extension
  Service
Office of 1890 Programs
South Agriculture Building, Room 3345
1400 Independence Avenue, S.W.
Washington, DC 20250-0910
(202) 720-2471   Fax: (202) 720-3398
E-mail: mmayes@reeusda.gov

Purpose To provide grants to colleges and universities for apprenticeships to minority high school students interested in pursuing postsecondary education in the food and agricultural sciences.

Eligibility This program is open to colleges and universities that apply for funding to encourage outstanding minority high school juniors and seniors to pursue their education in the food and agricultural sciences. Participants must be U.S. citizens and Alaskan Natives, American Indians, African Americans, Hispanic Americans, or Pacific Islanders who have completed their junior or senior year of high school and rank in the upper third of their high school class. No experience in or knowledge of agriculture is required, but may be considered in the determination of an appropriate research assignment.

Financial data Students receive at least the minimum hourly wage or stipend of equal value.

Duration Summer months.

Special features Students apply for this program through participating universities and colleges; for a list, contact the address above.

Number awarded Each summer, the United States Department of Agriculture (USDA) sponsors a minimum of 100 students nationwide.

Deadline Institutions may submit grant applications at any time; each institution sets its own deadlines for students.

[1767]
USDA SUMMER INTERN PROGRAM

Department of Agriculture
Attn: Agricultural Research Service
Civil Rights Staff, Special Programs Manager
South Agriculture Building, Room 3552
1400 Independence Avenue, S.W.
Washington, DC 20250-0300
(202) 720-6161   E-mail: taylorr@ars.usda.gov

Purpose To provide grants to colleges and universities for apprenticeships to underrepresented minority college undergraduates interested in pursuing postsecondary education in the food and agricultural sciences.

Eligibility This program is open to colleges and universities that apply for funding to encourage outstanding minority undergraduate students to pursue their education in the food and agricultural sciences. Participants must be U.S. citizens and Alaskan Natives, American Indians, African Americans, Hispanic Americans, or Pacific Islanders.

Financial data Students are employed at the GS-3 level.

Duration 8 weeks, during the summer.

Special features Students apply for this program through participating universities and colleges; for a list, contact the address above.

Deadline May of each year.

[1768]
VERY SPECIAL ARTS INTERNSHIPS

Very Special Arts
Attn: Director of Human Resources
John F. Kennedy Center for the Performing Arts
1300 Connecticut Avenue, N.W.
Washington, DC 20566
(202) 628-2800   (800) 933-8721
Fax: (202) 737-0725   TDD: (202) 737-0645

Purpose To provide work experience at the Very Special Arts program of the John F. Kennedy Center for the Performing Arts.

Eligibility This program is open to upper-level college and graduate students who intend to pursue careers in arts education, arts administration, and disability fields. They must be interested in assisting with the administration and management of Very Special Arts programs and special projects in Washington, D.C. Minorities and persons with disabilities are encouraged to apply.

Financial data The monthly stipend for a full-time assignment is $500; part-time interns receive a pro-rated salary.

Duration Assignments range from 20 to 40 hours per week, and are available for fall, spring, or summer semesters.

Special features Assignments are available in the following departments: national programs, state services, international, communications, marketing and development, and Very Special Arts Galleries.

Number awarded Varies each year.

Deadline June of each year for fall assignments, October of each year for spring assignments, and March of each year for summer assignments.

[1769]
VIRGINIA PRESS ASSOCIATION MINORITY INTERNSHIP

Virginia Press Association
c/o Ray Hall
P.O. Box 85613
Richmond, VA 23285-5613
(804) 550-2361

Purpose To provide work experience in journalism to minority students in Virginia.

Eligibility This program is open to minority students at the level of junior through graduate school who are residents of Virginia or attending a college or university in Virginia. Applicants must be seeking an internship in journalism.

Financial data The total stipend is $2,500.

Duration 10 weeks.

Number awarded 1 each year.

Deadline March of each year.

[1770]
WALT DISNEY STUDIOS FELLOWSHIP PROGRAM

Walt Disney Studios
Attn: Brenda Vangsness
500 South Buena Vista Street
Burbank, CA 91521-0880
(818) 560-1018

Purpose To provide work experience to minorities and women interested in script writing.

Eligibility Writers who are interested in writing for the film industry are eligible to submit scripts (either a completed motion picture screenplay, a full length 2- to 3-act play, or a half-hour television script). This program is open to all writers but focuses on hiring African Americans, Latinos, Asians, Native Americans, and women.

Financial data Fellows receive $30,000.

Duration 1 year.

Special features Fellows train with creative teams at the 3 divisions of Walt Disney Studios: Hollywood Pictures, Walt Disney Pictures, and Touchstone Pictures.

Number awarded Varies; generally, 10 to 15 each year.

Deadline April of each year.

[1771]
WAVE 3 TELECOMMUNICATIONS INTERNSHIP

WAVE TV 3
P.O. Box 32970
Louisville, KY 40232
(502) 585-2201   Fax: (502) 561-4115

Purpose To provide the opportunity for work experience to students interested in telecommunications.

Eligibility Full-time college students who are between their junior and senior years and majoring in communications or broadcast journalism are eligible to apply, if they reside in Louisville or are attending school in the area. Preference is given to minorities.

Financial data Interns earn at least minimum wage and work 40 hours per week.

Duration 8 to 12 weeks, beginning in June.

Special features Interns work in either the production department or news department.

Number awarded 4 each year, 2 in each department.

Deadline February of each year.

[1772]
WCVB-TV SUMMER MINORITY INTERNSHIP PROGRAM

WCVB-TV
Attn: Human Resources Department
5 TV Place
Needham Heights, MA 02194-2303
(617) 433-0462   Fax: (617) 449-0260

Purpose To provide work experience at WCVB-TV in Boston to minorities who are interested in broadcast journalism as a career.

Eligibility Applicants must have completed their junior year, be majoring in some field of broadcasting, be U.S. citizens, and be minorities or others disadvantaged by economic or social conditions.

Financial data Interns receive $150 per week.

Duration 12 weeks during the summer.

Special features This program provides an opportunity for participants to obtain an overview of the television broadcasting field in news, programming, public affairs, or sales.

Limitations Interns must provide their own transportation.

Number awarded 5 each year.

Deadline April of each year.

[1773]
WEST COAST CONFERENCE ATHLETIC ADMINISTRATION INTERNSHIP

West Coast Conference
Attn: Assistant Commissioner
400 Oyster Point Boulevard, Suite 221
South San Francisco, CA 94080
(415) 873-8622   Fax: (415) 873-7846

Purpose To provide work experience to minorities and others interested in college sports.

Eligibility This program is open to graduate students who are interested in working with administration of college athletics. Members of ethnic minority groups are strongly encouraged to apply.

Financial data A monthly stipend is paid; no housing or health benefits are provided.

Duration 10 months, beginning in August.

Special features Interns work for the West Coast Conference, in South San Francisco, California for 40 hours per week, with flexibility to accommodate class schedules. Responsibilities include, but are not limited to, assisting in the areas of marketing, promotions, and corporate sales, championships administration, officiating, and compliance.

Number awarded 1 each year.

Deadline May of each year.

[1774]
WILMINGTON STAR-NEWS INTERNSHIP

Wilmington Star-News
Attn: Managing Editor
1003 South 17th Street
P.O. Box 840
Wilmington, NC 28402
(910) 343-2000

Purpose To provide work experience at the *Wilmington Star-News* in North Carolina to college students who are interested in preparing for a career in journalism.

Eligibility This program is open to students from any state interested in working on a daily newspaper in news/editorial, photography, or advertising. Preference is given to juniors for the positions in news/editoral and photography, to recent graduates for the position in advertising. Minorities are especially encouraged to apply.

Financial data The salary is $300 per week.

Duration 10 to 12 weeks, during the summer, for news/editorial and photography; 1 year for advertising.

Number awarded 2 in news/editorial and 1 in photography each year; internships in advertising are available only occasionally.

Deadline Applications should be submitted early in the year for news/editorial and photography internships; applications for internships in advertising may be submitted at any time.

[1775]
W.K. KELLOGG COMMUNITY-BASED TRAINING FELLOWSHIP PROGRAM FOR MINORITY MEDICAL STUDENTS

National Medical Fellowships, Inc.
Attn: Scholarships and Programs
110 West 32nd Street, 8th Floor
New York, NY 10001-3205
(212) 714-1007

Purpose To encourage underrepresented minority medical school students to enter or establish organized, community-based primary care practices.

Eligibility Only nominations are accepted; students may not apply directly. Nominees must be underrepresented minority (African American, Native American, Mexican American, and mainland Puerto Rican) second- and third-year students attending accredited medical schools in the United States. Candidates must demonstrate academic achievement and motivation for careers as community-based primary care practitioners.

Financial data The stipend is $10,000; fellows may also apply for $1,000 travel stipends to attend approved professional meetings.

Duration The program requires 2 rotations of 8 to 12 weeks each.

Special features Fellows receive first-hand experience in community medicine under the guidance of senior staff at a participating community-based facility, assisting in health care delivery, community epidemiology, and health education as appropriate. On the first rotation, they receive an introduction to a community-based primary care facility. On the second rotation, they complete a clinical or research project at the same site. The program was created in 1995 with grant support from the W.K. Kellogg Foundation.

Number awarded 15 each year.

Deadline Nominations are requested from medical schools in late fall of each year.

[1776]
ZINA GARRISON/VISA MINORITY INTERNSHIP

Women's Sports Foundation
Eisenhower Park
1899 Hempstead Turnpike, Suite 400
East Meadow, NY 11554-1000
(516) 542-4700　　　　　　　　　　(800) 227-3988
Fax: (516) 542-4716　　　　　　　E-mail: wosport@aol.com

Purpose To provide women of color an opportunity to get a start in a sports-related career.

Eligibility Eligible to apply for these internships are women of color who are undergraduate students, college graduates, graduate students, or women in career change. The internships are conducted in the offices of the Women's Sports Foundation on Long Island, New York.

Financial data The salary is $5,000.

Duration 6 months.

Number awarded 2 each year.

Deadline Applications may be submitted at any time.

Annotated Bibliography of General Financial Aid Directories

Sources of Information on:
Scholarships, Fellowships, Loans ●
Grants ●
Awards and Prizes ●
Internships, Work Experience Programs,
and On-the-job Training Opportunities ●
Financial Assistance to Special Population Groups ●

Scholarships, Fellowships and Loans

[1777]
The A's & B's of Academic Scholarships. Alexandria, VA: Octameron Associates, 1985— . Annual.

Do you have a "B" average or better? Are your SAT/ACT scores 900/21 or better? If so, you might be able to qualify for a college merit scholarship. This pamphlet lists the major awards offered by 1,200 colleges to students in the top third of their class who have combined SAT scores of 900 or more. Most entries provide information—in tabular form—on number of awards, value range, class standing, study fields, renewability, restrictions, and application date. A short section (generally 4 pages) identifies some noninstitution-based awards. A companion annual pamphlet issued by Octameron Associates is *Don't Miss Out: The Ambitious Student's Guide to Scholarships and Loans*, which outlines strategies for seeking financial aid for college students; very brief information is provided for a number of sample or representative funding programs.

[1778]
Bear's Guide to Finding Money for College. By John B. Bear and Mariah P. Bear. Berkeley: Ten Speed, 1996.

This informal and sometimes irreverent introduction to financial aid for college students identifies a surprisingly large number of specific financial aid programs in addition to providing the usual chatty instructions and encouragement found in trade-oriented paperbacks. Over 100 athletic, military, and corporate scholarships are listed and very briefly described. In addition, 200 fellowships, grants-in-aid, and other special awards are mentioned. Addresses are given for these programs but, generally, telephone numbers are not. Nevertheless, there is much information here for the price.

[1779]
Chronicle Financial Aid Guide. Moravia, NY: Chronicle Guidance Publications, 1978— . Annual.

Information on financial aid programs offered nationally or regionally by approximately 700 private and public organizations is provided in this annual directory. The financial aid sponsors include private organizations, clubs, foundations, sororities and fraternities, federal and state governments, and national and international labor unions. The scope of the assistance programs listed extends from the incoming freshman through the baccalaureate, graduate, and postdoctoral levels. The programs are indexed by subject and sponsor.

[1780]
College Blue Book. New York: Macmillan, 1923— . Biennial.

Each volume in the latest edition of this multi-volume set provides information on a different area of higher education (e.g., tabular data on American colleges). Volume 5 of the set is devoted to scholarships, fellowships, loans, and grants available to undergraduate and graduate students. It identifies over $150 million offered by more than 2,500 programs. Arranged by discipline and subdivided by specific subject, the volume is indexed by sponsor, title, interest field, and levels of awards.

[1781]
College Student's Guide to Merit and Other No-Need Funding. By Gail A. Schlachter and R. David Weber. El Dorado Hills, CA: Reference Service Press, 1996— . Biennial.

Finally, there's a financial aid directory that's aimed at the middle class. Described here are more than 1,200 financial aid programs that are based on academic merit, personal characteristics, organizational affiliation, creative skills, or career interests--but never on income level. Each of these no-need scholarships is described in detail in this unique directory--a companion volume to the *High School Senior's Guide to Merit and Other No-Need Funding* (described elsewhere in this bibliography).

[1782]
Financial Aid for Study and Training Abroad. By Gail A. Schlachter and R. David Weber. El Dorado Hills, CA: Reference Service Press, 1992— . Biennial.

A companion volume to *Financial Aid for Research and Creative Activities Abroad* (described below), this comprehensive guide describes more than 800 scholarships, fellowships, loans, and grants that Americans can use to support study and training in other countries. The funding opportunities are arranged by target group (high school/undergraduate students, graduate students, postdoctorates, and professionals/other individuals) and indexed by program title, sponsoring organization, geographic coverage, subject, and deadline dates. Support is available for every course of study and in all major countries.

[1783]
Financial Aids for Higher Education. Prep. by Oreon Keeslar. Dubuque, IA: William C. Brown, 1963— . Biennial.

Each biennial edition of this directory contains detailed information on over 3,000 programs (scholarships, loans, and contests) sponsored by professional associations, national fraternal organizations, religious groups, charities, service organizations, national corporations, small businesses, labor unions, travel clubs, and state and national governments. The main section of each edition consists of an alphabetical listing of programs by official title. Each entry describes applicant eligibility and restrictions, remuneration, application process and deadlines, and sources of additional information. There is an index that provides access to sources of financial aid by sponsor, common name, field of specialization, type of program, and restrictions.

[1784]
Financial Assistance for Library Education. Chicago: American Library Association, 1970— . Annual.

This comprehensive summary of fellowships, scholarships, grants-in-aid, loans, and other financial aids for library education is available from the American Library Association (50 East Huron Street, Chicago, IL 60611) for $1 to cover postage. The booklet is an annually revised list of awards from state library agencies, national and state library associations, local libraries, and academic institutions offering undergraduate and graduate programs in library education in the United States or Canada. Scholarships of less than $200 are not listed. For each entry, the following information is given: granting body, level of program, type of assistance, number available, academic or other requirements, application deadline, and application address.

[1785]
High School Senior's Guide to Merit and Other No-Need Funding. By Gail A. Schlachter and R. David Weber. El Dorado Hills, CA: 1996— . Biennial.

Do you think you parents make too much money for you to qualify for financial aid? Not true! This unique guide identifies and describes more than 1,000 merit scholarships and other no-need funding programs (programs based on organization affiliation, personal characteristics, creative abilities, and career interests) that never consider income level when making awards to high school seniors interested in going on to college. The entries are grouped by discipline (humanities, sciences, social sciences, and any subject area) and indexed by sponsor, program title, geographic restrictions, subject coverage, and deadline date.

[1786]
The Journalist's Road to Success: A Career and Scholarship Guide. Princeton: Dow Jones Newspaper Fund, 1979— . Annual.

This booklet is a guide to available financial aid for students majoring in journalism or communications from news organizations, professional societies, journalism-related groups, colleges, and universities. Over $7 million in financial aid for more than 3,000 journalism students is also described. Scholarships under $100 are not included. The listing is arranged into 2 main sections: Part 1 deals with aid offered through schools and departments of journalism in American and Canadian colleges and universities (as well as by newspapers and professional societies). Part 2 lists miscellaneous sources of scholarships and those grants designed for minority students. An even more comprehensive list of minority opportunities is available in *Diversity and You*, a free booklet published by the Fund. Both booklets are available from the Fund (P.O. Box 300, Princeton, NJ 08540).

[1787]
Money for Graduate Students in the Social Sciences. By Gail A. Schlachter and R. David Weber. El Dorado Hills, CA: Reference Service Press, 1996— . Biennial.

This is the source to use if you are looking for money to help you pay for a master's or doctoral degree in accounting, advertising, anthropology or ethnology, business administration, criminology, demography, economics, education, geography, international relations, law, library/information science, marketing, political science, psychology, sociology, or any other social science. In all, nearly 1,000 funding opportunities are described in detail; information is provided on sponsor, purpose, eligibility, financial data, duration, special features, limitations, number awarded, and deadline date. Entries are grouped by purpose (study or research) and indexed by program title, sponsor, residency requirements, tenability, subject coverage, and deadline. Reference Service Press also issues two other titles aimed at graduate students in the other disciplines: *Money for Graduate Students in the Humanities* and *Money for Graduate Students in the Sciences*.

[1788]
Need a Lift? To Educational Opportunities, Careers, Loans, Scholarships, Employment. Prep. by the American Legion Educational and Scholarship Program. Indianapolis: American Legion, 1969— . Annual.

This annually revised guide to sources of financial aid is distributed for a $2 charge from the American Legion (P.O. Box 1055, Indianapolis, IN 46206). It is primarily intended as a source book for children of veterans, although it also contains general information of interest to any student pursuing postsecondary education. The booklet presents descriptions of scholarships, fellowships, loans, and state educational benefits valued at over $4 billion.

[1789]
Scholarships and Loans for Nursing Education. New York: National League for Nursing, 1984— . Biennial.

In addition to providing information about the general process of and requirements for applying for financial aid, this booklet describes 6 federal financial aid programs and more than 50 sources of private aid available to students interested in nursing. The descriptions for each of these programs specify purpose, eligibility, remuneration, number awarded, application process, and deadline.

[1790]
Scholarships, Fellowships and Loans. Detroit: Gale, 1949— . Irreg.

Issued irregularly since 1949, this comprehensive guide to student aid provides detailed information on scholarships, fellowships, grants, and loans available to undergraduate and graduate students. The latest edition provides information on over $1 billion awarded by 1,400 financial aid programs. The directory is arranged alphabetically by sponsoring agency and is indexed by field of interest. For an abbreviated but less expensive version of this title, see *Fund Your Way through College*, published by Visible Ink (a subsidiary of Gale Research).

[1791]
Selected List of Fellowships & Other Support Opportunities for Advanced Education for United States Citizens and Foreign Nationals. Arlington, VA: National Science Foundation. Annual.

Distributed without charge by the National Science Foundation, this booklet presents concise descriptions of 250 major undergraduate, graduate, and postdoctorate fellowships, loans, work-study assignments, and scholarship programs funded by various organizations, foundations, and government agencies. For each program, the following information is provided: remuneration, eligibility, restrictions, application process, and sources of additional information. A short bibliography of other publications listing fellowships, scholarships, and student loans completes this booklet.

[1792]

The Student Guide: Financial Aid from the U.S. Department of Education. Washington, DC: U.S. Department of Education. Annual.

In 1995, of the more than $24 billion that our nation spent on education, nearly half was given to postsecondary students who needed help in paying their higher education costs. These funds were supplied through the basic federal programs (Pell Grants, College Work-Study, Stafford Student Loans, etc.). *The Student Guide*, distributed without charge by the U.S. Department of Education, describes each of these programs in detail, indicating purpose, remuneration, application procedures, eligibilities, recipient responsibilities, and notification process. For a free copy, call (800) 4-FED AID.

Grants

[1793]

Annual Register of Grant Support: A Guide to Support Programs of Government Agencies, Foundations, and Business and Professional Organizations. New York: Bowker, 1969— . Annual.

Nearly 3,000 programs sponsored by government agencies, private foundations, corporations, unions, church groups, and educational and professional associations are described in the latest edition of this directory. The programs provide grant support in the humanities, international affairs, race and minority concerns, education, environmental and urban affairs, social sciences, physical sciences, life sciences, technology, and other areas. Each entry contains the following information: organization name; address and telephone number; major field(s) of organizational interest; name(s) of grant program(s); purpose; nature of support available; amount of support per award; number of applicants and recipients for most recent years; legal basis for program; eligibility requirements; application instructions; and deadline. The work is indexed by subject, sponsor, geographic requirements, and personnel.

[1794]

ARIS Funding Messenger: Creative Arts and Humanities Report. San Francisco: Academic Research Information System (ARIS), 1976— . 8 times/yr., plus supplements.

Up-to-date information on funding opportunities, agency activities, new programs, and funding policies in the creative arts and humanities is available from this current awareness service. Arts coverage includes funding for practicing artists and arts groups in both the performing and visual arts. Regional, national, and international competitions are highlighted. Humanities coverage includes information on funding for the academic study of the traditional humanistic disciplines as well as for projects emphasizing the broader social and community applications. Both public and private programs are described. Each entry provides address, telephone numbers, concise guidelines, and deadline dates. Reports are issued every 6 weeks and supplements are issued as needed.

[1795]

ARIS Funding Messenger: Medical Sciences Report. San Francisco: Academic Research Information System (ARIS), 1976— . 8 times/yr., plus supplements.

Covered in this current awareness service are grant and fellowship opportunities, agency activities, new programs, and funding policies in the medical science. The emphasis is on biomedical research, health care and services, and the general biological sciences. Both public and private programs are described. Each entry provides address, telephone numbers, concise guidelines, and deadline dates. Reports are issued every 6 weeks, and supplements are issued when appropriate.

[1796]

ARIS Funding Messenger; Social and Natural Sciences Report. San Francisco: Academic Research Information System (ARIS), 1976— . 8 times/year, plus supplements.

This current awareness service, begun in 1976, presents up-to-date information on public and private funding in the fields of 1) social sciences research, including business, education, law, and the behavioral sciences; 2) natural sciences research, including agriculture, computer sciences, engineering, environmental sciences, mathematics, and space sciences. Each entry provides address, telephone number, concise guidelines, and deadline dates. The reports are issued every 6 weeks, and supplements are issued as needed, to include deadlines and RFPs announced after a report's publication date.

[1797]

Awards Annual: An International Guide to Career, Research, and Educational Funds. Detroit: St. James Press (dist. by Gale), 1991— . Biennial.

The latest edition of this international directory (the emphasis is on English-speaking countries) describes over 2,000 grants, awards, scholarships/fellowships, and research funding in all disciplines available to professionals, scientists, researchers, artists and writers, faculty members, and individuals pursuing advanced degrees. Program entries are arranged alphabetically by sponsoring organization and provide information on purpose, area of study, requirements, deadline, financial data, duration, ratio of number of awards to applicants, and application procedures.

[1798]

Catalog of Federal Domestic Assistance. Prep. by the U.S. General Services Administration. Washington, DC: G.P.O., 1965— . Annual.

This is the "what's what" of government grant programs. It is *the* single source of information on programs administered at the federal level. Over 1,000 domestic assistance programs are described in this annual publication, including grants, loans, loan guarantees and shared revenue; provision of federal facilities; direct construction of goods and services; donation or provision of surplus property, technical assistance, and counseling; statistical and other information services; and service activities of regulatory agencies. These assistance programs are available to state and local governments, public and private organizations and institutions, and individuals. Each program entry contains information on purpose, availability, authorizing legislation, administering agency, and sources of additional information. The catalog is organized into 3 indexes: a functional index, a subject index, and an agency program index. The catalog is also available in online form as the Federal Assistance Program Retrieval System (FAPRS).

[1799]
Corporate Giving Directory: Comprehensive Profiles and Analyses of America's Private Foundations. Detroit: Taft, 1977— . Annual.

Taft is 1 of the oldest, largest, and best known of the grant information subscription services. This directory, first issued in 1977 and updated annually since then, contains over 600 corporate foundation profiles. The entries are arranged by program name and present information on sponsoring company, grant distribution, type of grants, areas of interest, contact persons, total assets, sample grants, corporate operating location, and Fortune 500 ranking (profiles average 1 page in length). Multiple indexes are provided (e.g., state, field of interest). Use Taft's monthly *Corporate Updates* and *Corporate Giving Watch* to supplement entries in the annual directory.

[1800]
Corporate 500: The Directory of Corporate Philanthropy. San Francisco: Public Management Institute (dist. by Gale), 1980— . Irreg.

This directory, first issued in 1980, summarizes and analyzes in detail information about the contributions programs of the most influential corporations in America. The latest edition provides not only a picture of each corporation's grant pattern, but an overview as well of the entire field of corporate giving (now well in excess of $2 billion a year). The more than 500 corporations described are those known to be the most active in supporting nonprofit organizations and public agencies. Arranged by corporation, each entry provides name, address, and phone number of the company; details of eligibility; geographic preferences; financial profile; application procedures; areas of funding interest; policy statement; restrictions and special requirements; number of grants given; amount and range of grants; sample grant recipients; contribution committee members; and special analyses by the research staff of the Public Management Institute. Additional access to the information is offered through a series of indexes, including areas of interest, activities, and geography.

[1801]
Directory of Research Grants. Phoenix: Oryx, 1975— . Annual.

In the latest edition, more than 4,000 grants, contracts, fellowships, and loan programs for research, training, and innovative effort sponsored by more than 600 organizations are described. The emphasis is on U.S. programs, although some sponsored by other countries are included. Entries are arranged by program title. Annotations include requirements, restrictions, financial data (but not for all entries), name and addresses, and application procedures. The programs are indexed by subject. The information presented in this publication is also available online (through Dialog) as GRANTS, on CD-ROM with monthly supplements, and in two derivative publications: *Directory of Grants in the Humanities* and *Directory of Biomedical and Health Care Grants.*

[1802]
Federal Grants & Contracts Weekly. Arlington, VA: Capitol Publications, 1974— . Weekly (51 issues).

Each week, close to $100 million in federal funding opportunities are announced. The *Federal Grants & Contracts Weekly* acts as an "early warning" system, to alert readers to all federal grant announcements as well as to research, training, and technical services contracts. Each 8-page issue is published on Monday and contains information on Requests for Proposals (FRPs), closing dates for grant programs, procurement-related regulatory news, contract awards, updates on federal budget action, and profiles on grant programs and federal agencies. Another weekly issued by Capitol Publications, *Health Grants and Contracts Weekly,* provides the same type of current awareness service for the medical field.

[1803]
Federal Register. Prep. by the U.S. Office of Federal Register. Washington, DC: G.P.O.: 1936— . Daily (Monday through Friday).

The *Federal Register* is issued every week day except holidays. It is the official source for the publication of public regulations and legal notices issued by federal executive agencies and independent agencies. Thus, this is an excellent place to check for the latest information (including deadline date) on federally funded programs. There is also a separately published *Federal Register Index* that is issued monthly; each issue is cumulative, with the December issue serving as the annual cumulative index.

[1804]
Financial Aid for Research and Creative Activities Abroad. By Gail A. Schlachter and R. David Weber. El Dorado Hills, CA: Reference Service Press, 1992— . Biennial.

This directory will help Americans tap into the millions of dollars available for research, lectureships, exchange programs, work assignments, conference attendance, professional development, and creative projects abroad. The 1,300 listings cover every major field of interest, are tenable in practically every country in the world, are sponsored by more than 500 different private and public organizations and agencies, and are open to all segments of the population, from high school students to professionals and postdoctorates. A companion volume (described above) identifies funding opportunities for study and training abroad.

[1805]
The Foundation Directory. New York: Foundation Center, 1960— . Annual; supplements issued mid-year.

The Foundation Center is the only nonprofit organization in the country that focuses on the activities of private foundations. This directory is the standard work on nongovernmental grantmaking foundations. It lists nonprofit, nongovernmental organizations with assets in excess of $2 million or which made grants in excess of $200,000 in 1 year. More than 6,000 foundations are identified. These represent only 10 percent of all grantmaking foundations but over 90 percent of all grant money distributed ($8 billion annually). For information on the more than 4,000 foundations that annually grant between $50,000 and $199,000, see the *Foundation Directory Part II.* Supplements are issued between editions of these directories and list foundations by state for which recent fiscal data are available on microfiche. The directory is also available to be searched online, through Dialog.

[1806]
The Foundation Grants Index. New York: Foundation Center, 1971— . Annual.

The *Foundation Grants Index* provides detailed subject access to the 60,000 grants made in excess of $10,000 during the year of record by approximately 950 major foundations with a total value of more than $1.8 million. This represents about 47 percent of all foundation giving. The grants are listed alphabetically by foundation under state division. Entries specify the amount and date of the grant, name and location of the recipients, a description of the grant, and any known limitations in the foundation's giving pattern. The entries are indexed by key word, subject category, and recipient. To update the information presented in this index, use the *Foundation Grants Index Quarterly* and/or the *Foundation Grants Index* database (available through Dialog).

[1807]
Foundation Grants to Individuals. New York: Foundation Center, 1977— . Irreg.

This is the only publication devoted entirely to foundation grant opportunities (including some scholarships and loans) for individual applicants. The latest edition provides full descriptions of nearly 2,250 foundations annually making grants of at least $2,000 to individuals. These foundations represent more than $8.5 billion in assets and together give over $96 million to individuals annually. The work is organized by type of grant awarded (e.g., scholarships, general welfare, medical assistance), subdivided by eligibility requirements and means of access (including "Grants to Foreign Individuals" and "Grants to Employees of Specific Companies"). Multiple avenues of access are provided through the following indexes: subject, state restrictions, travel provisions, company-related grants, student grants, and foundations.

[1808]
Foundation Reporter: Comprehensive Profiles and Analyses of America's Private Foundations. Detroit: Taft, 1977— . Annual.

Included annually in this definitive directory are 600 indepth profiles and analyses of America's private foundations. Lengthy entries provide information on history of the foundation, officers, directors, types of foundations, areas of interest, fiscal activities, types of grants awarded, grants distribution, sample grants, application requirements, and contact persons. The following indexes are supplied: state, type of grant, field of interest, and officers/directors by name, place of birth, and alma mater. To update the entries included here, use Taft Foundation's *Foundation Giving Watch* and *Foundation Updates*.

[1809]
The Foundation 1000. New York: Foundation Center, 1977— . Annual.

Of all the Foundation Center's directories, *The Foundation 1000* provides the most detailed treatment but covers the smallest number of foundations. In all, only 1,000 grantmaking organiza-

tions are treated, with entries averaging 3 to 6 pages each. These foundations account for 60 percent of the total annual giving of all U.S. foundations, more than $5 billion in grants annually. Each profile provides information on the foundation's areas of giving, types of grants, and types of recipients. Prior to 1993, this directory was published on a quarterly basis under the title *Source Book Profiles.*

[1810]
Grant Guides. New York: Foundation Center. Annual.

This is a series of computer-produced subject guides to foundation funding. The reports provide the same data that can be found in the *Foundation Grants Index Annual* (described elsewhere in this section of the bibliography), but the listing is arranged according to specific subjects. There are currently 30 available, covering such areas as library and information services, mentally retarded and disabled, science and technology, and social services.

[1811]
Grants and Fellowships of Interest to Philosophers. Newark, DE: American Philosophical Association, 1972— . Annual.

This annually-issued directory identifies grants and fellowships for graduate and postdoctoral study and research in the United States and abroad available from approximately 30 sources. Entries, arranged alphabetically by sponsoring organization, supply information on deadline, fields of study, purpose, qualifications, tenure, stipend, number, application procedures, and contact person.

[1812]
Grants, Fellowships, & Prizes of Interest to Historians. Washington, DC: American Historical Association, 1978— . Annual.

Begun as a 46-page pamphlet, this 260-page annual listing identifies and describes nearly 400 sources of funding for graduate students, postdoctoral researchers, and scholars in the history profession tenable in the United States and abroad. Covered here are fellowships, internships, awards, prizes, and travel grants. The entries are arranged in 3 sections: support for dissertation and postdoctoral research, support for dissertation study and research, and support for organizations working in the fields of historical research or education.

[1813]
The Grants Register: Postgraduate Awards in the English Speaking World. Ed. by Lisa Williams. New York: St. Martin's Press, 1969— . Biennial.

Despite its title, this directory is not restricted to grants listings only; it also includes fellowships, exchanges, vocational study, travel grants, grants-in-aid, competitions, prizes, and other awards (including awards for refugees, war veterans, minority groups, and students in unexpected financial difficulty). Published every 2 years, the directory provides fairly up-to-date information on awards sponsored by more than 2,000 awarding bodies other than universities; listed are awards offered by governmental agencies, international agencies, national organizations, and private agencies. Emphasis is on awards for nationals of the United

States, Canada, the United Kingdom, Ireland, Australia, New Zealand, South Africa, and the developing countries. The following information is provided for each program: remuneration, eligibility, deadline, application procedures, subject areas covered, purpose, number offered, where tenable, awarding organization, and address for application and/or further information. There are indexes by subject and awards/awarding bodies.

[1814]
Guide to Grants & Fellowships in Languages & Linguistics. Washington, DC: Linguistic Society of America, 1984— . Biennial.

Published biennially, this directory lists and describes grants and fellowships in the fields of language and linguistics sponsored by institutions, associations, foundations, and government agencies located in the United States. Nearly 200 programs are covered. They are arranged by sponsoring organization. In each entry, the following information is provided: program title, sponsoring organization name, address, and telephone number, purpose, eligibility, restrictions, duration, stipend, and application procedures.

[1815]
Guide to U.S. Foundations, Their Trustees, Officers, and Donors. New York: Foundation Center, 1972— . Annual.

This is the only publication that lists *all* foundations giving more than $1 per year. The most recent edition contains brief descriptions of over 33,000 currently active grantmaking foundations in the United States (5 times more than any other published source). A 2-volume set, the first volume arranges foundations by state and provides information for each on name, address, principal officers, market value of assets, grants paid, gifts received, fiscal period, and annual reports; the second volume, which features foundations listed by state, serves as an index to Volume One. The information included in the directory is also available to be searched online, through Dialog. Formerly, the directory was issued under the title *National Data Book.*

[1816]
Money for Visual Artists: A Comprehensive Resource Guide. Washington, DC: ACA Books, 1993. 200p.

This newly revised and expanded guide for visual artists seeking financial support describes hundreds of grants, fellowships, awards, artists colonies, emergency grants-in-aid, and technical assistance programs. Entries include name, address, telephone number, type of award and/or scope of service, eligibility requirements, application procedures, and deadlines. ACA Books also issues a number of similar titles, aimed at artists in other fields: *Money for Performing Artists* (1991), *Money for Film & Video Artists* (1993), and *Money for International Exchange in the Arts* (1992).

[1817]
The National Directory of Corporate Giving. 3d ed. New York: Foundation Center, 1993.

The third edition of this directory offers authoritative information on over 2,300 corporate philanthropic programs (1,700 corporate foundations plus more than 600 direct giving programs). Information is given for each of these programs on: key personnel, appli-

cation procedures, types of support generally awarded, giving limitations, financial data, and purpose/activities. As a new feature in the third edition, descriptions of recently awarded grants are included. A bibliography to guide further research on corporate funding and 6 indexes complete the volume. For more in-depth information on the 250 largest of the corporate foundations described here (those that grant at least $1.25 million annually), see *Corporate Foundation Profiles,* also published by the Foundation Center.

[1818]
The National Directory of Grants and Aid to Individuals in the Arts. 9th ed. Des Moines, IA: Washington International Arts Letter, 1995.

More than 3,000 grants, prizes, and awards for professional work in the United States and abroad are described here. The disciplines covered include architecture, arts management, crafts, dance, film and video, music, museum administration, theater, visual and plastic arts, and writing. The sources are arranged alphabetically by sponsor and indexed by discipline. Each entry contains information on the address, basic requirements, amount of grant or award, and restrictions, if any.

[1819]
The National Guide to Funding Series. New York: Foundation Center, various dates.

The Foundation Center issues a series of guides to funding in various subject areas, all of which start with the title *The National Guide to Funding.* Each volume provides essential information on the foundations and corporate direct giving programs in the subject covered and follows the same organization: grantmaker portraits, sample grants, and indexes. Currently, the titles in this series cover arts and culture, higher education, elementary and secondary education, libraries and information services, international and foreign programs, environment and animal welfare, health, youth and family, the economically disadvantaged, religion, women and girls, and aging.

Awards and Prizes

[1820]
Awards, Honors, and Prizes: An International Directory of Awards and Their Donors. 12th ed. Detroit: Gale, 1996. 2v.

The first volume of this widely-used reference work, *United States and Canada,* contains up-to-date information on more than 16,000 awards, honors, and prizes given in North America in the areas of advertising and public relations, art, business, government, finance, science, engineering, literature, technology, sports, religion, public affairs, law, publishing, international affairs, transportation, architecture, journalism, music, photography, theater, and the performing arts. Excluded from the listing are scholarships, fellowships, study awards to students, prizes received as a result of entering contests where something is achieved only for the purpose of the contest, and local and regional awards. The volume is divided into 4 sections: 1) the main listing for each award, where the following information is given: name, address, title of award, purpose, eligibility, form of award, frequency, date established, and who established the award; 2) a list of subjects and "see also" references (each award is indexed by subject and/or areas of interest); 3) an alphabetical index to the specific names of each award; and 4) an organization index. Volume 2 adds international coverage by describing organizations and awards given in countries other than the United States or Canada.

[1821]

Dramatists Sourcebook: Complete Opportunities for Playwrights, Translators, Composers, Lyricists, and Librettists. Ed. by M. Elizabeth Osborne. New York: Theatre Communications Group, 1982— . Annual.

While one half of this directory focuses on ""script opportunities" (theaters willing to review unpublished plays), there are separate sections that relate directly to financial aid programs: prizes, fellowships and grants, colonies and residencies, and emergency funds. The entries in these sections are arranged by sponsoring organization and subdivided by specific programs. The information presented includes eligibility, financial arrangements, purpose, application process, and deadlines. To update the listings in the sourcebook, use the Theatre Communications Group's monthly magazine, *American Theater.*

[1822]

Grants and Awards Available to American Writers. New York: P.E.N. American Center, 1973— . Annual.

Grants and awards in excess of $500, available to American writers for use in the United States and abroad, are described in this widely-used directory. According to the editors, this is the only reference work ""which combines both domestic and foreign grants for American writers." Additional sections identify grants and awards available to Canadian writers and state arts councils. The 600 to 700 entries included each year are arranged alphabetically by organization and indexed by award title, type of literature, and sponsoring organization. There is no subject index. Each listing specifies purpose of the award, amount available, eligibility, and application procedures. The programs covered are open to playwrights, poets, journalists, fiction writers, researchers, and scholars. Use the *P.E.N. American Center Newsletter* to update this listing.

[1823]

National Advisory List of Contests and Activities. Reston, VA: National Association of Secondary School Principals, 1940— . Annual.

This annually-issued advisory list of regional and national contests and activities suitable for inclusion in a school program or curriculum is prepared by the National Association of Secondary School Principals' Committee on National Contests and Activities. The contests and activities listed here are ""designed solely to benefit secondary school youth in educational, civic, social and ethical development." They are open to all secondary students regardless of race, creed, sex, or national origin. The programs are divided into national and regional categories, listed alphabetically by sponsoring organization, and indexed by program type. The following information is provided for each entry: sponsors' address, program title, date registration closes, and program dates. This listing is also available electronically, on America Online.

Internships

[1824]

Directory of International Internships. 3d ed. East Lansing, MI: Career Development Placement Services, Michigan State University, 1994.

An internship can serve as a bridge between education and preparation for a career. International internships can offer several additional advantages: cross-cultural exposure, an increase in foreign language competency, learning to adapt to different environments, and international contacts for the future. This directory identifies 500 international internships available to undergraduate and graduate students interested in preparing for an international career. Indexing is by subject and geographic location. Even a comprehensive sources like Peterson's *Internships* cannot match the number of international internships identified here.

[1825]

Directory of Residency Training Programs Accredited by the Accreditation Council for Graduate Medical Education. Chicago: American Medical Association, 1981— . Annual.

Over 5,000 residency programs accredited by the Accreditation Council for Graduate Medical Education are covered in this annual directory. Entries specify program name, name and address of director, specialities available, teaching hospitals' names, requirements, and length of program. For similar but more specialized listings of opportunities in the medical field, see the Association for the Care of Children's Health's *Directory of Student Placements in Health Care Settings in North America* and the American Academy of Family Physician's annual *Directory of Family Practice Residency Programs.*

[1826]

Earn & Learn: Your Guide to In-School Educational Employment Programs. By Joseph M. Re. Alexandria, VA: Octameron Associates, 1979— . Annual.

"Cooperative education" is a blend of classroom instruction and on-the-job work experiences related to formal instruction. The main part of this annually-issued pamphlet consists of a name/address list of over 800 colleges participating in cooperative education programs. Also included is a name/address list of federal agencies—from Agriculture to Treasury—that act as program sponsors.

[1827]

Internship Programs in Professional Psychology, Including Postdoctoral Training Programs. Knoxville, IA: Association of Psychology Internship Centers, 1967— . Annual.

Issued annually, this directory identifies institutions offering internship and postdoctoral training programs in psychology. The listing is arranged geographically. Program entries specify institution address, contact person, internship characteristics, number of internships available, stipend, and admissions requirements. For a similar listing of internship opportunities in psychiatry, see the American Psychiatric Association's biennial *Directory of Psychiatry Residency Training Programs.*

[1828]

Internships: On-the-Job Opportunities for All Types of Careers. Princeton, NJ: Peterson's Guides, 1981— . Annual.

Published annually since 1981, this publication identifies over 34,000 short-term career-oriented positions in major American firms. The jobs cover a wide range of fields, including architecture, business communications, and sciences. Program entries describe length and season of the position, rates of pay, desired qualifications, duties, training involved, availability of college credit, and application contacts, procedures, and deadlines. International internships are also listed, as well as specific information for interns working abroad and non-U.S. citizens applying for U.S. internships.

[1829]

Princeton Review-Student Access Guide to America's Top 100 Internships. By Mark Oldman and Samer Hamadeh. New York: Villard, 1995.

Unlike Peterson's *Internships* directory (described above), this listing is selective rather than comprehensive. It describes in detail the "top" 100 internships in America, as selected by the Princeton Review and Student Access. Each program entry (generally three pages) provides information on: application process, selection process, compensation, quality of the work experience, locations, duration, prerequisites, and sources of additional information.

[1830]

Summer Employment Directory of the United States. Princeton, NJ: Peterson's Guides, 1952— . Annual.

Summer employment opportunities often function as internships. For over 30 years, this directory has been providing college students, high school students, and teachers with detailed information on 50,000 summer jobs at resorts, campus, parks, businesses, and government offices in the United States. A short international section is also included. Arrangement is geographical and then by type of employer (camp, restaurant, etc.). Each listing specifies who to contact, application address, payment rates, qualifications needed, and number of openings available. For similar coverage of summer opportunities in foreign countries, see the annual *Directory of Summer Jobs Abroad* (published by Vacation-Work and distributed by Writer's Digest).

Financial Assistance to Special Population Groups

[1831]

AFL-CIO Guide to Union Sponsored Scholarships, Awards, and Student Financial Aid. Washington, DC: AFL-CIO. Annual.

This guide contains a selected list of AFL-CIO sponsored scholarships available from international and national unions, local unions, and AFL-CIO state and local central bodies. It is intended to aid union members, their dependents, and certain other students in the search for financial assistance to cover the cost of attending colleges and other postsecondary institutions. In all, over 2,000 scholarships worth more than $3 million are described.

[1832]

Directory of Financial Aids for Women. By Gail A. Schlachter. El Dorado Hills, CA: Reference Service Press, 1978— . Biennial (Directories of Financial Aid for Special Needs Groups).

First published in 1978, this is the only extensive and regularly updated list of scholarships, fellowships, loans, grants, internships, and awards/prizes designed primarily or exclusively for women. The directory is divided into 3 separate sections: a descriptive list of more than 1,700 national and international financial aid programs set aside for women, an annotated bibliography of 60 key sources that identify financial aid programs, and a set of indexes that provide access by program title, sponsoring organization, geographic coverage, deadline date, and subject.

[1833]

Federal Benefits for Veterans and Dependents. Prep. by the U.S. Veterans Administration. Washington, DC: G.P.O., 1969— . Annual.

This is one of the federal government's all-time best-selling publications. The booklet provides a comprehensive summary of federal government benefits available to veterans and their dependents. It is updated annually and contains information on alcoholism treatment programs, aid for the blind, burial assistance, clothing allowances, compensation for service-connected disabilities, death payments, dental treatment, dependents' education, education and training loans, etc.

[1834]

Financial Aid for the Disabled and Their Families. By Gail A. Schlachter and R. David Weber. El Dorado Hills, CA: Reference Service Press, 1988— . Biennial (Directories of Financial Aid for Special Needs Groups).

This is the first comprehensive and up-to-date listing of scholarships, fellowships, awards, and grants-in-aid that have been established for disabled individuals and their dependents. Each edition describes nearly 800 programs open to this special needs group. The following information is provided for each of these entries: program title, eligibility, financial data, duration, special features, limitations, number awarded, and deadline. Also included in the directory are a list of state sources of educational benefits, addresses of state agencies designed to help the disabled, 60 key sources listing general financial aid directories, and a set of indexes that provide access by program title, sponsoring organization, geographic coverage, subject, specific disability, and deadline date.

[1835]

Financial Aid for Veterans, Military Personnel, and Their Dependents. By Gail A. Schlachter and R. David Weber. El Dorado Hills, CA: Reference Service Press, 1988— . Biennial (Directories of Financial Aid for Special Needs Groups).

Veterans, military personnel, and their dependents (spouses, children, grandchildren, and dependent parents) make up more than one third of America's population today. Each year, public and private agencies set aside billions of dollars in financial aid for these groups. This is the only directory to identify, in one source, all the federal, state, and privately-funded scholarships, fellowships, loans, grants/grants-in-aid, awards, and internships set aside specifically for individuals with ties to the military. More than

950 programs are described in the latest edition. These opportunities are open to applicants at all levels (from high school through postdoctoral) for education, research, travel, training, career development, or emergency situations. The detailed entries are indexed by title, sponsoring organization, geographic coverage, subject, and deadline dates.

[1836]

Minority Funding Set. By Gail A. Schlachter and R. David Weber. El Dorado Hills, CA: Reference Service Press, 1997— . Biennial (Directories of Financial Aid for Special Needs Groups).

This new set replaces Reference Service Press' one-volume *Directory of Financial Aids for Minorities.* Each of the volumes in the set can be purchased separately and focuses on a different ethnic group: *Financial Aid for African Americans* (1,500 funding opportunities described); *Financial Aid for Asian Americans* (nearly 1,100 entries); *Financial Aid for Hispanic Americans* (more than 1,400 entries); and *Financial Aid for Native Americans* nearly 1,800 entries). All types of funding are covered: scholarships, fellowships, loans, grants, awards, and internships. Detailed program entries provide information on contact, purpose, eligibility, remuneration, duration, special features, limitations, number awarded, and deadline date.

Indexes

Program Title Index

Program titles are arranged alphabetically, word by word. To help users select only those programs within their scope of interest, each entry number is preceded by a two–character alphabetical code within parentheses. The first character (capitalized) in the code identifies program type: S = Scholarships; F = Fellowships; L = Loans; G = Grants; A = Awards; and I = Internships. The second character (lower cased) identifies eligible minority groups: i = American Indians; a = Native Alaskans; p = Native Pacific Islanders; n = Native Americans in General. For example, if a program is followed by (S–n, 241, the program is described in the Scholarships section under Native Americans, in entry number 241. If the same program title is followed by another entry number—for example, (L–n) 763—the program is also described in the Loans section, under Native Americans, in entry 763.

AAIA Displaced Homemaker Scholarships, (S–i) 1
AAJA Hawaii Chapter Scholarships, (S–p) 154, (F–p) 466
AAJA Los Angeles General Scholarships, (S–p) 155, (F–p) 467
AAJA–Newhouse National Scholarships, (S–p) 156, (F–p) 468
AAUW Dissertation Fellowships, (G–n) 859
AAUW Founders Distinguished Senior Scholar Award, (A–n) 1442
AAUW Selected Professions Fellowships. See Focus Professions Group Fellowships, entry (F–n) 553
AAUW Summer Fellowships, (G–n) 860
ABC Native American Grants, (S–n) 171, (F–n) 483
ABC Newspaper Internship Program, (I–n) 1521
Abe Fellowship Program, (G–n) 861
Academic Career Awards, (G–n) 862
Academic Excellence Awards in Bilingual Education, (G–n) 863
Academic Research Enhancement Award, (G–n) 864
ACE Fellows Program, (G–n) 865
ACLS Fellowships, (G–n) 866
ADHF/AGA Student Research Fellowships, (G–n) 867
Adolph van Pelt Scholarships, (S–i) 2, (F–i) 380
Adopt–A–Student Minority Scholarship Program. See SNPA Foundation Adopt–A–Student Minority Scholarship Program, entry (S–n) 341
Adoption Opportunities Program Grants, (G–n) 868
Adult Education Grants for Indian Education, (G–i) 788
Advanced Industrial Concepts Materials Science Program, (F–n) 484, (I–n) 1522
Advanced Nurse Education Grants, (G–n) 869
Advanced Technological Education Program, (G–n) 870
AEJMC Communication Theory and Methodology Division Minority Doctoral Scholarship, (F–n) 485
Aerospace Illinois Space Grant Consortium Program, (S–n) 172, (F–n) 486
Agency for Health Care Policy and Research Small Grant Program for Conference Support. See Small Grant Program for Conference Support, entry (G–n) 1323

Agency for Toxic Substances and Disease Registry Clinical Fellowships in Environmental Medicine, (G–n) 871
Agency for Toxic Substances and Disease Registry Faculty Research Participation Program, (G–n) 872
Agency for Toxic Substances and Disease Registry Postgraduate Research Program, (G–n) 873
Agency for Toxic Substances and Disease Registry Student Internship Program, (I–n) 1523
Ahahui Kalakaua Scholarships, (S–p) 157, (F–p) 469
AHCPR Small Project Grant Program, (G–n) 874
AIA Minority/Disadvantaged Scholarship Program, (S–n) 173
AIC Materials Science Program. See Advanced Industrial Concepts Materials Science Program, entries (F–n) 484, (I–n) 1522
AICPA Fellowships for Minority Doctoral Students, (F–n) 487
Air Force Office of Scientific Research Broad Agency Announcement, (G–n) 875
AISF Grants, (S–i) 3, (F–i) 381
AISF Loans, (L–i) 729
Al Medoro Scholarship, (S–n) 174
Al Qöyawayma Award for Excellence in Arts and Science, (S–i) 4, (F–i) 382
Alabama Space Grant Consortium Graduate Fellowship Program, (F–n) 488, (G–n) 876
Alabama Space Grant Consortium Teacher Education Scholarship Program, (S–n) 175
Alabama Space Grant Consortium Undergraduate Scholarship Program, (S–n) 176
Alaska Library Association Scholarship for Graduate Library Studies, (F–a) 452
Alaska Research Award. See John T. Dillon Alaska Research Award, entry (G–n) 1106
Alaska State Council on the Arts Career Opportunity Grants, (G–a) 831
Albert W. Dent Student Scholarship, (F–n) 489

S–Scholarships   F–Fellowships   L–Loans   G–Grants   A–Awards   I–Internships
i–American Indians   a–Native Alaskans   p–Native Pacific Islanders   n–Native Americans in General

529

Albuquerque Journal Publishers' Scholarship Fund for Minorities, (S–n) 177, (I–n) 1524

Alexander Hollaender Distinguished Postdoctoral Fellowship Program, (G–n) 877

Alexander Sisson Award, (G–n) 878

Alexander Thweatt Sales Internship Program, (I–n) 1525

All Indian Pueblo Council Jobs Training Partnership Act, (S–i) 5, (I–i) 1490

All Indian Pueblo Council Scholarship Grant Program, (S–i) 6

All Indian Pueblo Council Summer Youth Employment Program, (I–i) 1491

Allan & Joyce Niederman Award, (A–i) 1414

Allan V. Cox Award, (G–n) 879

Allen Fellowships. See Frances C. Allen Fellowships, entry (G–i) 801

Alliances for Minority Participation Grants, (G–n) 880

Alzheimer's Association Investigator–Initiated Research Grants, (G–n) 881

Amelia Kemp Memorial Scholarship, (S–n) 178, (F–n) 490

American Association of University Women Dissertation Fellowships. See AAUW Dissertation Fellowships, entry (G–n) 859

American Association of University Women Founders Distinguished Senior Scholar Award. See AAUW Founders Distinguished Senior Scholar Award, entry (A–n) 1442

American Association of University Women Selected Professions Fellowships. See Focus Professions Group Fellowships, entry (F–n) 553

American Association of University Women Summer Fellowships. See AAUW Summer Fellowships, entry (G–n) 860

American Baptist Church Native American Grants. See ABC Native American Grants, entries (S–n) 171, (F–n) 483

American Chemical Society Scholars Program, (S–i) 7, (S–a) 138

American Council of Learned Societies Fellowships. See ACLS Fellowships, entry (G–n) 866

American Council on Education Fellows Program. See ACE Fellows Program, entry (G–n) 865

American Dental Hygienists' Association Institute Minority Scholarship, (S–n) 179, (F–n) 491

American Digestive Health Foundation/AGA Student Research Fellowships. See ADHF/AGA Student Research Fellowships, entry (G–n) 867

American Economic Association/Federal Reserve System Minority Fellowship Program, (F–n) 492, (I–n) 1526

American Gastroenterological Association Student Research Fellowships. See ADHF/AGA Student Research Fellowships, entry (G–n) 867

American Heart Association Established Investigator Grant, (G–n) 882

American Heart Association Grant-in-Aid, (G–n) 883

American Heart Association Scientist Development Grant, (G–n) 884

American Heart Association Student Research Program, (I–n) 1527

American Indian, Alaska Native, and Native Hawaiian Mental Health Research Grants, (G–n) 885

American Indian Heritage Foundation Scholarship, (S–i) 8

American Indian Museum Studies Program, (G–i) 789, (G–a) 832, (I–i) 1492, (I–a) 1514

American Indian Program, (G–i) 790

American Indian Scholarship Fund Grants. See AISF Grants, entries (S–i) 3, (F–i) 381

American Indian Scholarship Fund Loans. See AISF Loans, entry (L–i) 729

American Indian Scholarships, (S–i) 9, (F–i) 383

American Indian Studies Postdoctoral and Visiting Scholars Fellowship Program, (G–i) 791

American Institute of Architects Minority/Disadvantaged Scholarship Program. See AIA Minority/Disadvantaged Scholarship Program, entry (S–n) 173

American Institute of Certified Public Accountants Fellowships for Minority Doctoral Students. See AICPA Fellowships for Minority Doctoral Students, entry (F–n) 487

American Library Association Minority Fellowship Program, (G–n) 886

American Meteorological Society Industry Graduate Fellowships, (F–n) 493, (I–n) 1528

American Meteorological Society Industry Undergraduate Scholarships, (S–n) 180

American Meteorological Society Minority Scholarships, (S–n) 181

American Meteorological Society 75th Anniversary Scholarship. See AMS 75th Anniversary Scholarship, entry (S–n) 183

American Nurses Association Research Training Fellowship for Minority Nurses. See Research Training Fellowship for Minority Nurses, entry (F–n) 690

American Philological Association Minority Scholarship, (S–n) 182

American Philosophical Society Library Mellon Resident Research Fellowships, (G–i) 792

American Political Science Association Ph.D. Fellowships for Minority Students, (F–n) 494

American Psychiatric Association/Glaxo Wellcome Fellowship Program. See APA/Glaxo Wellcome Fellowship Program, entry (I–n) 1532

American Society for Engineering Education Minorities in Engineering Award. See ASEE Minorities in Engineering Award, entry (A–n) 1453

American Society for Microbiology Faculty Fellowship Program, (G–n) 887

American Society for Microbiology/NIGMS Minority Undergraduate Research Fellowship. See ASM/NIGMS Minority Undergraduate Research Fellowship, entry (G–n) 905

American Society of Mechanical Engineers Graduate Teaching Fellowship. See ASME Graduate Teaching Fellowship, entry (F–n) 498

American Society of Mechanical Engineers Minority Leadership Program, (I–n) 1529

American Speech–Language–Hearing Foundation Young Scholars Award for Minority Students, (F–n) 495

AMS 75th Anniversary Scholarship, (S–n) 183

Anchorage Daily News Internship, (I–n) 1530

Anderson Memorial Scholarship Program. See A.T. Anderson Memorial Scholarship Program, entries (S–i) 11, (F–i) 385

Andrew W. Mellon Fellowships in Humanistic Studies, (F–n) 496

Andrew W. Mellon Postdoctoral Fellowships in the Humanities at Bryn Mawr College, (G–n) 888

Anisfield–Wolf Book Award in Race Relations, (A–n) 1443

ANL Laboratory–Graduate Research Appointments, (G–n) 889, (I–n) 1531

Annual Women of Color Psychologies Award, (A–n) 1444

Antarctic Research Program, (G–n) 890

Antoinette Lierman Medlin Scholarship Award, (G–n) 891

APA/Glaxo Wellcome Fellowship Program, (I–n) 1532

Aplan Award, (A–i) 1415

S–Scholarships   **F–Fellowships**   **L–Loans**   **G–Grants**   **A–Awards**   **I–Internships**

i–American Indians   **a–Native Alaskans**   **p–Native Pacific Islanders**   **n–Native Americans in General**

S–Scholarships	**F–Fellowships**	**L–Loans**	**G–Grants**	**A–Awards**	**I–Internships**
i–American Indians	**a–Native Alaskans**	**p–Native Pacific Islanders**		**n–Native Americans in General**	

S–Scholarships	F–Fellowships	L–Loans	G–Grants	A–Awards	I–Internships
i–American Indians	a–Native Alaskans		p–Native Pacific Islanders		n–Native Americans in General

Cox Minority Journalism Scholarship Program, (S–n) 217, (I–n) 1573

C.R. Bard Foundation Prize, (F–n) 526, (A–n) 1459

Crawford Minority Scholarship. See Shirley Crawford Minority Scholarship, entry (F–n) 698

Creation and Presentation Grants to Organizations, (G–n) 967

Creek Nation Higher Education Undergraduate Grant Program, (S–i) 24

Creek Nation Tribal Funds Grant. See Muscogee (Creek) Nation Tribal Funds Grant Program, entry (S–i) 75

Creek Nation Tribal Incentive Grant Program. See Muscogee (Creek) Nation Tribal Incentive Grant Program, entry (S–i) 76

Crusade Scholarship Program, (F–n) 527

C.S. Kilner Leadership Award, (A–n) 1460

CSU Forgivable Loan/Doctoral Incentive Program, (F–n) 528, (L–n) 751

CSWS Visiting Scholar Program, (G–n) 968

CT&M Division Minority Doctoral Student Scholarship, (F–n) 529

Cuffe Memorial Fellowships. See Paul Cuffe Memorial Fellowships, entry (G–i) 822

Culturally Diverse Institutions Undergraduate Student Fellowships, (S–i) 25, (I–i) 1496

Curry Award for Girls and Young Women. See Eleanor Curry Award for Girls and Young Women, entry (S–n) 229

Cutler Fellowship in Consumer Studies. See Carley—Canoyer—Cutler Fellowship in Consumer Studies, entry (F–n) 512

Damon Walsh Memorial Award, (A–n) 1461

D'Arcy McNickle Center Summer Institute for Secondary and Tribal College Teachers, (G–i) 796

David A. DeBolt Teacher Shortage Scholarships, (S–n) 218, (F–n) 530, (L–n) 752

David Oakerhater Merit Fellowship. See ECIM Scholarships, entries (F–i) 392, (F–a) 454

Davis Educational Fund. See Unto These Hills Educational Fund Scholarship, entry (S–i) 126

The Day Scholarship for Minority Journalists, (S–n) 219, (I–n) 1574

DeBolt Teacher Shortage Scholarships. See David A. DeBolt Teacher Shortage Scholarships, entries (S–n) 218, (F–n) 530, (L–n) 752

Decorah Memorial Award. See Diane Decorah Memorial Award, entries (A–i) 1420, (A–a) 1440

Delaware NASA Space Grant Undergraduate Tuition Scholarships, (S–n) 220

Delware Space Grant Consortium Graduate Student Fellowships. See NASA/DESGC Graduate Student Fellowships, entry (F–n) 638

Delware Space Grant Consortium Undergraduate Summer Scholarships. See NASA/DESGC Undergraduate Summer Scholarships, entry (G–n) 1191

Demonstration Grants for Indian Children, (G–i) 797

Denali Press Award, (A–n) 1462

Dent Student Scholarship. See Albert W. Dent Student Scholarship, entry (F–n) 489

Denver Metro Media Alliance Diversity Scholarship. See CHSPA/Denver Metro Media Alliance Diversity Scholarship, entry (S–n) 206

Department of Agriculture Research Apprenticeship Program for Minority High School Students. See USDA Research Apprenticeship Program for Minority High School Students, entry (I–n) 1766

Department of Agriculture Small Business Innovation Research Program. See USDA Small Business Innovation Research Program, entry (G–n) 1386

Department of Agriculture Summer Intern Program. See USDA Summer Intern Program, entry (I–n) 1767

Department of Defense Augmentation Awards for Science and Engineering Research Training, (F–n) 531, (G–n) 969

Department of Defense Infrastructure Support Program for Historically Black Colleges and Universities and Minority Institutions, (G–n) 970

Department of Defense Small Business Innovation Research Grants, (G–n) 971

Department of Defense Small Business Technology Transfer Grants, (G–n) 972

Department of Education Small Business Innovation Research Grants, (G–n) 973

Department of Energy Distinguished Postdoctoral Research Program, (F–n) 532, (G–n) 974

Department of Energy Faculty Research Participation Program, (G–n) 975

Department of Energy Graduate Student Research Participation Program, (G–n) 976

Department of Energy Laboratory Cooperative Postgraduate Research Training Program, (G–n) 977

Department of Energy Laboratory Graduate Participation Program, (G–n) 978

Department of Energy Minority Institution Research Travel Grants, (G–n) 979

Department of Energy Minority Technical Education Program, (S–i) 26, (S–p) 160

Department of Energy Research Travel Contracts, (G–n) 980

Department of Energy Small Business Innovation Research Grants. See DOE Small Business Innovation Research Grants, entry (G–n) 991

Department of Energy Small Business Technology Transfer Grants. See DOE Small Business Technology Transfer Grants, entry (G–n) 992

Department of Energy Student Research Participation Program, (I–n) 1575

Department of State Student Intern Program. See United States Department of State Student Intern Program, entry (I–n) 1759

Department of Transportation Short Term Lending Program. See DOT Short Term Lending Program, entry (L–n) 754

Department of Transportation Small Business Innovation Research Grants, (G–n) 981

DESGC Graduate Student Fellowships. See NASA/DESGC Graduate Student Fellowships, entry (F–n) 638

DESGC Undergraduate Summer Scholarships. See NASA/DESGC Undergraduate Summer Scholarships, entry (G–n) 1191

Detroit Free Press Minority Journalism Scholarship, (S–n) 221, (I–n) 1576

Developmental Grants for Minority Collaborative Projects, (G–n) 982

Diane Decorah Memorial Award, (A–i) 1420, (A–a) 1440

Diederich Award, (A–i) 1421

Diederich Improvement Award, (A–i) 1422

Diederich Landscape Awards, (A–i) 1423

S–Scholarships	F–Fellowships	L–Loans	G–Grants	A–Awards	I–Internships
i–American Indians	a–Native Alaskans	p–Native Pacific Islanders		n–Native Americans in General	

Environmental Management Research Participation Program for the U.S. Army Environmental Center, (G–n) 1007

Environmental Monitoring Systems Laboratory Research Participation Program, (G–n) 1008

Environmental Protection Agency Small Business Innovation Research Grants. *See* EPA Small Business Innovation Research Grants, entry (G–n) 1011

Environmental Protection Agency Tribal Lands Environmental Science Scholarship. *See* EPA Tribal Lands Environmental Science Scholarship, entries (S–i) 30, (F–i) 396

Environmental Science and Engineering Fellowships, (G–n) 1009

Environmental Science and Management Fellows Program, (F–n) 543, (G–n) 1010

EPA Small Business Innovation Research Grants, (G–n) 1011

EPA Tribal Lands Environmental Science Scholarship, (S–i) 30, (F–i) 396

Epidemiologic Research Studies of Acquired Immunodeficiency Syndrome (AIDS) and Human Immunodeficiency Virus (HIV) Infection in Selected Population Groups, (G–n) 1012

Epilepsy Foundation Health Sciences Student Fellowships, (G–n) 1013

Epilepsy Foundation of America Junior Investigator Research Grants, (G–n) 1014

Epilepsy Foundation of America Research Training Fellowships, (F–n) 544, (G–n) 1015

Epilepsy Foundation of America Research/Clinical Training Fellowships, (F–n) 545, (G–n) 1016

Episcopal Asian American Ministry Leadership Development Fund, (F–p) 472

Episcopal Council of Indian Ministries Scholarships. *See* ECIM Scholarships, entries (F–i) 392, (F–a) 454

Equal Rights Advocates Law Clerkships, (I–n) 1580

Equality Award, (A–n) 1465

Erickson Award. *See* Bonnie Erickson Award, entry (A–i) 1419

Establishment of Departments of Family Medicine Grants, (G–n) 1017

ETA Research and Demonstration Grants, (G–n) 1018

Ethnic Diversity Scholarships, (S–n) 230

Ethnic Leadership Supplemental Grants. *See* Racial Ethnic Leadership Supplemental Grants, entry (F–n) 686

Ethnic Materials Information Exchange Round Table Multicultural Award. *See* EMIERT/Gale Research Multicultural Award, entry (A–n) 1464

Ethnic Minority Bachelor's Scholarships, (S–n) 231

Ethnic Minority Master's Scholarships, (F–n) 546

Ethnic Minority Postgraduate Scholarship Program. *See* NCAA Ethnic Minority Postgraduate Scholarship Program, entry (F–n) 653

Ethnic Minority Researcher and Mentorship Grants. *See* Oncology Nursing Foundation Ethnic Minority Researcher and Mentorship Grants, entry (G–n) 1249

ETS Postdoctoral Fellowship Program, (G–n) 1019

ETS Summer Internships in Program Direction, (I–n) 1581

ETS Summer Program in Research for Graduate Students, (I–n) 1582

Evangelical Lutheran Church in America Educational Grant Program. *See* ELCA Educational Grant Program, entry (F–n) 541

Evangelical Scholars Program. *See* Pew Evangelical Scholars Program, entry (G–n) 1259

Evans Memorial Fund. *See* Blossom Kalama Evans Memorial Fund, entries (S–p) 159, (F–p) 471

Even Start Family Literacy Program for Federally Recognized Indian Tribes and Tribal Organizations, (G–i) 798

Excellence in Minority Fiction Award. *See* Charles H. and N. Mildred Nilon Excellence in Minority Fiction Award, entry (A–n) 1457

Extended Opportunity Programs and Services Grants, (S–n) 232

Extended Opportunity Programs and Services Loans, (L–n) 755

Extramural Associates Program: Faculty Research Enhancement Support Program. *See* Faculty Research Enhancement Support Program, entry (G–n) 1024

Extramural Associates Program: Sponsored Research Infrastructure Program. *See* Sponsored Research Infrastructure Program, entry (G–n) 1336

Faculty Awards for Research, (G–n) 1020

Faculty Development Awards. *See* MORE Faculty Development Awards, entry (G–n) 1179

Faculty Development Fellowship Program, (F–n) 547, (L–n) 756

Faculty Development in Family Medicine Grants, (G–n) 1021

Faculty Development in General Internal Medicine and General Pediatrics Grants, (G–n) 1022

Faculty Early Career Development Program, (G–n) 1023

Faculty Fellowship Program at the High Temperature Materials Laboratory. *See* High Temperature Materials Laboratory Faculty Fellowship Program, entry (G–n) 1069

Faculty Research Enhancement Support Program, (G–n) 1024

Faculty Research Participation Program at the Agency for Toxic Substances and Disease Registry. *See* Agency for Toxic Substances and Disease Registry Faculty Research Participation Program, entry (G–n) 872

Faculty Research Participation Program at the Bureau of Engraving and Printing. *See* Bureau of Engraving and Printing Faculty Research Participation Program, entry (G–n) 922

Faculty Research Participation Program at the National Center for Toxicological Research. *See* National Center for Toxicological Research Faculty Research Participation Program, entry (G–n) 1196

Faculty Research Participation Program at the Naval Air Warfare Center Training Systems Division. *See* Naval Air Warfare Center Training Systems Division Faculty Research Participation Program, entry (G–n) 1214

Fahnestock Memorial Award. *See* Robert K. Fahnestock Memorial Award, entry (G–n) 1297

Fairchild Minority Access Program, (I–n) 1583

Falmouth Institute Scholarship, (S–i) 31

Family Planning Services Grants, (G–n) 1025

Family Planning Services Training Grants, (G–n) 1026

Fannie Lou Hamer Award, (G–n) 1027

Faris Higher Education Fund. *See* Norman TeCube Sr. Higher Education Fund, entries (S–i) 88, (F–i) 430

Farm Ownership Loans for Socially Disadvantaged Persons, (L–n) 757

Fayetteville Observer–Times Internships, (I–n) 1584

Federal Reserve System Minority Fellowship Program. *See* American Economic Association/Federal Reserve System Minority Fellowship Program, entries (F–n) 492, (I–n) 1526

Federal Transit Administration Human Resources Program, (G–n) 1028

Fel–Pro Automotive Technicians Scholarship Program, (S–n) 233

S–Scholarships	F–Fellowships	L–Loans	G–Grants	A–Awards	I–Internships
i–American Indians	a–Native Alaskans	p–Native Pacific Islanders		n–Native Americans in General	

S–Scholarships	F–Fellowships	L–Loans	G–Grants	A–Awards	I–Internships
i–American Indians	a–Native Alaskans		p–Native Pacific Islanders		n–Native Americans in General

F33 Awards. *See* National Research Service Award Senior Fellowships, entries (F–n) 647, (L–n) 775

F36 Awards. *See* Minority Access to Research Careers (MARC) Visiting Scientist Fellowships, entry (G–n) 1162

F37 Awards. *See* Medical Informatics Research Training Awards, entry (F–n) 615

F38 Awards. *See* NLM Fellowship in Applied Informatics, entry (G–n) 1228

Gaius Charles Bolin Fellowships for Minority Graduate Students, (G–n) 1048

Gale Research Multicultural Award. *See* EMIERT/Gale Research Multicultural Award, entry (A–n) 1464

Garrison/Visa Minority Internship. *See* Zina Garrison/Visa Minority Internship, entry (I–n) 1776

Garth Reeves Jr. Memorial Scholarships, (S–n) 239, (F–n) 560

GEM M.S. Engineering Fellowship Program, (F–i) 398, (I–i) 1497

GEM Ph.D. Engineering Fellowship Program, (F–i) 399

GEM Ph.D. Science Fellowship Program, (F–i) 400, (I–i) 1498

Gentry Biodiversity Fellowship. *See* Science, Engineering, and Diplomacy Fellowships, entry (G–n) 1308

Geological Society of America General Research Grants Program, (G–n) 1049

George A. Strait Minority Stipend, (F–n) 561

George M. Brooker Collegiate Scholarship for Minorities, (S–n) 240, (F–n) 562

Georges Lurcy Research Fellowship in Economics, (G–n) 1050

Gerber Prize for Excellence in Pediatrics, (F–n) 563, (A–n) 1468

Geriatric Education Centers Grants, (G–n) 1051

Getty Grant Program Multicultural Internships, (I–n) 1601

Getz Fellows. *See* ARTS Jazz Competition Scholarships, entries (S–n) 185, (A–n) 1446

Giles Minority Scholarship. *See* Louise Giles Minority Scholarship, entry (F–n) 602

Gillespie Scholarship. *See* Shields–Gillespie Scholarship, entry (G–n) 1319

Gillihan Award. *See* Dr. and Mrs. Jim Gillihan Award, entry (A–i) 1424

Girls Sports Travel Fund, (G–n) 1052

Global Change Graduate Fellowships, (F–n) 564, (I–n) 1602

GOALS Fellowships, (F–n) 565

Golden State Minority Scholarships, (S–n) 241, (F–n) 566

Gough Scholarship. *See* Helen Gough Scholarship, entry (S–i) 43

Gowers Research/Clinical Training Fellowships. *See* William Gowers Research/Clinical Training Fellowships, entries (F–n) 723, (G–n) 1397

Graduate Fellowship Program in Bilingual Education, (F–n) 567

Graduate Fellowships for American Indian and Alaskan Native Students, (F–i) 401, (F–a) 455

Graduate Internship Program at the U.S. Army Center for Health Promotion and Preventive Medicine. *See* U.S. Army Center for Health Promotion and Preventive Medicine Graduate Internship Program, entry (I–n) 1763

Graduate Opportunities for Advanced Level Studies Fellowships. *See* GOALS Fellowships, entry (F–n) 565

Graduate Research Participation Program at the Naval Air Warfare Center Training Systems Division. *See* Naval Air Warfare Center Training Systems Division Graduate Research Participation Program, entry (I–n) 1677

Graduate Scholarship in Women's Studies. *See* Pergamon—NWSA Graduate Scholarship in Women's Studies, entry (G–n) 1258

Graduate Student Research Participation Program at the National Center for Toxicological Research. *See* National Center for Toxicological Research Graduate Student Research Participation Program, entry (I–n) 1669

Graduate Training in Family Medicine Grants, (G–n) 1053

Graef Memorial Scholarship. *See* Irving Graef Memorial Scholarship, entries (F–n) 587, (A–n) 1470

Grand Portage Critical Professions Program, (S–i) 35, (F–i) 402

Grand Portage Scholarship Program, (S–i) 36

Grant Foreman Scholarships. *See* Louie LeFlore/Grant Foreman Scholarships, entry (S–i) 59

Grant Foundation Faculty Scholars Program. *See* William T. Grant Foundation Faculty Scholars Program, entry (G–n) 1398

Grants for Health Services Dissertation Research, (G–n) 1054

Grants for Improving Doctoral Dissertation Research, (G–n) 1055

Grants for Research in American Indian Linguistics and Ethnohistory. *See* Phillips Fund Grants for Native American Research, entries (G–i) 823, (G–a) 849

Grants for Residency Training and Advanced Education in the General Practice of Dentistry, (F–n) 568

Grants for State Loan Repayment Programs, (G–n) 1056

Grants for the Minority Fellowship Faculty Program, (F–n) 569

Grants to Combat Violent Crimes against Women, (G–i) 802

Grants to Indian Tribal Organizations for Supportive and Nutritional Services for Older Indians, (G–i) 803

Grassroots Arts Program, (G–n) 1057

Grau Undergraduate Scholarship. *See* Dr. Pedro Grau Undergraduate Scholarship, entry (S–n) 223

Great Plains Film Festival Awards, (A–i) 1425

Greenebaum Fund Scholarship. *See* Edward deZulueta Greenebaum Fund Scholarship, entry (S–n) 228

Greensboro News & Record Summer Internships, (I–n) 1603

Gretchen L. Blechschmidt Award, (G–n) 1058

Guaranteed Farm Operating Loans for Socially Disadvantaged Persons, (L–n) 759

Gulf Coast Research Laboratory Minority Summer Grant Program, (S–n) 242, (F–n) 570

G12 Awards. *See* Research Centers in Minority Institutions Awards, entry (G–n) 1284

Hamer Award. *See* Fannie Lou Hamer Award, entry (G–n) 1027

HANA Scholars Program, (S–n) 243, (F–n) 571

Hanke Fellowship for Graduate Research on Community Associations. *See* Byron Hanke Fellowship for Graduate Research on Community Associations, entry (G–n) 924

Hanks, Jr. Scholarship in Meteorology. *See* Howard H. Hanks, Jr. Scholarship in Meteorology, entry (S–n) 248

Harold T. Stearns Fellowship Award, (G–n) 1059

Harris Fellowships. *See* Patricia Roberts Harris Fellowships, entry (F–n) 676

Harry and Bertha Bronstein Scholarship Fund, (S–n) 244

Hartford Courant Minority Internships, (I–n) 1604

Hartley Memorial Fellowship. *See* Robert W. Hartley Memorial Fellowship, entry (G–n) 1298

Hattiesburg American Internship, (I–n) 1605

Hawai'i Space Grant Consortium Graduate Fellowship Program, (G–n) 1060

S–Scholarships　　　**F–Fellowships**　　　**L–Loans**　　　**G–Grants**　　　**A–Awards**　　　**I–Internships**
i–American Indians　　　**a–Native Alaskans**　　　**p–Native Pacific Islanders**　　　**n–Native Americans in General**

S–Scholarships   **F–Fellowships**   **L–Loans**   **G–Grants**   **A–Awards**   **I–Internships**
i–American Indians   **a–Native Alaskans**   **p–Native Pacific Islanders**   **n–Native Americans in General**

"I Have a Dream" Foundation Scholarships, (S–n) 251

Ida M. Pope Memorial Trust Scholarships, (S–p) 162

Idaho Minority and "At Risk" Student Scholarship, (S–n) 252

Idaho Space Grant Consortium Higher Education and Research Program, (S–n) 253, (F–n) 576, (G–n) 1075

IHS Loan Repayment Program, (G–i) 805, (G–a) 838

Illinois Consortium for Educational Opportunity Program, (F–n) 577

Illinois Minority Graduate Incentive Program, (F–n) 578

Imamura Memorial Scholarship. See Peter Imamura Memorial Scholarship, entries (S–p) 168, (F–p) 478

Incentive Grants Program, (S–i) 52

Incentive Scholarship and Grant Program for Native Americans—Merit-Based Scholarships. See North Carolina Incentive Scholarship and Grant Program for Native Americans—Merit-Based Scholarships, entry (S–i) 89

Incentive Scholarship and Grant Program for Native Americans—Need-Based Grants. See North Carolina Incentive Scholarship and Grant Program for Native Americans—Need-Based Grants, entries (S–i) 90, (F–i) 431

Independent Colleges of Southern California Scholarship Program, (S–n) 254

Independent Scientist Awards, (G–n) 1076

Indian and Native American Employment and Training Program, (G–i) 806, (G–a) 839

Indian Child Welfare Act Grants for Off-Reservation Indian Organizations, (G–i) 807

Indian Environmental Regulatory Enhancement Projects, (G–i) 808, (G–a) 840

Indian Fellowship Program, (S–i) 53, (S–a) 146, (F–i) 410, (F–a) 459, (L–i) 731, (L–a) 743

Indian Health Service Loan Repayment Program. See IHS Loan Repayment Program, entries (G–i) 805, (G–a) 838

Indian Loan Guaranty Fund, (L–i) 732, (L–a) 744

Indian Nurse Scholarship Awards, (S–i) 54

Indian Professional Development Grants, (F–i) 411, (L–i) 733

Indian Tribal Loans for Purchase of Land, (L–i) 734, (L–a) 745

Indian Vocational Education Program, (G–i) 809

Indiana Professional Chapter of SPJ Minority Scholarship, (S–n) 255

Indiana Space Grant Consortium Fellowships, (S–n) 256, (F–n) 579

Indiana Space Grant Consortium Research Grants, (G–n) 1077

Indianapolis Star Minority Internship, (I–n) 1610

Individual Dentist Scientist Awards, (F–n) 580

Individual East European Language Training Grants, (F–n) 581

Individual Fellowships in Health Services Research. See National Research Service Award Individual Fellowships in Health Services Research, entries (L–n) 773, (G–n) 1209

Individual Predoctoral National Research Service Awards for M.D./Ph.D. Fellows, (F–n) 582

Industrial Hygiene Graduate Fellowship Program, (F–n) 583, (I–n) 1611

Industry Research Scholar Awards, (G–n) 1078

Industry-Based Graduate Research Assistantships and Cooperative Fellowships in the Mathematical Sciences, (G–n) 1079, (I–n) 1612

Informal Science Education Program, (G–n) 1080

Information Handling Services/SAE Women Engineers Committee Scholarship, (S–n) 257

Initiative for Minority Student Development, (G–n) 1081

Initiative for Minority Students: Bridges to the Baccalaureate Degree Program, (G–n) 1082

Initiative for Minority Students: Bridges to the Doctoral Degree Program, (G–n) 1083

Inner-City Ventures Fund, (L–n) 760

Inouye Memorial Scholarship. See Ken Inouye Memorial Scholarship, entries (S–n) 268, (F–n) 593

INROADS/College Internship, (I–n) 1613

Institute for Journalism Education Editing Program for Minority Journalists. See Maynard Institute Editing Program for Minority Journalists, entries (F–n) 612, (I–n) 1644

Institute for Journalism Education Management Training Program. See Maynard Institute Management Training Program, entry (F–n) 613

Institute for Women's Policy Research Fellowships, (I–n) 1614

Institute of Early American History and Culture Postdoctoral Fellowship, (G–n) 1084

Institution-Wide Reform of Undergraduate Education in Science Mathematics, Engineering, and Technology. See Course and Curriculum Development Program, entry (G–n) 966

Institutional Dentist Scientist Awards, (F–n) 584, (G–n) 1085

Institutional Development Awards, (G–n) 1086

Instructional Materials Development Program, (G–n) 1087

Instrumentation and Laboratory Improvement Program, (G–n) 1088

Integrating Undergraduate Education in Science and Humanities. See Course and Curriculum Development Program, entry (G–n) 966

Intern Investment Program. See USAID Intern Investment Program, entry (I–n) 1765

International Clinical Research Fellowships. See William G. Lennox International Clinical Research Fellowships, entry (F–n) 722

International Migration Dissertation Fellowships, (G–n) 1089

International Migration Minority Summer Dissertation Workshop, (G–n) 1090

International Migration Postdoctoral Fellowships, (G–n) 1091

International Migration Research Planning Grants, (G–n) 1092

International Order of the King's Daughters and Sons North American Indian Scholarship Program, (S–i) 55

International Predissertation Fellowship Program Advanced Disciplinary Training Fellowships, (F–n) 585

International Predissertation Fellowship Program Standard Fellowships, (F–n) 586

International Security and Arms Control Postdoctoral Fellowships, (G–n) 1093

International Security and Arms Control Predoctoral Fellowships, (G–n) 1094

International Security and Arms Control Science Fellows Program, (G–n) 1095

Internships for Diversity in the Museum Profession, (I–n) 1615

Introduction to Biomedical Research Program, (G–n) 1096

Irene Ryan Acting Scholarships, (S–n) 258, (A–n) 1469

Iron Cloud Family Award, (A–i) 1426

Irvine Minority Scholars, (G–i) 810, (G–n) 1097

Irving Graef Memorial Scholarship, (F–n) 587, (A–n) 1470

Ivy League–Public Information Internship, (I–n) 1616

IWPR Fellowships. See Institute for Women's Policy Research Fellowships, entry (I–n) 1614

S–Scholarships	F–Fellowships	L–Loans	G–Grants	A–Awards	I–Internships
i–American Indians	a–Native Alaskans	p–Native Pacific Islanders		n–Native Americans in General	

J. Hoover Mackin Research Grants, (G–n) 1098

J. Paul Getty Trust Fund for the Visual Arts, (G–n) 1099

J. Robert Oppenheimer Fellows Program, (G–n) 1100

Jackie Joyner Kersee/Ray Ban Minority Internship, (I–n) 1617

Jackie Robinson Scholarship, (S–n) 259

Jackson Award. See Sara Jackson Award, entry (G–n) 1305

Jackson Research/Clinical Training Fellowships. See John Hughlings Jackson Research/Clinical Training Fellowships, entries (F–n) 589, (G–n) 1104

Jackson Scholarship Award for Ethnic Minority Gifted/Talented Students with Disabilities. See Stanley E. Jackson Scholarship Award for Ethnic Minority Gifted/Talented Students with Disabilities, entry (S–n) 348

Jackson Scholarship Award for Ethnic Minority Students with Disabilities. See Stanley E. Jackson Scholarship Award for Ethnic Minority Students with Disabilities, entry (S–n) 349

Jacob K. Javits Gifted and Talented Students Education Program, (G–n) 1101

Jacobs Research Funds Small Grants Program, (G–i) 811, (G–a) 841

James A. Rawley Prize, (A–n) 1471

James B. Black College Scholarships, (S–n) 260

James Comer Minority Research Fellowship for Medical Students, (I–n) 1618

James E. Webb Internships, (I–n) 1619

James G.K. McClure Educational and Development Fund Scholarships, (S–n) 261

James H. Robinson Memorial Prize in Surgery, (A–n) 1472

Jane Whitman Women in the Workplace Fund. See Chicago Foundation for Women Grant Program, entry (G–n) 944

Jang Youth Leadership Fund. See Susan Jang Youth Leadership Fund, entry (G–n) 1349

Japan Advanced Research Grants, (G–n) 1102

Japan Studies Dissertation Workshop, (G–n) 1103

Jasco Tools Incentive Program, (S–n) 262

Jeanne Spurlock Minority Medical Student Clinical Fellowship in Child and Adolescent Psychiatry, (I–n) 1620

Jeanne Spurlock Research Fellowship in Drug Abuse and Addiction for Minority Medical Students, (I–n) 1621

Jessie Barrington Educational Fund. See Richard and Jessie Barrington Educational Fund, entry (S–i) 108

Jim Gillihan Award. See Dr. and Mrs. Jim Gillihan Award, entry (A–i) 1424

Jimmy A. Young Memorial Scholarships, (S–n) 263

JoAnne Katherine Johnson Award for Unusual Achievement in Mathematics or Science, (A–n) 1473

John and Muriel Landis Scholarship Award, (S–n) 264, (F–n) 588

John Carter Brown Library Associates Fellowship, (G–i) 812, (G–a) 842

John Carter Brown Library Long–Term Research Fellowships, (G–i) 813, (G–a) 843

John Carter Brown Library Short–Term Research Fellowships, (F–i) 412, (F–a) 460, (G–i) 814, (G–a) 844

John Hughlings Jackson Research/Clinical Training Fellowships, (F–n) 589, (G–n) 1104

John M. Olin Postdoctoral Fellowships in U.S. Military History and International Security, (G–n) 1105

John Ross Foundation Scholarships, (S–p) 163, (F–p) 473

John T. Dillon Alaska Research Award, (G–n) 1106

Johnny Strickland Memorial Scholarship, (S–i) 56

Johnson Award for Unusual Achievement in Mathematics or Science. See JoAnne Katherine Johnson Award for Unusual Achievement in Mathematics or Science, entry (A–n) 1473

Joint Seminars and Workshops. See NSF Joint Seminars and Workshops, entry (G–n) 1239

Jointly Sponsored NIH Predoctoral Training Program in the Neurosciences, (F–n) 590, (G–n) 1107

Joseph E. Murray Award, (G–n) 1108

Joseph Ehrenreich Scholarships, (S–n) 265

Joseph L. Fisher Dissertation Fellowships, (G–n) 1109

Joseph Shankman Award, (G–n) 1110

Journalism Career Development Workshop Scholarships. See Philadelphia Inquirer Journalism Career Development Workshop Scholarships, entry (S–n) 325

Joyce Niederman Award. See Allan & Joyce Niederman Award, entry (A–i) 1414

Kaiser Media Internships in Urban Health Reporting, (I–n) 1622

Kaiulani Home for Girls Trust Scholarship, (S–p) 164, (F–p) 474

Kala Singh Memorial Scholarship, (F–n) 591

Kamehameha Schools Bishop Estate Scholarships, (S–p) 165, (F–p) 475

Kansas Ethnic Minority Fellowship, (F–n) 592, (L–n) 761

Kansas Ethnic Minority Scholarship Program, (S–n) 266

Kansas Teacher Scholarship, (S–n) 267, (L–n) 762

Katrin H. Lamon Fellowship, (G–n) 1111

Kemp Memorial Scholarship. See Amelia Kemp Memorial Scholarship, entries (S–n) 178, (F–n) 490

Ken Inouye Memorial Scholarship, (S–n) 268, (F–n) 593

Kennedy Book Awards. See Robert F. Kennedy Book Awards, entry (A–n) 1485

Kennedy Fisheries Research and Development Grants. See Saltonstall–Kennedy Fisheries Research and Development Grants, entry (G–n) 1304

Kennedy Journalism Awards. See Robert F. Kennedy Journalism Awards, entry (A–n) 1486

Kentucky Foundation for Women Organizational Grants, (G–n) 1112

Kentucky Space Grant Consortium Graduate Fellowships, (F–n) 594

Kentucky Space Grant Consortium Research Grants, (G–n) 1113

Kentucky Space Grant Consortium Support for Teacher Workshops, (G–n) 1114

Kentucky Space Grant Consortium Undergraduate Scholarships, (S–n) 269

Kersee/Ray Ban Minority Internship. See Jackie Joyner Kersee/Ray Ban Minority Internship, entry (I–n) 1617

Kilner Leadership Award. See C.S. Kilner Leadership Award, entry (A–n) 1460

King, Chavez, Parks Visiting Professors Program. See Martin Luther King, Jr., Cesar Chavez, Rosa Parks Visiting Professors Program, entry (G–n) 1135

King, Jr. Memorial Scholarship Fund. See Martin Luther King, Jr. Memorial Scholarship Fund, entries (S–n) 284, (F–n) 607

Kittrell Fellowship for Minorities. See Flemmie P. Kittrell Fellowship for Minorities, entry (F–n) 550

Knight–Ridder Minority Scholarship Program, (S–n) 270, (I–n) 1623

Knight–Ridder Minority Specialty Development Program, (I–n) 1624

S–Scholarships	F–Fellowships	L–Loans	G–Grants	A–Awards	I–Internships
i–American Indians	a–Native Alaskans	p–Native Pacific Islanders		n–Native Americans in General	

Louisiana Space Consortium Research Enhancement Awards Program. *See* LaSPACE Research Enhancement Awards Program, entry (G–n) 1116

Louisiana Space Consortium Scholars Program. *See* LaSPACE Scholars Program, entry (S–n) 273

Louisville Community Foundation Educational Opportunity Scholarship Fund, (S–n) 279

LSSI Minority Scholarship. *See* LITA/LSSI Minority Scholarship, entry (F–n) 598

Lubbock Avalanche–Journal Internship, (I–n) 1634

Luce Foundation/ACLS Dissertation Fellowship Program in American Art. *See* Henry Luce Foundation/ACLS Dissertation Fellowship Program in American Art, entry (G–n) 1065

Lucent Technologies Training Program for Minority Medical Students and Medical Residents. *See* Training Program for Minority Medical Students and Medical Residents, entry (I–n) 1755

Lurcy Research Fellowship in Economics. *See* Georges Lurcy Research Fellowship in Economics, entry (G–n) 1050

Mackin Research Grants. *See* J. Hoover Mackin Research Grants, entry (G–n) 1098

Macon Telegraph Internships, (I–n) 1635

MAERC Student Fellowships, (S–n) 280, (I–n) 1636

Magnetic Fusion Energy Technology Fellowship Program, (F–n) 603, (I–n) 1637

Magnetic Fusion Science Fellowship Program, (F–n) 604, (I–n) 1638

Maine Arts Commission Traditional Arts Apprenticeship Program, (G–i) 816, (I–i) 1500

Maine Space Grant Consortium Research Acceleration Grant Program. *See* MSGC Research Acceleration Grant Program, entry (G–n) 1183

Maine Space Grant Consortium Travel Grant Program. *See* MSGC Travel Grant Program, entry (G–n) 1184

Malki Museum Scholarships, (S–i) 60

Management and Technical Assistance 7(j) Program Grants, (G–n) 1128

Manhattan Community Arts Fund Regrant Program, (G–n) 1129

Manhattan Theatre Club Playwriting Fellowships, (F–n) 605, (G–n) 1130

Manufacturing Opportunities through Science and Technology, (G–n) 1131

Many Voices Multicultural Collaboration Grants, (G–n) 1132

Many Voices Residencies, (G–n) 1133

MARC Faculty Predoctoral Fellowships. *See* Minority Access to Research Careers (MARC) Faculty Predoctoral Fellowships, entry (F–n) 623

MARC Predoctoral Fellowships. *See* Minority Access to Research Careers (MARC) Predoctoral Fellowships, entry (F–n) 624

MARC Senior Faculty Fellowships. *See* Minority Access to Research Careers (MARC) Senior Faculty Fellowships, entry (G–n) 1161

MARC Undergraduate Student Training in Academic Research (U–STAR) Program, (S–n) 281

MARC Visiting Scientist Fellowships. *See* Minority Access to Research Careers (MARC) Visiting Scientist Fellowships, entry (G–n) 1162

Marie F. Peters Ethnic Minorities Outstanding Achievement Award, (A–n) 1476

Marilyn Lloyd Fellowship Program, (F–n) 606, (I–n) 1639

Marilyn Lloyd Scholarship Program, (S–n) 282, (I–n) 1640

Marion Wright Edelman Scholarship, (G–n) 1134

Mark J. Schroeder Scholarship in Meteorology, (S–n) 283

Mark Ulmer Native American Scholarship, (S–i) 61

Marriage and Family Therapy Minority Fellowship Program. *See* MFT Minority Fellowship Program, entry (F–n) 620

Marriage and Family Therapy Minority Supervision Stipend Program. *See* MFT Minority Supervision Stipend Program, entry (G–n) 1150

Martin Luther King, Jr., Cesar Chavez, Rosa Parks Visiting Professors Program, (G–n) 1135

Martin Luther King, Jr. Memorial Scholarship Fund, (S–n) 284, (F–n) 607

Mary Litty Memorial Fellowship, (F–n) 608, (G–n) 1136

Mary's Pence Grant Program, (S–n) 285, (G–n) 1137

MASGC Graduate Fellowships, (F–n) 609

MASGC Summer Jobs Program, (I–n) 1641

MASGC Undergraduate Research Opportunity Program, (G–n) 1138

Mass Media Science and Engineering Fellows Program, (I–n) 1642

Massachusetts Home Mortgage Loan Program for Minority Households. *See* MHFA Home Mortgage Loan Program for Minority Households, entry (L–n) 765

Massachusetts Indian Association Scholarship Fund, (S–i) 62, (F–i) 415

Massachusetts Native American Tuition Waiver Program, (S–i) 63

Massachusetts Space Grant Consortium Graduate Fellowships. *See* MASGC Graduate Fellowships, entry (F–n) 609

Massachusetts Space Grant Consortium Summer Jobs Program. *See* MASGC Summer Jobs Program, entry (I–n) 1641

Massachusetts Space Grant Consortium Undergraduate Research Opportunity Program. *See* MASGC Undergraduate Research Opportunity Program, entry (G–n) 1138

Master Artist and Apprentice Grants in Traditional Native Arts, (I–a) 1515

MAT Internships, (I–n) 1643

Mathematical Sciences and Their Applications throughout the Curriculum. *See* Course and Curriculum Development Program, entry (G–n) 966

Mathematical Sciences Postdoctoral Research Fellowships, (F–n) 610, (G–n) 1139

Mathematical Sciences University–Industry Postdoctoral Research Fellowships, (F–n) 611, (G–n) 1140

Mathematical Sciences University–Industry Senior Research Fellowships, (G–n) 1141

Mathematics, Engineering, Science, Business, Education, Computers Program. *See* MESBEC Program, entries (S–n) 287, (F–n) 618, (L–n) 764

Maynard Institute Editing Program for Minority Journalists, (F–n) 612, (I–n) 1644

Maynard Institute Management Training Program, (F–n) 613

McClure Educational and Development Fund Scholarships. *See* James G.K. McClure Educational and Development Fund Scholarships, entry (S–n) 261

McCormick Tribune Minority Fellowship in Urban Journalism at the Chicago Reporter, (G–n) 1142

MCI International Scholarships, (S–n) 286

S–Scholarships	F–Fellowships	L–Loans	G–Grants	A–Awards	I–Internships
i–American Indians	a–Native Alaskans	p–Native Pacific Islanders		n–Native Americans in General	

Minority Access to Energy–Related Research Careers Student Fellowships. *See* MAERC Student Fellowships, entries (S–n) 280, (I–n) 1636

Minority Access to Research Careers (MARC) Faculty Predoctoral Fellowships, (F–n) 623

Minority Access to Research Careers (MARC) Predoctoral Fellowships, (F–n) 624

Minority Access to Research Careers (MARC) Senior Faculty Fellowships, (G–n) 1161

Minority Access to Research Careers (MARC) Student Training in Academic Research (U–STAR) Program. *See* MARC Undergraduate Student Training in Academic Research (U–STAR) Program, entry (S–n) 281

Minority Access to Research Careers (MARC) Visiting Scientist Fellowships, (G–n) 1162

Minority Advertising Intern Program, (I–n) 1653

Minority Advertising Training Program Internships. *See* MAT Internships, entry (I–n) 1643

Minority and "At Risk" Student Scholarship. *See* Idaho Minority and "At Risk" Student Scholarship, entry (S–n) 252

Minority Arts Administration Fellowships. *See* Arts Midwest Minority Arts Administration Fellowships, entry (I–n) 1537

Minority Biomedical Research Support Program, (G–i) 817, (G–a) 846

Minority Business Development Loan Program, (L–n) 766

Minority Career Advancement Awards. *See* Career Advancement Awards for Minority Scientists and Engineers, entry (G–n) 933

Minority Clinical Associate Physician Program, (G–n) 1163

Minority Dental Student Scholarship, (F–n) 625

Minority Dissertation Research Grants in Aging, (G–n) 1164

Minority Dissertation Research Grants in Mental Health, (G–n) 1165

Minority Editing Training Program/Editing. *See* METPRO/Editing Program, entry (I–n) 1647

Minority Editorial Training Program/Reporting. *See* METPRO/Reporting Program, entry (I–n) 1648

Minority Engineers Development Program. *See* Hercules Minority Engineers Development Program, entries (S–n) 246, (I–n) 1607

Minority Faculty Fellowship Program, (I–n) 1654

Minority Fellowship Faculty Program. *See* Grants for the Minority Fellowship Faculty Program, entry (F–n) 569

Minority Fellowship in Urban Journalism. *See* McCormick Tribune Minority Fellowship in Urban Journalism at the Chicago Reporter, entry (G–n) 1142

Minority Fellowship Program in General Sociology, (F–n) 626, (G–n) 1166

Minority Fellowship Program in Mental Health, (F–n) 627, (G–n) 1167

Minority Fellowship Program in Psychiatry, (L–n) 767, (I–n) 1655

Minority Fellowships in Transplantation, (G–n) 1168

Minority Geoscience Graduate Scholarships, (F–n) 628

Minority Geoscience Undergraduate Scholarships, (S–n) 290

Minority Initiative for K–12 Teachers and High School Students. *See* NCRR Minority Initiative for K–12 Teachers and High School Students, entry (G–n) 1219

Minority Institution Grants for Personnel Training for the Education of Individuals with Disabilities, (G–n) 1169

Minority Institution Research Travel Grants. *See* Department of Energy Minority Institution Research Travel Grants, entry (G–n) 979

Minority Institution Travel Award Program. *See* NCHGR Minority Institution Travel Award Program, entry (G–n) 1217

Minority Investigator Research Enhancement Award. *See* NIDDK and NIAMS Minority Investigator Research Enhancement Award, entry (G–n) 1227

Minority Investigators in Asthma and Allergy Research Awards. *See* Underrepresented Minority Investigators in Asthma and Allergy Research Awards, entry (G–n) 1372

Minority Journalism Educators Fellowship, (F–n) 629, (G–n) 1170

Minority Journalism Scholarship Program. *See* Cox Minority Journalism Scholarship Program, entries (S–n) 217, (I–n) 1573

Minority Medical Faculty Development Program, (F–n) 630, (G–n) 1171

Minority Medical Student Clinical Fellowship in Child and Adolescent Psychiatry. *See* Jeanne Spurlock Minority Medical Student Clinical Fellowship in Child and Adolescent Psychiatry, entry (I–n) 1620

Minority Oncology Leadership Award. *See* National Cancer Institute Minority Health Professional Training Initiative, entry (G–n) 1194

Minority Opportunities for Research Faculty Development Awards. *See* MORE Faculty Development Awards, entry (G–n) 1179

Minority Opportunities through School Transformation (MOST) Program Summer Institutes, (S–n) 291

Minority Participation in Legal Education (MPLE) Pre–Law Scholarship Program. *See* Florida Minority Participation in Legal Education (MPLE) Pre–Law Scholarship Program, entry (S–n) 236

Minority Participation in Legal Education (MPLE) Scholarship Program. *See* Florida Minority Participation in Legal Education (MPLE) Scholarship Program, entry (F–n) 551

Minority Postdoctoral Research Fellowships, (F–n) 631, (G–n) 1172

Minority Prequalification Pilot Loan Program, (L–n) 768

Minority Presence Grants (General Program II), (S–i) 72, (S–n) 292

Minority Research Centers of Excellence. *See* Centers of Research Excellence in Science and Technology, entry (G–n) 941

Minority Research Fellowship for Medical Students. *See* James Comer Minority Research Fellowship for Medical Students, entry (I–n) 1618

Minority Research Infrastructure Support Program Grants, (G–n) 1173

Minority Research Planning Grants. *See* Research Planning Grants for Minority Scientists and Engineers, entry (G–n) 1290

Minority Scholar Awards, (G–n) 1174

Minority Scholar–in–Residence Program, (G–n) 1175

Minority Scholarship Award for College Students in Chemical Engineering, (S–n) 293

Minority Scholarship Award for Incoming College Freshmen in Chemical Engineering, (S–n) 294

Minority Science Improvement Program, (G–n) 1176

Minority Specialty Development Program. *See* Knight–Ridder Minority Specialty Development Program, entry (I–n) 1624

Minority Student Administrative Summer Internship Program. *See* ORISE Minority Student Administrative Summer Internship Program, entry (I–n) 1697

Minority Teachers of Illinois Scholarship Program, (S–n) 295, (L–n) 769

Minority Travel Award Program. *See* NIDDK and NIAMS Minority Travel Award Program, entries (G–i) 819, (G–p) 856

Minority Travel Fellowship Program, (G–n) 1177

S–Scholarships   **F–Fellowships**   **L–Loans**   **G–Grants**   **A–Awards**   **I–Internships**
i–American Indians   **a–Native Alaskans**   **p–Native Pacific Islanders**   **n–Native Americans in General**

S–Scholarships F–Fellowships L–Loans G–Grants A–Awards I–Internships

i–American Indians a–Native Alaskans p–Native Pacific Islanders n–Native Americans in General

National Aeronautics and Space Administration Small Business Technology Transfer Grants. *See* NASA Small Business Technology Transfer Grants, entry (G–n) 1190

National Aeronautics and Space Administration/DESGC Graduate Student Fellowships. *See* NASA/DESGC Graduate Student Fellowships, entry (F–n) 638

National Aeronautics and Space Administration/DESGC Undergraduate Summer Scholarships. *See* NASA/DESGC Undergraduate Summer Scholarships, entry (G–n) 1191

National Assessment of Educational Progress (NAEP) Visiting Scholar Program, (G–n) 1192

National Association for Bilingual Education Outstanding Dissertations of the Year Competition, (A–n) 1479

National Association for Campus Activities Multicultural Scholarship Program. *See* NACA Multicultural Scholarship Program, entry (S–n) 301

National Association for Girls and Women in Sport Internship, (I–n) 1668

National Association of Schools of Public Affairs and Administration Diversity Doctoral Awards Program, (F–n) 639

National Cancer Institute Minority Enhancement Award, (G–n) 1193

National Cancer Institute Minority Health Professional Training Initiative, (G–n) 1194

National Cancer Institute Minority School Faculty Development Awards. *See* National Cancer Institute Minority Health Professional Training Initiative, entry (G–n) 1194

National Center for Atmospheric Research Postdoctoral Program, (G–n) 1195

National Center for Human Genome Research Minority Institution Travel Award Program. *See* NCHGR Minority Institution Travel Award Program, entry (G–n) 1217

National Center for Human Genome Research Visiting Investigator Program. *See* NCHGR Visiting Investigator Program, entry (G–n) 1218

National Center for Research Resources Minority Initiative for K–12 Teachers and High School Students. *See* NCRR Minority Initiative for K–12 Teachers and High School Students, entry (G–n) 1219

National Center for Toxicological Research Faculty Research Participation Program, (G–n) 1196

National Center for Toxicological Research Graduate Student Research Participation Program, (I–n) 1669

National Center for Toxicological Research Postgraduate Research Program, (G–n) 1197

National Center for Toxicological Research Undergraduate Program, (I–n) 1670

National Collegiate Athletic Association Ethnic Minority Postgraduate Scholarship Program. *See* NCAA Ethnic Minority Postgraduate Scholarship Program, entry (F–n) 653

National Collegiate Athletic Association Internship Program. *See* NCAA Ethnic Minority and Women's Internship Programs, entry (I–n) 1679

National Committee on Pay Equity Internship Program, (I–n) 1671

National Council of Teachers of English Regular Grants–in–Aid, (G–n) 1198

National Defense Science and Engineering Graduate Fellowship Program, (F–n) 640

National Foundation for the Improvement of Education Student Success Program, (G–n) 1199

National Health Service Corps Loan Repayment Program, (G–n) 1200

National Health Service Corps Scholarship Program, (S–n) 302, (F–n) 641, (L–n) 772

National Heart, Lung, and Blood Institute Minority Access to Research Careers Summer Research Training Program. *See* NHLBI/MARC Summer Research Training Program, entry (G–n) 1225

National Heart, Lung, and Blood Institute Minority Institutional Research Training Program, (F–n) 642

National Heart, Lung, and Blood Institute Minority School Faculty Development Award, (F–n) 643

National Heart, Lung, and Blood Institute Research Development Award for Minority Faculty, (G–n) 1201

National Heart, Lung, and Blood Institute Short–Term Research Training for Minority Students Program, (S–n) 303, (F–n) 644

National Institute of Allergy and Infectious Diseases Introduction to Biomedical Research Program. *See* Introduction to Biomedical Research Program, entry (G–n) 1096

National Institute of Arthritis and Musculoskeletal and Skin Diseases Minority Investigator Research Enhancement Award. *See* NIDDK and NIAMS Minority Investigator Research Enhancement Award, entry (G–n) 1227

National Institute of Arthritis and Musculoskeletal and Skin Diseases Minority Travel Award Program. *See* NIDDK and NIAMS Minority Travel Award Program, entries (G–i) 819, (G–p) 856

National Institute of Diabetes and Digestive and Kidney Diseases Minority Investigator Research Enhancement Award. *See* NIDDK and NIAMS Minority Investigator Research Enhancement Award, entry (G–n) 1227

National Institute of Diabetes and Digestive and Kidney Diseases Minority Travel Award Program. *See* NIDDK and NIAMS Minority Travel Award Program, entries (G–i) 819, (G–p) 856

National Institute of Diabetes and Digestive and Kidney Diseases Research Training of Underrepresented Minorities, (G–n) 1202

National Institute of Diabetes and Digestive and Kidney Diseases Summer Research Training Program for Undergraduate Minority Students, (G–n) 1203

National Institute of General Medical Sciences Minority Undergraduate Research Fellowship. *See* ASM/NIGMS Minority Undergraduate Research Fellowship, entry (G–n) 905

National Institute of Standards and Technology Small Business Innovation Research Grants, (G–n) 1204

National Institute on Aging Research Training of Underrepresented Minorities, (G–n) 1205

National Institute on the Education of At–Risk Students, (G–i) 818, (G–a) 847

National Institutes of Health Individual Research Project Grants, (G–n) 1206

National Institutes of Health Small Business Technology Transfer Grants, (G–n) 1207

National Institutes of Health Small Grant Program, (G–n) 1208

National Lawyers Guild Summer Projects, (F–n) 645, (I–n) 1672

National Library of Medicine Fellowship in Applied Informatics. *See* NLM Fellowship in Applied Informatics, entry (G–n) 1228

National Medical Fellowships Scholarships. *See* NMF Scholarships, entry (F–n) 658

National Museum of the American Indian Conservation Internships. *See* NMAI Conservation Internships, entries (I–i) 1504, (I–a) 1516

S–Scholarships **F–Fellowships** **L–Loans** **G–Grants** **A–Awards** **I–Internships**

i–American Indians **a–Native Alaskans** **p–Native Pacific Islanders** **n–Native Americans in General**

S–Scholarships   F–Fellowships   L–Loans   G–Grants   A–Awards   I–Internships
i–American Indians   a–Native Alaskans   p–Native Pacific Islanders   n–Native Americans in General

S–Scholarships F–Fellowships L–Loans G–Grants A–Awards I–Internships
i–American Indians a–Native Alaskans p–Native Pacific Islanders n–Native Americans in General

---

S–Scholarships   **F–Fellowships**   **L–Loans**   **G–Grants**   **A–Awards**   **I–Internships**

i–American Indians   **a–Native Alaskans**   **p–Native Pacific Islanders**   **n–Native Americans in General**

Training Program on Poverty, the Underclass and Public Policy, entries (F–n) 715, (G–n) 1375

Powers Award, (A–i) 1433

Powless Scholarship Fund. See Purcell Powless Scholarship Fund, entry (F–i) 438

Poynter Institute Writers Camp for Grade K–8 Teachers and Elementary and Middle School Students, (G–n) 1266

Poynter Institute Writers Camp for High School Students, (G–n) 1267

Pre–Law Summer Institute for American Indians and Alaska Natives, (F–i) 436, (F–a) 464

Precollege and Public Science Education Program. See Howard Hughes Medical Institute Precollege and Public Science Education Program, entry (G–n) 1071

Predoctoral Fellowship Awards for Minority Students, (F–n) 682

Predoctoral Fellowship Program for Minorities. See Ford Foundation Predoctoral Fellowship Program for Minorities, entry (F–n) 555

Predoctoral Fellowships in Biological Sciences. See Howard Hughes Medical Institute Predoctoral Fellowships in Biological Sciences, entry (F–n) 575

Predoctoral Research Fellowships in Economic Studies, (G–n) 1268

Predoctoral Research Fellowships in Foreign Policy Studies, (G–n) 1269

Predoctoral Research Fellowships in Governmental Studies, (G–n) 1270

Predoctoral Training in Family Medicine Grants, (G–n) 1271

Presenting Program of the New York State Council on the Arts, (G–n) 1272

Presidential Early Career Awards for Scientists and Engineers, (G–n) 1273

President's Postdoctoral Fellowship Program. See University of California President's Postdoctoral Fellowship Program, entry (G–n) 1374

Preventing Alcohol–Related Problems among Ethnic Minorities, (G–n) 1274

Principals' Program. See Bush Principals' Program, entry (F–n) 504

Prize for Excellence in Pediatrics. See Gerber Prize for Excellence in Pediatrics, entries (F–n) 563, (A–n) 1468

Procter & Gamble Graduate R&D Summer Program, (I–n) 1711

Procter & Gamble R&D Summer Program for Engineers, (I–n) 1712

Procter & Gamble Undergraduate R&D Summer Program, (I–n) 1713

Professional Associates Program for Minorities and Women at Brookhaven National Laboratory, (G–n) 1275

Professional Internship Program at Oak Ridge National Laboratory. See ORNL Professional Internship Program, entries (S–n) 321, (F–n) 674, (I–n) 1698

Professional Nurse Traineeships, (F–n) 683

Program for Minority Research Training in Psychiatry, (F–i) 437, (F–p) 479, (G–i) 824, (G–p) 857

Programs and Shelters for Battered Women, (G–n) 1276

Programs to Encourage Minority Students to Become Teachers, (G–n) 1277

Project SEED: Summer Educational Experience for the Disadvantaged, (I–n) 1714

PRSA Multicultural Affairs Scholarships, (S–n) 327

Public Health and National Health Service Corps Scholarship Training Program. See National Health Service Corps Scholarship Program, entries (S–n) 302, (F–n) 641, (L–n) 772

Public Health Service Small Business Innovation Research Program, (G–n) 1278

Public Health Special Project Grants, (G–n) 1279

Public Policy and International Affairs Graduate Fellowships, (F–n) 684

Public Policy and International Affairs Junior Year Summer Institutes, (S–n) 328

Public Policy and International Affairs Senior Year Summer Programs, (F–n) 685

Public Relations Society of America Multicultural Affairs Scholarships. See PRSA Multicultural Affairs Scholarships, entry (S–n) 327

Public Telecommunications Facilities Program Grants, (G–n) 1280

Pueblo of Acoma Higher Education Grant Program, (S–i) 107

Purcell Powless Scholarship Fund, (F–i) 438

Putnam International Visiting Professorship. See Merritt–Putnam International Visiting Professorship, entry (G–n) 1148

Putnam Research/Clinical Training Fellowships. See Merritt–Putnam Research/Clinical Training Fellowships, entries (F–n) 617, (G–n) 1149

QEM Network Internships, (I–i) 1509, (I–a) 1518

QEM Science Student Internships, (I–i) 1510, (I–a) 1519

Qöyawayma Award for Excellence in Arts and Science. See Al Qöyawayma Award for Excellence in Arts and Science, entries (S–i) 4, (F–i) 382

Qöyawayma Award. See Polingaysi Qöyawayma Award, entries (S–i) 106, (F–i) 435

Quality Education for Minorities Network Internships. See QEM Network Internships, entries (I–i) 1509, (I–a) 1518

Quality Education for Minorities Science Student Internships. See QEM Science Student Internships, entries (I–i) 1510, (I–a) 1519

Quinn Scholars Program. See Chips Quinn Scholars Program, entries (S–n) 204, (I–n) 1558

R. Robert & Sally D. Funderburg Research Scholar Award in Gastric Biology Related to Cancer, (G–n) 1281

Racial Ethnic Educational Scholarship Program, (S–n) 329

Racial Ethnic Leadership Supplemental Grants, (F–n) 686

Racine Education Council Awards, (S–n) 330, (I–n) 1715

Radio and Television News Directors Foundation Capitol Hill News Internships. See Capitol Hill News Internships, entry (I–n) 1553

Radio and Television News Directors Foundation Entry Level Internships. See RTNDF Entry Level Internships, entry (I–n) 1722

Radio and Television News Directors Foundation Summer Internships. See RTNDF Summer Internships, entry (I–n) 1723

Radisson Inn Scholarship. See Oneida Tribe/Radisson Inn Scholarship, entries (S–i) 102, (I–i) 1507

Ralph J. Bunche Award, (A–n) 1483

Ralph W. Ellison Prize, (F–n) 687, (A–n) 1484

Rawley Prize. See James A. Rawley Prize, entry (A–n) 1471

S—Scholarships	F—Fellowships	L—Loans	G—Grants	A—Awards	I—Internships
i—American Indians	a—Native Alaskans	p—Native Pacific Islanders		n—Native Americans in General	

Ray Ban Minority Internship. *See* Jackie Joyner Kersee/Ray Ban Minority Internship, entry (I–n) 1617

RCA Ethnic Scholarship Fund, (S–n) 331

Real Estate and Land Use Institute Scholarships for Minorities, (S–n) 332, (F–n) 688

REAP. *See* Research and Engineering Apprenticeship Program (REAP) for High School Students, entry (I–n) 1716

Red Cloud Indian Art Show Awards, (A–i) 1434

Reed Award. *See* Bruce L. "Biff" Reed Award, entry (G–n) 921

Reed Undergraduate Fellowship in Environmental Engineering. *See* Philip D. Reed Undergraduate Fellowship in Environmental Engineering, entries (S–i) 105, (I–i) 1508

Reeves Jr. Memorial Scholarships. *See* Garth Reeves Jr. Memorial Scholarships, entries (S–n) 239, (F–n) 560

Reformed Church in America Ethnic Scholarship Fund. *See* RCA Ethnic Scholarship Fund, entry (S–n) 331

Regents Health Care Opportunity Scholarships. *See* New York State Regents Health Care Opportunity Scholarships, entries (F–i) 427, (F–a) 462

Regents Professional Opportunity Scholarships. *See* New York State Regents Professional Opportunity Scholarships, entries (S–i) 86, (S–a) 150, (F–i) 428, (F–a) 463

Reproductive Rights Coalition Fund Grants, (G–n) 1282

Research and Engineering Apprenticeship Program (REAP) for High School Students, (I–n) 1716

Research Assistantships for Minority High School Students, (G–n) 1283

Research Centers in Minority Institutions Awards, (G–n) 1284

Research Experiences for Undergraduates Sites Program, (G–n) 1285

Research Experiences for Undergraduates Supplements Program, (G–n) 1286

Research Fellowship in Drug Abuse and Addiction for Minority Medical Students. *See* Jeanne Spurlock Research Fellowship in Drug Abuse and Addiction for Minority Medical Students, entry (I–n) 1621

Research in Undergraduate Institutions Faculty Research Projects. *See* RUI Faculty Research Projects, entry (G–n) 1301

Research in Undergraduate Institutions Research Instrumentation Grants. *See* RUI Research Instrumentation Grants, entry (G–n) 1302

Research Infrastructure in Minority Institutions Awards, (G–n) 1287

Research on the Mental Health of Minority Populations, (G–n) 1288

Research Opportunity Awards, (G–n) 1289

Research Partcipation Program at the Risk Reduction Engineering Research Laboratory. *See* Risk Reduction Engineering Research Laboratory Research Participation Program, entry (G–n) 1295

Research Participation Program at Directorate of Environment–Fort McClellan. *See* Directorate of Environment–Fort McClellan Research Participation Program, entry (G–n) 983

Research Participation Program at St. Louis District, U.S. Army Corps of Engineers. *See* St. Louis District, U.S. Army Corps of Engineers Research Participation Program, entry (G–n) 1338

Research Participation Program at the Environmental Monitoring Systems Laboratory. *See* Environmental Monitoring Systems Laboratory Research Participation Program, entry (G–n) 1008

Research Participation Program at the U.S. Army Construction Engineering Research Laboratory. *See* U.S. Army Construction Engineering Research Laboratory Research Participation Program, entry (G–n) 1383

Research Participation Program for the Tennessee Valley Authority. *See* Tennessee Valley Authority Research Participation Program, entry (G–n) 1359

Research Planning Grants for Minority Scientists and Engineers, (G–n) 1290

Research Proposal Development Program for Minority Nurses, (G–n) 1291

Research Supplements for Underrepresented Minority Graduate Research Assistants, (I–n) 1717

Research Supplements for Underrepresented Minority High School Students, (I–n) 1718

Research Supplements for Underrepresented Minority Individuals in Postdoctoral Training, (F–n) 689, (G–n) 1292

Research Supplements for Underrepresented Minority Undergraduate Students, (I–n) 1719

Research Training Fellowship for Minority Nurses, (F–n) 690

Research Training Fellowship in Psychology, (F–n) 691

Research Training Fellowships for Medical Students Program. *See* HHMI Research Training Fellowships for Medical Students Program, entry (G–n) 1067

Residency Training in General Internal Medicine and General Pediatrics Grants, (F–n) 692

Resources for the Future Summer Internships. *See* RFF Summer Internships, entry (I–n) 1720

RFF Summer Internships, (I–n) 1720

Richard and Jessie Barrington Educational Fund, (S–i) 108

Richard S. Smith Scholarship, (S–n) 333

RIDGE Initiative Postdoctoral Fellowships, (G–n) 1293

Ridge Inter–Discipliary Global Experiments Initiative Postdoctoral Fellowships. *See* RIDGE Initiative Postdoctoral Fellowships, entry (G–n) 1293

Risk Assessment Science and Engineering Fellowships, (G–n) 1294

Risk Reduction Engineering Research Laboratory Research Participation Program, (G–n) 1295

Robert A. Hine Memorial Scholarship, (S–n) 334

Robert C. Maynard Institute Editing Program for Minority Journalists. *See* Maynard Institute Editing Program for Minority Journalists, entries (F–n) 612, (I–n) 1644

Robert C. Maynard Institute Management Training Program. *See* Maynard Institute Management Training Program, entry (F–n) 613

Robert D. Watkins Minority Graduate Fellowship, (G–n) 1296

Robert F. Kennedy Book Awards, (A–n) 1485

Robert F. Kennedy Journalism Awards, (A–n) 1486

Robert K. Fahnestock Memorial Award, (G–n) 1297

Robert W. Brocksbank Leadership Award, (S–i) 109

Robert W. Brocksbank Scholarship, (S–i) 110, (F–i) 439

Robert W. Hartley Memorial Fellowship, (G–n) 1298

Robinson Scholarship. *See* Jackie Robinson Scholarship, entry (S–n) 259

Rock Hill Herald Internships, (I–n) 1721

Rocky Mountain NASA Space Grant Consortium Graduate Research Fellowships, (F–n) 693

Rollan D. Melton Fellowship, (F–n) 694, (G–n) 1299

Ronald E. McNair Postbaccalaureate Achievement Program Grants, (G–n) 1300

S–Scholarships   F–Fellowships   L–Loans   G–Grants   A–Awards   I–Internships
i–American Indians   a–Native Alaskans   p–Native Pacific Islanders   n–Native Americans in General

Roosevelt Teacher Fellowships. *See* Eleanor Roosevelt Teacher Fellowships, entries (F–n) 542, (G–n) 1002

Rosa Parks Visiting Professors Program. *See* Martin Luther King, Jr., Cesar Chavez, Rosa Parks Visiting Professors Program, entry (G–n) 1135

Rosemary & Nellie Ebrie Foundation Scholarships, (S–p) 169, (F–p) 480

Rosewood Family Scholarship Fund, (S–n) 335

Roslyn Fund for the Arts. *See* Chicago Foundation for Women Grant Program, entry (G–n) 944

Ross Foundation Scholarships. *See* John Ross Foundation Scholarships, entries (S–p) 163, (F–p) 473

Rostkowski Award. *See* Nicolaus Rostkowski Award, entry (A–i) 1430

RTNDF Capitol Hill News Internships. *See* Capitol Hill News Internships, entry (I–n) 1553

RTNDF Entry Level Internships, (I–n) 1722

RTNDF Summer Internships, (I–n) 1723

Rudwick Prize. *See* Elliott Rudwick Prize, entry (A–n) 1463

RUI Faculty Research Projects, (G–n) 1301

RUI Research Instrumentation Grants, (G–n) 1302

Rural Arts Projects Support Grants, (G–n) 1303

Ruth Chance Law Fellowship, (I–n) 1724

Ryan Acting Scholarships. *See* Irene Ryan Acting Scholarships, entries (S–n) 258, (A–n) 1469

R01 Awards. *See* National Institutes of Health Individual Research Project Grants, entry (G–n) 1206

R03 Awards. *See* National Institutes of Health Small Grant Program, entry (G–n) 1208

R29 Awards. *See* First Independent Research Support and Transition (FIRST) Awards, entry (G–n) 1032

R41 Awards. *See* National Institutes of Health Small Business Technology Transfer Grants, entry (G–n) 1207

R42 Awards. *See* National Institutes of Health Small Business Technology Transfer Grants, entry (G–n) 1207

SACNAS Conference Grants, (G–i) 825

SACNAS Summer Program for Latinos and Native Americans. *See* Cornell–SACNAS Summer Program for Latinos and Native Americans, entry (I–n) 1571

Sacramento Bee Minority Media Scholarships, (S–n) 336

Safe and Drug–Free Schools and Communities Program for Native Hawaiians, (G–p) 858

Sally D. Funderburg Research Scholar Award in Gastric Biology Related to Cancer. *See* R. Robert & Sally D. Funderburg Research Scholar Award in Gastric Biology Related to Cancer, entry (G–n) 1281

Saltonstall–Kennedy Fisheries Research and Development Grants, (G–n) 1304

Samuel R. Wallis Memorial Scholarship, (F–p) 481

San Angelo Standard–Times Internship, (I–n) 1725

San Jose Mercury News Minority Scholarship, (S–n) 337, (I–n) 1726

Santo Domingo Scholarship Program, (S–i) 111

Sara Jackson Award, (G–n) 1305

Savannah Morning News Internships, (I–n) 1727

Savannah River Site Professional Internship Program, (S–n) 338, (F–n) 695, (I–n) 1728

SBA Loans to Participants in the 8(a) Program, (L–n) 782

SBA Microloan Program, (L–n) 783

Scholarship Award for Ethnic Minority Gifted/Talented Students with Disabilities. *See* Stanley E. Jackson Scholarship Award for Ethnic Minority Gifted/Talented Students with Disabilities, entry (S–n) 348

Scholarship Award for Ethnic Minority Students with Disabilities. *See* Stanley E. Jackson Scholarship Award for Ethnic Minority Students with Disabilities, entry (S–n) 349

Scholarship for Minority Students in Memory of Edna Yelland. *See* CLA Scholarship for Minority Students in Memory of Edna Yelland, entry (F–n) 519

Scholarship Grants for Prospective Educators. *See* Phi Delta Kappa Scholarship Grants for Prospective Educators, entry (S–n) 324

Scholarship in Communications for Minorities. *See* Newsday Scholarship in Communications for Minorities, entry (S–n) 307

Scholarships at Presbyterian Colleges. *See* Charlotte W. Newcombe Scholarships at Presbyterian Colleges, entry (S–n) 202

Scholarships for Disadvantaged Students Grants, (S–n) 339, (F–n) 696

Scholarships for Minority Accounting Students, (S–n) 340, (F–n) 697

School, College and University Partnership Grants, (G–n) 1306

School–to–Work Opportunities Act Indian Program Grants, (G–i) 826

School–to–Work Opportunities Act Urban/Rural Program Grants, (G–n) 1307

Schroeder Scholarship in Meteorology. *See* Mark J. Schroeder Scholarship in Meteorology, entry (S–n) 283

Schultz Scholarship Fund. *See* Claire B. Schultz Scholarship Fund, entry (S–n) 209

Schuyler M. Meyer, Jr. Scholarship Fund, (S–i) 112, (F–i) 440

Science and Engineering Opportunity Program for Minorities and Women at Brookhaven National Laboratory, (I–n) 1729

Science and Technology Alliance Summer Student Program, (I–n) 1730

Science, Engineering, and Diplomacy Fellowships, (G–n) 1308

Science to Achieve Results Graduate Environmental Education Fellowships. *See* STAR Graduate Environmental Education Fellowships, entry (F–n) 705

Scientist Development Award for New Minority Faculty, (G–n) 1309

SCSU Summer Minority Teaching Fellows, (G–n) 1310

S.D. Bechtel Jr. Foundation Fellows, (S–i) 113

Secretary of Navy Doctoral Research Fellowships for Naval Readiness, (G–n) 1311

Sedimentary Geology Division Grant, (G–n) 1312

SEDL Minority Internship Program. *See* Southwest Educational Development Laboratory Minority Internship Program, entry (I–n) 1737

Seminole and Miccosukee Indian Scholarship Program, (S–i) 114, (F–i) 441

Seneca Nation of Indians Higher Education Program, (S–i) 115, (F–i) 442

Senior Scientist Awards, (G–n) 1313

Sequoyah Graduate Fellowships for American Indians and Alaskan Natives, (F–i) 443, (F–a) 465

Services Training Officers Prosecutors Violence against Women Formula Grant Program. *See* Grants to Combat Violent Crimes against Women, entry (G–i) 802

Seventh Generation Fund General Support Grants, (G–n) 1314

Sexuality Research Program Dissertation Fellowships, (G–n) 1315

S–Scholarships	F–Fellowships	L–Loans	G–Grants	A–Awards	I–Internships
i–American Indians	a–Native Alaskans	p–Native Pacific Islanders		n–Native Americans in General	

S–Scholarships   F–Fellowships   L–Loans   G–Grants   A–Awards   I–Internships
i–American Indians   a–Native Alaskans   p–Native Pacific Islanders   n–Native Americans in General

---

University of California at Santa Barbara Library Minority Fellowship Program. *See* UCSB Library Minority Fellowship Program, entry (I–n) 1756

University of California President's Postdoctoral Fellowship Program, (G–n) 1374

University of Michigan Research and Training Program on Poverty, the Underclass and Public Policy, (F–n) 715, (G–n) 1375

University of Minnesota Affirmative Action Residency Program, (I–n) 1761

University of Wisconsin Visiting Minority Scholar Lecture Program, (G–n) 1376

University Postdoctoral Fellowship Program, (G–n) 1377

University Research Expeditions Program Teacher Research Participation Program, (G–n) 1378

Unto These Hills Educational Fund Scholarship, (S–i) 126

Upjohn Minority Summer Fellow Program, (I–n) 1762

UPS Scholarship for Minority Students, (S–n) 364

Upward Bound Grants, (G–n) 1379

Upward Bound Math/Science Grants, (G–n) 1380

Urban and Rural School Improvement Program, (G–n) 1381

UREP Teacher Research Participation Program. *See* University Research Expeditions Program Teacher Research Participation Program, entry (G–n) 1378

U.S. Army Center for Health Promotion and Preventive Medicine Graduate Internship Program, (I–n) 1763

U.S. Army Center for Health Promotion and Preventive Medicine Postgraduate Internship Program, (G–n) 1382

U.S. Army Center for Health Promotion and Preventive Medicine Undergraduate Internship Program, (I–n) 1764

U.S. Army Construction Engineering Research Laboratory Research Participation Program, (G–n) 1383

U.S. Army Environmental Center Environmental Management Research Participation Program. *See* Environmental Management Research Participation Program for the U.S. Army Environmental Center, entry (G–n) 1007

U.S. Department of State Student Intern Program. *See* United States Department of State Student Intern Program, entry (I–n) 1759

U.S. Navy–ASEE Sabbatical Leave Program, (G–n) 1384

U.S. Navy–ASEE Summer Faculty Research Program, (G–n) 1385

USAID Intern Investment Program, (I–n) 1765

USDA Research Apprenticeship Program for Minority High School Students, (I–n) 1766

USDA Small Business Innovation Research Program, (G–n) 1386

USDA Summer Intern Program, (I–n) 1767

Utah Career Teaching Scholarships, (S–n) 365

VA Home Loans for Native Americans, (L–n) 787

van Pelt Scholarships. *See* Adolph van Pelt Scholarships, entries (S–i) 2, (F–i) 380

Vermont Space Grant Consortium Graduate Research Assistantships. *See* VSGC Graduate Research Assistantships, entries (F–n) 719, (G–n) 1394

Vermont Space Grant Consortium Undergraduate Scholarships. *See* VSGC Undergraduate Scholarships, entry (S–n) 369

Very Special Arts Internships, (I–n) 1768

Victor Horsley Research/Clinical Training Fellowships, (F–n) 716, (G–n) 1387

Vigil Awards, (A–i) 1438

Vincent Wilkinson Endowment Fund. *See* Museum Intern Partnership Program, entry (I–i) 1502

Violence and Traumatic Stress Research Grants, (G–n) 1388

Virgil Hawkins Fellows Scholarships, (F–n) 717

Virginia Press Association Minority Internship, (I–n) 1769

Virginia Space Grant Community College Scholarship Program, (S–n) 366

Virginia Space Grant Graduate Fellowships, (F–n) 718, (G–n) 1389

Virginia Space Grant Teacher Education Scholarship Program, (S–n) 367

Virginia Undergraduate Student Financial Assistance (Last Dollar) Program, (S–n) 368

Visa Minority Internship. *See* Zina Garrison/Visa Minority Internship, entry (I–n) 1776

Visiting Minority Scholar Lecture Program. *See* University of Wisconsin Visiting Minority Scholar Lecture Program, entry (G–n) 1376

Visiting Professorships for Women, (G–n) 1390

Visual Arts Program of the New York State Council on the Arts, (G–n) 1391

Vocational Rehabilitation Service Projects for American Indians with Disabilities, (G–i) 829

Vocational Rehabilitation Service Projects for Migratory Agricultural and Seasonal Farmworkers with Disabilities, (G–n) 1392

Volunteer/Donor Award, (G–n) 1393

Vouras Dissertation Research Grant. *See* Paul P. Vouras Dissertation Research Grant, entry (G–n) 1255

VSGC Graduate Research Assistantships, (F–n) 719, (G–n) 1394

VSGC Undergraduate Scholarships, (S–n) 369

W. Lincoln Hawkins Undergraduate Research Fellowship, (G–i) 830

Wade Journalism Fellowship. *See* Lawrence Wade Journalism Fellowship, entries (S–n) 274, (F–n) 596, (I–n) 1629

Waialua Hawaiian Civic Club Scholarships, (S–p) 170

Wallis Memorial Scholarship. *See* Samuel R. Wallis Memorial Scholarship, entry (F–p) 481

Walsh Memorial Award. *See* Damon Walsh Memorial Award, entry (A–n) 1461

Walt Disney Studios Fellowship Program, (I–n) 1770

Washington Chevron Merit Award, (S–n) 370

Washington State American Indian Endowed Scholarship Program, (S–i) 127, (F–i) 447

Washington State Need Grant, (S–n) 371

Washington State Tuition and Fee Waiver Program, (S–n) 372

Watkins Minority Graduate Fellowship. *See* Robert D. Watkins Minority Graduate Fellowship, entry (G–n) 1296

Watts Memorial Fellowship. *See* Charles H. Watts Memorial Fellowship, entries (G–i) 795, (G–a) 835

WAVE 3 Telecommunications Internship, (I–n) 1771

WCVB–TV Summer Minority Internship Program, (I–n) 1772

Webb Internships. *See* James E. Webb Internships, entry (I–n) 1619

Wertheimer Multilingual Award. *See* Leonard Wertheimer Multilingual Award, entry (A–n) 1474

West Coast Conference Athletic Administration Internship, (I–n) 1773

White Earth Critical Professions Program, (S–i) 128, (F–i) 448

S–Scholarships	**F–Fellowships**	**L–Loans**	**G–Grants**	**A–Awards**	**I–Internships**
i–American Indians	**a–Native Alaskans**		**p–Native Pacific Islanders**		**n–Native Americans in General**

Sponsoring Organization Index

Names of sponsoring organizations are arranged alphabetically, word by word. To help users select only those programs within their scope of interest, each entry number is preceded by a two–character alphabetical code within parentheses. The first character (capitalized) in the code identifies program type: S = Scholarships; F = Fellowships; L = Loans; G = Grants; A = Awards; and I = Internships. The second character (lower cased) identifies eligible minority groups: i = American Indians; a = Native Alaskans; p = Native Pacific Islanders; n = Native Americans in General. For example, if the name of a sponsoring organization is followed by (S–n, 241, a program sponsored by that organization is described in the Scholarships section under Native Americans, in entry number 241. If the same sponsoring organization's name is followed by another entry number—for example, (L–n) 763—the user is directed to either a different program sponsored by that organization or to the same program described in the Loans section, under Native Americans, in entry 763.

Abbott Laboratories, (G–n) 1372
ABC Newspaper Internship Program, (I–n) 1521
Academy for Educational Development, (F–n) 660–661
Academy of Applied Science, (I–n) 1716
ADA Endowment and Assistance Fund, (F–n) 625
Advertising Club of Los Angeles, (I–n) 1643
Aerospace Illinois Space Grant Consortium, (S–n) 172, (F–n) 486
Ahahui Kalakaua Association of Hawaiian Civic Clubs, (S–p) 157, (F–p) 469
Akron Beacon Journal, (I–n) 1545
Alabama Space Grant Consortium, (S–n) 175–176, (F–n) 488, (G–n) 876
Alaska Library Association, (F–a) 452
Alaska State Council on the Arts, (G–a) 831, (I–a) 1515
Albuquerque Journal, (S–n) 177, (I–n) 1524
All Indian Pueblo Council, Inc., (S–i) 5–6, (I–i) 1490–1491
Alzheimer's Association, (G–n) 881
American Academy of Allergy, Asthma & Immunology, (G–n) 1372
American Academy of Child & Adolescent Psychiatry, (I–n) 1618, 1620–1621
American Architectural Foundation, (S–n) 173
American Art Therapy Association, Inc., (F–n) 514
American Association for Cancer Research, (G–n) 1174
American Association for Marriage and Family Therapy, (F–n) 620, (G–n) 1150
American Association for the Advancement of Science, (G–n) 960, 1009, 1294, 1308, 1356, (I–n) 1642
American Association of Advertising Agencies, (I–n) 1653
American Association of Critical–Care Nurses, (S–n) 226
American Association of Family and Consumer Sciences, (F–n) 512, 550
American Association of Law Libraries, (F–n) 561

American Association of University Women, (F–n) 511, 542, 553, (G–n) 859–860, 952, 1002, 1004, 1265, (A–n) 1442
American Baptist Financial Aid Program, (S–n) 171, 212, (F–n) 483
American Bar Foundation, (G–n) 989, (I–n) 1628
American Chemical Society, (S–i) 7, (S–a) 138, (A–n) 1455, (I–n) 1714
American College of Healthcare Executives, (F–n) 489
American College of Neuropsychopharmacology, (G–n) 1177, (I–n) 1762
American Council of Learned Societies, (F–n) 581, 585–586, (G–n) 866, 963, 987, 1029, 1065
American Council on Education, (G–n) 865
American Dental Hygienists' Association, (S–n) 179, 210–211, (F–n) 491, 522–523
American Digestive Health Foundation, (F–n) 499, (G–n) 867, 1003, 1078, 1253, 1281, 1337
American Economic Association, (F–n) 492, (I–n) 1526
American Foundation for Pharmaceutical Education, (F–n) 539
American Fund for Dental Health, (F–n) 625
American Gastroenterological Association, (F–n) 499, (G–n) 867, 1003, 1078, 1281, 1337
American Geological Institute, (S–n) 290, (F–n) 628
American Heart Association, (G–n) 882–884
American Heart Association. California Affiliate, (I–n) 1527
American Indian Graduate Center, (F–i) 401, (F–a) 455
American Indian Heritage Foundation, (S–i) 8, 73, (A–i) 1428
American Indian Law Center, Inc., (F–i) 436, (F–a) 464
American Indian Scholarship Fund, (S–i) 3, (F–i) 381, (L–i) 729
American Indian Science and Engineering Society, (S–i) 4, 11, 16, 30, 87, 106, 110, 112, (F–i) 382, 385, 396, 429, 435, 439–440
American Institute of Architects, (S–n) 173

S–Scholarships   F–Fellowships   L–Loans   G–Grants   A–Awards   I–Internships
i–American Indians   a–Native Alaskans   p–Native Pacific Islanders   n–Native Americans in General

561

California Psychological Association Foundation, (F–n) 507
California School Library Association, (S–n) 275, (F–n) 597
California Space Grant Consortium, (F–n) 508
California State Library, (F–n) 509, (I–n) 1552
California State University, (F–n) 528, (L–n) 751
California State University. Real Estate and Land Use Institute, (S–n) 332, (F–n) 688
California Student Aid Commission, (F–n) 506
California Teachers Association, (S–n) 284, (F–n) 607
Camille and Henry Dreyfus Foundation, Inc., (A–n) 1455
Carnegie Institution of Washington, (G–n) 934–935
Carnegie Museum of Natural History, (I–n) 1554
Casualty Actuarial Society, (S–i) 118, (S–a) 151
Center for Advanced Study in the Behavioral Sciences, (F–n) 708
Center for Science in the Public Interest, (G–n) 1245
Charlotte Observer, (I–n) 1556
Charlotte W. Newcombe Foundation, (S–n) 202
Cherokee Nation of Oklahoma, (S–i) 18, 59, (F–i) 388
Chevron U.S.A. Inc., (S–n) 310, 320, 344, 370, (F–n) 701
Cheyenne and Arapaho Tribes of Oklahoma, (S–i) 19, (F–i) 389
Chiat/Day/Mojo, (I–n) 1643
Chicago Foundation for Women, (G–n) 944
Chicago Reporter, (G–n) 1142
Chicago Resource Center, (G–n) 1276
Chicago Sun-Times, (S–n) 203, (I–n) 1557
Chickasaw Nation, (S–i) 59
Chinese American Arts Council, (G–n) 1129
Choctaw Nation, (S–i) 21, 59, (F–i) 390
CH2M Hill, (F–n) 574
City University of New York. Bernard M. Baruch College, (F–n) 650, (G–n) 1211
Clarksville Leaf-Chronicle, (I–n) 1563
Cleveland Foundation, (A–n) 1443
Coca-Cola Foundation, (I–n) 1540
Colgate Oral Pharmaceuticals, (S–n) 211, (F–n) 523
Colgate-Palmolive Company, (S–n) 210, (F–n) 522, 625
College Art Association of America, (I–n) 1565
Colorado Commission on Higher Education, (S–n) 213
Colorado Council on Library Development, (F–n) 524
Colorado High School Press Association, (S–n) 206
Colorado Society of Certified Public Accountants, (S–i) 22, (S–n) 230, (F–i) 391
Columbia University. Center on Addiction and Substance Abuse, (I–n) 1564
Columbia University. Graduate School of Journalism, (A–n) 1482
Columbus Ledger-Enquirer, (I–n) 1567
Committee on Institutional Cooperation, (F–n) 517, (I–n) 1747
Commonwealth Fund of New York, (I–n) 1585
Community Associations Institute Research Foundation, (G–n) 924
Community Foundation for Palm Beach and Martin Counties, (S–n) 195, 209, 244, (G–n) 954
Concerned Parents of Novato, (S–n) 214
Connecticut Space Grant College Consortium, (G–n) 961–962
Consortium for a Strong Minority Presence at Liberal Arts Colleges, (G–n) 1175
Consortium for Graduate Study in Management, (F–n) 525, (I–n) 1569
Continental Society, Daughters of Indian Wars, (S–i) 23
Cornell University. Mathematical and Theoretical Biology Institute, (I–n) 1571
Corporation for Public Broadcasting, (G–n) 1187

Council for Exceptional Children, (S–n) 350, (F–n) 706
Council of Energy Resource Tribes, (S–i) 17, (F–i) 387, (I–i) 1494–1495
Council of Ivy Group Presidents, (I–n) 1616
Council on Career Development for Minorities, (S–i) 109
Council on Social Work Education, (F–n) 534–535, (L–n) 753
Cox Enterprises, Inc., (S–n) 217, (I–n) 1573
C.R. Bard, Inc., (F–n) 526, (A–n) 1459
Creek Nation of Oklahoma, (S–i) 24, 59, 75–76

Dallas Morning News, (I–n) 1622
Danforth Foundation, (F–n) 538
Dartmouth College, (F–n) 515, (G–n) 943
The Day Publishing Company, (S–n) 219, (I–n) 1574
Delaware Space Grant Consortium, (S–n) 220, (F–n) 638, (G–n) 1191
Denali Press, (A–n) 1462
Detroit Free Press, (S–n) 221, (I–n) 1576, 1622
Dow Jones Newspaper Fund, (S–n) 222, (I–n) 1577
Duke University, (F–n) 543, (G–n) 1010
Duracell USA, (S–n) 224, (I–n) 1578
Durham Herald-Sun, (I–n) 1579

Edna McConnell Clark Foundation, (S–n) 328, (F–n) 684–685
Educational Testing Service, (G–n) 1019, 1192, (I–n) 1581–1582
Eight Northern Indian Pueblo Council, Inc., (S–i) 27, (F–i) 393
Eli Lilly Company, (F–i) 395
Entomological Society of America, (S–n) 346, (F–n) 704
Epilepsy Foundation of America, (F–n) 501, 544–545, 589, 608, 617, 716, 720, 722–723, (G–n) 911, 1013–1016, 1104, 1136, 1148–1149, 1387, 1395, 1397
Episcopal Church Center, (F–i) 392, (F–a) 454, (F–p) 472
Equal Rights Advocates, Inc., (I–n) 1580, 1724
Evangelical Lutheran Church in America, (F–n) 541

Fairchild Publications, (I–n) 1583
Falmouth Institute, Inc., (S–i) 31
Fayetteville Observer-Times, (I–n) 1584
Fel-Pro Incorporated, (S–n) 233
Fermi National Accelerator Laboratory, (F–n) 548, (I–n) 1586
Fiction Collective Two, (A–n) 1457
Fine Arts Work Center in Provincetown, (G–n) 1031
Five Colleges, Incorporated, (G–n) 1033
Fleet Bank of Maine, (S–n) 235, (I–n) 1587
Florence TimesDaily, (I–n) 1588
Florida Arts Council, (G–n) 1034, 1036
Florida Department of Education, (S–i) 114, (S–n) 335, (F–i) 441, (F–n) 717
Florida Department of State, (G–n) 1034, 1036
Florida Education Fund, (S–n) 236, (F–n) 551, 614, (G–n) 1143
Florida Governor's Council on Indian Affairs, (S–i) 32, (S–a) 140, (S–p) 161
Florida Space Grant Consortium, (F–n) 552, (G–n) 1035, (I–n) 1589
Florida Today, (I–n) 1590
Fond du Lac Tribal Council, (S–i) 33–34, (F–i) 397

S–Scholarships	F–Fellowships	L–Loans	G–Grants	A–Awards	I–Internships
i–American Indians	a–Native Alaskans	p–Native Pacific Islanders		n–Native Americans in General	

Ford Foundation, (S–n) 291, 328, (F–n) 554–555, 585–586, 633, 684–685, 715, (G–n) 866, 953, 1039–1040, 1315–1316, 1375

Fort Lauderdale Sun–Sentinel, (I–n) 1592–1593

Fort Wayne News–Sentinel, (S–n) 238, (I–n) 1594

Fort Worth Star–Telegram, (I–n) 1595

Foundation for Exceptional Children, (S–n) 348–350, (F–n) 706

Frameline, (G–n) 1044

Fredrikson & Byron Foundation, (F–n) 558

Free Lance–Star, (I–n) 1598

Freedom Forum, (S–n) 204, (I–n) 1558

Fresno Bee, (I–n) 1599

Gale Research, Inc., (A–n) 1464

General Electric Foundation, (F–n) 517

Geological Society of America, (G–n) 878–879, 891, 898, 921, 1006, 1049, 1058–1059, 1074, 1098, 1106, 1122, 1235–1236, 1297, 1312, 1330–1332, 1343

George Bird Grinnell American Indian Children's Education Foundation, (S–i) 4, 112, (F–i) 382, 440

Getty Grant Program, (I–n) 1601

Glaxo Wellcome, (I–n) 1532

Golden State Minority Foundation, (S–n) 241, (F–n) 566

Grand Portage Tribal Council, (S–i) 35–36, (F–i) 402

Great Plains Film Festival, (A–i) 1425

Greenfield Review Literary Center, (A–i) 1420, 1427, (A–a) 1440–1441, (A–n) 1481

Greensboro News & Record, (I–n) 1603

Greenville Foundation, (G–n) 953

Hartford Courant, (I–n) 1604

Harvard Apparatus Foundation, (G–n) 1399

Harvard University. Graduate School of Design, (F–n) 600

Harvard University. Medical School, (I–n) 1597, 1745

Hattiesburg American, (I–n) 1605

Hawai'i Community Foundation, (S–p) 159, 163–164, 169, (F–p) 471, 473–474, 480

Hawai'i Space Grant Consortium, (G–n) 1060–1061

Hearst Broadcasting, (I–n) 1606

Helen Gough Scholarship Foundation, (S–i) 43

Henry J. Kaiser Family Foundation, (G–n) 1180, (A–n) 1480, (I–n) 1622

Henry Luce Foundation, (G–n) 1065

Hercules Incorporated, (S–n) 246, (I–n) 1607

Heritage Foundation, (S–n) 274, (F–n) 596, (I–n) 1629

Hewlett–Packard Company, (I–n) 1608

Holding Our Own, Inc., (G–n) 1322

Hopi Tribe, (S–i) 44–49, (F–i) 405–408

Horizons Foundation, (G–n) 955

Howard Hughes Medical Institute, (F–n) 575, (G–n) 1067–1068, 1071–1073

Howard Rock Foundation, (S–a) 145, (F–a) 458

Hualapai Tribal Council, (S–i) 50–51, (F–i) 409

Huntington Herald–Dispatch, (I–n) 1609

"I Have a Dream" Foundation, (S–n) 251

Idaho Board of Education, (S–n) 252

Idaho Space Grant Consortium, (S–n) 253, (F–n) 576, (G–n) 1075

Illinois State Board of Higher Education, (F–n) 578

Illinois Student Assistance Commission, (S–n) 218, 295, 377, (F–n) 530, 726, (L–n) 752, 769

Independent Colleges of Northern California, (S–n) 310

Independent Colleges of Southern California, (S–n) 344, (F–n) 701

Independent Colleges of Washington, (S–n) 370

Indiana Space Grant Consortium, (S–n) 256, (F–n) 579, (G–n) 1077

Indiana University. Minority Faculty Fellowship Program, (I–n) 1654

Indianapolis Star, (I–n) 1610

Industrial Relations Council on GOALS, (F–n) 565

Information Handling Services, Inc., (S–n) 257

INROADS, Inc., (I–n) 1613

Institute for the Study of World Politics, (F–n) 537, (G–n) 993

Institute for Women's Policy Research, (I–n) 1614

Institute of Early American History and Culture, (G–n) 1084

Institute of Industrial Engineers, (S–n) 364

Institute of Real Estate Management Foundation, (S–n) 240, (F–n) 562

International Association of Culinary Professionals Foundation, (S–n) 215

International Association of Jazz Educators, (S–n) 185, (A–n) 1446

International Order of the King's Daughters and Sons, (S–i) 55

Irene Ryan Foundation, (S–n) 258, (A–n) 1469

Jackie Robinson Foundation, (S–n) 259

James G.K. McClure Educational and Development Fund, Inc., (S–n) 228, 261

Japan Foundation, (G–n) 1103

Japan Foundation. Center for Global Partnership, (G–n) 861

Jasco Tools, (S–n) 262

Jeffrey Modell Foundation, (G–n) 1226

Jicarilla Apache Tribe, (S–i) 88, (F–i) 430

John D. and Catherine T. MacArthur Foundation, (F–n) 533, 680, (G–n) 985, 1263

Kamehameha Schools, (S–p) 162, 165, (F–p) 475

Kansas Board of Regents, (S–n) 266–267, (F–n) 592, (L–n) 761–762

Katrin H. Lamon Endowment for Native American Art and Education., (G–n) 1111

Kennedy Center American College Theater Festival, (S–n) 258, (A–n) 1469

Kentucky Foundation for Women, (G–n) 1112

Kentucky Space Grant Consortium, (S–n) 269, (F–n) 594, (G–n) 1113–1114

Knight–Ridder, Inc., (S–n) 270–271, (I–n) 1623–1625

KNTV Television, (S–n) 272, (I–n) 1626

Landmark Communications, Inc., (I–n) 1627

Landscape Architecture Foundation, (S–n) 227

Latino Media Association. Seattle Chapter, (S–n) 311

S–Scholarships	F–Fellowships	L–Loans	G–Grants	A–Awards	I–Internships
i–American Indians	a–Native Alaskans		p–Native Pacific Islanders		n–Native Americans in General

Lawrence Livermore National Laboratory, (I–n) 1710, 1741
Leech Lake Tribal Council, (S–i) 57–58, (F–i) 413
Leo Burnett Company, Inc., (S–n) 276
Lesbian Natural Resources, (G–n) 1120
Leukemia Society of America, (G–n) 1366
Library Systems & Services Inc., (F–n) 598
Lilly Endowment, (F–n) 517, (G–n) 939
Lisle Fellowship, (G–n) 1134
Los Alamos National Laboratory, (G–n) 1100, 1115, 1127, 1354, (I–n) 1632–1633, 1646, 1730, 1750, 1757
Los Angeles Philharmonic, (S–n) 278, (F–n) 601, (A–n) 1475
Los Angeles Times, (I–n) 1648
Louisiana Space Consortium, (S–n) 273, (F–n) 595, (G–n) 1116
Louisville Community Foundation, (S–n) 279
Lower Manhattan Cultural Council, (G–n) 1129
Lubbock Avalanche–Journal, (I–n) 1634
Lucent Technologies, (I–n) 1755

Macon Telegraph, (I–n) 1635
Maine Arts Commission, (G–i) 816, (I–i) 1500
Maine Space Grant Consortium, (G–n) 1183–1184
Malki Museum, Inc., (S–i) 60
Manhattan Community Arts Fund, (G–n) 1129
Manhattan Theatre Club, (F–n) 605, (G–n) 1130
Marion Merrell Dow, (F–n) 722
Mary's Pence, (S–n) 285, (G–n) 1137
Massachusetts AFL–CIO, (S–n) 250
Massachusetts. Higher Education Coordinating Council, (S–i) 63
Massachusetts Housing Finance Agency, (L–n) 765
Massachusetts Indian Association, (S–i) 62, (F–i) 415
Massachusetts Institute of Technology. Department of Urban Studies and Planning, (F–n) 633
Massachusetts Institute of Technology. Lincoln Laboratory, (I–i) 1501
Massachusetts Space Grant Consortium, (F–n) 609, (G–n) 1138, (I–n) 1641
MCI International, (S–n) 286
Medical Library Association, (F–n) 634
Memphis Commercial Appeal, (I–n) 1645
Menominee Indian Tribe of Wisconsin, (S–i) 64–65, (F–i) 416
Merck U.S. Human Health Division, (I–n) 1525
Mescalero Apache Tribe, (S–i) 66, (F–i) 417
Metrolina Native American Association, (S–i) 56, 67, (S–a) 147
Metropolitan Life Foundation, (F–n) 619, (A–n) 1477
Metropolitan Museum of Art, (I–n) 1649–1650
Miami Herald, (I–n) 1651
Michigan Commission on Indian Affairs, (S–i) 68, (F–i) 418
Michigan Space Grant Consortium, (G–n) 1152–1155
Michigan Women's Foundation, (G–n) 1156, 1408
Mid–American Athletic Conference, (I–n) 1652
Mille Lacs Tribal Council, (S–i) 69–70, (F–i) 419
Milwaukee Journal, (I–n) 1622
Minnesota Higher Education Services Office, (S–n) 288, (F–n) 621
Minnesota Historical Society, (G–n) 1159
Minnesota Space Grant Consortium, (S–n) 289, (F–n) 622
Minnesota State Department of Education, (S–i) 71, (F–i) 420
Minority Advertising Training Program, (I–n) 1643
Mississippi Office of State Student Financial Aid, (S–n) 242, (F–n) 570, (I–n) 1656

Missouri Department of Elementary and Secondary Education, (S–n) 296–297, (L–n) 770–771
Missouri School of Journalism, (A–n) 1478
Missouri Space Grant Consortium, (F–n) 632, (I–n) 1657–1658
Missouri Valley Conference, (I–n) 1659
Modesto Bee, (S–n) 298, (I–n) 1660
Money for Women/Barbara Deming Memorial Fund, Inc., (G–n) 1027
Montana Guaranteed Student Loan Program, (S–i) 74
Montana Space Grant Consortium, (S–n) 299, (F–n) 635, (G–n) 1178
Morris Scholarship Fund, (S–n) 300, (F–n) 636
Ms. Foundation for Women, (G–n) 1117, 1181–1182, 1282
Muskogee Daily Phoenix, (I–n) 1662
Myrtle Beach Sun News, (I–n) 1663
Mystic Seaport Museum, (G–i) 822

Naples Daily News, (I–n) 1664
Nashville Banner, (I–n) 1667
Nathan Cummings Foundation, (G–n) 963
National Abortion and Reproductive Rights Action League, (I–n) 1665
National Action Council for Minorities in Engineering, (S–i) 12, 52, 77–78, 105, 113, 123, 130, (G–i) 830, (A–i) 1435, (I–i) 1493, 1503, 1508
National Association for Bilingual Education, (A–n) 1479
National Association for Campus Activities, (S–n) 301
National Association for Girls and Women in Sport, (I–n) 1668
National Association of Black Journalists, (F–n) 613
National Association of Black Journalists. Seattle Chapter, (S–n) 311
National Association of Hispanic Journalists, (F–n) 613
National Association of Schools of Public Affairs and Administration, (F–n) 639
National Broadcasting Company, (F–n) 652
National Center for Atmospheric Research, (G–n) 1195, (I–n) 1731
National Collegiate Athletic Association, (F–n) 653, (I–n) 1679
National Committee on Pay Equity, (I–n) 1671
National Consortium for Graduate Degrees for Minorities in Engineering and Science (GEM), (F–i) 398–400, (I–i) 1497–1498
National Council of Teachers of English, (G–n) 1198
National Council on Family Relations, (A–n) 1476
National FFA Center, (S–n) 234, 276
National Foundation for Advancement in the Arts, (S–n) 184–191, (A–n) 1445–1452
National Foundation for the Improvement of Education, (G–n) 1199
National Gallery of Art, (I–n) 1615
National Kidney Foundation of Massachusetts and Rhode Island, (G–n) 1108, 1110, 1393
National Lawyers Guild, (F–n) 645, (I–n) 1672
National Medical Fellowships, Inc., (F–n) 526, 557, 563, 587, 619, 658, 687, 721, (A–n) 1459, 1467–1468, 1470, 1472, 1477, 1484, 1489, (I–n) 1564, 1585, 1755, 1775
National Organization for Women. Legal Defense and Education Fund, (I–n) 1686–1688
National Performance Network, (G–n) 1237–1238
National Physical Science Consortium, (F–n) 659, (I–n) 1689

S–Scholarships	F–Fellowships	L–Loans	G–Grants	A–Awards	I–Internships
i–American Indians	a–Native Alaskans		p–Native Pacific Islanders		n–Native Americans in General

S–Scholarships	F–Fellowships	L–Loans	G–Grants	A–Awards	I–Internships
i–American Indians	a–Native Alaskans		p–Native Pacific Islanders		n–Native Americans in General

Pacific 10 Conference, (I–n) 1700
Paducah Sun, (I–n) 1701
Palm Beach Post, (I–n) 1702
Peninsula Community Foundation, (S–n) 229
Pennsylvania Minority Business Development Authority, (L–n) 766
Pensacola News Journal, (I–n) 1704
Pergamon Press, (G–n) 1258
Pew Charitable Trusts, (G–n) 939, 1259, (I–n) 1564
Phi Delta Kappa International, (S–n) 324
Philadelphia Daily News, (I–n) 1705
Philadelphia Inquirer, (S–n) 325, (I–n) 1536, 1622, 1706–1707
Philip D. Reed Foundation, (S–i) 105, (S–n) 328, (F–n) 684–685,
    (I–i) 1508
Philip Morris Companies, (G–n) 1237
Playwrights' Center, (G–n) 1132–1133
Portland Oregonian, (I–n) 1622
Poynter Institute for Media Studies, (G–n) 1266–1267
Presbyterian Church (U.S.A.), (S–i) 79, 81, 122, (S–a) 148–149,
    153, (F–i) 422, (F–a) 461, (F–n) 559, 686, (G–n) 1361
Princeton University. Center for the Study of American Religion,
    (G–n) 939
Procter & Gamble Company, (I–n) 1711–1713, 1748
Public Relations Society of America, (S–n) 327
Pueblo of Acoma, (S–i) 107

Quality Education for Minorities (QEM) Network, (I–i) 1509–1511,
    (I–a) 1518–1520

Racine Education Council, (S–n) 330, (I–n) 1715
Radio and Television News Directors Foundation, (S–n) 201, 225,
    (F–n) 513, 540, (G–n) 1151, (I–n) 1553, 1722–1723
Radisson Inn, (S–i) 102, (I–i) 1507
RAND Critical Technologies Institute, (G–n) 1356
Red Cloud Indian Art Show, (S–i) 124, (A–i) 1414–1417, 1419,
    1421–1424, 1426, 1429–1431, 1433–1434, 1436–1437
Reformed Church in America, (S–n) 331
Resources for the Future, (G–n) 1109, (I–n) 1720
Robert C. Maynard Institute for Journalism Education, (F–n)
    612–613, (I–n) 1644
Robert F. Kennedy Memorial, (A–n) 1485–1486
Robert Wood Johnson Foundation, (F–n) 630, (G–n) 1171
Rochester Area Foundation, (S–n) 262, 373
Rock Hill Herald, (I–n) 1721
Rockefeller Family Fund, (G–n) 998
Rockefeller Foundation, (S–n) 328, (F–n) 684–685, (G–n) 866,
    1238
Rocky Mountain NASA Space Grant Consortium, (F–n) 693
Ronald and Nancy Reagan Research Institute, (G–n) 881

Sacramento Bee, (S–n) 336
San Angelo Standard-Times, (I–n) 1725
San Jose Mercury News, (S–n) 337, (I–n) 1726
Sandia National Laboratories, (F–n) 672, (G–n) 1354, (I–n) 1750
Santo Domingo Tribe, (S–i) 111
Sara Lee Foundation, (A–n) 1458
Savannah Morning News, (I–n) 1727

Savannah River Site, (S–n) 338, (F–n) 695, (I–n) 1691, 1728
Scarecrow Press, (A–n) 1465
School of American Research, (G–n) 1111
Seattle Times, (I–n) 1546
Seattle, Washington. Personnel Department, (I–n) 1570, 1661
Seminole Nation, (S–i) 59
Seneca Nation of Indians, (S–i) 115, (F–i) 442
Seventh Generation Fund, (G–n) 1314, 1363
Shell Oil Company Foundation, (G–n) 1318
Shoshone Higher Education Program, (S–i) 116, (F–i) 444
Sidney Hillman Foundation, (A–n) 1487
Sister Fund, (G–n) 1321
Sky People Higher Education, (S–i) 92
Smithsonian Environmental Research Center, (I–n) 1732
Smithsonian Institution. Center for Museum Studies, (G–i) 789,
    (G–a) 832, (G–n) 1324–1325, (I–i) 1492, 1502, (I–a) 1514
Smithsonian Institution. Conservation Analytical Laboratory, (G–n)
    892–893, (I–n) 1534–1535
Smithsonian Institution. National Museum of Natural History,
    (G–i) 790
Smithsonian Institution. National Museum of the American
    Indian, (I–i) 1504–1505, (I–a) 1516–1517
Smithsonian Institution. National Zoological Park, (I–n) 1600,
    1673–1674
Smithsonian Institution. Office of Equal Employment and Minority
    Affairs, (I–n) 1619
Smithsonian Institution. Office of Fellowships and Grants, (G–n)
    893, 1212, (I–n) 1535, 1733–1734
Social Science Research Council, (F–n) 533, 581, 585–586, 680,
    703, (G–n) 861, 985, 987, 1029, 1089–1092, 1102–1103,
    1263, 1315–1316, 1333–1334
Society for Advancement of Chicanos and Native Americans in
    Science, (F–i) 395, (G–i) 825, (A–i) 1432, 1438, (I–n) 1571
Society of Actuaries, (S–i) 118, (S–a) 151
Society of Automotive Engineers, (S–n) 257
Society of Professional Journalists. Indiana Chapter, (S–n) 255
Society of Professional Journalists. Los Angeles Chapter, (S–n)
    268, (F–n) 593
Society of Professional Journalists. South Florida Chapter, (S–n)
    239, (F–n) 560
Society of Professional Journalists. Tampa Bay Chapter, (S–n)
    352
Society of Women Engineers, (S–n) 205
Sociologists for Women in Society, (F–n) 710
South Carolina Arts Commission, (G–n) 1327–1329
South Carolina Space Grant Consortium, (S–n) 342–343, (F–n)
    700
South Dakota Board of Regents, (S–i) 10
South Dakota Space Grant Consortium, (S–i) 119, (F–i) 445, (I–i)
    1512
Southern California Edison Company, (S–n) 254, 334, 345
Southern Conference, (I–n) 1736
Southern Illinois University Carbondale, (F–n) 577–578
Southern Newspaper Publishers Association, (S–n) 341, (I–n)
    1735
Southwest Educational Development Laboratory, (I–n) 1737
Southwestern Bell Foundation, (S–n) 355
Special Libraries Association, (F–n) 702
St. Cloud State University. Academic Affairs Office, (G–n) 1310
St. Paul Pioneer Press, (I–n) 1738
Stanford University. Center for International Security and Arms
    Control, (G–n) 1093–1095

S–Scholarships   **F–Fellowships**   **L–Loans**   **G–Grants**   **A–Awards**   **I–Internships**
i–American Indians   **a–Native Alaskans**   **p–Native Pacific Islanders**   **n–Native Americans in General**

S–Scholarships   **F–Fellowships**   **L–Loans**   **G–Grants**   **A–Awards**   **I–Internships**
i–American Indians   **a–Native Alaskans**   **p–Native Pacific Islanders**   **n–Native Americans in General**

U.S. Department of Education. Office of Special Education and Rehabilitative Services, (G–i) 829, (G–p) 854, (G–n) 931, 1169, 1392

U.S. Department of Education. Office of Vocational and Adult Education, (G–i) 809, 826, 828, (G–p) 855, (G–n) 916–918, 1307

U.S. Department of Energy, (S–n) 280, 282, (F–n) 583, 606, (G–n) 871–873, 908, 922–923, 937–938, 975, 977, 983, 1007–1008, 1063, 1131, 1196–1197, 1214–1215, 1231, 1247, 1295, 1338, 1359, 1382–1383, (I–n) 1523, 1555, 1611, 1636, 1639–1640, 1669–1670, 1677–1678, 1697, 1763–1764

U.S. Department of Energy. Office of Civilian Radioactive Waste Management, (F–n) 518, (I–n) 1562

U.S. Department of Energy. Office of Defense Programs, (G–n) 1273

U.S. Department of Energy. Office of Economic Impact and Diversity, (S–i) 26, (S–p) 160, (G–n) 979

U.S. Department of Energy. Office of Energy Research, (F–n) 564, (G–n) 877, 889, 976, 978, 991–992, 1317, 1355, (I–n) 1531, 1575, 1602

U.S. Department of Energy. Office of Environment, Safety, and Health, (F–n) 497, (I–n) 1533

U.S. Department of Energy. Office of Fossil Energy, (S–n) 326, (F–n) 677, (G–n) 976, 978, 1041–1043, (I–n) 1596, 1708, 1760

U.S. Department of Energy. Office of Fusion Energy, (F–n) 603–604, (G–n) 1047, (I–n) 1637–1638

U.S. Department of Energy. Office of Nuclear Energy, (F–n) 664, (I–n) 1690

U.S. Department of Energy. Office of Science Education Programs, (F–n) 532, (G–n) 974, 980

U.S. Department of Energy. Office of Transportation Technologies, (G–n) 1069

U.S. Department of Health and Human Services, (G–i) 803

U.S. Department of Health and Human Services. Administration for Children and Families, (G–i) 799, 808, (G–a) 836, 840, 848, (G–n) 868, 1213, 1326

U.S. Department of Health and Human Services. Health Care Financing Administration, (G–n) 1062, 1144

U.S. Department of Health and Human Services. Office of Population Affairs, (G–n) 1025–1026

U.S. Department of Housing and Urban Development, (L–i) 735

U.S. Department of Interior, (G–n) 1250

U.S. Department of Justice, (G–i) 802

U.S. Department of Labor. Employment and Training Administration, (G–i) 806, 826, (G–a) 839, (G–n) 1018, 1157, 1307

U.S. Department of State, (S–n) 237, (F–n) 556, 581, (G–n) 987, 1029, 1308, (I–n) 1591, 1759

U.S. Department of the Treasury, (G–n) 922–923

U.S. Department of Transportation. Federal Aviation Administration, (G–n) 910

U.S. Department of Transportation. Federal Highway Administration, (S–i) 28, (F–i) 394

U.S. Department of Transportation. Federal Transit Administration, (G–n) 1028

U.S. Department of Transportation. Office of Small and Disadvantaged Business Utilization, (L–n) 754

U.S. Department of Transportation. Research and Special Programs Administration, (G–n) 981

U.S. Department of Veterans Affairs, (L–n) 787, (G–n) 1273

U.S. Environmental Protection Agency, (S–i) 25, 30, (F–i) 396, (F–n) 705, (G–n) 908, 1008–1009, 1011, 1247, 1294–1295, (I–i) 1496

U.S. Food and Drug Administration, (G–n) 937–938, 1196–1197, 1278, (I–n) 1669–1670

U.S. Health Resources and Services Administration, (S–i) 38, (S–a) 141, (S–p) 166, (S–n) 245, 302, 312–313, 339, (F–i) 403, (F–a) 456, (F–p) 476, (F–n) 549, 568–569, 572, 641, 649, 679, 683, 692, 696, (L–p) 746, (L–n) 758, 763, 772, (G–n) 869, 940, 984, 1017, 1021–1022, 1051, 1053, 1056, 1158, 1200, 1243–1244, 1260, 1271, 1279

U.S. Indian Health Service, (S–i) 39–40, 42, (S–a) 142–144, (F–i) 404, (F–a) 457, (L–i) 730, (L–a) 742, (G–i) 805, (G–a) 838

U.S. Library of Congress, (I–n) 1631

U.S. National Aeronautics and Space Administration, (S–i) 119, (S–n) 172, 175–176, 220, 253, 256, 269, 273, 289, 299, 305, 315–316, 322, 342–343, 357, 366–367, 369, 375, (F–i) 445, (F–n) 486, 488, 508, 552, 576, 579, 594–595, 609, 622, 632, 635, 637–638, 654, 656–657, 666–667, 675, 693, 700, 712, 718–719, 725, (G–n) 876, 961–962, 1020, 1035, 1060–1061, 1075, 1077, 1113–1114, 1116, 1138, 1152–1155, 1178, 1183–1184, 1188–1191, 1220–1223, 1229, 1233–1234, 1252, 1273, 1389, 1394, 1400–1402, (I–i) 1511–1512, (I–a) 1520, (I–n) 1589, 1641, 1657–1658, 1666, 1680–1681, 1685, 1744

U.S. National Endowment for the Arts, (G–n) 902, 967, 999, 1066, 1261, (I–n) 1649

U.S. National Endowment for the Humanities, (G–i) 796, 813, (G–a) 843, (G–n) 866, 966, 1084

U.S. National Institutes of Health, (S–n) 360, (F–n) 646, 682, 689, (L–n) 774, 776, 786, (G–n) 864, 1024, 1032, 1068, 1124, 1126, 1206–1208, 1210, 1273, 1278, 1292, 1320, 1336, (I–n) 1717–1719, 1746

U.S. National Institutes of Health. National Cancer Institute, (F–n) 616, 647, (L–n) 775, (G–n) 862, 1145, 1147, 1160, 1174, 1193–1194, 1366

U.S. National Institutes of Health. National Center for Human Genome Research, (G–n) 1147, 1217–1218

U.S. National Institutes of Health. National Center for Research Resources, (G–n) 1086, 1147, 1163, 1219, 1284, 1287

U.S. National Institutes of Health. National Eye Institute, (F–n) 616, (G–n) 1145

U.S. National Institutes of Health. National Heart, Lung, and Blood Institute, (S–n) 303, (F–n) 616, 642–644, (G–n) 1076, 1145, 1201, 1225, 1372

U.S. National Institutes of Health. National Institute of Allergy and Infectious Diseases, (F–n) 616, 647, (L–n) 775, (G–n) 1076, 1096, 1145, 1168, 1226, 1372

U.S. National Institutes of Health. National Institute of Arthritis and Musculoskeletal and Skin Diseases, (F–n) 616, 647, (L–n) 775, (G–i) 819, (G–p) 856, (G–n) 862, 897, 1076, 1145, 1147, 1227

U.S. National Institutes of Health. National Institute of Child Health and Human Development, (F–n) 590, 616, 647, (L–n) 775, (G–n) 1076, 1107, 1145, 1409

U.S. National Institutes of Health. National Institute of Dental Research, (F–n) 580, 584, 590, 616, 647, (L–n) 775, (G–n) 1076, 1085, 1107, 1145–1146, 1346

U.S. National Institutes of Health. National Institute of Diabetes and Digestive and Kidney Diseases, (F–n) 616, (G–i) 819, (G–p) 856, (G–n) 1076, 1145, 1202–1203, 1227, 1368

S–Scholarships   F–Fellowships   L–Loans   G–Grants   A–Awards   I–Internships

i–American Indians   a–Native Alaskans   p–Native Pacific Islanders   n–Native Americans in General

U.S. National Institutes of Health. National Institute of Environmental Health Sciences, (F–n) 616, (G–n) 862, 1076, 1145, 1147

U.S. National Institutes of Health. National Institute of General Medical Sciences, (S–n) 281, (F–n) 590, 623–624, (G–i) 817, (G–a) 846, (G–n) 905, 1081–1083, 1107, 1161–1162, 1179

U.S. National Institutes of Health. National Institute of Mental Health, (F–i) 437, (F–p) 479, (F–n) 535, 582, 590, 616, 627, 648, 655, 690–691, 699, (G–i) 824, (G–p) 857, (G–n) 862, 885, 964–965, 1076, 1107, 1145, 1147, 1165, 1167, 1173, 1177, 1288, 1309, 1313, 1388, 1409–1410

U.S. National Institutes of Health. National Institute of Neurological Disorders and Stroke, (F–n) 590, 616, (G–n) 950, 1107, 1145, 1147, 1342

U.S. National Institutes of Health. National Institute of Nursing Research, (F–n) 590, (G–n) 1107, 1147

U.S. National Institutes of Health. National Institute on Aging, (F–n) 536, 590, 616, 647, (L–n) 775, (G–n) 862, 1076, 1107, 1145–1147, 1164, 1205, 1409

U.S. National Institutes of Health. National Institute on Alcohol Abuse and Alcoholism, (F–n) 582, 616, 647–648, 699, (L–n) 775, (G–n) 862, 982, 995, 1076, 1145, 1147, 1274, 1313

U.S. National Institutes of Health. National Institute on Deafness and Other Communication Disorders, (F–n) 590, 616, 647, (L–n) 775, (G–n) 1076, 1107, 1145, 1369

U.S. National Institutes of Health. National Institute on Drug Abuse, (F–n) 582, 616, 648, 699, (G–n) 994–996, 1076, 1145, 1313

U.S. National Institutes of Health. National Library of Medicine, (F–n) 615, (G–n) 1228

U.S. National Science and Technology Council, (G–n) 1273

U.S. National Security Agency, (I–n) 1566, 1571

U.S. Navy, (S–n) 194, 198, (G–n) 1214–1215, (I–n) 1677–1678

U.S. Navy. Naval Research Laboratory, (G–n) 1216

U.S. Navy. Office of Naval Research, (F–n) 531, (G–n) 969–970, 1248, 1250, 1273, 1311, 1384–1385

U.S. Small Business Administration, (L–n) 768, 782–783, (G–n) 1128

U.S. Substance Abuse and Mental Health Services Administration, (F–i) 446, (F–p) 482, (F–n) 520–521, 534, 707, (L–i) 741, (L–p) 747, (L–n) 750, 753, 767, (I–n) 1655

U.S. Tennessee Valley Authority, (G–n) 1359

Utah State Office of Education, (S–n) 365

Vermont Space Grant Consortium, (S–n) 369, (F–n) 719, (G–n) 1394

Very Special Arts, (I–n) 1768

Virginia Press Association, (I–n) 1769

Virginia Space Grant Consortium, (S–n) 366–367, (F–n) 718, (G–n) 1389

Virginia. State Council of Higher Education, (S–n) 368

Waialua Hawaiian Civic Club, (S–p) 170

Walt Disney Studios, (I–n) 1770

Warner–Lambert Company, (G–n) 1148

Washington Higher Education Coordinating Board, (S–i) 127, (S–n) 371–372, (F–i) 447

Washoe Tribe of Nevada and California, (S–i) 108

Watts Health Foundation, Inc., (S–n) 196

WAVE TV 3, (I–n) 1771

WCVB–TV, (I–n) 1606, 1630, 1772

Wells Fargo Bank, (S–i) 108

West Coast Conference, (I–n) 1773

Western History Association, (G–n) 1305

Western States Advertising Agencies Association, (I–n) 1643

Whatcom Museum, (G–i) 811, (G–a) 841

White Earth Tribal Council, (S–i) 128–129, (F–i) 448

Wilcox Hospital Foundation, (F–p) 481

William and Flora Hewlett Foundation, (G–n) 1396

William Randolph Hearst Foundation, (S–i) 130, (G–n) 953

William T. Grant Foundation, (G–n) 1398

Williams College. Dean of the Faculty, (G–n) 1048

Wilmington Star–News, (I–n) 1774

Wisconsin Center for Education Research, (G–n) 1376

Wisconsin Higher Educational Aids Board, (S–i) 131, (S–n) 374, 376, (F–i) 449

Wisconsin Space Grant Consortium, (S–n) 375, (F–n) 725, (G–n) 1400–1402

W.K. Kellogg Foundation, (F–n) 633, (I–n) 1775

Woman in the Moon Publications, (A–n) 1454

Women of the Evangelical Lutheran Church in America, (S–n) 178, (F–n) 490, (G–n) 1045

Women's Community Foundation, (G–n) 1404

Women's Foundation, (S–n) 378, (G–n) 1349, 1405

Women's Fund of Greater Omaha, (G–n) 1406

Women's Funding Alliance, (G–n) 1407

Women's Sports Foundation, (G–n) 1052, 1352, (I–n) 1617, 1776

Women's Studio Workshop, (G–n) 900–901, (I–n) 1742–1743

Woodrow Wilson National Fellowship Foundation, (S–n) 237, 328, (F–n) 496, 556, 684–685, (I–n) 1591

Woods Hole Marine Biological Laboratory, (G–n) 1399

Woods Hole Oceanographic Institution, (G–n) 1347, 1412, (I–n) 1754

Xerox Corporation, (S–n) 379, (F–n) 728

Yakama Indian Nation, (S–i) 41, 132–135, (F–i) 450, (A–i) 1439

Yale University. International Security Studies, (G–n) 1105

Zuni Tribe, (S–i) 136–137, (F–i) 451

S–Scholarships	**F–Fellowships**	**L–Loans**	**G–Grants**	**A–Awards**	**I–Internships**
i–American Indians	**a–Native Alaskans**		**p–Native Pacific Islanders**		**n–Native Americans in General**

Residency Index

This index identifies the residency requirements of the programs listed in the directory. Index entries (city, county, state, province, region country, continent) are arranged alphabetically (word by word) and subdivided first by program type and then by availability group. Cross–references provide access to broader or more specific geographic index terms. The numbers cited refer to book entry numbers, not to page numbers.

Hawaii
 Scholarships: **Native Pacific Islanders,** 154, 159, 162–167, 169–170
 Fellowships: **Native Pacific Islanders,** 466, 471, 473–477, 480–481
 Loans: **Native Pacific Islanders,** 746
 Grants: **Native Pacific Islanders,** 850–855, 858; **Native Americans in General,** 1121, 1213, 1326
 See also United States; names of specific cities and counties
Helena, Montana
 Loans: **Native Americans in General,** 768
 See also Montana
Hendry County, Florida
 Scholarships: **Native Americans in General,** 195
 See also Florida
Hollywood, California. *See* Los Angeles, California
Houston, Texas
 Fellowships: **Native Americans in General,** 619
 Loans: **Native Americans in General,** 768
 Awards: **Native Americans in General,** 1477
 See also Texas

Idaho
 Scholarships: **Native Americans in General,** 252
 Grants: **Native Americans in General,** 1086
 See also United States; names of specific cities and counties
Illinois
 Scholarships: **Native Americans in General,** 172, 218, 295, 377
 Fellowships: **Native Americans in General,** 486, 530, 577, 726
 Loans: **Native Americans in General,** 752, 769
 See also Midwestern states; United States; names of specific cities and counties
Indiana
 Scholarships: **Native Americans in General,** 255
 See also Midwestern states; United States; names of specific cities and counties
Iowa
 Scholarships: **Native Americans in General,** 300
 Fellowships: **Native Americans in General,** 636
 See also Midwestern states; United States; names of specific cities and counties

Japan
 Grants: **Native Americans in General,** 861
 See also Foreign countries
Jefferson County, Kentucky
 Scholarships: **Native Americans in General,** 279
 See also Kentucky
Jefferson County, Ohio
 Scholarships: **Native Americans in General,** 329, 351
 See also Ohio

Kane County, Illinois
 Scholarships: **Native Americans in General,** 203

See also Illinois
Kansas
 Scholarships: **American Indians,** 16; **Native Americans in General,** 266–267
 Fellowships: **Native Americans in General,** 592
 Loans: **Native Americans in General,** 761–762
 Grants: **Native Americans in General,** 1086
 See also Midwestern states; United States; names of specific cities and counties
Kansas City, Missouri
 Loans: **Native Americans in General,** 768
 See also Missouri
Kentucky
 Grants: **Native Americans in General,** 1086, 1112
 See also Southern states; United States; names of specific cities and counties

Lake County, Illinois
 Scholarships: **Native Americans in General,** 203
 See also Illinois
Lake County, Indiana
 Scholarships: **Native Americans in General,** 203
 See also Indiana
Latin America. *See* Central America; Mexico
Lea County, New Mexico
 Scholarships: **American Indians,** 120
 Loans: **American Indians,** 740
 See also New Mexico
Livingston County, New York
 Scholarships: **Native Americans in General,** 262, 373
 See also New York
Los Angeles, California
 Scholarships: **Native Americans in General,** 286
 Loans: **Native Americans in General,** 768
 See also California
Los Angeles County, California
 Scholarships: **Native Pacific Islanders,** 158; **Native Americans in General,** 196, 268
 Fellowships: **Native Pacific Islanders,** 470; **Native Americans in General,** 593
 Grants: **Native Americans in General,** 920, 953, 1099, 1119
 See also California
Louisiana
 Scholarships: **American Indians,** 125
 See also Southern states; United States; names of specific cities
Louisville, Kentucky
 Scholarships: **Native Americans in General,** 279
 See also Kentucky
Lynn, Massachusetts
 Scholarships: **Native Americans in General,** 250
 See also Massachusetts

Maine
 Scholarships: **American Indians,** 125; **Native Americans in General,** 235
 Grants: **American Indians,** 816; **Native Americans in General,** 1183–1184

Fellowships: **American Indians,** 427–428, 442; **Native Alaskans,** 462–463; **Native Americans in General,** 709

Loans: **Native Americans in General,** 748–749

Grants: **Native Americans in General,** 903, 932, 1037, 1123, 1272, 1335, 1362, 1391

See also United States; names of specific cities and counties

New York, New York

Scholarships: **Native Americans in General,** 286, 307

Fellowships: **Native Americans in General,** 605, 619

Loans: **Native Americans in General,** 768

Grants: **Native Americans in General,** 1129–1130, 1224, 1321

Awards: **Native Americans in General,** 1477

See also New York

North Carolina

Scholarships: **American Indians,** 56, 61, 67, 72, 89–90, 121, 125–126; **Native Alaskans,** 147, 152; **Native Americans in General,** 228, 261, 292, 308–309

Fellowships: **American Indians,** 431; **Native Americans in General,** 502

Loans: **Native Americans in General,** 777

Grants: **Native Americans in General,** 1057, 1125, 1185, 1232

See also Southern states; United States; names of specific cities and counties

North Dakota

Scholarships: **American Indians,** 10, 16, 43, 91; **Native Americans in General,** 199

Fellowships: **Native Americans in General,** 503

Grants: **Native Americans in General,** 1086, 1233–1234

See also Midwestern states; United States; names of specific cities

Northern Marianas

Grants: **Native Americans in General,** 1213, 1326

See also United States

Novato, California

Scholarships: **Native Americans in General,** 214

See also California

Ocean County, New Jersey

Scholarships: **Native Americans in General,** 192

See also New Jersey

Ohio

Scholarships: **Native Americans in General,** 314

See also Midwestern states; United States; names of specific cities and counties

Oklahoma

Scholarships: **American Indians,** 16, 18–19, 21, 24, 59, 75–76, 104; **Native Americans in General,** 317–318

Fellowships: **American Indians,** 388–390, 434; **Native Americans in General,** 668–670

Loans: **Native Americans in General,** 778–779

Grants: **Native Americans in General,** 1086, 1252

See also Southern states; United States; names of specific cities and counties

Omaha, Nebraska

Grants: **Native Americans in General,** 1406

See also Nebraska

Ontario County, New York

Scholarships: **Native Americans in General,** 262, 373

See also New York

Orange County, California

Scholarships: **Native Pacific Islanders,** 158; **Native Americans in General,** 268

Fellowships: **Native Pacific Islanders,** 470; **Native Americans in General,** 593

See also California

Oregon

Scholarships: **American Indians,** 16

Fellowships: **Native Americans in General,** 673

Loans: **Native Americans in General,** 781

Grants: **Native Americans in General,** 1251

See also United States; names of specific cities and counties

Orleans County, New York

Scholarships: **Native Americans in General,** 262, 373

See also New York

Otero County, New Mexico

Scholarships: **American Indians,** 120

Loans: **American Indians,** 740

See also New Mexico

Palau

Grants: **Native Americans in General,** 1213, 1326

See also United States

Palm Beach County, Florida

Scholarships: **Native Americans in General,** 195, 209, 244

Grants: **Native Americans in General,** 954

See also Florida

Pennsylvania

Scholarships: **Native Americans in General,** 325, 329, 351

Loans: **Native Americans in General,** 766

See also United States; names of specific cities and counties

Philadelphia, Pennsylvania

Fellowships: **Native Americans in General,** 619

Loans: **Native Americans in General,** 768

Awards: **Native Americans in General,** 1477

See also Pennsylvania

Phoenix, Arizona

Fellowships: **Native Americans in General,** 619

Awards: **Native Americans in General,** 1477

See also Arizona

Pinellas County, Florida

Grants: **Native Americans in General,** 1266–1267

See also Florida

Pittsburgh, Pennsylvania

Fellowships: **Native Americans in General,** 619

Awards: **Native Americans in General,** 1477

See also Pennsylvania

Placer County, California

Scholarships: **Native Americans in General,** 336

See also California

Porter County, Indiana

Scholarships: **Native Americans in General,** 203

See also Indiana

Providence, Rhode Island

Fellowships: **Native Americans in General,** 619

Awards: **Native Americans in General,** 1477

See also Rhode Island

Tulsa, Oklahoma
Fellowships: **Native Americans in General,** 619
Awards: **Native Americans in General,** 1477
See also Oklahoma

United States
Scholarships: **American Indians,** 1–4, 6–9, 11–15, 17–31, 33, 35, 37–40, 42, 44–55, 57, 62, 64–66, 69, 73, 75–83, 87–88, 92–96, 98–101, 104–106, 109–113, 115–116, 118–119, 122–124, 126, 128, 130, 132–137; **Native Alaskans,** 138–139, 141–144, 146, 148–149, 151, 153; **Native Pacific Islanders,** 155–156, 160, 164, 168; **Native Americans in General,** 171, 173–174, 177–194, 197–198, 201–202, 204–205, 207–208, 210–212, 215–217, 220, 222–227, 231, 233–234, 236–237, 239–241, 243, 245–249, 251, 253, 256–259, 263–265, 268–271, 273–274, 276–277, 281–283, 285, 287, 289–291, 293–294, 299, 301–304, 310, 312–313, 315–316, 318, 320–324, 326–328, 331, 333, 335, 338–340, 342–344, 346–350, 354, 357, 359–364, 370, 379
Fellowships: **American Indians,** 380–413, 415–417, 419, 421–424, 429–430, 432, 434–437, 439–440, 442–446, 448, 450–451; **Native Alaskans,** 453–457, 459–461, 464–465; **Native Pacific Islanders,** 467–468, 472, 474, 478–479, 481–482; **Native Americans in General,** 483–485, 487, 489–501, 507–508, 511–518, 520–523, 525–529, 531–562, 564–569, 571–576, 578–591, 593–596, 598–600, 602–606, 608–613, 615–618, 620, 622–635, 637–653, 655–667, 669–672, 674–687, 689–708, 710, 712, 714–716, 719–724, 727–728
Loans: **American Indians,** 729–737, 739, 741; **Native Alaskans,** 742–745; **Native Pacific Islanders,** 747; **Native Americans in General,** 750–751, 753–754, 756–760, 763–764, 767, 772–776, 779–780, 782–783, 785–787
Grants: **American Indians,** 788–815, 817–830; **Native Alaskans,** 832–847, 849; **Native Pacific Islanders,** 856–857; **Native Americans in General,** 859–875, 877–901, 904–908, 910–918, 921–924, 931, 933–943, 945–952, 956–960, 962–1033, 1035, 1038–1056, 1058–1085, 1087–1098, 1100–1107, 1109, 1111–1118, 1120–1122, 1124, 1126–1128, 1130–1132, 1134–1142, 1144–1152, 1157–1177, 1179–1182, 1186–1220, 1225–1231, 1235–1250, 1253–1265, 1268–1271, 1273–1302, 1304–1321, 1323–1326, 1330–1334, 1336–1348, 1350–1353, 1355–1357, 1359–1361, 1363–1388, 1390, 1392, 1394–1399, 1403, 1409–1413
Awards: **American Indians,** 1414–1439; **Native Alaskans,** 1440–1441; **Native Americans in General,** 1442–1457, 1459–1467, 1469–1474, 1476, 1478–1487, 1489
See also names of specific cities, counties, states, and regions

Utah
Scholarships: **Native Americans in General,** 365
See also United States; names of specific cities

Ventura County, California
Scholarships: **Native Pacific Islanders,** 158; **Native Americans in General,** 268

Fellowships: **Native Pacific Islanders,** 470; **Native Americans in General,** 593
See also California

Vermont
Scholarships: **Native Americans in General,** 369
See also United States; names of specific cities and counties

Virgin Islands
Scholarships: **Native Americans in General,** 234, 343
Fellowships: **Native Americans in General,** 700
Grants: **Native Americans in General,** 1096
See also United States

Virginia
Scholarships: **Native Americans in General,** 366–368
Fellowships: **Native Americans in General,** 718
Grants: **Native Americans in General,** 1389
See also Southern states; United States; names of specific cities and counties

Warwick, Rhode Island
Fellowships: **Native Americans in General,** 619
Awards: **Native Americans in General,** 1477
See also Rhode Island

Washington
Scholarships: **American Indians,** 16, 41, 127, 132–135; **Native Americans in General,** 311, 371–372
Fellowships: **American Indians,** 447, 450
Grants: **Native Americans in General,** 1407
Awards: **American Indians,** 1439
See also United States; names of specific cities and counties

Washington, D.C.
Scholarships: **Native Americans in General,** 286
Fellowships: **Native Americans in General,** 619
Awards: **Native Americans in General,** 1477
See also Southern states; United States

Wayne County, New York
Scholarships: **Native Americans in General,** 262, 373
See also New York

West Virginia
Scholarships: **Native Americans in General,** 329, 351
Grants: **Native Americans in General,** 1086
See also Southern states; United States; names of specific cities

Wichita, Kansas
Fellowships: **Native Americans in General,** 619
Awards: **Native Americans in General,** 1477
See also Kansas

Will County, Illinois
Scholarships: **Native Americans in General,** 203
See also Illinois

Wisconsin
Scholarships: **American Indians,** 64–65, 95–103, 131; **Native Americans in General,** 199, 374–376
Fellowships: **American Indians,** 414, 416, 433, 438, 449; **Native Americans in General,** 503, 725
Loans: **American Indians,** 739
Grants: **American Indians,** 821; **Native Americans in General,** 1400–1402
See also Midwestern states; United States; names of specific cities and counties

Tenability Index

This index identifies the geographic locations where the programs listed in the directory may be used. Index entries (city, county, state, province, region, country, continent) are arranged alphabetically word by word and first subdivided by program type and then by availability group. Cross–references provide access to broader and more specific geographic index terms. The numbers cited refer to book entry numbers, not to page numbers.

Subject Index

This index is arranged by subject or program emphasis, subdivided first by program type and then by eligible minority group. Subject terms are arranged in alphabetical order, word by word. Cross–references provide access to related index terms. The numbers cited refer to book entry numbers, not page numbers.

General programs

Scholarships: **American Indians,** 1–3, 5–6, 8–9, 13–15, 18–21, 24, 27, 29, 31–32, 34, 36, 43–47, 49–51, 55–56, 58, 60–68, 70–76, 79, 82, 84–85, 88–96, 98–101, 103–104, 107–108, 111–112, 114–117, 121–122, 125–127, 129, 131–137; **Native Alaskans,** 139–140, 145, 147–148, 152–153; **Native Pacific Islanders,** 157–158, 161–165, 167, 169–170; **Native Americans in General,** 178, 194, 198, 202, 207, 209, 212–214, 218, 228–229, 232, 235, 243–244, 250–252, 254, 259, 261–262, 266, 279, 292, 301, 306, 308–309, 318–319, 329–331, 334–335, 348–349, 351, 358, 361–362, 368, 371–374, 376, 378

Fellowships: **American Indians,** 380–381, 383–384, 386, 388–390, 393, 401, 405–406, 408–409, 411, 414–418, 420, 423, 425–426, 430–434, 440–444, 447, 449–451; **Native Alaskans,** 453, 455, 458, 465; **Native Pacific Islanders,** 469–470, 473–475, 477, 480; **Native Americans in General,** 490, 506, 511, 515–516, 527–528, 530, 538, 547, 571, 577, 592, 614, 669, 671, 676, 709, 713

Loans: **American Indians,** 729, 733, 737–739; **Native Americans in General,** 751–752, 755–756, 761, 766, 777, 779–780

Grants: **American Indians,** 821; **Native Americans in General,** 859–860, 936, 943, 963, 1033, 1045, 1134–1135, 1143, 1175, 1224, 1231, 1265, 1283, 1300, 1310, 1335, 1349, 1363, 1373–1374, 1377

Awards: **American Indians,** 1418, 1425, 1428, 1439; **Native Americans in General,** 1442, 1460–1461

Internships: **American Indians,** 1490–1491, 1506, 1509; **Native Alaskans,** 1518; **Native Americans in General,** 1525, 1587, 1654, 1682, 1715, 1747

Directories: 1777–1783, 1785, 1788, 1790–1792, 1797–1810, 1813, 1815, 1817, 1819–1820, 1823–1824, 1826, 1828, 1830–1833, 1835–1836

Genetics

Fellowships: **Native Americans in General,** 575

Grants: **American Indians,** 792; **Native Americans in General,** 1067–1068, 1073, 1217–1218

Internships: **Native Americans in General,** 1673

See also General programs; Medical sciences

Geography

Grants: **Native Alaskans,** 833; **Native Americans in General,** 1055, 1255

Internships: **Native Americans in General,** 1559–1560

See also General programs; Social sciences

Geology

Scholarships: **Native Americans in General,** 290, 321, 326, 338, 343

Fellowships: **Native Americans in General,** 628, 637, 657, 659, 674, 677, 695, 703

Grants: **Native Americans in General,** 878–879, 890–891, 894, 898, 921, 957, 997, 1006, 1049, 1058–1061, 1074, 1098, 1106, 1122, 1235–1236, 1293, 1297, 1312, 1330–1332, 1343, 1412

Internships: **Native Americans in General,** 1689, 1698, 1708, 1728, 1760

See also Earth sciences; General programs; Physical sciences

Geosciences. See Earth sciences

German language. See Language, German

Gerontology. See Aged and aging

Gifted and talented. See Education, gifted/talented

Government. See Political science and politics; Public administration

Grade school. See Education, elementary

Graphic arts

Scholarships: **American Indians,** 124; **Native Americans in General,** 174, 189, 203, 219, 272, 341

Grants: **American Indians,** 811; **Native Alaskans,** 841; **Native Americans in General,** 900–901, 922–923, 1031, 1129

Awards: **American Indians,** 1436; **Native Americans in General,** 1450

Internships: **Native Americans in General,** 1521, 1530, 1539, 1541, 1545–1547, 1557, 1574, 1593–1594, 1600, 1610, 1626, 1631, 1651, 1683–1684, 1705, 1727, 1735, 1738, 1753

Directories: 1816

See also Art; Arts and crafts; General programs

Guidance. See Counseling

Gynecology

Scholarships: **Native Americans in General,** 302

Fellowships: **Native Americans in General,** 641

Loans: **Native Americans in General,** 772

Grants: **American Indians,** 805; **Native Alaskans,** 838; **Native Americans in General,** 1056, 1200

See also General programs; Medical sciences

Handicapped. See Disabilities

Hawaiian language. See Language, Hawaiian

Hawaiian studies

Scholarships: **Native Pacific Islanders,** 159

Fellowships: **Native Pacific Islanders,** 471

See also General programs; Native American studies

Health and health care

Scholarships: **American Indians,** 11, 16, 18, 25, 37–38, 40–42, 48, 59, 110; **Native Alaskans,** 141, 143–144; **Native Pacific Islanders,** 166; **Native Americans in General,** 196, 199, 228, 245, 261, 339

Fellowships: **American Indians,** 385, 403–404, 407, 439; **Native Alaskans,** 456–457; **Native Pacific Islanders,** 476; **Native Americans in General,** 489, 497, 503, 549, 569, 572, 616, 664, 696

Loans: **American Indians,** 730; **Native Alaskans,** 742; **Native Pacific Islanders,** 746; **Native Americans in General,** 758, 763, 773

Grants: **American Indians,** 805–806, 817; **Native Alaskans,** 838–839, 846; **Native Americans in General,** 862, 864, 869, 871–874, 927, 940, 944, 980, 984, 1007, 1013, 1024–1025, 1051, 1054, 1062–1064, 1076, 1081–1083, 1144–1147, 1157–1158, 1180, 1207, 1209, 1224, 1245, 1275, 1278–1279, 1284, 1287, 1308, 1313, 1323, 1336, 1361, 1378, 1382, 1398, 1408

Awards: **Native Americans in General,** 1480

Internships: **American Indians,** 1496, 1499; **Native Americans in General,** 1523, 1533, 1551, 1596, 1622, 1632–1633, 1690, 1699, 1707, 1763–1765, 1775

Directories: 1795, 1802, 1825

See also General programs; Medical sciences; Nurses and nursing

Hearing impairments

Fellowships: **Native Americans in General,** 495, 591

Grants: **Native Americans in General,** 973, 1369

Internships: **Native Americans in General,** 1582

Internships: **American Indians,** 1513; **Native Americans in General,** 1543, 1552, 1568, 1608
See also Computer sciences; General programs; Libraries and librarianship
Insurance. *See* Actuarial sciences
International affairs
Scholarships: **Native Americans in General,** 176, 237, 286, 328
Fellowships: **Native Americans in General,** 488, 533, 537, 556, 680, 684–685
Grants: **Native Americans in General,** 861, 876, 985, 993, 1093–1095, 1105, 1263, 1268–1269, 1308
Internships: **Native Americans in General,** 1559–1560, 1591, 1759, 1765
Directories: 1793
See also General programs; Political science and politics
International relations. *See* International affairs

Japanese language. *See* Language, Japanese
Japanese studies
Grants: **Native Americans in General,** 1102–1103
See also General programs
Jewelry
Scholarships: **Native Americans in General,** 189
Awards: **Native Americans in General,** 1450
Internships: **Native Alaskans,** 1515
See also Arts and crafts; General programs
Jobs. *See* Employment
Journalism
Scholarships: **Native Pacific Islanders,** 154–156, 168; **Native Americans in General,** 177, 192–193, 199, 201, 203–204, 206, 217, 219, 221–222, 225, 238–239, 255, 265, 268, 270–272, 274, 277, 298, 300, 304, 307, 311, 314, 325, 336–337, 341, 352
Fellowships: **Native Pacific Islanders,** 466–468, 478; **Native Americans in General,** 485, 503, 513, 529, 540, 560, 593, 596, 612–613, 629, 636, 652, 694
Grants: **Native Americans in General,** 1142, 1151, 1170, 1186, 1266–1267, 1299
Awards: **Native Americans in General,** 1478, 1482, 1486–1487
Internships: **Native Americans in General,** 1521, 1524, 1530, 1536, 1538–1539, 1541, 1545–1548, 1551, 1553, 1556–1558, 1563, 1567, 1573–1574, 1576–1577, 1579, 1583–1584, 1588, 1590, 1593–1595, 1598–1599, 1603–1606, 1609–1610, 1622–1627, 1629–1630, 1634–1635, 1644–1645, 1647–1648, 1651, 1660, 1662–1665, 1667, 1675, 1683–1684, 1696, 1701–1702, 1704–1705, 1707, 1721–1723, 1725–1727, 1729, 1735, 1738–1739, 1752–1753, 1769, 1771–1772, 1774
Directories: 1786, 1822
See also Communications; General programs; Radio; Television; Writers and writing
Junior college. *See* Education, higher
Jurisprudence. *See* Legal studies and services

Labor unions and members
Scholarships: **Native Americans in General,** 199
Fellowships: **Native Americans in General,** 503, 565
Awards: **Native Americans in General,** 1487

Internships: **Native Americans in General,** 1551
Directories: 1831
See also General programs; Social sciences
Landscape architecture
Scholarships: **American Indians,** 86; **Native Alaskans,** 150; **Native Americans in General,** 227
Fellowships: **American Indians,** 428; **Native Alaskans,** 463; **Native Americans in General,** 600
See also Botany; General programs; Horticulture
Language, Albanian
Fellowships: **Native Americans in General,** 581
See also General programs; Language and linguistics
Language and linguistics
Scholarships: **Native Americans in General,** 208, 267, 317
Fellowships: **Native Americans in General,** 495, 660–661, 668, 703
Loans: **Native Americans in General,** 762, 778
Grants: **American Indians,** 790, 792, 810–811, 823; **Native Alaskans,** 833, 841, 849; **Native Americans in General,** 1019, 1055, 1097, 1198, 1379
Awards: **Native Americans in General,** 1474, 1479
Internships: **American Indians,** 1499; **Native Americans in General,** 1559–1561, 1566, 1582, 1749
Directories: 1814
See also General programs; Humanities; names of specific languages
Language, Bulgarian
Fellowships: **Native Americans in General,** 581
See also General programs; Language and linguistics
Language, Chinese
Fellowships: **Native Americans in General,** 685
See also General programs; Language and linguistics
Language, Czech
Fellowships: **Native Americans in General,** 581
See also General programs; Language and linguistics
Language, English
Grants: **American Indians,** 810; **Native Americans in General,** 1097, 1198
See also English as a foreign language; English as a second language; General programs; Language and linguistics
Language, French
Fellowships: **Native Americans in General,** 685
See also General programs; Language and linguistics
Language, German
Fellowships: **Native Americans in General,** 685
See also General programs; Language and linguistics
Language, Hawaiian
Scholarships: **Native Pacific Islanders,** 159
Fellowships: **Native Pacific Islanders,** 471
Grants: **Native Pacific Islanders,** 851, 854; **Native Americans in General,** 1213
See also General programs; Language and linguistics
Language, Hungarian
Fellowships: **Native Americans in General,** 581
See also General programs; Language and linguistics
Language, Japanese
Fellowships: **Native Americans in General,** 685
See also General programs; Language and linguistics
Language, Macedonian
Fellowships: **Native Americans in General,** 581
See also General programs; Language and linguistics
Language, Native American
Grants: **Native Americans in General,** 1213

Novels
Awards: **American Indians,** 1427; **Native Alaskans,** 1441; **Native Americans in General,** 1481
See also Fiction; General programs; Writers and writing
Nuclear engineering. *See* Engineering, nuclear
Nuclear science
Scholarships: **Native Americans in General,** 264
Fellowships: **Native Americans in General,** 518, 588, 664
Grants: **Native Americans in General,** 1115
Internships: **Native Americans in General,** 1562, 1690
See also General programs; Physical sciences
Nurses and nursing
Scholarships: **American Indians,** 37, 40, 42, 50, 54, 59, 64, 86, 93, 99; **Native Alaskans,** 143–144, 150; **Native Pacific Islanders,** 166, 170; **Native Americans in General,** 197, 226, 228, 231, 261, 288, 302–303, 312–313, 339, 356
Fellowships: **American Indians,** 384, 404, 428, 446; **Native Alaskans,** 453, 457, 463; **Native Pacific Islanders,** 476, 482; **Native Americans in General,** 501, 520, 546, 615–616, 621, 641, 644, 683, 690, 696, 711
Loans: **American Indians,** 730, 741; **Native Alaskans,** 742; **Native Pacific Islanders,** 746–747; **Native Americans in General,** 750, 772
Grants: **American Indians,** 805; **Native Alaskans,** 838; **Native Americans in General,** 862, 864, 869, 911, 984, 1025–1026, 1051, 1056, 1064, 1076, 1145–1147, 1200, 1228, 1243–1244, 1249, 1291, 1313, 1315–1316
Internships: **Native Americans in General,** 1717
Directories: 1789
See also General programs; Health and health care; Medical sciences
Nutrition
Scholarships: **American Indians,** 40, 42; **Native Alaskans,** 143–144; **Native Americans in General,** 200
Fellowships: **American Indians,** 404; **Native Alaskans,** 457; **Native Americans in General,** 510
Loans: **American Indians,** 730; **Native Alaskans,** 742
Grants: **American Indians,** 803; **Native Americans in General,** 867, 1245
Internships: **Native Americans in General,** 1673
See also General programs; Home economics; Medical sciences

Obstetrics
Scholarships: **Native Americans in General,** 302
Fellowships: **Native Americans in General,** 641
Loans: **Native Americans in General,** 772
Grants: **American Indians,** 805; **Native Alaskans,** 838; **Native Americans in General,** 1056, 1200
See also General programs; Medical sciences; Pregnancy
Occupational therapy
Scholarships: **American Indians,** 38, 86; **Native Alaskans,** 141, 150; **Native Americans in General,** 245, 339
Fellowships: **American Indians,** 403, 428; **Native Alaskans,** 456, 463; **Native Americans in General,** 572, 696
See also Counseling; Employment; General programs

Oceanography
Scholarships: **Native Americans in General,** 180–181, 183, 223, 248–249, 283, 290, 323
Fellowships: **Native Americans in General,** 493, 564, 628, 637, 640
Grants: **Native Alaskans,** 833; **Native Americans in General,** 890, 945, 1058, 1060–1061, 1230, 1250, 1293, 1412
Internships: **Native Americans in General,** 1528, 1602, 1731
See also General programs; Marine sciences
Opera. *See* Music; Voice
Operations research
Grants: **Native Americans in General,** 910, 1311
Internships: **American Indians,** 1513
See also General programs; Social sciences
Optical engineering. *See* Engineering, optical
Optics
Fellowships: **Native Americans in General,** 640
Grants: **Native Americans in General,** 1100, 1127, 1189
Internships: **Native Americans in General,** 1632–1633
See also General programs; Physics
Optometry
Scholarships: **American Indians,** 38, 42, 86; **Native Alaskans,** 141, 144, 150; **Native Americans in General,** 245, 303, 339
Fellowships: **American Indians,** 403–404, 428; **Native Alaskans,** 456–457, 463; **Native Americans in General,** 569, 572, 644, 670, 696
Loans: **American Indians,** 730; **Native Alaskans,** 742; **Native Americans in General,** 763
Grants: **American Indians,** 805; **Native Alaskans,** 838; **Native Americans in General,** 864, 984, 1051
See also General programs; Medical sciences
Orchestras. *See* Music
Osteopathy
Scholarships: **American Indians,** 38, 42; **Native Alaskans,** 141, 144; **Native Pacific Islanders,** 166; **Native Americans in General,** 245, 302–303, 339
Fellowships: **American Indians,** 403–404; **Native Alaskans,** 456–457; **Native Pacific Islanders,** 476; **Native Americans in General,** 549, 569, 572, 641–642, 644, 649, 670, 696
Loans: **American Indians,** 730; **Native Alaskans,** 742; **Native Pacific Islanders,** 746; **Native Americans in General,** 758, 763, 772
Grants: **American Indians,** 805; **Native Alaskans,** 838; **Native Americans in General,** 940, 984, 1051, 1056, 1200
See also General programs; Medical sciences

Packaging engineering. *See* Engineering, packaging
Painting. *See* Fine arts
Pay equity. *See* Equal opportunity; Income
Peace studies
Fellowships: **Native Americans in General,** 533, 680
Grants: **Native Americans in General,** 985, 1093–1094, 1263
See also General programs; Political science and politics
Pediatrics
Scholarships: **Native Americans in General,** 302

Fellowships: **Native Americans in General,** 563, 641, 692

Loans: **Native Americans in General,** 772

Grants: **American Indians,** 805; **Native Alaskans,** 838; **Native Americans in General,** 1022, 1056, 1200, 1398

Awards: **Native Americans in General,** 1468

See also General programs; Medical sciences

Performing arts

Scholarships: **American Indians,** 4; **Native Americans in General,** 188, 258

Fellowships: **American Indians,** 382

Loans: **Native Americans in General,** 748

Grants: **American Indians,** 810; **Native Americans in General,** 902–903, 920, 944, 967, 999, 1037, 1057, 1066, 1097, 1112, 1123, 1125, 1129, 1185, 1232, 1237–1238, 1261, 1303, 1335, 1358, 1362

Awards: **Native Americans in General,** 1449, 1469

Internships: **Native Americans in General,** 1537

Directories: 1794, 1816, 1818, 1821

See also General programs; names of specific performing arts

Personnel administration

Grants: **Native Americans in General,** 1268

Internships: **Native Americans in General,** 1619, 1632, 1697, 1710, 1741

See also General programs; Management

Petroleum engineering. *See* Engineering, petroleum

Pharmaceutical sciences

Scholarships: **American Indians,** 37–38, 40, 42, 86; **Native Alaskans,** 141, 143–144, 150; **Native Americans in General,** 245, 303, 339

Fellowships: **American Indians,** 403–404, 428; **Native Alaskans,** 456–457, 463; **Native Americans in General,** 539, 569, 572, 575, 644, 696

Loans: **American Indians,** 730; **Native Alaskans,** 742; **Native Americans in General,** 763

Grants: **American Indians,** 805; **Native Alaskans,** 838; **Native Americans in General,** 864, 872–873, 940, 984, 1051, 1073, 1177, 1196–1197

Internships: **Native Americans in General,** 1523, 1525, 1669–1670, 1762

See also General programs; Medical sciences

Philanthropy

Grants: **Native Americans in General,** 906

See also General programs

Philology. *See* Language and linguistics

Philosophy

Fellowships: **Native Americans in General,** 703

Grants: **American Indians,** 810–811; **Native Alaskans,** 841; **Native Americans in General,** 963, 1097, 1111

Directories: 1811

See also General programs; Humanities

Photogrammetry

Grants: **Native Americans in General,** 1230

See also General programs; Photography

Photography

Scholarships: **Native Pacific Islanders,** 155, 168; **Native Americans in General,** 187, 203, 219, 221, 265, 304, 311, 325

Fellowships: **Native Pacific Islanders,** 467, 478

Grants: **Native Americans in General,** 1027, 1031, 1099, 1112, 1129

Awards: **Native Americans in General,** 1448, 1486

Internships: **Native Americans in General,** 1521, 1530, 1539, 1541, 1546–1548, 1557, 1567, 1574, 1576, 1579, 1584, 1593–1594, 1599, 1603, 1627, 1631, 1645, 1648, 1651, 1662–1664, 1667, 1675, 1683–1684, 1702, 1704, 1706, 1727, 1738–1739, 1753, 1774

See also Fine arts; General programs

Physical education. *See* Education, physical

Physical sciences

Scholarships: **American Indians,** 16, 25; **Native Americans in General,** 176, 321

Fellowships: **American Indians,** 426; **Native Americans in General,** 488, 517, 532, 554–555, 578, 603–604, 665, 674

Loans: **American Indians,** 738

Grants: **Native Americans in General,** 872–873, 876, 889, 908, 922–923, 937, 960, 974–978, 980, 983, 1007–1009, 1039–1042, 1081, 1246–1247, 1294–1295, 1308, 1338, 1359, 1374

Awards: **American Indians,** 1438

Internships: **American Indians,** 1496, 1509–1510; **Native Alaskans,** 1518–1519; **Native Americans in General,** 1523, 1531, 1559–1560, 1568, 1575, 1637–1638, 1698, 1729, 1754, 1763–1764

Directories: 1793

See also General programs; Sciences; names of specific physical sciences

Physical therapy

Scholarships: **American Indians,** 38, 40, 42, 86; **Native Alaskans,** 141, 143–144, 150; **Native Americans in General,** 245, 339

Fellowships: **American Indians,** 403–404, 428; **Native Alaskans,** 456–457, 463; **Native Americans in General,** 572, 696

Loans: **American Indians,** 730; **Native Alaskans,** 742

See also Disabilities; General programs; Health and health care; Rehabilitation

Physics

Scholarships: **Native Americans in General,** 180, 216, 290, 315–316, 326, 338, 343, 369, 379

Fellowships: **American Indians,** 400; **Native Americans in General,** 493, 497, 500, 548, 575, 614, 628, 637, 640, 659, 662–664, 666–667, 677, 695, 700, 703, 719, 728

Grants: **American Indians,** 792, 794, 810; **Native Americans in General,** 875, 879, 890, 896, 934, 938, 945, 957, 1060–1061, 1063, 1073, 1097, 1100, 1115, 1127, 1143, 1188, 1195, 1204, 1275, 1293, 1370, 1394, 1412

Internships: **American Indians,** 1498, 1501, 1513; **Native Americans in General,** 1528, 1533, 1543, 1550, 1572, 1596, 1632–1633, 1658, 1689–1690, 1699, 1708, 1710, 1728, 1730–1731, 1741, 1746, 1760

See also General programs; Mathematics; Physical sciences

Physiology

Fellowships: **Native Americans in General,** 575, 724

Grants: **American Indians,** 792; **Native Americans in General,** 1067, 1073, 1368, 1399

Internships: **Native Americans in General,** 1673

See also General programs; Medical sciences

Plays

Scholarships: **Native Americans in General,** 191

Fellowships: **Native Americans in General,** 605

Grants: **Native Americans in General,** 920, 1037, 1112, 1123, 1125, 1129–1130, 1132–1133, 1262, 1272, 1362

Awards: **Native Americans in General,** 1443, 1452, 1456

Directories: 1821–1822

See also General programs; Literature; Performing arts; Writers and writing

Podiatry

Scholarships: **American Indians,** 38, 42; **Native Alaskans,** 141, 144; **Native Americans in General,** 245

Fellowships: **American Indians,** 403–404; **Native Alaskans,** 456–457; **Native Americans in General,** 569, 572, 679

Loans: **American Indians,** 730; **Native Alaskans,** 742

Grants: **American Indians,** 805; **Native Alaskans,** 838; **Native Americans in General,** 984, 1051

See also General programs; Medical sciences

Poetry

Scholarships: **Native Americans in General,** 191

Grants: **Native Americans in General,** 920, 1027, 1031, 1034

Awards: **American Indians,** 1420; **Native Alaskans,** 1440; **Native Americans in General,** 1443, 1452, 1481

Directories: 1822

See also General programs; Literature; Writers and writing

Poisons. *See* Toxicology

Polar studies

Grants: **American Indians,** 792

See also General programs

Police science. *See* Criminal justice

Polish language. *See* Language, Polish

Political science and politics

Scholarships: **Native Americans in General,** 282

Fellowships: **Native Americans in General,** 494, 501, 537, 585–586, 606

Grants: **American Indians,** 810; **Native Alaskans,** 833; **Native Americans in General,** 911, 960, 993, 1055, 1097, 1270, 1298, 1315–1316, 1398

Internships: **American Indians,** 1509–1510; **Native Alaskans,** 1518–1519; **Native Americans in General,** 1559–1560, 1639–1640, 1665

See also General programs; Public administration; Social sciences

Pollution

Grants: **Native Americans in General,** 1011, 1382

See also Environmental sciences; General programs

Polymer science

Fellowships: **Native Americans in General,** 484

Internships: **Native Americans in General,** 1522

See also Chemistry; General programs

Population studies

Fellowships: **Native Americans in General,** 703

Grants: **Native Americans in General,** 1308, 1315–1316

Internships: **Native Americans in General,** 1765

See also Family planning; General programs; Social sciences

Posters. *See* Graphic arts

Poverty

Fellowships: **Native Americans in General,** 715

Grants: **Native Americans in General,** 927, 1182, 1375, 1404–1405

See also General programs; Social services; Social welfare

Pregnancy

Grants: **Native Americans in General,** 1026

See also Family planning; General programs; Midwifery; Obstetrics

Preschool education. *See* Education, preschool

Preservation

Grants: **Native Americans in General,** 1066

Internships: **Native Americans in General,** 1631

See also General programs; specific types of preservation

Preservation, historical. *See* Historical preservation

Press. *See* Journalism

Prints. *See* Art; Graphic arts

Psychiatry

Scholarships: **Native Pacific Islanders,** 166

Fellowships: **American Indians,** 437; **Native Pacific Islanders,** 476, 479; **Native Americans in General,** 520–521, 691

Loans: **Native Pacific Islanders,** 746; **Native Americans in General,** 750, 767

Grants: **American Indians,** 805, 824; **Native Alaskans,** 838; **Native Pacific Islanders,** 857; **Native Americans in General,** 1398

Internships: **Native Americans in General,** 1532, 1620, 1655

Directories: 1827

See also Behavioral sciences; Counseling; General programs; Medical sciences; Psychology

Psychology

Scholarships: **American Indians,** 38, 42, 53, 86; **Native Alaskans,** 141, 144, 146, 150; **Native Pacific Islanders,** 166; **Native Americans in General,** 245, 339

Fellowships: **American Indians,** 403–404, 410, 428; **Native Alaskans,** 456–457, 459, 463; **Native Pacific Islanders,** 476; **Native Americans in General,** 501, 507, 521, 536, 569, 572, 585–586, 614, 662–663, 691, 696, 707

Loans: **American Indians,** 730–731; **Native Alaskans,** 742–743; **Native Pacific Islanders,** 746

Grants: **American Indians,** 805, 810–811; **Native Alaskans,** 833, 838, 841; **Native Americans in General,** 911, 984, 1019, 1051, 1097, 1143, 1200, 1311, 1315–1316, 1398

Awards: **Native Americans in General,** 1444

Internships: **Native Americans in General,** 1581–1582, 1656

Directories: 1827

See also Behavioral sciences; Counseling; General programs; Psychiatry; Social sciences

Public administration

Scholarships: **Native Americans in General,** 176, 199, 282, 328

Fellowships: **Native Americans in General,** 488, 503, 543, 606, 639, 650, 684–685, 715

Grants: **Native Alaskans,** 848; **Native Americans in General,** 876, 899, 1010, 1050, 1118, 1211, 1245, 1270, 1298, 1326, 1375

Internships: **American Indians,** 1509; **Native Alaskans,** 1518; **Native Americans in General,** 1551, 1570, 1619, 1639–1640, 1661, 1674, 1692, 1697, 1720, 1765, 1768, 1772

See also General programs; Management; Political science and politics; Social sciences

Public affairs. *See* Public administration

Public health. *See* Health and health care

Public policy. *See* Public administration

Public relations

Scholarships: **Native Americans in General,** 272, 327

Calendar Index

The Calendar Index lists entry numbers for programs with established filing dates. It is divided into four major sections: American Indians, Native American Alaskans, Native Pacific Islanders, and Native Americans in General. Each section of the calendar is subdivided first by program type (Scholarships, Fellowships, Loans, Grants, Awards, or Internships) and then by month, beginning with January. Entry numbers follow sequentially. Remember, not all sponsoring organizations supplied deadline information, so not all programs are listed in this index.

American Indians

Scholarships:
January: 53, 62, 86, 133, 135
February: 6–7, 10, 14–15, 25, 27–28, 38, 64–65, 73, 88, 92–94, 107, 111
March: 14–16, 18–19, 21, 37, 39–40, 80, 82, 93–94, 99, 101, 122, 137
April: 13, 20, 31, 42, 55–56, 80, 82, 99, 101, 104, 116, 118, 125–126, 133, 135
May: 2, 19, 24, 43, 61, 66, 79, 85, 92, 96–97, 124, 127, 137
June: 4, 11, 13, 23, 30, 34, 36, 58–59, 70, 75–76, 84, 87, 104, 106, 110, 112, 114, 129, 133, 135
July: 9, 17, 85, 91, 102
August: 1, 99, 101, 103, 107
September: 62, 80, 82, 88, 93–94, 97, 137
October: 6, 13, 19, 27, 66, 102, 111, 133, 135
November: 9, 18, 22, 92, 103, 116
December: 85, 104
Any time: 3, 29, 33, 35, 44, 50, 57, 60, 69, 71, 83, 95, 98, 100, 115, 128, 131–132

Fellowships:
January: 410, 412, 415, 428, 446, 450
February: 393–394, 403, 416, 427, 430, 432
March: 389–390, 421, 423, 426, 432, 436–437, 451
April: 386, 404, 421, 423, 434, 444, 450
May: 380, 388–389, 392, 401, 414, 417, 447, 451
June: 382, 385–386, 396, 429, 434–435, 439–441, 450
July: 383, 387
August: 411, 433, 438
September: 415, 421, 423, 430, 432, 443, 451
October: 386, 389, 393, 417, 450
November: 383, 391, 398–400, 433, 437–438, 444
December: 434
Any time: 381, 397, 402, 413, 419–420, 424, 437, 442, 448–449

Loans:
January: 731, 741
March: 736, 738
April: 730, 736
August: 733
September: 736
Any time: 729, 732, 734, 737, 739

Grants:
January: 793–795, 801, 804, 812–814, 817–818
February: 796, 810–811, 823
March: 792, 799, 808, 824
April: 828
May: 817
June: 798, 822, 829
July: 807, 809, 815, 820, 826–827
August: 788, 797, 800, 816
September: 817
November: 799, 824
December: 791, 803
Any time: 790, 805, 819, 821, 824

Awards:
February: 1428
April: 1420, 1427
May: 1414–1417, 1419, 1421–1424, 1426, 1429–1431, 1433–1434, 1436–1437
Any time: 1418

Internships:
February: 1496, 1501–1502, 1505, 1509–1511
March: 1494, 1499
July: 1507
August: 1500
October: 1507
November: 1497–1498, 1513
Any time: 1506

Native Alaskans

Scholarships:
January: 146, 150
February: 138, 141, 145
March: 142–143, 153
April: 144, 151
May: 148
Any time: 139

Fellowships:
January: 452, 459–460, 463
February: 456, 458, 462
March: 464
April: 457
May: 454–455
September: 465

Loans:
January: 743
April: 742

Any time: 744–745

Grants:
January: 834–835, 837, 842–844, 846–847
February: 841, 849
March: 836, 840
May: 833, 846, 848
July: 845
September: 846
November: 836
December: 833
Any time: 831, 838

Awards:
April: 1440–1441

Internships:
February: 1517–1520
April: 1515
September: 1515

Native Pacific Islanders

Scholarships:
February: 159, 162–165, 169
March: 166
April: 154–157, 168, 170
June: 158
July: 167

Fellowships:
January: 482
February: 471, 473–475, 480
March: 476, 479
April: 466–469, 478, 481
May: 472

June: 470
July: 477
November: 479
Any time: 479

Loans:
January: 747
March: 746

Grants:
March: 857
May: 850–854
November: 857
Any time: 856–857

Native Americans in General

Scholarships:
January: 173, 181, 197, 204–206, 221, 226, 231, 250, 286, 290, 300, 315–316, 324, 334, 348–349
February: 176–177, 180, 182, 195, 199, 201, 209, 216, 219, 225, 230, 234, 237, 239, 244–245, 254, 264–265, 268, 274, 276–277, 297–298, 310, 313, 320–321, 326, 329, 338, 344–345, 347, 351, 357, 369–370, 377
March: 174, 178, 193, 200, 202–203, 220, 227, 229, 235, 240–241, 243, 259, 266–267, 269, 271, 280, 284, 287, 302, 314, 328, 335–336, 341, 363, 365–367, 375
April: 175, 192, 196, 198, 214, 217–218, 224, 228, 233, 261, 272, 278, 281, 287, 293–294, 301, 307, 327, 331–332, 362
May: 179, 184–191, 210–211, 215, 242, 275, 282, 311, 321, 326, 333, 338, 353, 359, 377
June: 183, 223, 248–249, 263, 283, 285, 317, 323, 330, 339–340

July: 295, 361, 377
August: 303, 346
September: 184–191, 287, 306, 318, 321, 326, 338, 379
October: 241, 247, 330, 371
November: 198–199, 222, 238, 257, 260, 364, 377
December: 173, 208, 281, 312, 337, 350, 361

Fellowships:
January: 497, 500, 512, 518, 520–521, 525–527, 536, 542, 546, 550, 553–554, 563–564, 580–581, 583, 600, 603–604, 614, 616, 628, 636, 640, 646, 655–656, 664, 666–667, 679, 687, 690–691, 699, 705, 707–708, 715, 718, 727
February: 484, 488, 492–493, 501, 503, 506, 513, 528, 534–535, 537, 539–540, 543, 548, 552, 556, 558, 560, 569, 572, 577–578, 588, 590, 593, 596, 605, 608, 612, 633, 645, 650, 653, 671, 674, 677, 695, 701, 712, 719, 726

Native Americans in General (Continued)

Native Americans in General (Continued)

1598, 1618–1619, 1621, 1628–1629, 1631, 1644, 1649–1650, 1667–1668, 1671–1672, 1679, 1691, 1697–1698, 1708, 1711–1713, 1716, 1722–1723, 1728, 1732–1734, 1744, 1748, 1756, 1759–1760, 1771

March: 1532, 1544, 1546, 1549, 1552, 1554, 1557, 1587, 1593, 1597, 1604–1605, 1618, 1620–1621, 1625, 1630, 1634–1636, 1655–1656, 1688, 1702, 1720–1721, 1729, 1731, 1735, 1743, 1754, 1758, 1762, 1769

April: 1538, 1552, 1573, 1578, 1606, 1608, 1615–1616, 1620, 1626, 1643, 1662, 1668, 1692–1693, 1696, 1700, 1703, 1752, 1770, 1772

May: 1529, 1552, 1592, 1639–1640, 1659, 1698, 1708, 1724, 1728, 1767, 1773

June: 1614, 1652, 1715, 1734, 1736, 1759

July: 1546, 1671, 1742

August: 1702

September: 1559, 1564, 1698, 1708, 1728, 1755

October: 1537, 1560, 1585, 1601, 1651, 1654, 1668, 1671, 1682, 1685, 1715, 1732, 1734, 1759, 1768

November: 1530, 1546, 1551, 1556, 1566, 1577, 1580, 1603, 1612, 1648, 1654, 1676, 1689, 1702, 1705, 1742, 1765

December: 1527, 1536, 1541, 1545, 1561, 1579, 1599–1600, 1613, 1624, 1641, 1643, 1647, 1673–1674, 1683–1684, 1687, 1701, 1726–1727, 1753

Any time: 1523, 1531, 1555, 1567–1568, 1580, 1583, 1596, 1608–1609, 1617, 1660, 1664–1665, 1669–1671, 1677–1678, 1686, 1688, 1699, 1704, 1710, 1739, 1741, 1751, 1754, 1763–1764, 1766, 1774, 1776

ABOUT THE AUTHORS

Dr. Gail Ann Schlachter has worked for more than two decades as a library administrator, a library educator, and an administrator of library-related publishing companies. Among the reference books to her credit are the biennially-issued *Directory of Financial Aids for Women* and two award-winning bibliographic guides: *Minorities and Women: A Guide to Reference Literature in the Social Sciences* (which was chosen as an "outstanding reference book of the year" by *Choice)* and *Reference Sources in Library and Information Services* (which won the first Knowledge Industry Publications "Award for Library Literature"). She was the reference book review editor for *RQ* for 10 years, is a past president of the American Library Association's Reference and User Services Association, and is the current editor of the *Reference and User Services Association Quarterly.* In recognition of her outstanding contributions to reference service, Dr. Schlachter has been awarded both the Isadore Gilbert Mudge Citation and the Louis Shores/Oryx Press Award.

Dr. R. David Weber teaches economics and history at East Los Angeles College, where he has been named "Teacher of the Year" for the last four years in a row. He has written a number of critically-acclaimed reference works, including *Dissertations in Urban History* and the three-volume *Energy Information Guide.* With Gail Schlachter, he is the author of Reference Service Press' *Financial Aid for the Disabled and Their Families,* which was selected by *Library Journal* as one of the "best reference books of the year," and a number of other financial aid titles, including the *College Student's Guide to Merit and Other No-Need Funding,* which was selected as one of the "outstanding reference books of the year" by *Choice.*